HILLIER'S MANUAL
OF
TREES & SHRUBS

HILLIER'S MANUAL OF TREES & SHRUBS

Fifth Edition

DAVID & CHARLES

Newton Abbot London North Pomfret (Vt)

Reprinted 1973
Reprinted 1974
Reprinted 1975
New edition 1977
Fifth edition 1981
Reprinted 1984
Reprinted 1988

British Library Cataloguing in Publication Data

Hillier's manual of trees and shrubs.—5th ed.
1. Trees—Dictionaries
2. Shrubs—Dictionaries
635.9′76′0321 SB435

ISBN 0-7153-8302-7

Set in 'Monotype' Old Style Series 2 and Grotesque Bold Condensed Series 15
by Yelf Brothers Limited Newport Isle of Wight
and printed in Great Britain
by Redwood Burn Limited Trowbridge, Wilts.
for David & Charles Publishers plc
Brunel House Newton Abbot Devon

Published in the United States of
America by David & Charles Inc
North Pomfret Vermont 05053 USA

CONTENTS of the MANUAL

LIST OF ILLUSTRATIONS

The majority of the photographs are by Michael Warren; additional pictures were provided by Pat Brindley, Brian Humphrey, Roy Lancaster and Dennis Woodland.

PREFACE

In 1864 Edwin Hillier bought a small nurseryman's and florist's business in Winchester trading under the name of Farthing. The business prospered to the extent that in 1874 the now famous West Hill Nursery was commenced. Edwin's two sons inherited from him; Edwin Lawrence built up the collection of trees and shrubs for which the name of Hillier is renowned throughout the horticultural and botanical world, whilst Arthur Richard acted as the firm's administrative head. Unfortunately, in 1913, the 120-acre Shroner Wood and nursery, part of which Edwin Lawrence had developed into one of the finest pineta in the country, was sold. However, even before the sale, the firm had bought a piece of land on the west side of Winchester where a very wide range of trees and shrubs, roses and fruit trees, was grown. The remarkable Edwin Lawrence died in 1944, and his brother Arthur retired two years later. Since that time the business has continued to develop under its present head, Harold G. Hillier, son of Edwin. Today, when economic pressures force more and more nurserymen to concentrate on growing more and more of fewer and fewer popular garden plants, the firm of Hillier continues to cultivate an enormously wide range of plant material and unquestionably is the greatest hardy tree and shrub nursery in the world.

It is good to know that the work is now being shared with his two sons, John and Robert, who before joining the firm gained practical experience in some of the leading nurseries in the U.S.A., France, Germany and Holland. I also understand that in the "Home Nursery" the fifth generation is under cultivation.

Hillier's cultivate, in all, some 14,000 different kinds of plants, and gradually these are being incorporated into the Hillier Gardens and Arboretum at Ampfield near Romsey, which now covers about 115 acres (48 hectacres). All these plants are named with the care and authority associated with the naming of the plants in the botanic gardens of the country. In fact the Hillier Gardens and Arboretum do constitute a great British botanical garden, established by the foresight and enterprise and immense knowledge and capacity for hard work of Harold Hillier.

It has always been the concern of Hillier's that the public be given the most up to date and accurate information possible about the plants sold by the horticultural trade; always their concern that the horticultural public be sold authentically named plants. Towards these ends over the years they have published a series of catalogues which for the accuracy of the information contained therein are unrivalled in my opinion. Certainly I know of nothing to compare with this present manual (it is far more than a mere catalogue) which succinctly describes, with (to quote from the introduction) "a blend of practical garden knowledge and botanical system and reasoning", approximately 8,000 trees, shrubs, climbers, conifers and bamboos hardy in the northern hemisphere. At a time when so much of the expensive horticultural literature being published is a waste of the paper on which it is printed, this latest Hillier publication—immensely readable and containing all kinds of information otherwise available only in numerous specialised and very costly books—is an absolutely essential reference work for anyone interested in hardy woody plants be he horticulturalist, arboriculturalist or botanist and by making it available at such an absurdly low cost Hillier's are performing a great public service.

HAROLD R. FLETCHER
Regius Keeper
Royal Botanic Garden
Edinburgh
(1956-1970)

INTRODUCTION

This manual was originally published in 1971 and contains brief descriptions of over 8,000 plants, representing 638 genera. We believe that no other nursery has ever offered such a wide and comprehensive range of trees and shrubs hardy in the northern hemisphere.

A number of rare items are included of which we may have no immediately saleable stock. In addition to those described, we maintain limited stocks of numerous other plants for which we welcome enquiries.

Every effort has been made to bring this manual up to date and in line with the requirements of the modern gardener. Its contents are a blend of practical garden knowledge and botanical system and reasoning.

We would like to draw your attention to the sections on Nomenclature and Classification (pp. 3 to 5), the Glossary (pp. 8 to 10) and to the lists of Recommended Trees and Shrubs for various soils, aspects and special features (end of manual).

We wish to acknowledge the help given us by several botanical friends, in particular Mr. Desmond Clarke, and the many useful comments and suggestions received from customers.

We also wish to place on record our appreciation of the research and detailed work done by Mr. Roy Lancaster and Mr. P. H. B. Gardner.

PLANT VALUES

For over a hundred years we have endeavoured to bring before the public as great a selection of hardy plants as was economically possible. Growing plants is a pleasure as well as a business, and today we offer what we believe to be a wider selection of plants than is obtainable elsewhere in the world.

A proportion of the plants are rare or little known and it is our objective, as plantsmen, that they should at least be "known about" and considered for inclusion in planting schemes.

Current fashion, accompanied and often dictated by economic reality, is forcing most nurserymen to reduce the choice of plants they offer and to grow only those which tolerate mechanical and mass production.

Although some will consider a few of our prices high and certain of our terms stringent, many of our customers have told us that by retaining and if possible extending our collection of plants we are doing a service to horticulture. This can only be continued if we maintain an economic price structure. A skilled horticultural craftsman should be able to enjoy the same living standards as his counterpart in other industries.

It costs many thousand pounds each week to propagate, cultivate and maintain the plants we offer, and our customers will appreciate that every plant purchased is not the result of an overnight assembly line but the culmination of a carefully planned operation lasting from 2 to 6 or more years and carried out by plantsmen who know and care about what they are doing.

Whether a plant is bought for the aesthetic or utility value, its initial cost is soon recovered and, unlike many manufactured goods, the value increases yearly, giving added pleasure.

It must be emphasised that we are not only specialists in the uncommon but that we also grow by the hundred thousand, the popular plants, and for these we shall be pleased to quote the keenest competitive prices for quantities.

DESCRIPTIONS

The descriptions in this manual have, wherever possible, been based upon typical plants growing in our nurseries. However, as species and varieties are often variable, particularly in cultivation, such characters as leaf shape, colour and texture, colour of flower, occurence of flower and fruit, habit of plant and autumn colour may vary (within the limitations of the species) from those described. Autumn colours are particularly influenced by local and seasonal conditions, but some clones of a species are more reliable than others.

NOMENCLATURE AND CLASSIFICATION

Plant nomenclature is controlled by two internationally accepted codes.

Wild plants are covered by the "International Code of Botanical Nomenclature", whilst cultivated plants (cultivars) are covered by the "International Code of Nomenclature for Cultivated Plants".

Advances in our knowledge both of plant variation and plant relationships has inevitably resulted in the re-classification of many plants. This, plus the remorseless application of the "Rule of Priority" (i.e. the use of the earliest legitimate name) has necessitated a number of name changes. For various reasons not all changes are accepted in this manual, but where a plant has been re-named it has been cross-referenced under its old name, which is also included as a synonym after the accepted name.

In order to assist our customers in understanding the use and arrangement of names etc. in this manual, the following explanatory notes are provided, but we wish to point out that not all the names, opinions, interpretations etc. in this manual are internationally accepted.

GENERA—These are shown in bold type and capital letters

e.g. **ACER, PRUNUS, PINUS**

FAMILIES—These are shown in bold type with a capital initial and follow the generic names

e.g. **MALUS—Rosaceae**
(genus) (family)

SPECIES—These are shown in bold type with a small initial and are listed under the genus to which they belong

e.g. **RHODODENDRON**
ponticum
racemosum
radicans

SUBSPECIES & VARIETIES—Wild varieties and subspecies are shown in bold type with a small initial and follow the species to which they belong

e.g. **SARCOCOCCA hookerana digyna**
(genus) (species) (variety)

CULTIVARS—Garden varieties and selected forms from the wild maintained in cultivation normally follow the species to which they belong. They are shown in bold type, spelt with a capital initial and are enclosed in single quotation marks

e.g. **CAMELLIA japonica 'Jupiter'**
FAGUS sylvatica 'Cristata'
(genus) (species) (cultivar)

CLONE—A group of individuals derived originally from a single individual and maintained in cultivation by vegetative propagation. All such individuals of a clone are exactly alike and are identical with the original. The majority of the cultivars in this manual are clonal in origin.

FORMS—Although *forma* is a recognised botanical category below variety, the term form is here used in a looser, more general manner and may refer to a variety, subspecies or cultivar.

HYBRIDS—Hybrids between two or more species, forms, etc., are normally given a collective name in latin form. These are shown as for a species but are preceded by a multiplication sign

e.g. **QUERCUS × hispanica**

Sometimes a hybrid group is given a collective name in English

e.g. **RHODODENDRON Lady Chamberlain**

which is then followed by the various named clones

e.g. **RHODODENDRON Lady Chamberlain**
'Gleam'
'Ivy'

Where no collective name is available for a hybrid consisting of a single clone, its clonal name is given and treated in the same way as a cultivar

e.g. **CISTUS 'Silver Pink'**
SORBUS 'Winter Cheer'

Where neither collective name nor clonal name exists or is known for a hybrid, the names of the parents are given, connected by a multiplication sign

e.g. **QUERCUS canariensis × robur**

Parents of hybrids, where known, are shown in italics and enclosed in parentheses after the name of the hybrid, or in a few instances are mentioned in the description. Unless otherwise indicated, the sequence of the parents is purely alphabetical

e.g. **VIBURNUM × hillieri** (*erubescens × henryi*)
(hybrid) (parents)

BI-GENERIC HYBRIDS—Natural (sexual) hybrids between species of two different genera are shown in bold type and are preceded by a multiplication sign

e.g. **× MAHOBERBERIS** (*MAHONIA × BERBERIS*)
(bi-generic hybrid) (parents)

Graft hybrids (chimeras) between species of two different genera are shown in bold type and are preceded by a plus sign

e.g. **+ LABURNOCYTISUS** (*LABURNUM+CYTISUS*)
(graft hybrid) (parents)

SECTIONS AND SERIES—The larger genera are normally sub-divided into Sections or Series. Where it is felt these may be of use as a reference they have been added in parentheses after the individual species

e.g. **FRAXINUS mariesii** (Ornus Sect.)
RHODODENDRON forrestii (s. Neriiflorum)

GROUPS—Where the named clones of a variable hybrid have been listed separately, reference to the hybrid is contained in parentheses after the clone concerned.

e.g. **COTONEASTER 'Cornubia'** (Watereri Group)

SYNONYMS—Old or invalid names (those by which a plant was previously known), also those names not accepted in this manual, are shown in italics and placed in parentheses after the accepted name.

e.g. **PONCIRUS trifoliata** (*Aegle sepiaria*)
THUJA plicata (*T. lobbii*)
(accepted name) (synonym)

Where a synonym is accompanied by the abbreviation HORT., it indicates that the plant in question is known by this name only in Horticulture (Gardens).

e.g. **HEBE brachysiphon** (*traversii* HORT.)

FOREIGN NAMES OF CULTIVARS—Names of cultivars enclosed in brackets as against parentheses, indicate prior names (correct names) of foreign origin which have been given an English equivalent

e.g. **HAMAMELIS × intermedia 'Magic Fire'** ['Feuerzauber']
(translation) (prior name)

COMMON NAMES—Common or colloquial names of common usage are included in double quotation marks before the description

e.g. **QUERCUS coccinea** "Scarlet Oak"
(botanical name) (common name)

In addition, the more familiar common names are included in the text and are cross referenced to the appropriate botanical name.

AUTHORITIES—Following the names of the species, subspecies and varieties etc., are the names in capitals, usually abbreviated, of the authority responsible for publishing that particular combination

e.g. **OSMANTHUS delavayi** FRANCH.—name given by the botanist Franchet

ILEX aquifolium L.—name given by Linnaeus

COTONEASTER salicifolius floccosus REHD. & WILS.—name given by Rehder and Wilson to a variety of *C. salicifolius.*

ORIGINS

The countries of origin of wild species and varieties where known, have been included, normally at the end of the description. Distribution of individual plants may vary depending on one's concept of a species.

DATES OF INTRODUCTION

The dates of introduction into Western Gardens of wild species and varieties where known, have been included at the end of each description, e.g. I. 1869.

Where no date of introduction is known, the earliest known date of cultivation is included, e.g. C. 1658.

AWARDS

Many plants of particular merit have been given awards by the Royal Horticultural Society. The most important awards, from the beginning up to and including 1980 are given at the end of the relevant descriptions.

HEIGHTS

The ultimate height of a tree or shrub is largely dependent on such factors as soil, aspect and local weather conditions. With British gardens in mind we have devised a height scale (see p. 18) to give the probable range of each plant growing under average conditions. Allowances must be made for specimens growing in shade, against walls and under exceptional circumstances.

FLOWERING PERIODS

Flowering periods in this manual should be taken as being approximate, as they will vary according to locality and from year to year depending on the vagaries of the season.

WORKS OF REFERENCE

The following is a selection from the many books, monographs, journals, etc. referred to during the compilation of this manual.

A California Flora—P. A. Munz (1959)
A Dictionary of the Flowering Plants and Ferns—J. C. Willis (8th edit., 1973)
A Glossary of Botanic Terms—B. D. Jackson (4th edit., 1928)
A Students Flora of Tasmania (3 pts.)—W. M. Curtis (1956/67)
Bamboos—A. H. Lawson (1968)
Berberis and Mahonia—L. W. A. Ahrendt (Journal of the Linnean Society, 1961)
Check List of the Trees of the United States—E. J. Little, Jnr. (U.S. Dept. of Agriculture Handbook No. 41, 1953)
Climbing Roses Old and New—Graham Thomas (1965)
Die Laubgeholze—G. Krussman (1965)
Dictionary of Gardening (5 vols.)—Royal Horticultural Society (1951/69)
Dwarf Conifers 2nd edit.)—H. J. Welch (1968)
Flora Europaea (2 vols.)—Edited by T. G. Tutin et al (1964/68)
Flora of the British Isles—A. R. Clapham, T. G. Tutin and E. F. Warburg (2nd edit. 1962)
Flora of Japan—J. Ohwi (1965)
Flora of New Zealand (Vol. I)—H. H. Allan (1961)
Handbook of Coniferae—W. Dallimore and A. B. Jackson (4th edit., 1966)
International Code of Botanical Nomenclature—(1971)
International Code of Nomenclature for Cultivated Plants—(1969)
Manual of Cultivated Conifers—P. den Ouden and B. K. Boom (1965)
Manual of Trees and Shrubs—A. Rehder (2nd edit. 1940)
Rhododendron Handbook (2 parts)—Royal Horticultural Society (1967)
Shrub Roses of Today—Graham Thomas (1962)
The Cultivation of New Zealand Trees and Shrubs—L. J. Metcalf (1972)
The International Rhododendron Register—Royal Horticultural Society (1958)
The Species of Rhododendron—The Rhododendron Society (1930)
Trees and Shrubs hardy in the British Isles (3 vols.)—W. J. Bean (7th edit. 1951) also 8th edit. Revised Vols. 1 (A-C), 2 (D-M) 1973 and 3 (N-RL) 1976.

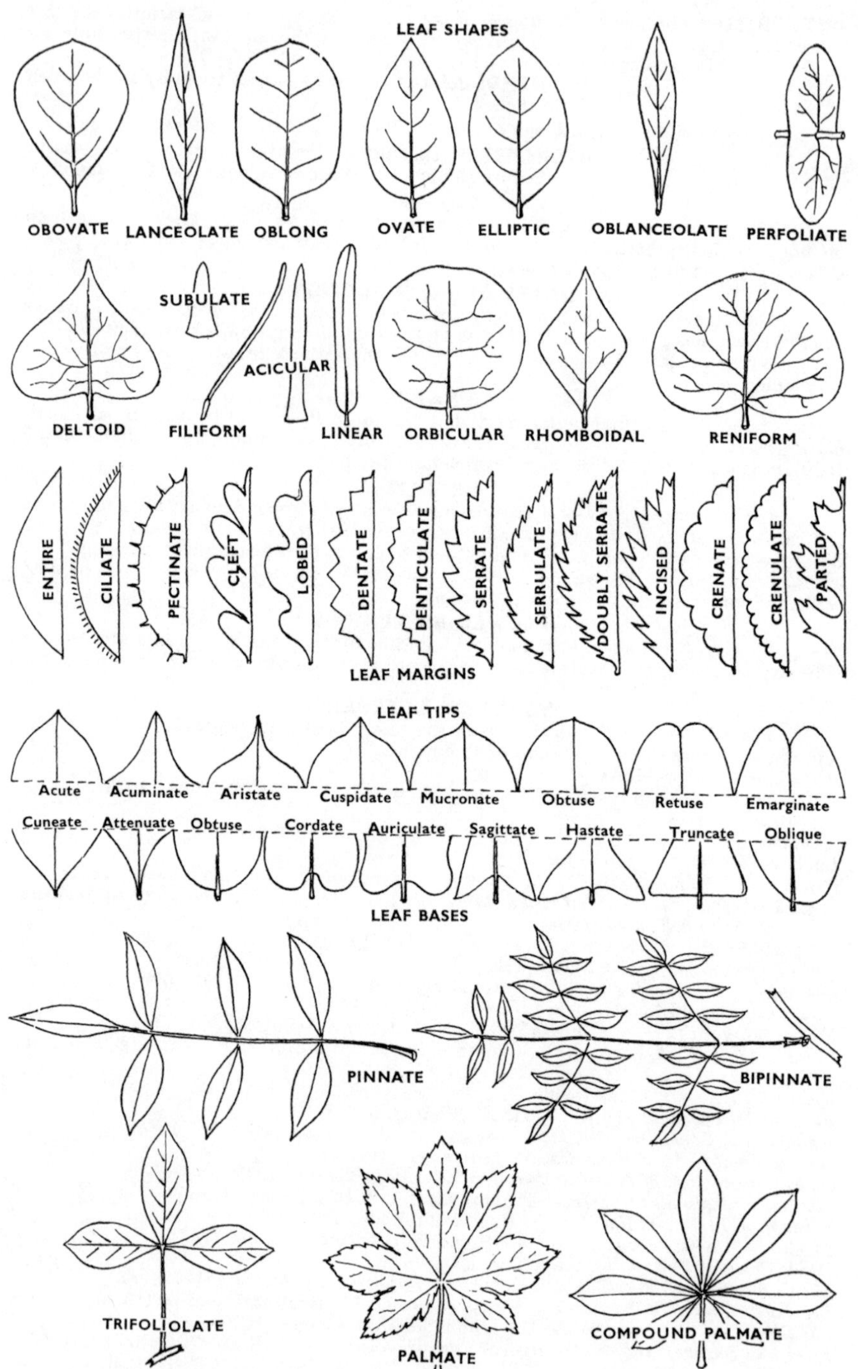
LEAF SHAPES
OBOVATE
LANCEOLATE
OBLONG
OVATE
ELLIPTIC
OBLANCEOLATE
PERFOLIATE
SUBULATE
ACICULAR
DELTOID
FILIFORM
LINEAR
ORBICULAR
RHOMBOIDAL
RENIFORM
ENTIRE
CILIATE
PECTINATE
CLEFT
LOBED
DENTATE
DENTICULATE
SERRATE
SERRULATE
DOUBLY SERRATE
INCISED
CRENATE
CRENULATE
PARTED
LEAF MARGINS
LEAF TIPS
Acute
Acuminate
Aristate
Cuspidate
Mucronate
Obtuse
Retuse
Emarginate
Cuneate
Attenuate
Obtuse
Cordate
Auriculate
Sagittate
Hastate
Truncate
Oblique
LEAF BASES
PINNATE
BIPINNATE
TRIFOLIOLATE
PALMATE
COMPOUND PALMATE

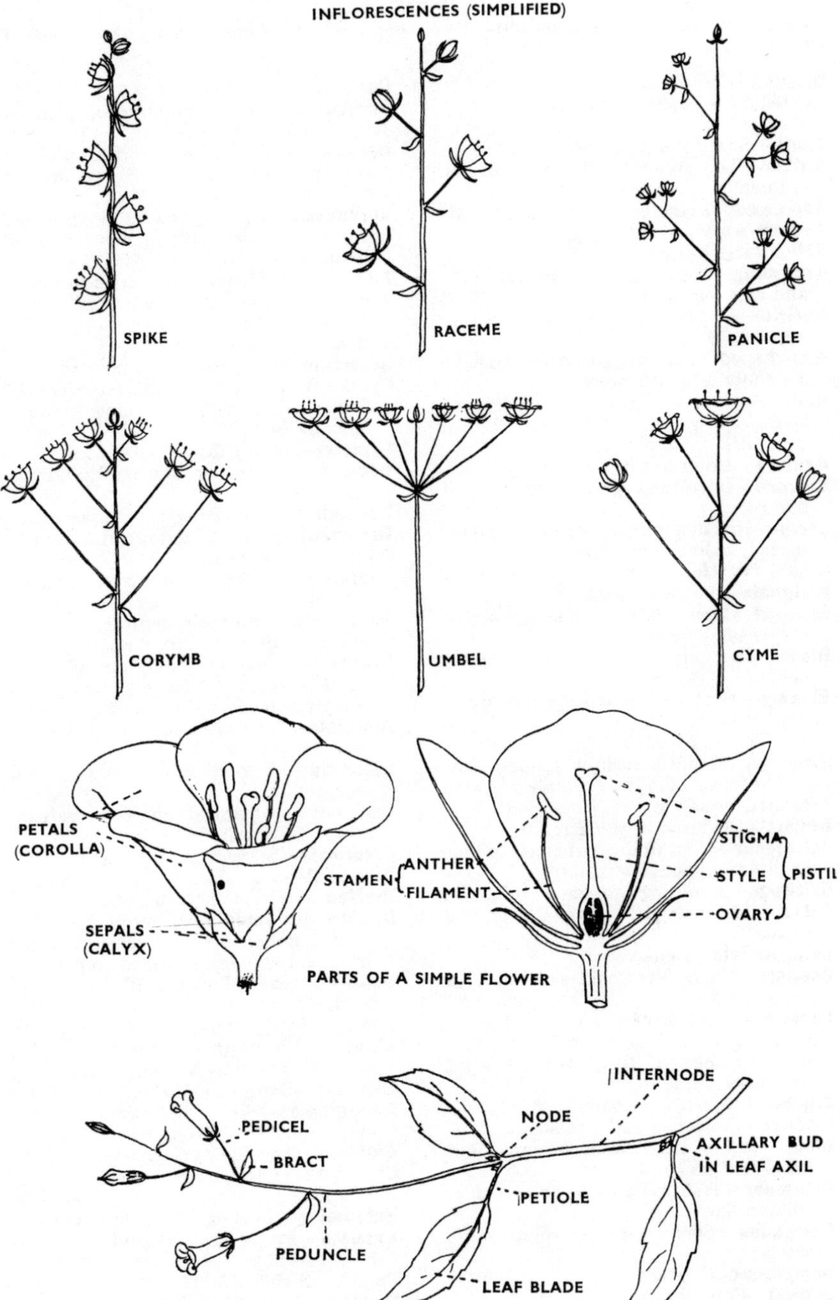
INFLORESCENCES (SIMPLIFIED)
SPIKE
RACEME
PANICLE
CORYMB
UMBEL
CYME
PETALS
(COROLLA)
SEPALS
(CALYX)
STAMEN
ANTHER
FILAMENT
STIGMA
STYLE
OVARY
PISTIL
PARTS OF A SIMPLE FLOWER
INTERNODE
NODE
PEDICEL
BRACT
AXILLARY BUD
IN LEAF AXIL
PETIOLE
PEDUNCLE
LEAF BLADE

GLOSSARY

Technical and botanical terms have been used only when necessary **for precision and brevity.**

Acicular—Needle-shaped
Acuminate—Tapering at the end, long pointed
Acute—Sharp pointed
Anther—The pollen-bearing part of the stamen
Adpressed—Lying close and flat against
Aristate—Awned, bristle-tipped
Articulate—Jointed
Ascending—Rising somewhat obliquely and curving upwards
Auricle—An ear-shaped projection or appendage
Awl-shaped—Tapering from the base to a slender and stiff point
Axil—The angle formed by a leaf or lateral branch with the stem, or of a vein with the midrib
Axillary—Produced in the axil
Bearded—Furnished with long or stiff hairs
Berry—Strictly a pulpy, normally several seeded, indehiscent fruit
Bifid—Two-cleft
Bipinnate—Twice pinnate
Bisexual—Both male and female organs in the same flower
Blade—The expanded part of a leaf or petal
Bloomy—With a fine powder-like waxy deposit
Bole—Trunk, of a tree
Bract—A modified, usually reduced leaf at the base of a flower-stalk, flower-cluster, or shoot
Bullate—Blistered or puckered
Calcareous—Containing carbonate of lime or limestone, chalky or limy
Calcifuge—Avoiding calcareous soils
Calyx—The outer part of the flower, the sepals
Campanulate—Bell-shaped
Capitate—Head-like, collected into a dense cluster
Capsule—A dry, several-celled pod
Catkin—A normally dense spike or spike-like raceme of tiny, scaly-bracted flowers or fruits
Ciliate—Fringed with hairs
Cladode—Flattened leaf-like stems
Clone—See under Nomenclature and Classification (p. 3)
Columnar—Tall, cylindrical or tapering, column-like
Compound—Composed of two or more similar parts
Compressed—Flattened
Conical—Cone-shaped
Cordate—Shaped like a heart, as base of leaf
Coriaceous—Leathery
Corolla—The inner normally conspicuous part of a flower, the petals
Corymb—A flat-topped or dome-shaped flower head with the outer flowers opening first
Corymbose—Having flowers in corymbs
Crenate—Toothed with shallow, rounded teeth, scalloped
Cultivar—Garden variety, or form found in the wild and maintained as a clone in cultivation
Cuneate—Wedge-shaped
Cuspidate—Abruptly sharp pointed
Cyme—A flat-topped or dome-shaped flower head with the inner flowers opening first
Cymose—Having flowers in cymes
Deciduous—Soon or seasonally falling, not persistent
Decumbent—Reclining, the tips ascending
Decurrent—Extending down the stem
Deltoid—Triangular
Dentate—Toothed with teeth directed outward
Denticulate—Minutely dentate
Depressed—Flattened from above
Diffuse—Loosely or widely spreading
Digitate—With the members arising from one point (as in a digitate leaf)
Dioecious—Male and female flowers on different plants
Dissected—Divided into many narrow segments
Distichous—Arranged in two vertical ranks: two-ranked
Divaricate—Spreading far apart
Divergent—Spreading
Divided—Separated to the base
Double—(flowers) with more than the usual number of petals, often with the style and stamens changed to petals
Doubly Serrate—Large teeth and small teeth alternating
Downy—Softly hairy
Elliptic—Widest at or about the middle, narrowing equally at both ends
Elongate—Lengthened
Emarginate—With a shallow notch at the apex
Entire—Undivided and without teeth
Evergreen—Remaining green during winter
Exfoliating—Peeling off in thin strips
Exserted—Projecting beyond (stamens from corolla)
Falcate—Sickle-shaped
Fascicle—A dense cluster
Fastigiate—With branches erect and close together

Fertile—Stamens producing good pollen or fruit containing good seeds, or of stems with flowering organs
Ferruginous—Rust-coloured
Filament—The stalk of a stamen
Filiform—Thread-like
Fimbriate—Fringed
Flexuous—Wavy or zig-zag
Floccose—Clothed with flocks of soft hair or wool
Florets—Small, individual flowers of a dense inflorescence
Floriferous—Flower-bearing
Gibbous—Swollen, usually at the base (as in corolla)
Glabrous—Hairless
Glandular—With secreting organs
Glaucous—Covered with a "bloom", bluish-white or bluish-grey
Glutinous—Sticky
Hermaphrodite—Bisexual, both male and female organs in the same flower
Hirsute—With rather coarse or stiff hairs
Hispid—Beset with rigid hairs or bristles
Hoary—Covered with a close whitish or greyish-white pubescence
Hybrid—A plant resulting from a cross between different species
Imbricate—Overlapping, as tiles on a roof
Impressed—Sunken (as in veins)
Incised—Sharply and usually deeply and irregularly cut
Indehiscent—Fruits which do not (burst) open
Indumentum—Dense hairy covering
Inflorescence—The flowering part of the plant
Internode—The portion of stem between two nodes or joints
Involucre—A whorl of bracts surrounding a flower or flower cluster
Keel—A central ridge
Lacerate—Torn, irregularly cut or cleft
Laciniate—Cut into narrow pointed lobes
Lanceolate—Lance-shaped, widening above the base and long tapering to the apex
Lanuginose—Woolly or cottony
Lateral—On or at the side
Lax—Loose
Leaflet—Part of a compound leaf
Linear—Long and narrow with nearly parallel margins
Lip—One of the parts of an unequally divided flower
Lobe—Any protruding part of an organ (as in leaf, corolla or calyx)
Lustrous—Shining
Membranous—Thin and rather soft
Midrib—The central vein or rib of a leaf
Monoecious—Male and female flowers separate, but on the same plant
Monotypic—Of a single species (genus)
Mucronate—Terminated abruptly by a spiny tip
Nectary—A nectar-secreting gland, usually a small pit or protuberance
Node—The place upon the stem where the leaves are attached, the "joint"
Nut—A non-splitting, one-seeded, hard and bony fruit
Oblanceolate—Inversely lanceolate
Oblique—Unequal-sided
Oblong—Longer than broad, with nearly parallel sides
Obovate—Inversely ovate
Obtuse—Blunt (as in apex of leaf or petal)
Orbicular—Almost circular in outline
Oval—Broadest at the middle
Ovary—The basal "box" part of the pistil, containing the ovules
Ovate—Broadest below the middle (like a hen's egg)
Ovule—The body which, after fertilisation, becomes the seed
Palmate—Lobed or divided in hand-like fashion, usually five or seven-lobed
Panicle—A branching raceme
Paniculate—Having flowers in panicles
Parted—Cut or cleft almost to the base
Pea-flower—Shaped like a sweet pea blossom
Pectinate—Comb-like (as in leaf margin)
Pedicel—The stalk of an individual flower in an inflorescence
Peduncle—The stalk of a flower cluster or of a solitary flower
Pellucid—Clear, transparent (as in gland)
Pendulous—Hanging, weeping ,
Perfoliate—A pair of opposite leaves fused at the base, the stem appearing to pass through them
Perianth—The calyx and corolla together; also commonly used for a flower in which there is no distinction between corolla and calyx
Persistent—Remaining attached
Petal—One of the separate segments of a corolla
Petaloid—Petal-like (as in stamen)
Petiole—The leaf-stalk
Pilose—With long, soft straight hairs
Pinnate—With leaflets arranged on either side of a central stalk
Pinnatifid—Cleft or parted in a pinnate way
Pistil—The female organ of a flower comprising ovary, style and stigma
Plumose—Feathery, as the down of a thistle
Pollen—Spores or grains contained in the anther, containing the male element
Polygamous—Bearing bisexual and unisexual flowers on the same plant
Procumbent—Lying or creeping
Prostrate—Lying flat on the ground

Pruinose—Bloomy

Puberulent—Minutely pubescent

Pubescent—Covered with short, soft hairs, downy

Punctate—With translucent or coloured dots or depressions

Pungent—Ending in a stiff, sharp point, also acid (to the taste) or strong smelling

Pyramidal—Pyramid-shaped (broad at base tapering to a point

Raceme—A simple elongated inflorescence with stalked flowers

Racemose—Having flowers in racemes

Rachis—An axis bearing flowers or leaflets

Recurved—Curved downward or backward

Reflexed—Abruptly turned downward

Reniform—Kidney-shaped

Reticulate—Like a network (as in veins)

Revolute—Rolled backwards, margin rolled under (as in leaf)

Rib—A prominent vein in a leaf

Rotund—Nearly circular

Rufous—Reddish-brown

Rugose—Wrinkled or rough

Runner—A trailing shoot taking root at the nodes

Sagittate—Shaped like an arrow-head

Scabrous—Rough to the touch

Scale—A minute leaf or bract, or a flat gland-like appendage on the surface of a leaf, flower or shoot

Scandent—With climbing stems

Scarious—Thin and dry, not green

Semi-evergreen—Normally evergreen but losing some or all of its leaves in a cold winter or cold area

Sepal—One of the segments of a calyx

Serrate—Saw-toothed (teeth pointing forward)

Serrulate—Minutely serrate

Sessile—Not stalked

Setose—Clothed with bristles

Sheath—A tubular envelope

Shrub—A woody plant which branches from the base with no obvious trunk

Simple—Said of a leaf that is not compound or an unbranched inflorescence

Sinuate—Strongly waved (as in leaf margin)

Sinus—The recess or space between two lobes or divisions of a leaf, calyx or corolla

Spathulate—Spoon-shaped

Spicate—Flowers in spikes

Spike—A simple, elongated inflorescence with sessile flowers

Spine—A sharp-pointed end of a branch or leaf

Spur—A tubular projection from a flower; or a short stiff branchlet

Stamen—The male organ of a flower comprising filament and anther

Staminode—A sterile stamen, or a structure resembling a stamen, sometimes petal-like

Standard—The upper, normally broad and erect petal in a pea-flower; also used in nurseries to describe a tall single stemmed young tree

Stellate—Star-shaped

Stigma—The summit of the pistil which receives the pollen, often sticky or feathery

Stipule—Appendage (normally two) at base of some petioles

Stolon—A shoot at or below the surface of the ground which produces a new plant at its tip

Striate—With fine, longitudinal lines

Strigose—Clothed with flattened fine, bristle-like, hairs

Style—The middle part of the pistil, often elongated between the ovary and stigma

Subulate—Awl-shaped

Succulent—Juicy, fleshy, soft and thickened in texture

Suckering—Producing underground stems; also the shoots from the stock of a grafted plant

Tendril—A twining thread-like appendage

Ternate—In threes

Tessellated—mosaic-like (as in veins)

Tomentose—With dense, woolly pubescence

Tomentum—Dense covering of matted hairs

Tree—A woody plant that produces normally a single trunk and an elevated head of branches

Trifoliate—Three-leaved

Trifoliolate—A leaf with three separate leaflets

Turbinate—Top-shaped

Type—Strictly the original (type) specimen, but used in a general sense to indicate the typical form in cultivation

Umbel—A normally flat-topped inflorescence in which the pedicels or peduncles all arise from a common point

Umbellate—Flowers in umbels

Undulate—With wavy margins

Unisexual—Of one sex

Urceolate—Urn-shaped

Velutinous—Clothed with a velvety indumentum

Venation—The arrangement of the veins

Verrucose—Having a wart-like or nodular surface

Verticillate—Arranged in a whorl or ring

Villous—Bearing long and soft hairs

Viscid—Sticky

Whorl—Three or more flowers or leaves arranged in a ring

PLANT SEXES

Most gardeners are aware that plants such as *Ilex* and *Aucuba* normally produce male and female flowers on different plants and to obtain fruits plants of both sexes are required.

Unfortunately the occurrence of male and female flowers on different plants is not always so straightforward, there are numerous variations and exceptions to the rule.

The majority of plants that we meet with in cultivation possess normal or perfect flowers, that is, male and female organs in the same flower on the same plant. This condition is known as BISEXUAL or HERMAPHRODITE.

Other plants have male and female organs in different flowers and these are known as UNISEXUAL flowers, that is, flowers of only one sex.

In some species the male and female flowers occur on the same plant or individual and this condition is termed MONOECIOUS (on the one plant).

In other species the male and female flowers occur on different plants or individuals and this condition is termed DIOECIOUS (on two plants).

Examples of plants with perfect (HERMAPHRODITE) flowers include—*Rose, Robinia, Rhododendron, Weigela, Prunus* and *Erica.*

Examples of plants with UNISEXUAL flowers include—*Alnus, Buxus, Akebia, Corylus, Sarcococca, Quercus, Pinus, Laurus, Populus, Salix, Garrya, Rhus* and *Taxus.* Of these *Alnus, Buxus, Akebia, Corylus, Sarcococca, Quercus* and *Pinus* are MONOECIOUS and *Laurus, Populus, Salix, Garrya, Rhus* and *Taxus* are DIOECIOUS.

As if things weren't complicated enough there exist plants whose flowers are POLYGAMOUS, that is, both Perfect (HERMAPHRODITE) and UNISEXUAL flowers may occur on the same or different individuals of the one species.

If this occurs on the *same* plant the following combinations may arise:—

Hermaphrodite and Male flowers on the same plant—
ANDRO-MONOECIOUS

Hermaphrodite and Female flowers on the same plant—
GYNO-MONOECIOUS

Hermaphrodite, Male and Female flowers on the same plant—
COENO-MONOECIOUS

If this occurs on *different* plants of the one species the following combinations may arise:—

Hermaphrodite and male plants occur—ANDRO-DIOECIOUS
Hermaphrodite and female plants occur—GYNO-DIOECIOUS
Hermaphrodite, male and female plants occur—TRIOECIOUS

Where a species of plant is known to have usually DIOECIOUS flowers, plants of both sexes should be planted together if fruits are required. Species with POLYGAMOUS flowers can occur in many genera and in such cases it is wiser to plant a group of plants. Examples include—*Pernettya mucronata, Decaisnea fargesii, Celastrus orbiculatus, Callicarpa* species, *Symplocos paniculata* and certain species of *Viburnum* such as *davidii, foetidum* and *rhytidophyllum.*

Many plants raised from seed do not flower until they have reached a particular size or age and until they do it is impossible to sex those that are known or suspected to have UNISEXUAL or POLYGAMOUS flowers.

When examining male or female flowers one will usually find vestiges of the other organ present in the flower. When this occurs it will be found that one or other of the organs is sterile and more often than not reduced in size—e.g. in the male flower of the English Holly the stamens are conspicuous and have large receptive yellow anthers, whereas the ovary is small and functionally useless. In the female flower the positions are reversed, the ovary is developed and completely formed whilst the stamens are small and the anthers empty and shrivelled.

Plants normally MONOECIOUS
Trees and Shrubs

Alnus (Alder)
Andrachne
Betula (Birch)
Buxus (Box)
Carpinus (Hornbeam)
Carya (Hickory)
Castanea (Sweet Chestnut)
Celtis (Nettle Tree)
Chrysolepis chrysophylla
Corylus (Hazel)
Fagus (Beech)
Decaisnea fargesii
Hemiptelea davidii
Juglans (Walnut)
Liquidambar (Sweet Gum)
Lithocarpus
Morus (Mulberry) (or dioecious)
Nothofagus (Southern Beech)

Pachysandra
Platanus (Plane Tree)
Pterocarya (Wing Nut)
Sarcococca (Christmas Box)
Sycopsis sinensis
Quercus (Oak)
Zelkova

Climbers

Akebia
Holboellia
Kadsura
Stauntonia

Conifers

Most are monoecious but a number are dioecious for which—see below.

Plants normally DIOECIOUS

Trees and Shrubs

Acer—certain spp. (many are polygamous)
Ailanthus spp. (Tree of Heaven) (also polygamous)
Aucuba japonica
Baccharis
Broussonetia
Cercidiphyllum
Chionanthus (Fringe Tree)
Comptonia peregrina (Sweet Fern)
Coprosma
Cotinus (Smoke Tree) (also polygamous)
Cudrania tricuspidata
Daphniphyllum
Diospyros
Empetrum nigrum (Crowberry)
Eucommia ulmoides
Garrya
Gymnocladus dioicus (Kentucky Coffee Tree)
Helwingia japonica
Hippophae rhamnoides (Sea Buckthorn)
Idesia polycarpa
Ilex (Holly) (occasionally polygamous)
Laurus (Bay)
Lindera (also polygamous)
Maclura pomifera (Osage Orange)
Morus (or monoecious)
Myrica (also monoecious)
Nyssa (also polygamous)
Orixa japonica
Osmanthus (also perfect or polygamous)
Osmaronia cerasiformis
Phellodendron
Phillyrea
Populus (Poplar)
Rhus (also polygamous)
Ribes—certain spp. including alpinum and laurifolium
Ruscus
Salix (Willow)
Sassafras albidum (occasionally perfect)
Securinega suffruticosa
Shepherdia (Buffalo-berry)
Skimmia (except **reevesiana**)
Zanthoxylum (also polygamous)

Climbers

Actinidia—certain spp. including **chinensis, coriacea and kolomitka**
Celastrus—certain spp. including **orbiculatus** and **scandens** (also polygamous)
Menispermum
Schisandra
Sinofranchetia chinensis
Sinomenium acutum
Smilax
Vitis (also polygamous)

Conifers

Araucaria (Monkey Puzzle)
Cephalotaxus
Diselma archeri
Ginkgo biloba (Maidenhair Tree)
Juniperus—certain spp. including **chinensis, communis** and **virginiana**
Podocarpus
Torreya—though apparently monoecious in cultivation
Taxus (Yew)

THE PLANT COLLECTORS

"Never has so much been done for so many by so few". These words of Winston Churchill have been used in more than one context since his famous wartime speech and one feels that they may justifiably be applied to the plant collectors who have enriched our gardens and parks with the treasures of other lands.

Much has been written about these men, their travels and introductions and here it will suffice to mention the names of just a few who have been responsible for collecting and introducing for the first time many of our now familiar trees and shrubs.

For each collector is given his main area of exploration followed by a selection his introductions.

It must be emphasised that the plants in these lists are *first* introductions. Many collectors introduced certain species several times after the original introduction and very often the plants in cultivation today are a result of these subsequent collectings.

No attempt has been made to mention the many botanical collectors whose primary and often only concern was pressed specimens for the herbarium.

John Fraser (1752-1811) North America
Aesculus parviflora; Abies fraseri; Magnolia fraseri; Pieris floribunda; Rhododendron maximum.

Philip F. von Siebold (1796-1866) Japan
Arundinaria japonica; Carya ovata; Hamamelis japonica 'Arborea'; Ilex latifolia; Ligustrum japonicum; Lespedeza thunbergii; Malus sieboldii; Spiraea nipponica; Trachycarpus fortunei; Wisteria floribunda.

David Douglas (1798-1834) North America
Abies grandis, A. procera (nobilis); Acer circinatum; Arbutus menziesii; Garrya elliptica; Gaultheria shallon; Pinus coulteri, P. ponderosa, P. radiata; Ribes sanguineum; Rubus spectabilis; Spiraea douglasii.

William Lobb (1809-1863) South America and California
Berberis darwinii; Desfontainea spinosa; Embothrium coccineum; Nothofagus obliqua; Fitzroya cupressoides; Sequoiadendron giganteum; Thuja plicata.

Robert Fortune (1812-1880) China and Japan
Weigela florida; Lonicera fragrantissima; Jasminum nudiflorum; Forsythia viridissima; Ilex cornuta; Prunus triloba; Cryptomeria japonica; Rhododendron obtusum; Mahonia bealii; Rhododendron fortunei; Skimmia reevesiana; Akebia quinata; Callicarpa dichotoma; Cephalotaxus fortuni.

Charles Maries (1851-1902) Japan and China
Acer carpinifolium, A. davidii, A. rufinerve; Carpinus cordata; Hamamelis mollis; Abies mariesii; A. veitchii; Enkianthus campanulatus; Styrax obassia; Rhododendron oldhamii; Fraxinus mariesii; Viburnum plicatum 'Mariesii'.

Pere Jean Delavay (1834-1895) China
Deutzia discolor; Berberis pruinosa; Osmanthus delavayi; Rhododendron ciliicalyx, R. racemosa, R. fictolacteum; Sorbus vilmorinii.

Ernest Wilson (1876-1930) China
Acer griseum; Arundinaria murielae; Berberis gagnepainii, B. verruculosa, B. wilsoniae; Clematis montana rubens; Cornus kousa chinensis; Cotoneaster dammeri, C. salicifolius floccosus; Davidia involucrata; Dipelta floribunda; Hydrangea sargentiana; Magnolia delavayi; Malus hupehensis; Lonicera nitida; Populus lasiocarpa; Rhododendron fargesii, R. williamsianum, R. lutescens, R. calophytum; Sorbaria arborea; Stranvaesia davidiana; Viburnum davidii, V. rhytidophyllum.

George Forrest (1873-1932) China
Acer forrestii; Abies delavayi forrestii; Berberis replicata; Buddleia fallowiana; Camellia reticulata (wild form), C. saluenensis; Cotoneaster lacteus; Deutzia monbeigii; Gaultheria forrestii; Hypericum forrestii; Jasminum polyanthum; Pieris formosa forrestii; Pyracantha rogersiana; Rhododendron griersonianum, R. sinogrande, R. forrestii, R. oreotrephes; Sorbus harrowiana; Syringa yunnanensis.

Frank Kingdon Ward (1885-1958) S.W. China; Upper Burma and Tibet
Acer wardii; Berberis calliantha, B. hypokerina; Cornus chinensis; Cotoneaster wardii, C. conspicuus; Gaultheria wardii; Rhododendron calostrotum, R. imperator, R. tsangpoense; R. wardii.

PREPARATION OF GROUND, PLANTING AND AFTER CARE

In preparing new beds for planting it is advisable to dig two spits deep, the subsoil being turned on its own level and not brought to the surface. Some really well-rotted old manure or compost may be dug in during the course of preparation. Fresh manure should not be used where it will come into close contact with the roots immediately following planting. Failing the availability of farmyard manure, compost or peat, a well balanced Plant Food may be used. In the case of hedges it is usually best to dig the line of the hedge about a metre wide and two spits deep, the hedge being planted along the centre of this prepared strip.

Planting Distances. In the descriptions, references are made to ultimate size, and in addition there are many remarks as to rate of growth, all of which should prove useful when planting.

One often sees shrub borders which present a solid mass to the eye. In such borders shrubs lead a crowded existence without being allowed to develop effectively.

As plants grow better in company, it is usually best to plant for present effect and a few years later thin out and transplant to avoid overcrowding.

If one plants at correct distances to allow for future development this will result initially in small subjects appearing isolated in large bare areas. Until the plants develop enough to occupy their alloted space this problem is easily solved by the use of ground cover, whilst attractive temporary displays may be created by the use of herbaceous perennials or annuals.

Ultimate sizes vary considerably with site, nature of soil, exposure and rainfall, and should a customer require advice on this subject we shall be pleased to help, providing we are given accurate details regarding local conditions.

Planting of most hardy subjects can be carried out safely at any time during "open weather" from late October to March for deciduous open-ground plants, and early October to May for evergreens, provided that proper attention is given after planting; open weather in the dead of winter is better for planting hardy subjects than a bad day in November or March. It is a mistake to think that evergreens can be planted only in autumn and spring; nursery-grown plants, which have been kept regularly transplanted, can be moved at any time while dormant. **Hardy pot-grown plants** may be planted at any time if after care is given. There are, however, some subjects which are not hardy until established and for these spring planting is advised.

When planting in grass, or in any position where the whole area is not prepared, it is recommended that circles of soil not less than 1·20m. across be prepared for each tree or large shrub, and ·9m. across for smaller subjects. Holes must be refilled following preparation, since it is an easy matter on receipt of the plants to take out holes in the prepared positions adequate to accommodate the roots, these areas should be kept cultivated for the first three years after planting.

In heavy "sticky" clay soils it is advisable to have some good friable compost available to place around the roots.

It is **important to plant firmly** and to the same depth as previously grown in the nursery, which may readily be seen by the "soil mark" at the base of the stem. Trees should be supported by a suitable stout stake, driven into the planting hole before the tree is positioned, so avoiding the possibility of damaging the roots. The tree is best secured to the stake by Rainbow, Tom's, or similar Tree Ties, one just below the head of the tree and one ·6 to ·9m. above the ground. Large specimen trees should be supported by three or more guy wires fixed to plugs driven into the ground. In gardens open to the public, it is sometimes necessary to avoid using guy wires and give support by underground methods; information on this subject is available on request.

Great care is taken when lifting plants which require a ball of soil. Such efforts are largely wasted if on arrival the planter removes the sacking and spreads the roots. A "balled" specimen, especially if of large size, should be placed in the hole to the correct depth before such sacking as may be readily cut away is removed; any sacking left beneath the plant will soon rot. Containers should be removed carefully prior to planting, care being taken to preserve the earth ball. With heavy specimens measure the depth and width of the root ball to ensure that the hole is prepared to the correct measurements before placing the plant in the hole.

In succeeding weeks occasional "treading up" is necessary when the ground is friable to avoid looseness at the roots caused by wind or frost.

In wet sites "mound planting" is recommended and **in dry areas** "basin planting", otherwise the soil over the roots of new plantings should be kept flat, cultivated and free from turf and weed for at least the first three years following planting. It is helpful to apply a 5cm. deep top mulch of strawy manure, peat, or compost in the spring before the ground becomes too dry. This will help in conserving essential moisture.

Evergreens planted in exposed situations should be afforded temporary protection on the windward side in the form of a wattle hurdle, or hessian screen.

Care should be taken to ensure that new plantings are not permitted to become dry in the first spring and summer, and **artificial watering is recommended during any dry spells.** In addition, evergreens benefit substantially by being sprayed overhead with water in the cool of the evening or in early morning during periods of drought until re-established.

PRUNING

For the pruning of individual trees and shrubs we recommend our customers to use the tables given in the R.H.S. Diary. The most comprehensive book on this subject is "The Pruning of Trees, Shrubs and Conifers" by George E. Brown, published in 1972.

Judicious pruning can improve a tree or shrub, conversely bad pruning can ruin it.

First and foremost, pruning should be used to remove dead and diseased wood and to maintain a healthy, balanced framework of branches, where air may circulate and the sun penetrate to ripen growths. Of course, not all trees and shrubs enjoy the direct influence of the sun and there are those that are naturally of dense habit. Such characteristics are mentioned in the descriptions and should be taken into account when pruning is contemplated.

A second reason for pruning is that certain shrubs possess qualities which are encouraged by the removal of certain growths. Shrubs with coloured, or otherwise attractive stems such as *Cornus alba, C. stolonifera* 'Flaviramea', and certain willows (*Salix* spp.) may have some or all of the old shoots cut to near ground level in winter or early spring so as to encourage the production of strong, brightly coloured new shoots. Many flowering shrubs may be induced to flower with greater freedom or to produce larger inflorescences by annual or bi-annual removal of old flowering wood.

In general, shrubs which flower on the previous year's wood, such as *Deutzia, Philadelphus, Syringa, Weigela,* etc., may be pruned immediately after flowering, whilst those which flower on the current year's wood, such as *Buddleia davidii, Caryopteris, Ceanothus* (deciduous kinds), etc., may be pruned in March. Some shrubs, such as rhododendrons and azaleas, heathers (*Calluna*) and heaths (*Erica*) benefit from the removal of the flower heads immediately after flowering.

The majority of shrubs require no regular pruning, other than the removal of dead, weak and straggly growths. With but few exceptions drastic pruning checks or retards flowering.

A third reason for pruning is to keep in check large-growing or otherwise vigorous trees and shrubs which are outgrowing their alloted space and threaten to be a nuisance or a danger.

Large evergreens, such as many rhododendrons, laurel (*Prunus laurocerasus*), viburnums, holly, yew and cotoneasters, which have become bare at the base and unsightly, if cut hard back into the old wood in April will sprout again and may then be encouraged to form a more shapely specimen.

Though most heavy pruning is often left until winter, July to early September is quite a good time to tidy up the shrub garden or remove the unwanted limb from a tree. When carried out at this time the healing process is enabled to get under way before the period of winter dormancy. **Large wounds** should be painted with a recommended wound dressing such as Arbrex which we would be pleased to supply.

THE HILLIER ARBORETUM

Jermyns Lane, Ampfield, Romsey, Hants.

History

When Mr. H. G. Hillier, C.B.E., came to live in Jermyns House in 1953 there was already in existence a small garden, mainly lawns and shrubbery plus several large specimen trees. These included numerous fine beech planted about 1840.

Immediately on settling in he began an ambitious programme of development and planting resulting in the creation of several distinct garden features. These included a large scree for alpines and carpeting shrubs, an herbaceous border, a woodland garden for magnolias and camellias, etc., a peat garden and a bog garden. In addition, a 10 acre (4 hectare) field first planted as a tree nursery was partially cleared and the remaining trees left to form the basis of an arboretum.

Each year since has witnessed further developments including a new scree, a pond, a heather garden and a Rhododendron Collection. In our Centenary year—1964—a massive double border 230m. long was made running diagonally across the original ten acres of the arboretum. This was planted with alternate bays of roses and herbaceous perennials backed by a representative selection of evergreen shrubs and rose species.

Today the Gardens and Arboretum total 115 acres (48 hectares) and contain many thousands of hardy woody plants plus collections of alpines, herbaceous perennials and aquatics. Semi-hardy plants are grown against the walls of the house and in other sheltered positions.

Purpose

The gardens and arboretum serve several important functions. It is primarily a collection constantly being added to by gifts from friends and enthusiasts, exchanges with botanic gardens and purchases from other nurseries both at home and abroad. It is also a show-case around which visitors may wander at leisure, observing plants in all their multiplicity of shape and form, colour and effect; an all-season garden, each month bringing its own wave of interests and surprises. As a living collection it is a botanist's paradise, containing one of the most diverse collections of trees and shrubs in the temperate regions of the world.

Another aspect of the collections, often overlooked, is one of conservation. Many of the plants represented are extremely rare in the wild state. In one or two cases they are on the verge of extinction and their continued presence in collections such as this offers their best, perhaps only, hope for survival.

Transfer of the Arboretum's Ownership

Mr. Harold Hillier has been most anxious to secure the future of this unique collection as both a national and international asset. This objective has been fully supported by the Hampshire County Council. It was finally achieved in October 1977 when Mr. Hillier presented the Arboretum as a generous gift to the County Council. A Charitable Trust has been established in which the County Council have responsibility for the Arboretum as corporate Trustee, advised by a committee of distinguished experts.

Official Opening

The most important day in the life of the Arboretum was May 9th 1978 when Mr. Hillier's gift of the Arboretum to the Hampshire County Council was officially accepted by Her Majesty Queen Elizabeth The Queen Mother on behalf of the County.

Opening Times

The Arboretum is open to the public from 9 a.m. to 4.30 p.m. Monday to Friday throughout the year and from 1 p.m. to 6 p.m. on Saturdays, Sundays and Bank Holidays from Easter until the last Sunday of October. A small charge is made for admission to help towards maintenance costs.

HOW TO FIND THE GARDENS

From Winchester take the Romsey Road (A31). Jermyns Lane is 9 miles S.W. of Winchester and the first turning on the right after passing through the village of Ampfield. This turning is signposted Braishfield and Timsbury. The Car Park is on the right hand side of the lane, one mile from the main road.

From Romsey, take the Winchester Road (A31), a mile beyond Rolfe's Garage turn left into the road signposted Braishfield, then three-quarters of a mile along this road turn right at the cross-roads into Jermyns Lane signposted Ampfield. The Car Park is on the left hand side of the lane, a quarter of a mile from the cross-roads.

Visitors travelling by bus (No. 66) from Winchester or Romsey, should alight at Jermyns Lane.

LANDSCAPE AND ADVISORY SERVICE

We very frequently receive requests for a representative to call and give advice on such subjects as garden construction, layouts and other horticultural matters, and with this object in view we are always pleased to meet clients by appointment. For such advisory visits, which can only be undertaken by qualified members of our staff, we charge a fee plus travelling and out-of-pocket expenses. **Plans,** when required, are prepared and an appropriate charge made according to the amount of detail involved. **When requesting a representative to call** please state as clearly as possible the purpose of the visit and the kind of advice sought.

EXHIBITIONS

We exhibit at the majority of the R.H.S. fortnightly shows, which are held throughout the year on Tuesdays and Wednesdays at the R.H.S. Hall, Vincent Square, London, S.W.1.

Also at the **Chelsea Flower Show** (annually at the end of May), at the principal Provincial Agricultural Shows, and at some of the leading **International Shows** in Europe.

TREES & SHRUBS

This section does not include CLIMBERS, CONIFERS or BAMBOOS, which are listed under separate headings at the end of this manual.

---

* Indicates that the plant is evergreen.
† Indicates that the plant is too tender for exposed positions in all but the mildest localities, though most of them are hardy on walls, or when given evergreen, woodland, or similar protection.
‡ Indicates that the plant requires lime-free or neutral soil, and will not tolerate alkaline or chalky conditions.
× Indicates that the plant is of hybrid origin.
+ Indicates that the plant is a chimera (graft hybrid).
I Indicates the date of original introduction into Western Gardens.
C Indicates the first recorded date of cultivation where the exact date of introduction is not known.

Plants which have received **awards** from the Royal Horticultural Society, London, are referred to by the following letters:—

A.G.M.—Award of Garden Merit. (Instituted 1921).
A.M.—Award of Merit. (Instituted 1888).
A.M.T.—Award of Merit after trial at the R.H.S. Gardens, Wisley, Surrey.
F.C.C.—First Class Certificate. (Instituted 1859).
F.C.C.T.—First Class Certificate after trial at the R.H.S. Gardens, Wisley.

HEIGHTS

The eventual height of an individual tree or shrub is partly dependent on local conditions.

For the British Isles the following scales have been devised to give the probable range of each species growing under average conditions, but allowances must be made for specimens growing in shade, against walls and under exceptional circumstances.

Trees
Large—Over 18m. (Over 60ft.)
Medium—10 to 18m. (35 to 50ft.)
Small—4·5 to 9m. (15 to 30ft.)

Shrubs
Large—Over 3m. (Over 10ft.)
Medium—1·5 to 3m. (6 to 10ft.)
Small—1 to 1·5m. (3 to 5ft.)
Dwarf—·3 to ·6m. (1 to 2ft.)
Prostrate—Creeping

FLOWERING PERIODS

Flowering periods given in this manual should be taken as being approximate as they will vary slightly depending on the vagaries of the season.

ABELIA—**Caprifoliaceae**—Beautiful small to large summer and autumn flowering shrubs, revelling in full sun.

chinensis R.BR. A small shrub with fragrant white, rose tinted flowers, freely produced. July to August. C. and E. China. C. 1844. A.M. 1976.

'Edward Goucher' (*grandiflora* × *schumannii*). Small, semi-evergreen shrub having flowers similar in colour to *A. schumannii* and produced with the freedom of *A.* ×*grandiflora*. A first class shrub for the small garden.

†**floribunda** DCNE. A medium sized, semi-evergreen shrub producing abundant tubular flowers up to 5cm. long, of a brilliant cherry-red in June. Best against a warm wall. Mexico. I. 1841.

graebnerana REHD. A rare species of medium size; flowers apricot with yellow throat. C. China. I. 1910.

'Vedrariensis'. A form with larger leaves and broader blotches in the throat of the flower.

×**grandiflora** REHD. (*chinensis* × *uniflora*). A small to medium sized semi-evergreen shrub, carrying its pink and white flowers over a long period. July to September. Origin unknown. A.G.M. 1962.

schumannii REHD. A small shrub giving an abundant and continuous display of lilac-pink flowers during late summer. Subject to injury in very cold winters. W. China. I. 1910. A.M. 1926.

ABELIA—*continued*

serrata SIEB. & ZUCC. A dwarf to small shrub of slow growth; flowers white or blush, tinged orange, May to June. Not recommended for shallow chalk soils. Japan. I. 1879.

triflora R.BR. A large erect shrub of graceful habit. Flowers produced in June in threes in dense clusters, white tinged pink, and exquisitely scented. N.W. Himalaya. I. 1847. A.M. 1959.

umbellata REHD. Medium sized shrub of spreading habit. The pure white flowers are produced in early June. C. and W. China. I. 1907.

ABELIOPHYLLUM—**Oleaceae**—A monotypic genus related to *Fontanesia* and *Fraxinus*, but very different in appearance.

distichum NAKAI. A small shrub of slow growth. The fragrant white, pink tinged flowers are produced on the leafless stems during February. Korea. I. 1924. A.M. 1937. F.C.C. 1944.

ABUTILON—**Malvaceae**—Handsome small to large shrubs for a south wall or cool greenhouse. Flowers often large, bell-shaped or open and saucer-shaped, produced over a long season.

†**'Ashford Red'.** A medium sized shrub with large apple-green leaves and flowers of good texture, size and substance, best described as a deep shade of crushed strawberry. An outstanding plant.

'Margherita Maans'. See *A. ochsenii.*

megapotamicum ST.HIL. & NAUD. (*vexillarium*). A small to medium sized shrub for a warm wall. The conspicuous pendulous flowers have a red calyx, yellow petals and purple anthers. Summer and autumn. Brazil. I 1864. A.M. 1949.

'Variegatum'. Leaves with mottled, yellow variegation.

† × **milleri** HORT. (*megapotamicum* × *pictum*). A medium sized shrub. Flowers bell-shaped, orange, with crimson stamens; leaves dark green. Continuous flowering.

'Variegatum'. Leaves mottled yellow.

†**ochsenii** PHIL. ('*Margherita Maans*'). A medium to large, slender shrub for a sunny wall, with cup-shaped flowers of a lovely lavender-blue, darker at centre. Chile. I. about 1957. A.M. 1962.

× **suntense** BRICKELL (*ochsenii* × *vitifolium*). This vigorous, extremely floriferous hybrid has been produced by several sources. A.G.M. 1973. A.M. 1977 (to a white-flowered form). We offer the following clone:—

'Jermyns'. A deliberate cross made at our Winchester nursery in 1969, using the form of *A. vitifolium* known as '*Veronica Tennant*'. Flowers clear, dark mauve.

vexillarium. See *A. megapotamicum.*

vitifolium PRESL. A large, handsome shrub needing a sunny sheltered site. Flowers saucer-shaped, pale to deep·mauve. May to July. The vine-shaped leaves are downy and grey. Chile. I. 1836. F.C.C. 1888.

'Album'. Flowers white. A.M. 1961.

'Veronica Tennant'. A free-flowering selection with large, mauve flowers.

†***ACACIA**—**Leguminosae**—"Wattle". The acacias are mostly winter or spring-flowering cool-greenhouse shrubs with yellow blossoms, but several species attain tree size out-of-doors in favoured localities. Most become chlorotic on chalk soils. Unless otherwise stated, all are native of Australia.

armata R.BR. "Kangaroo Thorn". A small leaved prickly species of dense bushy habit. Masses of yellow flowers all along the branches. Spring. I. 1803.

baileyana F. MUELL. "Cootamundra Wattle". Small tree or large shrub with attractive glaucous leaves and racemes of bright yellow flowers freely produced. Winter and spring. I. 1888. A.M. 1927, F.C.C. 1936.

dealbata LINK. (*decurrens dealbata*). "Silver Wattle". A large shrub or small tree for a sheltered wall. The fern-like leaves are silvery green. Flowers produced in late winter to early spring, fragrant. The popular golden "Mimosa" of florists. I. 1820. A.M. 1935. F.C.C. 1971.

decurrens dealbata. See *A. dealbata.*

diffusa KER. A large, lax, genista-like shrub; sulphur yellow flowers in small heads. I. 1818. A.M. 1934.

'Exeter Hybrid' (*longifolia* × *riceana*) ('*Veitchiana*'). A beautiful medium to large sized shrub which arose as a seedling from *A. riceana*, and like that species bears narrow leaves and spikes of rich yellow flowers. Garden origin. A.M. 1961.

ACACIA—*continued*

longifolia WILLD. "Sidney Golden Wattle". Large shrub with long, lance-shaped leaves and bright yellow flowers in 4 to 8cm. spikes. One of the hardiest species, and fairly lime tolerant. I. 1792.

sophorae F. V. MUELL. Leaves somewhat shorter and broader. Moderately hardy in favoured areas.

melanoxylon R.BR. "Blackwood Acacia". A tree-like species allied to *A. longifolia*, but with pinnate, juvenile foliage. I. 1808.

mucronata WILLD. A large shrub related to and resembling *A. longifolia*, but with much narrower leaves. A.M. 1933.

pendula A. CUNN. "Weeping Myall". Small tree with pendulous stems and cylindrical panicles of yellow flowers.

rhetinodes SCHLECHT. A small tree with narrow willow-like leaves. Flowers freely carried in large, loose panicles during the summer. One of the most lime tolerant species. I. 1871. A.M. 1925.

riceana HENSLOW. A large shrub or small tree of graceful habit. Leaves needle-like; flowers pale yellow. Tasmania. A.M. 1926.

verticillata WILLD. "Prickly Moses". A large shrub or small tree with whorled needle-like leaves and cylindrical spikes of bright yellow flowers. I. 1780. A.M. 1926.

"ACACIA, FALSE". See *ROBINIA pseudoacacia.*

ACANTHOPANAX—Araliaceae—Trees or shrubs often with attractive fruits. Flowers rarely of ornamental value.

henryi HARMS. A large shrub producing large spherical heads of black fruits resembling giant blackberries. When in flower besieged by insects of many kinds. C. China. I. 1901.

pentaphyllus. See *A. sieboldianus.*

ricinifolius. See *KALOPANAX pictus.*

sieboldianus MAK. (*pentaphyllus*) (*spinosus* HORT. not MIQ.). A medium sized shrub with numerous erect stems and clusters of three to five-parted leaves, each cluster with a small curved prickle at its base. China. I. 1874.

'Variegatus'. Leaflets edged creamy-white.

simonii SCHNEID. A medium sized shrub with spiny stems and bristly leaves. China. I. 1901.

spinosus HORT. See *A. sieboldianus.*

ACER—Aceraceae—The "Maples" are an extensive and very ornamental genus, mostly very hardy and of easy culture. Those referred to as "Japanese Maples" will be found under *A. japonicum* and *A. palmatum*. Unless otherwise mentioned the flowers are not conspicuous.

acuminatum WALL. A small tree closely related to *A. papilio*. Leaves on scarlet petioles, usually three-lobed, the lobes with slender tail-like points. W. Himalaya.

amplum REHD. A small tree with polished, green stems. Leaves like those of the "Norway Maple", five-lobed, bronze when young. C. China. I. 1901.

‡**argutum** MAXIM. A small tree with elegant, five-lobed, pale green leaves, made conspicuous by the reticulate venation. Japan. I. 1881.

buergeranum MIQ. (*trifidum* HOOK. & ARN. not THUNB.). Small, bushy tree with three-lobed leaves. E. China and Korea. C. 1890.

†**campbellii** HOOK. f. & THOMS. Medium sized tree with palmately lobed leaves, often colouring well in autumn. Only succeeding in mildest areas. E. Himalaya and S.W. China. I. about 1851.

yunnanense. See *A. flabellatum yunnanense.*

campestre L. "Field Maple"; "Hedge Maple". A picturesque medium sized tree frequently used in rustic hedges; foliage turns clear yellow, sometimes flushed red, in autumn. Europe (incl. British Isles), W. Asia.

'Pulverulentum'. Leaves thickly speckled and blotched with white.

'Schwerinii'. A form with purple leaves.

capillipes MAXIM. A small tree with striated bark; young growths coral red. Attractive autumn tints. Japan. I. 1892. A.G.M. 1969. A.M. 1975.

ACER—*continued*

cappadocicum GLEDITSCH. (*laetum*). A medium sized to large tree with broad, five to seven-lobed, glossy leaves turning to rich butter-yellow in autumn. Caucasus and W. Asia to Himalaya. I. 1838.

'Aureum'. Young leaves red, turning golden yellow, remaining so for many weeks. A.G.M. 1969.

'Rubrum'. Young growths blood red. A most attractive form. I. 1838.

sinicum REHD. A very attractive variety with smaller, usually five-lobed leaves; young growths coppery-red. China. I. 1901. A.M. 1958.

carpinifolium SIEB. & ZUCC. "Hornbeam Maple". Small to medium sized tree with leaves remarkably like those of the "Common Hornbeam" but opposite, turning gold and brown in autumn. Japan. I. 1879.

caudatum. See *A. papilio.*

multiserratum. See *A. multiserratum.*

ukurunduense. See *A. ukurunduense.*

circinatum PURSH. "Vine Maple". A large shrub, or occasionally a small tree, with almost circular leaves prettily tinted in summer, and turning orange and crimson in autumn. The wine red and white flowers in April are quite decorative. Western N. America. I. 1826.

cissifolium K. KOCH. A small tree with trifoliolate, bronze-tinted leaves which turn to red and yellow in autumn. Similar to *A. henryi*. Not very tolerant of chalk soils. Japan. I. before 1870.

×**coriaceum** TAUSCH. (*monspessulanum*×*pseudoplatanus*). Small tree of neat, rounded habit with rather leathery, three-lobed leaves which are often retained well into winter. C. 1790.

crataegifolium SIEB. & ZUCC. A small tree or large shrub with prettily marked bark and small leaves of variable shape; flowers mustard yellow in slender racemes. Japan. I. 1879.

creticum. See *A. sempervirens.*

dasycarpum. See *A. saccharinum.*

davidii FRANCH. A small tree with attractively striated green and white bark. The shining, dark green, ovate leaves colour richly in the autumn. The green fruits are often attractively suffused red and hang all along the branches in autumn. C. China. I. 1879.

'Ernest Wilson'. Rare in cultivation. A more compact tree with branches ascending then arching. Leaves pale green, rather cup-shaped at base, petioles pink at first. The original form from W. Hupeh and W. Yunnan, introduced by Maries and later by E. H. Wilson and Kingdon Ward.

'George Forrest' (*'Horizontale'*). This is the form most commonly met with in cultivation. An open tree of loose habit with vigorous spreading branches and large dark green leaves with rhubarb-red stalks. Introduced by George Forrest from Yunnan in 1921-22. A.M. 1975 (for fruit).

diabolicum K. KOCH. "Horned Maple". A medium sized tree with large, five-lobed leaves, pendulous corymbs of yellow flowers in April and distinctive bristly, reddish fruits. Japan. I. 1880.

purpurascens REHD. A most ornamental tree, its branches in spring draped with innumerable drooping clusters of salmon-coloured flowers. Japan. C. 1878.

×**dieckii** PAX (*lobelii*×*platanoides*). A medium sized to large tree of rapid growth. Leaves large, five-lobed, turning to dark red-brown or old gold in the autumn. Garden origin.

distylum SIEB. & ZUCC. A medium-sized tree with undivided leaves, which when unfolding are attractively tinted cream and pink. Rich yellow autumn colour. Japan. I. 1879.

divergens PAX (*quinquelobum* K. KOCH not GILIB.). Large shrub or small tree with small, polished five or occasionally three-lobed leaves. Related to *A. campestre*. Transcaucasus. I. 1923.

erianthum SCHWER. A small tree with five to seven-lobed leaves marked beneath by white tufts of hair in the vein axils. Often abundant crops of attractive pink winged fruits. Not very tolerant of chalk soils. China. I. 1907.

ACER—*continued*

†**flabellatum** REHD. A small, shrubby tree, resembling *A. campbellii*. Leaves broadly palmate, seven to nine-lobed, the lobes sharply serrate. Not hardy enough for coldest areas. C. China. Introduced by Ernest Wilson in 1907.

yunnanense FANG. (*campbellii yunnanense*). A slender tree with deeply five-lobed leaves and red petioles.

forrestii DIELS. A most beautiful small tree with striated bark; young stems and petioles an attractive coral red. Not very tolerant of chalk soils. China. I. 1906.

franchetii PAX. A small, slow-growing tree with large three-lobed leaves, suggesting kinship with *A. villosum*. C. China. I. 1901.

ginnala MAXIM. A large shrub or small tree of vigorous, spreading habit. The bright green, three-lobed leaves turn to orange and vivid crimson in autumn. China, Manchuria and Japan. I. 1860.

semenowii PAX. Shrubby variety with smaller occasionally five-lobed leaves. Turkestan. C. 1880.

giraldii PAX. A medium sized to large tree, similar to *A. villosum* but differing in its bloomy young stems and leaves which have broader, less acuminate lobes, coarser serrations and are glaucous and reticulate beneath. Yunnan.

glabrum TORR. "Rock Maple". A large shrub or small tree of upright habit with variable leaves which may be three to five-lobed or trifoliolate. Western N. America. I. about 1884.

douglasii DIPP. A variety with three-lobed leaves. I. 1902.

grandidentatum NUTT. Usually a small, rather slow growing tree with three-lobed leaves. Allied to *A. saccharum*. Attractive autumn tints of red and orange. Western N. America, N. Mexico. I. 1882.

griseum PAX. "Paperbark Maple". One of the most beautiful of all small trees. Leaves trifoliolate, gorgeously coloured red and scarlet in autumn. Old bark on trunk and primary branches flakes and curls back to reveal the cinnamon-coloured underbark. C. China. I. by Wilson in 1901. A.M. 1922. A.G.M. 1936.

grosseri PAX. One of the most beautiful of the "Snake-bark" maples. A small tree, the leaves of which colour magnificently in autumn. C. China. I. about 1923.

hersii. See *A. hersii*.

heldreichii BOISS. A very handsome, medium sized tree. Distinct on account of its deeply cleft three-lobed leaves which almost resemble those of the "Virginia Creeper". S.E. Europe. I. 1879.

henryi PAX. A small to medium sized spreading tree, having stems marked with bluish striations; young leaves beautifully tinted, resembling those of *A. cissifolium*, but leaflets nearly entire. Flowers yellow, in slender drooping catkins appearing with the unfolding leaves. C. China. I. 1903.

hersii REHD. (*grosseri hersii*). A small tree with wonderfully marbled bark. Leaves with or without lobes. Fruits in conspicuous long racemes. Rich autumn colour. C. China. I. 1921. A.G.M. 1969.

× **hillieri** LANCASTER (*cappadocicum* × *miyabei*). Small tree with five-lobed leaves turning butter-yellow in autumn.

†**hookeri** MIQ. Medium sized, semi-evergreen tree with red young shoots and large, usually entire leaves. Only suitable for the mildest areas. E. Himalaya. I. 1892.

× **hybridum** SPACH (*monspessulanum* × *opalus*). A medium sized to large tree with three-lobed leaves and drooping panicles of yellow-green flowers in May.

hyrcanum FISCH & MEY. Small tree of compact habit and slow growth allied to *A. opalus*. S.E. Europe, Crimea, Caucasus and Asia Minor. C. 1865.

japonicum THUNB. A small tree or large bush with foliage of a soft green, beautifully coloured in autumn. Flowers red, appearing in delicate drooping clusters with the young leaves. There are a number of forms, and all do best in a moist well drained position sheltered from cold winds. Japan. I. 1864.

'Aconitifolium' (*'Laciniatum'*) (*'Filicifolium'*). Leaves deeply lobed and cut, colouring rich ruby-crimson in autumn. A.G.M. 1957.

'Aureum'. Soft yellow leaves; slow-growing. Scorches in full sun. F.C.C. 1884. A.G.M. 1969.

'Filicifolium'. See *'Aconitifolium'*.

'Laciniatum'. See *'Aconitifolium'*.

'Vitifolium'. Broad, fan-shaped leaves with ten to twelve lobes. An extremely beautiful form colouring brilliantly in the autumn. F.C.C. 1974 (for autumn foliage).

ACER—*continued*

laetum. See *A. cappadocicum.*

†**laevigatum** WALL. A small, semi-evergreen tree with smooth green shoots, bloomy when young. Leaves oblong-lanceolate, acuminate, 15cm. or more long, bright green and lustrous, reticulate beneath; adpressed serrate, at least when young. This species has been received from various sources as *A. fargesii.* Himalaya, China. I. 1907.

laxiflorum PAX. A rare small tree with striated bark and dark green leaves. Inclined to be calcifuge. W. China. I. 1908.

leucoderme SMALL. A small tree with three to five-lobed leaves. Allied to *A. saccharum.* Lovely autumn tints. S.E. United States. C. 1900.

lobelii TEN. A medium to large tree related to *A. platanoides* and *A. cappadocicum.* It is distinguished by its habit of ascending branches, forming a compact, pyramidal head, broadening with age, well-furnished with rich green, palmate leaves. S. Italy. C. 1838.

macrophyllum PURSH. "Oregon Maple". A large tree with very large, handsome, dark, shining green leaves which turn a bright orange in the autumn. A striking tree for foliage and fruit effect. Western N. America. I. 1826.

mandshuricum MAXIM. A large shrub or small tree with trifoliolate leaves and red petioles. Allied to *A. nikoense* but leaves glabrous. Rich autumn colour. Manchuria, Korea. C. 1904.

maximowiczii PAX. An attractive small tree with striated stems and three or five-lobed leaves, which are attractively red tinted throughout the growing season, becoming more colourful as autumn approaches. C. China. I. 1910.

micranthum SIEB. & ZUCC. A large shrub or small tree. The small, five-lobed leaves are beautifully tinted throughout the growing season. Autumn foliage usually red. Japan. I. 1879.

miyabei MAXIM. A small to medium sized tree of rounded habit. The large, three to five-lobed leaves recall those of the "Norway Maple". Japan. I. 1892.

mono MAXIM. (*pictum*). A medium sized tree with palmately five to seven-lobed leaves, which usually turn bright yellow in autumn. Japan, China, Manchuria, Korea. I. 1881.

ambiguum REHD. A rare variety with leaves minutely downy beneath. Autumn colour usually yellow. Origin unknown. C. 1892.

tricuspis REHD. A variety with smaller, three-lobed, rather persistent, leaves. C. China. I. 1901.

monspessulanum L. "Montpelier Maple". Usually a small tree of neat habit; occasionally shrubby. In general appearance it resembles our native field maple but the three-lobed leaves are perfectly glabrous and glaucous beneath, and the stalks do not possess the milky juice of the common species. South Europe, West Asia. I. 1739.

multiserratum MAXIM. (*caudatum multiserratum*). A small tree with downy shoots and five to seven-lobed leaves, downy beneath. China. I. 1907.

neglectum. See *A.* ×*zoeschense.*

negundo L. "Box Elder". A fast-growing, bushy-headed tree of medium to large size. The young shoots are bright green and the leaves are pinnate with three to five, sometimes seven to nine, leaflets of a bright green above, paler beneath. A very popular Maple. North America. C. 1688.

'Auratum'. Leaves bright golden yellow. A.M. 1901.

californicum SARG. A form with downy shoots, large trifoliolate leaves and attractive pendulous racemes of pink-winged fruits. California. C. 1865.

'Elegans' (*'Elegantissimum'*). Leaves with bright yellow marginal variegation. Young shoots with white bloom. F.C.C. 1898.

'Variegatum' (*'Argenteovariegatum'*). Leaves with broad, irregular white margin. A most effective tree but tends to revert if not carefully pruned. A.G.M. 1973.

violaceum JAEG. Young shoots purple or violet covered by a white bloom. Leaflets usually five to seven. An attractive tree in spring when draped with its long pendulous reddish-pink flower tassels. A.M. 1975.

nigrum MICHX. f. (*saccharum nigrum*). A medium to large tree with deeply furrowed bark and large three sometimes five-lobed leaves of a dull, dark green, turning yellow in autumn. Eastern N. America. I. 1812.

ACER—*continued*

nikoense MAXIM. "Nikko Maple". A very hardy and beautiful tree of small to medium size. The hairy, trifoliolate leaves, glaucous beneath, turn a glorious orange and flame in autumn. Now a rare tree in its native lands. Japan. C. China. I. 1881. F.C.C. 1971.

†**oblongum** DC. A small tree or large shrub suitable only for mild areas. The oblong, semi-persistent leaves are entire though sometimes three-lobed on young trees, glabrous above, glaucous beneath. Himalaya, C. and W. China. I. 1824.

concolor PAX. Leaves green on both sides. Our stock is a hardier form introduced by Ernest Wilson from China.

oliveranum PAX. A handsome species forming a large shrub or small tree. Leaves five-lobed, somewhat resembling *A. palmatum* but cleaner cut. C. China. I. 1901.

opalus MILL. "Italian Maple". A medium sized tree of rounded habit with shallowly five-lobed leaves which are glabrous above, downy, occasionally glabrous beneath. The yellow flowers are conspicuous and appear in crowded corymbs on the leafless stems in March. S. Europe. I. 1752. A.M. 1967.

obtusatum HENRY. A variety with usually larger leaves softly downy beneath, the lobes short and rounded. S.E. Europe and Italy. I. 1805.

orientale. See *A. sempervirens.*

† × **osmastonii** GAMBLE (*campbellii* × *laevigatum*). Small tree, the young shoots covered by a conspicuous almost chalky white bloom changing to white striations on the pale green older bark. Leaves large, deeply five-lobed green on both surfaces, purplish when unfolding, petioles red.

palmatum THUNB. "Japanese Maple". Generally a large shrub or small tree with a low, rounded head. Leaves five or seven-lobed of a bright green. Japan, C. China, Korea. I. 1820. A.G.M. 1969.

Many cultivars have been raised from this species, which exhibit a wide range of forms both in leaf and habit. The majority attain the size of a large bush or occasionally a small tree, and give gorgeous red, orange or yellow autumnal colours. Though the type and certain stronger forms will tolerate chalk soils, the "Japanese Maples" are at their best in a moist but well drained loam, sheltered from cold winds especially from the east.

'Albomarginatum' (*'Argenteomarginatum'*). Leaves smaller than those of the type, green with a white marginal variegation. Liable to revert.

'Atropurpureum'. The most popular "Japanese Maple". A striking colour form; leaves bronzy crimson throughout the summer. A.G.M. 1928.

'Aureum'. Leaves suffused soft yellow becoming golden yellow in summer.

'Chitoseyama'. A superb clone with deeply cut greenish-bronze leaves which colour richly in autumn. Old plants possess a dense mound-like habit with gracefully drooping branches.

'Corallinum'. A rarely seen, most distinct cultivar of slow growth, forming a compact small shrub. Young stems soft coral pink; leaves usually less than 5cm. long, five-lobed, bright shrimp-pink when unfolding, changing to pale mottled green by midsummer.

coreanum NAKAI. A geographical form; leaves becoming rich crimson in autumn, lasting longer than most.

'Crippsii'. A slow-growing elegant form with bronze-red leaves finely cut into grasslike segments. A plant of weak constitution. A.M. 1903.

(**Dissectum Group**). A group of clones in which the leaves are divided to the base into five, seven or nine pinnatifid lobes. They are generally shrubby in habit, mushroom-shaped when young, ultimately a dense, rounded bush, the branches falling from a high crown.

'Dissectum'. Leaves green. A.G.M. 1956.

'Dissectum Atropurpureum'. Leaves deep purple. A.G.M. 1969.

'Dissectum Flavescens'. Leaves soft, yellow-green in spring.

'Dissectum Ornatum'. Leaves bronze tinted.

'Dissectum Palmatifidum'. More finely cut foliage than *'Dissectum'*, but not very constant. F.C.C. 1869.

'Dissectum Variegatum'. Leaves bronze-red, some tipped pink and cream.

'Flavescens'. See *'Reticulatum'*.

(**Heptalobum Group**) (*Septemlobum Group*). A group of clones having leaves larger than those of the type, and usually seven-lobed, the lobes finely doubly serrate, broadest about the middle.

ACER pseudoplatanus 'Brilliantissimum'
(*Young foliage*)

ARBUTUS unedo 'Rubra'

ABUTILON × suntense 'Jermyns'

AUCUBA japonica 'Salicifolia'

ANDROMEDA polifolia 'Compacta'

Colourful foliage of CALLUNA among dwarf conifers

CORNUS kousa chinensis

CALLISTEMON citrinus 'Splendens'

ACER—*continued*

palmatum 'Heptalobum Elegans'. Leaves up to 13cm. long, green, deeply and attractively toothed.

'Heptalobum Elegans Purpureum'. Leaves dark bronze crimson.

'Heptalobum Lutescens'. Leaves glossy green turning clear butter-yellow in autumn.

'Heptalobum Osakazuki'. Leaves green, turning in autumn to fiery scarlet, probably the most brilliant of all "Japanese Maples". A.G.M. 1969.

'Heptalobum Rubrum'. Large leaves blood-red in spring, paling towards late summer.

'Heptalobum Rufescens'. A distinct, wide-spreading shrub with broad, deeply cleft leaves, green in summer and attractively tinted in autumn.

koreanum. See *coreanum.*

'Linearilobum' (*'Scolopendrifolium'*). Leaves divided to the base into long, narrow, remotely serrate lobes. A.M. 1896.

'Linearilobum Atropurpureum'. Leaves bronze-red.

'Nigrum'. A form with leaves of deep purple.

'Reticulatum' (*'Flavescens'*). Leaves soft yellow green with green margins and dark veins.

'Ribesifolium' (*'Shishigashira'*). A slow growing form of distinctive upright growth almost fastigiate but with a broad crown. Leaves dark green, deeply cut, changing to old gold in autumn.

'Roseomarginatum'. Leaves pale green, irregularly edged with coral pink, Charming but not constant and liable to revert. F.C.C. 1865.

'Senkaki' (*'Sangokaku'*). "Coral Bark Maple". An invaluable shrub or small tree for winter effect, all the younger branches being of a conspicuous and attractive coral-red. Leaves turning soft canary-yellow in autumn. A.M. 1950. A.G.M. 1969.

'Septemlobum'. See *Heptalobum Group.*

'Sessilifolium' (*'Decompositum'*). A small tree of erect habit with short stalked, deeply cut leaves colouring well in autumn.

'Shishigashira'. See *'Ribesifolium'*.

'Versicolor'. Leaves green with white, pink-tinged blotches and spots. Liable to revert.

papilio KING (*caudatum*). A medium-sized tree with glabrous shoots and five-lobed, coarsely-toothed leaves, downy beneath. E. Himalaya.

†**paxii** FRANCH. A small, striking, semi-evergreen tree with three-lobed leathery leaves, glaucous beneath. China.

pensylvanicum L. (*striatum*). A small tree, young stems green, beautifully striped with white and pale jade green. Leaves up to 18cm. across, three-lobed, turning bright yellow in the autumn. Not very tolerant of chalk soils. Eastern N. America. I. 1755.

'Erythrocladum'. A lovely form in which the young shoots in winter are shrimp pink with pale striations. A plant of weak constitution. A.M. 1976. F.C.C. 1977.

pentaphyllum DIELS. A rare, handsome species making a small tree. Leaves on long, slender scarlet petioles, divided to the base into five linear-lanceolate segments which are green above, glaucous and reticulate below. China. I. 1929.

pictum. See *A. mono.*

platanoides L. "Norway Maple". A handsome, fast-growing tree of large size. The conspicuous clusters of yellow flowers are produced on the bare stems in April, usually following those of *A. opalus.* In autumn the foliage turns a clear bright yellow, occasionally red. Europe, Caucasus. Long cultivated. A.M. 1967. A.G.M. 1969.

'Columnare'. A large erect form of columnar habit.

'Crimson King'. A large, handsome tree; leaves of a deep crimson-purple. A.G.M. 1969.

'Cucullatum'. A large, erect tree. Leaves fan-shaped, with seven or nine pointed lobes. Similar in effect to *'Laciniatum'* but lobes not as pointed.

'Dissectum' (*'Palmatifidum'*). Almost identical with *'Lorbergii'*, but leaves darker green and lobes with crinkled margins and straight points. A.G.M. 1969.

'Drummondii'. A very striking cultivar, which tends to revert; leaves with a marginal white band. A.M. 1956. A.G.M. 1969.

'Erectum'. An erect usually slow growing cultivar of medium size with short ascending branches.

ACER—*continued*

platanoides 'Globosum'. A striking small tree, the short branches forming a dense mop-shaped head.

'Laciniatum'. "Eagle's Claw Maple". An erect growing, large tree, the leaves, smaller than in the type, are wedge-shaped at the base and have lobes reduced to claw-like points.

'Lorbergii'. Medium sized tree; leaves palmately divided, pale green; the lobes with entire margins and long pointed tips ascending from the leaf plane. A.G.M. 1969.

'Palmatifidum'. See '*Dissectum*'.

'Reitenbachii'. A medium sized tree. Leaves red on emerging, gradually turning to green and finally assuming red autumn tints.

'Schwedleri'. Leaves and young growths rich crimson-purple. Most effective when pruned hard every other autumn.

'Walderseei'. An unusual form in which the leaves are densely speckled with white flecks, greyish from a distance. A tree of rather weak constitution.

pseudoplatanus L. "Sycamore". A picturesque large tree, and one of the best for exposed situations in any soil. Long planted and naturalized in many parts of the British Isles. Native of Europe and W. Asia.

'Atropurpureum' ('*Purpureum Spaethii*'). A selected form with leaves purple beneath.

'Brilliantissimum'. A distinctive small tree of slow growth. The young leaves in spring are a glorious shrimp-pink later changing to pale yellow-green and finally green. A.M. 1925. A.G.M. 1973. F.C.C. 1977.

'Corstorphinense'. "Corstorphine Plane". This tree does not differ materially in leaf colour or otherwise from the common sycamore. Its interest is purely historical.

'Erectum' ('*Fastigiatum*'). A large tree with erect branches.

erythrocarpum PAX. A form with conspicuous and attractive red seed wings.

'Fastigiatum'. See '*Erectum*'.

'Leopoldii'. Leaves yellowish-pink at first, later green, speckled and splashed yellow and pink. F.C.C. 1865.

'Luteovirens'. Leaves variously marked yellow and cream.

'Nizetii'. Leaves heavily marked yellow and white, suffused pink, purplish beneath.

'Prinz Handjery'. A small slow growing tree similar to '*Brilliantissimum*' but slightly larger, and with leaves purple tinged beneath. F.C.C. 1890.

purpureum REHD. A large pictorial tree, the under-surfaces of the leaves being conspicuously coloured purple; effective in a breeze.

'Purpureum Spaethii'. See '*Atropurpureum*'.

'Simon-Louis Freres'. Leaves variegated with cream and purple; slow growing.

'Worleei'. "Golden Sycamore". Medium sized tree. Leaves soft yellow-green at first then golden, finally green.

quinquelobum K. KOCH. See *A. divergens*.

‡**rubrum** L. "Red Maple", "Canadian Maple". A free-growing, ultimately large tree. The palmate leaves are dark green above, glaucous beneath and turn rich red and scarlet in autumn. Although fairly lime-tolerant, it rarely colours as well on chalky soils. Eastern N. America. C. 1656. A.M. 1969.

'Columnare'. Eventually a tall tree of broad columnar habit. C. 1889

'Scanlon'. A medium-sized tree of American origin eventually, forming a broadly columnar, conical head of branches. Rich autumn colour.

'Schlesingeri'. A clone notable for its outstanding autumn colour which is a rich deep scarlet. C. 1888. A.M. 1976.

rufinerve SIEB. & ZUCC. A medium sized tree; young stems glaucous, older stems and trunk green with conspicuous white striations. Leaves three-lobed, recalling those of *A. pensylvanicum*. Bright red and yellow autumn colours. Japan. I. 1879.

albolimbatum SCHWER. Leaves mottled or margined white. Not always constant.

saccharinum L. (*dasycarpum*) (*eriocarpum*). "Silver Maple". A large, fast growing tree. Leaves deeply five-lobed, silvery-white beneath, creating a delightful effect when ruffled by the wind. Attractive autumn tints. Eastern N. America. I. 1725.

'Fastigiatum'. See '*Pyramidale*'.

laciniatum REHD. A graceful tree with pendulous branchlets and finely and deeply cut leaves.

'Lutescens'. Leaves soft yellow-green during summer.

'Pendulum'. A form with somewhat pendulous branches.

'Pyramidale' ('*Fastigiatum*'). An upright-growing form.

ACER—*continued*

saccharum MARSH. "Sugar Maple". An ornamental, ultimately large tree resembling the "Norway Maple". One of America's finest autumn-colouring trees. Orange, gold, scarlet and crimson being exhibited by different individuals. C. and E. North America. I. 1735.

'Temple's Upright' (*'Monumentale'*). A striking but exceedingly slow-growing form of columnar habit, in autumn turning into a pillar of orange. C. 1885.

sempervirens L. (*creticum*) (*orientale*). "Cretan Maple". A slow-growing large shrub or small tree. The leaves are of various shapes, ovate and entire to three-lobed, up to 4cm. long, glabrous and bright green and often retained until Christmas. Related to *A. monspessulanum*. E. Mediterranean Region. I. 1752.

sieboldianum MIQ. A small tree or large shrub similar to *A. japonicum* but flowers yellow not red and leaves finely toothed. Japan. C. 1880. A.M. 1966.

spicatum LAM. "Mountain Maple". A small tree or large shrub. Leaves three, sometimes five-lobed, colouring red and yellow in autumn. Flowers in erect racemes, later replaced by attractive red fruits. Not very tolerant of chalk soils. C. and E. North America. I. 1750.

stachyophyllum HIERN. A rare, small tree, the young shoots and petioles flushed scarlet. Leaves ovate, sharply three-lobed and dentate, ending in a long point. E. Himalaya, W. China.

sterculiaceum WALL. (*villosum*) WALL. A remarkable tree with very large palmately lobed leaves, and drooping clusters of large fruits. Often gives good autumn colour. Himalaya. I. before 1850.

striatum. See *A. pensylvanicum*.

syriacum BOISS. & GAILL. A large shrub or small bushy tree with ovate-entire or three-lobed leaves. Syria, Cyprus. C. 1903.

tataricum L. "Tatarian Maple". A large shrub or small tree of spreading habit. The leaves are dull, pale green and doubly toothed, tapering to a slender point. On young plants and vigorous shoots they may be lobed and resemble those of *A. ginnala*. Flowers greenish-white, produced in erect panicles in May and June. S.E. Europe, Asia Minor. I. 1759.

tetramerum PAX. Medium sized tree of graceful habit with ovate, incisely serrate leaves. China. I. 1901.

trautvetteri MEDWED. A medium-sized tree with large, deeply five-lobed leaves; flowers in upright panicles. A handsome foliage tree. Caucasus. I. 1866. A.M. 1975.

trifidum HOOK. & ARN. See *A. buergeranum*.

triflorum KOMAR. A very rare, slow-growing, small tree related and similar to *A. nikoense*, but with characteristic dark brown, furrowed bark. Leaves trifoliolate, glaucous beneath. One of the most consistent small trees for the brilliance of its autumn colour. Manchuria, Korea. I. 1923.

truncatum BGE. A small, round headed tree bearing five to seven-lobed leaves which are truncate or occasionally heart-shaped at the base. China. I. 1881.

tschonoskii MAXIM. A very rare, small tree or large shrub with five-lobed leaves which turn a lovely colour in autumn. Not very tolerant of chalk soils. Japan. I. 1902.

turkestanicum PAX. A large shrub or small bushy tree with three to five-lobed leaves. W. Asia.

ukurunduense TRAUTV. & MEY. (*caudatum ukurunduense*). A small tree with five-lobed leaves, deeply veined and pubescent beneath. Colourful autumn tints. Not very tolerant of chalk soils. E. Asia.

velutinum vanvolxemii REHD. A large tree remarkable for its enormous leaves which are three to five-lobed. Caucasus, N. Persia. I. 1873.

villosum. See *A. sterculiaceum*.

†**wardii** W.W.SM. A small, semi-evergreen tree with bloomy young stems, and oblong-lanceolate, slender pointed leaves which are similar to those of *A. laevigatum* but are more prominently veined, and with axillary tufts of hair beneath.

wilsonii REHD. A large shrub, or sometimes a small tree. Leaves generally three-lobed, occasionally with two small basal lobes, glabrous. Young foliage bright shrimp to coral pink, passing with age to soft pale green. S.W. China. I. 1907.

× **zoeschense** PAX. (*neglectum* LANGE not HOFFMANNS.) A medium-sized tree with five-lobed dark green, somewhat purple-tinged leaves. Clearly a hybrid of *A. campestre* but leaves larger and more angular. Garden origin.

***†ACRADENIA—Rutaceae**—A monotypic Tasmanian genus.

frankliniae KIPP. The only species of the genus; a small evergreen Tasmanian shrub succeeding well in mild areas. Dark green trifoliolate leaves and flat clusters of white flowers in May. I. 1845.

"ADAM'S NEEDLE". See *YUCCA gloriosa.*

***ADENOCARPUS—Leguminosae**—Very leafy, evergreen shrubs with broom-like, golden-yellow flowers. Natives of the Mediterranean Region.

†anagyrifolius leiocarpus MAIRE. Small to medium sized shrub with glandular stems and slightly glaucous trifoliolate leaves. Golden-yellow pea flowers in summer. Morocco.

decorticans BOISS. Essentially a shrub for a sunny wall. Vigorous, densely clothed with trifoliolate leaves. Flowering in May and June. A.M. 1947.

†foliosus DC. A small shrub with small hairy leaves densely crowded along the stems and numerous short, dense terminal racemes of yellow pea flowers in Spring.

AEGLE sepiaria. See *PONCIRUS trifoliata.*

AESCULUS—Hippocastanaceae—"Horse Chestnut"; "Buckeye". These are among the most ornamental of late spring and early summer flowering trees. All have compound, palmate leaves, and flowers in racemes, and all are easily cultivated, thriving in any soil.

arguta BUCKL. Small shrubby tree related to *A. glabra* but leaves with seven to nine leaflets which are deeply double toothed. Flowers soft cream. Oklahoma, Texas (U.S.A.). I. 1909.

×bushii SCHNEID. (*discolor×glabra*). A small to medium sized tree with individual flowers of red, pink and yellow in May or June. Mississippi, Arkansas (U.S.A.).

californica NUTT. A low, wide-spreading tree or shrub. The fragrant white or pink-tinted flowers are borne in dense, erect panicles up to 20cm. long. California. I. about 1850.

×carnea HAYNE (*hippocastanum×pavia*) (*rubicunda*). "Red Horse Chestnut". A large tree, much used for avenues and parks. Flowers rose-pink in panicles up to 20cm. long.

'Briotii'. A compact form with deeper coloured flowers. A.M. 1965.

'Plantierensis' (×*carnea*×*hippocastanum*). A sterile, pink flowered hybrid the result of a back-cross.

chinensis BGE. The "Chinese Horse Chestnut" is a very distinct small, slow-growing and rare tree with white flowers carried in long cylindrical racemes. N. China. I. 1912.

flava SOLAND. (*octandra*). "Sweet Buckeye". A medium sized or large tree; flowers nearest to yellow in a "Horse Chestnut"; leaves usually give good autumn tints. S.E. United States. I. 1764.

georgiana. See *A. neglecta georgiana.*

glabra WILLD. "Ohio Buckeye". A small tree with cream coloured flowers and good autumn leaf colour. S.E. and C. United States. C. 1809.

pallida SCHELLE. Habit of branching more erect. I. 1812.

glaucescens SARG. A small, slow-growing tree with yellow-green flowers and leaves glaucescent beneath. S.E. United States.

hippocastanum L. "Common Horse Chestnut". Possibly the most beautiful of large flowering trees hardy in the British Isles. Exceptionally attractive when covered with its stout "candles" of white flowers in May. Providing the familiar "conkers" of children's games in autumn. Native of the wild border region between Greece and Albania. I. into W. Europe in 1576 and to the British Isles early in the 17th century.

'Baumannii' (*'Flore Pleno'*). Flowers double, white; does not set seed.

'Flore Pleno'. See *'Baumannii'.*

laciniata SCHELLE. A slow-growing form with leaves narrowly, deeply and irregularly incised.

'Pumila'. A curious dwarf form with smaller, deeply incised leaves.

'Pyramidalis'. An unusual form of broadly pyramidal habit.

×hybrida DC. (*flava×pavia*) (*lyonii*) (*versicolor*). Small to medium-sized tree producing red and yellow flowers in panicles 10 to 18cm. long.

indica HOOK. "Indian Horse Chestnut". A magnificent large tree with panicles of pink-flushed flowers, occasionally as much as 40cm. long and 13cm. wide, in June and July. N.W. Himalaya. I. 1851. A.M. 1922. F.C.C. 1933. A.G.M. 1969.

'Sydney Pearce'. A free-flowering form of upright habit, with dark olive-green leaves. Flowers in large panicles with individual blossoms up to 2·5cm. across, petals white, marked yellow and prettily suffused pink. Raised at Kew in 1928. A.M. 1967. A.G.M. 1969.

AESCULUS—*continued*

× **mississippiensis** SARG. (*glabra* × *pavia*). Small tree with flowers dark red and yellow, the stamens protruding beyond the petals.

× **mutabilis** SCHELLE (*discolor mollis* × *neglecta*). A large shrub or small tree with red and yellow flowers in May and June.

'Harbisonii'. Flowers bright red.

'Induta' (*'Rosea Nana'*). Flowers apricot with yellow markings during summer. A.M. 1959.

neglecta LINDL. A medium sized tree bearing panicles of pale yellow flowers in May and June. Rich autumn colour. S.E. United States. C. 1826.

'Erythroblastos'. A slow-growing form in which the young leaves are a brilliant shrimp-pink changing to a pale yellow-green later in the season. A.M. 1962.

georgiana SARG. (*A. georgiana*). A shrubby form with broader and denser panicles of orange-red flowers. S.E. United States. I. 1905.

octandra. See *A. flava.*

parviflora WALT. (*Pavia macrostachya*). A spreading shrub 2·5m. or more high, flowering freely in July and August. Flowers white, with red anthers, in panicles 20 to 30cm. long. Leaves attractively coloured in autumn. S.E. United States. I. 1785. A.M. 1955. A.G.M. 1969.

pavia L. (*Pavia rubra*). "Red Buckeye". A beautiful small tree; flowers crimson, in panicles 15cm. long, opening in June. S. United States. I. 1711.

'Atrosanguinea'. Flowers a little deeper red.

'Humilis'. Of low, spreading growth; flowers red.

splendens SARG. A shrubby species, with long panicles of scarlet flowers in May. Perhaps the handsomest of the "Buckeyes".

turbinata BL. "Japanese Horse Chestnut". A large tree with outsize foliage attractively veined and tinted in autumn. Flowers in long panicles, yellowish-white with a red spot, appearing in June, a little later than those of *A. hippocastanum*. Japan. I. before 1880.

wilsonii REHD. A very rare tree with larger leaves than those of *A. chinensis.* Introduced by Wilson from China in 1908.

AGAPETES serpens. See *PENTAPTERYGIUM serpens.*

AILANTHUS—Simaroubaceae—Handsome, fast-growing trees with large, pinnate leaves. Extremely tolerant of atmospheric pollution.

altissima SWINGLE (*glandulosa*). "Tree of Heaven". A large imposing tree with distinct ash-like leaves which on young specimens are up to 1m. long. Female trees produce large conspicuous bunches of reddish "key"-like fruits. N. China. I. 1751. A.M. 1953.

'Pendulifolia'. A graceful tree with very large drooping leaves.

giraldii DODE. A large tree similar to *A. altissima* but leaves larger with more numerous and closer spaced leaflets. China.

glandulosa. See *A. altissima.*

vilmoriniana DODE. Very close to *A. altissima* from which it differs in the occasional bristly shoots, and sometimes rich red rachis. China. I. 1897.

ALANGIUM—Alangiaceae—Slow-growing, eventually tall shrubs with broad palmate leaves and small white flowers shaped like a miniature lily.

chinense HARMS. Handsome shrub with large maple-like leaves. The fragrant flowers have six recurved petals and open in June and July. They are about 3cm. long and carried in cymes. E. Asia. I. 1805.

platanifolium HARMS. Large shrub with three to five, occasionally seven-lobed leaves and cymes of white, yellow-anthered flowers in June and July. Japan, China; Korea; Manchuria; Formosa. I. 1879.

ALBIZIA—Leguminosae—Deciduous mimosa-like shrubs or small trees valuable for their handsome foliage and attractive fluffy heads of flowers. Full sun.

julibrissin DURAZZ. The hardiest species; flower heads pink, produced in summer. Withstands severe frost. Iran to China; Formosa. I. 1745.

'Rosea'. The dense heads of fluffy flowers are bright pink. Hardier than the type.

†**lophantha** BENTH. A large shrub or small tree with beautiful pinnate or doubly pinnate foliage and sulphur-yellow bottle-brush-like racemes of flowers, produced in spring or earlier under glass. Only suitable for the mildest localities. W. Australia. I. 1803.

"ALDER". See *ALNUS.*

"ALLSPICE". See *CALYCANTHUS.*

"ALMOND". See *PRUNUS dulcis.*

ALNUS (*ALNOBETULA* in part)—**Betulaceae**—The "Alders" will grow in almost any soil, except very shallow chalk soils, and are particularly useful for damp situations. The most lime tolerant species are *A. cordata, A. glutinosa* and *A. viridis.* Male and female flowers are borne on the same plant.

cordata DESF. (*cordifolia*). "Italian Alder". A splendid medium to large-sized conical-shaped tree for all types of soil, growing rapidly even on chalk soils; and notable for its bright green, glistening foliage. Corsica and South Italy. I. 1820. A.M. 1976.

crispa mollis FERN. "American Green Alder". A medium-sized shrub with downy young shoots. Leaves bright green, ovate or broad elliptic, pubescent beneath and sticky to the touch when young. N.E. North America. I. 1897.

firma SIEB. & ZUCC. A densely branched small tree or large shrub with occasionally downy branches and ovate, acuminate, sharply toothed leaves often remaining green until late autumn. Japan. The following variety is the plant most often cultivated.

hirtella FRANCH. & SAV. A graceful variety making a large shrub or small tree with handsome hornbeam-like foliage. Japan. I. 1894.

glutinosa GAERTN. "Common Alder". A small to medium sized bushy tree with sticky young growths and yellow catkins in March. Once used extensively in the manufacture of clogs in the north of England. Europe (incl. British Isles), W. Asia, North Africa.

'Aurea'. Leaves pale yellow, particularly noticeable in spring and early summer. F.C.C. 1867.

'Fastigiata'. See *'Pyramidalis'.*

'Imperialis'. An attractive form with deeply and finely cut leaves. A.M. 1973.

incisa KOEHNE. Leaves small, deeply cut or pinnate with broad, rounded, dentate lobes.

'Laciniata'. A stronger growing form of stiffer habit, leaves not so finely divided as those of *'Imperialis'.*

'Pyramidalis' (*'Fastigiata'*). A form with branches at an acute angle making a narrowly pyramidal tree.

hirsuta RUPR. (*tinctoria*). A medium sized tree similar in many respects to *A. incana* but the leaves are generally larger and more deeply lobed. N.E. Asia and Japan. I. 1879.

incana MOENCH. "Grey Alder". An exceptionally hardy tree or large shrub with leaves grey beneath. Ideal for cold or wet situations. Europe, Caucasus, E. North America. I. 1780.

'Acuminata'. See *'Laciniata'.*

'Aurea'. Young shoots and foliage yellow and catkins conspicuously red-tinted. A.G.M. 1973.

'Laciniata' (*'Acuminata'*). Leaves dissected. F.C.C. 1873.

'Pendula'. A handsome small tree forming a large mound of pendulous branches and grey-green leaves.

'Ramulis Coccineis'. This attractive tree does not appear to differ from *'Aurea'*, which see.

vulgaris SPACH. Large shrub or small tree with leaves pubescent beneath. The typical European form. Europe, Caucasus.

japonica SIEB. & ZUCC. A striking species in time making a medium sized to large tree. Leaves elliptic, relatively narrow and pointed. Korea, Manchuria, Japan, Formosa. I. before 1880.

maximowiczii CALLIER. A large shrub with rather thick twigs, broad leaves and clusters of short, fat, yellow catkins in late spring. Japan, Kamtchatka, Korea. I. 1914.

nitida ENDL. "Himalayan Alder". Medium sized tree with ovate, normally entire leaves. Distinct on account of its long male catkins being produced in autumn. N.W. Himalaya. I. 1882.

oregona. See *A. rubra.*

orientalis DCNE. "Oriental Alder". Medium-sized tree with sticky buds, glossy green, ovate, coarsely toothed leaves and clusters of yellow catkins in March. Syria, Cilicia, Cyprus. I. 1924.

rhombifolia NUTT. "White Alder". Medium sized to large tree of spreading habit with often diamond-shaped leaves. Western N. America. I. 1895.

ALNUS—*continued*

rubra BONG. (*oregona*). Medium sized, fast growing tree of graceful habit festooned in spring with the 10 to 15cm. long male catkins. Leaves large. Western N. America. I. before 1880.

rugosa HORT. See *A. serrulata*.

serrulata WILLD. (*rugosa* HORT.). "Smooth Alder". A large shrub or small tree with long catkins in spring before the leaves appear, related to *A. incana* but differing in its obovate leaves, green beneath. E. United States. I. 1769.

sinuata RYDB. (*sitchensis*). "Sitka Alder". A small tree or large shrub with broad leaves. The male catkins are conspicuous, up to 13cm. long, hanging in great profusion. Western N. America, E. Asia. I. 1903.

sitchensis. See *A. sinuata*.

×**spaethii** CALLIER (*japonica*×*subcordata*). A tree of medium size, with large leaves. Outstanding when in catkin. Garden origin.

subcordata C. A. MEY. "Caucasian Alder". A fast growing medium sized to large tree with broad leaves up to 15cm. long. Caucasus, Iran. I. 1838.

tenuifolia NUTT. Small tree or large shrub with oval leaves, cordate or rounded at the base. Western N. America. I. 1891.

tinctoria. See *A. hirsuta*.

viridis DC. "Green Alder". A medium sized to large shrub forming a clump of long, erect, hazel-like stems. The common alder of the Central European Alps. Europe, N. Asia. I. 1820.

ALOYSIA. See *LIPPIA*.

AMELANCHIER—Rosaceae—"Snowy Mespilus", "June Berry". A beautiful genus of very hardy small trees or shrubs, mainly natives of North America, thriving in moist, well drained, lime free soils, the most lime-tolerant species being *A. alnifolia, A. asiatica, A. florida* and *A. ovalis*. The abundant racemes of white flowers are produced in spring before the leaves are fully developed. The foliage is often richly coloured in the autumn.

alnifolia NUTT. A medium sized shrub with rounded leaves. Short, dense, terminal racemes of flowers in spring, followed by black fruits. Western N. America. I. 1918.

asiatica WALP. An elegant large shrub flowering in May and intermittently over a long period. Fruits like black currants. China. I. 1865.

canadensis MED. (*oblongifolia*) (*botryapium*). Medium to large sized suckering shrub with tall erect stems, oblong leaves and erect racemes. Grows well in moist situations. See also *A. lamarckii* and *A. laevis*. N. America. A.M. 1938.

cusickii FERN. Large shrub occasionally a small tree with few flowered racemes and fruits at first scarlet gradually turning black. N. America. C. 1934.

florida LINDL. A large shrub or small tree with rounded or oval leaves and purplish fruits. Autumn tints include a rich clear yellow. Western N. America. I. 1826.

×**grandiflora.** See under *A. lamarckii*.

'Rubescens'. See *A. lamarckii 'Rubescens'*.

humilis WIEG. Erect growing, suckering shrub of medium size. Shoots deep red, leaves elliptic oblong. Flowers in dense upright racemes in May. Fruits almost black, bloomy. Eastern U.S.A. I. 1904.

laevis WIEG. A small tree or occasionally large shrub usually grown, wrongly in English gardens, under the name of *A. canadensis*. A picture of striking beauty in early May, when the profusion of white fragrant flowers is interspersed with delicate pink young foliage. The leaves assume rich autumnal tints. N. America. C. 1870.

lamarckii SCHRODER. A large shrub or small tree of bushy, spreading habit. Leaves oval to oblong, coppery-red and silky when young, colouring richly in autumn. Flowers in lax, ample racemes scattered along the branches. The best species for general planting, a tree in full flower being a beautiful spectacle. This recently named species has been known in gardens and the wild for many years. It is naturalised in Belgium, Holland, N.W. Germany and several parts of England where it has been variously, but wrongly, referred to the following species:—*AA. canadensis, laevis and confusa*. The plant grown in gardens as *A.*×*grandiflora* also belongs here. A.M. 1976.

'Rubescens' (×*grandiflora 'Rubescens'*). Flowers tinged pink, darker in bud.

AMELANCHIER—*continued*

oblongifolia. See *A. canadensis.*

ovalis MED. (*vulgaris*). Medium sized to large shrub of upright habit. Flowers large in short erect racemes. Fruit red becoming black. C. and S. Europe. I. 1596.

sanguinea DC. Medium sized shrub with oval-oblong or rounded leaves and loose, lax racemes in May. Fruits black, bloomy. S.E. Canada, N.E. United States. I. 1824.

×**spicata** K. KOCH. (*canadensis* × *stolonifera*). A large suckering shrub of bushy habit. Flowers in short erect racemes. Fruits blue-black. N. America.

stolonifera WIEG. A small to medium-sized suckering shrub forming a dense thicket of erect stems. Flowers in short erect racemes. N. America. I. 1883.

vulgaris. See *A. ovalis.*

×**AMELASORBUS**—**Rosaceae**—An interesting natural hybrid between *Amelanchier* and *Sorbus*. Occurring in Idaho and Oregon, U.S.A.

jackii REHD. (*Amelanchier alnifolia* × *Sorbus scopulina*). This unusual shrub has oval to elliptic leaves. In spring 5cm. long clusters of white flowers are produced followed by dark red fruits which are covered with a blue "bloom".

†**AMICIA**—**Leguminosae**—A small genus of Central American sub-shrubs requiring a well drained soil and a warm sunny sheltered site.

zygomeris DC. A medium sized shrub of extremely vigorous habit, with erect, greenish, downy stems which are hollow and generally herbaceous in nature. Leaves pinnate, with four obovate notched leaflets, arising from a pair of inflated, purple-tinged leafy stipules. The yellow, purple-splashed, pea-flowers are produced in short axillary racemes during autumn, often too late to avoid the attention of early frosts. Mexico. I. 1826.

AMORPHA—**Leguminosae**—A genus of sun-loving shrubs or sub-shrubs with racemes of small violet or blue pea-flowers in summer.

canescens NUTT. "Lead Plant". A small sub-shrub from North America, with acacia-like foliage; flowers violet, produced in dense cylindrical racemes 10 to 15cm. long in the late summer and early autumn. Eastern N. America. I. 1812.

fruticosa L. "False Indigo". A variable shrub of medium height with pinnate leaves and slender racemes of purplish-blue flowers in July. S. United States. I. 1724.

'Pendula'. A form with pendulous branches.

AMPHIRAPHIS. See *MICROGLOSSA.*

AMYGDALUS. See *PRUNUS dulcis.*

†**ANAGYRIS**—**Leguminosae**—A genus of two tender sun-loving shrubs or small trees related to *Piptanthus.*

foetida L. A large shrub or small tree with sage-green trifoliolate leaves, which are foetid when crushed, and short racemes of yellow pea flowers in late spring. Mediterranean Region. C. 1750.

ANDRACHNE—**Euphorbiaceae**—A small genus of insignificant shrubs.

colchica BOISS. A small, dense shrub of botanical interest. Caucasus.

‡***ANDROMEDA**—**Ericaceae**—A small genus of low-growing slender stemmed shrubs for the peat garden or damp acid soils. Many species formerly included in this genus may now be found under the following: *CASSIOPE, CHAMAEDAPHNE, LEUCOTHOE, LYONIA, OXYDENDRUM* and *PIERIS.*

glaucophylla LINK. (*polifolia angustifolia*). A dwarf shrub with slender erect stems, narrow leaves and terminal clusters of pale pink pitcher-shaped flowers in late spring and early summer. Differs from *A. polifolia* in the leaves being minutely white tomentulose beneath. N.E. North America. C. 1879.

'Latifolia'. A form of looser, more straggly growth with broader leaves.

lucida. See *LYONIA lucida.*

polifolia L. "Bog Rosemary". A charming dwarf shrub, a rare native of the British Isles. The slender stems bear narrow glaucous-green leaves glabrous and white beneath, and terminal clusters of soft pink flowers in May or early June. Europe, N. Asia, N. America. C. 1768.

angustifolia. See *A. glaucophylla.*

'Compacta'. A gem for a cool peat bed; bears clusters of bright pink flowers from May onwards. Compact habit. A.M. 1964.

'Major'. A taller form with broader leaves.

'Minima'. A decumbent or nearly prostrate form with dark green linear leaves and pink flowers.

†***ANOPTERUS—Escalloniaceae**—A genus of two species related to *Escallonia*.

glandulosus LABILL. A rare, Tasmanian evergreen shrub or small tree, with coarsely toothed obovate, leathery leaves. A beautiful plant, producing terminal racemes of lily-of-the-valley like flowers in April and May. Hardy only in favoured localities. I. about 1840. A.M. 1926.

ANTHYLLIS—Leguminosae—A genus of mainly low-growing, sun-loving, deciduous or evergreen shrubs from Central and Southern Europe.

†***barba-jovis** L. "Jupiter's Beard". A medium sized shrub with pinnate, silvery leaves and cream coloured flowers borne in terminal clusters in early summer. S.W. Europe, Mediterranean Region. C. 1640.

hermanniae L. An attractive dwarf shrub suitable for the rock garden; masses of small, pea-shaped, yellow flowers with orange markings on the standards, in June and July. Mediterranean Region. I. early 18th century.

ARALIA—Araliaceae—American and Asiatic hardy or near hardy shrubs and trees mainly grown for the beauty of their large compound leaves.

chinensis L. "Chinese Angelica Tree". A tall, suckering shrub or small tree, with stout, spiny stems. Leaves doubly pinnate, 1 to 1·25m. long and ·6m. or more wide; flowers small, white, in huge panicles, the panicles with a central axis, appearing in August and September. N.E. Asia. I. about 1830.

elata SEEM. "Japanese Angelica Tree". Usually seen as a large suckering shrub but occasionally making a small sparsely branched tree. The huge, doubly pinnate leaves are gathered mainly in a ruff-like arrangement towards the tips of the stems. Flowers white, in large panicles, the panicles branched from base, in early autumn. Japan. I. about 1830. A.M. 1959.

'Aureovariegata'. Leaflets irregularly margined and splashed with yellow. The two variegated forms are distinct in the spring but later in the summer the leaves of both become variegated silver-white.

'Variegata'. A handsome form with leaflets irregularly margined and blotched creamy white. A.M. 1902. See note under '*Aureovariegata*'.

sieboldii. See *FATSIA japonica*.

spinosa L. "Hercules' Club", "Devil's Walking-stick". A North American species with viciously spiny stems. Panicles with a central axis, flowers greenish-white, much earlier than *elata* and *chinensis*, but less showy. July. In fruit when the other two are in flower. S.E. United States. I. 1688. A.M. 1974 (for fruit).

***ARBUTUS—Ericaceae**—The "Strawberry Trees" are amongst the most ornamental and highly prized of small evergreen trees, belonging to the Old and New worlds and attaining, with few exceptions, 3 to 6m. The dark, glossy green leaves, panicles of white, pitcher-shaped flowers and strawberry-like fruits are very attractive.

†**andrachne** L. The beautiful Grecian "Strawberry Tree". White pitcher-shaped flowers produced in the spring. Stems cinnamon-brown. Tender when young; hardy when mature, if rightly sited. S.E. Europe. I. 1724.

× **andrachnoides** LINK. (*andrachne* × *unedo*) (× *hybrida*). Intermediate between the "Killarney Strawberry Tree" and the Grecian species. Remarkably beautiful cinnamon-red branches and remarkably lime-tolerant. Quite hardy. Flowers during late autumn and winter. A.M. 1953. A.G.M. 1969.

‡**menziesii** PURSH. The noble "Madrona" of California, occasionally seen as a tree up to 18m. Flowers in conspicuous panicles in late spring, followed by small, orange-yellow fruits. Hardy in the home counties when rightly sited. One of the many fine introductions of David Douglas. Western N. America. I. 1827. A.M. 1926. A.G.M. 1973.

unedo L. "Killarney Strawberry Tree". A small tree often of gnarled appearance when old, bark deep brown and shredding. Flowers and fruits produced simultaneously in late autumn. Withstands gales in coastal districts. Unusual among ericaceous plants for its lime tolerance. Mediterranean Region, S.W. Ireland. F.C.C. 1933. A.G.M. 1969.

'Integerrima'. A slow growing shrubby form with entire leaves. White flowers occasionally produced.

'Quercifolia'. A distinct form with coarsely toothed leaves tapering to an entire base.

'Rubra'. A choice form with pink flushed flowers and abundant fruits. A.M. 1925.

‡***ARCTERICA**—**Ericaceae**—A monotypic genus.

nana MAK. (*Pieris nana*). A prostrate shrublet only a few inches in height. Leaves in pairs or whorls of three. The fragrant, white, urn-shaped flowers are produced in terminal clusters in April and May. Japan, Kamtchatka. I 1915.

‡***ARCTOSTAPHYLOS**—**Ericaceae**—Distinctive evergreens, varying from prostrate shrubs to small trees. Allied to *Rhododendron* they succeed under like soil conditions but love the sun.

manzanita PARRY. A beautiful tall-growing evergreen shrub, with attractive dark red brown stems, sea-green leaves and spikes of pink or white pitcher-shaped flowers. California. I. 1897. F.C.C. 1923.

myrtifolia PARRY. A rare, tiny Californian shrublet with white, bell-shaped flowers, tipped pink.

nevadensis A. GRAY. A prostrate, Californian species bearing its white urn-shaped flowers in racemes or panicles. Fruits red.

pumila NUTT. A very attractive prostrate species with small, downy, grey-green leaves. Flowers white or pinkish, followed by brown fruits. California. C. 1933.

†**tomentosa** LINDL. A small shrub with attractive shreddy bark and densely, grey tomentose branches. Leaves sage-green, densely hairy beneath; flowers white in spring. Western N. America. C. 1835.

uva-ursi SPRENG. "Red Bearberry". An interesting, native, creeping alpine shrub; flowers small, white tinged pink; fruits red. A good plant for sandy banks. Cool temperate regions of Northern Hemisphere.

‡**ARCTOUS**—**Ericaceae**—A small genus related to *Arctostaphylos* but differing in the deciduous, always toothed leaves. Low growing shrubs for cool, peaty soils.

alpinus NIED. (*Arctostaphylos alpina*). "Black Bearberry". A rare native shrublet forming a dense mat of prostrate reddish stems. Flowers in terminal clusters, urn-shaped, white flushed pink, in late spring. Fruits black. Northern latitudes of Europe (incl. Scotland), Asia, North America. C. 1789.

‡†***ARDISIA**—**Myrsinaceae**—A large genus of evergreen trees and shrubs.

japonica BL. An attractive dwarf evergreen for pot culture or a lime-free soil in very mild areas. Reaching 30cm. in height, it produces whorls of glossy leaves and bright-red berries. China, Japan. C. 1834.

ARISTOTELIA—**Elaeocarpaceae**—A small genus of mainly evergreen Australisian and South American shrubs needing some protection in cold districts. Male and female flowers often occur on separate plants.

†***chilensis** STUNTZ (*macqui*). An interesting evergreen attaining 5m. in mild districts. Leaves 13cm. long, lustrous green; berries small, black, on female plants. Suitable for maritime exposure. Chile. I. 1773.

'Variegata'. Leaves conspicuously variegated yellow.

***fruticosa** HOOK. f. A variable shrub recalling *Corokia cotoneaster;* leaves leathery, varying from linear to oblong obovate. The tiny flowers are followed by small berries variable in colour. New Zealand.

macqui. See *A. chilensis*.

†**serrata** W.R.OLIV. (*racemosa*). A graceful small tree from New Zealand, with heart-shaped, long-pointed leaves 5 to 10cm. long, which are jaggedly toothed, and downy when young, small rose-pink flowers and dark red berries. Well-developed specimens may be seen in mild areas. I. 1873.

ARONIA—**Rosaceae**—Attractive shrubs related to *Pyrus* and *Sorbus*, with white flowers in spring followed by conspicuous clusters of red or black fruits, and brilliant autumn colours. Not recommended for shallow chalk soils.

arbutifolia PERS. "Red Chokeberry". A medium sized shrub notable for its bright red fruits and exceptionally brilliant autumn colours. E. North America. C. 1700.

'Erecta'. A compact erect branched shrub with rich autumn colour. A.G.M. 1936. A.M. 1974.

floribunda. See *A. prunifolia*.

melanocarpa ELLIOTT. "Black Chokeberry". Small shrub with white, hawthorn-like flowers in spring followed by lustrous black fruits. E. North America. I. about 1700. A.M. 1972.

'Brilliant'. A form notable for its exceptionally fine autumn colour.

prunifolia REHD. (*floribunda*). Intermediate in character between the two preceding species. Fruits purple-black. S.E. United States. I. 1800.

ARTEMISIA—Compositae—Aromatic plants with attractive green or grey foliage.

abrotanum L. The "Southernwood" or "Lad's Love" of cottage gardens. A small erect grey-downy shrub with sweetly aromatic, finely divided leaves. S. Europe. C. in England since 16th century.

†**arborescens** L. A small shrub of rounded habit. The billowy filigree of its silvery leaves makes it a charming subject for the grey of blue border. S. Europe. I. 1640. A.M. 1966.

tridentata NUTT. A medium sized shrub of spreading habit. The grey, aromatic leaves are wedge shaped, three-toothed at the apex and occur in clusters along the stems. Western U.S.A. I. 1895.

"ASH". See *FRAXINUS.*

ASIMINA—Annonaceae—A small genus containing the following hardy species.

triloba DUN. In this country the "Pawpaw" forms a large deciduous shrub with obovate leaves up to 20cm. long. The bottle-shaped fruits are rarely developed in this country. S.E. United States. One of the first American plants to be introduced by Peter Collinson in 1736.

"ASPEN". See *POPULUS tremula.*

†***ASTELIA—Liliaceae**—A small genus of clump-forming perennials.

nervosa BANKS & SOLAND. Dense tufts of sedge-like, green, conspicuously veined leaves; flowers small, fragrant, in dense panicles; female plants bear orange berries. New Zealand.

ASTERANTHERA ovata. See under CLIMBERS.

ASTRAGALUS—Leguminosae—"Goat's Thorn". Dwarf, spiny shrubs suitable for a sunny border or rock garden.

angustifolius LAM. Very dwarf and slow-growing with branches densely set with spines and grey, pinnate leaves. Flowers pea-shaped, white, tinged blue, borne in clusters in May and June. A rock-garden shrub. Greece, Asia Minor.

‡**ATHEROSPERMA—Atherospermataceae**—A genus of two Australian species.

***moschatum** LAB. An interesting evergreen, Australasian small tree having lanceolate leaves, white downy beneath. The whole plant is very fragrant and yields an essential oil. Cream-coloured, solitary flowers. I. 1824.

ATRAPHAXIS—Polygonaceae—The shrubby Buckwheats are a small group of interesting, but not spectacular, usually low spreading plants for dry, sunny positions.

frutescens K. KOCH. A dwarf, semi-prostrate shrub with slender, wiry stems, narrow sea-green leaves and clusters of tiny pink and white flowers in late summer. S.E. Europe and Caucasus to Siberia and Turkestan. I. 1770.

ATRIPLEX—Chenopodiaceae—Shrubs which thrive in coastal districts and saline soil as well as inland. Flowers unattractive, but foliage of a striking silvery-grey.

canescens JAMES. A lax, semi-evergreen bush of medium size; leaves narrow, greyish-white. W. North America. Long cultivated.

halimus L. "Tree Purslane". A medium sized semi-evergreen shrub with silvery-grey leaves. S. Europe. C. since early 17th century.

***AUCUBA—Cornaceae**—Evergreen, shade loving shrubs, forming dense, rounded bushes 2 to 3m. high, thriving in almost any soil or situation, however sunless. Very handsome when well grown, especially the variegated forms (which retain their colour best in an open position), and the berrying (female) clones.

japonica THUNB. The wild type, a medium sized shrub with green leaves often referred to as *var. concolor* or *viridis*. The male plant is commonest in cultivation. Japan. I. 1861. F.C.C. 1864. A.G.M. 1969.

borealis MIYABE & KUDO. An extremely hardy dwarf variety from the forests of northern Japan.

concolor. See under *A. japonica.*

'Crassifolia'. A small to medium sized shrub with thick, broad, deep green leaves, toothed in the upper half. Male. A.G.M. 1969.

'Crotonifolia' (*'Crotonoides'*). Leaves large, boldly spotted and blotched with gold. The best golden variegated aucuba. Male. A.G.M. 1969.

'Dentata'. Leaves undulate, coarsely toothed in the upper half.

'Fructu-albo' (*'Fructuluteo'*). Leaves sparingly spotted and blotched pale green and gold. Fruits yellowish-white. F.C.C. 1883.

'Gold Dust'. Leaves conspicuously speckled and blotched gold. Female.

'Grandis'. A form with very large elliptic, deep green leaves. Male. F.C.C. 1867.

'Hillieri'. A noble form with large, lustrous dark green leaves and pointed fruits. Female.

'Lance Leaf'. A striking form with polished deep green lance-shaped leaves. A male counterpart of *'Longifolia'*.

AUCUBA—*continued*

japonica 'Longifolia'. Leaves long, lanceolate and bright green. Female. F.C.C. 1864.

'Maculata'. See *'Variegata'*.

'Nana Rotundifolia'. A small, free-berrying form. Leaves small, rich green with an occasional spot, and sharply toothed in the upper half. Stems an unusual shade of sea-green. Female. A.G.M. 1969.

'Salicifolia'. A free-berrying form differing from *'Longifolia'* in its narrower leaves, and sea-green stems. Female.

'Speckles'. A male counterpart to *'Variegata'*.

'Sulphurea'. A distinct form with sea green stems. Leaves green with a pale yellow margin. Inclined to revert in shade. Female. F.C.C. 1865.

'Variegata' (*'Maculata'*). Leaves speckled yellow. Female. It is this form which was first introduced from Japan in 1783. F.C.C. 1865.

viridis. See under *A. japonica*.

AZALEA and × **AZALEODENDRON.** See under *RHODODENDRON*.

procumbens. See *LOISELEURIA procumbens*.

†***AZARA**—**Flacourtiaceae**—Shrubs or small trees with attractive evergreen leaves and fragrant flowers in early spring. All are natives of Chile.

dentata RUIZ & PAV. Medium-sized shrub confused in cultivation with *A. serrata*, differing in its smaller leaves, dark glossy green above, felted beneath. It is also less hardy.. Chile. I. about 1830.

gilliesii. See *A. petiolaris*.

integrifolia RUIZ. & PAV. A tall wall shrub with oval leaves; the chrome yellow flower clusters are conspicuous in late winter and early spring. I. 1832. A.M. 1934.

browneae REICHE. This variety has larger, obovate leaves. An excellent wall shrub; flowers yellow.

'Variegata'. Leaves with pretty pink and cream variegation.

lanceolata HOOK. f. A medium sized or large shrub with attractive, narrow, bright green leaves; bears multitudes of small, mustard-yellow fragrant flowers in April or May. A.M. 1931.

microphylla HOOK. f. An elegant small tree with large sprays of dainty foliage; flowers yellow, vanilla scented, appearing on the undersides of the twigs in early spring. The hardiest species. I. 1861. F.C.C. 1872.

'Variegata'. Leaves prettily variegated with cream; slow growing.

petiolaris JOHNSTON (*gilliesii*). A tall shrub notable for the fragrance of its small yellow flowers, which appear in February and March. Leaves ovate to oblong, comparatively large, leathery, toothed, teeth with sharp mucro-points. Has withstood 15°C of frost without injury. I. 1859. A.M. 1933.

serrata RUIZ. & PAV. A large shrub for wall or sheltered site, with distinctive, oval, serrate leaves and conspicuous clusters of yellow flowers, produced in July. Small white berries are produced in a hot summer. Hardier than most. A.M. 1957 (as *A. dentata*).

BACCHARIS—**Compositae**—Rapid-growing and useful seaside shrubs with inconspicuous flowers.

halimifolia L. "Bush Groundsel". A useful seaside shrub up to 4m. Variable, sage-green leaves and white groundsel-like flowers in October. E. North America. I. 1683.

***patagonica** HOOK. & ARN. Medium-sized shrub with short, stalkless, evergreen, polished leaves. Flower-heads yellowish-white appearing singly in the upper leaf axils in May. Patagonia.

BALLOTA—**Labiatae**—Sub-shrubs requiring a sunny, well-drained position.

pseudodictamnus BENTH. A dwarf shrub entirely covered with greyish-white wool. Leaves orbicular-cordate. A most effective foliage plant particularly if pruned back each spring. An excellent addition to the grey garden. Lilac-pink flowers are produced in whorls in July. Mediterranean Region.

"BAMBOOS". See end of Manual.

†***BANKSIA**—**Proteaceae**—An interesting genus of Australian trees and shrubs with handsome foliage and cone-shaped flower heads recalling the "Bottle-Brushes". Only suitable for the mildest localities, or worthy of a conservatory.

integrifolia L.f. Medium sized shrub of dense habit. Leathery leaves, olive green above and white beneath; flowers yellow. I. 1788.

marginata CAV. Medium-sized shrub. Leaves, somewhat spiny, 5cm. long, deep green above, snowy-white beneath; flowers lemon-green.

serrata L. f. A tall shrub with long narrow leaves curiously squared at the apex; flowers silvery grey. Not very lime tolerant.

"BARBERRY". See *BERBERIS.*

†***BAROSMA—Rutaceae**—A small genus of attractive, heath-like evergreens, natives of South Africa.

pulchella BARTL. & WENDL. (*Diosma pulchella* HORT.). Aromatic heath-like shrub with terminal clusters of mauve flowers. A pleasing plant but only suitable for the mildest areas or cool greenhouse. I. 1787.

†***BAUERA—Baueraceae**—A small genus of tender evergreen shrubs.

rubioides ANDR. An attractive small late-spring flowering shrub suitable for mild gardens, also making an excellent pot plant for conservatory; flowers eight-petalled, white, with slight pink flush. Tasmania, S.E. Australia. A.M. 1941.

"BAY". See *LAURUS nobilis.*

"BEAUTY BUSH". See *KOLKWITZIA amabilis.*

"BEECH". See *FAGUS.*

"BEECH, SOUTHERN". See *NOTHOFAGUS.*

BENTHAMIA fragifera. See *CORNUS capitata.*

BENZOIN aestivale. See *LINDERA benzoin.*

BERBERIS—Berberidaceae—The "Barberries" as a group are of easy cultivation, thriving in sun or shade and in almost any soil that is not water-logged. They vary in habit from dwarf to large shrubs, but except where otherwise stated are of medium size. The flowers vary from pale yellow to orange and appear during spring. The fruits are usually very showy and many species give brilliant autumn colour. Apart from those listed we offer a varied range of mixed hybrids. See also *MAHONIA.*

***actinacantha** ROEM. & SCHULT. A remarkable small, Chilean evergreen. Fragrant chrome-yellow flowers. Leaves hard and rigid with an occasional spine, varying from orbicular ovate, 2·5cm. across carried on a long stalk to a tiny elliptic sessile leaf. I. about 1830.

aggregata SCHNEID. A dense habited bush, usually less than 1·5m. high. The numerous paniculate clusters of flowers are followed in the autumn by masses of red berries, backed by the rich coloration of the dying leaves. A parent of many hybrids. W. China. I. 1908. A.M. 1913.

amoena DUNN (*leptoclada*). A small shrub similar to *B. wilsoniae stapfiana.* Leaves sea-green, semi-persistent; most striking when displaying its coral-red ellipsoid fruits. China.

angulosa HOOK. f. & THOMS. Small shrub with large, solitary yellow flowers and dark purplish berries. Himalaya. I. about 1850.

***× antoniana** AHRENDT (*buxifolia × darwinii*). A small, rounded bush with almost spineless leaves; very pretty when bearing its single, long-stalked, deep yellow flowers, or blue-black berries. Garden origin.

aristata DC. (*chitria* LINDL.). S sub-evergreen species from Nepal, ultimately 3m. high. Flowers bright yellow, often tinged red, borne in racemes 5 to 10cm. long and followed by red berries covered with bloom. Nepal. I. 1818.

†***asiatica** ROXB. A striking, unmistakable and vigorous species. Leaves leathery, obovate, 3ins. or more long, sea-green above, white beneath, conspicuously veined. Berries red, finally blue-black. Nepal, Bhutan, Assam. I. 1820.

***atrocarpa** SCHNEID. Flowers freely borne on elegant arching branches, differing from *B. sargentiana* in its smaller, less prominently veined leaves. W. China. I. 1909.

'Barbarossa'. (Carminea Group). A vigorous shrub 1·5 to 2m. high which produces its red berries in such profusion that the branches are arched by their weight.

bealei. See *MAHONIA bealei.*

***bergmanniae** SCHNEID. A compact, pyramidal evergreen up to 3m. with clusters of large spiny leaves and blue-black berries. W. China. I. 1908.

'Bountiful'. (Carminea Group). A spreading bush about 1m. high. Very decorative in the autumn when laden with clusters of coral-red berries on arching branches.

brachypoda MAXIM. A rare, medium sized species with narrow, elongated racemes of yellow flowers in May, followed by bright red, oblong berries. The leaves, young shoots and spines are characteristically downy. China. I. 1907.

***× bristolensis** AHRENDT (*calliantha × verruculosa*). A small shrub of dense rounded habit with small prickly leaves, glossy dark green above, white pruinose beneath. An excellent dwarf hedge if clipped. Garden origin.

'Buccaneer'. (Carminea Group). A bush of erect growth, notable for the large size of its deep red berries which are carried in large clusters and last until December.

BERBERIS—*continued*

buxifolia LAM. (*dulcis*). A South American semi-evergreen species of medium size, with leaves glaucous-grey beneath; the early flowers are followed by purple-blue grape-like berries. Magellan Straits. I. 1830. A.M. 1961.

'Nana'. A slow-growing, dense, evergreen mound about ·5m. high.

***calliantha** MULLIGAN. A small shrub with small holly-like leaves conspicuously glaucous beneath. Young stems crimson. Flowers pale yellow, solitary or in pairs; fruits blue-black. S.E. Tibet. I. 1924. A.M. 1942.

***candidula** SCHNEID. (*hypoleuca* HORT.). A dense, dome-shaped bush up to 1m., with small, shining, dark green leaves, silvery-white beneath and single, bright yellow flowers. W. China. I. 1895.

× carminea AHRENDT (*aggregata* × *wilsoniae*). A colourful group of hybrids from an original cross made at Wisley. Vigorous, small to medium sized shrubs of semi-erect or spreading habit, sometimes forming large mounds, glorious in the autumn when fuming with their red, scarlet or pink berries. Several clones have been named.

'Chenaultii' (Hybrido-gagnepainii Group). A dense growing, small shrub with arching, verrucose stems and ovate-lanceolate leaves which are undulate and spiny at the margin, dull green above, pruinose grey at first beneath.

chillanensis SPRAGUE. A large-growing shrub with yellow and orange flowers displayed profusely in May. The small, glossy leaves, borne closely along slender, erect growths, make this an attractive shrub even when not in bloom. Andes of Chile and Argentina. A.M. 1932. The variety *hirsutipes* is the plant generally grown in cultivation.

chinensis POIR. Large shrub with red-brown stems, oblanceolate leaves, few flowered racemes and dark red berries. S.W. Russia. C. 1808.

chitria HORT. Large-growing, large-leaved species with long, drooping bunches of conspicuous dark red, bloomy berries each about 1·5cm. long. Himalaya. I. 1818. A.G.M. 1924.

***chrysosphaera** MULLIGAN. An evergreen shrub of small to medium size. Leaves narrow, borne in clusters, glossy green above, white beneath. Flowers canary-yellow, strikingly large for a *Berberis*. A Kingdon Ward introduction from S. Tibet in 1933-34.

†*comberi SPRAGUE & SANDWITH. A very distinct, small evergreen shrub difficult to establish. Leaves thick, holly-like; flowers solitary. Discovered in the Argentine Andes by Comber in 1925.

concinna HOOK. f. Small shrubs of compact habit with shining, dark green leaves which are white beneath. The solitary yellow flowers are followed by large oblong, red berries up to 2cm. long. Sikkim. I. about 1850. A.M. 1918.

***congestiflora** C. GAY. A large shrub. The flowers are produced in dense clusters at intervals along the stems. Closely related to *B. hakeoides*, but differing in its thinner textured leaves and shorter pedicels. Chile. I. 1925.

***coxii** SCHNEID. A handsome, medium sized species. Leaves leathery, 2·5 to 5cm. long, lustrous above, glaucous beneath. Berries blue-black. Upper Burma. I. 1919.

†*crispa C. GAY. A small shrub of dense wiry habit, the 1·5cm. long, spoon-shaped, green leaves are spiny toothed and occur in clusters along the stems. Chile. I. 1928.

***darwinii** HOOK. This early-flowering species is one of the finest of all flowering shrubs. Leaves three pointed, dark shining green above. Chile, Chiloe, Argentine. First discovered in 1835 by Charles Darwin on the voyage of the "Beagle". Introduced by William Lobb in 1849. A.G.M. 1930. F.C.C. 1967.

'Nana'. See *B.* × *stenophylla 'Nana'*.

'Prostrata'. See *B.* × *stenophylla 'Prostrata'*.

diaphana MAXIM. A shrub 1 to 2m. high giving good autumn colour. Berries bright red. N.W. China. I. 1872.

dictyophylla FRANCH. (*dictyophylla 'Albicaulis'*). A Chinese shrub to 2m., colouring well in autumn. Young stems red and covered with white bloom; leaves chalk white beneath. The large, solitary, red berries are also covered with white bloom. W. China. I. 1916.

approximata REHD. (*B. approximata*). A tall spreading shrub, colouring well in autumn.

epruinosa SCHNEID. Less bloomy in all its parts.

dielsiana FEDDE. A large vigorous shrub with slightly angled red-brown stems narrowly elliptic leaves and racemes of yellow flowers followed by red berries. W. China. I. 1910.

BERBERIS—*continued*

***dumicola** SCHNEID. An uncommon species allied to *B. sargentiana*. Its flowers are orange-tinged. Yunnan. I. 1914.

***empetrifolia** LAM. Dwarf shrub with slender arching stems, narrow leaves and small golden yellow flowers in May. Intolerant of shallow chalk soils. Chile. I. 1827.

formosana. See *B. kawakamii formosana*.

forrestii AHRENDT. Large shrub with loosely arching stems, obovate leaves and long racemes of yellow flowers followed by red berries. W. China. I. about 1910.

franchetiana macrobotrys AHRENDT. A large shrub with arching stems, yellow flowers and red berries. W. China. I. 1937.

francisci-ferdinandii SCHNEID. Vigorous, large shrub, producing large drooping bunches of sealing-wax red berries. W. China. I. 1900.

***gagnepainii** SCHNEID. A small shrub making a dense growth of erect stems closely set with narrow, undulate leaves. Berries black, covered by a blue bloom. Forms an impenetrable hedge. W. China. I. about 1904.

georgei AHRENDT. A rare and attractive shrub of medium height. The leaves colour well in autumn when the crimson berries in pendulous clusters are most conspicuous. China. A.M. 1979.

gilgiana FEDDE. Red-brown shoots with leaves 2·5 to 4cm. long, grey beneath; berries deep blood-red. China. I. 1910.

glaucocarpa STAPF. A large, semi-evergreen shrub notable for its profusion of blue-black berries heavily covered with a white bloom, carried in conspicuous clusters. Punjab. A.M. 1943.

gyalaica AHRENDT. Medium sized shrub related to *B. sherriffii*. Berries oblong-elliptic, blackish-purple with blue bloom. S.E. Tibet. I. about 1925.

***hakeoides** SCHNEID. A very distinct and quite remarkable Chilean species. It is of loose habit with shoots, often unbranched, up to 3m. high. Leaves usually in pairs, rounded and spiny. Flowers golden-yellow, produced in clusters all along the shoots, in April and May. I. 1861. A.M. 1901.

henryana SCHNEID. A distinct species with long, pear-shaped leaves and elliptic-oblong, red berries. C. China.

heteropoda sphaerocarpa AHRENDT. Medium sized shrub with few flowered racemes of orange-yellow flowers followed by globose black berries slightly blue bloomy. N.W. China.

hispanica BOISS. & REUT. (*australis*). An open-habited shrub about 2m. high. Leaves rather small, elliptic and light green; flowers orange-yellow; berries oval, blue-black. S. Spain, N. Africa.

***hookeri** LEM. (*wallichiana* HOOK. not DC.). A Himalayan species forming a dense, evergreen, compact shrub not more than 1 to 1·5m. high. Leaves glaucous beneath. Berries green at first then black. Nepal, Sikkim, Bhutan. I. 1848.

viridis SCHNEID. Leaves green beneath and small black berries. This is the commonest form in cultivation. Nepal, Bhutan, Assam.

*× **hybrido-gagnepainii** SURINGAR (*gagnepainii* × *verruculosa*). A small shrub of dense growth. Leaves ovate, with revolute, spiny margins, dull green above, green beneath. Ideal as a small hedge or as undercover.

'Chenaultii'. See *B. 'Chenaultii'*.

***hypokerina** AIRY-SHAW. An outstanding small shrub forming a thicket of purple stems. Leaves as much as 10cm. long, holly-like, silvery white beneath. Berries dark blue, with white bloom. Called "Silver Holly" by its discoverer, Kingdon Ward. Does not thrive in thin, chalky soil. Upper Burma. I. 1926. A.M. 1932.

***ilicifolia** FORST. "Holly-leaved Barberry". A very rare evergreen species of small to medium height. Leaves spiny and dark shining green. Flowers orange-yellow in short dense racemes in May. Chile. I. 1843.

ilicifolia HORT. See ×*MAHOBERBERIS neubertii*.

†***incrassata** AHRENDT. A medium sized shrub with reddish brown, thornless stems and large strongly spiny leaves often 13cm. long. The dense clusters of yellow flowers are followed by purple berries. N. Burma. I. 1931.

***insignis** HOOK. f. & THOMS. A noble Himalayan shrub of medium size forming a dense clump of erect smooth, yellowish stems which are remarkable for their lack of spines. Leaves usually in clusters of three, lanceolate, large, occasionally up to 18cm. long, with bold marginal spiny teeth, dark polished green above, yellowish-green and glossy beneath. Flowers large, in dense axillary clusters followed by

BERBERIS—*continued*

black, ovoid berries. This description applies to var. *tongloensis* SCHNEID. which is the only form in general cultivation. It is usually regarded as tender but is proving quite hardy in our arboretum. Sikkim, Nepal, Bhutan. Introduced from Sikkim by Sir Joseph Hooker in 1850.

*× **interposita** AHRENDT (*hookeri viridis × verruculosa*). A vigorous, small shrub, developing into a dense rounded mound of arching stems. Leaves 1·5 to 2cm. long, sharply spiny, glossy dark green above, pruinose below often green by autumn.

× **irwinii** and its cultivars. See under *B. × stenophylla*.

jamesiana FORR. & W.W.SM. A large, erect branched species giving rich autumn tints. Flowers in racemes, followed by pendulous clusters of translucent, coral-red berries. Yunnan. I. 1913. A.M. 1925.

***julianae** SCHNEID. An excellent dense evergreen to 3m. with strongly spiny stems and clusters of stiff narrow, spine-toothed leaves, copper tinted when young. Flowers yellow, slightly scented, in dense axillary clusters. A good screening or hedging plant. China. I. 1900.

***kawakamii** HAYATA. A short, spiny, evergreen species, densely furnished with short rather broad leaves, copper-tinted when young. Clusters of rich yellow flowers in March and April. Formosa. I. about 1919.

formosana AHRENDT (*B. formosana*). A dense, slow-growing, erect shrub with leathery leaves. Berries black with mauve bloom. Formosa. I. 1935.

koreana PALIB. An attractive species, its large leaves colouring well in autumn; flowers in drooping racemes; the red, waxen, ovoid berries are conspicuous. Korea.

***lempergiana** AHRENDT. A distinct Chinese species, akin to *B. julianiae*, but with broader, paler leaves. Berries oval and bloomy, produced in clusters. I. 1935.

leptoclada. See *B. amoena*.

†***levis** FRANCH. Bushy shrub up to 2m. with long, oblanceolate, glossy green leaves. Berries black. W. China. I. 1909.

liechtensteinii SCHNEID. A medium sized, semi-evergreen shrub. Berries ovoid, red, produced in short racemes. W. China. I. 1908.

***linearifolia** PHIL. An erect, medium sized shrub of rather ungainly habit, with dark, glossy green, spineless leaves. The orange-red flowers produced early in spring, and sometimes again in the autumn, are the richest coloured of the genus. Introduced from Argentine by Harold Comber in 1927. Native also of Chile. F.C.C. 1931.

'Orange King'. A selected form with larger flowers of a rich orange.

*× **lologensis** SANDW. (*darwinii × linearifolia*). A very beautiful, medium sized, evergreen shrub, offspring of two superb species. Leaves variable in shape, entire and spiny on the same bush; flowers apricot-yellow. A natural hybrid found with the parents in Argentine by Comber in 1927. A.M. 1931.

***lycium** ROYLE. A semi-evergreen species of medium height. Leaves up to 5cm. long, light sea-green; flowers bright yellow in elongated racemes, followed by purple "bloomy" berries. Himalaya. I. about 1835.

× **macracantha** SCHRAD. (*aristata × vulgaris*). A tall shrub up to 4m. high. The yellow flowers are produced in racemes of ten to twenty blooms and are followed by purple berries. Garden origin.

***manipurana** AHRENDT (*knightii*) (*xanthoxylon* HORT.) (*hookeri latifolia*). A vigorous species reaching about 3m. with large, lustrous leaves, yellow flowers and oblong, blue-black berries. An excellent hedging plant. Manipur. I. 1882.

× **mentorensis** L. M. AMES (*julianae × thunbergii*). A vigorous intermediate hybrid up to 2m., with obovate leaves and dark brown-red berries. Garden origin 1924.

micrantha AHRENDT. Medium sized shrub of dense habit. Berries dark red in dense racemes. Bhutan. I. 1838.

mitifolia STAPF. A distinct species with spike-like racemes of yellow flowers, pubescent leaves, and elongated crimson berries. W. China. I. 1907.

montana GAY. A large shrub remarkable for the large size of its flowers which are yellow and pale orange. Berries black. Andes of Chile and Argentina. I. 1925-7. A.M. 1935. A.G.M. 1969.

morrisonensis HAYATA. "Mt. Morrison Babrerry". A low, compact, free-flowering shrub with large bright red berries and brilliant autumn tints of scarlet and gold. Formosa. I. 1912.

BERBERIS—*continued*

mucrifolia AHRENDT. A dwarf shrub of dense, compact habit, with erect slender, spiny stems and small, mucronate leaves. Flowers usually solitary, berries bright red. Nepal. I. about 1954.

oblonga SCHNEID. Medium to large sized shrub. Flowers in densely packed racemes. Berries purple-black with white bloom. Turkestan. I. 1876.

orthobotrys SCHNEID. A medium sized shrub of vigorous, upright habit bearing large, bright red, oval berries. Bright autumn tints. Kashmir, Afghanistan, Nepal. A.M. 1919.

canescens AHRENDT (*B. 'Unique'*). A form with narrower leaves, pruinose beneath. Kashmir, Nepal.

× **ottawensis** SCHNEID. (*thunbergii* × *vulgaris*). A medium-sized shrub with green, rounded or oval leaves and red berries in drooping clusters.

'Purpurea'. A vigorous hybrid of medium to large size. A really first class shrub with rich vinous purple foliage, yellow flowers and red berries. Garden origin. A.M. 1978.

pallens FRANCH. A large shrub. Berries ovoid, bright red; leaves richly tinted in autumn. W. China. I. 1929.

***panlanensis** AHRENDT. A charming, small, compact evergreen of very neat growth. Leaves linear, sea-green and spine toothed. An ideal hedging plant. W. China. I 1908.

parisepala AHRENDT. Slow growing small sized shrub related to *B. angulosa*. Leaves often red tinted in autumn. Berries large, red. S.E. Tibet, Bhutan, Nepal. I. about 1928.

***'Parkjuweel'** (× *hybrido-gagnepainii 'Chenaultii'* × *thunbergii*). A small shrub of dense prickly habit. Leaves obovate, almost spineless, colouring richly in autumn, occasionally remaining until the following spring. Garden origin.

'Pirate King'. (Carminea Group). A small, dense shrub of vigorous growth, berries fiery orange-red.

poiretii SCHNEID. Attractive shrub up to 1·5m. with elegant drooping branches and abundant pale-yellow flowers followed by slender, bright red berries. N. China, Amurland. I. about 1860.

polyantha HEMSL. Medium sized, erect shrub with large and abundant drooping flower panicles, followed by grape-like clusters of red berries. One of the most constant in the vivid red of its autumn colour. W. China. I. 1904. A.M. 1917.

prattii SCHNEID. Medium sized to large shrub. Flowers in erect panicles followed by ovoid, bright coral berries. A lovely shrub of great ornamental beauty when heavy with fruits in the autumn. W. China. A.M. 1953. The plant we grow is the variety *laxipendula*.

***pruinosa** FRANCH. A vigorous Chinese evergreen of medium size with distinct spine-toothed, sea-green foliage, white beneath. The soft yellow flowers are followed by abundant crops of blue-black berries covered with white bloom. Yunnan. I. 1894. A.M. 1924.

longifolia AHRENDT. A form with longer, narrower leaves.

***replicata** W.W.SM. A graceful, slow-growing evergreen, attaining about 1·5m.; leaves narrow, recurved at the edges and glaucous beneath; berries ellipsoid, black-purple. Yunnan. I. 1917. A.M. 1923.

× **rubrostilla** CHITTENDEN (*aggregata* × *wilsoniae*). A beautiful, small sized shrub of garden origin; very showy in autumn with its large, oblong, coral-red berries. Fruits among the largest in the genus. Many clones of this hybrid have been named. Garden origin. F.C.C. 1916. A.G.M. 1969.

***sargentiana** SCHNEID. A hardy species up to 2m. The evergreen leaves are leathery, elliptic-oblong, net-veined and up to 13cm. long; berries blue-black. W. China. I. 1907. A.M. 1915. F.C.C. 1916.

sherriffii AHRENDT. An elegant, medium sized shrub with elliptic, entire leaves, conspicuous when bearing its large, drooping panicles of "bloomy" blue-black berries. S.E. Tibet. I. 1938.

sieboldii MIQ. A small suckering shrub of compact habit with oval leaves which colour richly in the autumn. Racemes of pale yellow flowers followed by globose, shining orange berries. Japan. I. 1892. A.G.M. 1935.

sikkimensis AHRENDT. A small shrub with angled shoots and short racemes of ovoid dark red berries. Sikkim. I. about 1924.

BERBERIS—*continued*

silva-taroucana SCHNEID. A large shrub of elegant habit, the young growths are attractively tinged reddish-purple. The long racemes of yellow flowers are followed by egg-shaped scarlet berries. China. I. 1912.

***soulieana** SCHNEID. A sparsely branched, medium sized evergreen of stiff habit. Leaves narrow, with pronounced spinose teeth. Flowers yellow borne in clusters in the leaf axils in May. Berries black, covered with a glaucous bloom. C. China. I. 1897.

***× stenophylla** LINDL. (*darwinii × empetrifolia*). An indispensable evergreen, ultimately a medium-sized graceful shrub, its long arching branches wreathed with yellow flowers in April. C. 1860. F.C.C. 1864. A.G.M. 1923.

'Autumnalis'. Small shrub of graceful habit producing a second crop of flowers in autumn. A.G.M. 1969.

'Coccinea' (× *irwinii 'Coccinea'*). A small shrub with crimson buds opening orange. A.M. 1925. A.G.M. 1969.

'Corallina' (× *irwinii 'Corallina'*). A small shrub of lax habit. Buds coral red opening yellow. A.G.M. 1969.

'Corallina Compacta' (× *irwinii 'Corallina Compacta'*). A dwarf shrub rarely exceeding 30cm. Buds coral red opening yellow. A.G.M. 1969.

'Etna'. A seedling raised in our nurseries. A small shrub with shining, dark green leaves. In April the whole bush erupts into flower and the leaves are hidden by clusters of fiery-orange blossoms.

'Gracilis' (× *irwinii 'Gracilis'*). A small shrub of lax habit. Leaves bright green. Flowers golden yellow.

'Gracilis Nana' (× *irwinii 'Gracilis Nana'*). A dwarf, slow-growing shrub of dense habit, with golden yellow flowers.

'Irwinii' (*B. × irwinii*). A small, compact shrub; flowers deep yellow. A.G.M. 1969.

'Nana' (*darwinii 'Nana'*). Small compact shrub with rich yellow flowers.

'Picturata' (× *irwinii 'Picturata'*). A small floriferous shrub; flowers deep yellow.

'Pink Pearl'. A curious form of chameleon nature. Leaves dark green or mottled and striped pink and cream. Flowers may be creamy-yellow, orange, pink or bicoloured on different shoots of the same bush.

'Prostrata' (*darwinii 'Prostrata'*). Attractive low shrub; the orange buds open golden yellow.

'Semperflorens'. Small shrub with red buds opening orange, still flowering when the type has finished.

†*sublevis W.W.SM. Medium sized shrub with ribbed, strongly spiny stems and narrow spine-edged leaves. Flowers primrose yellow, fragrant. W. China. C. 1935.

***taliensis** SCHNEID. A rigid, slow-growing, evergreen hummock, scarcely exceeding 1m. in height. Its lanceolate leaves are dark, glossy green. Flowers lemon-yellow. Berries blue-black. Yunnan. I. 1922.

taylorii AHRENDT. Medium sized shrub with densely packed panicles of greenish-yellow flowers. Berries ovoid, black with blue bloom. S.E. Tibet. I. 1939.

temolaica AHRENDT. One of the most striking barberries. A vigorous shrub up to 3m. with stout erect-spreading branches. Young shoots and leaves conspicuously glaucous, the shoots becoming a dark, bloomy, purple-brown with age. Berries egg-shaped, red, covered with bloom. Introduced from S.E. Tibet by Kingdon Ward in 1924.

thunbergii DC. An invaluable small shrub, compact in growth and unsurpassed in the brilliance of its autumn foliage and bright red berries. Japan. I. about 1864. F.C.C. 1890. A.G.M. 1927.

atropurpurea REHD. Foliage rich, reddish-purple, throughout spring and summer, and increasing in intensity as winter approaches. Rather taller growing than the type. A.M. 1926. A.G.M. 1932.

'Atropurpurea Nana'. A charming dwarf form of this popular purple-foliaged shrub, suitable for the rock garden or dwarf hedge. A.G.M. 1969.

'Aurea'. Leaves yellow, becoming pale green by late summer.

'Erecta'. A small, compact, fastigiate shrub forming a dense clump; excellent for low hedges. Superb autumn colours.

'Minor'. An interesting, dense-habited, dwarf shrub scarcely exceeding ·5m.

'Red Pillar'. A most attractive form of *'Erecta'* with reddish purple leaves.

'Rose Glow'. A very striking, small colourful shrub. The leaves of the young shoots are purple, mottled silver-pink and bright rose later becoming purple.

BERBERIS—*continued*

tsangpoensis AHRENDT. A most interesting species, forming a dwarf, wide-spreading mound, the slender yellow stems often extending several feet along the ground. Attractive autumn tints and red berries. S.E. Tibet. I. 1925.

umbellata G. DON. A medium sized, semi-evergreen except in severe winters; shoots bright red at first; yellow flowers in long-stalked corymbs followed by red, egg-shaped berries. Nepal. I. 1848.

'Unique'. See *B. orthobotrys canescens.*

***valdiviana** PHIL. A medium to large, stately species, like a smooth-leaved holly, distinct on account of its large, leathery, polished almost spineless leaves. Flowers saffron yellow in drooping racemes. A first class plant deserving wider planting. Chile. I. 1902 and again by Clarence Elliott in 1930. A.M. 1939.

validisepala AHRENDT. A medium sized species allied to *B. yunnanensis* and differing in its shorter spines and smaller flowers and berries. Yunnan. I. about 1930.

***veitchii** SCHNEID. (*acuminata*). An evergreen to about 2m. with long, lanceolate, spine-toothed leaves and red young shoots; flowers bronze-yellow, long-stalked in axillary clusters; berries black. C. China. I. 1900.

vernae SCHNEID. (*caroli hoanghensis*). A very graceful, medium-sized Chinese shrub; flowers in dense, slender racemes all along the stems; berries globose, salmon-red. I. 1910. A.M. 1926.

***verruculosa** HEMSL. & WILS. A very pleasing, compact, slow-growing Chinese shrub 1·5 to 2m. high, with rough, minutely warty stems densely covered with small, glossy, dark green leaves which are white beneath. Flowers usually solitary, golden-yellow. W. China. I. 1904. A.M. 1911. A.G.M. 1929.

virescens HOOK. f. A tall, erect branched shrub with red shoots and brilliant red autumn colour. Berries reddish, bloomy. Sikkim. I. 1849.

virgetorum SCHNEID. Shrub up to 2m. with comparatively large obovate spineless leaves and oblong-elliptic reddish berries. China. I. about 1909.

vulgaris L. The "Common Barberry", a medium-sized shrub producing pendulous clusters of egg-shaped, bright red, translucent berries. The bark and wood were once used in the treatment of jaundice. Europe (incl. British Isles), N. Africa, Temperate Asia. Naturalised in N. America.

'Atropurpurea' (*'Purpurifolia'*). "Purple-leaf Barberry". A striking shrub, its deep vinous-purple foliage contrasting with the nodding racemes of yellow flowers. A.M. 1905.

wilsoniae HEMSL. A splendid small shrub forming dense mounds of thorny stems. Leaves small, sea-green turning to attractive autumn shades which blend with the coral of the fruit clusters. W. China. I. about 1904 by Ernest Wilson and named after his wife. F.C.C. 1907. A.G.M. 1969.

'Globosa'. A dwarf compact globular form.

guhtzunica AHRENDT. This variety resembles *subcaulialata*, and has attractive, sea-green leaves and reddish-purple young shoots; berries in clusters, translucent white, changing to coral red. W. China. I. 1937.

stapfiana SCHNEID. This semi-evergreen shrub with its soft yellow flowers is a little taller than the type and has more glaucous sea-green spathulate leaves and elliptic coral red berries. W. China. I. 1896.

subcaulialata SCHNEID. A taller variety with larger leaves than the type. W. China. I. 1908.

*× **wintonensis** AHRENDT. A hybrid of *B. bergmanniae*. The flowers appearing in February are exceptionally freely borne and are followed by blue-black, bloomy berries. Raised in our nurseries.

yunnanensis FRANCH. An attractive, medium sized shrub of rounded habit with brilliant autumn colours and bright red berries. W. China. I. 1886.

zabeliana SCHNEID. A neat, compact bush of medium height with plum-red berries and good autumn colour. Kashmir, Afghanistan.

†***BESCHORNERIA—Amaryllidaceae**—A small genus related to *Agave*.

yuccoides K. KOCH. A striking, Mexican yucca-like plant. The flower stems attain about 2m. carrying drooping racemes of bright green flowers with red bracts. This remarkable plant has flourished here in our nursery on chalk at the foot of a south-facing wall for more than twenty years. Requires full sun and well drained position. I. before 1859. A.M. 1933.

BETULA—Betulaceae—The Birch family includes among its members some of the most elegant trees, many of which are noteworthy for their stem colour, and attractive yellow leaves in autumn. They succeed on most soils, both damp and dry, but do not reach maximum size on shallow chalk soils.

BETULA—*continued*

alba. See *B. pendula* and *B. pubescens.*

albo-sinensis BURK. Beautiful medium sized species, the pink and red bark being covered with a glaucous bloom. W. China. I. 1901.

septentrionalis SCHNEID. A Chinese tree with singularly beautiful bark, which is shining orange-brown with pink and grey "bloom". I. 1908.

alleghaniensis. See *B. lutea.*

× **aurata** BORKH. (*pendula* × *pubescens*). A small to medium sized tree, variable in shape and texture of leaf but generally intermediate between the parents. Frequent with the parents in the wild.

× **caerulea** BLANCHARD (*caerulea-grandis* × *populifolia*). A small tree with creamy-white, orange-tinted bark and ovate, sharply pointed leaves. Occurring with the parents in the wild. I. 1905.

caerulea-grandis BLANCH. This small birch has conspicuous white bark, large ovate leaves and showy catkins. N. America. I. 1905.

chinensis MAXIM. Large shrub occasionally a small tree without conspicuous bark. An uncommon small leaved species of neat habit. China. I. 1906.

costata TRAUTV. Medium to large tree with conspicuous creamy-white exfoliating bark. Rich yellow autumn colour. Certainly one of the best birches. N.E. Asia. C. 1880.

cylindrostachya LINDL. A rare, small tree of uncertain constitution. Young shoots downy, bearing large ovate to ovate-oblong downy leaves occasionally to 6ins. long. An interesting species with large leaves requiring a sheltered position and happiest in the milder areas of the British Isles. Himalaya.

davurica PALL. A medium sized tree with peculiarly rugged bark. Tends to be early leafing and perhaps more suited for northerly and colder areas. Manchuria, N. China, Korea. I. 1882.

ermanii CHAM. Tall growing species from N.E. Asia; trunk pinkish-white, branches orange brown. Glossy, parallel-veined leaves. A.G.M. 1969.

subcordata KOIDZ (*nipponica*). This Japanese variety is as beautiful as the type, with cream and white trunk and orange-brown branches.

× **fetisowii.** A hybrid of Polish origin, forming a graceful, narrow-headed tree notable for its peeling, chalk-white bark extending up the trunk to the branches.

glandulifera BUTLER (*pumila glandulifera*). Medium sized shrub. Leaves small, obovate, sometimes orbicular, gland dotted. Male catkins pink, passing to yellow. N. America.

grossa SIEB. & ZUCC. Medium size tree with smooth, dark grey bark and hornbeam-like leaves. The twigs have a distinctive smell when bruised. Japan. I. 1896.

humilis SCHRANK. A small to medium size shrub with hairy twigs and small leaves. Europe and N. Asia.

jacquemontii SPACH. Medium sized tree with attractively peeling bark and ovate, doubly serrate leaves. One of the loveliest birches, with dazzling white stems. W. Himalaya. C. 1880. A.G.M. 1969.

× **koehnei** SCHNEID. (*papyrifera* × *pendula*). Medium sized tree of graceful habit. Outstanding for its pure white bark.

lenta L. "Cherry Birch". Rarely a tall tree in this country, though attaining 25m. in its native land. Trunk smooth, dark, reddish-brown or purple. The young bark is sweet and aromatic. Leaves turn rich yellow in autumn. Eastern N. America. I. 1759.

luminifera WINKL. A remarkable large tree. The large, deep green lustrous leaves persist until sharp frost in late autumn. W. China. I. 1901.

lutea MICHX. (*alleghaniensis*). A medium sized tree with smooth, shining, amber coloured or golden-brown bark which peels prettily. Leaves ovate-oblong, downy, turning rich yellow in autumn. Eastern N. America. I. about 1767.

lyalliana. See *B. papyrifera commutata.*

mandschurica. See *B. platyphylla.*

japonica. See *B. platyphylla japonica.*

szechuanica. See *B. platyphylla szechuanica.*

maximowicziana REG. This, the largest-leaved birch, reaches 30m. in its native habitat. As seen in this country it is a fast growing wide-headed tree of medium height. Trunk orange-brown, finally greyish. Leaves heart-shaped, up to 15cm. long, turning a lovely clear butter yellow in the autumn. Japan. I. 1893.

medwediewii REG. A large shrub or small shrubby tree with stout erect branches. Distinct in its large terminal buds and large corrugated leaves which turn yellow in autumn. Transcaucasica. I. 1897. A.M. 1975 (for autumn colour).

BETULA—*continued*

middendorffii TRAUTV. & MEY. Medium to large shrub with usually resinous-glandular stems and small rounded leaves. Closely related to *B. humilis*. N.E. Asia. C. 1904.

nana L. "Dwarf Birch". A small native shrub with tiny, neat, rounded leaves. Northern Temperate Regions.

nigra L. "River Birch", remarkable for its shaggy bark. As its common name suggests, it is one of the finest trees for planting in damp ground. The soft-green diamond-shaped leaves are glaucous beneath. C. and E. United States. Introduced by Peter Collinson in 1736.

papyrifera MARSH. "Paper Birch", "Canoe Birch". A striking, large tree with white papery bark and yellow autumn foliage. N. America. I. 1750.

commutata FERN. (*papyrifera occidentalis* in part) (*B. lyalliana*) (*papyrifera macrophylla*). An attractive, large tree with white bark and broad, ovate leaves.

humilis FERN. & RAUP. (*neoalaskana*). "Yukon Birch". A handsome, large tree with red-brown, peeling bark. Alaska. I. 1905.

kenaica HENRY. A tree from the coast of Alaska with white bark tinged orange.

macrophylla. See *commutata*.

minor WATS. A shrubby form or occasionally a small bushy tree. N.E. North America. I. 1904.

neoalaskana. See *papyrifera humilis*.

pendula ROTH. (*verrucosa*) (*alba* in part). The "Common Silver Birch", aptly described as the "Lady of the Woods". A medium sized, white stemmed tree thriving in drier soils than *B. pubescens*, from which it is distinguished by its rough, warty shoots and sharply cut, diamond-shaped leaves. Europe (incl. British Isles), Asia Minor. A.G.M. 1969.

'Dalecarlica'. "Swedish Birch". A tall, slender, graceful tree with drooping branchlets and prettily cut leaves. Sweden. A.G.M. 1969.

'Dentata Viscosa'. A small, bushy tree with coarsely toothed leaves. Young growths sticky. Of no special horticultural merit.

'Fastigiata'. An erect form of medium size and rather stiff habit. A.G.M. 1969.

'Purpurea'. "Purple Leaf Birch". An extremely ornamental, slow growing tree with purple leaves. Rather weak constitution. F.C.C. 1874.

'Tristis'. A tall graceful tree with slender, pendulous branches, forming a narrow, symmetrical head. A tree of outstanding merit. A.G.M. 1969.

'Youngii'. "Young's Weeping Birch". Ultimately a beautiful dome-shaped or mushroom-headed, small weeping tree. A.G.M. 1969.

platyphylla SUK. (*mandschurica*). A large tree with white bark. Allied to *B. pendula* but differing in its larger leaves. Mandshurica, Korea.

japonica HARA (*mandschurica japonica*) (*B. tauschii*). "Japanese White Birch". A very beautiful form with white bark. Japan. C. 1887.

rockii. A Chinese form introduced by the American collector Joseph Rock.

szechuanica REHD. (*mandschurica szechuanica*). A vigorous, medium sized tree with chalky-white bark. W. China. I. 1908.

populifolia MARSH. The "Grey Birch" is the American counterpart of our "Silver Birch". A small tree with ashen-white bark, thriving equally well in dry or boggy ground. E. North America. I. 1750.

pubescens EHRH. (*alba* in part). "Common White Birch". This species thrives on a variety of soils and especially in damp localities; it is distinguished from *B. pendula* by the more reddish bark, smooth downy shoots, and more rounded leaves. Europe (incl. British Isles), N. Asia.

carpatica ASCH. & GRAEBN. (*B. coriacea*). A small tree with a wide distribution from Iceland to the Carpathians, forming a densely branched head. An extremely tough hardy tree, ideal for exposed windy situations.

pumila L. A small to large shrub of upright habit with downy young shoots and pointed, coarsely toothed leaves. Eastern N. America. I. 1762.

tatewakiana OKHI & WATANABE. A small to medium-sized shrub with densely glandular branches downy when young. Leaves leathery, ovate to obovate, serrate in the upper half and downy beneath, 1·5 to 2·5cm. long. A rare species, native of bogs in northern Japan.

utilis D. DON (*bhojpattra*). "Himalayan Birch". An attractive medium sized tree with orange-brown or dark, coppery-brown, peeling bark. We offer the Chinese form with brown bark. Himalaya. Introduced by Sir Joseph Hooker in 1849.

verrucosa. See *B. pendula*.

"BILBERRY". See *VACCINIUM myrtillus.*

"BIRCH". See *BETULA.*

"BLACKTHORN". See *PRUNUS spinosa.*

"BLADDER NUT". See *STAPHYLEA.*

"BLADDER SENNA". See *COLUTEA.*

BOENNINGHAUSENIA—Rutaceae—A monotypic genus allied to *Ruta.*

albiflora REICHENB. A late-flowering sub-shrub, in flower and foliage somewhat like a white *Thalictrum.* Flowers during late summer. Good on chalk soils. E. Asia.

"BOTTLE BRUSH". See *CALLISTEMON.*

†BOUVARDIA—Rubiaceae—A useful genus of late summer-flowering shrubs.

triphylla SALISB. A small, showy Mexican plant with orange-scarlet tubular flowers produced late in summer and autumn. Suitable for the conservatory. Against a sunny south wall this plant has survived several mild winters in Surrey. I. 1794.

†*BOWKERIA—Scrophulariaceae—A small genus of tender, evergreen, S. African shrubs.

gerardiana HARV. A tender, medium sized, South African shrub, producing white calceolaria-like flowers during summer. Requires conservatory cultivation except in the mildest areas. Natal. I. about 1890.

"BOX". See *BUXUS.*

"BOX ELDER". See *ACER negundo.*

†*BRACHYGLOTTIS—Compositae—A genus of two species related to *Senecio.*

repanda J. R. & G. FORST. A large shrub with very large, soft green leaves white beneath, and mignonette-scented flowers in large panicles. Creates a tropical effect. The leaves were used as primitive postcards by Maori tribes in remote areas of New Zealand. Only for the mildest areas or conservatory.

'Purpurea'. Leaves purple above, white beneath. .A.M. 1977.

"BRAMBLE". See *RUBUS.*

"BRIDAL WREATH". See *SPIRAEA arguta.*

"BROOM". See *CYTISUS* and *GENISTA.*

"BROOM, BUTCHER'S". See *RUSCUS aculeatus.*

"BROOM, HEDGEHOG". See *ERINACEA anthyllis.*

"BROOM, SPANISH". See *SPARTIUM junceum.*

BROUSSONETIA—Moraceae—A small genus of shrubs with dioecious flowers.

kazinoki SIEB. & ZUCC. A large, spreading shrub with ovate leaves variously one to three-lobed and toothed. A rare shrub mainly differing from *B. papyrifera* in its glabrous young shoots and leaves. China, Japan.

papyrifera VENT. "Paper Mulberry". A large shrub or small tree with variously lobed, hairy leaves. The female is decorative, with its peculiar globular heads of orange-red fruits. In Japan paper is made from its bark. Eastern Asia, naturalised in United States. I. early in the 18th century.

'Laciniata'. A dwarf form with curious, finely and deeply divided leaves.

‡*BRUCKENTHALIA—Ericaceae—A monotypic genus related to *Erica.*

spiculifolia REICHENB. A dwarf, heath-like plant up to 23cm. high. Terminal racemes of rose-pink bell-shaped flowers in June. E. Europe. Asia Minor.

‡*BRYANTHUS—Ericaceae—A monotypic genus.

gmelinii D. DON (*musciformis*). A rare shrublet related to *Phyllodoce,* having prostrate branches, closely set with small linear leaves. Flowers rose-pink borne three or more together upon slender, erect stalks. Japan, Kamchatka. C. 1834.

"BUCKEYE". See *AESCULUS.*

"BUCKTHORN". See *RHAMNUS.*

"BUCKTHORN, SEA". See *HIPPOPHAE rhamnoides.*

BUDDLEIA—Loganiaceae—A genus including several species of the greatest garden value, thriving in almost any soil and revelling in full sun. The flowering period is July to September unless otherwise stated. All have opposite leaves except *B. alternifolia.* Many species almost double their height when grown against a sunny wall.

BUDDLEIA—*continued*

albiflora HEMSL. A large shrub similar in general appearance to *B. davidii* but with stems rounded not four-angled as in the common species. Flowers pale lilac in long slender terminal panicles. Horticulturally inferior to *B. davidii*. China. I. 1900.

alternifolia MAXIM. A large shrub or occasionally a small tree, with graceful arching branches bearing long, narrow dark green, alternate leaves and wreathed in June with delicately fragrant, lilac flowers. China. I. 1915. A.M. 1922. A.G.M. 1924.

'Argentea'. An uncommon form having leaves covered with closely adpressed, silky hairs giving them a silvery sheen.

†***asiatica** LOUR. A large shrub or small tree with long, lax stems, narrowly lanceolate leaves, white beneath and terminal and axillary, drooping cylindrical panicles of sweetly sctnted white flowers during winter. India; Malaysia; Formosa. I. 1876. F.C.C. 1906.

†***auriculata** BENTH. A medium-sized shrub of open habit. Leaves white-felted beneath. Flowers in long, cylindrical panicles, strongly fragrant, creamy-white with yellow throat. Winter. Suitable for a warm wall. S. Africa. A.M. 1923.

†**candida** DUNN. A medium sized shrub distinguished by soft, flannel-like, fawn-grey leaves and small racemes of violet flowers. E. Himalaya. I. 1928.

caryopteridifolia W. W. SM. This seems to be the hardiest of a small group of spring-flowering species. A medium to large shrub with woolly, white leaves and shoots. The fragrant, lilac-coloured flowers are borne in late spring or early autumn. China. I. 1913.

colvilei HOOK. f. & THOMS. A large shrub or small tree of vigorous growth. Leaves dark green. The large, tubular, deep rose flowers are produced in terminal, drooping panicles in June. While tender as a young plant, mature specimens have withstood zero temperatures at Winchester and survived all winters since 1925. Himalaya. I. 1849. F.C.C. 1896.

'Kewensis'. A form with rich red flowers. A.M. 1947.

crispa BENTH. (*paniculata* HORT.). A medium sized to large shrub, the deeply toothed leaves and stems covered with a dense white felt. Flowers fragrant, lilac with an orange throat, produced in terminal cylindrical panicles in late summer. N. India. I. 1850. A.M. 1961.

farreri. See *B. farreri*.

davidii FRANCH. (*variabilis*). This universally grown medium-sized shrub gives the best results when hard pruned in March. The fragrant flowers, in long racemes, are very attractive to butterflies. Does well near the sea. Well naturalised in many towns and cities in the British Isles. Cent. and West China. C. 1890. A.M. 1898. A.G.M. 1941.

alba REHD. & WILS. White flowers.

'Amplissima'. Huge panicles, deep mauve.

'Black Knight'. Long trusses of very deep violet. A.G.M. 1969.

'Border Beauty'. Deep crimson-purple; compact habit.

'Charming'. Lavender pink.

'Dubonnet'. Strong growing with massive panicles of deep purple.

'Empire Blue'. Rich violet-blue with orange eye. A.G.M. 1969.

'Fascinating' (*'Fascination'*). Wide, full panicles of vivid lilac-pink.

'Fortune'. Long cylindrical racemes of soft lilac with orange eye. A.G.M. 1969.

'Fromow's Purple'. Deep purple-violet, in large handsome panicles.

'Harlequin'. Leaves conspicuously variegated creamy-white; flowers reddish purple. Lower growing than most cultivars. *'Variegata'* is a similar, but inferior clone.

'Ile de France'. Long, elegant racemes of rich violet.

magnifica REHD. & WILS. Bluish-purple. Petal lobes reflexed. A.M. 1905. F.C.C. 1905.

nanhoensis REHD. An elegant, slender branched variety with narrow leaves and long, narrowly cylindrical panicles of mauve flowers. Introduced by Reginald Farrer from Kansu in 1914.

'Alba'. A lovely form with white flowers.

'Pink Pearl'. Lilac-pink with soft yellow eye, in dense panicles.

'Royal Red'. Massive panicles of red-purple. A.M. 1950. A.G.M. 1969.

'Salicifolia'. A low growing form with linear leaves and slender, narrow racemes.

'Variegata'. See under *'Harlequin'*.

veitchiana REHD. Lavender, in large panicles. F.C.C. 1902.

BUDDLEIA—*continued*

davidii 'White Bouquet'. Fragrant white, yellow-eyed flowers in large panicles.

'White Cloud'. Pure white flowers in dense panicles.

'White Profusion'. Large panicles of pure white, yellow-eyed flowers. A.G.M. 1969.

fallowiana BALF. f. & W. W. SM. Medium sized to large shrub. Stems and leaves white woolly; flowers very fragrant, pale lavender-blue, in large panicles. Requires a sheltered position. China. C. 1921.

'Alba'. Flowers creamy white, with orange eye. A.M. 1978.

†**farreri** BALF. f. & W. W. SM. A noble, tall foliage shrub for a sheltered site in full sun. Leaves hastate, very large, densely woolly-white beneath, velvety above. Flowers fragrant, rose-lilac, appearing in April. China. I. 1915.

†**forrestii** DIELS. A large shrub, young leaves pubescent beneath. Flowers fragrant, usually pale lilac, produced in cylindrical racemes in late summer to early autumn. Requires a sheltered position. S.W. China. I. 1903.

globosa HOPE. The Chilean "Orange Ball Tree". A striking, erect, medium sized shrub with handsome foliage. In June, laden with orange-yellow, ball-like inflorescences. Chile, Peru. I. 1774.

japonica HEMSL. (*curviflora* ANDRE). A medium sized shrub of arching habit. Shoots four-winged producing drooping, dense terminal panicles of lavender woolly flowers during summer. Japan. I. about 1896.

†×**lewisiana** EVERETT (*asiatica*×*madagascariensis*) (×*madagasiatica*). Hybrids of garden origin between two floriferous species.

'Margaret Pike'. A large, strong growing shrub with wand-like, white woolly stems. Flowers of soft yellow carried in long, dense terminal racemes during winter. A.M. 1953. F.C.C. 1954.

lindleyana LINDL. Medium sized shrub with long, slender, curved racemes of purple-violet flowers, which are individually strikingly beautiful. China. I. 1843.

'Lochinch' (*davidii*×*fallowiana*). A medium sized shrub of bushy compact habit with grey pubescent young stems and leaves. Later the leaves become green and glabrous above, remaining white tomentose beneath. Flowers scented, violet-blue with deep orange eye, in dense conical panicles. A.G.M. 1969.

×**madagasiatica.** See *B.* ×*lewisiana.*

†***madagascariensis** LAM. Yellow flowers in long panicles during winter. A beautiful tall evergreen for the conservatory. Madagascar. I. 1827.

myriantha DIELS. A medium sized shrub with lanceolate leaves which are white or yellow tomentose beneath. Flowers purple, downy, in slender panicles in late summer. W. China, Burma. C. 1933.

nivea DUTHIE. A vigorous, medium sized shrub with large leaves, the whole plant woolly white with a thick white felted down. Flowers small, lilac-purple in August. China. I. 1901.

†**officinalis** MAXIM. Flowers throughout winter if given cool greenhouse treatment. Leaves clothed beneath with grey wool, semi-evergreen. Delicate mauve, fragrant flowers in panicles. China. I. 1908. A.M. 1911.

×**pikei 'Hever'.** (*alternifolia*×*caryopteridifolia*). A medium sized hardy hybrid with lilac-mauve flowers borne in terminal panicles 15 to 30cm. A.M. 1953.

†**pterocaulis** A. B. JACKS. A rare species from Yunnan and Burma having long pointed leaves and stout spiky lilac inflorescences.

†**salviifolia** LAM. "South African Sage Wood". A medium sized shrub, hardy in the south-west of England. Leaves sage-like; flowers white or pale lilac with orange eye. South Africa. C. 1783.

sterniana COTTON. A large shrub with very large hastate leaves, densely woolly white beneath, velvety above, making this an attractive foliage plant; flowers produced in spring, pale lavender with a deep orange eye. China. I. 1922.

tibetica W.W.SM. A medium sized, attractive shrub with heart-shaped, bullate leaves covered with soft white velvety down which also clothes the shoots. The leaf-stalks are winged. Flowers soft lilac during March and April. Tibet. I. 1931.

'West Hill' (*davidii*×*fallowiana*). A medium sized shrub of spreading habit. The long arching stems are thinly covered with a loose tomentum. The leaves are grey pubescent above, later almost glabrous and green, and white tomentose beneath. Flowers fragrant, pale-lavender with an orange eye, produced in large terminal, curved panicles in late summer. This attractive shrub has for many years been erroneously distributed as *B. fallowiana.*

×**weyerana** WEYER (*davidii magnifica*×*globosa*). An unusual hybrid with ball-shaped heads of orange-yellow, often mauve tinged, flowers borne in long slender panicles on the young wood in summer. Garden origin.

BUPLEURUM—Umbelliferae—A genus of about seventy-five species, mostly herbs and sub-shrubs, of which the following is the only woody species normally cultivated in the open in Britain.

***fruticosum** L. One of the best evergreen shrubs of medium size for exposed places near the sea and for all types of soil. Foliage sea-green; flowers yellow, July to September. S. Europe. Long cultivated. A.M. 1979.

†*BURSARIA—Pittosporaceae—A small genus related to *Pittosporum*.

spinosa CAV. An Australian and Tasmanian shrub growing to about 2·5m. It has dainty foliage and panicles of small, fragrant white flowers in summer. A.M. 1928.

"BUTCHER'S BROOM". See *RUSCUS aculeatus*.

"BUTTER NUT". See *JUGLANS cinerea*

"BUTTON BUSH". See *CEPHALANTHUS occidentalis*.

***BUXUS—Buxaceae**—Evergreen shrubs or occasionally small trees, thriving on most soils, in sun or shade. Many are useful for hedging purposes.

balearica LAM. "Balearic Islands Box". A large shrub or small erect growing tree with large, firm, bright green leathery leaves 4cm. long by 2cm. broad. Balearic Isles and S.W. Spain. I. before 1780.

harlandii HORT. not HANCE. A hardy, dwarf shrub of distinct habit, forming a dense, compact dome of bright green, oblanceolate leaves. Probably a form of *B. microphylla sinica*. The true *B. harlandii* HANCE is more tender and not in cultivation.

microphylla SIEB. & ZUCC. A dwarf or small shrub of dense rounded habit. Leaves narrowly oblong, thin in texture, up to 1·5cm. long. Of Japanese origin but unknown in the wild. I. 1860.

'Compacta'. A dwarf clone with tiny leaves, slowly forming a dense compact bun. Suitable for rock garden or trough.

'Green Pillow'. A slow growing clone of American origin forming a dense, compact hummock. Leaves larger than those of *'Compacta'* and of a brighter green.

japonica REHD. & WILS. (*B. japonica*). A distinct small to medium sized shrub of open spreading habit. Leaves broadly obovate of thick leathery texture. Twigs four-angled. Japan. I. 1860.

koreana NAKAI. A dwarf variety differing from *B. microphylla* in its loose, spreading habit and dark green, often bronze tinted leaves. Korea. I. 1919.

'Richard'. A dwarf cultivar from the U.S.A. The leaves are obovate, thick and firm with a deep apical notch, and of a bright green.

sinica REHD. & WILS. Taller and more spreading than the type, also looser in habit, with slightly larger leaves and pubescent branches. China. I. 1900.

empervirens L. "Common Box". A large shrub or small tree producing luxuriant masses of small dark green leaves. Distributed through Southern Europe, North Africa and Western Asia. Naturalized and possibly wild in Southern England. The "Common Box" has given rise to innumerable forms and variations, many of which are suitable for hedging and topiary.

'Agram'. A selection from the U.S.A. Described as a columnar form. Leaves elliptic, emarginate, medium to large, deep shining green.

'Arborescens'. A large shrub or occasionally a small tree with medium to large, dark green leaves. Excellent for screening.

'Argentea'. A wide spreading shrub. Leaves dark green shaded grey and margined creamy-white. Tends to revert.

'Aurea Maculata'. See *'Aureovariegata'*.

'Aurea Maculata Pendula'. See *'Aurea Pendula'*.

'Aurea Marginata'. See *'Marginata'*.

'Aurea Pendula' (*'Aurea Maculata Pendula'*). An attractive cultivar forming a large bush or a small tree with weeping branchlets and leaves mottled and blotched creamy-yellow.

'Aureovariegata' (*'Aurea Maculata'*). A medium to large shrub of dense bushy habit. Leaves green, variously striped, splashed and mottled creamy-yellow.

'Elata'. See *'Longifolia'*.

'Elegantissima'. A small to medium sized, slow growing shrub of dense, compact, dome-shaped habit. Leaves small often mis-shapen, green with irregular creamy-white margin. Makes an attractive specimen shrub. The best silver box.

'Gold Tip'. This is one of the most common forms of Box in commercial horticulture, and is generally made to do duty for the type. The upper leaves of the terminal shoots are often tipped with yellow.

BUXUS—*continued*

sempervirens 'Handsworthensis' (*'Handsworthii'*). A large shrub, initially of erect habit but spreading in maturity. Leaves thick, leathery, dark green, of rounded or oblong shape. Excellent as a tall hedge or screen.

'Hardwickensis'. A large strong-growing shrub of stiff habit. The stout shoots are well clothed with leathery leaves more rounded and bullate than those of the related *'Handsworthensis'*.

'Horizontalis'. See *'Prostrata'*.

'Japonica Aurea'. See *'Latifolia Maculata'*.

'Latifolia'. A large shrub of dense but spreading habit. Leaves comparatively large, of a deep shining green.

'Latifolia Bullata'. Similar in habit to *'Latifolia Macrophylla'* but with leaves blistered and puckered.

'Latifolia Macrophylla'. A medium to large shrub of loose, spreading habit. Leaves large, broadly ovate to rounded, dark shining green.

'Latifolia Maculata' (*'Japonica Aurea'*). A small to medium sized shrub of dense compact habit when young, forming a large mound. The large leaves are irregularly blotched dull yellow. When grown in the open the bright yellow young growths are attractive in spring. Makes an excellent hedge of dense habit.

'Longifolia' (*'Salicifolia'*) (*'Elata'*). A large shrub or small tree producing dense sprays of large, narrowly-oblong leaves. An attractive cultivar of elegant habit particularly when grown on a single stem.

'Marginata' (*'Aurea Marginata'*). A large growing cultivar of erect habit. The medium sized leaves, often puckered and mis-shapen, are green, irregularly splashed and margined yellow. Tends to revert when allowed to grow too freely. A branch sport of *'Hardwickensis'*.

'Myosotifolia'. An erect, slow growing small to medium sized shrub of compact twiggy habit, with small dark green leaves.

'Myrtifolia'. Usually seen as a small or medium sized shrub, but in time reaching a large size. Leaves small, narrow, occuring in characteristic dense, flattened sprays, sometimes becoming bronzed in winter.

'Pendula'. A large shrub of loose, open growth. The branchlets are pendulous and bear masses of dark green leaves. Makes an unusual small tree when trained to a single stem.

'Prostrata' (*'Horizontalis'*). A strong growing medium sized shrub with horizontally spreading branches.

'Rosmarinifolia' (*'Thymifolia'*). A dwarf shrub of neat habit. The small leaves are linear to linear-lanceolate in shape, of a distinct dark sage green and rough to the touch.

'Rotundifolia'. A small, slow-growing form with rounded leaves.

'Salicifolia'. See *'Longifolia'*.

'Suffruticosa'. "Edging Box". A dwarf or small shrub commonly used as an edging to paths and flower beds, particularly those of a formal nature. Leaves, of medium size, ovate, bright shining green.

'Thymifolia'. See *'Rosmarinifolia'*.

'Vardar Valley'. A dwarf geographical form from the Balkans making a low, compact mound. A specimen in the Arnold Arboretum, Mass., is said to have attained ·6m. high and 1·2m. across in twenty years.

wallichiana BAILL. A rare species in cultivation, usually of open, lax habit and of medium size. Leaves narrowly oblong-lanceolate, to 5cm. or more long. Subject to injury in our most severe winters. N.W. Himalaya. I. 1850.

"CABBAGE TREE". See *CORDYLINE*.

CAESALPINIA—Leguminosae—Spectacular shrubs for sunny, sheltered sites.

†gilliesii BENTH. (*Poinciana gilliesii*). A large South American shrub popularly known as "Bird of Paradise". Dainty leaflets, bipinnately arranged. Flowers borne as many as 30 to 40 together, in long, erect racemes and consisting of rich yellow petals and a cluster of scarlet stamens 5 to 8cm. long; opening in July and August. Requires a hot, sunny wall. Argentina. I. 1829. A.M. 1927.

japonica SIEB. & ZUCC. Handsome, large Japanese shrub armed with prominent spines. Flowers 20 to 30 in a raceme, bright yellow, with scarlet stamens, opening in June. Leaves acacia-like, of a refreshing shade of soft green. I. 1881. F.C.C. 1888.

CAESALPINIA—*continued*

†**tinctoria** DOMB. A strong-growing, scandent shrub with attractively divided leaves and elegant racemes of yellow flowers in summer. Columbia.

†**CALCEOLARIA**—**Scrophulariaceae**—The shrubby members of this large genus are sun-loving evergreen plants having "pouch"-shaped flowers in terminal panicles. All require a well-drained position at the foot of a sunny wall.

***integrifolia** MURR. Handsome small shrub bearing corymbs of large yellow flowers in late summer. Chiloe. I. 1822.

angustifolia LINDL. (*hayi*). A variety with narrow leaves. A.M. 1960.

hayi. See *angustifolia.*

violacea. See *JOVELLANA violacea.*

"CALICO BUSH". See *KALMIA latifolia.*

CALLICARPA—**Verbenaceae**—A family of neat shrubs notable for their soft rose-madder autumn colour and conspicuous violet or lilac-purple fruits which are freely produced where several plants are grown together. Flowers in cymes, small, pink.

bodinieri LEVL. Medium-sized shrub with long leaves and deep lilac fruits. Foliage deep rose-purple in autumn. C. and W. China. I. about 1845.

giraldii REHD. (*C. giraldiana*). A medium sized to large shrub with long, scurfy pubescent stems and elliptic to lanceolate long-pointed leaves. Flowers lilac, produced during late summer, and followed by masses of small dark lilac or pale violet fruits. E. to W. China. C. 1900. F.C.C. 1924.

dichotoma K. KOCH (*purpurea*) (*koreana* HORT.). A compact shrub to about 1·5m. Leaves ovate to obovate coarsely serrated; flowers pink in July, followed by deep lilac fruits. China, Korea, N. Formosa. I. 1857. A.M. 1962.

giraldiana. See *C. bodinieri giraldii.*

japonica THUNB. An attractive, small shrub of compact growth, with oval leaves, pale pink flowers and violet fruits. Japan. I. 1845.

angustata REHD. (*longifolia* HEMSL.). A form with narrow leaves attaining as much as 23cm. in length. China; Formosa. I. 1907.

'Leucocarpa'. Fruits white.

luxurians REHD. A form with larger leaves and flower clusters. Japan.

koreana. See *C. dichotoma.*

purpurea. See *C. dichotoma.*

†***CALLISTEMON**—**Myrtaceae**—The Australian "Bottle Brushes" are magnificent sun-loving evergreens, but only suited to the mildest districts. Flowers are produced during summer in cylindrical spikes. The long stamens are the colourful part of the flower. Not successful in shallow chalky soils.

citrinus SKEELS (*lanceolatus*). A vigorous spreading shrub of medium size with narrow, rigid leaves, lemon-scented when crushed. Flowers red, in dense spikes during summer. I. 1788.

'Splendens'. Flowers brilliant scarlet. A graceful shrub, 1·5 to 2m. in height, flowering throughout summer, and thriving in the open in the milder southern counties. A.M. 1926.

lanceolatus. See *C. citrinus.*

linearis DC. Small narrow leaves and long cylindrical spikes of scarlet flowers. Hardy in sheltered positions along the South Coast. I. 1788.

pallidus DC. A medium-sized shrub related to *C. salignus*. Leaves narrowly elliptic. Flowers cream-coloured. Tasmania.

rigidus R.BR. A medium-sized shrub with narrow, rigid leaves up to 13cm. long. Flowers dark red, densely crowded in spikes 8 to 10cm. long.

salignus DC. One of the hardiest of the "Bottle Brush" family, in favourable localities attaining a height and width of about 2·5m. Leaves narrow, willow like; flowers pale yellow. I. 1788. A.M. 1948.

speciosus DC. A medium sized shrub with narrow sharp-pointed leaves and deep scarlet flowers. I. 1823.

‡***CALLUNA**—**Ericaceae**—A genus of a single species, differing from *Erica* in its four-parted corolla and the large coloured four-parted calyx.

CALLUNA—*continued*

vulgaris HULL (*Erica vulgaris*). "Heather"; "Ling". One of our most familiar native shrublets, covering large tracts of mountain and moorland in northern and western parts of the British Isles, and equally well known on the heaths and commons of the south. A.G.M. 1969.

A great number of forms are cultivated in gardens, varying in colour of flower and foliage, time of flowering and habit. All are easily grown plants for lime-free soils even tolerating moist positions. Though tolerant of shade, they are freer flowering and happier in full sun. One of the most beautiful shrubs, especially the double flowered forms, for cutting for indoor decoration, the dried flowers retaining their colour indefinitely. Native of Europe and Asia Minor.

Pruning, consisting of the removal of the old inflorescences, may be carried out after flowering. In the case of cultivars with coloured foliage and those with attractive dried inflorescences, pruning is best left until late March.

Flowering times are indicated as follows:—

Early—July to August
Mid—August to September
Late—October to November

alba BRAUN-BLANQUET. "White Heather". A white flowered form of the type. Mid. ·5m. Popularly connected with Scotland but liable to appear wherever the species grows.

'Alba Aurea'. Bright green foliage with yellow tips; flowers white. Mid. 10cm.

'Alba Carlton'. Very floriferous, white. Mid. ·5m.

'Alba Elata'. Dense habit. Flowers white. Mid to Late. ·6m.

'Alba Minor'. Dwarf. Flowers white. Early. 15 to 23cm.

'Alba Plena' (*'Alba Flore Pleno'*). A popular free-flowering cultivar. Flowers white, double. Mid. ·5m. A sport of *'Alba Elegans'*. A.M. 1938. A.M.T. 1960. A.G.M. 1969.

'Alba Pumila'. Dwarf form of compact habit. Flowers white. Mid. 10cm.

'Alba Rigida'. An attractive plant with distinctive horizontal branching habit. Flowers white. Mid. 15cm. A.M.T. 1964.

'Alportii'. Tall erect growth. Flowers crimson. Mid. ·6m. A.G.M. 1947.

'Alportii Praecox'. Similar to *'Alportii'* but a little dwarfer and flowering two to three weeks earlier. Early. ·5m.

'Argentea'. Young shoots of a bright pale green in spring. Flowers mauve. Mid. ·3m.

'August Beauty'. Free flowering, white. Mid. ·5m. A.M.T. 1960.

'Aurea'. An attractive form. Foliage gold-tinted, turning bronze-red in winter. Flowers purple. Mid. ·3m. A.M.T. 1961.

'Barnett Anley'. Compact and erect, yellowish-green foliage. Flowers petunia-purple in densely packed racemes. Mid. ·5m. A.M.T. 1960. F.C.C.T. 1962. A.G.M. 1969.

'Blazeaway'. A startling foliage plant. The green foliage changes to rich red in winter. Flowers lilac-mauve. Mid. ·5m.

'Camla'. See *'County Wicklow'*.

'Coccinea'. Grey-green foliage. Flowers dark crimson contrasting with the pale grey young shoots. Mid. 23cm.

'County Wicklow' (*'Camla'*). Dwarf and spreading. Flowers shell pink, double. Mid. 23cm. A.M.T. 1960. F.C.C.T. 1961. A.G.M. 1969.

'Cuprea'. An old cultivar with young shoots golden in summer, ruddy bronze in autumn and winter. Flowers pale mauve. Mid. ·3m. F.C.C. 1873.

'C. W. Nix'. A choice plant with dark green foliage and long tapered racemes of dark glowing crimson flowers. Mid. ·6m. A.M.T. 1961.

'David Eason'. An unusual heather with reddish flowers which, however, never open. Late. ·5m.

'Drum-ra'. A pretty cultivar with white flowers. Mid. ·5m. A.M.T. 1961.

'Durfordii'. Very dark foliage and upright racemes of pale pink flowers. Late, often into December. ·3 to ·6m.

'Elsie Purnell'. Flowers of a lively silvery pink, double, deeper coloured in bud. Mid to Late. ·6 to ·8m. A.M.T. 1963.

'Flore Pleno'. An old cultivar with flowers lilac-pink, double. Mid. ·5m. A.M. 1929.

'Foxii'. A dwarf, compact cushion of soft green, studded with pink flowers. Mid. 15cm.

CALLUNA—*continued*

vulgaris 'Foxii Nana'. Dwarf, forming a dense cushion of green. Flowers, when produced, light purple. Mid. 10cm.

'Golden Feather'. A most attractive clone with golden feathery foliage changing to a gentle orange in winter. ·5m. A.M.T. 1965. F.C.C.T. 1967. A.G.M. 1973.

'Gold Haze'. Foliage of a bright golden hue. Flowers white. Mid. ·5 to ·6m. A.M.T. 1961. F.C.C.T. 1963. A.G.M. 1969.

'Goldsworth Crimson'. A strong growing plant. Flowers deep crimson. Mid to Late. ·6 to ·8m.

'Hammondii'. A strong growing cultivar with dark green foliage. Flowers white. Mid. ·8m. Useful as a low hedge. A.G.M. 1969.

'Hammondii Aureifolia'. Tips of young shoots coloured golden yellow in spring. Flowers white. Mid. ·5 to ·6m.

'Hammondii Rubrifolia'. Similar in habit to '*Hammondii Aureifolia*' but tips of young shoots red tinged in spring. Flowers purple. Mid. ·5 to ·6m.

'H. E. Beale'. A splendid cultivar producing very long racemes of double, bright rose-pink flowers, excellent for cutting. Mid to Late. ·6m. A.G.M. 1942. F.C.C. 1943.

'Hibernica'. A dwarf clone, extremely free-flowering, the mauve flowers often outnumbering and smothering the leaves. Late. 15cm.

'Hiemalis'. Erect growing, flowers of a soft mauve. Mid to Late. ·5m.

'Hirsuta Compacta'. See '*Sister Anne*'.

'Hookstone'. Erect growing; flowers salmon-pink in long racemes. Mid. ·5 to ·6m.

'Humpty Dumpty'. An amusing form of compact but uneven habit. Flowers white, not freely produced. Mid. 15cm.

'J. H. Hamilton'. A pretty dwarf with large, pink double flowers. Early. 23cm. Perhaps the finest double heather. A.M. 1935. A.M.T. 1960. F.C.C.T. 1961. A.G.M. 1962.

'Joan Sparkes'. Flowers mauve, double, occasionally producing single flowers. A sport of '*Alba Plena*'. Mid. 23cm. A.M. 1957.

'Joy Vanstone'. Golden foliage, deepening to rich orange in winter. Flowers orchid pink. Mid. ·5m. A.M.T. 1971.

'Kit Hill'. Dwarf, with curving racemes of white flowers. Mid. 23cm.

'Mair's Variety'. Tall, flowers white, especially suitable for cutting. Mid. ·8m. A.M.T. 1961. F.C.C.T. 1963.

'Minima'. A dwarf compact form. Flowers when produced are purple. Mid. ·8cm.

'Mrs. Ronald Gray'. A charming prostrate mat. Flowers reddish-purple. Mid. 5 to 8cm.

'Mullion'. Semi-prostrate, with numerous branches and densely packed racemes of deep pink flowers. Mid. 15 to 23cm. A.M.T. 1963.

'Orange Queen'. The young foliage in spring is gold and as the season advances turns to deep orange. Flowers pink. Mid. ·6m.

'Pallida'. An old cultivar of vigorous habit; flowers pale pink. Mid. ·3m.

'Penhale'. Compact mounds of dark green foliage becoming bronzed in winter. Flowers rose-purple. Mid. ·3m.

'Peter Sparkes'. Flowers deep pink, double, in long racemes. Useful for cutting. Mid to Late. ·5m. A.M. 1958. F.C.C.T. 1962. A.G.M. 1969.

'Pygmaea'. Very dwarf, spreading branchlets, and dark green foliage. Flowers purple, rarely produced. Mid. 8cm. A.M.T. 1962.

'Robert Chapman'. The spring foliage is gold and changes first to orange then finally red. Flowers soft purple. Mid. ·3 to ·6m. A.M.T. 1962. A.G.M. 1965.

'Rosalind'. Golden foliage and pink flowers. Mid. ·3 to ·6m. A.M.T. 1961.

'Ruth Sparkes'. Foliage bright yellow-green but inclined to revert. Flowers white, double. Sport of '*Alba Plena*'. Mid. 23cm.

CALLUNA—*continued*

vulgaris 'Serlei'. Erect growing with dark green foliage. Flowers white, in long racemes. Late. ·6m. A.M.T. 1961. F.C.C.T. 1962. A.G.M. 1969.

'Serlei Aurea'. Similar to '*Serlei*' but possesses foliage of a bright golden hue. ·6m. A.M.T. 1961.

'Serlei Rubra' ('*Serlei Grandiflora*'). Similar to '*Serlei*' but flowers dark reddish-purple. ·6m.

'Silver Queen'. A very beautiful plant. Foliage silvery-grey, flowers pale mauve. Mid. ·6m.

'Sister Anne' ('*Hirsuta Compacta*'). Compact mounds of pretty grey foliage; flowers pink. Mid. 8 to 10cm.

'Spitfire'. Golden foliage turning bronze-red in winter. Flowers pink. Mid. 23 to 30cm.

'Sunset'. Foliage variegated yellow, gold and orange. Flowers pink. Mid. 23 to 30cm. A.M.T. 1967. F.C.C.T. 1968.

'Tenuis'. Loose-growing; flowers red-purple in long racemes. Early to Mid. 23cm.

'Tib'. A lovely, floriferous cultivar. Flowers rosy-red, double. Early. ·3 to ·6m. A.M.T. 1960. F.C.C.T. 1962.

'Tricolorifolia'. Young growths in spring turning from bronze to red, finally deep green. Flowers pink. Mid. ·6m.

'Underwoodii'. The pale mauve buds remain closed and gradually change to an effective silvery-white colour which lasts well into winter. Mid to Late. ·3m. A.M.T. 1960.

'White Gown'. Long racemes of white flowers. Mid to Late. ·6 to ·8m.

CALOPHACA—Leguminosae—A small genus of low shrubs and herbs for sunny, well drained positions.

grandiflora REGEL. Dwarf often procumbent shrub with pinnate leaves and axillary racemes of bright yellow pea-flowers in June or July. Turkestan. I. 1880.

wolgarica FISCH. A very hardy prostrate shrub bearing yellow, pea-flowers in June and July. Leaves pinnate. Needs full sun and good drainage. S.E. Russia. I. 1786.

CALYCANTHUS—Calycanthaceae—"Allspice". A North American genus of aromatic medium-sized shrubs of easy cultivation, with conspicuous red-brown flowers during the summer and early autumn.

fertilis WALT. (*glaucus*). Glossy leaves and brown-crimson flowers throughout summer. I. 1806.

'Purpureus'. Leaves tinged purple beneath.

floridus L. "Carolina Allspice". A rare species much confused in gardens with *C. fertilis* but leaves normally downy beneath. I. 1726.

occidentalis HOOK. & ARN. (*macrophyllus* HORT.). A Californian species with larger flowers and leaves than *C. fertilis*, differing also from the previous two species in the exposed leaf buds. I. 1831.

praecox. See *CHIMONANTHUS praecox*.

‡*CAMELLIA—Theaceae—Camellias are magnificent flowering evergreens, the majority of which are as hardy as "Laurel". They are a little more lime tolerant than Rhododendrons, and thrive in a good acid or neutral peaty soil.

A woodland site with light overhead shade is ideal but they can be grown successfully and often flower more freely when planted open to full sun, as for example, when against a south or west facing wall. In such positions careful attention to watering and mulching is vital, or bud-dropping may result. Damage to open flowers will result from the effects of early morning spring sunshine following frost, so in some areas of the British Isles a north or west facing site is good unless light overhead shade of trees is available.

They are ideal plants for growing in tubs and for a cool greenhouse or conservatory.

Flowers:—

Single—One row of not over eight regular, irregular or loose petals and conspicuous stamens.

Semi-double—Two or more rows of regular, irregular or loose petals and conspicuous stamens.

CAMELLIA—*continued*

Anemone Form—One or more rows of large outer petals lying flat or wavy; the centre a convex mass of intermingled petaloids and stamens.

Paeony Form—A deep rounded flower consisting of a convex mass of petals, petaloids and sometimes stamens.

Double—Imbricated petals showing stamens in a concave centre when open.

Formal Double—Fully imbricated, many rows of petals with no stamens.

Flower sizes:—

Very large—Over 12·5cm. (5ins.) across
Large—10 to 12·5cm. (4 to 5ins.) across
Medium—7·5cm. to 10cm. (3 to 4ins.) across
Small—5 to 7·5cm. (2 to 3ins.) across

Flower size, form and colour are subject to some variation in certain cultivars; type of soil, aspect and general cultivation all playing a part.

† Indicates that the plant and its forms are too tender for exposed positions in all but the mildest localities though most of them are suitable for warm walls or when given evergreen, woodland, or similar protection in less favoured gardens. They also make excellent cool greenhouse or conservatory plants.

Cornish Snow (*cuspidata* × *saluenensis*). A delightful, free growing medium sized to large hybrid, bearing multitudes of small, white flowers along the branchlets. Garden origin about 1930. A.M. 1948. A.G.M. 1963.
'Michael'. A beautiful clone with larger single, white flowers. The best form of this attractive hybrid.
'Winton'. Soft almond pink.

cuspidata VEITCH. A large shrub with small leaves, copper tinted when young, and small creamy white flowers. South China. I. 1900. A.M. 1912.

†drupifera LOUR. A little known species, akin to *C. sasanqua*, discovered at 900m. on Lantan Island, near Hong Kong.

†granthamiana SEALY. A remarkable species from Hong Kong. A large shrub, having large parchment white flowers. The leaves are quite distinct with their conspicuously impressed venation, bronze when unfolding. A.M. 1974.

× **heterophylla** HU (*japonica* × *reticulata*). The original plant to which this name was given was found in a temple garden in Yunnan. It is thought to occur in the wild and very rarely in cultivation. The undermentioned clone most resembles *C. reticulata*, but possesses certain characteristics of *C. japonica*.
'Barbara Hillier'. A beautiful large shrub with large, handsome polished leaves and large, single, satin-pink flowers. A first class shrub.

†hongkongensis SEEM. A tender species making a large shrub, bearing 5cm. wide crimson flowers with prominent bright yellow anthers. Leaves large, up to 15cm. long, leathery and obscurely toothed, of an unusual metallic blue-brown when unfolding. Hong Kong. I. 1874.

†'Inamorata' (*reticulata* × *saluenensis*). Closely resembling *C. reticulata* in habit and leaf but the rose-pink flowers resemble those of *C. saluenensis*. Raised at Exbury by Francis Hanger.

'Inspiration' (*reticulata* × *saluenensis*). A medium sized shrub with large, semi-double flowers of a deep pink. A.M. 1954. F.C.C.T. 1980.

japonica L. "Common Camellia". A large evergreen shrub with characteristically, polished leaves. The wild species, a native of Japan and Korea, was originally introduced in 1739 and was later followed by various cultivars from China and Japan.

As the Rose has become the plaything of the commercial hybridist so the Camellia has become the toy of both the commercial and amateur gardener. Far too many scarcely separable sports (mutations) have been made separate entities. In fact a single bush may embrace three cultivars. At the present time named cultivars of this species are numbered in thousands and are constantly being added to.

CAMELLIA—*continued*

The majority are of medium size, the more vigorous clones reaching a large size after many years. In most areas **flowers** are normally produced from February to early mid-May, but their size and colour may vary depending on age of plant, growing conditions and season. A.G.M. 1930.

japonica 'Abundance'. White; medium, peony form. Growth slow and upright.

'Admiral Nimitz' (*'Kishu-tsukasa'*). Deep rose-pink; large, formal double. Growth vigorous, compact and erect.

'Adolphe Audusson'. Blood-red, conspicuous stamens; large, semi-double. Growth vigorous, compact. A first-class, well proved plant. A.M. 1934. F.C.C. 1956. A.G.M. 1969.

'Alba Plena' (*'Alba Grandiflora'*). White; large, formal double. Growth erect, bushy. Probably the best double white for general planting. A.M. 1948.

'Alba Simplex'. White with conspicuous stamens; large, single. The most proven single white. A.G.M. 1969.

'Albertii'. See *'Prince Albert'*.

'Althaeiflora'. Dark red; large, paeony form. Large specimens are to be found in old gardens. A.G.M. 1953.

'Anemoniflora'. Dark crimson; medium, anemone form. Growth vigorous and erect. A.M. 1950

'Apollo'. Rose-red, occasionally blotched white; medium, semi-double. Growth vigorous and open. One of the most satisfactory camellias for British Gardens. It is often confused with *'Jupiter'* from which it differs in its more numerous, deeper coloured petals, also in its longer, pointed leaves which possess a characteristic twisted tip. A.M. 1956. A.G.M. 1969.

'Apple Blossom' (*'Joy Sander'*). Pale blush-pink, deepening at margin; medium, semi-double. A.M. 1933.

'Are-jishi'. Rose-red; medium, paeony form. Growth vigorous and open. Distinct in its thick, coarsely toothed, tapering leaves.

'Augusto Pinto (*'Augusto Leal de Gouveia Pinto'*). Light lavender pink to carmine, each petal bordered white; large, semi-double to double. A.M. 1958.

'Beni-otome'. See *'Cheerful'*.

'Berenice Boddy'. Light pink, deeper beneath; medium, semi-double. Growth vigorous and erect.

'Betty Sheffield Blush'. Light pink with several darker markings; large, semi-double to loose paeony form. A sport of *'Betty Sheffield'*.

'Betty Sheffield Supreme'. White, each petal bordered deep pink to red; large, semi-double to loose paeony form. A sport of *'Betty Sheffield'*.

'Billie McCaskill'. Soft-pink; medium, semi-double with deeply fimbriated petals. Growth medium, compact and erect.

'Blood of China'. Deep salmon-red; large, semi-double to loose paeony form. Growth vigorous and compact.

'Bush Hill Beauty'. Rose-red, clouded white, medium; semi-double. Growth compact.

'Chandleri'. Bright red with occasional white blotch; large semi-double to anemone form.

'Chandleri Elegans'. See *'Elegans'*.

'Cheerful' (*'Beni-otome'*). Rose-red; medium, formal double. Growth vigorous, compact and erect.

'C. M. Hovey'. Carmine; medium, formal double. Growth vigorous and compact. F.C.C. 1879.

'C. M. Wilson'. Light pink; very large, anemone form. Growth slow, spreading. A sport of *'Elegans'*. A.M. 1956.

'Compton's Brow White'. White; medium, single. A.M. 1930.

'Comte de Gomer'. Pale pink, striped and speckled rose-pink; medium, double. Growth medium, compact.

'Contessa Lavinia Maggi'. White or pale pink with broad rose-cerise stripes; large, formal double. F.C.C. 1862. A.G.M. 1969.

'Coquetti'. Delft rose; medium, double. Growth slow, compact and erect. A.M. 1956. A.G.M. 1969.

'Daikagura'. Bright rose-pink blotched white; large, paeony form. Growth slow, compact.

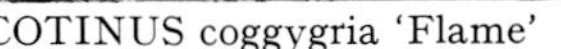

COTINUS coggygria 'Flame'

CORNUS florida 'Cherokee Chief'

CYTISUS × kewensis

CHAENOMELES speciosa 'Moerloosei'

DESFONTAINEA spinosa

FUCHSIA 'Mrs Popple'

CAMELLIA—*continued*

japonica 'Daikagura White'. See *'Shiro-daikagura'*.

'Daitairin' (*'Hatsu-zakura'*). Light rose-pink; large, single, with mass of petaloids in centre. Growth vigorous, erect. A.M. 1953.

'Debutante'. Light pink; medium, paeony form. Growth vigorous, erect.

'Devonia' (*'Devoniensis'*). White; medium, single rather cup-shaped. Growth vigorous, erect. A.M. 1900.

'Dobrei'. Geranium-lake with darker veins; medium, semi-double. Growth vigorous, erect.

'Donckelarii'. Red, often marbled white; large, semi-double. Growth slow and bushy. A first-class plant for the open garden. A.M. 1960. A.G.M. 1969.

'Drama Girl'. Deep salmon-rose pink; very large, semi-double. Vigorous, open slightly pendulous growth. A.M. 1966. F.C.C. 1969.

'Dr. H. G. Mealing'. Blood-red; large, semi-double. Growth vigorous and open.

'Dr. Tinsley'. Pale pink shading to deep pink at margins; medium, semi-double. Compact, upright growth.

'Elegans' (*'Chandleri Elegans'*). Deep peach pink; very large, anemone form. Growth spreading. A well proved cultivar for general cultivation. A.M. 1953. F.C.C. 1958. A.G.M. 1969.

'Fimbriata Superba'. See *'Fred Sander'*.

'Flora'. White; large, single with waxy petals.

'Frau Minna Seidel'. See *'Pink Perfection'*.

'Fred Sander' (*'Fimbriata Superba'*). Crimson with curled, fimbriated petals; medium, semi-double. Growth vigorous, compact and erect. A sport of *'Tricolor'*. A.M. 1921.

'Frizzle White'. White; large, semi-double with crinkled petals. Vigorous spreading growth.

'Furo-an'. Soft pink; medium, single. A.M. 1956.

'Gauntlettii'. See *'Lotus'*.

'Geisha Girl'. Light pink with darker stripes and blotches; large, semi-double. Open, upright growth.

'General Lamorciere'. See *'Marguerite Gouillon'*.

'Gloire de Nantes'. Rose-pink; large, semi-double. Growth medium, compact and erect. A splendid, well proved cultivar. A.M. 1956. A.G.M. 1969.

'Grand Sultan'. Dark red; large, semi-double to formal double.

'Guest of Honor'. Salmon-pink; very large, semi-double to loose paeony form. Growth vigorous, compact and erect. A.M. 1967.

'Guilio Nuccio'. Coral rose-pink; very large, semi-double. Growth vigorous, erect. A.M. 1962.

'H. A. Downing'. Rose-red with blood-red veins, large, semi-double. Growth vigorous, bushy.

'Haku-rakuten'. White; large, semi-double to loose paeony form with curved and fluted petals. Growth vigorous and erect.

'Hana-fuki'. Soft pink, sometimes splashed white; large, semi-double cup-shaped flowers. Growth medium and compact. A.M. 1956.

'Hatsu-zakura'. See *'Daitairin'*.

'High Hat'. Light pink; large, paeony form. Growth slow, compact. A sport of *'Daikagura'*.

'Hi-no-maru'. Pink with conspicuous yellow stamens; medium, single.

'Imbricata Rubra'. Light red; medium, formal double. Distinct leaves, inclined to curl.

'Imura'. White; large, semi-double. Growth vigorous, open and willowy.

'James Allan'. Fiery-red; large, variable in form, single, semi-double, paeony or anemone. Growth medium and open.

'Joshua E. Youtz'. White; large paeony form. Growth slow, compact.

'Joy Sander'. See *'Apple Blossom'*.

'Jupiter'. Bright scarlet, sometimes blotched white; medium, single to semi-double with conspicuous bunch of stamens. Growth vigorous, erect. One of the best camellias for general planting.

'Kelvingtoniana'. Red with conspicuous white variegations; large, semi-double to loose paeony form. A wide spreading, sparsely branched, well proved cultivar. F.C.C. 1869.

'Kenny'. Deep rose pink, blotched white; large, semi-double to paeony form. Growth slow and compact.

CAMELLIA—*continued*

japonica 'Kimberley'. Carmine, with red stamens; medium, single, cup-shaped flowers. Growth vigorous, compact and erect. A.M. 1934.

'Kishu-tsukasa'. See '*Admiral Nimitz*'.

'Kouron-jura'. Very dark self-red; medium, formal double. One of the darkest of all camellias. Growth medium, semi-erect. A.M. 1960.

'Kumasaka'. Rose-pink; medium, double to paeony form. Growth vigorous, compact.

'Lady Buller'. See '*Nagasaki*'.

'Lady Clare'. Deep, clear peach-pink; large, semi-double. Growth vigorous and spreading. Still one of the best of all camellias. A.M. 1927. A.G.M. 1969.

'Lady de Saumerez'. Bright red spotted white; medium, semi-double. Growth vigorous, compact. A well proved cultivar for English gardens. A sport of '*Tricolor*'.

'Lady McCulloch'. White blotched crimson; medium, semi-double.

'Lady Vansittart'. White, striped rose-pink; medium, semi-double, with wavy-edged petals. Growth slow, bushy, leaves undulate.

'Lady Vansittart White'. White; medium, semi-double, with wavy-edged petals. Growth slow, bushy; leaves undulate.

'Lallarook' ('*Laurel Leaf*'). Pink, marbled white; large, formal double. Growth slow and compact; foliage laurel-like.

'Lanarth'. Cardinal red; medium, nearly single. Growth vigorous and erect. A.M. 1960.

'Latifolia'. Soft rose-red; medium, semi-double. Growth vigorous and bushy. A broad-leaved, hardy cultivar succeeding well in the open.

'Laurel Leaf'. See '*Lallarook*'.

'Lawrence Walker'. Red; large, loose paeony to anemone form. Growth vigorous, compact and erect.

'Letitia Schrader'. Dark red; large, paeony to anemone form. Growth medium, compact.

'Lotus' ('*Gauntlettii*') ('*Sode-gashuki*'). White; very large, semi-double, of water-lily form. This vigorous cultivar with spreading branches, is of weak constitution.

'Madame Charles Blard'. White; medium, paeony form. Medium upright growth.

'Madame Victor de Bisschop'. White, medium, semi-double. Growth open and vigorous.

'Magnoliiflora'. Blush pink, with forward pointing petals rather like the expanding buds of *Magnolia stellata;* medium, semi-double. Growth medium, compact. A.M. 1953.

'Magnoliiflora Alba' ('*Yobeki-dori*'). White flushed pale pink.

'Margarete Hertrich'. White; medium, formal double with numerous small petals. Growth vigorous, compact and erect.

'Margherita Coleoni'. Dark red; medium, double to formal double. Growth vigorous, erect.

'Marguerite Gouillon' ('*General Lamorciere*'). Delicate pink, slightly striped and flecked deeper pink; medium, full paeony form. Growth vigorous, bushy.

'Mars'. Turkey-red; large semi-double with conspicuous bunch of stamens. Growth open and loose. Often confused in cultivation with both '*Apollo*' and '*Mercury*'.

'Mary Charlotte'. Light pink; medium, anemone form. Growth compact and upright.

'Mathotiana' ('*Mathotiana Rubra*'). Crimson; large, double to formal double. Growth compact and upright.

'Mathotiana Alba'. White, rarely with a pink spot; large, formal double. Not recommended for an exposed position.

'Mathotiana Rosea'. Clear pink; large, formal double. Vigorous, compact and erect. A sport of '*Mathotiana Alba*'. A.M. 1954.

'Mathotiana Rubra'.. See '*Mathotiana*'.

'Mercury'. Deep soft crimson with slightly darker veins; large, semi-double. Growth medium, compact. A.M. 1948.

'Morning Glow'. White; large, formal double. Growth vigorous, compact and erect.

CAMELLIA—*continued*

japonica 'Mrs. Bertha A. Harms'. Ivory white with faint pink tint; large, semi-double with wavy, crimpled petals. Open upright growth.

'Mrs. D. W. Davis'. Blush-pink, very large, semi-double. Growth vigorous, compact. Requires shelter but makes an excellent conservatory shrub. A.M. 1960. F.C.C. 1968.

'Nagasaki' (*'Lady Buller'*). Rose-pink, marbled white; large, semi-double. Leaves often mottled yellow. Growth spreading. A well proved cultivar for English gardens. A.M. 1953. A.G.M. 1969.

'Nobilissima'. White with yellow shading; medium, paeony form. Growth fairly erect. One of the earliest to flower.

'Paulette Goddard'. Deep red; large, semi-double to paeony form. Growth erect.

'Peach Blossom'. Light pink; medium, semi-double. Growth medium and compact. A shade deeper than *'Magnoliiflora'*.

'Pink Champagne'. Soft pink; large, semi-double to paeony form with irregular petals. Vigorous open growth. A.M. 1960.

'Pink Perfection' (*'Frau Minna Seidel'*). Shell-pink; small, formal double. Growth vigorous and erect.

'Preston Rose' (*'Duchesse de Rohan'*). Salmon-pink; medium, paeony form. Growth vigorous. A.G.M. 1969.

'Pride of Descanso' (*'Yuki-botan'*). White; large, semi-double to loose paeony form with irregular petals. Growth vigorous.

'Prince Albert' (*'Albertii'*). Pink, striped carmine and occasionally white; medium, paeony form. Growth vigorous, compact and upright.

'Purity'. White; medium, double to formal double. Growth vigorous and upright.

'Purple Emperor'. Deep pink slightly marked with white; large, semi-double.

'Quercifolia'. Crimson, large, single, fishtail foliage.

'R. L. Wheeler'. Rose-pink, large to very large, semi-double to anemone form. Growth vigorous. A.M. 1959. F.C.C. 1975.

'Rogetsu'. White with cream-coloured stamens; medium, single, with rounded petals frilled at the margins.

'Royal White'. White; large, semi-double to double. Growth vigorous, spreading.

'Rubens'. Deep rose-pink spotted white; medium, formal double. Spreading growth.

'Rubescens Major'. Crimson, with darker veining; large, double. Habit compact and bushy. A.M. 1959. A.G.M. 1969.

rusticana KITAMURA (*C. rusticana*). "Snow Camellia". A tough, hardy variety from the mountains of northern Japan (Hondo), differing from the type in its wide-spreading petals which open out flat, and its shorter stamens which are almost free to the base, not united into a tube as in *C. japonica*. Flowers red, comparatively small. I. 1954.

'Sabina'. Pink or pink and white; medium, semi-double.

'Shiro-daikagura' (*'Daikagura White'*). White; medium, loose paeony form. Growth medium, compact and erect.

'Sieboldii'. See *'Tricolor'*.

'Snowflake'. White; medium, single.

'Sode-gashuki'. See *'Lotus'*.

'Souvenir de Bahuaud Litou'. Light pink; large, formal double. Growth vigorous and erect. A sport of *'Mathotiana Alba'*.

'Splendens'. Red; large, semi-double.

'Sylvia'. Carmine red, flecked white; medium, single, of cupped form. A sport of *'Kimberley'*.

'Tomorrow'. Rose; very large, semi-double to paeony form. Vigorous, open, slightly pendulous growth. A.M. 1960.

'Tomorrow's Dawn'. Deep soft pink to light pink shading to white at margin, with occasional red streaks and white petaloids; very large, semi-double with irregular petals and large petaloids to full paeony form. Vigorous, open growth. A sport of *'Tomorrow'*.

'Tricolor' (*'Sieboldii'*). White, streaked carmine; medium, semi-double. Growth compact. A well proved cultivar for English gardens.

'Ville de Nantes'. Dark red, usually blotched white; large, semi-double with erect fimbriated petals. Growth slow and bushy. A sport of *'Donckelarii'*.

'Virgin's Blush'. White faintly flushed pink; medium, semi-double to paeony form. Growth vigorous.

CAMELLIA—*continued*

japonica 'Waiwhetu Beauty'. Light pink; medium, semi-double. Growth vigorous.

'Yobeki-dori'. See *'Magnoliiflora Alba'*.

'Yoibijin'. Pale pink; small, single. Growth medium, open.

'Yours Truly'. Pink, streaked deep pink and bordered white; medium, semi-double. Growth slow, bushy; leaves undulate. A sport of *'Lady Vansittart'*. A.M. 1960.

'Yuki-botan'. See *'Pride of Descanso'*.

'Leonard Messel' (*reticulata* × *williamsii 'Mary Christian'*). A very beautiful large shrub which originated at Nymans in Sussex, where it proves to be hardy. Flowers large rich clear pink; semi-double. The dark green leaves incline, like the flower, towards *C. reticulata*. A.M. 1958. F.C.C. and Cory Cup 1970.

maliflora LINDL. A large shrub showing kinship with *C. sasanqua* and like that species rather shy flowering. Flowers soft pink; small, double. Leaves small. Introduced from China in 1818 but not known in a wild state. A.M. 1977.

†**oleifera** ABEL. A medium-sized to large shrub with elliptic, toothed leaves to 6cm. long and small, fragrant, white, flowers in spring. E. Asia. I. 1811.

'Jaune'. White with large centre of yellow petaloids and a few stamens of darker yellow. Known as "Fortune's Yellow Camellia".

reticulata LINDL. One of the most beautiful of all flowering shrubs. The semi-double form *'Captain Rawes'* introduced by Robert Fortune in 1820 was, for a hundred years, regarded in Western gardens as the type plant to which Lindley gave the name *C. reticulata*, until that great plant collector George Forrest, sent home the single wild form from West China in 1924. It is this form (usually referred to as Wild Type) which we are offering. It makes a large compact shrub of much better constitution than the more popular named cultivars. It is hardy in all but the coldest and most exposed gardens and has been uninjured here since it was planted in 1954. There has been extremely little variation between the hundreds of plants raised from seed. The handsome rigid, leathery, net-veined leaves are an excellent foil for the large, single, rose-pink flowers, which are inclined to be trumpet-shaped before finally expanding, and are usually freely produced during late winter and early spring. A.M. 1944.

The following clones with single or semi-double flowers are large shrubs or small trees and are only suitable for the conservatory, except in mild areas.

† **'Buddha'.** Rose-pink, very large, semi-double with irregular upright wavy petals. Growth vigorous, erect. A.M. 1962.

† **'Butterfly Wings'.** Soft pink; very large, semi-double.

† **'Captain Rawes'** (*'Semi-plena'*). Carmine rose-pink; very large, semi-double. The original form, introduced in 1820 by Robert Fortune, is a magnificent shrub. F.C.C. 1963.

† **'Crimson Robe'.** Carmine-red, very large, semi-double with wavy, crinkled petals. F.C.C. 1967.

'Flore Pleno'. See *'Robert Fortune'*.

† **'Lion Head'.** Deep turkey red; large to very large, paeony form.

'Mary Williams'. Crimson to rose; large, single. A vigorous and hardy clone raised at Caerhays Castle by that great gardener J. C. Williams. A.M. 1942. F.C.C. 1964.

† **'Noble Pearl'** (*'Paochucha'*). A superb cultivar; flowers oriental-red, large to very large, semi-double. A.M. 1963.

'Pagoda'. See *'Robert Fortune'*.

'Paochucha'. See *'Noble Pearl'*.

† **'Professor Tsai'.** Rose-pink; semi-double with wavy petals.

† **'Purple Gown'** (*'Tzepao'*). Dark purple-red with narrow stripes of white or wine-red; large to very large, double to paeony form. A.M. 1966.

† **'Robert Fortune'** (*'Pagoda'*) (*'Flore Pleno'*). Deep crimson; large, double. Growth compact. F.C.C. 1865.

'Semi-plena'. See *'Captain Rawes'*.

† **'Shot Silk'.** Brilliant pink; large, semi-double with loose, wavy petals. F.C.C. 1967.

'Trewithen Pink'. Deep rose; large, semi-double. A vigorous, hardy clone selected by G. H. Johnstone who made Trewithen one of the great Cornish gardens, and wrote a standard work on Magnolias. A.M. 1950.

'Tzepao'. See *'Purple Gown'*.

Wild Type. See under *C. reticulata*.

rusticana. See *C. japonica rusticana*.

CAMELLIA—*continued*

†**saluenensis** STAPF. A beautiful medium to large shrub somewhat similar to *C. reticulata* but with smaller leaves and medium-sized flowers, the latter being a lovely soft-pink, single, carried in great profusion. W. China. I. 1924.

'Salutation' (*reticulata* × *saluenensis*). A deliberate cross raised at Borde Hill, Sussex, by Col. Stephenson Clarke, C.B., possibly the greatest "all round" amateur gardener of this century, who left to posterity one of the most complete arboretums. A splendid hybrid of medium to large size with matt green leaves and semi-double, soft silvery pink flowers, 13cm. across, during late winter and early spring. A.M. 1936.

sasanqua THUNB. An attractive winter and early spring flowering species producing small but fragrant, usually white flowers. This delightful species with its numerous progeny is worthy of wall protection. As the plants age and mature they withstand our winters with only a little occasional damage, but they are not so reliable as the Japonica Group, and require the Californian sun to do them justice. Japan. I. 1896.

'Blanchette'. White; single.
'Briar Rose'. Soft, clear pink; single.
'Crimson King'. Bright red; single.
'Duff Allan'. White; single.
'Hiryu'. Crimson; single to semi-double.
'Mine-no-yuki'. White; paeony form.
'Momozono-nishiki'. Rose, shaded white; semi-double with curled petals.
'Narumi-gata'. Large creamy-white, shaded pink towards the margin; fragrant. Perhaps the most reliable flowering of this species. A.M. 1953 (under the name *C. oleifera*).
'Rosea Plena'. Pink; double.
'Rubra'. Rich red; single.
'Tricolor'. White, striped pink and red; single.
'Usubeni'. Soft pink, occasionally marbled white; semi-double.
'Variegata'. Blush-white. Leaves grey-green, margined white.
'Versicolor'. White centre, edged lavender with pink in between; single.

†**sinensis** KTZE. (*thea*) (*Thea sinensis*). The "Tea Plant" of commerce, geographically a variable species in size and shape of leaf. The form we have been growing here for the past forty years has proved a slow growing, compact, rather small shrub with small, nodding white flowers in spring. Assam to China. I. 1740.

†**taliensis** MELCHIOR. An interesting species related to *C. sinensis*. A large shrub or small tree; leaves bright green, laurel-like; flowers small, axillary, cream with conspicuous yellow stamens. W. China. I. 1914.

thea. See *C. sinensis*.

†**tsaii** HU. A tender, very graceful large shrub resembling *C. cuspidata*. Flowers white, small but numerous; foliage copper-coloured when young. W. China, Burma, Indo-China. I. 1924. A.M. 1960.

× **vernalis** (*japonica* × *sasanqua*). Intermediate between its parents, this hybrid has pure white, slightly fragrant flowers with petals arranged in three rows. Flowering from February to May.

× **williamsii** W. W. SM. (*japonica* × *saluenensis*). One of the most valuable hybrid shrubs ever produced and perhaps the best Camellia for general planting in the British Isles. The cultivars originating from this cross are invaluable shrubs, exquisitely beautiful, and exceedingly free-flowering over a long period trom November to May. In foliage they tend towards the *japonica* parent and in flowers towards *saluenensis*. Raised by J. C. Williams at Caerhays Castle, Cornwall about 1925.

'Bartley Pink'. Bright cherry-pink; small, single.
'Bow Bells'. Bright rose; semi-double carried continuously over a long period.
'Caerhays'. Lilac-rose; medium, anemone form. Spreading, somewhat pendulous habit gained from its parent *C. japonica 'Lady Clare'*. A.M. 1969.
'C. F. Coates'. Deep rose; medium ,single; leaves peculiarly three-lobed at the apex, hence sometimes known as the "Fishtail Camellia".
'Charles Michael'. Pale-pink; large, semi-double with long petals.

CAMELLIA—*continued*

× **williamsii 'Citation'.** Silver blush pink; large, semi-double with irregular petals. Growth vigorous, open and erect. A.M. 1960.

'Coppelia'. Carmine-rose; single.

'Coppelia Alba'. White; medium single. Growth erect.

'Crinkles'. Rose-pink; large, semi-double with crinkled petals. Growth bushy and erect.

'Donation'. Orchid pink; large, semi-double. Perhaps the most beautiful Camellia raised this century. Growth vigorous, erect. A.M. 1941. A.M. 1952. A.G.M. 1958. F.C.C.T. 1974.

'E. G. Waterhouse'. Light pink, medium, formal double. Growth upright.

'Elizabeth Rothschild'. Soft rose-pink; medium, semi-double.

'First Flush'. Apple blossom pink; medium, semi-double. Free and early flowering.

'Francis Hanger'. White; single. Growth erect, inclined towards *C. japonica*. Leaves strongly undulate. A.M. 1953.

'Golden Spangles'. Phlox-pink; small, single; leaves with yellow-green central blotch.

'Hiraethlyn'. Palest pink; perfect single form. The *japonica* parent is said to be *'Flora'*.

'J. C. Williams'. Phlox-pink; medium single. The first clone of × *williamsii* to be named, and one of the most beautiful of all camellias. F.C.C. 1942. A.G.M. 1949. A.M.T. 1977.

'Jermyns'. Clear, self peach pink, with broad petals. A first class selection raised in our nurseries.

'Lady Gowrie'. Pink; large, semi-double. Growth vigorous and compact.

'Mary Christian'. Clear pink; small, single. A.M. 1942. F.C.C.T. 1977.

'November Pink'. Phlox-pink; medium, single. Usually the earliest of the group to flower. A.M. 1950.

'Parkside'. Clear pink; large, semi-double.

'Pink Wave'. Rhodamine pink; semi-double. A.M. 1957.

'St. Ewe'. Rose-pink; medium, single of cup form. A.M. 1947. F.C.C.T. 1974.

***CAMPHOROSMA—Chenopodiaceae**—A small genus of aromatic, heath-like shrubs.

monspeliaca L. A small, aromatic shrub with inconspicuous flowers and sage-green leaves. Suitable for sunny, dry positions in coastal areas. N. Africa, S. Europe to C. Asia.

†*CANTUA—Polemoniaceae—A small genus of South American trees and shrubs.

buxifolia JUSS. (*dependens*). A very beautiful small shrub with graceful drooping corymbs of bright cherry-red tubular flowers in April; semi-evergreen in mild localities. Requires a warm, sheltered wall. Andes of Bolivia, Peru and Chile. I. 1849. A.M. 1905.

"CAPE FIGWORT". See *PHYGELIUS capensis*.

CARAGANA—Leguminosae—Attractive, but not spectacular, shrubs or small trees with compound leaves, and normally yellow pea-flowers in early summer.

arborescens LAM. A small shrubby tree from Siberia and Manchuria. One of the toughest and most accommodating of all plants, succeeding in the most exposed areas on all types of soil. Flowers yellow. I. 1752.

'Lorbergii'. An extremely graceful, medium sized shrub with narrow, almost grass-like, leaflets. C. about 1906.

'Nana'. A remarkable dwarf shrub; an outstanding "dot plant" for the rock garden.

'Pendula'. A very attractive weeping form.

boisii SCHNEID. A yellow-flowered species from China and Tibet, attaining about 2m. Differs from *C. arborescens* in its downy seed pods.

chamlagu. See *C. sinica*.

decorticans HEMSL. A shrubby or tree-like species from Afghanistan, ultimately 5 to 5·5m. with tiny stipules. Flowers light yellow, about 2·5cm. long. I. 1879.

franchetiana KOMAR. A tall Chinese shrub of open spreading habit. The buff yellow flowers are 2·5cm. long, the pinnate leaves bright apple-green. I. 1913.

CARAGANA—*continued*

frutex K. KOCH (*frutescens*). A spineless, glabrous shrub up to 3m. producing bright yellow flowers in May. Widely distributed from Eastern Europe to Central Asia. I. 1752.

jubata POIR. A curious small slow growing shrub of irregular form, thickly covered with coarse brownish-grey hairs and slender spines. Large white pea flowers produced singly in late spring. Siberia, Mongolia. I. 1796.

maximowicziana KOMAR. A small semi-pendulous species, 1·2 to 2m. high, with spiny branchlets, bearing solitary yellow flowers 1in. long. China, Tibet. I. 1910.

microphylla LAM. A spreading shrub of medium height from Siberia and N. China; flowers bright yellow, usually in pairs. I. 1789.

pygmaea DC. A small shrub sometimes prostrate in habit with long slender somewhat pendulous branches. The 2·5cm. long yellow flowers hang on drooping stalks beneath the branches in May or June. China to Siberia. I. 1751.

sinica REHD. (*chamlagu*). A rounded bushy, Chinese shrub of medium size, displaying buff yellow, pea-shaped flowers in May and June. I. 1773.

× **sophorifolia** TAUSCH (*arborescens* × *microphylla*). Intermediate between its parents and of equal garden value.

tragacanthoides POIR. A low, spreading, very spiny shrub from Tibet, China and Siberia. The bright yellow flowers produced in June are followed by grey, silky seed-pods. I. 1816.

turkestanica KUM. An uncommon, spiny species of loose habit; yellow flowers.

CARMICHAELIA—**Leguminosae**—Erect or prostrate New Zealand, broom-like shrubs. Many have distinctive flattened stems which carry out the work normally performed by the leaves. All require a sunny, well-drained position.

†**australis** R.BR. A small to medium-sized shrub with flattened young stems and tiny pale purple pea-flowers during June and July. C. 1823. A.M. 1927.

enysii T. KIRK. Occasionally forms a hummock up to 20cm. with a dense mat of branchlets; flowers small, lilac-pink. I. 1892.

†**flagelliformis** COLENSO. Erect shrub 1m. or more high, with compressed branchlets. Flowers small, blue-purple with darker veining.

petriei T. KIRK. Distinguished by its stout branchlets and erect growth; fragrant, thickly clustered racemes of violet-purple flowers.

†**williamsii** T. KIRK. Distinguished from other cultivated species by its branchlets, being 6 to 12mm. wide, and by its larger flowers which are creamy-yellow; attains about 1·5m. Only for the mildest localities. I. 1925.

***CARPENTERIA**—**Philadelphaceae**—A monotypic genus for a warm sunny position.

californica TORR. A beautiful medium sized Californian evergreen, producing in July its large white flowers with golden anthers. Needs a sunny site, preferably backed by a wall. I. about 1880. F.C.C. 1888. A.G.M. 1935.

'Ladham's Variety'. A vigorous free-flowering clone with larger flowers often measuring 8cm. across. A.M. 1924. F.C.C. 1980.

CARPINUS—**Carpinaceae**—The "Hornbeams" are picturesque and easily grown trees, suitable for clay or chalky soils, and very attractive when laden with their hop-like fruit clusters.

americana. See *C. caroliniana*.

betulus L. "Common Hornbeam". Recommended both for single specimens and for hedging, resembling beech in the latter respect. A medium sized to large tree with a characteristic grey, fluted trunk and ovate, serrate, ribbed leaves. Europe (incl. British Isles); Asia Minor.

'Columnaris'. A small columnar tree of dense, compact growth, conical when young. Slower growing and smaller than '*Fastigiata*'.

'Fastigiata' JAEG. ('*Pyramidalis*'). A medium sized tree of erect, pyramidal habit. Quite narrow as a young tree but broadening as it matures. A.G.M. 1969.

'Incisa'. A form with small, narrow, deeply-toothed leaves, but inclined to revert. '*Quercifolia*' is similar.

'Pendula'. A small elegant tree, the wide spreading branches nodding at their extremities.

'Purpurea'. The young leaves have a purple tinge, but soon become green. Only a collector's plant.

'Pyramidalis'. See '*Fastigiata*'.

'Quercifolia'. See under '*Incisa*'.

'Variegata'. A form in which some leaves are splashed creamy white.

CARPINUS—*continued*

caroliniana WALT. The "American Hornbeam" or "Blue Beech", forms a beautiful small tree with grey fluted bark, but not so tall as our native species. Branches spreading, arching at their tips. Leaves polished apple-green, tinted as autumn approaches. Eastern N. America. I. 1812.

cordata BL. A slow growing, small tree with comparatively broad, deeply veined leaves, heart-shaped at the base. Fruits green, in large clusters. Japan, N.E. Asia, N. and W. China. I. 1879.

henryana WINKL. Medium sized tree. Leaves ovate lanceolate, up to 9cm. long. C. and W. China. I. 1907.

japonica BL. A very beautiful, wide spreading, small Japanese tree or large shrub, with prominently corrugated leaves and conspicuous fruiting catkins. In general appearance recalls *Alnus firma*. Japan. I. 1895.

laxiflora BL. Medium sized tree with rather drooping branches and ovate-oblong, slenderly-pointed leaves and conspicuous, loose clusters of green fruiting "keys". Japan. I. 1914.

macrostachya OLIV. A geographical variety differing from the type in its larger leaves and fruit clusters. Throughout the summer the young growths are bright red. W. and C. China. I. 1900.

orientalis MILL. Small bushy tree or shrub with small, sharply toothed leaves. S.E. Europe and Asia Minor. I. 1735.

tschonoskii MAXIM. Small ornamental tree, leaves varying in length from 4 to 8cm. Japan, Korea and China. I. 1901.

turczaninowii HANCE. An attractive small, shrubby tree recalling *Nothofagus dombeyi*, with slender stems and small leaves. The young emerging leaves are bright red. N. China, Korea. C. 1914.

ovalifolia WINKL. The form most often cultivated with slightly larger serrated leaves. I. 1889.

†**CARPODETUS**—**Escalloniaceae**—A small genus.

***serratus** FORST. A graceful, tall New Zealand evergreen with small, dark green leaves. Flowers small, white, in cymose panicles in summer; needs a sheltered site.

CARRIEREA—**Flacourtiaceae**—A small genus of four species. Small trees from S.E. Asia.

calycina FRANCH. A very rare large shrub or small tree forming a broad head. Leaves glabrous, shining dark green. Flowers cup shaped, creamy white in terminal candelabra-like racemes in June. Fruit an oblong or spindle-shaped woody capsule. W. China. I. 1908.

CARYA—**Juglandaceae**—"Hickory". A genus of fast growing, stately, large trees allied to the walnuts, mainly confined to North America. The large compound leaves, often over 30cm. long, turn a clear yellow before falling in the autumn and the picturesque grey trunks are attractive in winter. Difficult subjects to transplant, they are best planted when small.

alba K. KOCH. See *C. tomentosa*.

alba NUTT. See *C. ovata*.

amara. See *C. cordiformis*.

cordiformis K. KOCH (*amara*). "Bitter Nut". Eventually a large tree with thin, brown scaly bark. Characteristic yellow winter buds. Leaves with usually seven, occasionally five or nine, lanceolate leaflets. Perhaps the best "Hickory" for general planting. Eastern N. America. I. 1766.

glabra SWEET (*porcina*). A medium sized to large tree with smooth, regularly folded bark. Leaves composed of five to seven taper-pointed leaflets, the terminal one large, obovate, 13 to 18cm. long. Eastern N. America. I. 1799. A.M. 1967.

illinoensis K. KOCH (*pecan* ENGL. & GRAEBN.) (*olivaeformis*). A large and valuable nut-bearing tree in North America, but not so successful in the British Isles. Distinct by reason of its numerous leaflets—usually eleven to seventeen on each leaf. S.E. and South Central U.S.A. I. about 1760.

laciniosa LOUD. (*sulcata*). A medium sized tree in this country, with large handsome leaves, with usually seven, occasionally nine, ovate leaflets, the terminal one larger and obovate. Mature trees with shaggy bark. E. United States. I. 1804.

olivaeformis. See *C. illinoensis*.

CARYA—*continued*

ovata K. KOCH (*alba* NUTT. not K. KOCH). "Shagbark Hickory". The most valuable nut producing species in the U.S.A. A handsome tree of medium to large size. Leaves composed of five long pointed leaflets, the three upper ones large and obovate. Rich yellow autumn foliage. Eastern N. America. C. 1629.

pecan. See *C. illinoensis.*

porcina. See *C. glabra.*

sulcata. See *C. laciniosa.*

tomentosa NUTT. (*alba* K. KOCH not NUTT.). "Mockeinut"; "Big-bud Hickoiy". A medium-sized tree occasionally over 18m. with downy young shoots. Leaves over 30cm. long composed of seven, sometimes five or nine ovate leaflets, the terminal leaflet larger and obovate. All are downy and glandular beneath and turn rich butter-yellow in autumn. A stately tree easily recognised by its fragrant, ornamental foliage and large winter buds. S.E. Canada, E. United States. I. 1766.

CARYOPTERIS—Verbenaceae—Small, showy, late summer flowering shrubs with aromatic leaves, best grown in well drained soil and in full sun. Excellent for chalky soils.

×**clandonensis** SIMMONDS (*incana* × *mongolica*). A variable hybrid first raised by Mr. Arthur Simmonds (see below).

'Arthur Simmonds'. This attractive hybrid thrives almost anywhere, producing its bright blue flowers in August and September. An ideal subject for mass effect, and can be kept to a height of about ·6m. Deservedly one of the most popular small hybrid shrubs raised this century. A fitting plant to commemorate its raiser A. Simmonds, perhaps the greatest secretary ever to have served the Royal Horticultural Society. Previously distributed as *C.* ×*clandonensis.* A.M. 1933. F.C.C. 1941. A.G.M. 1942.

'Ferndown'. A seedling selection with slightly darker flowers of a blue-violet shade. A.M. 1953.

'Heavenly Blue'. A clone of American origin. The habit is a little more compact than *C. 'Arthur Simmonds'* and the colour perhaps a shade deeper.

incana MIQ. (*tangutica*) (*mastacanthus*). A small shrub covered by a greyish felt-like pubescence. Flowers violet-blue. The dominant parent of the popular hybrid *clandonensis.* Japan, Korea, China, Formosa. I. 1844. A.M. 1899.

mastacanthus. See *C. incana.*

mongolica BGE. Distinct in its dwarf habit, narrow leaves, and comparatively large, rich blue flowers. A plant of weak constitution. Mongolia, China. C. 1844. A.M. 1928.

tangutica. See *C. incana.*

CASSANDRA. See *CHAMAEDAPHNE.*

†**CASSIA—Leguminosae**—A huge genus of mainly tropical species. Both the following species from tropical South America require a warm, sheltered, sunny site or conservatory.

corymbosa LAM. Less robust than *C. obtusa,* with more slender growths. Leaves with narrower, acuminate leaflets, flowers also smaller and paler yellow, in late summer and autumn. I. 1796. A.M. 1933.

obtusa CLOS. (*corymbosa* HORT.). A very handsome and vigorous wall shrub with pinnate leaves. Flowers large, rich deep yellow, in terminal clusters during late summer and autumn. Wrongly distributed in the past as *C. corymbosa.*

***CASSINIA—Compositae**—Heath-like shrubs of dense habit, grown mainly for foliage effect. Those listed are from New Zealand and pass all but the severest winters more or less unharmed. Best given full sun and good drainage.

fulvida HOOK. f. (*Diplopappus chrysophyllus*). "Golden Heather". A small, erect, dense shrub, the small, crowded leaves give a golden effect; flowers white in dense terminal heads in July. Young growths sticky to the touch.

leptophylla R. BR. Erect, greyish shrub up to 2m. with tiny leaves, white or yellowish downy beneath. Flower heads white in terminal corymbs in August and September.

vauvilliersii HOOK. f. Similar to *C. fulvida* but taller with larger leaves, dark green and glabrous above and tawny-yellow or white beneath.

albida KIRK. "Silver Heather". An attractive variety with white hoary stems and leaves.

‡***CASSIOPE** (*ANDROMEDA* in part)—**Ericaceae**—Attractive shrublets for a moist peaty soil, and conditions simulating open moorlands. Natives of Northern arctic and mountain areas.

'Badenoch'. A slender hybrid, probably *C. fastigiata* × *C. lycopodioides*, forming a loose clump of narrow stems up to 10cm. bearing white bells on thread-like peduncles.

'Edinburgh' (*fastigiata* × *tetragona*). A chance seedling raised at the Royal Botanic Garden, Edinburgh. Slender, dark green stems up to 18cm. high. Flowers white, calyx green edged red; spring. Perhaps the most accommodating of a pernickety family. A.M. 1957.

fastigiata D. DON. A dwarf shrublet up to 30cm. high, with white-margined, adpressed leaves, giving a four-angled effect to the stems. The white bell-shaped flowers are carried on hair-like stalks in April and May. Himalaya. I. about 1849. F.C.C. 1863.

lycopodioides D. DON. A prostrate mat of thread-like branchlets above which little white bells dangle from the slenderest of stalks. N.E. Asia, N.W. America. A.M. 1937. F.C.C. 1962.

'Rigida' (*C. rigida* HORT.). Similar to the type, but with comparatively larger, white, semi-pendulous flowers. A.M. 1938.

mertensiana D. DON. Dwarf shrub 15 to 30cm. in height. Stems erect or spreading, four-angled. Flowers pure white in April. Mountains of Western N. America. I. about 1885. A.M. 1927.

'Muirhead' (*lycopodioides* × *wardii*). A tiny shrublet with characteristic, curved, repeatedly forked shoots and small nodding white flowers in spring. A.M. 1953. F.C.C. 1962.

'Randle Cooke' (*fastigiata* × *lycopodioides*). A mat forming shrublet with stems up to 15cm. high. The white, bell-flowers appear along the stems in late April. Garden origin 1957. A.M. 1964.

rigida HORT. See *C. lycopodioides 'Rigida'*.

tetragona D. DON (*Andromeda tetragona*). Forms tufts of erect shoots covered with closely imbricated, deep green leaves, from which the nodding, white-bell-shaped flowers appear in April and May. N. America, Asia, Europe. I. 1810.

Wardii Hybrid. An erect shrublet with white urn-shaped flowers in spring.

CASTANEA—**Fagaceae**—All possess a family likeness. Leaves mostly long, lance-shaped and toothed. A peculiarity of the twigs is the absence of a terminal bud. The tiny white flowers in slender racemes are individually not conspicuous. The "Chestnuts" are long lived, drought resistant trees thriving on well drained, preferably rather light soils. They are moderately lime tolerant and may be grown with fair success given deep soils over chalk, but become chlorotic on shallow chalky soils.

americana. See *C. dentata*.

arkansana. See *C. ozarkensis*.

crenata SIEB. & ZUCC. (*japonica*). "Japanese Chestnut". A small tree or large shrub with long bristle-toothed leaves. Japan. I. 1895.

dentata BORKH. (*americana*). The "American Sweet Chestnut", rare in cultivation and becoming so in its native haunts. Differs mainly from the European species in its narrower always glabrous leaves. Eastern N. America. C. 1800.

henryi REHD. & WILS. A native of Central and Western China, in nature a tree upwards of 70m. high. In cultivation in our area a rare and very distinct shrub, making late, unripened growth which is cut back by winter frost. Introduced by E. H. Wilson in 1900.

japonica. See *C. crenata*.

mollissima BL. "Chinese Chestnut". Medium to large size tree with ovate or oblong, coarsely serrate leaves. China, Korea. I. 1903.

× **neglecta** DODE (*ozarkensis* × *pumila*). Similar to *C. pumila*, but leaves less white pubescent beneath; fruits a little larger.

ozarkensis ASHE (*arkansana*). "Ozark Chestnut". Generally a medium-sized tree with long, coarsely serrate leaves. Central U.S.A. I. 1891.

pumila MILL. "Chinquapin". A rare North American species, seldom more than a large shrub in cultivation. Distinguished from the closely related *C. alnifolia* by its acute not obtuse leaves which are tomentose beneath. I. 1699.

CASTANEA—*continued*

sativa MILL. "Sweet Chestnut"; "Spanish Chestnut". A fast growing tree, a large specimen being extremely ornamental particularly in July when laden with its yellowish-green male and female catkins. Hotter than average summers are required to produce good crops of nuts. A valuable timber tree, and especially useful for coppicing. Native of S. Europe, N. Africa and Asia Minor. Long cultivated and naturalised in the British Isles, where it is believed to have been introduced by the Romans.

'Albomarginata'. Leaves with a creamy white margin. A.M. 1964.

'Aureomarginata'. Leaves bordered yellow.

'Heterophylla'. Leaves variously shaped, sometimes linear with irregular lobed margin. Inclined to revert.

'Marron de Lyon' (*'Macrocarpa'*). The best fruiting clone, bearing at a very early age.

seguinii DODE. Large shrub or small tree with long, coarsely serrate leaves. E. and C. China. I. 1853.

***CASTANOPSIS—Fagaceae**—Evergreen trees differing from *Quercus* in their erect male spikes, and from *Castanea* in their evergreen leaves and terminal buds, etc.

chrysophylla. See *CHRYSOLEPIS chrysophylla.*

cuspidata SCHOTTKY (*Quercus cuspidata*). A large shrub or small bushy tree with glabrous twigs. The leathery, shining, dark green leaves are oval in shape and possess a slenderly drawn out apex. Requires a sheltered position. Japan, Korea. I. 1830.

†*CASUARINA—Casuarinaceae—A small genus of evergreen trees and shrubs.

nana SIEB. "Dwarf Sheoke". Small, densely-branched Australian shrub with slender rush-like stems. Only for the mildest areas.

CATALPA—Bignoniaceae—A small family of beautiful late-summer flowering trees, mostly of low, wide-spreading habit. The foxglove-like flowers, which do not occur in young plants, are borne in conspicuous panicles. When planting avoid exposed areas, where the large leaves would become tattered. Suitable for all types of well drained soils.

bignonioides WALT. The "Indian Bean Tree". A medium sized tree. Flowers white with yellow and purple markings in July and August. E. United States. I. 1726. A.M. 1933. A.G.M. 1960.

'Aurea'. "Golden Indian Bean Tree". An outstanding form with large, velvety, soft-yellow leaves. A.M. 1974.

'Nana'. A compact rounded bush or a small round headed tree if grafted as a standard.

'Variegata'. Leaves variegated white, or creamy-yellow.

bungei C. A. MEY. A small Chinese tree Flowers white with purple spots, in clusters of 8 to 30cm. in July, are not freely produced. The broadly palmate leaves have slender acuminate lobes. N. China. I. 1905.

× **erubescens** CARR. (*bignonioides* × *ovata*) (× *hybrida*). A medium sized tree, intermediate between the parents. Leaves broad ovate, both three-lobed and entire on the same tree, purple when unfolding; flowers in late July, like those of *C. bignonioides*, but smaller and more numerous. C. 1874.

'Purpurea'. Young leaves and shoots dark purple, almost black, gradually becoming dark green. A.M. 1970.

fargesii BUR. One of the best of the mid-summer flowering trees. It is allied to its Chinese neighbour *C. bungei* and as seen in cultivation it forms a tree of medium size with leaves smaller than those of the Indian Bean Tree. The conspicuous flowers are of typical form, lilac-pink with red-brown spots and stained with yellow, carried seven to fifteen together in corymbs. China. C. 1901. A.M. 1973.

duclouxii GILMOUR (*C. duclouxii*). A tree equal in merit to the type and with similar flowers, but differs in the leaves being less pubescent and having more conspicuous acuminate lobes. A.M. 1934. China.

× **hybrida.** See *C.* × *erubescens.*

kaempferi. See *C. ovata.*

ovata G. DON (*kaempferi*). A Chinese species, forming a tree 11m. or more in height. Leaves usually three-lobed. Small, white flowers with yellow and red markings, produced in many-flowered narrowly pyramidal panicles in July and August. I. 1849. A.M. 1933.

CATALPA—*continued*

speciosa ENGELM. A tall tree with large heart-shaped leaves. The purple-spotted white flowers, appearing in July, are slightly larger than those of *C. bignonioides*, but are fewer in the panicle. Central U.S.A. I. 1880. A.M. 1956.

CEANOTHUS—Rhamnaceae—The species of this large and varied family almost all of which are native of California, are known collectively as "Californian Lilacs". In warm climates most are evergreen, but in the cooler temperate regions many are more or less deciduous. They vary from prostrate plants to very vigorous, tall shrubs, but are mostly of medium size and provide us with the best blue-flowered shrubs which can be grown out of doors in this country.

The Ceanothus require full sun and good drainage; all are to a point lime tolerant, but only a few give a good account of themselves in a really poor shallow chalky soil. Most are excellent for seaside gardens. The deciduous kinds may have the laterals cut back to within 8 or 10cm. of the previous years growth in March. The evergreen kinds need little, if any, pruning, but when desirable, light pruning should be carried out immediately after flowering.

americanus L. "New Jersey Tea". Small shrub bearing dense panicles of dull-white flowers in June and July. Eastern and Central U.S.A. I. 1713. The leaves are said to have been used as a substitute for tea, especially during the American Civil War.

†***arboreus** GREENE. A tall, large-leaved species. Flowers deep vivid blue, borne abundantly in large panicles in spring.

'Trewithen Blue'. An improved selection with large panicles of deep blue, slightly scented flowers. Originated at Trewithen Gardens, nr. Truro, home of one of the finest collections of trees and shrubs in Cornwall. A.M. 1967.

†***'A. T. Johnson'.** A floriferous hybrid, with rich blue flowers in spring and again in autumn. A.M. 1934.

***'Autumnal Blue'.** Possibly the hardiest evergreen hybrid Ceanothus; bears panicles of rich, dark blue flowers abundantly in late summer and autumn. A.M. 1930.

'Brilliant'. See *C. veitchianus*.

†***'Burkwoodii'** (*'Indigo'* × *floribundus*). A medium-sized, rounded shrub. Flowers rich, dark blue throughout summer and autumn. A.M. 1930.

†**caeruleus** LAG. "Azure Ceanothus". A tall shrub with semi-evergreen leaves and long panicles of sky blue flowers in summer and autumn. Mexico. I. 1818.

†***'Cascade'.** A lovely hybrid of the evergreen, spring flowered group, bearing its bright blue flowers in elongated, long stalked clusters. A.M. 1946.

'Ceres' (Pallidus Group). Panicles of lilac-pink flowers during summer.

'Charles Detriche' (Delilianus Group). A medium sized shrub with flowers of a rich dark blue during summer.

†***crassifolius** TORR. "Hoaryleaf Ceanothus". Medium-sized shrub with tomentose branches and thick, leathery, sharply toothed leaves. Flowers white in spring.

†***cyaneus** EASTW. Bright, green, shiny, ovate leaves, and intense blue flowers, borne in long-stalked panicles in early summer. I. 1925. A.M. 1934.

***'Delight'** (*papillosus* × *rigidus*). A splendid hybrid, and one of the hardiest. Flowers rich blue, in long panicles in spring. A.M. 1933. A.G.M. 1957.

× **delilianus** SPACH (*americanus* × *caeruleus*) (*arnouldii*). A small to medium deciduous shrub producing its panicles of soft blue flowers throughout summer. Many of the popular deciduous hybrids are selected clones of this cross.

†***dentatus** TORR. & GR. The true species, with tiny, glandular leaves and bright blue flowers in May. I. 1848. See also *C.* × *lobbianus* and *C.* × *veitchianus*.

†***'Dignity'.** A beautiful hybrid, somewhat similar to *'Delight'*, frequently flowering again in autumn.

†***divergens** PARRY. An attractive semi-prostrate evergreen. The rigid branches are smothered in spring with racemose inflorescences of deep blue flowers.

†***'Edinburgh'** (*'Edinensis'*). Rich blue flowers and olive-green foliage. An attractive plant.

***fendleri** A. GRAY. A low, spring flowering shrub with downy shoots; white or mauve-tinted flowers in terminal clusters. I. 1893.

†***foliosus** PARRY. Forms a spreading shrub with glossy leaves and heads of rich blue flowers in spring.

'Gloire de Plantieres' (Delilianus Group). A small shrub with panicles of deep blue flowers in summer.

'Gloire de Versailles' (Delilianus Group). The most popular deciduous Ceanothus. Large panicles of powder-blue flowers in summer and autumn. F.C.C. 1872. A.G.M. 1925.

CEANOTHUS—*continued*

†***gloriosus** J. T. HOWELL (*rigidus grandifolius*). A remarkable prostrate shrub bearing dark glossy-green leaves and clusters of lavender-blue flowers in April and May. Here it has formed a flat carpet 4m. across.

exaltatus J. T. HOWELL. A more upright growing variety.

***griseus** MCMINN. (*thyrsiflorus griseus*). Known in California as the "Carmel Ceanothus". The form cultivated in this country has pale lilac-blue flowers in May.

'Henri Desfosse' (Delilianus Group). A hybrid resembling '*Gloire de Versailles*', but with flowers a deeper almost violet-blue, summer. A.M. 1926.

†***impressus** TREL. A very distinct shrub in its small leaves, with deeply impressed veins. Flowers deep blue in spring. A.M. 1944. F.C.C. 1957. A.G.M. 1969.

***incanus** TORR. & GR. A spreading shrub with thorny whitish branches. Slightly fragrant, creamy-white flowers in April and May.

†**'Indigo'** (Delilianus Group). True indigo-blue; summer flowering. A.M. 1902.

†**integerrimus** HOOK. & ARN. "Deer Bush". Large semi-evergreen shrub. The three-nerved leaves are dull sea-green. Flowers pale blue in large panicles in June. I. 1853.

†***'Italian Skies'.** Medium sized shrub with deep blue flowers in spring.

†***jepsonii** GREENE. Small shrub with holly-like, leathery leaves and rich blue flowers in spring.

†*×**lobbianus** HOOK. (*dentatus×griseus*) (*dentatus* HORT.). A large shrub, excellent for covering a wall. Bright blue flowers in May and June. A.G.M. 1969.

'Russellianus'. This clone is distinguished by its very glossy, small leaves, and long-stalked, bright blue flower-heads.

'Marie Simon' (Pallidus Group). Pink flowers in panicles on the young growths in summer.

†***megacarpus** NUTT. Medium-sized shrub with small evergreen leaves and panicles of white flowers in spring.

*×**mendocinensis** MCMINN (*thyrsiflorus×velutinus laevigatus*). "Mendocino Ceanothus". A small to medium sized shrub with dark green rather sticky leaves and racemes of pale blue flowers in spring.

×**pallidus** LINDL. (? ×*delilianus×ovatus*). This very hardy, small to medium-sized garden hybrid of European origin has light blue flowers in summer. There are several named clones.

'Plenus' (*C. 'Albus Plenus'*). An equally hardy summer flowering hybrid with double white flowers, pink in bud.

†***papillosus** TORR. & GR. A distinct species, a large shrub with comparatively long narrow, viscid leaves. Gives a brilliant display of rich blue flowers in late spring. I. 1850.

roweanus MCMINN. A variety with darker flowers. A.M. 1980.

'Perle Rose' (Pallidus Group). Bright rose-carmine; summer.

'Pinquet-Guindon'. Lavender, suffused pink, a curious colour combination; summer.

***prostratus** BENTH. Known in California as "Squaw Carpet", this creeping evergreen makes a dense mat up to 1·5m. wide and bears quantities of bright blue flowers in spring. A.M. 1935.

***pumilus** GREENE. A creeping, alpine species; flowers pale blue in spring. Leaves narrower than those of *C. prostratus*.

†***purpureus** JEPSON. Small spreading shrub with small, leathery, holly-like leaves and lavender-purple flower-clusters in late spring.

†***rigidus** NUTT. Has distinctive, wedge-shaped leaves, and purple-blue flowers in spring. Growth compact. I. 1847.

pallens SPRAGUE. A variety with larger leaves and paler flowers.

†***sorediatus** HOOK. & ARN. A small to medium-sized shrub with rigid branches and glandular toothed, three-veined leaves, glossy dark green above. Flowers varying from pale to dark blue in spring.

***'Southmead'.** A dense-growing shrub of medium size with small oblong leaves, glossy dark green above. Flowers rich blue in May and June. A.M. 1964.

†***spinosus** NUTT. A large shrub, only rarely spiny in cultivation. Leaves leathery, entire, glossy green on both surfaces. Flowers rich blue in spring.

***thyrsiflorus** ESCHSCH. A large shrub, one of the hardiest evergreen species. Flowers bright blue in early summer. I. 1837. A.M. 1935.

repens MCMINN. "Creeping Blue Blossom". A vigorous, mound-forming, hardy form, producing early in its life, generous quantities of Cambridge-blue flowers.

'Topaz' (Delilianus Group). Light indigo-blue; summer flowering. A.M. 1961. A.G.M. 1969.

CEANOTHUS—*continued*

***×veitchianus** HOOK. (*rigidus×thyrsiflorus*) (*'Brilliant'*) (*dentatus floribundus* HORT.). Large evergreen with deep blue flowers in May and June. For hardiness, freedom of flowering and richness of colour, this shrub well merits its popularity. I 1853. A.G.M. 1925.

***velutinus laevigatus** TORR. & GRAY. A wide-spreading shrub with large glossy, somewhat viscid, leaves. Flowers grey-white in dense panicles in autumn. Here uninjured by our severest winters.

†*verrucosus NUTT. A vigorous, medium-sized shrub with rigid, verrucose stems and crowded leathery leaves which have a single vein and are sometimes notched at the apex. Flowers white, with darker centres, appearing in spring. A.M. 1977.

CEDRELA—Meliaceae—A small genus of mainly tropical species.

sinensis JUSS. (*Ailanthus flavescens* CARR.). A medium sized, fast growing tree with handsome, large pinnate leaves in which the terminal leaflet is sometimes absent, and fragrant white flowers in panicles often 30cm. long. Lovely yellow tints in Autumn. N. and W. China. I. 1862.

CELTIS—Ulmaceae—The "Nettle Trees" or "Hackberries" are elegant, fast-growing, medium-sized trees allied to the Elms.

australis L. Small to medium sized tree with characteristic broad lanceolate leaves, rough to the touch above. S. Europe, N. Africa, Asia Minor. I. 1796.

caucasica WILLD. "Caucasian Nettle Tree". Medium sized tree with ovate coarsely toothed leaves. E. Bulgaria, W. Asia. I. 1885.

glabrata PLANCH. Small tree or large shrub forming a rounded head. Distinct in its glabrous leaves which are markedly unequal at the base. W. Asia. C. 1870.

jessoensis KOIDZ. A small to medium-sized tree with narrowly, occasionally broadly ovate leaves, obliquely rounded at base, acuminate at apex, pale green or glaucous beneath. Japan, Korea. I. 1892.

labilis SCHNEID. Small tree with long acuminate leaves. China. I. 1907.

laevigata WILLD. (*mississippiensis*). "Mississippi Hackberry". A handsome large tree with lanceolate, entire or few-toothed leaves. S.E. United States. C. 1811.

occidentalis L. North American "Hackberry". Medium sized tree; mature specimens have rough, warted, corky bark, and produce black fruits in profusion. I. 1656.

crassifolia GRAY. A vigorous tree, the arching stems bearing heart-shaped leaves larger than those of the type.

pumila PURSH. A shrub of dense habit with ovate leaves. U.S.A. I. 1876.

reticulata TORR. Small to medium-sized tree with ovate, conspicuously reticulate leaves, which may be entire or coarsely toothed in the upper half. Fruits orange-red. S.W. United States. I. 1890.

sinensis PERS. A small tree, very striking in the polished surface of its foliage. E. China, Korea, Japan. I. 1910.

tournefortii LAM. A small "Hackberry" from the Orient with polished green leaves and red and yellow fruits. S.E. Europe, Asia Minor. I. 1738.

CEPHALANTHUS—Naucleaceae—A small genus of evergreen and deciduous trees and shrubs.

occidentalis L. The "Button Bush" is an easily cultivated but rarely grown shrub of medium height. Leaves ovate, 5 to 15cm. long; flowers creamy-white, produced during August, in small, globular heads. E. and S. United States, Mexico, Cuba. I. 1735.

'Angustifolius'. A form with lanceolate or narrow-elliptic leaves, often in whorls of three.

†CERATONIA—Leguminosae—A monotypic genus for sheltered positions.

***siliqua** L. "St. John's Bread". Supposedly the source of "locusts and wild honey". A large shrub with dark green pinnate leaves, extensively planted in the Mediterranean region where it forms a picturesque round-headed tree. Mediterranean Region.

CERATOSTIGMA—Plumbaginaceae—Small ornamental shrubs often referred to as "Hardy Plumbago", useful on account of their blue flowers in early Autumn. Suitable for dry well drained soil, preferably in full sun.

griffithii C. B. CLARKE. A beautiful Himalayan species with deep blue flowers. Leaves often turn conspicuously red in autumn. In our nurseries survived the hard winter of 1963.

†minus PRAIN (*polhillii*). A slender species resembling *C. willmottianum*, but smaller in all its parts. Flowers slate-blue. W. China.

CERATOSTIGMA—*continued*

willmottianum STAPF. Forms a shrub of about 1m. in height. The rich blue flowers appear in July and continue until autumn. Suitable either for the shrub border or herbaceous border. The foliage is tinted red in the autumn. W. China. I. 1908. A.M. 1917. A.G.M. 1928.

CERCIDIPHYLLUM—**Cercidiphyllaceae**—A small genus of autumn colouring trees.

japonicum SIEB. & ZUCC. An attractive Japanese tree with leaves similar to those of the "Judas Tree" (*Cercis*), but opposite and smaller. In this country forms a small to medium sized tree, assuming pale yellow or smoky pink autumnal colouring in favourable seasons when, at the same time a sweetly pungent scent like burnt sugar pervades the air. May be grown in any deep, fertile soil. Flowers small, dioecious. Japan, China. I. 1881.

sinense REHD. & WILS. A Chinese form introduced by E. H. Wilson in 1907. Stated to be more tree-like in habit but differing very little from the type.

magnificum NAKAI. A rare tree of medium size. Differs from *C. japonicum* in its smoother bark and its larger, more cordate leaves with coarser serrations. Lovely yellow autumn tints. Japan.

CERCIS—**Leguminosae**—Small trees with distinctive foliage and beautiful pea-flowers in spring. Requires full sun and drainage.

canadensis L. The North American "Redbud". A small tree with a broad, round head, unfortunately not very free-flowering in this country. Flowers pale rose in May and June. It may be distinguished from *C. siliquastrum* by its thinner, brighter green leaves. S.E. Canada, Eastern U.S.A., N.E. Mexico. I. 1730.

chinensis BGE. (*japonica*). A Chinese species having glossy-green, heart-shaped leaves up to 5ins. across; flowers bright pink in May. Not suitable for cold areas.

occidentalis GRAY. "Western Redbud". A deciduous shrub, or occasionally a small tree up to 5m. Leaves rounded or notched at apex; flowers rose-coloured, produced on short stalks in clusters. S.W. United States.

racemosa OLIV. A tree up to 11m. high. Flowers pink in drooping racemes, freely produced in May, but not on young trees. China. I. 1907. A.M. 1927.

reniformis S. WATS. (*canadensis texensis*). A small glossy-leaved tree akin to *C. occidentalis*, differing in the downy leaf undersurfaces and larger parts. Texas; Mexico.

siliquastrum L. "Judas Tree". Clustered, rosy-lilac flowers wreathe the branches in May. The purple-tinted seed pods are conspicuous from July onwards. E. Mediterranean Region. I. 16th century. Legend has it that this is the tree on which Judas hanged himself. A.G.M. 1927.

'Alba'. Flowers white and foliage a pale green. A.M. 1972.

'Bodnant'. A clone with deep purple flowers. F.C.C. 1944.

***CERCOCARPUS**—**Rosaceae**—Small trees or large shrubs from Western N. America known for their hard, heavy wood which has given rise to the Common name "Mountain Mahogany".

betuloides TORR. & GR. (*betulifolius*). A large graceful, lax shrub with small obovate leaves. Western U.S.A., Mexico.

ledifolius NUTT. Small tree or large shrub with furrowed bark. Leaves narrow lanceolate, thick and leathery. Western N. America. I. 1879.

montanus RAF. (*parvifolius*). A medium-sized shrub of open habit, with obovate, prominently veined leaves coarsely toothed at the apex. In common with other species it has no beauty of flower but the fruits possess a slender, twisted, silky white tail 5 to 10cm. long. Western N. America. C. 1913.

†*CESTRUM—**Solanaceae**—Showy medium sized shrubs suitable for warm wall or conservatory; mainly natives of Central and South America.

aurantiacum LINDL. Long, tubular flowers, deep orange-yellow in large terminal panicles. Guatemala. I. 1840. A.M. 1961.

elegans SCHLECHT. (*purpureum*). Clusters of bright red flowers over a long period. Mexico. I. 1840. A.M. 1975.

'Newellii'. A seedling resembling *C. elegans* in habit. Flowers large, orange-red. Garden origin. F.C.C. 1876. A.M. 1951.

parqui L'HERIT. A Chilean species. Flowers yellowish-green, fragrant at night, borne in June and July. Hardy in sunny sheltered places in the south and west. I. 1787.

purpureum. See *C. elegans*.

CHAENOMELES—Rosaceae—Better known as *Cydonia*, and familiarly as "Japonica", these ornamental "Quinces" are among the most beautiful and easily cultivated of early spring flowering shrubs. The saucer-shaped flowers varying in shades of red, orange and white are followed by large yellow quinces. Will thrive in the open border or against a wall even if shaded. When treated as a wall shrub, they may be cut back immediately after flowering.

×**californica** WEBER (*cathayensis* × *superba*). A group of small shrubs with stiff, erect, spiny branches, narrow leaves and pink or rosy-red flowers. Raised by Messrs. Clarke and Co. of California.

'Enchantress'. Flowers deep rose-pink, freely produced. A.M. 1943.

cathayensis SCHNEID. (*lagenaria wilsonii*). A large, sparsely branched shrub with formidable spines, and long, narrow, finely toothed eaves. Flowers white flushed salmon-pink appearing in spring; fruits very large, occasionally 15cm. or more long. C. China. I. about 1800.

japonica SPACH (*Cydonia japonica*) (*Cydonia maulei*). A small shrub, flowers bright orange-flame. Japan. I. about 1869. F.C.C. 1890. A.G.M. 1943.

alpina MAXIM. A dwarf form with ascending branchlets and procumbent stems. Flowers bright orange.

lagenaria. See *C speciosa*.

wilsonii. See *C. cathayensis*.

sinensis. See *PSEUDOCYDONIA sinensis*.

speciosa NAKAI (*lagenaria*) (*Cydonia speciosa*). The well-known, early-flowering "Japonica", a much-branched, spreading shrub of medium size. Seedling raised plants bear flowers of mixed colours, dominantly red. China. I. before 1800. A.G.M. 1927.

'Atrococcinea'. Deep crimson.

'Brilliant'. Clear scarlet; large.

'Cardinalis'. Crimson-scarlet. A.M. 1893. A.G.M. 1969.

'Eximia'. Deep brick-red.

'Falconnet Charlet'. Double flowers of an attractive salmon-pink.

'Kermesina Semiplena'. Scarlet; semi-double.

'Moerloosei'. Delicate pink and white, in thick clusters. A.M. 1957. A.G.M. 1969.

'Nivalis'. Pure white; large. A.G.M. 1969.

'Phylis Moore'. Clear almond pink in large clusters; semi-double. A.G.M. 1924. A.M. 1931.

'Red Ruffles'. Clear red; large, semi-double.

'Rosea Plena'. Rose-pink; double.

'Rubra Grandiflora'. Crimson; extra large. Low, spreading habit. A.G.M. 1969.

'Sanguinea Plena'. Red, double.

'Simonii'. Blood-red; flat, semi-double. Dwarf habit. An exceptionally beautiful cultivar. A.M. 1907. A.G.M. 1924.

'Snow'. Pure white; large.

'Spitfire'. Deep crimson-red; large. Erect habit.

'Umbilicata'. Deep salmon-pink.

'Versicolor Lutescens'. Pale creamy-yellow, flushed pink.

×**superba** REHD. (*japonica* × *speciosa*). Small to medium sized shrubs of vigorous habit.

Boule de Feu'. Orange-red.

'Crimson and Gold'. Deep crimson petals and golden anthers. A.G.M. 1969. A.M. 1979.

'Elly Mossel'. Orange-red; large. Somewhat spreading habit.

'Ernst Finken'. Fiery red, produced in abundance. Vigorous in growth.

'Etna'. Rich vermilion. Small shrub.

'Fire Dance'. Glowing signal-red. Spreading habit.

'Hever Castle'. Shrimp-pink.

'Incendie'. Orange-red of a distinct shade; semi-double.

'Knap Hill Scarlet'. Bright orange-scarlet, profusely borne throughout spring and early summer. A.M. 1961. A.G.M. 1969.

'Nicoline'. Scarlet-red. Spreading habit.

'Pink Lady'. Clear rose-pink, darker in bud. Spreading habit.

'Red Chief'. Bright red; large; double.

'Rowallane'. Blood-crimson; large. A.G.M. 1957.

'Vermilion'. Brilliant vermilion.

CHAMAEBATIARIA (*SPIRAEA* in part)—**Rosaceae**—A monotypic genus.

millefolium MAXIM. A small shrub with erect downy aromatic stems, sticky when young, and elegant finely divided leaves. White flowers in terminal panicles in summer. Requires a sunny position. Western N. America. I. 1891.

‡***CHAMAEDAPHNE** (*CASSANDRA*)—**Ericaceae**—A monotypic genus.

calyculata MOENCH. "Leather Leaf". A small wiry shrub for a lime-free soil. Flowers heath-like, white, borne all along the arching branches in March and April. Eastern N. America, N. Europe, N. Asia. I. 1748.

'Nana'. A dwarf, compact form.

CHAMAEPERICLYMENUM canadense. See *CORNUS canadensis.*

†***CHAMAEROPS**—**Palmaceae**—A genus of two species.

humilis L. The only palm wild in Europe. A most interesting miniature palm from S.W. Europe where it covers mountain sides in coastal areas. Rarely exceeds 1·5m. in height. Occasionally forms a short trunk. Hardy in mild localities. I. 1731.

"CHASTE TREE". See *VITEX agnus-castus.*

"CHERRY". See *PRUNUS.*

"CHERRY, CORNELIAN". See *CORNUS mas.*

"CHESTNUT, GOLDEN". See *CHRYSOLEPIS chrysophylla.*

"CHESTNUT, HORSE". See *AESCULUS hippocastanum.*

"CHESTNUT, SPANISH". See *CASTANEA sativa.*

"CHESTNUT, SWEET". See *CASTANEA sativa.*

"CHILEAN FIRE BUSH". See *EMBOTHRIUM coccineum.*

***CHILIOTRICHUM**—**Compositae**—A monotypic genus allied to *Olearia.*

diffusum KUNTZE (*amelloides*) (*rosmarinifolium*). A small shrub with evergreen linear leaves 2 to 5cm. long, white-tomentose beneath becoming brown. Conspicuous white, daisy flowers in summer. A variable species found over a wide area in Southern South America. Some forms are hardier than others.

CHIMONANTHUS—**Calycanthaceae**—"Winter Sweet". A monotypic genus. A medium sized, easily grown shrub best planted against a sunny wall to ripen growth. Succeeds in any well drained soil, and excellent on chalk. When treated as a wall shrub, long growths may be cut back immediately after flowering.

fragrans. See *C. praecox.*

praecox LINK. (*fragrans*) (*Calycanthus praecox*). Flowers sweetly scented, pale, waxy yellow, stained purple at the centre, appearing on the leafless branches during winter but not produced on young plants. China. I. 1766.

'Grandiflorus'. A form with deeper yellow flowers than the type and with a conspicuous red stain. A.M. 1928.

'Luteus'. Well distinguished by its rather larger unstained flowers which are a uniform clear waxy-yellow, and open later than those of the type. A.M. 1948. F.C.C. 1970.

CHIONANTHUS—**Oleaceae**—"Fringe Tree". This genus comprises two handsome species, one from the New and one from the Old Worlds. They are quite hardy and of easy cultivation, producing during June and July an abundance of white flowers, conspicuous by their four or five narrow, strap-shaped petals. Flowers not carried by young plants. Best in full sun.

retusus LINDL. "Chinese Fringe Tree". Given a continental climate, it is one of the most handsome of large shrubs, bearing a profusion of snow-white flowers in June and July, followed by damson-like fruits. China. I. 1845. F.C.C. 1885.

virginicus L. The North American "Fringe Tree", ultimately a large shrub with larger and more noteworthy leaves than its Chinese counterpart; flowers white, slightly fragrant. Eastern N. America. I. 1736. A.M. 1931.

†**CHLORANTHUS**—**Chloranthaceae**—A small genus of mainly tropical species.

***brachystachys** BLUME. Small evergreen shrub with oblong leaves and spikes of bright orange fruits. A conservatory plant in most areas. India to Japan.

***CHOISYA—Rutaceae**—A small genus of evergreen shrubs.

ternata H.B.K. "Mexican Orange Blossom". A medium sized shrub of rounded habit. The trifoliolate leaves are shining dark green, aromatic when crushed. Flowers white, sweetly-scented, throughout late spring and early summer. A useful shrub for sun or shade. Mexico. I. 1825. F.C.C. 1880. A.G.M. 1969.

"CHOKEBRRY, RED". See *ARONIA arbutifolia*.

CHORDOSPARTIUM—Leguminosae—A monotypic genus related to *Carmichaelia*.

stevensonii CHEESEM. A medium sized, rare broom-like, leafless New Zealand shrub, bearing racemes of lavender-pink flowers in summer. In habit resembles a miniature weeping willow. I. 1923. A.M. 1943.

CHOSENIA—Salicaceae—A rare monotypic genus closely related to the willows (*Salix*) but differing in its pendulous, not erect, male catkins, its glandless flowers and other minor, botanical characters.

arbutifolia SKVORTZ. (*bracteosa*) (*Salix arbutifolia*) (*Salix eucalyptoides*). Said to attain large tree size in its native habitats. Long willowy stems covered by a conspicuous white bloom. Leaves lanceolate, bright green and bloomy at first. A rare tree or large shrub of elegant habit. N. Asia. I. 1906.

bracteosa. See *C. arbutifolia*.

***CHRYSOLEPIS—Fagaceae**—A genus of two species related to *Castanopsis*.

chrysophylla HJELMQUIST (*Castanopsis chrysophylla*). "Golden Chestnut". A small to medium sized tree or large shrub. Leaves leathery and pointed, dark green above, yellow beneath. Fruits produced in dense green, prickly clusters. Succeeds best in a well drained acid or neutral soil. Western U.S.A. I. 1844. A.M. 1935.

'Obtusata'. A distinct form with obtuse leaves 5cm. or more long. Free fruiting. A small tree in our Chandler's Ford nursery has survived the severest winters without any ill-effect.

vacciniifolia. See *QUERCUS vacciniifolia*.

†*CINNAMOMUM—Lauraceae—A genus of trees of mainly economic importance.

camphora NEES. "Camphor Tree". A handsome foliage shrub, but too tender for any but the mildest localities. The wood yields the Camphor of commerce. Tropical Asia and Malaya to China and Japan. I. 1727.

glanduliferum MEISSN. A rare Chinese species. Leaves evergreen, broadly ovate, leathery, light green above and white beneath; aromatic when crushed.

***CISTUS—Cistaceae**—The Sun Roses revel in full sun and are excellent for dry banks, rock gardens and similar positions. The flowers are produced in June and July, and unless otherwise stated are white. Where no height is given it may be assumed to be about 1m. Native of S. Europe and N. Africa.

As a family most of the Cistus resent severe frost, but are remarkably wind tolerant and withstand maritime exposure. They do well on chalk.

†× aguilari PAU (*ladanifer × populifolius*). A vigorous plant with very large flowers.

'Maculatus'. Flowers with a central ring of crimson blotches. A most handsome plant. A.M. 1936.

albidus L. A small, compact shrub with whitish-hoary leaves. Flowers pale rose-lilac, with a yellow eye. S.W. Europe and N. Africa. C. 1640.

atchleyi WARBURG. A dwarf shrub of compact dome-shaped habit, with green reticulate leaves and racemes of white flowers. Found by W. Ingwersen and S. Atchley in northern Greece in 1929.

× canescens 'Albus' (*albidus × creticus*). A grey-leaved shrub with white flowers 5cm. across.

× corbariensis POURR. (*populifolius × salviifolius*). One of the hardiest. Crimson tinted buds, opening pure white.

creticus L. (*villosus*). An extremely variable small shrub with often shaggily, hairy stems, flowers varying from purple to rose, with yellow centre. C. 1650.

'Albus'. Flowers white.

crispus HORT. not L. See *C. × pulverulentus*.

× cyprius LAM. (*ladanifer × laurifolius*). A hardy, vigorous hybrid about 2m. high. Clusters of 8cm. wide, white flowers with crimson basal blotches. A.M.T. 1925. A.G.M. 1926.

'Albiflorus'. Flowers without blotches.

CISTUS—*continued*

†**'Elma'** (*laurifolius × palhinhae*). The beautifully formed, extra large, pure white flowers contrast with the deep green, polished, lanceolate leaves. Sturdy, bushy habit to 2m. A.M. 1949.

× **florentinus** LAM. (*monspeliensis × salviifolius*). A free, white flowered, natural hybrid, seldom above ·6m. high. A.M.T. 1925.

formosus. See *HALIMIUM lasianthum.*

× **glaucus** POURR. (*laurifolius × monspeliensis*). An attractive shrub up to 1·2m. high with slender shoots and white flowers 4 to 5cm. across.

hirsutus LAM. A dwarf floriferous species with white flowers stained yellow at base, and conspicuous yellow stamens. Portugal, W. Spain. C. 1634.

†**ladanifer** L. "Gum Cistus". A tall erect species with lance-shaped leaves. The flowers, up to 10cm. across, are white with a chocolate basal stain; petals crimpled. S.W. Europe and N. Africa. C. 1629.

'Albiflorus'. Flowers pure white.

laurifolius L. The hardiest species, sometimes exceeding 2m. in height. Leaves leathery, dark glaucous green; flowers white with yellow centre. S.W. Europe to C. Italy. I. 1731. A.G.M. 1969.

× **laxus** AIT. (*hirsutus × populifolius*). Intermediate in character between its parents. Flowers white with yellow centre. C. 1656.

libanotis L. (*bourgeanus*). A dwarf, lax shrub. Leaves linear, dark green, up to 5cm. long. Flowers small, white. S.W. Portugal, S.W. Spain.

× **loretii** ROUY. & FOUC. (*ladanifer × monspeliensis*). The large white flowers have crimson basal blotches. Dwarf habit.

× **lusitanicus** MAUND (*hirsutus × ladanifer*). Large white flowers with crimson basal blotches. C. 1830.

'Decumbens'. A wide-spreading form, growing 1·2m. or more across and ·6m. high.

†**monspeliensis** L. "Montpelier Rock Rose". A small shrub distinguished by its linear-oblong, sticky leaves and pure white flowers 1in. across. S. Europe. C. 1634.

† × **obtusifolius** SWEET (*hirsutus × salviifolius*). A dwarf shrub of rounded habit. Flowers 2·5 to 4cm. across, white with a yellow basal stain.

†**palhinhae** INGRAM (*ladaniferus latifolius*). This strikingly handsome and distinct species is proving remarkably hardy. Low-growing and compact, with glossy, sticky leaves, the pure white flowers are nearly 10cm. across. Collected in S.W. Portugal in 1939 by Captain Collingwood Ingram and Senhor Palhinha. A.M. 1944.

†**parviflorus** LAM. Shrub with small, grey felted leaves and clear pink flowers. Only suitable for the mildest localities. S.E. Italy, Greece. C. 1825.

'Pat' (*ladanifer × palhinhae*) (*'Paladin Pat'*). A beautiful hardy hybrid reminiscent of *C. ladanifer* in foliage and producing 13cm. wide white, maroon-blotched flowers. A.M. 1955.

'Peggy Sammons'. A small to medium-sized shrub of erect habit, with grey-green downy stems and leaves. Flowers of a delicate shade of pink.

× **platysepalus** SWEET (*hirsutus × monspeliensis*). Intermediate between its parents, flowers white stained yellow at base.

populifolius L. An erect shrub with small, hairy, poplar-like leaves and flowers white stained yellow at the base. One of the hardiest. S.W. Europe. C. 1634. A.M. 1930.

lasiocalyx WILLK. This variety has larger, wavy flowers with a conspicuous inflated calyx and is proving one of the hardiest.

† × **pulverulentus** POURR. (*albidus × crispus*) (*crispus* HORT.) (*'Roseus'*) (*'Warley Rose'*). A dwarf shrub of compact habit with sage-green wavy leaves. Flowers vivid cerise. S.W. Europe. C. 1929.

† × **purpureus** LAM. (*creticus × ladanifer*). Flowers large, rosy-crimson with chocolate basal blotches. I. 1790. A.M.T. 1925. A.G.M. 1927.

'Roseus'. See *C. × pulverulentus.*

†**salviifolius** L. A low shrub with sage-like leaves and white flowers with a yellow basal strain. S. Europe. C. 1548.

'Prostratus'. A dwarf form.

'Silver Pink'. An exceptionally hardy plant. The flowers, of a lovely shade of silver pink, are carried in long clusters. Originated as chance hybrid, possibly *C. creticus × laurifolius*, in our nurseries about 1910. A.M. 1919. A.G.M. 1930.

CISTUS—*continued*

†×**skanbergii** LOJAC. (*monspeliensis*×*parviflorus*). One of the most beautiful with clear pink flowers. Greece.

†**symphitifolius** LAM. (*vaginatus*). A very distinct, tall-growing plant for mildest localities with vivid magenta flowers and golden anthers. Canary Isles. I. 1799.

×**verguinii** COSTE & SOULIE (*ladanifer*×*salviifolius*). The large white flowers have maroon blotches.

villosus. See *C. creticus*.

CITHAREXYLUM—**Verbenaceae**—Sub-tropical American trees and shrubs related to *LANTANA*.

†***spicatum** RUSBY. (*bessonianum*). Evergreen shrub with leathery, lanceolate leaves. The fragrant, white, Verbena-like flowers are produced in drooping spikes. Only suitable for the mildest gardens. Bolivia.

"CITRANGE". See ×*CITRONCIRUS webberi*.

×**CITRONCIRUS webberi** J. INGRAM & H. E. MOORE. (*Citrus sinense*×*Poncirus trifoliata*). "Citrange". A large, semi-evergreen, vigorous shrub with long spines. Leaves large, trifoliolate with narrowly winged petioles; flow ers,when produced, large, up to 6cm. across, white, fragrant. Fruits the size of a golf ball or larger, orange or yellow. Hardy in the south of England. Garden origin 1897.

†**CITRUS**—**Rutaceae**—A genus of partially armed, semi-evergreen trees or shrubs of great economic importance for their fruits. A few may be grown against sunny walls in very warm, sheltered gardens, but most are best given conservatory treatment.

ichangensis SWINGLE. "Ichang Lemon". Small to medium sized shrub with ovate-elliptic, tapered leaves and conspicuously winged petioles, the wings as broad as the leaf blades. Flowers when produced, white. Fruits lemon shaped of good flavour. C. and S.W. China. I. about 1907.

japonica. See *FORTUNELLA japonica*.

'Meyer's Lemon'. A medium sized to large shrub with short-stalked, large, dark green elliptic leaves. Flowers white, fragrant, in clusters. Large fruits.

trifoliata. See *PONCIRUS trifoliata*.

‡**CLADOTHAMNUS**—**Ericaceae**—A monotypic genus related to *Elliottia* and *Ledum*.

pyroliflorus BONG. This sole representative of its genus is an erect, deciduous N. American shrub of about 1·2m., allied to *Elliottia* and so distinct as to be well worthy of inclusion in any collection of ericaceous plants. The curious flowers, borne in June, have five spreading petals of terra-cotta edged with yellow.

CLADRASTIS—**Leguminosae**—A small genus of very ornamental trees but the flowers, similar to those of the "False Acacia" (*Robinia pseudoacacia*), do not appear on young trees.

amurensis. See *MAACKIA amurensis*.

lutea K. KOCH (*tinctoria*). "Yellow Wood". A very handsome, medium sized tree producing, in June, long, drooping, wistaria-like panicles of fragrant white flowers. The leaves turn clear yellow before falling. S.E. United States. I. 1812. A.M. 1924.

sinensis HEMSL. The "Chinese Yellow Wood" is a remarkably beautiful and distinct July-flowering tree of medium size. The compound leaves are soft green above and glaucous beneath, and the pink tinged, white, slightly fragrant flowers are borne in large panicles. China. I. 1901. A.M. 1923. A.M. 1938.

tinctoria. See *C. lutea*.

CLERODENDRUM—**Verbenaceae**—Late flowering shrubs with foetid leaves.

bungei STEUD. (*foetidum*). A semi-woody, suckering shrub of medium height. Stems dark coloured, erect, bearing large heart-shaped leaves and large terminal corymbs of rosy-red fragrant flowers in August and September. China. I. 1844. A.M. 1926.

trichotomum THUNB. A strong-growing, large shrub valuable for autumn effects. The white, very fragrant flowers enclosed in maroon calyces, appear in August and September, and are followed by bright blue berries still with their colourful calyces. China, Japan. C. 1880. F.C.C. 1893.

fargesii REHD. Differs in having smooth leaves and stems, and usually fruits with greater freedom. W. China. I. 1898. A.M. 1911.

‡**CLETHRA**—**Clethraceae**—Shrubs requiring a lime-free soil, flowering in July and August, and notable for their fragrance. All have white flowers in long racemes or panicles and several forms have exfoliating bark.

CLETHRA—*continued*

acuminata MICHX. "White Alder". A large shrub, with racemes of fragrant, cream coloured flowers; leaves yellow in autumn. S.E. United States. I. 1806.

alnifolia L. The "Sweet Pepper Bush", usually not much exceeding 2m. in height. Flowers in erect, terminal racemes, white or nearly white, sweetly-scented in August. Eastern N. America. I. 1731. A.G.M. 1969.

'Paniculata'. A superior form with flowers in terminal panicles. A.M. 1956. A.G.M. 1969.

'Rosea'. A lovely clone with buds and flowers tinged pink. Also distinct in its leaves, which carry a very healthy gloss.

†***arborea** AIT. A magnificent large shrub or small tree with lily-of-the-valley like flowers produced in large terminal panicles; only suitable for the mildest counties. Madeira. I. 1784. A.M. 1912.

barbinervis SIEB. & ZUCC. (*canescens*). A medium sized handsome Japanese species with long racemes of fragrant flowers. Leaves red and yellow in autumn. Japan. I. 1870.

delavayi FRANCH. A magnificent large shrub of great beauty, requiring a sheltered site. The long, broad, many-flowered racemes of white "Lily of the-Valley" flowers are horizontally disposed over the whole plant. Injured only by exceptionally severe frost. W. China. I. 1913. F.C.C. 1927.

fargesii FRANCH. (*wilsonii*). A very beautiful Chinese species attaining about 2·5m., producing, in July, pure white, fragrant flowers in panicles up to 25cm. long. Rich yellow autumn colour. C. China. I. 1900. A.M. 1924.

†**monostachya** REHD. & WILS. A large shrub with long terminal racemes of pure white flowers. One of the most beautiful of late summer flowering shrubs. W. China. I. 1903.

tomentosa LAM. A beautiful, medium sized, summer-flowering shrub resembling *C. alnifolia*, but having greyer foliage and later flowers. S.E. United States. I. 1731.

wilsonii. See *C. fargesii*.

‡***CLEYERA**—**Theaceae**—A small genus of evergreen trees and shrubs related to *Eurya*, but differing in the bisexual flowers and normally entire leaves.

fortunei HOOK. f. (*Eurya fortunei*) (*E. latifolia 'Variegata'*). A most attractive evergreen for favoured loc alities where it forms a large shrub. The elliptic, glabrous leathery leaves have a slender, blunttip. In colour they are dark, shining green, marbled grey, with a cream margin which is occasionally flushed deep rose. Introduced from Japan in 1861. The green form is unknown. A.M. 1963.

japonica THUNB. (*ochnacea*) (*Eurya ochnacea*) (*Ternstroemia japonica*). A slow growing shrub up to 3m., distinctive in its habit of growth, the branches rigidly spreading and densely leafy. Leaves entire, leathery, dark shining green above often turning red in winter. Flowers small, white, very numerous in spring but not conspicuous. Japan, China, Korea, Formosa. C. 1870.

ochnacea. See *C. japonica*.

†**CLIANTHUS**—**Leguminosae**—A genus of two tender shrubs requiring a hot sunny position in a well drained soil. They make excellent conservatory shrubs.

puniceus BANKS & SOLAND. "Parrot's Bill"; "Lobster's Claw". A vigorous, semi-evergreen, scandent shrub of medium size with pinnate leaves 8 to 15cm. long composed of eleven to twenty-five oblong leaflets. The curious claw-like flowers are brilliant red and carried in pendulous racemes during early summer. When grown outside it succeeds best against a warm south or west facing wall. New Zealand. I. 1831. A.M. 1938.

'Albus'. Flowers white. A.M. 1938.

CNEORUM—**Cneoraceae**—A genus of two species.

†***tricoccon** L. A dwarf, evergreen shrub with small yellow flowers and three-sided brownish-red fruits. Sunny well-drained position. W. Mediterranean Region. C. 1793.

†***COLEONEMA**—**Rutaceae**—A small genus of tender, evergreen shrubs.

album BARTL. & WENDL. A small dainty, white-flowered, South African shrub for the mildest localities, with aromatic, heath-like foliage. An excellent pot plant.

COLLETIA—**Rhamnaceae**—Remarkably spiny South American shrubs producing scented flowers during summer and autumn.

armata MIERS. This robust shrub, attaining about 2·5m. in height, has strong, stout rounded spines. In late summer and autumn the branches are crowded with small, fragrant, pitcher-shaped, white flowers. Chile. I. about 1882. A.M. 1973.

'Rosea'. Flowers pink in bud; a delightful shrub. A.M. 1972.

COLLETIA—*continued*

cruciata GILLIES & HOOK. (*bictoniensis*). A remarkable, rather slow growing shrub, with branchlets transformed into formidable flat, triangular spines, crowded with small, pitcher-shaped white flowers in late summer and autumn. Uruguay, S. Brazil. I. 1824. A.M. 1959.

†**infausta** N. E. BR. Related to and resembling *C. armata* but completely glabrous. A spiny shrub of medium size. Flowers white or greenish-white, from March to June. Chile. I. 1823.

†**COLQUHOUNIA**—**Labiatae**—A genus of six species.

coccinea WALL. A showy, Himalayan shrub, with large downy leaves and bearing scarlet tubular flowers in autumn. Requires a sunny site, preferably against a wall where it will attain 2·5 to 3m. Occasionally cut back by sharp frost, but usually shoots again in early summer. I. before 1850.

mollis PRAIN (*vestita*). A form with slightly woolier leaves, and orange and yellow flowers. Nepal.

COLUTEA—**Leguminosae**—The "Bladder Sennas" have large inflated seed pods. They are easily grown shrubs with pinnate leaves and conspicuous, pea-flowers throughout the summer. If encroaching on other plants or getting out of hand they may be hard pruned in March.

arborescens L. A vigorous bush up to 4m. high; flowers yellow. S. Europe; Mediterranean Region. Often naturalised on railway embankments. I. in the 16th century.

'Bullata'. A slow-growing, dense-habited form.

× **media** WILLD. (*arborescens* × *orientalis*). A strong growing, medium sized shrub with greyish leaves and rich, bronze-yellow flowers. Garden origin.

orientalis MILL. Rounded shrub of medium size with attractive glaucous leaves and copper-coloured flowers. Caucasian Region. I. 1710.

‡**COMPTONIA**—**Myricaceae**—A genus of a single species related to and once included under *Myrica*.

peregrina COULT. "Sweet Fern". A small, suckering, aromatic shrub having downy stems and narrow downy leaves shaped somewhat like the fronds of a small "Spleenwort" fern; small glistening brown catkins in spring. Thrives in lime-free soil and, if given sufficient moisture, is best in full sun. E. North America. I. 1714.

CONVOLVULUS—**Convolvulaceae**—A large genus of mainly trailing perennials.

†***cneorum** L. A good rock-garden shrub with silvery-silky leaves and large pale pink and white, funnel-shaped flowers in May. Full sun and well drained position. S.E. Europe. C. 1640. A.M. 1977.

***COPROSMA**—**Rubiaceae**—An extensive Australasian genus of dioecious, mainly tender shrubs or small trees.

acerosa A. CUNN. One of the hardiest of the genus. A low, wiry shrub suitable for the rock garden, with small, linear leaves, female plants with translucent blue berries. New Zealand.

† × **cunninghamii** HOOK. f. (*propinqua* × *robusta*). Medium sized shrub, a natural hybrid from New Zealand, with linear-lanceolate, leathery leaves about 5cm. long. Pale-coloured, translucent berries.

†**lucida** J. R. & G. FORST. A medium sized shrub with large, glossy, obovate leaves; fruits, when produced, reddish-orange. New Zealand.

petriei CHEESEM. Creeping shrub forming dense mats, quite hardy on our rock garden. Female plants bear conspicuous blue berries. New Zealand.

propinqua A. CUNN. A wiry-stemmed shrub with small linear leaves; related to *C. acerosa*. Fruits blue. New Zealand.

"CORAL BERRY". See *SYMPHORICARPOS orbiculatus*.

"CORAL TREE". See *ERYTHRINA crista-galli*.

†***CORDYLINE** (*DRACAENA* in part)—**Agavaceae**—A small genus of trees and shrubs.

australis HOOK. f. The "Cabbage Tree" of New Zealand. A conspicuous feature of gardens in the south-west. A small tree, usually forming a single trunk and bearing several stout ascending branches. Each branch is crowned by a large dense mass of long sword-like leaves. Flowers small, creamy-white and fragrant, produced in large terminal panicles in early summer. I. 1823. A.M. 1953.

'Atropurpurea' (*lentiginosa*). A form with purple leaves.

CORDYLINE—*continued*

indivisa STEUD. A tender species differing from *C. australis* in its normally unbranched stem and dense head of broader leaves. New Zealand. I. about 1850. F.C.C. 1860.

CORIARIA—Coriariaceae—An interesting small genus of shrubs characterised by the frond-like arrangement of their leaves, and the persistence of their attractive flower petals which become thick and fleshy, enclosing the seeds. Of wide distribution.

japonica GRAY. A pleasing, small, low-growing Japanese shrub, the arching stems making good ground cover. The red fruits are most conspicuous and the autumn foliage is attractively tinted. I. before 1893. A.M. 1908.

myrtifolia L. A graceful shrub to 1·5m., with glistening black fruits. Both leaves and fruits are poisonous. Mediterranean Region. I. 1629.

†**napalensis** WALL. A small to medium sized, spreading shrub with black-purple fruits. Foliage attractively tinted in autumn. Himalaya. Upper Burma.

terminalis HEMSL. An attractive small sub-shrub from Sikkim and China. The frond-like leaves give rich autumn tints. Conspicuous black fruits. Sikkim, Tibet, China. I. 1897. A.M. 1931.

fructurubro HEMSL. A form with very effective translucent currant-red fruits. There seems no record of the origin of this attractive form which links the black-fruited Chinese type with the yellow-fruited Sikkim form.

xanthocarpa REHD. Translucent yellow fruits. Sikkim; E. Nepal. A.M. 1904. F.C.C. 1970.

thymifolia HUMB. A dwarf, suckering ground covering shrub throwing out graceful frond-like stems with pinnate leaves, the whole creating dense fern-like clumps. The insignificant flowers are followed in late summer by racemes of tiny black currant-like fruits. Mexico to Peru.

"CORNEL". See *CORNUS*.

CORNUS—Cornaceae—The extensive family of "Dogwoods" or "Cornels" ranges from creeping shrubs to trees, the majority being from 2 to 3m. high. They are ornamental in diverse ways, and mostly of easy cultivation. All have opposite leaves excepting *C. alternifolia* and *C. controversa*. Those grown for their attractive coloured stems should be hard pruned every other year in March.

A number of species including *C. alba, C. sanguinea* and *C. stolonifera* are included by some authories in a separate genus (*THELYCRANIA*).

alba L. "Red-barked Dogwood". This well known species, succeeding in wet or dry soils, forms a thicket of stems up to 3m. high, the young branches being rich red in winter. Leaves colour well in autumn. Fruits white or tinged blue. Siberia to Manchuria, N. Korea. I. 1741.

'Atrosanguinea'. See *'Sibirica'*.

'Aurea'. A charming form, the leaves suffused soft yellow.

'Elegantissima' (*'Sibirica Variegata'*). Leaves broadly margined and mottled white. A.G.M. 1969.

'Gouchaltii'. The plant grown under this name in cultivation does not differ from *'Spaethii'*.

'Kesselringii'. Stems almost black-purple. Very striking.

'Sibirica' (*'Atrosanguinea'*). "Westonbirt Dogwood". A less robust form with brilliant crimson winter shoots. There is very little of this plant now at Westonbirt. A.M. 1961. A.G.M. 1969.

'Spaethii'. A superb form with conspicuously golden-variegated leaves. F.C.C. 1889. A.G.M. 1969.

'Variegata'. Leaves greyish-green with an irregular creamy white margin.

alternifolia L. f. A large shrub occasionally a small tree with horizontally spreading branches. Leaves alternate, sometimes giving rich autumn tints. Eastern N. America. I. 1760.

'Argentea' (*'Variegata'*). One of the very best silver-variegated shrubs, forming a dense bush of 2·5 to 3m. Leaves small with a regular creamy-white margin. F.C.C. 1974.

amomum MILL. Medium sized shrub, notable for its rich blue fruits and for its purple winter shoots. Eastern N. America. I. 1683. A.M. 1968.

asperifolia HORT. See *C. drummondii*.

baileyi COULT. & EVANS. A vigorous shrub with erect reddish-brown branches up to 3m. high. The leaves, which colour brilliantly in the autumn, are glaucous beneath. Fruits white. E. North America. I. 1892.

bretschneideri L. HENRY. A medium-sized shrub with usually reddish shoots and ovate leaves. Flowers creamy-white in cymes, followed by bluish-black fruits. N. China. C. 1887.

CORNUS—*continued*

‡**canadensis** L. (*Chamaepericlymenum canadense*). The "Creeping Dogwood" is not strictly a shrub, the 6in. shoots being renewed from ground level annually. It forms attractive carpets starred in summer with white flowers, succeeded by tight heads of vivid red fruits. Does best in sandy peat or leaf-mould. N. America. I. 1774. A.M. 1937. So different is this plant in habit, it has been transferred to its own separate genus *Chamaepericlymenum*.

candidissima MARSH. See *C. racemosa*.

†***capitata** WALL. (*Benthamia fragifera*). In the mildest districts this beautiful species is a small tree. Flowerheads surrounded by attractive sulphur-yellow bracts in June and July, followed in October by large strawberry-like fruits. Himalaya. I. 1825. A.M. 1922 (for flowers). A.M. 1974 (for fruit).

†**chinensis** WANGER. (KW.19300). A large shrub or small tree not to be confused with *C. kousa chinensis*. Green young stems and large, conspicuously veined leaves. Flowers yellow, produced in large sessile clusters on the naked branches in late winter. Collected by Kingdon Ward in N. Assam in 1950. The species also occurs in W. China.

controversa HEMSL. A magnificent tree-like species with alternate leaves. The sweeping, tabulated branches are clothed during May with broad clusters of cream-coloured flowers. In autumn small black fruits are produced and at the same time the foliage often turns to a rich purple-red. Japan, China, Formosa. I. before 1880.

'Variegata'. A small tree, retaining the horizontal branching of the type, but slower growing and with a striking silver variegation.

drummondii C. A. MEY. (*asperifolia* HORT.). A large shrub or small tree with red brown twigs. Leaves ovate, slender pointed; fruits white. Eastern and Central U.S.A. C. 1836.

'Eddie's White Wonder' (*florida* × *nuttallii*). A superb hardy large shrub or small tree producing large white flowers in spring. Highly praised by its American raisers. A.M. and Cory Cup 1972. F.C.C. 1977.

florida L. (*Benthamidia florida*). The beautiful North American "Flowering Dogwood". A large shrub or small bushy tree. Each flower-head has four conspicuous, white, petal-like bracts in May. Foliage rich coloured in autumn. Not successful on poor shallow chalk soils. E. United States. C. 1730. A.M. 1951.

'Apple Blossom'. A cultivar of American origin. Flower bracts apple-blossom pink.

'Cherokee Chief'. An American selection with bracts of a beautiful deep rose-red.

'Pendula'. An unusual form with pendulous branches.

rubra SCHELLE. A beautiful form with rosy-pink bracts; young leaves reddish. F.C.C. 1927. A.G.M. 1937.

'Spring Song'. An American cultivar with bracts of a bright, deep rose-red.

'Tricolor'. Leaves green with an irregular creamy-white margin, flushed rose, turning bronze purple edged rosy-red in autumn. A superb variegated shrub.

'White Cloud'. An American selection with bronzed foliage, noted for its freedom of flowering and the whiteness of its floral bracts.

glabrata BENTH. A large shrub of dense habit. Leaves lanceolate, glossy green on both sides. Fruits white or tinged blue. Western N. America. I. 1894.

hemsleyi SCHNEID. & WANGER. A large vigorous shrub with reddish shoots and leaves greyish downy beneath; fruits blue-black. China. I. 1908.

kousa HANCE. (*Benthamia japonica*). A large, elegant shrub. The numerous flowers of which the white bracts are the conspicuous part, are poised on slender erect stalks covering the spreading branches in June. Fruits strawberry-like. Conspicuous tufts of dark coloured down in the axils of the leaf veins beneath. Rich bronze and crimson autumn colour. Not recommended for poor, shallow. chalk soils. Japan, Korea. I. 1875. F.C.C. 1892. A.M. 1958. A.G.M. 1969.

chinensis OSBORN. A taller, more open and equally beautiful geographical form. Leaves slightly larger and normally without tufts of down beneath. China I. 1907. F.C.C. 1924. A.M. 1956. A.G.M. 1969. A.M. 1975 (for foliage).

macrophylla WALL. A large-leaved, small tree or tall shrub. Flowers creamy-white in heads 10 to 15cm. across in July and August. Fruits blue-black. Himalaya, China, Japan. I. 1827. A.M. 1899.

CORNUS—*continued*

mas L. "Cornelian Cherry". A large shrub or small, densely branched tree producing an abundance of small yellow flowers on the naked twigs in February. Fruits bright red, cherry-like and edible; leaves reddish-purple in autumn. C. and S. Europe. Long cultivated. A.G.M. 1924. A.M. 1929.

'Aurea'. A large shrub; leaves suffused yellow.

'Elegantissima' (*'Tricolor'*). A slow growing, medium size bush best shaded from strong sun. Leaves variegated yellow and flushed pink. F.C.C. 1872.

'Macrocarpa'. A form with larger fruits than the type.

'Tricolor'. See *'Elegantissima'*.

'Variegata'. Leaves conspicuously margined with white. An outstanding variegated shrub or small tree. A.G.M. 1973.

nuttallii AUDUB. (*Benthamidia nuttallii*). A noble, medium-sized tree from Western N. America. Flowers appearing in May; floral bracts large, white, sometimes becoming flushed pink. Foliage turns yellow, occasionally red in autumn. Not recommended for poor, shallow chalk soils. I. 1835. F.C.C. 1920. A.M. 1971.

'Gold Spot'. An unusual form, the older leaves splashed, spotted and mottled yellow.

'North Star'. A selected form of strong, vigorous growth with dark purple young shoots and larger flowers.

obliqua RAF. (*purpusii*). Very similar to *C. amomum* but usually more loosely branched; the berries are blue or occasionally white. N. America. I. 1888.

†***oblonga** WALL. A rare evergreen species making a large shrub. Leaves narrowly elliptic, dark glossy green above, grey downy below. Flowers white, produced in late autumn in terminal corymbs. Himalaya, W. China. I. 1818.

officinalis SIEB. & ZUCC. A small tree or large shrub with attractive peeling bark and clusters of yellow flowers borne on the naked twigs in February. Red fruits and rich autumn tints. Resembles the closely related *C. mas* but coarser growing with exfoliating bark and earlier flowering, the individual flowers with longer pedicels. Japan, Korea. C. 1877. A.M. 1970.

paniculata. See *C. racemosa*.

paucinervis HANCE. A slow-growing, narrow-leaved, Chinese shrub, seldom exceeding 2m.; useful in producing its creamy-white flowers in 8cm. wide rounded clusters during July and August; fruits black. I. 1907. A.M. 1911.

pumila KOEHNE. A dense rounded bushy hummock. Flowers seldom seen but stated to be in dense, long stalked cymes in July. Fruits black. Origin unknown. C. 1890.

racemosa LAM. (*paniculata*) (*candidissima* MARSH). A medium-sized shrub. Flowers creamy-white, in panicles borne in June and July. Fruits white with bright rose-coloured stalks. Good autumn colour. E. and C. United States. I. 1758.

rugosa LAM. An erect-growing shrub of medium size from Eastern N. America. Distinct roundish leaves densely grey woolly beneath and conspicuous clusters of white flowers in June; fruits pale blue. I. 1784.

sanguinea L. "Common Dogwood". Our native hedgerow species, greenish, red flushed stems and rich purple autumn colour. Fruits black, bitter to the taste. Europe.

stolonifera MICHX. (*sericea*). A rampant suckering shrub with vigorous shoots up to 2·5m., in suitable situations forming a dense thicket of dark red stems. Fruits white. N. America. I 1656.

'Flaviramea'. Young shoots yellow to olive green, very effective in winter, particularly when planted with the red-stemmed sorts. Ideal for moist or wet situations.

walteri WANGER. An interesting tall shrub, or small tree from Central and West China. Leaves oval, slender-pointed; flowers white in 8cm. wide corymbs during June; fruit globose, black. Central and West China. I. 1907.

***COROKIA**—**Cornaceae**—A small but interesting genus of New Zealand evergreen shrubs with small, starry, yellow flowers and red or orange fruits.

†**buddleioides** A. CUNN. A medium sized shrub with slender stems and long, narrow, leathery leaves which are silvery white beneath. The small yellow star-like flowers are followed by dark red fruits. C. 1836.

linearis CHEESEM. A form with even narrower, linear leaves.

COROKIA—*continued*

cotoneaster RAOUL. "Wire-netting Bush". The tortuous tracery of its twiggy branchlets forms a curiously attractive small to medium sized bush, with tiny yellow flowers and orange fruits. Hardy except in cold areas. I. 1875. A.M. 1934.

†**macrocarpa** T. KIRK. A tall attractive shrub with comparatively large, lanceolate leaves, silvery beneath. Flowers in axillary racemes; large red fruits. Chatham Islands.

×**virgata** TURRILL (*buddleioides* × *cotoneaster*). A medium-sized shrub of erect habit, with oblanceolate leaves, white beneath; very small fruits, bright orange. Floriferous and free fruiting. Survives most winters uninjured. I. 1907. A.M. 1934.

CORONILLA—**Leguminosae**—Free-flowering shrubs producing bright yellow, pea flowers throughout the growing season.

emerus L. A hardy, medium sized, elegant shrub with clusters of flowers in the leaf axils; seed pods slender and articulated, like a scorpion's tail. C. and S. Europe. Long cultivated. A.G.M. 1930.

emeroides HAYEK. A small shrub, similar to the type but leaves with seven instead of nine leaflets and flower-heads more crowded and longer-stalked. C. and S.W. Europe.

†***glauca** L. A charming medium-sized shrub for a warm wall. Leaves glaucous. Most floriferous in April but bloom is produced intermittently throughout the year. S. Europe. I. 1722. A.M. 1957.

'Variegata'. Leaves conspicuously and prettily variegated with creamy-white.

†***valentina** L. A charming small glaucous shrub producing a mass of rich yellow flowers, with the fragrance of ripe peaches. Mediterranean Region, S. Portugal. C. 1596. A.M. 1977.

†***CORREA**—**Rutaceae**—A small genus of Australian and Tasmanian evergreens, suitable for the mildest gardens or for cool greenhouse cultivation. The attractive flowers are regularly and abundantly produced, in late winter when under glass.

alba ANDREWS. A small Australian shrub with oval leaves, grey beneath. Flowers funnel-shaped with reflexed lobes, creamy-white. Tasmania. I. 1793.

backhousiana HOOK. (*speciosa backhousiana*). Medium sized shrub with clusters of drooping, greenish-white flowers. Tasmania.

decumbens F. V. MUELL. A small shrub with narrow, grey-green leaves. Flowers narrowly tubular, crimson, with a greenish tip. The projecting anthers are yellow.

×**harrisii** PAXT. A beautiful, early-flowering, small shrub with rose-scarlet flowers about 1in. long. A hybrid of *C. speciosa*. A.M. 1977.

pulchella SWEET (*speciosa pulchella*). A small shrub with leaves green beneath. Flowers palest almond pink, borne throughout the winter.

CORYLOPSIS—**Hamamelidaceae**—This easily grown, exquisitely beautiful group of Asiatic shrubs should be much more widely planted. The conspicuous drooping racemes of fragrant primrose yellow, cup-shaped flowers are regularly carried just before the leaves in spring. They thrive on acid or neutral soils and with the exception of *C. pauciflora* will survive indefinitely on chalk soils, given ·6m. depth of soil.

glabrescens FRANCH. & SAV. A wide-spreading shrub of medium to large size with broadly ovate or orbicular leaves which are glaucescent beneath. Flowers in freely borne, slender tassels; fruits glabrous. Japan. I. 1905. A.M. 1960. F.C.C. 1968. A.G.M. 1969.

gotoana MAK. A medium-sized to large shrub of open spreading habit. Leaves large, orbicular and slightly convex, bluish-green above and pink-flushed when young, chalk-white beneath. Fruits glabrous. Closely related to *C. glabrescens* but the leaf colour (in our form at least) is shared by no other cultivated species. Japan.

‡**pauciflora** SIEB. & ZUCC. A densely branched shrub with slender stems, slowly reaching 2m. by as much across. The ovate, bristle-toothed leaves, 4 to 6cm. long, are the smallest in the genus, and are pink when young. Flowers primrose yellow and cowslip-scented, borne in short two to three-flowered racemes opening in March, generally before those of other species; fruits glabrous. Japan; Formosa. I. 1862. F.C.C. 1893. A.G.M. 1923.

CORYLOPSIS—*continued*

platypetala REHD. & WILS. A medium sized to large shrub of spreading habit. Leaves ovate to elliptic, the petioles, midrib beneath and the young shoots, with scattered, stalked glands. Flowers with broad petals of pale primrose, in dense, long racemes; fruits glabrous. W. China. I. 1907.

sinensis HEMSL. A large shrub or small tree to 4·5m. with young branches both pubescent and with scattered, stalked glands. Leaves obovate, glaucescent and densely pubescent beneath. Flowers lemon-yellow; fruits pubescent. Said to be the commonest species in China. C. and W. China. I. about 1901. A.M. 1967.

spicata SIEB. & ZUCC. A spreading, hazel-like shrub of medium size. Young shoots densely pubescent. Leaves broad ovate to rounded, glaucous and softly pubescent beneath. Flowers in rather narrow racemes, to 15cm. long, the petals long and bright yellow, anthers dark purple; fruits pubescent. Japan. I. about 1863. A.M. 1897.

veitchiana BEAN. A large, erect growing shrub with characteristic elongated, oblong-elliptic leaves of a bright green, edged with incurved teeth and glaucous beneath. Flowers in large racemes, primrose-yellow with conspicuous brick-red anthers; fruits pubescent. A very distinct species of upright habit, the leaves purplish when young. W. China. I. 1900. A.M. 1912. F.C.C. 1974.

willmottiae REHD. & WILS. A medium sized to large shrub with variable, but generally obovate leaves, often purple or reddish-purple when young, glaucescent and pubescent on the veins beneath. Flowers soft yellow, in dense showy racemes; fruits glabrous. W. China. I. 1909. A.M. 1912. F.C.C. 1965.

'Spring Purple'. A selection with most attractive plum-purple young growths.

wilsonii HEMSL. A large shrub or occasionally a small tree with stellately-pubescent young branches. Leaves ovate to elliptic, glaucous and pubescent beneath, mainly on the veins. Flowers in dense pendulous racemes; fruits glabrous. C. and S.W. China. I. 1900.

CORYLUS—Corylaceae—Large shrubs or trees native of the temperate regions of the Northern Hemisphere. Many are cultivated for their edible nuts.

americana WALT. "American Hazel". A medium-sized shrub with rounded heart-shaped leaves. Nuts 1·5cm. long, slightly flattened, concealed by the long, downy husks. Eastern N. America. I. 1798.

avellana L. "Hazel". Our native species, a large shrub or small many-stemmed tree, impressive when draped with its long yellow lambs tails in February. Useful as a tall screening shrub. Leaves yellow in autumn. Europe, W. Asia, N. Africa.

'Aurea'. A soft yellow-leaved form, excellent in contrast with the "Purple-leaf Filbert", but rather weak growing.

'Contorta'. "Corkscrew Hazel"; "Harry Lauder's Walking Stick". Curiously twisted branches; slow-growing to about 3m. A winter feature when in catkin. A.M. 1917.

'Heterophylla' (*'Laciniata'*) (*'Quercifolia'*). Leaves smaller and deeply lobed.

'Laciniata'. See *'Heterophylla'*.

'Quercifolia'. See *'Heterophylla'*.

'Pendula'. A form with weeping branches.

chinensis FRANCH. "Chinese Hazel". A large tree with spreading branches, and light coloured, furrowed bark. Allied to *C. colurna*. W. China. I. 1900.

colurna L. "Turkish Hazel". A remarkable, large tree of very symmetrical, pyramidal form. The striking, corky corrugations of the bark are an attractive feature. S.E. Europe, W. Asia. I. 1582.

cornuta MARSH. (*rostrata*). "Beaked Hazel". Medium-sized shrub interesting on account of the slender, bristly-hairy, beaked husk which covers the nut. E. and C. North America. I. 1745.

jacquemontii DCNE. A medium-sized tree related to *C. colurna*. W. Himalaya. C. 1898.

maxima MILL. "Filbert". A large shrub or small, spreading tree, with large, rounded, heart-shaped leaves. The nuts are larger and longer than those of *C. avellana* and are concealed by a large husk. Long cultivated for its nuts and parent of numerous cultivars. See also our Fruit Catalogue. Balkans. I. 1759. A.M. 1977.

'Purpurea' (*'Atropurpurea'*). "Purple-leaf Filbert". A large shrub rivalling the purple beech in the intensity of its colouring.

CORYLUS—*continued*

tibetica BATAL. "Tibetan Hazel". A small to medium sized tree of wide spreading habit, with usually numerous stems. Distinct in the spiny burr-like husks which enclose the nuts, the whole cluster resembling that of the Spanish Chestnut (*Castanea*). C. and W. China. I. 1901.

COTINUS (*RHUS* in part)—**Anacardiaceae**—A genus of two species now separated from *Rhus*, the "Smoke Trees" are among the most attractive of the larger summer flowering shrubs. The leaves give rich autumn tints.

americanus. See *C. obovatus*.

coggygria SCOP. (*Rhus cotinus*). "Venetian Sumach" or "Smoke Tree". This species from Central and Southern Europe attains from 2·5 to 4m. The smooth, rounded, green leaves give good autumn tints. The fawn-coloured, plume-like inflorescences, 15 to 20cm. long, produced in profusion in June and July, are persistent and turn smoky-grey by late summer. C. 1656. A.G.M. 1969.

'Atropurpureus'. See *purpureus*.

'Flame'. This is the best form for the rich colour of its autumn leaves which turn brilliant orange-red before falling. Flowers pink as in *purpureus*. Frequently masquerades in gardens as *Rhus cotinoides*. A.G.M. 1969.

'Foliis Purpureis'. The leaves, especially when young, are of a rich plum-purple colour, changing to light red shades towards autumn. A.M. 1921. A.G.M. 1930.

purpureus REHD. (*'Atropurpureus'*). "Burning Bush". Leaves green. The large panicles of purplish-grey flowers resemble puffs of pink smoke from a distance. A.M. 1948. A.G.M. 1969.

'Royal Purple'. A selected form with deep wine-purple leaves, translucent in sunshine, the colour reddening towards autumn. A.G.M. 1969. *'Notcutt's Variety'* is similar.

'Rubrifolius'. A form with deep wine-red leaves, translucent in sunshine.

obovatus RAF. (*americanus*) (*Rhus cotinoides*). A rare American shrub which, in favourable seasons and situations, is one of the most brilliantly coloured autumn shrubs. Larger in all its parts than *C. coggygria*. S.E. United States. I. 1882. A.M. 1904. A.M. 1976.

COTONEASTER—**Rosaceae**—This important genus includes amongst its members some of the most indispensable of hardy ornamental shrubs. Though mainly ranging in height from 2 to 3m., they vary from prostrate creepers to small trees, and while the majority are deciduous, many are evergreen. Brilliant autumn colour, either of leaf or fruit, are their main attributes, and their white or pink-tinged flowers often smother the branches in June, and are very attractive to bees. They are tolerant of almost all soils and conditions.

acuminatus LINDL. Large shrub of vigorous, erect habit, resembling *C. cooperi*. Leaves ovate-acuminate, fruits large, bright red. Himalaya. I. 1820.

acutifolius TURCZ. Medium-sized shrub with lax branches, pointed dull green leaves and ellipsoid fruits which are reddish at first finally black. N. China. C. 1883.

villosulus REHD. & WILS. Vigorous form with slightly larger leaves which colour well in autumn. C. and W. China. I. 1900.

adpressus BOIS. Dwarf, wide-spreading shrub, a gem for rock work, with bright red fruits, and small leaves which turn scarlet in autumn. W. China. I. 1896.

praecox BOIS. & BERTH. (*C. praecox*). A vigorous variety with arching branches, growing up to 1m. high and 2m. across. Fruits extra large, orange-red. Autumn colour brilliant red. Known in gardens as "Nan-shan". W. China. I. 1905.

affinis LINDL. A large, vigorous, Himalayan shrub or small tree related to *C. frigidus*, from which it differs in its sub-globose, purple-black fruits and usually more obovate leaves. I. 1828.

bacillaris SCHNEID. (*affinis obtusata*). A form with conspicuously blunt obovate leaves; striking in flower and when carrying masses of jet-black fruits. Himalaya.

* **'Aldenhamensis'** (Watereri Group). A medium-sized to large shrub of wide-spreading habit. The long branches are almost fan-like and carry narrow, ribbed leaves and loose clusters of small bright red fruits. A handsome shrub of distinctive habit. A.M. 1927.

ambiguus REHD. & WILS. A medium sized shrub akin to *C. acutifolius*. Dark purple-red obovoid fruits and good autumn colour. W. China. I. 1903.

amoenus WILS. A pretty, semi-evergreen shrub resembling *C. franchetti*, but with smaller leaves, and of more compact, bushy habit; fruits bright red. Yunnan. I. 1899.

COTONEASTER—*continued*

apiculatus REHD. & WILS. A small shrub occasionally attaining 2m., with arching branches and small rounded leaves and solitary red fruits. China. I. 1910.

applanatus. See *C. dielsianus*.

bullatus BOIS. Large shrub with large, handsome, conspicuously corrugated leaves, which colour richly in autumn, and clusters of large, bright red fruits early in the season. The foliage assumes rich autumnal colourings. One of the finest species in cultivation. W. China. I. 1898.

floribundus REHD. & WILS. The most beautiful form having more flowers and fruits in a cluster, and slightly larger leaves. China.

macrophyllus REHD. & WILS. An extremely handsome variety with large, dark-green corrugated leaves. A.M. 1912.

***buxifolius** LINDL. Dwarf shrub of dense habit with small dull green leaves and small obovoid red fruits. Suitable for the rock garden. Nilgiri Hills (S.W. India). I. 1919.

vellaeus FRANCH. Procumbent form from West China.

***congestus** BAKER (*microphyllus glacialis*) (*pyrenaicus*). A pretty, dense-habited, creeping evergreen forming a series of molehill-like mounds of small, bluish-green leaves. Fruits red. Himalaya. I. 1868.

***conspicuus** MARQUAND. A graceful medium-sized, small-leaved shrub with arching branches, wide-spreading. Flowers white, covering the plant in early summer, followed by equally numerous bright red fruits. S.E. Tibet. I. 1925. A.M. 1933. Regarded by some authorities as a variety of *C. microphyllus*.

'Decorus'. A low-growing, free-fruiting form, excellent for covering banks. A.G.M. 1947. F.C.C. 1953.

'Highlight'. A spectacular shrub of medium size forming a dense mound of arching shoots. The masses of white flowers in May are followed by large orange red fruits.

cooperi microcarpus MARQUAND. A large shrub with abundant red fruits. Allied to *C. frigidus* but with smaller, narrower leaves. Bhutan.

* **'Cornubia'** (Watereri Group). A vigorous semi-evergreen growing upwards of 6m. high. Among tall-growing kinds its red fruits are perhaps the largest, and borne in profusion, weigh down the branches. A.M. 1933. F.C.C. 1936. A.G.M. 1969.

***dammeri** SCHNEID. (*humifusus*). Quite prostrate, with long, trailing shoots studded in autumn with sealing-wax-red fruits. Leaves oval or obovate, 2·5 to 4cm. long. An ideal shrub for covering banks and ground cover beneath other shrubs. China. I. 1900.

radicans SCHNEID. A variety with smaller, generally obovate leaves and flowers generally in pairs. A.G.M. 1973.

dielsianus PRITZ. (*applanatus*). An elegant shrub of medium size crowded with sub-globose scarlet fruits and brilliantly tinted, small leaves in autumn. C. China. I. 1900. A.M. 1907.

elegans REHD. & WILS. Leaves smaller, more rounded, nearly glabrous; berries coral red. China. I. 1908.

distichus LANGE. (*rotundifolius* BAK. not LINDL.). An excellent ,slow-growing shrub of medium size, with stiff, rigid branches, small polished leaves and large, bright scarlet, elliptic fruits borne singly in the leaf axils; persisting until spring. Himalaya, S.W. China. I. 1825. A.G.M. 1927. This plant has in the past been erroneously distributed as *C. rotundifolius*.

tongolensis SCHNEID. A superb small to medium sized shrub, a mound of arching branches covered in autumn by the bright scarlet, obovoid fruits. Rich autumn colour. W. China.

divaricatus REHD. & WILS. A medium-sized shrub; one of the best and most reliable for autumn fruit and foliage. Fruits dark red. Excellent for hedging. W. China. I. 1904. F.C.C. 1912. A.G.M. 1969.

***'Exburiensis'** (Watereri Group). A large shrub with apricot-yellow fruits becoming pink tinged in winter. Almost identical with *C. 'Rothschildianus'*. A.G.M. 1969.

'Firebird'. A medium sized to large shrub of spreading habit. Leaves bullate, shining dark green above, fruits large, orange-red in dense clusters. A hybrid of *C. bullatus* probably with *C. franchetii*.

COTONEASTER—*continued*

foveolatus REHD. & WILS. A Chinese shrub to 2·5m. having comparatively large leaves which are shining, grass-green, turning orange and scarlet in autumn. Flowers pink; fruits black. I. 1908.

franchetii BOIS. A very graceful, medium-sized, semi-evergreen shrub, with sage green foliage and ovoid, orange-scarlet fruits. One of the most popular species. China. I. 1895.

sternianus TURRILL (*C. wardii* HORT.). This excellent shrub, one of the best of all *Cotoneasters*, has, in the past, been widely distributed wrongly under the name of *C. wardii*. Leaves sage-green above and silvery-white beneath. Fruits large, sub-globose, bright orange-red. Produced in great abundance. S. Tibet, N. Burma. I. 1913. A.M. 1939 (as *C. wardii*). A.G.M. 1953.

frigidus WALL. A small spreading tree or large shrub, fast-growing, loaded in autumn and throughout the winter with large, heavy clusters of crimson fruits. The true plant with its large, broad elliptic leaves is now seldom seen, hybrid seedlings of the Watereri Group being made to do duty for it. Himalaya. I. 1824. A.G.M. 1925. A.M. 1966.

'Fructuluteo' (*'Xanthocarpus'*). Large bunches of creamy-yellow fruits. A.M. 1932.

***glaucophyllus** FRANCH. A large-sized, July flowering shrub with oval leaves, correspondingly late in berrying. At all seasons a handsome species. W. China. C. 1915. A.M. 1924.

serotinus STAPF. (*C. serotinus*). A glabrous shrub, differing in its shorter, more leathery roundish leaves and even later orange-red fruits. I. 1907. F.C.C. 1919.

vestitus W.W.SM. This is the variety most frequently seen in gardens. A vigorous bush to 3m. or more. It flowers profusely in July and it is December before the fruits take on their red colour. Leaves tomentose beneath. W. China.

***harrovianus** WILS. A graceful, arching, evergreen attaining about 2m. and very conspicuous in bloom. The attractive red fruits are not fully coloured until late December. China. I. 1899. A.M. 1905.

harrysmithii FLINCK & HYLMO. Small shrub occasionally up to 2m., branchlets horizontally arranged. Closely related to *C. nitens* but less vigorous, and with smaller leaves, flowers and fruits. Collected in W. China in 1934 by the Swedish collector Dr. Harry Smith.

hebephyllus DIELS. Medium-sized shrub with long, arching branches, wreathed with white flowers followed by large, dark-red, globular fruits. China. I. 1910.

***henryanus** REHD. & WILS. A large, wide-growing evergreen or semi-evergreen shrub with long, dark green corrugated leaves, downy beneath; fruits crimson. It seems doubtful whether this plant is specifically different from *C. salicifolius*. C. China. I. 1901. A.M. 1920.

horizontalis DCNE. A low-growing shrub of spreading habit, with branches of characteristic "herring-bone" pattern. Invaluable for north or east walls or for covering banks, etc. giving rich autumnal colour of fruit and leaf. W. China. I. about 1870. F.C.C. 1897. A.G.M. 1925.

perpusillus SCHNEID. A charming dwarf form with smaller leaves. W. China. I. 1908. A.M. 1916.

'Saxatilis'. A flat growing, prostrate form with distinctive wide-spreading fan-like branches and small leaves.

'Variegatus'. Especially pleasing in autumn when the small, cream variegated leaves are suffused with red.

humifusus. See *C. dammeri*.

hupehensis REHD. & WILS. A medium sized shrub of dense yet graceful habit. The oval leaves are interspersed with numerous white flowers in May followed by large, solitary bright red fruits on long slender stalks. W. China. I. 1907.

***'Hybridus Pendulus'.** A very striking evergreen with glossy leaves, and long, prostrate branches which carry brilliant red fruits in abundance during autumn and winter. When grown on a stem makes an attractive small weeping tree. Garden origin. Variously claimed to be a hybrid of *C. dammeri* with either *C. frigidus* or *C. salicifolius*. A.M. 1953.

ignavus WOLF. Medium-sized shrub closely related to *C. melanocarpus*, with many-flowered drooping clusters of pink flowers. Fruits purple-black. E. Turkestan. I. 1880.

COTONEASTER—*continued*

* **'Inchmery'** (Watereri Group). A large shrub or small tree producing bunches of large, salmon-pink fruits yellow at first. In general appearance closely approaching *C. frigidus.*

integerrimus MED. (*vulgaris*). An erect-branched shrub, usually less than 2m. high, with roundish leaves, pink tinged flowers and red fruits. Widely distributed from Europe to N. Asia. It still survives on Great Orme Head above Llandudno, N. Wales, where it was first discovered in 1783.

* **'John Waterer'** (Watereri Group). A large, semi-evergreen shrub, its long spreading branches laden with bunches of red fruits in autumn. A.M. 1951. A.G.M. 1969.

***lacteus** W. W. SM. Distinct in its large, oval, leathery leaves which are grey tomentose beneath. Fruits red, rather small but carried in broad clusters, ripening late in the year and lasting well after Christmas. China. Introduced by George Forrest in 1913. A.M. 1935. A.G.M. 1969.

lindleyi STEUD. (*nummularia* LIND.). A tall, elegant, Himalayan shrub or small tree with long, sweeping branches. The leaves are round or oval, fruits blackish-purple. N.W. Himalaya. I. 1824.

lucidus SCHLECHT. An upright-growing, Siberian species of medium height, with pink and white flowers followed by lustrous, black fruits. The dark, glossy leaves give brilliant autumn colour. Altai Mts. I. 1840.

melanocarpus laxiflorus SCHNEID. (*C. polyanthemus*). This variety of a widely distributed species has pink flowers in large drooping clusters; fruits black; leaves colouring early in the autumn. Europe to Asia. C. 1826.

***microphyllus** LINDL. Dwarf, glossy-leaved evergreen with extra large, globose, scarlet fruits, much used for draping walls and banks. Extremely tough and hardy. Himalaya, S.W. China. I. 1824.

cochleatus REHD. & WILS. (*melanotrichus*). Charming, slow-growing, prostrate form, with paler, duller green, broader leaves. A.M. 1930. W. China, S.E. Tibet; E. Nepal.

thymifolius KOEHNE. Dainty shrub with extremely small, narrow, shining, deep green leaves. A superb rock plant. Himalaya.

moupinensis FRANCH. A medium-sized shrub similar to *C. bullatus*, but with fruits dark red, turning black. Leaves give rich autumn tints. W. China. I. 1907.

mucronatus FRANCH. An erect species of medium height with green, slenderly-pointed leaves and clusters of orange-red fruits. China. Closely related to *C. acuminatus* and perhaps merely a small leaved form.

multiflorus BGE. A large spreading shrub, as free in flower as "Hawthorn", but more graceful; fruits large, bright-red, ripening in August. N.W. China. I. 1837.

'Newryensis'. A rare, erect-branched shrub of medium to large size, closely related to *C. franchetii*; conspicuous orange-red fruits. Origin probably China. C. 1911.

nitens REHD. & WILS. A very graceful shrub up to 2m., the polished leaves being disposed in an almost frond-like arrangement and giving brilliant autumn colour; fruits elliptic, black. W. China. I. 1910.

nitidifolius MARQUAND. A medium-sized shrub of graceful habit with slender, lax stems and wavy edged, shining green leaves. The clusters of white flowers are followed by crimson fruits. A distinct and attractive species. Often rich crimson autumn colours. S.W. China. I. 1924.

nummularia. See *C. lindleyi* and *C. racemiflorus.*

obscurus REHD. & WILS. An uncommon species of medium size; leaves yellow-grey beneath; fruits obovoid, dark red. W. China. I. 1910.

orbicularis SCHLECT. A rare medium sized to large shrub of spreading habit. Leaves small, broad-elliptic, greyish hairy beneath. Fruits top-shaped red, singly or in pairs along the secondary twigs. Sinai Peninsular.

***pannosus** FRANCH. A medium sized shrub with long slender, arching branches. It resembles *C. franchetii* but has smaller sage green leaves and small fruits which are rounded, deep red and colour later. W. China. C. 1888.

* **'Pink Champagne'** (Watereri Group). A large, vigorous, dense growing shrub with slender arching branches and narrow leaves approaching the habit of *C. salicifolius.* Fruits small but plentifully produced, at first yellow becoming pink tinged.

praecox. See *C. adpressus praecox.*

COTONEASTER—*continued*

***prostratus** BAK. (*rotundifolius* LINDL.) (*microphyllus uva-ursi*). A small, vigorous, semi-prostrate Himalayan species with long arching branches clothed with small glossy leaves; fruits large, rose-red. I. 1825. A.G.M. 1927.

'Eastleigh'. A large, vigorous, much branched shrub with dark green leaves and large, deep ox-blood red fruits in profusion. Raised in our nurseries about 1960.

lanatus (*C. buxifolius* BAK.) (*C. wheeleri* HORT.). A medium-sized to large shrub with long arching branches. Taller and more vigorous than the type.

pyrenaicus. See *C. congestus*.

racemiflorus K. KOCH (*nummularia* FISCH. & MEY.). A widely-distributed variable species, characterised by its tall, slender arching branches and orbicular leaves, grey-white beneath. Fruits brick-red. The combination of the leaves and fruit in a September sun is most arresting. S. Europe, N. Africa to Himalaya and Turkestan. C. 1829.

microcarpus REHD. & WILS. A vigorous, Chinese variety differing in its narrow ovoid, sealing-wax-red fruits.

royleanus DIPP. Small shrub with rounded leaves and few-flowered cymes.

veitchii REHD. & WILS. A form with larger flowers and larger, dark red fruits. China. I. 1900.

roseus EDGEW. A small, loose-growing shrub related to *C. integerrimus*, occasionally reaching about 2m. Leaves oval, mucronate, quite smooth. Flowers pink-tinged in small clusters followed by small, red, obovoid fruits. N.W. Himalaya, Afghan. I. 1882.

***'Rothschildianus'** (Watereri Group). A large shrub possessing a distinctive, wide-spreading habit when young. Large clusters of creamy-yellow fruits. The cultivar *'Exburyensis'* is very similar. Both were raised at Exbury, Hants.

rotundifolius. See *C. distichus* and *C. prostratus*.

rubens W. W. SM. Small, free-berrying shrub of spreading habit. The solitary flowers have pink tinged petals followed by red fruits. W. China. I. 1927. A.M. 1924.

sabrina. See *C. splendens 'Sabrina'*.

* **'St. Monica'** (Watereri Group). A semi-evergreen hybrid with leaves which colour brightly before falling in late winter. It forms a large shrub and bears heavy crops of bright red fruits. Found in a convent garden near Bristol.

***salicifolius** FRANCH. An invaluable but variable evergreen, tall and graceful, carrying heavy crops of small, bright red fruits in autumn. A parent of innumerable hybrids. China. I. 1908. Available in the following clones:—

'Autumn Fire' ['Herbstfeuer']. A small to medium-sized, semi-evergreen shrub of lax almost pendulous habit. The bright orange-red fruits are produced in large quantities in autumn.

'Avondrood'. See *'Repens'*.

floccosus REHD. & WILS. A very graceful and distinct variety, with small, narrow, polished leaves, shining green above white woolly beneath, poised on slender, drooping, fan-like stems. Masses of tiny red fruits. China. I. 1908. A.M. 1920.

'Fructuluteo'. An interesting form with yellow fruits.

'Parkteppich'. A scrambling, partially prostrate shrub covered with small red fruits in autumn.

'Repens' (*'Avondrood'*). A prostrate shrub with very narrow leaves and small red fruits. An excellent ground cover.

rugosus REHD. & WILS (*C. rugosus*). A variety with broader and darker leaves than those of *floccosus*, tomentose beneath and with larger flowers and fruits. I. 1907. A.M. 1912.

***'Salmon Spray'** (Watereri Group). A medium-sized free-fruiting shrub producing large leafy sprays of salmon-red fruits, akin to *C. henryanus*. Raised in our nurseries.

serotinus. See *C. glaucophyllus serotinus*.

sikangensis FLINCK & HYLMO. Medium sized shrub related to *C. obscurus*, differing in its more upright habit, thicker leaves and its shiny orange-red fruits. Collected by Dr. Harry Smith in W. China in 1934.

simonsii BAK. A well-known, semi-evergreen, erect-growing shrub, much used in plantations and for hedges. Fruits large, scarlet. Khasia Mts. (Assam). I. 1865.

COTONEASTER—*continued*

***'Skogholm'.** A dwarf, evergreen shrub of wide-spreading habit. Leaves small; fruits large, obovoid, coral-red in autumn. W. China.

splendens FLINCK. & HYLMO. A handsome species up to 2m., related to *C. dielsianus*. The arching shoots with small, greyish-green rounded leaves, are studded with large, obovoid, bright orange fruits in autumn. W. China.

'Sabrina' (*C. 'Sabrina'*). A free berrying clone raised in the Somerset garden of Mr. Norman Hadden. A.M. 1950.

tomentosus LINDL. (*nebrodensis*). A rare, erect-branched shrub from the European Alps and W. Asia. The rotund leaves are white tomentose beneath, and perhaps the woolliest of the genus; flowers pink, fruits large, brick-red, colouring in August. I. 1759.

***turbinatus** CRAIB. An elegant, medium sized, July-flowering shrub; leaves white beneath; fruits red, top-shaped, downy, ripening in October. China. I. 1910.

uniflorus BGE. Small shrub closely related to *C. integerrimus* but with smaller leaves and usually solitary flowers. C. Asia, W. China. C. 1907.

'Valkenburg' (*horizontalis* × *salicifolius floccosus*). A dwarf or prostrate shrub with long spreading stems; leaves turn orange and scarlet in autumn.

wardii W. W. SM. A stiff, erect-branched shrub of moderate size. Leaves dark, glossy green above, white beneath. Berries bright orange-red, top-shaped. S.E. Tibet. I. 1913. (See also *C. franchetii sternianus*).

***× watereri** EXELL. Variable semi-evergreen hybrids between *Cotoneaster frigidus*, *C. henryanus* and *C. salicifolius* and their forms. All are completely hardy, medium to large shrubs or occasionally small trees of strong vigorous growth, with long leaves and heavy crops of normally red or orange-red fruits. There are many named clones. A.M. 1951.

zabelii SCHNEID. A medium-sized species of arching, spreading growth. Fruits obovoid, dark red in short stalked pendulous clusters. China. I. 1907. A.M. 1912.

"COTTONWOOD". See *POPULUS deltoides*.

"CRAB APPLE". See *MALUS*.

"CRANBERRY'. See *VACCINIUM oxycoccos*.

+CRATAEGOMESPILUS (*CRATAEGUS+MESPILUS*)—**Rosaceae**—Interesting graft hybrids (chimaeras) between hawthorn and medlar. Both the following originated on the same tree. They are ornamental, wide-spreading, small trees especially attractive for their comparatively large white flowers and yellow and orange autumn tints.

dardarii SIMON-LOUIS (*C. monogyna+M. germanica*). "Bronvaux Medlar". The original hybrid, consisting of a central core of hawthorn and an outer envelope of medlar. The shoots are occasionally thorny. Leaves like those of the medlar, but smaller. Fruits also medlar-like but smaller and in clusters. Occasional branches revert to either parent. Originated in the garden of Mons. Dardar at Bronvaux, near Metz, France, about 1895.

'Jules d'Asnières' (*+C. asnieresii*). Occurred at the same time and on the same tree as *+C. dardarii*, but in this case the medlar forms the central core and hawthorn the outer envelope. Young shoots woolly; leaves varying from entire to deeply lobed. Fruits similar to those of the hawthorn.

grandiflora. See *×CRATAEMESPILUS grandiflora*.

CRATAEGUS—**Rosaceae**—The "Thorns" are among the hardiest and most adaptable trees, giving a good account of themselves even in industrial areas, and in windswept coastal districts. When established they are tolerant of both dryness and excessive moisture.

Most are wide spreading, small trees or large shrubs with attractive autumn tints. Except where otherwise stated the flowers are white, and open in May and June, and the fruits are red.

altaica LANGE. "Altai Mountain Thorn". A small tree from Central Asia with strongly lobed, finely toothed leaves, bearing bright yellow fruits 1·5cm. in diameter. I. 1876.

arkansana SARG. A small elegant North American tree with often thornless branches. Fruits bright red, as much as 2·5cm. across. Arkansas. I. 1902.

arnoldiana SARG. A beautiful small tree with shallowly lobed leaves. Fruits large, like red cherries. N.E. United States. I. 1901. A.M. 1936.

CRATAEGUS—*continued*

azarolus L. "Azarole". A large shrub or small tree, native of North Africa and Western Asia which, although introduced in the 17th century, is still rare in cultivation. The comparatively large white flowers, produced in dense clusters, have purple anthers. The edible fruits are usually orange. Leaves rhomboid, wedge-shaped at the base. A.M. 1976.

calpodendron. See *C. tomentosa.*

canbyi SARG. Small bushy tree, leaves glossy green, serrate and shallowly lobed; fruits dark shining crimson, almost as large as cherries. N.E. United States. I. 1901.

×**carrierei.** See *C.* ×*lavallei.*

champlainensis SARG. Small tree related to *C. arnoldiana*, from which it differs in its more heart-shaped leaves. N. America. I. 1901.

chlorosarca MAXIM. A small, normally thornless tree, notable for its pyramidal habit and dark purple-brown shoots. Leaves shallowly lobed, dark and glossy above; fruits dark purple-black. Japan. C. 1880.

coccinea. See *C. intricata* and *C. pedicillata.*

coccinioides ASHE (*acutiloba*) (*speciosa*). A small, round-headed tree with large red fruits. The young leaves are tinged red when opening and in the autumn the foliage gives very good colouring. E. United States. I. 1883.

collina CHAPM. Related to *C. punctata.* Leaves nearly glabrous; fruits large and red. C. and E. United States. C. 1889.

cordata. See *C. phaenopyrum.*

crus-galli L. "Cockspur Thorn". A wide-spreading, small glabrous tree, with thorns often up to 8cm. long. Attractive in leaf, flower and fruits, the latter often lasting well into the New Year. E. and C. North America. I. 1691.

oblongata SARG. A horizontally branched small tree with narrow oblong-elliptic leaves and brighter coloured, oblong fruits.

pyracanthifolia AIT. Forms a small, picturesque, thornless, horizontally branched tree, with narrower leaves than the type. A mature standard specimen makes a perfect umbrella shape.

dahurica KOEHNE. An uncommon small species from S.E. Siberia, and one of the earliest to come into growth; fruits orange-red.

×**dippeliana** LANGE (×*leeana*). A free-flowering, small tree, a hybrid of *C. tanacetifolia.* Fruits light orange-red. Garden origin about 1830.

douglasii LINDL. (*rivularis*). Small tree with slender, often drooping branches and shining, dark green, often rounded leaves. Fruits black and shining. North America. I. 1828.

dsungarica ZAB. A small tree with spiny branches, large flowers and purplish-black fruits. S.E. Siberia, Manchuria. A.M. 1931.

durobrivensis SARG. A large shrub, one of the most ornamental of N. American thorns. The flowers are possibly the largest in the genus, and the large, red fruits remain until mid-winter. I. 1901.

ellwangerana SARG. Small tree with ascending branches and oval leaves. Large bright crimson fruits. N. America. C. 1900. A.M. 1922.

flabellata K. KOCH. A large shrub or small tree with thorny stems and fan-shaped, double toothed leaves. Fruits crimson. S.E. Canada, N.E. United States. C. 1830.

flava AIT. "Yellow Haw". A very distinct small tree with small leaves and conspicuous ellipsoid, orange-yellow fruits. S.E. United States.

×**grignonensis** MOUILLEF. A small tree, a hybrid of *C. stipulacea.* Late in flowering and ripening its large, bright red fruits. Leaves remain green until winter. Origin about 1873.

holmesiana ASHE. An outstanding small tree. The large white flowers are followed by conspicuously large, rather oblong red fruits. N.E. United States. I. 1903.

intricata LANGE (*coccinea* in part). Large shrub or small tree with erect or spreading branches. Fruits reddish-brown. Eastern N. America. I. 1730.

jackii SARG. Medium sized shrub with spiny stems and large, dark red fruits. Canada. I. 1903.

jonesiae SARG. A small tree particularly noted for its large, bright, glossy, red fruits. N.E. United States, S.E. Canada. A.M. 1977.

CRATAEGUS—*continued*

korolkowii. See *C. wattiana.*

laciniata UCRIA (*orientalis*). A beautiful, small oriental tree, distinguished by its deeply cut, downy leaves, dark green above and grey beneath. Fruits large, coral-red or yellowish-red. Orient. I. 1810. A.M. 1933. F.C.C. 1970. A.G.M. 1973.

× **lavallei** HERINQ. (*crus-galli* × *stipulacea*) (× *carrierei*). A small, dense headed tree, distinguished by its long, glossy, dark green leaves which often remain until December. Fruits orange-red persisting throughout the winter and very colourful against the dark foliage. Garden origin about 1870. A.M. 1924. A.G.M. 1925.

× **leeana.** See *C.* × *dippeliana.*

macracantha LOUD. A North American tree or shrub up to 5m. high. Leaves attractively coloured in autumn. Fruits bright crimson. Has the longest spines of all thorns sometimes up to 10 to 13cm. in length. I. 1819.

maximowiczii SCHNEID. (*sanguinea villosa*). A tree forming a compact cone with shallowly lobed leaves, distinct in its flower stalks, calyx, and young fruits being bristly-hairy. Fruits smooth when ripe. N.E. Asia.

× **media** BECHST. (*monogyna* × *oxyacantha*). A large shrub or small tree, intermediate in character between the parents. It is a variable plant found both in the wild and in cultivation. Several of the clones listed under *C. oxyacantha* belong here.

missouriensis ASHE. A shrub or small tree having distinctive, sharply toothed, pubescent leaves and orange-red fruits. S.E. United States. I. 1905.

mollis SCHEELE. "Red Haw". One of the best of the American species, forming a wide-spreading tree 10 to 12m. high. Leaves downy; fruits showy, like red cherries, carried in large clusters. C. North America. Long cultivated.

monogyna JACQ. "Common Hawthorn", "May", "Quick". A familiar native, extensively planted as a hedge throughout the country. A tree in full flower in May is a wonderful sight and is equal to any of the foreign species. In autumn its branches are often laden with red fruits—"haws". The flowers are white and strongly fragrant. Europe, N. Africa, W. Asia.

'Biflora' (*'Praecox'*). The "Glastonbury Thorn" produces leaves earlier than the type and occasionally an early but smaller crop of flowers during winter.

'Compacta' (*'Inermis Compacta'*). A remarkable dwarf form with stout, stiff, unarmed branches.

'Flexuosa' (*'Tortuosa'*). A curious and striking form with twisted corkscrew branches.

'Pendula'. "Weeping Thorn". A form with graceful, arching branches; flowers white.

'Pendula Rosea'. Graceful pendulous branches and pink flowers.

'Praecox'. See *'Biflora'*.

'Pteridifolia'. A form with deeply lobed and toothed leaves.

'Stricta' (*'Fastigiata'*). Branches erect. An excellent, small, tough tree for exposed places.

'Tortuosa'. See *'Flexuosa'*.

'Variegata'. Leaves splashed and mottled creamy-white.

nitida SARG. A small tree with spreading, usually thornless, branches and elliptic to oblong, shining leaves which change to orange and red in the autumn. Fruits red. E. United States. I. 1883.

orientalis sanguinea. See *C. schraderana.*

oxyacantha L. emend JACQ. (*oxyacanthoides*) (*laevigata*). Less common as a native than *C. monogyna.* Many of the following clones are probably hybrids (*C.* × *media*) between the two species, all making large shrubs or small trees, and are very showy when covered with flowers in May. N.W. and C. Europe (incl. British Isles).

'Aurea'. Fruits yellow.

'Coccinea Plena'. See *'Paul's Scarlet'*.

'Gireoudii'. Young leaves prettily mottled pink and white. A.M. 1972.

'Masekii'. Flowers double; pale rose.

'Paul's Scarlet' (*'Coccinea Plena'*). Flowers double; scarlet. Originated as a sport of *'Rosea Flore Pleno'* in a garden in Hertfordshire in 1858. F.C.C. 1867. A.G.M. 1969.

'Plena'. Flowers double; white. A.G.M. 1969.

CRATAEGUS—*continued*

'Punicea'. Flowers single; scarlet.

'Rosea'. Flowers single; pink.

'Rosea Flore Pleno'. Flowers double; pink.

pedicellata SARG. (*coccinea* in part). "Scarlet Haw". A small tree with wide-spreading head of thorny branches. Leaves with glandular teeth. Large bunches of scarlet fruits and often rich autumn colour. N.E. North America. I. 1683.

persistens SARG. A small tree. Leaves remain green during early winter and are accompanied by the long-persistent, red fruits. Possibly a hybrid of *C. crus-galli*.

phaenopyrum L. f. (*cordata*). "Washington Thorn". A striking, round-headed species up to 10m. and one of the most distinct of the genus, with its glossy, maple-like leaves and profusion of small, dark-crimson fruits. Good autumn tints. S.E. United States. I. 1738.

pinnatifida BGE. A small tree with large, conspicuously lobed leaves; thorns short or absent. Fruits crimson, minutely dotted. N.E. Asia. C. 1860.

major N. E. BR. The Chinese variety is one of the most ornamental thorns, with its glossy, crimson fruits. Among the best of all small trees for its rich red autumn colour. N. China. C. 1880. F.C.C. 1886.

prunifolia PERS. A small, compact, broad-headed tree, notable for its persistent, showy fruit, and polished, oval leaves. Rich autumn colour. Possibly a hybrid between *C. macracantha* and *C. crus-galli*. C. 1797. A.G.M. 1969.

punctata JACQ. An attractive tree up to 11m. producing great crops of white blossom. Fruits large, dull crimson with pale spots. East N. America. I. 1746.

'Aurea' (*'Xanthocarpa'*). Fruits yellow.

rivularis. See *C. douglasii*.

saligna GREENE. A shrub or small tree from Colorado. Fruits lustrous, at first red, finally black. I. 1902.

schraderana LEDEB. (*orientalis sanguinea*). A small, round-headed tree with deeply-cut, grey-green, downy leaves and large, dark purple-red fruits in autumn. Greece; Crimea.

stipulacea LOUD. A small but vigorous, semi-evergreen tree, remarkable as being one of the few Mexican trees hardy in this country. Leaves glossy-green above, pubescent beneath, fruits like yellow crab apples, very persistent. I. 1824.

submollis SARG. A small tree often grown as *C. mollis* but differing in its rather smaller leaves and bright orange-red fruits. N.E. United States, S.E. Canada. A.M. 1953.

tanacetifolia PERS. "Tansy-leaved Thorn". A small, usually thornless, tree with grey, downy-leaves, conspicuous in flower and fruit; the latter appear like small yellow apples. Asia Minor. I. 1789. A.M. 1976.

tomentosa L. (*calpodendron*). A North American species forming a small, round-headed tree, very floriferous and bearing orange-red, pear-shaped fruits. I. 1765.

uniflora MOENCH. A medium sized shrub with small rounded leaves and one to three flowers in a cluster. Fruits yellow or greenish-yellow. Eastern U.S.A. I. 1704.

wattiana HEMSL. & LACE. (*korolkowii*). Small, often thornless tree with sharply toothed leaves and translucent yellow fruits. Baluchistan.

wilsonii SARG. A small tree or large shrub. Leaves lustrous; fruits deep-red. C. China. I. 1907.

×**CRATAEMESPILUS** (*CRATAEGUS* × *MESPILUS*)—**Rosaceae**—A natural hybrid between the hawthorn and medlar, bearing clusters of attractive white flowers.

grandiflora E. G. CAMUS (*C. oxyacantha* × *M. germanica*) (*Crataegomespilus grandiflora*). An apparently sterile hybrid found wild in France, about 1800. A small, broad-headed tree with hairy leaves, occasionally lobed. Flowers in pairs or threes, 2·5cm. across; fruits like large, yellowish-brown haws. Orange and yellow autumn tints.

‡†***CRINODENDRON** (*TRICUSPIDARIA*)—**Elaeocarpaceae**—The two cultivated species of this genus are native of Chile, and are worthy additions to gardens in the milder areas of Great Britain. They require lime free soil and partial shade.

hookeranum GAY (*Tricuspidaria lanceolata*). This shrub is one of the gems of the garden. The flowers, like long stalked crimson lanterns, hang thickly along the branches in May. A large, dense shrub in mild localities. Introduced by William Lobb in 1848. F.C.C. 1916 (as *Tricuspidaria lanceolata*).

patagua MOL. (*Tricuspidaria dependens*). This is a strong-growing shrub or small tree, bearing its white, bell-shaped flowers in late summer. Requires wall protection in cold districts. I. 1901.

"CROWBERRY". See *EMPETRUM nigrum.*

"CUCUMBER TREE". See *MAGNOLIA acuminata.*

†CUDRANIA—Moraceae—A small genus related to *Morus.*
tricuspidata LAV. "Chinese Silkworm Thorn". A large shrub or small tree with ovate, entire or three-lobed leaves and stalked axillary clusters of tiny flowers. Rare in cultivation. China, Korea. C. 1872.

"CURRANT, FLOWERING". See *RIBES.*

"CURRY PLANT". See *HELICHRYSUM angustifolium.*

‡*CYATHODES—Epacridaceae—Heath-like Australian and New Zealand shrubs, with tiny white pitcher-shaped flowers and very attractive foliage. They require lime-free soil.
colensoi HOOK. f. A decumbent species with glaucous foliage; fruits white or red. A very beautiful prostrate shrub. Proving qutite hardy. A.M. 1962.
†robusta HOOK. f. Small, erect shrub with white fruits and narrow leaves, glaucous beneath. Chatham Islands.

CYDONIA—Rosaceae—A monotypic genus related to *Chaenomeles.*
japonica. See *CHAENOMELES speciosa.*
maulei. See *CHAENOMELES japonica.*
oblonga MILL. (*vulgaris*). The "Common Quince". Native of N. Persia and Turkestan. A small, unarmed tree occasionally up to 6m. high. Flowers white to pale rose; fruit golden-yellow, fragrant. Leaves often turn a rich yellow before falling. This and its named clones make characteristic single specimens for lawns. Also see our Fruit Tree Catalogue. For ornamental "Cydonias" see *CHAENOMELES.*

‡CYRILLA—Cyrillaceae—An interesting monotypic genus.
***racemiflora** L. "Leatherwood". A small, late-summer flowering evergreen shrub. Leaves lanceolate, turning crimson in autumn. Flowers white, borne in whorls of slender, cylindrical racemes at the base of the current year's shoots in late summer-autumn. Requires lime-free soil. S.E. United States, W. Indies, Mexico, Northern S. America. I. 1765. A.M. 1901.

CYTISUS—Leguminosae—The "Brooms" vary from prostrate shrublets to those attaining small tree size, all having typical pea-shaped flowers, and mostly late spring or early summer flowering, but there are a few which flower towards autumn. The species are native of Europe and have yellow flowers unless otherwise stated.

The majority of species are lime tolerant but *C. multiflorus* and *C. scoparius* and their mixed progeny, comprising the bulk of the hardy hybrid brooms, will not succeed for long on poor shallow, chalky soils, nor strange to relate, in extremely acid soils. They do best in neutral or acid soils, or deep soils over chalk, including stiff clay-loam. They are all sun loving, light demanders, and attain about 1·2 to 2m. high.

The more vigorous species and hybrids may be pruned immediately after flowering to prevent legginess, taking care not to cut into the old hard wood.
albus. See *C. leucanthus* and *multiflorus.*
ardoinii FOURNIER. A miniature, mat-forming alpine shrub from the Maritime Alps (S. France). Flowers bright yellow, April to May. I. 1866. A.M. 1955.
austriacus L. (*Chamaecytisus austriacus*). A valuable, late-flowering, dwarf shrub producing a succession of heads of bright-yellow flowers from July to September. Foliage covered with silky adpressed hairs. C. and S.E. Europe to C. Russia. I. 1741.
battandieri MAIRE. A tall shrub. Leaves laburnum-like, grey, with a silky sheen. Flowers in cone-shaped clusters, bright yellow, pineapple-scented, appearing in July. An excellent shrub for a high wall. Morocco. I. about 1922. A.M. 1931. F.C.C. 1934. A.G.M. 1938.
× beanii DALLIM. (*ardoinii × purgans*). Charming dwarf shrub up to ·35m. in height. Flowers golden yellow, May. Garden origin 1900. F.C.C. 1955. A.G.M. 1969.
'Burkwoodii'. A vigorous hybrid with flowers of cerise; wings deep crimson edged yellow. May to June. A.M.T. 1973.
candicans. See *C. monspessulanus.*

CYTISUS—*continued*

capitatus. See *C. supinus.*

'C. E. Pearson'. Flowers creamy-yellow flushed crimson on standard; wings rich flame. May to June.

'Daisy Hill'. Flowers deep rose in bud, opening to cream, flushed rose on standard; wings deep crimson. May to June.

×**dallimorei** ROLFE (*multiflorus* × *scoparius Andreanus'*). Medium sized shrub raised at Kew in 1900. Flowers deep rose flushed scarlet. A parent of some of the best hybrids. A.M. 1910.

decumbens SPACH. A prostrate, rock-garden shrublet; flowers bright-yellow in May and June. S. Europe. I. 1775.

demissus BOISS. A prostrate shrub no more than 10cm. high. A gem for the rock garden with exceptionally large yellow flowers with brown keels, May. Found on Mount Olympus in Greece at about 2,300m. A.M. 1932.

'Donard Seedling'. Flowers pale yellow with mauve-pink standard; wings flushed red. May to June.

'Dorothy Walpole'. Flowers dark cerise-red; wings velvety crimson; May to June. A.M. 1923.

elongatus. See *C. ratisbonensis.*

emeriflorus REICHB. (*glabrescens* SART.). A dwarf, compact shrub. Flowers bright golden yellow produced in small clusters in May and June. Switzerland, N. Italy. C. 1896.

frivaldskyanus DEGEN. A dwarf shrub often forming a low, compact mound of hairy, leafy stems. Flowers bright yellow in terminal heads in June and July.

glabrescens. See *C. emeriflorus.*

grandiflorus DC. (*Sarothamnus grandiflorus*). "Woolly-podded Broom". In its bright-yellow flowers, this species from South Spain and Portugal, resembles the "Common Yellow Broom", but is well distinguished by its grey-woolly seed pods. It grows 2·5 to 3m. high and is quite hardy. I. 1816.

hirsutus L. (*Chamaecytisus hirsutus*). An extremely variable, dwarf or small hairy shrub of loose habit, producing long leafy racemes of yellow or buff stained pea-flowers in May and June. S. and C. Europe. I. during 18th century.

'Hollandia'. Flowers pale cream, back of standard cerise; wings dark cerise. May to June. A.M.T. 1973.

ingramii BLAKELOCK (*Sarothamnus ingramii*). An interesting species discovered in the mountains of North-west Spain by Capt. Collingwood Ingram. A medium sized shrub of erect habit. Flowers yellow and cream, in June.

'Johnson's Crimson'. Flowers clear crimson. A fine hybrid, in habit resembling the "White Spanish Broom". A.M.T. 1972. F.C.C.T. 1973.

×**kewensis** BEAN (*ardoinii* × *multiflorus*). Sheets of cream-coloured flowers in May; growth semi-prostrate. Raised at Kew in 1891. A.G.M. 1951.

'Killiney Red'. Flowers rich red; wings darker and velvety. May to June.

'Lady Moore'. Flowers large, creamy-yellow, flushed rose on standard and flame on wings; larger and richer than those of *'C. E. Pearson'*. May to June. A.M. 1928.

leucanthus WALDST. & KIT. (*albus* HACQ.). A dwarf shrub with spreading downy stems. Flowers white or cream, borne in terminal heads in June and July. C. & S.E. Europe. I. 1806.

'Lord Lambourne'. Standard pale cream; wings dark red. May to June. A.M. 1927.

†***maderensis magnifoliosus** BRIQ. A large shrub with fragrant, bright yellow flowers in racemes in spring and early summer. A conservatory plant, except in very mild localities. Madeira.

'Minstead'. A charming hybrid derived from *C. multiflorus*, producing multitudes of small flowers which are white, flushed lilac, darker on wings and in bud. May to June. A.M. 1949.

†**monspessulanus** L. (*Teline monspessulanus*) (*candicans*). "Montpelier Broom". A medium sized, graceful, semi-evergreen species; clusters of yellow flowers from April to June. Subject to injury by severe frost. S. Europe, Asia Minor, N. Africa. C. 1735. A.M. 1974.

'Mrs. Norman Henry'. Similar in habit to *'Minstead'*, but flowers with darker coloured wings. May to June. A.M.T. 1972.

‡**multiflorus** SWEET (*albus* LINK.). "White Spanish Broom". An erect shrub of medium height, its stems studded with small white flowers in May and June. Parent of many hybrids. Spain, Portugal, N.W. Africa. C. 1752. A.G.M. 1926. A.M.T. 1974.

CYTISUS—*continued*

nigricans L. (*carlieri*) (*Lembotropis nigricans*). A most useful and elegant small, late-flowering shrub producing long terminal racemes of yellow flowers continiously during late summer. C. and S.E. Europe to C. Russia. I. 1730. A.G.M. 1948.

†**'Porlock'** (*monspessulanus* × *racemosus*). Quickly forms a large, semi-evergreen bush. Flowers in racemes, butter-yellow, very fragrant, appearing in April and May. A lovely conservatory shrub. Raised about 1922. A.M. 1931.

× **praecox** WHEELER (*multiflorus* × *purgans*). "Warminster Broom". A small shrub, a spectacular plant forming, in early May, a tumbling mass of rich cream. Garden origin about 1867. A.G.M. 1933.

'Albus'. Flowers white.

'Allgold'. An outstanding small shrub with arching sprays of long-lasting yellow flowers. A.G.M. 1969. F.C.C.T. 1974.

procumbens SPRENG. A dwarf shrub with prostrate branches. Flowers borne in the leaf axils in May and June. S.E. Europe. A.M. 1948.

purgans SPACH. A dense, usually leafless shrub forming a mass of erect branches 1m. high. Flowers fragrant, yellow, in April and May. S.W. Europe, N. Africa. C. mid 19th century.

purpureus SCOP. (*Chamaecytisus purpureus*). "Purple Broom". A pretty, low shrub about 45cm. high. Flowers lilac-purple, produced in May. C. and S.E. Europe. I. 1792. A.M. 1980.

albus ZAB. A slightly dwarfer form with white flowers.

'Atropurpureus'. Flowers deep purple. A superb dwarf shrub.

ratisbonensis SCHAEF. (*biflorus*) (*elongatus*) (*Chamaecytisus ratisbonensis*). An attractive small shrub of loose habit som(what resembling *C. hirsutus*. Flowers yellow or with a reddish stain, arranged in long arching, leafy racemes in May and June. C. Europe to Caucasus, W Siberia. I. about 1800.

scoparius LINK. (*Sarothamnus scoparius*). "Common Broom". A familiar, medium sized, native shrub, as conspicuous as the gorse but without its spines. Flowers rich butter-yellow in May. A parent of many named clones. See generic description for soil requirements. Europe. A.G.M. 1969.

'Andreanus'. A form in which the flowers are attractively marked with brown-crimson. F.C.C. 1890. F.C.C.T. 1973.

'Cornish Cream'. A most attractive form with cream-coloured flowers. A.M. 1923. A.G.M. 1969. F.C.C.T. 1973.

'Dragonfly'. Standard deep yellow; wings deep crimson. Strong growing. May to June.

'Firefly'. Standard yellow; wings with a bronze stain. A.M. 1907. A.G.M. 1969.

'Fulgens'. A late flowering clone of dense, compact habit. Flowers rufous in bud opening orange-yellow; wings deep crimson. June.

'Golden Sunlight'. A strong growing form with flowers of a rich yellow. A.G.M. 1969. A.M.T. 1973.

maritimus. See *prostratus*.

prostratus A. B. JACKS. (*maritimus*). A dwarf spreading shrub with large, yellow flowers. Found wild on sea cliffs in a few localities in the west of the British Isles. A.M. 1913.

sulphureus REHD. Flowers cream, tinged red in bud; wings and keel pale sulphur. A.G.M. 1969.

sessilifolius L. Elegant shrub of medium size, with short racemes of bright yellow flowers in June. Leaves usually sessile on flowering stems. C. and S. Europe, N. Africa. Long cultivated. A.M. 1919.

supinus L. (*capitatus*) (*Chamaecytisus supinus*). A compact shrub about ·6 to 1m., very variable in the wild. Flowers large, yellow, in terminal clusters from July onwards. C. and S. Europe. I. 1755.

supranubius. See *SPARTOCYTISUS nubigenus*.

'Toome's Variety'. A hybrid of *C. multiflorus* with long slender stems covered in May with multitudes of small creamy-white flowers, flushed lilac on the inside of the standard.

× **versicolor** DIPP. (*hirsutus* × *purpureus*). Of dwarf habit; flowers pale buff shaded lilac pink. May to June. Garden origin about 1850.

'Hillieri' (*hirsutus hirsutissimus* × *versicolor*). A low shrub with arching branches. The large flowers, yellow flushed pale bronze changing to buff-pink are borne in May and June. Raised in our nurseries. I. 1933.

'Zeelandia' (*'Burkwoodii'* × *praecox*). Standard lilac outside, cream inside; wings pinkish, keel cream. May-June. F.C.C.T. 1974.

‡***DABOECIA—Ericaceae**—A small genus of low-growing, lime-hating shrubs, related to *Erica*, but distinct on account of the usually large, glandular, deciduous corolla and broader leaves.

†**azorica** TUT. & E. F. WARB. A very pretty plant, less hardy and dwarfer than the "Connemara Heath", flowers also darker coloured, being of a rich crimson shade. Requires a sheltered position. Azores. I. 1929. A.M. 1932.

cantabrica K. KOCH (*Menziesia polifolia*). "Connemara Heath"; "St. Dabeoc's Heath". One of the most charming and useful of dwarf shrubs producing long racemes of very showy rose-purple, pitcher-shaped flowers from June to November. W. Europe (incl. Ireland). A.G.M. 1930.

'Alba'. Flowers white. A.G.M. 1969.

'Atropurpurea'. Rose-purple, darker than the type. A.G.M. 1969.

'Bicolor'. White, rose-purple and striped flowers often on the same raceme. A.G.M. 1969.

'Porter's Variety'. Dwarf, compact form with small, pinched rose-purple flowers.

'Praegerae'. Dwarf, spreading habit; flowers curiously narrowed, rich pink. A.M.T. 1970.

"DAISY BUSH". See *OLEARIA*.

†***DAMNACANTHUS—Rubiaceae**—A small genus of evergreen, spiny shrubs, suitable for sun or shade, and a well-drained soil.

indicus GAERTN. f. A dainty, spiny, small shrub, suitable for growing in pots. Small, fragrant, funnel-shaped white flowers followed by coral-red berries. China, Formosa, Japan, Himalaya. I. 1868.

***DANAË—Liliaceae**—A monotypic genus related to *Ruscus*, differing in its hermaphrodite flowers borne in short terminal racemes.

racemosa MOENCH. (*Ruscus racemosus*). "Alexandrian Laurel". A charming, small, shade-bearing evergreen with arching sprays of narrow polished green leaves. Orange-red fruits produced after hot summers. Excellent for cutting. Asia Minor to Persia. C. 1713. A.M. 1933.

DAPHNE—Thymelaeaceae—A genus of beautiful, usually fragrant shrubs, mostly of small size and suitable for the rock garden. Good loamy soil, moisture, and good drainage are essential for their success.

***acutiloba** REHD. A medium sized shrub with long leathery leaves and terminal heads of white, normally scentless flowers in July. Fruits large, bright scarlet W. China. I. 1908.

longilobata. See *D. longilobata*.

alpina L. A dwarf, deciduous species with grey-green leaves and fragrant white flowers in May and June; fruits orange-red. S. and C. Europe. C. 1759.

altaica PALL. Small, semi-evergreen shrub of upright habit. Flowers white, slightly. fragrant, in terminal clusters in May or June followed by red fruits. Altai Mts. I. 1796.

***arbuscula** CELAK. A dwarf, rounded, alpine shrublet from Eastern Czechoslovakia, with crowded, narrow leaves. Flowers rose-pink, fragrant; fruits brownish-yellow. A.M. 1915. F.C.C. 1973.

aurantiaca DIELS. "Golden-flowered Daphne". A small, very distinct and rare Chinese species of slow growth with fragrant, rich yellow flowers in May, and ovate-oblong, opposite leaves glaucous beneath. Szechwan, Yunnan. F.C.C. 1927.

bholua BUCH.-HAM. A rare, deciduous, or semi-evergreen shrub up to 2m., recalling *D. odora*, with stout, erect branches. Leaves oblanceolate. Flowers large, sweetly scented, deep reddish-mauve in bud, opening white, with reddish-mauve reverse, twenty or more in a terminal umbel, appearing continuously in January and February. Fruits black. We grow stocks of this species collected at different altitudes. Himalaya. A.M. 1946.

blagayana FREYER. A dwarf shrub with prostrate branches terminating in bunches of oval leaves and clusters of richly scented, creamy-white flowers from March to April; fruits whitish. A difficult plant succeeding best in deep leaf mould and half shade. From the mountain forests of S.E. Europe. I. about 1875. F.C.C. 1880.

× **burkwoodii** TURRILL (*caucasica* × *cneorum*). A fast-growing semi-evergreen shrub attaining 1m. in height. The pale-pink, deliciously fragrant flowers are borne in clusters on short leafy shoots all along the branches in May and June. A.M. 1935. The clone '*Somerset*' is almost identical.

caucasica PALL. A small, narrow-leaved, Caucasian shrub. Terminal clusters of fragrant white flowers in May and June; fruits yellow.

DAPHNE—*continued*

***cneorum** L. "Garland Flower". A great favourite on account of its fragrance, and the rose-pink flowers which are borne in clusters on prostrate branches during April and May; fruits brownish-yellow. A difficult plant to establish. C. and S. Europe. A.G.M. 1927.

'Alba'. A rare, white form of '*Pygmaea*'. A.M. 1920.

'Eximia'. A more prostrate form with larger leaves and flowers. The unopened flower buds are crimson opening to rich rose-pink. A.M. 1938. F.C.C. 1967.

'Pygmaea'. Free-flowering, its branches lying flat on the ground.

'Variegata'. A vigorous form; leaves attractively margined with cream.

verlotii MEISN. A rare, lax form from the Central and Southern Alps, differing from the type in its more prostrate growth and narrower, pointed leaves. A.M. 1916.

***collina** SMITH. A first rate rock garden shrub. Forms a shapely bush 28 to 35cm. high, each shoot clothed with blunt, deep green leaves and terminating in a cluster of fragrant, rose-purple flowers in May. Both this and the following variety are two of the most rewarding of daphnes. S. Italy. C. 1752. A.M. 1938. A.G.M. 1973.

neapolitana LINDL. A beautiful dwarf, hardy shrub rarely more than 1m. high, with blunt, ash-green leaves. Clusters of rose-pink, fragrant flowers are borne profusely from April to early June. A.G.M. 1969.

dauphinii. See *D.* ×*hybrida.*

genkwa SIEB. & ZUCC. There can be few lovelier shrubs than this oriental species, but it is difficult to establish. A small shrub with light green, mostly opposite leaves. Flowers clear lilac-blue, carried all along leafless branches in April and May. China; Formosa. Introduced by Robert Fortune from China in 1843. Long cultivated in Japan. F.C.C. 1885.

giraldii NITSCHE. An uncommon dwarf, erect shrub to about ·75m. It bears fragrant yellow flowers in clusters in May or June, followed by bright red fruits. N.W. China. I. 1911.

***gnidium** L. A small, erect, slender shrub with fragrant creamy-white flowers from June to August, and red fruits. S. Europe and N. Africa.

× **houtteana** LINDL. (*laureola* × *mezereum*). A small shrub of erect habit partially evergreen purplish leaves similar to the *laureola* parent in shape. Flowers dark red-purple in April. Subject to virus.

*× **hybrida** SWEET (*collina* × *odora*) (*dauphinii*). This charming small shrub has the beauty and fragrance of *D. odora,* and is hardier. Reddish-purple flowers are produced from late autumn through winter.

†***jasminea** SIBTH. & SM. A dwarf, cushion-forming shrublet with small, narrow glaucous leaves. Flowers rose-pink in bud, opening white, deliciously fragrant. A rare alpine gem growing on cliffs and rocks in Greece. Requires winter protection. A.M. 1968.

***julia** KOS.-POL. A rare dwarf, evergreen, mound forming shrub from S. Russia closely resembling and sometimes included under *D. cneorum* but flower-heads more crowded. I. 1960.

***laureola** L. "Spurge Laurel". A useful, small, shade-bearing native. Flowers fragrant, yellow-green in dense clusters beneath the leathery, polished green leaves. February and March. Fruits black. S. and W. Europe (incl. England).

philippi MEISSN. Dwarf variety with obovate leaves and smaller flowers. A very pleasing evergreen for the rock garden. Pyrenees. C. 1894.

longilobata TURRILL (*acutiloba longilobata*). A small erect, deciduous or semi-evergreen shrub up to 2m. with slender purplish stems, narrowly elliptic leaves and white flowers during summer. Closely related to *D. acutiloba.* Himalaya.

mezereum L. The well-known, sweet-scented, deciduous "Mezereon". A small shrub flowering in February and March. The purple-red flowers, covering the previous year's shoots, are followed by scarlet poisonous fruits. Thrives in chalk soils. Europe (incl. British Isles), Asia Minor and Siberia. A.G.M. 1929.

'Alba'. Flowers white; fruits translucent amber; branches more upright.

'Grandiflora' ('*Autumnalis*'). Flowers larger than the type and beginning to open as early as September.

'Rosea'. A selected form. Large, clear rose-pink flowers.

***odora** THUNB. (*indica* '*Rubra*'). This very fragrant, winter and early spring flowering, small shrub from China and Japan, should be given some protection, but is hardy enough to withstand frost of considerable severity. It makes a bush of 1·2 to 2m. in height. I. 1771.

DAPHNE—*continued*

odora 'Alba'. A form with white flowers.

'Aureomarginata'. Leaves with creamy-white marginal variegation. Hardier and stronger growing than the type. A.G.M. 1973. A.M. 1976.

***oleoides** SCHREB. (*buxifolia*). An uncommon dwarf species with thick leaves, terminating in a bristle-like tip; flowers cream or pale pink, fragrant, in terminal clusters; fruits red. S. Europe to the Himalaya.

brachyloba MEISN. Differs in its leaves which are rounded not pointed, and apressed pilose above; also in the shorter lobed white flowers in a lax head.

†***papyracea** STEUD. Little known species related to *D. odora*, and recognised by its long oblanceolate leaves. Flowers white; fruits dark red.

***petraea** LEYB. (*rupestris*). An alpine gem only 5 to 7·5cm. high with small linear leaves; flowers fragrant, rosy-pink, produced in terminal clusters in June. A choice gnarled little shrublet suitable for the alpine house or scree. N. Italy. C. 1894. A.M. 1906.

'Grandiflora'. A form with larger flowers. A.M. 1918. F.C.C. 1924.

***pontica** L. A small, free-growing, wide-spreading shrub which will thrive under drip and in heavy soil. Bright green, glossy leaves and loose clusters of elusively fragrant, spidery, yellow-green flowers in April and May; fruits blue-black. Asia Minor. I. 1752. A.M. 1977.

pseudo-mezereum GRAY. A rare species similar in habit and leaf to *D. mezereum* but with smaller, greenish-yellow, scentless flowers clustered around the tips of the shoots in April. Fruits red. Male and female flowers on separate plants (dioecious). Japan. C. 1905.

***retusa** HEMSL. A slow-growing, dwarf shrub with stout, stiff branches. Clusters of fragrant deep rose-purple flowers in May and June. W. China. I. 1901. A.M. 1927. A.G.M. 1946.

***'Rossetii'** (*cneorum* × *laureola philippii*). A natural hybrid found in the Pyrenees. It forms a compact, rounded bush usually less than ·6m. The reddish flowers are rarely seen. The oblanceolate leaves are intermediate between those of its parents.

rupestris. See *D. petraea*.

***sericea** VAHL. Differs from *D. collina* in the leaves being narrower, olive-green and the flowers paler pink. Fruits orange-red. S.E. Europe. A.M. 1931.

'Somerset'. See under *D.* × *burkwoodii*.

***tangutica** MAXIM. A small Chinese species closely related to and resembling *D. retusa*, but distinguishable by its longer, more acute leaves. Flowers in terminal clusters in March or April, fragrant, white tinged, purple on the inside, rose-purple outside. China. Introduced by Wilson in the early 1900's. A.M. 1929. A.G.M. 1949.

× thauma FARRER (*petraea* × *striata*). A dwarf, compact shrub forming a low mound, with narrow leaves densely crowding the branchlets. Flowers bright rose-purple, borne in terminal clusters in May and June. A natural hybrid introduced from the south Tyrol in 1911.

***DAPHNIPHYLLUM—Daphniphyllaceae**—A small genus of Asiatic evergreens. These aristocratic-looking shrubs have leaves recalling *Rhododendron decorum* but the flowers are not conspicuous. They thrive in half shade and a neutral loamy soil, but are lime tolerant.

humile MAXIM. A wide-spreading, much-branched, slow growing shrub of medium size. Leaves shining green above and glaucous beneath. Japan. I. 1879.

macropodum MIQ. (*glaucescens*). A large, striking evergreen shrub from China and Japan. Large rhododendron-like leaves pale green above, glaucous beneath. Flowers inconspicuous, pink and green, pungently scented in clusters beneath the leaves in late spring. Remarkably hardy. I. 1879. F.C.C. 1888.

"DATE PLUM". See *DIOSPYROS lotus*.

†**DATURA—Solanaceae**—Tender shrubs, natives mainly of Mexico and Tropical America. Grown outside only in the south west and the Isles of Scilly.

sanguinea RUIZ. & PAV. Tree-like shrub up to 3m., taller in the Isles of Scilly. Large softly hairy leaves and large orange-red trumpets hanging from the branches in May and June. Peru.

suaveolens HUMB. & BONPL. (*Brugmansia suaveolens*). "Angel's Trumpet". A large tree-like shrub with flannel-like leaves and large, pendulous, trumpet shaped, fragrant white flowers from June to August. An excellent conservatory subject. Mexico.

DAVIDIA—Davidiaceae—(Originally placed under Cornaceae). Medium sized trees recalling *Tilia*, the Davidias are perfectly winter hardy and will thrive in every kind of fertile soil. The small inconspicuous flowers are collected into a dense globular head up to 2·5cm. across. Each head is attended by an unequal pair of large, conspicuous white bracts which have been fancifully likened to handkerchiefs.

involucrata BAILL. "Pocket-handkerchief Tree". "Dove Tree". "Ghost Tree". This beautiful medium sized tree is most conspicuous in May when draped with its large, white bracts. C. and W. China. First discovered by the French missionary David in 1869, introduced by Wilson in 1904. A.G.M. 1969. A.M. 1972.

vilmoriniana WANG. The leaves on established trees are glabrous, not silky hairy beneath, and the fruits more elliptic and less russety. Horticulturally both this and the type are very similar and of equal merit. Introduced by Farges from China in 1897. F.C.C. 1911. A.G.M. 1969.

†**DEBREGEASIA—Urticaceae**—A small genus of tender trees and shrubs related to the nettles, but unlike them, harmless to the touch.

longifolia WEDD. A medium sized shrub of which the long, lance-shaped leaves, pale beneath, are the most striking feature. Produces yellow, mulberry-like fruits. S.E. Asia.

DECAISNEA—Lardizabalaceae—A genus of two species of deciduous shrubs. The following hardy species will grow in sun or semi-shade, and moist but well-drained soil.

fargesii FRANCH. A very distinct W. Chinese shrub attaining about 3m. Large, pinnate leaves ·6 to 1m. long; flowers often unisexual, yellow-green in racemes up to ·5m. long, followed by remarkable metallic-blue pods like those of the broad bean in shape. I. 1895.

†***DENDROMECON—Papaveraceae**—A genus of two species related to *Romneya*, but differing in their entire evergreen leaves and smaller, yellow flowers.

rigida BENTHAM. A large shrub, best grown against a warm sunny wall. Leaves narrow, rigid and glaucous. Flowers poppy-like, four petalled, bright buttercup-yellow, produced intermittantly over a long period. California. I. about 1854. A.M. 1913.

‡†***DESFONTAINEA—Potaliaceae**—Given a sheltered position and half-shade this beautiful evergreen is hardy in the home counties. Not successful on shallow chalk soils.

spinosa RUIZ. & PAV. (*hookeri*). Magnificent late-summer-flowering evergreen, slowly attaining 1·8 to 2m. Leaves small, holly-like; flowers tubular, scarlet with a yellow mouth. Chile, Peru. I. about 1843. A.M. 1931.

'Harold Comber'. A form collected by Comber with 5cm. long flowers varying in colour from vermilion to orient red. A.M. 1955.

DESMODIUM—Leguminosae—A large genus of herbs and shrubs differing from *Lespedeza* in their many-seeded pods, and leaflets with small subulate stipules.

penduliflorum. See *LESPEDEZA thunbergii*.

†**praestans** FORR. A large shrub with long scandent stems and large rounded leaves. The dense covering of silky hairs give the whole plant a silvery appearance. Flowers purple in compact, crowded racemes during late summer. A species requiring a well-drained position in the full sun preferably backed by a wall. S.W. China.

tiliifolium G. DON. A small to medium sized, semi-woody shrub with erect stems and trifoliolate leaves. In summer a profusion of pale-lilac pea-flowers in large panicles. Himalaya. C. 1883.

DEUTZIA—Philadelphaceae—A genus of easily cultivated shrubs, succeeding in all types of fertile soil. June-flowering and growing from 1·2 to 2m. high, unless otherwise described. Thin out and cut back old flowering shoots to within a few cms. of the old wood, immediately after flowering. Gardeners are indebted to Lemoine of Nancy, France, for the many attractive hybrid clones.

'Avalanche'. See *D.* ×*maliflora 'Avalanche'*.

×**candelabra** REHD. (*gracilis* × *sieboldiana*). This graceful shrub is similar to *D. gracilis*, but hardier and the flower panicles are broader and denser. Garden origin.

chunii HU. A very beautiful and remarkable July-blooming species. Flowers 12mm. across; petals pink outside, white within, reflexed, exposing the yellow anthers. Panicles to 10cm. long, produced all along the branches. Leaves narrow, grey beneath. This plant both in pink and white flowered forms is sometimes seen in cultivation under the name *D. ningpoensis*. E. China. I. 1935.

DEUTZIA—*continued*

compacta CRAIB. This rare, July-blooming Chinese species forms a neat bush. Flowers in 7·5cm. wide corymbs, pink in bud, opening to white, strongly resembling "Hawthorn" in size, form, and in their sweet scent. I. 1905.

'Lavender Time'. Flowers lilac at first, turning to pale lavender. A very distinct shrub, collected in the wild.

'Contraste'. (Hybrida Group). Flowers star-shaped, in loose panicles, soft lilac-pink; outside of petals rich vinous purple. A.M. 1931.

corymbosa R. BROWN. A medium sized shrub with ovate leaves and corymbs of white flowers in June. Not so good a garden plant as *D. setchuenensis corymbiflora*, but hardier.

discolor 'Major'. Flowers 2 to 2·5cm. across in corymbose clusters, white, pink-tinted outside. The best form of this handsome Chinese species.

×**elegantissima** REHD. (*purpurascens*×*sieboldiana*). Rose-pink tinted, fragrant, flowers in paniculate corymbs. Garden origin 1909. A.M. 1914. A.G.M. 1954.

'Fasciculata'. A very beautiful clone of medium size. Flowers bright rose-pink. A.M. 1949. F.C.C. 1972.

'Rosealind'. A lovely clone with flowers of a deep carmine-pink. A.M. 1972.

glomeruliflora FRANCH. A Chinese shrub usually less than 2m. high. Leaves grey beneath; flowers large, white, in denes clusters, in May and June. I. 1908.

gracilis SIEB.& ZUCC. An elegant, white-flowered, Japanese species, a parent of many good hybrids. Needs protection from late spring frosts. Much used for forcing. I. about 1840.

×**hillieri** (*longifolia 'Veitchii'*×*setchuenensis corymbiflora*). An attractive shrub of graceful habit raised in our nurseries. The star-like flowers are purple tinged in bud opening pink and fading to white. They are carried twenty to thirty together in compact clusters in late June or July.

hookerana AIRY-SHAW. This rare species with small leaves comes from Sikkim and W. China and is closely related to *D. monbeigii*. Dense corymbs of white flowers in late June.

×**hybrida** LEMOINE (*discolor*×*longifolia*). A variable hybrid of medium size, extremely floriferous. There are a number of named clones. Garden origin 1925.

hypoglauca. See *D. rubens*.

'Joconde' (Hybrida Group). A superb, strong-growing shrub, with very large flowers lined and shaded rose-purple outside. A.M. 1959.

×**kalmiiflora** LEMOINE. (*parviflora*×*purpurascens*). A charming, floriferous shrub, flowers large, white flushed carmine. Garden-origin 1900.

longifolia FRANCH. A handsome medium sized shrub with long, narrowly lanceolate leaves and large clusters of white or pink tinted flowers in June and July. W. China. I. 1905. A.M. 1912.

'Veitchii'. The large clusters of rich lilac-pink-tinted flowers in June and July, make this the most aristocratic of a popular group of shrubs. A.M. 1912. F.C.C. 1978.

'Magicien' (Hybrida Group). Large flowers, mauve-pink, edged, white and tinted purple on the reverse. A.G.M. 1969.

×**magnifica** REHD. (*scabra*×*vilmoriniae*) (*crenata magnifica*). A vigorous, medium-sized shrub with large panicles of double, white flowers. Garden origin 1909. A.M. 1916. A.G.M. 1926.

'Eburnea'. A very beautiful clone. Single white flowers in loose panicles.

'Latiflora'. Flowers up to 2·5cm. across, white, single.

'Longipetala'. White, long-petalled flowers. One of the best clones of this popular erect-branched shrub.

'Macrothyrsa'. White flowers in large clusters.

×**maliflora** REHD. (*lemoinei*×*purpurascens*). Strong growing, medium-sized shrub with large corymbs of white, purple flushed flowers in June. Garden origin 1905.

'Avalanche'. The slender erect branches are arched by the weight of the fragrant white flowers.

mollis DUTHIE. Small to medium sized shrub with leaves thickly felted beneath. Flowers white, in dense corymbs in June. W. China. I. 1901. A.M. 1931.

monbeigii W. W. SM. A very pretty shrub, distinct in its small leaves, white beneath. A profusion of small, glistening, star-like, white flowers; late. China. I. 1921. A.M. 1936.

DEUTZIA—*continued*

'Mont Rose'. (Hybrida Group). Flowers rose-pink with darker tints, very freely borne in paniculate clusters. A.G.M. 1957. A.M. 1971.

'Perle Rose'. (Hybrida Group). A medium-sized shrub with long, ovate-lanceolate leaves and soft rose flowers, borne in long stalked, corymbose panicles in June.

pulchra VIDAL. A magnificent, hardy, Formosan shrub of medium size. The racemes of white flowers are like drooping spikes of Lily-of-the-valley. I. 1918.

purpurascens REHD. A graceful species of medium height; flowers white tinted rich purplish-crimson, sweetly scented, in early June. Parent of many hybrids. Yunnan. I 1888.

× **rosea** REHD. (*gracilis* × *purpurascens*). This hybrid forms a compact shrub with arching branches and widely bell-shaped pink flowers. Garden origin 1898.

'Campanulata'. An erect clone with white petals contrasting with the purple calyx.

'Carminea'. Very attractive clone; flowers flushed rose-carmine. A.G.M. 1969.

'Floribunda'. Flowers pink tinged, in dense, erect panicles.

'Grandiflora'. Large white flowers with pink suffusion.

'Multiflora'. Free-flowering clone with white flowers.

'Venusta'. This clone leans towards *D. gracilis*, but has larger white flowers.

rubens REHD. (*hypoglauca*). A graceful, Chinese shrub with arching branches; leaves lanceolate, white on under-surface; flowers numerous, pure white, appearing in June. I. 1910.

scabra THUNB. (*crenata*). Tall, erect-branched shrub to 3 to 3·5m. producing in June and July large paniculate clusters of white flowers. Japan, China. I. 1822. A.G.M. 1928.

'Azaleiflora'. Flowers smaller than type, with reflexed petals.

'Candidissima'. Tall shrub; flowers double, pure white. A.M. 1980.

'Macrocephala'. Large bell-shaped white flowers.

'Plena'. Double, suffused rose-purple outside. F.C.C. 1863.

'Watereri'. Flowers single, white, tinted carmine.

schneiderana REHD. A medium sized shrub producing panicles of white flowers in June or July. W. China. I. 1907. A.M. 1938.

laxiflora REHD. A variety with somewhat narrower leaves and lax panicles.

setchuenensis FRANCH. A charming, slow-growing species up to 2m., producing corymbose clusters of innumerable small, white, star-like flowers during July and August. One of the very best summer-blooming shrubs, but not quite hardy enough for the coldest parts of the British Isles. China. I. 1895. A.M. 1945.

corymbiflora REHD. This equally beautiful and very floriferous form differs in its broader leaves. A.M. 1945.

sieboldiana MAXIM. An elegant shrub of loose habit, with ovate or elliptic leaves and panicles of white flowers produced in early June. Japan. C. 1890.

staminea R. BR. A Himalayan species of medium height; flowers white in 5cm. wide corymbs, produced in June. Requires a warm sheltered position. I. 1841.

vilmoriniae LEMOINE. A rapid growing, erect-branched, Chinese species, attaining 2·5 to 3m.; flowers white, in broad corymbose panicles. Leaves long lance-shaped, grey beneath. I. 1897. A.M. 1917.

× **wilsonii** DUTHIE (*discolor* × *mollis*). A handsome natural hybrid with brown exfoliating bark and panicles of large white flowers in June. W. and C. China. I. about 1901. A.M. 1908.

"DEVIL'S CLUB". See *OPLOPANAX horridus*.

"DEVIL'S WALKING STICK". See *ARALIA spinosa*.

†***DICHOTOMANTHES—Rosaceae**—A monotypic genus closely related to *Cotoneaster*, differing in the dry capsular fruits with persistent enlarged calyces. Suitable for a sheltered wall in any fertile soil.

tristaniicarpa KURZ. A large, cotoneaster-like Chinese shrub. Flowers white in terminal corymbs during June. Spring foliage prettily tinted. I. 1917.

DIERVILLA—Caprifoliaceae—A genus of easily-grown, small, summer-flowering shrubs allied to *Lonicera*. Frequently confused with Weigela but differing in the smaller, yellow, two-lipped flowers.

lonicera MILL. (*canadensis*). A small suckering shrub; flowers pale-yellow, honeysuckle-shaped, opening in June and July. Good autumn leaf colour in exposed positions. N. America. I. 1720.

rivularis GATT. A small shrub with lemon-yellow flowers in July and August, and attractive autumn tints. S.E. United States. C. 1898.

DIERVILLA—*continued*

sessilifolia BUCKL. Flowers sulphur-yellow, in short panicles, from June to August. S.E. United States. I. 1844.

× **splendens** KIRCHN. (*lonicera* × *sessilifolia*). A hybrid with short-petioled leaves and sulphur-yellow flowers.

DIOSMA pulchella. See *BAROSMA pulchella.*

DIOSPYROS—**Ebenaceae**—A large genus of mainly tropical evergreen and deciduous trees and shrubs, many of considerable economic importance. Male and female flowers on separate plants.

armata HEMSL. A remarkable, large, slow-growing, semi-evergreen, Chinese shrub with spiny spreading branches; leaves lustrous. I. 1904.

kaki L. f. (*chinensis*). "Chinese Persimmon". A large shrub or small tree long cultivated in the East for its edible fruits, and in this country for the glorious orange-yellow to orange-red and plum-purple autumn colour of its large, lustrous leaves. The orange-yellow, tomato-like fruits are carried here in the open most late summers. China. I. 1796.

lotus L. The "Date Plum" is a perfectly hardy small tree with tapered leaves dark polished green above, paler below. The female trees produce purple or yellow fruits like small tomatoes. E. Asia. C. 1597.

virginiana L. The N. American "Persimmon" forms an elegant, wide spreading tree of medium size, giving good autumn colour. Has rugged, tessellated bark. I. 1629.

DIOSTEA (*BAILLONIA*)—**Verbenaceae**—A genus of three species of South American shrubs.

juncea MIERS. A tall, elegant shrub, resembling the "Spanish Broom" in growth, but with opposite leaves. Clusters of pale-lilac, verbena-like flowers are borne in June, but seldom with sufficient profusion to be conspicuous. Andes of Chile and Argentine. I. 1890.

DIPELTA—**Caprifoliaceae**—A small genus of tall shrubs, native of China, bearing a general resemblance to *Weigela.*

floribunda MAXIM. A large shrub of first-class garden merit. Fragrant weigela-like flowers produced in great profusion in May, pink, flushed yellow at the throat. C. and W. China. I. 1902. A.M. 1927.

ventricosa HEMSL. A large, attractive, spring-flowering shrub. The conspicuous lilac-rose flowers have a curiously swollen base. W. China. I. 1904.

yunnanensis FRANCH. Large shrub; flowers cream-coloured with orange markings. Related to *D. ventricosa* but flowers narrowed at base. W. China. I. 1910.

DIPLACUS. See *MIMULUS.*

DIPLOPAPPUS chrysophyllus. See *CASSINIA fulvida.*

DIPTERONIA—**Aceraceae**—One of the only two genera of the family *Aceraceae*, the other being *Acer.*

sinensis OLIV. A large Chinese shrub with conspicuous, pinnate leaves. The flowers are inconspicuous but are followed, in autumn, by large clusters of pale green changing to red, winged seeds rather like those of the "Wych Elm", but more conspicuous. I. about 1900. A.M. 1922.

DIRCA—**Thymelaeaceae**—A genus of only two species, related to *Daphne*, but differing botanically in the exerted stamens. They thrive in moist soils particularly those of a calcareous nature.

palustris L. "Leatherwood". An interesting shrub of medium size. Flowers yellow, about 12mm. long, produced usually in threes on the leafless branches during March. The strong, flexible stems are used for basket making in some parts of the U.S.A. North America. I. 1750.

‡**DISANTHUS**—**Hamamelidaceae**—A monotypic genus requiring a moist, but well-drained soil in semi-shade.

cercidifolius MAXIM. A medium sized shrub resembling a "Witch Hazel" in habit, and "Judas Tree" in leaf, highly valued for its beautiful soft crimson and claret-red autumn tints. The tiny purplish flowers are produced in October. Japan, S.E. China. I. 1893. A.M. 1936. F.C.C. 1970.

DISCARIA—**Rhamnaceae**—A small genus of spiny shrubs from the southern hemisphere requiring a sunny, sheltered position in most, well-drained soils.

serratifolia BENTH. & HOOK. f. Large shrub with long, drooping, spiny branches and lustrous green leaves; flowers small, fragrant in dense clusters in June. Chile, Patagonia. C. 1842.

DISCARIA—*continued*

toumatou RAOUL. "Wild Irishman". A botanically interesting, small to medium sized, curious New Zealand shrub allied to *Colletia* but less formidably armed. Flowers small, green-white but numerous; leaves small, in opposite clusters or occasionally absent. Spines in pairs, slender, green, over an inch long. I. 1975.

***DISTYLIUM—Hamamelidaceae**—A small genus of evergreen shrubs and trees related to *Sycopsis*, but with flowers in racemes. They thrive best in conditions suitable to *Hamamelis*.

racemosum SIEB. & ZUCC. A wide-spreading, but slow-growing evergreen shrub reaching tree size in the wild, with glossy, leathery leaves. Its petal-less flowers consist of conspicuous red stamens produced in April. S. Japan; Taiwan; Korea. I. 1876.

DOCYNIA—Rosaceae—A group of small Oriental trees, resembling wild pears and allied to *Cydonia*.

delavayi SCHNEID. A Chinese tree; leaves persist into the winter; flowers in April, white, rose-tinted without; fruits apple-like, yellow. S.W. China. C. 1890.

rufifolia REHD. A species similar to *D. delavayi*, but with less persistent leaves. Young leaves reddish. S.W. China. I. 1903.

"DOGWOOD". See *CORNUS*.

DORYCNIUM—Leguminosae—A small genus of sub-shrubs and herbs, requiring a sunny, well-drained position in most soils.

hirsutum SER. A charming dwarf sub-shrub with erect annual stems and terminal heads of pink-tinged white pea-flowers during late summer and autumn. The whole plant is silvery hairy, a pleasant foil for the red-tinged fruit pods. Requires a position in full sun. Mediterranean Regions, S. Portugal. C. 1683.

"DOVE TREE". See *DAVIDIA involucrata*.

DRACAENA

australis. See *CORDYLINE australis*.

indivisa. See *CORDYLINE indivisa*.

†*DRIMYS—Winteraceae—Handsome evergreen shrubs or small trees for favoured localities.

andina. See *D. winteri andina*.

aromatica. See *D. lanceolata*.

colorata. See *PSEUDOWINTERA colorata*.

lanceolata BAILL. (*aromatica*). A medium sized to large, aromatic shrub of neat and pleasing habit. Attractive copper-tinted young growths, and numerous small, creamy-white flowers in April and May. Male and female on separate plants. Tasmania, S.E. Australia. I. 1843. A.M. 1926.

winteri J. R. & G. FORST. "Winter's Bark". A very handsome, tall shrub or small tree with large, leathery leaves glaucous beneath. Flowers fragrant, ivory-white, in loose umbels, opening in May. We grow two forms, one with shorter broader leaves than the other. S. America. I. 1827. A.M. 1971.

andina REICHE. (*D. andina*). A dwarf, compact, slow-growing variety. It flowers freely at ·3m. high.

***DRYAS—Rosaceae**—Carpeting plants with small evergreen oak-like leaves, dark shining green above, gleaming white beneath. Suitable for screes or wall tops, between paving or on the rock garden, in most soils.

octopetala L. "Mountain Avens". A native species. The white, yellow centred flowers like little dog roses are carried on 7·5cm. stalks, and cover the whole plant during May or early June. These are followed by silky tassels which later change to fluffy grey balls of down. N. America, Europe (including the British Isles), Asia. C. 1750. A.M. 1955.

'Minor'. A charming miniature, smaller in all its parts.

×**suendermanii** SUENDERM. (*drummondii* × *octopetala*). An uncommon hybrid similar in most respects to *D. octopetala*, but differing in its slightly larger, rather erect leaves and its nodding, creamy-white flower buds, those of the native plant being erect and white; flowering in May or early June. C. 1750. A.M. 1955. A.G.M. 1969.

ECHINOPANAX. See *OPLOPANAX*.

EDGEWORTHIA—**Thymelaeaceae**—A small genus of shrubs related to *Daphne*.

chrysantha LINDL. (*papyrifera*). A Chinese shrub attaining 1·2 to 1·5m. Terminal clusters of fragrant yellow flowers clothed on the outside with white, silky hairs. Used in Japan for the manufacture of a high class paper for currency. I. 1845. A.M. 1961.

EDWARDSIA chilensis. See *SOPHORA macrocarpa*.

EHRETIA—**Ehretiaceae**—Two species of this rare genus of small Asiatic trees are in cultivation and thrive in any fertile soil, including chalk soils. Both are of distinctive appearance having conspicuous leaves and corymbose panicles of small white flowers. Tender when young, ripened growth will withstand our coldest winters, but unripened growth is liable to frost damage.

dicksonii HANCE (*macrophylla* HORT.). An interesting, fast growing, small sturdy tree with conspicuously large, roughly hairy, lustrous leaves to 23cm. long. Broad corymbs of small, fragrant, white flowers in June. China, Formosa, Liukiu Isles. I. 1897.

thyrsiflora NAKAI (*acuminata* HORT.) (*serrata* HORT.). A small, slow growing tree; leaves smaller than those of *E. dicksonii* and glabrous, or nearly so, at maturity; flowers later, normally in August. China, Japan, Korea and Formosa. I. 1900.

ELAEAGNUS—**Elaeagnaceae**—A family comprising deciduous and evergreen, mostly fast growing shrubs or small trees. Excellent wind resisters; valuable for hedges and shelter belts particularly in maritime and exposed areas. The flowers, though small, are pleasantly scented and produced in abundance. They will thrive in any fertile soil except very shallow chalk soil.

angustifolia KUNTZE. "Oleaster". A large, spiny shrub or small tree with fragrant flowers in June and silvery-grey, willow-like leaves. Fruits silvery-amber, oval, 12mm. long. Easily mistaken for the "Willow-leaved Pear" (*Pyrus salicifolia*). Temperate Asia, widely naturalised in S. Europe. Cultivated in England in the 16th century. A.M. 1978.

orientalis L. (*E. orientalis*). A broader-leaved, greener, often spineless form.

commutata RYDB. (*argentea* PURSH. not MOENCH.). "Silver Berry". A medium sized, stoloniferous shrub, leaves intensely silver, flowers fragrant in May. Fruits small, egg-shaped, silvery. N. America. I. 1813. A.M. 1956.

*×**ebbingei** HORT. (*macrophylla×pungens*) (×*submacrophylla* SERVETT.). A large, hardy, fast-growing evergreen shrub, splendid for creating shelter, even near the sea. Leaves large, silvery beneath. Flowers in autumn, silvery-scaly and fragrant; fruits orange with silvery freckles in spring. Garden origin 1929. A.G.M. 1969.

***glabra** THUNB. A first class, vigorous, thornless evergreen shrub similar to *E. macrophylla*, but with narrower leaves. Flowers fragrant, in autumn; fruits orange with silvery freckles. China, Korea, Japan. C. 1888.

***macrophylla** THUNB. The broad, rotund leaves of this species are silvery on both surfaces, becoming green above as the season advances. Eventually a large spreading shrub. Flowers in autumn, fragrant. Korea, Japan. I. 1879. A.M. 1932. A.G.M. 1969.

multiflora THUNB. (*edulis*) (*longipes*). A wide-spreading shrub of medium size with leaves green above, silvery beneath. Most decorative in July when laden with its oblong, edible, ox-blood red fruits. Flowers fragrant, produced in April and May on the new shoots. Japan, China. I. 1862. A.M. 1976.

***pungens** THUNB. A vigorous, spreading, rarely spiny evergreen shrub up to 5m. A good shelter-making evergreen. Leaves green and shiny above, dull white speckled with brown scales beneath. Flowers in autumn, fragrant. Japan. I. 1830.

'Dicksonii' (*'Aurea'*). A rather slow-growing, erect clone, leaves with a wide irregular margin of golden yellow.

'Maculata'. Leaves with a central splash of gold, giving a very bright effect. A very handsome shrub of moderate growth. F.C.C. 1891. A.G.M. 1969.

reflexa. See *E.* ×*reflexa*.

'Simonii'. A handsome form of erect habit with broad, elliptic-oblong leaves.

'Variegata'. A large vigorous shrub, leaves with a thin creamy yellow margin.

*×**reflexa** MORR. & DCNE. (*glabra×pungens*) (*pungens reflexa*). A tall, vigorous, nearly spineless evergreen with elongated, reddish-brown, almost scandent branches. Leaves densely clad beneath with brown scales.

×**submacrophylla.** See *E.* ×*ebbingei*.

ELAEAGNUS—*continued*

umbellata THUNB. (*crispa*). A large, strong growing, wide spreading shrub with yellowish-brown shoots and soft green leaves, silvery beneath, giving a unique effect in autumn when heavily laden with its small, rounded orange fruits. Flowers delightfully fragrant in May and June. China, Korea, Japan. I. 1830. A.M. 1933.

parvifolia SCHNEID. (*E. parvifolia*). A geographical form from the Himalaya possessing all the good qualities of the type.

†***ELAEOCARPUS**—**Elaeocarpaceae**—A genus of mainly tropical trees thriving best in a peaty soil.

cyaneus SIMS. An Australian shrub of medium size, bearing in summer, racemes of white, fringed flowers, recalling those of *Chionanthus*, followed by conspicuous, turquoise-blue, marble-like fruits. For mildest localities only. I. 1803. F.C.C. 1912.

dentatus VAHL. An unusual species with purplish-grey fruits, of botanical interest, for sheltered gardens. New Zealand. I. 1883.

"ELDER". See *SAMBUCUS*.

"ELDER, BOX". See *ACER negundo*.

‡**ELLIOTTIA**—**Ericaceae**—A very rare monotypic genus requiring a lime-free soil and an open sunny position.

racemosa ELLIOTT. A beautiful medium sized, erect-branched, enkianthus-like shrub, scarcely known in European gardens. Leaves oblong-elliptic, 5-10cm. long. The four-petalled, white, slightly fragrant flowers are carried in erect terminal racemes or panicles during late summer. S.E. United States. I. 1813.

"ELM". See *ULMUS*.

"ELM, WATER". See *PLANERA aquatica*.

ELSHOLTZIA—**Labiatae**—A small genus of aromatic herbs and subshrubs valued for their late flowers. In cold districts or after severe frost the stems are usually cut to the ground in winter but reappear the following spring. Easily grown in any fertile soil, and an open position in full sun.

fruticosa REHD. (*polystachya*). A vigorous, pubescent shrub up to 2m. bearing elliptic-oblong to lanceolate leaves and long slender spikes of small white flowers during late summer and autumn. Himalaya, W. China. I. about 1903.

stauntonii BENTH. A small sub-shrub with rounded stems, the leaves lance-shaped, smelling of mint when crushed. Flowers lilac-purple, freely borne in panicles from August to October making a splendid splash of late colour. N. China. I. 1909.

'Alba'. Flowers white.

‡***EMBOTHRIUM**—**Proteaceae**—A small genus of evergreen trees or shrubs. Ideally sited when growing in a sheltered border or woodland clearing in a deep, moist but well-drained lime-free soil. Particularly suitable for gardens in the West and South-West.

coccineum FORST. "Chilean Fire Bush". This glorious species with its profusion of brilliant orange-scarlet flowers in May and early June is one of the most desirable garden treasures. Normally an erect, semi-evergreen slender, tall shrub or small tree with a measured span of life, but on Valencia Island, S.W. Ireland, there is a giant of 15m. Chile. I. 1846. A.M. 1928.

lanceolatum O. KUNTZE. This, the least evergreen form with linear-lanceolate leaves, is perfectly hardy. Collected by Mr. H. Comber. A.M. 1932. F.C.C. 1948 when exhibited by the late Lord Aberconway, who pointed out that the flower clusters touch one another, so that the whole branch is clad in scarlet. Our stock is the form sometimes referred to as "Norquinco Valley".

† **'Longifolium'.** Differs from the type in its longer, usually persistent, leaves. F.C.C. 1948.

EMMENOPTERYS—**Rubiaceae**—A small genus of two species of deciduous trees for a sheltered site. The following is the only species in general cultivation.

henryi OLIV. A rare small tree or large shrub of spreading habit. Leaves large, ovate, particularly decorative in spring when the bronze-coloured young growths unfold. Although this tree has yet to flower in this country, E. H. Wilson described it as being "one of the most strikingly beautiful trees of the Chinese forests, with its flattish to pyramidal corymbs of white, rather large flowers and still larger white bracts". It prefers a moist, deep loam but is chalk tolerant. China. I. 1907.

‡***EMPETRUM**—**Empetraceae**—Dwarf carpeting shrubs, natives of moors and mountains and wild, windswept places.

atropurpureum FERN. & WIEG. (*nigrum tomentosum*). A wiry-stemmed shrub covered with a white tomentum. Fruits reddish-purple. N. America. C. 1890.

hermaphroditum HAGERUP (*nigrum scoticum*). An hermaphrodite species similar to *E. nigrum* but growth more compact. High latitudes of northern hemisphere (incl. British Isles).

nigrum L. The "Crowberry" is a very widely distributed, procumbent evergreen forming wide-spreading dense carpets; inconspicuous purple-red flowers followed by black fruits. Requires a moist, lime-free soil. High latitudes of northern hemisphere (incl. British Isles).

scoticum. See *E. hermaphroditum*.

‡**ENKIANTHUS**—**Ericaceae**—An outstanding, distinct group of shrubs, requiring lime-free soil. The flowers, produced in May, are drooping, cup or urn-shaped, and prettily veined, while the exquisite colouring of the fading leaves is not excelled in any other genus.

campanulatus NICHOLS. An erect-branched Japanese species attaining 2·5 to 3m. A splendid shrub with variable yet subtle qualities and one of the easiest to grow of a lovely family. Flowers cup-shaped, sulphur to rich bronze carried in great profusion and lasting for three weeks; useful for cutting. Autumn foliage of every shade between yellow and red. Japan. I. 1880. A.M. 1890. A.G.M. 1932.

cernuus rubens MAK. The best form of a choice Japanese species noteworthy for its deep-red, fringed flowers and brilliant autumn colour. Of medium size. A.M. 1930.

chinensis FRANCH. (*himalaicus*) (*sinohimalaicus*). A remarkably beautiful small tree or tall narrow shrub, under favourable conditions reaching 6m. Flowers probably the largest of the genus, yellow and red with darker veins, carried in many-flowered umbels. Leaves comparatively large, usually with red petioles, giving attractive autumn tints. W. China, N.E. Upper Burma. I. 1900. A.M. 1935.

perulatus SCHNEID. (*japonicus*). A densely leafy, slow-growing, compact Japanese shrub to 2m. high. Masses of urn-shaped, white flowers appear with the leaves in spring. One of the most consistently good autumn shrubs for the intensity of its scarlet leaves. Japan. I. about 1870.

†***ENTELEA**—**Tiliaceae**—A monotypic genus requiring a sheltered site or conservatory.

arborescens R. BR. A shrub up to 3m. for the mildest localities. Leaves large, heart-shaped and double toothed. Flowers in erect open heads white, with central bunch of yellow stamens. May. The wood of this plant is one of the lightest known, lighter even than cork. New Zealand. I. 1820.

***EPHEDRA**—**Ephedraceae**—Curious shrubs with slender rush-like green stems. A genus of great botanical interest, providing a link between flowering plants and conifers.

andina C. A. MEY. A dwarf, spreading species from Chile. I. 1896.

distachya L. "European Shrubby Horsetail". Dwarf shrub with slender, erect stems forming large creeping patches. Fruits, when produced, red. S. and E. Europe. Cultivated in the 16th century.

gerardiana sikkimensis STAPF. A dwarf species with erect, many-branched stems forming extensive patches. Himalaya (E. Nepal; Sikkim). I. 1915.

‡***EPIGAEA**—**Ericaceae**—A genus of three species of creeping shrubs for peaty soils and semi-shade.

asiatica MAXIM. A dwarf, creeping, mat-forming evergreen for moist, peaty soils. Flowers rose-pink, urn-shaped, produced in terminal and axillary racemes in April. Japan. I. about 1930. A.M. 1931.

repens L. "May Flower". A creeping evergreen of a few cm. high. Dense terminal heads of fragrant white or rose tinted flowers in April. Eastern N. America. I. 1736. A.M. 1931.

***ERICA**—**Ericaceae**—"Heath". In Erica it is the corolla which is coloured and conspicuous, not the calyx as in the closely related *Calluna*.

Heaths are now very numerous, for apart from the species and older cultivars, scores of newly named cultivars are constantly swelling the ranks. Their popularity arises in part from their all-the-year-round effect when different cultivars are planted.

ERICA—*continued*

The seasons of flowering indicate that it is possible to have ericas in flower most months of the year. Those forms with long racemes are ideal for cutting for indoor decoration, and even when dead and brown they are not without beauty. All but tree heaths may be pruned immediately after flowering by removing the old inflorescences. When such species as *E. arborea* and *E. lusitanica* become too large and lanky they may be hard pruned into the old wood during April.

With few exceptions ericas are lime-hating and thrive best in acid soils, particularly those of a sandy nature. They are generally tolerant of semi-shade but flower best in full sun, combining most effectively with callunas (heathers), daboecias, dwarf rhododendrons and dwarf conifers.

For soils containing lime, a number of mainly winter flowering species and their cultivars are available, viz. *Erica carnea, E. mediterranea, E. terminalis* and also the several cultivars of *E.* × *darleyensis*.

‡ **arborea** L. "Tree Heath". A medium to large shrub which occasionally grows to 5m. high and through. Fragrant white, globular flowers are produced profusely in early spring. S. Europe, Caucasus, N. and E. Africa. I. 1658.

'Alpina'. A more hardy form, less tall, but more erect. Foliage brighter green. A.G.M. 1933. A.M. 1962.

‡**australis** L. "Spanish Heath". Medium sized shrub with rose-purple flowers during April and May. One of the showiest of "Tree Heaths". Not recommended for the coldest areas. Spain, Portugal. I. 1769. A.M. 1935. F.C.C. 1962. A.G.M. 1969.

'Mr. Robert'. A beautiful white form. A.M. 1929. A.G.M. 1941.

'Riverslea'. A lovely cultivar with flowers of fuchsia-purple. A.M. 1946.

‡†**canaliculata** ANDR. This beautiful "Tree Heath" has reached a height of 5·5m. in Cornwall. Flowers white or pink tinged, with protruding brown anthers. January and March. Needs a warm sheltered position. S. Africa. C. about 1802.

carnea L. (*herbacea*). One of the most widely planted dwarf shrubs in cultivation, orming dense hummocks and mats covered with rosy-red flowers throughout winter. Alps of Central Europe. A.G.M. 1924.

There are today innumerable cultivars available in a wide range ot shades through the white-pink-purple spectrum. The early cultivars begin flowering in November and the latest in April, but the majority are mid-season January to March. All are lime tolerant but not recommended for shallow chalk soils. Heights may be taken as 15 to 23cm. unless otherwise stated. This species has had a confused nomenclatural history and in accordance with the rules of Botanical Nomenclature the correct name should now be *E. herbacea* L.

'Alan Coates'. Low, spreading habit. Leaves dark. Flowers pale pink. Mid. A.M.T. 1965.

'Atrorubra'. Dark rose-pink. Late.

'Aurea'. Foliage bright gold during spring and early summer. Flowers deep pink paling to almost white. Mid to Late. A.M.T. 1971.

'Cecilia M. Beale'. A free-flowering, white form with erect shoots holding the flowers well above the ground. Mid.

'C. J. Backhouse'. Pale pink, deepening with age. Late.

'Eileen Porter'. Low growing, with rich carmine-red flowers from October to April. The dark corollas and the pale calyces produce a delightful bicoloured effect. A.M. 1956.

'Gracilis'. Bright rose-pink; compact. Early to Mid.

'James Backhouse'. Large flowers of soft pink. Late.

'King George'. See *'Winter Beauty'*.

'Loughrigg'. Rose-purple; dark green foliage. Mid. A.M.T. 1966.

'Mrs. Samuel Doncaster'. Rose-carmine; somewhat glaucous foliage. Mid to Late.

'Praecox Rubra'. Deep rose-red. Early to Mid. A.M.T. 1966. F.C.C.T. 1968.

'Prince of Wales'. Bright rose-pink. Late.

'Queen Mary'. Deepest rose-red. Early to Mid.

'Queen of Spain'. Pale madder pink. Late.

'Rosy Gem'. Bright pink flowers, neat bushy habit. Late.

'Rubra'. Flowers rose-red. Mid.

ERICA—*continued*

carnea 'Ruby Glow'. Large flowers, rich dark red; foliage bronzed. Late. A.M.T. 1967. A.G.M. 1969.

'Snow Queen'. Large pure white flowers held well above the foliage. Mid.

'Springwood Pink'. Clear rose-pink flowers. Good habit and foliage. Mid. A.M.T. 1964. A.G.M. 1969.

'Springwood White'. Still the finest white cultivar, its strong trailing growths packed with long, urn-shaped flowers. Mid. A.M. 1930. A.G.M. 1940. F.C.C.T. 1964.

'Startler'. Flowers soft coral-pink. Mid.

'Thomas Kingscote'. Pale pink. Late.

'Urville'. See *'Vivelii'*.

'Vivellii' (*'Urville'*). Deep, vivid carmine; bronzy red foliage in winter; a superb cultivar. Mid. A.M.T. 1964. F.C.C.T. 1965. A.G.M. 1969.

'Winter Beauty' (*'King George'*). Bright rose-pink, commencing to flower in December. A.M. 1922. A.G.M. 1927.

‡ciliaris L. "Dorset Heath". A low-spreading species up to ·3m. high. Flowers comparatively large, rosy-red, in short terminal racemes, from July to October. S.W. Europe (incl. British Isles).

'Maweana'. Similarly to the type but with larger, long lasting flowers borne on stiff erect stems.

'Mrs. C. H. Gill'. Dark green foliage and freely-produced clear red flowers.

'Stoborough'. Long racemes of white flowers. ·5 to ·6m.

'Wych'. Flesh-pink flowers in long racemes. ·5m.

‡cinerea L. The common native purple "Bell Heather", forming mats of wiry stems, and flowering from June to September. Height 23 to 30cm. unless otherwise stated. W. Europe (incl. British Isles).

'Alba Major'. White flowers in short racemes.

'Alba Minor'. Small and compact, 15cm. White. A.M.T. 1967. F.C.C.T. 1968.

'Atropurpurea'. Bright purple.

'Atrorubens'. Quite distinct, brilliant red flowers in long sprays. A.M. 1915.

'Atrosanguinea Smith's Variety'. Flowers of an intense scarlet; dark foliage. 15cm.

'C. D. Eason'. Glowing deep pink. F.C.C.T. 1966. A.G.M. 1969.

'Cevennes'. Lavender-rose, over a long period. A.M.T. 1968.

'C. G. Best'. Soft salmon-pink.

'Coccinea' (*'Fulgida'*). Of dwarf habit. 10cm. Dark scarlet.

'Colligan Bridge'. Long, erect racemes of vivid purple.

'Domino'. White flowers and ebony coloured calyces, a charming combination. A.M.T. 1970.

'Eden Valley'. Soft lilac-pink, paler at base. 15cm. A.M. 1933. A.G.M. 1969.

'Fulgida'. See *'Coccinea'*.

'Golden Drop'. Summer foliage golden-copper coloured turning to rusty-red in winter. Flowers pink, rarely produced. 15cm.

'Golden Hue'. Golden foliage turning red in winter. A most effective plant. ·5m.

'G. Osmond'. Pale mauve, dark calyces.

'Lilacina'. Pale lilac.

'Mrs. Dill'. Very neat, compact and low-growing; bright pink. 10cm.

'P. S. Patrick'. Long sprays of bright purple flowers. A.M.T. 1967. A.G.M. 1969.

'Romiley'. A smaller version of *'Atrorubens'*, flowers vivid rose-red. 15 to 20cm.

'Rosea'. Bright pink. A.G.M. 1928. A.M.T. 1966. A.G.M. 1969.

'Ruby'. Rose-purple.

'Sea Foam'. Pale mauve.

'Startler'. Bright gleaming pink.

'Velvet Night'. Blackish-purple, a most unusual colour.

'W. G. Notley' (× *Ericalluna 'W. G. Notley'*). Purple flowers, the corolla deeply divided.

corsica. See *E. terminalis*.

ERICA—*continued*

×**darleyensis** BEAN (*carnea*×*mediterranea*). A most useful hybrid in its several forms, and a natural companion to *E. carnea.* All the following clones average ·5 to ·6m. in height and flower throughout the winter. Lime tolerant, but not recommended for shallow chalk soils. See '*Darley Dale*'.

'Alba'. See under '*Silberschmelze*'.

'Archie Graham'. Compact growth, dark foliage and racemes of deep rose flowers.

'Arthur Johnson'. Long dense sprays of magenta flowers, useful for cutting. A.M. 1952. A.G.M. 1969.

'Darley Dale'. Pale pink flowers over a long period. One of the most popular of all ericas. This, the original plant, appeared in the Darley Dale Nurseries, Derbyshire, about 1890. Previously catalogued as *E.* ×*darleyensis.* A.M. 1905. A.G.M. 1924.

'George Rendall'. A superb form with rich pink flowers over a long period. A.G.M. 1969.

'Silberschmelze' ('*Molten Silver*'). Perhaps the best winter white, certainly the most rewarding. Sweetly scented flowers over a long period. Sometimes referred to as *E.* ×*darleyensis* '*Alba*'. A.M.T. 1968. A.G.M. 1969.

erigena. See under *E. mediterranea.*

herbacea. See under *E. carnea.*

hibernica. See *E. mediterranea.*

hybrida. This name refers correctly to various hybrids of South African species, but has erroneously been used for several European hybrids, including *E.* ×*darleyensis, E.* ×*praegeri, E.* '*Stuartii*', *E.* ×*watsonii* and *E.* ×*williamsii*'.

‡**lusitanica** RUDOLF (*codonodes*) "Portugal Heath". A fine "Tree Heath", resembling *E. arborea,* but earlier flowering. Large pale green plumose stems crowded with white tubular, fragrant flowers, pink in bud, from December onwards. Portugal. A.M. 1972.

‡**mackaiana** BAB. (*mackaii*). A rare, dwarf species with dark green foliage, and rose-crimson flowers in umbels from July to September. 15cm. W. Ireland, Spain.

'Lawsoniana'. Dwarf form with small pink flowers.

'Plena' ('*Crawfordii*'). Double, rosy-crimson.

mediterranea HORT. (*carnea occidentalis*) (*hibernica* SYME). A dense shrub of small to medium size, covered from March to May with fragrant rose-red flowers. Lime tolerant but not recommended for shallow chalk soils. The wild Irish form often referred to as *E. hibernica* differs in no way from the continental form. This species has an extremely confused nomenclatural history and in accordance with the rules of Botanical Nomenclature the correct name should be *E. erigena* R. ROSS. S. France; Spain; N. Ireland.

'Alba'. White, free-flowering, up to 1·2m.

'Brightness'. A low growing form; buds bronze-red, opening to rose-pink. ·6 to 1m. A.M. 1972.

'Coccinea'. Similar to '*Brightness*' but buds and flowers richer coloured. ·6 to 1m.

'Glauca'. An erect growing form of dense compact growth, foliage slightly glaucous. Flowers a pale flesh colour. 1 to 1·2m.

'Nana' ('*Compacta*'). A compact form only ·5m., with silvery-pink flowers.

'Rubra'. Compact habit, dark foliage and ruby-red flowers.

'Superba'. A fine pink-flowered form, up to 2m. or over. A.M. 1972. A.G.M. 1973.

'W. T. Rackliff'. A charming cultivar of dense, compact habit, with dark green foliage and pure white flowers with brown anthers. 1 to 1·2m. A.M. 1972.

‡†**pageana** BOLUS. A remarkable, small South African species. Erect growth and cylindrical clusters of bell-shaped, rich yellow flowers of a waxy texture in spring. In our arboretum it survives only the mildest winters. A.M. 1937.

‡×**praegeri** OSTENF. (*mackaiana*×*tetralix*). Hybrids between "Mackay's Heath" and the "Cross-leaved Heath". The following clone is the only one at present in general cultivation:—

'Connemara'. A dwarf shrub with terminal clusters of pale pink flowers during late summer. 6ins. This is the original plant collected in the wild in Connemara Previously catalogued as *E.* ×*praegeri.*

‡**scoparia** L. "Besom Heath". A medium sized shrub of loose habit. Flowers greenish, appearing in May and June. W. Mediterranean Region. I. 1770.

azorica D. WEBB. Similar to the type in habit, but smaller flowers. Azores.

'Pumila' ('*Nana*') ('*Minima*'). A dwarf form not above ·6m.

ERICA—*continued*

stricta. See *E. terminalis.*

‡**'Stuartii'.** A plant of uncertain origin found only once in Co. Galway, Ireland, in 1890. Some authorities believe it to be an abnormal form of *E.* ×*praegeri.* Flowers pinched and narrow, deep rose; June-September. ·3m.

terminalis SALISB. (*stricta*) (*corsica*). "Corsican Heath". Bushy, medium sized shrub with erect branches. The rose-coloured flowers, borne in late summer in terminal heads, fade to warm brown and remain throughout winter. Excellent on chalk soils. W. Mediterranean Region, naturalised in N. Ireland. I. 1765.

‡**tetralix** L. "Cross-leaved Heath". A native species growing ·2 to ·5m. high. Dense heads of rose-coloured flowers are produced from June to October. N. and W. Europe (incl. British Isles).

'Alba Mollis' (*'Mollis'*). Pretty grey foliage and white flowers. A.M. 1927. A.G.M. 1973.

'Alba Praecox'. Grey foliage and white flowers; earlier than *'Alba Mollis'*.

'Con Underwood'. Grey-green hummocks studded with crimson flower clusters. A.G.M. 1973.

'Lawsoniana'. See *E. mackaiana 'Lawsoniana'*.

'L. E. Underwood'. Silver-grey mounds; flowers pale pink, a striking terracotta in bud.

'Mary Grace'. Bright pink flowers set amid silvery foliage.

'Mollis'. See *'Alba Mollis'*.

'Pink Glow'. Grey foliage and bright pink flowers.

'Rosea'. Flowers rose-coloured.

†**umbellata** L. An attractive species of dwarf habit, proving fairly hardy. Flowers throughout summer, cerise-pink, with chocolate anthers. Lime tolerant. Spain, Portugal and Morocco. A.M. 1926.

‡**vagans** L. "Cornish Heath". A dwarf, spreading shrub, producing its flowers in long sprays from July to October. S.W. Europe (incl. British Isles).

'Alba'. A compact form, flowers white. ·6m.

'Cream'. White flowers in long racemes, an improvement on *'Alba'*. ·6m. A.M.T. 1968.

'Fiddlestone'. A superb form, throwing up long racemes of rose-cerise flowers over a long period. ·5 to ·6m.

'Grandiflora'. Very long sprays of rose-coloured flowers. 1m.

'Kevernensis'. See *'St. Keverne'*.

'Kevernensis Alba'. A compact form with small racemes of white flowers. ·3m. A.M.T. 1971.

'Lilacina'. Short racemes of lilac-pink flowers over a long period. ·5m.

'Lyonesse'. Pure white, with protruding brown anthers. ·5 to 1m. A.M. 1928. A.G.M. 1969.

'Mrs. D. F. Maxwell'. Deep cerise; a superb cultivar. ·5m. A.M. 1925. A.G.M. 1969. F.C.C.T. 1970.

'Pyrenees Pink'. Long racemes of pink flowers. ·5m.

'Rubra'. Rosy red. ·5m.

'St. Keverne' (*'Kevernensis'*). Flowers clear rose-pink. ·5m. A.M. 1914. A.G.M. 1927. F.C.C.T. 1971.

‡×**veitchii** BEAN (*arborea*×*lusitanica*). A hybrid "Tree Heath" of which the following is the only clone at present in general cultivation:—

'Exeter'. A beautiful shrub of medium size, with attractive bright green foliage, and great plumes of fragrant white flowers in spring. Not recommended for the coldest areas. A.M. 1905. This is the original clone raised by Messrs. Veitch at Exeter, before 1900. Previously catalogued as *E.* ×*veitchii.*

vulgaris. See *CALLUNA vulgaris.*

‡×**watsonii** BEAN (*ciliaris*×*tetralix*). Hybrids between two native species. We offer the following clones:—

'Dawn'. A spreading form with young foliage yellow in spring, and terminal clusters of large, rose-pink flowers; July to October, often continuing until November. 23cm.

'F. White'. Flowers white suffused pink. July to October. 20cm.

'H. Maxwell'. An attractive clone similar to 'Dawn' but taller and more upright in habit, and flowers slightly paler in colour; July to October. ·3m.

'Truro'. Rose-coloured flowers in short racemes; July to October. 23cm. The original clone, found wild in Cornwall. Previously catalogued as *E.* ×*watsonii*

ERICA—*continued*

‡ × **williamsii** DRUCE (*tetralix* × *vagans*). A variable hybrid of which the following are the only clones at present in general cultivation:—

'Gwavas'. A dwarf shrub of compact habit with yellowish-green foliage in spring. Flowers pink; July to October. ·5 to ·6m.

'P. D. Williams'. A pretty, late flowering heath. Young growths tipped yellow in spring, becoming bronze in winter. Flowers rose-pink in umbels; July to September. ·3 to ·6m. This is the original clone found in the wild in Cornwall. Formerly catalogued as *E.* × *williamsii*.

× **ERICALLUNA 'W. G. Notley'.** See *E. cinerea 'W. G. Notley'*.

ERINACEA—Leguminosae—A monotypic genus.

anthyllis LINK. (*pungens*). "Hedgehog Broom", "Blue Broom". A dwarf, slow growing spiny shrub requiring a well drained position in full sun. Flowers slate-blue, in April and May. Spain. I. 1759. A.M. 1922. F.C.C. 1976.

***ERIOBOTRYA—Rosaceae**—A small genus of evergreen trees native of eastern Asia.

japonica LINDL. "Loquat". An architectural plant normally seen as a large shrub in the British Isles, and best grown against a wall. One of the most striking evergreens on account of its firm, leathery, corrugated leaves often ·3m. long. The clusters of strongly fragrant, hawthorn-like flowers, produced only after a hot summer, open intermittently from November to April, and are sometimes followed by globular or pear-shaped, yellow fruits 4 to 5cm. across. China, Japan. Commonly cultivated in warmer countries for its edible fruits. I. 1787.

prinoides. See *PHOTINIA prionophylla*.

†**ERYTHRINA—Leguminosae**—A large genus of mainly tropical trees and shrubs with trifoliolate leaves, and often prickly stems.

crista-galli L. "Coral Tree". A very beautiful semi-woody plant from Brazil, with trifoliolate leaves. Flowers like waxen "Sweet-peas", deep scarlet, in large terminal racemes during summer. Needs a warm, sunny wall, and protection for the crown in winter. I. 1771. A.M. 1954.

***ESCALLONIA—Escalloniaceae**—This genus ranks high among flowering evergreens, and is all the more valuable for giving its display during summer and early autumn. Though not all are hardy inland, most can be grown successfully near the sea, and there make perfect hedges and wind-breaks. Unless otherwise stated they average 1·5 to 2·5m. in height. The species are native of South America. With rare exceptions they are lime-tolerant and drought resistant, thriving in all types of well-drained soil. No species have large leaves or large flowers, reference to size being only comparative within the group.

Pruning consisting of cutting back the old flowering growths may be carried out immediately after flowering and large unwieldy plants may be hard pruned at the same time.

'Alice'. A first-class hybrid with large leaves and large, rose-red flowers.

'Apple Blossom'. A very attractive, slow growing hybrid with pink and white flowers. A.M. 1946. A.G.M. 1951.

bellidifolia. See under *E.* × *stricta 'Harold Comber'*.

†**bifida** LINK & OTTO (*montevidensis*). Handsome large shrub from S. Brazil, requiring wall protection. Leaves large, flowers white, carried in large panicles, in late summer and autumn. A.M. 1915.

'C. F. Ball'. A seedling of *E. macrantha*. Large leaves, aromatic when bruised. Crimson flowers; vigorous growing up to 3m. Excellent for maritime exposure. A.M. 1926.

'C. H. Beale'. A strong-growing medium-sized shrub with crimson-red flowers borne in profusion.

'Crimson Spire'. A strong-growing shrub of erect growth up to 2m. Leaves comparatively large, dark glistening green. Flowers bright crimson. An excellent hedging shrub.

'Donard Beauty'. Rich rose-red, exceedingly free flowering shrub with large leaves, aromatic when bruised. A.M. 1930.

'Donard Brilliance'. Flowers rich rose-red, large. A shrub of graceful habit with arching branches and large leaves. A.M. 1928.

'Donard Gem'. Large pink, sweetly-scented flowers; growth compact, leaves small. A.M. 1927.

'Donard Radiance'. A magnificent strong growing shrub of compact habit and medium size. Large, brilliant, soft rose-red, chalice-shaped flowers. Leaves large, shining deep green. A.M. 1954.

ESCALLONIA—*continued*

'Donard Seedling'. A vigorous hybrid up to 3m.; flowers flesh-pink in bud, opening white, leaves large. A.M. 1916. A.G.M. 1969.

'Donard Star'. Medium sized shrub of compact upright habit. Large leaves and large flowers of a lovely rose-pink. A.M. 1967.

'Donard White'. Medium sized shrub of compact, rounded habit with small leaves. Flowers white, pink in bud, produced over a long period.

'Edinensis' (*rubra* × *virgata*). Of neat, bushy habit, 2 to 2·5m. high, leaves small. Flowers carmine in bud opening to clear shell pink. A.M. 1918. A.G.M. 1969.

'E. G. Cheeseman'. A vigorous hybrid of which *E. revoluta* is probably one parent. Flowers deep, bright cherry-red, bell-shaped, 12mm. long, nodding, carried in terminal leafy panicles. Leaves large, ovate to rotund obovate, coarsely serrated sage or grey-green. Downy in all its parts.

× **exoniensis** VEITCH (*rosea* × *rubra*). A vigorous shrub to 4m. high with downy, glandular shoots and large leaves; flowers white or blush. A.M. 1891.

'Gwendolyn Anley'. A small, very hardy shrub of bushy habit, leaves small, flowers flesh-pink. A.G.M. 1969.

illinita PRESL. Tall, strong smelling shrub up to 3m. with glandular shoots, large leaves and cylindrical panicles of white flowers. Chile. I. 1830.

'Ingramii' (*macrantha* × *punctata*). Flowers deep rose-pink; grows 4m. high and makes a good hedge; leaves large, aromatic when bruised. An excellent maritime shrub.

†**'Iveyi'** (*bifida* × *exoniensis*). A large, vigorous hybrid with large, handsome, glossy foliage and large panicles of white flowers in autumn. A.M. 1926.

†**laevis** SLEUM. (*organensis*). A small Brazilian shrub with large lustrous leaves, aromatic when bruised and large clear pink flowers. I. 1844.

'Langleyensis' (*punctata* × *virgata*). A hardy, graceful shrub up to 2·5m. in height with small leaves, the rose-pink flowers wreathing the arching branches. Garden origin 1893. A.M. 1897. A.G.M. 1926.

leucantha REMY. A tall graceful shrub recalling *Leptospermum stellatum*, with angular stems and large crowded panicles of white flowers in July. Chile. I. 1927.

macrantha HOOK. & ARN. Flowers rose-crimson, set amidst large, fine, glossy, aromatic leaves. Strong-growing up to 4m., and one of the best hedge plants to withstand sea gales. Parent of many hybrids. Chiloe. I. 1848.

montana. See under *E. rubra uniflora*.

montevidensis. See *E. bifida*.

'Newryensis' (*'Langleyensis'* × *rosea*). Vigorous, upright growth. Flowers white tinged pink. Leaves large, aromatic when bruised. Makes a good wind break.

organensis. See *E. laevis*.

'Peach Blossom'. Medium sized shrub, similar in habit to *'Apple Blossom'* but with flowers of a clear peach-pink. A.G.M. 1969.

'Pink Pearl'. Flowers soft pink stained bright rose-pink about 20mm. across, when wide open, carried in short dense racemes on arching branches. Rather small obovate leaves.

'Pride of Donard'. Flowers large, brilliant rose, somewhat bell-shaped, carried in terminal racemes from June onwards. Leaves large, dark polished green above.

pterocladon. See *E. rosea*.

punctata DC. (*sanguinea*). A tall, glandular shrub of robust habit. Leaves large, aromatic when bruised. Flowers deep crimson. An excellent sea wind-break. Chile.

†**revoluta** PERS. A large shrub with grey-felted shoots and foliage; soft pink to white flowers in terminal racemes from August to September. Chile. I. 1887.

rosea GRISEB. (*pterocladon*). Medium sized shrub with downy angled branches and small leaves. Flowers white, fragrant, in slender racemes. Parent of many hybrids. Patagonia. I. 1847.

rubra PERS. (*microphylla*). A medium sized shrub with loose panicles of red flowers in July. Leaves aromatic when bruised. Chile. I. 1827.

'Pygmaea'. See *'Woodside'*.

uniflora POEPP. & ENDL. A low, compact, dense growing shrub with long leaves. Flowers deep-red. Previously grown and catalogued as *E. montana*.

ESCALLONIA—*continued*

rubra 'Woodside' (*'Pygmaea'*). A small shrub of neat habit, the product of a witches broom, suitable for the large rock garden, its branches spreading over a considerable area. Flowers small, crimson.

'St. Keverne' (*kevernensis*). Medium sized shrub of arching habit, with small leaves and large, rich, pink flowers; free-flowering.

'Slieve Donard'. A medium sized, compact shrub. Leaves small and large panicles of apple-blossom pink flowers. Very hardy.

×**stricta** REMY. (*leucantha* × *virgata*). A variable, natural hybrid of which we offer the following clone:—

'Harold Comber'. One of the hardiest of the family. A dense shrub up to 1·5m., the slender stems crowded with small leaves and small white flowers. Introduced by Harold Comber from Chile as *E. bellidifolia* (Comber 988).

‡**virgata** PERS. (*philippiana*). A graceful, small-leaved deciduous shrub with arching branches and white flowers. Not suitable for chalky soils. A hardy species and parent of many hybrids. Chile. I. 1866. F.C.C. 1888.

viscosa FORBES. A tall, strong smelling shrub up to 3m., with sticky resinous shoots and large, glossy green leaves; flowers white in pendulous clusters. Chile.

'William Watson'. A medium-sized, small-leaved shrub of compact growth. Flowers bright red over a long period.

***EUCALYPTUS—Myrtaceae**—"Gum Tree". A large genus of fast-growing, evergreen trees, mainly native of Australia. In common with many other plants of wide distribution selections from high altitudes usually prove hardier than the same species from lower levels. Several species are hardy or nearly hardy in the British Isles, their lush foliage, unusual multi-stamened flowers (which are white unless otherwise stated) and attractive stems providing an impressive subtropical effect. The leaves of adult trees are often very different from those of young specimens, many providing excellent foliage for floral decoration. The common name refers to the quantity of gum that exudes from their trunks.

Eucalyptus will grow in a great variety of soils and many are tolerant of wet sites but some species tend to become chlorotic in very shallow chalk soils. As yet *E. parvifolia* is the only species which we have proved will grow indefinitely on a chalk soil.

They are best planted as small, pot-grown plants, preferably in the spring. If, due to over-rapid growth, there is a likelihood that a tall, young tree will blow over, we recommend cutting back to about 23 to 45cm. from the ground in the spring and selecting the strongest new growth, removing all other subsidiary shoots, unless a bushy plant with several stems is preferred. Strong cold winds are a greater danger to many eucalypts than hard frosts.

camphora R. T. BAKER (*ovata aquatica*). One of the hardiest species. A small to medium sized tree with rough bark, forming clumps. Leaves ovate to lanceolate. In its native habitat this species usually grows in wet areas, even in standing water. A.M. 1977.

†**cinerea** F. MUELL. A medium-sized tree with silver-grey leaves. Only hardy in the mildest localities.

†**citriodora** HOOK. "Lemon-scented Gum". Foliage sweetly scented. Only suitable for the mildest areas but worth a place in the conservatory.

coccifera HOOK. f. A large Tasmanian tree with striking glaucous leaves and stems, which quality is not apparent in young plants. Passes without injury all but the very severest winters in the home counties. A.M. 1953.

†**cordata** LABILL. A dense growing species making a small tree with grey-silver sessile leaves. The attractive white bark is marked with green or purplish patches. Tasmania.

coriacea. See *E. pauciflora*.

dalrympleana MAIDEN. A most attractive, very fast growing species of medium size, proving one of the hardiest. Attractive patchwork bark becoming white and handsome grey-green leaves which are bronze coloured when young. A.M. 1953.

†**ficifolia** F. MUELL. A superb small tree of lax habit. Leaves broad lanceolate up to 15cm. long. Flowers scarlet or flame coloured in large corymbs towards the ends of the branches, very effective against the glossy, green foliage. Very tender, best under glass. Both flowers and foliage are cut and sold in florists' shops. F.C.C. 1907.

EUCALYPTUS—*continued*

†**globulus** LABILL. "Tasmanian Blue Gum". In mild districts this species will make a large noble tree but is more usually seen as a sparsely branched shrub in sub-tropical bedding schemes. The large leaves are blue-green in colour, almost silvery on young specimens. Tasmania. C. 1829.

gunnii HOOK. f. This fine species is one of the hardiest. Leaves of adult tree sickle-shaped, sage-green, of young trees rounded and of a startling silver-blue. It will attain large tree size or will make an excellent bush if regularly pruned. Tasmania. A.M. 1950.

johnstonii MAIDEN. (*subcrenulata*). One of the hardier species. A large tree with reddish bark and bright, glossy, apple-green leaves. Closely related to *E. urnigera*. Tasmania.

mitchelliana CAMBAGE. A medium-sized tree known as "Weeping Sally" in Australia. Bark smooth and white with age. Leaves narrowly lanceolate, green.

niphophila MAIDEN & BLAKELY. "Snow Gum". A beautiful small tree of comparatively slow growth with large leathery, grey-green leaves. The trunk is a lovely green, grey and cream patchwork and has been likened to a python's skin. A tree planted in our arboretum has sustained no frost damage since it was planted in 1960. A.M. 1977.

nitens MAIDEN. "Silver Top". A large tree with long, ribbon-like glaucous leaves. Appears to be one of the more hardy species but not yet fully tested. A.M. 1975.

ovata aquatica. See *E. camphora*.

parvifolia CAMBAGE. An exceptionally hardy species, here making a handsome medium sized tree and surviving the severest winters. Will even tolerate chalk soils. Mature leaves narrow, blue-green.

pauciflora SIEB. (*coriacea*). "Cabbage Gum". A small high-mountain tree, and one of the hardiest species. When growing conditions are favourable will withstand up to 15°C of frost. The sickle-shaped leaves are up to 20cm. long; the trunk white.

pauciflora × salicifolia. A medium-sized tree with attractive bark and long, narrow, sickle-shaped, sage-green leaves. Hardier than *E. pauciflora*.

†**perriniana** RODWAY. A small silver-leaved tree. Stems white, with dark blotches. Juvenile leaves rounded; mature leaves oblanceolate, glaucous.

†**pulverulenta** SIMS. A handsome small tree resembling *E. cordata*, with attractive bluish, rounded leaves. Hardy in the south west and similar areas.

†**salicifolia** CAV. (*amygdalina*). A large shrub or medium sized tree with fibrous bark and long, narrow, aromatic, green leaves.

subcrenulata. See *E. johnstonii*.

urnigera HOOK. f. Small to medium sized, hardy, Tasmanian species with greyish, peeling bark and dark green leaves.

vernicosa HOOK. f. "Varnish-leaved Gum". A Tasmanian shrub or occasionally a small tree producing dense masses of thick, elliptic-lanceolate, shining green leaves.

EUCOMMIA—**Eucommiaceae**—A hardy monotypic genus thriving in all types of fertile soil.

ulmoides OLIV. The only hardy tree known to produce rubber. A vigorous and ornamental Chinese tree up to 9m. or more, with rather large, leathery, glossy elm-like leaves. If a leaf is torn gently in half, and the two halves are eased apart, then by holding the stalk the detached lower half will hang seemingly unconnected, but it is in fact attached by fine strands of latex almost invisible to the naked eye. I. about 1896.

‡**EUCRYPHIA**—**Eucryphiaceae**—A small genus of highly ornamental shrubs or trees flowering when sufficiently mature from July to September. All have white flowers with conspicuous stamens. They thrive best in sheltered positions and in moist loam, preferably non-calcareous. The roots should be shaded from hot sun.

billardieri. See *E. lucida*.

†***cordifolia** CAV. A very beautiful large evergreen shrub or, in favoured areas, a broad columnar tree of 9 to 12m. Leaves heart-shaped; flowers like a white "Rose of Sharon". Somewhat lime tolerant. Valdivia, Chiloe. I. 1851. A.M. 1936.

†***cordifolia × lucida.** A large, tall growing evergreen of vigorous growth. Leaves oblong-lanceolate, leathery, dark shining green above, glaucous beneath. Flowers white. Resembles *E. lucida* in general appearance but differs in its larger flowers and leaves which are wavy-edged, pointed and occasionally toothed.

EUCRYPHIA—*continued*

glutinosa BAILL. (*pinnatifolia*). One of the most glorious of woody plants. A large erect-branched deciduous shrub or small tree, with pinnate leaves; flowers 6cm. across, are borne profusely in July and August. Beautiful autumn tints. Chile. I. 1859. F.C.C. 1880. A.G.M. 1935. F.C.C. 1977.

†*× **hillieri** IVENS (*lucida*×*moorei*). An interesting chance hybrid between an Australian and a Tasmanian species. The following clone is the only one in general cultivation:—

'Winton'. This interesting hybrid originated as a self-sown seedling. Its pinnate leaves have fewer leaflets than those of *E. moorei* and it is also considerably hardier. Its beautifully formed, cup-shaped flowers resemble those of *E. lucida*.

*× **intermedia** BAUSCH (*glutinosa*×*lucida*). A lovely, fast growing hybrid. Leaves variable both simple and trifoliolate occuring on the same plant, glaucous beneath. Flowers smaller than those of *E. glutinosa*, crowding the branches. This hybrid first occured at Rostrevor, N. Ireland, the garden of the late Sir John Ross of Blandenburg.

'Rostrevor'. The form in general cultivation. An extremely floriferous, free-growing, small tree of compact, broadly columnar habit. The fragrant, white, yellow-centred flowers each 2·5 to 5cm. across smother the slender branches in August and September. Raised at Rostrevor, Co. Down. A.M. 1936. F.C.C. 1973.

***lucida** BAILL. (*billardieri*). A delightful species, a large, densely leafy shrub or small tree, with simple, oblong leaves, glaucous beneath. The charming, fragrant, pendulous flowers, up to 5cm. across, appear in June and July. Tasmania. I. 1820. A.M. 1936.

milliganii. See *E. milliganii*.

†***milliganii** HOOK. f. (*lucida milliganii*). A delightful miniature species eventually a small shrubby tree. Leaves tiny, neat, shining dark green. Buds exceptionally sticky. Flowers cup-shaped, similar to those of *E. lucida* but smaller. Even as a small shrub it flowers freely. Tasmania. Introduced by H. Comber in 1929. A.M. 1978.

†***moorei** F. MUELL. A rare small tree, having pinnate leaves, elegantly poised. The white flowers are rather smaller than those of *E. glutinosa*. Suitable only for the mildest localities. Australia. I. 1915. A.M. 1933.

*× **nymansensis** BAUSCH (*cordifolia*×*glutinosa*). A variable hybrid between two superb South American species. The leaves are intermediate between those of the parents, both simple and compound leaves appearing on the same plant.

'Mount Usher'. Resembling more *E. cordifolia* in general appearance. The flowers are often double. Raised at Mount Usher in Ireland.

'Nymansay'. A magnificent small to medium sized tree of rapid growth. Flowers 6cm. across, wreathing the branches in August and September. First raised about 1915 at Nymans, Sussex, by Mr. James Comber, head gardener to the late Lt. Col. L. C. R. Messel. A.M. 1924. F.C.C. 1926. A.G.M. 1973.

†***EUGENIA**—**Myrtaceae**—Evergreen trees and shrubs widely distributed but most prevelant in the tropics. Only possible in the mildest gardens. They will succeed in all types of well drained soil.

guayarillo BENTH. (*guavayi* HORT.). A small shrub producing white flowers and dark-coloured fruits. Requires a warm sheltered position.

myrtifolia SIMS. "Australian Brush Cherry". A large, vigorous, evergreen shrub with glossy, myrtle-like leaves and beautiful white flowers in late summer followed by globular red fruits. Makes a handsome conservatory specimen. Australia.

pungens BERG. A medium sized shrub with slender brown stems and pale green, spine-tipped privet-like leaves. Flowers white, solitary in the leaf axils. Brazil.

ugni. See *MYRTUS ugni*.

EUODIA (*EVODIA*)—**Rutaceae**—Deciduous or evergreen trees and shrubs with simple or compound leaves. Related and similar in general appearance to *Phellodendron* but differing in the freely exposed winter buds and the fruits consisting of dehiscent pods. Flowers normally unisexual. The hardy species in cultivation are deciduous trees succeeding in all types of soil.

daniellii HEMSL. Fast growing small to medium sized tree with large, pinnate leaves and corymbs of small, white pungently scented flowers in late summer, succeeded by lustrous black fruits. China, Korea. I. 1905.

EUODIA—*continued*

hupehensis DODE. A wide-spreading tree of medium height. Large compound leaves, whitish flowers and paniculate clusters of bright red fruits on female trees. Thrives in poor and shallow chalky soils. China. I. 1908. A.M. 1949. F.C.C. 1976.

velutina REHD. & WILS. A small tree with downy pinnate leaves and branches. Flowers yellowish-white in dense heads in August. China. I. 1908.

EUONYMUS—Celastraceae—A family of widely different shrubs, both evergreen and deciduous, used for a variety of purposes in gardens. They thrive in almost any soil, and are particularly "at home" on chalk. The flowers, in early summer, are normally green or purplish and of little ornament. The chief attraction is the often very showy, lobed sometimes winged, fruits which persist into winter. It is desirable to plant several specimens in close proximity to obtain cross pollination, as single specimens sometimes never fruit due to imperfect flowers. Many deciduous species give attractive autumn tints.

alatus SIEB. A slow-growing, much-branched shrub of medium size, distinguished by the broad corky wings on the branchlets under favourable conditions. One of the finest of all deciduous shrubs for autumn colour. China, Japan. I. 1860. A.G.M. 1932.

apterus REG. An unusual form differing from the type in its more lax habit and its scarcely winged or wingless stems. Equally colourful in autumn.

'Compactus'. A dense compact form; ideal for a low hedge.

americanus L. A medium sized shrub with four-angled branches and narrowly oval, glossy green leaves. The tiny flowers are succeeded by three to five lobed, red, warty capsules. E. United States. C. 1683.

bungeanus MAXIM. A large shrub or small tree of slender habit, with elliptic, slender-pointed leaves. Flowers yellowish-white in June; fruits four-lobed, cream to flesh pink, only produced after a hot summer. Autumn colour pale straw-yellow. N. and N.E. China. I. 1883. A.M. 1941.

semi-persistens SCHNEID. A distinct semi-evergreen shrub often retaining its leaves until the new year. Fruits pink. China.

cornutus HEMSL. A rare small to medium sized shrub of loose habit. The remarkable pink tinged fruits bear four to six slender, horn-like extensions, giving them the appearance of jester's caps. China.

europaeus L. "Spindle". A familiar native hedgerow shrub, particularly on chalk soils. A vigorous green-stemmed shrub occasionally a small tree, producing an abundance of scarlet capsules. Europe. A.G.M. 1969.

'Albus' (*'Fructu-albo'*). A conspicuous white-fruited form, showy in winter. A.G.M. 1969.

'Atropurpureus'. Leaves dull purple throughout spring and summer, passing to vivid shades of red in the autumn. A.G.M. 1969.

'Aucubifolius'. Leaves mottled with yellow and white and attractively tinted with pink in autumn.

'Fructu-coccineo'. Capsules bright red.

'Red Cascade'. A selected form, the arching branches often pendulous under the weight of the rosy-red fruits. A.M. 1949. A.G.M. 1969.

***fortunei** HAND-MAZZ. An extremely hardy, trailing evergreen, suitable for ground cover in sun or shade, or as a self clinging climber, the long stems rooting at intervals. Leaves generally elliptic, up to 6cm. long, distinctly veined beneath. Like the English Ivy, the creeping and climbing stems are barren and only when adult growths appear are flowers and fruits produced. Flowers small, pale green, produced in loose cymes during summer, followed in autumn by pinkish capsules with orange seeds. China. I. 1907.

'Carrierei'. A small shrub with larger leaves, reaching 2 to 2·5m. against a wall. This is regarded as the adult form of var. *radicans* and produces both flowers and fruits. A.M. 1936.

'Coloratus'. A trailing or climbing form reaching 8m. with support, leaves beautifully coloured sanguineous purple throughout winter, especially when the roots are starved or controlled. An unusual character is that the leaves which are coloured in winter may resume their summer green in spring.

'Gracilis'. See *'Variegatus'*.

'Kewensis'. A dainty form with slender prostrate stems and minute leaves. Suitable for the rock garden where it will form small hummocks or cover rocks. Climbing if support is available. Possibly a sport of *radicans*. I. 1893.

EUONYMUS—*continued*

fortunei radicans REHD. A trailing or climbing shrub with ovate or elliptic, shallowly-toothed leaves up to 3·5cm. long, rather leathery in texture. This is the commonest form in cultivation with smaller leaves than the type. Propagation of the adult growth has resulted in various shrubby forms such as '*Carrierei*'. Japan; Korea; China. I. about 1865. A.G.M. 1969.

'Silver Pillar' ('*Versicolor Albus*'). Leaves narrow with a broad marginal white variegation. Habit erect.

'Silver Queen'. A small shrub of compact habit, attaining 2·5 to 3m. against a wall. The unfolding leaves in spring are a rich creamy-yellow later becoming green with a broad creamy white margin. One of the loveliest of variegated shrubs. A sport of '*Carrierei*', producing flowers and fruits. A.M. 1977.

'Variegatus' ('*Gracilis*'). A trailing or climbing form, the leaves greyish-green, margined white, often tinged pink. An excellent plant for a wall or as ground cover. A sport of *radicans.*

vegetus REHD. A small, bushy, creeping form with both prostrate and erect stems, climbing if support is available. The leaves are quite distinct being broad ovate to orbicular, thick in texture and dull green. Flowers and fruits are normally freely produced. Probably a distinct form of var. *radicans.* Introduced from Japan in 1876.

†***frigidus** WALL. A rare, tender species of medium size, with small, chocolate-coloured flowers hanging on slender stalks. Leaves oblanceolate. E. Himalaya.

grandiflorus WALL. An erect, semi-evergreen shrub to 4m. high with conspicuous, comparatively large, straw-yellow flowers and yellow capsules with scarlet seeds. Leaves often give rich wine-purple autumn colour. Himalaya, China. I. 1824. A.M. 1927.

salicifolius STAPF. The form most usually grown, with longer, narrower leaves. W. China. C. 1922. A.M. 1953.

hians KOEHNE. A large shrub with obovate-oblong leaves and cymes of small, cream-petalled, red-based flowers which are followed by pink capsules, splitting to reveal the red seeds. Japan. I. about 1865.

†***ilicifolius** FRANCH. A remarkable Chinese species with thick, spiny, holly-like leaves. Capsules rounded, whitish; seeds orange-coloured. W. China. I. 1930. Only suitable for the mildest localities.

***japonicus** THUNB. A large, densely branched shrub, one of the best evergreens for coastal or town planting, and succeeding in sun or shade.

'Albomarginatus'. Leaves with a narrow white margin.

'Aureopictus' ('*Aureus*'). Leaves with golden centre and a broad green margin. Liable to revert.

'Duc d'Anjou' ('*Viridivariegatus*'). Leaves pale or yellowish green with a central splash of dark green.

'Macrophyllus' ('*Latifolius*'). Leaves larger than those of the type, elliptic. F.C.C. 1866.

'Macrophyllus Albus' ('*Latifolius Variegatus*'). Leaves with a conspicuous broad white margin. The most conspicuous variegated form.

'Microphyllus' ('*Myrtifolius*'). A small, slow growing form of dense, compact habit with small, narrow leaves. Somewhat resembling "Box" in general appearance.

'Microphyllus Pulchellus' ('*Microphyllus Aureus*'). Small golden variegated leaves.

'Microphyllus Variegatus'. Small leaves with a white margin.

'Myrtifolius'. See '*Microphyllus*'.

'Ovatus Aureus' ('*Aureovariegatus*'). Leaves margined and suffused creamy-yellow, particularly apparent in the young leaves; growth rather slow and compact. Requires a sunny site to retain its colour. The most popular golden euonymus.

robustus. A very hardy geographical form with rather thick, round ovate leaves and stiff compact growth. Under favourable conditions the first fruiting form of the species.

***kiautschovicus** LOES. (*patens*). Hardy, spreading, evergreen shrub of medium size, producing green-yellow flowers in early autumn, followed by late pink fruits. Akin to *E. japonicus* from which it differs in its wider inflorescence, thinner more pointed leaves and laxer habit. This plant should replace *E. japonicus* in the coldest areas. E. and C. China. I. about 1860. A.M. 1961.

EUONYMUS—*continued*

lanceifolius LOES. A deciduous or semi-evergreen small tree or large shrub from China; leaves 7·5 to 12·5cm. long, usually lanceolate-oblong; the pink four-lobed fruits open to disclose the scarlet-coated seeds. Unfortunately this species fruits too infrequently. C. and W. China. I. 1908. A.M. 1929.

latifolius MILL. A European species growing 3 to 4·5m. high. Has larger, scarlet fruits, and more brilliant autumn foliage than the common "Spindle Tree". I. 1730. A.M. 1916.

†***lucidus** D. DON (*pendulus*). A large, evergreen shrub for the mildest localities. In spring the young growths are crimson, passing to coppery-salmon, finally deep green. Confused in gardens with *E. fimbriatus*, which however is a deciduous species. Himalaya. I. 1850.

maackii RUPR. Large shrub, related to *E. europaeus*, giving beautiful autumn colour. Fruits pink, with orange seeds. N. China, Manchuria, Korea. C. 1880.

macropterus RUPR. A medium sized to large shrub of spreading habit, with oval or obovate leaves and attractive pink, four-winged capsules. Manchuria. I. 1905.

***myrianthus** HEMSL. A large, slow-growing evergreen shrub with rather long, tough, leathery leaves. Flowers greenish-yellow, in dense rounded heads of up 7·5cm. across. Fruits orange-yellow, splitting to expose the attractive orange-scarlet seeds. W. China. I. 1908. A.M. 1976.

nanus BIEB. (*rosmarinifolius* HORT.). A useful, dwarf, semi-evergreen shrub with narrow leaves and tiny, brown-purple flowers. Ideal as a ground cover and for banks. Caucasus to China. I. 1830. A.M. 1920.

turkestanicus KRISHT. (*nanus koopmanii*). A semi-erect form up to 1m. with longer leaves. The commonest form in cultivation. C. 1883.

obovatus NUTT. A prostrate shrub with long trailing stems. Peculiar in its three-lobed crimson fruits which are covered with prickly warts. Eastern N. America. I. 1820.

oresbius W. W. SM. An uncommon shrub to about 2m., with very narrow, linear leaves. The pendulous, rosy-red, scarlet-seeded fruits are seldom seen in cultivation. W. China. C. 1934.

oxyphyllus MIQ. A slow-growing, medium sized to large shrub; leaves pass to rich shades of red and purple-red in the autumn when at the same time the branches are strung with rich carmine red capsules. Japan, Korea and China. I. 1892.

patens. See *E. kiautschovicus*.

pendulus. See *E. lucidus*.

phellomanus LOES. A Chinese shrub of medium size, with shoots conspicuously corky-winged. Leaves oval to obovate, 5 to 10cm. long; the conspicuous, four-lobed, pink fruits are freely carried. N. and W. China. C. 1924. F.C.C. 1924.

planipes. See *E. sachalinensis*.

sachalinensis MAXIM. (*planipes*). A large, handsome species similar to *E. latifolius* and equally colourful in autumn. Large scarlet fruits. N.E. Asia. I. 1892. A.M. 1954. A.G.M. 1969.

sanguineus LOES. A medium sized, occasionally large, Chinese shrub, rare in cultivation. The young shoots and leaves are often flushed purple beneath. The red fruits and tinted leaves are attractive in autumn. I. 1900.

sargentianus LOES. & REHD. Medium-sized shrub with usually obovate, abruptly pointed leaves, dull greyish-green above. The four-angled, yellowish fruit capsules contain bright orange seeds. W. China. I. 1908.

semiexsertus KOEHNE. Large shrub with attractive pinkish-white fruits and red seeds. Japan. C. 1895. A.M. 1947.

sieboldianus BL. Large shrub with oblong, serrulate leaves, pale green flowers and pinkish-white fruits, opening to reveal the red seeds. Japan, China, Korea.

verrucosus SCOP. Medium sized shrub with densely warty branches. Flowers purple-brown in three to seven flowered cymes, followed after a hot summer by yellowish-red capsules. Attractive autumn tints. E. Europe, W. Asia. I. 1763.

***wilsonii** SPRAGUE. A large and striking, Chinese evergreen of lax habit. The lanceolate leaves are 7 to 15cm. long and one-third as wide. The four-lobed fruits are set with awl-shaped spines giving a remarkable hedgehog-like appearance. I. 1904.

EUONYMUS—*continued*

yedoensis KOEHNE. A strong-growing, large shrub bearing conspicuous rose-pink fruits, and large leaves turning yellow and red in early autumn. Japan, Korea. I. 1865. A.M. 1924. A.G.M. 1969.

†EUPATORIUM—Compositae—A huge genus of trees, shrubs and herbs.

***ligustrinum** DC. (*micranthum*) (*weinmannianum*). An evergreen Mexican shrub producing large, flat heads of small white flowers in late summer and autumn. In favoured districts grows to 2·5m. I. 1867.

micranthum. See *E. ligustrinum.*

EUPTELEA—Eupteleaceae—A small genus of two species. Large shrubs or small trees. The flowers, of which there are no petals, appear in dense clusters all along the leafless branches in spring and consist of bunches of red anthered stamens. Succeeds in all types of fertile soil.

franchetii. See *E. pleiosperma.*

pleiosperma HOOK. f. & THOMS. (*franchetii*) (*davidiana*). A small, multi-stemmed tree or large shrub with stout erect stems, attracting attention in spring when crowded with clusters of red anthers. Young growths copper-tinted. Autumn leaf colour is sometimes conspicuous. E. Himalaya, W. China. I. 1896.

polyandra SIEB. & ZUCC. A large shrub or small tree, differing from *E. pleiosperma* in its coarsely and irregularly toothed leaves; also notable for its pretty red and yellow autumn colours. Japan. C. 1877.

***EURYA—Theaceae**—A small genus of evergreen shrubs related to and often confused with *Cleyera*, but differing in the dioecious flowers and usually toothed leaves.

†emarginata 'Microphylla'. A small, spreading, densely-branched shrub recalling *Cotoneaster horizontalis* when young. The slender branches are grey above, brown beneath. Leaves arranged in two ranks on the shoots, leathery, obovate or orbicular, 6 to 8mm. long, notched at the apex, glossy green above, the margins toothed and slightly recurved. Flowers small, pale yellow-green, borne in the axils of the leaves in spring. The type is a native of coastal areas in Japan.

fortunei. See *CLEYERA fortunei.*

japonica THUNB. A small evergreen shrub with bluntly serrate, leathery leaves, dark green and lustrous above, pale green beneath. The inconspicuous greenish-yellow flowers formed in late summer open in spring and possess on objectionable smell. They are followed by purplish-black berries. Japan; Formosa; Korea. F.C.C. 1861.

'Variegata'. A charming dwarf shrub, compact in habit. Leaves two ranked, oblanceolate, toothed, pale green with a dark green margin. F.C.C. 1894.

latifolia 'Variegata'. See *CLEYERA fortunei.*

ochnacea. See *CLEYERA japonica.*

EURYBIA. See *OLEARIA.*

***EURYOPS—Compositae**—Evergreen shrubs from Africa with conspicuous yellow daisy flowers. The following require a warm sunny position and a well-drained soil.

acraeus M. D. HENDERSON (*evansii* HORT.). A dwarf shrub of rather neat habit, forming a low compact mound of grey stems and small, narrow, silvery-grey leaves. The canary-yellow flower-heads, 2·5cm. across, smother the plant during late May and June. Introduced sometime about 1945 from the Drakensburg Mountains, Basutoland. At first confused with *E. evansii*, a related species. Ideal for the rock garden or scree. Generally hardy if soil and aspect are suitable. A.M. 1952.

hybridus. See under *E. pectinatus.*

†pectinatus CASS. A small shrub with erect greyish downy shoots up to 1m. Leaves 5 to 7.5cm. long, deeply lobed (pectinate), grey-downy. Flower-heads rich yellow, 4cm. across, borne on long, slender, erect peduncles in late May and June. Plants we have grown under the name *E. hybridus* have proved to be this species. S. Africa. I. 1731.

†virgineus LESS. A small shrub forming a dense clump of erect glabrous shoots .6 to 1m. in height. The neat, tiny, green, pectinate leaves densely crowd the stems. Flowers 1.25cm. across, produced on slender stalks in the axils of the upper leaves during spring. S. Africa. I. 1821.

EVODIA. See *EUODIA.*

EXOCHORDA—Rosaceae—Beautiful, May-blooming shrubs with long, arching branches festooned with conspicuous racemes of comparatively large paper-white flowers. Generally inclined to become chlorotic on very shallow chalk soils.

giraldii HESSE. An excellent large free-flowering shrub similar to *E. korolkowii*, but not so erect in habit. N.W. China. I. 1907.

wilsonii REHD. This variety has the largest flowers in the genus, being 5cm. across. C. China. I. 1907. A.M. 1931.

korolkowii LAV. (*albertii*). A vigorous species from Turkestan, attaining about 4·6m.; one of the best for chalky soils. I. 1881. A.M. 1894. A.G.M. 1933.

× **macrantha** SCHNEID. (*korolkowii* × *racemosa*). Large shrub similar in habit to *E. racemosa*. Abundant racemes of large white flowers in late spring. Garden origin about 1900. A.M. 1917.

‡**racemosa** REHD. (*grandiflora*). The best-known species, a large shrub rather spreading in habit. Not suitable for shallow chalk soil. China. I. 1849. A.M. 1978.

serratifolia MOORE. An extremely free-flowering species which thrives in chalky soils, forming an elegant medium sized bush.

pubescens REHD. Leaves pubescent beneath.

***FABIANA—Solanaceae**—A monotypic heath-like shrub, belonging to the potato family. Succeeds best in a sunny position in moist, well-drained neutral or acid soil, but is sufficiently lime-tolerant to be well worth growing in all but very shallow soils over chalk.

†**imbricata** RUIZ & PAV. A charming shrub of medium size. In June its branches are transformed into plumes of white tubular flowers. Chile. I. 1838. A.M. 1934.

'Prostrata'. A small shrub, hardier than the type, forming a dense rounded mound of feathery branchlets which are usually covered with small, pale mauve-tinted flowers in May and June. Ideal for the large rock garden or wall top.

† **violacea** HORT. Similar to the type but with lavender-mauve flowers. F.C.C. 1932.

FAGUS—Fagaceae—"Beech". A small genus containing some of the most noble of trees. The European species reach their maximum size in deep well drained soils in the British Isles. The Asiatic species are also giving a good account of themselves, but the American Beech is disappointing as seen in cultivation and is less lime tolerant.

americana. See *F. grandifolia*.

crenata BL. (*sieboldii*). A large tree closely allied to the "Common Beech" (*F. sylvatica*) from which it differs in its rather more obovate leaves. Japan. I. 1892.

englerana SEEMEN. A rare tree of medium size with foliage of a glaucous sea-green hue. C. China. I. 1907.

ferruginea. See *F. grandifolia*.

grandifolia EHRH. (*americana*) (*ferruginea*). The "American Beech" does not form a large tree in this country. Distinguished from the "Common Beech" by its suckering habit and its longer, narrower leaves, with nearly twice as many veins. Eastern N. America. I. 1766. F.C.C. 1894.

pubescens FERN & REHD. Leaves pubescent beneath.

japonica MAXIM. "Japanese Beech". A small, often shrubby tree in British gardens, with ovate to elliptic, bright green leaves. Japan. I. 1905.

lucida REHD. & WILS. A small tree with ovate leaves which are often shining green on both surfaces. W. China. I. 1905.

orientalis LIPSKY. "Oriental Beech". A large tree differing from the "Common Beech" in its rather larger, obovate leaves, which in autumn turn a rich yellow. E. Europe; Asia Minor. I. 1904.

sieboldii. See *F. crenata*.

sylvatica L. "Common Beech". Our native beech is undoubtedly the most noble large tree for calcareous soils and is excellent for hedgemaking. The rich golden-copper of its autumn foliage is not excelled by any other tree. Given a well drained soil and avoiding heavy clay there is perhaps no other tree which will thrive in such extremes of acidity and alkalinity. Europe. There are many named cultivars, of which we offer the following:—

'Albovariegata' ('*Argenteovariegata*'). Leaves margined and streaked white.

'Ansorgei'. A remarkable form with very narrow lanceolate to almost linear dark purple leaves.

FAGUS—*continued*

sylvatica 'Asplenifolia'. See under *heterophylla.*

'Atropunicea'. See under *purpurea.*

'Atropurpurea'. See under '*Riversii*'.

'Atropurpurea Macrophylla'. See under '*Riversii*'.

'Aurea Pendula'. An extremely elegant form of tall slender growth, the branches hanging down almost parallel with the main stem. Leaves golden yellow, but will sometimes scorch in full sun, and in too deep shade lose their rich colour.

'Aureovariegata'. See '*Luteovariegata*'.

'Cochleata'. A slow growing, shrubby form with obovate leaves strongly toothed in the upper half.

'Cockleshell'. A tall columnar form, the leaves small and rounded. A sport of '*Rotundifolia*' raised in our nurseries in 1960.

'Cristata'. "Cock's Comb Beech". A slow-growing eventually large tree, with clustered leaves, deeply lobed and curled.

'Cuprea'. See under *purpurea.*

'Dawyck' ('*Fastigiata*' HORT.). "Dawyck Beech". A tall columnar tree broadening in maturity. A.G.M. 1969.

'Fastigiata'. See '*Dawyck*'.

'Grandidentata'. A form with leaves coarsely toothed; branches slender.

heterophylla LOUD. "Fern-leaved Beech"; "Cut-leaved Beech". One of the most effective of large ornamental trees. As used here this name covers several forms in which the leaves are narrow and variously cut and lobed. They include '*Asplenifolia*', '*Incisa*' and '*Laciniata*'. A.G.M. 1969.

'Incisa'. See under *heterophylla.*

'Laciniata'. See under *heterophylla.*

'Latifolia' ('*Macrophylla*'). Leaves much larger than in the type, often up to 15cm. long and 10cm. wide.

'Luteovariegata' ('*Aureovariegata*'). Leaves variegated with yellow.

'Macrophylla'. See '*Latifolia*'.

'Norwegiensis'. See under '*Riversii*'.

'Pendula'. "Weeping Beech". A spectacular large, weeping tree taking on various forms, sometimes the enormous branches hang close to and perpendicular with the main stem like an elephant's trunk, while in other specimens some primary branches are almost horizontal and draped with long hanging branchlets.

'Prince George of Crete'. A striking form with very large leaves.

purpurea AIT. "Purple Beech". This name covers several purplish-leaved forms which are normally selected from seed-raised plants. They include the forms '*Atropunicea*, and '*Cuprea*'. See also under '*Riversii*'.

'Purpurea Latifolia'. See under '*Riversii*'.

'Purpurea Pendula'. "Weeping Purple Beech". A superb small weeping tree with dark purple leaves. Usually a small mushroom-headed tree.

'Riversii'. "Purple Beech". A large tree with large, dark purple leaves. This tree and its variants are vegetatively propagated. '*Atropurpurea*', '*Atropurpurea Macrophylla*', '*Norwegiensis*' and '*Purpurea Latifolia*' are similar clones.

'Rohanii'. A purple-leaved form of the "Fern-leaved Beech". A remarkably beautiful, rather slow-growing tree.

'Roseomarginata'. An attractive cultivar with purple leaves edged with an irregular pale pink border. Not very constant.

'Rotundifolia'. Unusual cultivar with strongly ascending branches and small rounded leaves.

'Tortuosa'. A low, wide-spreading tree, with twisted and contorted branches which are pendulous at their extremities.

'Zlatia'. A slow growing tree. Leaves soft yellow at first becoming green in late summer.

†***FASCICULARIA—Bromeliaceae**—A small genus of stemless plants forming dense clumps of evergreen, strap-shaped, spiny leaves. They require a warm sunny, sheltered position in a well drained soil or rock fissure.

FASCICULARIA—*continued*

bicolor MEZ. (*Rhodostachys bicolor*). A hardy plant in mild areas and given winter protection almost so in colder areas. Leaves long, narrow and spine toothed, sage green above, glaucous beneath, produced in dense tufted rosettes. The shorter, central leaves are a rich crimson colour producing a delightful bicolor effect. Flowers tubular, sky-blue gathered together in a dense, tight, sessile head in the centre of the rosette. Whilst in bud the flower head is surrounded and concealed by conspicuous ivory coloured bracts which later open to enable the flowers to expand in summer. Chile. I. 1851. A.M. 1949.

***×FATSHEDERA** (*FATSIA×HEDERA*)—**Araliaceae**—An interesting and very useful evergreen bigeneric hybrid. Splendid shade bearing plant creating excellent ground cover. Tolerant of atmospheric pollution, maritime exposure and all types of soil. In constant demand as a house plant.

lizei GUILLAUM (*F. japonica×H. helix*). A small to medium sized shrub of loose habit with large, leathery palmate leaves. Said to be a hybrid between the "Irish Ivy" and *Fatsia japonica 'Moseri'*. Garden origin 1910.

'Variegata'. Leaves grey-green with an irregular creamy white margin.

***FATSIA**—**Araliaceae**—A monotypic genus succeeding in all types of well drained soil.

japonica DCNE. & PLANCH. (*Aralia sieboldii*). A handsome medium sized to large shrub of spreading habit. The very large polished, dark green, palmate leaves give a subtropical effect and are an admirable foil to the panicles of milk-white, globular flower-heads that terminate the stems in October. Succeeds best in semi-shade and is excellent for seaside gardens. Japan. I. 1838. F.C.C. 1966. A.G.M. 1969.

'Variegata'. Lobes of leaves white at tips. F.C.C. 1868.

†*FEIJOA—**Myrtaceae**—A monotypic, summer-flowering genus.

sellowiana BERG. A large shrub requiring a warm, sheltered position. Leaves grey-green, white-felted beneath; flowers with fleshy crimson and white petals and a central bunch of long crimson stamens. The large egg-shaped berries are sometimes produced after a long hot summer. Both petals and fruits are edible, having a rich, aromatic flavour. Brazil; Uruguay. I. 1898. A.M. 1927.

'Variegata'. A form with cream and white variegated leaves. A.M. 1969.

†FENDLERA—**Philadelphaceae**—A small genus of four species of shrubs with opposite leaves. They require a warm, sunny position in a well drained soil.

wrightii HELL. A beautiful but difficult plant to grow, forming a small to medium sized shrub for a warm sunny position. The small leaves are lanceolate, three-nerved and roughly hairy above. The white or pink-tinted four-petalled flowers are produced singly or in small clusters in the leaf axils during May and June. S.W. United States. N. Mexico. I. 1879.

FICUS—**Moraceae**—A vast genus numbering over 600 species, only a few of which may be grown outside in this country.

carica L. "Common Fig". A very handsome, large shrub, or small spreading tree in suitable districts. Often grown against a warm sunny wall where its handsome lobed leaves and peculiar edible fruits are an object of interest throughout the year. W. Asia. Cultivated in England since early 16th century.

See also our FRUIT TREE Catalogue.

†*nipponica FR. & SAV. (*radicans* HORT.). Similar to *F. pumila* in habit but with longer, narrower leaves which end in a long point. The veinlets are prominently reticulated beneath. Only suitable for the conservatory or for use in hanging baskets though it may survive outside for several years in a warm sheltered position in the milder counties. Japan; Ryukyus; Formosa; China; S. Korea.

'Variegata' (*radicans 'Variegata'*). An attractive form with leaves irregularly margined creamy-white.

†*pumila L. (*stipulata*). A scandent shrub, climbing the trunks of trees like ivy in its native habitat. The juvenile growths bear small, neat ovate or heart-shaped leaves 1·25 to 2cm. long. In time adult growths are formed which produce larger leaves up to 10cm. long, also, if conditions are suitable, flowers and fruits. A tender plant for the conservatory where it may be encouraged to cover walls or used in hanging baskets. It may also be grown in a sheltered corner outside in milder cistricts. Japan; Ryukyus; Formosa; China. I. 1721.

'Minima' (*stipulata 'Minima'*). A very slender creeper, forming close carpets of minute leaves 6mm. long. It is an ideal plant for clothing shady rocks and low walls and in such a situation has survived outside for over thirty-five years in our Winchester nursery.

"FIG, COMMON". See *FICUS carica.*

"FIRETHORN". See *PYRACANTHA.*

†**FIRMIANA—Sterculiaceae**—A small genus of mainly asiatic trees.

simplex WIGHT (*Sterculia platanifolia*). A noble foliage tree of medium size for the mildest localities. Large maple-like leaves. China, long cultivated in Japan; Formosa. I. 1757.

FONTANESIA—Oleaceae—A small genus of two species. Privet-like shrubs closely related to the Ash (*Fraxinus*), but with simple leaves.

fortunei CARR. A large shrub with lanceolate leaves. The minute, greenish-white flower clusters are produced in May and June. China. I. 1845.

phillyreoides LABILL. A medium-sized shrub with ovate or elliptic leaves. Flowers greenish-white in June. Asia Minor. I. 1787.

FORESTIERA—Oleaceae—A genus of mainly privet-like shrubs succeeding in any ordinary soil. The leaves are opposite and the small unisexual flowers greenish, of little or no ornament.

acuminata POIR. (*Adelia acuminata*). "Swamp Privet". A large shrub or small tree. Fruits narrow-oblong, dark purple. S.E. United States. I. 1812.

neo-mexicana GRAY. Medium-sized shrub of spreading habit. Flowers inconspicuous, followed by black, egg-shaped fruits covered with a blue bloom. S.W. United States. C. 1913.

FORSYTHIA—Oleaceae—The most colourful of early spring-flowering shrubs, all very hardy and easy to grow. The bell-shaped flowers which wreathe the branches, are golden-yellow unless otherwise described. Several large-flowered hybrids have been raised by Dr. Karl Sax at the Arnold Arboretum.

Thin out and cut back old flowering shoots to within a few cm. of the old wood, immediately after flowering.

'Arnold Dwarf' (*intermedia* × *japonica saxatilis*). An interesting hybrid raised at the Arnold Arboretum in 1941. It has value as a low, ground cover plant attaining a height of only ·6 to 1m., but a spread of 1·8 to 2·1m. Flowers few, yellow-green, of no merit.

'Arnold Giant' (Intermedia Group). A triploid hybrid raised at the Arnold Arboretum in 1939. A robust shrub of medium size with exceptionally large, nodding, rich yellow flowers.

'Beatrix Farrand'. The plant offered under this name is a tetraploid raised at the Arnold Arboretum in 1944. The deep, canary-yellow, nodding flowers are exceptionally large, being considerably more than 2·5cm. across when fully expanded. The habit is upright and dense. A.M. 1961.

europaea DEG. & BALD. "European Golden Ball". A medium-sized shrub with long, four-angled branches and ovate to ovate-lanceolate, usually entire leaves. Flowers pale yellow appearing in April. Albania; Jugoslavia; Bulgaria. I. 1899.

giraldiana LINGELSH. A large shrub of loose, graceful habit, the first species to begin flowering, its pale yellow blossoms sometimes appearing in late February. N.W. China. I. 1910.

× **intermedia** ZAB. (*suspensa* × *viridissima*). A vigorous hybrid of medium to large size, intermediate in habit and flower between its parents, flowering during late March and April. Leaves sometimes trifoliolate. C. before 1880. A.M. 1894. There are several named clones. See also '*Arnold Giant*' and '*Lynwood*'.

'Densiflora'. Habit of growth fairly compact. The flowers are carried in such profusion as to almost hide the branches. Garden origin 1899.

'Primulina'. Flowers pale yellow. Garden origin 1910.

'Spectabilis'. One of the best and most popular of early spring flowering shrubs. The flowers are so profuse as to create a mass of golden yellow. Garden origin 1906. A.M. 1915. A.G.M. 1923. F.C.C. 1935.

'Vitellina'. Strong and erect growth; flowers deep yellow. Garden origin 1899.

'Karl Sax'. A strong-growing, floriferous hybrid with deep canary-yellow flowers.

'Lynwood' (Intermedia Group). A lovely cultivar, found in a cottage garden in Northern Ireland in 1935. The large, broad-petalled, rich yellow flowers are borne profusely all along the branches. This clone together with '*Beatrix Farrand*' and '*Karl Sax*' is one of the most spectacular of the forsythias. A.G.M. 1956. F.C.C. 1966.

FORSYTHIA—*continued*

ovata NAKAI. An early-flowering Korean species growing only 1·2 to 1·5m. high. Leaves ovate, flowers amber yellow in early March. Associates well with heaths and *Rhododendron* '*Praecox*'. I. 1918. A.M. 1941. A.G.M. 1947.

'Robusta'. A strong-growing shrub probably of hybrid origin, attaining 1·8 to 2·7m. Flowers deep yellow. In the past wrongly catalogued as *F. ovata* '*Robusta*'.

suspensa VAHL. A rambling shrub attaining about 3·1m. but much higher against a wall, with slender interlacing branches. Flowers on slender pedicels produced in late March and early April. Leaves often trifoliolate. China. I. 1833.

atrocaulis REHD. Young stems almost black-purple, contrasting with the comparatively large, pale lemon-yellow flowers. A.M. 1934.

fortunei REHD. The largest and most vigorous form with stout arching branches. China. I. about 1860.

'Nymans'. A large shrub with bronze-purple branches and large, primrose-yellow flowers. A sport of *atrocaulis*.

sieboldii ZAB. A variety with slender, pendent almost prostrate branches. An excellent wall shrub for a north or east aspect, or for covering an unsightly bank. China; long cultivated in Japan. I. 1833.

viridissima LINDL. Erect, square stemmed shrub up to 2·4m. high, with lanceolate leaves. Normally the last Forsythia to flower, commencing in April, some time after *F. suspensa*. China. I. 1844.

'Bronxensis'. A dense and compact dwarf form with masses of twiggy branchlets. Garden origin 1928. A.M. 1958.

'Volunteer' (*ovata* × *suspensa*). A vigorous shrub of medium size, with dark coloured young shoots and thickly clustered, deep yellow flowers. An interesting hybrid which originated in the garden of the late Mr. Arthur Simmonds, V.M.H., at Clandon in Surrey.

FORTUNAEA chinensis. See *PLATYCARYA strobilacea*.

FORTUNEARIA—Hamamelidaceae—A monotypic genus differing from *Hamamelis* in its five-parted flowers, and from *Corylopsis* in its tiny, narrow petals.

sinensis REHD. & WILS. A large, rather slow growing shrub. Similar in general appearance to *Hamamelis*, but with tiny green flowers borne in terminal racemes during winter. Moderately lime tolerant but grows better in neutral or acid soil. W. China. I. 1907.

†***FORTUNELLA—Rutaceae**—A small genus formerly included under *Citrus*. Suitable only for the conservatory.

japonica SWINGLE. (*Citrus japonica*). "Round Kumquat". A large shrub with spiny green branches and ovate leaves. Flowers white; fruits the size of a cherry, golden yellow. Only known in cultivation. A.M. 1905.

‡**FOTHERGILLA—Hamamelidaceae**—A small genus of N. American shrubs conspicuous in spring with their bottle-brush-like flower spikes, and again in autumn for the rich colouring of their leaves. They require neutral or lime-free soil.

gardenii MURR. (*alnifolia*) (*carolina*). Pretty shrub usually less than 1m. high, conspicuous in April and May with its erect, fragrant inflorescences, composed of clusters of white stamens. S.E. United States. I. 1765.

major LODD. A slow-growing shrub of medium size. Conspicuous, white flower-clusters before the leaves. Leaves glaucous beneath. Brilliant autumn colours. Alleghany Mts. (U.S.A.). I. 1780. A.M. 1927. A.G.M. 1946. F.C.C. 1969.

monticola ASHE. Slow-growing, medium-sized shrub, with showy white inflorescences. Gives good autumn colour. S.E. United States. I. 1899. A.M. 1937. F.C.C. 1971.

FRANGULA. See under *RHAMNUS*.

‡**FRANKLINIA—Theaceae**—A gorgeous autumn flowering shrub given a hot continental summer, when its ripened growths will withstand a zero winter. Not a plant for our insular climate.

alatamaha MARSH. (*Gordonia alatamaha*) (*G. pubescens*). A remarkable and rare shrub or small tree from Georgia, U.S.A. but not found in a wild state since the 18th century. Large, lustrous, green, oblong leaves, turning crimson in autumn. The large Stewartia-like, cup-shaped snow-white flowers only open during a hot, late summer. Perhaps last seen in the wild by the American collector, Lyon, in 1803. I. 1770.

FRAXINUS—Oleaceae—"Ash". An extensive genus of hardy, fast-growing trees, which thrive in almost any soil. Tolerant of wind-swept and coastal localities, and smoke-polluted areas. Leaves pinnate. The Ornus Group are attractive flowering trees.

FRAXINUS—*continued*

americana L. (*alba*). "White Ash". A large species soon forming a noble shade tree. One of the fastest growing of American hardwoods. Winter buds brown. Eastern N. America. I. 1724.

angustifolia VAHL. A large, elegant, fast-growing tree with perfectly glabrous, slender pointed leaflets. Winter buds brown. S. Europe; N. Africa. C. 1800.

australis SCHNEID. A geographical form with undersides of leaves slightly hairy. S. Europe; N. Africa. C. 1890.

lentiscifolia HENRY. A beautiful variety with small, graceful leaves and semi-pendulous branches.

'Pendula'. A handsome tree with slender pendulous branches.

bungeana DC. (Ornus Sect.). A large shrub or small tree. Twigs and petioles downy but leaflets glabrous, five to seven in number. Flowers produced in terminal panicles in May. Winter buds black. N. China. I. 1881.

chinensis ROXB. (Ornus Sect.). "Chinese Ash". A free-growing, medium-sized tree with attractive leaves which sometimes give wine-purple autumn colours. Winter buds a conspicuous grey. Flowers sweetly scented. China. I. 1891.

acuminata LINGELSH. A variety having leaflets with longer tapering points. China. I. 1910.

rhyncophylla HEMSL. An outstanding, tall, Chinese variety; grows well in this country and is notable for the large size of its terminal leaflets. N.E. Asia. I. 1892.

†**dipetala** HOOK. & ARN. A medium-sized to large shrub with four-angled branches; leaves varying in number of leaflets, usually five. This species is particularly useful for the creamy-white flowers which are produced in conspicuous panicles on the previous year's growth in late spring. Requires a warm sheltered position as the young growths are subject to damage by late frosts. California; Mexico. I. 1878.

excelsior L. "Common Ash". A large, magnificent tree and one of the most valuable for timber. Winter buds black. Europe (incl. British Isles); Caucasus. There are several named clones.

'Aurea'. See under '*Jaspidea*'.

'Aurea Pendula'. A small tree of rather weak constitution, the young shoots yellow and drooping, forming an umbrella-shaped crown.

'Crispa'. Slow growing, shrubby form of stiff, upright growth. Leaves small, shining, dark green with curled and twisted leaflets.

'Diversifolia' ('*Monophylla*'). "One-leaved Ash". A vigorous tree, with leaves simple or sometimes three-parted and usually jaggedly toothed.

'Erosa'. A small tree with very narrow, deeply cut leaves.

'Jaspidea'. A vigorous clone, the young shoots golden-yellow, branches yellowish, conspicuous in winter. Leaves clear yellow in autumn. Often found in cultivation under the name '*Aurea*' which is a dwarf, slow-growing tree.

'Monophylla'. See '*Diversifolia*'.

'Nana'. A densely branched small rounded bush.

'Pendula'. "Weeping Ash". A strong growing tree forming an attractive wide-spreading mound of divergent, weeping branches.

†**floribunda** WALL. (Ornus Sect.). Striking small tree with purplish young wood. The large leaves bear a conspicuous polished sheen. Flowers white, in large terminal panicles. Himalaya. I. 1822.

†**griffithii** C. B. CLARKE (*bracteata*). (Ornus Sect.). A nearly-evergreen species with quadrangular green shoots and leathery, dark green and glabrous, entire leaflets. Flowers in large, loose panicles. Only suitable for the mildest areas. S.E. Asia. I. 1900.

holotricha KOEHNE. A small tree with downy young growths. Leaflets many, narrow, decidedly greyish. Balkan Peninsular. C. 1870.

latifolia BENTH. (*oregona*). "Oregon Ash". A medium-sized, fast-growing tree with large leaves. Winter buds brown. Western N. America. C. 1870.

longicuspis sieboldiana. See *F. sieboldiana*.

mandshurica RUPR. "Manchurian Ash". A large tree showing kinship with our native species. Winter buds dark brown. N.E. Asia. I. 1882.

mariesii HOOK. f. (Ornus Sect.). The most beautiful "Flowering Ash". A small, tree with creamy-white flowers in handsome panicles during June. C. China. I. 1878. A.M. 1962.

FRAXINUS—*continued*

nigra MARSH. "Black Ash". A small to medium-sized tree which in the wild is said to grow in wet situations. Winter buds dark brown; leaves with seven to eleven slender pointed leaflets. Not one of the best species in cultivation. Eastern N. America. I. 1800.

oregona. See *F. latifolia*.

ornus L. (Ornus Sect.). "Manna Ash". A pretty tree of medium size, flowering abundantly in May. This is the type plant of the Ornus Group popularly known as "Flowering Ashes". S. Europe; Asia Minor. I. before 1700. A.G.M. 1973.

oxycarpa WILLD. A rare, graceful, small-leaved tree akin to *F. angustifolia*. Winter buds dark brown. S. Europe to Persia and Turkestan. I. 1815.

'Raywood'. This form is especially attractive in the autumn when its leaves turn plum-purple. An excellent tree of relatively compact habit.

paxiana LINGELSH. (Ornus Sec.). A remarkable tree of medium size with glabrous twigs and large terminal winter buds coated with brownish down. Leaves about 30cm. long composed of seven to nine lanceolate, toothed, slender-pointed leaflets, the lowest pair much smaller than the rest. Petioles often enlarged at the base. Flowers white, produced in large panicles during May and June. W. and C. China. I. 1901.

pennsylvanica MARSH. (*pubescens*). "Red Ash". A fast-growing, shade-giving tree of medium size, with downy shoots and large leaves. Winter buds brown. Eastern N. America. I. 1783.

'Aucubifolia'. Leaves mottled golden-yellow.

lanceolata SARG. "Green Ash". A variety with bright-green, glabrous shoots and narrow leaflets. E. United States. I. 1824.

'Variegata'. A brightly variegated tree; leaves silver-grey, margined and mottled cream-white.

platypoda OLIV. A medium-sized tree, the leaves with seven to eleven sessile, finely-toothed leaflets and a conspicuously enlarged and swollen petiole base. W. and C. China. I. 1909.

potamophila. See *F. sogdiana*.

quadrangulata MICHX. Small tree with distinctly four-winged, square branchlets. Leaves with seven to eleven short-stalked leaflets. Central and Eastern U.S.A. I. 1823.

sieboldiana BL. (*longicuspis sieboldiana*) (Ornus Sect.). A medium sized tree. Leaflets five, rarely seven, often giving good autumn tints. Flowers white in terminal panicles in May. Japan; Korea. I. 1894.

sogdiana BGE. (*potamophila*). A small tree with greenish, glabrous shoots; leaves with seven to eleven lanceolate, glabrous leaflets conspicuously toothed, sessile or almost so. Turkestan. C. 1890.

spaethiana LINGELSH. A small to medium sized tree with conspicuously large leaves, remarkable for the large, swollen, often red-brown base of its petioles. Large panicles of flowers. Japan. C. 1873.

syriaca BOISS. "Syrian Ash". A rare small tree with crowded, whorled leaves of a bright apple-green. Winter buds brown. W. and C. Asia. C. 1880.

tomentosa MICHX. f. A medium-sized tree with downy young shoots and petioles. Leaves large, with usually nine stalked leaflets, downy beneath. Eastern U.S.A. C. 1912.

velutina TORR. "Arizona Ash". A neat and pretty tree of 9 to 12m. Remarkable for its leaves and shoots which are densely clothed with grey, velvety down. Winter buds brown. S.W. United States, N. Mexico. I. 1891.

coriacea REHD. A form with leaflets more leathery and less downy than in the type. California. C. 1900.

glabra REHD. Leaves with three to seven leaflets which are glabrous like the branches.

toumeyi REHD. A distinct variety of dense habit. Leaves smaller than in the type, with three to five downy leaflets. Arizona, New Mexico, Mexico. I. 1891.

xanthoxyloides DC. The "Afghan Ash" is a small tree or large shrub of unusual appearance, with small, rounded, close-set leaflets on a winged petiole. Winter buds brown. Himalaya to Afghanistan. C. 1870.

dimorpha WENZ. "Algerian Ash". A geographical form from N. Africa, differing in leaf shape and other minor characters. N. Africa. I. about 1855.

dumosa CARR. A curious small bush with interlacing branches and tiny leaflets. C. 1865.

†***FREMONTODENDRON** (*FREMONTIA*)—**Sterculiaceae**—A small genus of tall evergreen shrubs for the milder parts of the British Isles. The flowers have no petals but possess a large, coloured calyx. Requires full sun and good drainage, excellent on chalk soils.

californicum KOV. A beautiful large, semi-evergreen shrub with usually three-lobed leaves, and large yellow flowers borne freely throughout the summer. In most districts needs a south-facing wall. California; Arizona. I. 1851. F.C.C. 1866.

mexicanum DAVIDSON. Similar to, but differing from *F. californicum* in its generally five-lobed leaves which are often shiny above. Flowers with slightly narrower sepals, giving a "star-like" sppearance. California; Mexico. I. 1926. A.M. 1927.

†***FREYLINIA**—**Scrophulariaceae**—A small genus of evergreen South African shrubs.

lanceolata G. DON. (*cestroides*). A pretty, medium sized shrub for the mildest localities. Panicles of fragrant, creamy-white or yellow flowers in late summer. S. Africa. I. 1774.

"FRINGE TREE". See *CHIONANTHUS*.

FUCHSIA—**Onagraceae**—Most of the kinds listed below have passed successfully many winters out-of-doors in our nurseries. Although the tender sorts may be cut to ground level, they usually shoot up strongly again in spring. All have red sepals except where otherwise stated, and flower freely throughout summer and autumn. Remarkable in thriving alike in sun or shade in any well-drained soil.

'Alice Hoffman'. A small shrub with small purple tinged leaves in dense clusters. Flowers small, calyx scarlet, petals white.

†×**bacillaris** LINDL. (*microphylla*×*thymifolia*). A beautiful dwarf shrub with small flowers; calyx glowing crimson, petals reflexed, coral-red. The form we offer was previously wrongly catalogued as *F. parviflora*.

'Cottinghamii'. A charming shrub taller than the above described, the flowers similar in colour and shape but smaller, and succeeded by glossy, purple-brown, bead-like fruits.

†**'Brilliant'.** A small shrub with large flowers. Calyx rose-scarlet; petals broad, rose-purple. A.M.T. 1962.

'Chillerton Beauty'. A beautiful, small shrub with medium-sized flowers; calyx white, flushed deep rose, petals clear soft violet. A.G.M. 1973.

'Corallina'. A strong, robust shrub with large, deep green leaves and scarlet and violet flowers. Previously wrongly catalogued as *F. 'Exoniensis'* which is not in cultivation.

'Cottinghamii'. See *F.* ×*bacillaris 'Cottinghamii'*.

†**'Display'.** A small shrub with large flowers. Calyx carmine; petals and long protruding stamens rose-pink.

'Dunrobin Bedder'. Small shrub of spreading habit. Flowers similar to *F. magellanica*, scarlet and violet. A.M. 1890.

†**'Elsa'.** Small shrub with large flowers. Calyx white flushed pink; petals doubled, violet-rose.

†**excorticata** L. f. The largest of the three New Zealand species, making a very large tree-like shrub in the mildest localities, but here never more than a medium-sized bush. Flowers 2.5cm. long, resembling *F. procumbens* in colour, appearing in spring. I. 1824.

gracilis. See *F. magellanica gracilis*.

'Variegata'. See *F. magellanica 'Variegata'*.

†**'Madame Cornelissen'.** A large-flowered hybrid of *C. magellanica*, with red calyx and white petals. A.M. 1941. A.M.T. 1965. A.G.M. 1969.

magellanica LAM. A graceful South American shrub of medium size with long, slender flowers; calyx scarlet, petals violet. Leaves generally in whorls of three. I. 1823.

'Alba'. Flowers shorter, white, faintly tinged mauve. A.M. 1932.

gracilis BAILEY. A beautiful, floriferous shrub of slender habit, with leaves generally in pairs. Flowers small, scarlet and violet. A.G.M. 1930.

'Pumila'. A charming dwarf shrub with small, narrow leaves and tiny flowers of scarlet and deep violet.

'Riccartonii'. See *F. 'Riccartonii'*.

'Variegata' (*F. gracilis 'Variegata'*). A striking, variegated form. Leaves green, margined creamy-yellow flushed pink, against which the small scarlet and purple flowers appear most effectively. Less hardy than the type. A.G.M. 1969.

FUCHSIA—*continued*

magellanica 'Versicolor'. A small shrub of spreading habit. The slender stems sport leaves of a striking grey-green which are rose tinted when young and irregularly variegated creamy-white when mature. A lovely foliage shrub. A.M.T. 1965. A.G.M. 1969.

'Margaret'. A vigorous shrub producing an abundance of crimson and violet-purple, semi-double flowers. A.M.T. 1965.

'Margaret Brown'. A dwarf shrub of erect, compact habit with large flowers; calyx crimson, petals magenta.

'Mrs. Popple'. A small, large-flowered, hardy hybrid with spreading scarlet sepals, violet petals, and long protruding crimson stamens and style. A.M. 1934. A.G.M. 1958. A.M.T. 1962.

parviflora. See under *F.* ×*bacillaris*.

'Peter Pan'. A dwarf shrub producing an abundance of small red and purple flowers.

†**procumbens** A. CUNN. A trailing, small-leaved New Zealand species. Flowers small; erect, calyx tube yellow, sepals violet and green, stamens red and blue, petals absent. Fruits comparatively large, magenta. I. about 1854.

†**'Reflexa'.** A small shrub with tiny leaves and small, bright cerise flowers darkening with age; fruits black. Regarded by some authorities as a form of *F. thymifolia*, whilst others suggest it may belong to *F.* ×*bacillaris*.

'Riccartonii' (*magellanica 'Riccartonii'*). This common, hardy shrub attains a large size, and is often used as a hedging plant in mild districts. Differing from *F. magellanica* in its deeper coloured calyx and broader sepals. A.G.M. 1927. A.M.T. 1966.

'Tom Thumb'. A very free-flowering dwarf shrub; calyx rose-scarlet; petals violet. A.M.T. 1938. F.C.C.T. 1962. A.G.M. 1969.

"FURZE". See *ULEX*.

"FURZE, NEEDLE". See *GENISTA anglica*.

***GARRYA—Garryaceae**—Free-flowering evergreens, male and female flowers being borne on separate plants. Leathery leaves and conspicuous catkins. Excellent both in maritime exposure and atmospheric pollution, and useful for furnishing North or East facing walls. They succeed in all types of well drained soil, but require protection in cold areas.

congdonii EASTW. A shrub up to 1·8m. with narrowly oval leaves, rounded on juvenile plants. Male catkins up to 7·5cm. long in late spring. California.

elliptica LINDL. The male plant of this species is a magnificent evergreen, draped, during January and February, with long, greyish-green catkins. The female plant is scarcely less effective, with its long clusters of deep purple-brown fruits. California, Oregon. I. 1828. A.M. 1931. A.G.M. 1960 (male form). A.M. 1975 (for fruit).

'James Roof'. A strong, vigorous male form with large leathery leaves and extra long catkins. A.M. 1974.

†**flavescens** WATS. An erect, medium-sized shrub with leathery, elliptic, sharply-pointed leaves. Flowers in pendulous catkins during spring. A variable species, the typical form has leaves and young stems clothed with yellowish hairs but in their sage-green leaves and greyish-green appearance our plants approach the variety *pallida*. California.

†**fremontii** TORR. A rare medium to large size shrub similar to *G. elliptica* but with generally obovate leaves, glabrous or nearly so beneath, shorter male catkins and fruits which appear in the late spring. Western U.S.A.

†**laurifolia macrophylla** WANGER. A vigorous, medium sized to large shrub with large leaves up to 15cm. long. Catkins less spectacular than those of *G. elliptica*, appearing in late spring. Mexico. I. 1846.

×**thuretii** CARR. (*elliptica*×*fadyenii*). A vigorous hybrid, rapidly attaining 5·5m. and making a solid green wall. Leaves dark green, glossy, about 14cm. long. An excellent wind resister. Garden origin about 1862.

wrightii TORR. A medium sized shrub with slender, 5cm. catkins in summer. Leaves elliptic, firm and leathery with sharp, mucro point, sage green and conspicuously veined. S.W. United States. I. 1901.

‡*×**GAULNETTYA** (*GAULTHERIA*×*PERNETTYA*) (×*GAULTHETTYA*)—**Ericaceae**—Hybrids between these two genera are known to occur in the wild in New Zealand, but the following is of Garden origin:—

×**GAULNETTYA**—*continued*

wisleyensis HORT. (*G. shallon*×*P. mucronata*). An interesting hybrid which originated at Wisley about 1929. The following are the only clones in general cultivation:—

'Ruby'. A small shrub of vigorous habit forming a dense evergreen thicket. Leaves up to 2·5cm. long, dark green and leathery; flowers white, produced in late May and early June in dense terminal and axillary racemes. The fruits ripening in late autumn and winter, are ruby-red, each crowned by a similarly coloured swollen calyx like a tiny elf's cap.

'Wisley Pearl'. A small shrub with dull, dark green leaves 3·8cm. or more long and half as wide. The branches are laden during autumn and winter with short but crowded bunches of large ox-blood-red fruits. This is the original selected clone usually distributed as ×*Gaulthettya wisleyensis*. A.M. 1939.

‡***GAULTHERIA—Ericaceae**—An interesting genus, related to *Vaccinium*, differing in the superior ovary; thriving in moist, lime-free, preferably peaty soil, and a shady position. They are mainly tufted shrubs, spreading by underground stems. In the majority of species the calyx enlarges after flowering, becomes fleshy and coloured and encloses the true fruit. The white urn-shaped flowers are normally borne in late spring or early summer.

adenothrix MAXIM. A dainty dwarf creeping shrub forming a low carpet of zig-zag red-brown hairy stems furnished with small leathery dark green leaves. Flowers white suffused pink borne from May to July and followed by hairy crimson fruits. Japan. I. 1915.

antipoda FORST. f. An interesting New Zealand species, varying in habit between a prostrate shrub to an erect bush of 1·2m. Fruits red or white, globose, about 1·25cm. across. I. 1820.

caudata STAPF. A low-growing, wide-spreading shrub forming a dense mound. A specimen in our arboretum is at present ·75m. high and 2·5m. across. The narrowly elliptic to elliptic-oblong, sharply serrulate leaves which are reticulate and punctate beneath are widely spaced along the attractively arching, reddish shoots. Flowers in axillary racemes. Yunnan.

cuneata BEAN. A dwarf shrub of compact habit. Leaves narrowly oblanceolate. Fruits white, smelling of "Germolene" when crushed. A delightful species. W. China. I. 1909. A.M. 1924.

forrestii DIELS. An attractive, spreading, Chinese shrub having conspicuous, white-stalked axillary racemes of white, waxy, fragrant flowers, followed by blue fruits. I. about 1908. A.M. 1927. A.M. 1937.

fragrantissima WALL. A medium-sized species with narrowly elliptic toothed sub-glabrous leaves; flowers in racemes from the leaf axils, fragrant; fruits bright blue. Himalaya; Mts. of Burma; India and Ceylon. I. about 1850.

hispida R. BR. Small shrub with bristly young shoots. Leaves oblong, up to 6·3cm. long. Flowers white, in terminal panicles followed by succulent, berry-like white fruits. Australia; Tasmania. C. 1927. A.M. 1927.

hookeri C. B. CLARKE (*veitchiana*). A dwarf, densely spreading shrub with bristly arching stems. Leaves leathery and glandular toothed, elliptic to obovate 5 to 7·5cm. long. Flowers white in dense, axillary terminal clusters in May; fruits blue. Himalaya, W. China. I. 1907. A.M. 1943. F.C.C. 1945.

humifusa RYBD. (*myrsinites*). A dwarf shrub of dense compact habit and only a few cm. high, bearing small, rounded, wavy leaves. The small, pink tinged, bell-shaped flowers in summer are followed by small red fruits. N.W. North America. C. 1830.

itoana HAYATA. A rare, creeping species forming close mats of bright green, pernettya-like foliage. Fruits white. Taiwan. I. shortly before 1936.

miqueliana TAKEDA. A neat, dwarf, Japanese shrub, usually not above 30cm. high, with shining green, oblong leaves. The short racemes are conspicuous in June, and are followed by white or pink edible fruits. I. 1892. A.M. 1948.

†**nummularioides** D. DON. A neat, creeping, Himalayan species with small, broadly ovate, bristly leaves arranged in two ranks; fruits blue-black. Suitable for a sheltered shady bank. I. about 1850.

oppositifolia HOOK. f. A small, densely-branched shrub of spreading habit with arching, usually glabrous shoots. Leaves normally opposite, ovate to oblong, dark glossy green above and strongly reticulate. The white, bell-shaped flowers are borne in conspicuous terminal panicles during May and June. Fruits white. An extremely ornamental New Zealand species easily recognised by its opposite leaves. It requires a sheltered position. A.M. 1927.

GAULTHERIA—*continued*

procumbens L. "Checkerberry". A North American creeping evergreen, forming carpets of dark green leaves amongst which, in autumn and winter, the bright red fruits are freely intermixed. I. before 1762.

pyroloides HOOK. & THOMS. (*pyrolifolia*). A dwarf creeping shrub forming mats of short stems and bright green, obovate or rounded, reticulately-veined leaves, 2·5cm. long. The pink-tinged urn-shaped flowers are borne in short leafy racemes from mid-May often to July. Fruits blue-black. An interesting little plant recalling *Salix reticulata* in leaf. Himalaya. C. 1933.

semi-infera AIRY-SHAW. A dwarf shrub with hispid shoots and obovate to oblanceolate leaves 5-8cm. long, glossy green above. Flowers white, occasionally blush, followed by obovoid fruits variable in colour, often indigo-blue. Himalaya. A.M. 1950.

shallon PURSH. A vigorous species forming thickets up to 1·8m. high, an ideal undergrowth for game coverts, etc. Leaves broad and leathery; flowers pinkish-white, fruits dark purple, in large clusters. Western North America. I. 1826.

stapfiana AIRY-SHAW. A dwarf shrub with arching and erect stems and elliptic to oblanceolate leaves. Flowers white followed by bright blue fruits. Closely related to *G. hookeri* under which name it is usually found in gardens. It mainly differs from this species in its usually more erect, glabrous or appressed bristly stems. W. China.

tetramera W. W. SM. A dwarf shrub of compact habit forming a wide mound of arching stems. Leaves broadly oval to lanceolate-elliptic, reticulate and dark green above. Flowers white, borne in May and June and followed by blue or violet coloured fruits. W. China. C. 1933. A.M. 1950.

trichophylla ROYLE. A charming shrublet of tufted habit. Flowers pink followed by conspicuous large blue fruits. Himalaya; W. China. I. 1897. A.M. 1918.

veitchiana. See *G. hookeri*.

wardii MARQUAND & SHAW. A Kingdon Ward introduction from S.E. Tibet, distinct in its bristly nature and leathery, lanceolate leaves with deeply impressed veins. May or June blooming; flowers in racemes, white; fruits milky-blue. C. 1933. A.M. 1933.

×**GAULTHETTYA.** See ×*GAULNETTYA*.

GAYA lyallii. See *HOHERIA glabrata* and *lyallii*.

ribifolia. See *HOHERIA lyallii*.

‡**GAYLUSSACIA**—**Ericaceae**—The "Huckleberries" are evergreen or deciduous shrubs closely resembling *Vaccinium*, and requiring similar conditions.

baccata K. KOCH. "Black Huckleberry". A small shrub of erect habit. Leaves resinous beneath; flowers in May, dull red, in short dense racemes; fruits lustrous black, edible. Autumn tints of a soft crimson. Eastern N. America. I. 1772.

***brachycera** GRAY. Dwarf shrub with thick, leathery, glossy green leaves. Flowers white, produced in May and June. E. United States. I. 1796. A.M. 1940.

"GEAN". See *PRUNUS avium*.

GELSEMIUM sempervirens. See under CLIMBERS.

GENISTA—**Leguminosae**—A beautiful genus of shrubs closely allied to Cytisus, and requiring similar treatment. Some of the dwarf species are indispensable alpines, while the taller ones include some invaluable summer-flowering shrubs. They associate well with the heathers. All succeed in acid or neutral soil and are lime tolerant. All have yellow flowers unless otherwise described.

aetnensis DC. "Mount Etna Broom". A large, elegant shrub, free-flowering in July. Sardinia and Sicily. A.G.M. 1923. F.C.C. 1938.

anglica L. "Needle Furze", "Petty Whin". A dwarf, spiny, native shrub. Showy yellow flowers from May to July. W. Europe.

cinerea DC. One of the best early summer-flowering shrubs, growing 2·4 to 3·5m. high; an elegant and fragrant mass of golden-yellow during June and July. S.W. Europe. A.M. 1924. A.G.M. 1933.

dalmatica. See *G. sylvestris*.

delphinensis VILL. This tiny decumbent shrub is one of the best species for the rock garden. Deep yellow flowers in terminal or axillary clusters in July to August. Like a miniature *G. sagittalis*. S. France.

†**ephedroides** DC. An unusual, small, erect-branched shrub with very small leaves which soon fall, leaving the slender stems quite naked. The solitary, fragrant, yellow flowers are borne towards the end of the shoots in May and June. Sardinia; Sicily and S. Italy.

GENISTA—*continued*

†**falcata** BROT. A small gorse-like shrub. Slender branches, with spiny lateral shoots; flowers deep golden-yellow in long panicles in May. Portugal; W. Spain.

†**fasselata** DCNE. (*sphacelata*). A curious, small, rather gorse-like, spiny shrub with typical yellow flowers, from the E. Mediterranean region.

germanica L. A dwarf, spiny shrub covered with short racemes of yellow flowers in June. C. and W. Europe to C. Russia. C. 1588.

hispanica L. "Spanish Gorse". One of the best plants for sunny sites, dry banks etc. forming .6m. high dense, prickly mounds covered unfailingly in May and June with masses of yellow flowers. S.W. Europe. I. 1759. A.G.M. 1969.

horrida DC. (*Echinospartium horridum*). A dwarf, rigid, spiny shrub of silvery-grey hue. Flowers in small terminal heads from July to September. S.W. Europe. I. 1821.

januensis VIV. (*triquetra*). "Genoa Broom". A rare, procumbent shrub with somewhat winged branches. Flowers bright yellow in May. S.E. Europe. I. about 1840. A.M. 1932.

lydia BOISS. (*spathulata*). An outstanding dwarf shrub. Slender pendulous branchlets are smothered in golden-yellow flowers in May and June. E. Balkans. I. 1926. A.M. 1937. A.G.M. 1946. F.C.C. 1957.

†**monosperma** LAM. (*Lygos monosperma*). An unusual species up to 1·8m. with long, slender, rush-like stems. The young growths give the plant a silvery appearance. Flowers milky-white, fragrant. S. Europe and N. Africa. I. 1690.

pilosa L. A dwarf, native shrub, producing cascades of golden-yellow flowers in May. W. and C. Europe (incl. British Isles).

pulchella. See *G. villarsii.*

radiata SCOP. A slow-growing species, forming a dense shrub about 1m. high. Flowers in June, deep yellow. C. and S.E. Europe. I. 1758.

sagittalis L. (*Chamaespartium sagittale*). A dwarf shrub with broadly winged, prostrate branches, giving an evergreen appearance; flowers in June. Useful for dry walls etc. C. and S. Europe. C. 1588.

scorpius DC. A rare species, which has here reached a height of 1·8m. Branches spiny, like gorse but grey; flowers in bright yellow masses in April and May. S.W. Europe.

sphacelata. See *G. fasselata.*

sylvestris SCOP. (*dalmatica*). "Dalmatian Broom". A decumbent shrub forming hummocks 15 to 23cm. high, covered with terminal racemes of yellow flowers in June and July. An excellent plant for a well-drained ledge in the rock garden. W. Balkans; C. and S. Italy. I. 1893.

tenera O. KUNTZE (*virgata* LINK. not LAM.). A beautiful, hardy shrub attaining 3·7m. and as much through, flowering in June and July. Resembles *G. cinerea.* Madeira. I. 1777. A.G.M. 1923.

tinctoria L. "Dyer's Greenweed". A late flowering native shrub of about ·6m. with bright yellow flowers in long terminal racemes from June to September. Europe.

anxantica FIORI. A glabrous, dwarf form. Italy. I. 1818.

humilior SCHNEID. (*mantica*). A distinct, downy, erect variety with purple stems and deep yellow flowers. Italy. I. 1816.

'Plena'. Floriferous dwarf, semi-prostrate form with double flowers. A superb dwarf shrub for the rock garden. A.G.M. 1969.

'Royal Gold'. A small, free-flowering shrub, the stems thickly covered with rich yellow flowers through summer. A.G.M. 1969.

villarsii CLEMENTI (*pulchella*). A miniature rock garden shrub 7·5 to 10cm. high. Young shoots grey, hairy; flowers bright yellow, solitary in the axils of the terminal leaves in May. S.E. France; W. Balkans.

virgata LINK. See *G. tenera.*

‡†***GEVUINA**—**Proteaceae**—A genus of three species.

avellana MOL. "Chilean Hazel". An interesting species making, in favourable localities, a large shrub or small tree. The long branches are held rather loosely and carry handsome polished green pinnate leaves. Flowers white in panicles followed by bright red, cherry-like fruits, rarely produced in this country. It grows best in sheltered woodlands. S. Chile. I. 1826.

"GHOST TREE". See *DAVIDIA involucrata.*

GLEDITSIA (*GLEDITSCHIA*)—**Leguminosae**—A genus of extremely beautiful foliage trees. Mature trunks often formidably armed with long thorns. Leaves pinnate, resembling the "Mimosas". Flowers greenish and insignificant. Seeds produced in flattened pods of varying length. Succeeds in all types of well drained soils and tolerant of atmospheric pollution.

aquatica MARSH. "Water Locust". Small, shrubby tree with large branched spines and simply or doubly pinnate leaves. Pods, when produced, short, less than 5cm. long containing a solitary seed. S.E. United States. I. 1723.

caspica DESF. "Caspian Locust". A small tree, old specimens with trunks formidably armed with numerous spines 15cm. or more long. Leaflets larger than in most species. Transcaucasus; N. Iran. I. 1822.

delavayi FRANCH. A Chinese tree of medium height, with dark green, lustrous leaves, coppery red young growths and enormous spines. Unripened growths are cut back in very cold winters. I. 1900.

horrida. See *G. japonica* and *G. sinensis*.

japonica MIQ. (*horrida* MAK.). A graceful, medium sized Japanese tree of somewhat pyramidal habit, its trunk being armed with branched spines. The fern-like leaves are composed of up to thirty small leaflets. Quite hardy even in a young state. I. 1894.

macracantha DESF. A tall, medium sized, spiny tree from Central China, particularly notable for the variable size of its leaflets; flowers in downy racemes followed by long seed-pods. C. 1800.

sinensis LAM. (*horrida* WILLD.). "Chinese Honey Locust". A handsome medium-sized tree with branched spines and fern-like foliage. China. I. 1774.

× **texana** SARG. (*aquatica* × *triacanthos*). A natural hybrid making eventually a large tree with smooth bark and spineless branches. Similar in general appearance to *G. triacanthos*. S.E. United States. I. 1900.

triacanthos L. "Honey Locust". This elegant large sized tree, with frond-like leaves, is very tolerant of industrially polluted atmosphere. A large specimen is quite effective when strung with its long, shining-brown seed pods. C. and E. United States. I. 1700.

'Bujoti' ('*Pendula*'). A shrubby form or occasionally small tree, with narrower leaflets and slender pendulous branchlets.

'Elegantissima'. A beautiful, compact, slow-growing shrub attaining 3·5 to 4·6m. with large, fern-like foliage.

inermis ZAB. A form which bears no thorns.

'Inermis Aurea'. See '*Sunburst*'.

'Pendula'. See '*Bujoti*'.

'Sunburst' ('*Inermis Aurea*'). A striking, medium sized tree, having thornless stems and bright yellow young leaves. A.G.M. 1973.

†**GLOCHIDION**—**Euphorbiaceae**—A large genus of trees and shrubs mainly native of tropical areas.

sinicum HOOK. & ARN. (*fortunei*). A rare and interesting, shrubby Chinese member of the *Euphorbia* family, with handsome, frond-like leaves composed of many leaflets of variable shape.

"GOLDEN RAIN". See *LABURNUM*.

‡†***GORDONIA**—**Theaceae**—An Asiatic and American genus of camellia-like trees or shrubs, conspicuous both in leaf and flower. Require a lime-free soil.

alatamaha. See *FRANKLINIA alatamaha*.

axillaris D. DIETR. (*anomala*). A rare evergreen, large shrub or small tree. Large, leathery, dark, glossy-green leaves; flowers 7·5 to 15cm. across, creamy-white, appearing from November to May. China and Formosa. I. 1818. A.M. 1929.

chrysandra COWAN. A large, Chinese shrub. Flowers creamy-white, fragrant, 2ins. across during late winter. Yunnan. I. 1917.

lasianthus ELLIS. "Loblolly Bay". A beautiful, but tender, magnolia-like species attaining small tree size in this country. Flowers white, 7·5cm. across, in July and August. S.E. United States. I. 1768.

"GORSE, COMMON". See *ULEX europaeus*.

"GORSE, SPANISH". See *GENISTA hispanica*.

‡†***GREVILLEA**—**Proteaceae**—Beautiful shrubs from Australia and Tasmania. The flowers, superficially like those of honeysuckle, but smaller, are produced over a long period. Good drainage essential and avoid overhead shade and chalk soils.

alpina LINDL. A charming, compact, low shrub for the mildest parts, freely producing its curious, red and cream flowers over a long season. Grey-green, needle-like leaves. An excellent pot plant. S. E. Australia. I. before 1857. A.M. 1936.

glabrata MEISSN. An erect glabrous shrub with attractive lobed leaves and long, pyramidal panicles of white flowers with pink stigmas in spring. A conservatory plant except in the mildest localities.

ornithopoda MEISSN. A medium sized to large shrub for the conservatory. The pendulous branches carry long, flat, pale green, trifid leaves. The thick clusters of creamy-white flowers cascade down the stems in April. I. 1850.

rosmarinifolia A. CUNN. A beautiful shrub for mild districts, where it will attain 1·8m. The conspicuous, crimson flowers are produced in long terminal racemes during summer. Deep green, needle-like leaves. I. about 1822. A.M. 1932.

× **semperflorens** (*sulphurea* × *thelemanniana*). An interesting and beautiful hybrid of garden origin. The flowers are a combination of yellow suffused rose-pink and tipped at the apex with green during summer. Leaves needle-like. Attains about 1.8m. in sheltered areas of S.W. England. Garden origin 1927.

sulphurea A. CUNN. A beautiful, medium-sized shrub for mild districts. Terminal racemes of bright, canary-yellow flowers in summer. Bright green needle-like leaves. A.M. 1974.

GREWIA—**Tiliaceae**—A large genus of mainly tropical or subtropical trees and shrubs.

†**occidentalis** L. A little known South African shrub or small tree allied to the "Lime". Leaves oval; flowers in stalked clusters, pink. I. 1690.

GRINDELIA—**Compositae**—A small genus of shrubs and herbaceous plants.

***chiloensis** CABRERA (*speciosa*). This surprisingly hardy, small evergreen subshrub, is a really handsome plant. The narrow leaves with undulate, toothed margins are hoary, affording a harmonious contrast with the large, rich cornflower-like yellow flowers, which appear from June to October, carried singly on stout tall stems. Buds covered with a milk-white, sticky varnish. Requires full sun and acute drainage. Argentina. I. about 1850. A.M. 1931.

†***GRISELINIA**—**Cornaceae**—A small genus of trees and shrubs, native of New Zealand and Chile. Flowers inconspicuous, male and female on separate plants.

littoralis RAOUL. This densely leafy, large, evergreen shrub, which is tree-like in mild localities, is an excellent hedge plant for maritime exposures. Leaves leathery, apple-green. Succeeds in all types of fertile soil. Liable to frost damage in cold inland areas. New Zealand. I. about 1850.

'Dixon's Cream'. An attractive form with leaves splashed and marked creamy white. Occurred as a sport of '*Variegata*' in the garden of Major W. G. M. Dixon in Jersey.

'Variegata'. Conspicuous white variegated foliage. A.M. 1978.

lucida FORST. f. A very handsome, tender species with large leaves which have a noticeably oblique base and an almost varnished upper surface. New Zealand.

"GUELDER ROSE". See *VIBURNUM opulus*.

"GUM TREE". See *EUCALYPTUS*.

GYMNOCLADUS—**Leguminosae**—A genus of two species from America and China of pod-bearing trees.

canadensis. See *G. dioicus*.

dioica K. KOCH (*canadensis*). "Kentucky Coffee Tree". This medium-sized, slow growing tree is one of the most handsome of all hardy trees. Young twigs light grey, almost white, specially noticeable in winter. The large compound leaves are pink tinted when unfolding, and turn clear yellow before falling. The seeds were used as a substitute for coffee by the early settlers in North America. E. and C. United States. I. before 1748.

'Variegata'. Leaflets with a creamy-white variegation.

"HACKBERRY". See *CELTIS*.

***HAKEA**—**Proteaceae**—A remarkable genus of Australiasian, evergreen shrubs, some suggesting kinship with the conifers. A few species are hardy and make excellent subjects for sunny, arid positions. Not good on chalk soils.

acicularis. See *H. sericea*.

HAKEA—*continued*

microcarpa R. BR. An interesting medium to large-sized shrub of dense rounded habit. The fragrant, creamy-white flowers are produced in clusters in the axils of needle-like leaves in May and are followed by chestnut-brown seed capsules.

sericea SCHRAD. & J. WENDL. (*acicularis*). A tall shrub or small, bushy tree creating an effect which might be associated with the desert. Flowers white in the axils of the awl-shaped leaves which vary from 2·5 to 7·5cm. long. May to July. Proving hardy in favoured sites.

‡**HALESIA**—**Styracaceae**—A very beautiful small genus of shrubs or small trees allied to *Styrax* and, like them, thriving in a lime-free soil. All the following are natives of North America and produce snowdrop-like flowers along naked branches in May followed by small, green, winged fruits.

carolina L. (*tetraptera*). "Snowdrop Tree". A large shrub or occasionally small spreading tree, very beautiful in spring when the branches are draped with white, nodding, bell-shaped flowers in clusters of three or five. Fruits pear-shaped, four-winged. S.E. United States. I. 1756. A.G.M. 1946. A.M. 1954. F.C.C. 1980.

diptera ELL. This species is similar to *H. carolina*, but is more shrubby in habit and less free-flowering. It is also distinguished by its broader leaves and two-winged fruits. S.E. United States. I. 1758. A.M. 1948.

monticola SARG. A magnificent small spreading tree differing from *H. carolina* in its greater size and its larger flowers and fruits, the latter up to 5cm. long. Mts. of S.E. United States. I. about 1897. A.M. 1930.

'Rosea'. Flowers very pale pink.

vestita SARG. A magnificent variety which in gardens produces larger flowers up to 3cm. across, white sometimes tinged rose. Leaves more or less downy beneath at first, becoming glabrous. A.M. 1958.

tetraptera. See *H. carolina*.

*×**HALIMIOCISTUS** (*HALIMIUM*×*CISTUS*)—**Cistaceae**—Pretty and interesting hybrids surviving, when given full sun and good drainage, all but the coldest winters. See also *CISTUS*, *HALIMIUM* and *HELIANTHEMUM*.

'Ingwersenii' (*Helianthemum clusii*). Discovered in Portugal, and believed to be *H. umbellatum*×*C. hirsutus*. A free-growing, dwarf, spreading shrub, with pure white flowers, borne over a long period. I. about 1929.

revolii DANSEREAU. A beautiful low evergreen producing a long succession of white, yellow-centred flowers.

sahucii JANCHEN (*H. umbellatum*×*C. salviifolius*). A dwarf spreading shrub with linear leaves and pure white flowers from May to September. S. France. I. about 1929. A.G.M. 1969.

†**wintonensis** O. & E. F. WARB. This beautiful hybrid originated in our nurseries, and is believed to be *H. ocymoides*×*C. salviifolius*. Flowers 5cm. across, pearly white with a feathered and pencilled zone of crimson-maroon, contrasting with yellow stains at the base of the petals; May to June. An attractive dwarf grey-foliaged shrub. I. about 1910. A.M. 1926 (as *Cistus wintonensis*).

***HALIMIUM**—**Cistaceae**—A small genus of mostly low, spreading shrubs, akin to *Helianthemum*, and referred to it by some authorities. They require full sun, and are subject to injury by severe frost. Natives of the Mediterranean region. See also *CISTUS*, ×*HALIMIOCISTUS* and *HELIANTHEMUM*.

†**atriplicifolium** SPACH. A beautiful small, silver shrub of spreading habit. Flowers golden yellow, up to 3·8cm. across in June; leaves broad, silvery-grey. Requires a sheltered sunny site. C. and S. Spain. C. in the mid 17th cent.

†**halimifolium** WILLK & LANGE. A small, erect shrub with narrow grey leaves. From May onwards the bright yellow flowers, up to 3·8cm. across, appear in erect, few-flowered panicles. Each petal has a dark spot at its base. Mediterranean Region. C. since middle of 17th century.

lasianthum SPACH (*Cistus formosus*). A low, spreading shrub, ultimately ·6 to 1m. high, with greyish leaves, and golden yellow flowers with a dark blotch at the base of each petal; May. S. Portugal; S. Spain. I. 1780. A.M. 1951.

'Concolor'. Petals without blotches.

libanotis WILLK. X LANGE (*commutatum*) (*Helianthemum rosmarinifolium*). Dwarf shrub of semi-erect habit with linear leaves and golden-yellow flowers 2·5cm. across; June. Mediterranean Region.

HALIMIUM—*continued*

ocymoides WILLK. & LANGE. (*Helianthemum algarvense*). Charming, compact shrub of ·6 to 1m. with small, grey leaves and bright yellow flowers, with blackish-brown basal markings. Portugal and Spain. C. 1800. A.G.M. 1932.

umbellatum SPACH. A dwarf species, very similar to *H. libanotis*, from which it differs in its white flowers; June. Mediterranean Region. I. 1731.

HALIMODENDRON—Leguminosae—Succeeds in any well-drained, open site.

halodendron SCHNEID. (*argenteum*). "Salt Tree". An attractive, spiny, silvery-leaved shrub up to 1·8m. Masses of purplish-pink pea-flowers in June and July. An excellent sea-side plant. Grows in dry saltfields in Siberia. S.E. Russia, C. and S.W. Asia. I. 1779.

HAMAMELIS—Hamamelidaceae—"Witch Hazel". A most distinct and beautiful genus of mainly winter flowering shrubs or small trees. In the majority, the spider-like yellow or reddish flowers appear on the normally leafless branches from December to March. The curious strap-shaped petals withstand the severest weather without injury, and the hazel-like foliage usually gives attractive autumn colour.

Size of flower
- Large—over 3cm. (1¼in.) across
- Medium—2 to 3cm. (¾ to 1¼in.) across
- Small—up to 2cm. (¾in.) across

× **intermedia** REHD. (*japonica* × *mollis*). Large shrubs of variable nature generally intermediate between the parents. Leaves often large particularly on vigorous shoots. Flowers medium to large, rarely strongly scented, with petals somewhat folded and crimpled, appearing from December to March. All the following clones have arisen in cultivation.

'Adonis'. See '*Ruby Glow*'.

'Allgold'. Leaves varying from elliptic to obovate-orbicular. Flowers deep yellow with reddish calyces, forming thick clusters on the ascending branches. Autumn colour yellow.

'Carmine Red' (*japonica 'Carmine Red'*). A strong growing clone of somewhat spreading habit, raised in our nurseries. Leaves large, almost round in shape with strongly oblique base, and dark shining green above. Flowers large, pale bronze, suffused copper at tips, appearing red. Autumn colour yellow.

'Copper Beauty'. See '*Jelena*'.

'Diane'. Claimed by its raiser to be one of the best red-flowered seedlings yet raised, and superior in this respect to '*Ruby Glow*'. The large leaves colour richly in autumn. Originated in the Kalmthout Arboretum, Belgium. A.M. 1969.

'Feuerzauber'. See '*Magic Fire*'.

'Hiltingbury' (*japonica 'Hiltingbury'*). A large shrub of spreading habit, raised in our nurseries. The large leaves give brilliant autumn autumn tints of orange, scarlet and red. Flowers medium to large, pale copper, suffused red.

'Jelena' ('*Copper Beauty*'). A superb clone of vigorous spreading habit. Leaves large, broad and softly hairy. Flowers large, in dense clusters, yellow suffused a rich coppery-red, appearing orange. Lovely autumn colours of orange, red and scarlet. Raised at Kalmthout Arboretum, Belgium, and named after a great gardener, Jelena de Belder. A.M. 1955.

'Magic Fire' ['*Feuerzauber*']. A vigorous clone with strong ascending branches, and large rounded leaves. Flowers medium to large, bright coppery-orange suffused red.

'Moonlight'. A large shrub with ascending branches. Flowers medium to large, petals folded and crimpled, pale sulphur-yellow with a claret-red tinge at base; scent strong and sweet. As effective a shrub as *H. mollis 'Pallida'*, but differing from this clone in its narrower, more crimpled and paler petals. Autumn colour yellow.

'Ruby Glow' (*japonica 'Rubra Superba'*) ('*Adonis*'). A strong-growing cultivar of somewhat erect habit. Flowers coppery-red. Rich autumn colour.

japonica SIEB. & ZUCC. "Japanese Witch Hazel". A variable species, commonly a large spreading shrub. Leaves generally obovate or somewhat diamond-shaped, smaller than those of *H. mollis* and becoming glabrous and shining. Flowers small to medium with much twisted and crimpled petals, appearing from December to March. Rich autumn colour. Japan. I. 1862.

HAMAMELIS—*continued*

japonica 'Arborea'. A tall-growing form occasionally making a small wide-spreading tree. The almost horizontal arrangement of the branches is most characteristic. Flowers normally small but plentifully produced in dense clusters, rich deep yellow with red calyces; sweet scent but faint. Autumn colour yellow. F.C.C. 1881.

'Carmine Red'. See *H.* ×*intermedia 'Carmine Red'*.

flavopurpurascens REHD. A large shrub developing in time a spreading habit similar to *H. japonica 'Arborea'*. Flowers small to medium, sulphur-yellow suffused red at base. Autumn colour yellow. Japan.

'Hiltingbury'. See *H.* ×*intermedia 'Hiltingbury'*.

'Rubra Superba'. See *H.* ×*intermedia 'Ruby Glow'*.

'Sulphurea'. A large, spreading shrub with ascending branches. Flowers small to medium, petals much crimpled and curved, pale sulphur yellow; scent sweet but faint. Autumn colour yellow. A.M. 1958.

'Zuccariniana'. A large shrub distinctly erect in growth, at least in the young stage, but flattening out later. Flowers small, pale sulphur-yellow, with greenish-brown calyces; scent variously described as sweet to pungent. One of the latest witch hazels to flower, usually in March. Autumn colour yellow. F.C.C. 1891.

macrophylla PURSH. A rare species closely allied to *H. virginiana* of which it is sometimes regarded as a variety. A large shrub or small tree. Leaves obovate, sinuately lobed in the upper half, bright green, turning a startling butter-yellow in autumn. Flowers small to medium, with narrow, crimpled, pale yellow petals, normally opening in December or January, or earlier if the weather permits. S.E. United States. I. 1828.

mollis OLIV. "Chinese Witch Hazel". Perhaps the handsomest of all witch hazels and certainly the most popular. A large shrub with large, softly hairy, rounded leaves and clusters of large, sweetly fragrant, golden-yellow, broad-petalled flowers from December to March. Autumn colour yellow. China. First introduced by C. Maries in 1879 (see *'Coombe Wood'*) and much later by E. H. Wilson. F.C.C. 1918. A.G.M. 1922.

'Aurantiaca'. See *'Brevipetala'*.

'Brevipetala' (*'Aurantiaca'*). An upright form with rounded, softly hairy leaves which are characteristically glaucous beneath, and thick clusters of deep yellow, short-petalled flowers, appearing orange from a distance. Scent heavy and sweet. Autumn colour yellow. A.M. 1960.

'Coombe Wood'. A choice form more spreading in habit than the type and with slightly larger flowers. Scent strong and sweet. Autumn colour yellow. The original form introduced by C. Maries in 1879.

'Goldcrest'. A selected form with large flowers of a rich golden yellow suffused claret red at base. The red suffusion occurs also on the backs of the rolled petals in bud creating a characteristic orange cluster effect. Scent strong and sweet. Generally later flowering than other *H. mollis* clones. Autumn colour yellow. A.M. 1961.

'Pallida'. Deservedly one of the most popular witch hazels. The large, sulphur-yellow flowers are borne in densely crowded clusters along the naked stems. Scent strong and sweet, but delicate. Autumn colour yellow. A.M. 1932. F.C.C. 1958. A.G.M. 1960.

vernalis SARG. "Ozark Witch Hazel". A medium sized to large shrub producing tall, erect stems. The flowers though very small are produced in large quantities during January and February, varying in colour from pale yellow to red, but generally of a pale orange or copper. The scent is heavy and pungent, but not unpleasant. Autumn tints usually butter yellow. Central U.S.A. I. 1908.

'Red Imp'. A selection with petals claret-red at base, paling to copper at tips. Calyces claret-red. Originated in our nurseries in 1966.

'Sandra'. Young unfolding leaves suffused plum-purple, becoming green and purple flushed on undersides. In autumn the whole bush ignites into orange, scarlet and red. Flower petals cadmium-yellow. Originated in our nurseries in 1962. A.M. 1976.

'Squib'. A selection with petals of cadmium yellow; calyces green. Originated in our nurseries in 1966.

tomentella REHD. Leaves glaucescent and pubescent beneath.

HAMAMELIS—*continued*

virginiana L. The commercial source of "Witch Hazel". A large shrub, occasionally a small broad crowned tree. Often used as an understock for the larger flowered witch hazels but produces lovely golden yellow autumn tints and myriads of small to medium-sized yellow flowers from September to November. Scent sweet but faint. Eastern N. America. I. 1736.

HARTIA sinensis. See *STEWARTIA pteropetiolata.*

"HAWTHORN". See *CRATAEGUS monogyna* and *C. oxyacantha.*

"HAZEL". See *CORYLUS.*

"HEATH". See *ERICA.*

"HEATH, CONNEMARA". See *DABOECIA cantabrica.*

"HEATHER". See *CALLUNA.*

"HEATHER, BELL". See *ERICA cinerea.*

"HEATHER, GOLDEN". See *CASSINIA fulvida.*

"HEATHER, SILVER". See *CASSINIA vauvilliersii albida.*

***HEBE** (*VERONICA* in part)—**Scrophulariaceae**—Evergreen shrubs, formerly included under *VERONICA*. All but a few are native of New Zealand. They are ornamental spring to autumn flowering shrubs and are invaluable for seaside and industrial planting. Most of those which do not thrive inland may be safely planted along the south and west coasts, even in exposed places where few other shrubs will survive. They will succeed in all types of well-drained soil. Flowers white unless otherwise stated.

albicans CKN. A very splendid, dwarf, dense, rounded, glaucous shrub. Perfectly hardy in our arboretum.

†**'Alicia Amherst'** (*'Veitchii'*) (*'Royal Purple'*). A magnificent *Speciosa* hybrid. A small shrub with long racemes of deep purple-blue flowers in late summer.

†×**andersonii** CKN. (*salicifolia*×*speciosa*). A vigorous shrub to 1·8m. Leaves about 10cm. long. Long racemes of soft-lavender-blue flowers, fading to white; August to September. C. 1845.

'Variegata'. A very attractive form with leaves broadly margined and splashed creamy-white.

angustifolia. See *H. parviflora angustifolia.*

anomala CKN. A compact, slow-growing shrub up to 1·5m., with small, bright green crowded leaves. Flowers June to July. Probably a form of the variable *H. odora.* I. 1883. A.M. 1891.

'Aoira'. See *H. recurva.*

armstrongii CKN. & ALLAN. A dwarf "whipcord" species with erect densely branched stems of an olive-green colour, sometimes yellow-tinged at tips. Flowers appearing in July and August. The plant commonly grown under this name in gardens is *H. ochracea.* A.M. 1925 (possibly to *H. ochracea*).

'Compacta'. See under *H. propinqua.*

'Autumn Glory'. A small shrub of loose habit. Flowers intense violet, borne continuously in short dense racemes in late summer and autumn. A.G.M. 1969.

balfouriana CKN. A dwarf shrub of compact growth with small, obovate, pointed, yellowish-green leaves, purple-edged in bud, densely crowding the dark coloured stems. Flowers purplish-blue during summer. Raised at Edinburgh Botanic Garden from New Zealand seed. It is believed to be a hybrid of *H. vernicosa* with perhaps *H. pimeleoides.*

'Bowles' Hybrid'. A charming, dwarf shrub for the rock garden. The flowers, both in spring and summer, crowd the short branches in pretty, mauve-coloured racemes. Moderately hardy.

brachysiphon SUMMERHAYES (*traversii* HORT. not CKN. & ALLAN). A popular shrub growing 1·5m. high or sometimes considerably more, and flowering profusely in June or July. I. 1868.

'White Gem'. A hardy compact shrub rarely above ·5m. high, producing a profusion of white flowers in June.

buchananii CKN. & ALLAN. A dwarf shrub with tiny, rounded, leathery, closely imbricated leaves. Flowers June and July. Suitable for the rock garden.

HEBE—*continued*

buxifolia CKN. & ALLAN. A small, erect shrub with rich green polished leaves and small white flowers; June to July. Probably a form of the variable *H. odora.*

patens CHEESEM. (*myrtifolia* HORT.). A dense, erect branched shrub attaining about ·3m., with small, polished green, imbricated leaves.

canterburiensis MOORE. A dwarf shrub forming a neat, rounded hummock covered by short racemes of white flowers in June to July. I. 1910.

'Carl Teschner' (*elliptica* × *pimeleiodes*). A hardy, dwarf, summer-flowering shrub of compact habit with small leaves and abundantly produced, short racemes of violet flowers with a white throat; June to July. A splendid free-growing ground cover. Garden origin. A.M. 1964. A.G.M. 1969.

†**'Carnea'.** An attractive shrub growing about 1·2m. high, with long racemes of rose-pink flowers which fade to white, produced plentifully from May to late summer. A.M. 1925.

carnosula CKN. (*pinguifolia carnosula*). Dwarf to prostrate in habit; leaves small, glaucous, shell-like. Flowers white; July to August. Suitable for the rock garden. Possibly of hybrid origin.

ciliolata CKN. & ALLAN. A miniature shrublet with congested, greyish-green stems and closely imbricated leaves.

colensoi 'Glauca'. A dense-habited shrub with attractive glaucous-blue foliage; height .6 to 1m. Flowers July to August.

†**cookiana** CKN. & ALLAN. Small, dense floriferous shrub with elliptic fleshy leaves and long dense racemes of white, mauve-tinged, flowers from August to October.

cupressoides CKN. & ALLAN. Normally a small shrub, but occasionally reaching as much as 2m., of very distinct appearance. The long, slender, green or grey branches are remarkably like those of a *Cupressus*. Flowers small, pale blue, produced quite freely in June and July. F.C.C. 1894.

darwiniana. See *H. glaucophylla.*

†**dieffenbachii** CKN. & ALLAN. A small, wide-spreading, irregular shrub with long, lance-shaped leaves distinctly tiered. Flowers lilac-purple, in long showy racemes in September. Chatham Islands.

× **divergens** CKN. (possibly *H. elliptica* × *gracillima*). Forms a neat, rounded shrub to 1·2m., well characterised by its short, elliptic-oblong, flat-spreading leaves, and dense racemes of white or pale lilac flowers with violet anthers.

'Edinensis' (*muscoidea* HORT.). A charming, dwarf shrub suitable for the rock garden. Leaves tiny, bright green, imbricated. Originated in 1904.

elliptica FORST. (*decussata*) (*magellanica*). A rare, small to medium-sized shrub with oval or obovate, pale green leaves, downy at the margins. Flowers comparatively large, white, fragrant, borne in racemes. New Zealand, Chile, Tierra del Fuego, Falkland Isles. I. 1776.

epacridea CKN. & ALLAN. A tiny, conifer-like shrublet, densely clothed with recurved scale-like leaves. Flowers white in short terminal racemes in July. A miniature carpeting evergreen suitable for the rock garden or scree. I. 1860.

'Ettrick Shepherd'. A small, moderately hardy hybrid with violet-coloured flowers in long racemes.

× **franciscana** SOUSTER (*elliptica* × *speciosa*) (*lobelioides*). A first rate and most popular hybrid. We offer the following clones:—

'Blue Gem'. A small, compact dome-shaped shrub producing dense racemes of bright blue flowers. One of the hardiest hebes and resistant to salt-laden winds. This is perhaps the most commonly planted *Hebe* and is hardy anywhere along the English coast, except in the very coldest areas. Excellent for low hedges. Raised at Edinburgh before 1862. F.C.C. 1869.

'Variegata'. Leaves broadly edged with creamy-white.

gibbsii CKN. & ALLAN. A dwarf shrub, the stout branches almost hidden by the comparatively large, glaucous, reflexed leaves which are noticeably ciliate and densely arranged in four ranks. Flowers white, produced in short, dense racemes during late summer. An easily recognised species, rare both in the wild and in cultivation.

glaucophylla CKN. (*darwiniana*). A small, bushy shrub with slender branches bearing small, narrow, greyish-green leaves. Flowers white, borne in slender racemes towards the ends of the branches in July and August. Usually found in gardens under the synonym.

HEBE—*continued*

glaucophylla 'Variegata' (*darwiniana 'Variegata'*). A small, neat-habited shrub with slender wiry shoots. Leaves greyish-green, margined creamy-white. A most attractive form.

†**'Gloriosa'** (*'Pink Pearl'*). A most attractive Speciosa hybrid. A small, compact shrub with bright pink flowers carried in conspicuous long racemes.

'Great Orme'. A compact bush to 1m. high. Leaves lance-shaped, 5 to 7·5cm. long. Flowers bright pink in long tapering racemes. Reasonably hardy. A.G.M. 1961.

haastii CKN. & ALLAN. A very hardy, dwarf species, its stems densely covered with small overlapping leaves. Flowers forming a terminal head; July to August.

†**'Headfortii'.** An attractive, purple-blue flowered Speciosa hybrid, growing about ·6 to 1m. high.

hectoris CKN. & ALLAN. An interesting hardy, dwarf shrub of erect habit, having thick rounded, stiffly cord-like branches thickly covered by yellowish-green closely adpressed leaves. Flowers white or pale pink in a crowded terminal head in July.

'Hielan Lassie'. A moderately hardy, compact, narrow-leaved shrub. Flowers rich blue-violet, in racemes 5 to 7·5cm. long, from July to September.

hulkeana CKN. & ALLAN. Perhaps the most beautiful species of *Hebe* in cultivation. A small shrub of loose habit occasionally reaching 1·8m. against a sheltered wall. Glossy green, toothed, ovate leaves and large panicles of delicate lavender-blue flowers in May and June. It survived uninjured at Winchester the severe winter of 1962-63. I. about 1860. F.C.C. 1882.

insularis CKN. & ALLAN. Dwarf shrub, resembling *H. diosmifolia*, but differing in its rather broader, somewhat oblong leaves, and less densely branched inflorescence. Flowers pale lavender-blue in June and July.

×**kirkii** CKN. & ALLAN (*salicifolia kirkii*). One of the hardiest of large-flowered *Hebes*, similar to *H. salicifolia* but with shorter leaves. A hybrid of *H. salicifolia*, possibly with *H. rakaiensis*.

†**'La Seduisante'** (*'Diamant'*). A very attractive Speciosa hybrid. A small shrub with large bright crimson racemes of flowers. A.M. 1897.

†**lavaudiana** CKN. & ALLAN. A small shrublet closely related to *H. hulkeana*, but with smaller leaves. Inflorescence a compact corymb of spikes. Flowers lilac-pink in May. I. 1880.

leiophylla CKN. & ALLAN. One of the hardiest of the New Zealand species forming a shrub about 1·2m. high. Leaves narrow, resembling those of *H. parviflora*. Flowers in 10cm. long racemes in July and August.

×**lewisii** ARMSTR. (*elliptica* × *salicifolia*). A small to medium sized shrub of erect habit. Pale blue flowers are borne in 5 to 6·5cm. racemes at the end of the stems; July and August.

'Lindsayi' (*amplexicaulis* × *pimeleoides*). A very hardy shrub to about 1m. high and of equal width. Leaves rather rotund; flowers pink in short conspicuous racemes.

loganioides J. B. ARMST. (*selaginoides* HORT.). A dwarf shrublet only a few inches high, its slender stems clothed with tiny, spreading, scale-like leaves. Flowers white, borne in short terminal racemes during summer. A peculiar, almost conifer-like plant which may well be of hybrid origin.

lycopodioides CKN. & ALLAN. A dwarf shrub with slender, erect four-sided stems of a yellow-green colour. Leaves scale-like, with a sharp horn-like point, densely clothing the branches. Flowers white in July. F.C.C. 1894.

'MacEwanii' (*pimeleoides* × ?). A dwarf shrub with glaucous foliage and blue flowers.

†**macrantha** CKN. & ALLAN. A very valuable dwarf shrub, noteworthy on account of its leathery, toothed leaves, and its pure white flowers which are as much as 2cm. across. A.M. 1952.

macroura. See *H. stricta macroura*.

'Marjorie'. A shrub of remarkable hardiness for a *Hebe*. Forms a neat bush about 1m. high, and produces racemes 5 to 7·5cm. long of light violet and white flowers from July to September.

matthewsii CKN. An erect growing shrub to 1·2m. Leaves thick, and leathery, oblong or oval; flowers white or pale purple in July, in racemes 5 to 10cm. long. A.M. 1927.

HEBE—*continued*

'Midsummer Beauty'. A handsome small shrub with conspicuous reddish underside to the leaves. Flowers in long lavender racemes throughout summer. Moderately hardy. A.M. 1960. F.C.C. 1975.

'Mrs. E. Tennant'. A comparatively hardy small shrub. Flowers light violet, in racemes 7·5 to 12·5cm. long, from July to September.

'Mrs. Winder'. A small to medium sized, moderately hardy hybrid with purple foliage and bright blue flowers. A.M. 1978.

muscoidea. See *H. 'Edinensis'*.

ochracea M. B. ASHWIN. A dwarf, densely branched shrub with erect, glossy cord-like stems of a characteristic ochre or old gold colour. Flowers appearing in July and August. This plant is commonly found in gardens under the name *H. armstrongii* which differs in its greener branches and its sharply keeled and pointed leaves.

odora CKN. A small to medium sized shrub with crowded leaves and white flowers during summer. Extremely variable. Both *H. anomala* and *H. buxifolia* probably belong here.

†**parviflora** CKN. & ALLAN (*arborea*). An erect-branched shrub to about 1·5m., but considerably taller in its native habitat. Leaves long and narrow; flowers white, tinged lilac-pink in July and August. I. 1822.

angustifolia MOORE. A variety with linear, grass-like leaves and purple-brown stems.

pimeleoides 'Glaucocaerulea'. A semi-prostrate shrub with small, glaucous-blue leaves and pale lavender flowers; June and July.

minor CKN. & ALLAN. A minute shrub forming loose mounds 5 to 7·5cm. high, the slender stems clothed with narrow glaucous leaves 5mm. long. A choice little plant for the scree or trough.

pinguifolia carnosula. See *H. carnosula*.

'Pagei' (*Veronica pageana*). Wide mats of small, glaucous-grey leaves which are attractive throughout the year. The small white flowers are borne in quantity in May. Excellent ground cover or rock garden plant. A.M. 1958. A.G.M. 1969.

propinqua CKN. & ALLAN. A dwarf, many-branched shrublet forming a low mound of rounded, green or yellowish green, thread-like stems. Sometimes found in gardens, quite wrongly, under the names *H. armstrongii 'Compacta'* and *H. salicornioides 'Aurea'*.

†**'Purple Queen'.** An outstanding Speciosa hybrid. A small shrub with large racemes of purple flowers. A.M. 1893.

rakaiensis CKN. (*subalpina* HORT.). A dwarf shrub forming dense, compact mounds of crowded stems bearing small, neat, pale green leaves. Flowers white, borne in short, crowded racemes in June and July. A splendid ground cover in full sun. Usually found in gardens wrongly as *H. subalpina*. A.G.M. 1973.

raoulii CKN. & ALLAN. A dwarf shrub with spathulate leaves which are toothed and often reddish at the margins. Flowers lavender or almost white, borne in crowded terminal spikes during summer.

recurva SIMP. & THOM. (*'Aoira'*). A small, slender-branched shrub of open, rounded habit up to 1m. Leaves narrow, lanceolate, glaucous above. Flowers white, in slender racemes. The clone in general cultivation has in the past been referred to as *'Aoira'*. A.M. 1972.

salicifolia PENNELL. A medium sized shrub for maritime districts. Leaves lanceolate, bright green; flowers white, or lilac-tinged in long racemes; June to August. Withstands most winters with only superficial injury. A parent of many hybrids.

'Spender's Seedling'. A small, very hardy, free-flowering shrub. Its fragrant white flowers are produced over a long period. A.M. 1954.

'Variegata'. Leaves with creamy-white margins.

salicornioides 'Aurea'. See under *H. propinqua*.

selaginoides. See *H. loganioides*.

†**'Simon Delaux'.** Small rounded shrub with rich crimson flowers in large racemes. One of the best of the Speciosa hybrids.

†**speciosa** R. CUNN. A small shrub of dense rounded habit with handsome leathery leaves and dark, reddish-purple flowers. Represented in cultivation by innumerable colourful hybrids and cultivars, many of which are only suitable for seaside gardens.

HEBE—*continued*

stricta macroura L. B. MOORE. Small shrub to 1·2m. with long, dense racemes of white flowers; leaves long, elliptic-lanceolate.

subalpina. See under *H. rakaiensis.*

subsimilis astonii M. B. ASHWIN. Miniature, much branched shrublet forming a compact hummock of thin, rounded green stems.

tetrasticha CKN. & ALLAN. A miniature shrublet forming tiny patches of green, four-sided stems, thickly clothed with the closely adpressed scale-like leaves.

traversii HORT. See *H. brachysiphon.*

venustula L. B. MOORE (*laevis*). Dwarf or small shrub forming a rounded hummock. The small 1·25cm. long, yellowish-green leaves have a thin yellowish margin. Flowers white in short racemes crowding the branches in summer.

'Waikiki'. A moderately hardy shrub of medium size with bluish flowers. The young growths are bronze tinted.

HEDYSARUM—Leguminosae—A large genus of easily grown perennials and shrubs.

multijugum MAXIM. A small Mongolian shrub of lax habit with sea green pinnate leaves and producing long racemes of rose-purple, pea-flowers throughout summer. I. 1883. A.M. 1898.

HEIMIA (*NESAEA*)—**Lythraceae**—A small genus of shrubs or herbs related to the familiar "Loosestrife".

salicifolia LINK. An interesting shrub attaining 1·2m. Leaves narrow; flowers yellow, 1·25cm. across, produced in the leaf axils from July to September. N. and S. America. I. 1821.

***HELIANTHEMUM—Cistaceae**—"Rock Rose"; "Sun Rose". Evergreen shrubs of dwarf habit, producing multitudes of flowers in brilliant colours throughout summer. They are excellent for dry, sunny situations.

The many colourful forms generally seen in cultivation are mainly hybrids and cultivars of a group of three species—*H. apenninum, H. nummularium* and *H. croceum.* Between them they have produced a great variety of silver and green leaved plants with flowers ranging in colour from orange, yellow or white, to rose, red and scarlet, both single and double. See under *nummularium.* See also *CISTUS,* ×*HALIMIOCISTUS* and *HALIMIUM.*

algarvense. See *HALIMIUM ocymoides.*

alpestre DC. A very dwarf species with grey-green foliage and bright yellow flowers in June and July. Mts. ot S. and C. Europe. I. 1818. A.M.T. 1925.

apenninum MILL. "White Rockrose". A dwarf shrublet forming mats of slender, spreading shoots crowded with narrow, grey leaves. Flowers white with a yellow eye, borne in profusion from May to July. W. and S. Europe. A rare native species found only in two localities, one in Devon another in Somerset.

" roseum SCHNEID. (*H. rhodanthum*). An attractive dwarf form with hoary foliage and silvery-rose flowers.

canadense MICHX. (*Crocanthemum canadense*). A rare dwarf shrublet with downy stems and small, alternate leaves, greyish-tomentose beneath. Flowers bright yellow, usually solitary in the leaf axils during early summer. Of little ornamental merit, this rare species is being grown by us mainly because of its importance in medical research. We are indebted to Dr. Henry Skinner of the National Arboretum, Washington, for locating this plant in the wild and sending us some seeds. Eastern U.S.A. C. 1825.

chamaecistus. See *H. nummularium.*

clusii. See ×*HALIMIOCISTUS 'Ingwersenii'.*

lunulatum DC. A dainty, cushion-like alpine with yellow flowers having a small orange spot at the base of each petal; June to July. Italy. A.G.M. 1973.

nummularium MILL. (*chamaecistus*) (*vulgare*). The following is a select list of the cultivars and hybrids of this, the "Common Sun Rose". Splendid ground cover plants for full sun and poor dry soil. Europe (incl. British Isles).

'Afflick'. Bright deep-orange-bronze, with bronze-copper centre; foliage green.

'Amy Baring'. Deep buttercup-yellow; dwarf, compact habit; foliage green. A.G.M. 1969.

'Ben Dearg'. Deep copper-orange, with darker centre; foliage green.

'Ben Fhada'. Golden yellow, with orange centre; foliage grey-green. A.G.M. 1969.

'Ben Hope'. Carmine, with deep orange centre; foliage light grey-green. A.G.M. 1969.

HELIANTHEMUM—*continued*

'Ben Ledi'. Bright, deep tyrian-rose; foliage dark green.

'Ben More'. Bright, rich orange, with darker centre; foliage dark green.

'Ben Nevis'. Deep buttercup-yellow, with conspicuous bronze-crimson central zone; foliage green. A.M. 1924. A.M.T. 1924.

'Coppernob'. Deep glowing copper, with bronze-crimson centre, foliage grey-green.

'Golden Queen'. Bright golden-yellow; foliage green.

'Jock Scott'. Bright, deep rose-cerise, with darker centre; foliage green.

'Jubilee'. Drooping, primrose yellow, double; foliage green. A.G.M. 1969. A.M.T. 1970.

'Mrs. Croft'. Pink, suffused orange; foliage silver-grey.

'Mrs. C. W. Earle'. Scarlet, with yellow basal flush, double; foliage dark green. A.G.M. 1969.

'Red Dragon'. Scarlet, with yellow centre; foliage green.

'Rhodanthe Carneum'. Pale rhodamine-pink, with orange centre; foliage silver-grey.

'Rose of Leeswood'. Rose-pink, double; foliage green.

'Snowball'. Creamy-white, with pale yellow centre; double; foliage green.

'Supreme'. Crimson; foliage grey-green.

'The Bride'. Creamy-white, with bright yellow centre; foliage silver-grey. A.M. 1924. A.M.T. 1924. A.G.M. 1969.

'Watergate Rose'. Rose-crimson, with orange tinged centre; foliage grey-green. A.M.T. 1932. A.G.M. 1969.

'Wisley Primrose'. Primrose-yellow, with deeper yellow centre; foliage light grey-green. A.G.M. 1969. A.M.T. 1970.

rhodanthum. See *H. apenninum roseum.*

rosmarinifolium. See *HALIMIUM libanotis.*

vulgare. See *H. nummularium.*

***HELICHRYSUM—Compositae**—The shrubby members of this extensive, widely distributed genus provide some interesting, mainly low-growing, often aromatic plants with attractive foliage. Most are reasonably hardy given full sun and well drained poor soil.

angustifolium. See *H. serotinum.*

antennarium. See *OZOTHAMNUS antennaria.*

diosmifolium. See *OZOTHAMNUS thyrsoideus.*

ericeteum. See *OZOTHAMNUS ericifolius.*

italicum G. DON (*rupestre* HORT.). A variable species. The form we offer is proving hardy here, and is a superb, dwarf shrub with long, narrow grey leaves and terminal, long-stalked clusters of bright yellow flower heads during summer. One of the best of all silvery-grey shrubs. Mediterranean region. Plants we have received under the name *H. rupestre* belong here.

ledifolium. See *OZOTHAMNUS ledifolius.*

†petiolatum D. DON. A dwarf, often trailing shrublet with white woolly stems and long-stalked, ovate grey woolly leaves. Flowers yellow in late summer. Normally a tender species but may overwinter in the milder areas if given good drainage and overhead protection. S. Africa.

†plicatum DC. (*anatolicum*). An attractive, dwarf, silvery-white shrub, with long, narrow, downy leaves and terminal clusters of bright yellow flowers in July. S.E. Europe. I. 1877.

rosmarinifolium. See *OZOTHAMNUS rosmarinifolius.*

rupestre HORT. See *H. italicum.*

†scutellifolium BENTH. A curious dwarf, Tasmanian species. Slender, antler-like shoots clothed with white down through which the circular, grey-green, appressed leaves peep. Flowers yellow in terminal clusters. A plant for the rock garden.

†selago BENTH. & HOOK. f. not KIRK. A dwarf shrublet of variable growth. The slender, erect or ascending stems are rather stiffly held and much branched. The tiny, green, scale-like leaves are closely adpressed to the stems. They are smooth on the outside, but coated white on the inside, and give the stems a chequered appearance. New Zealand. A plant for the rock garden or alpine house.

'Major'. A more robust selection with thicker stems and larger leaves.

serotinum BOISS. (*angustifolium*). "Curry Plant". Dense, dwarf shrub with narrow, sage-green leaves with a strong curry-like smell. Heads of yellow flowers in mid-summer. S. Europe.

HELICHRYSUM—*continued*

splendidum LESS. (*triliniatum* HORT. not DC.) (*aveolatum* HORT. not DC.). A small, globular shrub to about 1m. Leaves silvery grey, with three longitudinal ridges. The everlasting flowers remain a good yellow into the New Year. One of the very few South African plants hardy in the home counties.

†**stoechas** DC. "Goldilocks". A dwarf shrub. Leaves silvery-white; flowers bright yellow, in corymbs during summer. S. Europe. C. 1629.

thyrsoideum. See *OZOTHAMNUS thyrsoideus.*

triliniatum HORT. See *H. splendidum.*

HELWINGIA—**Cornaceae**—A small genus of three species, interesting on account of the peculiar position of the insignificant flowers which due to the fusion of the pedicel with the petiole and leaf midrib, appear on the upper surface of the leaf.

japonica F. G. DIETR. (*rusciflora*). A small shrub, bearing its pale green flowers, and later its black berries, upon the upper surface of the leaves. Japan. I. 1830.

HEMIPTELEA—**Ulmaceae**—A monotypic genus closely related to *Zelkova* but differing in its spiny branches and winged fruits.

davidii PLANCH. A small, dense, shrubby tree with spine-tipped branchlets and oval, toothed leaves. China; Korea. I. 1908.

"HERCULES' CLUB". See *OPLOPANAX horridus.*

HESPERALOE. See under *YUCCA.*

HESPEROYUCCA whipplei. See *YUCCA whipplei.*

†***HETEROMELES**—**Rosaceae**—A monotypic genus formerly included in *Photinia.*

arbutifolia M. ROEM. (*Photinia arbutifolia*). "Christmas Berry"; "Tollon". A large shrub in favoured areas. Leaves thick and leathery, lanceolate to obovate, 5 to 10cm. long. Flowers white, produced in flattened terminal panicles in late summer. Fruits bright red, like haws. California. I. 1796.

HIBISCUS—**Malvaceae**—Of this extensive genus, few are hardy in our climate, but of these the following provide us, in favourable seasons, with some of the most effective late summer and early autumn flowering shrubs. They need full sun.

†**hamabo** SIEB. & ZUCC. Small to medium-sized shrub with neatly-toothed, rounded leaves, stellate hairy above, densely so beneath. Flowers yellow, with a dark red eye; July and August. Only possible in the mildest gardens. Japan, Korea.

sinosyriacus L. H. BAILEY. A very handsome, vigorous species making a medium sized to large shrub. The leaves are broader than those of *H. syriacus* and are sage-green in colour. The flowers, too, are slightly larger, and the petals thicker, appearing September and October or until the frosts. It enjoys similar conditions to *H. syriacus* but is best in a really warm, sunny sheltered position. C. China. Introduced by Hillier and Sons in 1936.

It is variable in habit and colour and is available in the following clones:—

'Autumn Surprise'. Petals white with attractively feathered cerise base.
'Lilac Queen'. Petals white, flushed lilac with garnet-red base.
'Ruby Glow'. Petals white with a cerise base.

syriacus L. Given a position in full sun and a favourable season, no late-flowering shrub is more beautiful than this shrubby "Mallow". The large, trumpet-shaped flowers open in succession between July and October according to the season. It is generally seen as a medium to large sized shrub, occasionally a small tree. E. Asia. It is not known when this species was introduced into cultivation but it existed in England in the late 16th century. A.G.M. 1934.

Many clones are in cultivation of which we offer the following:—

'Ardens'. Pale rosy-purple with maroon blotch at base; double, large. Erect, compact habit, spreading later. *'Caeruleus Plenus'* is a similar clone.
'Blue Bird' ['Oisseau Bleu']. Violet-blue with a darker eye; single. The best single blue, an improvement on *'Coelestis'*. A.M. 1965. A.G.M. 1969.
'Caeruleus Plenus'. See under *'Ardens'*.
'Coelestis'. Light violet blue with reddish base; single. A.M. 1897.
'Duc de Brabant'. Deep rose-purple; double.

HIBISCUS—*continued*

'Elegantissimus'. See *'Lady Stanley'*.

'Hamabo'. Pale blush with crimson eye; single, large. One of the best of the cultivars. A.M. 1935. A.G.M. 1969.

'Jeanne d'Arc'. White; semi-double.

'Lady Stanley' (*'Elegantissimus'*). White, shaded blush pink with maroon base; almost double.

'Meehanii'. Lilac-mauve with maroon eye; single. Leaves with an irregular creamy-white margin.

'Monstrosus'. White with maroon centre; single.

'Monstrosus Plenus'. Similar in colour to *'Monstrosus'* but double.

'Puniceus Plenus'. See under *'Violet Clair Double'*.

'Roseus Plenus'. See under *'Violet Clair Double'*.

'Snowdrift'. White; single. Large and early flowering. A.M. 1911. *'Totus Albus'* is scarcely different.

'Totus Albus'. See under *'Snowdrift'*.

'Violet Clair Double' (*'Violaceus Plenus'*). Wine-purple, deep reddish-purple at base within; double. *'Puniceus Plenus'* and *'Roseus Plenus'* are scarcely different.

'William R. Smith'. Pure white; single, large. A.G.M. 1969.

'Woodbridge'. Rich rose-pink with carmine centre; single, large. The best single red, an improvement on *'Rubis'*. A.M. 1937. A.G.M. 1969.

"HICKORY". See *CARYA*.

HIPPOPHAE—Elaeagnaceae—A genus of three species of hardy shrubs or small trees with slender, willow-like, silvery or sage-green leaves. Attractive orange berries are produced on female plants. Excellent wind resisters for maritime exposure.

rhamnoides L. "Sea Buckthorn". A tall shrub, sometimes a small tree, succeeding in almost any soil. Attractive in summer with its narrow, silvery leaves, and in winter with its orange-yellow berries which contain an intensely acrid yellow juice, which are normally avoided by birds, although pheasants are said to eat them. Plant in groups to contain both sexes. Europe (incl. British Isles), Temperate Asia. A.M. 1944.

salicifolia D. DON. A rare species making a small to medium sized tree. Differing from *H. rhamnoides* in its taller habit, pendulous branches which are less spiny and its sage green leaves. Himalaya. I. 1822.

HOHERIA—Malvaceae—A beautiful New Zealand genus of floriferous, mid to late summer flowering shrubs or small trees belonging to the "Mallow" family. All have white flowers. The evergreen species need a specially selected site, or wall protection except in mild districts. The leaves of juvenile plants are often deeply toothed and lobed and are smaller than those of adult plants.

***angustifolia** RAOUL (*microphylla*). An elegant, slender, small tree with roundish to narrowly lanceolate leaves up to 5cm. long. Juvenile plants are dense and bushy with slender interlacing branches and minute, obovate, shallowly-toothed leaves. Flowers 1·25cm. across. A.M. 1967.

glabrata SPRAGUE & SUMMERH. (*Gaya lyallii* KIRK) (*Plagianthus lyallii* HOOK. f.). A magnificent large shrub or small tree, possibly a little hardier than *H. lyallii*. In June and July its flexible branches are bent with the weight of masses of fragrant, almost translucent, white flowers. A.M. 1911. F.C.C. 1946.

'Glory of Amlwch' (*glabrata* × *sexstylosa*). A large shrub or small tree, retaining its foliage during mild winters. Flowers of pure white, 3·75cm. across, densely crowded on the stems. Originated in the garden of Dr. Jones, Amlwch, Anglesey. A.M. 1960.

lyallii HOOK. f. (*Gaya lyallii* BAKER) (*Gaya lyallii ribifolia*) (*Plagianthus lyallii* GRAY). A beautiful but variable large shrub or small tree. The more or less glabrous juvenile leaves change to grey tomentose adult foliage. Clusters of cherry-like, white flowers crowd the branches in July, normally later than *H. glabrata*. A.G.M. 1926. A.M. 1955. F.C.C. 1964.

†*populnea A. CUNN. Beautiful large shrub or small tree with broadly ovate leaves; blooming in late summer or autumn. Flowers about 2cm. across, in dense clusters. A.M. 1912.

'Foliis Purpureis'. Leaves plum-purple on the lower surface. A.M. 1977.

lanceolata. See *H. sexstylosa*.

'Osbornei'. Flowers with blue stamens. Leaves purple tinged beneath.

'Variegata'. Leaves yellow-green, edged deep green.

HOHERIA—*continued*

†***sexstylosa** COL. (*populnea lanceolata*). This splendid floriferous, tall, vigorous shrub or small tree differs from *H. populnea* in its greater hardiness, more upright growth and narrower adult leaves. Those of young trees are extremely variable. F.C.C. 1924 (under the synonym). A.M. 1964.

'Crataegifolia'. The juvenile form with small, coarsely toothed leaves, maintained as a bush by vegetative propagation.

"HOLLY". See *ILEX*.

HOLODISCUS—Rosaceae—A small genus of hardy spiraea-like shrubs.

discolor MAXIM. (*Spiraea discolor*). A handsome and elegant North American shrub to 3·7m. high, blooming in July when its long, drooping, feathery panicles of creamy-white flowers are most conspicuous. Leaves greyish-white tomentose beneath. Introduced by David Douglas in 1827. A.G.M. 1949 (as *Spiraea discolor*). We grow the variety *ariifolius* which to all intents and purposes is the same. A.M. 1978.

"HONEY LOCUST". See *GLEDITSIA triancanthos*.

"HONEYSUCKLE". See *LONICERA*.

"HOP HORNBEAM". See *OSTRYA carpinifolia*.

"HOP TREE". See *PTELEA trifoliata*.

"HORNBEAM". See *CARPINUS*.

"HORSE CHESTNUT". See *AESCULUS hippocastanum*.

HOVENIA—Rhamnaceae—A small genus of trees and shrubs native of Eastern Asia.

dulcis THUNB. "Japanese Raisin Tree". A large shrub or small tree, native of China and the Himalaya, grown for its handsome, polished foliage. The fleshy, reddish branches of the inflorescences are edible. China. Cultivated in Japan and India. I. 1812.

HYDRANGEA—Hydrangeaceae—The numerous species, varieties and cultivars of this genus are easily cultivated, but all require generous treatment and resent dryness at the roots. For the larger leaved species some shade is essential. Summer and autumn is the flowering period unless otherwise stated.

The majority of species and their forms produce flowers in a flattened or dome-shaped terminal head. These heads are composed of flowers of two kinds. The majority are fertile and though coloured are rather small and often insignificant. The second type are sterile but possesses rather large, conspicuous, coloured sepals. These sterile flowers or ray-florets occur on the outside of the head and in some instances completely surround the fertile flowers, hence the popular name "Lace Cap". Some hydrangeas, in particular the Hortensia group of *H. macrophylla*, have flower heads which are composed entirely of ray-florets.

acuminata. See under *H. serrata 'Bluebird'*.

anomala. See under CLIMBERS.

arborescens L. A small shrub of loose bushy growth, with ovate, slender pointed, serrated leaves. Flowers in corymbs up to 15cm. across, bearing several long-stalked, creamy-white marginal ray florets. They are borne in succession from July to September. It differs from the related *H. cinerea* and *H. radiata* in the usually glabrous leaves. E. United States. I. 1736.

'Grandiflora'. The commonly cultivated form with large globular heads of creamy-white sterile florets. I. 1907. A.M. 1907. A.G.M. 1969.

aspera D. DON. A magnificent, but variable, large-leaved species of medium size covered in June and July with large heads of pale porcelain-blue flowers, with a ring of lilac-pink or white ray florets. Himalaya; W. and C. China; Formosa.

'Ayesha' (*'Silver Slipper'*). A most distinct and unusual hydrangea of puzzling origin. It is usually placed in the Hortensia group of *H. macrophylla* but its appearance is very different from the usual "mop-headed" hydrangea. The leaves are bold and glossy green above. The rather flattened dense heads are composed of thick petalled ,cup-shaped florets resembling those of a large lilac. They possess a faint but distinct fragrance and in colour are greyish-lilac or pink. A.M. 1974.

bretschneideri. See *H. heteromalla 'Bretschneideri'*.

chinensis MAXIM. A rare, small shrub with oval or lanceolate-oblong, denticulate leaves. Flowers produced in corymbs, composed of bluish fertile flowers and a few slender-stalked white ray florets. Requires a sheltered position. S.E. China; Formosa. C. 1934.

HYDRANGEA—*continued*

cinerea SMALL. A small, spreading shrub. Leaves grey tomentose beneath; flowers with a few white ray florets in corymbs in June and July. S.E. United States. I. 1908.

'Sterilis'. A form with globular heads of sterile creamy-white florets. Orig. before 1908.

dumicola W. W. SM. A large shrub, sometimes tree-like, with shoots rough to the touch. The large, ovate to ovate-lanceolate, pale green leaves are adpressed white pubescent beneath. Flowers white, borne in large flattened heads. Closely related to *H. xanthoneura*. W. China. C. 1934.

heteromalla D. DON. A medium sized Himalayan species resembling *H. bretschneideri*. The leaves are dark green above and whitish beneath. Flowers in broad corymbs, white, with conspicuous marginal ray florets. I. 1821.

'Bretschneideri' (*H. bretschneideri*). A medium sized July blooming species, with broad, flattened white lacecaps. Bark chestnut brown, exfoliating. Hardy in full exposure. China. I. about 1882.

'Snowcap'. A superb shrub of stately habit with large heart-shaped leaves and white flowers in large flattened corymbs 20 to 25cm. across. A hardy shrub, tolerant of wind, sun and drought. For many years this plant was grown by us under the name *H. robusta,* which species is now regarded as a ssp. of *H. aspera*. Although collected in the Himalaya our plant is sufficiently distinct and ornamental as to deserve the above clonal name.

hirta SIEB. A small, much-branched shrub with dark coloured stems and ovate, deeply-toothed leaves. Dense compact corymbs of blue-purple fertile flowers. Ray florets absent. Japan.

integerrima. See under CLIMBERS.

involucrata SIEB. A pretty, dwarf species. Flowers blue or rosy-lilac, surrounded by white or variously tinted ray florets. Japan; Formosa. C. 1864.

'Hortensis'. A remarkable and attractive form with double, creamy-white, florets which become rose tinted in the open. A.M. 1956.

longipes FRANCH. A medium-sized, spreading shrub of loose habit, remarkable in the genus for the length of the leaf-stalks. Flowers white, the outer ray florets as much as 4cm. across. W. China. I. 1901.

macrophylla SER. This name covers a large and varied group of hydrangeas, many of which are possibly of hybrid origin, and may be divided into two groups, namely the **Hortensias** and the **Lacecaps** (see below).

acuminata. See under *H. serrata 'Bluebird'*.

normalis WILS. (*normalis rosea*) (*maritima*). A small to medium-sized shrub producing flat corymbs of fertile flowers with a few pink, marginal ray florets. The wild form, a native of the coastal regions of Central Japan, first introduced by E. H. Wilson in 1917. See also *'Seafoam'* under Lacecaps below.

normalis rosea. See *H. macrophylla normalis*.

serrata. See *H. serrata*.

HORTENSIAS

The familiar mop-headed hydrangeas. Their average height in most gardens ranges from 1·2 to 1·8m. (4 to 6ft.), but in sheltered gardens and woodlands in mild localities some cultivars will reach as much as 3·5m. (10ft.). They are admirable for seaside planting and many are seen at their best in coastal gardens.

The florets are sterile, forming large globular heads of white, pink, red, blue or a combination of these colours which in some cultivars give a wonderful almost metallic lustre which creates, when dead, marvellous everlasting flowers for the floral artist.

In very shallow chalk soils *H. macrophylla* and its forms may become chlorotic; this can be counteracted by generous mulching and feeding. In all alkaline soils it is impossible to retain without treatment, the blue shades of colour. By treatment it is comparatively easy to control the colour of container-grown plants and plants in soils which are only slightly alkaline. Where its use is desirable Blueing Powder should be applied every seven or fourteen days during the growing season at the rate of 85gm. (3oz.) being dissolved in 13.5 litres (3 gallons) of water.

Thin out and cut back immediately after flowering (except in cold areas) old flowering shoots to within a few cm. of the old wood.

HYDRANGEA—*continued*

HORTENSIAS

'Altona'. Rose coloured; large florets. Blues well when treated. Best in shade. A.M. 1957.

'Ami Pasquier'. Deep red; dwarf habit. A.M. 1953.

'Ayesha'. See *H. 'Ayesha'*.

'Baardse's Favourite'. Rich pink; dwarf.

'Blue Prince' ['Blauer Prinz']. Rose-red; cornflower-blue when treated.

cyanoclada. See *'Nigra'*.

'Deutschland'. Deep pink; attractive autumn tints. A.M. 1927.

'Domotoi'. Loose irregular heads of large double, pale pink or blue florets.

'Europa'. Deep pink; large florets.

'Garten-Baudirektor Kuhnert'. Rose coloured; vivid blue if treated.

'Generale Vicomtesse de Vibraye'. Vivid rose; good blue when treated. A.M. 1947.

'Gertrude Glahn'. Deep pink to purple.

'Goliath'. Deep pink or purplish blue; very large florets in small heads. One of the finest cultivars for seaside gardens.

'Hamburg'. Deep rose or purplish; large florets.

'Heinrich Seidel'. Glowing red to purple; large, fringed florets. Best in semi-shade.

'Holstein'. Pink; sky-blue in acid soils. Free-flowering, large florets with serrated sepals.

'Joseph Banks'. A medium sized shrub of vigorous growth, of particular value for coastal planting. Very large heads which are cream at first, passing to pale pink or pale hyacinth blue. Said to be a branch sport of the wild Japanese type. Introduced via China in 1789.

'King George'. Rose-pink; large florets with serrated sepals. A.M. 1927.

'La France'. Phlox pink to mid-blue in huge heads.

'La Marne'. Pale pink or blue in enormous heads, sepals prettily feathered. Excellent by the sea.

'Loreley'. Carmine to deep blue; free flowering.

'Madame Emile Mouilliere'. Florets large, with serrated sepals; white, with pink or blue eye. Perhaps the best white cultivar and certainly one of the most popular. A.M. 1910.

'Mandshurica.' See *'Nigra'*.

'Marechal Foch'. Rich rosy-pink, purple to vivid deep gentian blue in an acid soil. Very free flowering. A.M. 1923.

'Miss Belgium'. Rosy-red; dwarf.

'Munster'. Florets violet, crimson or deep blue turning to bright autumn tints ot red and scarlet; dwarf.

'Niedersachsen'. Pale pink; good blue when treated. A.M. 1968.

'Nigra' (*cyanoclada*) (*'Mandshurica'*). A distinct cultivar with stems black or almost so; florets rose or occasionally blue. C. 1870. F.C.C. 1895.

'Queen Elizabeth'. A lovely shade of rose-pink. A cultivar which lends itself readily to blueing.

'Queen Emma'. Large heads of crimson.

'Silver Slipper'. See *H. 'Ayesha'*.

'Souvenir de Madame E. Chautard'. Clear pale pink, mauve or blue; dwarf, eaıly flowering.

'Souvenir de President Doumer'. Dark velvety red, purple to dark blue. Dwarf habit.

'Strafford'. Light red.

LACECAPS

A smaller group than the Hortensias, but similar in growth and requirements. Producing large, flattened corymbs of fertile flowers around which are borne a ring of coloured ray florets.

'Blue Wave'. A strong growing shrub of medium size producing beautifully shaped heads of blue fertile flowers surrounded by numerous large ray florets, varying in colour from pink to blue. In suitable soils the colour is a lovely gentian blue. Best in semi-shade. Raised by Messrs. Lemoine from seed of *'Mariesii'* about 1900. A.M. 1956. F.C.C. 1965.

HYDRANGEA—*continued*

'Lanarth White'. Compact growing, and with large flattened heads of bright blue or pink fertile flowers surrounded by a ring of white ray florets. A superb cultivar. A.M. 1949.

'Maculata' (*'Variegata'*). A medium sized shrub of erect habit; flower heads with a few small white ray florets. Grown for its attractive leaves which have a broad creamy-white margin.

'Mariesii'. Wide flat corymbs of rosy-pink flowers, the ray florets very large. When grown in suitable soil the flowers turn a very rich blue. Introduced by Maries from Japan in 1879. F.C.C. 1881. A.G.M. 1938.

'Mariesii Alba'. See *'White Wave'*.

'Sea Foam' (*maritima 'Seafoam'*). A small to medium-sized shrub with blue fertile flowers surrounded by white ray florets. A handsome shrub succeeding best in seaside and sheltered gardens. Said to be a clone of the wild coastal hydrangea *H. macrophylla normalis* and to have arisen as a reversion on the Hortensia *'Joseph Banks'*.

'Tricolor'. A choice, strong growing cultivar with leaves which are most attractively variegated green, grey and pale yellow. Flowers pale pink to white, large, freely produced. Said to be a branch sport of *'Mariesii'*. F.C.C. 1882.

'Veitchii'. A medium sized shrub with rich, dark green leaves, growing best in semi-shade. Flowers in flattened corymbs, the sterile outer florets white fading to pink. Very hardy and very lime tolerant. Introduced from Japan about 1880. A.M. 1974.

'White Wave' (*'Mariesii Alba'*) (*'Mariesii Grandiflora'*). A small shrub which originated in the nursery of Messrs. Lemoine of Nancy as a seedling of *'Mariesii'*, about 1902. It is a strong growing clone with flattened heads of bluish or pinkish, fertile flowers margined by large, beautifully formed, pearly-white ray florets. Free-flowering in an open position. A.M. 1948.

maritima. See *H. macrophylla normalis*.

'Seafoam'. See under LACECAPS.

paniculata SIEB. A medium sized to large shrub with both fertile and large, creamy-white sterile florets in dense terminal panicles in late summer and autumn. For large panicles, the laterals should be cut back to within 5 or 7·5cm. of the previous year's growth. Japan; China; Formosa. I. 1861. A.G.M. 1936. A.M. 1964.

'Grandiflora'. One of the showiest of hardy large shrubs. The massive panicles of sterile florets, appearing in summer and autumn, are white fading to pink. When cut make excellent winter decoration. Introduced by Siebold from Japan about 1867. F.C.C. 1869. A.G.M. 1969. Available both in bush and standard forms.

'Praecox'. A form with smaller panicles of dentated ray florets, flowering generally in early July and hardy in the coldest areas of Europe. A.M. 1956. A.G.M. 1960. F.C.C. 1973.

petiolaris. See under CLIMBERS.

'Preziosa'. See *H. serrata 'Preziosa'*.

quercifolia BARTR. The value of this medium sized, white-flowered shrub lies in the magnificent autumnal tints of its large, strongly lobed leaves. S.E. United States. I. 1803. A.M. 1928.

radiata WALL. (*nivea*). An erect shrub up to 1·8m., remarkable for the snow-white under-surfaces of the leaves. Flowers creamy-white, sweetly scented, produced in broad corymbs in July. Carolina (U.S.A.). I. 1786.

robusta HORT. See under *H. heteromalla 'Snowcap'*.

rosthornii. See under *H. villosa*.

sargentiana REHD. A noble shrub of medium size. The shoots are thickly clothed with a curious moss-like covering of hairs and bristles. Leaves very large and velvety. The large inflorescences in July and August are bluish, with white ray florets. Suitable for a sheltered shrub border or woodland. Winter hardy, but requires shade and wind protection. China. I. 1908. A.M. 1912. Considered by some authorities to be a subspecies of *H. aspera*.

serrata SER. (*macrophylla serrata*) (incl. *H. thunbergii*). A charming dwarf shrub rarely exceeding 1m. Flattened corymbs of blue or white flowers surrounded by a pretty circle of white, pink, or bluish ray florets often deepening to crimson in autumn. A variable species. Japan; Korea. I. 1843.

HYDRANGEA—*continued*

serrata acuminata. See under *'Bluebird'*.

'Bluebird' (*H. acuminata 'Bluebird'*). A small, robust shrub with stout shoots and abruptly acuminate leaves. The blue fertile flowers are borne in slightly dome-shaped corymbs surrounded by large ray florets which are reddish-purple on chalk soils, and a lovely sea-blue on acid soils. Reputedly a selected form of *H. serrata acuminata*, but in our experience the two are identical. Plants seen under either name would suggest by their robust nature a hybrid origin with *H. macrophylla* as one parent. A.M. 1960. A.G.M. 1969.

chinensis HORT. A charming, dwarf shrub of dense habit with rathery wiry branches and short-stalked downy leaves. Flowers in flattened corymbs, ray florets lilac-blue on chalk soils, powder blue on acid soils. The origin and botanical status of this shrub is something of a conundrum. It has every appearance of being a wild species though it does not fit any available description. It is sometimes found in cultivation under the name *H. chinensis acuminata*, but bears no resemblance to the plants generally grown in gardens as *H. serrata acuminata*. Our stock plant has only attained ·3× ·6m. after many years. See also *H. serrata koreana*.

'Grayswood'. An attractive small shrub. Flattened corymbs of blue fertile flowers surrounded by a ring of ray florets which are white at first, changing to rose and finally deep crimson. A.M. 1948.

'Intermedia'. Small shrub with flat corymbs of pinkish fertile flowers surrounded by a ring of ray florets which are white at first turning to shades of crimson.

koreana HORT. A delightful dwarf shrub, with slender branches and slender, acuminate, almost sessile leaves. Ray florets lilac on chalk soils, sky-blue on acid soils. Similar in habit to *chinensis* but even smaller with longer, smoother, thicker-textured leaves. Our stock plant has only attained ·3m.× ·3m. after many years. Origin unknown, possibly Korea.

'Preziosa'. A handsome shrub with purplish-red stems up to 1·5m. high. Leaves purple-tinged when young. Attractive globular heads of large rose-pink florets deepening to reddish-purple in autumn. A hybrid between *H. macrophylla* and *H. serrata*. Garden origin. A.M. 1963. F.C.C. 1964. A.G.M. 1973.

'Rosalba'. A small shrub distinguished by its larger leaves, and ray florets which are white at first, quickly turning to crimson. A.M. 1939.

strigosa REHD. A striking, rare, slow-growing, medium sized shrub. The lilac and white flowers appear in the autumn after all the other Hydrangeas are over. Leaves lance-shaped, conspicuously adpressed hairy, as are the shoots. Subject to damage by late spring frosts. C. China. I. 1907. Considered by some authorities to be a subspecies of *H. aspera*.

thunbergii. See *H. serrata*.

villosa REHD. One of the loveliest of late summer flowering species. A medium sized shrub of spreading habit, with stems, leaf and flower stalks densely villous. The large inflorescences are lilac-blue with prettily-toothed marginal sepals. Requires half-shade. A variable species, forms of which are sometimes found in cultivation under the name *H. rosthornii*. W. China. I. 1908. A.M. 1950. Considered by some authorities to be a form of *H. aspera*.

xanthoneura DIELS. A large shrub of loose habit. Leaves toothed, glabrous above, whitish hairy beneath. Flowers in a large flat head in June. Ray florets creamy white. C. China. I. 1904. Considered by some authorities to be a form of *H. heteromalla*.

wilsonii REHD. A large, vigorous often tree-like Chinese shrub with large lustrous leaves and white florets. Hardy in full exposure. I. 1909.

***HYMENANTHERA—Violaceae**—A small genus of evergreen or semi-evergreen shrubs of rigid habit, related to the "Pansy" and "Violet" but completely different in appearance. Natives of Australia, New Zealand and Tasmania.

angustifolia DC. (*dentata angustifolia*). A small, erect growing, Tasmanian shrub with smooth, oblanceolate leaves. Flowers small, yellow, often unisexual; berries white with purple markings. I. 1820.

crassifolia HOOK. f. A semi-evergreen New Zealand shrub of spreading habit, usually less than 1·5m. high. Leaves obovate. Bears quantities of white berries on the underside of the branches. C. about 1875. F.C.C. 1892.

obovata T. KIRK. An erect, medium-sized, New Zealand species, with obovate, occasionally toothed, leathery leaves up to 5cm. long; berries purplish.

HYPERICUM—Guttiferae—The shrubby hypericums will thrive in almost any well-drained soil. They are very desirable summer and autumn blooming shrubs, producing their conspicuous bright yellow flowers in great abundance. They are happy in full sun or semi-shade.

Many of the asiatic species have for many years been mixed or mis-named in cultivation. The species described below have been revised in accordance with the research recently carried out by Dr. N. K. B. Robson of the British Museum.

acmosepalum ROBSON (*oblongifolium* HORT.) (*kouytchense* HORT.). A splendid, very hardy, small, semi-evergreen shrub of erect habit, distinguished by its close-set, narrowly oblong leaves which often turn orange or scarlet in late autumn and winter. Flowers 5cm. across, golden yellow, freely-borne from June to October, followed by bright red capsules. Previously wrongly catalogued as *H. kouytchense*. China (Yunnan, Kweichow).

androsaemum L. "Tutsan". A good shade-bearing shrub, seldom above .75m. high, continuous and free-flowering. Flowers rather small but with conspicuous anthers, followed in autumn by erect, red, finally black, berry-like capsules. W. and S. Europe (incl. British Isles). C. before 1600.

augustinii ROBSON. A rare, small, densely-branched shrub with arching branches and sessile, ovate to oblong-lanceolate leathery leaves, the upper leaves amplexicaule. Flowers golden-yellow, 4 to 6cm. across, clustered at the ends of the branches during autumn. Named in honour of Augustine Henry who first discovered this species. China (Yunnan).

aureum. See *H. frondosum*.

†***balearicum** L. A dwarf, erect-branched shrub with very distinctive winged stems and small, curiously warted leaves. Flowers small, yellow, fragrant, borne from June to September. Balearic Isles. I. 1714.

beanii ROBSON. (*patulum henryi* BEAN). A small shrub related to *H. patulum*. Branches gracefully arching, producing slightly drooping flowers up to 6cm. across. Named in honour of W. J. Bean who first described it. China (Yunnan and Kweichow). A.M. 1904. Often grown in cultivation under the name *H. patulum henryi*. See also *H. forrestii* and *H. pseudohenryi*.

'Gold Cup'. A graceful form differing from the type in its attractive lanceolate leaves arranged along the arching branches in two opposite rows. Flowers deep yellow, cup-shaped, 6cm. across.

bellum LI (L.S. & E. 15737). A small, elegant, densely branched shrub with broadly ovate to orbicular, wavy-edged leaves and deep yellow, slightly cup-shaped flowers 3·5cm. across. Capsules puckered. A rare species related to *H. forrestii*. E. Himalaya. I. about 1908.

'Buttercup'. See *H. uralum*.

***calycinum** L. "Rose of Sharon". A dwarf, evergreen shrub with large leaves and large golden flowers. Excellent as a ground cover in dry and shaded places, but if left unchecked can become a weed. Occasionally naturalised. S.E. Europe; Asia Minor. I. 1676.

†**chinense** L. A pretty, semi-evergreen shrub, not above 1m. high, with oblong-oval leaves and 6cm. wide golden flowers with conspicuous stamens. A choice shrub for mild localities. China; Formosa. I. 1753.

***coris** L. A dwarf or prostrate evergreen shrublet with slender stems and linear leaves, arranged in whorls of three to six. The golden yellow flowers, 1.25 to 2cm. across, are borne in terminal panicles up to 12cm. long during summer. Ideal for the rock garden, scree or dry wall. C. and S. Europe. C. 1640.

densiflorum PURSH. A small, densely branched shrub with linear-oblong leaves and corymbs of small, abundantly produced deep yellow flowers in July and August. Eastern U.S.A. I. 1889.

dyeri HORT. not REHD. See *H. stellatum*.

'Eastleigh Gold'. A small semi-evergreen shrub of loose, spreading habit with drooping, reddish-brown branchlets. Leaves elliptic, slightly leathery, dark shining green above, 4 to 5cm. long. Flowers 6cm. across, slightly cup-shaped, golden-yellow with comparatively short stamens, freely borne from late June to October. Capsules puckered. This plant occured as a seedling in our nurseries about 1964. It may possibly be a hybrid *H. beanii* × *H. stellatum* or merely a form of *H. beanii*.

elatum. See *H.* ×*inodorum* MILL.

'Elstead'. See *H.* ×*inodorum 'Elstead'*.

HYPERICUM—*continued*

***empetrifolium oliganthum** RECH. f. A dwarf or prostrate evergreen shrublet with slender stems and small linear leaves. Flowers golden-yellow, 1·25 to 2cm. across, borne in small, erect panicles during summer. Requires a warm, sunny, well-drained position on the rock garden or scree. Crete. I. 1788. A.M. 1937.

forrestii ROBSON (*patulum forrestii*) (*calcaratum*) (*patulum henryi* HORT.). A hardy shrub of neat habit usually attaining 1 to 1·2m. in height. Leaves persist into the early winter giving rich autumn tints. The saucer-shaped, golden yellow flowers, 5 to 6cm. across, rounded in bud, are profusely borne throughout summer and autumn. S.W. China, Assam, Burma. Introduced by George Forrest in 1906. A.M. 1922. A.G.M. 1924. Previously distributed by us under the name of *H. patulum henryi.*

frondosum MICHX. (*aureum*). An attractive North American shrub up to 1·2m. high, often giving the effect of a miniature tree. Leaves sea-green; flowers in clusters, bright yellow with a large boss of stamens, appearing in July and August. The sepals are large and leaf-like. A beautiful and unmistakable species. S.E. and S. United States.

'Hidcote' (*patulum 'Hidcote'*) (*'Hidcote Gold'*). A superb hardy, semi-evergreen shrub of compact habit, attaining approximately 2m. in height and 2m. to 2·5m spread. The golden-yellow saucer-shaped flowers, which are the largest of any hardy *Hypericum*, are produced with gay abandon from July to October. The origin of this plant is uncertain, suggestions ranging from a wild plant collected in Yunnan to a garden hybrid. Whatever its history it is now one of the most popular of all flowering shrubs. A.M. 1954. A.G.M. 1954.

hircinum L. A compact shrub to about 1m. Leaves emitting a strong, pungent odour when bruised. Flowers 2·5cm. across, bright yellow with conspicuous stamens, borne freely from July to September. C. and S. Europe. Naturalised in the British Isles. I. 1640.

hookeranum WIGHT & ARN. A small semi-evergreen shrub, distinguishable by its leathery, ovate-oblong, sea green leaves on pale green, stout rounded branchlets, and clusters of large cup-shaped, pale yellow flowers from August to October. These are followed by puckered fruits. Nepal to Burma and Thailand, S. India. I. before 1853. A.M. 1890. Our stock is of the hardy Himalayan form.

leschenaultii. See *H. leschenaultii.*

×inodorum MILL. (*androsaemum×hircinum*) (*elatum*) (*multiflorum* HORT.) (*×persistens*). An erect-growing shrub up to 1·5m. Leaves ovate to ovate-oblong. The small, pale yellow flowers are produced in terminal cymes and are followed by attractive red fruits. A variable hybrid, some forms tending more to one parent than the other. Formerly catalogued as *H. elatum.* France?, Madeira?, naturalised in the British Isles.

'Elstead' (*elatum 'Elstead'*). A selected form with brilliant salmon-red fruits. A.M. 1933.

inodorum WILLD. not MILL. See *H. xylosteifolium.*

kalmianum L. A slender-branched shrub of dense, compact habit up to 1m. high. Main stems often gnarled, with pale brown, flaky bark. Leaves narrow, 2·5 to 5cm. long, sea-green when young. Flowers 1·25 to 2cm. across, bright yellow produced in the axils of the terminal leaves. N.E. United States; E. Canada. I. 1759.

kouytchense LEVL. (*penduliflorum*) (*patulum grandiflorum*) (*patulum 'Sungold'*). A small, semi-evergreen shrub of rounded, compact habit. Leaves ovate. Flowers up to 6cm. across, golden-yellow, with conspicuous long stamens, freely borne from late June to October. The bright-red, long-styled capsules resemble colourful upturned stork's heads. China (Kweichow). Previously catalogued as *H. penduliflorum.*

kouytchense HORT. See *H. acmosepalum.*

†*leschenaultii CHOISY (*hookeranum leschenaultii*). A beautiful but tender shrub of lax habit and medium size. Leaves sessile ovate-oblong. The rich yellow flowers, 6 to 7·5cm. across, are borne singly or in clusters at the ends of the shoots. Only suitable for the mildest localities or conservatory. Sumatra to Lombok and S.W. Celebes. I. 1853.

lysimachioides HORT. See *H. stellatum.*

×moseranum ANDRE (*calycinum×patulum*). A first-rate, dwarf shrub, usually not more than ·5m. high, making excellent ground cover. Stems arching, reddish. Flowers 5 to 6cm. across with conspicuous reddish anthers, borne from July to October. Garden origin about 1887. F.C.C. 1891.

HYPERICUM—*continued*

× **moseranum 'Tricolor'.** Leaves prettily variegated white, pink and green. Succeeds best in a sheltered position. A.M. 1896.

multiflorum HORT. See *H.* × *inodorum* MILL.

× **nothum** REHD. (*densiflorum* × *kalmianum*). A curious small shrub distinguished by its slender, interlacing stems with brown peeling bark, narrow leaves and numerous small flowers in late summer. Originated in 1903.

oblongifolium HORT. See *H. acmosepalum.*

patulum THUNB. The true species of this name is a tender plant from S.W. China and is doubtfully in cultivation in the British Isles. It was originally introduced from Japan (where it was widely cultivated) by Richard Oldham in 1862, and became popular in European gardens. The subsequent introduction of closely related, but hardier species from China, such as *H. beanii, H. forrestii* and *H. pseudohenryi* saw its gradual replacement.

forrestii. See *H. forrestii.*

grandiflorum. See *H. kouytchense* LEVL.

henryi. See *H. beanii, H. forrestii* and *H. pseudohenryi.*

'Hidcote'. See *H. 'Hidcote'.*

'Sungold'. See *H. kouytchense* LEVL.

uralum. See *H. uralum.*

penduliflorum. See *H. kouytchense* LEVL.

prolificum L. A small, densely-branched shrub of rounded bushy habit. Main stems often gnarled, with attractive grey and brown peeling bark. Leaves narrow, 2·5 to 5cm. long, shining above. Flowers 1·25 to 2cm. across, bright yellow, borne in terminal clusters from July to September. E. & C. United States. I. about 1750.

pseudohenryi ROBSON (*patulum henryi* HORT.). A small, mound-forming shrub with arching stems and narrowly ovate to lanceolate-oblong leaves. Flowers 3 to 5cm. across, with spreading petals and conspicuous stamens, abundantly produced in July and August. First introduced by Ernest Wilson in 1908. China (Yunnan, Szechwan, Sikang). Often grown under the name *H. patulum henryi.* See also *H. beanii* and *H. forrestii.*

reptans HOOK. f. & THOM. A slender shrublet with prostrate stems rooting at intervals and forming small mats. Leaves ·6 to 2cm. long, crowding the stems. Flowers terminal, solitary, rich golden yellow, 4·5cm. across, borne from June to September. A choice alpine species for the rock garden or scree. Himalaya. C. 1881. A.G.M. 1927.

†**'Rowallane'** (*hookeranum 'Rogersii'* × *leschenaultii*). This magnificent, semi-evergreen plant is the finest of the genus, but needs a sheltered site. The 5 to 7·5cm. wide, bowl-shaped flowers are of an intensely rich golden-yellow colour, of firm texture, and beautifully moulded. Graceful in habit, and as much as 2m. high in mild districts. A.M. 1943. Often wrongly grown under the name *H. rogersii.*

stellatum ROBSON (*dyeri* HORT. not REHD.) (*lysimachioides* HORT.). An elegant, semi-evergreen species of semi-pendulous habit 1 to 1·2m. in height and greater in width. Flowers 4cm. across. The slender-pointed sepals give the prettily red tinted calyces a delightful star-like effect, hence the name. The young growths are similarly tinted. Capsules puckered. China (Yunnan, Szechwan, Sikang). I. 1894. Previously catalogued wrongly as *H. dyeri.*

uralum D. DON (*patulum uralum*) (*'Buttercup'*). A delightful, hardy, semi-evergreen shrub attaining ·6 to 1m., with arching stems and ovate or oval, often wavy-edged leaves, 2·5 to 4cm. long, smelling faintly of oranges when crushed. The golden-yellow flowers, 2·5cm. across, are borne in terminal cymes during August and September. Nepal. I. 1820.

wilsonii ROBSON. A small shrub with spreading branches and ovate to ovate-lanceolate leaves. Flowers 4 to 5cm. across, golden-yellow, with spreading petals and conspicuous stamens. Discovered by Ernest Wilson in 1907. China (Hupeh, Szechwan).

xylosteifolium ROBSON (*inodorum* WILLD. not MILL.). A small suckering shrub, forming a dense thicket of erect, slender, usually unbranched stems 1 to 1·2m. high. Leaves ovate or oblong, 2·5 to 5cm. long. Flowers rather small, 2 to 2·5cm. across, solitary or in terminal clusters at the ends of the shoots opening intermittently from July to September. Previously distributed as *H. inodorum.* Caucasus (Georgia), N.E. Turkey. C. 1870.

HAMAMELIS mollis 'Pallida'

HYDRANGEA serrata 'Preziosa'

ITEA ilicifolia

LOMATIA myricoides

KALMIA latifolia

LINDERA benzoin

LIGUSTRUM japonicum

IDESIA—Flacourtiaceae—A monotypic genus. It succeeds best in a deep neutral or somewhat acid soil, but may be grown quite well given ·76m. of loam over chalk. Some geographical forms are subject to damage in severe weather whilst others seem quite hardy.

polycarpa MAXIM. An ornamental, medium-sized tree with large, ovate, long-stalked leaves, glaucous beneath, recalling those of *Populus wilsonii*. The tiny yellowish-green, often dioecious flowers are borne in large terminal panicles in summer, but not on young trees. Large bunches of pea-like, bright red berries are borne on female trees in autumn. Japan, China. I. about 1864. A.M. 1934.

vestita DIELS. A particularly hardy, Chinese form with leaves tomentose beneath. W. China. I. 1908.

ILEX—Aquifoliaceae—A large genus of evergreen and deciduous trees and shrubs occurring in temperate and tropical regions of both hemispheres. The evergreen species and their forms provide some of the handsomest specimen trees hardy in our climate. The European and Asiatic species are adaptable to most soils and are indifferent to sun or shade, but most of the North American species require a neutral or preferably an acid soil.

Certain species are invaluable for hedge making and will withstand polluted atmosphere and maritime exposure. As a group they display a great variety of form and colour of leaf excelled by few other genera. Male and female flowers are borne usually on separate plants, and in a favourable season female plants fruit abundantly. Well-rooted and balled nursery stock may be moved throughout the dormant season. In a damp spring evergreen hollies move well in May.

*×**altaclarensis** DALLIM. This name was originally used to describe the "Highclere Holly" which was said to be the result of a cross between *I. aquifolium* and *I. perado*. In the present work the name is used to cover a number of similar but variable hybrids in which *I. platyphylla* may also have played a part. Most are large shrubs or small to medium-sized trees of vigorous growth, with handsome, normally large leaves. The majority are excellent for tall hedges or screens. They are quite tolerant of industrial conditions and seaside exposure.

'Atkinsonii'. A green-stemmed clone with large, handsome, rugose leaves, glossy dark green above and with regular spiny serrations. A bold holly with leaves amongst the finest in the group. Male.

'Balearica' (*I. balearica* HORT.) (*platyphylla balearica* HORT.) (*aquifolium balearica* HORT.). A hardy, vigorous, medium-sized tree of erect, somewhat conical habit when young. Leaves ovate to elliptic, flat, leathery, shining green, entire or with a few small spines, always spine-tipped. Free fruiting. Both this plant and *'Maderensis'*, as grown in gardens, are, in our opinion, clones of hybrid origin despite their geographical attributions. *'Purple Shaft'* and *'Silver Sentinel'* are similar clones.

'Camelliifolia' (*aquifolium 'Camelliifolia'*). A beautiful large-fruiting clone of pyramidal habit, and with purple stems. The long, large, mainly spineless leaves are a lovely shining dark green, reddish-purple when young. A.G.M. 1931.

'Camelliifolia Variegata'. Leaves dark polished green, marbled paler green and margined gold. Sometimes half or complete leaves are gold.

'Golden King' (*aquifolium 'Golden King'*). One of the best golden-variegated hollies and one of the few plants to have received two awards in the same year. The broad, almost spineless leaves are green, with a bright yellow margin. Said to be a branch sport of *'Hodginsii'*, but in our opinion *'Hendersonii'* is the more likely. Female. A.M. and F.C.C. 1898. A.G.M. 1969.

'Hendersonii'. Compact in growth, the comparatively dull green leaves are generally entire though occasionally shortly spiny. A female clone, producing often heavy crops of large fruits.

'Hodginsii'. A strong, vigorous, male clone with purple stems. The large, dark-green rounded or oval leaves are variably armed, some boldly spiny others few-spined, the latter more prevalent on older specimens. It forms a noble specimen tree for a lawn and is especially suitable for coastal and industrial areas where, particularly in the north of England, it has been extensively planted in the past. Sometimes described wrongly as a female clone. The clones *'Nobilis'* and *'Shepherdii'* are very similar. A.G.M. 1969.

ILEX—*continued*

× **altaclarensis 'Jermyns'.** A strong-growing, green-stemmed clone with polished green, almost spineless leaves. Ideal for hedging. Male.

'Lawsoniana'. A branch sport of *'Hendersonii'* with large, generally spineless leaves splashed yellow in the centre. Female. Tends to revert. Such shoots should be removed. F.C.C. 1894.

'Maderensis' (*I. maderensis* HORT.). A vigorous, medium-sized tree with dark stems and regularly spined, flat leaves. A male clone which probably originated in a similar way to *'Balearica'*. *I. maderensis* LAM. is a synonym of *I. perado.*

'Maderensis Variegata'. A striking clone with reddish-purple stems. Leaves dark green, with irregular central yellow splash. Male.

'Moorei'. A vigorous large leaved clone with stems green, tinged reddish-purple. Leaves large, approaching those of *'Wilsonii'*, but rather longer in outline, polished dark green above, boldly and regularly spined. Male.

'Mundyi'. A most pleasing green-stemmed clone. Leaves large, broadly oval, regularly spiny and with a prominent venation. Male. One of the most magnificent of this group.

'N. N. Barnes' (*aquifolium 'N. N. Barnes'*). Distinct purple shoots and large, dark, shining green leaves. Female.

'Purple Shaft'. A striking cultivar with strong, dark purple, young shoots and abundant fruit. Fast growing and making a fine specimen tree. A sport of *'Balearica'*.

'Silver Sentinel'. One of the handsomest variegated hollies. A vigorous, erect-growing, female clone. The firm, flat, sparsely spiny leaves are often 8·25 to 10cm. long, and in colour deep green with pale green and grey mottling, and an irregular, but conspicuous creamy-white or creamy-yellow margin. Often grown in gardens under the name *I. perado 'Variegata'* and on the continent as *'Belgica Aurea'*. It is probably a sport of the clone *'Balearica'* which it resembles in habit and leaf shape.

'Wilsonii'. A compact, dome-shaped clone with green stems and large, evenly spiny, prominently veined leaves. Female. Deservedly one of the most popular of this group. F.C.C. 1899. A.G.M. 1969.

'W. J. Bean' (*aquifolium 'W. J. Bean'*). A dense, compact-growing clone with large, spiny, dark green leaves and bright red fruits.

***aquifolium** L. "Common Holly". There is no more beautiful or useful evergreen for this climate. It is usually seen as a small tree or large bush, but in favourable positions may reach 18 to 21m. It is native over a wide area from W. and S. Europe (incl. the British Isles), North Africa to China. Cultivated since ancient times.

Innumerable cultivars have arisen with variously shaped and coloured leaves and of different habits. Unless otherwise stated all will eventually make large shrubs or small trees. Both the type and many of its clones are excellent for hedge-making and are excellent both in industrial and coastal areas.

'Amber'. An interesting clone, which occurred in our nurseries before 1955; attractive, large bronze-yellow fruits.

'Angustifolia'. A slow-growing cultivar of neat pyramidal habit. Stems purple; leaves varying to 3·75cm. long by 1·25cm. wide, long pointed and with ten to sixteen slender marginal spines. Female. *'Serratifolia'*, *'Hascombensis'* and *'Pernettiifolia'* are similar clones.

'Argentea Marginata'. "Broad-leaved Silver Holly". This name covers a group of cultivars with white margined leaves. Both male and female. We offer a handsome free-fruiting female with green stems. A.G.M. 1969.

'Argentea Pendula'. "Perry's Silver Weeping Holly". A small, graceful tree with strongly weeping branches, forming in time a compact mushroom of white margined leaves. It is a female clone and fruits freely.

'Argentea Mediopicta'. See *'Silver Milkboy'*.

'Argentea Regina'. See *'Silver Queen'*.

'Aurea Mediopicta Latifolia'. See *'Golden Milkboy'*.

'Aurea Marginata'. This name covers a group of cultivars with yellow margined leaves. Excellent for hedging.

ILEX—*continued*

aquifolium 'Aurea Marginata Ovata'. A strong-growing clone with deep purple shoots. Leaves ovate, strongly and evenly spined, green mottled grey, with an irregular yellow margin. Male.

'Bacciflava' (*'Fructuluteo'*). "Yellow-fruited Holly". A handsome cultivar with heavy crops of bright yellow fruits.

balearica. See *I.* ×*altaclarensis 'Balearica'*.

'Bicolor'. See *'Muricata'*.

'Calamistrata'. See *'Crispa'*.

'Camelliifolia'. See *I.* ×*altaclarensis 'Camelliifolia'*.

chinensis. See *I. centrochinensis*.

'Crassifolia'. A curious slow-growing clone with very thick, curved, strongly spine-edged leaves, and purple young shoots. Male.

'Crispa' (*'Tortuosa'*) (*'Calamistrata'*). A peculiar clone with twisted and curled, thick leathery leaves, tipped with a sharp, decurved spine. A sport of *'Scotica'*. Male.

'Crispa Aureopicta'. Similar to *'Crispa'* but the dark green leaves have a central splash of yellow and pale green. Male.

'Donningtonensis'. Dark blackish purple stems and purple flushed, spiny young leaves. Male.

'Elegantissima' (Argenteomarginata Group). A green-stemmed clone with boldly spined, wavy-edged leaves, green with faint marbling and creamy-white margins. Male.

'Ferox'. "Hedgehog Holly". A distinctive clone with small leaves, th eupper surfaces of which are puckered and furnished with short, sharp spines. Male. Lower and slower-growing than most, making an excellent hedge. This is said to be the oldest indentifiable cultivar of holly still in cultivation, having been known at least since the early 17th century.

'Ferox Argentea'. "Silver Hedgehog Holly". Rich purple twigs, the leaves with creamy-white margin and spines. A very effective combination. Male.

'Ferox Aurea'. "Gold Hedgehog Holly". Leaves with a central deep gold or yellow-green blotch. Male.

'Flavescens' (*'Clouded Gold'*). "Moonlight Holly". Leaves suffused canary yellow, shaded old gold. Particularly effective on a dull winter afternoon or in spring when the young leaves appear. Female.

'Foxii'. A purple-stemmed clone with shining green, ovate leaves bearing evenly spaced marginal spines. Resembles a long spined *'Ovata'*. Male.

'Fructuluteo'. See *'Bacciflava'*.

'Golden King'. See *I.* ×*altaclarensis 'Golden King'*.

'Golden Milkboy' (*'Aurea Mediopicta Latifolia'*). A striking and most ornamental holly with large flattened, spine-edged leaves which are green with a large splash of gold in the centre. Reverting shoots should be removed. Male.

'Golden Queen' (*'Aurea Regina'*) (Aureomarginata Group). A striking cultivar, young shoots green or reddish-tinged. Leaves broad, spiny, dark green with pale green and grey shading and a broad yellow margin. Male. A.G.M. 1969.

'Golden van Tol'. A sport of *'J. C. van Tol'* with attractive golden-margined leaves.

'Grandis'. See under *'Silver Queen'*.

'Green Pillar'. An erect-growing form with upright branches and dark green, spiny leaves. Female. An excellent specimen or screening tree.

'Handsworthensis'. A green or dusky-stemmed cultivar of compact habit, with small, regularly and sharply spined leaves. Male.

'Handsworth New Silver' (Argenteomarginata Group). An attractive purple-stemmed clone, distinguished by its comparatively long leaves which are deep green mottled grey, with a broad, creamy-white margin. Female. A.G.M. 1969.

'Hastata' (*'Latispina Minor'*). A remarkable, dense, slow-growing cultivar with deep purple shoots and small, rigid, undulating leaves with an occasional stout spine towards the base. Male.

heterophylla LOES. This name covers the numerous wild forms with variously spined and entire leaves on the same plant. We offer a handsome purple-stemmed female clone.

'Heterophylla Aureomarginata' (*'Pyramidalis Aurea'*). "Egham Holly". A strong-growing, green-stemmed clone. Leaves deep shining green with an irregular but conspicuous golden margin. Female.

ILEX—*continued*

aquifolium 'J. C. van Tol' (*'Polycarpa'*). A superb cultivar with dark, shining, almost spineless green leaves, and producing large, regular crops of red fruits. A.G.M. 1969.

'Laurifolia'. A striking cultivar with glossy, usually spineless leaves and deep purple shoots. Male.

'Laurifolia Aurea' (*'Laurifolia Variegata'*). Dark green leaves thinly edged yellow. Very effective with the deep purple twigs. Male. F.C.C. 1883.

'Madame Briot' (Aureomarginata Group). An attractive purple-stemmed clone with strongly spiny leaves which are green, mottled and margined dark yellow. Female. A.G.M. 1969.

'Monstrosa' (*'Latispina Major'*). An easily-recognised cultivar of dense habit with bright green stems and broad, viciously spiny leaves. Male.

'Muricata' (*'Bicolor'*) (Aureomarginata Group). An effective green-stemmed clone. Leaves flattened, dark green with a dark old gold margin. Female.

'Myrtifolia'. A neat-growing cultivar with purple shoots; leaves small, dark green, variably edged with sharp spines or entire. Intermediate in leaf between *'Ovata'* and *'Angustifolia'*. Male.

'Myrtifolia Aurea' (*'Myrtifolia Variegata'*). Dark purple stems and strongly spined leaves, dark mottled green with a narrow deep yellow margin. Male.

'Myrtifolia Aureomaculata'. A dense compact form with small, evenly spined leaves. In colour they are dark green with a pale green shading and an irregular central splash of gold.

'N. N. Barnes'. See *I.* ×*altaclarensis 'N. N. Barnes'*.

'Ovata' (*'Ovalifolium'*). A slow-growing cultivar with purple shoots and distinct, neat ovate leaves, shallowly scalloped along the margin. Male.

'Ovata Aurea'. The thick, short-spined leaves are margined gold, and contrast beautifully with the deep purple twigs. One of the brightest and neatest of variegated hollies. Male.

'Pendula'. An elegant, free-fruiting, small tree forming a dense mound of weeping stems thickly clothed with dark green, spiny leaves. Female.

'Polycarpa'. See *'J. C. van Tol'*.

'Pyramidalis' (Heterophylla Group). A handsome, free-fruiting clone with green stems and bright green, variously spined leaves. Conical in habit when young, broadening in maturity. A.G.M. 1969.

'Pyramidalis Fructuluteo'. Similar to *'Pyramidalis'*, but with bright yellow fruits.

'Recurva'. A slow-growing clone of dense habit with purplish twigs and strongly spined, recurved leaves, 2·5 to 3·75cm. long. Male.

'Scotica'. A distinctive cultivar with thick, leathery deep green leaves which are spineless and slightly twisted, with a cup-shaped depression below the apex. Female.

'Silver Milkboy' (*'Argentea Mediopicta'*). An attractive cultivar with strongly spiny leaves which are dark green with a central blotch of creamy-white. Male. Inclined to revert. Green shoots should be removed.

'Silver Queen' (*'Argentea Regina'*). A striking clone with blackish-purple, young shoots and broadly ovate dark green leaves faintly marbled grey and bordered creamy-white. Male. *'Grandis'* is a similar clone.

'Smithii'. A dense-growing clone with purplish twigs and narrow, often spineless leaves. Male.

'Tortuosa'. See *'Crispa'*.

'Watererana' (*'Waterer's Gold'*). (Aureomarginata Group). Dense, compact, slow-growing shrub with green stems striped greenish-yellow. The small, rounded, generally spineless leaves are mottled yellow-green and grey, with an irregular yellow margin. Male.

'W. J. Bean'. See *I.* ×*altaclarensis 'W. J. Bean'*.

* ×**attenuata** ASHE (*cassine* × *opaca*) (×*topeli*). "Topal Holly". A tall, slender shrub or small tree of rather conical habit, with narrow, normally entire leaves 5 to 10cm. long, and clusters of red fruits. A natural hybrid found with the parents in southern U.S.A. Not suitable for chalky soils. Ours is a female clone.

'East Palatka'. A female clone of upright conical habit. Leaves pale glossy green, obovate, entire except for a sharp terminal point and an occasional spine.

'Foster'. An attractive clone of compact habit, with narrow, variously spined, glossy-green leaves bronze when young, and red fruits.

balearica. See *I.* ×*altaclarensis 'Balearica'*.

ILEX—*continued*

*× **beanii** REHD. (*aquifolium* × *dipyrena*). A variable hybrid with leaves generally of a matt green. Superficially closer to the *aquifolium* parent. C. 1900.

bioritsensis. See *I. pernyi veitchii*.

‡***cassine** L. not WALT. "Dahoon Holly". An extremely variable species making a large shrub, or rarely a small tree. The lanceolate leaves are occasionally 10cm. long. Fruits red. S.E. United States. Not suitable for chalky soils. I. 1726. We offer the following clone:—

'Angustifolia'. A selection with longer, narrower leaves.

†***centrochinensis** HU (*aquifolium chinensis*). A medium-sized shrub with slender purple twigs and shining deep green, oblong-lanceolate, strongly spiny leaves. C. China, in the same areas where *Metasequoia* was discovered.

***ciliospinosa** LOES. Large shrub bearing small, neat, leathery, spine-toothed leaves up to 5cm. long. Fruits egg-shaped, red. Related to *I. dipyrena*, but differs in its smaller, more regularly spiny leaves and rounded shoots. C. and W. China. I. 1908.

†***corallina** FRANCH. A small, variable, graceful tree with slender stems and narrowly elliptic to elliptic-lanceolate, slender pointed and serrated leaves. Small red fruits produced in axillary clusters. W. China. I. about 1900.

pubescens HU (YU 10918). A more robust variety with stouter stems. Leaves broader, spine-toothed and of thicker texture. W. China.

***cornuta** LINDL. A dense, slow-growing species, rarely 2·4m. high. Leaves of a peculiar, rectangular form, mainly five-spined. The large red fruits are rarely abundant. China. I. 1846.

'Burfordii'. A small, very free-fruiting shrub of compact growth with shining green, leathery leaves which, except for a short terminal spine, are entire. Extensively planted in the United States as a low evergreen hedge. Female.

'Dwarf Burford'. A dwarf female form of slow growth and dense, compact habit. Leaves varying from entire to spiny.

'Kingsville Special'. A strong-growing shrub with large, leathery, almost spineless leaves.

'Rotunda'. Dwarf selection with compact, rounded habit, and strongly spined, oblong leaves.

***crenata** THUNB. A tiny-leaved holly of slow growth reaching 4 to 6m. Fruits small, shining black. A variable species particularly in cultivation. Excellent as a dwarf clipped hedge. Japan. I. about 1864.

'Aureovariegata' (*'Variegata'*). Leaves suffused yellow in spring, becoming pale green.

'Convexa'. A free-fruiting, low, bushy shrub, with glossy bullate or convex leaves. A superb low hedge.

fukasawana MAK. A distinct, comparatively large-leaved variety of dense, erect habit with strong, angular shoots and lanceolate or narrowly-elliptic, blunt-toothed leaves up to 5cm. long, bright or yellowish-green when young. Japan.

'Golden Gem'. A dwarf, compact shrub with flattened top and yellow leaves, particularly attractive during winter and spring.

'Helleri'. Perhaps the most attractive dwarf, small-leaved form, making a low, dense, flattened hummock.

'Latifolia'. A form with larger elliptic leaves 2 to 3cm. long. I. 1860.

'Mariesii' (*'Nummularia'*). A dwarf, most unholly-like clone of very slow growth, with crowded, tiny round leaves. Ideal for troughs or Bonsai culture. Female. Introduced by Maries in 1879.

paludosa HARA. (*radicans*). A low-growing variety with broad elliptic leaves. Found in damp places in Japan.

'Stokes'. A dwarf shrub, forming a dense, compact mound of tiny leaves.

‡**decidua** WALT. "Possumhaw Holly". A medium-sized to large shrub with slender stems and obovate to oblanceolate, crenately-toothed leaves. Fruits bright orange or red, lasting well into winter, but not very prolific on young plants. Not suitable for chalky soils. S.E. United States. I. 1760.

***dipyrena** WALL. A large shrub or small tree, conical in outline, with angled young shoots. Leaves dark green, with a short purplish petiole; variably spined. Fruits deep red, slightly two-lobed. E. Himalaya. I. 1840.

***'Dr. Kassab'.** A neat-growing shrub, a seedling of *I. cornuta* with conspicuous yellow-green stems and very dark green, oblong, five-spined leaves.

ILEX—*continued*

***fargesii** FRANCH. A large shrub or occasionally a small tree, easily recognised by its narrow, oblong or oblanceolate leaves up to 12·5cm. long. Fruits small, red. C. China. I. 1900. A.M. 1926.

sclerophylla HORT. A form with slender leaves.

†fragilis HOOK. f. A large shrub or occasionally a small tree with thinly textured, elliptic-ovate, slender-pointed, serrated leaves which are prettily tinted when young. Only for the mildest areas. E. Himalaya.

†*franchetiana LOES. A large shrub or small tree related to *I. fargesii*. Leaves oblanceolate to elliptic, acuminate, serrated. Female trees produce small red fruits. W. China.

geniculata MAXIM. A large, deciduous shrub or small tree, with slender, greyish branches. Leaves ovate to elliptic, shallowly toothed and thin in texture. Fruits red. Japan. I. 1894.

†*georgei COMBER. A rare species making a medium-sized to large shrub of compact habit. Leaves elliptic-lanceolate, up to 5cm. long, thick and spinose. Fruits small, sealing-wax red. Not hardy in the home counties. Discovered by George Forrest in S.W. China.

‡*glabra GRAY. "Inkberry". A small to medium-sized shrub forming a dense rounded bush. Leaves small, dark shining green. Fruits small, black. Not suitable for chalky soils. Eastern N. America. I. 1759.

leucocarpa F. W. WOODS. An unusual form with white fruits.

***hookeri** KING. This species has succeeded outside in our nursery for a number of years, sheltered by surrounding shrubs. Leaves ovate to lanceolate, acute to acuminate, prominently and regularly spine-toothed, 5 to 7·5cm. long, terminating, like the conspicuous serrations, in a sharp mucro-point. Closely related to *I. dipyrena*. Himalaya.

insignis. See *I. kingiana*.

***integra** THUNB. A medium-sized to large shrub, tender in the young stage. Leaves obovate to broad elliptic, spineless and leathery. Fruit 1·25cm. long, red. Japan. I. 1864.

***'Jermyns Dwarf'.** A dwarf shrub with arching stems forming a low, dense mound. Leaves polished dark green, strongly spine-toothed. Of hybrid origin, a seedling of *I. pernyi*. Female.

***'John T. Morris'** (*cornuta 'Burfordii × pernyi*). Small shrub of dense, compact habit. Leaves strongly spiny similar to but smaller than *I. cornuta*. Male.

***kingiana** COCKERELL (*insignis*) (*nobilis*). A remarkable species with stout shoots and elliptic-lanceolate, leathery, few-toothed leaves 15 to 20cm. long. Fruits large, red. Leaves of juvenile plants are smaller and markedly spiny. We appear to have two forms, one of which is proving surprisingly hardy in our arboretum. It makes a small tree or large shrub. E. Himalaya. A.M. 1964.

*** × koehneana** LOES. (*aquifolium × latifolia*). An interesting evergreen hybrid of American origin. A large shrub or small tree with purple-flushed young shoots. Leaves elliptic to oblong-lanceolate, slightly undulate, dark polished green above and evenly spiny throughout. Female plants bear large red fruits.

'Chestnut Leaf' (*castaneifolia* HORT.). A robust clone of French origin. The thick, leathery, yellowish-green leaves are boldly margined with strong, spiny teeth.

***latifolia** THUNB. A magnificent species, in this country usually making a small tree or large shrub. Leaves nearly equal in size to those of *Magnolia grandiflora*, dark glossy green, leathery, oblong with serrated margins. Although quite hardy it succeeds best in a sheltered position. Orange-red fruits often abundantly produced. Japan. I. 1840. A.M. 1952. A.M. 1977.

***'Lydia Morris'** (*cornuta 'Burfordii' × pernyi*). A small, compact, pyramidal shrub up to 1·8m. with polished green, strongly spiny leaves, a little smaller than those of *I. cornuta*. Large red fruits. A female counterpart to *I. 'John T. Morris'*.

macrocarpa OLIV. A small to medium-sized, deciduous tree with ovate, serrated leaves up to 15cm. long. Remarkable on account of the size of its fruits, which resemble small black cherries. C. China. I. 1907.

macropoda MIQ. A large shrub or small tree with ovate to broad elliptic, sharply-toothed leaves. Fruits red. Related to and resembling the American *I. montana*. China, Japan, Korea. I. 1894.

maderensis HORT. See *I. × altaclarensis 'Maderensis'*.

maderensis LAM. See *I. perado*.

ILEX—*continued*

***× makinoi** HARA (*leucoclada × rugosa*). A dwarf evergreen shrub similar in general appearance to *I. rugosa* but larger in all its parts. Leaves narrowly oblong, less conspicuously veined. Fruits red. Japan.

†*melanotricha MERRILL. A small tree or large shrub related to *I. franchetiana*. Leaves oblong-elliptic, up to 8·75cm. long. Fruits red. Only suitable for sheltered gardens. S.W. China.

‡*myrtifolia WALT. (*cassine myrtifolia*). A medium-sized to large, evergreen shrub with narrow leaves, 2·5 to 5cm. long. Fruits normally red. Not suitable for chalky soils. S.E. United States.

***'Natalie Webster'.** A large shrub, possibly a form or hybrid of *I. opaca*. Leaves dull green, entire or few spined.

***'Nellie R. Stevens'** (*aquifolium × cornuta*). Medium-sized shrub with dark green, corrugated, softly spiny leaves. Female.

‡*opaca AIT. "American Holly". In this country, a large shrub or small tree. Leaves variously spiny, of a distinctive soft olive green or yellow green. Not suitable for chalky soils. Fruits red. E. and C. United States. I. 1744.

'Xanthocarpa'. Fruits yellow.

‡*pedunculosa MIQ. A large shrub or small tree with dark, glossy-green, entire leaves. Fruits bright red, carried on slender stalks 2·5 to 3·75cm. long. Not suitable for chalky soils. China; Japan; W. Formosa. I. 1893.

continentalis LOES. A Chinese variety, larger in its various parts.

†*perado AIT. (*maderensis* LAM.). "Azorean Holly". A small to medium-sized tree which is doubtless one parent of many of the *Altaclarensis Hybrids*. It is distinguished from our native "Holly" mainly by its distinctly winged leaf stalks and flatter leaves which are variously short-spined, occasionally entire, and rounded at the tip. Rather tender except in sheltered gardens and mild districts. Canary Isles; Azores. C. 1760.

platyphylla LOES. (*I. platyphylla*). "Canary Island Holly". A handsome species of bushy habit making a small tree in mild districts. The leaves are large and broad, occasionally 12·5 to 15cm. long by half or more as wide. They are dark green, leathery, short stalked and shortly toothed. The fruits are deep red. Canary Isles. C. 1760.

***pernyi** FRANCH. A distinguished large shrub or small tree with small, peculiarly spined leaves, almost triangular in shape. Fruits small, bright red. C. and W. China. I. 1900. F.C.C. 1908.

veitchii BEAN (*I. bioritsensis*). Similar in general appearance to the type, but with larger leaves. Fruits small, red. W. China; Formosa. A.M. 1930.

platyphylla. See *I. perado platyphylla*.

balearica HORT. See *I. × altaclarensis 'Balearica'*.

maderensis HORT. See *I. × altaclarensis 'Maderensis'*.

†*rotunda THUNB. A small tree with ovate or broad elliptic, entire leaves up to 10cm. long, recalling those of *Ligustrum japonicum*. Fruits small, red, borne in clusters on the current year's growth. S.E. Asia. I. 1849.

‡*rugosa SCHMIDT. A dwarf shrub occasionally prostrate, forming a dense low mound. Young stems sharply angled almost quadrangular; leaves elliptic to lanceolate, acute and toothed, slightly rugose above. Fruits red. Not suitable for chalky soils. Japan, Sakhalin, Kuriles. I. 1895.

***'San Jose'.** An attractive, vigorous, small tree or large shrub of American origin, reputedly a hybrid between *I. × altaclarense 'Wilsonii'* and *I. sikkimensis*. Young shoots purple-flushed; leaves elliptic to ovate-lanceolate, dark polished green above, paler beneath, conspicuously and evenly spined.

‡serrata THUNB. (*sieboldii*). A deciduous, slow-growing, small to medium-sized shrub of dense twiggy habit. Leaves small and thin, attractively tinted in autumn. The tiny red fruits of the female plants are produced in abundance and last throughout the winter or until eaten by birds. Not recommended for chalky soils. Japan. I. 1893.

'Leucocarpa'. A form with white fruits.

sieboldii. See *I. serrata*.

***sugerokii** MAXIM. A rare, small to medium-sized shrub of dense, compact, upright habit. Leaves elliptic, 2·5 to 3·75cm. long, shallowly toothed in upper half, leathery and glossy dark green. Fruits red, solitary in the leaf axils of the current year's growths. Closely related to *I. yunnanensis*, differing in its generally glabrous shoots and few toothed leaves. In the wild it is often found with *I. crenata*, and like that species is suitable as a dense hedge. Japan. I. 1914.

ILEX—*continued*

‡**verticillata** GRAY (*Prinos verticillatus*). A deciduous large shrub with purple-tinged leaves, especially in the spring, turning yellow in the autumn. Fruits bright red and long-persisting. Not suitable for chalky soils. Eastern N. America. I. 1736. A.M. 1962.

'Aurantiaca'. Fruits yellowish.

'Christmas Cheer'. A selected female clone of American origin bearing masses of bright red fruits which normally last through the winter months.

***yunnanensis** FRANCH. A medium-sized to large shrub of bushy habit. Leaves small; ovate to ovate-lanceolate, acute or obtuse, crenately toothed, glossy green above, neatly arranged on the slender, densely pubescent twigs. The small, slender-stalked, bright red fruits are conspicuous on female plants. W. China. I. 1901.

gentilis LOES. An attractive variety; the young emerging leaves are brownish-red, maturing to a deep dull green. Subject to damage by late spring frosts.

***ILLICIUM**—**Illiciaceae**—A small genus of aromatic evergreen shrubs allied to *Magnolia* and thriving under conditions congenial to *Rhododendron*, though tolerant of a little lime. A small group of outstanding evergreens with unusual, many-petalled flowers.

anisatum L. (*religiosum*). A medium-sized to large aromatic shrub of slow growth. Leaves obovate or oval, abruptly pointed, thick and fleshy, glossy deep green. Flowers pale yellow, about 2·5cm. across, in spring, carried even on young plants. Japan, Formosa. I. 1790. A.M. 1930.

floridanum ELLIS. A medium-sized, aromatic shrub with deep green, broadly oval, leathery leaves; flowers maroon-purple in May and June. Southern U.S.A. I. 1771.

henryi DIELS. A medium-sized shrub with glossy, leathery leaves and flowers of a bright rose. W. China.

"INDIAN BEAN TREE". See *CATALPA bignonioides*.

INDIGOFERA—**Leguminosae**—A very attractive genus of shrubs which, owing to their racemes being produced from leaf-axils of growing shoots, flower continuously throughout summer and autumn. All have elegant, pinnate leaves and require full sun. They thrive in all types of soil and are especially good on dry sites. Some species may be cut back during severe winters but these usually throw up a thicket of strong shoots the following spring. Old, poorly shaped specimens may also be hard pruned to achieve the same effect.

amblyantha CRAIB. Similar to and with all the good qualities of *I. potaninii*. In our experience they are, for garden purposes, identical. Flowers a delightful shrimp pink. China. I. 1908.

decora LINDL. (*incarnata*). A rare and pretty, dwarf shrub from China and Japan, producing long racemes of pink pea-flowers. I. 1846. A.M. 1933.

alba REHD. An attractive form with white flowers. I. about 1878. A.M. 1939.

heterantha BRANDIS (*gerardiana*). Flowers bright purplish rose, foliage very elegant. Grows ·9 to 1·2m. in the open, but much higher against a wall. Plants we have received under the name *I. divaricata* are almost identical with this species and it is perhaps merely a geographical form. N.W. Himalaya. C. 1840.

hebepetala BENTH. A medium-sized, wide-spreading shrub with flowers of distinct colouring, being rose with a deep crimson standard. N.W. Himalaya. C. 1881.

incarnata. See *I. decora*.

kirilowii PALIB. (*macrostachya*). A small shrub with flowers of bright almond-pink in long, dense racemes, but rather hidden by the leaves. N. China, Korea. I. 1899.

potaninii CRAIB. A splendid, medium-sized shrub. Flowers clear pink in racemes 12 to 20cm. long produced continuously from June to September. N.W. China. C. 1925.

pseudotinctoria MATSUM. A vigorous species from China and Japan, attaining about 1·5m. Related to *I. amblyantha*, it has pink flowers in dense racemes up to 10cm. long. I. 1897. A.M. 1965.

†**pulchella** ROXB. (*rubra*) (*violacea*). A small shrub bearing long, axillary racemes of purple-red flowers. Only for the mildest areas or conservatory. East Indies. I. 1819.

"IRONWOOD". See *OSTRYA virginiana*.

ITEA—**Iteaceae**—A small genus of attractive and unusual, summer flowering shrubs thriving in half shade. The evergreen species will take full sun against a south or west wall, providing the soil is not too dry.

ITEA—*continued*

***ilicifolia** OLIV. A lax, evergreen, holly-like shrub up to 3m. or more in height, charming in appearance when, in late summer, it is laden with long, drooping, catkin-like racemes of fragrant greenish-white flowers. C. China. I. 1901. A.M. 1911.

‡virginica L. An attractive, small, erect-branched, deciduous shrub, producing upright cylindrical racemes of fragrant, creamy-white flowers in July. Foliage often colours well in the autumn. Eastern U.S.A. I. 1744. A.M. 1972.

†*yunnanensis FRANCH. Closely resembles *I. ilicifolia*, but has longer leaves. Flowers white in racemes 15 to 18cm. long. Yunnan, China. I. about 1918.

JAMESIA—Philadelphaceae—A monotypic genus related to *Deutzia*, but flowers with a superior ovary. Any ordinary soil in full sun.

americana TORR. & GRAY. A small to medium-sized erect shrub, with greyish leaves and slightly fragrant, white flowers produced in cymose clusters during May and June. Western N. America. I. 1862.

"JASMINE". See *JASMINUM*.

"JASMINE, WINTER". See *JASMINUM nudiflorum*.

JASMINUM—Oleaceae—"Jasmine", "Jessamine". The jasmines are popular as climbing plants but too little planted as self-supporting shrubs. All the shrubby species have yellow flowers and are more or less deciduous in a hard winter but their usually green stems create an evergreen effect. Their soil requirements are cosmopolitan. For climbing species see under CLIMBERS at end of Manual.

fruticans L. A small to medium-sized, semi-evergreen shrub with erect stems. Leaves normally trifoliolate; flowers yellow, in clusters at the end of the stems from June to September. Fruits black. Mediterranean Region. C. 1517.

humile L. (*farreri*) (*pubigerum*). A small to medium-sized, semi-scandent, half evergreen shrub, with normally trifoliolate leaves. Flowers bright yellow, in terminal clusters in June or July. This extremely variable species is distributed over a wide area from Afghanistan to Yunnan and Szechwan. C. 1650.

glabrum. See *wallichianum*.

***'Revolutum'** (*J. revolutum*). A quite remarkable and beautiful medium-sized shrub with deep green persistent leaves of good texture, composed of usually five to seven leaflets. These create a splendid setting for the comparatively large deep yellow, slightly fragrant flowers in cymbose clusters during summer. Originally introduced from China in 1814. A.M. 1976.

wallichianum P. S. GREEN (*glabrum*). A form of tall, scandent growth, the leaves with normally seven to eleven leaflets, the terminal one long and acuminate. Flowers yellow, in pendant clusters. N.E. Nepal. I. 1912.

nudiflorum LINDL. "Winter Jasmine". One of the most tolerant and beautiful of winter flowering shrubs. Flowers bright yellow appearing on the naked green branches from November to February. Makes strong, angular growths up to 4·5m. long. Excellent for covering unsightly walls and banks. When grown as a wall shrub, long growths may be cut back immediately after flowering. W. China. Introduced by Robert Fortune in 1844. A.G.M. 1923.

parkeri DUNN. A dwarf or prostrate shrub normally forming a low mound of densely crowded, greenish stems; bearing small, pinnate leaves and tiny yellow flowers in summer. Suitable for the rock garden. W. Himalaya. I. 1923. A.M. 1933.

revolutum. See *J. humile 'Revolutum'*.

subhumile. See under CLIMBERS.

"JERUSALEM SAGE". See *PHLOMIS fruticosa*.

†JOVELLANA—Scrophulariaceae—Attractive small shrubs, sometimes listed under *Calceolaria*, but their flowers lack the pouched lip of the latter.

sinclairii KRANZL. A very distinct New Zealand species of dwarf habit, suitable for a rock garden in a mild locality, with white or pale lavender, purple spotted flowers in June. I. 1881.

***violacea** G. DON (*Calceolaria violacea*). A charming, small, Chilean shrub with erect branches and small neat leaves. Flowers pale violet with darker markings, produced in June and July. I. 1853. A.M. 1930.

"JUDAS TREE". See *CERCIS siliquastrum*.

JUGLANS—Juglandaceae—The "Walnuts" are mostly fast-growing, ornamental trees which are not particular as to soil, but should not be planted in sites subject to late frosts. Their leaves are pinnate, like those of the "Ash" and, in some species, are large and ornamental.

JUGLANS—*continued*

ailantifolia CARR. (*sieboldiana*). An erect-growing tree of medium size with large, handsome leaves often as much as 1m. long. Japan. I. 1860.

cordiformis REHD. A form differing only in the shape of its fruits.

californica S. WATS. A distinct, large shrub or small tree, with attractive leaves composed of eleven to fifteen oblong-lanceolate leaflets. S. California. C. 1889.

cathayensis DODE. A handsome, medium-sized tree with conspicuous, large leaves bearing eleven to seventeen leaflets. C. and W. China; Formosa. I. 1903.

cinerea L. "Butternut". A handsome, fast-growing species of medium size with shoots sticky to the touch, and large, hairy leaves and exceptionally large fruits. Eastern N. America. C. 1633.

hindsii R. E. SMITH. Medium-sized tree with handsome foliage. Central California. C. 1878.

major. See *J. microcarpa major.*

mandshurica MAXIM. Medium-sized tree with stout, glandular-hairy young shoots. Leaves up to ·6m. long, sometimes longer on young trees, composed of eleven to nineteen taper-pointed leaflets. Manchuria, N. China. I. 1859.

microcarpa BERL. (*rupestris*). "Texan Walnut". A very graceful, small, shrubby tree similar to *J. californica,* but with numerous small, thin, narrow leaflets. Texas, New Mexico. C. 1868.

major BENSON (*J. major*). A medium-sized tree differing from the type in its larger size, generally larger, more coarsely-toothed leaflets and larger fruits. New Mexico to Arizona. I. about 1894.

nigra L. "Black Walnut". A large, noble, fast-growing tree, with deeply furrowed bark and large leaves. Fruits large and round, generally in pairs. E. and C. United States. C. 1686. Named, vegetatively produced clones are also available. See our Fruit Catalogue.

regia L. "Common Walnut". A slow-growing, medium-sized to large tree with a characteristic rounded head. S.E. Europe, Himalaya and China. Cultivated in England for many centuries. The timber is highly prized and very valuable.

Normally grown from seed, the quality of its nuts are uncertain. Young grafted trees of named clones selected for the quality of their nuts and earlier fruiting are also available, as per our Fruit Catalogue.

'Laciniata'. "Cut-leaved Walnut". A form with somewhat pendulous branchlets and deeply cut leaflets. A.M. 1960.

rupestris. See *J. microcarpa.*

sieboldiana. See *J. ailantifolia.*

×**sinensis** DODE (*mandshurica*×*regia*) (*regia sinensis*). A large tree, similar to *J. regia* in general appearance, but leaflets oblong-obovate and slightly toothed. N. and E. China.

"JUNE BERRY". See *AMELANCHIER.*

‡**KALMIA—Ericaceae**—Charming spring and early summer flowering shrubs luxuriating under conditions similar to those required by *Rhododendron.* The conspicuous flowers are saucer-shaped; for maximum flowering, plant in full sun and moist soil.

***angustifolia** L. A low growing shrub up to 1m. high, slowly spreading and forming thickets. Leaves variable in shape, normally ovate-oblong, in pairs or threes. Flowers rosy-red; June. Eastern N. America. I. 1736.

ovata PURSH. A form with broader, ovate leaves of a bright green.

'Rubra'. Foliage deep green; flowers deep rosy-red, carried over a long period.

'Rubra Nana'. A dwarf form with flowers of a rich garnet-red.

***carolina** SMALL. A species closely resembling *K. angustifolia,* but differing by reason of the normally grey-downy undersurfaces of its leaves. Flowers purple-rose. S.E. United States. I. 1906.

cuneata MICHX. A small, semi-evergreen shrub rarely above 1m. high. Small, alternate, dark green leaves sessile or nearly so; flowers white, cup-shaped in clusters along the stems during summer. S.E. United States. I. 1820.

***latifolia** L. "Calico Bush". A magnificent rhododendron-like shrub of medium size. Apart from roses and rhododendrons possibly the best June-flowering shrub for acid soils. The glossy, alternate leaves 5 to 13cm. long make a pleasing setting for the clusters of bright-pink, saucer-shaped flowers which open in June, giving the impression of sugar-icing when in bud. Eastern N. America. I. 1734. A.G.M. 1948.

'Clementine Churchill'. The best red-flowered Kalmia. A lovely clone. A.M. 1952. A.G.M. 1969.

KALMIA—*continued*

latifolia 'Myrtifolia'. A very slow growing, small bush of compact habit, with smaller leaves and flowers. A.M. 1965.

***polifolia** WANGENH. (*glauca*). A small, wiry shrub ·3 to ·6m. high with narrow leaves, dark shining green above, glaucous beneath, in pairs or threes. Flowers in large terminal clusters, bright rose-purple, opening in April. In its native land this species grows in swamps and boggy places. Eastern N. America. I. 1767.

‡*KALMIOPSIS—Ericaceae—A monotypic genus.

leachiana REHD. A choice and rare, dwarf shrub of considerable beauty. Pink kalmia-like blooms in terminal, leafy racemes from March to May. Quite hardy. A protected plant in S.W. Oregon. I. 1931. A.M. 1937.

KALOPANAX—Araliaceae—A monotypic genus differing from *Acanthopanax* in its lobed but not compound leaves.

pictus NAKAI (*septemlobus*) (*Acanthopanax ricinifolium*). A small to medium-sized tree in cultivation, superficially resembling an *Acer*. The branches and sucker growths bear scattered, stout prickles. Leaves five to seven lobed, in young plants over 30cm. across. The small clusters of white flowers are borne in large, flattish heads ·3 to ·6m. across in autumn. Japan. C. 1874.

maximowiczii LI. Leaves deeply lobed.

"KENTUCKY COFFEE TREE". See *GYMNOCLADUS dioicus*.

KERRIA—Rosaceae—A monotypic genus differing from *Rhodotypos* in its alternate leaves and yellow flowers. A suckering shrub which has adorned our gardens since Victorian days. May be thinned and pruned immediately after flowering.

japonica DC. A graceful shrub up to 1·8m. high, or more against a wall. In April and May its arching branches are wreathed with rich yellow flowers, like large buttercups. Its green stems are most effective in winter. China, Japan. I. 1834. A.G.M. 1928.

'Picta'. See '*Variegata*'.

'Pleniflora' ('*Flore Pleno*'). The well known double flowered form. Taller and more vigorous than the type. Introduced from China by William Kerr in 1804. A.G.M. 1928. A.M. 1978.

'Variegata' ('*Picta*'). A pleasing and elegant creamy-white, variegated form of lower spreading habit, up to 1·5m. in height.

KOELREUTERIA—Sapindaceae—Very attractive, wide-spreading trees, 9 to 12m. high, with long, pinnate leaves and large panicles of small yellow flowers in July and August. Of easy cultivation on all soils. Flowering best in hot, dry summers.

apiculata. See *K. paniculata apiculata*.

paniculata LAXM. The best-known species, given such names as "Pride of India", "China-tree" and "Goldenrain-tree", etc. A broad-headed tree with normally pinnate leaves comprising nine to fifteen ovate leaflets. The yellow flowers are followed by conspicuous bladder-like fruits. The leaves turn yellow in autumn. China. I. 1763. A.M. 1932.

apiculata REHD. (*K. apiculata*). An uncommon variety which flowers more freely as a young tree than *K. paniculata* from which it differs in its normally doubly-pinnate leaves with more numerous leaflets. China. I. 1904.

'Fastigiata'. A rare and remarkable, slow-growing form of narrowly columnar habit, attaining 8m. high by 1m. wide.

KOLKWITZIA—Caprifoliaceae—A monotypic genus.

amabilis GRAEBN. "Beauty Bush". This lovely and graceful, very hardy and adaptable, medium-sized shrub forms a dense, twiggy bush. In May and June its drooping branches are draped with masses of bell-shaped flowers, soft pink with a yellow throat. The calyces and pedicels are conspicuously hairy. One of the many lovely shrubs introduced by Ernest Wilson. W. China. I. 1901. A.M. 1923.

'Pink Cloud'. A lovely pink flowered seedling selected and raised at Wisley. F.C.C. 1963. A.G.M. 1965. '*Rosea*' is a similar clone.

+**LABURNOCYTISUS** (*LABURNUM+CYTISUS*)—**Leguminosae.**

adamii SCHNEID. (*Laburnum anagyroides+Cytisus purpureus*). A remarkable small tree, a graft hybrid (chimera) with laburnum forming the core and broom the outer envelope. Some branches bear the yellow flowers of the laburnum, whilst other branches bear dense, congested clusters of the purple-flowered broom. To add to the "confusion" most branches produce intermediate flowers of a striking, coppery-pink shade. Originated in the nursery of Mons. Adam near Paris in 1825.

LABURNUM—Leguminosae—"Golden Rain". Small, ornamental trees of easy cultivation, suitable for almost all types of soil. The yellow pea-flowers are produced in drooping racemes during late spring and early summer. All parts of the plant are poisonous, particularly the seeds.

alpinum BERCHT. & PRESL. "Scotch Laburnum". A small, broad-headed tree producing long, drooping racemes of fragrant flowers in early June. Leaves trifoliolate, deep shining green above, paler and with a few hairs beneath. Pods flattened, glabrous and shining. C. and S. Europe. C. 1596.

'Pendulum'. A slow-growing form developing a low, dome-shaped head of stiffly weeping branches.

'Pyramidale'. A form with erect branches.

anagyroides MED. (*vulgare*). "Common Laburnum". A small tree flowering in late May or early June, the drooping racemes crowded along the branches. This species differs from *L. alpinum* in its earlier flowering, shorter racemes, smaller, dull green leaves which are densely appressed hairy beneath and in its rounder, appressed hairy pods. C. and S. Europe. C. 1560.

'Aureum'. "Golden-leaved Laburnum". Leaves soft yellow during summer; sometimes liable to revert. F.C.C. 1875.

'Autumnale' (*'Semperflorens'*). A form which frequently flowers for a second time in the autumn.

'Erect'. An excellent small tree with stiffly ascending branches. Originated as a seedling in our nurseries.

'Pendulum'. A low, elegant tree with long, slender, drooping branches.

'Quercifolium'. A curious, small tree with leaflets deeply lobed.

×**vossii.** See *L.* ×*watereri 'Vossii'*.

vulgare. See *L. anagyroides*.

×**watereri** DIPP. (*alpinum*×*anagyroides*) (*'Parkesii'*). A small tree with glossy leaves and long, slender racemes in June. Resembles *L. alpinum* in general habit, but leaves and pods slightly more hairy, the latter usually only partially developed.

'Alford's Weeping'. A vigorous, small tree with a wide-spreading head of long, drooping branches. Originated as a seedling in our nurseries.

'Vossii' (*L.* ×*vossii*). A lovely form, very free-flowering, with long racemes. A.G.M. 1928.

"LABURNUM, EVERGREEN". See *PIPTANTHUS laburnifolius*.

†**LAGERSTROEMIA—Lythraceae**—A genus of evergreen and deciduous trees and shrubs often with exotic flowers.

indica L. "Crape Myrtle". A beautiful, large shrub or small tree requiring more hot sun than we can anticipate in our insular climate. The main stem is attractively mottled grey, pink and cinnamon. Flowers usually lilac-pink with crinkled petals, borne in terminal panicles in autumn, only opening outside after a warm, late summer. Best planted against a south-facing wall. China, Korea. I. 1759. A.M. 1924.

'Rosea'. Flowers deep rose.

"LAUREL, ALEXANDRIAN". See *DANAE racemosa*.

"LAUREL, CALIFORNIAN". See *UMBELLULARIA californica*.

"LAUREL, COMMON" or "CHERRY". See *PRUNUS laurocerasus*.

"LAUREL, PORTUGAL". See *PRUNUS lusitanica*.

†***LAURELIA—Atherospermataceae**—A small genus of three evergreen species.

serrata BERTERO (*aromatica*). "Chilean Laurel". A handsome, large evergreen shrub or small to medium-sized, lime-tolerant tree. The leathery, serrated leaves are of a bright green and are strongly aromatic. Only suitable for mild areas. Chile. I. before 1868.

***LAURUS—Lauraceae**—A genus of only two or three species of evergreen shrubs or small trees. The small, yellowish-green, dioecious flowers cluster the branches in April and are followed, on female trees, by shining black fruits. Suitable for all types of well-drained soil.

†azorica FRANCO (*canariensis*) (*maderensis*). "Canary Island Laurel". In this country a large, evergreen shrub. A handsome species, differing from *L. nobilis* in its larger, broader leaves and its downy young twigs; leaves of older trees become narrower. Suitable only for the mildest gardens. There appear to be two forms in cultivation; one with hairy leaves and another with glabrous leaves, the latter being more tender. Canary Islands, Azores.

nobilis L. "Bay Laurel". The "Laurel" of the ancients, now grown for its aromatic foliage and for its usefulness as a dense, pyramidal evergreen shrub or tree. Stands clipping well, and thrives in coastal regions where it will form good hedges. Subject to frost damage in cold areas. Mediterranean Region. C. 1562.

angustifolia MARKG. (*'Salicifolia'*). "Willow-leaf Bay". A remarkably hardy form with long, narrow, pale green, leathery, wavy-edged leaves.

'Aurea'. Leaves golden yellow, particularly attractive in winter and spring.

"LAURUSTINUS". See *VIBURNUM tinus*.

LAVANDULA—Labiatae—"Lavender" is perhaps the most highly prized of all aromatic shrubs. It is a favourite for dwarf hedges, associating well with stonework or rose beds, and as a component of grey or blue borders. It succeeds in all types of well drained soil preferably in full sun. An excellent maritime plant.

angustifolia MILL. (*spica* L. in part) (*officinalis*). "Old English Lavender". It has been pointed out by various authorities that all the clones generally grown in gardens under this name are hybrids between *L. angustifolia* and *L. latifolia*. Both species are native of the Mediterranean Region and have been cultivated since the mid 16th century. A.M.T. 1962. The flowers are borne in dense spikes on long slender stems.

'Alba'. A robust form with long, narrow, grey-green leaves producing erect stems from ·9 to 1·2m. high. Flowers white, opening in late July.

'Folgate'. A compact form with narrow, grey-green leaves and stems from ·6 to ·75m. high. Flowers lavender-blue, opening in early July. A.M.T. 1963.

'Grappenhall'. A robust form with comparatively broad, grey-green leaves and strong stems from ·9 to 1·2m. high. Flowers lavender-blue, opening in late July.

'Hidcote'. A compact form with narrow, grey-green leaves and stems from ·6 to ·8m. high. Flowers violet in dense spikes, opening in early July. One of the best and most popular cultivars. A.M. 1950. F.C.C.T. 1963. A.G.M. 1965. *'Nana Atropurpurea'* is a similar, though older clone.

'Hidcote Giant'. Similar in habit and appearance to *'Grappenhall'*, but flowers a little darker in colour.

'Loddon Pink'. A compact form with narrow grey-green leaves and stems from ·6 to ·75m. high. Flowers pale pink opening in early July. A.M.T. 1963.

'Munstead'. A compact form with narrow, green leaves and stems from ·6 to ·75m. high. Flowers lavender-blue, bluer than in most, opening in early July. A.M.T. 1963.

'Nana Alba'. A dwarf, compact form with comparatively broad, grey-green leaves and stems up to ·3m. Flowers white, opening in early July.

'Rosea'. A compact form with narrow leaves, greener than those of *'Loddon Pink'*. Stems ·6 to ·75m. high, bearing lavender-pink flowers in early to mid July.

'Twickel Purple'. A compact form with comparatively broad, grey-green leaves and stems from ·6 to ·75m. high. Flowers lavender-blue, opening in early July. A.M.T. 1961.

'Vera'. A robust form with comparatively broad, grey leaves and stems from 1 to 1·2m. high. Flowers lavender-blue, opening in late July. Usually referred to in cultivation as "Dutch Lavender". A.M.T. 1962.

†lanata BOISS. A small, white-woolly perennial or sub-shrub producing long-stalked spikes of fragrant, bright violet flowers from July to September. Spain.

spica. See *L. angustifolia*.

stoechas L. "French Lavender". A dwarf, intensely aromatic shrublet with narrow leaves. Flowers dark purple borne in dense, congested terminal heads during summer. It requires a warm, dry, sunny position. Mediterranean Region. Cultivated since mid 16th century. A.M. 1960.

LAVATERA—Malvaceae—The shrubby-mallows have typical mallow flowers and palmate leaves. Succeeding in all types of soil preferably in full sun. Excellent for maritime exposure.

bicolor. See under *L. maritima.*

†**maritima** GOUAN. An elegant species attaining 1·5 to 1·8m. against a sunny wall. Both the stems and the palmate leaves are greyish and downy. Flowers large, saucer-shaped, pale lilac with purple veins and eye, produced continuously from mid-summer to late autumn. Needs a warm, sheltered position. S. France. We grow the form previously known as *L. bicolor.*

olbia L. A vigorous subshrub up to 2·1m. high, the whole plant conspicuously softly grey downy. Large, pink or reddish-pink flowers throughout summer. Best in a warm, sunny position. S. France. C. 1570. A.M. 1912.

"LAVENDER". See *LAVANDULA.*

"LEATHERWOOD". See *CYRILLA racemiflora* and *DIRCA palustris.*

‡***LEDUM—Ericaceae**—Low-growing, evergreen inhabitants of swamp moors in Northern latitudes. All have neat foliage, usually covered below with white or rust-coloured woolly tomentum, and terminal clusters of white flowers. They require a lime-free soil.

buxifolium. See *LEIOPHYLLUM buxifolium.*

glandulosum NUTT. (*columbianum*). A useful, dwarf species, occasionally up to 1m. Leaves oblong, oval or ovate, glandular and scaly beneath; flowers in terminal clusters 2·5 to 5cm. across in May. Western N. America.

groenlandicum OED. (*latifolium*). "Labrador Tea". The best known of the genus, a dwarf, upright evergreen occasionally to 1m. Flowers white, produced from April to June in conspicuous terminal clusters. N. America, Greenland. I. 1763.

'Compactum'. A compact form developing into a neat shrub ·3 to ·46m. high, with broader leaves on shorter branches, and smaller flower clusters than in the type. A.M. 1980.

latifolium. See *L. groenlandicum.*

minus HORT. A dwarf shrub possibly only a form of *L. palustre.* Narrow leaves and clusters of white flowers in May. N.E. Asia.

palustre L. "Wild Rosemary". A variable species up to 1m. high, closely related to *L. groenlandicum,* producing terminal clusters of white flowers in April and May. Arctic regions of Europe, Asia and America. I. 1762.

dilatatum WAHLBG. (*hypoleucum*) (*nipponicum*). A form with slightly broader leaves. Japan, Korea, E. Siberia. C. 1902. A.M. 1938.

‡***LEIOPHYLLUM—Ericaceae**—A monotypic genus requiring the same conditions as *Ledum* from which it differs in the small, glabrous, box-like leaves.

buxifolium ELL. (*Ledum buxifolium*). A dwarf shrub of neat, compact, rounded habit, producing in May and June clusters of white flowers, pink in bud. Leaves opposite and alternate. An attractive species requiring lime-free soil. Eastern N. America. I. by Peter Collinson in 1736. A.M. 1955.

hugeri SCHNEID. Leaves mostly alternate, longer than in the type.

prostratum GRAY. A very dainty, prostrate or loosely spreading, dwarf shrub. Leaves mostly opposite. A.M. 1945.

‡**LEITNERIA—Leitneriaceae**—A rare monotypic genus of botanical interest closely related to *Myrica,* but very different in general appearance. It requires a moist, lime-free soil.

floridana CHAPM. "Corkwood". A medium-sized to large, suckering shrub, occasionally a small tree. Leaves narrow-elliptic to elliptic-lanceolate, 12·7 to 20·3cm. long. Flowers small, appearing in slender, greyish catkins in spring, male and female borne on separate plants. S.E. United States. I. 1894.

"LEMON PLANT". See *LIPPIA citriodora.*

†**LEONOTIS—Labiatae**—An easily grown shrub in all types of soil but only suitable for a sunny wall in very mild localities. Excellent for the conservatory.

leonurus R. BR. "Lion's Ear". A small, square-stemmed shrub with downy, lanceolate, opposite leaves and dense axillary whorls of 5cm. long, downy, bright orange-scarlet, two-lipped flowers in late autumn. S. Africa. I. 1712.

LEPTODERMIS—**Rubiacae**—Interesting and subtly attractive small to medium-sized shrubs for all soils in moderately sheltered gardens.

kumaonensis PARKER. An uncommon small shrub with downy leaves. Flowers small, trumpet-shaped, white becoming lilac or purplish, borne in clusters in the leaf axils from July to October. N.W. Himalaya. I. 1923.

pilosa DIELS (*Hamiltonia pilosa*). A medium-sized shrub with smaller leaves than *L. kumaoensis*. Flowers lavender, produced from July to September. Yunnan. I. 1904.

***LEPTOSPERMUM**—**Myrtaceae**—An attractive genus of small-leaved, Australasian shrubs related to the "Myrtles" and of about equal merit to the Tree Heaths. In warm maritime and mild localities many form large shrubs up to 4·6m. high, but elsewhere most require the protection of a wall. They succeed best in full sun in well-drained acid or neutral soils. Flowers white unless otherwise stated, and borne in May and June.

cunninghamii SCHAU. An Australian species to about 2m. with attractive silvery-grey leaves and reddish stems. Flowering in July, several weeks later than those of *L. lanigerum*. Exceptionally hardy. A.M. 1959.

humifusum SCHAU. (*rupestre*) (*scoparium prostratum* HORT.). A remarkably hardy, prostrate shrub, forming an extensive carpet of reddish stems and small, blunt, leathery leaves. Small, white flowers stud the branches of mature specimens in early summer. Tasmania. Introduced by H. Comber in 1930.

†**laevigatum** F. MUELL. A vigorous species with comparatively large, glossy, glabrous leaves and flowers 2cm. across. Australia, Tasmania. A.M. 1927.

lanigerum SMITH (*pubescens*). A beautiful small shrub, similar to *L. cunninghamii*, but with long, more silvery, leaves, often bronzed towards autumn, flowering earlier. In the southern counties there are bushes which have grown splendidly in open borders for more than twenty years. Australia, Tasmania. I. 1774.

liversidgei R. T. BAKER & H. G. SMITH (*thymifolia*). An Australian species with numerous small, crowded leaves, lemon-scented when crushed. Flowers white in graceful sprays. One of the hardier species which has here survived many winters in the open.

myrtifolium. See *L. sericeum*.

†**rodwayanum** SUMMERHAYES & COMBER. Tasmanian species bearing flowers as much as 3cm. across, the largest of the genus, borne in late summer. Introduced by Harold Comber in 1930.

†**scoparium** J. R. & G. FORST. The common "Manuka" or "Tea-tree" of New Zealand. A variable species which has given rise to numerous forms. Flowers white. Australia, Tasmania, New Zealand. I. 1772. A.M. 1972.

'Album Flore Pleno'. Flowers white, double; habit compact and erect.

'Boscawenii'. Flowers up to 2·5cm. across, rich pink in bud opening white with reddish centre. Compact habit. A.M. 1912.

'Chapmanii'. Leaves brownish green, flowers bright rose. C. 1889.

'Decumbens'. A semi-prostrate form, with pale pink, long-lasting flowers, freely produced.

'Keatleyi'. An outstanding cultivar with large, waxy-petalled flowers of a soft pink. Young shoots and leaves crimson and silky. A.M. 1961.

'Nanum'. A charming, dwarf form, attaining about ·3m.; rose-pink flowers produced with great freedom. An excellent alpine-house shrub. A.M. 1952.

'Nichollsii'. Flowers carmine red; foliage dark purplish-bronze. F.C.C. 1912. A.M. 1953.

'Nichollsii Grandiflorum'. A selected form of '*Nichollsii*' with larger flowers.

prostratum HORT. See *L. humifusum*.

'Red Damask'. Very double, deep red, long-lasting flowers. A.M. 1955.

'Roseum Multipetalum'. Double, rose-pink flowers in profusion. A.M. 1928.

sericeum LABILL. (*myrtifolium*). A moderately hardy Tasmanian shrub of medium height. Leaves small, bright green, pointed; flowers white; young stems red.

stellatum CAV. A medium-sized shrub; leaves bright green; only injured by the severest weather. Australia.

LESPEDEZA—**Leguminosae**—"Bush Clover". The cultivated species of this extensive genus are very useful, late-flowering shrubs, their racemes of small, pea-flowers being borne profusely and continuously along the shoots which are bowed by their weight. All have trifoliolate leaves and given full sun are of the easiest cultivation.

LESPEDEZA—*continued*

bicolor TURCZ. A medium-sized shrub of semi-erect habit. The bright rose-purple flowers are borne in racemose inflorescences in late summer. Korea, Manchuria, China, Japan. Introduced by Maximowicz in 1856.

buergeri MIQ. A medium-sized shrub of spreading habit. Flowers purple and white in dense racemes. Japan, China.

cyrtobotrya MIQ. A small shrub throwing up annually, erect, woody stems. In late summer rose-purple pea-flowers crowd the ends of each shoot. Japan, Korea. I. 1899.

kiusiana NAKAI. Of uncertain identity, but a distinct and very attractive small shrub with soft-green, clover-like leaves, and light rose-purple flowers in large compound leafy panicles.

thunbergii NAKAI (*sieboldii*) (*Desmodium penduliflorum*). One of the best autumn flowering shrubs. The arching 1·2 to 1·5m. stems, are bowed to the ground in September by the weight of the huge terminal panicles of rose-purple pea-flowers. Japan, China. I. about 1837. F.C.C. 1871.

‡***LEUCOPOGON**—**Epacridaceae**—A large genus of evergreen shrubs and trees requiring the same conditions as *Erica*.

fraseri A. CUNN. A dwarf, New Zealand shrublet related to *Cyathodes* and requiring similar treatment. The decumbent branchlets are clothed with close-set, imbricated, shining green leaves. Flowers small, white or lavender, tubular, fruits orange-yellow.

‡**LEUCOTHOE**—**Ericaceae**—An attractive and useful genus of shade-bearing shrubs for lime-free soils. They are natives of North America and Japan.

catesbaei. See *L. fontanesiana*.

***davisiae** TORR. (*Andromeda davisiae*). A pretty shrub, usually less than 1m. high, with dark green, glossy leaves and erect panicles of pure white flowers in June. California. Introduced by William Lobb in 1853. F.C.C. 1883.

***fontanesiana** SLEUM. (*catesbaei* HORT.). A small to medium-sized shrub of elegant habit. An excellent ground cover for acid soils. The graceful arching stems carry lanceolate, leathery, green leaves which, in autumn and winter, especially in exposed positions, become tinged a rich beetroot-red or bronze purple. The short, pendant racemes of white, pitcher-shaped flowers, appear all along the stems in May. S.E. United States. I. 1793. A.M. 1972. For many years this plant has been grown as *L. catesbaei* which name rightly belongs to another, closely related, species (*L. axillaris*).

'Nana'. A lower growing, more compact form.

'Rainbow' (*'Multicolor'*). Leaves variegated with cream, yellow and pink.

'Rollissonii'. A selection with narrower leaves.

grayana MAXIM. A remarkable, small, semi-evergreen shrub with stout, green, ascending stems becoming an attractive, deep polished red in winter, and large, broadly oval leaves usually turning bronze-yellow tinted purple in autumn. Flowers pale green, produced in July and August in ascending one-sided racemes. Japan. I. 1890.

oblongifolia OHWI. A slightly dwarfer variety of stiffer, more upright habit; stems dark polished reddish-purple in winter. Leaves markedly oblong, smaller and darker than those of the type, turning to yellow and flame in the autumn. Japan.

***keiskei** MIQ. A small, glabrous, evergreen shrub with arching red-tinged shoots. Leaves ovate to ovate-elliptic, slender pointed, glossy green above, and 5 to 10cm. long. The comparatively large, cylindrical, white flowers are borne in nodding, terminal and axillary racemes in July. Japan. I. 1915. A.M. 1933.

***populifolia** DIPP. A vigorous, medium-sized shrub of considerable quality. Leaves lanceolate to ovate-lanceolate, up to 10cm. long. Flowers white, in short racemes. Subject to injury in the coldest areas. S.E. United States. I. 1765.

LEYCESTERIA—**Caprifoliaceae**—A small genus of hollow-stemmed shrubs. Suitable for any reasonably fertile soil.

†**crocothyrsos** AIRY-SHAW. An interesting and attractive, medium-sized shrub, suitable only for mild districts. Leaves large, slender pointed. The yellow flowers are borne in terminal racemes in April and are followed by small, gooseberry-like, green fruits. Assam. Introduced by Kingdon Ward in 1928. A.M. 1960.

LEYCESTERIA—*continued*

formosa WALL. A medium-sized erect shrub with stout, hollow, sea-green shoots covered at first with a glaucous bloom. Flowers white, carried in dense terminal, drooping panicles of claret-coloured bracts, appearing from June to September. These are followed by large, shining, reddish-purple berries which are attractive to pheasants. Himalaya. I. 1824.

LIGUSTRUM—Oleaceae—The "Privets" are mostly fast-growing, evergreen or semi-evergreen shrubs, not particular as to soil and shade tolerant. Many produce conspicuous flower heads and fruits.

acuminatum. See *L. tschonoskii.*

acutissimum KOEHNE. A Chinese shrub of medium height akin to *L. obtusifolium.* I. about 1900.

amurense CARR. "Amur Privet". A large shrub of tough constitution. Similar in most respects to *L. ovalifolium,* but with twigs and leaves below, pubescent. N. China. C. 1860.

chenaultii HICKEL. A remarkable semi-evergreen small tree or large shrub worthy of a place in every large garden. Leaves conspicuously long, lance-shaped and slender. Flowers white in large lilac-like panicles in late summer. S.W. China. I. 1908.

compactum BRANDIS (*yunnanense*). A striking, large, semi-evergreen shrub or small tree with glossy, bright green, lanceolate leaves up to 12·5cm. long. Bears large panicles of white flowers in June and July followed by blue-black fruits. Himalaya, S.W. China. I. 1874.

†confusum DCNE. A conspicuous, but rather tender, Himalayan species, forming a large shrub in mild districts. Flowers white, very freely borne in wide panicles in June and July. The clusters of bloomy black fruits are very striking. I. 1919.

***delavayanum** HARIOT (*ionandrum*) (*prattii*). A rather variable, small-leaved evergreen, spreading shrub of medium size. Flowers in dense panicles, white with violet anthers, fruits black. A good hedging plant but not for the colder counties. Yunnan. I. 1890.

***henryi** HEMSL. A medium-sized to large shrub of compact growth. Leaves small, roundish, dark almost black-green and glossy. Flowers in August. C. China. I. 1901. A.M. 1910.

ibota SIEB. & ZUCC. Small to medium-sized shrub of spreading habit, similar to but more elegant than *L. ovalifolium.* Japan. I. 1860.

ionandrum. See *L. delavayanum.*

***japonicum** THUNB. "Japanese Privet". A compact, medium-sized, very dense evergreen shrub with camellia-like foliage, of a shining olive-green. Bears large panicles of white flowers in late summer. An excellent evergreen for screening or hedging. N. China; Korea; Formosa; Japan. Introduced by Siebold in 1845.

'Macrophyllum'. A splendid form with broad, glossy, black-green, camellia-like leaves. Sometimes wrongly referred to as a form of *L. lucidum.* An outstanding evergreen.

'Rotundifolium' (*'Coriaceum'*). A very slow-growing, rigid, compact form with round, leathery, black-green leaves.

***lucidum** AIT. f. A large, evergreen shrub or small to medium-sized tree with large, glossy green, long pointed leaves and large, handsome panicles of white flowers in autumn. Occasionally seen as a beautiful, symmetrical tree up to 12m. or more high with an attractive fluted trunk. A worthy street tree for restricted areas. China. I. 1794. A.M. 1965. A.G.M. 1973.

'Excelsum Superbum'. A very striking, variegated form, the leaves being margined and mottled deep yellow and creamy white. Will attain small tree size. A.G.M. 1973.

'Latifolium'. A conspicuous form with large, camellia-like leaves. A.G.M. 1973.

'Tricolor'. Leaves rather narrow with an irregular border of white; tinged pink when young. A.G.M. 1973.

obtusifolium regelianum REHD. A low shrub with spreading branches. White flowers in terminal, nodding clusters, very freely produced in July; leaves rose-madder in autumn persisting for several weeks. Japan. C. 1885.

***ovalifolium** HASSK. "Oval-leaf Privet". The ubiquitous "Privet" is one of the commonest of cultivated shrubs, much used for hedging, but when unpruned will reach a large size. It tolerates most soils and aspects, only losing its leaves in cold districts. Useful for game coverts. Japan. C. 1885.

LIGUSTRUM—*continued*

ovalifolium 'Argenteum'. Leaves with creamy-white margin. A.G.M. 1973.

'Aureum'. "Golden Privet". A brightly coloured shrub with rich yellow, green-centred leaves, often completely yellow. A.G.M. 1973. A.M. 1977.

pekinensis. See *SYRINGA pekinensis.*

quihoui CARR. A medium-sized shrub of elegant habit. Florally, this Chinese species is one of the best of the genus, producing, in August and September, panicles up to ·5m. long. China. I. about 1862.

sempervirens. See *PARASYRINGA sempervirens.*

sinense LOUR. This free-flowering, Chinese species is perhaps the most floriferous of deciduous privets. A large shrub of spreading habit; leaves oval; flowers white, produced in long, dense sprays in July, followed by equally numerous black-purple fruits. I. about 1852.

'Pendulum'. A medium sized to large shrub with pendulous branches.

'Variegatum'. An attractive form. The soft grey-green and white leaves combining with the sprays of white flowers will lighten the dullest corner.

***strongylophyllum** HEMSL. Large shrub or small tree with small, rounded or ovate-lanceolate leaves and loose panicles of white flowers in late summer. C. China. I. 1879.

tschonoskii DCNE. (*acuminatum*). Medium-sized shrub of upright habit with large, slender-pointed leaves. Flowers white in June followed by lustrous black fruits. Japan. I. 1888.

'Vicaryi'. Medium-sized shrub with leaves suffused golden yellow. Said to be a hybrid between *L. ovalifolium 'Aureum'* and *L. vulgare.* Garden origin. C. about 1920.

vulgare L. The partially evergreen "Common Privet" is a familiar native of our hedgerows and woodlands particularly in chalk areas. Its long clusters of shining black fruits are conspicuous during autumn. Europe.

'Aureum'. A form with dull yellow leaves.

'Chlorocarpum'. Mature fruits yellowish-green.

'Glaucum'. Leaves a metallic blue-green.

'Insulense'. Leaves longer; inflorescences and fruits larger.

italicum VAHL (*sempervirens*). Leaves almost evergreen.

'Pyramidale' (*'Fastigiatum'*). A form with erect branches.

'Sempervirens'. See *italicum.*

'Xanthocarpum'. A form with yellow fruit.

yunnanense. See *L. compactum.*

"LILAC". See *SYRINGA.*

"LIME". See *TILIA.*

‡LINDERA—Lauraceae—Deciduous and evergreen aromatic trees and shrubs related to the "Bay" (*Laurus nobilis*), requiring lime-free soil. Flowers unisexual, small but sometimes conspicuous in the mass. Grown primarily for their attractive, variably shaped leaves which in the deciduous species give rich autumn tints. Fruit a berry.

benzoin BL. (*Benzoin aestivale*). "Spice Bush". A medium-sized to large shrub with large obovate leaves turning clear yellow in the fall. The small, greenish-yellow flowers in spring are followed, on female plants, by red berries. E. United States. I. 1683.

cercidifolia HEMSL. A large shrub or small tree with ovate or rounded, entire leaves. Flowers sulphur-yellow, in clusters on the leafless stems in March. Berries red. Leaves turn yellow in autumn. China. I. 1907.

glauca BL. A large shrub with narrow-elliptic leaves, glaucous beneath and turning to purple, orange and red in November. In China this and several other species are used in the manufacture of incense-sticks (joss-sticks). Japan, China, Korea, Formosa.

†*megaphylla HEMSL. A large, handsome, evergreen shrub or small tree recalling *Daphniphyllum.* Leaves up to 22cm. long by 6·5cm. wide, dark, shining green above, glaucous beneath. Flowers dioecious, the females producing plum-like fruits. S. China; Formosa. I. 1900.

obtusiloba BL. A magnificent, medium-sized to large shrub of erect or compact habit. The large, three-nerved, broadly ovate to obovate leaves are entire or three-lobed at the tip, turning in autumn from their bright summer green to a glorious butter-yellow, with rich pink tints. The flowers, in early spring, are the colour of newly-made mustard. Japan, China, Korea. I. 1880. A.M. 1952 (as *L. triloba*).

LINDERA—*continued*

praecox. See *PARABENZOIN praecox.*

†**rubronervia** GAMBLE. A handsome, medium-sized shrub with oblong-elliptic leaves which are shining green above, paler or glaucous below, turning orange and red in late autumn. S.W. China.

umbellata THUNB. A semi-erect-growing, medium-sized shrub with slender branches and elliptic to obovate, thin-textured leaves 6·5 to 14cm. long, glaucescent beneath. Flowers appearing with the leaves, yellow, in short umbels. Yellow is the dominant autumn colour. Japan, C. & W. China. I. 1892.

"LING". See *CALLUNA.*

‡***LINNAEA**—**Caprifoliaceae**—A monotypic genus named in honour of Carl Linne (Linnaeus). It requires a peaty woodland soil.

borealis L. "Twinflower". A charming little shrublet, its slender stems carpeting the ground, in moist acid soils forming extensive colonies. The small, delicate, nodding, pinkish-bell-like flowers are carried in pairs on thread-like stems from June to early August. A large patch in full flower in a Scottish woodland, a slight breeze wafting through the pink bells is an unforgettable sight. Throughout the N. Hemisphere (incl. British Isles). C. 1762.

LINUM—**Linaceae**—Attractive plants many of which are suitable for the rock garden. They require full sun and good drainage.

***arboreum** L. Dwarf, spreading shrub with narrow, glaucous leaves. Flowers golden yellow, in loose terminal clusters during summer. Eastern Mediterranean Region. C. 1788.

campanulatum L. A dwarf shrub with erect stems and glaucous, slender pointed leaves. Flowers yellow in terminal corymbs during summer. S. Europe. C. 1795. F.C.C. 1871.

†**LIPPIA** (*ALOYSIA*)—**Verbenaceae**—A large genus of tender shrubs and herbs.

citriodora H.B.K. "Lemon Plant". A medium-sized to large shrub with lanceolate, lemon-scented leaves normally in whorls of three. The tiny, pale purple, insignificant flowers are borne in terminal panicles in August. Best against a warm wall. Chile. I. 1784.

‡**LIQUIDAMBAR**—**Hamamelidaceae**—Handsome trees with maple-like leaves, which usually colour well in autumn. Not suitable for shallow chalky soil. The leaves of juvenile and adult trees are sometimes variable.

formosana HANCE. A beautiful Formosan tree surviving, uninjured, all but our severest winters. The leaves are attractively red tinted in spring and again in autumn. Differing from *L. styraciflua* in its duller, green, three to five-lobed leaves which are hairy beneath, and its normally hairy shoots. S. China; Formosa. I. 1884.

monticola REHD. & WILS. This Chinese form, discovered by E. H. Wilson, is perfectly hardy. It has remarkably large, normally three-lobed, glabrous leaves which colour richly in autumn. I. 1908. A.M. 1958.

orientalis MILL. A slow-growing, large bush or small bushy tree. Leaves small, glabrous, deeply five-lobed, attractively tinted in autumn. In warmer, drier climates it attains large tree size. Asia Minor. I. about 1750.

styraciflua L. "Sweet Gum". A beautiful, large tree, conspicuous at all times, especially in autumn when, if happily placed, the deeply five to seven-lobed, shining green, maple-like leaves assume their gorgeous crimson colouring. In winter, the corky bark of the older twigs is often a feature. It is occasionally confused with the maples (*Acer*), but its alternate leaves easily identify it. E. United States. I. in the 17th century. A.M. 1952. A.G.M. 1969. F.C.C.T. 1975.

'Aurea'. Leaves striped and mottled yellow.

'Lane Roberts'. A selected clone and one of the most reliable for its autumn colour which is a rich black crimson-red. Bark comparatively smooth.

'Variegata'. Leaves attractively margined creamy-white, flushed rose in late summer and autumn.

LIRIODENDRON—**Magnoliaceae**—The North American "Tulip Tree" was considered monotypic until, at the beginning of this century, a second and very similar species was discovered in China. Fast-growing trees succeeding in all types of fertile soil, they are made conspicuous by their curiously shaped, fore-shortened, three-lobed leaves, which turn clear yellow in autumn.

chinense SARG. A rare tree of medium size, similar to *L. tulipfera*, but leaves more glaucous beneath and narrower waisted. Flowers smaller, green without, yellowish within. China. Introduced by Wilson in 1901. A.M. 1980.

LIRIODENDRON—*continued*

tulipifera L. "Tulip Tree". A beautiful, large tree characterised by its distinctive, oddly shaped leaves which turn a rich butter-yellow in autumn. The peculiar flowers, appearing in June and July, are tulip-shaped, yellow-green with orange internal markings. Flowers are not produced on young trees. North America. C. 1688. A.M. 1970. A.G.M. 1973.

'Aureomarginatum'. Leaves bordered with yellow or greenish-yellow. A.M. 1974.

'Contortum'. A form with somewhat contorted, undulating leaves.

'Fastigiatum' (*'Pyramidale'*). An erect tree of broadly columnar habit. A magnificent medium-sized tree where height is required and space confined.

'Integrifolium'. An unusual form, the leaves without side lobes.

‡*LITHOCARPUS—Fagaceae—Evergreen trees, all but one native of E. and S. Asia. Differing from *Quercus* in the erect male spikes. They require a lime-free soil.

†densiflorus REHD. (*Quercus densiflora*). "Tanbark Oak". A small, evergreen tree native of California and Oregon. The shoots and the sharply toothed oblong, leathery leaves are covered with milk-white down when young, the leaves becoming dark shining green above and whitish or tawny downy below, finally glabrous. The bark of this tree is a source of tannin. Only for the most sheltered gardens in the south and west. I. 1874.

echinoides ABRAMS (*montanus*) (*Quercus echinoides*). "Dwarf Tanbark". A small to medium-sized, comparatively hardy shrub of open habit with glabrous, greyish-brown twigs. Leaves leathery, entire, ovate-elliptic to oblong-elliptic, 1·25 to 3·75cm. in length, green above, paler below, petioles yellow. A neat-growing bush proving quite hardy in our arboretum. California.

edulis NAKAI (*Quercus edulis*) (*Pasania edulis*). A small bushy tree or large shrub with glabrous young shoots. Leaves glabrous, leathery, tapered at both ends, yellowish-green above, scaly when young. Requires a sheltered position. Japan. I. early 19th century.

henryi REHD. & WILS. (*Quercus henryi*). An outstanding, small, evergreen tree with very long, lanceolate, slender-pointed leaves. Fruits when produced, in dense heads. This remarkable evergreen has grown slowly but successfully here for the past 20 years. China. I. 1901.

†pachyphyllus REHD. (*Quercus pachyphylla*). A small tree with a low, spreading head of branches. Leaves elliptic to elliptic-lanceolate 10 to 20cm. long, abruptly acuminate, dark glossy green above, pale metallic silvery-green beneath. A rare species only suitable for the milder counties. A fine tree at Caerhays, Cornwall, produces shillalah-like clusters of strangely contorted fruits which appear to be infertile. E. Himalaya.

LITHOSPERMUM—Boraginaceae—The shrubby or sub-shrubby members of this genus are delightful, low-growing, blue flowered plants particularly when associated with the rock garden. With the exception of *L. diffusum* all are lime tolerant.

‡*diffusum LAG. (*prostratum*). A prostrate shrub, forming large mats covered with lovely blue flowers in late spring and early summer. Not recommended for shallow chalky soils. S. Europe. I. 1825.

'Album'. Flowers white.

'Grace Ward'. A form with larger flowers. A.M. 1938.

'Heavenly Blue'. The form in general cultivation. The name is self-explanatory. A.M. 1909. A.G.M. 1925.

***oleifolium** LAPEYR. A choice and rare, evergreen, semi-prostrate shrub for sheltered rock garden or alpine house; beautiful, azure-blue, bell-shaped flowers from June to September. Spain (Pyrenees). I. about 1900. A.M. 1938.

petraeum. See *MOLTKIA petraea*.

†rosmarinifolium TENORE. A lovely dwarf, erect, rosemary-like shrub with narrow leaves and bright-blue flowers, during winter and early spring. A rock garden shrub for the milder counties, otherwise an excellent plant for the alpine house. Central Italy.

LITSEA glauca. See *NEOLITSEA sericea*.

"LOBSTER'S CLAW". See *CLIANTHUS puniceus*.

‡*LOISELEURIA—Ericaceae—A monotypic genus.

procumbens DESV. (*Azalea procumbens*). "Mountain Azalea". A charming, prostrate, native shrub, forming large mats or low mounds of procumbent stems and tiny leaves, studded in May with clusters of small, pink flowers. Requires moist, peaty conditions, best in full exposure. Alpine Arctic regions of the Northern Hemisphere (incl. Scotland). C. 1800.

‡***LOMATIA**—**Proteaceae**—A small genus of striking Australasian and Chilean evergreens. Attractive both in foliage and flower, they should be better known and more widely planted. Whilst hardy or near hardy in all but the coldest areas they cannot be recommended for shallow, chalky soils and succeed best in partial shade. A splendid group of plants for the flower arranger though some are a little too slow in growth for cutting.

†**dentata** R. BR. A medium-sized to large shrub in cultivation with elliptic to obovate, holly-like leaves, coarsely-toothed except at the base, shining dark green above pale green or glaucescent beneath. Flowers greenish-white. Chile. Introduced by Harold Comber. Reintroduced in 1963.

†**ferruginea** R. BR. A magnificent Chilean foliage plant. A large shrub or small, erect tree with large, deep green, much divided, fern-like leaves and red-brown, velvety stems. Flowers buff and scarlet in short racemes. Hardy only in mild localities. Chile, Patagonia. I. about 1846. A.M. 1927.

hirsuta DIELS. (*obliqua*). A little-known Chilean species, here proving hardy in a sheltered woodland. It is a remarkable, large shrub, with rather large, leathery, broadly and obliquely ovate leaves. The cream flowers are borne in May. Chile, Peru. I. 1902. A.M. 1956.

longifolia. See *L. myricoides*.

myricoides DORRIEN (*longifolia*). This species has proved hardy and long-lived in our nurseries, making a well-furnished, wide-spreading shrub 1·8 to 2·4m. high. Leaves long and narrow, distantly-toothed. Flowers white, grevillea-like, very fragrant, borne freely in July. An excellent evergreen for the flower arranger. S.E. Australia. I. 1816. A.M. 1955.

obliqua. See *L. hirsuta*.

silaifolia R. BR. A small, wide-spreading shrub with ascending stems, finely divided leaves and large panicles of creamy-white flowers in July. Leaves less finely divided than those of the very similar *L. tinctoria*. E. Australia. I. 1792.

tinctoria R. BR. Small, suckering shrub forming in time a dense thicket. Leaves pinnate or doubly pinnate with long, narrow segments. Flowers sulphur yellow in bud changing to creamy white, in long spreading racemes at the ends of the shoots. Tasmania. I. 1822. A.M. 1948.

"LOMBARDY POPLAR". See *POPULUS nigra 'Italica'*.

"LONDON PLANE". See *PLATANUS* × *hispanica*.

LONICERA—**Caprifoliaceae**—The shrubby honeysuckles are very different in appearance from the climbing species to which their colloquial name properly belongs. Their flowers are borne in pairs normally on slender peduncles and are followed by partially or completely fused berries. All are of easy cultivation in any ordinary soil. Most are extremely hardy continental plants. In our insular climate they generally flower well but are seldom spectacular in fruit as they are in colder climes. Thin out and cut back immediately after flowering, old flowering shoots to within a few cm. of the old wood. For climbing species see CLIMBERS at end of Manual.

albertii REG. (*spinosa albertii*). A low-growing shrub of prostrate or spreading habit attaining ·9 to 1·2m. Leaves linear, glaucous; flowers fragrant, lilac-pink in May. Berries purplish-red. Turkestan. I. about 1880.

alpigena L. Erect, medium-sized shrub. Leaves oval, oblong or obovate, 5 to 10cm. long, half as wide. Flowers in pairs, yellow, tinged red, produced in May. Berries red, drooping, cherry-like. C. Europe. C. since the 16th century.

× **amoena 'Rosea'** (*korolkowii* × *tatarica*). An attractive, medium-sized shrub producing an abundance of pink flowers in May and June. Garden origin before 1895.

angustifolia WALL. An elegant, narrow leaved, Himalayan species of medium size. The small, fragrant, pale pink flowers produced in April and May are followed by red, edible berries. I. about 1849.

caerulea L. A variable species, typically a stiff, compact shrub attaining about 1·5m. with orbicular-ovate, sea-green leaves, yellowish white flowers and conspicuous, dark blue berries. N. and C. Europe, N. Asia, Japan. Long cultivated.

chaetocarpa REHD. A pretty, erect-growing shrub 1·8 to 2·1m. in height with bristly stems and leaves. Flowers primrose yellow, comparatively large, subtended by two large, conspicuous bracts; May and June. Berries bright red. A shrub of quality and interest for every well-stocked garden. W. China. I. 1904.

LONICERA—*continued*

chrysantha TURCZ. A tall, hardy shrub up to 3·7m., blooming in May and June; flowers cream, becoming yellow. Berries coral-red. N.E. Asia. C. 1880.

'Clavey's Dwarf'. A small shrub up to 1m. possibly a hybrid of *L. xylosteum*. Flowers creamy-white; berries large, translucent red.

discolor LINDL. A medium-sized shrub with elliptic leaves, dark green above, glaucous beneath. Flowers yellowish-white or tinged rose. Kashmir to Afghanistan. C. 1847.

fragrantissima LINDL. & PAXT. A partially evergreen, Chinese shrub of medium size, producing its sweetly fragrant, cream-coloured flowers during late winter and spring. Red berries in May. Introduced by Robert Fortune in 1845.

iberica BIEB. Densely-branched shrub up to 3m. high. Flowers cream, borne on short stalks and enclosed by the cup-shaped, united bracts. Its unusual orbicular leaves make this a distinctive species. Caucasus, Persia. I. 1824.

'Microphylla'. A looser-growing form with smaller leaves.

involucrata BANKS (*ledebourii*). A vigorous, spreading, distinct shrub of medium size, blooming in June. Flowers yellow subtended by two conspicuous red bracts, which persist during fruiting; berries shining black. A robust, adaptable species growing equally well in seaside gardens and industrial areas. Western N. America. I. 1824.

korolkowii STAPF. A very attractive, vigorous, large shrub of graceful, arching habit, the downy shoots and pale, sea-green, downy leaves giving the shrub a striking grey-blue hue. Pink flowers are produced in June and are followed by red berries. Turkestan. C. 1880.

zabelii REHD. A beautiful variety with deeper rose-pink flowers. Leaves usually glabrous and broader than the type.

ledebourii. See *L. involucrata*.

ligustrina yunnanensis. See under *L. nitida 'Fertilis'*.

maackii MAXIM. A large shrub bearing fragrant, white flowers which turn yellow as they age. Berries dark red, long lasting. Manchuria, Korea. I. 1880.

podocarpa FRANCH. A tall, graceful, wide spreading shrub, attaining 3m., beautiful when bearing its white to yellow flowers, or loaded with red berries. The form here offered is considered superior to the type. I. 1900. A.M. 1907.

microphylla ROEM. & SCHULT. A small shrub of stiff habit with tiny leaves, producing pale yellow flowers followed by bright red berries. C. Asia. I. 1818.

morrowii A. GRAY. A vigorous, medium-sized shrub of spreading habit; leaves grey-green; flowers in early summer, creamy white changing to yellow followed by dark red berries. Japan. I. 1875.

myrtillus HOOK. f. & THOMS. In general appearance this remarkable Himalayan species resembles a *Ledum*. A dense, rounded shrub about 1m. high with small, conspicuously veined, ovate leaves glaucous beneath and small, fragrant, pitcher-shaped, creamy-white flowers produced in pairs in May. Berries orange-red. Himalaya, Afghanistan.

***nitida** WILS. This dense habited, small-leaved evergreen reaching a height of 1·5 to 1·8m., has long been used extensively for hedging, being quick in growth and responding well to clipping. W. China. I. 1908. It is slightly variable in cultivation and we offer the following clones:—

'Baggesen's Gold'. A form with yellow leaves during summer, turning yellow-green in autumn.

'Ernest Wilson'. This, the commonest form, has been the one most extensively used for hedging and is the "nitida" of the trade. Its habit is rather spreading with arching or drooping branches and tiny, ovate leaves. Flowers and fruits poorly produced in the British Isles. A.M. 1911 (as *L. nitida*).

'Fertilis'. A strong-growing clone of erect habit, with long arching branchlets and ovate or elliptic leaves. It differs from *'Ernest Wilson'* in its more erect habit, larger, narrower-based leaves, fragrant flowers and rather more freely produced translucent violet fruits. It has in the past been catalogued under the names *L. pileata yunnanensis* and *L. ligustrina yunnanensis*. A.M. 1924.

'Yunnan'. Similar to *'Ernest Wilson'*, but stouter and more erect in habit. Its leaves are also slightly larger and rather more freely produces both flowers and fruits. It has in the past been distributed under the name *L. yunnanensis*. Excellent for hedging.

LONICERA—*continued*

pileata OLIV. A dwarf, semi-evergreen, horizontally-branched shrub, occasionally 1·5m. high, most suitable for under-planting and ground cover particularly in shade. Leaves small, elliptic, bright green; berries in clusters, translucent violet. Very pretty in spring when the bright green young leaves appear among the dark green old leaves. China. I. 1900. A.M. 1910.

yunnanensis. See under *L. nitida 'Fertilis'*.

× **purpusii** REHD. (*fragrantissima* × *standishii*). A vigorous hybrid of medium size, producing its fragrant, cream-coloured flowers in winter. A.M. 1971.

pyrenaica L. This is perhaps the choicest shrubby honeysuckle, attaining about 1m. Small, sea-green leaves and nodding, comparatively large, funnel-shaped, cream and pink flowers in May and June, followed by orange-red berries. Central and Eastern Pyrenees, Balearic Isles. Perhaps the least easy shrubby honeysuckle to propagate. I. 1739. A.M. 1928.

quinquelocularis HARDW. A large shrub with oval leaves. Flowers white, changing to yellow, freely borne from the leaf axils in June and followed by translucent white berries. Himalaya, China. C. 1840.

transluscens ZAB. Leaves longer, heart-shaped at base. Flowers with distinctly gibbous corolla tube. C. 1870.

rupicola HOOK. f. & THOMS. A low, dense, globular shrub with interlacing branches. Flowers fragrant, lilac-pink in May and June. Related to *L. syringantha*. Himalaya. C. 1850.

ruprechtiana REG. A vigorous species forming a shapely bush of 2·4m. or more. The oblong-ovate to lanceolate leaves are downy beneath; flowers, in axillary pairs, white changing to yellow, May and June. N.E. Asia. I. about 1860.

sachalinensis NAKAI (*maximowiczii sachalinensis*). A medium-sized shrub of erect habit. Flowers dark violet-purple in May and June, followed by dark purple berries. Japan, Sakhalin, N. Korea, Manchuria, Ussuri.

setifera FRANCH. (Rock 13520). A rare and beautiful shrub of medium size. The erect stems are densely bristly. The tubular, sweetly scented, daphne-like white and pink flowers appear in short clusters on the naked stems during late winter and early spring. Berries red, bristly. China. A.M. 1980.

spinosa albertii. See *L. albertii*.

standishii JACQUES. A charming, deciduous or semi-evergreen, medium-sized, fragrant, winter-flowering species, resembling *L. fragrantissima*, differing in its bristly stems and more elliptic hairy leaves. Bears red berries in June. China. Introduced by Robert Fortune in 1845.

lancifolia REHD. A narrow-leaved form of more distinct appearance. China. I. 1908.

syringantha MAXIM. A graceful, intricately branched shrub of rounded habit 1·2 to 1·8m. in height. Leaves small, sea-green. Flowers tubular, soft lilac, fragrant, appearing in May and June. Berries red. We offer the clone which we selected and which in our earlier catalogues was distinguished as var. *grandiflora*. China, Tibet. I. about 1890.

tatarica L. A vigorous, variable shrub up to 3m., producing multitudes of pink flowers in May and June. Berries red. Central Asia to Russia. I. 1752.

'Alba'. A form with white flowers.

'Arnold Red'. Flowers rose-pink; berries larger. This cultivar originated as a seedling of *'Latifolia'* in the Arnold Arboretum in 1947.

'Hack's Red'. A first-class selection with rose-pink flowers.

sibirica REHD. Flowers rosy-pink. A.M. 1947. The forms *punicea*, *pulcherrima* and *rubra* are very similar.

thibetica BUR. & FRANCH. A vigorous species up to 1·8m. high, resembling *L. syringantha* in its lilac-pink, fragrant flowers, but differing in its leaves being dark glossy green above, white-tomentose beneath. Flowering in May and June. Berries red. Tibet. I. 1897.

tomentella HOOK. f. & THOMS. An elegant, small to medium-sized shrub with small, neat leaves and tubular, white, pink-tinged flowers in June. Berries small, black with a blue bloom. Sikkim. I. 1849.

trichosantha BUR. & FRANCH. A medium-sized, spreading Chinese shrub. The pale-yellow flowers produced in axillary pairs are followed by dark red berries. W. China. I. about 1908.

LONICERA—*continued*

× **vilmorinii** REHD. (*deflexicalyx × quinquelocularis*). A floriferous small-flowered, hybrid attaining 2·7m. Flowers yellow, berries pink suffused yellow, minutely speckled red. Garden origin about 1900.

xylosteum L. "Fly Honeysuckle". A presumed native shrub attaining about 3m.; flowers yellowish-white; attractive when bearing its red berries in late summer. Europe (incl. S.E. England), W. Siberia.

yunnanensis. See under *L. nitida 'Yunnan'*.

LOPHOMYRTUS bullata. See *MYRTUS bullata.*

obcordata. See *MYRTUS obcordata.*

"LOQUAT". See *ERIOBOTRYA japonica.*

†***LOROPETALUM**—**Hamamelidaceae**—A genus of one or two species, differing from Hamamelis in their evergreen leaves, inferior ovary and white petals. Unsuitable for shallow chalky soils.

chinense OLIV. A distinct evergreen shrub attaining 1·5 to 2m. and recalling *Sycopsis*. The white, witch-hazel-like flowers are freely produced during February and March. An interesting and attractive shrub in mild localities. China. Introduced by Charles Maries in 1880. F.C.C. 1894.

†**LUCULIA**—**Rubiaceae**—A small genus of very beautiful shrubs or small trees from temperate E. Asia. They are mainly suitable as winter-flowering shrubs for the conservatory or the mildest gardens out of doors.

grandifolia GHOSE. A beautiful shrub to 2m. from Bhutan, where it was discovered by Kingdon Ward growing at an altitude of 2,500m. indicating its probable greater hardiness than others of the genus. Fragrant trusses of snow-white flowers in June or July, and large, prominently veined leaves which give rich autumn colours. A.M. 1955.

gratissima SWEET. A semi-evergreen, free-growing shrub producing sweetly fragrant, almond-pink flowers in winter. Himalaya. I. 1816. A.M. 1938.

pinceana HOOK. A beautiful semi-evergreen plant with deliciously-scented almond-pink flowers from May to September. Leaves narrower and flowers larger than those of *L. gratissima*. Khasia Hills (Assam). I. 1843. A.M. 1930. F.C.C. 1935.

***LUETKEA**—**Rosaceae**—A rare monotypic genus differing from the closely related *Spiraea* in its dissected leaves.

pectinata KUNTZE (*Spiraea pectinata*). A dwarf, evergreen, mat-forming shrublet with tiny pectinate leaves and small racemes of white flowers in May and June. A choice little shrublet resembling a "mossy saxifrage" (*Saxifraga hypnoides*). Suitable for a cool moist pocket on the rock or peat garden. Western N. America. C. 1890.

LUPINUS—**Leguminosae**—The majority of lupins are herbaceous in nature, but amongst the shrubby species are several worthy garden plants.

***arboreus** SIMS. "Yellow Tree Lupin". A comparatively short-lived, more or less evergreen, fast-growing shrub up to 2m. Flowers normally yellow, but variable from seed, delicately scented, produced in dense racemes continuously throughout summer. Thrives in full sun in a well-drained position and easily naturalises in sandy soils, particularly by the sea. California. C. 1793.

'Golden Spire'. A form with deeper yellow flowers.

'Snow Queen'. Flowers white. A.M. 1899.

chamissonis ESCHS. A densely-branched silvery Lupin up to 1m. Ideal for "grey" borders; flowers clouded purple-blue, borne during early summer. Requires a sunny, preferably well-drained position. California. I. about 1826.

†***LUZURIAGA**—**Philesiaceae**—A small genus of half-hardy plants.

radicans RUIZ. & PAV. A shrubby evergreen of creeping habit and but a few cm. high. Leaves ovate, flowers star-shaped, glistening white, with prominent yellow anthers; summer; berries bright orange. Requires shade and moist conditions. Native of Chile and Peru where it is often found growing on the trunks of forest trees. I. before 1850.

LYCIUM—**Solanaceae**—Rambling shrubs, excellent for maritime exposures and for fixing sandy banks. Flowers small, usually violet, followed by conspicuous berries.

barbarum L. (*halimifolium*) (*chinense*) (*europaeum* HORT. not L.). "Duke of Argyll's Tea Tree". A vigorous, medium-sized shrub with long, often spiny, scrambling, arching stems. Flowers purple, in clusters of 5 to 7·5cm. diameter in the leaf axils from June to September followed by small, egg-shaped orange or scarlet berries. The form we offer is *'Carnosum'*, with pink flowers. Excellent by the sea. Long cultivated. China; extensively naturalised in Europe and W. Asia. I. about 17) .

LYCIUM—*continued*

chilense BERT. (*gracillianum*). A medium-sized, lax shrub with spineless, spreading branches, slender, almost linear, fleshy leaves and yellowish-white and purple, funnel-shaped flowers from June to August. Chile.

chinense. See *L. barbarum.*

europaeum HORT. See *L. barbarum.*

gracile. See *L. chilense.*

halimifolium. See *L. barbarum.*

‡**LYONIA**—**Ericaceae**—Attractive shrubs or occasionally small trees, closely related to *Pieris*, and requiring lime-free soil.

ligustrina DC. (*Andromeda paniculata*). A deciduous, small to medium-sized shrub with oval or obovate leaves. Flowers pitcher-shaped, white, carried in panicles during July and August. Thrives in a moist, peaty or sandy loam. Eastern N. America. I. 1748.

foliosiflora FERN. An unusual variety with leafy flower panicles.

***lucida** K. KOCH. (*Andromeda lucida*) (*Pieris lucida*). Small to medium-sized shrub with rather lax, sharply angled stems. Leaves broadly elliptic to ovate, entire, leathery and shining dark green above. Flowers white to pink, in axillary clusters in May and June. S.E. United States. I. 1765.

mariana D. DON. "Stagger Bush". A small shrub somewhat resembling *Gaultheria shallon.* Stems erect, flexuous and shiny; leaves oval, dark green and leathery. Flowers white or pink-tinged, nodding, borne in axillary panicles in May or early June. Eastern U.S.A. I. before 1736.

ovalifolia elliptica HAND.-MAZZ. Medium-sized to large shrub with slender, reddish shoots and elliptic, slender-pointed leaves, bronze when unfolding. Flowers small, white, occurring in axillary racemes in June and July. Japan, China. I. 1829.

‡†***LYONOTHAMNUS**—**Rosaceae**—A monotypic genus.

floribundus asplenifolius BRANDEGEE. A small, graceful, fast-growing evergreen tree of slender habit soon forming a remarkable slender trunk, like a miniature Redwood, with attractive chestnut brown and grey shreddy bark. Leaves fern-like, pinnate, the leaflets divided to the base into oblong lobes, glossy green above, grey hairy below. Flowers creamy-white in slender, spiraea-like panicles in early summer. Except in the milder counties needs the shelter of a warm, sunny wall. California (Santa Catalina Island). I. 1900.

MAACKIA—**Leguminosae**—A small genus of very hardy, attractive, small, slow growing deciduous trees related to *Cladrastis* but differing in the solitary, exposed leaf buds, opposite leaflets and densely packed, more or less erect racemes. All the species succeed in most soils including deep soil over chalk.

amurensis K. KOCH (*Cladrastis amurensis*). A small tree with pinnate leaves; flowers white, tinged palest slate-blue, in erect racemes, appearing in July and August, even on young plants. Manchuria. I. 1864.

buergeri SCHNEID. A variety with obtuse leaflets, usually pubescent beneath. Japan. I. 1892.

chinensis TAK. (*hupehensis*). A small, broad-headed tree producing downy terminal panicles of dull white pea-flowers in July and August. The dark bluish young shoots which, like the young leaves are densely covered with silvery-silky down, are particularly outstanding in late spring. China. Introduced by Ernest Wilson in 1908.

‡***MACHILUS**—**Lauraceae**—A large genus of evergreen trees of which the following is exceedingly rare in cultivation. Not recommended for shallow chalky soils.

ichangensis REHD. & WILS. A small tree, semi-evergreen in this country. Leaves oblong-lanceolate to lanceolate, long pointed, 10 to 20cm. long, leathery, of an attractive coppery colour when young. Flowers small, white, produced in short axillary panicles in late spring or early summer, followed by small shining black fruits. A rare species from W. Hupeh (China), introduced by E. H. Wilson about 1901.

†× **MACLUDRANIA** (*CUDRANIA* × *MACLURA*)—**Moraceae**—An interesting bigeneric hybrid for a mild locality and a sunny sheltered site on any well drained, fertile soil.

×**MACLUDRANIA**—*continued*

hybrida ANDRE. Small to medium sized tree with spiny branches and long, taper-pointed leaves. The inconspicuous flowers are followed by large, orange-like fruits. Garden origin in France before 1905.

MACLURA—Moraceae—A monotypic genus. Male and female flowers on separate trees.

pomifera SCHNEID. (*aurantiaca*). "Osage Orange". A hardy, free growing small to medium sized tree with thorny branches and fleshy yellow roots. Remarkable for its large, pale yellow, orange-like fruits which are borne on mature trees. Yellow autumn leaf colour. Used as an impenetrable hedge in the United States. Any well drained soil; excellent on chalky soils. S. and C. United States. I. 1818.

MADDENIA—Rosaceae—A small genus of botanically interesting small trees and shrubs related to *Prunus*, but the inconspicuous flowers differ in having ten, not five, sepals, and small petals which are sometimes absent. Any fertile soil.

hypoleuca KOEHNE. An unusual shrub or small tree, with cherry-like leaves, glaucous beneath, and small black fruits. China. I. 1907.

"MADRONA". See *ARBUTUS menziesii*.

MAGNOLIA—Magnoliaceae—Though not of equal merit, the "Magnolias" embrace the most magnificent of flowering trees hardy in the temperate regions. On the whole their cultural requirements are not difficult to provide; they need a reasonable depth of good soil, and respond to rich living, good drainage and plenty of moisture. The early flowering kinds need a sheltered site giving protection from spring frosts and cold winds; those with large leaves should be given shelter from gales, while partial shade provided by woodland or similar sites is beneficial to many species.

With the exception of *M. salicifolia*, the larger tree magnolias do not flower when small, and unless otherwise stated the flowers of the deciduous species appear before the leaves. The fruit-clusters of some species are colourful in autumn.

Magnolias are very tolerant of heavy clay soils and atmospheric pollution. The most lime tolerant are *MM. acuminata, cordata, delavayi, ×highdownensis, kobus, ×loebneri* and *wilsonii*.

acuminata L. "Cucumber Tree". A vigorous species rapidly growing into a large, spreading tree. Flowers with the leaves (not produced on young trees) greenish, metallic-blue and yellow, in May and June. The popular name refers to the shape and colour of the young fruit-clusters. Eastern U.S.A. I. 1736.

cordata. See *M. cordata*.

‡**ashei** WEATHERBY. A medium-sized to large shrub, in all respects a miniature *M. macrophylla*, but flowers appearing with the leaves and produced even on young specimens. It is strange that a plant of this quality growing in a country enjoying western civilization was not recorded in cultivation until 1933. Florida, Texas.

auriculata. See *M. fraseri*.

‡**campbellii** HOOK. f. & THOMS. The giant Himalayan "Pink Tulip Tree" attains its greatest dimensions in the warmer counties. The very large flowers, opening in February and continuing into March, are goblet-shaped at first, later spreading wide, like water lilies; petals usually pink within, deep rose-pink without. Flowers are not normally produced until the tree is between twenty to thirty years old. A large tree carrying many hundreds of blooms is an unforgettable sight. When raised from seed the flowers are usually pink, but many vary between white and deep rose-purple. There is also considerable variation in the degree of hardiness, the deeper coloured forms being usually the least hardy. E. Nepal; Sikkim; Bhutan. I. about 1865. F.C.C. 1903.

alba HORT. This is the form most common in the wild and would have become the type had not the pink-flowered form been discovered first. The plants offered have been raised from seed, so we cannot be sure they will produce pure white blossoms. First planted in Western gardens by J. C. Williams, and now the most glorious tree when in flower in the great garden he made at Caerhays Castle, Cornwall. F.C.C. 1951.

MAGNOLIA—*continued*

campbellii 'Charles Raffill'. A vigorous hybrid between the type and var. *mollicomata*, inheriting the early flowering habit of the latter. The large flowers are deep rose-pink in bud and when expanded are rose-purple on the outside, white with a pinkish-purple marginal flush on the inside. Grown at Windsor and one of the original seedlings raised by Charles Raffill at Kew in about 1946. The same cross had also arisen many years earlier in the garden of the late Sir Charles Cave, Bart. See *'Sidbury'*. A.M. and Cory Cup 1963. F.C.C. 1966.

'Darjeeling'. A superb clone with flowers of the darkest rose. Our stock was vegetatively propagated from the original tree in Darjeeling Botanic Garden, India.

'Ethel Hillier'. A vigorous, hardy form raised in our nurseries from wild collected seed, with very large flowers; petals white with a faint pink flush at the base on the outside.

'Kew's Surprise'. One of Charles Raffill's seedlings, grown at Caerhays, Cornwall. The magnificent flowers are larger than those of *'Charles Raffill'* and the outside of the petals of a richer pink colouring. F.C.C. and Cory Cup 1967.

'Lanarth' (*williamsiana 'Lanarth'*). A striking form of spp. *mollicomata* raised at Lanarth from seed collected by Forrest (F.25655). Flowers very large, of cyclamen-purple with even darker stamens. F.C.C. 1947.

mollicomata F. K. WARD (*M. mollicomata*). Similar in many respects to the type, but hardier and more dependable in this climate, also flowering at an earlier age, sometimes within ten to fifteen years. The flowers are like large, pink to rose-purple water lilies. Differing from the type in the hairy internodes on the peduncles (those of the type being glabrous) and often more hairy leaves. S.E. Tibet, Yunnan. I. 1920. F.C.C. 1939.

'Sidbury'. A medium-sized to large tree of vigorous habit, flowering earlier in life than *M. campbellii*, and equally spectacular in flower. This cross between *M. campbellii* and ssp. *mollicomata* occurred some years prior to 1946 at Sidbury Manor, Devon, the home of the late Sir Charles Cave, Bart. It therefore precedes those made by Charles Raffill at Kew.

'Wakehurst'. A magnificent hybrid differing from *'Charles Raffill'* in its darker-coloured flowers.

'Werrington'. A form of ssp. *mollicomata* originating from the same Forrest collection as *'Lanarth'* and of similar garden merit.

‡**'Charles Coates'** (*sieboldii × tripetala*) (*coatesii* HORT.). A distinct and interesting hybrid making a large bush or small tree. Flowers fragrant, creamy-white with a conspicuous centre of reddish stamens, resembling those of *M. tripetala*, and produced with the leaves in May and June. Raised at Kew. A.M. 1973. A.G.M. 1973.

†***coco** DC. (*pumila*) (*Talauma coco*). A small, evergreen or semi-evergreen shrub with smooth, net-veined leaves and nodding creamy-white, fragrant (particularly at night) flowers, produced intermittently during summer. Requires conservatory treatment except in the mildest localities. Java. I. 1876.

conspicua. See *M. denudata*.

cordata MICHX. (*acuminata cordata*). Resembles *M. acuminata*, but usually a smaller, compact, round-headed tree or large shrub. Flowers soft canary-yellow, borne with the leaves in summer and again in early autumn, even on young plants. S.E. United States. I. 1801.

‡**cylindrica** WILS. A very rare, small tree or large shrub. The white flowers are very similar to those of *M. denudata* but more elegant, appearing on the naked stems in April. The name refers to its cylindrical fruits. We believe we were the first to introduce this species to Britain via the United States. China. C. 1936. A.M. 1963.

‡**dawsoniana** REHD. & WILS. A rare and magnificent species from West China, attaining a small to medium-sized tree or large shrub. Leaves nearly 15cm. long, leathery, bright green above, rather glaucous beneath; flowers in spring, large, pale rose, suffused purple without, not produced on young trees. Szechwan. Introduced in 1908 by E. H. Wilson, perhaps the greatest ever plant collector. A.M. 1939.

MAGNOLIA—*continued*

†***delavayi** FRANCH. With the exception of *Rhododendron sinogrande* and *Trachycarpus fourtnei* and its allies, this magnificent species has probably the largest leaves of any evergreen tree or shrub grown out of doors in this country. A large shrub or bushy tree up to 14m., leaves sea-green, matt above, glaucous beneath. Bark of old trees buff-white, corky and fissured. The parchment coloured, creamy-white, slightly fragrant flowers in late summer and early autumn are 18 to 20cm. across, but the individual blossom seldom survives for more than two days. Requires wall protection except in favoured localities. Does well in soils over chalk. China (S. Yunnan). Introduced by E. H. Wilson in 1899. F.C.C. 1913.

‡**denudata** DESROUSS. (*conspicua*). "Yulan", "Lily Tree". A large shrub or small rounded tree usually below 9m. high. The fragrant, pure white, cup-shaped flowers open in early spring. The broad petals are thick and fleshy. China. I. 1789. A.G.M. 1936. F.C.C. 1968.

'Purple Eye'. A large, wide-spreading shrub, one of the most beautiful of this aristocratic family. Flowers large, fragrant, pure white with a purple stain at the base of the inner petals. Probably of hybrid origin.

‡**fraseri** WALT. (*auriculata*). A rare, medium-sized tree allied to *M. macrophylla*. Leaves up to 40cm. long, with two distinct auricles at the base, clustered at the ends of the branches. Flowers with the leaves large, parchment coloured, slightly fragrant, produced in May and June, and followed by attractive rose-coloured fruit-clusters. Mts. of S.E. United States. I. 1786. A.M. 1948

fuscata. See *MICHELIA figo*.

glauca. See *M. virginiana*.

globosa HOOK. f & THOMS. (*tsarongensis*). A large shrub, or rarely a small tree, with ferruginous-felted young shoots and buds. The nodding, creamy-white, rather globular, fragrant flowers are produced on stout brown-felted stalks during June. The leaves differ from those of the related *M. wilsonii* and *M. sinensis* on account of the red-brown pubescence beneath. Requires a protected site in colder areas E. Himalaya to W. China. I. 1919. A.M. 1931.

sinensis. See *M. sinensis*.

***grandiflora** L. One of the most magnificent evergreens, generally grown as a wall shrub, for which purpose it is admirably suited. It is, however, hardy in the open if given shelter and full sun, making a massive round-headed shrub or short stemmed tree. Leaves leathery, glossy green above, often reddish-brown beneath, at least when young. The delightfully fragrant, creamy-white flowers are sometimes up to 25cm. across, and are produced throughout summer and early autumn. Lime tolerant if given a good depth of rich loam. S.E. United States. I. 1734.

'Angustifolia'. Leaves lanceolate to oblanceolate, 15 to 20cm. long by 3·5 to 5cm. wide, glossy green above, cinnamon pubescent beneath, becoming glabrous. Flowers typical.

'Exmouth' (*'Exoniensis'*) (*'Lanceolata'*). A splendid clone with elliptic to elliptic-obovate leaves, polished, soft green above, reddish-brown felted beneath, becoming glabrous. Flowers very large, and richly fragrant, appearing at an early age. A.G.M. 1969.

'Ferruginea'. A form of erect, compact habit with typical flowers. Leaves elliptic-obovate, dark shining green above, richly ferruginous tomentose beneath, becoming glabrous; veins indistinct.

'Goliath'. A form with shorter, broader leaves than the type, dark glossy green above; green beneath, or thinly pubescent when very young. Flowers globular, very large, produced at an early age. A.M. 1931. F.C.C. 1951. A.G.M. 1969.

'Lanceolata'. See *'Exmouth'*.

'Undulata'. A distinct form with typical flowers. Leaves elliptic-oblong to oblong-obovate, margins strongly undulate, distinctly veined; glossy green above and green beneath, even when young.

***grandiflora × virginiana.** An interesting evergreen, large shrub or small tree, intermediate between two distinguished parents, most closely resembling *M. grandiflora*, but usually with smaller leaves and flowers. *'Freeman'* and *'Maryland'* are named clones of this hybrid.

MAGNOLIA—*continued*

‡**Gresham Hybrids.** In 1955 Dr. Todd Gresham, a noted Magnolia enthusiast of Santa Cruz, California, made a series of crosses involving *M.* ×*veitchii* with *M. liliiflora* on the one hand and *M.* ×*soulangiana 'Lennei Alba'* on the other. Of the hundred or so seedlings produced, twenty-four of each cross were selected and grown on. All proved vigorous in growth, developing into strong trees in the manner of *M.* ×*veitchii*. We are indebted to Dr. Gresham for several of his named clones including 'Peppermint Stick', 'Raspberry Ice' and 'Royal Crown', all *M. liliiflora* × *M.* ×*veitchii*, and 'Crimson Stipple', 'Delicatissima', 'Rouged Alabaster' and 'Sayonara', which are *M.* ×*soulangiana 'Lennei Alba'* ×*M.* ×*veitchii*. All these clones are growing in our arboretum, some having already flowered at 1·8m., and those which prove satisfactory will be propagated.

×**highdownensis** DANDY. A large shrub, said to be a hybrid between *M. sinensis* and *M. wilsonii*, and combining the good qualities of these species. Large pendant, white, fragrant flowers with purple central cone, appearing with the leaves in early summer. Succeeds on chalky soils. Grown in the late Sir Frederick Stern's garden, Highdown, Sussex, from seedlings received from Caerhays Castle in 1927. It is our opinion that this plant should be regarded as a clone of *M. wilsonii*. A.M. 1937.

‡**hypoleuca** SIEB. & ZUCC. (*obovata*). A handsome, medium-sized tree with often purple-tinged young shoots, and very large, obovate leaves. The creamy-white, fragrant flowers, borne in June, are 20cm. across, and have a central ring of crimson stamens; fruit-clusters attractive and large. Japan. I. 1865. F.C.C. 1893.

'Kewensis' (*kobus* × *salicifolia*). A small, slender, broadly conical tree, intermediate in habit and appearance between its parents. Flowers white, 6cm. long, in April before the leaves. Raised at Kew. A.M. 1952.

kobus DC. A very hardy Japanese small tree or large shrub which does not produce its slightly fragrant, white flowers until it has attained an age of about twelve to fifteen years, when they are regularly borne with magnificent freedom during April. Excellent for all types of soil including chalky soils. I. 1865. A.G.M. 1936. A.M. 1942.

borealis SARG. The largest tree form of the species, chiefly renowned for its lack of flower. A.M. 1948.

stellata. See *M. stellata*.

×**lennei.** See *M.* ×*soulangiana 'Lennei'*.

‡**liliiflora** DESROUSS. (*discolor*) (*purpurea*). A wide-spreading medium-sized shrub, occasionally to 4m., with obovate to broad elliptic leaves of a shining dark green above. Flowers erect, like slender tulips, gradually opening wide; purple flushed on the outside, creamy-white within, appearing in late April and continuing until early June, and intermittently during the summer. One of the best species for the smaller garden, thriving in all but chalky soils. C. China, long cultivated in Japan. I. 1790. A.G.M. 1973.

'Nigra' (×*soulangiana 'Nigra'*). A slightly more compact form with slightly larger flowers, deep vinous purple outside, creamy-white stained purple inside, borne freely over a long period from spring to summer. Introduced from Japan in 1861. A.M. 1907. A.G.M. 1969.

‡**liliiflora** × **stellata.** We are grateful to the U.S. National Arboretum, Washington, for eight named clones of the above parentage. Raised at the Arboretum in 1955/56, they are said to be superior to their parents in size, colour, fragrance and abundance of flower. The original plants are described as being multiple-stemmed, rounded or conical, erect-growing and 2 to 3m. in height. We are growing clones in our arboretum and should they prove equally outstanding under English conditions we shall propagate them for distribution. The clones received are as follows:—'Ann', 'Betty', 'Jane', 'Judy', 'Pinkie', 'Randy', 'Ricki' and 'Susan'.

×**loebneri** KACHE (*kobus* × *stellata*) (*kobus 'Loebneri'*). A variable hybrid uniting the best qualities of its two distinguished parents, and making a small tree or large shrub, flowering with profusion even on small plants. Flowers with numerous white, strap-shaped petals, fragrant, appearing in April. Succeeds well on all types of soil including chalk soil. Garden origin prior to 1910. A.G.M. 1969.

MAGNOLIA—*continued*

×**loebneri 'Leonard Messel'.** A magnificent tall shrub or small tree; flowers lilac-pink, deeper in bud. A chance hybrid between an unusual *M. kobus* which has a pale purple line along the centre of its petals, and *M. stellata 'Rosea'*. Originated at Nymans, Sussex, a great garden made by the late Col. Messel. A.M. 1955. F.C.C. 1969. A.G.M. 1973.

'Merrill'. An outstanding selection with large, white, fragrant flowers, freely produced. Raised at the Arnold Arboretum in 1939.

'Neil McEacharn'. A vigorous small tree with pink-flushed flowers. A cross between *M. kobus* and *M. stellata 'Rosea'* raised at Windsor from seed received from Neil McEacharn of the Villa Taranto. A.M. 1968.

'Snowdrift'. We have adopted this name for a clone descended from one of the original seedlings. It has larger flowers than *M. stellata* with about twelve petals; leaves also a little larger.

‡**macrophylla** MICHX. An awe-inspiring small tree when seen alone in its grandeur ideally placed in a site sheltered from the prevailing wind, but open to the sun and backed by dark evergreens. It has perhaps larger leaves and flowers than any other deciduous tree or shrub hardy in the British Isles. The leaves are of rather thin texture, glaucous beneath and sometimes exceed ·6m. in length. The very large, fragrant flowers are parchment coloured with purple markings in the centre and appear in early summer. S.E. United States. I. 1800. F.C.C. 1900.

‡**'Michael Rosse'.** A hybrid of uncertain origin believed to be a seedling of *M. sargentiana robusta*. A beautiful tree grown at Nymans, Sussex, having large soft purple flowers. A.M. 1968.

mollicomata. See *M. campbellii mollicomata.*
nicholsoniana HORT. See *M. sinensis.*
nicholsoniana REHD. & WILS. See *M. wilsonii.*

‡†***nitida** W. W. SM. An evergreen shrub or small tree of dense, fairly compact growth. Leaves leathery, ovate to elliptic, of a dark shining green above. Flowers creamy-white, scented, 5 to 7·5cm. across, borne in late spring or early summer. The young growths have an almost metallic lustre. A charming but tender species, only suitable for a sheltered garden or woodland in the mildest localities. One of the finest specimens is growing in the woods at Caerhays, Cornwall. S.W. China, S.E. Tibet. A.M. 1966.

'Norman Gould'. An attractive large shrub of uncertain origin, raised in the R.H.S. Gardens at Wisley. It is reputedly a colchicine-induced polyploidal form of *M. stellata*, resembling that species in general habit and leaf. The white flowers are also similar. F.C.C. 1967.

obovata. See *M. hypoleuca.*

‡**officinalis** REHD. & WILS. A small to medium-sized tree, closely related to *M. obovata*, with usually yellowish-grey young shoots, and large obovate leaves up to ·5m. long. The large, saucer-shaped flowers are white and fragrant, appearing at the end of leafy young growths in early summer. C. China. I. 1900.

biloba REHD. & WILS. A very rare Chinese tree, introduced by us to British gardens from the Botanic Garden, Lushan in 1936. Its large, obovate leaves are pale green above, glaucous and finely downy beneath; deeply notched at the apex. Flowers cup-shaped, 15 to 20cm. across, parchment coloured with maroon centre, fragrant. A.M. 1975.

parviflora. See *M. sieboldii.*

‡×**proctoriana** REHD. (*salicifolia×stellata*). A large, very floriferous shrub or small tree with shortly pubescent leaf-buds, and leaves which are green beneath. Flowers white, with six to twelve petals, appearing in April. Garden origin 1928.

pumila. See *M. coco.*
purpurea. See *M. liliiflora.*

‡**pyramidata** BARTR. A very rare, small, conical tree allied to *M. fraseri*, but differing in its smaller, thinner leaves and smaller flowers in June. S.E. United States. C. 1825.

MAGNOLIA—*continued*

‡†**rostrata** W. W. SM. A rare, medium sized, gaunt tree for woodland shelter, with broad, obovate, conspicuously veined leaves up to ·5m. long. Young foliage and buds clothed with tawny, velvety hairs. Flowers appearing with the leaves in June; petals fleshy, creamy-white or pink, followed by conspicuous pink cone-like fruits. Yunnan, S.E. Tibet, Upper Burma. A.M. 1974 (for foliage).

‡**salicifolia** MAXIM. A small, broadly conical tree or large shrub with slender branches. Leaves usually narrow and willow-like, occasionally ovate, normally slightly glaucous beneath; flowers, usually produced on young plants, white, fragrant, with mostly six narrow petals, produced on the leafless stems in April. The leaves, bark and wood are pleasantly lemon scented when bruised. Japan. I. 1892. A.M. 1927. A.G.M. 1941. F.C.C. 1962.

'Jermyns'. A slow-growing shrubby form, with broader leaves conspicuously glaucous beneath and larger flowers appearing later. One of the best flowering clones of this beautiful magnolia.

‡**sargentiana** REHD. & WILS. A noble, medium sized tree from W. China. Flowers like enormous water lilies, rose-pink without, paler within, produced on mature specimens in April and May in advance of the leathery, obovate leaves. Introduced by E. H. Wilson in 1908. F.C.C. 1935.

robusta REHD. & WILS. This magnificent variety has longer, narrower leaves and larger fruits. Flowers 23cm. in diameter, rosy-crimson without, paler within, and usually with more petals than the type, but not produced until tree size is attained. W. China. F.C.C. 1947.

‡**sieboldii** K. KOCH (*parviflora*). A large, wide-spreading shrub with ovate to obovate leaves, glaucous and hairy beneath. The nodding flowers in bud are egg-shaped, but turn outwards as the petals expand; flowers white and fragrant, appearing intermittently with the leaves from May to August. The crimson fruit-clusters are spectacular. Japan; Korea. I. 1865. F.C.C. 1894. A.G.M. 1935.

sinensis STAPF. (*globosa sinensis*) (*nicholsoniana* HORT.). A large, wide-spreading shrub resembling *M. wilsonii*, but easily distinguished by its broader, obovate leaves, tomentose beneath, and wider, more strongly lemon-scented, white, nodding flowers, 10 to 13cm. wide, which appear with the leaves, in June. The paper-white, fragrant flowers contrast with the central red staminal cone. Before 1930 this plant was distributed by Chenault of Orleans, France as *M. nicholsoniana*. W. China. I. 1908. A.M. 1927. F.C.C. 1931. A.G.M. 1969.

‡×**soulangiana** SOULANGE-BODIN (*denudata* × *liliiflora*). In its numerous forms, the best and most popular magnolia for general planting. Usually seen as a large shrub with several wide-spreading stems. Flowers, before the leaves, large, tulip-shaped, white, stained rose-purple at the base, appearing during April to early May. The best magnolia for tolerating indifferent clay soils and atmospheric pollution, but only moderately lime tolerant, and no good for shallow chalk soils. Originally raised by Mons. Soulange-Bodin at Fromont, near Paris, early in the 19th century. A.G.M. 1932. There are a number of named clones all of which have the useful habit of flowering when young.

'Alba'. See *'Alba Superba'* and *'Amabilis'*.

'Alba Superba' (*'Alba'*). One of the first of the group to produce its white scented, flowers, closely resembling those of *M. denudata*. A.G.M. 1969.

'Alexandrina'. One of the most pouplar clones, vigorous, erect and free-flowering; the large, erect flowers are white, flushed purple at the base.

'Amabilis' (*'Alba'*). A superb clone resembling *M. denudata* in general habit and flowers. The faint purplish flush at the base of the inner petals is generally quite concealed and the beautifully formed flowers appear ivory-white.

'Brozzonii'. The aristocrat of the "Soulangianas". Large, elongated white flowers, shaded purple at the base. One of the largest-flowered and latest of the group. F.C.C 1929. A.G.M. 1969.

'Lennei' (*M.* ×*lennei*). One of the finest clones. A vigorous, spreading, multi-stemmed shrub with large, broadly obovate leaves up to 25cm. long. The flowers, like enormous goblets, have thick fleshy petals which are rose-purple outside and creamy-white, stained soft purple inside, and appear during April and May, and sometimes again in the autumn. Said to have originated in a garden in Lombardy, Italy, sometime before 1850. F.C.C. 1863. A.G.M. 1969.

'Lennei Alba'. Flowers ivory-white, very like those of *M. denudata*.

'Nigra'. See *M. liliiflora 'Nigra'*.

'Norbertii'. A free-flowering clone with white flowers, flushed purple on the outside. Similar to *'Alexandrina'*, but flowers slightly smaller. A.M. 1960.

MAGNOLIA—*continued*

×**soulangiana 'Picture'.** A vigorous, erect-branched clone of Japanese origin, with large leaves and long, erect flowers, vinous purple on the outside, white on the inside. Flowers when quite young, and said by its raisers to be *M. denudata* ×*M. liliiflora 'Nigra'*. An excellent magnolia. A.M. 1969.

'Rubra'. See *'Rustica Rubra'*.

'Rustica Rubra' (*'Rubra'*). A vigorous clone, one of the best for general planting, with oval leaves and cup-shaped flowers of a rich rosy-red. A sport of *'Lennei'*. A.M. 1960. A.G.M. 1969.

'Speciosa'. A clone with leaves smaller than those of the type, and nearly white flowers abundantly produced.

'Triumphans'. Flowers white within, reddish-purple without, paling towards the tips.

'Verbanica'. Tepals pink on the outside. One of the last of the group to flower.

‡**sprengeri** PAMPAN. (*sprengeri diva*) (*denudata purpurascens*). A small to medium sized tree occasionally up to 13m., bearing in April fragrant, rose-carmine flowers resembling, and as rich as, those of *M. campbellii* but smaller. Leaves up to 18cm. long, obovate with a wedge-shaped base. Introduced by E. H. Wilson from W. Hupeh in 1901. A.M. 1942.

diva. See *M. sprengeri*.

elongata JOHNSTONE. Small bushy tree or large shrub. Flowers pure white, with narrower petals than those of the type. W. China. I. 1904. A.M. 1955.

stellata MAXIM. (*halliana*) (*kobus stellata*). A distinct and charming, slow-growing, Japanese shrub, forming a compact, rounded specimen usually wider than high, seldom exceeding a height of 3m. Winter buds grey-hairy. The white, fragrant, many-petalled flowers are profusely borne in March and April. Considered by some authorities a variety of *M. kobus*. Japan. I. 1862. F.C.C. 1878. A.G.M. 1923.

'Rosea'. Flowers flushed pink, deeper in bud. A.M. 1893.

'Rubra'. Flowers similar to those of *'Rosea'*, but slightly deeper in colouring. A.M. 1948.

'Water Lily'. An outstanding form of Japanese origin, with larger flowers and more numerous petals.

×**thompsoniana** C. DE VOS (*tripetala*×*virginiana*). A large, wide-spreading shrub resembling *M. virginiana*, but with larger leaves, up to 25cm. long, which persist into early winter. The large, fragrant, parchment-coloured flowers are carried intermittently throughout the summer even on young plants. Garden origin about 1808; an instance of two American species mating in London. A.M. 1958.

‡**tripetala** L. "Umbrella Tree". A very hardy North American tree sometimes attaining 9 to 12m., with an open head. Leaves large, 30 to 50cm. long and 15 to 25cm. wide. The cream-coloured flowers, 18 to 25cm. across, in May and June are strongly and pungently scented. They are followed by attractive, red, cone-shaped fruit-clusters. Eastern U.S.A. I. 1752.

tsarongensis. See *M. globosa*.

‡×**veitchii** BEAN (*campbellii*×*denudata*). A very vigorous, medium-sized to large tree, hardy and attractive both in leaf and flower. We offer the following clones:—

'Isca'. One of the original seedlings; flowers white in April.

'Peter Veitch'. A first class hardy magnolia with white, flushed purple-pink, goblets produced on the naked branches in April, as soon as it attains small tree size. We are indebted to Veitch's nursery of Exeter for this splendid magnolia. Garden origin 1907. F.C.C. 1921.

virginiana L. (*glauca*). "Sweet Bay"; "Swamp Bay". A partially evergreen shrub or small tree. The fragrant, creamy-white, rather small, globular flowers are produced from June to September. Leaves up to 13cm. long, glossy above, blue-white beneath. Eastern U.S.A. Probably the first magnolia to be grown in England. C. late 17th century.

'Wada's Memory'. A selected clone out of a number of seed raised plants supplied in 1940 to the University of Washington Arboretum, Seattle, by Mr. K. Wada of Yokohama, Japan. A small tree. The fragrant white flowers are larger than those of *M. kobus* and are borne in abundance. In our opinion it belongs to the same parentage as *M. 'Kewensis'* (*kobus*×*salicifolia*).

LIRIODENDRON tulipifera

MAHONIA aquifolium

MAHONIA 'Charity'

POTENTILLA dahurica 'Manchu'

MAGNOLIA 'Heaven Sent'

PIERIS 'Forest Flame'

PYRUS salicifolia 'Pendula'

NEILLIA thibetica

PHOTINIA glabra 'Rubens'

MAGNOLIA—*continued*

‡× **watsonii** HOOK. f. (*hypoleuca* × *sieboldii*). A rare shrub or small tree of rather indifferent constitution, with leathery, obovate leaves. Flowers in June and July, upward facing, creamy-white with prominent, rosy-crimson anthers and pink sepals, saucer-shaped, 13cm. wide, and with a fragrance almost overpowering. Garden origin in Japan. C. 1889. A.M. 1917. F.C.C. 1975.

wilsonii REHD. (*nicholsoniana* REHD. & WILS.). A large, wide-spreading shrub with elliptic-lanceolate leaves, pointed at the apex. In May and June, flowers pendulous, saucer-shaped, white with crimson stamens. A lovely species differing from *M. sinensis* in its narrower leaves and rather smaller flowers. Best in a partially shaded position. W. China. I. 1908. A.M. 1932. F.C.C. 1971.

*× **MAHOBERBERIS** (*MAHONIA* × *BERBERIS*)—**Berberidaceae**—Hybrids of botanical interest and some of horticultural merit between two closely related genera. In each case the *Mahonia* is the mother parent. Any soil and any exposure.

aquicandidula KRUSSMANN (*M. aquifolium* × *B. candidula*). A dwarf, slow-growing, unhappy looking shrublet of weak growth. The densely clustered leaves are ovate to ovate-elliptic, varying in size from 1 to 4cm. long, lustrous, dark green above and at first pruinose beneath, entire of spine toothed; many are compound, with two small leaflets at their base. Flowers yellow. Garden origin in Sweden, 1943.

aquisargentii KRUSSMANN (*M. aquifolium* × *B. sargentiana*). A really splendid and remarkable, small, dense-growing evergreen shrub with rather erect stems. Leaves varying in shape, either slender stalked, elliptic-lanceolate, up to 21cm. long, and regularly spine toothed; or short stalked, ovate-lanceolate and margined with 2cm.-long, vicious spines. Some leaves are compound, with two leaflets at their base. All are shining dark green above, paler beneath. Flowers soft yellow, in terminal clusters, followed by black berries. Garden origin in Sweden. ×*M. miethkeana* is a similar hybrid raised in the State of Washington, U.S.A., in 1940.

miethkeana. See under ×*M. aquisargentii*.

neubertii SCHNEID. (*M. aquifolium* × *B. vulgaris*) (*B. ilicifolia* HORT.). A small, loose habited shrub forming a rounded bush. Leaves both simple and compound, either obovate and finely toothed as in the *Berberis* parent; or ovate, acute and coarsely toothed. The young foliage is an attractive sea-green, becoming bronze or purple tinged. For many years distributed, quite wrongly as *Berberis ilicifolia*. Originated in the nursery of Mons. Baumann, at Bolwiller in Alsace, France, in 1854.

***MAHONIA**—**Berberidaceae**—Often listed under *Berberis*, from which they are well distinguished by their pinnate leaves and spineless stems. They are grown for their attractive evergreen foliage and yellow flowers in winter or spring, followed by usually blue-black berries. They thrive in most types of well drained soils, including chalk soil.

†**acanthifolia** G. DON. A magnificent large shrub, or small tree in mild areas, of erect habit. The enormous, pinnate leaves are arranged in dense collars at the summit of each stem, ideal backing for the bunches of long, spreading racemes of mimosa yellow, faintly scented flowers which appear in the autumn and continue into winter. Nepal, Sikkim, Assam. A.M. 1953. F.C.C. 1958.

'Aldenhamensis'. A splendid, strong-growing, medium sized erect shrub, with distinctive sea-green pinnate leaves and fascicles of rich yellow flowers along the stems in late winter. Of hybrid origin, possibly *M. pinnata* × *M. aquifolium*.

aquifolium NUTT. "Oregon Grape". A small shrub, valuable for under-planting or for game coverts, in sun or shade. Leaves pinnate, polished green sometimes turning red in winter. Flowers rich yellow, in dense racemes, borne in terminal clusters, opening in early spring; berries blue-black, very decorative. Parent of many hybrids. Western N. America. I. 1823. A.G.M. 1930.

'Atropurpurea'. A selected form in which the leaves are a rich reddish-purple during winter and early spring.

'Heterophylla'. See *M.* '*Heterophylla*'.

'Moseri'. A small shrub with attractive bronze-red young leaves turning to apple green and finally dark green.

bealei CARR. A medium to large siz, winter flowering shrub, related to *M. japonica*, from which it differs mainly in its stiffer, shorter, erect racemes, and its broad-based often overlapping leaflets. Now much rarer in cultivation than *M. japonica*, with which it has often been confused. China. I. 1845. A.M. 1916.

MAHONIA—*continued*

bealei × napaulensis. In our opinion this is probably the parentage of a Mahonia which we have long grown as *M. japonica trifurca*. It is a distinct shrub of upright habit, bearing large ruffs of pinnate leaves and erect, clustered racemes of yellow flowers in late winter.

'Buckland' (Media Group). A handsome clone raised by Mr. Lionel Fortescue at the Garden House, Buckland Monachorum, Devon. In leaf it tends towards *M. lomariifolia;* the racemes are long and lax.

'Charity' (Media Group). A superb medium sized to large shrub of upright, stately habit. Leaves ·5 to ·6m. long, bearing two-ranked long, spiny leaflets. The fragrant, deep yellow flowers are borne in long spreading and ascending racemes, in large terminal clusters during autumn and early winter. A.M. 1959. F.C.C. 1962. A.G.M. 1969.

eutriphylla FEDDE. A rare, small, slow-growing shrub. Leaves small, with three to five thick, rigidly spiny, dark green leaflets. Clusters of yellow flowers in spring followed by bloomy, black berries. An interesting shrub related to and perhaps only a form of *M. schiedeana*. Collected by E. K. Balls in Mexico to whom we are indebted for this plant.

fascicularis. See *M. pinnata*.

fortunei FEDDE. A slender, erect shrub, slowly attaining 1·8 to 2m., with distinctive matt green, linear-lanceolate leaflets. Flowers bright yellow, in erect narrow terminal racemes, from September to November. China. I. 1846.

fremontii FEDDE. A very beautiful blue-green, small to medium sized shrub, for a well drained site in full sun. The pinnate leaves are composed of small glaucous, crisped and spiny leaflets. Small clusters of flowers in May and June are followed by inflated, dry, yellowish or red berries. S.W. United States.

†haematocarpa FEDDE. An attractive species related to *M. fremontii*, but with smaller plum-coloured berries and longer, narrower, greener leaflets. Requires a sunny site. S.W. United States, N. Mexico. I. 1916.

'Heterophylla' (*aquifolium heterophylla*) (*toluacensis* BEAN not J.J.). A small shrub of loose, open habit with leaves composed of five to nine long, narrow, glossy-green, wavy-edged leaflets which often turn reddish-purple during winter. Flowers in racemes, clustered at the tips of the shoots in spring. Origin uncertain, but most likely a seedling of the original *M. toluacensis* J.J.

japonica DC. This beautiful species is deservedly one of the most popular of all evergreen shrubs; it has in the past been confused with *M. bealei*. It is one of the most ornamental of all known shrubs, having magnificent deep green, pinnate leaves and bearing from late autumn to early spring, terminal clusters of long pendulous, or laxly held, racemes of fragrant, lemon-yellow flowers. Some plants in cultivation are probably hybrids with *M. bealei* or *M. napaulensis*. China, long cultivated in Japan. A.M. 1916. A.G.M. 1962.

trifurca. See under *M. bealei × napaulensis*.

japonica × napaulensis. An attractive hybrid with good foliage and erect racemes of yellow flowers in late winter.

†lomariifolia TAKEDA. A very imposing species, but only sufficiently hardy for gardens in the milder counties. A large shrub, branches erect, stout, closely beset with long leaves composed of fifteen to nineteen pairs of rigid, narrow leaflets. Flowers deep yellow, borne during winter in dense terminal clusters of erect racemes 15 to 25cm. long, each raceme carrying as many as 250 small flowers. Yunnan, Formosa. I. 1931. A.M. 1938. F.C.C. 1939.

× media BRICKELL (*japonica × lomariifolia*). A vigorous shrub of medium to large size, with ruffs of handsome pinnate leaves and terminal clusters of long, lax racemes in late autumn and early winter. This magnificent hybrid has been independently raised in several places and a number of clones have been named. See *'Buckland'*, *'Charity'* and *'Winter Sun'*.

'Moseri'. See *M. aquifolium 'Moseri'*.

†napaulensis DC. A handsome medium-sized to large shrub allied to *M. acanthifolia*. Leaves large, with numerous glossy-green narrow leaflets. Flowers borne in slender, lax racemes in March to April. Nepal. I. 1858. A.M. 1974.

nervosa NUTT. A dwarf, suckering species, with lustrous leaves which often turn red in winter. Racemes 15 to 20cm. long in May and June; berries blackish-blue. Not the best of Mahonias on chalk. Western N. America. I. 1822.

MAHONIA—*continued*

†**nevinii** FEDDE. A small shrub with small, pinnate leaves. Leaflets five, flattened, grey-green above and attractively veined, pruinose beneath. Flowers in small clusters followed by black or deep purple berries. California. I. 1928.

pinnata FEDDE (*fascicularis*). A strong-growing shrub of medium size. Leaves short stalked, leaflets prickly and sea-green. The rich yellow racemes appear in clusters along the stems during late winter. California. A.G.M. 1947. A.M. 1948. Much confusion surrounds this plant in cultivation due to the existence of hybrids. The plant we grow is quite hardy and extremely floriferous, though probably itself a hybrid. I. before 1838.

pumila FEDDE. A rare, dwarf shrub of neat habit. Leaves with five to seven, flattened, spine-edged, sea-green, somewhat glaucous leaflets; flowers in spring; fruits bloomy-black in large clusters. S.W. Oregon and California.

repens G. DON. A dwarf suckering shrub, in time making small colonies. Leaflets matt green; flowers in terminal clusters followed by bloomy black berries. W. North America. I. 1822.

rotundifolia FEDDE. A small shrub of distinct appearance. Leaves ovate or rounded, sea-green, spineless; large plumes of rich yellow flowers borne in May, followed by black, bloomy berries. Probably a hybrid between *M. aquifolium* and *M. repens*.

†**swaseyi** FEDDE. Medium-sized shrub related to *M. fremontii*, differing in its leaflets, which are pruinose beneath and closely reticulate, also in its small leaf-like bracts. Berries yellowish-red. Texas (U.S.A.).

toluacensis BEAN not J.J. See *M. 'Heterophylla'*.

trifoliolata FEDDE. An attractive, medium sized evergreen for a well-drained sunny position against a warm sunny wall, where it will attain up to 4 to 5m. Leaves composed of three spiny, conspicuously veined, leaflets. Clusters of flowers in spring followed by redcurrant-like berries. S.E. Texas. We grow the following variety:—

glauca I. M. JOHNSTON. The form in general cultivation with leaflets conspicuously glaucous above. W. Texas to Arizona, N. Mexico. I. 1839.

'Undulata'. An ornamental medium sized shrub, taller than *M. aquifolium*, with lustrous dark green leaves, the leaflets with undulate margins. Flowers deep yellow in spring. Probably a hybrid between *M. aquifolium* and *M. pinnata*. A.G.M. 1960. A.M. 1971

×**wagneri** REHD. A variable small shrub resembling *M. aquifolium*, producing its racemes of flowers in spring. Believed to be a hybrid between *M. aquifolium* and *M. pinnata*.

'Winter Sun' (Media Group). A selected form raised by the Slieve Donard Nursery, N. Ireland. Racemes erect, densely packed with fragrant yellow flowers.

"MAIDENHAIR TREE". See *GINKGO biloba* under CONIFERS.

†**MALLOTUS—Euphorbiaceae**—Interesting, lime tolerant shrubs or small trees requiring full sun and a well drained soil. Only possible in the mildest areas of the British Isles.

japonicus MUELL.-ARG. A large shrub with large, handsome, roundish leaves. Flowers small, in large pyramidal panicles; male and female on different plants. Japan, Formosa, China, Korea.

MALUS—Rosaceae—The "Flowering Crabs" may be included with the "Ornamental Cherries", as together being unexcelled in floral charm by any other trees. With few exceptions they are easily grown, small to medium sized trees, and their flowering season is April and May, the flowers having five styles as against the solitary ones of *Prunus*. Many bear very attractive fruits in autumn, persisting in several sorts late into winter. Unless otherwise stated, all are small trees, thriving in all types of fertile soil. Straggly or untidy specimens may be hard pruned immediately after flowering.

E indicates crabs with edible fruits most suitable for using in preserves.

'Aldenhamensis' (Purpurea Group). A small tree or tall shrub of loose growth. Leaves purplish becoming bronze-green in late summer. Flowers single or semi-double, deep vinous red followed by reddish-purple fruits. Resembles *M. ×purpurea*, but flowering about a fortnight later. A.M. 1916.

'Almey'. An early, free flowering small tree of broad, rounded habit. Young leaves reddish-bronze. Flowers large, soft red with white centre; fruits orange-red with a crimson flush, persisting into winter. C. 1945.

MALUS—*continued*

angustifolia MICHX. An uncommon tree up to 10m. related to *M. coronaria*. The leaves on vigorous shoots are ovate and sharply lobed; on mature shoots, narrow and toothed. Flowers salmon-pink, violet-scented; fruits yellowish-green. E. United States. I. 1750.

×**arnoldiana** SARG. (*baccata*×*floribunda*). An extremely floriferous small round-headed tree or large shrub with somewhat drooping branches. Flowers fragrant, red in bud; opening white; fruits yellow, with reddish flush. Originated in the Arnold Arboretum, U.S.A. in 1883.

×**atrosanguinea** SCHNEID. (*halliana*×*sieboldii*). A small, mushroom-shaped tree with glossy green leaves. Flowers crimson in bud opening rose. Fruits yellow with a red cheek.

baccata BORKH. The true "Siberian Crab" is a small to medium sized tree of rounded habit. Flowers white, fragrant, followed by small red or yellow, berry-like fruits. Widely distributed throughout Asia. I. 1784.

mandshurica SCHNEID. An extremely hardy, round-headed tree up to 12m. Flowers early, during late April and May, white, fragrant; fruits slightly larger than those of the type. N.E. Asia. I. 1824. A.M. 1962. F.C.C. 1969.

'Cashmere'. A beautiful small hybrid tree having pale-pink flowers followed by yellow fruits in abundance.

'Chilko'. A small tree of Canadian origin developing a spreading head with large, purplish-red flowers up to 4·5cm. across. Fruits ovoid, 4cm. long, brilliant crimson with a shiny skin. E. C. 1920. A.M. 1967.

coronaria MILL. A beautiful, strong growing, American Crab up to 10m. Large fragrant flowers of a delightful shade of shell pink, produced with the foliage towards the latter end of May. Leaves often richly tinted in autumn. Eastern N. America. I. 1724.

'Charlottae' (*'Flore Pleno'*). A most excellent small tree with large, lobed leaves which colour richly in the autumn. Flowers large, semi-double, shell pink and violet-scented during late May and early June. Originated about 1902.

'Cowichan'. A vigorous tree up to 9m. or more with large, light red flowers. The large, reddish-purple fruits are accompanied by red tinted foliage. C. 1920.

crataegifolia. See *M. florentina.*

'Crittenden'. An excellent small, compact tree with attractive pale pink flowers. Particularly notable for its heavy crops of bright scarlet fruits which persist throughout autumn and winter. E. A.M. 1961. F.C.C. 1971.

'Dartmouth'. An attractive hybrid producing abundant, white flowers and equally plentiful reddish-purple fruits. E. Raised before 1883.

diversifolia. See *M. fusca.*

domestica BORKH. "Orchard Apple". A familiar tree ot hybrid origin probably derived from *M. dasycarpa*, *M. praecox* and *M. sylvestris*, as well as several asiatic species. It is cultivated for its fruit throughout the temperate regions of the world. Forms are often found naturalised or as garden escapes in wild situations, but they may always be distinguished from our native "Wild Crab" (*M. sylvestris*) by their larger, often sweet fruits. There are said to be over a thousand cultivars. For a selection of the best modern cultivars as well as some of the older favourites, see our Fruit Tree Catalogue. E.

'Dorothea'. A small tree, raised at the Arnold Arboretum, and possibly a hybrid between *M.* ×*arnoldiana* and *M. halliana 'Parkmanii'*. Flowers semi-double, 4 to 5cm. across, pale crimson, darker in bud; fruits folden yellow. C. 1943.

'Echtermeyer' (*'Exzellenz Thiel'*×*niedwetzkyana*) (*'Oekonomierat Echtermeyer'*) (*purpurea 'Pendula'*). A graceful, low, wide-spreading tree with weeping branches and purplish or bronze-green leaves. Flowers rose-crimson, deeper in bud, followed by reddish-purple fruits. C. 1914.

'Eleyi' (Purpurea Group). Resembles *M.* ×*purpurea* in leaf and flower, but slightly darker in both, the flowers opening slightly later. Carries very decorative purplish-red fruits in autumn. Garden origin before 1920. A.M. 1922. F.C.C. 1922. A.G.M. 1925, also see *M. 'Profusion'*, a more recent clone.

'Elise Rathke' (*pumila 'Pendula'*). A small tree with stiffly pendulous branches. Flowers large, pink in bud opening white, followed by large, sweet yellow fruits. E.

'Exzellenz Thiel' (Scheideckeri Group). A small, weeping tree or shrub raised by Spaeth about 1909. Flowers semi-double, pink in bud, opening white. C. 1909.

MALUS—*continued*

florentina SCHNEID. (*crataegifolia*). A small, round-headed tree with hawthorn-like foliage, white tomentose beneath, which turns orange and scarlet in autumn. Flowers white, fruits small, red. Italy, S. Yugoslavia, N. Greece. C. 1877. A.M. 1956.

floribunda VAN HOUTTE. "Japanese Crab". A most popular flowering small tree or large shrub with long arching branches. Remarkably beautiful when in flower, the crimson buds opening to white or pale blush. Fruits small, red and yellow. One of the earliest crabs to flower. Introduced from Japan in 1862. A.G.M. 1923.

fusca SCHNEID. (*diversifolia*) (*rivularis*). "Oregon Crab". A small tree or large shrub of dense, vigorous growth. Leaves serrate, often three lobed; flowers like apple blossom; fruits red or yellow. Western N. America. I. 1836.

'Gibbs' Golden Gage'. A small tree of unusual charm when carrying masses of medium sized, waxy, almost translucent yellow fruits. C. before 1923.

glaucescens REHD. A distinct small, round-headed tree with branches sometimes spiny, and lobed leaves, glaucous beneath, turning yellow and purple in autumn. Flowers pink; fruits waxy, green to yellow. N. America. C. 1902.

'Golden Hornet'. A small tree producing white flowers followed by large crops of bright yellow fruits which are retained until late in the year. One of the best fruiting crabs for general planting. C. before 1949. A.M. 1949. F.C.C. 1961. A.G.M. 1969.

halliana KOEHNE. A small tree up to 5m. Leaves narrow, dark, glossy green; flowers carmine in bud, opening shell-pink; small purple fruits. Originated in China where it is known only in cultivation. Introduced via Japan in 1863. A.M. 1935.

'Parkmanii'. A lovely form with pendulous clusters of partly semi-double flowers, rose-red in bud, opening shell-pink, borne on deep crimson pedicels.

× **hartwigii** KOEHNE. (*baccata* × *halliana*). A delightful small tree, intermediate between the parents. Flowers almost semi-double up to 5cm. across, pink in bud opening white.

'Hillieri' (Scheideckeri Group). A very attractive, late flowering tree, like *M.* × *scheideckeri*, but of better constitution. Flowers semi-double, crimson in bud, opening bright pink, wreathing the arching stems in clusters of five to eight. C. before 1928.

'Hopa'. A hybrid between *M. baccata* and *M. niedwetzkyana*, up to 10m., with large, purple-red flowers, followed by orange and red fruits. E. C. 1920.

hupehensis REHD. (*theifera*). A free-growing small tree with stiff, ascending branches. Flowers fragrant, soft pink in bud, opening white, produced in great abundance during May and June. Fruits yellow, tinted red. China, Japan. Introduced by E. H. Wilson in 1900. A.M. 1928. A.G.M. 1930.

'Rosea'. Differs from the type in its pale pink flowers and rather more spreading branches. A lovely tree in full bloom. A.M. 1938.

'Hyslop'. An openly branched, small tree with white flowers 1 to 4cm. across, followed by relatively large red-cheeked fruits 5 to 8cm. across. E.

‡**ioensis** BRITT. The "Prairie Crab" is a very attractive North American species closely allied to *M. coronaria*. Branches downy, and leaves persistently woolly beneath; flowers fragrant, 4 to 5cm. across, white usually flushed pink, in corymbs of four to six. C. United States.

'Plena'. "Bechtel's Crab". Large, semi-double soft pink, fragrant flowers. At its best perhaps the most beautiful flowering crab apple, but a tree of weak constitution and unsuitable for chalk soils. A.M. 1940. F.C.C. 1950.

'Jay Darling'. A most ornamental tree. Large wine-red flowers produced before or with the crimson-tinted foliage; fruits purplish-red.

'John Downie'. Perhaps the best fruiting "Crab". Flowers white; fruits comparatively large, conical, bright orange and red, of refreshing flavour. E. Garden origin before 1891. A.M. 1895. A.G.M. 1969.

'Kaido'. See *M.* × *micromalus*.

kansuensis SCHNEID. A large shrub or small tree with ovate, usually three-lobed leaves. Flowers small, creamy-white; fruits elongated, red and yellow. Good autumn colour. W. China. I. 1904. A.M. 1933.

'Katherine' (Hartwigii Group). A small tree with a regular, densely-branched, globular head. Deep pink buds open to semi-double pink flowers over 5cm. in diameter which gradually fade white. Even though the flowers are many petalled they are followed by bright red fruits flushed yellow. C. about 1928. A.M. 1967.

MALUS—*continued*

'Lady Northcliffe'. An attractive, small, densely-branched, broad-headed tree with flowers carmine-red in bud opening blush then white. Very free-flowering. Fruits small and round, yellow. A most ornamental tree for a small garden. C. before 1929.

lancifolia REHD. A small tree with variously shaped leaves, those of the flowering shoots lanceolate. Flowers shell pink followed by round, green fruits 2·5cm. across. U.S.A. I. 1912.

'Lemoinei' (Purpurea Group). This fine hybrid is more erect in growth than *M.* ×*purpurea*, and has larger, but fewer flowers, deep wine-red in colour. Garden origin 1922. A.M. 1928. A.G.M. 1937.

'Magdeburgensis'. A small, broad-headed tree like the domestic apple, with somewhat spreading branches and beautiful, large, semi-double flowers which are deep red in bud opening to purplish-pink clouded white. Fruits light green to yellow. A.M. 1933.

× **micromalus** MAK. (*baccata* × *spectabilis*) (*'Kaido'*). A small, erect-branched tree with clear, deep pink flowers, very showy in the mass. Fruits small, red or yellow. Introduced from Japan before 1856.

'Montreal Beauty'. A small tree of erect, open habit. Flowers white, slightly fragrant, freely borne along the branches and followed by comparatively large, conical yellow to orange, scarlet-flushed fruits. E.

'Neville Copeman' (Purpurea Group). A seedling from *M. 'Eleyi'*, developing into a small tree with green leaves shaded purple throughout summer. Flowers light purple followed by conical orange-red fruits. A.M. 1953.

niedzwetzkyana DIECK (*pumila niedzwetzkyana*). A small tree with red young growths. Flowers purple-red in dense clusters followed by large conical, dark red fruits covered with a plum-purple bloom. Parent of many notable hybrids. S.W. Siberia, Turkestan. I. about 1891.

orthocarpa LAV. A large shrub or small tree with pale pink flowers followed by orange and scarlet fruits. China.

platycarpa REHD. A low-spreading tree allied to *M. coronaria*. Flowers large, soft pink followed by large, fragrant, flattened, pale yellow fruits. N. America. I. 1912.

prattii SCHNEID. A distinct Chinese tree up to 10m., with very pleasing, large, red-veined leaves which give good autumn colour. Flowers white, followed by red or yellow fruits. China. I. 1904.

'Prince George's'. Originating in the Arnold Arboretum, this tree is probably a hybrid between *M. angustifolia* and *M. ioensis 'Plena'*. The flowers are fully double, 5cm. in diameter, and light pink in colour. C. 1919.

'Professor Sprenger' (Zumi Group). A small, dense-headed tree flowering in great profusion. Flowers pink in bud, opening white, followed by large quantities of shining, amber coloured fruits which usually remain until late December. Introduced by Mr. Doorenbos of the Hague, Holland in 1950.

'Profusion' (*'Lemoinei'* × *sieboldii*). A first class hybrid flowering a little later than *M. 'Lemoinei'*. Flowers in great profusion, wine-red, slightly fragrant, about 4cm. across, borne in clusters of six or seven. Fruits small, ox-blood red. Young leaves coppery-crimson. A tree of good constitution and probably the best of all the crabs with wine-red flowers and red young growths. A.G.M. 1969.

prunifolia BORKH. A small tree with oval, unequally toothed leaves. Flowers rose-crimson in bud opening white flushed pink, produced in April and followed by red conical fruits which retain their calyces. N.E. Asia. C. 1758.

'Fastigiata'. Branches ascending, forming a columnar head, becoming spreading with age. Fruits yellow and red.

'Pendula'. A form with pendulous branches.

rinki REHD. (*M. ringo*). A variety with almond-pink flowers; fruits bright yellow. W. China.

pumila MILL. This name which correctly belongs to the "Paradise Apple" of gardens has long been used to cover several apples including *M. dasyphylla, M. domestica* and *M. sylvestris*. The latter is the wild crab of the British Isles whilst *M. domestica* is the orchard apple.

niedzwetzkyana. See *M. niedzwetzkyana*.

'Pendula'. See *M. 'Elise Rathke'*.

MALUS—*continued*

× **purpurea** REHD. (× *atrosanguinea* × *niedzwetzkyana*). A beautiful hybrid, producing a wealth of rosy crimson flowers and dark purplish-green shoots and leaves. Fruits light crimson purple. Many clones have been named. Garden origin before 1900. We regard *M. 'Profusion'* as a tree of better constitution. A.M. 1914. A.G.M. 1923.

'Pendula'. See *M. 'Echtermeyer'*.

'Red Jade'. A lovely, small tree or shrub with weeping branches. Young leaves bright green; flowers white and pink; fruits red, the size of cherries, long persistent. C. 1935.

'Red Sentinel'. An excellent fruiting tree with white flowers and large clusters of deep red fruits which remain on the branches throughout winter. A.M. 1959.

'Red Tip' (*ioensis* × *niedzwetzykana*). An exciting hybrid worthy of inclusion in every representative group of crabs. Flowers red-purple, leaves broad, slightly lobed, young foliage bright red, fruits red flushed.

ringo. See *M. prunifolia rinki.*

rivularis. See *M. fusca.*

× **robusta** REHD. (*baccata* × *prunifolia*). Popularly, though incorrectly, known as "Siberian Crab", the clones of this variable hybrid have white or pinkish flowers and more or less globular, cherry-like red or yellow fruits without calyces. C. about 1815. A.M. 1957. A.G.M. 1958.

'Red Siberian'. Fruits red.

'Yellow Siberian'. Fruits yellow.

sargentii REHD. A delightful shrubby species up to 2·8m. high, with leaves often three-lobed. Smothered in spring with pure white flowers with golden anthers, and in autumn with small, bright red, cherry-like fruits. Closely related to *M. sieboldii* of which it is by some authorities regarded as a form. Japan. I. 1892. A.M. 1915. A.G.M. 1927.

'Rosea'. Flowers blush, rose in bud; slightly more vigorous than the type.

× **scheideckeri** ZAB. (*floribunda* × *prunifolia*). A very free-flowering, slow-growing shrub or miniature tree with masses of slightly fragrant, semi-double, pink and white blossoms. Not suitable for shallow, chalky soils. C. 1888. A.M. 1896.

sieboldii REHD. (*toringo*). A small, picturesque, semi-weeping, Japanese "Crab", rarely more than 3m. high. Leaves simple or variously lobed. Flowers pink in bud, fading to white, smaller than those of *M. floribunda;* fruits small, red or yellowish. Japan. I. 1856.

sikkimensis SCHNEID. A distinct, small, erect-branched tree from the Himalayas. Flowers white, followed by somewhat pear-shaped, dark red fruits. Easily recognised by the excessive development of stout, branching spurs on the trunk around the base of the branches. I. 1849.

'Simcoe'. A small but strong-growing tree of Canadian origin. Young growths copper-tinted. Flowers comparatively large, light purplish-pink produced in large quantities, followed by purplish-red fruits. C. 1920. A.M. 1940.

× **soulardii** BRITT. (*domestica* × *ioensis*). A very beautiful hybrid with large, clear, almond-pink flowers and yellow, red-flushed fruits. C. 1868.

spectabilis BORKH. A small tree with upright branches. The flowers are deep rose-red in bud, opening to blush, 5cm. wide. One of the loveliest flowering crabs, at its best during late April and early May. China, but not known in the wild. C. 1780.

'Albiplena'. Large, semi-double, white, delicately violet-scented flowers. Probably of hybrid origin, although some authorities regard it as a form of *M. sylvestris*.

'Riversii' (*'Rosea Plena'*). A tree with upright branches. The semi-double flowers are deep rose-red in bud, opening to rosy-pink. Introduced by the English nurseryman, Thomas Rivers, in 1872.

× **sublobata** REHD. (*prunifolia* × *sieboldii*). A small pyramidal tree. Leaves narrow-elliptic with an occasional lobe. Flowers pale pink; fruits yellow. Introduced from Japan about 1892.

MALUS—*continued*

sylvestris MILL. (*pumila* HORT. in part) (*acerba*). "Common Crab Apple". A small tree or a large shrub, often with spurs. Leaves ovate to broad elliptic, shallowly toothed, glabrous at maturity. Flowers white or suffused pink followed by yellowish-green or red flushed fruits, crowned by the persistent calyx and measuring 2 to 4cm. across. A parent of the orchard apple (*M. domestica*), also of several "Ornamental Crabs". Sometimes wrongly referred to in cultivation as *M. pumila*, which name rightly belongs to the "Paradise Apple" of gardens. Europe. The true species is wild in most parts of the British Isles, but is less frequent than the forms of *M. domestica* which are commonly planted and naturalised.

theifera. See *M. hupehensis*.

toringo. See *M. sieboldii*.

toringoides HUGHES. A very beautiful, small, shrubby tree with graceful, slender, wide-spreading branches and deeply lobed leaves. Flowers creamy white, slightly fragrant, in May, followed by rounded or pear-shaped red and yellow fruits which are particularly conspicuous. Attractive autumn tints. W. China. I. 1904. A.M. 1919. A.G.M. 1929.

transitoria SCHNEID. A slender, small tree resembling *M. toringoides* but more elegant, differing in its leaves being usually smaller, more narrowly lobed and more pubescent. Fruits smaller, rounded, yellow. Very beautiful in autumn colour. N.W. China. I. 1911.

trilobata SCHNEID. A comparatively rare and very distinct, erect-branched tree to about 13m. Leaves maple-like, deeply three-lobed, the lobes themselves often sharply lobed and toothed, attractively tinted in autumn. Flowers white; fruits yellowish but seldom produced. This little known tree is worthy of more extensive public planting where space is confined. E. Mediterranean Region, N.E. Greece. C. 1877.

tschonoskii SCHNEID. An attractive, strong-growing tree up to 12m. of erect, conical habit, and with ovate, irregularly incised leaves. Flowers white, tinged pink; fruits globose, yellowish-green, tinged reddish purple. One of the best trees for autumn colour, with its bold foliage of yellow, orange, purple and scarlet. A splendid tree for public planting in confined spaces. Japan. Introduced by Sargent in 1897. A.M. 1962.

'Van Eseltine'. A small tree of distinctive columnar habit, the branches stiffly erect. The semi-double flowers, 3·5 to 5cm. across, are rose-scarlet in bud opening shell-pink, clouded white on the inner petals; fruits yellow. An excellent crab for a small garden. C. 1930.

'Veitch's Scarlet'. An outstanding crab with white flowers followed by conspicuous bright red fruits. E. A.M. 1904. A.M. 1955.

'Wintergold'. A shapely, small, round-headed tree with white, pink-budded flowers and an abundance of clear yellow fruits which are carried well into winter.

'Wisley'. A vigorous seedling of *M. niedzwetzkyana*. Leaves bronzy-red; flowers large, vinous red, slightly scented, followed by large, purple-red fruits. A.M. 1924.

yunnanensis SCHNEID. A notable tree of small to medium size, with ovate, occasionally lobed leaves, turning crimson and orange in autumn. Flowers white; fruits deep red. W. China. I. 1900.

veitchii REHD. A comparatively tall, erect branched variety, distinguished by its cordate, lobulate leaves and more brightly coloured fruits. C. China. I. 1901. A.M. 1912.

×**zumi** REHD. (*baccata mandshurica* × *sieboldii*). A small pyramidal tree resembling, and often included as a variety of *M. sieboldii*, but differing in its rarely lobed leaves, and larger flowers and fruits. Flowers pink in bud, opening white, fragrant; fruits bright red. Japan. I. 1892. A.M. 1933.

'Calocarpa'. A form of spreading habit and with smaller leaves and flowers. Bright red fruits persist throughout the winter. Japan. I. 1890.

‡†*MANGLIETIA—Magnoliaceae—A small genus of evergreen trees closely related to *Magnolia*. They require a moist, lime-free soil and are only suitable for the mildest localities.

insignis BL. A small tree with stout twigs and leathery, oblanceolate to narrowly oval leaves 10 to 20cm. long, dark glossy green above, pale green or slightly glaucous beneath. The erect, solitary, creamy-white, tinged pink or deep rose, magnolia-like flowers 7·5cm. across are borne during May. Himalaya, Burma, W. China. I. about 1912.

"MANUKA". See *LEPTOSPERMUM scoparium.*

"MAPLE". See *ACER.*

***MARGYRICARPUS—Rosaceae**—A small genus of South American small shrubs or sub-shrubs with pinnate leaves. Any well-drained soil.

pinnatus KUNTZE (*setosus*). "Pearl Berry". A charming, prostrate or slightly erect, white-berrying shrub from the Chilean Andes. Leaves evergreen, deep green and finely cut. Suitable for the rock garden. I. 1829.

MARSDENIA—Asclepiadaceae—Interesting in being a genus of mainly tropical shrubs, with one hardy representative. Easily grown in full sun in any well-drained soil.

erecta R. BR. (*Cionura erecta*). An interesting lax shrub up to 2m. with attractively marbled, silvery-green, cordate-ovate leaves, and cymes of fragrant, white flowers from May to July. Sap milky white. Requires a warm border or wall. E. Mediterranean Region. C. since the 16th century.

"MAY". See *CRATAEGUS monogyna.*

"MAY FLOWER". See *EPIGAEA repens.*

***MAYTENUS—Celastraceae**—A large genus of evergreen trees and shrubs with only one or two species hardy in most parts of the British Isles. Any well-drained soil, acid or alkaline.

boaria MOL. (*chilensis*). A large, evergreen shrub, occasionally a small tree, recalling *Phillyrea latifolia* but more graceful, with slender branches and narrow elliptic, finely toothed leaves. The flowers are small and insignificant. An unusual species with pleasant, shining green foliage. Chile. I. 1829.

"MAZZARD". See *PRUNUS avium.*

MEDICAGO—Leguminosae—A genus of mainly clover-like herbs with trifoliolate leaves. Any well-drained soil; full sun.

†*arborea L. "Moon Trefoil". A small, semi-evergreen shrub with clusters of yellow pea-flowers produced continuously, though often sparsely, from May to September; seed pods resembling snail shells. Excellent for maritime exposure, elsewhere it requires the shelter of a warm wall. S. Mediterranean Region. I. 1596.

"MEDLAR". See *MESPILUS germanica.*

†*MELALEUCA—Myrtaceae—Elegant Australasian shrubs as cultivated in this country but some attain tree size in their native haunts. Resembling *Callistemon* ("Bottle Brush"). Only suitable for the mildest localities, and needing full sun but wind resistant. Not tolerant of chalk soils.

gibbosa LABILL. A small to medium sized, wiry shrub, with small, crowded, opposite leaves. Flowers light purple in short dense terminal "bottle-brushes" during summer. Tasmania, S. and S.E. Australia.

hypericifolia SMITH. Large shrub of graceful habit. Leaves small, aptly described by the specific epithet. Flowers bright red in summer. S.E. Australia. I. 1792.

squamea LABILL. Small to medium sized, erect shrub with narrow, alternate leaves crowded along the branches. Flowers variable in colour, usually purplish, in dense terminal heads in late spring. Tasmania, S. and S.E. Australia. I. 1805.

squarrosa SM. An erect, rigid shrub. Leaves ovate-lanceolate to ovate, sharply pointed; flowers pale yellow in crowded, oblong spikes during summer. Tasmania, S. and S.E. Australia. I. 1794.

wilsonii F. MUELL. An elegant shrub up to 2m., with linear-lanceolate leaves and conspicuous red or pink flowers in clusters along the shoots during late spring or summer. W. Australia. I. 1861.

†MELIA—Meliaceae—A small genus of sun-loving, deciduous, small trees or large shrubs of which the following species is the only one which sometimes succeeds in the mildest parts of the British Isles. Its bead-like seeds are used in necklaces, etc.

azedarach L. "Bead Tree". A small tree or large shrub best grown against a warm sheltered wall or in a conservatory. Large, elegant, doubly pinnate leaves and small fragrant lilac flowers in loose panicles during summer. In warm countries clusters of rounded, yellow, bead-like fruits are produced in autumn which remain long after the leaves have fallen. Commonly planted as a street tree in warmer countries, particularly in the Mediterranean region. It requires hot sun to ripen growth. N. India, C. and W. China. C. in England since the 16th century.

†***MELIANTHUS—Melianthaceae**—A small genus of sun-loving evergreen sub-shrubs, with attractive foliage and unusual flowers. Only possible in the mildest parts of the British Isles.

major L. A handsome, evergreen sub-shrub with spreading, hollow stems. Its glaucous, deeply-toothed, pinnate leaves, 30 to 45cm. long, give a striking sub-tropical effect. The tubular flowers are tawny-crimson, in dense, erect terminal racemes up to 15cm. long in summer. Hardy in Cornwall and Southern Ireland and similar favoured areas, where it will attain 2m. or more. Occasionally used as a "dot plant" in sub-tropical bedding. S. Africa. I. 1688. F.C.C. 1975.

†**MELICOPE—Rutaceae**—A genus of small trees and shrubs native of Australasia, Pacific Isles and Tropical Asia. One species is occasionally grown in the mildest parts of the British Isles.

ternata J. R. & G. FORST. A large, semi-evergreen shrub for the mildest localities. Leaves trifoliolate. Flowers greenish-white in cymose inflorescences in autumn. New Zealand. I. 1822.

MELICYTUS—Violaceae—A small genus of trees and shrubs bearing small, often dioecious flowers.

ramiflorus J. R. & G. FORST. As seen in this country a large shrub with lanceolate-oblong or narrow elliptic, coarsely toothed leaves. The clusters of tiny greenish-yellow flowers are followed by violet or dark blue berries. New Zealand. A.M. 1925.

MELIOSMA—Sabiaceae—An uncommon genus of summer-flowering, oriental shrubs or small trees, handsome in leaf, which may be simple or compound, and producing spiraea-like, paniculate inflorescences, crowded with small, white flowers. Although lime tolerant, they succeed best in a deep neutral soil.

cuneifolia FRANCH. A large shrub with simple, obovate, bristle-toothed leaves 8 to 18cm. long, bearing spiraea-like plumes of creamy white flowers with hawthorn-like fragrance in July. Fruit globose, about the size of a peppercorn, black. W. China. I. 1901.

meliantha SIEB. & ZUCC. (*stewardii*). The plants grown under this name were raised from seed received from China. A shrub 1·5 to 2m. high, with elliptic leaves and bearing wide panicles of white flowers at the tips of short, lateral branches.

oldhamii MIQ. A rare, small tree with handsome pinnate, ash-like leaves up to ·5m. long. Flowers white in large erect terminal panicles in June. China, Korea. I. 1900.

parviflora LECOMTE. Medium sized shrub of semi-erect habit with small, obovate, denticulate leaves. So far proving hardy in our nurseries. China. I. 1936.

pendens REHD. & WILS. A large shrub with simple, obovate, bristle-toothed leaves, up to 15cm. long. Flowers fragrant, white, in pendulous, terminal panicles in July. China. I. 1907.

†**pungens** WALP. Medium sized, semi-evergreen shrub with greyish stems and rather leathery, oblanceolate leaves conspicuously toothed in the upper half and with a tail-like apex, decurrent at the base.

stewardii. See *M. meliantha*.

tenuis MAXIM. A large shrub with slender, dark brown stems and coarsely-toothed, obovate leaves to 15cm. long. The tiny, creamy-yellow flowers are carried in pyramidal, nodding panicles in May and June. Japan. I. 1915.

veitchiorum HEMSL. A rare, small tree of architectural quality, remarkable for its very large, pinnate leaves, stout, rigid branches and prominent winter buds. Flowers creamy-white, fragrant, in 30 to 45cm. long panicles, in May; fruits violet. W. China. I. 1901.

‡**MENZIESIA—Ericaceae**—Small, slow-growing, deciduous shrubs recalling *Enkianthus*, requiring lime-free soil and, if possible, a position affording protection from late frosts. Flowers in terminal clusters, resembling *Daboecia*, but waxy in texture. This small genus embracing at least two exquisite shrubs of top quality, deserves greater recognition.

ciliicalyx MAXIM. A beautiful, small shrub with oval or obovate, ciliate leaves and clusters of nodding, pitcher-shaped flowers in May, varying in colour from cream to soft purple. Japan. I. 1915. A.M. 1938.

multiflora. See *M. multiflora*.

purpurea MAK. (*M. purpurea* HORT. not MAXIM). A superb, slow-growing variety with obovate, mucronate leaves. The striking, rose-purple flowers are larger than those of the type and appear slightly later. Usually grown in gardens wrongly as *M. purpurea* which is doubtfully in cultivation. Japan.

MENZIESIA—*continued*

ferruginea SM. A small to medium-sized shrub with peeling bark. The small, cylindrical, pink-tinged flowers are borne in nodding clusters during May. Western N. America.

glabella GRAY. A small shrub with obovate leaves and clusters of small, orange-flushed, pitcher-shaped flowers in late May and June. N. America. I. about 1885.

multiflora MAXIM. (*ciliicalyx multiflora*). A small shrub similar to *M. ciliicalyx*, but with shorter, more urn-shaped corollas, the colour varying from pale purple to near white, with deeper coloured lobes. Japan.

pilosa JUSS. A small shrub of erect habit and modest charm. Young shoots and leaves glandular downy. The pendulous, urn-shaped flowers are 6mm. long, creamy-yellow, flushed red and are carried in glandular-stalked, nodding clusters during May. E. United States. I. 1806.

purpurea HORT not MAXIM. See *M. ciliicalyx purpurea*.

MESPILUS—Rosaceae—A monotypic genus related to *Crataegus*.

germanica L. "Medlar". A small, picturesque, wide-spreading tree rivalling the "Black Mulberry" as an isolated specimen for an architectural feature. The large, hairy leaves turn a warm russet in the autumn. Large white flowers are produced singly in May and June, followed by brown fruits, 2 to 3cm. across. S.E. Europe, Asia Minor. Long cultivated in England and naturalised in some counties. For named clones selected for their fruits please see our Fruit Tree Catalogue.

"MESPILUS, SNOWY". See *AMELANCHIER*.

†*METROSIDEROS—Myrtaceae—A genus of handsome, evergreen trees, shrubs and aerial-rooted climbers, natives of the Antipodes. The brilliantly coloured "bottle-brush" flowers, composed largely of stamens, are often spectacular. All require protection and can only be grown outside in the mildest areas of the British Isles. Moderately lime-tolerant but not suitable for shallow chalk soils.

diffusa SMITH. In cultivation in this country an exceedingly slow-growing small to medium-sized, lax or scandent shrub with cymes of pink-petalled flowers with long pinkish stamens in April and May. New Zealand. I. 1910. A.M. 1931.

excelsa SOL. (*tomentosa*). Called the "Christmas Tree" in New Zealand, where it is abundant in parts of North Island and described as a "noble and picturesque tree". Its large "bottle-brush" flowers are brilliant crimson and smother the branches in summer. The finest examples in the British Isles are to be found in the Tresco Abbey Gardens. Elsewhere it is more usually a conservatory plant. I. 1840.

hypericifolia HORT. Under this name we are growing a small, slender-branched shrub with angular reddish-brown shoots, small, ovate-oblong leaves and clusters of red flowers.

kermadecensis W. R. B. OLIVER (*villosa* KIRK). Resembling *M. excelsa*, but a little smaller in all its parts; flowers scarlet. Suitable only for the very mildest areas. New Zealand, Polynesian Isles.

lucida A. RICH. One of the hardiest species, thriving in Cornwall and similarly favoured districts where it forms a large shrub or small tree of dense bushy habit. The small, polished, myrtle-like leaves are coppery when young. On mature specimens the clusters of bright crimson-stamened flowers are produced in late summer illuminating the dark green foliage. New Zealand.

robusta A. CUNN. The "Rata" of New Zealand. A magnificent, small to medium-sized, evergreen tree, for mild, maritime districts. Leaves dark green, thick and rounded, narrower on juvenile plants. Flowers coppery-scarlet appearing in late summer. Flowering at an earlier state than *M. lucida*, but less hardy. A.M. 1959.

tomentosa. See *M. excelsa*.

villosa. See *M. kermadecensis*.

"MEXICAN ORANGE BLOSSOM". See *CHOISYA ternata*.

"MEYER'S LEMON". See *CITRUS 'Meyer's Lemon'*.

"MEZEREON". See *DAPHNE mezereum*.

‡MICHELIA—Magnoliaceae—Evergreen trees or shrubs closely related to *Magnolia*, but differing most noticeably in the flowers being borne in the axils of the leaves. Only suitable for the milder lime-free areas.

MICHELIA—*continued*

***compressa** SARG. A rare, slow-growing shrub or occasionally a small tree with ovate to obovate, glossy-green, leathery leaves, 5cm. long. Flowers fragrant, pale yellow, or whitish, with a purplish-red centre, opening during late spring. Most often seen growing against a south or west wall or in the sheltered corner of a house. Uninjured by the long severe winter of 1962/63. Japan, Ryukyus, I. 1894.

†doltsopa BEAN. A magnificent small to medium-sized, semi-evergreen tree in the South West. Leaves 15 to 18cm. long, leathery, glaucous beneath; flowers formed in autumn, opening in spring, multipetalled, white and heavily scented. W. Yunnan, Tibet, E. Himalaya. I. about 1918. A.M. 1961.

†*figo SPRENG. (*fuscata*) (*Magnolia fuscata*). A medium-sized to large shrub, best treated as a greenhouse plant. Leaves small, dark glossy-green; flowers small, brown-purple and strongly scented of "pear drops", produced in a long succession during spring and summer. China. I. 1789.

MICROGLOSSA (*AMPHIRAPHIS*)—**Compositae**—A small genus of shrubs related to *Aster*. Any well-drained soil in a sunny position.

albescens C. B. CLARKE (*Aster albescens*). A small shrub up to 1m. high, producing its pale lilac-blue, daisy-like flowers in terminal corymbs in July. Himalaya; China. I. about 1840.

MIMULUS (*DIPLACUS*)—**Scrophulariaceae**—A large genus of mainly annual and perennial herbs, but embracing one or two woody plants suitable for favoured sunny positions. Lime tolerant.

†*aurantiacus CURT. (*glutinosus*). The "Shrubby Musk" is a pretty shrub for mild localities, especially near the sea, growing about 1·2m. high. Stems sticky to the touch. Flowers orange or salmon-yellow, borne throughout summer and autumn. California, Oregon. I. in the late 18th century. A.M. 1938.

glutinosus. See *M. aurantiacus*.

†*puniceus STEUD. (*aurantiacus puniceus*). A small shrub closely related to *M. aurantiacus*, differing mainly in its smaller, brick-red or orange-red flowers. California.

‡*MITCHELLA—**Rubiaceae**—A genus of only two species of evergreen, creeping plants suitable for a cool spot on the rock garden, or as ground cover in shade. They require a lime-free soil.

repens L. "Partridge Berry". A charming mat-forming sub-shrub with procumbent, rooting stems. The tiny, ovate or rounded leaves are dark glossy-green and borne in pairs. The small, fragrant, white or pink flowers are borne in terminal pairs in June and July. Fruits scarlet, 12mm. across. E. and C. North America. I. about 1761. A.M. 1951.

†*MITRARIA—**Gesneriaceae**—A monotypic genus.

coccinea CAV. A low, spreading evergreen with small, glossy, leathery leaves and large, bright orange-scarlet tubular flowers borne singly in the leaf-axils from late spring through summer. A charming plant for a partially shaded, sheltered position. Unsuitable for shallow chalk soils. Chile; Chiloe. I. 1848. A.M. 1927.

"MOCKERNUT". See *CARYA tomentosa*.

"MOCK ORANGE". See *PHILADELPHUS*.

MOLTKIA—**Boraginaceae**—A small genus of herbaceous perennials and sub-shrubs related to *Lithospermum*, differing in the exserted stamens. A well-drained site in full sun on scree or rock garden.

petraea GRISEB. (*Lithospermum petraeum*). A lovely sub-shrub forming a neat bush 30 to 45cm. high. Flowers tubular, pink in bud opening to violet-blue, in June and July. Greece. I. about 1840. F.C.C. 1871.

"MONKEY PUZZLE". See *ARAUCARIA araucana* under CONIFERS.

MORUS—**Moraceae**—The Mulberries form small to medium-sized picturesque trees. Although succeeding in any well-drained soil, they respond to liberal treatment and are particularly suitable for town or coastal gardens. In winter the twigs may be recognised by the absence of a terminal bud. The brittle fleshy roots call for special care in planting.

acidosa. See *M. australis*.

alba L. "White Mulberry". A small to medium-sized tree of rugged appearance. Leaves heart-shaped, or ovate-lanceolate, often up to 15cm. wide. Fruits whitish changing to reddish-pink, sweet and edible. Silkworms are traditionally fed on the leaves of this tree. China. Said to have been introduced into England in 1596.

MORUS—*continued*

alba 'Laciniata' (*'Skeletoniana'*). A curious form, the leaves deeply divided into narrow, long-pointed lobes.

'Macrophylla'. A remarkable form with large, often lobed, leaves 18 to 22cm. long, recalling those of a fig.

'Nana'. A small shrubby form of compact habit.

'Pendula'. A striking, small weeping tree with closely packed, perpendicularly falling branches. A.M. 1897. A.G.M. 1973.

'Pyramidalis'. An erect-branched form, resembling a Lombardy Poplar in habit.

'Skeletoniana'. See *'Laciniata'*.

tatarica SER. A small, bushy-headed geographical variety with smaller leaves and fruits. Withstands very low temperatures.

'Venosa'. Leaves slenderly tapered at both ends, green with conspicuous, pale veins.

australis POIR. (*acidosa*). A small bushy tree or large shrub with variously shaped leaves. Fruits dark red, sweet. China, Japan, Korea, Formosa. I. 1907.

bombycis KOIDZ. (*kagayamae*). A large shrub or small tree with ovate, irregularly toothed leaves 10 to 20cm. long. Fruits purplish-black. The leaves are much used for feeding silk worms. Japan, Korea, Sakhalin.

cathayana HEMSL. A remarkable, small tree with large, heart-shaped, slenderly pointed leaves and black, red or white fruits 2·5cm. long. C. and E. China. I. 1907.

kagayamae. See *M. bombycis*.

†**microphylla** BUCKL. In cultivation a very slow-growing bushy shrub, differing from *M. rubra* in its tiny leaves, also smaller catkins and fruits. This distinct species has not succeeded out-of-doors in our nurseries. Southern U.S.A. and Mexico. I. 1926.

nigra L. "Black Mulberry". A small, very long-lived architectural tree with wide-spreading head, becoming gnarled and picturesque with age. Leaves heart-shaped, rough above, downy below. Fruits dark almost black-red, with an agreeable taste. W. Asia. Said to have first been grown in England early in the 16th century.

rubra L. "Red Mulberry". A rare species in cultivation. A small to medium-size tree with rounded downy leaves, turning bright yellow in autumn. Very like the "White Mulberry". Fruit red. E. and C. United States. I. 1629.

'Nana'. A dwarf, slow-growing form of compact habit, broader than high. Leaves smaller and prominently three to five-lobed.

"MOUNTAIN ASH". See *SORBUS aucuparia*.

"MULBERRY". See *MORUS*.

"MULBERRY, PAPER". See *BROUSSONETIA papyrifera*.

†***MYOPORUM**—**Myoporaceae**—A genus of evergreen trees and shrubs, native of Japan and Australasia. Only one or two species will surive in the mildest localities. Lime tolerant.

laetum FORST. f. (*perforatum*). "Ngaio". An evergreen shrub or small tree notable for its dark, sticky buds and its lanceolate leaves, conspicuously studded with pellucid glands. Flowers small, white, purple-spotted. Will survive only in the mildest parts of the British Isles. Excellent for maritime exposure. New Zealand.

‡**MYRICA**—**Myricaceae**—A genus of interesting aromatic shrubs embracing species tolerant of dry sterile soil and those which delight in an acid bog. Flowers unisexual.

***californica** CHAM. & SCHLECT. "Californian Bayberry". A glossy leaved, hardy, evergreen shrub of medium to large size, occasionally a small tree. The oblanceolate, serrated leaves are polished apple green on both surfaces, less aromatic than in other species. Fruits dark purple, clustered like small black berries on short spurs and persisting until mid-winter. Tolerant of both moist and acid conditions. W. United States. I. 1848.

***cerifera** L. (*caroliniensis*). "Wax Myrtle". A North American evergreen shrub or small tree, with narrow obovate or oblanceolate leaves. A pleasing subject for a damp site. The glaucous wax which covers the fruits is made into fragrantly burning candles. E. United States, Carribean Isles. I. 1669.

MYRICA—*continued*

gale L. "Sweet Gale", "Bog Myrtle". A small, native, deciduous shrub of dense habit. Male and female catkins, of a warm golden brown colour which glisten in the sunlight, are produced on separate plants during April and May. The whole plant is strongly aromatic and may be grown in acid, boggy swamps where few other plants will exist. Europe to N.E. Asia, N. America. C. 1750.

pensylvanica LOIS. "Bayberry". A hardy, valuable plant for acid soils. The oblong or obovate aromatic leaves fall late in autumn. Conspicuous in winter with its tiny grey-white fruits. An excellent maritime plant, good for dry arid conditions. Eastern N. America. I. 1727.

MYRICARIA—Tamaricaceae—A small genus closely related to, and requiring the same conditions as *Tamarix*, differing in the flowers which have more numerous stamens, united in the lower half.

germanica DESV. (*Tamarix germanica*). Wand-like stems 1·2 to 2m. high, carry feathery, blue-green foliage and light pink, fluffy flowers throughout the summer. Succeeds best in neutral or acid soil but is lime tolerant. C. and S. Europe, W. Asia. C. 1582.

"MYROBALAN". See *PRUNUS cerasifera*.

†*MYRSINE (including *SUTTONIA*)—**Myrsinaceae**—A large genus of chiefly tropical trees and shrubs primarily of botanical interest; the females sometimes produce attractive fruits. Moderately lime tolerant, but not recommended for a shallow, chalky soil.

africana L. A small shrub with aromatic myrtle-like leaves and axillary clusters of tiny reddish-brown flowers. On female plants blue-black, pea-like fruits are produced. Resembling in general appearance *Pachistima myrsinites*, differing in its alternate leaves and dioecious flowers. Himalaya, China, Azores, Formosa, Mts. of E. and S. Africa. I. 1691. A.M. 1927.

retusa DC. A variety with more rounded-obovate leaves.

†australis ALLAN (*Suttonia australis*). A small to medium-sized shrub with slender orange-red branchlets and oblong or elliptic leaves with strongly undulate margins. For a sheltered position in mild gardens. New Zealand.

nummularia HOOK. f. (*Suttonia nummularia*). A prostrate, evergreen shrub with wiry stems and densely-set, small, orbicular, brownish-green leaves. On female plants small blue-purple fruits are produced. New Zealand.

"MYRTLE". See *MYRTUS*.

***MYRTUS—Myrtaceae**—The "Myrtles" are an easily cultivated and effective group of mostly white-flowered, aromatic evergreens for mild climates. They succeed best in full sun on any well-drained soil, including chalk soils and are excellent for maritime exposure.

†apiculata NIEDENZ. (*luma* HORT.). A lovely species attaining small tree size in mild localities. The cinnamon-coloured outer bark of even quite young trees peels off in patches, exposing the beautiful, cream-coloured inner surface. Leaves dark, dull green, oval, ending in a short abrupt point. The solitary, white flowers bedeck the branches during late summer and early autumn. The red and black fruits, when produced, are edible and sweet. In some southern Irish gardens it has become naturalized and reproduction is prolific. Chile. I. 1843.

†bidevillei BENTH. A small, erect shrub with dainty leaves rather like those of *Lonicera nitida* in shape and size.

†bullata A. CUNN. not SALISB. (*Lophomyrtus bullata*). The New Zealand "Ramarama". A large bush or small tree, with distinct round, leathery, coppery-green or reddish-brown, bullate leaves. Flowers white followed by blackish-red berries; suitable only for the mildest localities. C. 1854.

†chequen SPRENG. A Chilean "Myrtle" proving to be one of the hardiest, and ultimately forming a small, densely leafy tree, flowering in summer and autumn. Leaves aromatic, bright green, undulate. I. 1847.

†communis L. The "Common Myrtle", hardy in many localities, particularly by the sea. An aromatic, densely leafy shrub, attaining 3 to 4·5m. against a sunny wall. The white flowers are borne profusely in July and August, followed by purple-black berries. Mediterranean Region, S.W. Europe, W. Asia; thoroughly naturalised in S. Europe particularly in the Mediterranean region. Cultivated in England in the 16th century. A.M. 1972.

'Flore Pleno'. An uncommon form with double flowers.

'Microphylla'. An attractive form, smaller in all its parts.

MYRTUS—*continued*

tarentina L. (*'Jenny Reitenbach'*). A very pretty, compact, free-flowering form with small narrow leaves and white berries. Mediterranean Region. A.M. 1977.

'Variegata'. Leaves variegated creamy-white. A pretty plant.

†**lechlerana** SEALY. A large shrub or small tree of dense habit, well furnished to the ground. Leaves recalling those of *Vaccinium ovatum*, strikingly copper-coloured when young, ovate, dark polished green with reddish stalks. The clusters of fragrant blossoms appear in May; berries red then black, edible. Chile. I. 1927. A.M. 1945.

luma. See *M. apiculata*.

nummularia POIR. The only hardy Myrtle is a tiny prostrate shrublet with wiry, reddish stems. The tiny, neat rounded leaves are borne in two opposite ranks. Flowers white, borne at the end of the stems in May or June followed by pink berries. S. Argentine, S. Chile, Falkland Isles. I. before 1927. A.M. 1967.

†**obcordata** HOOK. f. (*Lophomyrtus obcordata*). A graceful, medium-sized to large shrub, the thin branches clothed with small, notched leaves. Berries dark red or violet. New Zealand.

†×**ralphii** HOOK. f. (*bullata*×*obcordata*) (*Lophomyrtus*×*ralphii*). A medium-sized to large shrub, occasionally a small tree, with ovate or rounded, puckered leaves. Flowers almond-pink, solitary in the axils of the leaves; berries dark red. A variable hybrid ranging in characters between the parents. New Zealand.

†**ugni** MOL. (*Eugenia ugni*). "Chilean Guava". A slow-growing, small to medium-sized, leathery-leaved shrub, rather stiff and erect in habit, bearing waxy, pink bells followed by edible and delicious, aromatic, mahogany-red berries. Chile. I. 1844. A.M. 1925.

'Variegata'. Leaves green shaded grey, with creamy-yellow margin.

***NANDINA**—**Berberidaceae**—A curious monotypic genus looking somewhat like a bamboo, but related to *Berberis*. Should be given a sheltered position in full sun in any well-drained soil.

domestica THUNB. "Sacred Bamboo". An extremely decorative, bamboo-like shrub of medium size, with long, erect, unbranched stems. The large, compound green leaves are attractively tinged red in spring and autumn. Flowers small, white, in large terminal panicles during summer. Hardy in all but the coldest districts. India, C. China, Japan. I. 1804. A.M. 1897.

'Nana Purpurea'. A small shrub of more compact habit, with less compound leaves and broader leaflets. The young foliage reddish-purple throughout the season.

NEILLIA—**Rosaceae**—A small genus of deciduous shrubs related to *Spiraea* and, like them, of the easiest cultivation in all but very dry soils.

longiracemosa. See *N. thibetica*.

malvacea. See *PHYSOCARPUS malvaceus*.

ribesoides REHD. Medium-sized shrub closely related to *N. thibetica*. Leaves deeply and incisely toothed. Flowers pink, borne in dense racemes in early summer. W. China. C. 1930.

thibetica FRANCH. (*longiracemosa*). A very attractive medium-sized shrub with erect, downy stems bearing ovate, slender-pointed, often three-lobed leaves and slender terminal racemes of pink, tubular flowers in May and June. W. China. Introduced by E. H. Wilson in 1904. A.M. 1931.

thyrsiflora D. DON. Small to medium-sized shrub of spreading habit with long, arching stems. Leaves three-lobed, slender-pointed and sharply toothed. The small, white flowers are borne on branched racemes at the ends of the shoots during summer. E. Himalaya.

torreyi. See *PHYSOCARPUS malvaceus*.

†***NEOLITSEA**—**Lauraceae**—A genus of evergreen aromatic trees and shrubs with attractive foliage; mainly native of Tropical Asia. Flowers dioecious. A few species succeed in the mildest parts of the British Isles. Not recommended for shallow chalk soil.

sericea KOIDZ. (*glauca*) (*Litsea glauca*). A rare and distinguished member of the *Lauraceae*, forming a medium to large shrub. This remarkable shrub has succeeded here in a sheltered position for the past six years with but little frost damage. The unfolding fawn-brown leaves are most attractive in colour and texture like soft suede above and white silk beneath, becoming with age leathery and dark glossy green above, glaucous beneath; aromatic when crushed. Flowers greenish-yellow in dense clusters in October. Japan, China, Formosa, Korea.

†***NERIUM—Apocynaceae**—A small genus of tender, ornamental, sun-loving evergreens related to, but very different from the "Periwinkle". Lime tolerant, but not recommended for shallow chalk-soil.

oleander L. "Oleander". A superb evergreen along the Mediterranean seaboard of Southern Europe where it rivals *Camellia japonica* of more northern gardens. An erect-branched evergreen shrub of medium to large size with pairs or whorls of leathery, long, lance-shaped leaves. Flowers like large periwinkles, available in white, yellow, buff and pink, appearing from June to October. In the British Isles the "Oleander" is one of the best evergreens for tub culture standing out of doors in full sun in the summer and protected in the conservatory during winter. Mediterranean Region. I. 1596.

"NETTLE TREE". See *CELTIS*.

NEVIUSIA—Rosaceae—A monotypic genus, mainly of botanical interest, related to *Kerria*. The petals are absent, but the white stamens are so numerous as to be conspicuous. Any well-drained soil.

alabamensis GRAY. "Alabama Snow Wreath". A spiraea-like shrub up to 2m. with arching branches, covered during April and May with clusters of fluffy white flower heads. Enjoys a sunny position. Alabama (U.S.A.). I. about 1860.

"NEW ZEALAND FLAX". See *PHORMIUM tenax*.

"NORWAY MAPLE". See *ACER platanoides*.

*†**NOTELAEA—Oleaceae**—A small genus of evergreen shrubs or small trees related to the "Olive". Only suitable for the milder areas of the British Isles.

excelsa WEBB. & BERT. (*Olea excelsa*). A large shrub or small tree with glabrous, grey, flattened shoots. Leaves opposite, elliptic to elliptic-lanceolate, 7·5 to 12·5cm. long. Flowers fragrant, white, borne in short terminal or axillary racemes during spring or summer. Trees like enormous evergreen oaks (*Quercus ilex*) are growing in the Abbotsbury Subtropical Gardens near Weymouth. With us it grows slowly and survives uninjured all but the coldest winters. The wood is extremely hard and heavy. Canary Isles. I. 1784.

‡**NOTHOFAGUS—Fagaceae**—A small genus of very ornamental, fast-growing evergreen and deciduous trees or large shrubs, from South America and Australasia. Related to *Fagus*, but differing in the normally small leaves, closely spaced along the branchlets, and in the male and female flowers appearing singly or in clusters of three. They vary in degree of hardiness and many are of rapid growth but are poor wind-resisters. They do not survive on chalk-soils.

antarctica OERST. "Antarctic Beech". An elegant, fast-growing tree of medium size. Leaves small, rounded and heart-shaped, irregularly toothed, dark green and glossy, turning yellow in autumn. Trunk and primary branches often curiously twisted. Chile. I. 1830.

'Benmore' (*'Prostrata'*). A low spreading form growing into a dense mound of interlacing branches.

uliginosa A.DC. A variety with rather larger, somewhat pubescent leaves. Chile.

***betuloides** BL. A medium-sized to large, densely leafy, evergreen tree. Leaves ovate or roundish, usually less than 2·5cm. long, dark shining green and toothed, closely arranged on the branchlets. Chile. I. 1830.

***cliffortioides** OERST. (*solandri cliffortioides*). "Mountain Beech". An elegant, small to medium-sized, fast growing tree, closely related to and perhaps only a variety of *N. solandri*, differing in its generally smaller, ovate leaves with curled edges and raised tip. New Zealand.

†***cunninghamii** OERST. A rare, small evergreen tree in mild gardens. The wiry shoots are clothed with tiny, almost diamond-shaped, closely set, glabrous leaves which are bluntly toothed in the upper half. Tasmania.

***dombeyi** BL. A medium to large evergreen tree of vigorous habit. Leaves 2·5 to 4cm. long, doubly-toothed, dark shining green. A fairly hardy tree which may lose its leaves in cold winters. In leaf very like *N. betuloides* but usually a faster growing, wider spreading tree with a more loosely open arrangement of its branches. Chile, Argentina. I. 1916.

***fusca** OERST. "Red Beech". Somewhat tender when young but developing into a beautiful, hardy, small to medium-sized evergreen tree. The rounded or oval, coarsely-toothed leaves, 2·5 to 4cm. long, often turn copper in the autumn. The bark on old trees becomes flaky. New Zealand.

NOTHOFAGUS—*continued*

†***menziesii** OERST. A graceful, small to medium-sized evergreen tree akin to *N. cunninghamii*. Leaves up to 12mm. long, rotund-ovate, dark-green, double toothed. Hardy in the southern counties if well sited. Bark of young wood cherry-like. New Zealand.

†***moorei** KRASSER. "Australian Beech". A small to medium-sized, evergreen tree with comparatively large, hard, leathery, dark green leaves, 4 to 8cm. long, which are an attractive copper colour when young. Not hardy here and only suitable for the mildest localities. New South Wales. I. 1892.

obliqua BL. "Roblé Beech". A large, elegant, very fast-growing tree, forming a handsome specimen in a few years. Leaves broadly ovate or oblong, 5 to 8cm. long, irregularly toothed, glabrous. Introduced from Chile by H. J. Elwes in 1902.

procera OERST. A fast-growing tree of large size, distinguished by its comparatively large, prominently veined leaves 4 to 10cm. long, resembling those of the "Hornbeam". Usually gives rich autumn tints. Chile. I. 1913.

***solandri** OERST. "Black Beech". A tall, slender, medium-sized evergreen tree with ascending fan-like branches. Branchlets wiry, bearing neatly arranged, tiny, oblong or elliptic, entire leaves. New Zealand.

cliffortioides. See *N. cliffortioides.*

NOTHOPANAX arboreum. See *PSEUDOPANAX arboreus.*

davidii. See *PSEUDOPANAX davidii.*

laetum. See *PSEUDOPANAX laetus.*

NOTOSPARTIUM—**Leguminosae**—A small genus embracing some moderately hardy, sun-loving, broom-like shrubs from New Zealand. They succeed in full sun in any well-drained soil.

carmicheliae HOOK. f. The "Pink Broom" of New Zealand is a charming, medium-sized shrub of graceful habit, its arching, leafless stems wreathed in July with lilac-pink, pea-flowers. Only injured in the coldest winters. I. 1883. F.C.C. 1889.

glabrescens PETRIE. A large shrub, a tree in its native habitat. Branches long and whippy; flowers rose, carried in loose racemes during May and June. I. 1930.

NUTTALLIA. See *OSMARONIA.*

‡**NYSSA**—**Nyssaceae**—A small genus of deciduous trees with insignificant monoecious or dioecious flowers followed by equally inconspicuous blue-black fruits. Noted for their rich autumn tints. They require moist, lime-free soil, and are best planted when small as they resent disturbance.

aquatica L. (*uniflora*). "Water Tupelo". A rare, small tree with ovate-oblong leaves, downy beneath as are the young shoots. S.E. United States. I. 1735.

sinensis OLIV. A rare, large shrub or small tree proving quite hardy here. Leaves narrowly ovate up to 15cm. long. A magnificent introduction. The young growths are red throughout the growing season and in autumn the leaves change to every shade of red. China. C. 1902. F.C.C. 1976.

sylvatica MARSH. (*multiflora*). "Tupelo". A handsome, slow-growing, medium-sized to large tree of broadly columnar outline. Leaves variable in shape generally obovate or oval, pointed, up to 15cm. long, dark glossy green, occasionally dull green above. A dense headed tree with handsome foliage turning rich scarlet, orange and yellow in the autumn. S. Canada, E. United States, C. and S. Mexico. I. 1750. A.M. 1951. F.C.C. 1968. A.G.M. 1969.

biflora SARG. A variety with usually narrower leaves and bearing the female flowers in pairs. S.E. United States.

"OAK". See *QUERCUS.*

†**OCHNA**—**Ochnaceae**—A large genus of warm temperate or tropical evergreen and deciduous trees and shrubs. The following is the only species occasionally met with in cultivation, requiring conservatory treatment.

***serrulata** WALP. (*multiflora*). A small shrub for the conservatory. Flowers yellow followed by curious, pendant, black, pea-like fruits, beautifully set-off by the bright crimson, waxy calyces. Natal (S. Africa). I. 1860. F.C.C. 1879.

†***OLEA**—**Oleaceae**—A genus of tender evergreen trees and shrubs with opposite, leathery leaves. One or two species survive in the mildest localities. Any well-drained soil.

OLEA—*continued*

europaea L. The "Olive" is only hardy in the mildest areas of the British Isles where it forms a large shrub or small tree, with grey-green, leathery leaves, glaucous beneath, and axillary racemes of fragrant, small white flowers in late summer. The olive oil of commerce is extracted from the fruits. Mediterranean Region, widely naturalised in warm temperate countries. Cultivated from time immemorial.

excelsa. See *NOTELAEA excelsa.*

fragrans. See *OSMANTHUS fragrans.*

verrucosa LINK. A small tree or large shrub with greyish, warty shoots and linear-lanceolate leaves. S. Africa. I. 1814.

"OLEANDER". See *NERIUM oleander.*

***OLEARIA** (including *EURYBIA*)—**Compositae**—The Daisy Bushes or Tree Daisies are of Australasian origin. As a genus they are attractive, evergreen, easy to grow, wind-resistant and sun-loving shrubs. They include some of the finest of all evergreens for maritime exposure. All have daisy-like flower-heads, which are white or creamy-white (unless otherwise stated), and the average height attained in this country is 1·2 to 2·5m. Straggly or untidy specimens may be hard pruned in April. Some species are very tolerant of atmospheric pollution. They will succeed in any well-drained soil and are especially recommended for chalky soils.

†albida HOOK. f. (*albiflora* HORT.). A medium-sized shrub with oblong-elliptic, undulate, pale green leaves, white beneath. A tender species, hardy plants in cultivation under this name being referable to *O. avicenniifolia.* New Zealand.

†arborescens CKN. & LAING (*nitida*). A vigorous large shrub or small tree up to 4m. Broadly ovate leaves, shining dark green above, with a silvery, satiny sheen beneath, slightly toothed. Flower-heads in large corymbs in May or June. New Zealand.

capillaris. See *O. capillaris.*

avicenniifolia HOOK. f. A medium-sized to large shrub with pointed leaves, whitish or buff beneath. Flower-heads sweetly fragrant, borne in wide corymbs, in August and September. Often erroneously grown in gardens as *O. albida,* which is a tender species with larger, wavy-edged leaves. A good dense hedge-making shrub, especially in maritime exposure or industrial areas. New Zealand.

'White Confusion'. A form with larger, slightly wavy leaves, and masses of white flower-heads in summer.

†capillaris BUCHAN. (*arborescens capillaris*). A small, compact, rounded shrub up to 1·2m., with leaves similar to those of *O. arborescens,* but much smaller and entire or minutely toothed. Flower-heads in corymbs in June. New Zealand.

†chathamica KIRK. A beautiful, small shrub up to 1·2m. resembling *O. semidentata,* but with broader, green leaves inclined to be obovate, three-veined, beneath. Flower-heads up to 5cm. across, solitary on long stalks, pale violet with purple centres in June. Chatham Isles. I. 1910. A.M. 1938.

†colensoi HOOK. f. A large shrub with obovate or oblong-obovate, leathery leaves, shining green above, white woolly beneath; flower-heads brownish-purple in July. Makes an excellent tall, evergreen shrub in favoured localities. New Zealand.

cymbifolia. See *O. nummulariifolia cymbifolia.*

dentata HOOK f. not HORT. See *O. macrodonta* BAKER.

dentata MOENCH not HORT. See *O. tomentosa* STEUD.

†erubescens DIPP. A small, spreading shrub with reddish shoots and conspicuously toothed, shining dark green leaves; flowering in May or June. Tasmania.

ilicifolia DC. A form with larger leaves occasionally 7·5cm. long by 2·5cm. wide. Flower-heads also larger. S.E. Australia.

†×excorticata BUCHAN. (*arborescens × lacunosa*). A remarkable shrub up to 3m. with narrow, leathery leaves up to 10cm. long; shining dark green above, thickly buff felted beneath. New Zealand.

†floribunda BENTH. A slender, Tasmanian species up to 2m., having the appearance of a "Tree Heath". The branches are crowded with minute, deep green leaves and in June are wreathed with small, white flower-heads. Tasmania, S. and S.E. Australia. A.M. 1935.

forsteri. See *O. paniculata.*

OLEARIA—*continued*

†**frostii** J. H. WILLIS. A small, downy shrub with sage-green, shallowly-toothed leaves. Flower-heads solitary on long peduncles, large, double, mauve, recalling the best forms of the modern michaelmas daisy. Usually wrongly cultivated as *O. gravis*. S.E. Australia.

†**furfuracea** HOOK. f. A large shrub or small tree with attractive, glossy, leathery leaves 5 to 10cm. long, grey-white beneath. Flower-heads borne in wide corymbs in August. New Zealand.

gunniana. See *O. phlogopappa*.

'Splendens'. See *O. stellulata 'Splendens'*.

× **haastii** HOOK. f. (*avicenniifolia* × *moschata*). A rounded bush of medium size with small, entire leaves, white felted beneath, and smothered with fragrant, white flower-heads in July and August. Hardy almost everywhere in the British Isles, and tolerant of town conditions. An excellent, well-proved hedging plant. New Zealand. I. 1858. F.C.C. 1873. A.G.M. 1928.

ilicifolia HOOK. f. A dense, medium-sized shrub with thick, leathery, linear-oblong, grey-green leaves which are sharply and coarsely toothed and whitish felted beneath. Flower-heads fragrant in June. The whole plant possesses a musky odour. One of the best of the hardier species. New Zealand. A.M. 1972.

insignis. See *PACHYSTEGIA insignis*.

lineata. See *O. virgata lineata*.

macrodonta BAKER (*dentata* HOOK. f.). "New Zealand Holly". A strong-growing, medium-sized shrub up to 3m., with sage-green, holly-like leaves 6 to 9cm. long, silvery-white beneath. Flower-heads fragrant, in broad panicles in June. One of the best screening or hedging shrubs for exposed coastal gardens. The whole plant possesses a musky odour. New Zealand. F.C.C. 1895.

'Major'. A form with larger leaves and flower corymbs.

'Minor'. A dwarf form, smaller in all its parts.

× **mollis** HORT not CKN. (*ilicifolia* × *moschata*). A small shrub of rounded, compact habit, with wavy-edged, silvery-grey, slightly toothed leaves, up to 4cm. long. Flower-heads in large corymbs in May. One of the hardiest of the genus. New Zealand.

moschata HOOK. f. A slow-growing, small to medium-sized shrub with small, flat, entire, grey-green leaves 2cm. long, white felted beneath. Flowers in July. The whole plant possesses a musky odour. New Zealand.

†**nernstii** BENTH. Both the stems and the long, narrow, shining-green leaves are clammy to the touch. A plant of botanical interest.

nitida. See *O. arborescens*.

nummulariifolia HOOK. f. One of the hardiest species. A medium-sized, stiffly-branched shrub of unusual appearance, with small, thick, yellow-green leaves, thickly crowding the stems. Flower-heads small, solitary in the axils of the leaves in July, fragrant. New Zealand.

cymbifolia HOOK. f. (*O. cymbifolia*). A form with rather sticky young shoots and leaves with strongly revolute margins. New Zealand.

odorata PETRIE. An elegant, medium-sized shrub of loose habit, with long, wiry stems and narrow-obovate leaves. Of no floral beauty, but worth growing for its fragrance in July. New Zealand.

× **oleifolia** KIRK (*avicenniifolia* × *odorata*). A slow-growing, medium-sized shrub of compact habit, suitable for windswept coastal gardens. It most resembles *O. haastii*, but the leaves are longer, up to 8cm. New Zealand.

†**pachyphylla** CHEESEM. Medium-sized shrub with large, entire, wavy-edged leaves, brown or silvery beneath. Flower-heads in large corymbs in July. New Zealand.

†**paniculata** DRUCE (*forsteri*). Large shrub or small tree. A distinct and pleasing species with bright olive-green, undulate leaves, reminding one of *Pittosporum tenuifolium;* flower-heads inconspicuous, but fragrant in November and December. Used for hedge-making especially in favoured maritime districts. New Zealand. I. 1816.

†**phlogopappa** DC. (*gunniana*) (*stellulata* BENTH.). The popular May-flowering Tasmanian "Daisy Bush". An extremely variable shrub in the wild. Of medium size; leaves aromatic, toothed and narrow, 1 to 3·5cm. long, thickly crowding the erect stems. Flower-heads 2cm. across produced in crowded panicles along the stems. Tasmania, S.E. Australia. I. 1848. F.C.C. 1885.

subrepanda J. H. WILLIS (*O. subrepanda*). Differs from the type in its smaller, narrower, grey-tomentose leaves and denser habit.

OLEARIA—*continued*

†**ramulosa** BENTH. Small, twiggy shrub with slender, arching stems and small linear leaves. Flower-heads small, crowding the stems in August. Tasmania, S. Australia. A.M. 1927.

†**rani** HORT. not DRUCE (*cunninghamii*). A medium-sized shrub with narrow leaves, dark green above, covered with a buff or whitish tomentum beneath. Flower-heads fragrant, in large branched corymbs, in May. Possibly *macrodonta* × *moschata*.

†**'Rossii'** (*argophylla* × *macrodonta*). A strong-growing shrub of medium size. Leaves elliptic, green above silvery downy beneath. Garden origin, in Ireland.

† × **scilloniensis** DORRIEN-SMITH (*lyrata* × *phlogopappa*). A compact, rounded, grey-leaved shrub up to 2·5m. An exceedingly free-flowering hybrid, the plant being literally covered with bloom in May. Garden origin. Tresco (Isles of Scilly). A.M. 1951.

†**semidentata** DECNE. One of the loveliest of all shrubs for the more favoured coastal gardens. A medium-sized shrub with lanceolate grey-green leaves, silvery beneath. The large, pendant, aster-like flower-heads are lilac, with a purple centre and appear in June. Chatham Isles. I. 1910. A.M. 1916.

†**solandri** HOOK. f. A dense, heath-like shrub of medium size giving a yellowish effect, rather like *Cassinia fulvida*. Leaves linear, 6mm. long in clusters. Flower-heads small, sweetly scented in August. Requires wall protection except in mild localities. New Zealand.

†**speciosa** HUTCH. A small shrub with brown woolly shoots and thick, leathery, glossy dark green leaves, thickly pale-brown felted beneath. Flower-heads large, white or blue during summer. S.E. Australia.

†**stellulata** DC. A variable, rather lax, small to medium-sized shrub recalling *O. phlogopappa* but taller and less compact, and with rather longer leaves. Flower-heads white, borne in panicles in May. Tasmania. A.M. 1893.

'Splendens' (*gunniana 'Splendens'*). We owe a debt to the late Harold Comber for the introduction of several good garden plants including this lovely form with flower-heads resembling michaelmas daisies. Introduced from Tasmania in 1930. Available in the following colours:—Blue, Lavender and Rose.

subrepanda. See *O. phlogopappa subrepanda*.

†**tomentosa** DC. (*dentata* MOENCH.). An uncommon tender species usually less than 1m., of special interest on account of its large, mauve, aster-like flower-heads, borne singly and continuously over a long period. Leaves oval, leathery, dark green and serrated. It seldom survives a winter in our area. S.E. Australia. I. 1793.

†**traversii** HOOK. f. Considered to be one of the best and fastest growing evergreens for wind-breaks in Cornwall and similar maritime localities, growing to 6m. high even in exposed positions on poor sandy soils. Shoots four-angled, covered as are the leaf-undersurfaces, in a dense white felt. Leaves broad, leathery, opposite, polished green above, silvery-white beneath. Flower-heads insignificant, in summer. Chatham Isles. I. 1887.

virgata HOOK. f. (*Eurybia virgata*). A variable, medium-sized to large shrub of dense habit with long, wiry, four-angled stems. Leaves 1 to 2cm. long, narrowly obovate to linear, arranged in pairs or in small clusters. Flowers in June small and of little or no ornamental value. New Zealand.

lineata KIRK (*O. lineata*). A large, very graceful shrub of loose habit, with long, slender, angular, pendulous branches. Leaves narrow linear. New Zealand.

†**viscosa** BENTH. Small shrub up to 2m. with sticky young shoots and shiny green lanceolate leaves, silvery white beneath. Flower-heads small, in August. A collectors plant. Tasmania. S.E. Australia.

'Waikariensis'. A small, attractive shrub with lanceolate leaves, olive-green above and gleaming white beneath. White flower-heads produced in axillary clusters. Origin unknown, probably New Zealand.

†**'Zennorensis'** (*ilicifolia* × *lacunosa*). A striking foliage plant up to 2m., with narrow, pointed, sharply-toothed leaves about 10cm. long and 12mm. wide, dark olive-green above and white beneath. Young stems and leaf stalks heavily coated with pale brown tomentum. Originated in the garden of that splendid gardener Arnold Foster at Zennor, Cornwall. A first class shrub for the less cold gardens. Excellent in maritime exposure.

"OLEASTER". See *ELAEAGNUS angustifolia*.

'OLIVE". See *OLEA europaea*.

ONONIS—**Leguminosae**—The shrubby members of this genus come from Southern and Central Europe, and make useful dwarf subjects for border or rock garden. All have trifoliolate leaves and pea-shaped flowers. They require full sun and succeed in any well-drained soil including shallow chalk-soils.

arvensis L. (*hircina*). A small, moderately hardy, sub-shrub producing in summer dense leafy racemes of pink flowers. Europe.

fruticosa L. A splendid small shrub forming a compact mound to 1m. high. Flowers bright rose-pink, borne in small clusters throughout summer. Leaflets narrow. W. Mediterranean Region. I. 1680. A.M. 1926.

hircina. See *O. arvensis.*

rotundifolia L. A vigorous but none-too-persistant, sub-shrubby species, rather dwarfer than *O. fruticosa,* and with larger, rounded leaflets. Flowers bright rose-pink, very continuous during summer. C. and S. Europe. Cultivated in England since the 17th century.

OPLOPANAX (*ECHINOPANAX*)—**Araliaceae**—A genus of only three species, differing from *Acanthopanax* in the simple leaves.

horridus MIQ. (*Echinopanax horridus*). "Devil's Club". A small to medium-sized shrub with stout spiny stems and broad, palmate, maple-like leaves which are prickly along the veins beneath. Flowers greenish-white, in panicles, followed by scarlet fruits. Western N. America. I. 1828.

ORIXA—**Rutaceae**—A monotypic genus with insignificant, dioecious flowers. Any well-drained soil.

japonica THUNB. A pungently aromatic, medium-sized shrub, with bright green leaves which change to palest lemon or white in autumn, contrasting with the more prevalent reds and purples of that season. Flowers inconspicuous in April. Japan, China, Korea. I. 1870.

'Variegata'. Leaves shaded silvery-grey, with an irregular creamy-white margin. We are indebted to Mons. Robert de Belder for this interesting and rare form.

"OSAGE ORANGE". See *MACLURA pomifera.*

"OSIER, COMMON". See *SALIX viminalis.*

***OSMANTHUS**—**Oleaceae**—An attractive and useful genus of evergreen, somewhat holly-like shrubs, doing well in almost all soils. Flowers small, white or cream, usually fragrant.

†**americanus** BENTH. & HOOK. f. "Devil Wood". A large shrub or small tree with obovate to oblanceolate, leathery, glossy green, entire leaves up to 15cm. long. The fragrant white flowers are borne in short axillary panicles in spring. Fruits dark blue. Requires a warm sheltered position or conservatory. S.E. United States. C. 1758.

aquifolium. See *O. heterophyllus.*

armatus DIELS. A handsome, large shrub of dense habit. Leaves elliptic or oblong-lanceolate, thick and rigid, up to 18cm. long, edged with stout, often hooked, spiny teeth. Flowers in autumn, sweetly scented. Thrives in sun or shade. A splendid evergreen worthy of more extensive planting. W. China. Introduced by E. H. Wilson in 1902.

delavayi FRANCH. (*Siphonosmanthus delavayi*). One of China's gems; a very beautiful, small-leaved species, slowly growing to 2m. high and more in diameter, and bearing its fragrant, white, jessamine-like flowers profusely in April. Yunnan. Introduced by the Abbé Delavay in 1890. A.M. 1914. A.G.M. 1923. F.C.C. 1931.

'Latifolius'. A distinct, taller-growing form with broader, more rotund leaves.

forrestii. See *O. yunnanensis.*

× **fortunei** CARR. (*fragrans* × *heterophyllus*). A large, comparatively vigorous evergreen shrub of dense habit. Leaves large, broad ovate, dark polished green and conspicuously veined above, edged with spiny teeth, giving them a holly-like appearance. Flowers delightfully fragrant, produced during autumn. Japan. I. 1856.

†**fragrans** LOUR. (*Olea fragrans*). A large shrub or small tree with large oblong-lanceolate, finely-toothed leaves. Flowers deliciously and strongly fragrant; summer. A wall shrub for the mildest localities, but this plant will not survive our average winter here. China, Japan. I. 1771.

aurantiacus P. S. GREEN. An unusual form with yellowish-orange flowers.

OSMANTHUS—*continued*

heterophyllus P. S. GREEN (*aquifolium*) (*ilicifolius*). A rather slow-growing, holly-like shrub, occasionally a small tree. Leaves almost as variable as in the common holly, entire or coarsely spine-toothed, dark, shining green. Flowers sweetly scented, in autumn. Often mistaken for a holly but readily distinguished by its opposite leaves. Makes a useful dense hedge. Japan. Introduced by Thomas Lobb in 1856. F.C.C. 1859.

'Argenteomarginatus'. See '*Variegatus*'.

'Aureomarginatus' ('*Aureovariegatus*') ('*Aureus*'). Leaves margined deep yellow.

'Gulftide'. Leaves somewhat lobed or twisted and strongly spiny; of dense habit. A remarkable and well worth-while shrub.

'Latifolius Variegatus'. A silver-variegated, broad-leaved form.

'Myrtifolius'. A neat, slow-growing, compact form with small, spineless leaves.

'Purpureus'. Growths at first purple, later green, slightly tinged purple.

'Rotundifolius'. A curious, slow-growing form of neat, compact habit, with short, thick, black-green, leathery leaves which are spineless but bluntly-toothed and occasionally twisted.

'Variegatus' ('*Argenteomarginatus*'). Leaves bordered creamy-white.

ilicifolius. See *O. heterophyllus*.

serrulatus REHD. A medium-sized, slow-growing shrub of compact habit. Leaves large, ovate-lanceolate, sharply-toothed or entire, glossy dark green. The clusters of white, fragrant flowers are borne in the leaf axils in spring. Himalaya.

†**suavis** C. B. CLARKE (*Siphonosmanthus suavis*). An erect-growing shrub up to 4m., related to *O. delavayi*, but differing in its 8cm. long, oblong-lanceolate, sharply-toothed, shining green leaves. Flowers fragrant, in spring. Needs a sheltered position. It is growing well here in a mixed shrub border. Himalaya.

yunnanensis P. S. GREEN (*forrestii*). A remarkable large shrub or small tree. Leaves lanceolate, dark olive green, up to 15cm. long, varying from undulate and coarsely-toothed to flat and entire, both on the same plant. Flowers ivory-white, fragrant, produced during late winter. Related to *O. armatus* but differing in its glabrous young shoots and lanceolate, less rigid leaves. This splendid, comparatively fast-growing evergreen is proving hardy here. If you belong to the old school of gardeners, 1920-1930 vintage, it is the "done thing" to "sniff" at this plant because its magnificent leaves conjure up thoughts of spectacular flowers which fail to materialise. China (Yunnan, Szechwan). Introduced by George Forrest in 1923. A.M. 1967.

*× **OSMAREA** (*OSMANTHUS* × *PHILLYREA*)—**Oleaceae**—This interesting and useful, conspicuous-flowering, bi-generic hybrid was raised by Burkwood and Skipwith about 1930. Excellent on all fertile soils, including shallow chalk-soils.

burkwoodii BURKWOOD & SKIPWITH (*O. delavayi* × *P. decora*). This is a first-class, hardy shrub of compact growth, slowly attaining 2·5 to 3m. Leaves oval 2·5 to 5cm. long, dark shining green, leathery and toothed. The white flowers borne in April or May are very fragrant. A.G.M. 1950. A.M. 1978.

OSMARONIA (*NUTTALLIA*)—**Rosaceae**—A monotypic genus related to, but superficially very different from, Prunus, with male and female flowers usually on different plants. Easily cultivated in all types of fertile soil, but sometimes inclined to become chlorotic in very poor shallow chalk soils.

cerasiformis GREENE. "Oso Berry". A suckering shrub, forming a thicket of erect stems 2 to 2·5m. or more high; producing its pendant racemes of fragrant, white, ribes-like flowers in February and March. Fruits plum-like, brown at first, purple when ripe. Leaves sea-green, conspicuous on vigorous young growths. California. I. 1848. A.M. 1927 (as *Nuttallia cerasiformis*).

†***OSTEOMELES**—**Rosaceae**—A genus of probably three species of small to medium-sized, evergreen shrubs. Pinnate leaves with tiny leaflets and corymbs of small, white flowers followed by small fruits. They need the protection of a sunny wall, when they will succeed in any well-drained soil.

subrotunda K. KOCH. A pretty, small, slow-growing shrub with small, dainty, pinnate, fern-like leaves covered with silky hairs. Flowers hawthorn-like appearing in June. Fruits reddish. Requires wall protection in cold districts. E. China. I. 1894.

OSTRYA—**Carpinaceae**—A small genus of medium-sized to large deciduous trees, resembling the "Hornbeam" and notable in autumn when arrayed with their hop-like fruits. Of easy cultivation in any fertile soil.

carpinifolia SCOP. (*vulgaris*). "Hop Hornbeam". A round-headed tree of medium size, with ovate, double-toothed leaves 8 to 13cm. long, which give clear yellow autumn tints. Fruits 3·5 to 5cm. long, each nutlet contained in a flat, bladder-like husk. Enchanting in spring when the many branches are strung with numerous long, drooping male catkins. S. Europe, Asia Minor. I. 1724.

japonica SARG. "Japanese Hop Hornbeam". A small to medium-sized tree with ovate to ovate-oblong leaves 7 to 13cm. long, velvety hairy beneath. Conspicuous when bearing its multitudes of green, hop-like fruits 4 to 5cm. long. Japan, N.E. China. I. 1888.

virginiana K. KOCH. "Ironwood". A rare and attractive, small tree of elegant, rounded or pyramidal habit, differing from *O. carpinifolia* in its glandular-hairy shoots and fewer-veined leaves. Rich, warm yellow autumn tints. Eastern N. America, N. Mexico. I. 1692.

vulgaris. See *O. carpinifolia.*

OSTRYOPSIS—**Carpinaceae**—A rare genus of two species of medium to large shrubs of botanical interest differing from *Ostrya* in the clustered, not racemose, fruits. Any fertile soil.

davidiana DCNE. A medium-sized, somewhat suckering shrub with the general appearance of the common hazel, but with sessile red glands on the under-surface of the leaves and long-stalked fruit clusters. N. and W. China. I. about 1865.

OXYCOCCUS macrocarpus. See *VACCINIUM macrocarpum.*

palustris. See *VACCINIUM oxycoccos.*

‡**OXYDENDRUM**—**Ericaceae**—A monotypic genus succeeding in shade or sun given a lime-free soil.

arboreum DC. (*Andromeda arborea*). "Sorrel Tree". A beautiful large shrub or small tree grown chiefly foı its exquisite crimson and yellow autumn colourıng. The white flowers in slender, drooping racemes are produced in clusters from the tips of the shoots in July and August. The leaves possess a pleasant acid flavour. Thrives under conditions suitable for Rhododendrons. E. United States. I. 1752. A.G.M. 1947. A.M. 1951 (for autumn colour). A.M. 1957 (for flowers). F.C.C. 1972 (for autumn foliage).

†***OXYLOBUS**—**Compositae**—A genus of five species succeeding in any well-drained soil but only in mild gardens.

arbutifolius A. GRAY. A small shrublet with roughly glandular-hairy shoots. Flower heads white, borne in erect, slender-stalked corymbs from June onwards. Mexico.

OXYPETALUM caeruleum. See under CLIMBERS.

***OZOTHAMNUS**—**Compositae**—Evergreen, summer-flowering shrubs related to *Helichrysum* under which name they are sometimes found. They require full sun and a well drained position.

†**antennaria** HOOK. f. (*Helichrysum antennaria*). A small to medium sized, dense-growing evergreen with narrowly obovate or spathulate, leathery leaves, grey beneath, glossy green above. Flower-heads white, in dense terminal clusters opening in June. Tasmania. I. before 1880.

†**ericifolius** HOOK. f. (*Helichrysum ericeteum*). An erect, pleasantly aromatic shrub of medium size. Leaves narrow like those of a "Rosemary", sticky to the touch; flowers white in terminal heads. Tasmania.

ledifolius HOOK. f. (*Helichrysum ledifolium*). A small, globular, dense, aromatic shrub. Leaves broadly linear with recurved margins, yellow-backed; flowers comparatively large, their inner bracts with conspicuous white-spreading tips, reddish in bud. Seed heads emit a sweet honey-like aroma. A superb shrub displaying its incurved terminal yellow leaves. Uninjured by the severe winter of 1962/63. Tasmania. I. 1930.

†**rosmarinifolius** DC. (*Helichrysum rosmarinifolium*). A medium-sized shrub for the mildest districts, with white-woolly stems and dark green, linear, verrucose leaves. The dense corymbs of red buds are spectacular for ten days or more before they open to white, scented flowers. In a sheltered border in our gardens this plant has thrived uninjured for over five years. Tasmania; S.E. Australia. I. 1827. A.M. 1968.

OZOTHAMNUS—*continued*

†**thyrsoideus** DC. (*O. rosmarinifolius* HORT.) (*Helichrysum thyrsoideum*) (*H. diosmifolium*). "Snow in Summer". This delightful plant was well known to our grandparents long before the related and somewhat similar species were introduced from Tasmania by Harold Comber. A medium-sized shrub with slender, spreading, angular branches and spreading linear leaves. Flower heads white, in large terminal corymbs during summer. Australia; Tasmania. A.M. 1925.

***PACHISTIMA** (*PACHYSTIMA*) (*PAXISTIMA*)—**Celastraceae**—A genus of two species of interesting, but not conspicuous dwarf, evergreen shrubs of neat habit, with tiny leaves and quadrangular stems. Not recommended for shallow chalk soils. They do best in a moist shady position.

canbyi GRAY. Leaves narrow, small greenish flowers during summer. Fruits white. Makes an unusual dwarf hedge or ground cover. Eastern U.S.A. C. 1800.

myrsinites RAF. Leaves small, leathery, toothed in upper half; opposite. Flowers tiny, four petalled, red, produced in March. Western N. America, N. Mexico. C. 1879.

PACHYSANDRA—**Buxaceae**—A small genus of dwarf shrubs or sub-shrubs, with monoecious flowers. Suitable for ground cover in moist, shaded sites. They do not luxuriate in shallow chalk-soils.

***axillaris** FRANCH. A dwarf, tufted, evergreen shrublet, with comparatively large leaves. Less spreading than *P. terminalis*. Flowers white, produced in short axillary spikes in April. China. I. 1901.

procumbens MICHX. A dwarf, creeping, semi-evergreen sub-shrub bearing terminal clusters of ovate to obovate leaves. Flowers with conspicuous pale stamens, borne in crowded cylindrical spikes on the lower halves of the shoots during spring. S.E. United States. I. 1800.

***terminalis** SIEB. & ZUCC. A very useful dwarf evergreen, carpeting shrublet for covering bare places under trees. Leaves clustered at the ends of the stems, rather diamond-shaped and toothed in the upper half. Spikes of greenish-white flowers are produced at the ends of the previous year's shoots in February and March. Japan. I. 1882. A.G.M. 1969.

'Variegata'. Leaves attractively variegated white.

†***PACHYSTEGIA**—**Compositae**—A monotypic New Zealand genus at one time united with *Olearia*.

insignis CHEESEM. (*Olearia insignis*). A dwarf shrub of remarkably distinct appearance, suitable for mild districts, and especially for maritime exposures where it will take the full blast of sea winds. Leaves obovate, up to 15cm. long, dark green above, white felted beneath. The large, white, yellow-centred, aster-like flowers are carried singly on stiff, erect, white-tomentose stems during late summer. I. 1850. A.M. 1915.

minor CHEESEM. Smaller in all its parts and less tomentose. Suitable for the rock garden, in a sunny, well-drained position. A distinct and interesting form of recent introduction.

PACHYSTIMA. See *PACHISTIMA*.

PAEONIA—**Paeoniaceae**—The "Tree Paeonies" are represented in the garden by a few species and their varieties and hybrids, but the term is most commonly applied to those which have originated from *P. suffruticosa*. These are amongst the most gorgeously coloured of all shrubs. They pass uninjured, our severest winters, but on account of their early growth they should be protected against spring frosts. Such species as *P. delavayi* and *P. lutea* have splendid foliage of architectural quality. Given full sun and a sheltered site they will thrive in any well-drained soil.

arborea. See *P. suffruticosa*.

delavayi FRANCH. A handsome, suckering shrub, attaining 2m. Flowers, in May, deepest crimson with golden anthers, followed by large, black-seeded fruits surrounded by conspicuously coloured, persistent sepals. The large, deeply cut leaves place this plant in the category of shrubs grown for the quality of their leaves. An excellent shrub for chalky soils. W. China. I. 1908. A.M. 1934.

angustiloba. See *P. potaninii*.

×**lemoinei** REHD. (*lutea*×*suffruticosa*). By this cross "Tree Paeonies" with enormous yellow flowers have been produced and also cultivars showing gorgeous colour combinations. Most will reach 1·5 to 2m. in height and flower in May or June. They appreciate a rich soil and do well in chalk-soil. First raised by Messrs. Lemoine about 1909. We offer the following clones:—

PAEONIA—*continued*

×**lemoinei 'Alice Harding'.** Flowers large, fully double, canary-yellow. A.M.T. 1960.

'Chromatella'. Flowers large, double, sulphur yellow. A sport of *'Souvenir de Maxime Cornu'*.

'Souvenir de Maxime Cornu'. Flowers fragrant, very large, double, bright yellow edged with carmine.

lutea FRANCH. A bold shrub of about 2m., possessing the foliage qualities of *P. delavayi*, in fact from leaf only they are difficult to tell apart. Flowers, borne in May or June are cup-shaped, 6cm. across, resembling those of the "King Cup" or "Marsh Marigold" (*Caltha palustris*). Yunnan. I. 1886. F.C.C. 1903.

ludlowii STERN & TAYLOR (*'Sherriff's Variety'*). This splendid variety, first collected by Kingdon Ward and subsequently by Ludlow and Sherriff in S.E. Tibet, has larger golden-yellow, saucer-shaped flowers, opening as the large and conspicuous leaves are beginning to expand. A.M. 1954. A.G.M. 1963.

moutan. See *P. suffruticosa*.

potaninii KOMAR. (*delavayi angustiloba*). A suckering shrub up to ·6m., forming small patches of glabrous stems and deeply divided, narrowly-lobed leaves. Flowers deep maroon, 5 to 6cm. across, nodding, appearing in May. W. China. I. 1904.

suffruticosa ANDR. (*moutan*) (*arborea*). "Moutan Peony". A branching shrub up to 2m. with large flowers 15cm. or more across in May. In 1943 an F.C.C. was given to a beautiful type introduced by Joseph Rock, which possessed large, single, palest flesh-pink flowers passing to silver-white marked at the base of each petal with a maroon splash. We are indebted to this untiring American collector for the introduction of several new species and many good hardy forms of hitherto tender subjects.

We also offer the following clones, but occasionally when certain of them are not available, a substitute is carefully selected:—

'Godaishu'. White with yellow centre; semi-double to double.

'Hanakishoi'. Deep cherry-red; double, large.

'Higurashi'. Vivid crimson; semi-double, large.

'Hodai'. Rosy-red; double, large.

'Jitsugetsu Nishiki'. Bright scarlet with deeper sheen; semi-double to double.

'Kumagai'. Deep pink turning to magenta; double.

'Renkaku'. Pure white, irregularly cut petals; double, large.

'Sakurajishi'. Lustrous pink, irregularly cut petals; double, large.

'Shunkoden'. Rosy-violet; semi-double.

'Taiyo'. Brilliant red with satin sheen of maroon; semi-double.

'Yachiyo-tsubaki'. Phlox pink, shading to soft neyron rose at tips, long petals ruffled and fringed at edges; semi-double to double.

CULTURAL NOTES

Whilst the above are winter hardy, the young growth is susceptible to damage by night frost in the spring and it is wise to provide artificial protection at this time. A sacking screen may be erected on a tripod of bamboos, the covering being positioned nightly during periods of frost, and removed after frost has gone off in the morning. Once growth has been hardened the screen may be removed entirely and stored for use the following year.

"PAGODA TREE". See *SOPHORA japonica*.

PALIURUS—Rhamnaceae—A small genus of deciduous trees and shrubs, requiring plenty of sun and good drainage. *P. spina-christi* is one of the plants from which the "Crown of Thorns" is said to have been made. Any fertile soil.

spina-christi MILL. (*aculeatus*). "Christ's Thorn". A medium-sized to large straggling shrub, the long thin stems armed with innumerable pairs of unequal thorns. The ovate leaves turn yellow in autumn. Flowers small, greenish-yellow in late summer. The curious fruits are circular, and remind one of miniature cardinal's hats. S. Europe to Himalaya, and N. China. C. 1597.

"PALM, HARDY". See *CHAMAEROPS* and *TRACHYCARPUS*.

‡**PARABENZOIN—Lauraceae**—A small genus of deciduous shrubs related to *Lindera* and requiring similar conditions, differing in the dry, five to six-lobed fruits.

praecox NAKAI (*Lindera praecox*). A large shrub or small tree of upright habit. Leaves light green turning a glorious yellow in autumn. The greenish-yellow flowers occur in short-stalked clusters along the bare twigs in March or early April. Japan. I. 1891.

PARAHEBE—**Scrophulariaceae**—A small genus of semi-woody, dwarf plants intermediate between *Hebe* and *Veronica*, formerly included under the latter. All are natives of Australasia and are suitable for the rock garden in all types of soil.

catarractae W. R. B. OLIVER (*Veronica catarractae*). A dwarf plant forming low-spreading mounds, making excellent ground cover in full sun. Leaves small, ovate or lanceolate, acute, coarsely-serrate. Flowers white to rose-purple with a central zone of crimson, in slender, erect racemes during late summer. A variable species. We offer a selected form with blue flowers.

'Diffusa'. A smaller-leaved clone, forming dense mats. Flowers white, veined rose-pink.

decora M. B. ASHWIN. Creeping sub-shrub forming low hummocks and patches. Leaves tiny, ovate or rounded, with one or two pairs of teeth. Flowers white or pink, borne in long-stalked racemes during summer. New Zealand. Usually grown as *P.* ×*bidwillii*, which is possibly not in cultivation.

lyallii W. R. B. OLIVER (*Veronica lyallii*). A low, prostrate shrublet with small, rounded or ovate leaves which are leathery and slightly crenate. Flowers white, prettily veined pink, anthers blue, appearing in slender racemes from July to August. I. 1870.

†perfoliata E. BRIGGS & EHREND. (*Veronica perfoliata*). "Digger's Speedwell". A dwarf sub-shrub, herbaceous in most areas, with erect stems usually about 30 to 45cm. Leaves perfoliate, greyish-green. Flowers violet-blue, borne in long axillary racemes in late summer. An unusual plant for a sunny, well-drained spot in mild areas. Australia. I. 1834.

***PARASYRINGA**—**Oleaceae**—A monotypic genus related to *Ligustrum* and *Syringa*. It resembles the former in habit and flower, also in the fruit which is fleshy at first, later becoming a dry capsule as in *Syringa*.

sempervirens W. W. SM. (*Ligustrum sempervirens*). A striking, evergreen shrub of small to medium size with dark green, leathery, rounded leaves. The small, white flowers are produced in conspicuous, dense panicles in August and September. W. China. I. 1913. A.M. 1930.

PARROTIA—**Hamamelidaceae**—A monotypic genus, remarkably lime-tolerant for the *Hamamelis* family.

jacquemontiana. See *PARROTIOPSIS jacquemontiana*.

persica C. A. MEY. A large shrub or small tree of wide-spreading habit. Bark of older stems delightfully flaking like that of the "London Plane". Leaves turning crimson and gold in autumn. Flowers consisting of clusters of crimson stamens, appearing in March. One of the finest small trees for autumn colour, even on chalk. N. Persia to the Caucasus. C. 1840. F.C.C. 1884. A.G.M. 1969.

'Pendula'. A form with pendulous branches, slowly developing into a dome-shaped mound 1·8 to 3m. high. Becoming a richly-coloured pile in autumn.

PARROTIOPSIS—**Hamamelidaceae**—A monotypic genus best in an acid or neutral soil, but moderately lime-tolerant. May be grown over chalk given ·6m. of good soil.

jacquemontiana REHD. (*Parrotia jacquemontiana*). A large shrub of erect habit. Leaves rounded or broadly ovate, usually turning yellow in autumn. The flower clusters, which remind one of *Cornus florida*, being subtended by conspicuous white bracts, are produced during April and May and intermittently throughout summer. W. Himalaya. I. 1879.

"PARTRIDGE BERRY". See *MITCHELLA repens*.

PASANIA edulis. See *LITHOCARPUS edulis*.

"PASSION FLOWER". See *PASSIFLORA* under Climbers.

PAULOWNIA—**Scrophulariaceae**—A small genus of Chinese trees. The species here listed are amongst the grandest of ornamental flowering trees. Their foxglove-shaped flowers, which are not borne on very young trees, are carried in erect panicles and, though formed in autumn, do not open until the following spring. The leaves of mature trees are large, whilst on vigorous, pruned plants they are enormous. Owing to the colour of their flowers, these trees are best planted where they can be viewed from above; the sites should be in full sun, but sheltered from gales. All types of deep, well-drained soil.

fargesii FRANCH. A magnificent tree of 18 to 21m. which, though more recently introduced, seems to be better adapted to our climate than the better known *P. tomentosa*, and flowers at a comparatively early age. Flowers fragrant, heliotrope, freely speckled dark purple in the throat and with a creamy basal stain. W. China. I. about 1896.

fargesii HORT. See *P. lilacina*.

PAULOWNIA—*continued*

fortunei HEMSL. A rare, small tree, similar in habit to *P. tomentosa*. Flowers fragrant, creamy-white, heavily marked with deep purple on the inside, flushed lilac on the outside. China; Formosa.

imperialis. See *P. tomentosa*.

lilacina SPRAGUE (*fargesii* HORT. not FRANCH.). Closely related to *P. tomentosa* this species differs mainly in its unlobed leaves and lilac flowers, pale-yellow in the throat, in June. C. about 1908. F.C.C. 1944.

tomentosa STEUD. (*imperialis*). This well-known species forms a round-topped tree 9 to 12m. high. The flowers are heliotrope, slightly darker than those of *P. fargesii*, and providing they come through the winter and escape a late frost, give a wonderful display in May. Alternatively, young plants may be pruned to the ground in spring and the resultant suckers thinned to a single shoot. Such is its vigour the shoot will reach 2·5 to 3m. in a single season and clothe itself with huge leaves up to ·6m. or more across. China. Introduced via Japan in 1834. A.M. 1934.

"PAWPAW". See *ASIMINA triloba*.

PAXISTIMA. See *PACHISTMA*.

"PEACH". See *PRUNUS persica*.

"PEAR". See *PYRUS*.

"PEARL BERRY". See *MARGYRICARPUS pinnatus*.

PENSTEMON (*PENTSTEMON*)—**Scrophulariaceae**—A large genus of mostly sub-shrubs and herbaceous plants, mainly from N.W. America and Mexico. There are a few woody species requiring the shelter of a sunny wall, and others which make excellent rock garden plants. Full sun and good drainage. See also our Hardy Perennial Catalogue.

†cordifolius BENTH. A slender-branched, semi-evergreen shrub up to 2m. high against a wall. Leaves heart-shaped, coarsely-toothed, dark glossy green. Flowers in panicles, orange-scarlet, from June to August. California. Discovered by David Douglas in 1831; introduced by Hartweg in 1848.

†corymbosus BENTH. A small, semi-evergreen shrub, closely related to *P. cordifolius*, differing in its smaller stature, its ovate leaves and its shorter flowers in flattened racemes. California.

heterophyllus 'Blue Gem'. Dwarf, erect shrublet with long, narrow leaves and lovely azure-blue, tubular flowers in long racemes during summer.

***menziesii** HOOK. A dwarf, or prostrate, evergreen shrublet for the rock garden with shortly-stalked, shallowly-toothed leaves and erect racemes of large, tubular, purple flowers in May and June. N.W. North America. C. 1902.

***newberryi** GRAY (*roezlii* HORT.). A dwarf shrub suitable for the rock garden similar to *P. menziesii*, but with longer, pointed leaves and scarlet flowers in profusion in June. Western U.S.A. C. 1872.

scouleri LINDL. A charming, dwarf sub-shrub with narrow, lanceolate leaves and large, lilac-coloured blossoms, arranged in erect racemes in June. Suitable for the rock garden. Western N. America. I. 1828. A.M. 1951.

'Albus'. A form with white flowers.

‡*PENTACHONDRA—**Epacridaceae**—A small genus of low-growing, evergreen shrubs for lime-free soils.

pumila R. BR. A tiny shrublet, a few cm. high. Stems procumbent; leaves bronze-tinted, very small; crowded on the stems. The small, cylindrical, white flowers are produced singly in the axils of the uppermost leaves in summer and are followed by red fruits. Tasmania, S.E. Australia, New Zealand.

†*PENTAPERA—**Ericaceae**—A monotypic genus related to and resembling *Erica*, differing in the five-lobed calyx and corolla. It requires a position in sun or semi-shade, and a lime-free soil.

sicula KLOTZSCH. An evergreen dwarf shrub with erect, downy stems clothed with linear heath-like leaves arranged in whorls of four. The pitcher-shaped white or pink flowers are borne in terminal clusters during May and June. Sicily, Malta, Syria. I. 1849. A.M. 1951.

‡†*PENTAPTERYGIUM—**Ericaceae**—A small genus of somewhat bristly, epiphytic shrubs, native of the East Himalayan and Khasia Mountains. Suitable for cool, conservatory cultivation or for a sheltered shaded wall in favoured areas.

PENTAPTERYGIUM—*continued*

'Ludgvan Cross' (*rugosum* × *serpens*). A striking hybrid, intermediate in size and character between its parents. Flowers large, pale pink, conspicuously veined with deeper pink, and with a crimson calyx. Garden origin.

rugosum HOOK. A handsome, small shrub from the Khasia Hills, Assam. Stems rather stiff and upright; leaves larger and broader than those of *P. serpens*, 7·5 to 10cm. long, rugose and toothed. Flowers 2·5cm. long, white marbled purple or red, nodding; fruits purple. A.M. 1934.

serpens KLOTZSCH (*Agapetes serpens*). A beautiful, long-flowering, Himalayan shrub up to 2m. with long sinuous arching branches. Leaves lanceolate 12mm. long. Flowers bright red with darker markings, pendulous, borne all along the slender, arching branches like curious Japanese lanterns. E. Himalaya. A.M. 1900.

‡**PERAPHYLLUM**—**Rosaceae**—A monotypic genus related to *Amelanchier*, but differing in its narrow leaves, long calyx tube and rounded petals. It is hardy and grows best in a hot, sunny position. Not recommended for chalk-soils.

ramosissimum NUTT. A small to medium-sized shrub with clusters of narrowly oblanceolate leaves, which are obscurely toothed in their upper halves, and umbels of pink and white flowers in April and May. The cherry-like fruits are rarely produced in this country. Western N. America. I. 1870.

"PERIWINKLE". See *VINCA*.

‡***PERNETTYA**—**Ericaceae**—Very attractive, mostly hardy, ornamental evergreens of dense habit for a lime-free soil. They extend from Mexico to the Magellan region, at the southern end of South America. Though small in flower, they are so very floriferous as to be conspicuous. The masses of pure white or vividly coloured, marble-like berries are some of the showiest fruits of the plant world and in some species last the whole winter. Whilst tolerant of shade they fruit best in full sun and when planted in groups to ensure cross-pollination. Some plants are hermaphrodite, whilst other are unisexual. Most Pernettyas make splendid ground cover.

buxifolia MART. & GAL. A dwarf shrub with slender but rigidly arching, sparsely bristly and downy stems forming low mounds. Leaves elliptic-lanceolate, dark glossy green and toothed, borne in two ranks. Flowers pitcher-shaped, white, produced in May and June and followed by large white, pink or lavender-flushed berries. Closely resembles *P. ciliata*, but our plants (E. K. Balls 4868) tend to have much larger berries. Mexico.

ciliata SMALL. A dwarf or prostrate shrub very closely resembling *P. buxifolia*, but with normally brighter green leaves and smaller berries in which the calyx lobes are hardly swollen in fruit. Mexico.

empetrifolia. See *P. pumila*.

leucocarpa DC. A dwarf shrub of compact habit. The small, neat, leathery leaves are densely arranged on the erect, wiry stems. Berries white, edible and sweet. S. Chile. I. 1926. A.M. 1929.

'Harold Comber'. A selection with comparatively large, attractive, deep rose berries. Originally collected by Harold Comber in the Chilean Andes.

mucronata GAUD. The showiest of all dwarf evergreens in fruit and one of the hardiest of South American shrubs. Forms dense thickets of wiry stems about ·6 to ·9m. high or occasionally more. The myriads of small, white, heath-like flowers in May to June are followed by dense clusters of long-persistent, marble-like berries, ranging from pure white to mulberry-purple. Though not strictly dioecious it is best to plant in groups of three or more and to ensure berry production include a proven male form. A marvellous plant which should be mass planted for ground cover. Chile to Magellan region. I. 1828. A.G.M. 1929. A.M. 1961.

'Alba'. Berries medium-sized, white with a faint pink tinge, which deepends with age. F.C.C. 1882.

'Atrococcinea'. Berries large, deep, shining ruby-red.

'Bell's Seedling'. An hermaphrodite form with reddish young stems and dark, shining green leaves; berries large, dark red. A.M. 1928. A.G.M. 1969.

'Cherry Ripe'. Similar in general appearance to *'Bell's Seedling'*, but berries medium to large, of a bright cherry-red.

Davis's Hybrids. A first rate selection of large berried forms in a mixture of colours. A.G.M. 1969.

PERNETTYA—*continued*

mucronata 'Edward Balls'. A very distinct male form of erect habit. Shoots stout and stiff, reddish and shortly hispid. Leaves broadly ovate or rounded. Collected in the wild by E. K. Balls.

'Lilacina'. A free-berrying form; berries medium-sized, reddish-lilac. F.C.C. 1878.

(Male). A selected male form.

'Mulberry Wine'. Young stems green; berries large, magenta ripening to deep purple.

'Pink Pearl'. Berries medium-sized, lilac-pink.

'Rosie'. Young stems red, leaves dark sea-green; berries large, pink with a deep rose flush.

rupicola REICHE. A distinct wild variety of loose habit with relatively narrow, obscurely toothed leaves and medium-sized berries, variably coloured. Chile, Argentine.

'Sea Shell'. Berries medium to large, shell-pink, ripening to rose.

'Thymifolia'. A charming, small, male form of neat habit. Leaves smaller than in the type; smothered in white flowers during late May and early June.

'White Pearl'. A selection of '*Alba*', with medium to large berries of a gleaming white.

prostrata SLEUMER. A dwarf or prostrate shrub forming low mounds of arching, downy and sparsely bristly stems and narrow glossy, bright green leaves. Flowers produced singly or in small racemes in May and June; pitcher-shaped, white, followed by usually black berries. Venezuela to Chile. I. about 1870.

pentlandii B. L. BURTT. A variety of more vigorous growth with strong, bristly young shoots and bold leathery elliptic or oblong-elliptic leaves up to 2·5cm. long. Berries black slightly larger than those of the type. A.M. 1957.

pumila HOOK. (*empetrifolia*). A dwarf, almost prostrate species with slender wiry stems and tiny leaves. Berries white or pink tinged. Magellan Straits, Falkland Isles.

tasmanica HOOK. f. A slender, fragile dwarf shrub a few centimeters high, often prostrate. Leaves very small and leathery. Berries up to 1cm., solitary, normally red, produced in the axils of the upper leaves. Tasmania. A.M. 1971.

PEROVSKIA (*PEROWSKIA*)—**Labiatae**—A small genus of late flowering, aromatic sub-shrubs with deeply-toothed or finely-cut leaves. They associate well with lavender for the blue and grey border, and succeed in a sunny position in all types of well-drained soil.

abrotanoides KAREL. Small shrub with grey-hairy branching stems and deeply-cut, grey-green leaves. Flowers violet-blue in terminal panicles during late summer and autumn. Afghanistan to W. Himalaya. C. 1935.

atriplicifolia BENTH. A beautiful, small, Himalayan shrub for the grey or blue border, the long, narrow panicles of lavender-blue flowers, produced in late summer, blending perfectly with the grey foliage and whitish stems. Afghanistan, W. Himalaya to Tibet. C. 1904. A.M. 1928. A.G.M. 1935.

'Blue Spire'. A beautiful selection with deeply cut leaves and even larger panicles of lavender-blue flowers. A.M. 1962. A.G.M. 1969.

'Hybrida' (*abrotanoides* × *atriplicifolia*). An admirable plant for late summer effect, having deeply-cut, grey-green leaves, and very long panicles of deep lavender-blue flowers. Originated in our nurseries before 1937.

†**PERSEA**—**Lauraceae**—A genus of shrubs and trees of which *P. gratissima*, the "Avocado Pear", is the most commonly grown species.

***borbonia** SPRENG. (*carolinensis*). "Red Bay". A handsome, small evergreen tree with leaves glossy above and glaucous beneath, fruits dark blue on red stalks. The wood is used in cabinet making. Only possible to grow in the mildest areas. E. United States. I. 1739.

"PERSIMMON, CHINESE". See *DIOSPYROS kaki*.

PERTYA—**Compositae**—A small genus of hardy, deciduous shrubs of botanical interest, succeeding in all types of soil.

sinensis OLIV. A Chinese shrub up to 1·5m. high. Leaves, bitter to the taste, 2·5 to 7·5cm. long, taper-pointed and borne in rosettes. Flower-heads purplish-pink, daisy-like, about 12mm. across, produced in June and July. I. 1901.

PETTERIA—**Leguminosae**—A monotypic genus of restricted distribution. In the wild it seldom exceeds 1·2 to 1·5m. It succeeds in all types of well-drained soil.

ramentacea PRESL. An unusual shrub with trifoliolate leaves attaining about 1·8 to 2·5m. May be likened to a shrubby, erect-flowered "Laburnum", producing its racemes of fragrant yellow flowers in May and June. Yugoslavia, N. Albania. I. 1838. A.M. 1976.

†***PEUMUS**—**Monimiaceae**—A monotypic genus of economic importance in South America. It will succeed in all well-drained soils, but only in the mildest gardens.

boldus MOLINA. A small, Chilean evergreen tree with leathery leaves and white dioecious flowers in terminal cymes. The bark is used in tanning and dyeing; the leaves are used medicinally to aid digestion and the fruits are sweet and edible. I. 1844.

PHELLODENDRON—**Rutaceae**—A small genus of small to medium-sized, wide-spreading trees resembling *Ailanthus* in their large, handsome, pinnate leaves and graceful habit. Related to *Euodia*, but differing in the enclosed winter buds and the fruit which is a drupe. They grow well on chalky soil, their attractive, aromatic leaves usually turning clear yellow before falling. Flowers yellow-green, small, in cymes, followed by small black, viscid fruits.

amurense RUPR. The "Amur Cork Tree", so called on account of the corky bark of older trees. Leaves 25 to 38cm. long with five to eleven leaflets. Distinguished by its bright green leaves and silvery-hairy, winter buds. Japan, Korea, N. China, Ussuri, Amur, Manchuria. I. 1885.

japonicum OHWI (*P. japonicum*). A Japanese variety with nine to fifteen leaflets. The black fruits are most attractive after a warm summer. I. 1863.

sachalinense F. SCHMIDT (*P. sachalinense*). A very hardy, Japanese variety with seven to eleven leaflets, and without corky bark.

chinense SCHNEID. A handsome tree with leaves up to 38cm. long, composed of seven to thirteen acuminate, glossy leaflets, and densely packed fruiting clusters. C. China. I. 1907.

glabriusculum SCHNEID. A variety differing in its almost glabrous leaflets. C. & W. China. I. 1907.

japonicum. See *P. amurense japonicum.*

sachalinense. See *P. amurense sachalinense.*

PHILADELPHUS—**Philadelphaceae**—"Mock Orange". Often erroneously called "Syringa". An indispensable genus of shrubs, giving a good display even on the poorest chalk soils. The flowers, produced in June and July, are fragrant in most and are pure white unless otherwise described. To prune, thin out and cut back, immediately after flowering, old flowering shoots to within a few cm. of the old wood. Many of the finest hybrids and cultivars were raised by the French nursery firm, Lemoine during the early years of the present century. Unless otherwise stated the cultivars reach a height of 1·8 to 2·4m.

'Albâtre' (Cymosus Group). A small shrub with double white, slightly fragrant flowers in large racemes.

'Amalthée' (Cymosus Group). A medium-sized shrub with long branches and single, sweetly-scented, rose-stained flowers.

argyrocalyx WOOTON. A very beautiful, distinct and graceful shrub, 1·5 to 1·8m. in height, related to *P. microphyllus*. The fragrant, evenly-spaced flowers are 3·5 to 4cm. across, and have large, silky-pubescent calyces. New Mexico (U.S.A.). I. 1916.

'Atlas'. A medium-sized shrub of loose habit with long arching branches. Flowers large, 5 to 6cm. across, single, white, slightly scented. Leaves often with faint yellow mottling. A.M. 1927.

'Avalanche' (Lemoinei Group). A small, semi-erect shrub with small leaves. In summer the masses of small, single, richly fragrant flowers weigh down the slender branches. A.G.M. 1936.

'Beauclerk' (Purpureo-maculatus Group). A splendid medium-sized shrub raised by the Hon. Lewis Palmer, with single broad-petalled flowers, 6cm. across, milk-white with a zone of light cerise around the stamens. A hybrid between *'Burfordensis'* and *'Sybille'*. A.M. 1947. F.C.C. 1951. A.G.M. 1955.

'Belle Etoile'. A beautiful compact shrub up to 2m. The single, 5cm. wide, flowers are flushed maroon at the centre, and are delightfully fragrant. A triploid hybrid. A.M. 1930. A.G.M. 1936.

PHILADELPHUS—*continued*

'Bicolore'. Small shrub. The single, cup-shaped flowers are creamy-white with a purple basal stain. A triploid hybrid.

'Boule d'Argent' (Polyanthus Group). A small shrub with large, double, pure white flowers freely produced in dense clusters, slightly fragrant. F.C.C. 1895.

'Bouquet Blanc' (Cymosus Group). Small shrub with double, orange-scented flowers in large crowded clusters. A.M. 1912.

brachybotrys KOEHNE (*pekinensis brachybotrys*). An elegant, medium-sized to large Chinese shrub with delicately fragrant, creamy-white flowers.

'Burfordensis' (Virginalis Group). A magnificent, erect-branched, medium-sized shrub raised by Sir William Lawrence. The large, single flowers are cup-shaped and have conspicuous yellow stamens. A.M. 1921. F.C.C. 1969.

'Burkwoodii' (*'Etoile Rose'* × *'Virginal'*). A slender, medium-sized shrub with single, fragrant flowers. The long narrow petals are arranged in windmill fashion, white, with a purple basal stain.

californicus BENTH. A vigorous, medium-sized shrub attaining 3m. Fragrant flowers, 2·5cm. across, are produced in large panicles. California (U.S.A.). I. 1885.

'Conquete' (Cymosus Group). A small shrub with slender, arching branches carrying clusters of large, fragrant, single and semi-double, pure white flowers with long, narrow petals intermixed with shorter petaloid stamens.

coronarius L. A strong-growing, medium-sized shrub with creamy-white, richly scented flowers. The most commonly cultivated species, particularly suitable for very dry soils. Origin obscure, perhaps wild in N. and C. Italy, Austria and C. Rumania. Long cultivated.

'Aureus' (*caucasicus 'Aureus'*). Leaves bright yellow when young, becoming greenish-yellow.

'Variegatus' (*caucasicus 'Variegatus'*). Leaves with a creamy-white margin. C. 1770.

'Coupe d'Argent' (Lemoinei Group). A rather frail aristocrat, and a small shrub of superb quality. The large, single, fragrant flowers have a very slight stain at the base of the petals. They are rather square in outline and beautifully poised at regular intervals. A.M. 1922.

× **cymosus** REHD. (*floribundus*). A group of variable hybrids with flowers in cyme-like racemes. There are numerous named clones. See *'Albatre'*, *'Amalthee'*, *'Bouquet Blanc'*, *'Conquete'*, *'Monster'*, *'Rosace'*, *'Velleda'* and *'Voie Lactee'*.

delavayi L. HENRY. A large vigorous shrub with large leaves, grey felted beneath. Flowers heavily scented, 3 to 4cm. across, in dense racemes. China, Tibet, Upper Burma. Discovered and introduced by the Abbé Delavay in 1887.

calvescens. A delightful form with purple calyces.

'Enchantment' (Virginalis Group). A small to medium-sized shrub, producing terminal clusters of double, sweetly scented flowers in profusion. A.M. 1966.

'Erectus' (Lemoinei Group). A small shrub of erect habit, with small leaves and flowers, extremely floriferous, and richly scented. Very like *'Avalanche'*. A.G.M. 1946.

'Etoile Rose' (Purpureo-maculatus Group). Flowers large, single, the petals elongated, white with a carmine-rose blotch at base. Fragrant.

× **falconeri** SARG. A large shrub. The slightly fragrant white flowers, 3 to 4cm. across, are very distinct on account of their narrow, lance-shaped petals. Origin uncertain.

'Favourite' (Polyanthus Group). An attractive cultivar up to 2m. Single, very large, cup-shaped flowers, pure white with serrated petals and a central cluster of yellow stamens.

floribundus. See *P.* × *cymosus*.

'Frosty Morn'. A small shrub with fragrant, double flowers.

'Girandole' (Virginalis Group). A showy shrub with clusters of very double, fragrant flowers. A.M. 1921.

'Glacier' (Virginalis Group). A small, late-flowering shrub, bearing crowded clusters of very double, fragrant flowers.

incanus KOEHNE. A medium-sized to large shrub, well distinguished by its hairy leaves and late blossoming. Flowers fragrant, in late July. C. China. I. 1904. A.M. 1980.

'Innocence' (Lemoinei Group). Flowers single, fragrant, borne with extraordinary freedom. Leaves often with creamy-white variegation.

PHILADELPHUS—*continued*

insignis CARR. A vigorous shrub 3 to 3·6m. high. Flowers about 3cm. wide, rather cup-shaped, scented, produced in panicles of fifteen to twenty. One of the last to flower, the blossoms remaining until mid-July. California (U.S.A.). A.M. 1929.

intectus BEADLE (*pubescens intectus*). A very vigorous shrub, growing 4·5m. or more high. Outstanding when laden with masses of slightly fragrant flowers. S.E. United States. C. before 1890.

× **lemoinei** LEMOINE (*coronarius* × *microphyllus*). Raised in 1884 by M. Lemoine, this was the original hybrid of which there are now numerous named clones. A small shrub; flowers very fragrant, 2·5cm. wide, produced in clusters of three to seven on short side branches. A.M. 1898. See '*Avalanche*', '*Coupe d'Argent*', '*Erectus*', '*Innocence*' and '*Manteau d'Hermine*'.

lewisii PURSH. A medium-sized to large shrub of erect habit with racemes of white flowers. Western N. America. I. 1823.

†**maculatus** HU. A beautiful medium-sized shrub with richly fragrant flowers which are white, with a purple blotch in the centre. Sometimes wrongly grown in gardens under the name *P. coulteri*, which differs in its exposed buds and pure white flowers. A parent of many fine hybrids and perhaps itself of hybrid origin. Mexico, Arizona (U.S.A.). I. early in the 19th century. A.M. 1961.

'Manteau d'Hermine' (Lemoinei Group). A popular dwarf, compact shrub; attaining about ·75 to 1·2m.; flowers fragrant, creamy-white, double. A.M. 1956. A.G.M. 1969.

microphyllus GRAY. A very dainty, small-leaved species, forming a twiggy bush about 1 to 1·2m. high. Flowers richly fragrant. S.W. United States. I. 1883. F.C.C. 1890.

'Minnesota Snowflake' (Virginalis Group). An American cultivar, 1·5 to 1·8m. high, with arching branches bowed by the weight of the double, fragrant flowers.

'Monster' (Cymosus Group). A vigorous, large shrub, quickly attaining 4·5m. Flowers nearly 5cm. across.

'Norma' (Polyanthus Group). Flowers single, 5cm. across, slightly fragrant, on long slender branches. A.M. 1913. A.G.M. 1949.

pekinensis brachybotrys. See *P. brachybotrys*.

× **pendulifolius** CARR. Medium-sized shrub with racemes of cup-shaped flowers. Probably a hybrid of *P. pubescens*.

× **polyanthus** REHD. A variable group of erect shrubs of which there are several named clones. See '*Favourite*' and '*Norma*'.

pubescens intectus. See *P. intectus*.

verrucosus HU (*P. verrucosus*). A vigorous shrub up to 3m. high. Flowers about 3 to 4cm. across, slightly fragrant, in racemes of five to seven. S.E. United States.

purpurascens REHD. A small-leaved species making a medium-sized shrub, with spreading and arching branches, wreathed with sweet-scented flowers, the white petals contrasting with the purple calyces. W. China. I. 1911.

× **purpureo-maculatus** LEMOINE (× *lemoinei* × *maculatus*). A small to medium-sized shrub. The arching stems are weighted with white, purple-stained, scented blossoms. There are several named clones. See '*Beauclerk*', '*Etoile Rose*', and '*Sybille*'.

'Pyramidal' (Virginalis Group). Strong-growing shrub with semi-double, fragrant flowers.

'Rosace' (Cymosus Group). Large, semi-double, fragrant flowers in large sprays. A.M. 1908.

satsumanus MIQ. (*satsumi*) (*acuminatus*). A slender, erect shrub with rather small, slightly scented flowers in racemes of five to eleven. Japan. I. 1851.

schrenkii RUPR. A large shrub of upright habit akin to *P. coronarius*. Flowers very fragrant. E. Siberia, Manchuria, Korea. I. 1874.

sericanthus KOEHNE. A spreading shrub of medium to large size. Late flowering, with racemes of small cupped flowers. C. China. Introduced by Paul Farges in 1897.

× **splendens** REHD. A large, spreading shrub, forming a wide mound of arching branches. Flowers large in crowded clusters, white, filled with bright yellow anthers. Origin unknown, possibly *P. gordonianus* × *P. grandiflorus*.

subcanus KOEHNE (*wilsonii*). A large shrub producing long racemes of fragrant, somewhat bell-shaped flowers. C. and W. China. I. 1908.

PARROTIA persica

PHILADELPHUS microphyllus

QUERCUS robur 'Fastigiata'

PONCIRUS trifoliata

RHODODENDRON lutescens

RHODODENDRON yakushimanum

RHODODENDRON scintillans

PHILADELPHUS—*continued*

'Sybille' (Purpureo-maculatus Group). A superb small shrub with arching branches bearing single, almost square, purple-stained, orange scented flowers. A triploid hybrid. A.M. 1954. A.G.M. 1955.

tomentosus G. DON. A medium-sized shrub with slender-pointed, hairy leaves, grey-felted beneath. Flowers fragrant, 2·5 to 3·5cm. across, borne in slender racemes in June. Himalaya. I. 1822.

'Velleda' (Cymosus Group). A pretty cultivar with single, perfectly shaped, fragrant flowers about 3 to 4cm. across, petals crimped at the edges.

verrucosus. See *P. pubescens verrucosus.*

'Virginal' (Virginalis Group). A strong-growing, erect-branched shrub to 3m., with flowers 2·5 to 3·5cm. across, richly fragrant. Still probably the best double flowered cultivar. F.C.C. 1911. A.G.M. 1926.

×**virginalis** REHD. A group of hybrids with double flowers of which the type is *'Virginal'*. See *'Burfordensis'*, *'Enchantment'*, *'Girandole'*, *'Glacier'*, *'Minnesota Snowflake'* and *'Pyramidal'*.

'Voie Lactee' (Cymosus Group). Flowers single, 5cm. across, their broad petals having slightly reflexed edges. A.M. 1912.

wilsonii. See *P. subcanus.*

‡†*×**PHILAGERIA** (*LAPAGERIA* × *PHILESIA*)—**Philesiaceae**—An exceedingly rare bigeneric hybrid for a cool, moist, peaty soil in a mild garden or conservatory. A difficult plant to establish.

veitchii MAST. (*Lapageria rosea* × *Philesia buxifolia*). A small scrambling shrub with wiry branches and small, narrow, leathery leaves. Flowers solitary in the axils of the leaves, drooping, pale rose-purple outside, bright rose inside, appearing in late summer and autumn. Raised by Messrs. Veitch about 1870, *Lapageria* being the mother parent.

‡†***PHILESIA**—**Philesiaceae**—A monotypic genus related to *Lapageria.*

magellanica GMEL. (*buxifolia*). One of the choicest, most remarkable and beautiful of dwarf, suckering, evergreen shrubs, forming wide thickets of wiry stems and narrow, rigid leaves which are green above, glaucous beneath; producing crimson tubular flowers, 5cm. long, in summer and autumn. Requires a moist, peaty, half shady site, well-drained soil and a sheltered position. S. Chile. Introduced by William Lobb in 1847. A.M. 1937.

'Rosea'. Flowers paler, almost rose-red.

***PHILLYREA**—**Oleaceae**—Handsome evergreen shrubs or small trees allied to *Osmanthus*, and sometimes mistaken for the "Holm Oak". The growths of the smaller-leaved kinds develop, at maturity, into elegant plumose masses of foliage. Succeed in all types of soil.

angustifolia L. A compact, rounded bush of medium size. Leaves narrow, normally entire, dark green and glabrous. Flowers small, fragrant, creamy-yellow, in axillary clusters in May and June. Excellent for maritime exposure. N. Africa, S. Europe. C. before 1597.

rosmarinifolia SCHELLE. A most attractive, neat, compact form with even narrower leaves.

decora VILM. (*vilmoriniana*) (*medwediewii*). A dome-shaped bush up to 3m. usually wider than high, with comparatively large, leathery leaves which are more or less entire, glossy green above. The clusters of small, fragrant, white flowers are borne freely in spring and followed by purplish-black fruits like miniature plums. A very distinct, tough evergreen worthy of more extensive planting. W. Asia. I. 1866. F.C.C. 1888. Now regarded as a species of *Osmanthus.*

'Latifolia'. A form with larger leaves.

latifolia L. An elegant, olive-like small tree or large shrub suitable for planting where the "Holm Oak" would grow too large. Its branches are bowed by the weight of luxuriant masses of small, glossy, dark green, opposite leaves. Flowers dull white in late spring, followed by tiny, blue-black fruits which are seldom produced in this country. S. Europe; Asia Minor. C. 1597.

'Rotundifolia'. Leaves broadly ovate or rotund.

spinosa REHD. (*latifolia ilicifolia*). Narrow, serrated leaves.

***PHLOMIS**—**Labiatae**—A valuable genus of mainly low-growing Mediterranean shrubs or sub-shrubs, usually densely hairy or woolly and producing attractive flowers in axillary whorls. They require full sun and good drainage.

chrysophylla BOISS. A pleasing, small shrub, differing from *P. fruticosa* in the yellow tinge of its sage-like foliage. Flowers golden yellow in June. Lebanon.

PHLOMIS—*continued*

'Edward Bowles'. An attractive, small, front row sub-shrub, with large, hoary, heart-shaped leaves, and whorls of sulphur-yellow flowers, in late summer and autumn.

fruticosa L. "Jerusalem Sage". A small, grey-green shrub, hardy in all but the coldest districts. Its whorls of bright yellow flowers are attractive in summer. A good plant for a sunny bank. Mediterranean Region. C. 1596. A.M. 1925. A.G.M. 1929.

†**italica** L. A very desirable dwarf shrub from the Balearic Isles. Stems and leaves white-hairy, flowers pale lilac in terminal spikes in summer. I. about 1800.

***PHORMIUM**—**Agavaceae**—A small genus of New Zealand evergreens with handsome, sword-like leaves. They have much the same garden value as the Yuccas and associate well with them. They thrive in a variety of soils and are good plants for maritime exposure and for industrial areas. They are more or less hardy in all but the coldest areas.

cookianum LE JOLIS (*colensoi*). Differs from *P. tenax* in its smaller stature and its thinner, greener leaves which are laxer and more flexible. Flowers yellowish, in panicles up to 1m. during summer. F.C.C. 1868.

tenax FORST. The "New Zealand Flax" is a striking evergreen for foliage effect, forming clumps of rigid, leathery, somewhat glaucous, sword-like leaves, varying from 1 to 3m. in length. Flowers bronzy-red in panicles up to 4·5m. high in summer. A superb architectural plant for creating contrasting and diverse effects. It possesses something of the subtropical, the arid desert, and the waterside. It may be grown in all types of fertile soil and in all aspects. It is tolerant of sea wind and industrial pollution. Its leaves contain one of the finest fibres known. New Zealand. Often found naturalised in the west of Ireland. I. 1789.

'Purpureum'. Leaves bronzy-purple. A striking plant contrasting with grey foliage subjects.

'Variegatum'. Leaves with a creamy-white margin. F.C.C. 1864.

'Veitchii'. Leaves striped creamy-yellow.

PHOTINIA—**Rosaceae**—A group of large, Asiatic shrubs or small trees allied to *Crataegus*. The flowers are white, produced during spring in corymbose clusters, followed in autumn by red fruits. The foliage of some deciduous species colours well before falling, and in some evergreen sorts the bronze-red unfolding leaves rival Forrest's *Pieris*. The deciduous species are inclined to be calcifuge, whilst the evergreens are lime-tolerant. Unfortunately the evergreen species seldom flower or fruit with any sort of freedom due presumably to lack of sun and warmth.

arbutifolia. See *HETEROMELES arbutifolia*.

beauverdiana SCHNEID. This Chinese species has proved to be a very desirable small tree up to 6m. high, conspicuous in late May or early June, when covered with corymbs of hawthorn-like flowers, and in autumn when bedecked with dark red fruits and richly tinted leaves. Moderately lime tolerant. W. China. I. 1900.

notabilis REHD. & WILS. Distinguished from the type by its larger leaves, up to 12·5cm. long, broader corymbs and taller habit. Excellent in autumn when its leaves colour before falling, leaving clusters of orange-red fruits. C. and W. China. I. 1908. A.M. 1960.

†***benthamiana** HANCE. This species from China has proved fairly hardy here, but does not succeed in poor, chalky soils. The oblanceolate, serrulate leaves are copper-tinted when unfolding.

†***davidsoniae** REHD. & WILS. Closely related to *P. glabra* but resembling more a *Stranvaesia*. In sheltered positions will form a tall, thorny, evergreen shrub or small tree, especially notable in spring when producing its reddish young growths. Leaves obovate to oblanceolate, leathery, dark glossy green and serrulate. Flowers in May. Fruits orange-red but seldom produced. C. China. I. 1900.

*×**fraseri** DRESS (*glabra*×*serrulata*). A variable hybrid, a large vigorous, evergreen shrub with dark, glossy-green, leathery leaves and attractive coppery, young growths. Proving hardy in a sheltered position. We offer the following clones:

'Birmingham'. An American raised clone with generally obovate, abruptly pointed leaves, bright coppery-red when young. Tending towards the *glabra* parent.

PHOTINIA—*continued*

×**fraseri 'Red Robin'** (*glabra 'Red Robin'*). A most spectacular clone raised in New Zealand, with sharply toothed, glossy-green leaves and brilliant red, young growths, equal to *Pieris formosa forrestii*. A.M. 1977.

'Robusta' (*glabra 'Robusta'*). A strong-growing clone tending toward the *serrulata* parent with its thick, leathery oblong to obovate leaves. Young growths brilliant coppery-red. This is proving the hardiest clone in our arboretum. A seedling raised in Hazlewood's Nursery, Sydney, Australia. A.M. 1974.

***glabra** MAXIM. (*prunifolia*). A medium-sized to large shrub with oblong to obovate, dark green, minutely serrulate, leathery leaves and bronze young growths. Flowers in May or June followed by red fruits. Japan. C. about 1903.

'Rubens'. A choice cultivar, the young leaves of a brilliant sealing-wax red. A.M. 1972.

'Robusta'. See *P. ×fraseri 'Robusta'*.

†**glomerata** REHD. & WILS. A tender, medium-sized to large shrub with lanceolate leaves up to 12·5cm. long. Young foliage bright red. Yunnan.

†***integrifolia** LINDL. Medium-sized shrub with slender pointed, entire, leathery, oblanceolate leaves up to 15cm. long. It is sad that this outstanding evergreen is too tender for our area. It is lime tolerant.

koreana LANCASTER (*villosa maximowicziana*). A large shrub of robust, spreading habit with densely, grey-pubescent young shoots. Leaves almost sessile, obovate, pale green, rather leathery in texture, the veins strongly impressed above giving the leaf a bullate appearance. The white flowers in May are followed in autumn by attractive orange-red, later red, fruits and the leaves turn a rich golden yellow. Regarded by Rehder as a form of *P. villosa*, this distinct shrub is here treated as a species in its own right.Not recommended for shallow chalk soils. Previously wrongly catalogued and distributed as *P. amphidoxa*. Korea (Quelpaert). Introduced via Japan in 1897.

†***prionophylla** SCHNEID. (*Eriobotrya prinoides*). A stiff-habited, medium-sized evergreen from China, with hard, leathery, obovate leaves with prickly margins. The white flowers appearing in July, are borne in corymbs 5 to 7·5cm. across; fruits crimson. Not hardy in our area. W. China. I. 1916.

***serrulata** LINDL. A very handsome, large, evergreen shrub or small tree. Leaves oblong, up to 15cm. long, shining dark green and leathery with coarsely-toothed margins. The young leaves throughout the whole of its long growing season are bright, coppery-red. Flowers in large corymbs during April and May; fruits red, the size of haws. One of the most splendid lime-tolerant evergreens. It is remarkable how the young growths withstand spring frost. China; Formosa. I. 1804.

villosa DC. (*variabilis*) (*Pourtheia villosa*). A deciduous species forming a large shrub or small, broad-headed tree, with obovate, shortly acuminate leaves. It bears hawthorn-like flowers in May, followed by small, egg-shaped, bright red fruits, and is one of the most effective autumn-colouring subjects, the leaves turning to scarlet and gold. It does not thrive on shallow, chalky soil. Japan, Korea, China. I. about 1865. A.M. 1932. A.G.M. 1969.

maximowicziana. See *P. koreana*.

sinica REHD. & WILS. A small tree or occasionally a large shrub, differing from the type in its more spreading habit, elliptic or elliptic-oblong leaves and its larger almost cherry-like fruits in pendulous clusters. C. China. I. 1908.

PHYGELIUS—**Scrophulariaceae**—Attractive penstemon-like sub-shrubs from South Africa. *P. capensis* is remarkable as being one of the very few South African shrubs hardy in the British Isles. They reach their greatest height against a sunny wall, but look well towards the front of the shrub or herbaceous border. They succeed in full sun in all types of well-drained soil.

aequalis HIERN. A small sub-shrub up to 1m., with four-angled stems. Flowers tubular, 2·5 to 3cm. long, salmon-pink on the outside, orange or dull purple within, produced in panicles in late summer and early autumn. Not so hardy as *P. capensis* and requires wall protection. A.M. 1936.

capensis BENTH. "Cape Figwort". A small shrub, occasionally up to 2m. in mild areas. Flowers tubular, nodding, scarlet with yellow throat, elegantly borne in erect panicles during summer and autumn. I. about 1855. A.G.M. 1969. We offer the following clone:—

'Coccineus'. Flowers crimson-scarlet. A.M. 1926.

†***PHYLICA**—**Rhamnaceae**—A large genus of evergreen shrubs mainly found in South Africa. Only suitable for sunny positions in the mildest areas.

superba. A remarkable, small, helichrysum-like shrub with crowded, small, silver-green leaves. Inflorescences, composed of tiny, green-white flowers, open in late autumn, emitting a strong fragrance like "Meadow-sweet". Only suitable for the mildest areas, but makes an attractive conservatory shrub. Lime tolerant. S. Africa.

‡***PHYLLODOCE**—**Ericaceae**—A genus of dainty, dwarf, heath-like shrubs, thriving in cool, moist, moorland conditions, and in lime-free soil. April to July flowering.

aleutica HELLER. A dwarf, carpeting shrublet, 15 to 23cm. high. Flowers pitcher-shaped (urceolate), creamy-white, or pale yellow, in terminal umbels during May and June. Aleutian Isles, Kamtchatka, N. Japan. I. 1915. A.M. 1939.

breweri HELLER. A dwarf, tufted species, 23 to 30cm. high. Flowers comparatively large, saucer-shaped, of a delightful rose-purple, produced in long terminal racemes in May and June. California. I. 1896. A.M. 1956.

caerulea BAB. (*taxifolia*). A rare, native alpine found wild in Perthshire. A dwarf cushion-forming shrublet up to 15cm.; flowers pitcher-shaped, bluish-purple, borne in delicate terminal umbels in May and June. Alpine-Arctic regions of N. Europe, N. America, N. Asia. C. 1800. A.M. 1938.

empetriformis D. DON. A dwarf, tufted shrublet, 15 to 25cm. high. Flowers bell-shaped, bright reddish-purple, produced in umbels during April and May. Western N. America. C. 1830.

× **intermedia** RYDB. (*empetriformis* × *glanduliflora*) (*hybrida*). A variable dwarf hybrid of vigorous growth, soon forming large mats up to 30cm. high and four times as much wide. Often wrongly grown in gardens as *P. empetriformis*, from which it differs in its pitcher-shaped flowers, puckered at the mouth. Western N. America. A.M. 1936.

'Fred Stoker' (*pseudoempetriformis* HORT.). This is the form in general cultivation. Named after that keen amateur gardener the late Dr. Fred Stoker. A.M. 1941.

nipponica MAK. One of the most perfect rock-garden shrublets for peaty soils. A dwarf, erect-growing species of neat, compact habit, 15 to 23cm. high. Flowers bell-shaped, white, or pink-tinged, appearing in terminal umbels in May. N. Japan. I. 1915. A.M. 1938. F.C.C. 1946.

taxifolia. See *P. caerulea*.

‡* × **PHYLLOTHAMNUS** (*PHYLLODOCE* × *RHODOTHAMNUS*)—**Ericaceae**—An interesting bi-generic hybrid raised by Cunningham and Fraser, nurserymen of Edinburgh. Suitable for a lime-free, moist, peaty or leafy soil.

erectus SCHNEID. (*P. empetriformis* × *R. chamaecistus*). A dwarf shrublet, 30 to 45cm. in height, its stems crowded with narrow leaves. Flowers shallowly funnel-shaped of a delicate rose, produced in terminal umbels in April and May. Garden origin about 1845. A.M. 1958. F.C.C. 1969.

PHYSOCARPUS—**Rosaceae**—A small genus of tall shrubs related to *Neillia*, and, like it, thriving in open moist positions. Tend to become chlorotic on a dry shallow chalk-soil.

amurensis MAXIM. Medium-sized shrub of compact habit with rounded, three to five-lobed leaves. Flowers white, with reddish-purple anthers, in clusters in summer. Manchuria, Korea.

capitatus KTZE. Medium-sized shrub with three-lobed, double-toothed leaves and clusters of white flowers in summer. Western N. America. I. 1827.

malvaceus KTZE. (*Neillia torreyi*) (*Neillia malvacea*). An elegant, spiraea-like shrub of medium size, bearing umbels of white flowers in June. Western N. America. I. 1896.

monogynus COULT. Small shrub with small, ovate, three to five-lobed leaves and clusters of white or pink-tinged flowers in summer. C. United States. I. 1879.

opulifolius MAXIM. (*Spiraea opulifolia*). "Nine Bark". A vigorous, medium-sized shrub, thriving almost anywhere. Leaves three-lobed; flowers white, tinged pink, produced in dense clusters along the stems in June. Eastern N. America. I. 1687.

'Luteus'. Young growths of a clear yellow, very effective when planted with purple-leaved shrubs.

PHYTOLACCA—Phytolaccaceae—A small genus of mainly herbs. Easy plants to grow in diverse types of soil. For *P. americana* and *P. clavigera* see our Hardy Perennial Catalogue.

†**dioica** L. (*arborea*). A large, semi-evergreen shrub of vigorous growth, making a small, heavy-limbed tree in its native habitat. Leaves poplar-like, up to 15cm. long. Flowers dioecious, greenish, in racemes 5 to 7·5cm. long, followed by dark purple, berry-like fruits. A conservatory shrub, only growing outside in the mildest areas. There is or was a thick-trunked tree in the public gardens at Gibraltar. Native of S. America.

PICRASMA—Simaroubaceae—A genus of mainly tropical trees and shrubs related to *Ailanthus*. Succeeding in a cool, well-drained loam, in sun or semi-shade.

quassioides BENNETT (*ailanthoides*). A very ornamental, small hardy tree with attractive, pinnate leaves 15 to 25cm. long, turning orange and scarlet in the autumn. All parts are bitter to the taste. Flowers green, in axillary corymbs, followed by red, pea-like fruits. Lime tolerant but succeeding best in neutral or acid soils. Japan, Formosa, China, Korea, India.

‡***PIERIS—Ericaceae**—Highly ornamental, dense-growing evergreen shrubs requiring similar treatment to rhododendrons. The flower panicles are formed in autumn, and those with red-tinged buds are attractive throughout winter. The flowers eventually open during April and May. They are white and pitcher-shaped, rather like lily-of-the-valley. Several have very attractive red or bronze young growth which is vulnerable to late spring frost and, for that reason, light overhead shade and protection on the north and east sides is desirable for *P. formosa* in all its forms.

floribunda BENTH. & HOOK. (*Andromeda floribunda*). A very hardy, slow-growing shrub forming a dense, rounded mound 1·2 to 2m. high. Flowers produced in numerous erect, terminal panicles during March and April. S.E. United States. I. 1800. A.G.M. 1946.

'Elongata' (*'Grandiflora'*). A distinct form with longer panicles, also flowering later than the type. Garden origin about 1935. A.M. 1938.

'Forest Flame' (*formosa forrestii 'Wakehurst'* × *japonica*). A superb large shrub, combining the hardiness of *P. japonica* with the brilliant red young growths of *'Wakehurst'*. The leaves pass from red, through pink and creamy-white to green. Flowers in large terminal, drooping panicles. Originated as a chance seedling in Sunningdale Nurseries about 1946. A.M. 1973. A.G.M. 1973.

formosa D. DON (*Andromeda formosa*). A magnificent large evergreen shrub for mild climates. The large leaves are leathery, finely-toothed and of a dark glossy green. The clustered flower panicles are produced in May. Young growths copper-tinted. E. Himalaya. C. 1858. A.M. 1894. F.C.C. 1969.

forrestii AIRY-SHAW. In its best forms this is one of the most beautiful of all shrubs, the young growths being brilliant red, and the large, slightly fragrant flowers borne in long, conical panicles. A handsome-foliaged shrub 2·5m. or more high, blooming in April. S.W. China, N.E. Upper Burma. Introduced by George Forrest about 1910. A.M. 1924. F.C.C. 1930. A.G.M. 1944.

Available in the following clones:—

'Charles Michael' (F.27765). A striking form raised at Caerhays Castle from Forrest's seed. The individual flowers are the largest of any form and occur in large panicles.

'Jermyns'. A superb clone, selected in our nursery. Young shoots vinous red. The whole inflorescence, including the sepals, is of the same rich colouring as the young stems and contrasts strikingly with the white flowers. A.M. 1959.

'Wakehurst'. A lovely selection, strong and vigorous, differing from the type in its relatively shorter, broader leaves. The vivid red young foliage contrasts beautifully with the glistening white flowers. A.M. 1957.

japonica D. DON (*Andromeda japonica*). A medium-sized shrub differing from *P. floribunda* in its more attractive, glossy foliage, coppery when young and its larger, white, more waxy flowers borne in drooping panicles during March and April. Japan. C. 1870. F.C.C. 1882. A.G.M. 1924.

'Bert Chandler' (*'Chandleri'*). An unusual form of Australian origin. The young foliage is salmon-pink changing to cream then white, finally green. Raised in Chandler's Nurseries in Victoria, Australia. A.M. 1977.

'Blush'. A beautiful form with flowers rose in bud, opening a pale blush pink.

PIERIS—*continued*

japonica 'Christmas Cheer'. An exceedingly hardy form from Japan. The flowers are flushed with deep rose at the tip, creating a delightful bicolor effect. The pedicels are also deep rose. Abundantly produced even on young plants and often appear during winter.

'Daisen' (*'Rosea Daisen Form'*). A selection from Mount Daisen in Japan. Flowers pink, deeper in bud. An improvement on *'Rosea'*.

'Purity'. A selected seedling from Japan bearing trusses of comparatively large, snow white flowers.

pygmaea YATABE. A curious dwarf form of slow growth almost unrecognizable as a *Pieris*, with leaves 1·2 to 2·5cm. long, linear-lanceolate, shallowly-toothed. Resembling a rather loose-leaved *Phyllodoce*. Flowers white, in simple racemes rarely produced.

'Variegata'. A slow-growing form of medium size. The leaves are prettily variegated with creamy-white, flushed pink when young. One of the most attractive of all silver variegated shrubs. A.G.M. 1969.

nana. See *ARCTERICA nana*.

taiwanensis HAYATA. A medium-sized shrub most resembling *P. japonica*, but differing in its rather larger, more matt foliage and its somewhat larger, more erect panicles of beautiful lily-of-the-valley-like, white flowers in March and April. Young growths bronze or bronze-red. Formosa. Introduced by E. H. Wilson in 1918. A.M. 1922. F.C.C. 1923. A.G.M. 1963.

'Crispa'. A small shrub of slow growth with matt leaves strongly curled or wavy-edged. Flowers in large, lax panicles which cover the whole bush. Young growths an attractive copper.

PILEOSTEGIA viburnoides. See under CLIMBERS.

***PIMELEA—Thymelaeaceae**—Attractive, small-leaved evergreens closely allied to *Daphne*, and requiring similar cultural treatment. All are Australasian in origin. Not recommended for shallow chalk-soils.

†drupacea LABILL. A small, erect shrub with ovate or narrow leaves 2·5 to 5cm. long. Terminal clusters of white flowers in summer, followed by black fruits. S.E. Australia, Tasmania. I. 1817.

†ferruginea LABILL. A dwarf, erect shrub of excellent quality, flowering in late spring and early summer. The heads of clear deep peach-pink flowers are borne at the tips of the branchlets, which are continuously produced. Leaves in rows, small and neat, shining green. May be kept in a cool house during winter, and out-of-doors in summer. W. Australia. I. 1824. A.M. 1959.

prostrata WILLD. (*laevigata*). A pretty and interesting carpeting species having prostrate or sub-erect branches clothed with small, glabrous, grey-green leaves. The fragrant white flowers produced in clusters in summer are followed by fleshy, white fruits. An excellent scree plant which has succeeded here for many years. New Zealand. A.M. 1955.

PIPTANTHUS—Leguminosae—A small genus of deciduous and evergreen, large shrubs with trifoliolate leaves and comparatively large, showy, yellow, pea flowers. They succeed in any drained soil, including chalk-soils.

***laburnifolius** STAPF. (*nepalensis*). "Evergreen Laburnum". An attractive, nearly evergreen Himalayan shrub 2·4 to 3·5m. high, with large, bright yellow, laburnum-like flowers, opening in May. Deciduous in severe winters. May be grown in the open but an excellent wall plant. I. 1821. A.M. 1960.

(**L. & S. 17394**). A medium-sized shrub with greyish-green, silky leaves and clusters of attractive yellow flowers during April and May. A most attractive, and as yet unnamed form, collected by Ludlow and Sherriff in Bhutan. It is slightly more tender than the type.

nepalensis. See *P. laburnifolius*.

"PISTACHIO". See *PISTACIA vera*.

PISTACIA—Anacardiaceae—A small genus of evergreen and deciduous shrubs, or occasionally small trees, related to *Rhus*, differing in the petal-less flowers. *P. chinensis* is the only fully hardy species. Best in sun they will succeed in all types of soil.

chinensis BGE. "Chinese Pistachio". A hardy, large shrub with elegant, glossy green, pinnate leaves assuming gorgeous colours in autumn. Flowers unisexual, in dense terminal clusters; fruits seldom appearing, small, reddish at first then blue. Central W. China. I. 1897.

PISTACIA—*continued*

†**terebinthus** L. "Chian Turpentine Tree". A small tree or large shrub with aromatic, dark glossy green, pinnate leaves. The unisexual flowers are greenish; fruits small, reddish, turning purplish-brown. Asia Minor, Mediterranean Region. I. 1656.

†**vera** L. "Pistachio". A small tree with pinnate leaves, the leaflets large and downy. The dense panicles of inconspicuous flowers are followed by small, reddish fruits—the "pistachio-nuts" of commerce, which are rarely developed outside in this country. Requires a hot, dry, sheltered position, or greenhouse. W. Asia, long cultivated. Introduced to England in 1770.

***PITTOSPORUM**—**Pittosporaceae**—A large genus of mostly Australasian evergreen shrubs or small trees, the majority only suitable for mild districts, where they will thrive especially well near the sea. Several have small, fragrant flowers, but they are chiefly grown for their foliage which is useful for cutting. All types of well-drained soil.

P. dallii and *P. patulum* are the only species which have never been injured outside here during their stay of thirty years.

†**bicolor** HOOK. A large shrub or small tree of erect habit with narrow, revolute, entire leaves which are dark green above, white becoming brownish tomentose beneath. Flowers bell-shaped, maroon and yellow in clusters during spring. A useful tall hedge in mild areas. Tasmania, S.E. Australia.

chinense. See *P. tobira*.

†**colensoi** HOOK. f. A medium-sized to large shrub, excellent in maritime districts. Leaves 3·5 to 10cm. long, oblong or oval, leathery and dark glossy green above. Flowers dark red, comparatively large, appearing in April. New Zealand.

†**cornifolium** A. CUNN. A distinct New Zealand species to 1·8m. high; leaves 5 to 7·5cm. long, whorled. Flowers purple, musk-scented in terminal umbels of two to five, in February and March. Often epiphytic on tree trunks in its native habitat, but succeeds in ordinary, well-drained soil in favoured areas of the British Isles.

crassifolium A. CUNN. The New Zealand "Karo", one of the hardiest species, passing many years here uninjured. Leaves 5 to 7·5cm. long, oval or obovate, thick and leathery, deep green above, white felted beneath. Flowers deep purple, in terminal clusters. An excellent dense-growing screen or shelter-belt in coastal areas.

dallii CHEESEM. A perfectly hardy, large, spreading New Zealand shrub or rarely a small tree of rounded shape. Shoots and petioles dark reddish-purple. Leaves elliptic to elliptic-lanceolate, leathery and jaggedly-toothed or occasionally entire, matt green. The fragrant, white flowers are borne in crowded terminal clusters during summer but we have yet to see flowering specimens in this country.

†**daphniphylloides** HAYATA. A remarkable large shrub or small tree, notable for the large size of its dark green, obovate or oblanceolate leaves, which may be 15 to 23cm. long. Flowers cream, deliciously scented, in large terminal clusters from April to July. Fruits small, red. Only suitable for the mildest areas or for the conservatory. There are large specimens in Cornwall. W. China; Formosa. Introduced by E. H. Wilson in 1904.

divaricatum CKN. A small to medium-sized shrub with rigid, wiry branches forming a dense, tangled mass. Leaves variable, 12 to 20mm. long, those of juvenile plants narrow lanceolate to obovate, deeply-toothed or pinnatifid, leaves of adult plants obovate to elliptic, entire or deeply-toothed or lobed. The small, dark maroon flowers are produced at the ends of the shoots, in May. A curious species and reminding one of *Corokia cotoneaster* in habit. Proving hardy. New Zealand.

†**eugenioides** A. CUNN. "Tarata". A large shrub or small tree with dark twigs and oval or oblong, glossy green, undulate leaves 5 to 10cm. long, and pleasantly aromatic. Flowers pale yellow, honey-scented, produced in terminal clusters in spring. New Zealand.

'Variegatum'. One of the prettiest and most elegant of variegated shrubs for very mild climates. Leaves margined creamy-white.

mayi. See *P. tenuifolium*.

nigricans. See *P. tenuifolium*.

PITTOSPORUM—*continued*

patulum HOOK. f. A large, slender, sparsely-branched, hardy shrub or small erect tree to 4·5m. Leaves variable, those of juvenile plants are 2·5 to 5cm. long, narrow and conspicuously lobed, those of adult plants 12mm. long, toothed or entire. Flowers bell-shaped, fragrant, dark crimson, in terminal clusters during May. New Zealand.

ralphii T. KIRK. This medium-sized to large shrub appears hardy, having stood many years uninjured here in our nursery. Related to *P. crassifolium* from which it differs in its larger, more oblong, less obovate leaves which are flat, not recurved, at the margins. Flowers dark crimson with yellow anthers. New Zealand.

†**tenuifolium** GAERTN. (*nigricans*) (*mayi*). A charming large shrub or small tree, with bright, pale green, undulate leaves, prettily set on black twigs. One of the hardier species, and now extensively used as a cut evergreen for floristry. A good hedging plant for mild localities. Flowers small, chocolate-purple, honey-scented, appearing in spring. New Zealand. A.M. 1931.

'Garnettii'. Leaves variegated white and flushed pink.

'James Stirling'. A charming form with small, dainty silvery-green rounded or oval leaves crowding the slender, blackish-purple branchlets.

'Purpureum'. An attractive selection in which the pale green leaves gradually change to a deep bronze-purple. More tender than the type.

'Silver Queen'. Leaves suffused silvery-grey. Forms a neat and handsome specimen shrub. A.M. 1914.

'Variegatum'. Leaves margined creamy-white.

'Warnham Gold'. Young leaves greenish-yellow, maturing to golden yellow, particularly attractive during autumn and winter. A selected seedling raised at Warnham Court, Sussex, in 1959.

†**tobira** AIT. (*chinense*). A rather slow-growing species from Japan and China eventually a large shrub with obovate, bright, glossy green leaves in whorls amidst which are set in summer the conspicuous, cream coloured, orange-blossom-scented flowers. An excellent wall shrub. Used extensively in Southern Europe for hedging, very drought-resistant. China; Formosa; Japan. I. 1804.

'Variegatum'. Leaves with an irregular, but conspicuous creamy-white margin. Plants under glass often flower during winter.

turneri PETRIE. A large shrub or small tree of erect habit. Leaves 2·5 to 4cm. long, obovate; flowers in terminal clusters pink or purple in May and June. On juvenile plants the slender, tortuous branches are formed in a dense tangled mass. One of the hardier species. New Zealand.

†**undulatum** VENT. A large shrub with dark, shining green, wavy-edged leaves 7·5 to 15cm. in length. Flowers creamy-white, fragrant, produced in terminal clusters in May and June even on young plants. Only suitable for the mildest localities. Australia. I. 1789.

'Variegatum'. A very beautiful silver-variegated form.

PLAGIANTHUS—Malvaceae—A small genus of graceful trees or shrubs, natives of Australasia, succeeding well in the south and south-west, in all types of fertile soil. The flowers are very small and normally unisexual. Not to be confused with the plant widely grown as *P. lyallii* and now transferred to *Hoheria*, which see.

betulinus A. CUNN. A graceful, slender, small to medium-sized tree. Leaves petioled, ovate to ovate-lanceolate, up to 7·5cm. long, crenate-serrate. Flowers inconspicuous, white, in large dense panicles during May. Juvenile plants present a dense bush of slender, flexuous, interlacing branches with short-stalked leaves 1 to 4cm. long, crenate-serrate or deeply and irregularly lobed. A curious tree passing through several stages of growth. New Zealand. I. 1870.

divaricatus J. R. & G. FORST. An interesting shrub forming a densely-branched bush 2m. high. Leaves alternate or in small clusters, those of young plants linear or spathulate, 2 to 3·5cm. long, of adult plants spathulate or narrow obovate, 6 to 20mm. long. Flowers small, yellowish-white, solitary or in short clusters in May. New Zealand. I. 1820.

lyallii. See *HOHERIA glabrata* and *H. lyallii.*

"PLANE". See *PLATANUS.*

PLANERA—Ulmaceae—A rare monotypic genus, of easy cultivation in all types of soil; related to *Ulmus*, but differing in its warty, nut-like fruits.

aquatica GMEL. (*ulmifolia*). "Water Elm". A small to medium-sized, wide-spreading tree with oval, simply or doubly serrate leaves which are from 2·5 to 7·5cm. in length and slightly rough to the touch. Flowers monoecious, inconspicuous. A native of swampy forests in S.E. United States. I. 1816.

PLATANUS—Platanaceae—A small genus of magnificent, large, maple-like trees with alternate leaves and attractive flaking bark. They may be grown in all types of fertile soil, but will not reach their maximum proportions in chalky soil and may become chlorotic in very shallow chalk-soils.

× **acerifolia.** See *P.* × *hispanica*.

× **hispanica** MUENCHH. (× *acerifolia*) (× *hybrida*). "London Plane". A large, noble, park tree with attractive mottled or patchwork flaking bark, and large, palmate leaves. The rounded, burr-like, fruit clusters are produced in strings of two to six and hang like baubles on the branches, from early summer through to the following spring. Extensively planted as a street tree owing to its tolerance of atmospheric pollution and severe pruning. First recorded about 1663. It has long been considered a hybrid between *P. occidentalis* and *P. orientalis*, though some opinion suggests that it may be a form of the latter.

'Pyramidalis'. A large, erect-growing form, making an excellent tree for a broad thoroughfare.

'Suttneri'. A striking form with large leaves boldly variegated creamy-white.

occidentalis L. The "Buttonwood" or "American Sycamore" is a difficult tree to cultivate successfully in this country. It differs from *P.* × *hispanica* in its shallowly lobed leaves and its smoother fruit clusters which are normally produced singly on long stalks. S. Ontario (Canada), Eastern U.S.A., N.E. Mexico. I. 1636.

orientalis L. "Oriental Plane". "Chennar Tree". A large, stately, long-lived tree, developing a wide-spreading head of branches. Bark attractively dappled and flaking; leaves deeply five-lobed, the lobes reaching half-way or more to the base. Fruit clusters bristly, two to six on a stalk. One of the most magnificent of all large trees and attaining a great age. S.E. Europe. Cultivated in England in the early 16th century. A.M. 1966. A.G.M. 1973.

digitata JANKO (*laciniata*). Leaves deeply divided into three to five finger-like lobes.

insularis A. DC. (*P. cretica*) (*P. cyprius*). "Cyprian Plane". A smaller tree with smaller leaves of variable shape, usually deeply divided, with narrow lobes and cuneate at the base.

†**racemosa** NUTT. (*californica*). A rare species, attaining a large size in California but much smaller in England. Leaves three or five-lobed to below the middle, tomentose beneath. Fruit clusters sessile, two to seven on each stalk. California, N.W. Mexico. I. 1870.

PLATYCARYA (*PETROPHYLLOIDES*)—**Juglandaceae**—A monotypic genus related to *Pterocarya*, differing in the erect inflorescences and twigs with a solid pith.

strobilacea SIEB. & ZUCC. (*Fortunaea chinensis*). A beautiful small tree recalling *Juglans rupestris*, with pinnate leaves composed of seven to fifteen sessile, lanceolate toothed leaflets. Flowers small, monoecious, the males in cylindrical catkins, the females in erect, green, cone-like clusters at the end of the current year's growth in July or August. China, Japan, Korea, Formosa. I. 1845.

"PLUMBAGO, HARDY". See *CERATOSTIGMA willmottianum*.

"POCKET HANDKERCHIEF TREE". See *DAVIDIA involucrata*.

POLIOTHYRSIS—Flacourtiaceae—A monotypic genus related to *Idesia*, differing in the capsular fruits. It is quite hardy and succeeds in all types of fertile soil.

sinensis OLIV. An interesting, small tree or large shrub with ovate, slender-pointed, attractively tinted leaves 10 to 15cm. long. Flowers monoecious, cream-coloured, borne in slender panicles in July. China. I. before 1908. A.M. 1960.

***POLYGALA—Polygalaceae**—A large genus of annual or perennial herbs and shrubs with colourful pea-flowers. The woody species thrive in most types of soil, but are not recommended for shallow chalk-soils.

‡**chamaebuxus** L. A dwarf, evergreen, alpine shrublet forming large tufts a few centimeters high. Flowers creamy-white tipped bright yellow, appearing in profusion from April to June. Suitable for a cool, moist position on the rock garden or in the peat garden. Mts. of C. Europe; a common plant in the Alps. C. 1658.

POLYGALA—*continued*

chamaebuxus 'Angustifolia'. A form with narrow leaves up to 2·5cm. long by 3mm. across. Flowers purple, tipped yellow.

grandiflora GAUD. (*purpurea*). A very beautiful form with purple wing-petals and yellow keel. A.M. 1896.

'Rhodoptera'. A form with smaller leaves. Flowers similar to *grandiflora*, but slightly smaller and of richer colouring.

†**'Dalmaisiana'** (*myrtifolia 'Grandiflora'* HORT.). A small, almost continuously flowering shrub for the conservatory, with bright purple pea-flowers. S. Africa.

‡**vayredae** COSTA. A choice, creeping alpine shrublet, somewhat resembling *P. chamaebuxus*, but with narrower leaves. Flowers reddish purple, tipped bright yellow in March and April. Suitable for a cool, moist position on the rock garden or in the peat garden. Pyrenees of Spain. C. 1923.

†**virgata** THUNB. An erect-growing shrub to 2m. with reed-like stems and narrow leaves. Flowers purple, very conspicuous in long racemes. Suitable for the conservatory. S. Africa. I. 1814. A.M. 1977.

POLYGONUM—Polygonaceae—A large genus of mainly herbs containing a few woody climbers and shrubs. See also under CLIMBERS.

equisetiformis SIBTH. & SM. A small subshrub of interesting and unusual growth. The long, slender, reed-like stems are usually devoid of leaves and bear a remarkable resemblance to those of a "Horsetail" (Equisetum sp.). The small, creamy-white flowers are borne in numerous, axillary clusters during late summer. Requires a warm, sunny, well-drained position. Usually cut back during a severe winter. Mediterranean Region, S. Bulgaria.

†***POMADERRIS—Rhamnaceae**—A genus of evergreen, small trees and shrubs, natives of Australasia. All require a warm, sheltered position or conservatory treatment. They succeed in all types of well-drained soil, but are not recommended for very shallow chalk-soils.

apetala LABILL. A large shrub with oblong-lanceolate, toothed leaves, wrinkled above, densely tomentose beneath; flowers small, mustard-yellow in large panicles in summer. S.E. Australia; Tasmania; New Zealand. I. 1803.

phylicifolia LODD. A small heath-like shrub having densely, woolly shoots, small, narrow leaves, and cream-coloured flowers borne very abundantly in April. S.E. Australia, Tasmania, New Zealand. I. 1819.

"POMEGRANATE". See *PUNICA granatum*.

PONCIRUS—Rutaceae—A hardy monotypic genus related to *Citrus*. It will succeed in all types of well-drained soil, preferably in full sun.

trifoliata RAF. (*Aegle sepiaria*) (*Citrus trifoliata*). "Japanese Bitter Orange". A stout, slow-growing, medium-sized shrub with green stems armed with stout spines and trifoliolate leaves. Beautiful in spring when carrying its white, sweetly-scented flowers, like orange blossom. The individual flowers are almost as large as those of *Clematis montana*. Fruits globular, like miniature oranges, 3·5 to 5cm. across, green ripening to yellow. N. China. I. 1850.

"POPLAR". See *POPULUS*.

POPULUS—Salicaceae—"Poplar". A large and useful genus which includes some of the fastest growing of all trees. Many are well adapted for quickly forming an effective, tall summer or permanent windbreak, but by reason of their rapid growth and surface-rooting they are unsuitable for small gardens, and should not be planted near buildings. The majority thrive in all types of soil, even when wet or boggy, but in wet sites mound planting is desirable. With a few exceptions poplars do not thrive on shallow chalky soils and most of the Black Poplars tend to become chlorotic and even die within 30 years. Many poplars are tolerant of atmospheric pollution and several are excellent in maritime exposure. Some of the poplars, especially the newer hybrids, are valuable for timber production and give comparatively quick returns. The Balsam poplars have pleasantly aromatic young leaves, whilst many of the Black poplars have attractive, copper-coloured growths in spring. The catkins of certain species are long, and drape the bare branches in spring, male and female catkins appearing on separate trees (dioecious). Some species and their hybrids are prone to canker.

×**acuminata** RYBD. (*angustifolia* × *sargentii*). A medium-sized balsam poplar with rounded twigs and ovate to rhomboid, acuminate, shining green leaves, aromatic when unfolding. Western N. America. I. 1898.

POPULUS—*continued*

alba L. "White Poplar"; "Abele". A large, suckering tree, conspicuous on account of the white-woolly undersurfaces of the leaves which are particularly noticeable when ruffled by the wind. The leaves variable in shape, some ovate and irregularly lobed or toothed, others larger and distinctly three to five-lobed like a maple. Leaf-stalks round or slightly flattened. Autumn colour yellow. An excellent tree in exposed sites, particularly valuable in coastal areas where if cut severely and retained as a shrub it is effective planted by the sea with similarly pruned red and yellow stemmed willows and *Spartium junceum*. The species grows well on chalky soil. C. & S. Europe to W. Siberia and W. Asia. Long cultivated and naturalised in the British Isles.

'Bolleana'. See *'Pyramidalis'*.

'Paletzkyana'. A form with deeply lobed and toothed leaves.

'Pyramidalis' (*'Bolleana'*). A large tree with erect branches, resembling in habit the "Lombardy Poplar", but slightly broader in relations to height. C. about 1872.

'Richardii'. A smaller growing, less vigorous tree with leaves bright golden yellow above, white beneath. A delightful form, very effective at a distance. A.M. 1912.

'Andover' (*nigra betulifolia × trichocarpa*). A robust, slow-growing, large tree of American origin; a hybrid between a black poplar and a balsam poplar.

'Androscoggin' (*maximowiczii × trichocarpa*). A large, extremely vigorous hybrid of American origin. Specimens growing in the Quantock Forest in Somerset have attained 30m. in seventeen years.

angulata AIT. "Carolina Poplar". A large, open-headed tree, with prominently angled twigs and large heart-shaped leaves. Origin uncertain, probably North America. C. about 1789.

balsamifera L. (*tacamahacca*). "Balsam Poplar". A large, erect-branched tree, grown mainly for the balsamic odour of its unfolding leaves. Twigs rounded, glabrous; buds large and sticky. Leaves ovate to ovate-lanceolate, whitish and reticulate beneath. The sticky buds and balsamic odour is possessed by a number of poplars notably *P. × candicans*. North America. Introduced before 1689.

michauxii HENRY. A minor form with petioles and veins of leaf beneath minutely hairy.

balsamifera × trichocarpa. A large tree of extremely fast growth, with white-backed leaves and fragrant buds.

× **berolinensis** DIPP. (*laurifolia × nigra 'Italica'*). "Berlin Poplar". A large, broadly columnar tree with slightly angled, downy twigs and ovate to rhomboid, acuminate leaves, pale beneath. Much used for street planting on the continent and for wind breaks on the North American prairies. A male clone.

× **canadensis** MOENCH. A large group of hybrids between the American *P. deltoides* and forms of the European *P. nigra*. They are known collectively as Hybrid Black Poplars. All are vigorous trees and are excellent for screening purposes. The wood of several clones is used in the match industry. The first clone originated possibly in France about 1750. The name *P. × euramericana* GUINIER is used by some authorities to cover all the Black Poplar hybrids between *P. angulata*, *P. deltoides* and *P. nigra*.

× **candicans** AIT. (*balsamifera × deltoides missouriensis*). "Ontario Poplar"; "Balm of Gilead Poplar". A medium-sized, broad-headed tree with stout, angled downy twigs and broad-ovate leaves which are greyish-white beneath, strongly balsam-scented when unfolding. Origin uncertain, probably North America. Only the female tree is known. C. 1773.

'Aurora'. A conspicuously variegated form. The leaves, especially when young, are creamy-white, often pink tinged. Older leaves green. To obtain the best results, hard prune the shoots in late winter. A.M. 1954.

POPULUS—*continued*

× **canescens** SM. (*alba* × *tremula*). A medium-sized to large, suckering tree sometimes forming thickets. Frequently planted on the continent as a roadside tree. Mature specimens develop an attractive creamy-grey trunk. Leaves variable in shape, rounded or deltoid, dentate and slightly toothed, more or less grey tomentose beneath. The smaller basal leaves eventually become green and glabrous. One of the best poplars for chalk-soils, giving attractive yellow and sometimes red autumn colour. The male catkins in late winter are most decorative, being woolly and crimson, up to 10cm. long. Female trees are rare in this country. W.C. & S. Europe (including England). Extensively planted and naturalised.

'Macrophylla'. "Picart's Poplar". A large-leaved form, very vigorous in growth.

'Carrierana' (Canadensis Group). A large, erect tree of vigorous growth. Proving lime tolerant.

cathayana REHD. A rare balsam poplar of vigorous growth. A medium-sized to large tree. The upright branches with rounded twigs carry large, white-backed leaves. N.W. China to Manchuria and Korea. I. about 1908. Subject to canker.

× **charkoviensis** SCHROED. A hybrid of Russian origin, probably between *P. nigra* and *P. nigra 'Italica'*. A large tree of broadly pyramidal habit.

deltoides MARSH. (*monilifera*). "Cottonwood"; "Necklace Poplar". A large, broad-headed, black poplar with rounded or angled twigs and broadly heart-shaped, slender pointed, bright green leaves. Now almost displaced in cultivation by its hybrid progeny. Eastern N. America.

'Eugenei' (Canadensis Group). A narrow tree with short, ascending branches; young leaves coppery in colour. Among the best poplars to grow commercially in this country. A hybrid between *P. nigra 'Italica'* and *P. 'Regenerata'*. Ours is a canker resistant form introduced by the late Lt. Col. Pratt, from Simon Louis' nursery in France.

× **euramericana.** See under *P.* × *canadensis*.

'Gelrica' (Canadensis Group). A vigorous male tree of continental origin, with whitish bark and coppery young growths. A hybrid between *P. 'Marilandica'* and *P. 'Serotina'*, usually breaking into leaf after the former and before the latter.

× **generosa** HENRY (*angulata* × *trichocarpa*). We were the first to distribute this remarkably vigorous hybrid, raised by Augustine Henry in 1912. Young trees sometimes increase in height at the rate of 2m. a year. Male and female trees are available, the males with long crimson-anthered catkins in April. Leaves conspicuously large on young trees, bright soft green above, turning yellow in autumn.

grandidentata MICHX. "Large-toothed Aspen". Medium-sized tree with rounded or ovate, deeply and broadly toothed leaves which are greyish-tomentose beneath at first, later glabrous and glaucous. Differing from *P. tremula* in its downy young shoots and from *P. tremuloides* in its large-toothed leaves. Eastern N. America. I. 1772.

'Henryana' (Canadensis Group). A large tree with wide-spreading, rounded head of branches. A male clone. Origin unknown.

'Hiltingbury Weeping' (*tremula 'Pendula'* × *tremuloides 'Pendula'*). A small tree with long, weeping branches forming a curtain of greyish-green trembling leaves. The result of a deliberate cross made in our Chandlers Ford nursery in 1962.

koreana REHD. A handsome balsam poplar of medium size, with conspicuous, large, bright apple-green leaves, white beneath and with red mid-ribs. One of the first trees to come into leaf in the early spring. Korea. Introduced by E. H. Wilson in 1918.

lasiocarpa OLIV. A magnificent medium-sized tree with stout angled, downy twigs. The leaves, often up to 30cm. long and 23cm. wide, are bright green with conspicuous red veins and leaf stalks. C. China. Discovered by Augustine Henry in 1888, introduced by E. H. Wilson in 1900. F.C.C. 1908.

laurifolia LEDEB. A slow-growing balsam poplar, making a medium-sized tree of elegant habit. The young shoots are strongly angled. Leaves narrowly ovate or lanceolate, whitish beneath. Siberia. I. about 1830.

POPULUS—*continued*

'Lloydii'. A large, spreading, female tree of moderate growth, a hybrid between *P. angulata* and *P. nigra betulifolia*.

'Maine' (*berolinensis* × *candicans*). An interesting American-raised, multiple hybrid of moderate growth.

'Marilandica' (Canadensis Group). A large, densely-branched female tree, with a wide head. Resembles *P. 'Serotina'*, but usually earlier leafing and its young leaves green. One of the best poplars for chalk-soils.

maximowiczii HENRY. A conspicuous, rapid growing balsam poplar of medium size, distinguished by its rounded, downy young twigs and its roundish, leathery, deeply-veined leaves with white undersurfaces and a twisted tip. Japan; Korea; Manchuria; Amur; Kamchatka. I. about 1890.

monilifera. See *P. deltoides*.

nigra L. "Black Poplar". A large, heavy-branched tree with characteristic burred trunk and glabrous twigs. Leaves rhomboid to ovate, slender-pointed, bright, shining green. C. & S. Europe; W. Asia. Long cultivated and naturalised in many countries. Often referred to as var. *typica*.

betulifolia TORR. "Manchester Poplar"; "Wilson's Variety". A picturesque, bushy-headed tree characterised by its downy shoots and young leaves. Tolerant of smoke pollution and formerly much planted in the industrial North of England. Native of eastern and central England.

'Italica' (*'Pyramidalis'*). "Lombardy Poplar". A large, narrow, columnar tree with close, erect branches. A male tree and one of the most effective of its habit, particularly suitable for forming a tall screen. Origin before 1750. Introduced to England in 1758.

'Italica Foemina'. The female form, a broader tree than *'Italica'* but of similar outline. The orange twigs are effective in winter.

'Plantierensis'. A fastigiate tree like the "Lombardy Poplar", which it has largely replaced in this country. It differs from the latter in its downy twigs, stronger lower branching and bushier, broader head. Appears to have the amalgamated characters of *betulifolia* and *'Italica'*.

'Pyramidalis'. See *'Italica'*.

'Thevestina'. A strong-growing, columnar tree, similar to the Lombardy Poplar, but female and with downy young shoots. In the Middle East and hotter climes than the British Isles, it is renowned for its white trunk.

viadri ASCHERS. & GRAEBN. A slender, erect-growing wild form. Introduced to England in 1893.

'Oxford' (*berolinensis* × *maximowiczii*). A vigorous growing large tree of American origin.

'Pacheri' (Canadensis Group). A fast-growing, large tree.

× **petrowskyana** SCHNEID. A very hardy hybrid between *P. deltoides* and possibly *P. laurifolia*. Branches angled and pubescent, leaves ovate, pale beneath. Origin before 1882.

'Regenerata' (Canadensis Group). A large, female tree with twiggy branches arching outwards. Branchlets slender; young leaves green, appearing about a fortnight earlier than those of *P. 'Serotina'*. Originated in a nursery near Paris in 1814 and now universally planted in industrial areas.

'Robusta' (Canadensis Group). A large, vigorous, male tree forming an open crown with a straight bole to summit. Young twigs minutely downy; young leaves an attractive coppery-red. A hybrid between *P. angulata* and *P. nigra 'Plantierensis'* raised by Messrs. Simon-Louis at Plantieres, near Metz (France) in 1895.

'Rumford'. A moderately vigorous tree of American origin, considered to be *P. angulata* × *P. nigra 'Plantierensis'*.

'Serotina' (Canadensis Group). A very vigorous, large, openly branched male tree with a usually uneven crown and glabrous twigs. Leaves late in appearing, copper-red when young. Catkins 7·5 to 10cm. long, with conspicuous red anthers. This commonly planted tree is said to have originated in France early in the 18th century.

'Serotina Aurea' (*'Van Geertii'*). (Canadensis Group). "Golden Poplar". Leaves clear golden-yellow in spring and early summer, becoming yellowish-green later then golden yellow in autumn. Originated as a sport in Van Geert's nursery at Ghent in 1871.

'Serotina Erecta' (Canadensis Group). A large, columnar form.

POPULUS—*continued*

sieboldii MIQ. "Japanese Aspen". Medium-sized tree with downy shoots and ovate, minutely-toothed, deep green leaves. Japan. C. 1881.

simonii CARR. A medium-sized, early-leafing, balsam poplar with slender, angled, glabrous, red-brown twigs and rhomboid leaves, pale beneath. Liable to canker. N. China. I. 1862.

'Fastigiata'. A columnar tree, the branches long and upright. Makes an excellent dense hedge or screen.

suaveolens FISCH. A very ornamental, medium-sized balsam poplar with rounded twigs and ovate-lanceolate, slender-pointed leaves pale beneath. E. Siberia. I. 1834.

szechuanica SCHNEID. A strikingly handsome balsam poplar making a large tree. Leaves large, whitish-glaucescent beneath, with crimson mid-rib, reddish when young. Fast-growing, but needs shelter from late spring frosts. W. China. I. 1908.

tibetica SCHNEID. One of the most ornamental poplars, differing from the type in its larger leaves, which resemble those of *P. lasiocarpa*. W. China. I. 1904.

tacamahacca. See *P. balsamifera*.

tremula L. "Aspen". A medium-sized, suckering tree. Leaves prominently-toothed, late in appearing and hanging late in the autumn when they turn a clear butter yellow. Petioles slender, compressed, causing the leaves to tremble and quiver in the slightest breeze. Catkins long and grey draping the branchlets in late winter or early spring. One of the commonest sources of wood for the match industry. Widely distributed in Europe and Asia extending to N. Africa.

'Pendula'. The "Weeping Aspen"; one of the most effective, small, weeping trees, especially attractive in February with its abundance of long purplish-grey, male catkins.

tremuloides MICHX. "American Aspen". A small to medium-sized tree, mainly distinguished from our native species *P. tremula*, by the pale yellowish bark of its young trunks and branches, and by its smaller, finely and evenly toothed leaves. Its catkins are also more slender. One of the most widely distributed of North American trees, being found in the mountains of N. Mexico northwards to Alaska. C. 1812.

'Pendula'. "Parasol de St. Julien". A small, pendulous, female tree which originated in France in 1865.

trichocarpa HOOK. "Black Cottonwood". The fastest and tallest growing of the balsam poplars, reaching a height of over 30m., and up to 60m. in its native habitat. Bark of young trees characteristically peeling. Buds large and sticky; leaves pale and reticulate beneath, strongly balsam-scented when unfolding. Autumn colour rich yellow. Liable to canker. Alaska; Canada; W. United States; Mexico. I. 1892.

violascens DODE. A large, vigorous and very ornamental tree related to *P. lasiocarpa*, resembling that species in its large conspicuous leaves. China. C. 1921.

wilsonii SCHNEID. A highly ornamental, medium-sized species, somewhat resembling *P. lasiocarpa*. Leaves large, up to 20cm. long, bright sea-green in colour. Branchlets thick, rounded, of a polished violet-green shade. C. and W. China. I. 1907.

yunnanensis DODE. A fast-growing, medium-sized balsam poplar similar to *P. szechuanica*. Leaves with white under-surfaces and reddish stalks and mid-ribs. S.W. China. I. before 1905.

"PORTUGAL LAUREL". See *PRUNUS lusitanica*.

POTENTILLA—Rosaceae—The shrubby potentillas are rich in good qualities. They are very hardy, dwarf to medium-sized shrubs, thriving in any soil, and in sun or partial shade. Their flowers, like small, single white or yellow roses, are displayed over a long season, beginning in June and in some forms lasting until November. Though they are shade tolerant they reach the zenith of their flowering when growing in full sun.

arbuscula D. DON (*fruticosa arbuscula*). A dwarf shrub related to *P. fruticosa*, but very distinct with shaggy branches due to the presence of large, brown stipules. Sage-green leaves with five leaflets. Large, rich yellow flowers are produced continuously from mid-summer to late autumn. Himalaya. A.M. 1925. A.M.T. 1965. A.G.M. 1969.

'Beesii' (*fruticosa 'Beesii'*) (*'Nana Argentea'*). A delightful dwarf shrub which displays its golden flowers on mounds of silvery foliage. A.G.M. 1956. A.M.T. 1966.

POTENTILLA—*continued*

bulleyana FLETCHER. A small shrub with silky-hairy leaves and bright yellow flowers. Taller growing and more erect than the type.

rigida HAND.-MAZZ. (*P. rigida*). A small, compact shrub with bristly stems covered with conspicuous papery stipules and leaves with only three leaflets; flowers bright yellow. Himalaya. I. 1906. Apart from the above described (*rigida*), we also grow an attractive form with smaller, silvery leaves and slightly smaller flowers.

'Beanii' (Friedrichsenii Group) (*fruticosa 'Beanii'*) (*'Leucantha'*). A dwarf shrub with dark foliage and white flowers.

dahurica NESTL. (*glabra*) (*glabrata*) (*fruticosa glabra*). A very variable species, rarely more than 1·5m. in height, usually much less. Both stems and leaves may be glabrous or hairy, depending on the form. The flowers are white and freely produced. N. China; Siberia. I. 1822. It has given rise to several forms of which we offer the following:—

'Abbotswood'. Dwarf shrub of spreading habit with dark foliage. Flowers white, plentifully and continuously produced. A.M.T. 1965.

'Farrer's White' (*fruticosa 'Farrer's White'*). A small shrub of somewhat erect habit, with multitudes of white flowers during summer.

'Hersii' (*fruticosa hersii*). A free-flowering, small shrub of erect habit. Leaves sage-green; flowers white. The same clone or a seedling of it, is offered on the Continent under the name 'Snowflake'.

'Manchu' (*fruticosa mandshurica* HORT.). A charming, dwarf, low-spreading shrub, bearing a continuous succession of white flowers on mats of greyish foliage. A.M. 1924. A.G.M. 1969.

'Mount Everest' (*fruticosa 'Mount Everest'*). A small, robust shrub up to 1·5m. of dense, rounded habit. Flowers white, produced intermittently throughout summer.

rhodocalyx (*fruticosa rhodocalyx*). A small, upright shrub of subtle, gentle quality, the aristocrat of a popular group. The rather small, somewhat cup-shaped flowers with reddish calyces, nod on slender stems.

'Subalbicans' (*fruticosa subalbicans*). A robust shrub up to 1·5m., with stiff, hairy stems, and clusters of comparatively large, white flowers.

veitchii JESSON (*fruticosa veitchii*). A small, graceful bush, about 1m. high, with arching branches bearing pure white flowers. W. and C. China. A.G.M. 1969.

'Dart's Golddigger'. A splendid, dwarf shrub of Dutch origin. Dense and compact habit, with light grey-green foliage and large butter-yellow flowers. A seedling probably of *P. arbuscula*.

'Daydawn'. A small shrub with flowers of an unusual shade of peach-pink suffused cream.

'Eastleigh Cream' (*parvifolia 'Gold Drop'* × *sulphurascens*). A small shrub of dense habit, spreading to form a low mound. Leaves green; flowers cream, 2·5cm. across. Raised in our Eastleigh Nursery in 1969.

'Elizabeth' (Sulphurascens Group) (*arbuscula* × *dahurica 'Manchu'*) (*fruticosa 'Elizabeth'*). A magnificent hybrid raised in our nurseries about 1950, forming a dome-shaped bush 1m. × 1·2m. and studded from late spring to early autumn with large, rich canary-yellow flowers. This plant is wrongly distributed throughout European nurseries as *P. arbuscula*. A.M.T. 1965. A.G.M. 1969.

× friedrichsenii SPAETH (*dahurica* × *fruticosa*). A vigorous shrub up to 2m., with slightly grey-green foliage and light yellow flowers. Originated as a seedling in Spaeth's Nursery in Berlin, in 1895. The clone in cultivation is sometimes referred to under the name *'Berlin Beauty'*. Other clones include *'Beanii'* and *'Ochroleuca'* which see. Both the latter and the present plant are excellent as informal hedges.

fruticosa L. A dense bush averaging 1 to 1·5m. high, producing yellow flowers from May to September. Leaves small, divided into five to seven, narrow leaflets. This is generally treated as a variable species, being distributed throughout the northern hemisphere, including the North of England and the West of Ireland. It is a parent of numerous hybrids.

grandiflora SCHLECHT. A shrub up to 1·5m., of strong erect growth with sage-green leaves and dense clusters of large, canary-yellow flowers. The clone *'Jackman's Variety'* is a seedling of this variety. F.C.C.T. 1966. A.G.M. 1969.

'Northman'. A small, erect shrub with sage-green leaves and small, rich yellow flowers.

POTENTILLA—*continued*

tenuiloba HORT. Erect growing shrub up to 1·5m., with narrow leaflets and bright yellow flowers. The clone in cultivation is probably of North American origin.

glabra. See *P. dahurica.*

'Hurstbourne' (*fruticosa 'Hurstbourne'*). Small shrub with bright yellow flowers.

'Jackman's Variety'. See under *P. fruticosa grandiflora.*

'Katherine Dykes' (*fruticosa 'Katherine Dykes'*). A shrub up to 2m., producing an abundance of primrose yellow flowers in summer. A.M. 1944. A.G.M. 1969.

'Lady Daresbury' (*fruticosa 'Lady Daresbury'*). A small shrub forming a broad, dome-shaped bush of arching branches; flowers large, yellow, continuously produced, but especially abundant in late spring and autumn.

'Logan' (Sulphurascens Group). A small shrub up to 1·5m., of bushy habit, producing masses of pale yellow flowers during summer.

'Longacre' (Sulphurascens Group) (*fruticosa 'Longacre'*). A dense, dwarf, mat-forming shrub. Flowers large, of a bright, almost sulphur-yellow. A.M.T. 1965

'Maanelys' (*'Moonlight'*) (*fruticosa 'Maanelys'*). A small shrub of Scandinavian origin, producing a continuous succession of soft yellow flowers from May to November.

'Milkmaid'. Small shrub with slender, upright stems and leaves with three to five leaflets. Flowers flattened, 2·5 to 3cm. wide, creamy-white, nodding or inclined on slender peduncles. A hybrid of *P. dahurica rhodocalyx*, raised in our nurseries in 1963.

'Minstead Dwarf' (*fruticosa 'Minstead Dwarf'*). A dwarf shrub forming a low hummock of green leaves and masses of bright yellow flowers.

'Ochroleuca' (Friedrichsenii Group) (*fruticosa 'Ochroleuca'*). A small, erect shrub up to 2m., similar to *P.×friedrichsenii*, but with cream-coloured flowers. Both make an excellent informal hedge.

parvifolia LEHM. (*fruticosa parvifolia*). A dense, compact shrub of semi-erect habit, seldom exceeding 1m. in height. Leaves small, with seven leaflets, the lower two pairs forming a whorl. Flowers golden yellow, comparatively small but abundantly produced during early summer, and more sparingly until October. C. Asia. A.G.M. 1969. A very popular species which has given rise to several forms in cultivation, of which we offer the following:—

'Buttercup' (*fruticosa 'Buttercup'*). A small shrub of compact habit producing small, deep yellow flowers over a long period.

'Gold Drop' (*fruticosa 'Gold Drop'*). A dwarf shrub of compact habit, with small, neat leaves and small, bright golden-yellow flowers. Often wrongly grown under the name *P. fruticosa farreri.*

'Klondike' (*fruticosa 'Klondike'*). A first-rate shrub of dwarf habit, similar to 'Gold Drop', but with larger flowers. A.M.T. 1965.

'Primrose Beauty' (*fruticosa 'Primrose Beauty'*). A small, spreading, free-flowering shrub with arching branches, grey-green foliage and primrose-yellow flowers with deeper yellow centres. A.M.T. 1965. A.G.M. 1969.

'Ruth' (*fruticosa 'Ruth'*). A small shrub of upright habit with nodding, slightly cup-shaped, creamy-yellow flowers with red-flushed calyces. A hybrid of *P. dahurica rhodocalyx*, raised in our nurseries in 1960.

salesoviana STEPHEN. An unusual, dwarf shrub with erect, hollow, reddish-brown stems, bearing large, dark green, pinnate leaves, white beneath. Flowers nodding, white, occasionally tinged pink, produced in terminal corymbs in June and July. Siberia. I. 1823.

'Stoker's Variety' (*fruticosa 'Stoker's Variety'*). A small shrub up to 1·5m., of upright habit. Small, densely-crowded leaves and abundantly produced rich yellow flowers.

×**sulphurascens** HAND.-MAZZ. (*arbuscula×dahurica*). A rather variable hybrid which has given rise to several of the best garden potentillas, including *'Elizabeth'*, *'Longacre'* and *'Logan'*, which see.

'Sunset'. A small shrub with flowers of an unusual colour varying between deep orange and brick red. Best grown in partial shade.

'Tangerine'. A dwarf, wide-spreading shrub forming a dense mound. Flowers of a pale coppery-yellow, which is best developed on plants growing in partial shade.

tridentata AIT. A prostrate sub-shrub forming low tufts or mats. Leaves trifoliolate, with oblanceolate leaflets, three-toothed at the apex. Flowers white during summer. An excellent plant for paving or scree. Eastern N. America. C. 1789.

POTENTILLA—*continued*

'Vilmoriniana' (*fruticosa 'Vilmoriniana'*). A splendid, erect-branched shrub up to 2m., with very silvery leaves and cream coloured flowers. The best tall, erect *Potentilla*. A.G.M. 1926. A.M.T. 1965.

'Walton Park' (*fruticosa 'Walton Park'*). A small, very floriferous shrub, forming a low compact bush with large, bright yellow flowers.

'William Purdom' (*fruticosa purdomii* HORT.). A small shrub of semi-erect growth up to 1·5m., with an abundance of light yellow flowers. F.C.C.T. 1966. A.G.M. 1969.

PRINOS verticillatus. See *Ilex verticillata*.

PRINSEPIA—Rosaceae—A small genus of uncommon and interesting, usually spiny shrubs. All do best in an open position, and succeed in any fertile soil.

sinensis BEAN. A rare, lax-habited shrub up to 2m. Flowers slender stalked, produced in clusters of two to five in the leaf axils of the previous year's wood, buttercup yellow, 12 to 20mm. across, clustering the arching stems in early spring. Fruits red, produced in August. Manchuria. I. 1908.

uniflora BATAL. A spreading shrub 1·5 to 2m. high, with spiny grey stems and linear leaves. Flowers white, in axillary clusters of one to three on the previous year's wood, in late April or early May. Fruits, purplish-red, like-short-stalked Morello cherries, rarely produced except during a hot summer. N.W. China. Introduced by William Purdom in 1911.

utilis ROYLE. An attractive, vigorous, small to medium-sized shrub with strongly spiny, arching, green stems. Flowers white, in axillary racemes during late March and early April. Himalaya. C. 1919.

"PRIVET". See *LIGUSTRUM*.

†***PROSTANTHERA—Labiatae**—A beautiful genus of small to medium-sized, floriferous, aromatic shrubs, native of Australasia. Ideal for the cool conservatory or in a warm sheltered corner in the milder counties. Inclined to become chlorotic on a shallow chalky soil. Established specimens are best pruned back hard immediately after flowering.

aspalathoides BENTH. A small, compact shrub with tiny, almost linear, dark green, aromatic leaves and red flowers. Australia.

lasianthos LABILL. Medium-sized to large shrub of erect growth. Leaves comparatively large, lanceolate. The purple tinted white flowers appear in branched, terminal racemes during spring. Tasmania; Australia. I. 1808. F.C.C. 1888.

melissifolia parvifolia SEALY. This pretty shrub has been confused with *P. sieberi*; flowers bright lilac, nearly 2·5cm. across, borne abundantly in early spring.

ovalifolia R. BR. An elegant, small to medium-sized shrub with small, olive-green leaves and soft lilac-mauve or purple flowers on long, drooping branches in spring. Australia. A.M. 1952.

rotundifolia R. BR. A beautiful small to medium-sized shrub of dense habit, with tiny rounded or ovate leaves. The attractive heliotrope flowers innundate the branches during spring. The massed effect of the flowers is quite staggering. I. 1824. A.M. 1924.

PRUNUS—Rosaceae—This large genus includes many of the most beautiful flowering trees suitable for temperate regions. The flowers of *Prunus* have solitary styles as against those of *Malus* and *Pyrus* which have five. Under *Prunus* are included the following:—Almond (*P. dulcis*); Apricot (*P. armeniaca*); Bird Cherry (*P. padus*); Common Laurel (*P. laurocerasus*); Peach (*P. persica*) and Portugal Laurel (*P. lusitanica*). For "Japanese Cherries" see end of this section.

With the exception of most of the evergreen species, all require an open, preferably sunny position, in any ordinary soil, being particularly happy in soils containing lime or chalk. It must, however, be emphasised that the Cherry Laurel (*P. laurocerasus*) will tend to become chlorotic in poor, shallow chalk-soils, and, as an alternative, the Portugal Laurel (*P. lusitanica*) should be planted.

'Accolade (*sargentii* × *subhirtella*). An outstanding cherry; a small tree with spreading branches and semi-double, rich-pink flowers 4cm. in diameter in pendulous clusters, produced in great profusion in early spring. A.M. 1952. F.C.C. 1954. A.G.M. 1961.

americana MARSH. "American Red Plum". A small tree of graceful habit. Flowers white, 2·5cm. across, borne in clusters of two to five; fruits up to 2·5cm. wide, yellow, finally bright red, but not freely produced in the British Isles. United States; S. Canada. I. 1768.

PRUNUS—*continued*

×**amygdalo-persica** REHD. (*dulcis*×*persica*). A hybrid between the Peach and Almond, first recorded about 1623. We offer the following clone:—

'Pollardii' (*P.* ×*pollardii*). This beautiful, small tree differs from the Almond in its larger, richer pink flowers. Said to have originated in Australia about 1904. Our stock tree bears fruit which leaves us in no doubt as to its hybrid origin. F.C.C. 1935. A.G.M. 1937.

amygdalus. See *P. dulcis*.

armeniaca L. "Apricot". The wild species. A small, round-headed tree with white or pink-tinged, single flowers in March and April, followed by yellow, red-tinged fruits. C. Asia; China. Widely cultivated and naturalised in S. Europe. The fruiting clones are widely cultivated; please see our Fruit Catalogue.

ansu MAXIM. (*P. ansu*). A small tree with rounded leaves and pink flowers in April; fruits red. Often confused in gardens with *P. mume* from which it differs in its darker, usually purple-flushed shoots and its larger flowers with strongly reflexed sepals. N. China, long cultivated in Japan and Korea. A.M. 1944.

'Flore Pleno' (*mume 'Grandiflora'*) (*mume 'Rosea Plena'*). A beautiful form with semi-double flowers, carmine in bud opening to pink, densely clustered on purple-flushed shoots in March or April. Usually found in gardens under one or other of the above synonyms. A.M. 1934.

avium L. "Gean"; "Mazzard"; "Wild Cherry". One of the most attractive of our native woodland trees. A medium-sized to large tree with smooth grey bark turning mahogany red, peeling and deeply fissured with age. The white cup-shaped flowers are borne in clusters and open with the leaves in late April or early May. Fruits small and shiny, reddish-purple, bitter or sweet to the taste. Autumn foliage crimson. From this species are derived most of the Sweet Cherries. Europe (including British Isles); W. Asia.

'Decumana' (*P. macrophylla*). An unusual form with large flowers 2·5cm. across, and very large leaves up to 23cm. long.

'Pendula'. A form with semi-pendulous, rather stiff branches.

'Plena' (*'Multiplex'*). "Double Gean". One of the loveliest of all flowering trees, its branches wreathed with masses of drooping, double-white flowers. Cultivated since 1700. A.G.M. 1924. F.C.C. 1964.

besseyi BAILEY (*pumila besseyi*). "Sand Cherry". A small shrub with greyish-green leaves turning rusty-purple in autumn. Clusters of tiny white flowers are massed along the branches in May. Fruits rounded, black with purplish bloom, rarely produced in the British Isles. Central United States. I. 1892.

×**blireana** ANDRE (*cerasifera 'Pissardii'*×*mume 'Alphandii'*). A beautiful large shrub or small tree with leaves of a metallic coppery-purple. Flowers double, over 2·5cm. across, slightly fragrant, rose-pink, with the leaves in April. Garden origin 1895. A.M. 1914. F.C.C. 1923. A.G.M. 1928.

'Moseri'. Differs from *P.* ×*blireana* in its slightly smaller, pale pink flowers, and paler foliage. A.M. 1912.

†**campanulata** MAXIM. "Formosan Cherry". A delightful, small, round-headed tree. The dark, rose-red flowers are produced in dense clusters during early spring. Only suitable outside in the mildest areas. S. China; Formosa; S. Japan. C. 1899. A.M. 1935.

'Plena'. A form with small, double red flowers.

canescens BOIS. A shrubby, medium-sized cherry with attractive dark mahogany peeling bark and slender, willowy branches. The polished dark brown inner bark is exposed on the older branches. Leaves greyish-green, downy, coarsely-toothed; flowers small, pink tinted, in early April; fruits red, pleasantly flavoured. China. I. 1898.

canescens×**serrula.** An unusual and not unattractive hybrid. A small tree, retaining the ornamental bark of *P. serrula* and possessing the long, willowy stems of *P. canescens* which, like the leaves, are downy. The flowers also resemble those of the latter, but are slightly larger. Flowering during April.

cappolin. See *P. serotina salicifolia*.

cerasifera EHRH. (*myrobalana*) (*korolkowii*) (*divaricata*). "Myrobalan"; "Cherry Plum". A small tree with greenish young shoots. The myriads of small white flowers crowd the twigs in March, sometimes earlier or later. Mature trees sometimes bear red or yellow "cherry-plums". An excellent dense hedging shrub. Balkans; Caucasus; W. Asia. C. during the 16th century. A.M. 1977.

PRUNUS—*continued*

cerasifera 'Atropurpurea'. See *'Pissardii'.*

'Diversifolia' (*'Aspleniifolia'*). Leaves bronze-purple, varying in shape from ovate to lanceolate, often irregularly toothed or lobed. Flowers white. A sport of *'Pissardii'.*

'Feketiana'. See *'Pendula'.*

'Hessei'. A medium-sized shrubby form with leaves pale green on emerging, becoming bronze-purple and mottled creamy-white. Flowers snow-white, crowding the slender purple shoots in late March.

'Lindsayae'. An attractive tree of graceful habit with flat, almond-pink flowers. Introduced from Iran by Miss Nancy Lindsay. A.M. 1948.

'Nigra'. Leaves and stems blackish-purple; flowers very prolific, pink fading to blush. A very effective, small tree flowering in March and April. F.C.C. 1939. The clone *'Vesuvius'* is almost, if not, identical.

'Pendula' (*'Feketiana'*). A form with pendulous, interlacing stems, green leaves and white flowers.

'Pissardii' (*'Atropurpurea'*). "Purple-leaved Plum". A very popular form with dark red young foliage turning to a deep purple. Flowers in great profusion, white, pink in bud, appearing in late March and early April; fruits purple, only occasionally produced. If grown as shrubs, both this and the clone *'Nigra'* are excellent hedging plants. Originally discovered as a sport, sometime before 1880 by Mons. Pissard, gardener to the Shah of Persia. F.C.C. 1884. A.G.M. 1928.

'Rosea'. Leaves bronze-purple at first, becoming bronze-green, then green in late summer. Flowers of a clear salmon pink, paling with age, crowding the slender purple stems. Distributed by Messrs. B. Ruys Ltd., of Holland, who believe the plant to be of hybrid origin (*P. cerasifera 'Nigra'* × *P. spinosa*). Sometimes found in gardens under the name *spinosa 'Rosea'.* It is looser and more open in habit than *P. spinosa* with slightly larger flowers less densely crowded on the branchlets, which are sparsely spiny.

'Trailblazer'. Similar in flower to *'Pissardii'.* Leaves larger, becoming bronze-green above.

'Vesuvius'. See under *'Nigra'.*

†**cerasoides rubea** INGRAM. "Kingdon Ward's Carmine Cherry". A lovely tree of small to medium size, related to *P. campanulata.* Flowers rose-pink, deeper in bud, but not generally free-flowering in the British Isles. W. China; Upper Burma. Introduced by Kingdon Ward in 1931.

cerasus L. "Sour Cherry". Of interest as being one of the parents of the "Morello Cherries". A small bushy tree with comparatively dark slender stems and producing dense clusters of white flowers in late April or May followed by red or black fruits, acid to the taste. S.W. Asia. Widely cultivated and naturalised in Europe.

'James H. Veitch'. See *P. 'Fugenzo'* under Japanese Cherries.

'Rhexii' (*P. ranunculiflora*). A form with very showy, double white flowers, 2·5 to 4cm. across. Known to have been in cultivation in England since the 16th century.

'Semperflorens'. "All Saints Cherry". A floriferous, and somewhat pendulous, small tree producing its white flowers intermittently throughout the spring and summer.

×**cistena** KOEHNE. (*'Cistena'*) "Purple-leaf Sand Cherry". A beautiful shrub, up to 2m., with rich red leaves and white flowers in spring; fruits black-purple. An excellent hedging plant. Garden origin before 1910.

communis ARCANGELI not HUDS. See *P. dulcis.*

concinna KOEHNE. A very beautiful, shrubby, small-leaved cherry of medium size, producing its white or pink-tinted flowers profusely before the purplish young leaves, in March or early April. China. Introduced by Wilson in 1907.

conradinae KOEHNE. This early flowering Cherry is a small tree of elegant habit. In a sheltered position its fragrant, white or pinkish flowers, which are produced very freely, give a welcome foretaste of spring, usually during the latter half of February. China. Introduced by E. H. Wilson in 1907. A.M. 1923.

'Malifolia'. Carmine buds and pink flowers about 3cm. across; slightly later-flowering than the type.

'Semiplena'. A form with a few extra petals, longer-lasting than those of the type, appearing in late February and March. A.M. 1935.

PRUNUS—*continued*

cornuta STEUD. (Padus Section). "Himalayan Bird Cherry". A medium-sized tree differing from *P. padus* in its larger leaves and fruits, the latter being glossy, brown-crimson and carried in drooping, grape-like clusters 10 to 13cm. long from mid-August onwards. Flowers white, carried in long, cylindrical racemes in May. Himalaya. I. 1860.

cyclamina KOEHNE. A delightful cherry, forming an elegant, small tree. The bright pink flowers profusely borne in April, have reflexed sepals. Unfolding leaves bright copper. C. China. Introduced by E. H. Wilson in 1907.

×**dasycarpa** EHRH. (*armeniaca*×*cerasifera*). The "Purple" or "Black Apricot". A small tree with purple twigs and a profusion of white flowers, appearing before the leaves in March. Fruits black, with a purple bloom, apricot-flavoured, rarely produced in the British Isles.

davidiana FRANCH. This Chinese peach is one of the earliest trees to bloom, and on that account should be given a sheltered position. A small, erect tree with finely-toothed, long-pointed leaves. The white or rose-coloured flowers open any time between January and March. Like all deciduous trees and shrubs which flower early on the leafless branches, it is very desirable to select a site with a suitable background. China. Introduced by the Abbe David in 1865.

'Alba'. Flowers white. F.C.C. 1892. A.G.M. 1927.

'Rubra'. Flowers pink.

dawyckensis SEALY. A small tree with shining, dark brown bark and downy young shoots and leaves, glaucous beneath. Flowers pale pink in April, followed by amber-red cherries. A tree of uncertain origin, first discovered in the famous gardens at Dawyck, Scotland, and thought to have been introduced by E. H. Wilson in 1907. Rehder suggested that it might be the hybrid *P. canescens*× *P. dielsiana*.

dehiscens. See *P. tangutica*.

dielsiana SCHNEID. (*dielsiana laxa*). A small floriferous tree related to *P. cyclamina*, but later flowering and never so tall. The trunk and primary branches are a dark mahogany-red. Flowers white or pale pink, with conspicuous stamens, borne on long, downy pedicels before the leaves in April or early May; fruits red. C. China. Introduced by E. H. Wilson in 1907.

laxa. See *P. dielsiana*.

domestica insititia POIR. (*P. insititia*). "Bullace". A small tree with occasionally spiny, brownish, pubescent branches and small white flowers in early spring, followed by rounded, purple, red, yellow or green fruits. Caucasus. Widely naturalised in hedges and woods, including the British Isles.

dulcis D. A. WEBB (*amygdalus*) (*communis*). "Common Almond". A universal favourite and one of the best spring flowering trees. A small tree with lanceolate, long-pointed, finely-toothed leaves. Flowers 2·5 to 5cm. across, pink, borne singly or in pairs in March and April. The edible almonds of commerce are mainly imported from South Europe. Distributed in the wild from North Africa to West Asia, but widely grown and extensively naturalised in the Mediterranean region. Cultivated in England since the 16th century or earlier.

'Alba'. Flowers white, single.

'Erecta'. A broadly columnar form up to 6m. or more, with erect branches and pink flowers.

'Macrocarpa'. Flowers very pale pink or white, up to 5cm. across. One of the best of the edible cultivars with large fruits. A.M. 1931.

nana. See *P. tenella*.

'Praecox'. A form with pale pink flowers opening two weeks earlier than the type, very often in late February. F.C.C. 1925.

'Roseoplena'. "Double Almond". Flowers pale pink, double.

×**dunbarii** REHD. (*americana*×*maritima*). A large shrub with sharply serrate, acuminate leaves, white flowers and purple fruits. Origin about 1900.

×**effusa.** See *P.* ×*gondouinii*.

emarginata EATON. A small, elegant, deciduous tree with a dense, spreading head. Flowers small, creamy-white, produced in dense clusters at the end of the branches in May, followed by small, dark fruits. We grow the variety *mollis* with downy, pointed leaves. The bark is bitter to the taste. Western N. America. I. 1865.

PRUNUS—*continued*

fenzliana FRITSCH. A small, wide-spreading, shrubby Almond, closely related to *P. dulcis*, but with narrower, sea-green leaves. The flowers, carmine in bud opening soft pink, are conspicuous on the naked branches during March. Caucasus. C. 1890.

fruticosa PALL. "Ground Cherry". A small, spreading shrub with small, white flowers and dark red fruits. When grown as a standard it forms a neat mop-headed miniature tree. C. and E. Europe to Siberia. C. 1587.

'Pendula'. A form with slender pendulous branches.

'Variegata'. Leaves variegated yellowish-white, but not very constant.

glandulosa THUNB. "Chinese Bush Cherry". A small, bushy shrub of neat habit with slender, erect shoots covered in April by numerous, small, pink or white flowers. Grows best in a warm, sunny position. C. and N. China, long cultivated in Japan. C. 1835.

'Albiplena'. A very beautiful shrub, each shoot pendant with a wealth of comparatively large, double, white flowers in early May. Excellent for forcing. C. 1852. A.M. 1950.

'Sinensis' (*japonica 'Flore Roseoplena'*). Flowers double, bright pink. A very popular shrub in Victorian and Edwardian gardens. C. 1774. A.M. 1968. Excellent for forcing.

× **gondouinii** REHD. (*avium* × *cerasus*) (× *effusa*). "Duke Cherry". A variable medium-sized tree producing white flowers in spring, followed by somewhat acid, red fruits. Several clones are grown for their fruits.

grayana MAXIM. (Padus Section). A small, Japanese bird cherry. Leaves coarsely-toothed, flowers white in erect, glabrous racemes 7·5 to 10cm. long, produced in June; fruits small, black. Japan. I. 1900.

'Hally Jolivette' ((*subhirtella* × *yedoensis*) × *subhirtella*) (Yedoensis Group). A small, graceful tree or large shrub raised at the Arnold Arboretum, U.S.A. Its slender, willowy stems are inundated in early spring with small, semi-double, blush-white flowers which continue over a long period.

× **hillieri** HILLIER (*incisa* × *sargentii*). Raised in our nurseries before 1928, the original is now a broad-crowned tree 10m. high, and in spring is like a soft pink cloud. In favourable seasons the autumn colour is gorgeous. A.M. 1959.

'Spire'. Possibly the best small street tree raised this century. A conical tree attaining 8m. high, and with a basal width of about 3m. Flowers soft pink; leaves with rich autumn tints.

'Hilling's Weeping'. A small tree with long, slender, almost perpendicularly weeping branches, wreathed with pure white flowers in early April.

†***ilicifolia** WALP. "Holly-leaved Cherry". A dense, medium-sized to large shrub. Leaves broadly ovate to orbicular, undulate, leathery and edged with spreading spines. Flowers white, in short racemes 5cm. long, in June and July, followed by red fruits. California (U.S.A.).

incana BATSCH. "Willow Cherry". A small to medium-sized, erect-branched shrub of loose habit. The slender leaves are white woolly beneath. Flowers pink occasionally followed by red, cherry-like fruits. S.E. Europe and Asia Minor. I. 1815.

incisa THUNB. "Fuji Cherry". A lovely Japanese species, generally shrubby, but occasionally a small tree, blooming with the greatest freedom in March. Leaves small, incisely-toothed, beautifully tinted in autumn. Flowers small, white, pink-tinged in bud and appearing pink at a distance; fruits only occasionally produced, small, purple-black. Makes an unusual hedge and long used by the Japanese for Bonsai. C. 1910. A.M. 1927. A.G.M. 1930.

'February Pink'. An early-flowering form with pale pink flowers in February or earlier.

'Moerheimii'. See *P. 'Moerheimii'*.

'Praecox'. A winter-flowering form with white flowers, pale pink in bud. A.M. 1957. F.C.C. 1973.

integrifolia SARG. See *P. lyonii*.

jacquemontii HOOK. f. A small to medium-sized shrub of straggling habit, with small leaves. Flowers pink, opening in April. Fruits only occasionally produced, small, red. Happiest in a well-drained, sunny position. N.W. Himalaya; Tibet; Afghanistan. I. 1879.

PRUNUS—*continued*

japonica THUNB. A small shrub with slender, wiry branches. The small, single white or pale pink flowers appear with the leaves in April; fruits only occasionally produced, dark red. C. China east to Korea. Long cultivated in Japan. I. 1860.

nakaii REHD. A geographical form introduced from Korea in 1918.

× **juddii** E. ANDERSON (*sargentii* × *yedoensis*). A small tree with leaves copper-tinted when unfolding, deep crimson in the fall. Flowers pale pink in late April or early May. Originated at the Arnold Arboretum, U.S.A., in 1914.

kansuensis REHD. Small tree akin to *P. persica*, with long, spray-like branches carrying pink-tinged, white blossoms in January or February. N.W. China. I. 1914. A.M. 1957.

korolkowii. See *P. cerasifera*.

kurilensis MIYABE (*nipponica kurilensis*). Small, bushy shrub of slow growth, related to *P. nipponica*, with coarsely-toothed leaves, rusty brown when young. Flowers in April, before the leaves, comparatively large, white or pink-tinged; fruits purplish black. Japan. I. 1905.

'Ruby'. A lovely form, its erect branches a mass of pale pink blossoms with conspicuous purplish-red calyces in early April.

Kursar (*campanulata* × *kurilensis*). A very beautiful small tree raised by Capt. Collingwood Ingram, the leading western authority on Japanese Cherries. The flowers, though small, are coloured a rich deep pink and are borne in great profusion with, or just before, the reddish-bronze, young leaves, in March or early April. A.M. 1952.

lanata MACK. & BUSH. Small tree with a rounded head of branches. Leaves obovate, downy beneath; flowers small, white, occasionally followed by red or yellow fruits. C. United States. I. 1903.

lannesiana WILS. (*serrulata lannesiana*) (*serrulata hortensis*). Under this name Ernest Wilson described a pink, single-flowered Japanese Cherry of garden origin. The wild type with fragrant white flowers he named *P. lannesiana albida* (now *P. speciosa*). Japanese botanists use the name *P. lannesiana* to cover the numerous garden cherries with large single or double flowers many of which are hybrids between *P. speciosa* and *P. serrulata spontanea*.

albida. See *P. speciosa*.

speciosa. See *P. speciosa*.

latidentata pleuroptera INGRAM. A small, round-headed tree with a peculiar mottled trunk. Flowers small, white, in drooping clusters with the leaves in April. China. I. 1908.

***laurocerasus** L. "Common Laurel"; "Cherry Laurel". A vigorous, wide-spreading, evergreen shrub attaining 6m. or more in height, by as much, or more, across. Leaves large, leathery, dark shining green. Mainly grown for screening purposes or for shelter in game coverts, but attractive in April when bearing its erect axillary and terminal racemes of small, white flowers, followed by cherry-like fruits, red at first, finally black. Not at its best on shallow, chalk-soils. E. Europe; Asia Minor. Extensively planted and naturalised in the British Isles. I. 1576. Although some of the forms appear to have a distinct geographical distribution we have treated all as cultivars.

There are few other evergreens more tolerant of shade and drip from overhanging trees than the laurel in its many forms. Several of the more compact, erect-growing cultivars make excellent tub specimens where *Laurus nobilis*, the "Bay", is insufficiently hardy.

'Angustifolia'. A form with ascending branches and narrow leaves similar to those of '*Zabeliana*'.

'Camelliifolia'. A large shrub or small tree. Leaves dark green twisted and curled.

'Caucasica'. A vigorous form of upright growth with rather narrow leaves.

'Herbergii'. Erect-growing form of dense, compact habit, with oblanceolate, polished green leaves. Excellent for hedging.

'Latifolia' ('*Macrophylla*'). A tall, vigorous, large-leaved form.

'Magnoliifolia'. An imposing evergreen with glossy leaves up to 30cm. long and 10cm. wide. The largest-leaved laurel.

'Mischeana'. A most ornamental clone slowly forming a dense, rather flat topped mound of dark, lustrous green, oblong leaves. A superb lawn specimen. Attractive also when in flower, the short, erect racemes packed along the stems.

PRUNUS—*continued*

laurocerasus 'Otinii'. A large, compact bush with large, very dark green, lustrous leaves.

'Otto Luyken'. A low, compact shrub with erect stems and narrow, shining green leaves. An outstanding clone in both leaf and flower. A.M. 1968. A.G.M. 1973.

'Reynvaanii'. A small, slow-growing form of compact habit, with stiff branches.

'Rotundifolia'. A bushy form, excellent for hedging. Leaves half as broad as long.

'Rufescens'. For over thirty years we have grown under this name a rather slow-growing, small, rather flat-topped bush with small, neat, oval to obovate leaves.

'Schipkaensis'. An extremely hardy, free-flowering, narrow-leaved form of spreading habit. I. 1888. A.M. 1959.

'Schipkaensis Macrophylla'. A German clone of open habit having ascending branches up to 2m. Leaves oblong-elliptic up to 18cm. long. Free fruiting.

'Serbica'. "Serbian Laurel". More upright than *'Schipkaensis'*, and with obovate, rugose leaves.

'Variegata'. Leaves heavily mottled and variegated creamy white. A rather curious yet conspicuous plant.

'Zabeliana'. A low, horizontally branched form, with long, narrow, willow-like leaves; very free flowering. Makes an excellent ground cover, even under the shade and drip of trees, also useful for breaking the regular outline of a border or bed in the same way as the "Pfitzer Juniper". A.G.M. 1973.

litigiosa SCHNEID. (*pilosiuscula barbata*). A splendid small, somewhat conical tree with small white flowers appearing in drooping clusters with the unfolding leaves in April. Worthy of more extensive planting where a fastigiate shape is required. Attractive autumn tints. C. China. I. 1907.

***lusitanica** L. "Portugal Laurel". An indispensable, large, evergreen shrub or small to medium-sized tree. A beautiful specimen tree when allowed to develop naturally. Leaves ovate, dark green with reddish petioles. Flowers small, white, hawthorn-scented, carried in long slender racemes, in June. Fruits small, red turning to dark purple. Hardier than the Cherry Laurel. Useful as game cover and a splendid hedging plant. Happy even on shallow chalk-soils, where it may be used instead of *P. laurocerasus*. Spain; Portugal. I. 1648.

'Angustifolia'. See *'Myrtifolia'*.

azorica FRANCO. A magnificent, large evergreen shrub or small tree with larger, thicker leaves of a bright green, reddish when unfolding and with reddish petioles. Azores. I. about 1860. F.C.C. 1866.

'Myrtifolia' (*'Angustifolia'*) (*'Pyramidalis'*). Forms a dense cone up to 5m., with polished, deep green leaves, smaller and neater than those of the type. In cold areas may be used as a formal evergreen to replace the conical "Bay".

'Variegata'. An attractive form with leaves conspicuously white variegated, sometimes pink flushed in winter.

†*lyonii SARG. (*integrifolia* SARG.). "Catalina Cherry". A rare evergreen shrub closely related to *P. ilicifolia*, but differing in its flat, mostly entire leaves, longer racemes and nearly black fruits. California. Our stock has toothed, slightly undulate leaves and may be a hybrid with *P. ilicifolia*.

maackii RUPR. "Manchurian Cherry". A rare, vigorous, small tree with attractive, shining, golden-brown, flaking bark. Flowers small, white, carried in irregular racemes on the previous year's shoots in April; fruits small, black. Manchuria; Korea. I. 1878.

macradenia KOEHNE. A small tree or large shrub related to *P. maximowiczii*. Flowers small, white, carried in few-flowered corymbose racemes in May. China. I. 1911.

macrophylla. See *P. avium 'Decumana'*.

mahaleb L. "St. Lucie Cherry". A very attractive, small to medium-sized tree of spreading or rounded habit, smothered with myriads of small white, fragrant blossoms in late April and early May, but not very free-flowering when young. Fruits black. Cherrywood pipes and walking sticks are made from this species. C. and S. Europe. I. 1714.

'Pendula'. An elegant form with gracefully arching branches. F.C.C. 1874.

mandshurica KOEHNE. "Manchurian Apricot". An uncommon small tree. Its pale pink flowers, which open in February and March, are of a lively peach-pink colour before expanding. Fruits rounded, yellow. Manchuria; Korea. C. 1900. A.M. 1977.

PRUNUS—*continued*

maritima MARSH. "Beach Plum". A small shrub of fairly compact habit, occasionally reaching 2 to 2·5m. Flowers small, white, produced in May. Fruits rounded, red or purple. Native of the eastern United States where it frequently grows in sandy places near the sea. Introduced by Farrer in 1800.

maximowiczii RUPR. A small, dense-headed tree with small, coarsely-toothed leaves and erect, corymbose racemes of small, creamy-white flowers in May. Fruits red turning black. Manchuria; Ussuri; Korea; Japan. I. 1892.

'Moerheimii' (*incisa 'Moerheimii'*). A small, picturesque, weeping tree of wide-spreading, dome-shaped habit. Flowers blush-white, pink in bud, in late March and early April.

mugus HAND.-MAZZ. "Tibetan Cherry". Described as growing prostrate in the wild but the plant in general cultivation is a stiff, thick-stemmed, rather compact small bush. The flowers are more curious than beautiful, shell pink with inflated reddish calyces, usually disposed singly or in pairs. W. China. I. before 1962.

mume SIEB. & ZUCC. "Japanese Apricot". A delightful small tree with green young shoots and single, almond-scented, pink flowers paling with age. Normally in flower during March, occasionally as early as late January or as late as early April. China; Korea; extensively cultivated in Japan. I. 1844.

'Alba'. A vigorous form with usually single, pure white flowers studding the branches in late March or early April.

'Alboplena'. Flowers semi-double, white, appearing in late winter and early spring.

'Alphandii' (*'Flore Pleno'*). A beautiful form with semi-double pink flowers in March, sometimes earlier.

'Beni-shidon'. A striking form with strongly fragrant, double, cup-shaped flowers which are a rich madder pink, darker in bud and paling slightly with age, appearing in late March or early April. A.M. 1961.

'Grandiflora'. See *P. armeniaca ansu 'Flore Pleno'*.

'O-moi-no-wac'. A charming form with semi-double, cup-shaped, usually white flowers in late March or early April. Occasional petals and sometimes whole flowers are pink.

'Pendula'. A small, weeping tree with single or semi-double flowers of a pale pink, in late February or March.

'Rosea Plena'. See *P. armeniaca ansu 'Flore Pleno'*.

munsoniana WIGHT & HEDR. "Wild Goose Plum". Small tree with lanceolate, shining green leaves and clusters of white flowers in spring, occasionally followed by red fruits. S.E. United States. C. 1911.

mutabilis. See *P. serrulata spontanea*.

myrobalana. See *P. cerasifera*.

nana STOKES not DU ROI. See *P. tenella*.

nigra AIT. "Canada Plum". A small, narrow-headed tree or large shrub, producing in spring, clusters of fragrant white flowers which later turn pink. Red or yellowish plum-like fruits. Canada and E. United States. I. 1773.

nipponica MATSUM. "Japanese Alpine Cherry". A dense shrub or bushy tree 2·5 to 3m., with chestnut-brown branches. Leaves coarsely-toothed; flowers white or pale pink in May. Fruits small, black. Japan. I. 1915.

kurilensis. See *P. kurilensis*.

'Okame' (*campanulata × incisa*). A small tree, one of the numerous hybrids raised by Capt. Collingwood Ingram. This is a very lovely cherry, with masses of carmine-rose flowers opening throughout March. Foliage attractively tinted in autumn. A.M. 1947. A.G.M. 1952.

padus L. "Bird Cherry". A small to medium-sized native tree widely distributed in the northern hemisphere. Flowers small, white, almond-scented, produced in slender, drooping or spreading racemes in May after the leaves; fruits black, bitter to taste. Europe (including British Isles); N. Asia to Japan.

'Albertii'. A very free-flowering form of medium size, strong and erect in growth.

'Colorata'. A remarkable clone with dark purplish shoots, coppery-purple young foliage and pale pink flowers. The leaves in summer are a sombre green with purple-tinged veins and undersurfaces. A.M. 1974.

commutata DIPP. (*seouliensis*). A geographical form from eastern Asia. A small to medium-sized tree of spreading habit. One of the first heralds of spring, the fresh green leaves appearing before winter has passed. A.M. 1956.

'Plena'. A form with longer-lasting, larger, double flowers.

seouliensis. See *commutata*.

PRUNUS—*continued*

padus 'Watereri' (*'Grandiflora'*). A medium-sized tree with conspicuous racemes up to 20cm. long. A.G.M. 1930. A.M. 1969.

'Pandora' (*subhirtella 'Ascendens Rosea'* × *yedoensis*) (Yedoensis Group). A splendid small tree with ascending branches which, in March or early April, are flooded with pale, shell-pink blossoms 2·5cm. across. Leaves bronze-red when unfolding, and often colouring richly in autumn. A.M. 1939. A.G.M. 1959.

pensylvanica L. f. A fast-growing, small to medium-sized tree with bright green, finely-toothed leaves and clusters of white flowers in late April and early May. Fruits small, red. North America. I. 1773.

persica BATSCH. "Peach". A small bushy tree or large shrub with pale pink flowers, 2·5 to 4cm. wide, in early April. Differing from the Almond in its smaller flowers which appear two to three weeks later, and in its fleshy, juicy fruits. Native probably of China, but cultivated since ancient times.

We offer here a selection of the best ornamental cultivars. For fruiting clones see our Fruit Tree Catalogue. It is essential, as a routine control for "Peach Leaf Curl", to spray all ornamental and fruiting Peaches and Almonds with "Medela" or a similar fungicide, in mid-February and again in early March.

'Alba'. Flowers white.

'Alboplena'. Flowers white, double. F.C.C. 1899.

'Alboplena Pendula'. A weeping form with double, white flowers.

'Atropurpurea'. See *'Foliis Rubis'*.

'Aurora'. Dense clusters of double, rose-pink flowers with frilled petals. A.M. 1950.

'Cardinal'. Flowers glowing red, semi-double, rosette-like.

'Crimson Cascade'. Weeping branches; flowers crimson, double.

'Foliis Rubris' (*'Atropurpurea'*). Leaves rich purplish-red when young, becoming bronze-green. Flowers single, pink; fruits reddish-purple. A.M. 1939.

'Helen Borchers'. A strong-growing form with large, semi-double, rose-pink flowers. A.M. 1949.

'Iceberg'. A very free-flowering form with large, semi-double, pure white flowers. A.M. 1950.

'Klara Mayer' (*'Flore Roseoplena'*). Flowers double, peach-pink. The best double peach for general planting. A.G.M. 1939.

'Prince Charming'. A small, upright-growing tree; flowers double, rose-red.

'Russell's Red'. Flowers double, crimson. A.M. 1933.

'Windle Weeping'. A very distinct weeping form with broad leaves and semi-double, cup-shaped flowers of purplish-pink. A.M. 1949.

pilosiuscula KOEHNE. Small tree or large shrub producing in April clusters of small, white or pink-tinged flowers with conspicuous protruding anthers in April, followed by red fruits in June. W. China. I. 1907.

'Pink Shell'. One of the loveliest of cherries in a genus full of floral treasures. A small, elegant tree, the slender, spreading branches drooping beneath a wealth of cup-shaped, delicate, shell-pink blossoms, which blend beautifully with the pale green of the emerging leaves in early April. A seedling of uncertain origin. A.M. 1969.

pleiocerasus KOEHNE. Small tree with small, white flowers in spring. W. China. I. 1907.

× **pollardii.** See *P. amygdalo-persica 'Pollardii'*.

prostrata LABILL. "Rock Cherry". A dwarf, spreading shrub usually forming a delightful, low, gnarled hummock reaching ·7m. high by 2m. wide in twenty-five years. Flowers bright pink borne along the wiry stems in April. S.E. Europe; Mediterranean Region; W. Asia. I. 1802.

pseudocerasus LINDL. A small tree, the leafless stems wreathed in clusters of white flowers in early March. Cultivated in China, but unknown in a wild state. I. 1819.

'Cantabrigiensis'. This interesting, small tree is well worth growing for its early display of fragrant pink blossoms, commencing as early as mid-February. The original plant is growing in the University Botanic Garden, Cambridge. A.M. 1925.

pubigera KOEHNE (Padus Section). A distinct and attractive bird cherry forming a medium-sized tree. Flowers small, creamy-white, in drooping racemes up to 18cm. long and 2·5cm. wide. W. China. A.M. 1957.

PRUNUS—*continued*

pumila L. "Sand Cherry". A spreading shrub to 2m. In May the naked branches are wreathed with multitudes of tiny white flowers. The greyish-green, narrowly obovate leaves become bright red in autumn. Fruits dark red. N.E. United States. I. 1756.

besseyi. See *P. besseyi.*

rufa HOOK. f. "Himalayan Cherry". A small tree with rusty-hairy young shoots and small clusters of pale pink flowers. Some forms have superb, peeling, reddish-brown or amber bark. Himalaya. I. 1897.

salicina LINDL. (*triflora*). "Japanese Plum". A small, bushy tree or large shrub with shining dark twigs. Leaves turning bright red in autumn. The small, white flowers crowd the leafless branches in early April. China. Long cultivated in Japan. I. 1870. A.M. 1926.

sargentii REHD. (*serrulata sachalinensis*). Considered by many to be the loveliest of all cherries. A round-headed tree, attaining 15 to 18m. in Japan, but rather less in this country. Bark dark chestnut brown. Young foliage bronze-red. Flowers single, pink, opening late March, or early April. One of the first trees to colour in the autumn, its leaves assuming glorious orange and crimson tints, usually in late September. One of the few cherries that bullfinches appear to ignore. Japan; Sakhalin; Korea. I. 1890. A.M. 1921. F.C.C.1925. A.G.M. 1928.

×schmittii REHD. (*avium × canescens*). This fast-growing, narrowly conical tree of medium size should have a great future for public planting. The polished brown trunk is a greater attraction than the pale pink flowers in spring. Garden origin in 1923.

†scoparia SCHNEID. A remarkable, rare, large shrub, with slender, broom-like branches recalling those of *Spartium junceum*, sparsely furnished with small, narrow leaves, reddish-bronze at first becoming bronze-green and finally green. Flowers pale pink, almond-like, in early spring. Persia. C. 1934.

scopulorum KOEHNE (*vilmoriniana*). A rare tree of upright habit, reaching 11 to 12m. Flowers tiny, fragrant, white flushed pink in March or April. China.

serotina EHRH. (Padus Section). In its native environs a large tree, but of small to medium size in this country. The attractive, glossy leaves, recalling those of the Portugal Laurel (*P. lusitanica*) turn clear yellow in the autumn. Flowers white, in racemes up to 15cm. long, produced during May and June. Eastern N. America; E. and S. Mexico; Guatemala. I. 1629.

'Asplenifolia'. An unusual form of graceful habit, with slender leaves strongly-toothed and less than 12mm. wide.

salicifolia KOEHNE. (*P. cappolin*). A form with lanceolate, long persisting glabrous and long-pointed leaves and stouter racemes. Remarkably hardy considering its native distribution. Mexico to Peru. I. 1820.

serrula FRANCH. (*serrula tibetica*). A small, but vigorous tree whose main attraction is the glistening surface of its polished red-brown, mahogany-like new bark. Leaves narrow, willow-like; flowers small, white, produced with the foliage in late April. W. China. Introduced by E. H. Wilson in 1908. A.M. 1944.

serrulata LINDL. (*serrulata alboplena*). A small, flat-topped tree with wide-spreading branches, green unfolding leaves and clusters of white, double flowers in late April and early May. An interesting tree of ancient garden origin, introduced from Canton in 1822. It has been suggested by some authorities that this tree may have arisen as a branch sport on the wild Chinese Hill Cherry (*P. serrulata hupehensis*). It was the first Japanese Cherry to be planted in European gardens and is the plant designated by Lindley as the type species.

alboplena. See *P. serrulata.*

'Autumn Glory'. A form of the "Korean Hill Cherry" selected by Capt. Collingwood Ingram for its consistent, rich, deep crimson and red autumn colours. Flowers pale blush, very prolific. A.M. 1966.

erecta. See '*Amanogawa*' under Japanese Cherries.

hupehensis INGRAM. (*mutabilis stricta*). "Chinese Hill Cherry". Considered to be the prototype of the cultivated double white cherry, to which Lindley gave the name *P. serrulata*. A medium-sized tree with ascending branches bearing clusters of white or blush flowers in April and early May. Young leaves bronze, and autumn foliage attractively tinted. C. China. Introduced by E. H. Wilson in 1900.

PRUNUS—*continued*

serrulata longipes. See '*Shimidsu Sakura*' under Japanese Cherries.

serrulata pubescens WILS. (*leveilleana*). "Korean Hill Cherry". A medium-sized tree with bronze-green, young foliage and white or pink flowers in late April and early May. Often producing rich autumn tints. Intermediate between the varieties *hupehensis* and *spontanea*, differing from both in its hairy petioles and leaf undersurfaces. China; Korea; Japan. I. 1907.

rosea. See '*Kiku-shidare Sakura*' under Japanese Cherries.

sachalinensis. See *P. sargentii*.

sieboldii. See '*Takasago*' under Japanese Cherries.

spontanea WILS. (*P. mutabilis*) (*P. jamasakura*). "Hill Cherry". A medium-sized tree, differing from var. *hupehensis* in its more spreading habit, greyer bark and bronze-coloured young foliage. Flowers white or pink in late April and early May. A beautiful cherry, said to be the most adored tree in Japan, one which has inspired her poets and artists and is a prototype of most of the Japanese Cherries. It is extremely variable, the best form havings rich, coppery-red young foliage and pure white flowers. Fruit dark purplish-crimson. Japan. I. about 1914. A.M. 1936.

simonii CARR. "Apricot Plum". Small tree or large shrub of erect, conical habit, producing white flowers in March and April. Fruits very conspicuous, tomato-shaped, red and yellow, fragrant, edible. N. China. I. 1863.

sinensis. See *P. glandulosa* '*Sinensis*'.

'Snow Goose'. A small tree with ascending branches crowded in spring with pure white, well-formed flowers. A seedling of similar parentage (*incisa* × *speciosa*) to '*Umineko*', but differing from that cultivar in its broader crown and its larger leaves which appear after the flowers.

speciosa INGRAM (*lannesiana speciosa*) (*lannesiana albida*). "Oshima Cherry". A medium-sized tree with ovate-elliptic leaves with aristate teeth and usually terminating in a slender, acuminate apex, bronze-green when unfolding soon turning bright green. In April the fragrant white flowers are carried on long pedicels. This species is regarded as the ancestor of many of the "Japanese Cherries", as for example '*Shirotae*'. Japan. C. 1909.

spinosa L. "Blackthorn"; "Sloe". A large, dense-habited shrub or small bushy tree with dark, spiny branches, crowded in March or early April with small white flowers. Fruits like small damsons, blue-bloomy at first, later shining black. A familiar native shrub in hedges, its fruits are used in preserves, for wine-making and for flavouring gin, whilst its branches provide the traditional black-thorn sticks and Irish shillalahs. Europe; N. Africa; W. Asia. Long cultivated.

'Plena'. An attractive form with double flowers. A.M. 1950.

'Purpurea'. A neat, compact bush with rich purple leaves and white flowers. One of the elite of purple-leaved shrubs. A.G.M. 1973.

'Rosea'. See *P. cerasifera* '*Rosea*'.

subhirtella MIQ. "Spring Cherry". An extremely variable small to medium-sized tree. It includes among its many forms some of the most delightful of early spring flowering trees, and in a good year most forms produce attractive autumn tints. Flowers small, pale pink in March and April. The type is unknown in the wild and some authorities regard it as a hybrid between *P. incisa* and *P. subhirtella ascendens*. Japan. I. 1894. A.G.M. 1927. A.M. 1930.

ascendens WILS. (*P. pendula ascendens*). The wild type which as seen in cultivation in this country is a small, semi-erect tree, but is much larger in Japan. Flowers white or pale pink, opening towards the end of March. Japan. C. 1916.

'Ascendens Rosea'. A lovely form with flowers of a clear shell-pink, enhanced by the red-tinged calyces. A.M. 1960.

'Autumnalis'. "Autumn Cherry". A small tree up to 7·6m. producing its semi-double, white flowers, intermittently from November to March. Flowers may be found on this tree on almost any winter's day and a few cut sprays are a welcome indoor decoration. C. 1900. A.M. 1912. A.G.M. 1924. F.C.C. 1966.

'Autumnalis Rosea'. Flowers semi-double, blush. A.M. 1960.

'Flore Pleno'. A rare and splendid form with flattish, many-petalled or double flowers, about 2·5cm. across, rich pink in bud, opening white. A.M. 1935.

'Fukubana'. This very striking small tree with its profusion of semi-double, rose-madder flowers is certainly the most colourful of the "Spring Cherries". I. 1927.

PRUNUS—*continued*

subhirtella 'Pendula' (*P. pendula*). Raised from Japanese seed, this forms a lovely slender weeping tree of medium size, recalling the most graceful forms of weeping birch. The tiny blush flowers in late March to early April are not conspicuous. I. 1862. A.M. 1930.

'Pendula Plena Rosea'. A weeping shrub or small tree. Flowers semi-double, rosette-like, rose-madder, similar to those of '*Fukubana*', but slightly paler. I. 1928. A.M. 1938.

'Pendula Rosea'. "Weeping Spring Cherry". A small weeping, mushroom-shaped tree. Flowers rich pink in bud passing to pale blush, wreathing the graceful drooping branches in late March and early April. This is the form widely distributed by European nurseries as '*Pendula*' for the past 75 years.

'Pendula Rubra' ('*Lanceata*'). Flowers single, deep rose, carmine in bud, wreathing the long pendulous branches.

'Stellata'. A very beautiful form of the Ascendens Section with larger, clear pink, star-shaped flowers produced in crowded clusters along the branches. I. about 1955. A.M. 1949.

tangutica KOEHNE (*dehiscens*). A large, bushy shrub with spiny branches. The carmine pink, almond-like flowers appear from March onwards. W. China. I. 1910.

tenella BATSCH (*nana*) (*Amygdalus nana*). The "Dwarf Russian Almond" is a charming, small shrub with long glabrous stems. Flowers borne in April, bright pink. S.E. Europe; W. Asia to E. Siberia. I. 1683. A.M. 1929.

'Alba'. Flowers white.

'Fire Hill'. Perhaps the best dwarf Almond. An outstanding small shrub, a selection of var. *gesslerana* from the Balkan Alps. The erect stems are wreathed with brilliant, rose-red flowers. A.M. 1959. A.G.M. 1969.

georgica HORT. A tall-growing, geographical form, up to 2m. with larger leaves. Flowers pink.

gesslerana REHD. A small shrub with bright pink flowers darker in bud.

tomentosa THUNB. "Downy Cherry". A very variable shrub of medium size and usually erect habit. Young shoots and leaves beneath tomentose. Flowers white or more usually pale pink, produced in late March or early April. Fruits red. N. and W. China; Korea; Himalaya. C. 1870.

triloba LINDL. (*triloba multiplex*). A medium-sized to large shrub with small, coarsely-toothed, three-lobed leaves. Flowers large, double, rosette-like, clear peach pink, produced in great profusion at the end of March or early April. Of garden origin, introduced by Robert Fortune from China in 1855. It makes a splendid wall shrub, if the old flowering shoots are pruned back immediately after flowering. A.G.M. 1935.

multiplex. See *P. triloba*.

simplex REHD. The wild form, with single, pink flowers. China. I. 1884.

triflora. See *P. salicina*.

'Umineko' (*incisa* × *speciosa*). A narrow-growing, upright tree of considerable merit. Flowers white, single, produced in April with the leaves which tint beautifully in autumn. A.M. 1928.

vilmoriniana. See *P. scopulorum*.

virginiana L. (Padus Section). "Choke Cherry". A small tree with glossy green leaves and densely packed racemes of small white flowers in May. Fruits dark red. Eastern N. America. I. 1724.

demissa TORR. "Western Choke Cherry". A small, bushy tree or shrub, mainly of botanical interest. W. United States. I. 1892.

'Wadai' (*pseudocerasus* × *subhirtella*). A small twiggy tree or large shrub with bristly-hairy young shoots, the trunk inclined to produce aerial roots. The pale pink flowers, deep rose in bud are produced in March and are scented of ripe peaches. Garden origin in Japan and named after Mr. K. Wada of Yokohama.

× **yedoensis** MATSUM. (*speciosa* × *subhirtella*). "Yoshino Cherry". A graceful, early-flowering, small to medium-sized tree with arching branches. Highly valued for the profusion of its almond-scented, blush-white flowers in late March and early April. Unknown in the wild; introduced from Japan in 1902, possibly earlier. A.M. 1927. A.G.M. 1930.

PRUNUS—*continued*

× **yedoensis 'Ivensii'.** Raised in our nurseries from seed of *P.* ×*yedoensis* in 1925. A quite remarkable small, vigorous, weeping tree with long, tortuous branches and long, slender, drooping branchlets which, in late March to early April, are transformed into snow-white cascades of delicately fragrant blossom. Named to commemorate our late manager, Arthur J. Ivens, F.L.S.

'Shidare Yoshino' (*perpendens*) (*'Pendula'*). A small tree with horizontal and arching branches often weeping to the ground. Flowers pale pink in late March and early April.

JAPANESE CHERRIES
of Garden Origin

The "Sato Zakura" of Japan are a large group of extremely ornamental flowering Cherries. Most are of obscure origin. Some are hybrids, whilst others are undoubtedly derived from the Chinese *P. speciosa* and the Japanese *P. serrulata spontanea.* No doubt other species have also contributed to their development.

The majority are small trees of easy cultivation, varying from low and spreading to tall and erect in habit. The leaves of some clones are bronze in spring,l providing a delightful backing to the emerging flowers. The flowers themseves may be single, semi-double or double, and vary in colour from rich pink to white or cream. With few exceptions the leaves turn to shades of yellow or tawny-orange in autumn. Like the edible cherries, they succeed in all types of well-drained soils, including chalk-soils. During the dormant period the buds are often subject to bird damage, when it is necessary to use a repellant to ensure blossom. Pruning of any kind is rarely necessary, but when unavoidable it is best carried out in late summer so that the cuts heal before winter. Flowering periods are indicated as follows:—

Early—Late March to early April
Mid—Mid to late April
Late—Late April to mid May

'Amanogawa' (*serrulata erecta*). A small, columnar tree with erect branches and dense, upright clusters of fragrant, semi-double, shell pink flowers. Mid to late. Young leaves greenish-bronze. A.M. 1931. A.G.M. 1931.

'Asagi' (*serrulata luteoides*). Similar to *'Ukon'*, but flowers single or nearly so and paler in colour, opening earlier. Early to Mid.

'Asano' (*serrulata geraldiniae*). A small tree with ascending branches, bearing dense clusters of deep pink, very double flowers. Early. Young leaves greenish-bronze. A beautiful tree, in effect an upright form of *'Kiku-shidare Sakura'*. I. 1929.

'Benden' (*serrulata rubida*). A vigorous tree with ascending branches, similar in size and habit to *'Kanzan'*. Flowers single, pale pink. Early. Young leaves reddish-brown or coppery-red.

'Benifugen'. See *'Daikoku'*.

'Botan Zakura' (*serrulata moutan*). A small tree with ascending and spreading branches. Flowers large, nearly 5cm. across, single or semi-double, fragrant, lilac-pink in bud opening pale pink or white. Mid. Young leaves bronze-green. Similar to *'Mikuruma-gaeshi'* and *'Ojochin'* in flower.

"Cheal's Weeping Cherry". See under *'Kiku-shidare Sakura'*.

'Daikoku' (*'Benifugen'*). A small tree with strong ascending branches. Flowers large up to 5cm. across, double, purplish-red in bud opening deep lilac-pink, with a central cluster of small green carpels, carried in loose, drooping clusters. Late. Young leaves yellowish-green. I. 1899.

'Fudanzakura' (*serrulata fudanzakura*) (*serrulata semperflorens*). A small, round-headed tree opening its single, pink-budded, white flowers during spells of mild weather between November and April. Especially useful for cutting for indoor decoration. Young leaves coppery-red or reddish-brown. A.M. 1930.

'Fugenzo' (*cerasus 'James H. Veitch'*) (*serrulata fugenzo*). Resembling *'Kanzan'* in some respects, but smaller and with a broader, flat-topped head. Flowers large, double, rose-pink, borne in drooping clusters. Very Late. Young leaves coppery-red. An old cultivar, introduced about 1880. F.C.C. 1899.

'Fukubana'. See *P. subhirtella 'Fukubana'*.

'Gioiko' (*serrulata tricolor*). A strong-growing tree with ascending branches; flowers semi-double, creamy-white, streaked green and often tinged with pink, opening a little later than *'Ukon'*. Young leaves reddish-brown. I. about 1914. A.M. 1930.

PRUNUS—*continued*

'Hatazakura'. "Flag Cherry". Branches ascending. Flowers fragrant, single, white or pink-flushed. Early. Young leaves green or bronze-tinged. The Japanese name refers to the peculiar tattered edges of the petals.

'Hisakura' (*serrulata splendens*). A beautiful, small tree with single, deep pink flowers, the calyces attractively tinted purplish-brown. Mid. Young leaves reddish-brown or coppery-red.

'Hokusai' (*serrulata spiralis*). One of the earliest and most popular introductions. A vigorous, wide-spreading tree, its branches hidden in spring by the large clusters of large, semi-double, pale pink flowers. Mid. Young leaves brownish-bronze. An old cultivar of good constitution, ideally suited to English gardens. I. about 1866.

'Horinji' (*serrulata decora*). A small, upright tree with ascending branches. Flowers semi-double, mauve-pink in bud opening soft pink, contrasting with the purplish-brown calyces, freely borne along the branches. Mid. Young leaves greenish-bronze. I. about 1905. A.M. 1935.

'Ichiyo' (*serrulata unifolia*). A beautiful tree with ascending branches and double, shell-pink flowers which have a circular, frilled appearance and are borne in long-stalked corymbs. Mid. Young leaves bronze-green. A.M. 1959.

'Imosé'. A free-growing tree with double, mauve-pink flowers, abundantly produced in long, loose clusters. Mid. Leaves reddish copper when young, glossy bright green at maturity, turning yellow in November. Fruits often produced in pairs on the same stalk. I. 1927.

'Ito-kukuri' (*serrulata fasciculata*). A small tree with ascending branches. Flowers semi-double, pale pink or white. Mid. Young leaves greenish bronze.

'Jo-nioi' (*lannesiana affinis*). A strong-growing cherry of spreading habit. The single, white, deliciously-scented blossoms wreath the branches in spring. The white petals contrast with the purple-brown sepals. Mid. Young leaves pale golden-brown. I. about 1900.

'Kanzan' (*'Sekiyama'*) (*serrulata purpurascens*). One of the most popular and commonly planted ornamental cherries. A strong-growing, medium-sized tree with characteristic stiffly ascending branches when young, later spreading. Flowers large and showy, double, purplish-pink. Mid. Young leaves coppery-red or reddish-brown. Often wrongly grown in cultivation under the name *'Hisakura'*, from which it differs in its taller stature and double flowers opening generally a week later. I. about 1913. A.M. 1921. A.G.M. 1930. F.C.C. 1937.

'Kiku-shidare Sakura' (*serrulata rosea*). A small tree with arching or drooping branches, very attractive when wreathed with clear deep pink, very double flowers. Early. Young leaves bronze-green, later green and glossy. A.M. 1915. Often wrongly referred to as "Cheal's Weeping Cherry".

'Kiku-zakura' (*serrulata chrysanthemoides*). A small, slow-growing cultivar. Flowers double, each flower being a congested, rounded mass of soft pink petals. Late. Young leaves bronze-green.

'Kojima'. See *'Shirotae'*.

'Kokonoye Sakura' (*serrulata homogena*). A small tree, producing large, semi-double, shell-pink blossoms in great profusion. Early-Mid. Young leaves bronze-green.

'Mikuruma-gaeshi' (*serrulata diversifolia*) (*serrulata temari*). A distinct tree with long, ascending, rather gaunt, short-spurred branches along which large, mostly single, blush-pink flowers are densely packed. Mid. Young leaves bronze-green. Similar to *'Ojochin'* and *'Botan Zakura'* in flower. A.M. 1946.

'Mount Fuji'. See *P. 'Shirotae'*.

'Ojochin' (*'Senriko'*). A striking tree easily distinguished by its large leaves and stout growth. Flowers single, 5cm. across, pink in bud opening blush, profusely borne in long-stalked clusters of as many as seven or eight. Mid. Young leaves bronze-brown becoming rather tough and leathery when mature. Similar to *'Botan Zakura'* and *'Mikuruma-gaeshi'* in flower. I. before 1905. A.M. 1924. A.G.M. 1926.

'Okiku-zakura'. A small tree of rather stiff habit. Flowers large, double, pale pink, passing to white. Mid. Young leaves bronze-green. A.M. 1934.

'Oku Miyako'. See under *'Shimidsu Sakura'*.

'Oshokun' (*serrulata conspicua*). A small tree of weak growth, but with very lovely, single flowers, carmine-red in bud opening to blush-pink, very freely produced. Mid to Late. Young leaves bronze-green.

PRUNUS—*continued*

'Pink Perfection'. A very striking cultivar raised in this country from *'Shimidsu Sakura'*, presumably pollinated by *'Kanzan'*. Habit is intermediate. Flowers bright rosy-pink in bud, opening paler, double, carried in long, drooping clusters. Mid to Late. Young leaves bronze. I. 1935. A.M. 1945.

'Sekiyama'. See *'Kanzan'*.

'Senriko'. See *'Ojochin'*.

'Shimidsu Sakura' (*'Shogetsu'*) (*serrulata longipes*). One of the loveliest of Japanese Cherries. A small tree with wide-spreading branches forming a broad, flattened crown. The large, fimbriated, double flowers are pink-tinted in bud, opening to pure white, and hang all along the branches in long stalked clusters. Mid to Late. Young leaves green. Wrongly called *'Oku Miyako'* in the past. A.M. 1930. A.G.M. 1933.

'Shirofugen' (*serrulata alborosea*). A strong-growing, wide spreading tree up to 10m. Flowers large, double, dull purplish-pink in bud opening white, then fading to purplish-pink, produced in long-stalked clusters and contrasting superbly with the copper-coloured young leaves. Very late. One of the best clones for general planting, the flowers are late and long-lasting. I. about 1900. A.M. 1951. A.G.M. 1959.

'Shirotae' (*serrulata albida*) (*'Mount Fuji'*) (*'Kojima'*). This beautiful cherry is one of the most distinct clones. A small vigorous tree with wide-spreading, horizontal or slightly drooping branches, often reaching to the ground. Flowers very large, single or semi-double, fragrant, snow-white, bursting from the soft green young foliage in long, drooping clusters. Mid. The leaves have a distinctive fringed appearance. I. about 1905.

'Shogetsu'. See *'Shimidsu Sakura'*.

'Shogun'. A vigorous cherry with deep pink, semi-double flowers, becoming abundant as the tree ages. Mid. Rich autumn colours.

'Shosar'. A strong-growing, rather fastigiate tree. Flowers single, clear pink. Early. Usually good autumn colour.

'Shujaku' (*serrulata campanuloides*). A small tree with double, slightly cup-shaped, pale pink flowers, freely produced. Mid. Young leaves yellowish-bronze. I. about 1900.

'Tai Haku'. "Great White Cherry". A superb, robust tree up to 12m. Flowers very large, single, of a dazzling white, enhanced by the rich coppery-red of the young leaves. Mid. One of the finest cherries for general planting and perhaps the best of the whites. It is one of the many lovely cherries which owes its popularity to Capt. Collingwood Ingram. A.M. 1931. F.C.C. 1944. A.G.M. 1964.

'Taizanfukun' (*serrulata ambigua*). A distinct, erect-growing cherry of twiggy habit, with leathery leaves. Flowers double, pale pink. Mid. Young leaves bronze.

'Takasago' (*serrulata sieboldii*) (*pseudocerasus watereri*). A small, spreading cherry with downy leaves. Flowers semi-double, pale pink. Mid. Young leaves varying from yellowish-brown to reddish-bronze. I. about 1864.

'Taki-nioi' (*serrulata cataracta*). A strong, vigorous, medium-sized tree with spreading branches. The honey-scented, single, white flowers are rather small, but are produced in great abundance and contrast effectively with the reddish-bronze, young leaves. Late.

'Taoyama Zakura'. A floriferous, small tree of slow growth and spreading habit. Flowers fragrant, semi-double, shell-pink becoming pale blush with purplish-brown calyces, effectively backed by the reddish-brown or coppery emerging leaves. Mid. I. 1929.

'Ukon' (*serrulata grandiflora*) (*serrulata luteovirens*). A robust tree of spreading habit. Flowers semi-double, pale yellowish, tinged green, occasionally pink-flushed, freely borne and very effective against the brownish-bronze young leaves. Closely akin to *'Asagi'*. Mid. The large, mature leaves turn rusty-red or purplish-brown in autumn. I. about 1905. A.M. 1923. A.G.M. 1969.

'Umineko'. See *P. 'Umineko'*.

'Washi-no-o' (*serrulata wasinowo*). A strong-growing tree with white, slightly fragrant, single flowers. Early. Young leaves soft bronze-green.

'Yae-murasaki Zakura' (*serrulata purpurea*). A small, free-flowering tree of slow growth. Flowers semi-double, purplish-pink. Mid. Young leaves coppery-red.

'Yedo Zakura' (*serrulata nobilis*). Small upright tree; flowers semi-double, carmine in bud, almond-pink when expanded. Mid. Young leaves golden-coppery. I. about 1905.

PRUNUS—*continued*

'Yokihi'. A small tree with widely ascending or spreading branches and large, semi-double, pale pink flowers in loose clusters, freely produced. Late. Young leaves bronze-green.

"Yoshino". See *P. ×yedoensis*.

PSEUDOCYDONIA—Rosaceae—A rare, monotypic genus formerly included under *CYDONIA*.

sinensis SCHNEID. (*Cydonia sinensis*). A small, occasionally semi-evergreen tree or large shrub with flaky bark. Shoots hairy when young, bearing obovate to ovate leaves 5 to 10cm. long. Flowers in spring, solitary, pink, followed by large egg-shaped yellow fruits 5 to 18cm. long, which in this country are rarely fully developed. China.

PSEUDOCYTISUS. See *VELLA*.

†***PSEUDOPANAX—Araliaceae**—A small genus of evergreens mainly from New Zealand, with remarkable leaves of variable form, often sword-shaped but varying depending on age of plant. Flowers small, greenish of little or no garden merit. Hardy in mild localities, and succeeding in all types of well-drained soil. Some make useful house plants.

arboreus W. R. PHILIPSON (*Neopanax arboreum*) (*Nothopanax arboreum*). A handsome large shrub in cultivation but often a small tree in its native habitat. The large, glossy green leaves are divided into five to seven coarsely toothed, stalked leaflets. Flowers in dense rounded clusters, replaced by decorative black fruits. Only suitable for the mildest areas. New Zealand. I. 1820.

crassifolius K. KOCH. A small, evergreen tree with leaves varying extraordinarily according to the age of the plant. In young unbranched specimens they are rigid and sharply toothed, up to ·6m. long, 12mm. wide, dark green with red mid-rib and purple under-surface. New Zealand. I. 1846.

davidii W. R. PHILIPSON (*Nothopanax davidii*). A somewhat hardier medium-sized large, slow-growing shrub, with variable leaves, simple or divided into two or three lanceolate leaflets. The flower clusters are followed by black fruits. China. Introduced by E. H. Wilson in 1907.

ferox T. KIRK. A small, slender-stemmed tree resembling *P. crassifolius* but leaves of juvenile and mature plants always simple. The leaves of young plants are pendant, greyish-green, with strongly hooked teeth. New Zealand.

laetus W. R. PHILIPSON (*daviesii* HORT.) (*Neopanax laetum*) (*Nothopanax laetum*). A very handsome species, related to but differing from *P. arboreus* in its much larger, drooping, three-lobed, glossy green leaves. New Zealand.

lessonii C. KOCH. A small tree or large shrub with bright green, compound leaves composed of three to five, coarsely toothed or entire, leathery leaflets. New Zealand.

†***PSEUDOWINTERA—Winteraceae**—A small New Zealand genus related to *Drimys*. Not suitable for shallow chalk-soils.

colorata DANDY (*Drimys colorata*). A small to medium-sized shrub. Unusual in the colouring of its aromatic, oval, leathery leaves, which are pale yellow-green above, flushed pink, edged and blotched with dark crimson-purple, glaucous beneath. The small greenish-yellow flowers are borne in axillary clusters. Fruits dark red to black, rarely produced in the British Isles. Grows best in sheltered woodland conditions. A.M. 1975.

†**PSORALEA—Leguminosae**—A large genus of herbs and shrubs with usually compound leaves. The following species is only suitable for the very mildest areas, but it makes an attractive conservatory shrub.

pinnata L. Medium-sized to large shrub with very beautiful pinnate leaves. Masses of lovely blue and white pea-flowers cluster the branches in May or June. S. Africa. I. 1690. A.M. 1903.

PTELEA—Rutaceae—North American aromatic shrubs or small trees of which the "Hop Tree" (*P. trifoliata*) is the best known. All possess gland-dotted, trifoliolate leaves and monoecious flowers. Suitable for all types of fertile soil.

baldwinii TORR. & GR. (*angustifolia*). Large shrub related to *P. trifoliata*, but differing in its smaller leaves with narrow leaflets and its larger individual flowers. S.W. United States; Mexico. I. 1893.

nitens GREENE. A rare species with lustrous leaves, strongly aromatic when crushed. S.W. United States. C. 1912.

polyadenia GREENE. A rare species akin to *P. trifoliata*. S.W. United States. I. 1916.

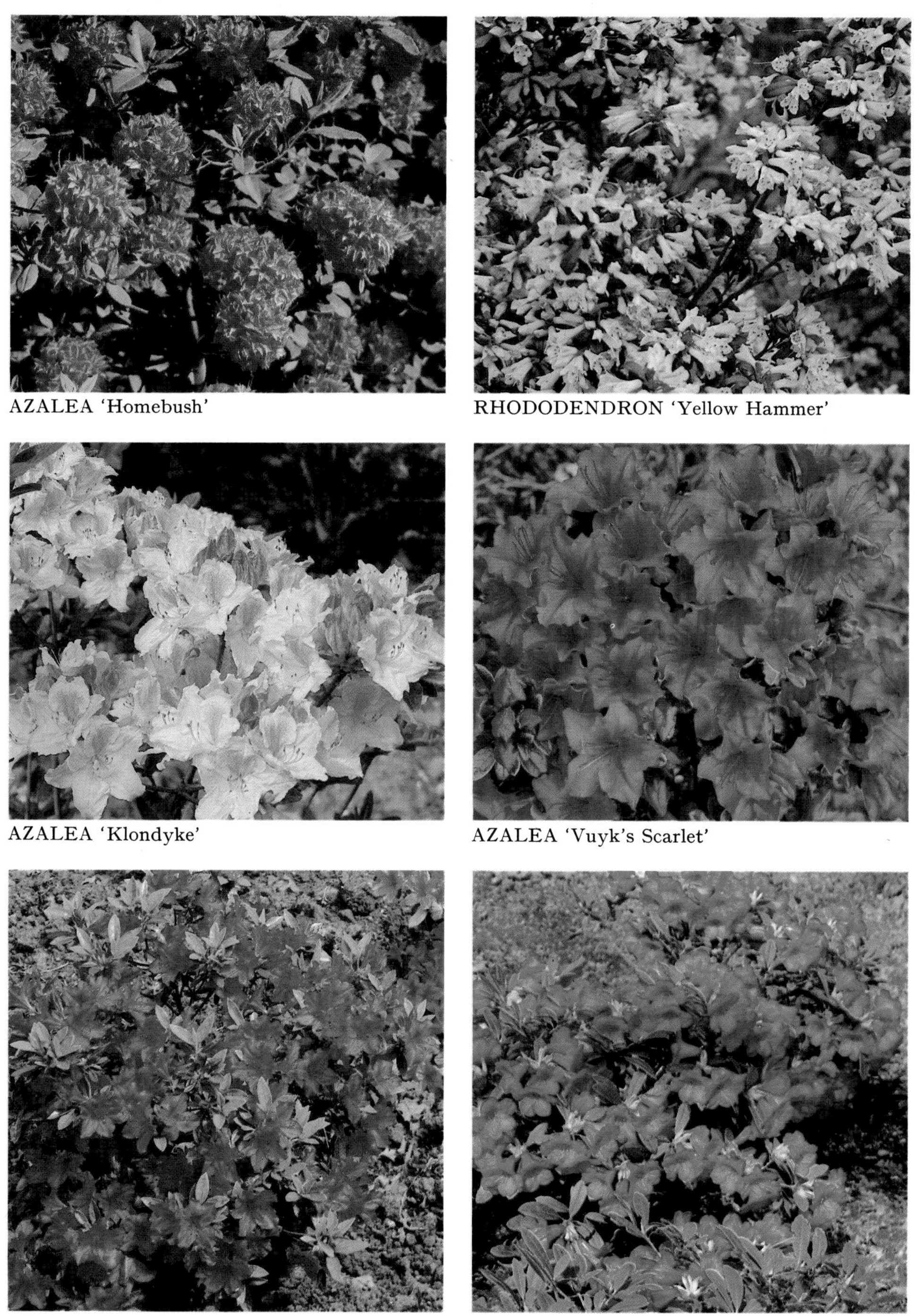

AZALEA 'Homebush'

RHODODENDRON 'Yellow Hammer'

AZALEA 'Klondyke'

AZALEA 'Vuyk's Scarlet'

AZALEA 'Blue Danube'

RHODODENDRON 'Elizabeth'

ROBINIA 'Hillieri'

ROSA 'Madame Pierre Oger'

ROSA 'Scarlet Fire'

ROSA pimpinellifolia 'Glory of Edzell'

ROSA 'Canary Bird'

ROSA rugosa 'Frau Dagmar Hastrup'

PTELEA—*continued*

trifoliata L. "Hop-tree". A low, spreading tree or large shrub. The corymbs of small, yellowish flowers, open in June and are probably the most fragrant of any hardy tree, being equal to those of the best scented honeysuckle. They are followed by dense green clusters of persistent, winged, elm-like fruits. Eastern N. America; Mexico. I. 1704.

'Aurea'. Leaves soft yellow, contrasting well with purple and dark green-leaved shrubs. F.C.C. 1980.

'Fastigiata'. A form with erect branches.

PTEROCARYA—Juglandaceae—"Wing Nut". Fast growing, often wide-spreading trees of the "Walnut" family, with handsome, pinnate leaves and monoecious catkin-like inflorescences. The pith of the stems is characteristically chambered. They succeed in all types of fertile soil.

caucasica. See *P. fraxinifolia*.

fraxinifolia SPACH (*caucasica*). A large, wide-spreading tree, occasionally forming large thickets of suckering stems, and usually with a short trunk and deeply furrowed bark. Leaves ·3 to ·6m. long, composed of numerous, oblong, toothed leaflets. Flowers greenish, in pendulous catkins, the females up to 50cm. long, draping the branches in summer. Fruits winged. A hardy, fast-growing tree, happiest in a moist, loamy soil, and particularly suitable for planting by lakes or rivers. Caucasus to N. Persia. I. 1782.

'Dumosa'. A remarkable medium to large shrub, with smaller leaflets.

×**rehderana** SCHNEID. (*fraxinifolia* × *stenoptera*). A large suckering tree, raised in the Arnold Arboretum in 1879. In general, it is intermediate in character between its parents. The rachis of the leaf is winged but never so pronounced nor toothed as in *P. stenoptera*. It is a first-class, hardy tree tolerant of all kinds of soils. The long drooping catkins which later support the fruits are an attractive feature for several months.

rhoifolia SIEB. & ZUCC. "Japanese Wing Nut". A large, fast-growing tree with leaves about 30cm. long, composed of eleven to twenty-one finely-toothed leaflets; female catkins 20 to 30cm. long. Japan. I. 1888.

stenoptera C. DC. (*sinensis*). A large, vigorous tree. Leaves 25 to 40cm. long, the rachis prominently winged. Female catkins 20cm. long; wings of fruit narrow and erect. China. I. 1860.

PTEROSTYRAX—Styracaceae—A small genus of interesting, large Asiatic shrubs or small trees, conspicuous in their halesia-like leaves and long panicles of small, interesting but not showy flowers. They succeed in all types of good deep soil, even over chalk, but cannot be recommended for poor, shallow, chalk-soils.

corymbosa SIEB. & ZUCC. A rare, small tree or large spreading shrub with bristle-toothed, ovate leaves and nodding, corymbose panicles of fragrant, white flowers in May and June. Fruits obovoid, five-winged. China; Japan. I. 1850.

hispida SIEB. & ZUCC. A large shrub or small tree with oval or obovate leaves. The fragrant, white flowers are borne in June and July in drooping panicles up to 23cm. long, followed by spindle-shaped, five-ribbed fruits. Japan; China. I. 1875. A.M. 1964.

†**PUNICA—Punicaceae**—A small genus of two species. The following is the only species in general cultivation.

granatum L. "Pomegranate". A large shrub, or occasionally a small bushy tree, requiring a warm, sunny wall and good drainage in the southern counties. Leaves oblong, deep shining green, coppery when young, changing to yellow in autumn. Flowers funnel-shaped, scarlet or orange-red with crumpled petals, produced during late summer and early autumn. The familiar, large, many-seeded fruits require a long, hot summer in which to develop and ripen. Naturalised in S.E. Europe it is a spectacular shrub when carrying its brilliant orange-red flowers, as showy as any Rose or Camellia. In the Mediterranean Region it is often seen as a dense hedge. S.W. Asia. Long cultivated in S. Europe.

'Albopleno' (*'Multiplex'*). Flowers double, creamy-white. Young leaves green.

'Flore Pleno' (*'Rubroplena'*). A showy form with double, orange-red flowers.

'Multiplex'. See *'Albopleno'*.

'Nana' (*'Gracillisima'*). A charming, dwarf form, with narrow leaves, plants of 15 to 23cm. producing many orange-scarlet flowers in September and October. Suitable for a selected sunny site on the rock garden. A.M. 1936.

***PYRACANTHA**—**Rosaceae**—The "Firethorns" are related to *Cotoneaster*, but are easily distinguished by their thorny branches and toothed leaves. They are frequently grown as wall shrubs, and will attain a height of 5m. or more and, when grown as such, their long growths may be cut back immediately after flowering. They are equally effective, though less tall, grown as specimen shrubs. Their masses of hawthorn-like flowers are borne in early summer, and their red, orange or yellow fruits in autumn and winter. All are hardy, and include some of the best evergreen flowering and fruiting shrubs for north and east walls. They are tolerant of all exposures and pollution and will grow in all kinds of fertile soil.

angustifolia SCHNEID. Medium-sized shrub, occasionally up to 4m. high. Very distinct with its narrow, oblong leaves, grey-felted beneath, and conspicuous clusters of orange-yellow fruits which are retained throughout winter. W. China. I. 1899. F.C.C. 1904.

atalantioides STAPF. (*gibbsii*)· A large, robust shrub, occasionally a small tree, with large, oval, dark glossy green leaves. Flowers in May or early June. Fruits scarlet, long-lasting. Excellent on a sunless wall. China. Introduced by E. H. Wilson in 1907. F.C.C. 1918. A.G.M. 1922.

'Aurea' ('*Flava*'). Fruits rich yellow. A.M. 1936. A.G.M. 1969.

'Buttercup'. A hybrid of spreading habit with small fruits of a rich yellow.

coccinea ROEM. A large shrub with narrowly obovate or oval, finely-toothed leaves. Flowers, in downy corymbs, in June followed by rich red fruits in dense clusters all along the branches. S. Europe; Asia Minor. I. 1629.

'Lalandei'. Perhaps the most popular Firethorn. Stronger growing and more erect than the type with broader leaves and larger, orange-red fruits thickly covering the branches in autumn and winter. Raised in France in 1874 by Mons. Lalande. A.G.M. 1925.

crenatoserrata REHD. (*yunnanensis*). A large shrub related to *P. atalantioides*. The obovate to oblanceolate leaves, 2·5 to 8cm. long have a broad, rounded apex with shallow, rounded teeth in their upper halves. Flowers in June, followed by innumerable clusters of small, red fruits which often persist until March. C. and W. China. I. 1906.

crenulata ROEM. A variable species related to *P. coccinea*, differing in its blunt-tipped leaves, and its smaller flowers and fruits, which are orange-red. Himalaya. I. about 1844. A.M. 1915.

rogersiana. See *P. rogersiana*.

gibbsii. See *P. atalantioides*.

koidzumii REHD. A rare Formosan species akin to *P. crenulata*, with oblanceolate leaves and loose clusters of red fruits.

'Orange Glow'. A vigorous shrub of dense habit, its branches inundated each autumn with bright, orange-red fruits which last well into winter. Probably *P. coccinea* × *crenatoserrata*.

rogersiana CHITT. (*crenulata rogersiana*). A large, free-fruiting shrub related to, but distinguished from, *P. crenulata* by its smaller, oblanceolate leaves and reddish-orange fruits. W. China. I. 1911. A.G.M. 1937. A.M. 1953.

'Flava'. Fruits bright yellow. F.C.C. 1919. A.G.M. 1969.

'Shawnee'. A densely-branched, spiny shrub of medium to large size, widely spreading at the base. The masses of white flowers are replaced by an equal abundance of yellow to light orange fruits which begin to colour as early as August. An American cultivar raised at the U.S. National Arboretum as a second generation seedling of the hybrid *P. crenatoserrata* × *koidzumii*. It is claimed by its raisers to be resistant to Fireblight and Scab.

'Watereri' (*atalantioides* × *rogersiana*). A very free-fruiting hybrid of compact growth, smothered annually with clusters of white flowers, followed by bright red fruits. Garden origin. A.M. 1955. A.G.M. 1969.

'Waterer's Orange'. A strong growing, free-fruiting shrub with orange-yellow fruits. A.M. 1959.

yunnanensis. See *P. crenatoserrata*.

× **PYRACOMELES** (*PYRACANTHA* × *OSTEOMELES*)—**Rosaceae**—A remarkable bigeneric hybrid, succeeding in all types of fertile soil. Tolerant of maritime exposure and air pollution.

vilmorinii REHD. (*P. crenatoserrata* × *O. subrotunda*). A small, semi-evergreen shrub with slender, thornless branches. Leaves 2 to 3cm. long, pinnate in the lower half, pinnatisect in the upper half. Flowers 1cm. across, white in corymbs in May, followed by small, coral-red fruits. Garden origin 1922.

***×PYRAVAESIA** LANCASTER (*PYRACANTHA×STRANVAESIA*). A deliberate hybrid made by our propagator Peter Dummer in 1967, in which the flowers of *Stranvaesia davidiana* were pollinated by pollen of *Pyracantha atalantioides*.

+PYROCYDONIA (*+PIROCYDONIA*) (*PYRUS+CYDONIA*)—**Rosaceae**—Interesting graft hybrids (chimeras) between Pear and Quince.

danielii REHD. (*Cydonia oblonga+Pyrus communis 'Williams' Bon Chretien'*). A remarkable quince-like tree or shrub with ovate, downy leaves and white flowers which are succeeded by large, apple-like fruits which are brown with paler spotting. First recorded in 1902 at the junction of a pear grafted onto a quince in a garden at Rennes in France.

×PYRONIA (*CYDONIA×PYRUS*)—**Rosaceae**—A remarkable bi-generic hybrid intermediate between a Quince and a Pear and succeeding in all types of fertile soil. Tolerant of polluted atmosphere.

veitchii GUILL. (*C. oblonga×P. communis*). A large shrub or small tree with oval, entire leaves. Flowers white, nearly 5cm. across, borne usually three together at the tips of branchlets; anthers violet. Fruit ellipsoid, 8cm. long, greenish-yellow, spotted red. Raised by Messrs. Veitch about 1895. Also known as *×P. 'John Seden'*.

'Luxemburgiana'. Leaves larger. Flowers about 4cm. across, pale rose. Fruits resembling small pears.

PYRUS—**Rosaceae**—The generic name, here applied only to the Pears, has been used in the past for Apples and Crabs (*Malus*); Chokeberries (*Aronia*); Japanese Quinces (*Chaenomeles*); and Mountain Ashes and Whitebeams (*Sorbus*), all of which are listed under their respective headings in this manual. The ornamental pears are small to medium-sized, deep rooted trees with green to silvery-grey leaves, and white flowers in April. They are quite tolerant both of drought and moisture, and are excellently suited for cold areas. They are also tolerant of smoke pollution and succeed in all types of fertile soil. All are native of the Old World.

amygdaliformis VILL. A rare and quaint species from the northern shores of the Mediterranean. A large shrub or small tree with occasionally spiny branches. Leaves narrow, shallowly toothed or entire, at first silvery, becoming sage green. Fruits small, globose, yellow-brown. I. 1810.

'Cuneifolia'. A form with smaller, narrower leaves than the type.

betulifolia BGE. A graceful, slender, small tree of rapid growth. Leaves ovate or rounded, with a slender point, strongly toothed, greyish-green at first, becoming green and glossy above. Fruits small, the size of a large pea, brown. N. China. I. 1882.

calleryana DCNE. Medium-sized tree with normally thorny branches and oval or broadly ovate, finely-toothed, glossy green leaves. Fruits small, like large brown peas, on slender stalks. China. I. 1908.

'Bradford'. A selected, non-thorny seedling, raised at the Plant Introduction Station, Glenn Dale, Maryland (U.S.A.), forming a vigorous, medium-sized, dense-headed tree, flowering profusely in late March or early April, and in suitable conditions the leaves colouring attractively in autumn. Highly praised as an ornamental in the United States and commonly planted as a street tree. The original tree is now said to be over 15m. high and 9m. across after forty-four years.

×canescens SPACH (*nivalis×salicifolia*). A small tree attractive when in flower. Leaves lanceolate or narrowly oval, finely-toothed, greyish-white, downy when young, eventually becoming green and glossy above. Fruits small, roundish, pale green. A most attractive silvery-foliage tree.

communis L. The common or garden pear. A medium-sized tree with oval or rounded, glossy green leaves which often give rich autumn tints. The branches in April are smothered with blossom, to be followed by sweet tasting pears. Long cultivated and said to be a hybrid of multiple parentage. Over a thousand cultivars are known.

elaeagrifolia PALL. A small tree or large shrub with erect, thorny branches and narrow, greyish leaves. Flowers over 2·5cm. across, followed by small, rounded or top-shaped fruits. A most attractive grey foliage tree. S.E. Europe. I. 1800.

PYRUS—*continued*

× **lecontei** REHD. (*communis* × *pyrifolia*). A small tree with glossy green, finely-toothed leaves and yellow fruits. Rich autumn colour. The cultivars '*Kieffer*' and '*Le Conte*' originated from this cross. Originated before 1850.

longipes COSS. & DUR. A small tree or large shrub with rounded or ovate, finely-toothed leaves which are glossy green above. Small, rounded, brown fruits. Algeria. I. before 1875.

× **michauxii** POIR. (*amygdaliformis* × *nivalis*). A small, round-headed tree with entire, ovate or oval, greyish leaves which later become glossy-green above. Fruits rounded or top-shaped, greenish-yellow, spotted brown.

nivalis JACQ. A small tree with stout, ascending branches, most conspicuous in April when the pure white flowers are abundantly produced simultaneously with the white-woolly young leaves. Leaves oval or obovate, entire. Fruits small, rounded, yellowish-green, becoming sweet when over-ripe. A most attractive silvery-foliage tree. S. Europe. I. 1800.

pashia D. DON. A small, round-headed tree with ovate, finely-toothed leaves sometimes three-lobed on vigorous shoots. Flowers pink-flushed in bud opening white with red anthers. Rounded fruits 2 to 2·5cm. across, brown with paler speckles. Himalaya; W. China. I. 1825.

pyraster BURGSD. (*communis pyraster*). "Wild Pear". A small to medium-sized tree with occasionally thorny branches. Leaves ovate or rounded, crenulate-serrulate, glossy green above. Fruits small, globose or pear-shaped, yellow or brown. The wild counterpart of *P. communis*. Europe; W. Asia; doubtfully wild in the British Isles.

pyrifolia NAKAI (*serotina*). A small to medium-sized tree. Leaves ovate-oblong, toothed, glossy-green above, 8 to 12cm. long, often giving rich autumn colour. Fruits small, rounded, brown. China. C. 1909.

culta NAKAI. A form with larger leaves and much larger fruits which are hard and gritty. Long cultivated in China and Japan. I. 1880.

salicifolia PALL. "Willow-leaved Pear". A graceful, small, often weeping tree with silvery, narrow, willow-like leaves eventually becoming greyish-green and shining above. Flowers creamy-white. Fruits small, top-shaped, brown. Caucasus. I. 1780. We offer the following clone:—

'Pendula'. A very elegant and attractive silvery-grey tree with weeping branches. This is the form in general cultivation. A.G.M. 1969.

serotina. See *P. pyrifolia*.

syriaca BOISS. A small, round-headed tree with usually thorny branches. Leaves oblong-lanceolate, finely-toothed, glossy-green. Fruits small, globular or top-shaped. S.W. Asia; Cyprus. I. before 1874.

ussuriensis MAXIM. A vigorous small to medium-sized tree with ovate or rounded, bristle-toothed leaves, turning bronze-crimson in autumn. The most important of the wild Chinese pears, and one of the earliest in flower. Fruits small, yellow-green. N.E. Asia. I. 1855.

QUERCUS—**Fagaceae**—A very large genus of deciduous and evergreen trees, or occasionally shrubs, extending from cold temperate to tropical regions. Two species are native to the British Isles and are valued for their timber. Many reach noble proportions and live to a great age. Several species possess large or attractively-cut leaves and quite a few give rich autumn tints. The flowers of the oak are monoecious, the drooping male catkins appearing with the leaves in spring. They thrive in deep, rich soils and, apart from the North American Red and White oaks, are mostly lime-tolerant, given a deep soil over chalk, but very few succeed on a shallow chalk-soil. One may judge the quality and depth of soil by the rate of growth and ultimate size of our native oaks.

‡***acuta** THUNB. (*laevigata*). A small, slow-growing evergreen tree or large bushy shrub. Leaves leathery, elliptic, slender pointed, glossy, dark green above. Most attractive when the bright, green, young leaves emerge in late spring and early summer. Japan. I. about 1878.

acutissima CARRUTH. (Cerris Section) (*serrata* SIEB. & ZUCC.). Medium-sized, free-growing tree with narrowly oblong, chestnut-like, bright, polished green leaves which persist into winter, margined with bristle-tipped teeth. They are downy at first, becoming glabrous above and glabrate beneath, with axillary tufts of hairs. Japan; Korea; China. I. 1862.

QUERCUS—*continued*

acutissima chenii CAMUS. A Chinese variety with obovate, glossy green leaves. Late-made, unripened growth is subject to frost damage in cold areas. Not satisfactory on shallow chalk soils.

aegilops. See *Q. macrolepis.*

***agrifolia** NEE. A small, round-headed, evergreen tree or large shrub occasionally reaching 12m., with smooth, black bark becoming rough and squared with age. Leaves oval or rounded, shortly-stalked, 2·5 to 5cm. long, hard in texture, armed with spine-tipped, marginal teeth; smooth, shiny green above, glabrous except for axillary tufts of hair beneath. Acorns sessile, cone-shaped, 2·5cm. long. California; Mexico. Introduced by Hartweg, in 1843.

‡alba L. (Prinus Section). "White Oak". In the British Isles, generally a medium-sized tree with obovate, deeply and irregularly lobed, soft-green leaves, reddish when unfolding, turning purple-crimson in autumn. S.E. Canada; E. United States. I. 1724.

repanda MICHX. Leaves with broad, shallow lobes.

aliena BL. (Prinus Section). A small tree with large, obovate to oblong-lanceolate, coarsely-toothed leaves, 15 to 20cm. long, shining dark green above, paler and pubescent beneath. Japan. I. 1908.

acuteserrata MAXIM. A form with smaller, narrower leaves with gland-tipped teeth. C. China; Korea; Formosa; Japan. I. 1905.

†*alnifolia POECH (Suber Section). "Golden Oak". A rare and interesting, slow-growing, medium to large shrub in cultivation. Leaves rounded or broad obovate, hard in texture, hooded at apex, glossy green above and yellow-felted beneath. Hardy in sheltered gardens in the home counties. Cyprus. I. 1815.

alpestris. See *Q. faginea.*

ambrozyana. See *Q. ×hispanica 'Ambrozyana'.*

aquatica. See *Q. nigra.*

†arizonica SARG. A large shrub or small tree in cultivation. Leaves long persistent, obovate to oblong-lanceolate, shortly spine-toothed, 5 to 10cm. long. S. Central U.S.A.; N. Mexico.

bambusifolia FORT. not HANCE. See *Q. myrsinifolia.*

‡bicolor WILLD. (Prinus Section). A medium-sized tree, with characteristic flaking bark, particularly noticeable on young specimens. Leaves obovate, 13 to 18cm. long, shallowly lobed, polished green above, thinly whitish or greyish felted beneath, or sometimes only inconspicuously pubescent. S.E. Canada; Eastern U.S.A. I. 1800.

borealis maxima. See *Q. rubra.*

‡×bushii SARG. (*marilandica×velutina*). Medium-sized tree with leaves intermediate in character between those of the parents, generally obovate and strongly three to seven lobed, clothed with a pale yellowish pubescence beneath. Eastern U.S.A.

canariensis WILLD. (Robur Section) (*mirbeckii*). "Algerian Oak". A handsome, large tree with very dark grey, deeply fissured bark and a dense rounded head of branches; much narrower as a young tree. The large, obovate or oval, shallowly-lobed leaves are dark shining green above, paler or slightly glaucous beneath and remain on the tree until the New Year. An excellent fast growing tree succeeding equally well on heavy clay or shallow chalky soil, easily recognised in winter by its bold, persistent foliage. N. Africa; S. Portugal; Spain. I. about 1845.

canariensis×robur. A fast-growing tree, intermediate in character between the parents, leaves never as large as in *Q. canariensis.* When home-grown seed of *Q. canariensis* is raised, the progeny is almost invariably this hybrid.

castaneifolia C. A. MEY. (Cerris Section). "Chestnut-leaved Oak". A magnificent medium-sized to large tree resembling the "Turkey Oak" in general appearance. Leaves oblong or narrowly oval, tapered at both ends and margined with coarse, triangular, sharply-pointed teeth, shining dark green above, minutely greyish pubescent beneath. Caucasus; Persia. I. 1846.

'Green Spire'. A broadly columnar form of compact habit, raised in our nurseries. A vigorous, tall tree.

QUERCUS—*continued*

cerris L. "Turkey Oak". A large tree and possibly the fastest growing oak in this country. Excellent in chalky soils and in maritime exposure. Leaves oval or oblong; coarsely-toothed or shallowly-lobed, covered with stellate hairs and slightly rough to the touch. Both the winter buds and the acorn cups are furnished with long, narrow, downy scales. The leaves of sucker shoots and vigorous growths are often variable in size and shape. S. Europe; Asia Minor. I. 1735.

ambrozyana. See *Q.* ×*hispanica 'Ambrozyana'*.

'Laciniata'. Leaves pinnatisect, with narrow, spreading, mucronate lobes.

'Variegata'. Leaves with a conspicuous, creamy-white margin. A most effective variegated tree.

***chrysolepis** LIEBM. (Ilex Section). "Californian Live Oak"; "Maul Oak". A variable, small, slow-growing evergreen tree or large shrub. Leaves oval or ovate, spine-toothed, often entire on mature trees, resembling those of *Q. coccifera*, but normally larger and greyish or yellowish downy and minutely gland-dotted beneath, becoming sub-glabrous during the second year. S.W. United States; Mexico. I. 1877.

vacciniifolia. See *Q. vacciniifolia*.

***coccifera** L. (Suber Section). "Kermes Oak". A very slow-growing, dense evergreen shrub 1 to 2m. high, occasionally more in its native habitat. The polished, green leaves are very variable and may be small and prickly or flat and nearly smooth. This is the host plant to the Kermes insect, from which is obtained cochineal, a once common scarlet dye. A splendid back-cloth for the rock garden. In the South of France it may frequently be seen growing in stony arid ground in company with scrubby *Quercus ilex*, *Phillyrea angustifolia*, *Juniperus oxycedrus* and *J. phoenicea*. Mediterranean Region; Portugal. Cultivated in England since 17th century.

‡coccinea MUENCHH. "Scarlet Oak". A large tree with attractive, broad, deeply-lobed leaves, each lobe furnished with several bristle-tipped teeth; glossy dark green above during summer, turning in autumn, branch by branch, to a glowing scarlet. Some leaves persist on a few lower branches until Christmas. One of the finest trees for autumn colour, but variable in this respect. S.E. Canada; E. United States. I. 1691.

'Splendens'. A selected form vegetatively propagated. Leaves rich scarlet in autumn. F.C.C. 1893. A.G.M. 1927.

conferta. See *Q. frainetto*.

cuspidata. See *CASTANOPSIS cuspidata*.

densiflora. See *LITHOCARPUS densiflorus*.

‡dentata THUNB. (Prinus Section) (*daimio*). "Daimyo Oak". A rare species generally making a small, angular tree or large irregular shrub in the British Isles. Remarkable for its very large, obovate, broadly-lobed leaves which are occasionally over 30cm. long and 18cm. wide. Japan; Korea; China. I. 1830. A.M. 1901.

'Pinnatifida'. A striking but slow-growing form in which the leaves are deeply cut into narrow lobes.

douglasii HOOK. & ARN. "Blue Oak". A small, Californian tree or large shrub with oblong, occasionally lobed leaves which are sea-green above, paler beneath.

***dumosa** NUTT. "Californian Scrub Oak". An evergreen, intricately-branched shrub, with slender stems and tiny, dark green, oblong or rounded, spiny leaves. California; Mexico.

edulis. See *LITHOCARPUS edulis*.

‡ellipsoidalis E. J. HILL. A medium-sized to large tree, related to *Q. palustris*, usually with a short trunk and spreading head. The deeply-lobed leaves, on slender petioles, turn deep crimson in autumn, equal to the best forms of *Q. coccinea*. C. North America. I. 1902.

faginea LAM. (*alpestris*). A large shrub or small spreading tree. Leaves very variable in shape with mucronate teeth, shining green above, grey tomentose beneath; long persistent. Spain; Portugal; Balearic Isles.

QUERCUS—*continued*

frainetto TEN. (Robur Section) (*conferta*) (*farnetto*) (*pannonica*). "Hungarian Oak". A magnificent, large, fast-growing tree with fissured bark. Leaves obovate, occasionally as much as 20cm. long, deeply and regularly lobed with large oblong lobes. This fine species ought to be more widely planted. For all types of soil including chalk soils, this exotic species, together with *Q. cerris* and *Q. canariensis* is equal to, or even superior in rate of growth to, our two native species. S.E. Europe. I. 1838.

fruticosa BROT. A semi-evergreen shrub of small to medium size. Leaves leathery, obovate-oblong with mucronate teeth. A scrub oak in Portugal, S.W. Spain and N. Africa. I. about 1829.

fulhamensis. See *Q.* ×*hispanica 'Fulhamensis'*.

gambelii NUTT. (Prinus Section). A small tree or large shrub with leathery, obovate, deeply-lobed, glossy leaves. S.W. United States; N. Mexico. I. 1894.

×**ganderi** C. WOLF (*agrifolia oxyadenia* × *kelloggii*). A small semi-evergreen tree with leathery, obovate, shallowly and irregularly-lobed leaves with bristle-tipped teeth. California (San Diego).

garryana HOOK. (Prinus Section). "Oregon Oak". A medium-sized tree in the British Isles with short, stout trunk and wide-spreading head. Leaves shining green, obovate, deeply cut into oblong lobes. W. North America. I. 1873.

glandulifera BL. (Prinus Section) (*serrata* THUNB.). A small, slow-growing tree. Leaves variable, oblong-obovate to ovate-lanceolate, up to 18cm. long, margined with gland-tipped teeth, bright apple-green above, greyish-white beneath, remaining late in the year. Japan; Korea; China. I. 1877.

‡***glauca** THUNB. A rare, small, evergreen tree or more usually a large, bushy shrub with stout, leafy branches. Leaves leathery, elliptic to obovate-oblong with an abrupt point and usually several teeth, glossy green above, glaucous beneath. Japan; Formosa; China.

grosseserrata. See *Q. mongolica grosseserrata*.

haas HORT. See *Q. pedunculiflora*.

henryi. See *LITHOCARPUS henryi*.

‡×**heterophylla** MICHX. f. (*phellos* × *rubra*). A medium-sized to large tree with oblong or oval leaves varying from entire to strongly-toothed, glabrous except for axillary tufts beneath. Occurring with the parents in the wild. C. 1822.

×**hispanica** LAM. (*cerris* × *suber*). A variable hybrid between the Cork Oak and the Turkey Oak but always a magnificent tree and sometimes nearly evergreen, occuring with the parents in the wild, in southern Europe. The same hybrid has also arisen a number of times in cultivation. All are hardy, semi-evergreen trees of medium to large size, inheriting some of the Turkey Oak's vigour. The bark is thick and fissured, but never as corky as that of the Cork Oak. A very lime tolerant tree. We offer the following clones:—

'Ambrozyana' (*cerris ambrozyana*). A distinct and attractive semi-evergreen tree differing from the Turkey Oak in its darker leaves which are white beneath and remain on the tree until the following spring. When established, unless in a very exposed position or in an extremely severe winter, this tree remains evergreen. A specimen in our arboretum is nearly as large as the original tree growing in Mylnany Arboretum, Czechoslovakia, the home of the late Count Ambrozy. When we visited this splendid arboretum under the guidance of the distinguished Director Bencat and his charming interpreter Dr. F. Botka we were shown this tree as well as many other exciting plants.

'Fulhamensis' (*Q. fulhamensis*) (*'Dentata'*). "Fulham Oak". A large tree with grey, corky bark and a dense head of drooping branchlets. Leaves grey beneath, coarsely-toothed. Raised at Osborne's nursery at Fulham about 1760.

'Lucombeana' (*Q. lucombeana*). "Lucombe Oak". A large, ornamental tree raised by Mr. Lucombe in his nursery in Exeter about 1762. The original form is a tall-stemmed tree resembling *Q. cerris*, with pale grey, shallowly-fissured bark and long leaves which mostly fall around the New Year. The form we offer, which originated in 1792 as a seedling of the above, is a shorter-stemmed tree with a low, broad crown and dark grey, corky bark with deep, wide fissures. The leaves are variously shaped, but in general are shorter and remain dark green on the tree until spring, except in the hardest winters.

×**hybrida.** See *Q.* ×*rosacea*.

QUERCUS—*continued*

***hypoleuca** ENGELM. A large, tender shrub, attaining tree-size in its native habitat. Leaves leathery, lanceolate pointed at apex, entire or with occasional teeth, greyish downy at first becoming green above white beneath. S. United States.

***hypoleucoides** CAMUS. A very rare and remarkable large, spreading shrub with grey tomentose branches. Leaves thick and leathery, narrowly oblong to lanceolate, 5 to 8cm. long, grey, downy beneath. Mexico.

***ilex** L. "Evergreen Oak"; "Holm Oak". A large tree with attractive corrugated bark and rounded head of branches, the ends of which become pendulous with age. Leaves leathery, dark glossy green above, greyish downy beneath or glabrous, entire or toothed, variable both in shape and size depending on age of tree and growing conditions. Leaves on young bushy specimens in shade are often completely green and glabrous. Thrives in all classes of well-drained soil, and is particularly valuable for coastal planting, but is not recommended for the very coldest inland areas. Responds well to clipping and tolerates shade.

Excepting certain conifers, this is probably the most majestic evergreen tree cultivated in the British Isles. A large tree with its lush piles of dark green foliage is a striking sight, particularly in June when the tawny or white woolly young shoots and pendulous, yellow catkins are emerging. There can be few species which exhibit such an extraordinary variation in shape, size and texture of leaf. The "Evergreen Oak" will make a magnificent rigid hedge resistant to sea winds. Mediterranean Region; S.W. Europe. Cultivated in England since the 16th century.

'Bicton'. A form with large, broad leaves. There is a remarkable old specimen at Bicton, South Devon.

'Fordii' (*'Angustifolia'*). A distinct small leaf form of dense, broadly conical habit. Leaves narrow, 2·5 to 4cm. long, and 8 to 12mm. wide.

gramuntia L. A slow-growing compact shrubby form with spine-toothed leaves.

‡**ilicifolia** WANGH. "Bear Oak". A spreading shrub or small tree rarely exceeding 5m., with obovate, deeply-lobed leaves that are white felted beneath, and persist into early winter. Young growths attractively pink-flushed. E. United States. I. about 1800.

‡**imbricaria** MICHX. "Shingle Oak". A medium-sized tree, occasionally reaching 20m. Leaves oblong or narrowly oval, 10 to 18cm. long, usually entire, shining dark green, displaying rich autumn colours. The English name refers to the use of the wood by early settlers for shingles on roofs. Eastern U.S.A. Introduced by John Fraser in 1786.

†***incana** ROXB. A very striking, small evergreen tree or large shrub for the mildest areas. Leaves narrowly oval, slender-pointed and conspicuously toothed, dark green above, white-felted beneath. It attains a large size in the Himalaya where it is accompanied by *Rhododendron arboreum*. Large, old specimens are said to have attractive flaking bark. I. about 1815.

infectoria OLIVIER. A large, semi-evergreen shrub or small tree, closely related to *Q. lusitanica* from which it differs chiefly in its glabrous or nearly glabrous, spine-toothed leaves and branches. S.W. Asia; Cyprus; Greece. I. 1850.

‡**kelloggii** NEWB. "Californian Black Oak". A medium-sized to large tree with deeply-lobed, bristle-toothed, shining green leaves. California and Oregon. I. 1878.

*× **kewensis** OSBORN (*cerris* × *wislizenii*). A small to medium-sized, vigorous tree, with dense compact head and almost persistent, small dark green, angularly-lobed leaves. Raised at Kew in 1914.

laevigata. See *Q. acuta*.

lanuginosa. See *Q. pubescens*.

‡**laurifolia** MICHX. "Laurel Oak". Medium-sized, semi-evergreen tree of dense, rounded habit. Leaves glossy green, oblong or oblong-obovate, entire or occasionally shallowly-lobed. Differing from the closely related *Q. nigra* in its narrower, less obovate and usually longer leaves. Eastern U.S.A. I. 1786.

‡× **leana** NUTT. (*imbricaria* × *velutina*). A medium-sized to large tree with oblong, entire or occasionally lobed leaves 10 to 18cm. long, firm and leathery in texture. Occuring with the parents in the wild. C. 1850.

libani OLIVIER (Cerris Section). "Lebanon Oak". A small, elegant tree with slender branches and long, persistent, oblong-lanceolate leaves which are glossy green above and margined with triangular, bristle-tipped teeth. Closely related to *Q. trojana*. Syria; Asia Minor. I. about 1855.

QUERCUS—*continued*

lobata NEE. "Valley Oak". A slow-growing, small to medium-sized tree in the British Isles. Leaves elliptic to obovate, with broad, rounded lobes, dark green above, pale downy beneath. California. I. 1874.

lucombeana. See *Q.* ×*hispanica 'Lucombeana'*.

‡×**ludoviciana** SARG. (*falcata pagodifolia*×*phellos*). A most attractive, large, semi-evergreen tree of vigorous habit. Leaves obovate to oblanceolate, usually deeply and irregularly lobed, shining green above. Rich autumn tints. Occurs with the parents in S.E. United States. I. 1880.

lusitanica LAM. "Portuguese Oak". Usually a small, broad-headed tree. Leaves varying from oval to obovate, strongly-toothed and grey felted beneath. Closely related to *Q. faginea* and *Q. canariensis*. Excellent on all soil types including chalk. Portugal; Spain. I. 1824.

macedonica. See *Q. trojana*.

macranthera FISCH. & MEY. (Robur Section). A splendid, fast-growing tree of medium size, striking on account of its large, broad-obovate, acute, strongly lobed leaves up to 15cm. long. It is easily distinguished from related species by its stout twigs which, like the slender-scaled winter buds and leaf under-surfaces, are clothed with pale grey velvety tomentum. An excellent tree, which may be grown in deep soils over chalk. Caucasus; N. Persia. I. 1873.

‡**macrocarpa** MICHX. (Prinus Section). "Burr Oak"; "Mossy-Cup Oak". A remarkable and handsome N. American species of medium size. On vigorous young trees the conspicuously-lobed, obovate leaves are sometimes up to 40cm. long. Young shoots, buds and under-surfaces or leaves covered by a pale down. Not a tree for the plantsman who wants a perfect specimen with a gun-barrel-like stem. N.E. and N. Central North America. I. 1811.

macrolepis KOTSCHY (Cerris Section) (*aegilops*). "Valonia Oak". A small to medium-sized tree with grey tomentose twigs. Leaves somewhat greyish-olive-green, oblong, sharply-lobed, the lobes bristle-tipped and occasionally toothed, grey tomentose beneath. The acorns, ripening the second year, are set in large cups with reflexed, slender scales. S. Balkans; S.E. Italy; W. Asia. I. 1731.

pyrami (*aegilops pyrami*). A small tree of neat habit with rugged bark and deeply cut, often fiddle-shaped leaves.

‡**marilandica** MUENCHH. "Black Jack Oak". A remarkable, small, slow-growing tree of low, spreading habit. Leaves sometimes almost triangular, broadly obovate, tapered to the base, more or less three-lobed at the broad apex, up to 18cm. long and often as much across, glossy green above, tawny-yellow beneath, turning yellow or brown in autumn. Eastern U.S.A. C. 1739.

‡**michauxii** NUTT. (Prinus Section) (*prinus* in part). "Swamp Chestnut Oak"; "Basket Oak". A medium to large round-headed tree with obovate, coarsely-toothed, bright green leaves. Rich yellow autumn colour. Eastern U.S.A. I. 1737.

mirbeckii. See *Q. canariensis*.

‡**mongolica** FISCH. (Prinus Section). "Mongolian Oak". A striking, irregular, small to medium-sized tree with thick glabrous branches. Leaves large, shortly-stalked, obovate to obovate-oblong, strongly lobed, auricled at the base, borne in dense clusters at the ends of the branches. Japan; Manchuria; Korea; Mongolia; E. Siberia. I. 1879.

grosseserrata REHD. & WILS. (*Q. grosseserrata*). A form with usually narrowly obovate, pointed leaves with rather acute, forward-pointing teeth. Japan.

montana. See *Q. prinus*.

‡**muehlenbergii** ENGELM. "Yellow Chestnut Oak". Medium-sized tree with oblong to oblong-lanceolate, coarsely-toothed leaves, yellowish-green above, pale pubescent beneath, mid-rib and petioles yellow. Rich autumn tints. S. Canada; E. United States; N.E. Mexico. I. 1822.

‡***myrsinifolia** BLUME (*bambusifolia*) (*vibrayeana*). A small, densely-branched evergreen tree of compact habit. The smooth, somewhat shining leaves are lanceolate with finely tapered points, remotely-toothed, dark green above, paler beneath, purple-red when unfolding. China; Japan. Introduced by Robert Fortune in 1854.

‡**nigra** L. (*aquatica*). "Water Oak". A medium-sized tree, native of the southern U.S.A., where it frequents moist areas. Leaves normally obovate, occasionally oblong, variously lobed, particularly on young plants, sometimes entire, glossy, deep rich green on both sides, often persisting into early winter. I. 1723.

QUERCUS—*continued*

pachyphylla. See *LITHOCARPUS pachyphyllus.*

‡**palustris** MUENCHH. "Pin Oak". A free-growing, large, dense-headed tree resembling *Q. coccinea*, but more elegant with the slender branches drooping gracefully at their extremities. Leaves deeply and sharply-lobed, shining green on both surfaces and with conspicuous tufts of down in the axils below. They are smaller than those of the "Scarlet Oak", but often turn the same rich scarlet in autumn. S.E. Canada; Eastern U.S.A. I. 1800.

pedunculata. See *Q. robur.*

pedunculiflora K. KOCH (*haas* HORT.). A rare, medium-sized to large tree related to and resembling *Q. robur*, but leaves somewhat glaucous-green above and pubescent beneath. S.E. Europe.

petraea LIEBL. (Robur Section) (*sessiliflora*). "Sessile Oak"; "Durmast Oak". One of our two large native species replacing the "Common Oak (*Q. robur*) in many damper districts or soils, notably in the west. It is distinguished by its often rather larger, long-stalked leaves which are usually pubescent beneath along the midrib, and cuneate, not auricled at the base; also in its sessile fruits. Good for maritime exposure. W., C. and S.E. Europe; Asia Minor.

'Acutifolia'. Leaves with pronounced and regular lobes.

'Columnaris'. A densely-branched, columnar tree of medium size. A sport of '*Mespilifolia*'.

'Laciniata'. Leaves up to 15cm. long, narrow, deeply incised with forward-pointing lobes, occasionally reduced almost to the midrib.

'Mespilifolia'. A form with irregular and crinkled, narrow leaves, 15 to 20cm. long, tapered at both ends and entire or shallowly-lobed.

'Purpurea' ('*Rubicunda*'). Leaves very similar in colour to those of the "Purple Beech".

'Salicifolia'. Leaves ovate-oblong to oblong-lanceolate, entire or with an occasional shallow lobe. Propagated from the tree in the Trompenburg Arboretum, Rotterdam, whose director, Mr. van Hoey Smith, is an authority on oaks.

‡**phellos** L. "Willow Oak". A large tree with slender branches and narrow, entire, willow-like leaves which are glossy green above, turning yellow and orange in autumn. The leaves of young trees are often lobed. An attractive species, broad-headed when young. Requires a lime-free soil. Eastern U.S.A. I. 1723.

***phillyreoides** GRAY (Ilex Section). A rare, evergreen shrub recalling *Phillyrea latifolia*, generally seen as a dense, rounded bush below 5m., but occasionally a small tree. Leaves oval or obovate, leathery, glossy green on both surfaces, sharply but minutely toothed, usually bronze-tinted when unfolding. A useful, bright looking, small-leaved evergreen rarely seen in gardens. China; Japan. Introduced by Richard Oldham in 1861.

‡**pontica** K. KOCH (Robur Section). "Armenian Oak". An unmistakable species, usually shrubby, but occasionally a small tree. Shoots stout; leaves large, oval to obovate, sometimes as much as 25cm. long and 12cm. wide, strongly ribbed and toothed. The mid-rib and petiole are yellow. Rich yellow autumn colour. Armenia; Caucasus. I. 1885.

‡**prinus** L. (*montana*). "Chestnut Oak". Medium-sized to large tree with an open, spreading crown. Leaves obovate to oblong-obovate, crenately-dentate, turning rich yellow in autumn. S.E. Canada; Eastern U.S.A. C. 1688.

×**pseudoturneri.** See *Q.* ×*turneri.*

pubescens WILLD. (Robur Section) (*lanuginosa*). A small to medium-sized tree, occasionally shrubby, with densely hairy twigs. Leaves obovate, with wavy margins, deeply-lobed and covered with a thick greyish down. W., C. and S. Europe.

palensis SCHWARZ. Differing from the type in its usually shrubby habit and smaller leaves.

QUERCUS—*continued*

pyrenaica WILLD. (Robur Section) (*toza*). "Pyrenean Oak". A medium to large-sized tree with a wide-spreading head of pendant branches, tomentose branchlets, and bark of pale grey, deeply fissured into knobbly squares. Leaves variable in size, obovate or broadly oblong, with long, narrow, usually pointed lobes, glossy green above, grey felted beneath. Its long, drooping, male catkins are attractive in June, turning from grey to gold. S.W. Europe; N. Italy. I. 1822.

'Pendula'. An elegant form with drooping branches. There are good examples of this tree both at Westonbirt Arboretum and Holland Park, London.

†***reticulata** HUMB. & BONPL. (Ilex Section). A rare, evergreen species. A large shrub or small, slow-growing tree with densely hairy branches and obovate, spine-toothed, leathery leaves, which are sea-green above, paler, shortly pubescent and strongly reticulate beneath. S. Arizona; New Mexico (U.S.A.). C. 1883.

robur L. (*pedunculata*). "Common Oak"; "English Oak". This is the better known and more widely distributed of our two native species, the other being *Q. petraea*. A large, long-lived tree, developing a broad head of rugged branches when growing in the open. Leaves sessile or almost so, shallowly-lobed and auricled at the base. Fruits one to several on a slender stalk. Almost all the ancient "named" oaks in the British Isles belong to this species rather than *Q. petraea*. Europe; Caucasus; Asia Minor; N. Africa.

'Atropurpurea'. A curious, slow-growing form with leaves and shoots a rich vinous purple, becoming greyish-purple at maturity.

'Concordia'. "Golden Oak". A small, rounded tree of very slow growth. Leaves suffused golden-yellow throughout spring and summer. Raised in Van Geert's nursery at Ghent in 1843. F.C.C. 1868.

'Cristata'. A curious form in which the short, broad, deeply-lobed leaves are folded and curled.

'Cucullata'. Leaves long and relatively narrow, the margins variously lobed and inrolled.

'Fastigiata'. "Cypress Oak". A large, imposing tree of columnar habit.

'Fastigiata Purpurea'. Smaller than *'Fastigiata'* with young leaves reddish-purple throughout the growing season. This is probably the cultivar *'Purpurascens'* of De Candolle.

'Filicifolia'. See *Q.* ×*rosacea 'Filicifolia'*.

'Pectinata'. See *Q.* ×*rosacea 'Filicifolia'*.

'Pendula'. "Weeping Oak". A small to medium-sized tree with pendulous branches.

'Strypemonde'. A curious form with relatively narrow, jaggedly lobed leaves, mottled yellow.

'Variegata'. Leaves with an irregular, creamy-white margin.

×**rosacea** BECHST. (Robur Section) (*petraea*×*robur*) (×*hybrida*). A variable hybrid, generally intermediate in character between the parents but sometimes leaning more to one than the other. Occurs with the parents in the wild.

'Filicifolia' (*robur 'Filicifolia'*) (*robur 'Pectinata'*). Leaves pinnately divided into narrow, forwardly pointing segments; petioles long and under-surfaces downy as in *Q. petraea*. Fruits peduncled. As effective as the better known "Fern-leaved Beech", though never so large a tree.

‡**rubra** L. (*borealis maxima*). "Red Oak". This large, fast-growing, broad-headed tree thrives in most parts of the British Isles, even in industrial areas, and in some places has reached a height of over 30m. Its large, oval or obovate, lobed, dull green leaves turn red and finally red-brown before falling, but on some trees they turn ruby-red or mixed yellow and brown or russet. It differs from the closely related *Q. coccinea* in its stout, more horizontal primary branches and in its usually less deeply-lobed, matt, not glossy, leaves. Eastern N. America. I. 1724. A.M. 1971. A.G.M. 1973.

'Aurea'. A small to medium-sized tree, the young leaves in spring of a bright yellow, later turning to yellow-green, finally green. A lovely clone which requires a sheltered position in partial shade otherwise the leaves are inclined to scorch in strong sun. A.M. 1971

‡***sadlerana** R. BR. A rare and distinct species collected in the Siskiyou Mountains, California. A small, stoutly-branched shrub with conspicuously scaly buds and prominently veined, serrately-toothed leaves. California; S.W. Oregon.

QUERCUS—*continued*

‡ × **schochiana** DIECK (*palustris × phellos*). A medium-sized tree of spreading habit, with glossy green, often willow-like leaves, few-toothed or lobed or occasionally entire. A most attractive hybrid, colouring bright yellow in the autumn. Semi-evergreen in sheltered positions. Occurs both in the wild and in cultivation. C. 1894.

serrata. See *Q. acutissima* and *Q. glandulifera.*

sessiliflora. See *Q. petraea.*

‡**shumardii** BUCKL. (*schumardii schneckii*). A small to medium-sized tree with attractive, deeply-cut leaves turning red or golden-brown in the autumn. S. and C. United States. I. 1897.

‡**stellata** WANGEN. A medium-sized tree with obovate, conspicuously and deeply lobed leaves which are rough to the touch above and densely clothed beneath with a stellate tomentum. W. and C. United States. I. 1819

***suber** L. "Cork Oak". Normally a short-stemmed, wide-spreading tree of medium size, but occasionally reaching 20m. Its bark is thick, rugged and corky and provides the cork of commerce. Leaves oval or oblong, broadly-toothed, leathery, lustrous green above, greenish-grey felted beneath. Though very frost resistant, it is not satisfactory in the coldest counties. S. Europe; N. Africa. Extensively cultivated in Spain and Portugal. I. 1699.

tinctoria. See *Q. velutina.*

toza. See *Q. pyrenaica.*

trojana WEBB (Cerris Section) (*macedonica*). "Macedonian Oak". A small to medium-sized, densely branched, usually deciduous tree. The rather shiny, obovate-oblong, taper-pointed leaves are margined with large, incurved triangular teeth, and are often retained until the end of the year. Balkans; S.E. Italy. I. about 1890.

× **turneri** WILLD. (*ilex × robur*) (*pseudoturneri*). "Turner's Oak". A distinctive, small to medium-sized, semi-evergreen tree with a compact, rounded head of dark green leaves, which are oblong-obovate to oblanceolate, with four to six broad, mucronate teeth on each margin. Good on calcareous soils. Raised in the nursery of a Mr. Turner in Essex, during the late 18th century.

***vacciniifolia** KELLOGG (Ilex Section) (*chrysolepis vacciniifolia*). "Huckleberry Oak". A slow-growing, small to medium-sized evergreen shrub of dense, bushy habit. Leaves 1·5 to 2·5cm. long, pointed, undulate and spine-toothed or entire, greyish-green beneath. Quite hardy in our arboretum. S.W. United States.

variabilis BL. (Cerris Section). A large, elegant tree which develops an attractive, corky bark. Leaves chestnut-like, narrow, oval or oblong, margined with small, bristle-tipped teeth, green above, densely greyish or yellowish-white pubescent beneath and persisting late into the autumn. China; Korea; Formosa; Japan. I. 1861.

‡**velutina** LAM. (*tinctoria*). "Black Oak"; "Yellow-bark Oak". A large tree with downy buds and young shoots. Leaves large, hard and often 30cm. long, deeply and irregularly-lobed, dark green and glossy above, covered by a pale pubescence beneath. The inner bark is a bright yellow, from which is extracted the dye "quercitron". Rich autumn tints. E. and C. United States. I. 1800.

'Rubrifolia' (*'Albertsii'*). One of the most striking of all oaks with its enormous hooded leaves measuring up to 40cm. long and 23cm. wide. Colours in autumn warm reddish-brown and yellowish.

vibrayeana. See *Q. myrsinifolia.*

‡***virginiana** MILL. "Live Oak". A small, wide-spreading, evergreen tree with tomentose twigs and elliptic or oblong, leathery leaves which are normally entire, or rarely with a few spiny teeth, glossy dark green above, greyish or whitish, pubescent beneath. S.E. United States; N.E. Mexico; W. Cuba. I. 1739.

warburgii A. CAMUS. A rare, large tree of uncertain origin. The large obovate, shallowly-lobed leaves are remarkably like those of *Q. robur*, but are slightly longer-stalked and semi-evergreen in nature, often remaining on the branches until the following March. Our stock is propagated from the original tree growing in the University Botanic Garden, Cambridge.

***wislizenii** A. DC. A large shrub or small, rounded tree of slow growth. Leaves holly-like, polished, leathery, oblong to ovate, edged with slender spiny teeth. Related to and resembling *Q. agrifolia*, but leaves almost sessile, and glabrous, with acorns maturing the first (not second) autumn. California; Mexico. I. 1874.

QUERCUS—*continued*

wislizenii frutescens ENGELM. A shrubby variety with smaller, rigidly spiny leaves. California.

"QUICK". See *CRATAEGUS monogyna*.

†***QUILLAIA**—**Rosaceae**—A small genus of tender, evergreen, South American trees or large shrubs, succeeding in all kinds of well-drained, fertile soil.

saponaria MOLINA "Soap Bark Tree". A small Chilean tree. Leaves oval, toothed, thick, leathery and shining green. Flowers usually solitary in April, rather large, white with purple centre. The bark contains saponin, as well as several minerals used for washing purposes in parts of Chile. Only suitable for the mildest localities. I. 1832.

"QUINCE". See *CYDONIA oblonga*.

***RAPHIOLEPIS**—**Rosaceae**—A small genus of rather slow-growing, evergreen shrubs with firm, leathery leaves. They require a warm, sunny position in a well-drained, fertile soil.

† × **delacourii** ANDRE (*indica* × *umbellata*). A charming shrub usually less than 2m., of rounded habit. Leaves obovate, glossy green, toothed in upper half. Flowers of a lovely rose-pink borne in erect, terminal panicles in spring or summer. Only injured by severe frosts. It makes an attractive wall shrub. Raised by Mons. Delacour, near Cannes, France, towards the end of 19th century. A.M. 1932.

'Coates' Crimson'. A choice selection with rose-crimson flowers.

†**indica** LINDL. A small shrub with narrow, toothed leathery leaves 5 to 7·5cm. long. Flowers white, flushed pink, borne in racemes intermittently during spring and summer. Only suitable for the mildest localities or the conservatory. S. China. C. 1806.

umbellata MAK. (*japonica*). A delightful, dense, slow-growing shrub of rounded habit, usually attaining about 1·2m. in the open or higher against a wall. Leaves oval, thick and leathery, inconspicuously toothed. Terminal clusters of slightly fragrant, white flowers in June, followed by bronzy-black fruits. Normally hardy, but injured in the severe winter 1962-63. Japan; Korea. I. about 1862.

†***REEVESIA**—**Sterculiaceae**—A small genus of trees and shrubs, with monoecious flowers. Only suitable for sheltered woodland gardens in the mildest areas, but excellent conservatory subjects. They require a moist, deep, preferably lime-free, loam and sun or semi-shade.

pubescens MAST. A rare, small, evergreen tree; leaves ovate, rather leathery with the veins impressed above. Flowers creamy-white, fragrant, borne in terminal corymbs during summer. E. Himalaya; W. China. A splendid specimen, like a large Bay tree (*Laurus nobilis*) grew for many years at Caerhays Castle, Cornwall. and a smaller specimen in a more exposed position at Wakehurst, Sussex, but both succumbed to the severe winter of 1962-63. A.M. 1954.

thyrsoidea LINDL. A tall, evergreen shrub or small tree with ovate-lanceolate leaves. Flowers fragrant, creamy-white, produced in dense terminal clusters 5 to 7·5cm. across, in July. S. China. I. 1826.

‡**REHDERODENDRON**—**Styracaceae**—A small genus of deciduous trees, natives of China and only known since 1930.

macrocarpum HU. A small tree with elliptic to oblong-ovate, finely serrate leaves, 7·5 to 10cm. long, usually attractively tinted before falling. Flowers white, with conspicuous yellow anthers, produced in lax, axillary racemes with the leaves, in May. The pendulous fruits are oblong, 8 to 10 ribbed, bright red. A magnificent species, in garden merit equal to the best *Styrax*. Requires a moist, lime-free soil. Discovered on Mt. Omei, W. China by Mr. F. T. Wang in 1931, and introduced by Professor Hu in 1934. A.M. 1947.

RHAMNUS—**Rhamnaceae**—A large genus of deciduous and evergreen trees and shrubs, mainly grown for their foliage effect. The flowers which may be perfect, dioecious or polygamous, are small but numerous in axillary clusters and generally inconspicuous. They will grow in all types of soils in sun or semi-shade.

RHAMNUS—*continued*

***alaterna** L. A useful, large, bushy, fast-growing evergreen shrub. Leaves alternate, small, dark glossy green; flowers yellowish-green in April; fruits red, becoming black. Mediterranean Region; Portugal. I. early in the 17th century. This evergreen should be pot-grown in nurseries. It is splendid for maritime exposure and industrial areas. In warmer, more sunnier climes, it rivals the English holly in fruit. Not recommended for the coldest inland areas.

'Angustifolia'. A small, compact bush of dense, rounded habit, with narrow, conspicuously-toothed leaves.

'Argenteovariegata'. Leaves green, marbled grey with an irregular, creamy-white margin. One of the best of all variegated shrubs, but a little less hardy than the type. A.M. 1976.

alpina L. "Alpine Buckthorn". A slow-growing, small to medium-sized shrub of compact habit, producing numerous erect stems. Leaves broad elliptic, finely-toothed, glossy green and attractively veined. Fruits black. S.W. Europe; C. Alps, Italy. I. 1752.

***californica** ESCH. (Frangula Section). "Coffee-berry". An interesting, more or less evergreen shrub of medium size with oblong or oval leaves about 5cm., occasionally to 10cm. long. Fruits red changing to purple-black. Western N. America. C. 1871.

crassifolia C. B. WOLF. A remarkable variety with larger leaves which, like the shoots are conspicuously grey velvety pubescent.

cathartica L. "Common Buckthorn". A large, native shrub or small tree, a common hedge or woodland shrub on chalk. Branches spiny, quite attractive in autumn, when laden with masses of shining black fruits. Europe.

davurica PALL. "Dahurian Buckthorn". A large shrub or small tree with slender-pointed, oblong leaves and black fruits in autumn. Siberia; Manchuria; N. China. I. 1817.

frangula L. (*Frangula alnus*). "Alder Buckthorn". A large shrub or small tree with ovate leaves turning yellow in autumn. Fruits red, changing to black. Its wood makes the best charcoal for gunpowder. Europe (including British Isles).

'Asplenifolia'. A curious form in which the leaf blade is reduced to a mere thread 3 to 5mm. wide.

***× hybrida billiardii** DIPP. (*alaterna × alpina*). A medium-sized, usually semi-evergreen shrub with small, narrow, coarsely-toothed leaves.

imeretina KIRCHN. The most outstanding of the buckthorns. A medium-sized to large shrub with stout shoots and large, handsome corrugated leaves which are dark green above, downy beneath, usually becoming bronze-purple in autumn. Some leaves may be as much as 30 to 35cm. long and 10 to 15cm. wide. A splendid shrub for a damp, shaded site. W. Caucasus. I. 1858.

infectoria L. "Avignon Berry". A spreading shrub to 2m., with spine-tipped branches and ovate or obovate leaves. The black fruits were once used by dyers. S. Europe.

japonica MAXIM. Medium-sized shrub with glossy, pale-green obovate leaves, crowded at the ends of the branchlets. The small, faintly-scented, yellowish-green flowers are produced in dense clusters in May. Fruits black. Japan. I. 1888.

parvifolia BGE. A spiny, medium-sized shrub with elliptic, dark green polished leaves and black fruits in autumn. It hasn't grown very successfully in our area. N.E. Asia. I. 1910.

procumbens EDGE. A prostrate species from the Himalaya, making a low mound of intricate stems, small, shining, bright green leaves, and producing black fruits. Most suitable for the rock garden.

pumila TURRA. "Dwarf Buckthorn". A dwarf, sometimes prostrate shrub, only a few inches high. Fruits blue-black. Suitable for the rock garden. Mts. of S. Europe; Alps. I. 1752.

purshiana DC. (Frangula Section). A small tree or large shrub worthy of inclusion in a representative arboretum. The rather large leaves are prominently veined, and downy beneath. Fruits red turning black. The drug "Cascara Sagrada" is obtained from the bark of this tree. Western N. America. C. 1870.

RHAMNUS—*continued*

rupestris SCOP. (Frangula Section). A small, spreading, sometimes procumbent shrub. Leaves elliptic or rounded. Fruits small, red at first, finally black. W. Balkans. C. 1800.

utilis DCNE. A medium-sized shrub with slender branches and oblong, polished-green leaves. Fruits black. Long cultivated for the dye known as "China Green". C. and E. China; Japan.

RHAPHITHAMNUS—Verbenaceae—A small genus of trees and shrubs, all native of Chile.

†*spinosus MOLDENKE (*cyanocarpus*). A medium-sized to large, evergreen, myrtle-like shrub of dense habit. Each pair or cluster of small, sharply-toothed leaves is accompanied by two or three sharp, needle-like spines. Flowers small, tubular, 1cm. long, pale blue, in April, berries deep blue. Requires a warm sunny wall. Introduced by William Lobb in about 1843.

RHODODENDRON (including *AZALEA*)—**Ericaceae.** The rhododendrons are one of the most important and diverse groups of ornamental plants in cultivation. They include many of the most spectacular as well as some of the noblest of flowering trees and shrubs. Late spring and early summer is the height of their flowering season and about nine-tenths flower during the months of April, May and June. The remainder are, nevertheless, an important group, bringing colour to the garden sometimes as early as January, or as late as August. Many are notable for their handsome foliage and a number of deciduous kinds for their autumn tints. For landscaping, the rhododendrons are unsurpassed. When massed, no other shrub gives such a wealth of colour. The variations in form, colour, texture and size of leaf is so remarkable that even if they never flowered, some species would still be the outstanding evergreens of the temperate world. Those with large leaves are subject to wind damage and should, if possible, be planted in woodland or similar shelter. The dwarf, small flowered species should be mass planted. They are particularly effective in the open heather garden. The same is true of almost all of the Lapponicum Series.

Rhododendrons may be grown in a moist, yet well drained, fertile soil, so long as no free lime is present. Few rhododendrons will tolerate even a trace of free lime, although applications of Iron Sequestrene to the soil often improves performance in such situations. A sheltered, semi-shaded position is appreciated by all rhododendrons but many, especially the alpine species and that wide range of hybrids popularly known as the Hardy Hybrids will luxuriate in full exposure to wind and sun. They are also remarkably tolerant of atmospheric pollution. It is better to give an annual mulch, not too deep, up to 8cm. preferably in early autumn, to protect and nourish the root system which, in rhododendrons, develops close to the soil surface, rather than loosen the top-soil by annual forking, and for this purpose, decaying leaves, bracken, peat or spent hops are excellent. Rhododendrons require no regular pruning, but the removal of the faded trusses immediately after flowering is extremely beneficial. The group of rhododendrons known as Hardy Hybrids, specimens of which have become straggly or too large may be hard pruned in April.

Hardiness. To indicate the relative hardiness of rhododendrons the system used in the Royal Horticultural Society's "Handbook of Rhododendrons" (Parts 1 and 2) has been adopted, and one or other of the symbols below will be found at the end of each individual description, except where whole groups of similar clones are of the same hardiness, in which case the symbol will be found at the end of the group description. Certain species may vary in hardiness and where this occurs, the symbol is arranged accordingly, e.g. H2-3.

H4 represents a rhododendron hardy anywhere in the British Isles.

H3 represents a rhododendron hardy in the South and West, also along the seaboard and in sheltered gardens inland.

H2 represents a rhododendron which requires protection in the most sheltered gardens.

H1 represents a rhododendron which can usually be grown only as a greenhouse plant.

RHODODENDRON—*continued*

Sections. To facilitate easy reference, the rhododendrons have been treated under five main headings, as follows:—

Rhododendron Species (including the *Azalea* series). See below.
Rhododendron Hybrids. See page 294.
Azaleodendrons. See page 317.
Deciduous Hybrid Azaleas. See page 318.
Evergreen Hybrid Azaleas. See page 321.

‡RHODODENDRON SPECIES (including the AZALEA series)

The genus Rhododendron is one of the largest, numbering over five hundred species. It is represented mainly in the northern hemisphere, reaching its greatest density in the vast expanse of mountain ranges and gorges bordering China, Tibet and Upper Burma. It is thanks to such men as George Forrest, Joseph Rock, Kingdon Ward and Ernest Wilson that our gardens have such a wide representation of species and forms. Had it not been for the late J. B. Stevenson, many of these would have been lost to cultivation during and after the first world war. Gardeners throughout the world owe to him a debt of gratitude for raising and maintaining at Tower Court, Ascot, the most complete set of Rhododendron species. After his death this work was bravely continued by his widow (who later became Mrs. Harrison) assisted by the Head Gardener, Mr. Keir. Fortunately before her death she sold the bulk of her collection to the Commissioner of Crown Lands, so that these plants have been saved for posterity in the Valley Garden made in Windsor Great Park, by Sir Eric Savill, that past master of informal gardening. Mention must also be made of Sir Joseph Hooker (1817-1911) who first introduced from the Sikkim Himalaya several of our finest species, including *R. barbatum*, *R. cinnabarinum*, *R. griffithianum*, *R. falconeri* and *R. thomsonii*.

The species offered below range from tiny, prostrate alpines to tree with enormous leaves. The dwarf species are charming rock-garden shrubs, those belonging to the *Lapponicum* and *Saluenense* series associating well with heaths. The massed planting of dwarf and alpine rhododendrons, with all their various colours ranging from white through pink and red to yellow, purple and blue, exhibit a greater colour range than that of the finest heather garden. The large-leaved species require shelter, especially from wind and will not tolerate very dry conditions for long periods. An ideal site for these is provided by thin oak woodland, with some evergreen shelter.

In compiling these notes we have been greatly assisted by the work done by Dr. Harold Fletcher in the rating of merit of Rhododendron species. Since the beginning of this century The Royal Botanic Garden, Edinburgh, has led the world in work on Rhododendrons, and such men as Sir Isaac Bayley Balfour, Sir William Wright Smith, and more recently Mr. Davidian, have been responsible for much research work, including the identification and describing of many new species.

Evergreen and Deciduous. Except where otherwise stated, the following species and their forms are evergreen.

Series. The series or section to which each species belongs is indicated in parentheses after the name.

Awards. Many awards have been given to unnamed forms of species, and these are indicated in the text as follows:—A.M.(F.) or F.C.C.(F.). This does not necessarily mean to indicate that we are offering that particular form.

aberconwayi COWAN (s. Irroratum). A small to medium-sized shrub with loose trusses of flat, saucer-shaped flowers, white, tinged pink, usually heavily spotted maroon; May and June. Leaves rather rigid and leathery, of medium size. Yunnan. H3.

adenogynum DIELS. (s. Taliense). Small to medium-sized shrub with woolly young shoots; leaves leathery covered with a tawny, suede-like felt beneath. Flowers funnel-shaped, deep rose in bud opening white, shaded rose; April to May. Yunnan; Szechwan; S.E. Tibet. C. 1917. H3.

adenophorum BALF. f. & W. W. SM. (s. Taliense). Medium-sized shrub with oblanceolate leaves covered beneath with a thick, cinnamon or fulvous tomentum. Flowers funnel-shaped, rose with scattered crimson spots; April. Yunnan. H4.

RHODODENDRON—*continued*

adenopodum FRANCH. (s. Ponticum). A medium-sized shrub with long, narrow leaves covered beneath by a dense, grey or pale fawn tomentum. Flowers bell-shaped, pale rose, with darker spots within, borne in loose trusses; April to May. Szechwan; Hupeh. I. 1901. A.M. 1926. H4.

aechmophyllum. See *R. yunnanense.*

aemulorum. See *R. mallotum.*

aeruginosum. See *R. campanulatum aeruginosum.*

aganniphum BALF. f. & WARD (s. Taliense). A medium-sized to large shrub with leaves 5 to 10cm. long, covered beneath with a smooth white or yellowish-white indumentum. Flowers bell-shaped, varying from white to deep rose, spotted crimson; May and June. S.E. Tibet; N.W. Yunnan. H4.

agastum BALF. f. & W. W. SM. (s. Irroratum). A large shrub or occasionally a small tree, the leaves clad beneath with a thin pale fawn indumentum. The narrowly-bell-shaped flowers are white, tinged rose with darker spots; February and March Yunnan. H4.

albrechtii MAXIM. (*Azalea albrechtii*) (s. Azalea). A very beautiful, medium-sized, deciduous shrub of open habit. Leaves obovate or oblong-obovate, clustered at the ends of the branches, turning yellow in autumn. Flowers deep rose, 5cm. across, appearing before or with the leaves; April and May. Japan. I. 1914. A.M. 1943. A.G.M. 1969. H4.

alutaceum BALF. f. & W. W. SM. (s. Taliense). A medium-sized to large shrub with oblong leaves up to 15cm. long, clothed beneath with a pale brown, woolly indumentum. Flowers in a loose truss, bell-shaped, rose, spotted and blotched crimson within; April. Yunnan. H4.

amagianum NEMOTO (*Azalea amagiana*) (s. Azalea). An outstanding medium-sized to large, deciduous shrub with broad-obovate leaves in clusters of three at the ends of the branches. Flowers funnel-shaped, orange-red, three to four in a truss; June and July. A.M. 1948. Japan. H4.

ambiguum HEMSL. (s. Triflorum). An attractive, medium-sized to large shrub, with 5 to 7·5cm. long leaves and clusters of three to six funnel-shaped flowers of greenish-yellow, spotted green. April and May. Szechwan. I. 1904. H4.

annae FRANCH. (s. Irroratum). Medium-sized to large shrub with rather small, narrow leaves; flowers bell-shaped, white to rose-flushed with or without purple spots; June and July. Kweichow. H3-4.

anthopogon D. DON (s. Anthopogon). A dwarf shrub of compact habit with brown, scaly branchlets and leaves up to 3cm. long, densely scaly below. Flowers in a tight, terminal cluster, narrowly tubular, varying in colour from cream to deep pink; April. Nepal; Sikkim; Assam. I. 1820. A.M. 1955. H4.

anhweiense WILS. (s. Barbatum). Medium-sized shrub with ovate-lanceolate leaves 5 to 7·5cm. long. Rounded heads of bell-shaped, white flowers, usually with a pink flush and reddish-purple spots; April and May. Anwhei Province (China). A.M. 1976. H4.

apodectum. See *R. dichroanthum apodectum.*

arborescens TORR. (*Azalea arborescens*) (s. Azalea). A large, deciduous shrub with obovate or oval, glossy green leaves, pale green or glaucous beneath usually attractively tinted in autumn. Flowers fragrant, funnel-shaped, white, occasionally pink flushed, style red, long and protruding; June and July. Eastern N. America. I. 1818. H4.

arboreum W. W. SM. (s. Arboreum). A magnificent large shrub or small tree, in its less hardy forms requiring woodland shelter. Leaves up to 20cm. long, green above, whitish to brownish-red below, primary veins conspicuously impressed. The bell-shaped, 5cm. long flowers are carried in dense, globular heads and vary in colour from white to blood red; January to April. It usually flowers very early and in cold districts is often ruined by frost. Many of its progeny are, however, hardier. This magnificent species was the first rhododendron introduced from the Himalaya and is the parent of many of our hardy hybrids and is itself hardy in all but the coldest localities. Temperate Himalaya; Kashmir to Bhutan; Khasia Hills. I. about 1810. H2-4.

'Album'. Flowers white. H4.

'Blood Red'. Flowers of a striking blood red. H3.

kingianum. See *R. zeylanicum.*

'Roseum'. Flowers rich pink, with darker spots; a lovely form. A.M. 1973. F.C.C. 1974. H4.

RHODODENDRON—*continued*

arboreum 'Sir Charles Lemon'. A magnificent, large shrub or small tree with handsome leaves, rust-red beneath and dense trusses of white flowers. H3. Now regarded as a probable hybrid between *R. arboreum* and *R. campanulatum.*

argenteum. See *R. grande.*

argyrophyllum FRANCH. (s. Arboreum). A beautiful large, densely leafy shrub of slow growth, with long leaves, silvery or white felted beneath. Flowers in a loose head, bell-shaped, white or pink with darker spots. May. Szechwan. I. 1904. A.M.(F.) 1934. H4.

'Roseum'. A selection with flowers of a clear rose.

arizelum BALF. f. & FORREST. (s. Falconeri). A large shrub or small tree for moist woodland with magnificent large leaves, covered with a cinnamon indumentum beneath. Compact heads of creamy-yellow bells, sometimes rose-tinted, and with dark crimson blotch. April. Yunnan; Upper Burma. A.M.(F.) 1963. H3-4.

atlanticum REHD. (*Azalea atlantica*) (s. Azalea). A charming, small, deciduous, stoloniferous shrub with obovate or oblong-obovate, bright green leaves. Flowers fragrant, funnel-shaped, white or white flushed pink, occasionally with a yellow blotch; May. Mid-eastern United States. I. about 1916. H4.

aucklandii. See *R. griffithianum.*

augustinii HEMSL. (s. Triflorum). A large, small-leaved shrub. In its best forms this beautiful, blue-flowered, Chinese species is one of the finest of all Rhododendrons. It is fairly quick-growing, making an ideal woodland shrub. The plants offered are from cuttings of selected forms from the best collections. April and May. The name commemorates Augustine Henry who first found this species. Hupeh; Szechwan; Yunnan; S. Tibet. I. 1899. A.G.M. 1924. A.M. 1926. H3-4.

chasmanthum DAVIDIAN (*R. chasmanthum*). A splendid variety with pale lavender to deep lavender-mauve flowers, a little later than the type, and borne in rather larger trusses. Yunnan; S.E. Tibet. A.M. 1930. F.C.C. 1932. H3.

'Electra'. A magnificent shrub when bearing clusters of violet-blue flowers marked with greenish-yellow blotches. The flowers are a startling colour, particularly when seen en masse on a large bush. Raised by Lionel de Rothschild at Exbury in 1937. It is a hybrid between the type and var. *chasmanthum.* A.M. 1940. H3.

auriculatum HEMSL. (s. Auriculatum). A large shrub, occasionally a small tree. Though very distinct and handsome in leaf, this Chinese species is chiefly remarkable for its late flowering, which occurs normally in July and August, but sometimes later. The large, white, funnel-shaped flowers, long-tapered in bud are borne in huge trusses and are richly scented. Hupeh. Introduced by E. H. Wilson in 1900. A.M. 1922. H4.

†**auritum** TAGG. (s. Boothii). A small shrub with dark-green leaves, 2·5 to 6cm. long. Flowers bell-shaped, 2·5cm. long, pale yellow slightly flushed pink on the lobes; April. S.E. Tibet. A.M. 1931. H2-3.

baileyi BALF. f. (s. Lepidotum). A small, Tibetan shrub sometimes reaching 2m., the young shoots and small leaves beneath coated with reddish-brown scales. Flowers saucer-shaped, red-purple, usually with darker markings; May. S.E. Tibet; Bhutan. I. 1913. A.M. 1960. H3-4.

bakeri HUME (s. Azalea). A deciduous shrub varying in height from dwarf to medium-size. Leaves obovate, glaucous beneath. Flowers in terminal clusters, funnel-shaped, varying in colour from orange to yellow or red; June. S.E. United States. H4.

barbatum G. DON (s. Barbatum). A beautiful, large, spreading shrub or small tree with coloured stems and attractively peeling bark. The branchlets and petioles are clad with conspicuous bristles. Leaves elliptic-lanceolate, 12 to 20cm. long, with conspicuously impressed primary veins. Flowers bell-shaped, of a glowing crimson-scarlet, carried in dense, globular heads; March. Nepal; Sikkim; Bhutan. C. 1829. A.M. 1954. H3-4.

basilicum BALF. f. & W. W. SM. (s. Falconeri). A large shrub or small tree succeeding best in woodland conditions. The young shoots clothed in a striking rufous tomentum. The large, handsome leaves have winged petioles and are a rich cinnamon beneath. Flowers pale yellow, sometimes crimson tinged and with a deep crimson basal blotch; April. Yunnan; N.E. Upper Burma. A.M.(F). 1956. H3-4.

RHODODENDRON—*continued*

bathyphyllum BALF. f. & FORR. (s. Taliense). Small, densely leafy shrub, the leaves 5 to 7·5cm. long, clothed beneath with a rust-coloured indumentum. Flowers 4 to 5cm. long, bell-shaped, white, spotted crimson; April-May. S.E. Tibet; Yunnan; Szechwan. H4.

bauhiniiflorum WATT. & HUTCH. (s. Triflorum). Medium-sized shrub related to *R. triflorum*, with reddish-brown stems, small leaves and clusters of two to three flat, saucer-shaped, lemon-yellow flowers; May and June. Assam. H3-4.

beanianum COWAN (s. Neriiflorum). Medium-sized shrub of open habit, with chestnut-brown or yellowish-brown, woolly tomentum on the undersides of the leaves; flowers in loose trusses, bell-shaped, waxy, usually red, sometimes pink; March to May. N.W. Burma; S.E. Tibet; Assam. Named after W. J. Bean, one of the greatest ever authorities on woody plants. A.M. (F.) 1953. H3-4.

bodinieri FRANCH. (s. Triflorum). A very hardy, medium-sized shrub with narrow, acuminate leaves. Flowers funnel-shaped, white or pale rose, with purple spots; March and April. Closely related to *R. yunnanense*. Yunnan. C. 1933. H3-4.

brachyanthum FRANCH. (s. Glaucophyllum). A dwarf or small shrub of neat habit, with aromatic leaves and bell-shaped, pale yellow flowers; June and July. Yunnan; S.E. Tibet. Discovered by the Abbé Delavay in 1884, introduced by George Forrest in 1906. H4.

brachycarpum G. DON (s. Ponticum). An attractive, hardy species of medium size with leaves covered with a fawn or brownish indumentum beneath. Flowers funnel-shaped, creamy-white, flushed pink; June and July. N. and C. Japan. H4.

brachystylum. See *R. trichocladum*.

brevistylum FRANCH. (s. Heliolepis). A medium-sized shrub with scaly shoots and leaves. Leaves strongly aromatic, shining green above. Flowers funnel-shaped, rose, stained crimson at the base within; late June and July. Yunnan; S.E. Tibet. I. 1906. A.M. 1933. H4.

†**bullatum** FRANCH. (s. Edgworthii). Medium-sized shrub, its branches coated with a soft fawn or brown, woolly tomentum as are the dark green, bullate leaves beneath. Flowers funnel-shaped, white or pink tinged, richly scented; April and May. Some forms of this beautiful species may be grown in the open in very mild districts, where it forms a rather straggly shrub. Yunnan; S.E. Tibet; N.E. Upper Burma. First found by the Abbé Delavay in 1886, introduced by George Forrest in 1904. A.M.(F.) 1923, F.C.C. (F.) 1937, A.M.(F.) 1946. H2-4.

bureavii FRANCH. (s. Taliense). Medium-sized shrub with attractive, dark, glossy green leaves, covered beneath with a rich red woolly indumentum. Flowers bell-shaped, rose, with crimson markings, ten to fifteen in a tight truss; April and May. This outstanding species is well worth growing if only for the attractive colours of its young growths which vary between pale fawn and a warm rusty red. Yunnan. I. by Wilson in 1904. A.M. 1939. (for flowers). A.M. 1972 H4.

caeruleum. See *R. rigidum*.

caesium HUTCH. (s. Trichocladum). Small shrub with attractive, shining, pale brown bark and aromatic leaves, green above, bluish-grey and scaly below. Flowers small, two or three together, funnel-shaped, greenish-yellow, with green flecks within; May. Yunnan. H4.

calendulaceum TORR. (*Azalea calandulacea*) (s. Azalea). A medium sized to large, deciduous shrub with elliptic or obovate-oblong leaves, turning orange and red in autumn. Flowers funnel-shaped, 5cm. across, varying in rich colours from yellow to orange or scarlet, hence the specific epithet (like a marigold); May and June. One of the most vividly coloured of all wild azaleas. Eastern N. America. I. 1806. H4.

callimorphum BALF. f. & W. W. SM. (*cyclium*) (s. Thomsonii). A dainty, medium-sized shrub with small, round leaves, green above, glaucous below. Flowers in loose trusses, bell-shaped, soft pink, deep rose in bud, occasionally with a crimson basal blotch; April to June. Yunnan; N.E. Burma. I. 1912. H4.

RHODODENDRON—*continued*

calophytum FRANCH. (s. Fortunei). One of the noblest of Chinese species and one of the hardiest of those species with conspicuous large leaves. A large shrub or small tree with thick shoots capped with rosettes of long, narrow, oblanceolate leaves. Large trusses of white or pink, bell-shaped flowers, each with a maroon basal blotch; March and April. Szechwan. First found by the Abbé David, introduced by E. H. Wilson in 1904. A.M.(F.) 1920. F.C.C. (F.) 1933. H4.

calostrotum BALF. f. & WARD (*riparium*) (s. Saluenense). A very attractive, dwarf shrub with grey-green foliage and comparatively large, flat or saucer-shaped, bright magenta-crimson flowers; May and June. A fine rock-garden species. N.E. Upper Burma; Yunnan; S.E. Tibet; Assam. I. 1919. A.M.(F.) 1935. H4.

'Gigha' (*'Red Form'*). A very splendid selection with flowers of a deep claret-red, contrasting with the grey-green young leaves. The name recalls the lovely garden made by Col. Sir James Horlick on the Isle of Gigha off the coast of Argyllshire. A.G.M. 1969. F.C.C. 1971.

caloxanthum BALF. f. & FARRER (s. Thomsonii). Charming, small, free-flowering shrub with small, rounded leaves and clusters of bell-shaped, citron-yellow flowers, tipped orange-scarlet in bud; April and May. One of Reginald Farrer's prettiest introductions. Burma; Tibet; Yunnan. I. 1919. A.M.(F.) 1934. H3-4.

campanulatum D. DON (s. Campanulatum). A large shrub, the unfolding leaves covered with a suede-like, fawn or rust-coloured indumentum. Flowers bell-shaped, varying in colour from pale rose to lavender-blue; April and May. A lovely species, said to be one of the commonest rhododendrons in the Himalayan forests. Kashmir to Bhutan. I. 1825. H4.

aeruginosum NICHOLS. (*R. aeruginosum*). A slow-growing compact shrub with the young growths a striking metallic blue-green. Nepal.

'Album'. Flowers white. See also 'White Campanula' under Hybrids.

'Knap Hill'. An attractive selection with lavender-blue flowers. A.M. 1925.

campylocarpum HOOK. f. (s. Thomsonii). A small to medium-sized shrub with ovate leaves, glossy green above, glaucous green below. Flowers bell-shaped, of a clear yellow; April and May. The best of its colour for general planting and one of the choicest of all hardy shrubs. In common with others of this series it does not flower when young. E. Nepal; Sikkim; Bhutan; Assam; Tibet. Introduced by Sir Joseph Hooker about 1849. F.C.C. 1892. H3-4.

elatum HORT. Taller and looser in growth than the type. Flowers usually with a crimson basal blotch, orange-vermillion in bud. Collected at a lower elevation than the type. H3-4.

campylogynum FRANCH. (s. Campylogynum). A delightful, dwarf shrub with small lustrous green leaves and producing long-stalked, nodding, rose-purple to almost mahogany, bell-shaped, waxy flowers when only a few cms. high. We also offer a choice form with flowers of a charming shade of pink; May and June. Suitable for the rock garden. Yunnan; S.E. Tibet; W. Burma. I. 1912. H3-4.

cremastum DAVIDIAN (*R. cremastum*). A delightful dwarf shrub of erect habit, suitable for the rock garden. Flowers waxy, rose-purple. Yunnan.

'Crushed Strawberry'. A selection made in our nurseries; flowers pink, a pleasant shade of crushed strawberry.

myrtilloides DAVIDIAN (*R. myrtilloides*). A charming shrublet, with smaller, delightful, waxy, plum-purple flowers. Burma; Tibet; Yunnan. A.M. 1925. F.C.C. 1943. H3-4.

camtschaticum PALLAS (s. Camtschaticum). A dwarf, spreading, deciduous shrublet, up to 30cm., with curious, comparatively large, saucer-shaped, rose-purple flowers in May. A curious feature is the corolla tube which on the lower side is split almost to the base. Leaves up to 5cm. long, giving attractive autumn tints. Requires an open, well drained situation. Alaska; N.E. Asia. I. 1799. A.M. 1908. H4.

canadense TORR. (*Rhodora canadensis*) (s. Azalea). A small, deciduous shrub of erect, twiggy habit. Leaves narrowly oval, sea-green. Flowers appearing before the leaves, saucer-shaped or bell-shaped, rose-purple; April. Thriving in moist situations. N.E. North America. I. 1767. A.M. 1928 (as *Rhodora canadensis*). H4.

'Album' Flowers white.

RHODODENDRON—*continued*

canescens SWEET (*Azalea canescens*)(s. Azalea). A medium to large, deciduous shrub with oblong or oblanceolate leaves, densely hairy beneath. Flowers funnel-shaped, sweetly-scented, white or pink-flushed with pink or reddish, gland covered tube; April and May. S.E. United States. I. 1810. H4.

cantabile. See *R. russatum*.

carolinianum REHD. (s. Carolinianum). A very attractive, free-flowering species attaining 2m. Leaves densely scaly beneath: flowers tubular, soft rose-purple; May and June. N. Carolina (U.S.A.). I. 1812. A.M.(F.) 1968. H4.

album REHD. Flowers white, with a yellow blotch; leaves also narrower and more pointed. I. 1895.

catacosmum BALF. F. & TAGG. (s. Neriiflorum). Handsome, medium-sized shrub with woolly twigs and leaves thickly clad with cinnamon-brown tomentum below. Flowers in a loose truss, bell-shaped, deep crimson, with a large petaloid calyx; March and April. S.E. Tibet to Yunnan. H4.

catawbiense MICHAUX (s. Ponticum). An extremely hardy, medium-sized to large shrub of dense habit, with oval or oblong, glossy green leaves up to 15cm. long. An old plant will develop into a dense thicket of layering stems. Flowers borne in a large truss, bell-shaped, varying in colour from lilac-purple to pink or white; June. A parent of many hardy hybrids. S.E. United States (Alleghany Mts.). I. 1809. H4.

caucasicum PALL. (s. Ponticum). A slow-growing, dome-shaped shrub of medium size. Leaves elliptic to oblanceolate, clad with a thin, fawn tomentum beneath. Flowers in a compact truss, widely funnel-shaped, pale sulphur-yellow with pale green markings within; May, occasionally again in late summer. A parent of many of the old hardy hybrids. The type is now rare in cultivation, the form here described being the plant previously known as '*Cunningham's Sulphur*'. Caucasus; N.E. Turkey. I. 1803. H4.

cephalanthum FRANCH. (s. Anthopogon). A very beautiful small, slender, aromatic shrub, with small leaves, densely scaly beneath, and dense terminal heads of tubular, white or pinkish, daphne-like flowers; May. Yunnan; Szechwan; S.E. Tibet; Upper Burma. I. 1908. H4.

crebreflorum COWAN & DAVIDIAN (*R. crebreflorum*). A choice dwarf form from Assam, with pink flowers. A gem for the peat garden. A.M. 1934.

cerasinum TAGG (s. Thomsonii). A medium-sized to large shrub with elliptic leaves 5 to 10cm. long and drooping trusses of long, bell-shaped flowers varying in colour from white with marginal band of cherry red to self red or crimson. It was to the former that Kingdon Ward gave the name "Cherry Brandy"; May. Burma; Tibet; Assam. A.M.(F.) 1938. H4.

chaetomallum BALF. f. & FORREST (s. Neriiflorum). A very splendid, medium-sized shrub with obovate leaves densely covered beneath with a brown, woolly indumentum. Flowers in loose trusses, blood red, waxy, bell-shaped; March and April. S.E. Tibet; Yunnan. I. 1918. A.M.(F.) 1959. H4.

hemigymnum TAGG & FORREST. Small shrub, the leaves beneath with only a thin veil of indumentum. Flowers bell-shaped, bright crimson; March and April. S.E. Tibet; Upper Burma. A.M. 1957.

chamaethomsonii COWAN & DAVIDIAN (*repens chamaethomsonii*) (s. Neriiflorum). Dwarf, semi-prostrate or spreading shrub producing trusses of five to six bell-shaped, crimson or rose-crimson flowers; March to April. Yunnan; S.E. Tibet. H4.

chamaethauma COWAN & DAVIDIAN (*repens chamaethauma*) (*repens chamaedoron*). A form with smaller leaves. A.M. 1932.

chameunum BALF. f. & FORREST (*charidotes*) (*cosmetum*) (s. Saluenense). Dwarf shrub with erect stems and bristle-clad branchlets. The small leaves are brown-scaly beneath. Flowers saucer-shaped, with wavy margin, rose-purple, with crimson spots, borne in loose clusters of up to six; April and May. Yunnan; Burma; Tibet; Szechwan. H4.

chapmanii GRAY (s. Carolinianum). Small shrub of stiff habit, occasionally reaching 2m.; leaves scaly below. Flowers in tight clusters, funnel-shaped, pink, with greenish spots, and conspicuous chocolate-coloured anthers; April and May. W. Florida (U.S.A.). I. 1936. H4.

charianthum. See *R. davidsonianum*.

charidotes. See *R. chameunum*.

RHODODENDRON—*continued*

charitopes BALF. f. & FORR. (s. Glaucophyllum). A charming shrublet rarely as much as 1·2m., with obovate leaves, glaucous and densely scaly below. Flowers bell-shaped, apple blossom-pink, speckled crimson; April and May. Upper Burma; Yunnan. H4.

chartophyllum. See *R. yunnanense*.

chasmanthum. See *R. augustinii chasmanthum*.

chrysanthum PALLAS (s. Ponticum). Prostrate or dwarf shrub up to 30cm. Leaves oblanceolate to obovate 4 to 7·5cm. long. Flowers bell-shaped, pale-yellow; May and June. Siberia; Manchuria south to Japan. I. 1796. H4.

chryseum BALF. f. & WARD (*muliense*) (s. Lapponicum). A dwarf, small-leaved alpine shrub with small, aromatic leaves and small trusses of funnel-shaped, bright-yellow flowers; April and May. Suitable for the rock garden. Yunnan; S.E. Tibet; Szechwan. H4.

ciliatum HOOK. f. (s. Maddenii). A beautiful, dome-shaped shrub about 1·2 to 1·5m., with attractive peeling bark and conspicuously ciliate leaves. Flowers nodding, fragrant, bell-shaped, rose-lilac, borne at an early age; March and April. E. Nepal; Sikkim; S.E. Tibet; Bhutan. I. 1850. A.M.(F.) 1953. H3-4.

cinnabarinum HOOK. f. (s. Cinnabarinum). This beautiful, medium-sized to large shrub with obovate-elliptic, scaly leaves and tubular flowers of bright cinnabar red, is one of the choicest of the Himalayan species, blooming in May and June. Sikkim; Bhutan; S.E. Tibet. Introduced by Sir Joseph Hooker in 1849. H4.

blandfordiiflorum HOOK. f. Flowers red outside, yellow within. E. Nepal; Sikkim. A.M. 1945.

'Mount Everest'. A lovely form from the Tower Court collection. Flowers pale apricot, freely produced, less tubular than in the type.

roylei HOOK. f. (*R. roylei*). Leaves glaucous, flowers rose-red to purple-red, shorter than those of the type. A splendid variety. Bhutan; S.E. Tibet.

citriniflorum BALF. f. & FORR. (s. Neriiflorum). A small shrub with obovate or oblong leaves covered with a thick fawn or dark brown indumentum. Flowers in trusses of four to six, bell-shaped, lemon-yellow or occasionally rose-flushed, shaded orange at base, calyx coloured and conspicuous; April and May. Yunnan; S.E. Tibet. Introduced by George Forrest in 1917. H4.

complexum BALF. f. & W. W. SM. (s. Lapponicum). A dwarf shrub of dense, tangled habit bearing tiny scaly leaves and small trusses of funnel-shaped, deep rosy-purple flowers; April and May. Yunnan. H4.

concatenans HUTCH. (s. Cinnabarinum). A distinct and lovely shrub of medium size. Leaves oval to oblong, densely scaly beneath, 4 to 6cm. long, glaucous blue when young; flowers bell-shaped, waxy, apricot-yellow faintly purple tinged on outside and sometimes conspicuously veined; April and May. S.E. Tibet. F.C.C. 1935. H3.

concinnum HEMSL. (*yanthinum*) (s. Triflorum). Medium-sized to large shrub with elliptic or obovate-elliptic, scaly leaves, and clusters of funnel-shaped, purplish flowers; April and May. Szechwan. I. 1904. H4.

benthamianum DAVIDIAN. A form with lavender-purple flowers.

pseudoyanthinum DAVIDIAN (*R. pseudoyanthinum*). A lovely variety with deep ruby-red or purple-red flowers. A.M. 1951.

coreanum. See *R. poukhanense*.

coriaceum FRANCH. (s. Falconeri). A large shrub or small tree with large, narrowly elliptic leaves, silvery at first beneath, later greyish to pale brown. Flowers in large, loose trusses, bell-shaped, white, or rose flushed, with a crimson basal blotch; April. Yunnan; S.E. Tibet; Upper Burma. H3-4.

coryanum TAGG & FORREST (s. Arboreum). A large shrub, with long, leathery, cinnamon-backed leaves and lax trusses of bell-shaped, creamy-white, crimson-spotted flowers; April and May. Named after that keen amateur gardener Reginald Cory. Yunnan; S.E. Tibet. H4.

coryphaeum BALF. f. & FORREST (s. Grande). An uncommon species forming a large shrub or small tree up to 4·5 or 6m. The large leaves have white or grey under-surfaces. Flowers creamy-white with basal crimson blotches, produced in April in heads of twenty or more. Yunnan; S.E. Tibet. H3-4.

cosmetum. See *R. chameunum*.

cowanianum DAVIDIAN (s. Trichocladum). A small, deciduous shrub, the leaves covered with yellow scales beneath. Flowers in clusters of two to four, bell-shaped, reddish-purple; calyx large; May. Central Nepal. H3-4.

RHODODENDRON—*continued*

†**crassum** FRANCH. (s. Maddenii). A medium-sized to large shrub with stout, scaly young shoots. Leaves lanceolate or oblanceolate, 5 to 12cm. long, thick and rigid, glossy dark green above, densely rusty scaly below. Flowers funnel-shaped, 5 to 8cm long, varying in colour from white to pink, with or without a yellow blotch, sweetly-scented; June and July. In some forms, one of the hardiest members of the Maddenii series. A beautiful, late-flowering shrub, worth growing as a conservatory shrub in cold districts. Yunnan; S.E. Tibet; Upper Burma. Introduced by George Forrest in 1906. A.M.(F.) 1924. A.M. 1938. H2-4.

crebreflorum. See *R. cephalanthum crebreflorum.*

cremastum. See *R. campylogynum cremastum.*

crinigerum FRANCH. (s. Barbatum). A medium-sized shrub with glandular-hairy shoots and glossy green, rather bullate leaves, covered beneath with a creamy-yellow or buff tomentum. The attractive, bell-shaped flowers are white or blush, with a blood-red basal blotch; April and May. Yunnan; S.E. Tibet. First found by the Abbé Soulie in 1895, introduced by George Forrest in 1914. A.M.(F.) 1935. H4.

croceum. See *R. wardii.*

cuneatum W. W. SM. (s. Lapponicum). Medium-sized shrub with 2·5cm. long, densely scaly leaves and 2·5cm. long, widely funnel-shaped flowers in varying shades of rose-lilac; April. Yunnan. I. 1913. H4.

cyanocarpum W. W. SM. (s. Thomsonii). A large shrub, well distinguished by its rigid, rounded, glaucous leaves and trusses of widely funnel-shaped flowers, varying in colour from white, pink to soft rose; March and April. Yunnan. A.M.(F.) 1933. H4.

cyclium. See *R. callimorphum.*

dasycladum BALF. f. & W. W. SM. (s. Thomsonii). Medium-sized shrub with glandular hairy, young shoots and leaves varying from 3 to 8cm. long. The small, funnel-shaped flowers may be white or rose, with or without a dark basal stain; April and May. Yunnan; S.E. Tibet. H4.

dauricum L. (s. Dauricum). A charming, early flowering, semi-evergreen shrub of medium size, with elliptic leaves 2 to 3cm. long and one to three-flowered trusses of funnel-shaped, bright rose-purple flowers 2·5 to 3·5cm. across from January to March. Closely related to *R. mucronulatum*, differing in its smaller, blunter, partially evergreen leaves and its smaller flowers. Japan; Korea; N. China; E. Siberia. C. 1780. H4.

'Midwinter'. A deciduous or semi-evergreen clone with flowers of phlox-purple. A.M. 1963. F.C.C. 1969.

sempervirens SIMS. A form with persistent leaves.

davidsonianum REHD. & WILS. (*charianthum*). (s. Triflorum). A medium to large-sized shrub, with lanceolate leaves. Flowers in both terminal and axillary clusters, funnel-shaped, extremely variable in colour from soft pink to purplish-rose, sometimes spotted. We offer various forms including a good pink form; April and May. Szechwan; Yunnan. Introduced by E. H. Wilson in 1908. A.M.(F.) 1935. F.C.C. (F.) 1955. A.G.M. 1969. H3-4.

decorum FRANCH. (s. Fortunei). This large and beautiful Chinese species should be in every representative collection. Leaves glabrous, oblong-obovate, pale beneath, up to 15cm. long. Flowers large, funnel-shaped, fragrant, in lax trusses, white or shell pink, sometimes spotted; May and June. Yunnan; Szechwan. I. 1904. H3-4.

degronianum CARRIERE (*pentamerum*) (*metternichii pentamerum*) (s. Ponticum). A very hardy, small, dome-shaped bush with dark green leaves up to 15cm. long, covered below with a fawn or rufous tomentum. Attractive, bell-shaped, soft pink flowers; May. Japan. I. 1870. H4.

†**delavayi** FRANCH. (s. Arboreum). A handsome large shrub or small tree with white-woolly young shoots; leaves glossy dark green above with a greyish-white tomentum beneath. Flowers usually blood red, bell-shaped, in a round, compact truss; March to May. Yunnan; Burma. F.C.C. 1936. H2-3.

deleiense. See *R. tephropeplum.*

desquamatum BALF. f. & FORREST (s. Heliolepis). A large shrub or small tree, the aromatic leaves oblong-elliptic, dark brown-scaly beneath. Flowers funnel-shaped or almost flat, mauve with darker markings; March and April. Yunnan; Szechwan; Burma; S.E. Tibet. A.M.(F.) 1938. H4.

RHODODENDRON—*continued*

detonsum BALF. f. & FORREST (s. Taliense). A rather slow-growing, medium-sized shrub. Leaves cinnamon to brown below; flowers bell-shaped, rose-pink with crimson markings; May. Yunnan. H4.

†**diaprepes** BALF. f. & W. W. SM. (s. Fortunei). A magnificent woodland species. A large shrub or small tree with light green, oblong-elliptic leaves up to 30cm. long. Flowers in loose trusses, bell-shaped, fleshy, white with a faint rose flush, slightly fragrant; June and July. A parent of *'Polar Bear'*. Yunnan; S.E. Tibet. I. 1913. A.M. 1926. H3.

dichroanthum DIELS. (s. Neriiflorum). A slow-growing, dome-shaped shrub 1·2 to 2m. Leaves 6 to 10cm. long, oblong-obovate to oblanceolate, with white or grey indumentum beneath. Bearing loose trusses of variably coloured, usually deep orange, bell-shaped flowers in May and June. Calyx large and fleshy, coloured as the corolla. Parent of many hybrids. Yunnan. First found by Forrest in 1906. A.M.(F.) 1923. H4.

apodectum COWAN. A colourful variety from the Yunnan, with orange-yellow flowers flushed rose or crimson.

herpesticum COWAN (*R. herpesticum*). A dwarf shrub with dull yellow to orange-red flowers. N. Burma.

scyphocalyx COWAN (*R. scyphocalyx*). Flowers in clusters of three to five, of an unusual coppery-orange, the lobes suffused red, calyx similarly coloured. N. Burma. I. by Forrest in 1919.

didymum. See *R. sanguineum didymum.*

dilatatum. See *R. reticulatum.*

diphrocalyx BALF. f. (s. Barbatum). Large shrub with bristle-clad young shoots. Leaves oblong-oval to obovate 10 to 15cm. long. Flowers bell-shaped, rose-crimson with darker spots and basal blotch, calyx large and fleshy, red; April. Yunnan. H3.

discolor FRANCH. (s. Fortunei). A superb, late-flowering species making a large shrub. Leaves oblong-elliptic to oblanceolate up to 20cm. long. The funnel-shaped, fragrant, pink flowers, with seven-lobed corollas are borne in huge trusses, giving a magnificent display; June and July. A parent of many distinguished hybrids. Szechwan; Hupeh. Introducedby E. H. Wilson in 1900. A.M. 1921. A.M.(F.) 1922. F.C.C.(F.) 1922. A.G.M. 1969. H4.

doshongense TAGG (s. Taliense). A small, dense shrub up to 1m. with small leaves which are silvery-white, later, fawn-felted beneath. The bell-shaped, pink, purple spotted flowers are borne in trusses of up to fifteen; March to May. S.E. Tibet. H4.

dryophyllum BALF. f. & FORREST (s. Lacteum). A variable, medium-sized to large shrub or small tree, with 5 to 7·5cm. long leaves coated on the underside with a suede-like fawn, brown or buff indumentum. Flowers bell-shaped or funnel-shaped, varying in colour from white through pink to rose-purple, sometimes with crimson spots or blotch; April and May. Yunnan; Szechwan; S.E. Tibet; Bhutan; Burma. H4.

eclecteum BALF. f. & FORREST (s. Thomsonii). An early flowering shrub of medium size with distinctive, short stalked oblong or obovate-oblong leaves. Flowers in loose trusses, bell-shaped, fleshy, varying in colour from white to rose-red; Feb. to April. Differing from the closely related *R. stewartianum* in the leaves, which are glabrous beneath. Yunnan; Szechwan; S.E. Tibet. A.M.(F.) 1949. H3.

edgarianum REHD. & WILS. (s. Lapponicum). A small shrub ·6 to 1m. high with small, densely scaly, sage-green leaves and a wealth of attractive, small, blue-purple flowers; May and June. Szechwan; Yunnan; S.E. Tibet. H4.

elaeagnoides. See *R. lepidotum.*

†**elliottii** WATT. & W. W. SM. (s. Irroratum). Large shrub or small tree requiring woodland conditions, with glossy-green leaves and large, bell-shaped, scarlet or crimson flowers; May to July. One of the best red flowered species and the parent ot many good hybrids. Manipur. I. 1927. A.M. 1934. F.C.C. 1937. H1-2.

eriocarpum. See *R. indicum eriocarpum.*

†**eriogynum** BALF. f. & W. W. SM. (*facetum*) (s. Irroratum). A superb, large shrub of tree-like habit requiring woodland conditions; leaves glaucous below. Flowers bell-shaped, up to 7·5cm. long and wide, scarlet or crimson; June and July. The parent of many excellent hybrids. Yunnan. I. 1915. A.M. 1924. H1-2.

RHODODENDRON—*continued*

eritimum BALF. f. & W. W. SM. (s. Irroratum). A variable, medium-sized to large shrub or small tree with leaves up to 18cm. long. Flowers in a large truss, bell-shaped, dark crimson, with a dark basal blotch; April. Yunnan; S.E. Tibet. H3.

erubescens HUTCH. (s. Fortunei). Medium-sized to large shrub, closely related to and very similar in general appearance to *R. fargesii*. Leaves oblong-elliptic, 7·5 to 12cm. long. Flowers funnel-shaped, 5cm. long, deep rose-pink on the outside, paler within, up to about eight in a truss; April. Szechwan. I. 1902. H4.

erythrocalyx BALF. f. & FORR. (s. Thomsonii). A medium-sized shrub with ovate to elliptic leaves. Flowers bell-shaped, white or pink, with or without crimson spots and basal blotch; April and May. S.E. Tibet; Yunnan. H3.

euchaites. See *R. neriiflorum euchaites*.

exasperatum TAGG (s. Barbatum). A large shrub forming an attractive trunk and having bronze-coloured, densely glandular-bristly young growths. Leaves 10 to 18cm. long by 5 to 10cm. wide. Flowers bell-shaped, brick red; April to May. Assam; S.E. Tibet. H3-4.

eximium NUTT. (s. Falconeri). A magnificent, large shrub or small tree, the young growths covered with orange-brown indumentum, as are the large leaves, up to 30cm. long and 7·5cm. wide. The 5cm. long, bell-shaped, fleshy flowers are pink or rose; April to May. Bhutan. A.M. 1973. H3-4.

exquisetum. See *R. oreotrephes*.

faberi HEMSL. (s. Taliense). Large shrub or small tree, the young shoots clothed with rust-red, woolly indumentum. Leaves up to 15cm. or more long, pale to rusty-brown beneath. Loose trusses of white, bell-shaped flowers; May. Szechwan. H4.

facetum. See *R. eriogynum*.

falconeri HOOK. f. (s. Falconeri). This magnificent, Himalayan rhododendron may be grown in sheltered gardens in most parts of the British Isles, where it makes a large shrub or small tree. Its large, broadly obovate leaves with deeply impressed veins separate it from most related species other than *R. eximium* which, however, has darker, rust-coloured tomentum. It has huge, dome-shaped trusses of waxy, creamy-yellow, purple-blotched, bell-shaped flowers; April and May. E. Nepal; Sikkim; Bhutan. Introduced from Sikkim by Sir Joseph Hooker in 1850. A.M. 1922. H3-4.

fargesii FRANCH. (s. Fortunei). An exceedingly floriferous shrub of large size, in leaf and flower very like *R. erubescens* and is closely related to *R. oreodoxa*. Flowers bell-shaped, usually rosy-lilac, sometimes spotted; March and April. Hupeh; Szechwan; Yunnan. I. 1901. A.M.(F.) 1926. H4.

fastigiatum FRANCH. (s. Lapponicum). A dense, small, dome-shaped bush ·6 to 1m., high with small, scaly leaves, sea-green when young. Flowers lavender-purple, funnel-shaped; April and May. Yunnan. A.M.(F.) 1914. H4.

fauriei FRANCH. (s. Ponticum). Medium-sized shrub with oblong-elliptic or obovate leaves and rounded trusses of bell-shaped, white flowers, each with a pink flush and green spots; June. Many Japanese authorities now unite this species with the closely related *R. brachycarpum*. Japan. H4.

ferrugineum L. (s. Ferrugineum). The "Alpen Rose" of Switzerland. A small, flattish-dome-shaped or spreading shrub, with eaves reddish-scaly beneath. Flowers rose-crimson, tubular, borne in small trusses in June. Pyrenees and Alps of C. Europe. C. 1752. H4.

album D. DON. Flowers white. I. 1830. A.M. 1969.

'Coccineum'. A charming form with crimson flowers.

fictolacteum BALF. f. (s. Falconeri). A very handsome, large shrub or small tree, with cinnamon-tomentose young shoots and long leaves dark green above, brown-tomentose beneath, occasionally as much as 30cm. long. Flowers bell-shaped, creamy-white, with a crimson blotch, in large trusses; April and May. One of the hardiest of the large-leaf species. Yunnan; Szechwan; S.E. Tibet. I. about 1885. A.M.(F.) 1923. A.G.M. 1969. H4.

RHODODENDRON—*continued*

fimbriatum HUTCH. (s. Lapponicum). A dwarf shrub. Leaves oblong-lanceolate 2·5 to 5cm. long. Flowers bell-shaped, violet-mauve or purple in comparatively large clusters at the tips of twiggy branchlets; April and May. Szechwan. H4.

fittianum BALF. f. (s. Dauricum). A small to medium-sized shrub. Generally considered synonymous with *R. dauricum*, but quite distinct as we have it, the 2·5cm. wide, mauve-pink flowers not opening until mid-April. H4.

flavidum FRANCH. (*primulinum*) (s. Lapponicum). A pretty, erect shrub ·6 to 1m. high, with small, glossy, aromatic leaves, and funnel-shaped, primrose-yellow flowers; March. W. Szechwan; S.E. Tibet. I. 1905. A.M. 1910 (as *R. primulinum*). H4.

'Album'. Differs from the type in its laxer habit and larger, white flowers.

flavorufum BALF. f. & FORR. (s. Taliense). Small shrub up to 2m. Leaves 7·5 to 12cm. long, clothed below with a pale yellow indumentum which later becomes rusty-brown. Flowers narrowly bell-shaped, white or soft rose, spotted crimson; April and May. Yunnan; S.E. Tibet. H4.

fletcheranum DAVIDIAN (s. Maddenii). Small, bristly shrub, with usually oblong-lanceolate, 5cm. long leaves, pale brown-scaly beneath. Flowers widely funnel-shaped, nearly 5cm. long, pale yellow, with deeply five-lobed calyx; March and April. Perhaps the hardiest member of the Maddenii series, distinguished by its decurrent leaf base, narrowly winged petioles, and crenulate leaf margin. Collected by Joseph Rock in S.E. Tibet in 1932, and for long grown under the name *R. valentinianum* to which species it is closely related. Named after Dr. Harold Fletcher, Regius Keeper, Royal Botanic Garden, Edinburgh, 1956-70. H4.

floccigerum FRANCH. (s. Neriiflorum). A small shrub; leaves oblong-elliptic, glaucous below and covered by a loose tomentum. The trusses of narrowly bell-shaped flowers are usually waxy and scarlet but may vary from rose to crimson, to yellow, margined rose; March and April. Yunnan; S.E. Tibet. I. 1914. H4.

floribundum FRANCH. (s. Arboreum). A pleasing large shrub with dense foliage, the leaves rich green and bullate above and white-felted beneath. Flowers bell-shaped, usually magenta-purple, or lavender purple, or rose, with crimson blotch and spots; April. Szechwan. I. 1903. H4.

forrestii DIELS. (s. Neriiflorum). A slow-growing, prostrate shrub, occasionally up to 30cm. high, forming mats or low hummocks of dark green, broadly obovate to rounded leaves which are 2·5 to 3·5cm. long and purple beneath. The comparatively large, bell-shaped, bright scarlet flowers are borne singly or in pairs from the tips of short branchlets; April and May. Requires moist soil and partial shade. S.E. Tibet; Yunnan; Burma. Discovered by George Forrest in 1905 and introduced by him in 1914. H4.

repens COWAN & DAVIDIAN (*R. repens*). A choice creeping variety, differing in its leaves which are pale or glaucous-green below. F.C.C.(F.) 1935. A parent of the F.C.C. clones '*Ethel*', '*Elizabeth*' and '*Little Ben*'. We also offer the clones **'Scarlet Pimpernel'** (K.W.5845) and **'Scarlet Runner'** (K.W.5846), both of which were introduced by Kingdon Ward, and are very similar to var. *repens*.

fortunei LINDL. (s. Fortunei). A large shrub or small tree, leaves elliptic, 10 to 18cm. long. Flowers bell-shaped. produced in loose trusses of six to twelve, lilac-pink, fragrant in May. Probably the first hardy Chinese species to be introduced. A parent of numerous hybrids. Chekiang. Introduced by Robert Fortune in 1855. A.G.M. 1969. H4.

'Mrs. Charles Butler'. Flowers blush, fading to almost white.

fulgens HOOK. f. (s. Campanulatum). Medium-sized shrub with broad leaves, dark shining green above, covered with reddish-brown indumentum below. The tight, rounded trusses contain ten to twelve, bell-shaped flowers of a bright scarlet; Feb. to April. The young shoots are adorned with attractive crimson bracts. Bark in some forms attractively peeling. E. Nepal; Sikkim; Bhutan; Assam; Tibet. I. about 1849. A.M. 1933. H4.

fulvum BALF. f. & W. W. SM. (*fulvoides*) (s. Fulvum). A large shrub or small tree, attractive on account of its large, polished dark green leaves which are clothed beneath with a conspicuous, cinnamon indumentum. Flowers bell-shaped, blush to deep rose with or without a crimson blotch; March and April. Yunnan; Szechwan; Burma; Assam; S.E. Tibet. Discovered and introduced by George Forrest in 1912. A.M.(F.) 1933. H4.

RHODODENDRON—*continued*

galactinum BALF. f. (s. Falconeri). A large shrub or small tree with large, leathery leaves, clothed beneath with buff-grey or pale cinnamon indumentum. Flowers bell-shaped, white to deep rose, with a crimson blotch and spots within; April and May. Szechwan. Discovered and introduced by E. H. Wilson in 1908. H4.

glaucophyllum HOOK. f. (*glaucum*) (s. Glaucophyllum). A small, aromatic shrub with lanceolate leaves, white beneath and bearing attractive, bell-shaped flowers of a pale old-rose to lilac shade; calyx large and leafy; April and May. E. Nepal; Sikkim; Bhutan; S.E. Tibet. I. 1850. H3-4.

luteiflorum DAVIDIAN. A lovely form from northern Burma, with lemon-yellow flowers. A.M.(F.) 1960.

glischroides TAGG & FORR. (s. Barbatum). Large shrub with bristly young shoots. Leaves oblong-lanceolate 10 to 15cm. long, bristle-clad on the undersurface. Flowers bell-shaped, white or creamy-white, flushed rose, with a crimson basal blotch; March and April. N.E. Upper Burma. I. 1925. H3-4.

glischrum BALF. f. & W. W. SM. (s. Barbatum). Large shrub or small tree. Leaves oblanceolate 10 to 25cm. long. The twigs and petioles covered with gland-tipped bristles. Flowers bell-shaped, varying in colour from white to deep rose, with crimson blotch and spots; April and May. Yunnan; Upper Burma; S.E. Tibet. I. 1914. H3.

glomerulatum HUTCH. (s. Lapponicum). A small shrub ·6 to 1m. high resembling *R. russatum*. Leaves ovate-elliptic 1 to 2cm. long, densely scaly. The clusters of light purple-mauve, funnel-shaped flowers are encircled by semi-persistent bud-scales; March to May. Yunnan. H4.

†**grande** WIGHT (*argenteum*) (s. Grande). A small tree or large shrub of imposing appearance. The handsome leathery, oblong to oblanceolate leaves are 15 to 30cm. long, dark green and shining above, silvery-white or buff tomentose beneath. Flowers bell-shaped, 5 to 7·5cm. across, ivory-white, with purple basal blotch within, pink in bud, borne in dense rounded trusses; Feb. to April. One of the most spectacular species but only suitable for sheltered woodland gardens in the milder counties. There exist some fine examples in Cornwall. E. Nepal; Sikkim; Bhutan. Introduced by Sir Joseph Hooker in 1849. F.C.C.(F.) 1901. H2-3.

griersonianum BALF. f. & FORR. (s. Griersonianum). A splendid, distinct and striking, medium-sized, Chinese Rhododendron. Leaves lanceolate, 10 to 20cm. long, matt green above, buff woolly beneath. The brilliant geranium-scarlet, narrowly bell-shaped flowers appear in June and are unlike any others in the genus. It is a prolific parent and its hybrid progeny are now innumerable. Distinct on account of its long, tapered flower-buds, a character possessed by only one other species, i.e. *R. auriculatum*. Yunnan; N. Burma. Discovered and introduced by George Forrest in 1917. F.C.C. 1924. H3-4.

†**griffithianum** WIGHT (*aucklandii*) (s. Fortunei). A magnificent, large shrub or small tree, the parent of innumerable award winning hybrids. Unfortunately, only suitable for the most sheltered gardens in the mildest areas. Bark of branches reddish-brown, attractively peeling. Leaves up to 30cm. long. Flowers widely bell-shaped, 7·5cm. long, and up to 15cm. across, carried in a loose truss of three to six, white, with faint green speckles, sweetly scented; May. Sikkim; Bhutan. Introduced by Sir Joseph Hooker in 1849. F.C.C. 1866. H1-3.

gymnocarpum BALF. f. & TAGG (s. Taliense). A very hardy, small shrub of compact habit, the thick, leathery leaves 6 to 11cm. long, covered on the underside with a fawn indumentum. Flowers bell-shaped, pale to deep crimson, with darker markings; April. S.E. Tibet. A.M.(F.) 1940. H4.

habrotrichum BALF. f. & W. W. SM. (s. Barbatum). Medium-sized to large shrub with reddish-bristly young shoots, dark green leaves up to 18cm. long, and compact trusses of funnel-shaped flowers of white to deep rose; April and May. Yunnan. I. 1912-13. A.M.(F.) 1933. H3.

haematodes FRANCH. (s. Neriiflorum). Generally considered one of the finest of Chinese Rhododendrons. A compact, small to medium-sized, slow-growing bush. Leaves oblong-obovate, 4 to 7·5cm. long, dark green, thickly rufous felted beneath; flowers bell-shaped, brilliant scarlet-crimson; May and June. A parent of several good hybrids. Yunnan. Introduced by George Forrest about 1911. F.C.C. 1926. H4.

RHODODENDRON—*continued*

hanceanum HEMSL. (s. Hanceanum). A dainty, small shrub with bronze-coloured young growths and ovate-lanceolate to obovate leaves which are finely scaly below. Flowers funnel-shaped, 2·5cm. long, creamy-white or pale yellow, slightly scented; April. Szechwan. H4. We offer the following clone:—

'Nanum'. A slow-growing shrub making a neat compact hummock up to 35cm. A choice rock-garden shrublet.

heliolepis FRANCH. (s. Heliolepis). Medium-sized shrub. Leaves elliptic-oblong, 6 to 10cm. long, intensely aromatic. Flowers in small, loose trusses, funnel-shaped, purple-rose; May and June, sometimes later. Yunnan. I. 1912. A.M.(F.) 1954. H4.

hemitrichotum BALF. f. & FORR. (s. Scabrifolium). A small shrub. Leaves oblanceolate about 2·5cm. long. Very attractive in April with its numerous small, funnel-shaped flowers, bright red in bud, opening white or pale pink with darker edges. Szechwan. Introduced by Forrest in 1919. H4.

hemsleyanum WILS. (s. Fortunei). A large shrub or occasionally a small tree with auricled leaves up to 20cm. long. Flowers trumpet-shaped 8 to 10cm. long, white; May and June. Named after the English botanist H. B. Hemsley (1843-1924) who named and described numerous plants of Chinese origin. Szechwan. H4.

hippophaeoides BALF. f. & W. W. SM. (s. Lapponicum). A small, erect, leafy shrub with small, greyish-green, oblanceolate leaves and usually lavender, lilac or rose coloured, or occasionally lilac-pink, funnel-shaped flowers; March and April. A fairly tolerant species which will grow even in semi-bog conditions. Yunnan. I. 1913. A.G.M. 1925. A.M.(F.) 1927. H4.

'Inshriach'. A choice form raised by Jack Drake in Scotland. Flowers lavender-mauve, darker at margins, in comparatively large, dense clusters.

hirsutum L. (s. Ferrugineum). Small, twiggy shrub, with bristly shoots and bristle-fringed leaves. Clusters of tubular rose-pink flowers in June. Alps of Central Europe. This species has the distinction of being the first rhododendron to be introduced into cultivation. I. 1656. H4.

'Album'. Flowers white.

hodgsonii HOOK. f. (s. Falconeri). A large Himalayan shrub or small tree, grown for its very handsome foliage. Leaves up to 30cm. long and 13cm. wide, dark green above, grey- or fawn-tomentose beneath. Flowers bell-shaped, dark magenta, carried in dense trusses; April. E. Nepal; Sikkim; Bhutan. I. 1849. H4.

†**hookeri** NUTT. (s. Thomsonii). An unusual species of medium to large size. Leaves pale glaucous-green beneath, the veins studded with small, isolated but conspicuous tufts of hooked hairs, a character possessed by no other known species. Flowers bell-shaped, blood red or pink, calyx often similarly coloured; March and April. Bhutan; Assam. I. 1850. F.C.C.(F.) 1933. H3.

hormophorum BALF. f. & FORREST (s. Triflorum). A small to medium-sized, floriferous shrub, the leaves lanceolate, 2·5 to 7·5cm. long, covered with pale yellow scales below; flowers funnel-shaped, rose lilac or lavender, usually with a ray of brown markings; May. Yunnan; Szechwan. A.M.(F.) 1943. H4.

houlstonii HEMSL. & WILS. (s. Fortunei). A choice species making a small tree or large shrub. Leaves oblong-oblanceolate 7·5 to 15cm. long. Flowers bell-shaped, usually soft lilac or pale pink, faintly lined and spotted; May. A parent of the A.M. hybrid named after our late manager Arthur J. Ivens. Hupeh; Szechwan. I. about 1900. H4.

hunnewellianum REHD. & WILS. (s. Arboreum). An attractive, large shrub or small tree neat and compact in growth, with long, narrow leaves with conspicuously impressed venation above and loosely grey-felted beneath. Flowers bell-shaped, white, tinted pink; March and April. Named in honour of a well known New England family of great gardeners. W. Szechwan. I. 1908. H4.

hypenanthum BALF. f. (s. Anthopogon). Dwarf shrub of dense, twiggy habit with small leaves which are densely scaly beneath. The small. tubular, yellow flowers are carried in tight rounded heads; April and May. N.W. and C. Himalaya. H3-4.

RHODODENDRON—*continued*

hyperythrum HAYATA (s. Ponticum). Small shrub with usually oblong, curiously rigid, polished green leaves, the lower surfaces dotted with reddish specks. Flowers funnel-shaped, pure white or with purple spots; April and May. Formosa. H3-4.

impeditum BALF. f. & W. W. SM. (s. Lapponicum). A dwarf, alpine shrub only a few cm. high with tiny leaves, forming low, tangled mounds of scaly branches. Flowers funnel-shaped, light purplish-blue; April and May. Frequently confused with *R. fastigiatum*. Most suitable for the rock garden. Yunnan; Szechwan. Introduced by George Forrest in 1911. A.M.(F.) 1944. A.G.M. 1969. H4.

imperator HUTCH. & WARD (s. Uniflorum). A dwarf shrub, often creeping, with small, narrow leaves and normally solitary, funnel-shaped flowers of pink or rose-purple, 2·5cm. across appearing even on very young plants; May. Best in an open sunny position and very suitable for the rock garden. Burma. Introduced by Kingdon Ward. A.M.(F.) 1934. H3-4.

indicum SWEET (*macranthum*) (*Azalea indica*) (*A. macrantha*) (s. Azalea). A small, dense, semi-evergreen bush rarely reaching medium size. Leaves small, narrow, lanceolate to oblanceolate, often turning crimson or purple in autumn. Flowers single or in pairs, widely funnel-shaped, varying in colour from red to scarlet; June. A variable species with numerous forms. Both this species and *R. simsii* and their forms are often referred to as "Indian Azaleas". S. Japan. I. 1883. A.M.T. 1975. H2-3.

'Balsaminiflorum' (*R. rosiflorum*) (*Azalea rosiflora*). Charming dwarf form with double, salmon-pink flowers. F.C.C. 1882.

'Coccineum'. Low, spreading shrub, with large, single, scarlet-red flowers; late.

'Double Rose'. Flowers double, rose-pink.

eriocarpum WILS. (*simsii eriocarpum*) (*R. eriocarpum*) (*tamurae*). A slow-growing, dwarf shrub of dense, compact habit. Flowers pink to lavender, large and frilled, opening in June and July. A variable shrub with several clones. Some authorities regard it as a distinct species. S. Japan; Formosa.

'Album Grandiflorum'. Flowers very large, white with green markings.

'Gumpo'. Large, wavy-petalled white flowers, occasionally flecked red. A.M. 1934.

'Jitsugetsuse'. Flowers pale mauve.

'Pink Gumpo'. Large flowers, peach-pink with deeper flecks.

'Terra Cotta Beauty'. Small flowers of terra-cotta pink.

'Hakatashiro'. A low shrub with very large, ivory-white flowers. Earlier flowering and more tender than the type.

'Kok-in-shita'. Dwarf shrub with rose-salmon flowers opening in June and July.

'Misomogiri'. A form with semi-double, salmon-coloured flowers.

'Salmonea'. Low-growing habit, large, single, salmon-red flowers.

'Zangetsu'. Flowers pale crimson with white throat.

insigne HEMSL. & WILS. (s. Arboreum). An exceptionally hardy and unmistakable, slow-growing Chinese species eventually attaining a large size. Leaves leathery, oblong-lanceolate, 6 to 13cm. long, rich glossy green above and silvery-white beneath when young, assuming a metallic lustre. Large trusses of bell-shaped flowers, soft pink with dark markings; May and June. Szechwan. A.M. 1923. H4.

intricatum FRANCH. (s. Lapponicum). Small, densely twiggy shrub, ·6 to 1m. high, with small, olive-green, aromatic leaves. Flowers funnel-shaped, lavender-blue, in small, rounded trusses; April and early May. Suitable for the rock garden. A parent of the A.M. clone '*Bluebird*'. Szechwan. Introduced by E. H. Wilson in 1904. F.C.C. 1907. H4.

irroratum FRANCH. (s. Irroratum). A large shrub or small tree. Leaves oblanceolate or elliptic, 6 to 13cm. long, green on both surfaces. Flowers narrowly bell-shaped, variously coloured, usually white, pink, or creamy-yellow with a more or less broad ray of dark crimson markings or sometimes heavily spotted; March to May. Yunnan; Szechwan. A.M.(F.) 1957. I. about 1886. H3.

'Polka Dot'. A very remarkable clone, the white flowers being densely marked with purple dots. It received an A.M. when exhibited by Exbury in 1957.

RHODODENDRON—*continued*

japonicum WILS. (*molle* SIEB. & ZUCC. not G. DON) (*sinense* MAXIM.) (*Azalea mollis*) (s. Azalea). A tall, deciduous shrub of medium size with ovate-oblong ciliated leaves 5 to 10cm. long, often giving rich autumn tints. Flowers usually appearing before the leaves, fragrant, funnel-shaped, orange-red or salmon-red, with basal blotch, borne in conspicuous trusses of six to twelve; May. This is a dominant parent of many named garden hybrids. Japan. I. 1861. H4.

†**johnstoneanum** HUTCH. (s. Maddenii). Large shrub with leaves elliptic to obovate, ciliate, 5 to 10cm. long, densely scaly below. The large, fragrant, funnel-shaped flowers are borne in clusters of three or four. They are creamy-white or pale yellow in colour, with red spots and a yellow blotch; May. There are forms with double flowers. Assam; Manipur. A.M.(F.) 1934. H2-3.

kaempferi PLANCH. (*obtusum kaempferi*) (s. Azalea). A very beautiful and very hardy deciduous or semi-evergreen shrub of medium size. Leaves 4 to 7·5cm. long and like the young shoots strigose pubescent. Flowers in clusters of two to four, funnel-shaped, varying in colour from biscuit to salmon-red to orange-red, or rose-scarlet; May and June. A parent of many of the Kurume azaleas. Japan. Introduced by Professor Sargent in 1892. A.M. 1953. A.G.M. 1969. H4.

'Daimio'. Salmon-pink flowers appearing as late as July.

'Highlight'. A striking form raised in our nurseries; flowers bright salmon-orange.

'Mikado'. Flowers an exquisite shade of apricot-salmon, late June and July.

keiskei MIQ. (s. Triflorum). A very attractive, free-flowering, semi-evergreen, dwarf species suitable for the rock garden. Leaves 2·5 to 7·5cm. long, lanceolate. Flowers widely funnel-shaped in trusses of three to five, lemon-yellow; March to May. Japan. I. 1908. A.M. 1929. H3-4.

keleticum BALF. f. & FORR. (s. Saluenense). A dwarf species forming mats or hummocks of small, densely scaly leaves from which the saucer-shaped, purple-crimson flowers arise, singly or in pairs; May and June. S.E. Tibet; Yunnan; Upper Burma. A.M.(F.) 1928. H4.

keysii NUTT. (s. Cinnabarinum). An interesting, medium-sized to large shrub with oblong-lanceolate, densely scaly leaves; very attractive when bearing its clusters of remarkable tubular, cuphea-like flowers of bright orange-red, tipped yellow and 2cm. long; June. S.E. Tibet; Bhutan; Assam. I. 1851. H3-4.

kingianum. See *R. zeylanicum*.

kiusianum MAK. (*Azalea kiusiana*) (*obtusum japonicum*) (s. Azalea). "Kyushu Azalea". A dwarf, evergreen or semi-evergreen shrub, occasionally up to 1m., of dense, spreading habit. Leaves small, oval. Flowers in clusters of two to five, funnel-shaped, varying in colour from salmon-red to crimson or purple, but usually lilac-purple; May and June. This is generally regarded as one of the species from which the Kurume Azaleas were developed. It is restricted in the wild to the tops of high mountains on the island of Kyushu (Japan). H3-4.

'Hillier's Pink'. A lovely form with flowers of a clear lilac-pink.

kongboense HUTCH. (s. Anthopogon). A dwarf shrub, occasionally up to 1m., the slender twigs covered with small, oblong leaves. Flowers 1cm. long, tubular, bright rose, borne in small tight heads; April and May. Tibet-Bhutan border. H4.

kotschyi SIMK. (s. Ferrugineum). Dwarf shrub of dense habit, the 1cm. long leaves are crenulate and are densely scaly below. Flowers tubular, with spreading lobes, rose-pink, appearing in clusters of three to eight from May to July. C. Europe (Carpathians). I. 1846. H3-4. The correct name for this species is now considered to be *myrtifolium* SCHOTT. x KOT.

lacteum FRANCH. (s. Lacteum). A beautiful large shrub or rarely a small tree of slow growth. Leaves oblong to oblong-elliptic, covered with a thin, suede-like fawn or brown tomentum below. Flowers bell-shaped, normally clear soft yellow, sometimes with a pink stain or crimson blotch; April and May. Unfortunately of rather weak constitution. Yunnan; Szechwan; Burma. I. 1910. F.C.C.(F.) 1926. H4.

lanatum HOOK. f. (s. Campanulatum). A small to medium-sized, unusual and attractive shrub. Leaves thick, inclined to obovate, 5 to 10cm. long, brown-felted beneath. Flowers bell-shaped, pale yellow with crimson-purple markings; April and May. Sikkim; Bhutan; Assam; Tibet. Discovered by Sir Joseph Hooker in 1848. I. 1850. H4.

RHODODENDRON—*continued*

lanigerum TAGG (*silvaticum*) (s. Arboreum). Large shrub or small tree, the young shoots grey tomentose and the large, oblong-lanceolate leaves 10 to 23cm. long, covered with white, grey or cinnamon-brown tomentum beneath. Flowers in a round, compact truss of twenty-five or more, bell-shaped up to 5cm. long, rose-purple to dark magenta; March and April. Assam; S.E. Tibet A.M. 1949. A.M. 1951 (as *R. silvaticum*). H.4 Several clones have received names including *'Chapel Wood'*. A.M. 1961, F.C.C. 1967; *'Silvia'*. A.M. 1954; and *'Round Wood'*. A.M. 1951.

lapponicum WAHLENB. (s. Lapponicum). A dwarf shrub of dense, compact habit. The tiny leaves are densely scaly. Flowers in clusters of two or three, funnel-shaped, purple; Jan. and Feb. A difficult plant to keep in cultivation. Arctic regions of Europe, Asia and America. I. 1825. H4.

ledifolium. See *R. mucronatum*.

ledoides. See *R. trichostomum*.

lepidostylum BALF. f. & FORREST (s. Trichocladum). A dwarf, deciduous or semi-evergreen shrub occasionally to 1m., of dense, compact habit. The small, bristly, ovate leaves are a conspicuous blue-green above until the winter months. Flowers funnel-shaped, pale yellow, produced singly or in pairs during May and June. A choice shrub for the peat garden or shady rock garden. The most glaucous leaved of the dwarf rhododendrons. Yunnan. A.M. 1969. H4.

lepidotum G. DON (*obovatum*) (*elaeagnoides*) (s. Lepidotum). A variable dwarf shrub with conspicuously scaly oblanceolate leaves 2 to 4cm. long. Flowers one to three in a small truss, saucer-shaped, scaly on the outside, varying in colour from pink to purple, occasionally yellow or white; June. N.W. Himalaya to Szechwan and Yunnan. I. 1829. H3-4.

leucaspis TAGG (s. Boothii). Dwarf shrub occasionally to 1m., with elliptic to obovate 4 to 6cm. long hairy leaves and scaly stems. The 5cm. diameter, lovely saucer-shaped flowers are milky-white, with contrasting chocolate-brown anthers, in clusters of two or three; Feb. and March. It should be given a sheltered site. A parent of several fine hybrids. Burma-Tibet frontier. Introduced by Kingdon Ward in 1925. A.M.(F.) 1929. F.C.C. 1944. H3-4.

linearifolium. See *R. macrosepalum 'Linearifolium'*.

macrosepalum. See *R. macrosepalum*.

litangense HUTCH. (s. Lapponicum). Dwarf shrub with small, aromatic leaves and clusters of small, funnel-shaped, plum-purple flowers; April and May. Szechwan; Yunnan. H4.

litiense BALF. f. & FORREST (s. Thomsonii). A very beautiful, medium-sized shrub similar to *R. wardii* with densely glandular young shoots. Leaves oblong up to 7·5cm. long, glaucous when young. Flowers widely bell-shaped or saucer-shaped, clear soft yellow without markings; May. Similar to *R. wardii*, differing in oblong leaves, waxy-glaucous beneath. Yunnan. A.M. 1931. F.C.C. 1953. H3.

lochmium BALF. f. (s. Triflorum). A medium-sized shrub of loose, open habit with leaves densely scaly beneath. Flowers funnel-shaped, white, flushed rosy-purple; May. Regarded by some authorities as a probable hybrid (*R. davidsonianum* × *trichanthum*). H4.

†**lopsangianum** COWAN (s. Thomsonii). A small shrub up to 2m. Leaves 3 to 6cm. long, glaucous beneath. Flowers narrowly bell-shaped, fleshy, deep crimson; April. Named after the late Dalai Lama of Tibet. S.E. Tibet. H2.

lowndesii DAVIDIAN (s. Lepidotum). A dwarf, deciduous shrublet of compact habit. Leaves bright green, obovate, bristly, up to 2·5cm. long. Flowers solitary or in pairs, widely bell-shaped, 2·5cm. across, pale yellow with light reddish spots; June and July. A charming diminutive species for the peat garden or rock garden. Discovered in Central Nepal by Col. Donald Lowndes in 1950. H3-4.

ludlowii COWAN (s. Uniflorum). A charming, dwarf shrub for the peat garden. Leaves obovate about 12mm. long. Flowers borne singly or in pairs, 2·5cm. long and wide, saucer-shaped, yellow, with reddish-brown spots in the centre; calyx large and leafy; April and May. Parent of A.M. clone *'Chikor'*. S.E. Tibet. H3-4.

RHODODENDRON—*continued*

lutescens FRANCH. (s. Triflorum). A lovely, but variable Chinese species up to 3·6m., requiring shelter on account of its early flowering. Leaves lanceolate, 4 to 7·5cm. long. Its primrose-yellow, funnel-shaped flowers and bronze-red young leaves are especially effective in thin woodland. Feb. to April. We grow the Exbury F.C.C form with lemon-yellow flowers. Szechwan; Yunnan. Discovered by the Abbé Delavay and introduced by E. H. Wilson in 1904. F.C.C.(F.) 1938. A.G.M. 1969. H3-4.

luteum SWEET (*Azalea pontica*) (s. Azalea). The well-known, common, fragrant, yellow azalea. A medium-sized, deciduous shrub, occasionally reaching 3·5m. high and as much or more across. Winter buds and young shoots sticky. Leaves oblong to oblong-lanceolate, 5 to 10cm. long, turning to rich shades of crimson, purple and orange in autumn. Flowers in a rounded truss, funnel-shaped, yellow, viscid on the outside, richly and strongly fragrant; May. Caucasus; E. Europe, occasionally naturalised in the British Isles. I. 1793. A.G.M. 1930. H4.

lysolepis HUTCH. (s. Lapponicum). An intricately branched, small shrub of stiff, erect habit, with small, bright shiny green leaves. Flowers funnel-shaped, rosy-mauve, lavender-blue or purple, in three-flowered trusses; April and May. Szechwan. H4.

macabeanum BALF. f. (s. Grande). A magnificent species for woodland conditions. A large, rounded shrub or small tree. The handsome leaves up to 30cm. long are dark, shining green and conspicuously veined above, greyish or greyish-white tomentose beneath. The large trusses of bell-shaped, pale-yellow, purple-blotched flowers are borne in March or April. In some forms the flowers are deep canary yellow. Assam; Manipur. Introduced by Kingdon Ward about 1928. A.M. 1937. F.C.C. 1938. H3-4.

macranthum. See *R. indicum*.

macrophyllum G. DON (*californicum*) (s. Ponticum). A large shrub with strong, stout stems and leaves like those of *R. ponticum*. Flowers bell-shaped, up to twenty, in a compact truss, rose-purple with reddish-brown spots. Opening in May and June. W. North America. H4.

macrosepalum MAXIM. (*linearifolium macrosepalum*) (s. Azalea). A small shrub of loose, spreading habit with often densely glandular hairy young shoots. Leaves ovate to ovate-elliptic or lanceolate, densely hairy, some leaves often turn rich crimson in autumn. Flowers fragrant, funnel-shaped, 5cm. across, lilac-pink to rose-purple; calyx lobes long and narrow; April and May. Japan. I. 1863. H3.

'Linearifolium' (*R. linearifolium*). An unusual clone with narrower leaves up to 7·5cm. long by 6mm. wide. The pink flowers are deeply divided into five narrow segments. Long cultivated in Japan, but unknown in the wild. H3-4.

maculiferum FRANCH. (s. Barbatum). A medium-sized to large shrub or small tree. Leaves 7·5 to 13cm. long, oval to obovate, sea-green beneath. Flowers in a loose truss, bell-shaped, white or rose-flushed, with a dark black-purple basal blotch; April. Szechwan; Hupeh. I. 1901. H3.

†**magnificum** WARD (s. Grande). A magnificent, large shrub or small tree for very sheltered woodland site with leaves 30 to 45cm. long, covered with a white or greyish-white indumentum beneath. Flowers in a dense truss, bell-shaped, 5cm. long, rose-purple; Feb. and April. Flowers not produced on young plants. Burma-Tibet frontier. I. 1931. A.M.(F.) 1950. H2-3.

makinoi TAGG (*metternichii angustifolium*) (s. Ponticum). A very hardy, medium sized shrub. The young growths are clothed with a white or tawny woolly indumentum and appear in late summer. Leaves narrow lanceolate, somewhat bullate above, thickly fawn or tawny-woolly tomentose beneath. Flowers bell-shaped, soft pink, sometimes with crimson dots; June. Japan. H3-4.

mallotum BALF. f. & WARD (*aemulorum*) (s. Neriiflorum). A distinct and beautiful large shrub or small tree, with obovate leaves 7·5 to 15cm. long, covered beneath with red-brown, woolly indumentum. Flowers bell-shaped, dark crimson; March and April. Yunnan; Upper Burma. I. 1919. A.M. 1933. H4.

mariesii HEMSL. & WILS. (s Azalea). An medium-sized to large, deciduous shrub. Leaves 3 to 7·5cm. long, prominently reticulate beneath, borne in clusters of two or three at the ends of the branches. Flowers saucer-shaped or shallowly funnel-shaped, 5cm. across, lilac or pale rose, with reddish spots on upper lobes; April. S.E. and C. China; Formosa. H3.

RHODODENDRON—*continued*

maximum L. (s. Ponticum). The "Great Laurel" or "Rose Bay" of the U.S.A. A useful and very hardy, large, evergreen shrub, or small tree, with leaves 10 to 30cm. long. Flowers in compact trusses, funnel-shaped, varying in colour from purple-rose to white, slightly fragrant; July. Eastern U.S.A. I. 1736. H4.

maxwellii. See *R. pulchrum 'Maxwellii'*.

meddianum FORREST (s. Thomsonii). Medium-sized to large shrub with glaucous young shoots and obovate or oval leaves, 5 to 18cm. long. Flowers bell-shaped, fleshy, deep crimson or bright scarlet; April. A parent of the A.M. clones *'Queen of Hearts'* and *'Rocket'*. Yunnan. I. 1917. H2-4.

atrokermesinum TAGG. A variety with usually larger, darker flowers and glandular branchlets. Burma. A.M. 1954.

megeratum BALF. f. & FORR. (s. Boothii). A charming but fastidious, dwarf species. Leaves glaucous and scaly below; flowers bell-shaped, rich yellow, calyx large; March and April. Yunnan; Tibet; Assam; Burma. A.M. 1935. A.M. 1970. H3.

melinanthum BALF. f. & WARD (s. Trichocladum). A small to medium-sized deciduous shrub. Leaves 4cm. long, obovate to oblanceolate, sea-green. Flowers funnel-shaped, yellow, appearing before the leaves; April and May. The best garden plant of this series. Upper Burma. H4.

metternichii SIEB. & ZUCC. (s. Ponticum). A very hardy, Japanese species of medium size, rare in cultivation. Leaves oblong-lanceolate 7·5 to 15cm. long, almost whorled, glossy above, tawny or rusty-brown-tomentose beneath. Flowers bell-shaped, seven-lobed, rose coloured; April and May. Japan. Introduced by Fortune and Siebold in 1860. H4.

angustifolium. See *R. makinoi*.

'Wada'. An interesting form with leaves which are deep cinnamon-brown beneath, habit more compact.

micranthum TURCZ. (s. Micranthum). A very distinct and interesting Chinese species which has racemes of tiny white, bell-shaped flowers resembling those of *Ledum* and entirely different from nearly all other rhododendrons; May to July. A free-growing, small-leaved shrub up to 2m. high. Hupeh; Szechwan; Kansu. I. 1901. H4.

microgynum BALF. f. & FORR. (s. Taliense). Small shrub with leaves 5 to 7·5cm. long, clad with buff tomentum beneath. Flowers bell-shaped, soft rose, spotted crimson; April. S.E. Tibet. H4.

microleucum HUTCH. (s. Lapponicum). Dwarf, densely leafy shrub with brown scaly twigs and small clusters of funnel-shaped, white flowers; April. Suitable for the rock garden. Yunnan. F.C.C. 1939. H4.

mimites TAGG & FORREST (s. Taliense). Medium-sized shrub with leaves elliptic to oblong, 6 to 10cm. long, buff-coloured beneath. Flowers funnel-shaped, white, tinged pink and flecked crimson, in loose trusses; May. S.W. Szechwan. H4.

molle SIEB. & ZUCC. not G. DON. See *R. japonicum*.

mollicomum BALF. f. & W. W. SM. (s. Scabrifolium). A small to medium-sized shrub of straggling habit with small, narrow-lanceolate, softly pubescent leaves and rose-coloured, tubular flowers from axillary buds, all along the branchlets; April. Yunnan; S.W. Szechwan. Introduced by Forrest in 1913. A.M.(F.) 1931. H3-4.

mollyanum COWAN & DAVIDIAN (s. Grande). Large shrub or small woodland tree of noble proportions; leaves inclined to oblong, 15 to 30cm. long, silvery white beneath; flowers in large trusses, bell-shaped, pink with a crimson basal blotch; April and May. Named after the late Duchess of Montrose. S.E. Tibet. H3-4.

monosematum HUTCH. (s. Barbatum). Medium-sized to large shrub of compact habit, with broadly oblong leaves, shining green beneath. Flowers 5cm. long, widely funnel-shaped, varying in colour from white to deep rose; April. Szechwan. I. 1904. H4.

morii HAYATA (s. Barbatum). A medium-sized to large shrub. A rare and beautiful rhododendron from Formosa. Leaves oblong-lanceolate, 7·5 to 13cm. long, green on both surfaces. The bell-shaped flowers white, with a ray of crimson spots; April and May. Introduced by Wilson in 1919. A.M.(F.) 1956. H4.

RHODODENDRON—*continued*

moupinense FRANCH. (s. Moupinense). A delightful, early flowering, small shrub with bristly branchlets. Leaves ovate-elliptic, densely scaly below. Flowers funnel-shaped, white, pink or deep rose, sometimes spotted red, sweetly scented; Feb. and March. Szechwan. This lovely species was introduced by E. H. Wilson in 1904. It should have some shelter, especially on the east side against early morning frost whilst in flower. It is a parent of the following A.M. clones: *'Bo-Peep', 'Bric-a-Brac', 'Tessa', 'Tessa Roza', 'Seta'* and several others. A.M.(F.) 1914. A.M.(F.) 1937. H4.

mucronatum G. DON (*ledifolium*) (*Azalea ledifolia*) (s. Azalea). A very lovely small evergreen or semi-evergreen shrub of wide-spreading, dome-shaped habit. Leaves elliptic-lanceolate, dull green and hairy. Flowers fragrant, funnel-shaped, pure white; May. Long cultivated in Japan, but unknown in the wild. It is now generally considered to be of hybrid origin, possibly *R. macrosepalum* × *R. ripense*. I. 1819. A.M.T. 1958. A.G.M. 1969. H4.

'Bulstrode'. A floriferous shrub; large white flowers with a faint yellowish-green stain.

'Lilacinum'. Flowers soft lilac-mauve.

'Noordtianum'. A form with slightly larger white flowers green at the throat.

mucronulatum TURCZ. (s. Dauricum). A slender, medium-sized, normally deciduous shrub. Leaves elliptic-lanceolate up to 5cm. long. Flowers 4 to 5cm. long, bright rose-purple, funnel-shaped; Jan. to March. Japan; Korea; China; Ussuri. A.M.(F.) 1924. A.M.(F.) 1935. A.G.M. 1969. H4.

muliense. See *R. chryseum*.

myiagrum BALF. f. & FORREST (s. Thomsonii). Small shrub related to *R. callimorphum*, with rounded leaves dark green above, glaucous below. The white, bell-shaped flowers are carried in trusses of four or five; May. Yunnan; Upper Burma. I. 1919. H4.

myrtilloides. See *R. campylogynum myrtilloides*.

nakaharae HAYATA (s. Azalea). A very attractive and rare dwarf shrub of creeping habit, suitable for the rock garden, with densely appressed-hairy shoots. Leaves small, oblanceolate, persistent. Flowers in small clusters, funnel-shaped, up to 2·5cm. long, of an unusual dark brick red; June and July or even later. Native of mountains in N. Formosa. H4.

neriiflorum FRANCH. (s. Neriiflorum). One of the most desirable species. A medium-sized shrub with narrow leaves, gleaming white beneath and trusses of fleshy, bell-shaped flowers which vary in colour from deep rose to scarlet or crimson; calyx large, coloured like the corolla; April and May. Yunnan; S.E. Tibet; Burma-Tibet frontier. First discovered by the Abbé Delavay and introduced by George Forrest in 1906. H3-4.

euchaites BALF. f. & FORREST (*R. euchaites*). A lovely form, differing from the type in its taller growth and larger, crimson-scarlet flowers in April. Often considered the finest of its series. N.E. India; Yunnan; Upper Burma. A.M. 1929. I. 1913.

phaedropum BALF. f. & FARRER. A form with variably coloured flowers; in the form we offer they are straw yellow tipped scarlet. N.E. Upper Burma; Siam.

nigropunctatum BUR. & FRANCH. (s. Lapponicum). A dwarf, aromatic shrub of dense, twiggy habit, with minute, densely scaly leaves. Flowers solitary or in pairs, small, widely funnel-shaped, pale purple; May and June. Szechwan. H4.

niphargum. See *R. uvariifolium*.

nipponicum MATSUM. (*Azalea nipponica*) (s. Azalea). A rare, small, deciduous shrub of stiff, erect habit; older stems with attractive, peeling, cinnamon-brown bark. Leaves large up to 15cm. long and 7·5cm. wide, obovate, turning rich orange or crimson in autumn. Flowers in clusters, appearing with or after the leaves, tubular, white; May and June. Japan. Introduced by E. H. Wilson in 1914. H4.

nitens HUTCH. (s. Saluenense). A dwarf, erect shrublet with aromatic leaves and usually deep purple flowers, widely funnel-shaped or saucer-shaped, up to 5cm. across; June and July. The last of its series to flower. Burma. H4.

niveum HOOK. f. (s. Arboreum). An attractive, large Himalayan shrub for woodland. Leaves obovate-lanceolate, to 15cm. long, young leaves covered with white indumentum, persisting and turning pale brown on the undersurfaces. Flowers bell-shaped, smokey-blue to rich purple, in tight globular heads; April and May. Sikkim; Bhutan. I. 1849. A.M.(F.) 1951. H4.

RHODODENDRON—*continued*

niveum 'Clyne Castle'. A form with larger leaves and rich purple flowers. H4.

nudiflorum TORR. (*Azalea nudiflora*) (s. Azalea). Medium-sized, deciduous shrub with oblong or obovate, bright green leaves. Flowers in clusters; fragrant, funnel-shaped, pale pink with reddish tube; May. A parent of many of the Ghent hybrid azaleas. Eastern N. America. Introduced by Peter Collinson in 1734. H4.

†**nuttallii** BOOTH (s. Maddenii). A superb species, but too tender for all but the mildest areas. A medium-sized to large shrub, often epiphytic in nature, of rather straggling habit. Leaves up to 20cm. long, bullate and reticulate above, densely scaly beneath, of an enchanting metallic purple when unfolding. The fragrant, funnel-shaped, lily-like flowers are 13cm. or more long and appear in loose trusses of three to nine, yellow or white flushed yellow within, tinged pink on the lobes; April and May. An ideal conservatory shrub. S.E. Himalaya. I. 1850. F.C.C. 1864. H1-2.

oblongifolium MILLAIS (*Azalea oblongifolia*) (s. Azalea). A deciduous shrub up to 2m. with obovate to oblanceolate leaves pale or glaucous beneath. Flowers appearing after the leaves, funnel-shaped, slightly clove-scented, white or occasionally pale pink; June and July. Southern C. United States. I. 1917. H3.

obtusum PLANCH. (*Azalea obtusa*) (s. Azalea). "Kirishima Azalea". A dwarf, densely-branched, evergreen or semi-evergreen, wide-spreading shrub seldom reaching 1m. Branches densely hairy, clothed with small, oval, glossy green leaves and flowering with prodigious freedom in spring. Flowers in clusters of one to three, 2·5cm. across, funnel-shaped; bright red, scarlet or crimson; May. Said by some authorities to be wild on a few high mountains on the island of Kyushu (Japan), but certain Japanese authorities consider it to be of hybrid origin. Long cultivated, both in Japan and China, and a parent of many of the Kurume azaleas. Introduced from China by Robert Fortune in 1844. A.M. 1898. H4.

'Amoenum' (*Azalea amoena*). The hardiest form. A rather taller, wide-spreading shrub. Flowers hose-in-hose, brilliant magenta or rose-purple. Introduced from Japanese gardens in 1845. A.M. 1907. A.M.T. 1965. A.G.M. 1965.

'Amoenum Coccineum'. A branch sport of *'Amoenum'* with carmine-rose, hose-in-hose flowers. Tends to revert. A.G.M. 1969.

'Amoenum Splendens'. A low, wide-spreading shrub with single, pale mauve flowers.

kaempferi. See *R. kaempferi*.

'Macrostemon'. Low spreading bush with single, salmon-orange flowers; 4cm. wide.

occidentale A. GRAY (*Azalea occidentalis*) (s. Azalea). Medium-sized, deciduous, summer-flowering shrub, with oval or obovate, glossy-green leaves, turning yellow, scarlet or crimson in autumn. Flowers normally appearing with the leaves, widely funnel-shaped, fragrant, creamy-white to pale pink with pale yellow or orange-yellow basal stain; June. A parent of many beautiful hybrids. Western N. America. Introduced by William Lobb about 1851. A.M.(F.) 1944. H4.

ochraceum REHD. & WILS. (s. Barbatum). A rare, medium-sized shrub with glandular hairy shoots and petioles. Flowers bell-shaped, crimson, in trusses of eight to twelve; March and April. W. Szechwan. H3-4.

†**oldhamii** MAXIM. (*Azalea oldhamii*) (s. Azalea). "Formosan Azalea". A medium-sized, evergreen shrub with densely, glandular hairy young shoots and elliptic, glossy-green leaves thickly covered with rust-coloured hairs. Flowers in clusters of one to three, funnel-shaped, bright brick-red; May. Formosa. First discovered by Richard Oldham in 1864, introduced by Charles Maries in 1878 and later by E. H. Wilson in 1918. H2-3.

oleifolium FRANCH. (s. Virgatum). A small to medium-sized shrub occasionally up to 2m., with slender branches and narrow leaves, scaly beneath. Flowers bell-shaped, pink, produced in the leaf axils; April and May. Not to be confused with *R. racemosum oleifolium* which is glaucous-white on the leaf undersurfaces. Yunnan; S.E. Tibet. I. 1906. H3.

oporinum BALF. f. & WARD (s. Heliolepis). Medium-sized shrub with aromatic leaves 2·5 to 7·5cm. long, pale reddish-brown beneath. Flowers narrowly bell-shaped 2cm. long, rose-pink or white, with or without crimson spots and basal blotch; June and July. Upper Burma. H4.

RHODODENDRON—*continued*

orbiculare DCNE. (s. Fortunei). An outstanding Chinese species forming a symmetrical, dome-shaped bush up to 3m. high. The rounded, heart-shaped leaves held rigidly horizontal are matt green above, glaucous beneath. Flowers bell-shaped, seven-lobed, rose-pink, sometimes with a bluish tinge; March and April. W. Szechwan. Introduced by E. H. Wilson in 1904. A.M. 1922. H4.

oreodoxa FRANCH. (*haematocheilum*) (s. Fortunei). A very floriferous large shrub, or small tree with oblanceolate-elliptic leaves glaucous beneath. Loose trusses of bell-shaped, pink flowers, deep red in bud; March and April. Closely related and very similar in appearance to *R. fargesii*. W. Szechwan; Mupin; Kansu. I. about 1904. A.M.(F.) 1937. H4.

oreotrephes W. W. SM. (*artosquameum*) (*exquisitum*) (*timetium*) (s. Triflorum). A free-flowering, large shrub with glaucous young growths and usually oblong-elliptic leaves which are scaly and glaucous beneath. Flowers generally funnel-shaped varying in colour from mauve, mauve-pink, purple to rose, with or without crimson spots; April and May. Several forms originally classed as species are now included here. (See synonyms above). Semi-deciduous in cold gardens. Yunnan; Szechwan; Tibet; Burma. First introduced by George Forrest in 1913. A.M.(F.) 1932 (as *R. timeteum*). A.M.(F.) 1937 (as *R. exquisitum*). H4.

orthocladum BALF. f. & FORR. (s. Lapponicum). A small, neat, Chinese shrub with densely scaly branches, and small, greyish, scaly leaves. Flowers small, funnel-shaped, mauve, purplish-blue or lavender-blue, produced with great profusion in April. Yunnan; Szechwan. I. 1913. H4.

†**ovatum** PLANCH. (s. Ovatum). A medium-sized to large shrub with pale bark and broadly ovate leaves up to 2·5cm. long. Flowers solitary, saucer-shaped, white, pink or purple, with purple spots; May and June. E. & C. China; C. Formosa. Introduced by Robert Fortune in 1844. H3.

pachytrichum FRANCH. (s. Barbatum). A slow-growing, medium-sized to large shrub, the young shoots thickly covered with shaggy, brown hairs. Leaves oblong to oblanceolate, 6 to 13cm. long shining green beneath. Flowers bell-shaped, up to 5cm. long, usually soft pink but varying in colour from white to deep pink, with a purple blotch; March and April. W. Szechwan. I. 1903. H4.

panteumorphum BALF. f. & W. W. SM. (s. Thomsonii). Medium-sized to large shrub with leaves oblong-elliptic, 5 to 10cm. long, and trusses of bell-shaped flowers of a lovely pale yellow; April and May. S.E. Tibet; Yunnan. H4.

paradoxum BALF. f. (s. Taliense). Medium-sized shrub, leaves oblong 5 to 13cm. long, producing loose trusses of bell-shaped, white flowers with a deep crimson basal blotch; April and May. Szechwan. H4.

parmulatum COWAN (s. Neriiflorum). Small shrub with leaves 3·5 to 7·5cm. long, glaucous below. Flowers about 5cm. long, bell-shaped, creamy-yellow or white, sometimes tinged pink, spotted crimson; April and May. S.E. Tibet. H4.

pemakoense WARD (s. Uniflorum). A beautiful, dwarf, suckering, alpine species from Tibet, only a few cm. high. Small leaves and comparatively large, funnel-shaped, lilac-pink or purple flowers; March and April. A very floriferous species provided the flower-buds escape frost damage. A.M.(F.) 1933. A.G.M. 1969. H3-4.

pentamerum. See *R. degronianum*.

pentaphyllum MAXIM. (s. Azalea). A very lovely, medium-sized to large, deciduous shrub. Leaves oval to elliptic-lanceolate, in whorls of five at the ends of the branches, turning orange and crimson in autumn. Flowers single or in pairs, appearing before the leaves, saucer-shaped or shallowly bell-shaped, rich clear peach pink; March and April. Japan. Introduced by E. H. Wilson in 1914. A.M.(F.) 1942. H4.

planetum BALF. f. (s. Fortunei). A large shrub with oblong leaves up to 20cm. long. Flowers bell-shaped, pink, eight to ten in a truss; March and April. Szechwan. H4.

pleistanthum. See *R. yunnanense*.

pocophorum BALF. f. (s. Neriiflorum). A medium-sized shrub with oblong-ovate leaves up to 15cm. long, covered beneath with brown, woolly indumentum. Flowers bell-shaped, crimson, in a tight head; March and April. S.E. Tibet. H3-4.

RHODODENDRON—*continued*

polylepis FRANCH. (s. Triflorum). A medium-sized to large shrub. Leaves narrowly elliptic-lanceolate, aromatic, densely scaly beneath. Flowers widely funnel-shaped, varying from pale to dark purple, often with yellow spots; April. S.W. Szechwan. Introduced by E. H. Wilson in 1904. H4.

ponticum L. (s. Ponticum). The commonest and most extensively planted *Rhododendron* in the British Isles, where it has become naturalised, and has inter-bred with garden cultivars to such an extent that the true species has become obscured. Large shrub with mauve to lilac-pink flowers which can look lovely especially in the fading light of evening. Its floral display in May and June is a feature of many districts. Invaluable for shelter belts and forming hedges. It is one of the few shrubs which will grow even under beech trees. Asia Minor; Caucasus; Armenia. I. 1763. H4.

'Cheiranthifolium'. A curious form with narrow, wavy leaves.

'Flore Pleno'. An unusual form with double flowers.

'Variegatum'. One of the few variegated rhododendrons. Leaves margined creamy-white.

poukhanense LEV. (*yedoense poukhanense*) (*coreanum*) (s. Azalea). "Korean Azalea". A small, usually deciduous shrub of dense, spreading habit. Leaves narrow, up to 8cm. long, dark green, turning to orange and crimson in autumn. Flowers in clusters of two or more, appearing before or with the leaves, 5cm. wide, fragrant, funnel-shaped, lilac-rose to pale lilac-purple; May. Korea; Japan. I. 1905. A.M. 1961. H4.

praestans BALF. f. & W. W. SM. (s. Grande). A large woodland shrub or small tree, bearing immense, leathery, obovate-oblong leaves which are dark green above and covered with a greyish-white or fawn plastered indumentum beneath, borne on large-winged petioles. Flowers in a dense truss, bell-shaped, deep magenta-rose or pink, with a crimson basal blotch; April and May. Yunnan; W. Burma; S.E. Tibet. Originally discovered by George Forrest on the mountains between the Mekong and the Yangtze rivers, in 1914. H3-4.

praevernum HUTCH. (s. Fortunei). An early flowering, medium-sized to large shrub. Leaves elliptic to oblanceolate, 10 to 18cm. long. Flowers up to 6cm. long, bell-shaped, white or rose flushed, with a large, reddish-purple basal blotch. Produced in trusses of eight to fifteen; February to April. Regarded by some authorities as a form of *R. sutchuenense*, from which it differs in the blotched flowers and glabrous leaf midrib. Hupeh. A.M. 1954. H4.

prattii FRANCH. (s. Taliense). Medium-sized to large shrub. Its leathery, ovate leaves, 10 to 15cm. long, are coated beneath with a fawn or brown indumentum. Flowers bell-shaped, white, with pink spots, calyx conspicuous and leafy; April and May. One needs patience to wait for this species to reach flowering age. Szechwan. I. 1904. A.M. 1967. H4.

preptum BALF. f. & FORREST (s. Falconeri). Medium-sized to large shrub with obovate leathery leaves, 10 to 18cm. long, clothed with pale buff indumentum beneath. Flowers in a dense truss, bell-shaped, creamy-white, with a crimson blotch. April and May. Upper Burma; Yunnan. H3-4.

primuliflorum BUR. & FRANCH. (s. Anthopogon). A twiggy, small to medium-sized, aromatic shrub. Leaves small, oblong-elliptic, densely scaly and white beneath. The small, tubular, daphne-like flowers, borne in small, rounded heads are usually white with a yellow tube; April and May. Differing from the very similar *R. cephalanthum* in the deciduous leaf-bud scales. Yunnan; Szechwan; Kansu. H4.

primulinum. See *R. flavidum.*

pronum TAGG & FORR. (s. Taliense). A dwarf, slow-growing shrub of gnarled appearance. Leaves 5 to 7cm. long, sea-green when young, covered with a dull grey or fawn indumentum below. The bell-shaped crimson or deep purple-rose flowers are carried in clusters of two or three; April and May. Yunnan; S.E. Tibet; Szechwan. H4.

prostratum W. W. SM. (s. Saluenense). A dwarf, bristly shrub generally of prostrate habit with small leaves, densely brown scaly beneath. Flowers in small clusters, widely funnel-shaped, crimson or deep purple-rose, with crimson spots; April and May. Yunnan; Szechwan; Tibet. Introduced by George Forrest in 1910. H4.

RHODODENDRON—*continued*

proteoides BALF. f. &. W. W. SM. (s. Taliense). Small shrub of slow growth. Leaves small, narrowly oblong, with revolute margins and thick, woolly, rufous tomentum below. Flowers in a compact truss, bell-shaped, creamy-yellow or white with crimson spots; April. Yunnan; Szechwan; S.E. Tibet. H4.

prunifolium MILLAIS (*Azalea prunifolia*) (s. Azalea). A remarkable late flowering, deciduous, medium-sized to large shrub. Leaves elliptic to obovate, up to 13cm. long. Flowers appearing after the leaves, four or five in a truss, funnel-shaped, 4 to 5cm across, colour normally brilliant orange-red; July and August. Georgia-Alabama border (U.S.A.). Introduced by Professor Sargent in 1918. H3-4.

pruniflorum. See *R. tsangpoense pruniflorum.*

pseudochrysanthum HAYATA (s. Barbatum). A slow-growing, medium-sized, dome-shaped shrub of compact habit. Leaves ovate-elliptic 5 to 7·5cm. long, when young covered with a woolly indumentum. Flowers bell-shaped, pale pink or white, with darker lines and spots; April. Formosa. A.M.(F.) 1956. H4.

pseudoyanthinum. See *R. concinnum pseudoyanthinum.*

pubescens BALF. f. & FORREST (s. Scabrifolium). An attractive, small shrub of straggling habit, with bristly stems and densely hairy narrowly lanceolate leaves. Flowers funnel-shaped, pink, produced in clusters of one to four; April and May. Closely related to *R. spiciferum*. Szechwan; Yunnan. H4.

'Fine Bristles'. Flowers white, suffused rose, deep pink in bud. A.M. 1955.

pulchrum SWEET (*phoenicium smithii*) (s. Azalea). A small to medium-sized shrub, with densely hairy twigs and elliptic to obovate leaves. Flowers in clusters of one to four, funnel-shaped, 5 to 6cm. across, rose-purple, with dark spots; May. Unknown in the wild and possibly of hybrid origin, perhaps *R. scabrum* × *R. mucronatum*. Long cultivated in Japan and China. I. early in the 19th century. H3.

'Maxwellii' (*R. maxwellii*). A form with larger flowers of a bright rose-red with a darker blotch. A.M.T. 1960.

'Tebotan' (*R. tebotan*). Flowers double, soft purple, with tiny, undeveloped, green leaves in centre.

pumilum HOOK. f. (s. Uniflorum). A dwarf or prostrate shrub of neat habit with small leaves which are narrow, scaly and usually glaucous beneath. The small pink or rose, bell-shaped flowers are borne in two- or three-flowered clusters; May and June. E. Nepal; Sikkim; Tibet. A.M.(F.) 1935. H4.

puralbum BALF. f. & W. W. SM. (s. Thomsonii). Medium-sized shrub related to *R. wardii*, and very similar in general appearance, but the saucer-shaped flowers are white; May. Leaves oblong-elliptic, 5 to 7·5cm. long, dark green. Yunnan. H3.

purdomii REHD. & WILS. (s. Taliense). A medium-sized shrub with oblong-lanceolate to oblong leaves 6 to 9cm. long. Flowers bell-shaped, white or pink; April and May. Named after William Purdom who collected for the Arnold Arboretum in China during the years 1909-11, and with Reginald Farrer in 1914. Shensi (China). H4.

quinquefolium BISSET & MOORE (s. Azalea). An exquisitely beautiful azalea, a medium-sized to large, deciduous shrub. Leaves broadly obovate or diamond-shaped, in whorls of four or five at the ends of the shoots. They are green bordered reddish-brown when young, colouring richly in autumn. Flowers in small clusters, appearing after the leaves, pendulous, saucer-shaped, 4 to 5cm. across, pure white, with green spots; April and May. Japan. I. about 1896. A.M. 1931. A.M.(F).) 1958 H4.

racemosum FRANCH. (s. Scabrifolium). A variable but invaluable Chinese species, normally a dense, small to medium-sized shrub, a suitable subject for the heather garden. Leaves oblong-elliptic, leathery, glaucous beneath. Flowers funnel-shaped, pale to bright pink, very numerous from axillary buds, forming racemes along the branchlets; March and April. Yunnan; Szechwan. Introduced by the Abbé Delavay about 1889. F.C.C. 1892. A.G.M. 1930. A.M. 1974. H4.

'Forrest's Dwarf' (F.19404). A dwarf form with red branchlets and bright pink flowers, originally collected by George Forrest. Admirable shrub for the rock garden.

RHODODENDRON—*continued*

radicans BALF. f. & FORR. (s. Saluenense). A prostrate, Tibetan alpine, forming carpets or low mounds of creeping stems and tiny, bright green leaves. The normally solitary, flattish, rose-purple flowers appear in May and June. Suitable for the rock garden. S.E. Tibet. Introduced by George Forrest in 1921. A.M.(F.) 1926. H4.

ravum BALF. f. & W. W. SM. (s. Lapponicum). Small shrub with densely scaly young shoots and small, scaly leaves. Flowers funnel-shaped, deep rose, occasionally purple, in terminal clusters; May. Yunnan; Szechwan. I. 1913. H4.

recurvoides TAGG & WARD (s. Taliense). Small shrub of dense, compact habit. Leaves narrowly lanceolate, 5 to 7·5cm. long, tawny-tomentose beneath, margins recurved; flowers in a compact truss, bell-shaped, white or rose with darker spots; April and May. Upper Burma. A.M.(F.) 1941. H4.

repens. See *R. forrestii repens.*

reticulatum G. DON (*Azalea reticulata*) (*dilatatum* MIQ.) (*rhombicum* MIQ.) (*wadanum*) (s. Azalea). A medium-sized to large, deciduous shrub. Leaves broad obovate, or diamond-shaped, conspicuously reticulate beneath, purplish when young, turning vinous purple in autumn. Flowers appearing before the leaves, solitary or in pairs, funnel-shaped, bright purple; April and May. Japan. I. 1865. A.M. 1894 (as *R. rhombicum*). H4.

rex LEVL. (s. Falconeri). A large shrub or small tree very like *R. fictolacteum*, with large, shining dark green leaves covered with grey to pale buff tomentum beneath. Flowers in large trusses, bell-shaped, rose or white, with a crimson basal stain and spots; April and May. Szechwan. F.C.C.(F.) 1935. A.M.(F.) 1946. A.G.M. 1969. H4.

rhantum. See *R. vernicosum.*

rhombicum. See *R. reticulatum.*

rigidum FRANCH. (*caeruleum*) (s. Triflorum). A beautiful, medium-sized shrub of twiggy habit. Leaves 2·5 to 6cm. long, oblong-elliptic. Flowers funnel-shaped, varying in colour from white to pink; March to May. Yunnan; Szechwan. A.M.(F.) 1939 (as *R. caeruleum*). H4.

'Album'. A form with white flowers.

riparium. See *R. calostrotum.*

ririei HEMSL. & WILS. (s. Arboreum). A large, early-flowering shrub with oblong-elliptic leaves, 10 to 15cm. long, silvery-white or greyish beneath. Flowers bell-shaped, purplish-blue; Feb. and March. Szechwan. I. 1904. A.M.(F.) 1931. H4.

roseum REHD. (*Azalea rosea*) (s. Azalea). A lovely, medium to large sized deciduous shrub with oval or obovate leaves. Flowers appearing in clusters with the leaves, clove-scented, funnel-shaped, pale to deep pink; May. Eastern N. America. I. 1812, perhaps earlier. A.M.(F.) 1955. H4.

rosiflorum. See *R. indicum 'Balsaminiflorum'.*

roxieanum FORREST (s. Taliense). A variable, slow-growing, small to medium-sized shrub of compact habit. The narrow leaves, 5 to 10cm. long, are coated below with a fawn or rust-red indumentum. The bell-shaped flowers are creamy-white usually rose flushed, appearing ten to fifteen together in a tight truss; April and May. It takes some time to reach flowering age but is well worth growing for its leaves alone. Yunnan; S.E. Tibet; Szechwan. I. 1913. H4.

roylei. See *R. cinnabarinum roylei.*

rubiginosum FRANCH. (s. Heliolepis). A floriferous, large shrub with ovate to elliptic aromatic leaves, 4 to 6cm. long, covered with rust-coloured scales beneath. Flowers funnel-shaped, pink or rosy-lilac, with brown spots; April and May. Szechwan; Yunnan; S.E. Tibet. Introduced by the Abbé Delavay in 1889. H4.

'Album'. A lovely form with white flowers.

rude TAGG & FORREST (s. Barbatum). Medium-sized shrub with bristly twigs and dark green, broad oblong to oblanceolate, 13 to 20cm. long leaves which are hispid above and covered with crisped hairs beneath. Flowers bell-shaped, purplish-crimson, with darker lines; April and May. Yunnan. H4.

rufum BATAL. (s. Taliense). Medium-sized to large shrub, the elliptic-oblong to obovate leaves red-brown beneath. Flowers narrowly bell-shaped, white or pinkish-purple, with crimson spots; April. Szechwan; Kansu. A.M. 1980. H4.

RHODODENDRON—*continued*

russatum BALF. f. & FORR. (*cantabile*) (s. Lapponicum). A first-rate garden plant, making compact growth up to 1 or 1·2m. high. Leaves oblong-lanceolate, densely scaly below and about 2·5cm. long. Flowers funnel-shaped, deep blue-purple or violet with a white throat; April and May. N.W. Yunnan; Szechwan. I. 1913. A.M.(F.) 1927. F.C.C.(F.) 1933. A.G.M. 1938. H4.

saluenense FRANCH. (s. Saluenense). Small, densely matted shrub of variable habit. The small, ovate-elliptic, aromatic leaves are hidden by clusters of funnel-shaped, rose-purple or purplish crimson flowers; April and May. S.E. Tibet; Yunnan; Szechwan. I. 1914. A.M.(F.) 1945. H4.

sanguineum FRANCH. (s. Neriiflorum). A very variable, dwarf or small shrub, with 4 to 6cm. long, obovate or narrow oblong leaves, greyish-white beneath. Flowers bell-shaped, bright crimson, in trusses of three to six not produced on young plants; May. Yunnan; S.E. Tibet. H4.

didymum BALF. f. & FORR. (*R. didymum*). Flowers of an unusual black-crimson. A parent of several good hybrids. S.E. Tibet.

roseotinctum BALF. f. & FORREST. A medium-sized shrub with rose or yellowish-red flowers. Yunnan; S.E. Tibet; Upper Burma.

sargentianum REHD. & WILS. (s. Anthopogon). Dwarf, twiggy shrub of dense, compact habit. Leaves small, aromatic when bruised. Flowers small, tubular, lemon-yellow or white; April and May. A gem for a cool spot on the rock garden but not an easy plant to grow. Szechwan. I. 1903-4. A.M.(F.) 1923. H4.

†scabrifolium FRANCH. (s. Scabrifolium). A small to medium-sized, straggly shrub with oblanceolate leaves, 4 to 5cm. long, roughly hairy above, tomentose and reticulate beneath. Flowers funnel-shaped, varying in colour from white to deep rose; March and April. Yunnan. I. 1885. H3.

†scabrum G. DON (s. Azalea). A small to medium-sized shrub of bushy habit. Leaves elliptic to oblanceolate, 6 to 10cm. long. Flowers with a large, green calyx, funnel-shaped, rose-red to brilliant scarlet; April and May. Islands of Japan. I. about 1909. A.M. 1911. H2.

'Red Emperor'. A striking form with large, scarlet flowers, usually a little later than those of the type.

schlippenbachii MAXIM. (*Azalea schlippenbachii*) (s. Azalea). This exquisitely beautiful azalea, though winter hardy, is subject to injury by late spring frosts. A medium-sized to large, deciduous shrub of rounded habit. The large, broadly obovate leaves are produced in whorls of five at the ends of the branches. They are suffused purplish-red when young, turning to yellow, orange and crimson in autumn. Flowers appearing before or with the leaves, saucer-shaped, 7·5cm. across, pale pink to rose-pink, occasionally white; April and May. Korea; Manchuria. First discovered by Baron Schlippenbach in 1854, introduced by James Veitch in 1893. A.M.(F.) 1896. F.C.C.(F.) 1944. A.G.M. 1969. H4.

scintillans BALF. f. & W. W. SM. (s. Lapponicum). In many ways this species is the best of the series, and one of the best of all small shrubs. The tiny oblanceolate leaves are very scaly. Flowers funnel-shaped, lavender-blue, or purple-rose; April and May. Yunnan. I. 1913. A.M.(F.) 1924. A.G.M. 1969. H4.

(**F.C.C. Form**). Flowers deep violet. F.C.C. 1934.

†scottianum HUTCH. (s. Maddenii). A beautiful but tender shrub of medium size, with densely, scaly branches. Leaves obovate, densely scaly beneath. Flowers widely funnel-shaped, up to 10cm. long and across, white, occasionally flushed rose, strongly and sweetly scented; May and June. Only suitable for conservatory treatment. Yunnan. H1.

scyphocalyx. See *R. dichroanthum scyphocalyx*.

searsiae REHD. & WILS. (s. Triflorum). An attractive, medium-sized shrub with leaves densely scaly and glaucous beneath. Flowers freely produced, widely funnel-shaped, white, rose or pruplish mauve, with pale green spots; April and May. Szechwan. Introduced by E. H. Wilson in 1908. H4.

selense FRANCH. (s. Thomsonii). Medium-sized shrub with oblong to obovate, dark green leaves and bell-shaped, pink or rose flowers, occasionally with a crimson basal blotch, in April and May. Tibet; Yunnan; Szechwan. I. 1917. H4.

semibarbatum MAXIM. (s. Semibarbatum). Medium-sized to large, deciduous shrub, often giving rich orange-yellow and crimson autumn colour. Leaves elliptic, 2·5 to 5cm. long. Flowers small, solitary, funnel-shaped, white or yellowish-white, flushed pink, spotted red; June. A very unusual species. Japan. H4.

RHODODENDRON—*continued*

serotinum HUTCH. (s. Fortunei). A large, late flowering shrub related to *R. decorum*, with leaves up to 15cm. long. Flowers bell-shaped, swwetly scented, 5cm. long, white flushed pink on the outside, spotted pink within and with a yellow basal stain. With its flowers opening in August and September it is one of the last rhododendrons to flower. W. China. C. 1889. A.M.(F.) 1925. H4.

serpyllifolium MIQ. (*Azalea serpyllifolia*) (s. Azalea). A remarkable, small, deciduous shrub, in fact a true mini azalea, of dense habit with slender, interlacing stems and very tiny leaves. Flowers appearing after the leaves, solitary or in pairs, small and funnel-shaped, rose-pink; April and May. Japan. C. 1880. H4.

setosum D. DON (s. Lapponicum). A small shrub with densely bristly branches and bristly, scaly, aromatic leaves. Flowers funnel-shaped, reddish-purple; May. Nepal; Sikkim; S.E. Tibet. I. 1825. H4.

†**shepherdii** NUTT. (s. Irroratum). Medium-sized shrub with oblong-elliptic, deep green leaves. Flowers in a compact, rounded truss, bell-shaped, deep scarlet, with dark red spots; March and April. Bhutan. I. 1850. H2-3.

sherriffii COWAN (s. Campanulatum). A medium-sized shrub with elliptic to oblong-elliptic leaves, 7·5cm. long, covered with a thick dark brown indumentum beneath. Flowers bell-shaped, deep rich carmine, with crimson, bloomy calyx. March and April. S. Tibet. A.M. 1966. H4.

shweliense BALF. f. & FORREST (s. Glaucophyllum). Dwarf, aromatic shrub, with densely scaly twigs and leaves oblong-obovate, 2·5 to 5cm. long. Flowers bell-shaped, pink with yellow flush and purple spots, scaly on the outside; May. Yunnan. H4.

silvaticum. See *R. lanigerum*.

†**simsii** PLANCH. (*Azalea indica* SIMS not L.) (s. Azalea). A tender evergreen or semi-evergreen shrub up to 2m., of dense, spreading habit. Leaves up to 5cm. long, broadly oval. Flowers funnel-shaped, 5 to 6cm. across, in cluster of two to six, rose-red to dark red, with darker spots; May. A parent of many of the greenhouse "Indica" hybrid azaleas. China; Formosa. I. early in the 19th century. F.C.C.(F.) 1933. H2.

eriocarpum. See *R. indicum eriocarpum*.

'Queen Elizabeth'. A beautiful form reminiscent of the greenhouse azaleas, but hardier. Flowers large, 7·5 to 9cm. across, double, white, edged rose-opal.

'Queen Elizabeth White'. Flowers double, pure white.

†**sinogrande** BALF. f. & W. W. SM. (s. Grande). A large shrub or small tree for woodland. Magnificent as a foliage plant, the shining dark green leaves being sometimes as much as ·8m. long and 30cm. wide, the lower surface with the silvery-grey or fawn indumentum. Flowers in huge trusses, creamy-white with a crimson blotch; April. Yunnan; Upper Burma; S.E. Tibet. Discovered and introduced by George Forrest in 1913. A.M.(F.) 1922. F.C.C.(F.) 1926. H3-4.

smirnowii TRAUTV. (s. Ponticum). A very hardy, compact, slow-growing shrub of medium to large size, with oblong-obovate leaves, 10 to 15cm. long, grey or pale brown felted beneath. Flowers bell-shaped, rose-purple or rose-pink; May and June. Caucasus; N.E. Asia Minor. I. 1886. H4.

smithii NUTT. & HOOK. (s. Barbatum). Large shrub or small tree with attractive plum-coloured bark and bristly-hairy shoots. Leaves oblong-lanceolate, 10 to 15cm. long, loosely tomentose below. Flowers bell-shaped, scarlet-crimson, in compact trusses; March. E. Sikkim; Bhutan. I. 1850. H3.

souliei FRANCH. (s. Thomsonii). A beautiful, hardy, medium-sized shrub with almost round leaves, 5 to 7·5cm. long, and saucer-shaped, white or soft pink flowers; May to June. Said to do best in the eastern counties. Szechwan; Tibet. I. 1905. F.C.C.(F.) 1909. H4.

sperabile BALF. f. & FARRER (s. Neriiflorum). A small shrub, occasionally reaching 2m. Leaves elliptic-lanceolate, 6 to 10cm. long, with a thick, tawny or cinnamon tomentum beneath. Flowers bell-shaped, fleshy scarlet or deep crimson; April and May. N.E. Upper Burma. Discovered and introduced by Reginald Farrer in 1919. A.M.(F.) 1925. H3-4.

sphaeranthum. See *R. trichostomum*.

spiciferum FRANCH. (s. Scabrifolium). A small, moderately hardy shrub from Yunnan with wiry, bristly stems and bristly, narrowly oblanceolate leaves. Flowers borne in profusion, funnel-shaped, rose or pink; April and May. Yunnan. H3.

RHODODENDRON—*continued*

†**spinuliferum** FRANCH. (s. Scabrifolium). A quite remarkable, medium-sized shrub, one of the many discovered by the Abbé Delavay. Leaves oblanceolate and bullate, 5 to 7·5cm. long, and like the stems softly pubescent; flowers in erect clusters, produced in the axils of the upper leaves, tubular, 2·5cm. long, red, with protruding stamens; April. Yunnan. I. 1907. H2-3.

stewartianum DIELS. (s. Thomsonii). An early flowering, medium-sized to large shrub with loose trusses of bell-shaped flowers, varying in colour from white to yellow, rose or crimson; Feb. to April. Differing from the very similar *R. eclecteum* in its leaves, the undersurfaces of which are minutely hairy and covered by a thin, creamy-yellow, farinose indumentum. S.E. Tibet; Upper Burma; Assam. A.M. 1934. H4.

stictophyllum BALF. f. (s. Lapponicum). A dwarf, densely branched shrub with tiny, densely-scaly leaves and clusters of small, funnel-shaped, lilac-mauve flowers; April. W. Szechwan. H4.

strigillosum FRANCH. (s. Barbatum). A large, Chinese shrub with bristly young shoots. Leaves oblong-lanceolate, 10 to 18cm. long, bristly-hairy. Magnificent when bearing its trusses of brilliant crimson, bell-shaped flowers in February and March. A sheltered woodland site is necessary. Szechwan. Introduced by E. H. Wilson in 1904. A.M.(F.) 1923. H3-4.

suberosum. See *R. yunnanense*.

sutchuenense FRANCH. (s. Fortunei). An outstanding, large, Chinese shrub, with stout shoots and drooping, oblong-oblanceolate leaves, up to 30cm. long. In favourable seasons its floral display is magnificent, the flowers, 7cm. long, bell-shaped, varying from palest pink to rosy-lilac, with purple spots; Feb. and March. Szechwan; Hupeh. Introduced by E. H. Wilson in 1901. H4.

'Geraldii' (*R. 'Geraldii'*). A large shrub with splendid foliage. Flowers white, with a deep purplish basal blotch; Feb. and March. A.M. 1945. H3-4.

tapetiforme BALF. f. & WARD (s. Lapponicum). A dwarf, scaly-branched shrub with terminal clusters of two or three pale mauve-pink or purple, funnel-shaped flowers; April. Szechwan; Yunnan. H4.

tashiroi MAXIM. (s. Azalea). A medium-sized to large, evergreen or semi-evergreen shrub with hairy branches. Leaves obovate-elliptic, usually in clusters of three at the ends of the branches, leathery, deep glossy green above. Flowers borne in clusters of two or three, funnel-shaped, pale rose-purple, spotted maroon-purple; April and May. Japan; Formosa. H3.

tebotan. See *R. pulchrum 'Tebotan'*.

telmateium BALF. f. &. W. W. SM. (s. Lapponicum). A small, erect shrub with small, oblanceolate, scaly leaves and branches. Flowers solitary or in clusters of two or three, small, funnel-shaped, deep rose-purple, with white throat; April and May. Suitable for the rock garden. Introduced by George Forrest in 1914. Yunnan; Szechwan. H4.

telopeum BALF. f. & FORREST (s. Thomsonii). Small to medium-sized shrub, with rounded leaves about 2·5 to 3·5cm. long, glaucous below. The bell-shaped flowers are yellow, sometimes with a faint reddish blotch; May. Similar to *R. caloxanthum*, but leaves smaller. S.E. Tibet; Yunnan. H4.

tephropeplum BALF. f. & FARRER (*deleiense*) (s. Boothii). A dwarf or small shrub occasionally to 1·5m., narrow, oblong-lanceolate leaves, 3·5 to 10cm. long, glaucous and dark scaly beneath. Flowers in profusion, bell-shaped, varying in colour from pink to carmine-rose; April and May. Young leaves an attractive plum purple beneath. Burma; Yunnan; S.E. Tibet; Assam. A.M.(F.) 1929. A.M. 1935 (as *R. deleiense*). H3-4.

thomsonii HOOK. f. (s. Thomsonii). A well-known and desirable Himalayan species. A large shrub or small tree with attractive, smooth, plum-coloured or cinnamon bark and rounded or oval leaves, 3·5 to 8cm. long, which are glaucous when young. Flowers in loose trusses, bell-shaped, deep blood red, calyx large, cup-shaped; April to May. Even after flowering the fruiting clusters are most attractive, with apple-green calyces and glaucous capsules. Because of its often consistent and prodigious flowering this magnificent species appreciates an annual feeding and mulching. E. Nepal; Sikkim· Bhutan; Tibet. Introduced by Sir Joseph Hooker in 1849. A parent of many fine hybrids. A.G.M. 19.25 A.M. 1973. H3.

RHODODENDRON—*continued*

tosaense MAK. (s. Azalea). A densely-branched, semi-evergreen shrub, occasionally reaching 2m. Leaves narrow, pubescent, turning crimson-purple in autumn. Flowers in clusters of one to six, funnel-shaped, 2·5 to 3cm. across, lilac-purple; April to May. Japan. I. 1914. H3-4.

'Barbara'. A lovely selection with flowers of a clear pink. Raised in our nurseries.

trichanthum REHD. (*villosum*) (s. Triflorum). Large shrub, the branches densely beset with bristles. Leaves ovate-elliptic, 5 to 10cm. long, pubescent. Flowers widely funnel-shaped, usually dark violet-purple, sometimes paler, three to five in a truss; May and June. Szechwan. I. 1904. H4.

trichocladum FRANCH. (*brachystylum*) (s. Trichocladum). Small, deciduous shrub with hairy twigs. Leaves ovate-oblong, 2·5 to 3·5cm. long. Flowers funnel-shaped, greenish-yellow, spotted dark green; April and May. E. Nepal; N.E. Upper Burma. I. 1910. H4.

trichostomum FRANCH. (*ledoides*) (*sphaeranthum*) (s. Anthopogon). A small, twiggy, aromatic shrub, with slender shoots bearing small, narrow leaves about 2·5cm. long and tight terminal heads of tubular, white, pink or rose, daphne-like flowers; May and June. Yunnan; Szechwan. A.M. 1925 (as *R. ledoides*). A.M. 1925 (as *R. sphaeranthum*). H3-4.

radinum COWAN & DAVIDIAN. Flowers more scaly, of equal garden merit. A.M. 1972.

triflorum HOOK. f. (s. Triflorum). A slender shrub of medium to large size, with attractive peeling bark. Leaves ovate-lanceolate, 5 to 7·5cm. long. Flowers funnel-shaped, lemon yellow with a ray of green spots borne in trusses of three; May and June. E. Nepal; Assam; Tibet; Burma-Tibet frontier. I. 1850. H4.

mahogani HUTCH. Flowers with a mahogany-coloured blotch or suffused mahogany. Discovered and introduced by Kingdon Ward, from S.E. Tibet.

triplonaevium BALF. f. & FORR. (s. Taliense). A small shrub up to 2m., the young growths covered with a conspicuous rufous tomentum. Leaves up to 15cm. long, clothed below with a rust-coloured indumentum. Flowers bell-shaped, white or rose-flushed, with a crimson basal blotch within; April and May. N.W. Yunnan. H4.

tsangpoense HUTCH. & WARD (s. Glaucophyllum). A variable dwarf to small, aromatic shrub. The leaves are obovate-oblong, 2·5 to 5cm. long, glaucous scaly below, interspersed with pale-green or pink scales which, when viewed through a lens, appear like glistening jewels set in a white satin cloth. Flowers produced very freely, semi-bell-shaped, varying in colour from crushed strawberry to deep-crimson or violet; May and June. Tibet; Burma; Assam. A.M.(F.) 1972. H4.

pruniflorum COWAN & DAVIDIAN (*R. pruniflorum*). Differs in its more densely scaly leaf-undersurfaces. Flowers usually plum-purple.

tsariense COWAN (s. Campanulatum). A small shrub with yellow-tomentose young shoots and obovate to elliptic-obovate leaves, covered with a dense woolly indumentum beneath. Flowers in a loose truss, bell-shaped, varying in colour from pale blush to cream or white, spotted red within; April and May. S.E. Tibet; Bhutan. H4.

tsusiophyllum. See *TSUSIOPHYLLUM tanakae.*

ungernii TRAUTV. (s. Ponticum). Large shrub notable for its hardiness and late flowering, producing its trusses of funnel-shaped, pinky-white flowers in July. Handsome, oblong-oblanceolate leathery leaves, 12 to 20cm. long, greyish-white to fawn, tomentose beneath. Caucasus; N.E. Asia. I. 1886. A.M. 1973. H4.

uvariifolium DIELS. (*niphargum*) (s. Fulvum). A large shrub or small tree, the young growths in spring of a beautiful silvery appearance. Leaves up to 25cm. long, oblanceolate to obovate, dark shining green above, white or grey tomentose beneath. Flowers bell-shaped, white or pale rose, with or without crimson spots, produced in March or April. Yunnan; Szechwan; S.E. Tibet. A.M. 1976. H4.

valentinianum FORREST (s. Maddenii). A small shrub with densely scaly and bristly young shoots. Leaves about 3cm. long, oval or obovate, densely scaly beneath, clustered at the ends of the branches; flowers narrowly bell-shaped, 3·5cm. long, pubescent and scaly on the outside, bright buttercup-yellow; April. N.W. Yunnan. Introduced by George Forrest in 1917 and later by Joseph Rock. Remarkably hardy for the Maddenii series. A.M. 1933. H3-4.

RHODODENDRON—*continued*

vaseyi A. GRAY (*Azalea vaseyi*) (s. Azalea). A beautiful, medium-sized to large deciduous shrub with narrowly oval leaves up to 13cm. long, often turning fiery-red in autumn. Flowers appearing before the leaves, widely funnel-shaped, 3·5 to 5cm. across, pale pink, rose-pink or white, with orange-red spots; April and May. North Carolina (U.S.A.). I. about 1880. A.G.M. 1927. H4.

†**veitchianum** HOOK. (s. Maddenii). A tender, small to medium-sized shrub with densely scaly leaves up to 13cm. long. Flowers comparatively large, widely funnel-shaped, fragrant, deeply five-cleft, with crinkled petals, white, with a faint green tinge; May to July. Only suitable for the conservatory. Burma; Tenasserim; Siam. I. 1850. H1.

vellereum HUTCH. (s. Taliense). A large shrub or small tree to 5m. Leaves silvery-white to fawn tomentose beneath. Flowers in a compact truss, bell-shaped, white or blush with purple or carmine spots; March and April. S.E. Tibet. H4.

venator TAGG (s. Irroratum). A medium-sized shrub of bushy habit with glandular hairy young shoots. Leaves oblong-lanceolate, 10cm. long. Scarlet, bell-shaped flowers in trusses of four or six; May and June. S.E. Tibet. A.M.(F.) 1933. H3.

vernicosum FRANCH. (*sheltonae*) (*rhantum*) (s. Fortunei). A variable, large shrub with oblong-elliptic leaves, 7·5 to 13cm. long, dull and wax covered above becoming shiny when rubbed. Flowers funnel-shaped, varying in colour from white to rose-lavender, sometimes with crimson spots; April and May. Yunnan; Szechwan. I. 1904. H4.

villosum. See *R. trichanthum.*

violaceum REHD. & WILS. (s. Lapponicum). A small, compact shrub with small, narrow glistening green leaves and terminal clusters of violet, funnel-shaped flowers; April and May. W. Szechwan. H4.

†**virgatum** HOOK. f. (s. Virgatum). A small to medium-sized, leggy shrub with ovate leaves, 3·5 to 6cm. long, scaly below. Flowers inclined to be tubular, varying from purple through pink to white, usually lilac-purple; April and May. E. Nepal; Sikkim; Bhutan. Introduced by Sir Joseph Hooker in 1849. A.M.(F.) 1928. H2-3.

viridescens HUTCH. (s. Trichocladum). A small, semi-evergreen shrub with oblong-elliptic leaves, about 2·5 to 3·5cm. long, glaucous beneath. Flowers funnel-shaped, yellowish-green, spotted green within; June. S.E. Tibet. H4.

viscosum TORR. (*Azalea viscosa*) (s. Azalea). "Swamp Honeysuckle". A medium-sized, deciduous, summer-flowering shrub of bushy habit. Leaves up to 3·5cm. long, dark green above, glaucous-green beneath. Flowers appearing after the leaves, narrowly funnel-shaped, 2·5 to 3·5cm. across, viscid on the outside, delightfully and spicily fragrant, white, sometimes with a pink stain; June and July. Eastern N. America. I. 1734. A.M.(F.) 1921. A.G.M. 1937. H4.

wallichii HOOK. f. (s. Campanulatum). Medium-sized to large shrub with elliptic-obovate leaves, 5 to 10cm. long, dark green and glabrous above, paler and dotted with tiny, powdery tufts of reddish-brown hair below. Flowers bell-shaped, lilac with rose spots, six to ten in a truss; April. E. Nepal; Sikkim; Bhutan; Assam. I. 1850. Closely related to *R. campanulatum.* H4.

wardii W. W. SM. (*croceum*) (s. Thomsonii). A compact, medium-sized to large Chinese shrub, with oblong-elliptic or rounded leaves, 5 to 10cm. long. Flowers in loose trusses, saucer-shaped, clear yellow, sometimes with a crimson basal blotch; May. Yunnan; Szechwan; S.E. Tibet. A beautiful species discovered and introduced by Kingdon Ward after whom it is named. A parent of several superb hybrids. A.M.(F.) 1926. A.M.(F.) 1931. A.G.M. 1969. H4.

wasonii HEMSL. & WILS. (s. Taliense). A small to medium-sized shrub of compact growth with stout, greyish-white young shoots. Leaves 5 to 10cm. long, usually oval, glossy green above, white beneath becoming reddish-brown. Flowers bell-shaped, varying in colour from white to pink, rose or rarely yellow, with crimson spots; May. W. Szechwan. Introduced by E. H. Wilson in 1904. H4.

weyrichii MAXIM. (s. Azalea). A very splendid, medium-sized to large, deciduous shrub with broad ovate or rounded leaves in clusters of two to three at the ends of the branches. Flowers opening before the leaves, widely funnel-shaped, variable in colour, usually bright brick-red, with a purple blotch; April and May. Japan and the island of Quelpaert (Korea). I. 1914. H4.

RHODODENDRON—*continued*

wightii HOOK. f. (s. Lacteum). A large, usually rather lax shrub, the oblong-elliptic leaves up to 20cm. long, covered with a fawn or rust-coloured suede-like tomentum below. Flowers in a loose, one-sided truss, bell-shaped, cream or pale yellow, spotted crimson, rarely white; May. C. and E. Nepal; Sikkim; Bhutan. A.M.(F.) 1913. I. 1850. H3-4.

williamsianum REHD. & WILS. (s. Thomsonii). A charming, Chinese shrub with attractive, bronze young growths, small, round, heart-shaped leaves and delightful, bell-shaped, shell-pink flowers; April. It is generally of dwarf, spreading habit, but may reach a height of 1 to 1·5m. Szechwan. Discovered and introduced by E. H. Wilson in 1908. A parent of several good hybrids including '*Arthur J. Ivens*'. A.M. 1938. H3.

wiltonii FRANCH. (s. Taliense). A medium-sized to large shrub with distinct, dark green, deeply veined, oblong-obovate leaves, 7·5 to 13cm. long, white turning to cinnamon-felted beneath. The bell-shaped flowers are usually pale pink with red markings; April and May. W. Szechwan. I. 1904. A.M.(F.) 1957. H4.

wongii HEMSL. & WILS. (s. Triflorum). A rare, small shrub with densely scaly twigs and terminal clusters of pale-yellow, funnel-shaped flowers; May and June. Similar to, but differing from *R. ambiguum* in its smaller stature, smaller, obtuse leaves and flowers without scales. Szechwan. H4.

xanthocodon HUTCH. (s. Cinnabarinum). An interesting aromatic species related to *R. cinnabarinum*. A medium-sized to large shrub with golden-scaly young shoots and glaucous young foliage. Leaves oblong-elliptic, 5 to 7·5cm. long, densely scaly. Clusters of waxy, yellow, bell-shaped to funnel-shaped flowers; May and June. Flowers best when given some form of shelter. Bhutan; S.E. Tibet. A.M.(F.) 1935. H4.

yakushimanum NAKAI (*metternichii yakushimanum*) (s. Ponticum). A remarkable species, forming a compact, dome-shaped bush up to 1·3m. high and equal width. Young growths silvery. Leaves leathery, recurved at the margins, dark glossy green above, densely brown-tomentose beneath. Flowers in a compact truss, bell-shaped, rose in bud, opening to apple-blossom pink and finally white; May. Only found on the windswept, rain-drenched, mountain peaks of Yakushima Island, Japan. I. 1934. This splendid, free-flowering species may well give rise to a new race of hardy hybrids. F.C.C. 1947. A.G.M. 1969. H4.

yanthinum. See *R. concinnum.*

yedoense MAXIM. ('*Yodogawa*') (s. Azalea). A small, usually deciduous shrub of dense, spreading habit. Leaves narrow, 5 to 9cm. long, often colouring prettily in autumn. Flowers funnel-shaped, double, rosy-purple; May. Long cultivated in Japan and Korea, probably a clone of a wild species, such as *R. poukhanense.* H4.

poukhanense. See *R. poukhanense.*

yunnanense FRANCH. (*aechmophyllum*) (*chartophyllum*) (*pleistanthum*) (*suberosum*) (s. Triflorum). A very hardy and exceedingly floriferous Chinese shrub up to 4m. Leaves lanceolate or oblanceolate, semi-deciduous in cold or exposed gardens. Flowers funnel-shaped, usually pink, with darker spots; May. Several forms originally classed as species are now included here. (See synonyms above). Szechwan; Yunnan; Burma; S.E. Tibet; Kweichow. Introduced by the Abbé Delavay in about 1889. A.M. 1903. A.G.M. 1934. H4.

'Praecox'. An early-flowering form.

zaleucum BALF. f. & W. SM. (s. Triflorum). A large shrub with lanceolate to obovate leaves, white beneath. Flowers in terminal and axillary trusses, widely funnel-shaped, varying in colour from white to purple, usalluy lilac-mauve, with or without crimson spots; April. Burma; Yunnan. Introduced by Forrest in 1912. A.M.(F.) 1932. H3-4.

†**zeylanicum** COWAN (*kingianum*) (s. Arboreum). A large shrub or small tree superb in the milder parts of the British Isles. Leaves elliptic-oblong, bullate, very dark green, covered with a dense fawn or tawny indumentum below. Flowers in a dense truss, bell-shaped, red; April and May. One of the most beautiful foliage rhododendrons. Ceylon. H2-3.

‡*RHODODENDRON HYBRIDS

The earliest hybrids began to appear about 1825, when *R. arboreum* flowered for the first time in this country. From this date up to the beginning of the present century, a large number of hybrids were raised, derived mainly from *RR. catawbiense* and *maximum* (U.S.A.); *arboreum* (Himalaya); *caucasicum* (Caucasus); *ponticum* (Turkey); and to a lesser extent, and somewhat more recently, *fortunei* (China) and *griffithianum* (Himalaya). Most of the hybrids produced from these species have several things in common, namely hardiness, ample foliage, firm and full flower trusses, and an ability to withstand exposure, and hence they are often referred to as the "Hardy Hybrids" (HH). As a group they are indispensable for planting in cold or exposed districts and are unsurpassed for landscape effect, whilst many are ideal as informal hedges or screens.

With the exploration of China and the eastern Himalaya during the first thirty years of the present century, a vast wealth of new and exciting species flooded British gardens. From this glorious palette has been raised a whole range of colourful and ornamental hybrids which continue to flow unabated. They show a much greater variation in foliage, flower and habit than the older hybrids and though most are hardy, few will tolerate the extreme conditions often weathered by the "Hardy Hybrids".

Among the many raisers of hybrid rhododendrons mention must be made of the following, whose names will always remain in association with this great genus, namely the late Lord Aberconway of Bodnant, North Wales; Sir Edmund Loder of Leonardslee, Sussex; the late Edward Magor of Lamellan, Cornwall; Lionel de Rothschild, creator of the Exbury Gardens, Hampshire; Mr. and Mrs. J. B. Stevenson of Tower Court, Ascot, Berks.; and J. C. Williams of Caerhays, Cornwall. In more recent years many fine hybrids have been raised in the Saville Gardens, Windsor, and in the R.H.S. Gardens, Wisley.

The following hybrids, all of which are evergreen, vary from prostrate alpines to small trees, and unless otherwise stated may be taken as averaging 1·8 to 3m. in height. The date of introduction of a hybrid (when known) is given in parenthesis at the end of each description. A number of the descriptions represent original work done by our late manager Arthur J. Ivens.

Dates in parentheses indicate the approximate year of introduction into commerce.

Flowering seasons are indicated as follows:—

Early—April
Mid—May to mid June
Late—Mid June onwards

'Adder' (*diphrocalyx × thomsonii*). Beautiful blood-red, bell-shaped flowers with large petaloid calyces. Early. (1933). H3.

'Adriaan Koster' (*campylocarpum* Hybrid × *'Mrs. Lindsay Smith'*). A robust, leafy shrub with bold foliage and well-filled, globular trusses of bell-shaped, creamy-yellow flowers. Mid. (1920). A.M.T. 1935. H4.

'A. Gilbert' (*campylogynum × discolor*). An exceedingly free-flowering hybrid, similar to *'Lady Bessborough'*, but more compact. Flowers fragrant, apricot yellow in bud, opening to pale cream with two small crimson "flashes". Mid. (1925). A.M. 1925. H3.

'Aladdin' (*auriculatum × griersonianum*). A very beautiful clone with large, widely expanded, brilliant salmon-cerise flowers in loose trusses. Late. (1930). A.M. 1935. H3.

Albatross (*discolor × Loderi*). One of the glories of Exbury. A large, robust shrub or a small tree with terminal clusters of large leaves and magnificent, lax trusses of richly fragrant, trumpet-shaped flowers 13cm. across. Mid. (1930). A.M. 1934. A.M.T. 1953. A.G.M. 1969. H3. We offer the following clones:—

'Townhill Pink' (*discolor × Loderi 'King George'*). Flowers in enormous trusses, deep pink in bud, opening shell pink. Mid. Both this and the white form were raised by Frederick Rose from seed given to him by Lionel de Rothschild. (1945). A.M. 1945.

'Townhill White'. A lovely clone differing only in its comparatively shorter, broader leaves and white flowers, which are pale yellowish-green within. Mid.

'Alice' (HH) A hybrid of *R. griffithianum*, large, vigorous and upright in habit. Flowers funnel-shaped, rose-pink with lighter centre, borne in tall, conical trusses. Mid. (1910). A.M. 1910. H4.

RHODODENDRON—*continued*

'Alison Johnstone' (*concatenans* × *yunnanense*). A dainty hybrid with oval leaves and trusses of slender-tubed flowers, amber flushed pink. Mid. (1945). A.M. 1945. H4.

'Alpine Glow' (Avalanche Group). A handsome, large shrub with long, rich green leaves and large trusses of enormous, widely funnel-shaped, delicate pink flowers. Mid. (1938). A.M. 1938. H3.

'Amaura' (*griersonianum* × *'Penjerrick'*). A lovely hybrid with loose trusses of funnel-shaped flowers which are rose-red in bud opening white flushed rose at base and with conspicuous crimson stamens. Mid. (1933). H3.

'Amor' (*griersonianum* × *thayeranum*). Flowers eight to ten in a truss, white, stained pink. Late. (1927). A.M. 1951. H3.

'Angelo' (*discolor* × *griffithianum*). A magnificent hybrid raised by Lionel de Rothschild at Exbury. We offer the clone known as *'Exbury Angelo'*. A large shrub or small tree with handsome foliage. Huge, shapely trusses of large, fragrant, trumpet-shaped, white flowers, 14cm. across, with green markings within. Mid. (1933). A.M. 1935. F.C.C. 1947. H3. See also *'Solent Queen'* and *'Solent Swan'*.

'Anita' (*campylocarpum* × *griersonianum*). Deep salmon-pink in bud, opening apricot-pink and fading to cream with a faint pink tinge. Mid. (1941). H3.

'Antonio' (*discolor* × *'Gill's Triumph'*). A splendid, large hybrid, notable for the rich scent of its beautiful, funnel-shaped, pink flowers which are blotched and spotted crimson within; rich pink in bud. Mid. (1933). A.M. 1939. H3.

'April Chimes' (*hippophaeoides* × *mollicomum*) (*'Hippomum'*). A charming, small shrub of upright habit, similar in leaf to *R. hippophaeoides*. Flowers appearing in the axils of the upper leaves and in terminal umbels, the whole forming a compact ball of funnel-shaped, rosy-mauve flowers, normally at their best during late April. A floriferous hybrid of neat habit, excellent as a cut bloom for indoor decoration. Raised as a chance seedling from seed of *R. hippophaeoides* in 1938. H3-4.

'Argosy' (*auriculatum* × *discolor*). A vigorous, large shrub or small tree with handsome, large leaves and very fragrant, trumpet-shaped, white flowers with a ray of dull crimson at base of throat. Late. (1933). H3-4.

'Ariel' (*discolor* × *'Memoir'*). A large shrub with freely-produced pale-pink flowers. Mid. (1933). H3.

'Armistice Day' (Griffithianum Hybrid × *'Maxwell T. Masters'*). A dome-shaped bush bearing large, rounded trusses of bell-shaped, scarlet-red flowers. Mid. (1930). H4.

'Arthur Bedford'. A charming hybrid of unknown parentage, possibly *R. ponticum* × mauve seedling. Compact, conical trusses of pale mauve flowers spotted with dark rose-madder within. Mid. (1936). A.M. 1936. F.C.C.T. 1958. H4.

'Arthur J. Ivens' (*houlstonii* × *williamsianum*). A medium, dome-shaped bush, resembling *R. williamsianum* in leaf-shape and the attractive coppery-red tints of its young foliage. Flowers shallowly bell-shaped, 7·5cm. across, deep pink in bud, opening delicate rose-pink with two small crimson "flashes". Early. Raised by and named after our late manager. (1938). A.M. 1944. H4.

'Arthur Osborn' (*griersonianum* × *sanguineum didymum*). A small, late flowtring shrub with small, narrowly oblong leaves, pale cinnamon beneath. Flowers drooping, funnel-shaped, ruby-red with orange-scarlet tube. Late. Sometimes continuing until early autumn. A useful, low-growing shrub, flowering when quite small. (1929). A.M. 1933. H3.

'Arthur Stevens' (*'Coronation Day'* × *souliei*). A lovely hybrid of rounded habit. Young shoots, petioles and buds bright yellow. The loose trusses of bell-shaped flowers are pale pink fading to white, with a deep rose-red basal stain. A seedling raised in our nurseries and named in memory of our late foreman. Mid. (1960). A.M. 1976. H3.

'Ascot Brilliant'. A hybrid of *R. thomsonii* with an unknown garden hybrid. Lax trusses of funnel-shaped, rose-red flowers, darker at margins. Early to Mid. Requires woodland treatment for the best results. (1861). H4.

'Aspansia' (*'Astarte'* × *haematodes*). A dwarf, spreading shrub raised at Bodnant. Flowers brilliant red, in loose trusses; calyces large, petaloid; Early. (1945). A.M. 1945. H4.

RHODODENDRON—*continued*

Augfast (*augustinii*×*fastigiatum*). A small, dense, rounded shrub with small scattered leaves and scaly young shoots. Flowers small, funnel-shaped, in terminal clusters. Forms of our own raising vary in colour from dark lavender-blue to heliotrope. Early. (1921). H4.

'Auriel' (*griersonianum*×*'Polar Bear'*). A large shrub with large trusses of striking pink flowers. Late. (1942). H3.

'Aurora' (*'Kewense'*×*thomsonii*). A large, fast-growing shrub or small tree of rather open habit. The fragrant, trumpet-shaped, rose-coloured flowers are borne in flat trusses 20cm. across. Early to Mid. (1922). A.M. 1922. H3.

'Avalanche' (*calophytum*×*Loderi*). A large shrub with bold foliage and large trusses of enormous, fragrant, widely funnel-shaped, snow-white flowers which are pink flushed in bud and possess a red basal stain within. The conspicuous red pedicels and bracts contrast superbly with the white of the flowers. Early. (1933). A.M. 1934. F.C.C. 1938. H3. See also *'Alpine Glow'*.

'Axel Olsen'. A small shrub with both prostrate and erect stems forming a low mound. Flowers funnel-shaped, blood red. Mid.

'Azor' (*discolor*×*griersonianum*). A large shrub bearing trusses of large, trumpet-shaped flowers of soft salmon-pink; Late. (1927). A.M. 1933. H3-4.

'Bad Eilsen' (*'Essex Scarlet'*×*forrestii repens*). Dwarf shrub of spreading habit, free flowering. Flowers funnel-shaped, red, with waved and crinkled margins; Mid. H4.

'Bagshot Ruby'. A vigorous hybrid of *R. thomsonii*, raised by John Waterer, Sons & Crisp, producing dense rounded trusses of widely funnel-shaped, ruby-red flowers; Mid. (1916). A.M. 1916. H4.

Barclayi (*'Glory of Penjerrick'*×*thomsonii*). A beautiful hybrid raised by Robert Barclay Fox at Penjerrick, Cornwall in 1913. Unfortunately, it is somewhat tender and is only seen at its best in Cornwall and similarly favourable areas. H2. We offer the following clones:—

'Helen Fox'. Flowers deep scarlet; Early.

'Robert Fox'. Flowers of a glowing deep crimson; Early. A.M. 1921.

'B. de Bruin'. (HH) A floriferous shrub, rather sprawling in habit at first. Perfectly formed, large conical trusses of bell-shaped, dark scarlet flowers; Mid to Late. (Before 1915). H4.

'Beau Brummell' (*eriogynum*×*'Essex Scarlet'*). Scarlet, funnel-shaped flowers, with conspicuous black anthers, as many as thirty in a neat globular truss; Late. (1934). A.M. 1938.

'Beauty of Littleworth'. (HH) One of the first *griffithianum* hybrids. A very striking, large shrub with immense conical trusses of white, crimson-spotted flowers; Mid. Still one of the best hardy hybrids. Raised by Miss Clara Mangles at Littleworth, Surrey, about 1900. F.C.C. 1904. F.C.C.T. 1953. H4.

'Beauty of Tremough' (*arboreum 'Blood Red'*×*griffithianum*). A fine, free-growing hybrid with handsome foliage and large trusses of blush-pink flowers with a bright pink margin; Early. (1902). F.C.C. 1902. H2.

'Beefeater' (*elliottii*×*'Fusilier'*). A superb Wisley hybrid with well-filled, flat-topped trusses of geranium-lake flowers; Mid. A.M. and Cory Cup 1958. F.C.C. 1959. H3.

'Bellerophon' (*eriogynum*×*'Norman Shaw'*). An Exbury hybrid of neat, leafy habit, bearing trusses of bright crimson flowers with great freedom; Late. (1934). H3.

'Betty Wormald' (*'George Hardy'*×red garden hybrid). (HH) A magnificent hybrid with immense trusses of large, widely funnel-shaped, wavy-edged flowers which are rich crimson in bud opening to deep rose-pink, lighter in the centre and with a broad pattern of blackish-crimson markings within; Mid. (Before 1922). A.M.T. 1935. F.C.C.T. 1964. A.G.M. 1969. H4.

'Bibiani' (*arboreum*×*'Moser's Maroon'*). A large shrub with good foliage, producing compact trusses of rich crimson, funnel-shaped flowers with a few maroon spots; Mid. (1934). A.M. 1934. H4.

'Billy Budd' (*elliottii*×*'May Day'*). A Wisley hybrid. Flowers turkey-red in a loose flat-topped truss; Early. (1954). A.M. 1957. H3.

'Biskra' (*ambiguum*×*cinnabarinum roylei*). A large, slender, floriferous shrub carrying rather flat trusses of pendant, narrowly funnel-shaped, vermilion flowers; Early. (1934). A.M. 1940. H3.

RHODODENDRON—*continued*

'Bluebird' (*augustinii × intricatum*). A neat, dwarf, small-leaved shrub suitable for the rock garden or the front row of borders. Flowers of a lovely violet blue borne in small, compact trusses; Early. Raised by the late Lord Aberconway at Bodnant in 1930. A.M. 1943. A.G.M. 1969. H4.

'Blue Diamond' (*augustinii × 'Intrifast'*). A slow-growing, compact bush, up to 1m. high or more, with terminal clusters of rich lavender-blue flowers; Early. Raised by Mr. J. J. Crosfield at Embley Park, Hampshire. (1935). A.M. 1935. F.C.C. 1939. A.G.M. 1969. H4.

'Blue Peter'. (HH) A vigorous, very free-flowering hybrid of upright habit. Flowers in compact, conical trusses, funnel-shaped, frilled at the margin, cobalt violet, paling to white at throat, with a ray of maroon spots; Mid. (1930). A.M.T. 1933. F.C.C.T. 1958. A.G.M. 1969. H4.

'Bluestone' (*augustinii × 'Bluebird'*). A Bodnant hybrid with terminal clusters of deep blue flowers; Early. (1950). H4.

'Blue Tit' (*augustinii × impeditum*). A Caerhays hybrid very similar to *Augfast*, forming dense bushes ·8 to 1m. high, and as much in width. The small, widely funnel-shaped flowers are borne in clusters at the tips of branchlets. They are a lovely lavender-blue in colour, which intensifies with age, as in *'Blue Diamond'*; Early. A first-class shrub for the rock garden or heather garden. (1933). H4.

'Boddaertianum' (*'Bodartianum'*). (HH) A large, fast-growing hybrid, developing into a small tree. Leaves long and narrow. Flowers in a compact, rounded truss, widely funnel-shaped, lavender-pink in bud, opening white, with a wide ray of crimson-purple markings; Early. Said to be *R. arboreum × campanulatum*, but in our opinion *R. arboreum album × ponticum album* is more likely. (1863). H4.

'Bodnant Yellow' (Lady Chamberlain Group). A beautiful rhododendron with flowers of orange-buff, flushed red on the outside; Mid. F.C.C. 1944. H3.

'Bonito' (*discolor × 'Luscombei'*). Flowers pink in bud opening to white, with a basal chocolate coloured blotch within; Mid. (1934). A.M. 1934. H4.

'Bo-peep' (*lutescens × moupinense*). A small Exbury hybrid of slender, loose habit. Flowers primrose-yellow with a darker ray within, borne in clusters of one or two, in March. (1934). A.M. 1937. H3.

'Bow Bells' (*'Corona' × williamsianum*). A charming shrub of bushy, compact habit, with bright coppery young growths. Flowers widely bell-shaped, deep cerise in bud, opening to soft pink within, shaded rich pink outside, borne in loose trusses; Early to Mid. (1934). A.M. 1935. H4.

'Bray' (Griffithianum Hybrid × *'Hawk'*). A Windsor hybrid in which the flowers deep pink in bud open mimosa yellow, shaded pale pink on the outside; Mid. A.M. 1960. H3.

'Break of Day' (*'Dawn's Delight' × dichroanthum*). A beautiful, small, compact-growing shrub, an Exbury hybrid, with loose trusses of drooping, funnel-shaped flowers which are deep orange at base, orange-red at the mouth, with a large orange-red calyx; Mid. (1934). A.M. 1936. H4.

'Bric-a-brac' (*leucaspis × moupinense*). A small, neat, floriferous shrub, bearing pure-white, wide-open flowers, 6cm. across, with bright chocolate-coloured anthers. Although hardy, it is best given a sheltered position to protect its flowers which appear in March or earlier in a mild season. Raised by Lionel de Rothschild, at Exbury. (1934). A.M. 1945. H3.

'Britannia' (*'Queen Wilhelmina' × 'Stanley Davies'*). (HH) A superb shrub of slow growth, forming a compact, rounded bush generally broader than high. Flowers gloxinia-shaped, of a glowing crimson-scarlet, carried in compact trusses backed by bold, handsome foliage; Mid. One of the most popular of all hardy hybrids and an excellent wind resister. Raised by C. B. van Nes & Sons of Boskoop, Holland. (1921). A.M. 1921. F.C.C.T. 1937. A.G.M. 1965. H4.

'Brocade'. A dome-shaped shrub, strongly resembling *'Arthur J. Ivens'* in habit and foliage. Flowers in loose trusses, bell-shaped, with frilly margins, vivid-carmine in bud, opening to peach-pink; Early to Mid. This pretty shrub was raised at Exbury and is stated to be a cross between *'Vervaeniana'* and *R. williamsianum.* The latter parent is obvious, but there seems little evidence of the other. H4.

'Brookside' (*'Goshawk' × griersonianum*). A Windsor hybrid of flamboyant appearance. The tubular campsis-like flowers are ochre yellow, shaded paler yellow and flame, blood red in bud; Mid. A.M. 1962. H3-4.

RHODODENDRON—*continued*

'Burning Bush' (*dichroanthum* × *haematodes*). Small shrub of compact habit, with narrow, bell-shaped flowers of a fiery tangerine-red; Mid. (1934). H4.

'Butterfly' (*campylocarpum* × *'Mrs. Milner'*). A very pretty hybrid bearing rounded trusses of widely funnel-shaped, primrose-yellow flowers with a broad ray of crimson speckles; Early to Mid. (1940). A.M.T. 1940. H4.

'Caerhays John' (*cinnabarinum* × *concatenans*). Medium sized shrub of erect, bushy habit. Flowers funnel-shaped, deep apricot, up to 6cm. across; Mid. Flowering later than *'Caerhays Lawrence'*. H4.

'Caerhays Lawrence' (*cinnabarinum* × *concatenans*). Similar in habit to *'Caerhays John'*, and bearing waxy flowers of a rich orange-yellow; Early to Mid. H4.

'Caerhays Philip' (*cinnabarinum blandfordiiflorum* × *concatenans*). A beautiful, medium-sized shrub with elliptic leaves and loose trusses of funnel-shaped yellow flowers 6cm. across; Early. A.M. 1966. H4.

'Calomina' (*calophytum* × *'Queen Wilhelmina'*). A medium-sized to large shrub bearing trusses of pink flowers with a darker basal blotch; Early. (1934). H3.

'Calrose' (*calophytum* × *griersonianum*). A Bodnant hybrid. A large shrub with bold foliage and dense trusses of funnel-shaped flowers which are deep rose in bud, opening pink with a deep rose basal stain; Early to Mid. (1939). H3-4.

'Carex White' (*fargesii* × *irroratum*). A tall, pyramidal, very free-flowering hybrid from Exbury. Flowers in a lax truss, bell-shaped, fragrant, pink-flushed in bud, opening white, freely spotted maroon within, opening in March or April. (1932). H4.

Carita (*campylocarpum* × *'Naomi'*). A beautiful Exbury hybrid bearing well-filled trusses of large, bell-shaped flowers of the palest shade of lemon, with a small basal blotch of cerise within; Early. (1935). A.M. 1945. H3-4.

'Charm'. Deep pink in bud, opening to cream, flushed and overlaid deep peach-pink.

'Golden Dream'. Flowers deep cream, flushed and shaded pink, becoming ivory white at maturity.

'Pink'. Flowers soft lilac-pink.

'Carmania' (*eriogynum* × *'Souvenir of Anthony Waterer'*). A first-class Exbury hybrid with bright pink flowers; Mid. (1935). H3.

'Carmen' (*forrestii repens* × *sanguineum didymum*). A dwarf or prostrate shrub carrying waxy, bell-shaped flowers of a glistening dark crimson; Mid. (1935). H4.

'C. B. van Nes' (*'Queen Wilhelmina'* × *'Stanley Davies'*). (HH) A very symmetrical and compact shrub with ample foliage and loose trusses of bell-shaped flowers of a glowing crimson-scarlet; Early. H4.

'Chanticleer' (*eriogynum* × *thomsonii*). A large, free-flowering shrub, raised at Exbury. Flowers of a magnificent, glowing crimson-scarlet, large and waxen; Early to Mid. (1935). H3.

'Chaste' (*campylocarpum* × *'Queen o' the May'*). A lovely hybrid with loose clusters of bell-shaped flowers of a soft primrose yellow; Mid. (1939). H3.

'Chikor' (*chryseum* × *ludlowii*). A choice dwarf shrub with small leaves and clusters of yellow flowers; Mid. Raised by E. H. M. and P. A. Cox at Glendoick, Perthshire. A.M. 1962. F.C.C.T. 1968. H4.

'China' (*fortunei* × *wightii*). A strong-growing plant with particularly handsome foliage and large, loose trusses of creamy-white flowers with a basal blotch of rose-carmine; Mid. (1936). A.M. 1940. A.M.T. 1948. H4.

'Chink' (*keiskei* × *trichocladum*). An early-flowering, dwarf shrub raised at Windsor Great Park, bearing lax trusses of drooping, bell-shaped flowers of an unusual chartreuse-green, with occasional darker spotting on the lower lobe, opening in March. (1961). A.M. 1961. H4.

'Choremia' (*arboreum* × *haematodes*). A medium-sized shrub resembling *R. haematodes* in habit and in its brilliant waxen, crimson-scarlet, bell-shaped flowers; Early. (1933). A.M. 1933. F.C.C. 1948. H3.

'Christmas Cheer'. (HH) An old *caucasicum* hybrid of rather dense, compact habit. Flowers pink in bud, fading to white. Normally flowering in March, occasionally February, the name referring to the one-time practice of forcing this plant for Christmas decoration. H4.

RHODODENDRON—*continued*

Cilpinense (*ciliatum* × *moupinense*). A beautiful, free-flowering, Bodnant hybrid forming a neat rounded bush up to 1m. high. Flowers in loose trusses, shallowly bell-shaped, 6cm. across, sparkling white, flushed pink, deeper in bud, opening in March. (1927). A.M. 1927. F.C.C. 1968. A.G.M. 1969. H4.

'Cinnandrum Tangerine' (*cinnabarinum roylei* × *polyandrum*). Flowers in loose trusses, trumpet-shaped, pale apricot within, flushed deep rose-pink without; Mid. (1937). A.M. 1937. H3.

Cinnkeys (*cinnabarinum* × *keysii*). A choice hybrid with oval, glossy green leaves. Flowers tubular, orange-red, shading to yellow in the lobes, produced in dense clusters; Mid. (1926). A.M. 1935. H4.

'Concessum'. (HH) Compact trusses of widely funnel-shaped, bright pink flowers with paler centres; Mid to Late. (Before 1867). H4.

Conroy (*cinnabarinum roylei* × *concatenans*). Loose, flat-topped trusses of pendant, narrowly trumpet-shaped, waxen flowers which are light orange with a rose tinge; Mid. (1937). A.M. 1950. H3.

'Cool Haven' (*'Chaste'* × *litiense*). A lovely hybrid named by us and raised at Embley Park, Hants. in 1945. Flowers in a well-filled, rounded truss, widely funnel-shaped, pale Dresden yellow, flushed pink on the outside, with a broad ray of crimson spots; faintly fragrant; Mid. H3.

'Coral Reef' (*'Fabia'* × *'Goldsworth Orange'*). A lovely hybrid, raised at Wisley. Flowers in a lax, open truss, narrowly bell-shaped with large lobes, salmon-pink tinged apricot in the throat and pink at the margin; Mid. A.M. 1954. H4.

'Cornish Cross' (*griffithianum* × *thomsonii*). A large shrub of rather open habit, producing lax trusses of narrowly bell-shaped, waxy flowers which are mottled rose-pink, shaded darker on the outside; Early to Mid. A lovely hybrid raised at Penjerrick in Cornwall. (Before 1930). H3.

'Cornubia' (*arboreum 'Blood Red'* × *'Shilsonii'*). A rather sparsely-leaved, large shrub or small tree. The blood-red, bell-shaped flowers are produced in compact, rounded trusses during March and April. A magnificent Penjerrick hybrid only suitable for sheltered gardens. (Before 1911). A.M. 1912. H3.

'Corona'. (HH) Forms a very charming, slow-growing compact mound. Flowers funnel-shaped, rich coral-pink, in rather elongated trusses; Mid. (Before 1911). A.M. 1911. H4.

'Coronation Day' (*Loderi* × *'Pink Shell'*). A striking hybrid when in flower. The enormous, fragrant flowers are 8 to 13cm. long and as much across. They are a delicate, mottled china rose in colour with a crimson basal blotch, and are carried in large, loose trusses; Mid. Raised at Embley Park, Hampshire. (1937). A.M. 1949. H3.

'Corry Koster'. (HH) A strong-growing hybrid of uncertain origin. Perfectly formed, conical trusses of frilly-edged, widely funnel-shaped flowers, which are rich pink in bud opening pink, paling to white at the margin and with a ray of brownish-crimson spots; Mid. (1909). H4.

'Countess of Athlone' (*'Catawbiense Grandiflorum'* × *'Geoffrey Millais'*). (HH) An attractive hybrid of compact growth, well furnished with glossy, olive-green leaves. Flowers widely funnel-shaped, wavy-edged, purple in bud, opening mauve with greenish-yellow markings at base; carried in conical trusses; Mid. (1923). H4.

'Countess of Derby' (*'Cynthia'* × *'Pink Pearl'*). (HH) A large shrub bearing perfectly formed, conical trusses of large, widely funnel-shaped flowers which are a striking pink in bud, opening pink, paling slightly on the lobes and marked with reddish-brown spots and streaks within; Mid. (1913). A.M. 1930. H4.

†**'Countess of Haddington'** (*ciliatum* × *dalhousiae*). A beautiful but tender hybrid of rather straggling habit. Leaves usually five in a terminal cluster, glaucous-green and gland-dotted beneath. Flowers richly fragrant, borne in umbels of two to four, trumpet-shaped, white, flushed pale rose; Early. A charming conservatory shrub. (1862). F.C.C. 1862. H1.

'Cowslip' (*wardii* × *williamsianum*). A small shrub of neat, rounded habit. Flowers bell-shaped, 5 to 6cm. across, cream or pale primrose with a pale pink flush when young, carried in loose trusses; Mid. (1937). A.M. 1937. H4.

'C. P. Raffill' (*'Britannia'* × *griersonianum*). An excellent hybrid raised at Kew, bearing large trusses of deep orange-red flowers; Mid. (1949). H3.

'Creeping Jenny'. See *'Jenny'*.

RHODODENDRON—*continued*

'Cremorne' (*campylocarpum* × *'Luscombei'*). A very beautiful, free-flowering, Exbury hybrid bearing trusses of apple blossom-pink flowers which are creamy-white within; Early to Mid. (1935). H3.

'Crest' (Hawk Group). A magnificent, Exbury hybrid, bearing large trusses of bell-shaped, primrose-yellow flowers which have a slight darkening in the throat. The individual flowers are 10cm. across; Mid. (1953). F.C.C. 1953. H3.

'Crossbill' (*lutescens* × *spinuliferum*). A slender shrub with tubular yellow flowers, tinged apricot, with long protruding stamens, opening in March and April. Raised at Caerhays. (1933). H3.

'Cunningham's Album Compactum'. (HH) A sturdy rather slow-growing bush of dense, leafy habit. Flowers in a compact truss, funnel-shaped, blush in bud opening white, with a narrow ray of greenish-brown markings within; Mid. A hybrid of *R. caucasicum* differing from *'Cunningham's White'* in its slower growth and narrower leaves which bear indumentum on their lower surfaces. H4.

'Cunningham's Blush'. (HH) Freer-growing than *'Cunningham's Album Compactum'*. Flowers in a lax truss, funnel-shaped, lilac-pink with a ray of crimson and brown markings within; Mid. H4.

'Cunningham's Sulphur'. See under *R. caucasicum* under Species.

'Cunningham's White (*caucasicum* × *ponticum album*). (HH) An extremely hardy, robust hybrid producing rather lax trusses of funnel-shaped flowers, which are mauve before expanding, opening white, with a ray of pale purple and brown markings within; Mid. A popular rhododendron in smoky, industrial areas in the Midlands and North of England where it was once extensively planted. Raised by James Cunningham of Edinburgh about 1830. H4.

'Cynthia' (*catawbiense* × *griffithianum*). (HH) One of the best rhododendrons for general planting, thriving in a great variety of situations. A large, vigorous, dome-shaped bush bearing magnificent conical trusses of widely funnel-shaped, rose-crimson flowers, each with a narrow ray of blackish-crimson markings within; Mid. Raised by Messrs. Standish and Noble of Bagshot before 1870. A.G.M. 1969. H4.

'Dairy Maid'. A hybrid of *R. campylocarpum*. A dense, slow-growing shrub bearing compact trusses of pale cream-coloured flowers with a small ray of crimson markings within; Mid. (1930). A.M.T. 1934. H4.

Damaris (*campylocarpum* × *'Dr. Stocker'*). A broadly dome-shaped bush with oval leaves. Flowers in a lax truss, widely bell-shaped, glossy pale canary-yellow, shading to ivory at the margin; Early to Mid. (1926). H3.

'Logan'. A lovely clone with Dresden-yellow flowers, admirably set-off by the rich green, glossy foliage. Early to Mid. (1948). A.M. 1948.

'Dame Nellie Melba' (*arboreum* × *'Standishii'*). (HH) A strong-growing, large shrub or small tree, bearing conical trusses of broadly funnel-shaped, pale pink flowers, darker on the outside, with two rays of brownish-crimson spots; Mid. (1926). A.M. 1926. H3.

'Damozel'. A wide-spreading hybrid of *R. griersonianum*. Dome-shaped trusses of funnel-shaped, ruby-red flowers, with darker spots within; Mid. (1936). A.M. 1948. H3-4.

'Daphne Daffarn'. (HH) A hybrid of *R. griffithianum* with an unnamed garden hybrid. Rounded trusses of narrowly bell-shaped flowers which are bright rose-pink shading to white on the lobes, with light crimson speckles within; Mid. (Before 1884). H4.

'David' (*'Hugh Koster'* × *neriiflorum*). Compact, rounded trusses of funnel-shaped, frilly-margined, deep blood-red flowers, slightly spotted within; Mid. (1939). F.C.C. 1939. A.M.T. 1957. H4.

'Dawn's Delight'. (HH) A hybrid between *R. griffithianum* and an unnamed *R. catawbiense* hybrid. Leaves long and dark glossy green. Flowers in a handsome conical truss, widely bell-shaped, carmine-ruby before expanding, opening to bright pink, soft pink with paler veins within, shading to white in the tube and with bright crimson markings; Mid. A lovely hybrid, raised by J. H. Mangles at Valewood, Nr. Haslemere, Surrey, before 1884. A.M. 1911. H4.

'Daydream' (*griersonianum* × *'Lady Bessborough'*). A beautiful Exbury hybrid with large, loose trusses of broadly funnel-shaped flowers which are rich crimson in bud, opening to pink, flushed crimson and fading to creamy-white, flushed pale pink on tube; Mid. (1936). A.M. 1940. H3.

RHODODENDRON—*continued*

'Diane' (Campylocarpum Hybrid × '*Mrs. Lindsay Smith*'). A sturdy, leafy bush of compact habit. Flowers in a compact truss, widely bell-shaped, primrose-yellow, delicately marked with a ray of crimson in the tube; Early to Mid. A beautiful hybrid raised by M. Koster and Sons of Boskoop, Holland in 1920. A.M.T. 1948. H4.

'Dido' (*decorum* × *dichroanthum*). A compact shrub. Flowers salmon-pink with darker veins; Mid. H4.

'Diva' (*griersonianum* × '*Ladybird*'). A hardy, free-flowering, Exbury hybrid with compact rounded trusses of widely funnel-shaped flowers of carmine-scarlet with brownish spots within; Mid. (1936). A.M. 1937. H3.

'Doncaster'. (HH) A very popular, distinct and easily recognised hybrid of *R. arboreum*. A small shrub, broadly dome-shaped in habit, with somewhat glossy, very dark green, leathery leaves, held very stiffly on the shoots. Flowers in a dense truss, funnel-shaped, brilliant crimson-scarlet, with a ray of black markings within; Mid. Raised by Anthony Waterer at Knap Hill. H4.

'Dormouse' ('*Dawn's Delight*' × *williamsianum*). A small to medium-sized, compact, dome-shaped bush with loose clusters of delicate pink, bell-shaped flowers set amid kidney-shaped leaves, which are copper-coloured when young; Mid. (1936). H4.

'Dr. Stocker' (*caucasicum* × *griffithianum*). (HH) A dome-shaped bush, broader than high, bearing loose trusses of large, widely bell-shaped flowers, which are milk-white tinged cream and delicately marked brown-crimson; Early to Mid. (1900). A.M. 1900. H3.

'Dusky Maid' (*discolor* × '*Moser's Maroon*'). A tall, erect bush of robust habit. Tight rounded trusses of very attractive dark, dusky red flowers; Mid to Late. (1936). H4.

'Earl of Athlone' ('*Queen Wilhelmina*' × '*Stanley Davies*'). A splendid hybrid from the same pod as '*Britannia*', but less hardy. Compact trusses of glowing, deep blood-red, bell-shaped flowers; Early to Mid. F.C.C.T. 1933. A.G.M. 1969. H3.

'Earl of Donoughmore'. A hybrid of *R. griersonianum*, produced by M. Koster and Sons in 1953. Flowers bright red, with an orange glow; Mid. H4.

'Earl of Morley' (*arboreum album* × *campylocarpum*). A slow-growing, but ultimately large shrub or small tree of pyramidal habit. The glistening, ivory-white, crimson-spotted flowers are borne in rounded trusses; Early. An exceedingly handsome hybrid, raised at Westonbirt about 1910. H3.

'East Knoyle' (*griersonianum* × *Loderi*). Flowers large, widely funnel-shaped, carmine in bud opening to rose, paler within and dark throated; in attractive loose trusses; Mid. (1930). H3.

†**'Eldorado'** (*johnstoneanum* × *valentinianum*). A small shrub of loose growth; young shoots softly bristly; leaves glaucous and densely brown scaly beneath. Flowers appearing in April in terminal clusters, funnel-shaped, primrose-yellow, scaly on the outside. (1937). H1.

'Eleanore' (*augustinii* × *desquamatum*). A large, pretty shrub with pale mauve flowers nearly 7·5cm. across. Early to Mid. Suitable for woodland planting. (1937). A.M. 1943. H3.

'Electra'. See *R. augustinii* '*Electra*' under Species.

'El Greco'. Flowers funnel-shaped, saffron-yellow, changing to azalea-pink at margins, flushed carmine rose, calyx large and similarly coloured; Mid. A.M.T. 1961. H4.

'Elisabeth Hobbie' ('*Essex Scarlet*' × *forrestii repens*). A dwarf shrub; loose umbels of six to ten translucent, scarlet-red, bell-shaped flowers; Early. (1945). H4.

'Elizabeth' (*forrestii repens* × *griersonianum*). A dwarf or small, spreading shrub raised at Bodnant. Flowers trumpet-shaped, 7·5cm. across, rich dark red, carried in clusters of five or six in April. (1939). A.M. 1939. F.C.C. 1943. A.G.M. 1969. H4.

'Emerald Isle' ('*Idealist*' × '*Naomi*'). An unusual hybrid with bell-shaped flowers of Chartreuse-green; May. (1956). A.M. 1956. H4.

'Erebus' ('*Fabia*' × *griersonianum*). An outstanding Bodnant hybrid of compact habit. Flowers funnel-shaped, brilliant deep scarlet, in loose trusses; Mid. (1936). H3.

RHODODENDRON—*continued*

'Ethel' (*'F. C. Puddle' × forrestii repens*). A dwarf Bodnant hybrid of low spreading habit. Large trumpet-shaped flowers of crimson-scarlet; Early. (1940). F.C.C. 1940. H3.

'Exbury Isabella' (*auriculatum × griffithianum*). A large shrub or small tree with large trusses of enormous, fragrant, trumpet-shaped white flowers; Late. (1948). H3.

Fabia (*dichroanthum × griersonianum*). A very beautiful, widely-dome-shaped bush bearing loose, flat trusses of funnel-shaped flowers which are scarlet, shaded orange in the tube and freely speckled with pale brown markings; Mid. Raised at Bodnant. (1934). A.M. 1934. H4.

'Tangerine'. Flowers vermilion in colour, shaded geranium-red around the mouth and poppy-red in the throat. As in *Fabia*, the calyx is large and petaloid, with incised margin; Mid. A.M. 1940.

'Waterer'. Salmon-pink, with a tint of orange; Late. Compact habit. A splendid selection.

'Faggetter's Favourite'. A hybrid of *R. fortunei* raised by W. C. Slocock of Woking. A tall grower, with fine foliage and producing large trusses of sweetly-scented, shell-pink flowers with white shading; Mid. (1933). A.M. 1933. A.M.T. 1955. H4.

'Fastuosum Flore Pleno' (*catawbiense × ponticum*). (HH) A very hardy hybrid, forming a large, dome-shaped bush. Flowers in a lax truss, funnel-shaped with wavy margins, rich mauve with a ray of brown-crimson markings within, filament unevenly petaloid; Mid. Raised at Ghent, Belgium sometime before 1846. A.G.M. 1928 (as *R. catawbiense 'Fastuosum Flore Pleno'*) and 1959. H4.

'F. C. Puddle' (*griersonianum × neriiflorum*). An excellent hybrid carrying trusses of slightly pendulous, brilliant scarlet flowers; Mid. Raised by and named after the late Mr. F. C. Puddle, Head Gardener at Bodnant. (1932). A.M. 1932. H3.

'Fireball' (*'Ascot Brilliant' × barbatum*). An early flowering shrub requiring woodland conditions. Flowers bell-shaped, with frilly margins, glowing carmine-scarlet, carried in rounded trusses in March. Raised by Richard Gill and Sons of Penryn, Cornwall, before 1925. A.M. 1925. H3-4.

'Fire Bird' (*griersonianum × 'Norman Shaw'*). A tall, vigorous shrub, producing large trusses of glowing salmon-red flowers. The bright green young leaves are strikingly set against long crimson bracts; Mid. (1938). H3-4.

'Fire Glow'. A hardy and extremely free-flowering hybrid of involved parentage, including *R. griersonianum* and *R. griffithianum*. Leaves ovate, wavy and twisted. Flowers racemose, trumpet-shaped, faintly fragrant, turkey-red, with a ray of dark brown markings; Mid. Raised at Embley Park, Hampshire, in 1920. (1935). A.M. 1935. H3.

'Firetail' (*'Britannia' × eriogynum*). An excellent, free-flowering hybrid for the woodland garden. The funnel-shaped, deep scarlet flowers are spotted brown within and are borne in fairly compact trusses; Mid. (1934). A.M. 1934. F.C.C. 1937. H3.

Fittra (*fittianum × racemosum*). A very free-flowering, dwarf, compact shrub, raised in our nurseries. The vivid, deep rose-pink flowers are borne in dense trusses of up to thirty blooms, often completely covering the plant; Early to Mid. (1938). A.M. 1949. H4.

†**'Fragrantissimum'** (*edgworthii × formosum*). A beautiful hybrid of medium size with attractive, dark green, corrugated leaves, paler beneath. Flowers appearing in terminal umbels of four, extremely fragrant, widely funnel-shaped up to 7·5cm. long, white, flushed rose without and greenish within at base; stamens with brown anthers; Early. Requires conservatory treatment except in the mildest areas. F.C.C. 1868. H1.

'Francis B. Hayes'. (HH) An old hardy hybrid derived, in part, from *R. maximum*, forming a strong leafy bush. Flowers in a conical truss, trumpet-shaped, mauve in bud, opening to blush and finally pure white, with an intense and well-defined ray of maroon, overlaid black; Mid to Late. (Before 1922). H4.

'Francis Hanger' (*dichroanthum × 'Isabella'*). Flowers with frilly margins, chrome-yellow, edged with a delicate tinge of pale rose; Mid. (1942). A.M. 1950. Raised at Exbury and named after the late Curator of the R.H.S. Gardens, Wisley. A.M. 1950.

RHODODENDRON—*continued*

Fulgarb (*arboreum 'Blood Red' × fulgens*). A large shrub or tree bearing small compact trusses of rich crimson flowers in February. A.M. 1937. H3.

'Furnivall's Daughter'. Similar to '*Mrs. Furnivall*' but stronger growing, with larger leaves and flowers, which are widely funnel-shaped, light rose-pink with a bold splash of dark markings; Mid to Late. A.M.T. 1958. F.C.C.T. 1961. H4.

'Fusilier' (*elliottii × griersonianum*). A magnificent Exbury hybrid, furnished with long, narrow leaves and bearing large trusses of brilliant red, bell-shaped flowers, individually 8cm. across; Mid. (1938). A.M. 1938. F.C.C. 1942. H3.

'Gaul' (*elliottii × 'Shilsonii'*). An Exbury hybrid with compact trusses of widely funnel-shaped, ruby-red flowers; Early. (1939). A.M. 1939. H3.

'Gauntlettii' (*'Album Elegans' × griffthianum*). (HH) A vigorous hybrid of the same parentage as '*Loder's White*', forming a stout, symmetrical bush with handsome, glossy, dark green foliage. Flowers in a fine, upstanding truss, widely bell-shaped, rich pink in bud opening to blush-white, lightly speckled crimson at the base within; nectaries crimson; Mid. (Before 1934). H4.

'Geisha' (*dichroanthum × 'Pineapple'*). An Exbury hybrid with narrowly bell-shaped, cream-coloured flowers; Mid. (1939). H4.

'General Eisenhower'. A hybrid of *R. griffithianum*, bearing large trusses of deep carmine flowers; Mid. (1946). H4.

'General Sir John du Cane' (*discolor × thomsonii*). A very fine hybrid producing large, lax trusses of fragrant, widely funnel-shaped flowers which are rose-madder, fading to pink, with a dark crimson basal flash within; Mid. (1933). H4.

'Geoffrey Millais'. (HH) A strong-growing *griffithianum* hybrid of upright habit, at least when young. Flowers fragrant, in a conical truss, bell-shaped, mauve-pink in bud, opening to glistening white flushed pink, with a ray of brown markings within; Mid. (1892). A.M. 1922. H4.

'Geraldii'. See *sutchuenense 'Geraldii'*.

'Gilian' (*griffithianum × thomsonii*). A beautiful hybrid, very similar to '*Dame Nellie Melba*'. The large bell-shaped flowers are a striking shade of cardinal-red; Early. (1923). A.M. 1923. H3.

'Gill's Crimson'. A handsome *griffithianum* hybrid with bold foliage and compact, rounded trusses of wax-like, bell-shaped flowers of a glowing blood-crimson; Early. H3.

Gladys (*campylocarpum × fortunei*). A shapely bush bearing firm, well-shaped trusses of widely funnel-shaped flowers which are creamy-yellow in bud, opening to pale cream with a few purple markings on a dark ground within, faintly fragrant; Mid. First raised by Brig. Gen. Clarke at Chilworth Manor, Nr. Southampton. (1926). A.M. 1926. H4.

'Rose'. A lovely clone. Flowers funnel-shaped, light rosy-pink in bud, opening to pale cream, with a crimson basal blotch within; Early to Mid. A.M. 1950.

'Goblin' (*'Break of Day' × griersonianum*). A small, neat, Exbury hybrid bearing loose trusses of salmon-pink, funnel-shaped flowers, calyx large, irregularly lobed, coloured as the corolla; Mid. A.M. 1939. H3-4.

'Golden Horn' (*dichroanthum × elliottii*). A brilliantly-coloured, small, Exbury hybrid. Flowers drooping, bell-shaped, salmon-orange, freely speckled with brownish markings within; calyx large, double, same colour as corolla; Mid. (1939). A.M. 1945. H3-4.

'Golden Horn Persimmon'. See '*Persimmon*'.

'Goldfort' (*fortunei × 'Goldsworth Yellow'*). Flowers pink in bud, opening creamy-yellow, tinted with apricot pink; Mid. (1937). H4.

'Goldsworth Orange' (*dichroanthum × discolor*). A low, spreading bush bearing large trusses of pale orange flowers, tinged with apricot-pink; Late. (1938). A.M.T. 1959. H4.

'Goldsworth Pink'. A hardy shrub raised from *R. griffithianum* crossed with an unnamed garden hybrid. Lax, conical trusses of widely funnel-shaped flowers which are deep rose in bud, opening to mottled rose-pink and fading to white; Mid. (1933). A.M.T. 1958. H4.

RHODODENDRON—*continued*

'Goldsworth Yellow' (*campylocarpum* × *caucasicum*). A leafy, dome-shaped bush, broader than high and very hardy. Flowers in a well filled, rounded truss, funnel-shaped, apricot pink in bud, opening primrose yellow, with a large ray of warm brown markings. Usually flowering at "bluebell time"; Mid. Raised by W. C. Slocock at Goldsworth Nurseries, Woking. (1925). A.M. 1925. H4.

'Goliath'. Flowers in a compact truss, large, widely funnel-shaped with frilled margins, glowing carmine-rose with paler mottling and with a few greenish-brown speckles within. Mid. H4.

'Gomer Waterer'. (HH) A large bush, a hybrid of *R. catawbiense*. Leaves large and leathery, oval or oblong-obovate, with deflexed margins. The buds in the leaf axils are reddish and rather conspicuous. Flowers in a large, dense, rounded truss, funnel shaped, but deeply divided, white, flushed pale mauve towards the edges, with a mustard-coloured basal blotch; Mid to Late. (Before 1900). A.M. 1906. A.G.M. 1969. H4.

'Grenadier' (*elliottii* × *'Moser's Maroon'*). An Exbury hybrid, a tall shrub of compact growth, bearing magnificent trusses of deep blood-red flowers; Mid to Late. (1939). F.C.C. 1943. H3.

'Griersims' (*'G. A. Sims'* × *griersonianum*). Loose trusses of funnel-shaped flowers of a deep scarlet with a few darker speckles within; Mid. H3.

'Grosclaude' (*eriogynum* × *haematodes*). An Exbury hybrid of neat, compact habit, producing lax trusses of bell-shaped, waxen, blood-red flowers, with wavy margins; Mid. (1941). A.M. 1945. H3-4.

'Gwillt-King' (*griersonianum* × *zeylanicum*). A vigorous and attractive shrub for woodland planting. Flowers bell-shaped, rich Turkey red; Mid. (1938). A.M. 1952. H2-3.

'Halcyone' (*'Lady Bessborough'* × *souliei*). A lovely hybrid bearing rather lax, flat-topped trusses of delicate pink, wide-open flowers with a basal flash of crimson spots; Mid. (1940). H4.

'Harvest Moon' (Campylocarpum Hybrid × *'Mrs. Lindsay Smith'*). A lovely hybrid with bell-shaped, creamy-white flowers marked with a broad ray of carmine spots within. Mid. A.M.T. 1948. H4.

'Hawk' (*'Lady Bessborough'* × *wardii*). A magnificent Exbury hybrid bearing loose, flat-topped trusses of large, sulphur-yellow, funnel-shaped flowers, apricot in bud; Mid. (1940). A.M. 1949. H3. See also *'Crest'*.

'Hebe' (*'Neriihaem'* × *williamsianum*). Small shrub with bell-shaped flowers of deep rose-pink; Mid. (1927). H3.

'Hecla' (*griersonianum* × *thomsonii*). A Bodnant hybrid with red flowers; Mid. (1941). H3.

'Hélène Schiffner'. A small, dense, rounded bush of German origin, bearing rounded trusses of widely funnel-shaped flowers which are mauve in bud, opening to pure white, occasionally with an inconspicuous ray of greenish markings within. Mid. F.C.C. 1893. H4.

'Helen Webster' (Discolor Hybrid × *'Richard Gill'*). Flowers widely bell-shaped, borne in a large, dome-shaped truss, phlox pink, darkening towards the lobes; Mid. A.M. 1954. H3.

'Hermes' (*dichroanthum apodectum* × *'Lady Bessborough'*). Spreading and compact in habit. Attractive, bell-shaped flowers of chrome yellow with pink markings; Mid. (1940). H4.

'Hesperides' (*'Ayah'* × *griersonianum*). A tall, erect, Exbury hybrid, producing large trusses of rose-pink flowers; Mid. (1940). H3.

'Hill Ayah' (*discolor* × *eriogynum*). Flowers rose-madder, darker in bud, funnel-shaped, borne in a compact truss; Late. A.M. 1965. H3-4.

'Hugh Koster' (Doncaster Hybrid × *'George Hardy'*). (HH) A sturdy, leafy bush with stiff, erect branches. Flowers in a well-formed truss, funnel-shaped, glowing crimson-scarlet, with black markings within; Mid. A fine, hardy hybrid resembling *'Doncaster'*, but foliage slightly wavy at the margins and flowers lighter in colour. (1915). A.M.T. 1933. H4.

'Humming Bird' (*haematodes* × *williamsianum*). A small, compact dome-shaped bush of distinctive appearance. Flowers half nodding, widely bell-shaped, carmine, shaded glowing scarlet inside the tube; Early. (1933). H3.

RHODODENDRON—*continued*

'Ibex' (*griersonianum* × *pocophorum*). An Exbury hybrid with leaves brown-felted below. Dome-shaped trusses of funnel-shaped, rose-carmine flowers, with darker spots within; Early to Mid. (1941). A.M. 1948. H3-4.

'Icarus' (*'A. Gilbert'* × *dichroanthum herpesticum*). A small, low-growing shrub producing flat-topped trusses of bell-shaped flowers which are deep rose-red in bud, opening to an unusual biscuit colour, shaded rose; Mid. (1941). A.M. 1947. H4.

'Idealist' (*'Naomi'* × *wardii*). A striking shrub when in flower. The large, pale cream, bell-shaped flowers, with a dark red basal blotch are coral-pink in bud and are borne in bold trusses; Early to Mid. (1941). A.M. 1945. H3.

Impeanum (*hanceanum* × *impeditum*). A dwarf, spreading shrub with small crowded leaves. Smothered with small clusters of saucer-shaped flowers of a striking Cobalt violet; Mid. An excellent shrub for the rock garden or heather garden. Cross made at Kew in 1915. F.C.C. 1934. H4.

'Impi' (*'Moser's Maroon'* × *sanguineum didymum*). Small trusses of funnel-shaped flowers of a very dark almost black-red, brilliant when viewed by transmitted light; Late. A.M. 1945. H4.

'Indomitable' (*'General Sir John du Cane'* × *souliei*). A lovely Exbury hybrid producing large trusses of widely funnel-shaped flowers which are white, flushed rose; Mid. (1942). H4.

Intrifast (*fastigiatum* × *intricatum*). A dwarf shrub of dense habit producing innumerable clusters of small, violet-blue flowers; Mid. H4.

'Isabella' (*auriculatum* × *griffithianum*). A beautiful Leonardslee hybrid. A large shrub or small tree bearing large trusses of enormous, fragrant, trumpet-shaped, frilly-edged, white flowers; Late. (1934). H3.

'Isabella Mangles'. (HH) A magnificent tall growing *griffithianum* hybrid with large leaves and tall trusses of large, trumpet-shaped, frilly-edged flowers of soft pink; Mid. Raised by J. H. Mangles before 1880. H4.

'Ispahan' (*'Fabia'* × *wardii*). A small shrub of low, spreading habit, bearing loose trusses of showy flowers, varying in colour from tangerine to yellow; Mid. (1941). H3.

'Ivanhoe' (*'Chanticleer'* × *griersonianum*). A tall shrub of loose habit. Flat-topped trusses of exceedingly brilliant, scarlet, funnel-shaped flowers with darker markings within; Early to Mid. (1941). A.M. 1945. H3.

'Jacksonii' (*caucasicum* × *'Nobleanum'*). (HH) A broadly dome-shaped, slow-growing, medium-sized bush. Flowers in a well-formed truss, widely funnel-shaped, bright rose-pink, with maroon markings and paler spotting within; normally opening in April, occasionally in March. One of the earliest raised hybrids, tolerant of industrial pollution and thriving where many other rhododendrons would fail. (1835). H4.

'Jacquetta' (*facetum* × *griersonianum*). A large shrub for woodland conditions. Leaves dull, dark green, covered with a loose brown floss beneath when young. Flowers red, funnel-shaped, borne in a loose truss; Mid. (1953). H3.

Jalisco (*'Dido'* × *'Lady Bessborough'*). A most attractive hybrid raised at Exbury. Flowers straw-coloured, tinted orange-rose at the tips; Late. (1942). H3-4.

'Eclipse'. Flowers primrose-yellow, streaked crimson on the outside and blotched and spotted crimson at the base within. A.M. 1948.

'Elect'. Flowers primrose-yellow, with paler lobes, marked with brownish-red spots within. A.M. 1948.

'Emblem'. Flowers pale yellow, with a dark basal blotch within. (1948).

'Janet'. Flowers apricot-yellow. (1948).

'Jamaica' (*'Break of Day'* × *eriogynum*). A small to medium-sized, wide-spreading shrub, bearing trusses of deep orange, bell-shaped flowers; Early to Mid. (1942). H3.

'Jenny' (*'Creeping Jenny'*) (Elizabeth Group). A prostrate shrub raised at Bodnant, carrying large, deep red, bell-shaped flowers; Mid. H4.

'Jersey Cream' (Zuiderzee Group). An Embley Park hybrid bearing compact, rounded trusses of funnel-shaped, cream-coloured or pale primrose flowers with a ray of crimson markings; Mid. A.M. 1939. H4.

'Jervis Bay' (Hawk Group). A superb clone bearing firm, rounded trusses of widely funnel-shaped, primrose-yellow flowers, with crimson basal flash; Mid. A.M. 1951. H3.

RHODODENDRON—*continued*

'J. G. Millais' (*'Ascot Brilliant'* × *'Pink Pearl'*). A fast-growing, vigorous hybrid raised by Waterer, Sons & Crisp at Bagshot. Flowers in a rather open-centred truss, bell-shaped, waxy, scarlet, spotted and streaked almost black on a lighter ground within; Early to Mid. H4.

'Jibuti' (*'Gill's Triumph'* × *griersonianum*). Tall and erect, bearing conical trusses of glaucous, bell-shaped, deep pink flowers, with darker beins; Mid. (1942). A.M. 1949. H3.

'J. J. de Vink' (Doncaster Hybrid × Griffithianum Hybrid). A handsome shrub for a position sheltered from prevailing wind. Flowers of a wonderful glowing crimson, borne in large trusses; Mid. A.M.T. 1946. H4.

'July Fragrance' (*diaprepes* × *'Isabella'*). A strong-growing bush, young leaves flushed bronze. Flowers in a large, loose truss, trumpet-shaped, white with a crimson basal stain within, deliciously fragrant; Late. Raised in our nurseries (1967). H3.

'Jutland' (*'Bellerophon'* × *elliottii*). Flowers in a large, dome-shaped truss, widely bell-shaped, geranium lake, flecked darker red; Late. (1942). A.M. 1947. H3.

'Karkov' (*griersonianum* × *'Red Admiral'*). A vigorous-growing, Exbury hybrid bearing large, globular trusses of widely funnel-shaped, frilly-edged flowers which are carmine-rose, faintly and evenly spotted; Early to Mid. (1943). A.M. 1947. H3.

'Kiev' (*Barclayi 'Robert Fox'* × *elliottii*). Loose, flat-topped trusses of large, blood-red, bell-shaped flowers, with wavy margins and distinct heavy spotting within. Early to Mid. (1943). A.M. 1950. H3.

'Kilimanjaro' (*'Dusky Maid'* × *elliottii*). A superb Exbury hybrid, with compact, globular trusses of funnel-shaped, currant-red, wavy-edged flowers, spotted chocolate within; Mid to Late. (1943). F.C.C. 1947. H3.

'Kingcup' (*'Bustard'* × *dichroanthum*). A small, low-growing shrub bearing loose flat-topped trusses of tubular, waxy flowers coloured a lovely Indian yellow; Mid. A.M. 1943. H4.

'Kluis Sensation' (*'Britannia'* × unnamed seedling). A hardy shrub with flowers of a bright scarlet, with darker spots on upper lobes; Mid. (1948). A.G.M. 1973. H4.

'Kluis Triumph'. A splendid griffithianum hybrid with outstanding deep red flowers; Mid. A.M.T. 1969. F.C.C.T. 1971. H4.

'Lady Berry' (*'Rosy Bell'* × *'Royal Flush'*). An erect-growing Exbury hybrid, with loose trusses of pendulous, fleshy, funnel-shaped flowers. In colour they are an attractive rose-opal on the inside and jasper-red on the outside; Early to Mid. (1935). A.M. 1937. F.C.C. 1949. H3.

Lady Bessborough (*campylocarpum elatum* × *discolor*). A tall, erect-branched hybrid bearing trusses of funnel-shaped, wavy-edged flowers which are apricot in bud, opening to creamy-white, with a flash of maroon on a deeper cream ground within; Mid. Raised at Exbury. F.C.C. 1933. H4.

'Roberte'. A beautiful clone with loose trusses of daintily fringed flowers of a bright salmon-pink colour, tinged with apricot and spotted with crimson in the throat; Mid. F.C.C. 1936.

'Ladybird' (*'Corona'* × *discolor*). A tall, vigorous shrub producing enormous trusses of large, frilly-edged, coral-pink flowers, freckled yellow within; Mid. A.M. 1933. H4.

Lady Chamberlain (*cinnabarinum roylei* × *'Royal Flush'*, orange form). Undoubtedly one of the loveliest rhododendrons grown in gardens. It forms a stiffly branched shrub with neat, sea-green leaves, and bears with the utmost freedom clusters of drooping, waxy, long, narrowly bell-shaped flowers. The typical colour is mandarin-red, shading to orange-buff on the lobes; Mid. It was raised by Lionel de Rothschild at Exbury. (1930). F.C.C. 1931. H3. It is a variable hybrid and we also offer the following clones:—

'Chelsea'. Flowers orange-pink.

'Exbury'. Flowers yellow, overlaid salmon-orange. F.C.C. 1931.

'Gleam'. Flowers orange-yellow, with crimson tipped lobes.

'Ivy'. Flowers orange.

'Salmon Trout'. Flowers salmon-pink.

'Seville'. Flowers bright orange.

RHODODENDRON—*continued*

'Lady Clementine Mitford'. (HH) A large shrub, a hybrid of *R. maximum*, with large, glossy green leaves. Flowers in a firm truss, widely funnel-shaped, peach-pink, shading to white in centre, with a V-shaped pattern of pink, olive-green and brown markings within; Mid to Late. (1870). A.M.T. 1971. H4.

'Lady Digby' (*facetum* × *strigillosum*). A beautiful large shrub for woodland planting similar to *R. strigillosum* in form and foliage. Leaves up to 25cm. long, tomentose beneath. Flowers bell-shaped, blood-red; Mid. A.M. 1946. H3-4.

'Lady Eleanor Cathcart' (*arboreum* × *maximum*). (HH) A magnificent large, dome-shaped bush or small tree with handsome and very distinctive foliage. Flowers in a rounded truss, widely funnel-shaped, bright clear rose with slightly darker veins and a conspicuous maroon basal blotch within; Mid to Late. Said to have originated at Sandleford Park, near Oxford, before 1844. H4.

'Lady Longman'. An excellent hardy hybrid with large vivid rose flowers with a chocolate eye; Mid to Late. H4.

'Lady Primrose'. A compact shrub, a hybrid between *R. campylocarpum* and a hardy hybrid. Flowers in a well-formed truss, funnel-shaped, with spreading lobes, pale primrose yellow, prettily speckled crimson within, rose-tipped in bud; Early to Mid. A.M.T. 1933. H4.

Lady Roseberry (*cinnabarinum roylei* × *'Royal Flush'* pink form). Similar to *'Lady Chamberlain'*, except in colour, pink shades predominating. Typical colour is deep pink graduating to a lighter shade at the margins; Mid. Raised by Lionel de Rothschild at Exbury. (1930). A.M. 1930. F.C.C. 1932. H3. We also offer the following clones:—

'Dalmeny'. Flowers soft pink.

'Pink Beauty'. A lovely pink form. (1955).

'Pink Delight'. A beautiful clone with flowers of a glistening pink, paler within.

'Lamellen' (*campanulatum* × *griffithianum*). A large shrub with splendid foliage and trusses of large, bell-shaped flowers which are lilac-rose in bud, opening blush and fading to creamy-white, with a few crimson spots within; Early. (1943). H3.

'Langley Park' (*'Queen Wilhelmina'* × *'Stanley Davies'*). (HH) A slow-growing bush of compact habit. Flowers in a loose truss, bell-shaped, glowing crimson, with a few inconspicuous blackish-crimson markings within; Mid. (Before 1922). H4.

'Lascaux' (*'Fabia'* × *litiense*). An unusual hybrid producing bell-shaped, fleshy flowers of barium-yellow, with a crimson basal blotch within, buds a blended shade of red and orange; calyx petaloid, colour as the corolla; Mid to Late. Raised at Wisley. (1954). A. M. and Cory Cup 1954. H3.

'Laura Aberconway' (*'Barclayi'* × *griersonianum*). A lovely Bodnant hybrid, bearing loose trusses of funnel-shaped, frilly-edged flowers coloured geranium lake; Mid. (1941). A.M. 1941. F.C.C. 1944. H3.

'Lavender Girl' (*fortunei* × *'Lady Grey Egerton'*). A vigorous, free-flowering hybrid of compact habit producing dome-shaped trusses of fragrant, funnel-shaped flowers which are lilac-mauve in bud opening pale lavender, darker at margins with pinkish yellow throat; Mid. (1950). A.M.T. 1950. F.C.C.T. 1967. A.G.M. 1969. H4.

'Leda' (*apodectum* × *griersonianum*). A remarkable Bodnant hybrid. A medium-sized shrub with vermilion flowers; Mid. (1933). H3-4.

'Lee's Dark Purple'. (HH) A compact rounded bush resembling *R. catawbiense* in habit and foliage. Flowers in a dense rounded truss, widely funnel-shaped, royal purple, with a ray of greenish-brown or ochre markings within; Mid. H4.

'Leonardslee Giles' (*griffithianum* × *'Standishii'*). A large hybrid, producing large, dome-shaped trusses of funnel-shaped flowers which are pink in bud, opening to pale pink and fading to white; Early to Mid. A.M. 1948. H3.

'Letty Edwards' (*campylocarpum elatum* × *fortunei*). (Gladys Group). Free-flowering shrub of compact habit. Flowers funnel-shaped, pale sulphur yellow with a deeper flush, pale pink in bud; Mid. A.M.T. 1946. F.C.C.T. 1948. A.G.M. 1969. H4.

'Lionel's Triumph' (*lacteum* × *'Naomi'*). An outstanding Exbury hybrid with long leaves and large trusses of bell-shaped flowers of Dresden yellow, spotted and blotched crimson at the base within; individual flowers are 10cm. across; Early to Mid. A.M. 1954. F.C.C. 1974. H3.

RHODODENDRON—*continued*

'Little Ben' (*forrestii repens* × *neriiflorum*). A dwarf, spreading shrub producing an abundance of waxy, bell-shaped flowers 4cm. long, of a brilliant scarlet, in March or April. (1937). F.C.C. 1937. H4.

'Little Bert' (*euchaites* × *forrestii repens*). Small shrub up to 1m. of outstanding merit; clusters of four to five nodding, shining, crimson-scarlet, bell-shaped flowers, 5cm. long. Neat, compact habit; Early. (1939). A.M. 1939. H4.

'Lochinch Spinbur' (*burmanicum* × *spinuliferum*). Loose-growing shrub with narrowly, elliptic leaves up to 7·5cm. long, scaly beneath. Flowers tubular, whitish-yellow, stained pink, borne in a loose truss; Early. A.M. 1957. H2-3.

Lodauric (*auriculatum* × '*Loderi*). Magnificent in leaf and flower. A large shrub or small tree, bearing nodding trusses of richly-scented, trumpet-shaped, pure white flowers, with two streaks of brownish-crimson at base within; Late. (1939). H3.

Loderi (*fortunei* × *griffithianum*). Generally considered to be the finest hybrid rhododendron. A strong-growing, large, rounded bush or small tree bearing enormous trusses of very large, lily-like, trumpet-shaped, richly scented flowers 13 to 15cm. across, varying in colour from white to cream and soft pink; Early to Mid. Raised by Sir Edmund Loder at Leonardslee in 1901. H3. From the original and subsequent crosses a great number of slightly different clones have been raised.

'Helen'. Pale pink, fading to white.

'Julie'. Cream, suffused sulphur. The nearest to a yellow Loderi. A.M. 1944.

'King George'. Perhaps the "best of the bunch". Flowers soft pink in bud, opening to pure white, with a basal flash of pale green markings within. A.M. 1968. A.G.M. 1969. F.C.C. 1970.

'Patience'. Flowers carmine-rose in bud, opening to white with a faint flash of crimson and green at the base within.

'Pink Diamond'. Flowers similar to those of '*King George*', but slightly smaller and a delicate pink in colour, with a basal flash of crimson, passing to green flushed brown. F.C.C. 1914. A.G.M. 1969.

'Pink Topaz'. Soft pink with a basal flash of green within.

'Sir Edmund'. Blush-white. A.M. 1930.

'Venus'. Deep pink in bud, opening to rhodamine pink, passing to pale pink with a very faint greenish flash at the base within. A.G.M. 1969.

'White Diamond'. Pure white, pink flushed in bud. F.C.C. 1914.

'Loder's White' ('*Album Elegans*' × *griffithianum*). (HH) A large, dome-shaped shrub, clothed to the ground with handsome foliage. Flowers in a magnificent, conical truss, widely funnel-shaped, mauve pink in bud, opening to pure white, edged with pink and marked with a few scattered crimson spots; Mid. Raised by J. H. Mangles before 1884. A.M. 1911. A.G.M. 1931. H4.

'Logan Damaris'. See *Damaris* '*Logan*'.

'Lord Roberts'. (HH) An old hybrid of erect growth. Flowers in a dense, rounded truss, funnel-shaped, dark crimson with an extensive V-shaped pattern of black markings; Mid to Late. H4.

'Louis Pasteur' ('*Mrs. Tritton*' × '*Viscount Powerscourt*'). (HH) A leafy bush of good habit. Flowers in a large, conical truss, widely funnel-shaped, brilliant light crimson at the edges, shading to glistening white in the centre, outer surface dark pink; Mid. (1923). H4.

'Luscombei' (*fortunei* × *thomsonii*). A large shrub forming a broadly dome-shaped bush. Flowers in a loose truss, trumpet-shaped, deep rose, with a well-defined ray of crimson markings within; Early to Mid. (1875). H3.

'Madame Albert Moser'. A vigorous, free-flowering hybrid raised by Anthony Waterer. Leaves glossy green, up to 15cm. long. Flowers in a conical truss, funnel-shaped, with wavy margins, mauve fading to white at base, heavily spotted yellow on upper petal; Mid. A.M.T. 1954. H4.

'Madame de Bruin' ('*Doncaster*' × '*Prometheus*'). (HH) A vigorous, leafy hybrid with dark green leaves marked by the conspicuous pale green midrib. Conical trusses of cerise; red flowers; Mid. (1904). H4.

'Madame Masson' (*catawbiense* × *ponticum*). (HH) An old hybrid, bearing trusses of white flowers, with a yellow basal blotch within; Mid. (1849). H4.

'Marcia' (*campylocarpum* × '*Gladys*'). A free-flowering hybrid, making compact trusses of primrose-yellow, bell-shaped flowers; Early to Mid. F.C.C. 1944. H3.

RHODODENDRON—*continued*

'Margaret'. A *griffithianum* hybrid producing large trusses of widely funnel-shaped flowers which are rose in bud opening white, with a conspicuous blackish-crimson basal flash; Mid. H4.

'Margaret Dunn' (*discolor* × *'Fabia'*). A vigorous, free-flowering hybrid bearing flowers of an unusual shade, apricot, flushed shell-pink; Mid. A.M. 1946. H4.

'Margaret Findlay' (*griersonianum* × *wardii*). A lovely hybrid raised by Col. Sir James Horlick. Flowers almost white, with a deep red stain at base of throat; Mid. (1942). H3.

'Mariloo' (*'Dr. Stocker'* × *lacteum*). A handsome, woodland rhododendron with bold foliage and bearing large trusses of lemon-yellow flowers, flushed green; Early to Mid. Named after Mrs. Lionel de Rothschild, one of the greatest experts on Rhododendron hybrids, a subject she loves and shared with her most distinguished husband. (1941). H3.

'Marinus Koster'. A magnificent, hardy, free-flowering shrub, a hybrid of *R. griffithianum*. Flowers in large trusses, deep pink in bud, opening to white shading to pink at the margins, with a large purple blotch within; Mid. (1937). A.M.T. 1937. F.C.C.T. 1948. H4.

'Mars'. (HH) A *griffithianum* hybrid with compact trusses of widely bell-shaped, rich crimson flowers; Early to Mid. (Before 1875). A.M. 1928. F.C.C.T. 1935. H4.

'Marshall' (*elliottii* × *haematodes*). A spreading shrub bearing trusses of waxy, funnel-shaped, blood-red flowers; Mid. (1947). H3.

'Mary Swaythling' (Gladys Group). Similar to *'Gladys'*, but differing in its soft, sulphur-yellow flowers, without markings; Mid. A.M. 1934. H3.

'Matador' (*griersonianum* × *strigillosum*). A Bodnant hybrid of spreading habit with leaves hairy beneath. Flowers in a large, loose truss, funnel-shaped, brilliant, dark orange-red; Early to Mid. (1945). A.M. 1945. F.C.C. 1946. H3.

'May Day' (*griersonianum* × *haematodes*). A magnificent, comparatively low, wide-spreading shrub bearing loose trusses of slightly-drooping, funnel-shaped flowers which are a brilliant signal-red or orange-red; calyces large and similarly coloured; Mid. (1932). A.G.M. 1969. H3.

'Medusa' (*griersonianum* × *dichroanthum scyphocalyx*). A low spreading shrub. Flowers funnel-shaped, in colour Spanish orange, shading to Mandarin red on the lobes, profusely speckled pale brown within; Mid. (1936). H3.

'Michael Waterer'. (HH) A slow-growing, free-flowering *ponticum* hybrid of compact habit. Flowers in a well-formed truss, funnel-shaped, crimson-scarlet, fading to rose-crimson; Mid to Late. (Before 1894). H4.

'Midsummer Snow' (*diaprepes* × *'Isabella'*). A handsome hybrid, raised in our nurseries. Buds and young shoots bright yellow-green. Flowers in a large, loose truss, large, trumpet-shaped, pure white, richly fragrant; Late. (1967). H3.

'Mohamet' (*dichroanthum* × *eriogynum*). An Exbury hybrid producing brilliant, rich orange-coloured flowers, with frilly margins and large, coloured, petaloid calyces; Mid. A.M. 1945. H3.

'Montreal' (Lady Bessborough Group). A tall shrub bearing clusters of funnel-shaped, wavy-edged flowers which are pink in bud turning to cream; Mid. H4.

'Moonshine Supreme' (*'Adriaan Koster'* × *litiense*). A Wisley hybrid with compact, dome-shaped trusses, saucer-shaped, primrose-yellow flowers, with a darker staining on upper segment and indistinct spotting; Early to Mid. (1953). A.M. 1953. H4.

'Moonstone' (*campylocarpum* × *williamsianum*). A small, dome-shaped bush, bearing attractive, bell-shaped flowers which are rose-crimson in bud opening cream or pale primrose; Early to Mid. (1933). H3.

'Moser's Maroon'. A vigorous, tall-growing hybrid of French origin, with coppery-red young growths. Flowers maroon-red, with darker markings within; Mid to Late. Used by the late Lionel de Rothschild as a parent for many of his hybrids. A.M. 1932. H4.

'Mother of Pearl'. A lovely hybrid, a sport of *'Pink Pearl'*, raised in the Bagshot nursery of Messrs. Waterer, Sons & Crisp, before 1914. Flowers rich pink in bud, opening to a delicate blush and fading to white, with a few external pink streaks; Mid. A.M. 1930. A.G.M. 1969. H4.

RHODODENDRON—*continued*

'Mount Everest' (*campanulatum* × *griffithianum*). A large shrub of vigorous growth and very free flowering. Conical trusses of narrow, bell-shaped flowers of pure white, with reddish-brown speckling in throat; large yellow stigma; Early. (1930). A.M.T. 1953. F.C.C.T. 1958. A.G.M. 1969. H4.

'Mrs. A. M. Williams'. (HH) A superb *griffithianum* hybrid. A large shrub of dense habit with dark green foliage and well-filled, rounded trusses of bright crimson-scarlet, funnel-shaped flowers with wavy margins and a broad ray of blackish spots; Mid. (1896). A.M. 1926. A.M.T. 1933. F.C.C.T. 1954. H4.

'Mrs. A. T. de la Mare' (*'Halopeanum'* × *fortunei 'Mrs. Charles Butler'*). (HH) A free-flowering, hardy hybrid of vigorous, upright, compact habit. Flowers in a compact, dome-shaped truss, funnel-shaped, with frilly margins, white, with greenish-yellow spotting in throat, pink-tinged in bud; Mid. A.M.T. 1958. A.G.M. 1969. H4.

'Mrs. Charles Butler'. See *R. fortunei 'Mrs. Charles Butler'* under Species.

'Mrs. Charles E. Pearson' (*'Catawbiense Grandiflorum'* × *'Coombe Royal'*). (HH) A robust hybrid with stout, erect branches. Flowers in a large, conical truss, widely funnel-shaped, mauve-pink in bud, opening pale pinky-mauve passing to nearly white, with a ray of burnt Sienna within; Mid. (1909). A.M.T. 1933. F.C.C.T. 1955. A.G.M. 1969. H4.

'Mrs. C. Whitner' (*Loderi 'Sir Edmund'* × *'Snow Queen'*). A large shrub bearing conical trusses of large, trumpet-shaped white flowers, suffused magenta, with a darker basal stain within; Mid. A.M. 1963. H.3-4.

'Mrs. Davies Evans'. (HH) A vigorous, free-flowering hybrid of upright, compact habit. Flowers in a compact globular truss, funnel-shaped, with frilly margins, Imperial purple, with a white basal blotch and yellow spots within; Mid. (Before 1915). A.M.T. 1958. H4.

'Mrs. E. C. Stirling'. (HH) A widely, dome-shaped bush, a hybrid of *R. griffithianum*, bearing handsome, conical trusses of flattened, crinkly-edged, mauve-pink flowers, with a paler centre, rich rose in bud; Mid. A.M. 1906. H4.

'Mrs. Furnivall' (Caucasicum Hybrid × Griffithianum Hybrid). (HH) A magnificent, dense-growing bush, producing compact trusses of widely funnel-shaped, light rose-pink flowers, with a conspicuous blotch of Sienna and crimson markings within; Mid to Late. One of the finest hardy hybrids ever produced. (1920). A.M.T. 1933. F.C.C.T. 1948. A.G.M. 1969. H4.

'Mrs. G. W. Leak' (*'Chevalier Felix de Sauvage'* × *'Coombe Royal'*). (HH) A splendid hybrid of Dutch origin. Flowers in a rather lax, conical truss, widely funnel-shaped, mottled light rosy-pink, darkening in tube and with a conspicuous splash of blackish-brown and crimson markings within, nectaries blood-red; Mid. (1916). F.C.C.T. 1934. A.G.M. 1969. H4.

'Mrs. J. C. Williams'. A tall, rounded bush bearing trusses of white flowers with a ray of crimson markings within, pink in bud; Mid to Late. A.M.T. 1960. H4.

'Mrs. Lionel de Rothschild'. A compact, erect-branched shrub with large, firm trusses of fleshy, widely funnel-shaped flowers, white, edged with apple-blossom pink and marked with a conspicuous ray of dark crimson; Mid. A.M. 1931. H4.

'Mrs. Mary Ashley' (*campylocarpum* × hardy hybrid). A compact bush, producing trusses of funnel-shaped, pink flowers, shaded cream; Early to Mid. H4.

'Mrs. P. D. Williams'. A free-flowering hybrid. Flowers in a compact flattened truss, ivory-white with a large brown blotch on the upper lobes; Mid to Late. A.M.T. 1936. H4.

'Mrs. Philip Martineau'. A vigorous hybrid of erect growth. Flowers in a well-formed truss, widely funnel-shaped, soft rose-pink, delicately marked with a ray of light green on a white ground; Mid to Late. A.M.T. 1933. F.C.C.T. 1936. H4.

'Mrs. R. S. Holford'. (HH) A Knap Hill hybrid of vigorous growth, apt to become leggy with age. Flowers in a large truss, widely funnel-shaped, salmon-rose, with a small pattern of crimson spots within; Mid to Late. (1866). H4.

'Mrs. Walter Burns' (*griffithianum* × *'Standishii'*). A beautiful hybrid with pink flowers marked by a basal bright red blotch within; Mid. A.M. 1931. H3.

'Mrs. W. C. Slocock'. A dense growing bush, a hybrid of *R. campylocarpum*. Flowers apricot pink, shading to buff; Mid. (1929). A.M. 1929. H4.

RHODODENDRON—*continued*

'Myrtifolium' (*hirsutum* × *minus*). A small shrub, occasionally up to 2m., of broadly dome-shaped habit. Leaves small, dark green and glossy above, scaly beneath. Flowers in terminal racemes, purplish-rose, spotted crimson; Late. (Before 1824). One of the earliest rhododendron hybrids. H4.

Naomi (*'Aurora'* × *fortunei*). A wonderful Exbury hybrid. A large shrub producing large, shapely trusses of fragrant, widely-expanded flowers which are a lovely soft lilac-mauve shading to greenish-yellow in the tube, with a ray of faint brown markings; Early to Mid. (1926). A.M. 1933. H3-4. Also available in the following clones:—

'Astarte'. Flowers pink shaded yellow, with a yellow throat.

'Early Dawn'. Pale pink.

'Exbury'. Lilac, tinged yellow.

'Glow'. Bright pink, deepening in throat.

'Hope'. Pink, tinged mauve.

'Nautilus'. Large frilled flowers of deep rose, flushed pale orange-yellow on the tube, becoming paler with age. A.M. 1938.

'Nereid'. Lavender and yellow.

'Pink Beauty'. Satiny pink.

'Stella Maris'. Buff, shaded lilac-pink, slightly larger and fuller in the truss than other clones and longer in leaf. F.C.C. 1939.

'Nehru' (*griersonianum* × *'Huntsman'*). A beautiful Exbury hybrid producing trusses of rich scarlet flowers; Early to Mid. (1946). H3.

'Nereid' (*dichroanthum* × *neriiflorum*). A natural hybrid, apparently introduced from the wild with seed of the former parent. Low and compact in habit. Flowers in a loose umbel, nodding, bell-shaped, waxy, salmon-pink, faintly spotted orange within, calyx coloured as the corolla; Mid. (1934). H3.

'New Comet' (*'Idealist'* × *'Naomi'*). An attractive hybrid producing large, heavy, globular trusses of shallowly funnel-shaped, Mimosa yellow flowers flushed pale pink; Early to Mid. A.M. 1957. H3.

Nobleanum (*arboreum* × *caucasicum*). (HH) A large, slow-growing shrub or small tree with dull, dark green leaves covered beneath with a thin, plastered, buff indumentum. Flowers in a compact truss, widely funnel-shaped, brilliant rose-scarlet in bud, opening to rich rose, flushed white within and with a few crimson spots; nectaries dark crimson. One of the earliest rhododendron hybrids, first raised by Anthony Waterer at Knap Hill about 1832. It is also one of the first to flower, opening from January to March, or earlier in sheltered gardens. A.G.M. 1926. H4.

'Album' (*arboreum 'Album'* × *caucasicum*). (HH) A dense bush of compact habit. Flowers in a compact truss, pink in bud, opening to white or blush, faintly marked with small ray of yellowish-green. Jan. to March. Raised by Messrs. Cunningham & Fraser of Edinburgh. A.G.M. 1969.

'Coccineum'. (HH) A large conical bush bearing trusses of bell-shaped flowers of a deep rose, marked with a few dark crimson spots at the base within. January to March.

'Venustum' (*arboreum venustum*). (HH) A very old hybrid, a densely leafy bush of broadly, dome-shaped habit, up to 2m. high and 3m. across. Flowers in a compact truss, funnel-shaped, glistening pink, shading to white in the centre, with a small pattern of dark crimson markings at base within; nectaries crimson. Flowering in late winter, but occasionally opens in December in a mild season. Raised by William Smith at Norbiton Common, near Kingston, Surrey in 1829. A.G.M. 1969. A.M. 1973.

'Norman Shaw' (*'Baron de Bruin'* × discolor). A tall shrub producing firm trusses of widely funnel-shaped, Phlox-pink flowers; Late. (1919). A.M. 1926. H4.

'Old Port'. (HH) A vigorous, leafy, dome-shaped bush with very glossy foliage, a hybrid of *R. catawbiense*. Flowers in a dense truss, widely funnel-shaped, of a rich plum colour, with a well-defined pattern of blackish-crimson markings; Mid to Late. Raised at Knap Hill in 1865. H4.

Oreocinn (*cinnabarinum* × *oreotrephes*). A delightful Lamellen hybrid of slender, twiggy habit, with sea-green leaves and pastel flowers of a soft apricot; Mid. We were fortunate to obtain the original plant for our collection. (1926). H4.

'Oudijk's Sensation'. A small shrub forming a dense mound. Flowers bell-shaped, of a striking bright pink, borne in loose trusses; Mid. H4.

RHODODENDRON—*continued*

'Pallescens' (*davidsonianum* × *racemosum*). A small, slender shrub of thin, open habit with lanceolate leaves, glaucous and scaly below. The funnel-shaped flowers occur in terminal clusters and in the upper leaf axils. They are pale pink in colour, with a white or carmine flush about the margin; Mid. A natural hybrid from W. China. A.M.(F.) 1933. H4.

Penjerrick (*compylocarpum elatum* × *griffithianum*). One of the choicest of all hybrid rhododendrons. Loose trusses of bell-shaped, fragrant, creamy-yellow, or pale pink flowers, with crimson nectaries; Early. Both colour forms are available. A.M. 1923. H3. One of the many fine hybrids raised by Mr. Smith, Head Gardener at Penjerrick.

'Persimmon' (Golden Horn Group). A colourful hybrid of medium size, more compact in habit than *'Golden Horn'*. Flowers orange-red, with a large calyx of similar colour; Mid. (1939). H3-4.

'Peter Koster' (Doncaster Hybrid × *'George Hardy'*). (HH) A handsome shrub of sturdy, bushy habit. Flowers in a firm truss, trumpet-shaped, rosy-crimson, paling towards the margins, darker in bud; Mid to Late. (1909). A.M.T. 1946. H4.

'Philip Waterer' (Maximum Hybrid × *'Mrs E. C. Stirling'*). (HH) A handsome hybrid producing conical trusses of widely funnel-shaped flowers which are a delicate soft rose, with darker veins, wavy at margins; Mid to Late. A.M. 1924. H4.

'Phoebus' (*'F. C. Puddle'* × *haematodes*). A medium-sized, spreading shrub with shortly-racemose inflorescences of nodding, bell-shaped flowers which are scarlet, shaded glowing blood-red, nectaries dark blood-red, calyx petaloid, coloured as the corolla; Early. (1941). H3.

'Pilgrim' (*fortunei* × *'Gill's Triumph'*). A tall-growing hybrid with large leaves, bearing trusses of large, trumpet-shaped flowers of rich pink, with a few dark markings within; Mid. A.M. 1926. H4.

'Pink Bride' (*griffithianum* × *'Halopeanum'*). A tall hybrid with trusses of bell-shaped, pale blush flowers; Early to Mid. A.M. 1931. H3-4.

'Pink Drift' (*calostrotum* × *scintillans*). A dwarf shrub of neat, compact habit with small, aromatic leaves and clusters of soft lavender-rose flowers; Mid. (1955). Suitable for the rock garden. H4.

'Pink Glory' (*irroratum* × *'Loderi'*). A large shrub producing handsome trusses of large, trumpet-shaped, blush-pink flowers, stained rose-madder; Early. A.M.T. 1940. H3.

'Pink Pearl' (*'Broughtonii'* × *'George Hardy'*). (HH) One of the most popular of all rhododendrons. A strong-growing shrub, ultimately tall, and bare at the base. Flowers in a magnificent, large, conical truss, widely funnel-shaped, rose-coloured in bud, opening to deep lilac-pink, fading to white at the margins, with a well-defined ray of crimson-brown markings; Mid. Raised by J. Waterer & Sons at Bagshot. A.M. 1897. F.C.C. 1900. A.G.M. 1952. H4.

'Polar Bear' (*auriculatum* × *diaprepes*). A superb, late-flowering hybrid forming a large shrub or small tree with handsome, large leaves. Flowers in large trusses, trumpet-shaped, richly fragrant, like pure white lilies, with a light green flash within; Late. Raised by J. B. Stevenson at Tower Court, Ascot in 1926. This lovely rhododendron is most suitable to woodland conditions. Unfortunately, flowers are not produced on young specimens. F.C.C. 1946. H3.

'Praecox' (*ciliatum* × *dauricum*). An extremely popular, small, early-flowering hybrid of compact growth. Leaves sometimes partially deciduous, aromatic when crushed. Flowers produced in twos and threes at the tips of the shoots. They are widely funnel-shaped in appearance, purplish-crimson in bud, opening to glistening rosy-purple, slightly darker on the outside. February to March. Raised by Isaac Davies of Ormskirk, Lancashire, about 1855. (1860). A.G.M. 1926. F.C.C. 1978. H4.

'Princess of Orange' (*campylocarpum* × *'Prince Camille de Rohan'*). A hybrid of neat, rounded habit. Flowers in a loose truss, funnel-shaped, with crinkled margins, mottled waxy pink with a well-defined ray of crimson markings, nectaries crimson; Early. H4.

'Professor Hugo de Vries' (*'Doncaster'* × *'Pink Pearl'*). Similar in habit to *'Countess of Derby'*. Flowers in a large, conical truss, widely funnel-shaped, rich-rose in bud, opening to lilac-rose, with a ray of reddish-brown markings on a light ground; Mid. A.M. 1975. H4.

RHODODENDRON—*continued*

Prostigiatum (*fastigiatum* × *prostratum*). A dwarf shrub of dense habit resembling *R. impeditum*, producing clusters of violet-purple flowers; Early. (1924). A.M. 1924. H4.

'Purple Splendour'. (HH) A sturdy, leafy bush with erect branches, a hybrid of *R. ponticum*. Flowers in a well-formed truss, widely funnel-shaped, rich royal purplish-blue, with a well-defined ray of black, embossed markings on a purplish-brown ground; Mid to Late. A fine hybrid, looking well against *'Goldsworth Yellow'*, which flowers about the same time. (Before 1900). A.M. 1931. A.G.M. 1969. H4.

'Queen of Hearts' (*meddianum* × *'Moser's Maroon'*). One of the last hybrids raised by Lionel de Rothschild. A striking shrub, producing dome-shaped trusses of widely funnel-shaped flowers of a deep, glowing crimson, speckled black within, enlivened by the white filaments; Early to Mid. A.M. 1949. H3.

'Queen Wilhelmina'. A tall-growing, stiffly-branched *griffithianum* hybrid. Flowers in a lax truss, widely bell-shaped, carmine in bud, opening to deep rosy-scarlet and fading to rose-pink, wavy at the margins; Early to Mid. (1896). H3.

Racil (*ciliatum* × *racemosum*). A small, free-flowering shrub, with small leaves and clusters of blush-pink flowers; Early. (1937). H4.

'Red Admiral' (*arboreum* × *thomsonii*). A superb large shrub raised at Caerhays. Flowers bell-shaped of a glowing red; Early. H3.

'Red Cap' (*didymum* × *eriogynum*). A dwarf, splendid Tower Court hybrid producing blood-red flowers until the end of summer; Late. (1935). H3.

'Red Riding Hood' (*'Atrosanguineum'* × *griffithianum*). A tall-growing shrub bearing large, conical trusses of brilliant deep red flowers; Mid. (1933). H4.

'Remo' (*lutescens* × *valentinianum*). A Tower Court hybrid of compact habit. Flowers in loose trusses, bright yellow; Early. (1943). H3.

'Repose' (*discolor* × *lacteum*). A beautiful hybrid raised at Exbury. The deeply bell-shaped flowers are whitish-cream, with a faint greenish suffusion and greenish-crimson speckling in the throat; Mid. (1956). A.M. 1956. H4.

'Review Order' (*euchaites* × *'May Day'*). A dense, medium-sized shrub of spreading habit. Leaves densely tomentose beneath; flowers in a lax truss, bell-shaped, blood-red, faintly brown-spotted within; Mid. (1954). A.M. 1954. H3.

'Rocket' (*meddianum* × *strigillosum*). A superb, Tower Court hybrid bearing a flat-topped truss of bell-shaped flowers. In colour they are a rich glowing blood red, spotted brown on the upper lobes, appearing in late March or early April. (1954). A.M. 1954. H3-4.

'Romany Chai' (*griersonianum* × *'Moser's Maroon'*). A lovely hybrid raised at Exbury, the name meaning "Gypsy Children". Large compact trusses of rich terra-cotta, with a dark maroon basal blotch; Mid to Late. A.M. 1932, when it was also awarded the Cory Cup. H3-4.

'Romany Chal' (*eriogynum* × *'Moser's Maroon'*). Another Exbury hybrid, the name meaning "Gypsy Girl". A tall bush, bearing lax trusses of bell-shaped, cardinal-red flowers, with a ray of black markings within; Mid to Late. Magnificent in a woodland setting. A.M. 1932. F.C.C. 1937. H3.

'Rosabel' (*griersonianum* × *'Pink Shell'*). A most attractive Knap Hill hybrid, with large, loose trusses of large, trumpet-shaped flowers which are rose-red in bud, opening pale pink with darker veining and speckled red within. When fully open pale salmon-pink with a dark eye; Mid. (1865). A.M. 1936. H3.

'Rosenkavalier' (*eriogynum* × *'Tally Ho'*). A Wisley hybrid, producing large, heavy trusses of funnel-shaped, scarlet flowers with red spotting on the upper lobes; Mid. Succeeds best in woodland. A.M. 1959. H3.

'Rosy Bell' (*ciliatum* × *glaucophyllum*). A charming, small shrub occasionally to 2m., bearing loose terminal clusters of bell-shaped, rose-pink flowers; Early to Mid. Bark dark brown and flaky. (1894). A.M. 1894. H4.

†**'Royal Flush'** (*cinnabarinum* × *maddenii*). An attractive hybrid raised at Caerhays. The clusters of tubular flowers are variable in colour. We offer both a pink and a yellow form; Mid. H3.

'Roza Stevenson' (*'Rosa Harrison'*). A superb hybrid raised by, and named in memory of one who was a great lover of rhododendrons; (see note under Rhododendron species). Flowers saucer-shaped, 10 to 12cm. across, deep lemon-yellow, darker in bud, borne in attractive trusses. F.C.C. 1968. H3.

RHODODENDRON—*continued*

'Rubina' (*didymum* × '*Tally Ho*'). A low-growing, spreading shrub, the leaves covered beneath with a suede-like, fawn-coloured indumentum. Flowers nodding, trumpet-shaped, blood-red, shaded dark maroon at base continuing into late summer; Late. (1938). H3-4.

Russautinii (*augustinii* × *russatum*). A first class compact shrub, combining the best features of its distinguished parents. Flowers deep lavender-blue; Mid. (1937). H4.

'Russellianum' (*arboreum* × *catawbiense*) ('*Southamptonia*'). (HH) An old hybrid. A large shrub or occasionally a small tree to 9m. or above, bearing rounded trusses of crimson-red flowers, paler at base; Early to Mid. (1831). H4.

'Saffron Queen' (*burmanicum* × *xanthostephanum*). A beautiful hybrid with narrowly elliptic leaves, glossy green above, with scattered brown scales beneath. Flowers tubular, sulphur-yellow, with darker spotting on the upper lobes; Mid. (1948). A.M. 1948. H3.

'Saint Breward' (*augustinii* × *impeditum*). A beautiful, small, compact, rounded shrub bearing tight, globular trusses of shallowly bell-shaped flowers of a soft lavender, darker at the margins, anthers pale blue; Early to Mid. F.C.C. 1962. H4.

'Saint Tudy' (*augustinii* × *impeditum*). A small shrub of dense, bushy habit, bearing dense trusses of shallowly bell-shaped, lobelia-blue flowers; Early to Mid. Raised by Maj. Gen. Harrison at Tremeer, St. Tudy, Cornwall. A.M. 1960. F.C.C.T. 1973. H4.

'Sapphire' ('*Blue Tit*' × *impeditum*). A dwarf, small-leaved shrub of open habit, resembling *R. impeditum*. Flowers of a pale, lavender-blue; Early. A.M.T. 1967. H4.

'Sappho'. (HH) A very free-growing bush of rounded or dome-shaped habit. Flowers in handsome, conical trusses, widely funnel-shaped, mauve in bud, opening to pure white, with a conspicuous blotch of rich purple overlaid black; Mid. Raised by Anthony Waterer at Knap Hill, before 1867. A.G.M. 1969. A.M.T. 1974. H4.

'Sarita Loder' (*griersonianum* × '*Loderi*'). An outstanding hybrid producing loose trusses of large, bright pink flowers, deep crimson in bud; Mid. (1934). A.M. 1934. H3.

Sarled (*sargentianum* × *trichostomum ledoides*). A dwarf shrub suitable for the rock garden with tiny leaves and rounded trusses of small flowers pink in bud, opening creamy white; Mid. A.M. 1974. H4.

'Scarlett O'Hara' ('*Langley Park*' × *thomsonii*). A handsome shrub, bearing loose trusses of waxy, blood-red, bell-shaped flowers; Mid. (1942). H3.

'Scarlet Wonder'. A very hardy, dwarf shrub forming a compact mound of dense foliage. Flowers trumpet-shaped, frilly-margined, ruby-red, borne in loose trusses at the ends of the shoots; Mid. This very useful shrub was raised by Mr. Dietrich Hobbie of Germany. A.G.M. 1973. H4.

'Seta' (*moupinense* × *spinuliferum*). An exceedingly pretty, medium-sized Bodnant hybrid of erect habit producing umbels of narrowly bell-shaped flowers which are white at base, shading to vivid pink in the lobes. One of the first hybrids to flower, in March or April. (1933). A.M. 1933. F.C.C. 1960. A.G.M. 1969. H3-4.

'Seven Stars' (*Loderi* '*Sir Joseph Hooker*' × *yakushimanum*). A large, vigorous, free-flowering hybrid raised at Windsor Great Park. Flowers bell-shaped, with wavy margins, white, flushed pink, reddish in bud; Mid. A.M. 1967. F.C.C.T. 1974. H3-4.

'Shilsonii' (*barbatum* × *thomsonii*). A strong-growing, rounded, symmetrical bush or small tree with attractive metallic coloured stems; intermediate in habit and foliage between the parents. Flowers in a loose truss, bell-shaped, blood-red, with darker veins and inconspicuous dark brown markings; calyx large, cup-shaped, pale green, flushed crimson; Early. Raised by Richard Gill before 1900. A.M. 1900. H3–4.

'Siren' ('*Choremia*' × *griersonianum*). A Bodnant hybrid, with bell-shaped flowers of a brilliant red, with darker spots; Mid. (1942). A.M. 1942. H3.

'Sir Frederick Moore' (*discolor* × '*St. Keverne*'). A tall, hardy hybrid, with long leaves and bearing large, compact, rounded trusses of large, widely funnel-shaped, wavy-edged flowers which are clear pink, heavily spotted crimson at base within; Mid. (1935). A.M. 1937. F.C.C.T. 1972. H3-4.

RHODODENDRON—*continued*

'Sir John Ramsden'. A large shrub of vigorous, loose habit, a cross between *R. 'Corona'* and either *R. campylocarpum* or *R. wardii*. Lax trusses of up to ten large, widely funnel-shaped, wavy margined flowers, which are carmine, with pale pink margins; Early to Mid. A.M. 1926. A.M.T. 1948. F.C.C.T. 1955. H3-4.

'Snow Queen' (*'Halopeanum'*×*'Loderi'*). A lovely, free-flowering Leonardslee hybrid. A large, compact bush, bearing dome-shaped trusses of large, funnel-shaped flowers which are dark pink in bud, opening to pure white, with a small red basal blotch within; Mid. (1926). A.M. 1934. A.M.T. 1946. F.C.C.T. 1970. H3-4.

'Solent Queen' (Angelo Group). A large Exbury hybrid producing magnificent trusses of large, widely funnel-shaped, fragrant flowers each about 13cm. across; white flushed pink at margins and with a central ray of green; Mid. A.M. 1939. H3.

'Solent Swan' (Angelo Group). A large shrub similar to *'Solent Queen'*, but the flowers are pure white; Mid. (1955). H3.

'Songbird' (*'Blue Tit'*×*russatum*). A charming, small shrub producing clusters of violet, bell-shaped flowers; Early. Raised by Col. Sir James Horlick, at Gigha, Argyllshire, Scotland. (1954). A.M. 1957. H4.

'Songster' (*'Blue Tit'*×*russatum*). A small, compact shrub covered with blue flowers. One of the best of its kind; Early. H4.

Souldis (*discolor*×*souliei*). A beautiful tall hybrid shrub, bearing loose trusses of large, bowl-shaped, blush-pink flowers fading to white, with a small crimson basal blotch; Mid to Late. (1927). H4.

'Southamptonia'. See *'Russellianum'*.

'Souvenir de Dr. S. Endtz' (*'John Walter'*×*'Pin k Pearl'*). A compact bush showing the influence of the former parent in its habit and that of the latter parent in its foliage and flowers. Flowers in a dome-shaped truss, widely funnel-shaped, rich rose in bud, opening to rich, mottled pink, paler in the centre and marked with a ray of crimson, nectaries crimson; Mid. Raised by L. J. Endtz & Co. of Boskoop before 1924. A.M. 1924. A.G.M. 1969. F.C.C.T. 1970. H4.

'Souvenir of Anthony Waterer'. (HH) A tall, upright-growing shrub with large trusses of deep salmon-pink, yellow-blotched flowers; Mid to Late. H4.

'Souvenir of W. C. Slocock'. A hybrid between *R. campylocarpum* and an unnamed hardy hybrid. Vigorous in growth bearing bell-shaped flowers which are a deep apricot-pink in bud, opening to creamy-white or pale yellow, occasionally lightly flushed pink on the outside; Mid. A.M.T. 1935. H4.

Spinulosum (*racemosum*×*spinuliferum*). An erect shrub, bearing compact trusses of narrowly bell-shaped, deep-pink flowers, with protruding anthers; Mid. Raised at Kew. (1926). A.M.(F.) 1944. H4.

'Sunrise' (*griersonianum*×*griffithianum*). A tall, Bodnant hybrid. Flowers in a generous truss, soft vermilion in bud, opening to deep pink and fading until only the margins and the base remain pink; Mid. (1933). F.C.C. 1942. H3.

'Susan' (*campanulatum*×*fortunei*). A tall, bushy hybrid bearing large trusses of bluish-mauve flowers, darker at margins and spotted purple within; Early to Mid. A.M. 1930. A.M.T. 1948. F.C.C. 1954. A.G.M. 1969. H4.

'Sussex Bonfire'. A small shrub up to 1·5m. Flowers deep blood-red, with darker calyces; Early to Mid. Raised at Leonardslee. A.M. 1934. H4.

'Tally Ho' (*eriogynum*×*griersonianum*). A broadly, dome-shaped bush bearing compact, rounded trusses of brilliant scarlet, funnel-shaped flowers; Mid to Late. A superb woodland plant raised by J. J. Crossfield at Embley Park. (1933). F.C.C. 1933. H3.

'Temple Belle' (*orbiculare*×*williamsianum*). A charming shrub of neat, rounded habit, much resembling the former parent. The rounded leaves are attractively glaucous beneath. Flowers in a loose cluster, bell-shaped, of a uniform Persian-rose without markings; Early to Mid. (1916). H3.

'Tensing' (*'Fabia'*×*'Romany Chai'*). A Wisley hybrid bearing large trusses of narrowly bell-shaped, rose-coloured flowers, tinged orange in the throat; Mid. (1953). A.M. 1953. H3.

'Tessa' (*moupinense*×*'Praecox'*). A small bush up to 1m. Flowers in loose flattened umbels, soft, slightly purplish-pink, with a ray of crimson spots, opening in March or early April. (1935). A.M. 1935. A.G.M. 1969. H4.

RHODODENDRON—*continued*

'The Master' (*'China'* × *'Letty Edwards'*). Huge globular trusses of large, funnel-shaped, pink flowers with a dark red basal blotch within; Mid. A.M.T. 1966. H3-4.

'Titness Park' (*barbatum* × *calophytum*). An attractive hybrid with large, globular trusses of bell-shaped, frilly-margined flowers which are pale pink, with a chocolate brown basal blotch within; Early. (1954). A.M. 1954. F.C.C. 1974. H4.

'Topsvoort Pearl'. A sport of *'Pink Pearl'*, resembling it in all but the colour of the flowers which are pale pink, with a red frilly margin; Mid. H4.

'Tortoiseshell Orange' (*'Goldsworth Orange'* × *griersonianum*). A Goldsworth hybrid bearing large, deep orange flowers; Mid to Late. (1945). H3-4.

'Touchstone'. A magnificent hybrid bearing large, loose trusses of very large, bell-shaped flowers, which are a mottled deep pink; Mid. A seedling of *R. griffithianum* raised at Embley Park, Nr. Romsey, Hampshire. (1937). A.M. 1937. F.C.C. 1939. H3.

'Treasure' (*forrestii repens* × *williamsianum*). Dwarf, mound-forming shrub with gnarled branches and neat oval or rounded leaves, bronze when young. Flowers bell-shaped, deep rose, 5cm. across; Early to Mid. H3-4.

'Trewithen Orange' (*concatenans* × *'Full House'*). A remarkable hybrid, bearing loose, pendant trusses of deep orange-brown flowers with a faint rosy blush; Early to Mid. Raised at Trewithen, near St. Austell, Cornwall. F.C.C. 1950. H3 4.

'Unique'. A leafy, dense-habited bush, a hybrid of *R. campylocarpum*. Flowers in a dense, dome-shaped truss, funnel-shaped, creamy white with a faint blush and marked by scattered, faint, crimson spots within. We offer both forms; Early to Mid. A.M.T. 1934. F.C.C.T. 1935. H4.

'Unknown Warrior' (*'Queen Wilhelmina'* × *'Stanley Davies'*). A compact shrub of the same origin as *'Britannia'*. Flowers in a compact truss, widely bell-shaped, crimson-scarlet in bud, opening to deep rose, with a few dark brown markings; Early to Mid. Raised by C. B. van Nes & Sons of Boskoop, before 1922. H4.

Valaspis (*leucaspis* × *valentianum*). A small shrub with densely brown tomentose stems and clusters of widely bell-shaped, bright yellow flowers in March or April. (1935). A.M. 1935. H2-3.

Vanessa (*griersonianum* × *'Soulbut'*). A spreading, rather shapely bush bearing loose trusses of soft pink flowers spotted carmine at the base within; Mid to Late. Raised at Bodnant, this was the first hybrid of *R. griersonianum* to be exhibited at the R.H.S. Cross made in 1924. (1929). F.C.C. 1929. H3-4.

'Pastel'. A lovely clone of spreading habit. Flowers cream, flushed shell-pink, stained scarlet on the outside; Mid to Late. (1946). A.M. 1946. F.C.C.T. and Cory Cup 1971.

'Vanguard' (*griersonianum* × *venator*). A floriferous hybrid of bushy habit, producing flattened trusses of funnel-shaped, crimson scarlet flowers; Mid. (1940). H3.

'Vanity Fair' (*eriogynum* × *'Vanessa'*). A Bodnant hybrid, bearing trusses of funnel-shaped, deep rose flowers with darker speckling within; Mid. (1941). H3.

'Westward Ho' (*discolor* × hardy hybrid). Flowers deep pink, crimson in throat; Mid. (1932). H3-4.

'W.F.H.' (*haematodes* × *'Tally Ho'*). A small, spreading shrub bearing clusters of brilliant scarlet, funnel-shaped flowers; Mid. Named after Mr. W. F. Hamilton, one time Head Gardener at Pylewell Park near Lymington, Hampshire. (1941). H3.

'White Campanula'. A seedling hybrid from *R. campanulatum* with white flowers of good substance and broad, dark green leaves.

'White Glory' (*irroratum* × *'Loderi'*). Loose, globular trusses of fifteen to eighteen large, funnel-shaped flowers, which are cream in bud opening white; Early. A.M. 1937. H3.

'Winsome' (*griersonianum* × *'Humming Bird'*). A lovely Bodnant hybrid, bearing loose, pendant trusses of long, wavy-edged, deep-pink flowers; Mid. Deep coppery young growths. (1939). A.M. 1950. H3-4.

'W. Leith' (*decorum* × *'Loderi'*). A beautiful hybrid of sturdy, erect habit, with large leaves, and bearing upright trusses of large, slightly drooping, greenish-ivory flowers which have a suggestion of pale lemon-yellow; Early to Mid. Raised by and named after the Head Gardener at Clyne Castle, Swansea. (1935). A.M. 1935. H3.

RHODODENDRON—*continued*

'Wonderland' (*'Alice' × auriculatum*). A large bush of vigorous growth and very free-flowering. Flowers in compact trusses, funnel-shaped, with a frilly margin, 9cm. across, creamy-pink in bud, opening to white with yellowish tinge and light spots in throat; Late. (1958). A.M.T. 1958. H3.

'Yellow Hammer' (*flavidum × sulfureum*). A charming, rather slender hybrid raised at Caerhays. Flowers in pairs from terminal and axillary buds, tubular or narrowly bell-shaped, bright yellow; Early. (Before 1931). H3-4.

'Yvonne' (*'Aurora' × griffithianum*). A tall-growing Exbury hybrid with large leaves and loose trusses of large bell-shaped flowers of pale pink with transparent veins, white within; Early to Mid. H3.

‡AZALEODENDRONS

A group of attractive hybrids between deciduous species of the Azalea series and evergreen species of other series. Very hardy, mostly semi-evergreen shrubs of small to medium size, flowering in May or June. H4.

***'Azaleoides'** (*nudiflorum × ponticum*). A dense-habited, slow-growing shrub with slender branches. Leaves oblanceolate, dull, dark green above, pale green or faintly glaucous beneath; flowers in rounded trusses, funnel-shaped, deliciously scented, purplish-lilac in bud, opening white, edged purplish-lilac and faintly spotted within; June. The first recorded rhododendron hybrid, which occurred as an accidental cross in the nursery of a Mr. Thompson, at Mile End, London, about 1820.

'Broughtonii Aureum' (*(maximum × ponticum) × molle*) (*'Norbitonense Broughtonianum'*). A small shrub of rounded habit. Leaves elliptic to oblanceolate, persistent, 7·5 to 10cm. long, dark green above, paler beneath, often bronze-flushed in winter. Flowers in a compact truss, widely funnel-shaped, deep creamy-yellow, with light brown markings, flushed pink in bud; June. Raised in the village of Broughton, Peebleshire, Scotland, about 1830. F.C.C. 1935.

'Dot'. Small to medium-sized shrub. Leaves green, oblanceolate to elliptic-obovate, 6 to 10cm. long. Large clusters of rose-crimson flowers. A.M. 1945.

'Galloper Light'. A most pleasing, leafy bush raised at Exbury, bearing loose trusses of funnel-shaped flowers which are cream in the tube shading to soft salmon-pink in the lobes, with a chrome-yellow blotch (general effect creamy-pink); Late. May to early June. A.M. 1927.

'Gemmiferum'. A small shrub of loose, open habit. Leaves elliptic to obovate, 3 to 5cm. long, leathery, dark green above, paler beneath. Flowers in a compact, rounded truss, funnel-shaped, dark crimson in bud, opening to rose, heavily flushed crimson; late May to early June. Brought into cultivation by T. Methven & Son, of Edinburgh, in 1868. Of similar origin to *'Azaleoides'*.

'Glory of Littleworth'. A superb, small, azalea-like, semi-evergreen shrub of stiff, erect habit. Leaves oblong to oblong-lanceolate, 7·5 to 11cm. long, often curled and undulate. Flowers funnel-shaped, cream at first becoming milk-white with conspicuous coppery blotch, fragrant; May. Raised by H. J. Mangles. A.M. 1911.

'Govenianum'. An erect, densely-branched bush up to 2m. or more in height. Leaves crowded at the tips of the shoots, elliptic to oblanceolate, leathery, 5 to 6cm. long, smooth, dark green and reticulate above, pale green beneath. Buds red in winter. Flowers funnel-shaped, fragrant, delicate lilac-purple, slightly paler on lobes, stained crimson on the ridges outside and faintly green spotted within; June. Brought into cultivation by T. Methven & Son, of Edinburgh, about 1868. Said to be a hybrid rhododendron (*catawbiense × ponticum*) crossed with an unknown azalea.

'Martine' (*racemosum × ?'Hinomayo'*). A small, densely branched shrub of Dutch origin. Leaves elliptic to elliptic-oblong, 1 to 2cm. long, bright glossy green. Flowers funnel-shaped, shell pink, abundantly produced; Mid.

'Nellie' (*occidentale × 'The Monitor'*). A small, azalea-like shrub, resembling the former parent in habit, but much broader in outline. Leaves narrowly elliptic to oblanceolate, dull green above, paler beneath. Flowers in a rounded truss, fragrant, funnel-shaped, pure white with a conspicuous deep yellow blotch; May.

'Norbitonense Aureum'. See *'Smithii Aureum'*.

'Norbitonense Broughtonianum'. See *'Broughtonii Aureum'*.

***'Odoratum'** (*nudiflorum × ponticum*). A small, dense, bushy shrub. Leaves obovate to obovate-elliptic, 5 to 6cm. long, green above, glaucous at first beneath. Flowers blush or pale lilac, fragrant. I. before 1875.

AZALEODENDRON—*continued*

'Smithii Aureum' ((*maximum* × *ponticum*) × *molle*) ('*Norbitonense Aureum*'). A small shrub resembling '*Broughtonii Aureum*', but differs in the leaves which are oblanceolate, 7 to 9cm. long, glaucous beneath, and the paler yellow flowers; late May to early June. The leaves assume a distinctive purplish or plum colour in winter. Raised by W. Smith, at Norbiton, Surrey, about 1930.

'Torlonianum'. An azalea-like shrub to 2m. high. Leaves elliptic, 5 to 10cm. long, dark shining green. Flowers in a neat rounded truss, funnel-shaped, lilac-rose, darker at the margins, with a conspicuous orange blotch; late May to early June.

DECIDUOUS HYBRID AZALEAS

The first deciduous hybrid azaleas began to appear in the early part of the 19th century and today number in hundreds. Their average height varies from 1·5 to 2·5m., but many clones may reach greater heights in moist, woodland gardens. Flowers are normally trumpet-shaped and single, though a number of clones have double flowers. Colours range from the delicate pastel shades of the Occidentale Hybrids to the riotous reds, flames and golds of the Mollis Azaleas and Knap Hill Hybrids. The flowers of such groups as the Ghent Azaleas and the Occidentale Hybrids are deliciously fragrant, particularly in the evening. All are deciduous and many exhibit rich autumn colours.

Ghent Hybrids (Gh)—Known by the collective name *R.* ×*gandavense*. A popular group of azaleas which originated mainly in Belgium, but also in England, between 1830 and 1850. More recently cultivars of this group have been produced in the U.S.A. Among the species involved are *RR. atlanticum, calendulaceum, luteum, nudiflorum, roseum, speciosum* and *arborescens*. They are distinguished by their usually fragrant, long-tubed, honeysuckle-like flowers. In growth they are taller and more twiggy than the Mollis Azaleas, and their flowering season is later, commencing about the end of May. Average height when growing in an open position 1·8 to 2·5m. H4.

Knap Hill Hybrids (Kn)—A large and colourful group of hardy azaleas probably derived from *R. calendulaceum* × *molle*, Ghent Hybrids × *R. molle* as well as *RR. occidentale*, '*Albicans*' and *arborescens*. Originally developed in the Knap Hill Nursery by Anthony Waterer, and more extensively by the late Lionel de Rothschild at Exbury, Hants. (the latter are often referred to as the Exbury Azaleas) they were further developed by Edgar Stead at Christchurch, New Zealand. New cultivars from several sources continue to appear, swelling the ranks of an already formidable assemblage. Members of the group are characterised by their trumpet-shaped, usually scentless flowers in a wide range of colours, opening in May. Average height when growing in an open position 1·8 to 2·5m. H4.

Mollis Azaleas (M)—This attractive group originated as selections of *R. japonicum*, made by L. van Houtte in 1873, and later on by other Belgium nurserymen. At a later date this species was crossed with *R. molle* to produce a range of seedlings with flowers of more intense and diverse colouring. Their large, scentless flowers are borne in handsome trusses usually in early May, before the leaves. Average height when growing in an open position 1·2 to 1·8m. H4.

Occidentale Hybrids (O)—A group of hybrids derived mainly from *R. molle* × *occidentale* (*R.* ×*albicans* WATERER) and *R.* ×*kosteranum* × *occidentale*. All have delicate, pastel coloured, fragrant flowers, opening in late May, usually a fortnight later than the Mollis Azaleas. Average height when growing in an open position 1·8 to 2·5m. H4.

Rustica Hybrids (R) (*rustica 'Flore Pleno'*)—A group of double-flowered hybrid azaleas produced by crossing double-flowered forms of Ghent azaleas with *R. japonicum*. They are compact in habit, with attractive, sweetly-scented flowers, opening in late May and early June. Average height when growing in an open position 1·2 to 1·5m. H4.

'Aida' (R). Deep peach pink with a deeper flush, double. (1888).

'Altaclarense' (M). Orange-yellow with darker flash, flushed pink in bud, fragrant, in a large, globular head. F.C.C. 1862.

'Annabella (Kn). Orange and yellow in bud, opening to golden-yellow, overlaid and flushed orange rose. (1947).

'Avon' (Kn). Pale straw-yellow, with golden yellow flare. (1958). A.M.T. 1958.

'Babeuff' (M). Bright salmon shaded orange. (1918).

'Ballerina' (Kn). White, with orange flash, suffused flesh-pink in bud: large flowers with frilled edges.

'Balzac' (Kn). Nasturtium red with orange flash; fragrant. A.M. 1934.

AZALEA—*continued*

'Basilisk' (Kn). Rich creamy-yellow in bud, opening to cream with bright orange flare. A.M. 1934.

'Beaulieu' (Kn). Deep salmon-pink in bud, opening soft salmon-pink, with deep orange flash; young foliage bronze-red.

'Berryrose' (Kn). Rose-pink with a yellow flash; young foliage coppery. A.M. 1934.

'Brazil' (Kn). Bright tangerine-red, darkening with age; frilly margins. (1934).

'Buzzard' (Kn). Pale straw-yellow, edged and tinted pink, with deep yellow flare. (1947).

'Byron' (R). White with faint pink tinge on outside; double. One of the loveliest of the group. (1888). A.M.T. 1953.

'Cam' (Kn). Deep pink, deepening towards the frilled margins, with golden yellow blotch; semi-double; compact, rounded truss. (1959). A.M.T. 1959.

'Cecile' (Kn). Dark salmon-pink in bud, opening to salmon-pink with yellow flare; large. (1947). A.G.M. 1969.

'Chevalier A. de Reali' (M). Pale yellow, fading quickly to off-white, with orange flare. (1875).

'Christopher Wren' (M) (*'Goldball'*). Orange-yellow flushed flame, with dark orange spotting; flushed red in bud.

'Clarice' (Kn). Pale salmon-pink, with an orange flare; flushed pink outside.

'Coccinea Speciosa' (Gh). Brilliant orange-red. Still one of the best of the old azaleas. (Before 1846). A.G.M. 1969.

'Comte de Gomer' (M). Rose-pink with orange flare. (1872). F.C.C. 1879.

'Comte de Papadopoli' (M). Bright pink, illuminated orange. (1873).

'Corneille' (Gh). Cream, flushed deep pink on outside, pink in bud; double. Especially good autumn leaf colour. A.M.T. 1958. A.G.M. 1969.

'Corringe' (Kn). Flame.

'Daviesii' (Gh). White with yellow flare, fragrant; a hybrid between *R. molle* and *R. viscosum*. (About 1840).

'Devon' (Kn). Orange-red. A.M.T. 1952.

'Directeur Moerlands' (M). (*'Golden Sunlight'*). Golden yellow, deepening in throat, with orange flare; buds Chinese white.

'Dracula' (Kn). An unusual colour; blackish-red in bud opening to a smouldering nasturtium red, overlaid crimson; margins frilled. Young leaves bronze tinted. The buds appear almost black from a distance. Raised in our nurseries. (1970).

'Dr. M. Oosthoek' (M). Deep orange-red. (1920). A.M. 1920. A.M.T. 1940. A.G.M. 1969.

'Dr. Reichenbach' (M). Pale salmon-orange, with orange flare; red flushed in bud. (1892).

'Eisenhower' (Kn). Fiery-red with orange blotch. (1952).

'Embley Crimson' (Kn). Crimson; compact habit. A seedling from Embley Park, Hampshire.

'Evening Glow' (M). Brilliant deep red. (1920).

'Exquisitum' (O). Flesh pink, flushed deep pink on outside, orange flare and frilly margins. Fragrant. (1901). A.M.T. 1950. F.C.C.T. 1968.

'Fanny' (Gh) (*'Pucella'*). Deep rose-magenta, with darker tube and orange flare, becoming rose with age.

'Fawley' (Kn). Flushed pink in bud, opening white flushed pink at margins with orange flare. (1947).

'Fireball' (Kn). Deep orange-red. Young foliage deep copper red. (1951).

'Firefly' (Kn). Rose-red with faint orange flare. (1947).

'Fireglow' (Kn). Orange-vermilion. (1926).

'Floradora' (M). Orange-red, deeply spotted. (1910). A.M. 1910.

'Frans van der Bom' (M). Orange, flushed salmon-pink. (1892).

'Freya' (R). Pale pink tinted orange-salmon; double. (1888). A.M. 1897. A.M.T. 1953.

'Frills' (Kn). Orange-red, semi-double with frilly margins. (1951).

'Frome' (Kn). Saffron yellow, overlaid fiery-red in throat, margins waved and frilled. (1958). A.M.T. 1958.

'Gallipoli' (Kn). Rose-red buds, opening pale tangerine, flushed pink with a warm yellow flare; very large. (1947).

'George Reynolds' (Kn). Deep butter yellow with chrome-yellow and green spotting, pink flushed in bud. A tall clone with large flowers. A.M. 1936.

AZALEA—*continued*

'Gibraltar' (Kn). Large, flame-orange flowers with warm yellow flash and crinkly petals; deep crimson-orange in bud. (1947).

'Ginger' (Kn). Orange-carmine in bud, opening to brilliant orange with warm golden upper petal. (1947).

'Gloria Mundi' (Gh). Bright orange with yellow flare, frilled at the margins. (1846).

'Gog' (Kn). Orange-red with yellow flash, flushed dark red on outside. (1926).

'Goldball'. See *'Christopher Wren'*.

'Gold Dust' (Kn). Pale yellow with gold flare. (1951).

'Golden Girl' (Kn). Yellow, with deeper blotch. (1951).

'Golden Horn' (Kn). Flowers straw-yellow with deep yellow flash tinged rose on the outside, and in bud, fading to ivory. Leaves bronze-tinted, greyish, hoary. (1947).

'Golden Oriole' (Kn). Deep golden-yellow, with orange flare; young leaves bronze tinted. (1939). A.M. 1947.

'Harvest Moon' (Kn). Straw yellow with chrome-yellow flare; slightly scented. (1938). A.M.T. 1953.

'Heron' (Kn). Deep red. (1952).

'Hollandia' (M). Yellow with orange flare. An excellent clone. (1902).

'Homebush' (Kn). Rose madder, with paler shading, semi-double, in tight rounded heads. A most attractive azalea. (1926). A.M.T. 1950. A.G.M. 1969.

'Hortulanus H. Witte' (M). Bright orange-yellow, red tinged in bud. (1892).

'Hotspur' (Kn). Dazzling flame-red with darker markings on upper petals. A.M. 1934.

'Hugh Wormald' (Kn). Deep golden-yellow, with a darker flare.

'Hugo Hardyzer' (M). Bright deep scarlet.

'Hugo Koster' (M). Salmon-orange, flushed red. (1892).

'Il Tasso' (R). Rose-red, tinted salmon; double. (1892).

'Irene Koster' (O). Rose-pink with small yellow blotch; late.

'J. C. van Tol' (M). Clear red; compact and erect in growth.

'Kathleen' (Kn). Salmon-pink with orange blotch, darker in bud. (1947).

'Kestrel' (Kn). Orange-red. (1952).

'Klondyke' (Kn). A wonderful glowing orange-gold, large flowers, tinted red on back and flushed red in bud; young foliage coppery-red. One of the most striking of its group. (1947).

'Knighthood' (Kn). Dusky orange buds, opening to brilliant orange, flushed red. A.M. 1943.

'Koningin Emma'. See *'Queen Emma'*.

'Koster's Brilliant Red' (M). Glowing orange-red. Perhaps the best of its colour. Very close to typical *R. japonicum*. (1918).

'Lemonara' (M). Apricot-yellow, tinged red on outside. (1912).

'Magnificum' (O). Creamy-white, flushed pink, with orange flare; rose flushed in bud. Fragrant. (1910).

'Marconi' (M). Brilliant red with orange flare. (Before 1924).

'Marina' (Kn). White flushed pale yellow, with conspicuous orange flash. (1951).

'Marion Merriman' (Kn). Chrome-yellow with large orange flash, petals with crimpled margins. A.M. 1925. A.M.T. 1950.

'Medway' (Kn). Pale pink with darker edges and orange flash, margins frilled; large (1959). A.M.T. 1959.

'Mrs. A. E. Endtz' (M). Rich deep yellow, flushed orange-red; orange in bud. (1900). A.M. 1900.

'Mrs. Peter Koster' (M). Deep red, with orange glow. A.M.T. 1953.

'Multatuli' (M). Deep glowing orange-red. (1918).

'Nancy Buchanan' (Kn). Pale straw-yellow, flushed pink with orange flare. (1947).

'Nancy Waterer' (Gh). Brilliant golden-yellow; large. (Before 1876). A.G.M. 1969.

'Narcissiflorum' (Gh). Pale yellow, darker in centre and on outside; double; sweetly scented; vigorous, compact habit. (Before 1871). A.M.T. 1954. A.G.M. 1969.

'Norma' (R). Rose-red with salmon glow; double. (1888). A.M. 1891. A.M.T. 1959. A.G.M. 1969.

'Orange Truffles' (Kn). Apricot, illuminated chrome-yellow within, flushed nasturtium-red on the outside, double, with frilly margins, borne in a tight, compact, rounded truss. Young foliage coppery-red. Raised in our Nurseries in 1966.

AZALEA—*continued*

'Orwell' (Kn). Geranium-red. (1962). A.M.T. 1966.
'Pallas' (Gh). Orange-red, with orange-yellow flare. (Before 1875).
'Peregrine' (Kn). Rich orange-red, darker in bud. (1949).
'Persil' (Kn). White, with orange-yellow flare.
'Peter Koster' (M). Orange, with darker blotch. (1895).
'Phidias' (R). Reddish-pink in bud, opening to cream, flushed rose; double. (1888).
'Pucella'. See *'Fanny'*.
'Queen Emma' (M) (*'Koningin Emma'*). Deep orange, with salmon glow.
'Raphael de Smet' (Gh). White, flushed rose, double; excellent autumn colour. (Before 1889). A.M. 1893.
'Royal Lodge' (Kn). Deep vermilion-red, becoming crimson-red with age, long protruding stamens. (1947).
'Salmon Queen' (M). Apricot yellow, edged pink, fading to salmon-pink.
'Sang de Gentbrugge' (Gh). Bright signal-red. (1873).
'Satan' (Kn). Geranium-red, darker in bud. (1926).
'Scarlet Pimpernel' (Kn). Flowers dark red in bud opening to red, with a faint orange flare; young foliage coppery-tinted. (1947).
'Seville' (Kn). Intense orange; late. (1926).
'Silver Slipper' (Kn). White flushed pink, with orange flare; young foliage copper tinted. (1948). A.M.T. 1962. F.C.C.T. 1963.
'Snowdrift' (M). White with deep yellow flash, deepening to orange with age; slender tubed.
'Spek's Orange' (M). Orange, deeper in bud. Late flowering for its group. A.M.T. 1948. F.C.C.T. 1953. A.G.M. 1969.
'Stour' (Kn). Mandarine red, with blotch of tangerine-orange, margins waved. (1958). A.M.T. 1958.
'Strawberry Ice' (Kn). Flesh-pink, mottled deeper pink at margins with a gold flare, deep pink in bud. (1947). A.M.T. 1963. A.G.M. 1969.
'Sunbeam' (M). A form of *'Altaclarense'* with larger flowers which are bright yellow, with an orange blotch. (1895). A.M.T. 1952.
'Superbum' (O). Pink, with apricot blotch, petals fringed. Fragrant. (1901).
'Tamar' (Kn). Chrome-yellow, upper petal saffron yellow tinged Chinese coral, margins waved. (1962).
'Tangiers' (Kn). Tangerine, flushed pink; large with frilly margins.
'Tay' (Kn). Chinese yellow, with orange blotch and crinkled margins. (1959). A.M.T. 1959.
'Thames' (Kn). Neyron rose, with darker veins and apricot blotch, margins frilled. (1958). A.M.T. 1958.
'Toucan' (Kn). Pale straw-yellow, with conspicuous saffron-yellow flare, fading with age; pink tinged margins. (1941).
'Trent' (Kn). Chrome-yellow, tinged salmon at margins, with golden yellow flare; buds pink tinged. (1958). A.M.T. 1958.
'Tunis' (Kn). Deep crimson with orange flare, darker in bud. (1926).
'Unique' (Gh). Vivid orange-red in bud, opening to yellowish-orange, in a dense, ball-like truss. (Before 1875). A.M.T. 1952.
'Von Gneist' (M). (*'Edward Henry'*) Orange-red, with salmon glow.
'Westminster' (O). Clear rich almond-pink, with faint orange flash. Fragrant.
'White Swan' (Kn). White with yellow flare.
'Whitethroat' (Kn). Pure white, double, with frilly margins; compact habit. (1941). A.M.T. 1962.
'Wryneck' (Kn). Straw-yellow, darker at margins deeper yellow flash, darker and pink-tinged in bud.
'Wye' (Kn). Apricot-yellow darker in throat, with orange flare and crinkled margins; pink flushed in bud.

‡*EVERGREEN HYBRID AZALEAS

The hardy evergreen and semi-evergreen species of the *Azalea* series have given rise to a prodigious number of hybrids, many of which have arisen in Europe and the U.S.A. The majority, however, have been received from Japan, from whence E. H. Wilson introduced the beautiful "Kurume" azaleas. In woodland glades, a close planting of dwarf, evergreen Kurume azaleas creates a spectacular effect, like a colourful patchwork quilt.

Evergreen azaleas will thrive in full sun if their roots are kept moist, but some shelter from cold winds is desirable and partial shade should be provided if possible, as in some clones the flowers are liable to bleach. The flowering season is April and May (the majority in May) when their blossom is often produced with such freedom that the foliage is completely hidden. Individual flowers are normally single but certain clones possess "hose-in-hose" flowers (one flower within another). Unless otherwise stated, their average height is ·6 to 1·2m. The date of introduction of a hybrid where known is given in parentheses at the end of each description.

The main groups are as follows:—

Gable Hybrids (G)—A large group of hybrids developed by Joseph B. Gable at Stewartstown, Pennsylvania, U.S.A., and introduced about 1927. Many are the result of *R. kaempferi* × *R. poukhanense* but several other species and named hybrids have been used. Flowers medium-sized—4 to 6cm. across.

Glenn Dale Hybrids (GD)—A large and varied group of hybrids in which innumerable species and hybrids have been used. They have been developed since 1935 by B. Y. Morrison of the United States Department of Agriculture at Glenn Dale, Maryland. Flowers vary from medium to very large—5 to 10cm. across.

Indian or Indica Azaleas (I)—A large group of mainly tender hybrids developed in Belgium and England and to a lesser extent in France and Germany during the 19th century. Several species are involved in their parentage including *R. indicum*, *R. mucronatum* and *R. simsii*. The numerous greenhouse azaleas forced for Christmas and offered by florists belong here. The flowers of this group are large—6 to 7·5cm. across.

Kaempferi Hybrids (Kf)—A large group of hybrids which originated in Holland about 1920. They were produced by crossing *R. kaempferi* with *R. 'Malvaticum'*. At a later date several new clones were raised using *R. pulchrum 'Maxwellii'*. The flowers of this group are usually of medium size—4 to 5cm. across.

Kurume Azaleas (K)—The Kurume azaleas originated in Kurume, Japan, during the last century. That great plant collector, E. H. Wilson, was responsible for their introduction into the West when, in 1920, he introduced his famous "Wilson's Fifty". Since the original introduction, numerous other clones have been raised, particularly in the U.S.A. The main species responsible for the original Kurumes are *RR. kaempferi*, *kiusianum* and *obtusum*. The flowers of this group are characteristically small, being 2·5 to 3·5cm. across.

Oldhamii Hybrids (O)—Hybrids between *R. kaempferi* and *R. oldhamii*, raised by Lionel de Rothschild at Exbury, about 1933. The flowers of this group are normally large, being 6 to 7·5cm. across.

Sander Hybrids (Sr)—Hybrids between Indian Azaleas and Kurume Azaleas. Developed originally in 1890 by Charles Sander of Brookline, Massachusetts. The flowers of this group are medium to large.

Satsuki Hybrids (S)—Introduced by the Chugai Nursery, Kobe, Japan to America during 1938-39. They are mainly the result of *R. indicum* × *R. simsii*, but various Belgian hybrids have also played a part. They are notorious for their tendency to sport and produce flowers of various colours. The flowers of this group are medium to large.

Vuyk Hybrids (V)—A group of hybrids which originated in the Vuyk van Nes Nursery, Boskoop, Holland, in 1921. The flowers of this group are normally large, being 5 to 7·5cm. across.

Wada Hybrids (W)—Hybrids of mixed parentage, raised by K. Wada, of Yokohama, Japan, before 1940. The flowers of this group are medium to large.

'Addy Wery' (K). Deep vermilion-red. (1940). A.M.T. 1950. H4.

'Alice' (Kf). Salmon-red with dark flash. (1922). H4.

'Ambrosia' (GD). Begonia-rose paling to apricot with age. (1948). H4.

'Anny' (Kf). Orange-red. (1922). A.M.T. 1948. H4.

'Appleblossom'. See *'Hoo'*.

'Arendsii' (Kf). Pale purple with flash of reddish spots; low spreading habit. H4.

'Atalanta' (Kf). Soft lilac. H4.

'Aya-kammuri' (K). Rose or salmon-red with white stain. (Wilson 19). H4.

'Azuma-kagami' (K). Phlox pink with darker shading, hose-in-hose. A tall-growing clone—to 1·8m., best in semi-shade. (Wilson 16). A.M.T. 1950. A.G.M. 1969. H3.

AZALEA—*continued*

'Beethoven' (V). Orchid purple, with deeper blotch; petals fringed. (1941). H4.

'Bengal Fire' (O). Fiery orange, ultimately 1·8m. high. (1934). H4.

'Benigiri' (K). Bright crimson. (1910). H4.

'Betty' (Kf). Salmon-pink with deeper centre. (1922). A.M.T. 1940. F.C.C.T. 1972. H4.

'Blaauw's Pink' (K). Salmon-pink with paler shading, early. (1953). H4.

'Black Hawk' (Sr). Very deep scarlet. H4.

'Blue Danube' (V). Bluish violet. A most distinctive and striking colour. A.M.T. 1970. F.C.C.T. 1975.

'Bungo-nishiki' (W). Orange-scarlet, semi-double; late. H4.

'Carmen' (Kf). Pink with reddish throat. (About 1920). H4.

'Challenger' (GD). Orange-red, suffused pale lavender, with conspicuous red blotch. (1947). H4.

'Chanticleer' (GD). Amaranth purple, brilliant in effect, very floriferous. Bushy, dense habit. H4.

'Charlotte' (Kf). Dark orange-red. H4.

'Christmas Cheer'. See '*Ima-shojo*'.

'Darkness' (GD). Brownish-red, with dark carmine blotch. Bushy, compact habit. H4.

'Dauntless' (GD). Aster-purple, base of tube scarlet. Dwarf habit. H4.

'Eddy' (Kf). Deep salmon-red; ultimately 1·5m. high. (1933). A.M. 1944. H3.

'Elizabeth' (GD). Begonia-rose, with darker stain. Spreading habit. H4.

'Esmeralda' (K). Pale pink; hose-in-hose. Dwarf habit. H4.

'Favorite' ('*Hinodegiri*' × *kaempferi*). Deep rosy pink. (1920). H4.

'Fedora' (Kf). Pale pink with darker flash. (1922). A.M. 1931. F.C.C.T. 1960. H4.

'Firefly'. See '*Hexe*'.

'Fudesute-yama' (K). Light poppy red. (Wilson 35). H4.

'Garden Beauty' (Kf). Soft pink with darker flash. (1922). H4.

'Hana-asobi' (K). Bright rose-carmine, with white anthers. (Wilson 50). H4.

'Harbinger' (GD). Rose, with darker blotch. Spreading habit. H4.

'Hatsugiri' (K). Bright crimson purple; dwarf. A.M.T. 1956. F.C.C.T. 1969. H4

'Heiwa' (S) ('*Peace*'). Purple, with deep purple spotting; large. H4.

'Hexe' (I) ('*Firefly*'). Glowing crimson; hose-in-hose. (1885). A.M. 1907. H4. Used in some continental nurseries as an understock.

'Hinodegiri' (K). Bright crimson. A popular clone. (Wilson 42). A.M.T. 1965. A.G.M. 1969. H4.

'Hinode-no-taka' (K). Crimson, with red anthers. (Wilson 48). H4.

'Hinomayo' (K). Clear pink, a most lovely clone up to 1·5m. in height. Obtained by C. B. van Nes & Sons from the Emperor's Garden in Tokyo, Japan, about 1910. A.M. 1921. F.C.C.T. 1945. A.G.M. 1954. H4.

'Hoo' (K) ('*Appleblossom*'). Pale pink with white throat. (Wilson 9). A.M.T. 1950. H4.

'Ima-shojo (K) ('*Christmas Cheer*'). Bright red; hose-in-hose. (Wilson 36). A.M.T. 1959. H4.

'Irohayama' (K). White, margined pale lavender, with faint chestnut-brown eye. (Wilson 8). A.M.T. 1952. H4.

'Izayoi' (W). Large, shell-pink; late; dwarf, spreading habit. (1955). H4.

'Izumigawa' (K). Rose-lilac, paler at base and with small reddish flash; hose-in-hose. (Before 1938). H4.

'Jeanette' (Kf). Phlox pink, with darker blotch. (1920). A.M.T. 1948. H4.

'Johann Sebastian Bach' (V). Cyclamen-purple. H4.

'Johann Strauss' (V). Salmon-pink, with deeper blotch. H4.

'John Bock' (Kf). Magenta mauve. H4.

'John Cairns' (Kf). Dark orange-red. A.M.T. 1940. A.G.M. 1952. H4.

'Kathleen' (Kf). Rosy-red. (1922). A.M.T. 1962. H4.

'Kirin' (K). Deep rose, shaded silvery-rose, hose-in-hose. (Wilson 22). A.M. 1927. A.M.T. 1952. A.G.M. 1969. H4.

'Kirishima Mauve' (K). Mauve. H4.

'Kirishima Pink' (K). Pink. H4.

'Kiritsubo' (K). Rosy-mauve. (Wilson 24). A.M.T. 1974. H4.

'Koningin Wilhelmina' (V). ('*Queen Wilhelmina*'). Vermilion-red; dwarf; best in semi-shade. H4.

AZALEA—*continued*

'Kure-no-yuki' (K) (*'Snowflake'*). White, hose-in-hose. Dwarf habit. (Wilson 2). A.M.T. 1952. A.G.M. 1969. H4.

'Kusudama' (S). Deep purplish-red, with white throat; large. H4.

'Leo' (O). Bright orange; late; dwarf and spreading in habit. (1933). H4.

'Louise'. (Kf). Salmon-scarlet. H4.

'Louise Dowdle' (GD). Brilliant Tyrian-pink with Tyrian-rose blotch; large. A.M.T. 1974. F.C.C.T. 1976. H4.

'Malvaticum'. Mauve with darker streaks and ray of purple speckles, large. A seedling of *'Hinodegiri'* raised by Koster & Co. of Boskoop, about 1910. H4.

'Miyagino' (K). Deep rose-pink, hose-in-hose; low, spreading habit. (1929). H4.

'Mother's Day'. Rose-red. A cross between a Kurume hybrid and an Indian azalea. A.M.T. 1959. A.G.M. 1969. F.C.C.T. 1970. H4.

'Naomi' (Kf). Salmon-pink, very late; ultimately to 1·8m. high. (1933). H4.

'Nora' (Kf). Orange-red. H4.

'Orange Beauty' (*'Hinodegiri* × *kaempferi*). Salmon-orange. (1920). A.M.T. 1945. F.C.C. 1958. A.G.M. 1969. H4.

'Palestrina' (V). White, with faint ray of green; very distinct and attractive. (1926). A.M. 1944. F.C.C. 1967. A.G.M. 1969. H4.

'Polar Sea' (GD). White, with pale green blotch; frilled. H4.

'Prinses Juliana' (V). Light orange-red. H4.

'Purple Queen' (I) (*'Formosa'* × *'Snow'*). Deep fuchsia-purple, hose-in-hose with frilly margins. (1954). H2.

'Purple Triumph' (V). Deep purple. (1951). A.M.T. 1960. H4.

'Queen Wilhelmina'. See *'Koningin Wilhelmina'*.

'Rashomon' (K). Scarlet. (Wilson 37). H4.

'Rosebud' (K). Rose-pink, hose-in-hose; late. Low spreading habit. A.M.T. 1972. H4.

'Sakata Red' (*Kurume Hybrid* × *kaempferi*). Fiery red. A.M.T. 1952. H4.

'Sakata Rose' (*Kurume Hybrid* × *kaempferi*). Rose. H4.

'Salmon Beauty' (K). Salmon-red with ray of darker spots. (1920). H4.

'Satsuki' (I). Pink, with dark blotch. H4.

'Shinnyo-no-hikari' (S). White, with deep reddish-purple spotting; large. H4.

'Shin-seikai' (K). White, hose-in-hose; dwarf habit. (Wilson 3). A.M. 1921. A.M.T. 1952. H4.

'Silver Moon' (GD). White, with pale green blotch, frilled. Broad spreading habit. H4.

'Snow' (K). White, with faint green tinge in throat; single or hose-in-hose. (1920). H4.

'Snowflake'. See *'Kure-no-yuki'*.

'Suga-no-ito' (K). Lavender pink with white throat. (Wilson 31). A.M.T. 1952. H4.

'Surprise' (K). Light orange-red. (1939). H4.

'Takasayo' (K). Cherry-blossom pink, hose-in-hose. (Wilson 11). H4.

'Tanager' (GD). Brilliant red, with dark blotch on upper lobe. H4.

'Tatsumi-no-hikari' (S). White, with pink on purple spots; very large. H4.

'Ukamuse' (K). Pale salmon-rose with darker flash, hose-in-hose. (Wilson 47). A.M.T. 1952. H4.

'Vida Brown' (K). Clear rose-pink, hose-in-hose. A.M.T. 1960. H4.

'Vuyk's Rosy Red' (V). Deep satiny-rose with darker flash. (1954). A.M.T. 1962. H4.

'Vuyk's Scarlet' (V). Bright red with wavy petals. (1954). A.M.T. 1959. F.C.C.T. 1966. A.G.M. 1969. H4.

'Waka-kayede' (K). Red. (Wilson 38). H4.

'Willy' (Kf)· Soft pink. H4.

'Yachiyo' (W). Lavender, hose-in-hose. H3.

'Zampa' (Kf). Orange-red. (1922). H4.

***RHODODENDRON maximum** × **KALMIA latifolia.** An unusual bi-generic hybrid of American origin, slow-growing but probably attaining medium size. Terminal buds concealed by slender pale brown scales. Leaves crowding the stems, dark glossy green above, leathery, lanceolate-oblong to oblanceolate, 7 to 10cm. long, sometimes twisted, the apex either retuse or mucronate, decurrent at base into a long slender petiole. This plant has not yet flowered with us.

‡†***RHODOLEIA—Hamamelidaceae**—A small genus of trees with the general habit of a rhododendron. A warm, sheltered position in woodland conditions is preferred, but only suitable for the mildest areas.

championii HOOK. A beautiful shrub or occasionally a small tree, with large, thick, shining green leaves, glaucous beneath, crowding the tips of the stems. The drooping flower clusters consist of numerous silky-hairy, multi-coloured bracts through which emerge the bright, rose-madder petals and black anthers. These are borne in the axils of the leaves in spring. Only suitable for the very mildest gardens, but a superb conservatory shrub. S. China. First introduced in 1852 and more recently by Kingdon Ward.

RHODORA canadensis. See *RHODODENDRON canadense.*

RHODOSTACHYS bicolor. See *FASCICULARIA bicolor.*

‡***RHODOTHAMNUS—Ericaceae**—A monotypic genus requiring a cool, moist pocket on the rock garden.

chamaecistus REICHENB. A charming, dwarf, evergreen shrublet rarely above 25cm. high. The pale rose, saucer-shaped flowers resemble those of *Rhododendron calostrotum*, and are produced during April and May. In common with others of the family it is not suited to chalky soil in cultivation, though it grows on hard limestone formations in the wild. E. European Alps. I. 1786. A.M. 1925.

RHODOTYPOS—Rosaceae—A monotypic genus most closely related to *Kerria*, differing, among other things, in its opposite leaves and white flowers. All types of soil, in sun or half shade.

scandens MAK. (*kerrioides*). A free-flowering shrub with erect branches to 1·2m. The paper-white flowers, 4 to 5cm. across, appear from May to July like white dog roses and are followed by conspicuous, shining black fruits. China; Korea; Japan. I. 1866.

RHUS—Anacardiaceae—The "Sumachs" are an easily cultivated genus of shrubs and trees, thriving in any fertile soil. The dioecious or monoecious flowers are small and rarely of merit, but in several species are succeeded by fruits which are colourful in the mass. The genus is mainly grown for its often striking foliage and rich autumn colours. The sap of some species is a severe irritant to the skin of those so allergic. The genus includes the "Poison Ivy" of N. America (*Rhus toxicodendron*). Both *R. glabra* and *R. typhina* make handsome foliage plants when pruned to the ground each or every other year in February.

aromatica AIT. (*canadensis*). A small, spreading, downy shrub with coarsely-toothed, trifoliolate leaves, aromatic when bruised. The yellowish flowers, though small, are produced in conspicuous clusters in April. Eastern U.S.A. I. 1759.

chinensis MILL. (*javanica* AUCT.) (*osbeckii*). A small, dioecious, broad-headed tree or large irregular shrub here attaining about 6m. The pinnate, coarsely-toothed leaves colour richly in autumn, and have a peculiarly winged rachis. Flowers yellowish-white, produced in large, terminal panicles in late summer. Late made, unripened growths are often cut back by winter frosts. Manchuria; Japan; China; Korea to Malaysia. I. 1737.

copallina L. A small to medium-sized, downy shrub. The lustrous leaves are pinnate; the usually entire leaflets being attached to a strongly winged rachis. The dense, erect clusters of small, greenish-yellow flowers are of little beauty, but the autumn colour of the foliage is rich red or purple and combines well with the red fruit clusters. Eastern N. America. I. 1688. A.M. 1973.

coriaria L. A small to medium-sized shrub or small tree. Leaves pinnate, with 7 to 21 ovate to oblong, coarsely-toothed leaflets, the rachis winged or partially so. The greenish-white, female flowers are followed by brownish-purple, hispid fruits. This species is extremely rare in cultivation in Britain. The "Sumach" of commerce is obtained from the leaves, and tannin from both leaves and shoots is used in the preparation of morocco leather. It requires a warm, sunny position in a well-drained soil. S. Europe.

cotinoides. See *COTINUS obovatus.*

cotinus. See *COTINUS coggygria.*

glabra L. "Smooth Sumach". A wide-spreading, medium-sized shrub with glabrous, glaucous stems and attractive glabrous, pinnate leaves which are glaucous beneath and usually turn an intense red or orange-yellow in autumn. The erect, scarlet, hairy, plume-like fruit clusters of the female plant are also conspicuous in autumn. Eastern N. America. C. 1620.

RHUS—*continued*

glabra 'Laciniata'. A splendid foliage plant, the fern-like leaves with deeply incised leaflets, turning to orange, yellow and red in autumn. Inclined to revert to the type. F.C.C. 1867.

potaninii MAXIM. (*henryi*). A small, round-headed tree which, planted at the beginning of the century, has reached 20m. on chalk soil in our Winchester nursery. Leaves pinnate, colouring richly in autumn. The greenish-white flowers and red fruits have not yet appeared on our tree. C. and W. China. Discovered by Augustine Henry in 1888 and introduced by E. H. Wilson in 1902. A.M. 1932.

× pulvinata GREENE (*glabra × typhina*) (× *hybrida*). A medium-sized to large shrub with downy stems, intermediate between the parents. Leaves turning to rich scarlet, orange and flame in autumn. Occurs with the parents in the wild. I. 1923.

†succedanea L. "Wax Tree". A small tree with large, pinnate leaves which are a lustrous, dark green above, paler beneath, colouring richly in autumn. Succeeds only in the mildest areas. The fruits of the female tree yield a wax which was once used for making candles in Japan. Formosa; China; Japan; Malaysia; India. I. 1862.

sylvestris SIEB. & ZUCC. A small to medium-sized shrubby tree, with pinnate leaves, giving conspicuous autumn colour. Fruits brownish-yellow. Formosa; China; Korea; Japan. I. 1881.

trichocarpa MIQ. A splendid large shrub or small tree with large, pinnate, downy leaves coppery pink when young, turning deep orange in autumn. Fruits yellow, bristly, borne in drooping clusters on female plants in autumn. Japan; Korea; China. I. 1894. A.M. 1979.

trilobata NUTT. A small shrub occasionally to 2m., closely related to *R. aromatica*, but more erect in growth and leaves with smaller leaflets and an unpleasant scent. Western N. America. I. 1877.

typhina L. "Stag's-horn Sumach". A wide-spreading, sparsely-branched, small tree or an irregular large shrub, developing a gaunt, flat-topped appearance, particularly noticeable in winter. The thick, pithy branches are covered, when young, with a dense coat of reddish-brown hairs. The large, pinnate leaves are downy at first and turn to rich orange, yellow, red or purple in autumn. Large, erect, green clusters of male flowers and smaller, female clusters are borne on separate plants. The dense conical clusters of crimson-hairy fruits are most decorative at the end of the year. Sometimes forming small thickets of suckering stems. Eastern N. America. C. 1629. A.G.M. 1969.

'Laciniata'. A striking, female form with deeply incised leaflets, creating a fern-like effect; orange and yellow autumn colours. A.M. 1910. A.G.M. 1969.

verniciflua STOKES. "Varnish Tree". Medium-sized tree with large, handsome, pinnate leaves; flowers in large, drooping panicles, followed on female trees by yellowish fruits. This is the source of the famous varnish or lacquer of Japan where it is cultivated in the warmer areas. The sap has been known to cause a severe rash when exposed to the skin. Japan; China; Himalaya. C. before 1862. F.C.C. 1862.

RIBES—**Grossulariaceae**—The flowering currants and ornamental gooseberries are a group of evergreen and deciduous, mainly spring-flowering shrubs of easy cultivation in all types of soil. Some are very showy in flower. The majority are extremely hardy. Leaves mostly three or five lobed, rarely of special merit. Straggly or untidy specimens may be hard-pruned immediately after flowering.

alpinum L. A small to medium-sized, semi-erect shrub of neat, densely-twiggy habit suitable for hedging. Flowers greenish-yellow, small, usually dioecious; berries red. Extremely shade tolerant. N. and C. Europe (including British Isles).

'Aureum'. A small shrub usually wider than high with leaves yellow when young. F.C.C. 1881.

'Pumilum'. A very dense, compact, rounded bush slowly reaching up to 1m., wider than high, with small, neat leaves.

ambiguum MAXIM. A small, sparsely-branched shrub with shortly lobed or toothed, orbicular leaves. Flowers greenish, solitary or in pairs in spring. Fruits rounded, green and glandular, hispid. In the wild it is found as an epiphyte on tree trunks and branches in mountain forests, but it is growing quite happily, though slowly, in an open border in our garden. Japan. I. 1915.

RIBES—*continued*

americanum MILL. "American Blackcurrant". A small shrub up to 1·8m., resembling the common blackcurrant in habit, leaf and smell, but differing in its longer, funnel-shaped, rather insipid yellowish flowers. The foliage turns to gorgeous crimson and yellow shades in autumn. Eastern N. America. I. 1729.

'Variegatum'. Leaves mottled pale green and cream.

aureum. See under *R. odoratum.*

× **culverwellii** MACFARL. (*grossularia* × *nigrum*). A small, thornless shrub of spreading habit with leaves and flowers resembling those of the gooseberry. Fruits like small, rounded gooseberries, green becoming dark red. First raised by Mr. Culverwell of Yorkshire, about 1880.

emodense REHD. Small shrub with leaves glandular beneath; flowers greenish, with purplish tinge, berries red or black. Himalaya; C. China. I. 1908.

verruculosum REHD. Differing from the type in its smaller leaves, which are dotted on the petiole and on the veins beneath with small wart-like glands. Berries red. N. China. I. 1921.

fasciculatum SIEB. & ZUCC. A small to medium-sized, dioecious shrub with coarsely-toothed leaves. Flowers fascicled, dioecious, creamy-yellow and fragrant but not showy; female plants bear scarlet berries which persist well into winter. Japan; Korea; China. C. 1884.

chinense MAXIM. A taller, more vigorous variety with larger, longer persistent leaves of a distinctive bright green. N. China to Korea. C. 1867. A.M. 1976.

***gayanum** STEUD. A small suckering, evergreen shrub with soft green velvety leaves. The bell-shaped, pale yellow flowers are honey-scented and densely packed into erect, cylindrical racemes, in early June. Chile. C. 1858.

glutinosum. See *R. sanguineum glutinosum.*

× **gordonianum** BEATON (*odoratum* × *sanguineum*). An extremely hardy, vigorous and rather pleasing shrub, intermediate in habit between its parents. Flowers in drooping racemes, bronze-red on the outside, yellow within. Garden origin 1837.

***henryi** FRANCH. A rare and very worthy, almost prostrate, evergreen shrub with glandular-bristly, young shoots and large, obovate to orbicular, pale green leaves. Flowers in drooping racemes, dioecious, greenish-yellow, produced with the new growths in February and March. It is related to *R. laurifolium,* differing in its dwarfer habit, hairy shoots and broader, thinner-textured leaves. Native of C. China; introduced inadvertently by E. H. Wilson in 1908, with seed of *Sinowilsonia henryi.*

lacustre POIR. "Swamp Currant". A subtly attractive, small shrub with slender, erect stems, which are closely beset with rich brown bristles. Flowers disc-like, small, but numerous, in long drooping racemes; petals pale yellow or white, spotted with red or pink, opening from late May to June or July. Growing in wet situations in its native environs. North America. I. 1812.

***laurifolium** JANCZ. (*vicarii*). An excellent, dwarf, evergreen shrub with large, leathery, narrow-elliptic, glabrous leaves and drooping racemes of dioecious, greenish-white flowers in February and March. Berries red then blackish. An interesting early-flowering shrub for the rock garden. The male form is sometimes referred to as *R. vicarii.* W. China. Discovered and introduced by E. H. Wilson in 1908. A.M. 1912.

menziesii PURSH. A small shrub with erect, bristly and spiny stems to 2m. The small, fuchsia-like flowers appear in pairs in the axils of the leaves in May, petals white, calyx reddish-purple, a delightful contrast; berries reddish, bristly. Western N. America. I. 1830.

odoratum WENDL. (*aureum* HORT. not PURSH.). "Buffalo Currant". A small to medium-sized shrub of loose, erect habit. Leaves glabrous, shining green, colouring richly in autumn. Lax racemes of golden-yellow flowers in April, deliciously clove-scented. Berries black. Long cultivated in gardens as *R. aureum,* which is a rarer, less ornamental species with smaller flowers. Central U.S.A. I. 1812.

roezlii REG. A small, spiny, loosely-branched shrub with pubescent young shoots. Flowers one to three in the leaf axils, petals rosy-white, calyx purplish, pubescent. Berries globular, purple, densely beset with slender bristles. California and S. Oregon (U.S.A.). C. 1899.

RIBES—*continued*

sanguineum PURSH. The popular "Flowering Currant", extensively planted throughout Britain. A medium-sized shrub with a characteristic pungent smell. Flowers deep rose-pink, petals white, produced during April in racemes which are drooping at first, later ascending. Berries black, bloomy. Useful for cutting for the home and easily forced, but tending to pale in colour. Western N. America. First discovered by Archibald Menzies in 1793 and introduced in 1817. The following clones are also available:—

'Albescens'. Flowers whitish, tinged pink.

'Album'. Flowers white.

'Atrorubens' (*'Atrosanguinea'*). Flowers deep blood-crimson.

'Brocklebankii'. A small, slower-growing shrub with attractive golden-yellow leaves and pink flowers. Tends to "burn" in full sun. A.M. 1914. A.G.M. 1973.

'Carneum' (*'Grandiflorum'*). Flowers of a deep flesh-pink.

glutinosum LOUD. (*R. glutinosum*). A Californian variety, differing little from the type, but in cultivation flowering two to three weeks earlier. I. 1832.

'Albidum'. Flowers white, tinged pink, similar in effect to *R. sanguineum 'Albescens'*, but earlier.

'King Edward VII'. Flowers of an intense crimson. Rather lower-growing than the type. A.M. 1904. A.G.M. 1969.

'Lombartsii'. Flowers larger than those of the type, rose-pink with white centre.

'Plenum'. Flowers double.

'Pulborough Scarlet'. A selected clone with deep red flowers the same colour as *Spiraea 'Anthony Waterer'*. A.M. 1959. A.G.M. 1969.

'Splendens'. Flowers rosy-crimson, in larger, longer racemes. A.G.M. 1928.

speciosum PURSH. An attractive medium-sized, semi-evergreen shrub with reddish-bristly stems and fruits and shining green leaves. The beautiful, slender, fuchsia-like, rich-red flowers are borne in pendulous clusters during April and May. In cold areas it is best grown against a sunny wall. California. I. 1828. A.G.M. 1925.

†***viburnifolium** GRAY. A medium-sized, evergreen shrub with long scandent stems. Leaves shining green, emitting a pleasant turpentine-like odour when crushed. Flowers small, terra-cotta red, in short, erect racemes in April; berries red. Requires a warm wall in all but the mildest areas. It is not hardy with us. California. I. 1897.

vicarii. See *R. laurifolium*.

vilmorinii JANCZ. A medium-sized, densely branched shrub of botanical interest, closely related to and resembling *R. alpinum*. The greenish or brown-tinted flowers are dioecious. Berries black. W. China. I. 1902.

‡***RICHEA**—**Epacridaceae**—A small genus of very distinct and subtly attractive evergreen shrubs, natives mainly of Tasmania. The following species require a moist preferably acid soil.

†**dracophylla** R. BR. An erect, small to medium-sized shrub, with long thick, spreading, lanceolate leaves crowded at the ends of the bare stems almost suggesting *Liliaceae*. Flowers in terminal, crowded panicles, white, the branches subtended by brown, rigidly pointed bracts. Tasmania.

scoparia HOOK. f. An unusual, hardy, small spreading shrub, resembling a dwarf, shrubby "Monkey Puzzle". The stems are clothed with stiff, sharply pointed leaves. Flowers pink, produced in erect, terminal, spike-like panicles, 5 to 10cm. long, in May. Tasmania. A.M. 1942.

ROBINIA—**Leguminosae**—A small genus of fast growing trees and shrubs, confined in the wild to the U.S.A. and N. Mexico. They are characterised by their attractive, pinnate leaves, often spiny stems and pendulous racemes of pea-flowers. All are hardy and suitable for any ordinary soil, being especially useful in dry, sunny situations. All species are tolerant of atmospheric pollution. As suckering trees and shrubs they are useful for fixing sand banks and shifting soil.

×**ambigua** POIR. (*pseudoacacia* × *viscosa*). A small tree with slightly viscid, young shoots and racemes of pale pink flowers in June. Garden origin before 1812.

'Bella-rosea'. An elegant form with slightly stickier shoots and rather large, pink flowers.

'Decaisneana' (*pseudoacacia 'Decaisneana'*). A vigorous form of medium-size, producing large racemes of pale pink flowers. F.C.C. 1865. A.G.M. 1969.

ROBINIA—*continued*

boyntonii ASHE. Medium-sized shrub generally with smooth, spineless branches and loose racemes of pink flowers in May and June, pods glandular-bristly. Eastern U.S.A. I. 1914.

elliottii ASHE (*hispida 'Rosea'*). A small to medium-sized shrub. Flowers large, rose-lilac, appearing in May and June; pods bristly. Branches rather brittle. S.E. United States. I. about 1901.

fertilis ASHE. A small to medium-sized, suckering shrub with bristly stems and rosy-pink flowers in June; pods densely bristly. Closely related to *R. hispida*, differing in its smaller flowers and pubescent leaflets. Branches rather brittle. S.E. United States. C. 1900.

'Monument'. A more compact form up to 3m.

hartwigii KOEHNE. A large shrub, the downy shoots are liberally sprinkled with glandular hairs. Flowers varying in colour from pale lilac to soft rose, borne twenty to thirty together in dense racemes during June and July, pods glandular-bristly. S.E. United States. C. 1904.

× **hillieri** HORT. (*kelseyi* × *pseudoacacia*). An elegant, small tree developing a rounded head of branches. Flowers slightly fragrant, lilac-pink in June. An excellent tree for the small garden; raised in our nurseries. A.M. 1962. A.G.M. 1973.

hispida L. "Rose Acacia". A medium-sized, suckering shrub of irregular habit with long, glandular-bristly branches. Short racemes of large, deep rose flowers, 2·5 to 4cm. long, in May and June; pods, when produced, glandular-bristly. An excellent small tree when grafted onto stems of *R. pseudoacacia*, but rather brittle and requires a sheltered position. It may also be grown effectively against a sunny wall. S.E. United States. I. 1743. A.M. 1934.

'Macrophylla'. A less bristly form with larger leaflets and larger flowers, resembling a pink wisteria.

× **holdtii** BEISSN. (*luxurians* × *pseudoacacia*). Resembling the latter parent in habit and vigour and bearing long, loose racemes of pale pink flowers in June or July, followed by attractive red seed pods. Garden origin about 1890.

'Britzensis' A form with nearly white flowers.

kelseyi HUTCHINS. A graceful shrub or small tree with slender branches and elegant foliage, producing its slightly fragrant, lilac-pink flowers in June; pods glandular-bristly. Branches somewhat brittle. S. Allegheny Mts. (U.S.A.). I. 1901. A.M. 1910. F.C.C. 1917.

luxurians SCHNEID. A vigorous large shrub or small tree with spiny stipules, producing short racemes of pale rose flowers in June, frequently again in August; pods bristly. S.E. United States; N. Mexico. I. 1887.

pseudoacacia L. "Common Acacia"; "False Acacia"; "Black Locust". A large, suckering tree, often of picturesque "oriental" appearance. Bark rugged and deeply furrowed, twigs with spiny stipules. Flowers slightly fragrant, white, with a yellow stain at the base of the standard, produced in long racemes in June; pods smooth. A commonly planted tree thriving in any well-drained soil and tolerant of industrial pollution. Its flowers are especially attractive to bees. Native of the eastern United States, introduced to France in 1601 and now widely naturalised both in that country and elsewhere in Europe especially in the vicinity of railways. The following clones are also available:—

'Aurea'. Leaves soft yellow in early summer, becoming green later. F.C.C. 1873. Now superseded by *'Frisia'*.

'Bessoniana'. A small to medium-sized, compact, round-headed tree, usually spineless. Perhaps the best clone for street planting.

'Coluteoides'. Flowers and racemes smaller than those of the type, but abundantly produced.

'Decaisneana'. See *R.* × *ambigua 'Decaisneana'*.

'Erecta' (*'Monophylla Fastigiata'*). A medium-sized tree of narrow, upright habit, leaves with one to three leaflets.

'Fastigiata'. See *'Pyramidalis'*.

'Frisia'. An outstanding, small to medium-sized tree with leaves which are a rich golden-yellow from spring to autumn, creating a brilliant splash of colour in the shrub border or arboretum. It associates particularly well with *Cotinus coggygria 'Royal Purple'*. Raised at the nursery of W. Jansen in Holland, in 1935. A.M. 1964. A.G.M. 1969.

ROBINIA—*continued*

pseudoacacia 'Inermis'. "Mop-head Acacia". A small tree with a compact, rounded head of spineless branches. A commonly planted street tree, but requires protection from strong winds. Flowers are rarely produced. A.G.M. 1969.

'Microphylla' (*'Angustifolia'*). A small to medium-sized, slow-growing tree with dainty, small, fern-like leaves with small leaflets; flowers rarely produced while young.

'Monophylla'. See *'Unifoliola'*.

'Pyramidalis' (*'Fastigiata'*). A slender, columnar tree of medium size, with spineless, closely erect branches.

'Rehderi'. A large bush or small bushy tree with rather erect, spineless branches.

'Rozynskyana'. An elegant and beautiful, large shrub or small spreading tree, the branches drooping at their tips and bearing large, drooping leaves.

'Semperflorens'. Flowers produced intermittently throughout summer.

'Tortuosa'. A picturesque, slow-growing, small to medium-sized tree with somewhat contorted branches.

'Unifoliola' (*'Monophylla'*). A curious form with leaves reduced to a single large leaflet or accompanied by one or two normal-sized leaflets.

viscosa VENT. "Clammy Locust". A small tree, occasionally to 12m., with characteristic viscid young shoots and leaf-stalks. Flowers in short racemes towards the end of June, pale rose, stained yellow on the standard. S.E. United States. I. 1791.

"ROCK ROSE". See *HELIANTHEMUM* and *CISTUS*.

ROMNEYA—Papaveraceae—"Tree Poppy". Two species of sub-shrubby, Californian perennials with glaucous stems and deeply-cut leaves and producing large, white, poppy-like flowers with a central mass of golden-yellow stamens. Sometimes difficult to establish, but once settled they spread quickly by underground stems (rhizomes). Best in a warm, sunny position.

coulteri HARVEY. Small to medium-sized perennial bearing large, solitary, fragrant flowers, 10 to 15cm. across, from July to October. Flower buds smooth, slightly conical and somewhat beaked. I. 1875. F.C.C. 1888. A.G.M. 1929.

× **hybrida 'White Cloud'** (*coulteri* × *trichocalyx*). A strong-growing, large-flowered clone of American origin.

trichocalyx EASTWOOD. Closely resembling *R. coulteri*, but stems more slender, peduncles leafy, buds bristly and rounded, not beaked.

ROSA—Rosaceae—The wild rose species possess a beauty and charm rarely to be found in the vast assemblage of today's popular garden hybrids. Indeed their often graceful elegance, plus their floral and fruiting qualities are a refreshing change from the comparatively vivid blowsiness of many Hybrid Tea and Floribunda roses. Not that the species are without colour. Their flowers vary from the most delicate pastels, to reds and scarlets of exceptional brilliance, and unless otherwise colourful fruits (heps) bring a welcome bonus which sometimes lasts well into winter, brightening the doleful days which follow Christmas. Their leaves are normally pinnate and deciduous and their stems beset with prickles.

They are of the easiest cultivation, thriving in most soils except those which are wet and acid. Most flower better when planted in full sun and the more ornamental species react favourably to an annual or bi-annual manuring.

The species and hybrids here described range in habit from trailing, or low, suckering shrubs (excellent as ground cover) to large shrubs and tall climbers. The more vigorous shrubs are best planted as isolated specimens in lawns or borders, whilst the climbing species are useful for training over fences, pergolas, against walls and into trees.

Pruning. Once established the species require very little pruning, except to remove dead wood or to thin out dense and overcrowded specimens which threaten to destroy their support. This may be carried out immediately after flowering unless fruits are expected, in which case prune in February.

We record our appreciation of the work done in popularising these roses by Mr. Graham Thomas, author of several books on the subject, which we have freely consulted.

We also grow a wide selection of modern and old-fashioned hybrid roses, and for details of these, as well as prices, please see our Rose Catalogue.

ROSA—*continued*

acicularis LINDL. A small, vigorous shrub rarely above 1·3m. high, with densely bristly stems and leaves with five to nine sea-green leaflets. Flowers 5 to 6cm. across, bright rose-pink; fruits 2·5cm. long, pear-shaped, bright rose. N. America; N. Europe; N.E. Asia; Japan. I. 1805.

'Agnes' (*foetida 'Persiana' × rugosa*). An erect shrub of Canadian origin, with arching branches and densely arranged, bright green leaves. The amber tinted, double, butter yellow flowers are deliciously and intriguingly scented. A.M. 1951.

× **alba** L. The "White Rose of York"; "Jacobite Rose". A medium-sized shrub with strong, prickly stems. Leaves with five to seven broad, greyish-green leaflets. Flowers 7·5cm. across, white, usually semi-double, richly scented; fruits oblong, red. The origin of this famous rose is still a source of argument. Its hybrid origin is generally agreed and many authorities now believe its parentage to be a *R. canina* form × *R. damascena*. It is known to have been in cultivation since before 1600 and research by the late Dr. C. C. Hurst confirms the opinions of those who claim that it was grown by the Greeks and Romans. During the Wars of the Roses it was traditionally adopted as an emblem by the Yorkists. It is the type of a group of old hybrids and in one or more of its forms is cultivated in S.E. Europe for Attar of Roses. Please also see our Rose Catalogue under Old Fashioned Roses.

'Albert Edwards' (*hugonis × pimpinellifolia altaica*). A medium-sized shrub, the arching branches wreathed in May with fragrant lemon-yellow flowers 5 to 6cm. across. A choice hybrid raised in our Sarum Road nursery, Winchester in about 1938 and named after our then rose-foreman.

alpina. See *R. pendulina*.

altaica. See *R. pimpinellifolia altaica*.

'Andersonii'. A medium-sized, strong-growing shrub with arching, prickly stems and leaves with usually five long-pointed leaflets, downy beneath. Flowers 5 to 7·5cm. across, rich, clear, rose-pink, scented, freely produced and showy over a long period. Fruits urn-shaped, scarlet, similar to those of the "Dog Rose" (*R. canina*). A hybrid of unknown origin possibly *R. canina* × *R. gallica*. C. 1912.

anemoniflora FORT. (*triphylla*). A rambling or climbing shrub with trifoliolate or five-foliate leaves. Flowers 2·5 to 4cm. across, double and anemone-like, blush-white. Introduced from a garden in Shanghai by Robert Fortune in 1844. It is not known in the wild and is most probably a hybrid of the group *R. banksiae*, *R. laevigata*, *R. multiflora*. It is subject to frost damage and is best grown against a sunny wall.

"Apothecary's Rose". See *R. gallica 'Officinalis'*.

arkansana PORTER. "Arkansas Rose". A small, densely-prickly shrub usually less than 1m. high. Leaves with five to eleven leaflets. Flowers 3 to 4cm. across, pink, followed by small, globular red fruits. Central U.S.A. C. 1917.

'Arthur Hillier' (*macrophylla × moyesii*). A vigorous, large shrub with semi-erect branches. The multitudes of large, rose-crimson flowers in June and July are followed in autumn by conspicuous, bright red, flask-shaped fruits. Occurred in our Sarum Road nursery, Winchester, in about 1938. A.M. 1977.

arvensis HUDS. "Field Rose". A trailing or climbing species forming dense mounds or drapes of slender stems. Leaves with five to seven shining green leaflets persisting late into winter. Flowers 4 to 5cm. across, white, with little or no fragrance, appearing in July; fruits rounded or oval, dark red. A common native species of woodlands and hedgerows. Europe.

'Splendens'. "Myrrh-scented Rose". A charming form, or possibly a hybrid, with long-persisting leaves. The small, double, soft pink flowers are scented of myrrh.

"Austrian Briar". See *R. foetida*.

"Austrian Copper". See *R. foetida 'Bicolor'*.

"Austrian Yellow". See *R. foetida*.

ROSA—*continued*

banksiae AIT. (*banksiae 'Alboplena'*). "Banksian Rose"; "Lady Banks' Rose". A tall-growing, vigorous, semi-evergreen climber reaching 7·5m. or above in a suitable position. The slender shoots are thornless or nearly so and the leaves are composed of three to five leaflets. Flowers 3cm. across, double and rosette-like, white and delicately fragrant of violets, borne in densely-packed umbels during May and June. This beautiful and well-known rose and its several forms do not flower when young. They thrive best on a warm wall in full sun which is needed to ripen growths. Plants grown in cold areas or in shady positions elsewhere are liable to frost damage which reduces, if not prevents flowering. The present form was introduced to Kew from a garden in Canton, China, by William Kerr in 1807 and was named after Lady Banks, wife of Sir Joseph Banks, one of the greatest ever directors of the Royal Botanic Garden, Kew.

'Alboplena'. See *R. banksiae*.

'Lutea'. "Yellow Banksian". Flowers double yellow, rosette-like. A few sensitive noses are reputed to detect in this beautiful rose a delicate fragrance. It was introduced from China via the Calcutta Botanic Garden by J. D. Parks some time before 1824. A.M. 1960.

lutescens VOSS. Flowers single, yellow, sweetly fragrant. I. before 1870.

normalis REGEL. Flowers single, creamy-white, sweetly fragrant. The wild form, said to have been introduced to Megginch Castle, Strathtay, Scotland, by Robert Drummond in 1796. It remained in obscurity until 1909 when E. H. Woodall, who had four years previously obtained cuttings, flowered it in his garden in Nice. Ernest Wilson has described his finding of this plant in C. and W. China, where it is abundant in glens and ravines, forming tangled masses on low trees and scrub.

"Banksian Rose". See *R. banksiae*.

banksiopsis BAK. A vigorous, medium-sized shrub with leaves composed of seven to nine leaflets. Flowers 2·5cm. across, rose-red, borne in corymbs and followed by flask-shaped, orange-red fruits. W. China. I. 1907.

bella REHD. & WILS. An attractive, small to medium-sized shrub with slender-spined stems and leaves with seven to nine, small, glaucescent leaflets. The bright, cherry-red flowers 3 to 4cm. across are slightly fragrant and appear singly or in clusters along the branches in June. Fruits small, orange-scarlet. N. China. I. 1910.

blanda AIT. "Smooth Rose"; "Meadow Rose". A small shrub with nearly thornless stems and leaves with five to seven, pale green leaflets. Flowers 6 to 7·5cm. across, rose-pink. Fruits small, globular or pear-shaped, red. North America. I. 1773.

†*bracteata WENDL. "Macartney Rose". A medium-sized to large evergreen shrub with rambling stems which are thick and stout and clothed with prickles and dense brownish down. Leaves deep green, composed of five to eleven closely set shining leaflets. Flowers 7·5 to 10cm. across, lemon-scented, white, with attractive golden anthers; each head surrounded by conspicuous leaf-like bracts. Fruits globose, orange-red. A most ornamental species, requiring a warm, sunny, sheltered wall. China; Formosa. I. 1793.

brunonii LINDL. (*moschata* HORT.). "Himalayan Musk Rose". A rampant climbing species reaching 9 to 12m. on a building or tree. Leaves limp, composed of five to seven, narrow, sea green leaflets. (Plants found in East Nepal 1972, possess glossy, dark green leaflets). The richly fragrant, white flowers, 2·5 to 5cm. across are carried in tight, downy-stalked corymbs; June and July. This vigorous species thrives best in full sun and a warm climate. Often wrongly grown in cultivation as *R. moschata*. Himalaya. I. 1822.

'La Mortola' (*moschata 'La Mortola'*). A superb hardier selection raised at the celebrated Hanbury garden, La Mortola in Italy. Its leaves are larger and more greyish-downy and the larger pure-white flowers are borne in more ample clusters. Richly fragrant. It requires a sheltered position and full sun to ripen growth.

"Burgundian Rose". See *R. centifolia 'Parvifolia'*.

"Burnet Rose". See *R. pimpinellifolia*.

"Burr Rose". See *R. roxburghii*.

"Cabbage Rose". See *R. centifolia*.

"Cabbage Rose, Crested". See *R. centifolia 'Cristata'*.

ROSA—*continued*

californica CHAM. & SCHLECHT. A medium-sized shrub with stout-prickled stems and leaves composed of five to seven leaflets. Flowers 3cm. across, pink, borne in corymbs. Fruits globose, usually with a prominent neck, red. Western U.S.A. C. 1878. We offer the following clone:—

'Plena'. A most attractive, free-flowering form bearing corymbs of semi-double, rich dark pink flowers fading to rose and purple. A.M. 1958.

'Canary Bird'. A beautiful shrub of medium size with arching stems and fresh-green, small, fern-like leaves. The bright canary-yellow flowers wreath the branches during late May and early June. The parents of this hybrid are almost certainly *R. hugonis* × *R. xanthina.*

canina L. "Dog Rose". A familiar native rose of hedgebanks and downs. A medium-sized to large shrub with strong prickly stems and leaves with five to seven leaflets. Flowers 4 to 5cm. across, white or pink, scented, followed by bright red, egg-shaped fruits. Perhaps the most variable of all roses, countless varieties and subspecies having received names. Europe; W. Asia.

× **cantabrigiensis** S. WEAVER (*hugonis* × *sericea*). A medium-sized shrub with densely bristly, arching stems and fragrant, fern-like leaves composed of seven to eleven leaflets. Flowers 5cm. across, soft yellow, passing to cream. A lovely hybrid raised in the University of Cambridge Botanic Garden. It received the Award of Merit in 1931, in which year it was also awarded the Cory Cup by the R.H.S. as the best intentional hardy hybrid shrub exhibited that year. A.M. 1931. A.G.M. 1969.

carolina L. A small, suckering shrub forming dense thickets of erect stems. Leaves composed of five to seven leaflets. The fragrant, rose-pink flowers 5 to 6cm. across, are produced in clusters from June to August. Fruits orange-shaped, red and glandular hairy. Eastern N. America. C. 1826.

centifolia L. "Cabbage Rose"; "Provence Rose". A small shrub with erect prickly stems and fragrant leaves with five to seven, broadly oval leaflets. Flowers large, double, rose-pink and richly fragrant. *R. centifolia* or a form of it is also known as the "Rose des Peintres" in recognition of its association with the old Dutch painters. The "Cabbage Rose" had long been regarded as the most ancient of roses until the late Dr. C. C. Hurst proved otherwise. It appeared in its present familiar form in the 18th century. Dr. Hurst further proved that it was borne of complex hybrid origin in which the following species played a part, *R. canina*, *R. gallica*, *R. moschata* and *R. phoenicea*. There are many forms of *R. centifolia* and it is a parent of numerous hybrids, for which see our Rose Catalogue under Old Fashioned Roses.

'Cristata'. "Crested Cabbage Rose"; "Crested Moss". A charming form of the "Cabbage Rose" in which the sepals are beautifully crested to such an extent that the flower buds are completely enveloped. Flowers large, rosy-pink. Said to have been found in the crevice of a wall at Fribourg, Switzerland, in 1820.

'Muscosa' (*R. muscosa*). "Moss Rose". A well known rose similar in habit to *R. centifolia*. It differs however in the dense, moss-like, glandular-bristly covering of the stems, branches, petioles, flower-stalks and calyx tubes. This unusual and characteristic clothing is sticky to the touch and gives off a resinous or balsam-like odour when bruised. The clear-pink, globular, double flowers later open flat and are richly scented. See also our Rose Catalogue, under Old Fashioned Roses.

'Parvifolia' (*R. burgundica*). "Burgundian Rose". A slow-growing, small, almost thornless rose of erect habit, its stems densely leafy. The small flat, pompon flowers are deep rose, suffused claret. Cultivated at least since 1764.

'Cherokee Rose'. See *R. laevigata*.

'China Rose'. See *R. chinensis*.

chinensis JACQ. (*indica* LINDL.). "China Rose". A small to medium-sized shrub with stout branches and leaves with three to five shining green leaflets. Flowers 5cm. across, crimson or pink, occasionally white, appearing continuously from June to September. Fruits scarlet, obovoid. This rose more than any other holds claim to being the ancestor of most of our modern garden hybrids. It was first introduced in the late 1700's and early 1800's in several garden forms and not until about 1900 was the wild form discovered in Central China by Dr. Augustine Henry. The form we offer is known as 'Old Blush'. See also our Rose Catalogue under China Roses.

ROSA—*continued*

chinensis 'Minima'. "Fairy Rose". A miniature shrub up to 15cm. high, bearing small leaves and small, single or double, pink or red flowers, 2 to 3cm. across. A variable rose which has given rise to a number of named clones for which see our Rose Catalogue, under Miniature Roses. All are delightful and dainty subjects suitable for growing in pots, troughs or window boxes, as edging to lawns, paths or on rock gardens.

'Mutabilis' (*'Tipo Ideale'*). A vigorous small to medium-sized, few-spined shrub of slender habit, with deep purplish young shoots and coppery young foliage. The slender-pointed, vivid-orange buds open to buff, shaded carmine flowers, changing to rose and finally crimson. They are richly tea-scented and expand to 7·5 to 10cm. An unusual and very versatile rose. A.M. 1957.

'Old Blush' (*R. semperflorens* in part) (*chinensis 'Semperflorens'* in part). The "Monthly Rose" is an old favourite of compact habit and small to medium size. Flowers scented of sweet peas, pink with darker veins, deepening with age. They are produced over a very long period and after a mild autumn may even be present at Christmas.

'Semperflorens'. See *R. chinensis 'Old Blush'*.

'Viridiflora'. The so called "Green Rose". A curious small shrub with double flowers consisting of numerous crowded, greenish, petal-like scales. Said to have been in cultivation as early as 1743.

cinnamomea L. A strong-growing, medium-sized shrub with leaves composed of five to seven, coarsely-toothed leaflets, glaucous beneath. Flowers 5cm. across, deep lilac-pink but variable, spicily fragrant. Fruits small, red. Europe; N. and W. Asia. C. before 1600.

'Complicata'. A lovely, medium-sized shrub which will, if allowed, clamber into small trees, or cover fences and hedges. The multitudes of very large, clear, deep peach-pink, white-eyed flowers are delicately fragrant. A flowering shrub of unsurpassing beauty, a hybrid of *R. gallica*. A.M. 1951. F.C.C. 1958. A.G.M. 1965.

× **coryana** HURST (*macrophylla* × *roxburghii*). A strong-growing, medium-sized shrub resembling more *R. roxburghii* in general appearance. Flowers 5 to 6cm. across, deep pink appearing in June. Raised at the University Botanic Garden, Cambridge in 1926 and named after Mr. Reginald Cory.

corymbifera BORKH. (*dumetorum*). A medium-sized shrub with stout-prickled stems and leaves with five to nine, hairy leaflets. Flowers 4 to 5cm. across, white or pale pink; fruits ovoid, orange-red. Closely related to *R. canina*, but differing mainly in its rather more sea-green, hairy leaves. Europe; W. Asia; N. Africa. C. 1838.

corymbulosa ROLFE. A small shrub with erect or somewhat climbing, almost spineless stems and leaves with three to five downy leaflets, which often turn reddish-purple beneath in autumn. Flowers 4 to 5cm. across, rose-pink with a whitish eye. Fruits globose, coral-red. C. and W. China. I. 1908.

damascena MILL. "Damask Rose". A small shrub with densely thorny stems and greyish-green leaves with five to seven leaflets. Flowers large, usually in corymbs, fragrant, varying in colour from white to red, followed by obovoid, red, bristle-clad fruits. An ancient rose probably of garden origin in Asia Minor, introduced to Europe in the 16th century. Its petals are used in the perfume industry, particularly those of the clone *'Trigintipetala'*, which are used more than any other in the production of "Attar of Roses" in Bulgaria. It is represented in cultivation by numerous named forms and hybrids, for which see our Rose Catalogue, under Old Fashioned Roses.

That distinguished geneticist and rosarian, the late Dr. C. C. Hurst, regarded the Damask Rose as being of hybrid origin. He further regarded it as constituting two distinct groups, i.e. *R. damascena* BLACKW., the "Summer Damask" (*gallica* × *phoenicea*) and *R.* × *bifera* HURST (*damascena semperflorens*), the "Autumn Damask" (*gallica* × *moschata*).

'Trigintipetala'. A form with rather small, loosely double flowers of a soft pink, richly scented. See also description under *R. damascena*.

'Versicolor'. "York and Lancaster Rose". An unusual form with loosely-double flowers which are white, irregularly but lightly flaked pink or blotched rose. Often confused with *R. gallica 'Versicolor'*. Cultivated prior to 1629.

"Damask Rose". See *R. damascena*.

ROSA—*continued*

davidii CREP. A strong-growing, medium-sized shrub of erect, open habit. Leaves composed of seven to nine, conspicuously-veined leaflets. Flowers 4 to 5cm. across, bright rose-pink, carried in large, many-flowered corymbs. The ovoid, scarlet, pendulous fruits have a distinctly long neck. Originally discovered in W. Szechwan, China, by the great French missionary and naturalist Armand David, it was later introduced by E. H. Wilson in 1903. A.M. 1929.

elongata REHD. & WILS. A variety with rather longer leaflets, fewer flowers and larger fruits. W. China. I. 1908.

persetosa. See *R. persetosa.*

"Dog Rose". See *R. canina.*

dumetorum. See *R. corymbifera.*

× **dupontii** DESEGL. (*moschata nivea*). A strong-growing, medium-sized shrub of loose habit, sometimes needing a little support, with leaves composed of three to seven leaflets, downy beneath. Flowers large, fragrant, 7·5cm. across, blush, passing to creamy-white, borne in corymbose clusters in July. A magnificent rose of hybrid origin possibly *R. gallica* crossed with *R. moschata* or one of its old hybrids. C. 1817. A.M. 1954.

'Earldomensis' (*hugonis* × *omeiensis pteracantha*). A quite distinct and pleasing, medium-sized, rather wide-spreading shrub with conspicuously flattened reddish thorns, small fern-like leaves and canary yellow flowers in early June.

ecae AITCH. A small shrub of dainty appearance and comparactively compact, with very prickly, slender, arching, dark chestnut brown branches. The small leaves 2 to 2·5cm. long are composed of five to nine oval leaflets. The small, buttercup-yellow flowers 2·5cm. across are borne all along the branches during late May and June. Fruits small, globular, red. Afghanistan. Introduced by Dr. Aitchison in 1880 and named after his wife, using her initials E.C.A. A.M. 1933.

eglanteria. See *R. foetida* and *R. rubiginosa.*

"Eglantine". See *R. rubiginosa.*

ernestii. See *R. rubus.*

fargesii. See *R. moyesii fargesii.*

farreri STAPF. A charming species up to 2m. high, with spreading branches and dainty fern-like leaves composed of seven to nine leaflets. The pale-pink or white flowers, 2 to 2·5cm. across, in June are followed by bright coral-red ovoid fruits which are effectively set against the purple and crimson autumn foliage. Introduced from Southern Kansu (China) in 1915 by Reginald Farrer, one of the greatest and most descriptive of horticultural writers. We offer the following variety:—

persetosa STAPF. "Threepenny-bit Rose". The form in general cultivation, originally selected from a batch of Farrer's seedlings by that great gardener and plantsman, E. A. Bowles. It differs from the type in its smaller leaves and smaller flowers which are coral red in bud opening soft pink.

fedtschenkoana REGEL. An erect-growing, medium-sized shrub with sea-green leaves composed of five to seven leaflets. The white flowers, 5cm. across, are produced continuously throughout summer. These are replaced by orange-red, bristly, pear-shaped fruits. An interesting and ornamental species with distinctive foliage. Turkestan.

ferruginea. See *R. rubrifolia.*

filipes REHD. & WILS. A strong-growing, rambling or climbing species forming large curtains over suitable support. Leaves with five to seven leaflets. The fragrant, white flowers, 2·5cm. across, are borne in large panicles in late June and July. Fruits globose, red. W. China. Introduced by E. H. Wilson in 1908. We offer the following clone:—

'Kiftsgate'. An extremely vigorous clone with light green foliage, which is richly copper tinted when young. Its panicles may contain as many as a hundred or more sweetly scented flowers, and it is almost as spectacular when bearing its numerous small, red fruits. It should be grown wherever space allows.

ROSA—*continued*

foetida HERRM. (*lutea*) (*eglanteria* MILL. not L.). "Austrian Yellow"; "Austrian Briar". A small shrub with erect, slender, prickly chestnut-brown stems and bright green leaves composed of five to nine leaflets. Flowers rich yellow, 5 to 6cm. across. Plant in full sun and in a well-drained site. Cultivated since the 16th century this species and its forms has figured in the ancestry of many of our modern garden roses. Though naturalised in S. and C. Europe (including Austria), it is a native of S.W. Asia.

'Bicolor'. "Austrian Copper". A remarkably beautiful plant requiring plenty of sun and a good, rich, well-drained soil. The flowers brilliant coppery-red, with brilliant yellow reverse. Very rarely completely yellow flowers are produced on the same bush. Cultivated since at least 1590.

'Persiana'. "Persian Yellow Rose". A beautiful form with golden yellow, double flowers. First introduced to the west in 1838, it has since been used as a parent for innumerable garden hybrids.

foliolosa NUTT. A low-growing, suckering shrub rarely exceeding 1m. in height. Leaves with seven to nine narrow, glossy green leaflets. Flowers fragrant, bright pink, 4 to 5cm. across, appearing usually in late July and continuing often into September. Fruits orange-shaped, red. Often good autumn colour. S.E. United States. C. 1888.

forrestiana BOULENGER. A strong-growing, medium-sized shrub with arching stems up to 2m. Leaves with five to seven oval or rounded leaflets. The rose-crimson, strongly fragrant flowers, 3 to 4cm. across, are borne in clusters surrounded by leafy bracts. These are followed by equally attractive pillar-box red, bottle-shaped fruits, which appear like highly coloured nuts encircled by the persistent green bracts. W. China. I. 1918.

"Fortune's Yellow". See *R.* ×*odorata 'Pseudindica'*.

×**fortuniana** LINDL. A tall-growing climber, reputedly a hybrid between *R. banksiae* and *R. laevigata*. It resembles the former in general appearance, but differs in its larger leaflets and bristly pedicels. The flowers, too, are larger, 6 to 7·5cm. across, double and white. This rose seldom flowers with sufficient freedom to be conspicuous. It requires a south-facing, sunny wall. Introduced from Chinese gardens by Robert Fortune in 1850.

gallica L. (*rubra*). "French Rose". A small, suckering shrub with erect, slender stems densely covered with prickles and bristles, and leaves composed of three to seven leaflets. Flowers deep pink, 5 to 7cm. across, followed by rounded or top-shaped, brick-red fruits. A native of C. and S. Europe, but cultivated in one form or another from time immemorial. It is a parent of countless hybrids and is the probable ancestor of the modern garden rose in Europe. Please see our Rose Catalogue for a selection of clones.

'Officinalis' (*R. officinalis*). The "Apothecary's Rose", also known as the "Red Rose of Lancaster". A small shrub producing richly fragrant, semi-double, rosy-crimson flowers, with prominent yellow anthers. An old rose known in cultivation since at least 1310. Its petals retain their fragrance even when dried and powdered and gave rise to a once important industry in preserves and confections. The centre of this industry was the town of Provins in France where the apothecaries were instrumental in its development. Sometimes referred to as the "Old Red Damask".

'Versicolor'. "Rosa Mundi". An old and well-loved rose which arose as a branch sport of the "Apothecary's Rose". Flowers semi-double, usually rose-red, striped white, and carrying a few entirely red blossoms. Some seasons all the flowers may be of a self red. A.M. 1961. Sometimes confused with *R. damascena 'Versicolor'*, the "York and Lancaster Rose".

gigantea COLLETT (×*odorata gigantea*). A vigorous, tall-growing, semi-evergreen climber. Leaves with five to seven leaflets. Flowers white, 5 to 7·5cm. across, fragrant followed by globose, bright red fruits. S.W. China; Burma. I. 1889. We offer the following clone:—

'Cooperi'. "Cooper's Burmese Rose". A beautiful rose reaching 12m. in a suitable position. The glossy green leaves resemble those of *R. laevigata*. Flowers large, slightly fragrant, pure white, occasionally with a pink stain and with golden anthers. Best grown against a south-facing wall.

giraldii CREP. A strong-growing, medium-sized shrub with leaves composed of seven to nine leaflets. Flowers pink, 1·5 to 2·5cm. across, followed by globular or ovoid, red fruits. N. and C. China. C. 1897.

ROSA—*continued*

glauca. See *R. rubrifolia.*

glaucophylla. See *R. hemisphaerica.*

'Golden Chersonese' (*'Canary Bird'* × *ecae*). A beautiful shrub of medium size, with slender arching stems and delightful, small, frond-like leaves. The deep buttercup-yellow flowers are sweetly scented, wreathing the branches during late May. Raised in 1963 by the distinguished rosarian E. F. Allen who kindly permitted us to be the first distributors under Licence Grant No. 269 (Plant Breeders Rights). It was awarded an A.M. at the Chelsea Show of 1966.

"Green Rose". See *R. chinensis 'Viridiflora'.*

haematodes. See *R. pendulina oxyodon.*

× **hardii** PAXT. (*clinophylla* × *persica*) (× *Hulthemosa hardii*). One of the most remarkable and beautiful of all roses. A small to medium-sized shrub with slender stems and leaves composed of one to seven oblanceolate leaflets. Flowers 5cm. across, yellow, with a red blotch at the base of each petal. Requires a warm, sunny position and perfect drainage;ideal for a sunny, south-facing wall, or sprawling over rock in a scree garden. A difficult plant to establish. Garden origin, Paris in 1836.

'Harrisonii' (*lutea hoggii*). "Harrison's Yellow"; "Hogg's Double Yellow". A small, free-flowering shrub occasionally reaching 2m. A hybrid of *R. pimpinellifolia*, probably with *R. foetida.* It bears brilliant yellow, semi-double flowers which possess a similar odour to those of *R. foetida.* These are followed by small blackish fruits. Raised by George Harison of New York in 1830. A.M. 1949.

'Headleyensis'. A vigorous but graceful, medium-sized shrub, thought to be the hybrid (*R. hugonis* × *pimpinellifolia altaica*). Leaves neat and fern-like. The primrose-yellow, fragrant flowers are carried along the arching branches in May. Garden origin about 1922. Raised by that distinguished botanist and amateur gardener Sir Oscar Warburg.

helenae REHD. & WILS. A vigorous rambling or climbing species reaching 6m. or more in a tree. Leaves with seven to nine leaflets. The creamy-white, fragrant flowers 2 to 4cm. across are borne in dense corymbs in June and are followed in autumn by large, drooping bunches of narrowly ovoid, orange-red fruits. W. and C. China. Introduced by Ernest Wilson in 1907 and named after his wife, Helen.

hemisphaerica HERRM. (*sulphurea*) (*glaucophylla*). The "Sulphur Rose" is a rare, medium-sized shrub of rather loose growth requiring a little support. The leaves are composed of five to nine sea-green leaflets. Flowers double, sulphur-yellow and sweetly scented, 5cm. across. This beautiful rose does best when given a warm, sheltered wall and even then it only flowers well during a warm summer. W. Asia. C. before 1625.

hemsleyana TACKHOLM. A vigorous, medium-sized shrub related to *R. setipoda*, with leaves composed of seven to nine leaflets. Flowers rose-pink, 4 to 5cm. across, in several-flowered corymbs, followed by hispid, bottle-shaped, red fruits. C. China. I. 1904.

× **hibernica** TEMPLETON (*canina* × *pimpinellifolia*). A vigorous, medium-sized shrub producing delightful, clear, bright shell-pink flowers 5cm. across, followed by globose, red fruits. First found near Belfast in 1802.

'Highdownensis'. A medium-sized shrub resembling in general appearance *R. moyesii*, of which it is a seedling. The dainty leaves are somewhat glaucous beneath. Flowers 6cm. across, light velvety crimson, with a ring of pale buff anthers, freely borne on the stout, semi-erect branches. Fruits flagon-shaped, orange-scarlet. Raised by that great amateur gardener the late Sir Frederick Stern at Highdown, nr. Goring, Sussex, before 1925. A.M. 1928.

× **hillieri.** See *R.* × *pruhoniciana 'Hillieri'.*

hispida. See *R. pimpinellifolia hispida.*

horrida FISCH. (*ferox* BIEB.). A dwarf, dense shrub with rigid, prickly stems. Leaves small, composed of five to seven rounded, coarsely-toothed leaflets. The white flowers 2·5 to 4cm. across are followed by globose, red fruits. The curious nature of this species reminds one of a small Gooseberry bush. S.E. Europe; W. Asia. I. 1796.

ROSA—*continued*

hugonis HEMSL. (*xanthina* CREP. not LINDL.). A very graceful shrub up to 2m. The long, arching branches are clothed with neat, fern-like leaves composed of five to eleven fresh green leaflets, often becoming bronze-hued in autumn. By mid-May the branches are wreathed with hundreds of soft yellow flowers, 5cm. across. These are followed by small, rounded, dark red fruits. Deservedly the most popular single yellow rose. It may be used to make a most delightful, informal hedge. C. China. I. 1899. A.M. 1917. A.G.M. 1925.

'Flore Pleno'. Flowers double. Not so graceful a plant as the type.

indica LINDL. See *R. chinensis*.

"Jacobite Rose". See *R.* ×*alba*.

"Lady Banks' Rose". See *R. banksiae*.

"Lady Penzance". See *R.* ×*penzanceana*.

laevigata MICHX. (*sinica* AIT. not L.). "Cherokee Rose". A strong-growing, semi-evergreen rambler or climber with beautiful, dark glossy green leaves composed of three coarsely-toothed, glabrous leaflets. Flowers white, fragrant, 7·5 to 10cm. across, borne singly on bristly stalks during late May and June. Fruits large and bristly. An attractive species with impressive foliage. Requires a warm, sheltered wall. A native of China, but long naturalised in the S. United States from whence the common name arose. A.M. 1954.

'Anemonoides'. A lovely rose, probably a hybrid, producing over several weeks, single, 10cm. wide, silver-pink flowers shaded rose, like a pink 'Mermaid'. Garden origin about 1895. A.M. 1900. Less vigorous than *R. laevigata*, but requiring similar conditions.

latibracteata BOULENGER. A medium-sized shrub which has been confused with *R. multibracteata* from which it differs in its larger, cherry-pink flowers, 4cm. across, carried in many-flowered corymbs. The conspicuous leafy flower bracts are three times the size of those of *R. multibracteata*. The leaves, sepals and thorns are also distinctly larger. W. China. I. 1936.

longicuspis BERTOL. (*lucens*). A remarkable, semi-evergreen rambler or climber of rampant growth. Leaves 12 to 28cm. long, composed of five to nine slender-pointed, glabrous, dark glossy green leaflets. The white, banana-scented flowers, 5cm. across, are borne in large terminal panicles. Fruits ovoid, scarlet or orange-red. A distinguished species with bold foliage and polished, dark reddish-brown shoots and copper tinted young growths. E. Nepal, N.E. India and W. China. C. 1915. A.M. 1964. A.G.M. 1969. Often confused with the closely related and similar *R. sinowilsonii*.

lucens. See *R. longicuspis*.

lucida. See *R. virginiana*.

lutea. See *R. foetida*.

'Lutea Maxima'. See *R. pimpinellifolia 'Lutea'*.

lutescens. See *R. pimpinellifolia hispida*.

"Macartney Rose". See *R. bracteata*.

'Macrantha'. A small, variable, wide-spreading shrub with prickly, arching branches neatly set with conspicuously-veined leaves composed of five to seven leaflets. Flowers large, 7 to 10cm. across, pink in bud opening clear almond pink, changing to almost white, deliciously fragrant and with conspicuous stamens. Fruits rounded, red. A magnificent rose of mound-like habit with loose, often procumbent stems, ideal for clothing banks, covering stumps, etc. A hybrid of uncertain origin.

macrophylla LINDL. A vigorous, distinctive, medium-sized to large shrub with large leaves composed of five to eleven leaflets. Flowers 5 to 7·5cm. across, bright cerise-pink, carried singly or in clusters of two to three. Fruits pear-shaped, glandular-bristly, bright red. Himalaya. I. 1818. A.M. 1897.

'Glaucescens' (FORREST 14958). In this form the flowers are rose-purple and the leaves conspicuously glaucous on both surfaces. The leaflets are more narrowly elliptic than those of '*Rubricaulis*'. The stems are also glaucous.

'Master Hugh'. A superb form collected in the wild by Messrs. Stainton, Sykes and Williams under the number 7822. The deep pink flowers are followed by large orange-red, changing to bright red, fruits, possibly the largest fruited rose in cultivation. When exhibited by that distinguished amateur gardener, Mr. Maurice Mason, it was given an Award of Merit in 1966.

ROSA—*continued*

macrophylla 'Rubricaulis' (FORREST 15309). A name adopted to distinguish a very distinct form which is conspicuous by its red stems overlaid with a plum-like bloom. The peduncles, petioles, bracts and the primary veins are also usually red. The flowers have more lilac-blue in them than those of the type and the plant is noticeably glaucous. It is unfortunate that this distinct form is less hardy than the type.

marginata WALLROTH. A vigorous, erect shrub of medium size with few-prickled stems and leaves composed of five to eleven glandular-toothed leaflets. Flowers 5 to 7·5cm. across, pink changing to white, followed by dark scarlet fruits. W. Asia. C. 1870. A.M. 1964.

× mariae-graebneriae ASCHERS. & GRAEBN. A beautiful, low, spreading shrub reputedly a hybrid between *R. virginiana* and possibly *R. palustris*. Leaves with shining, coarsely-toothed leaflets often colouring well in autumn. Flowers bright rose-pink, 5cm. across, carried often in many-flowered corymbs from June to August. Fruits orange-shaped, red. C. 1880.

'Max Graf' (*rugosa × wichuraiana*). A superb rose with long, trailing stems, excellent as a ground cover for sunny banks. The fragrant, rose-pink, golden-centred flowers, 5cm. across, are borne over a long period. A.M. 1964.

'Mermaid'. A beautiful, free-growing evergreen rose of rambling habit, with long stems and glossy green, ample foliage. Flowers 13 to 15cm. across, sulphur yellow with deep amber stamens, colourful even after the petals have fallen. Seen at its best in warmer, southern areas of the British Isles. A hybrid of *R. bracteata* and like that species best grown on a warm sheltered wall. Raised by Messrs. W. Paul of Waltham Cross. A.M. 1917. A.G.M. 1933.

microphylla ROXB. See *R. roxburghii*.

× micrugosa HENKEL (*roxburghii × rugosa*). Medium-sized shrub of dense bushy habit resembling *R. rugosa* in its foliage. Flowers pale pink followed by bristly, rounded, orange-red fruits. Garden origin before 1905.

mirifica. See *R. stellata mirifica*.

mollis SM. An erect-stemmed, native shrub up to 2m. Leaves composed of five to seven downy leaflets. Flowers rose-red, 4 to 5cm. across, in short clusters, followed by rounded, scarlet, bristle-clad fruits. Europe (including British Isles); Caucasus.

"Monthly Rose". See *R. chinensis 'Old Blush'*.

moschata HERRM. "Musk Rose". A strong-growing rather lax shrub up to 3·5m. Leaves composed of five to seven dark green, polished leaflets. The sweetly musk-scented, creamy-white flowers 5cm. across, are carried in large branching heads during late summer and autumn. A rare species in cultivation, other roses often bearing its name (see *R. brunonii*). It is a parent of many old garden hybrids and in particular that group known as Hybrid Musks. It is notable for its richly fragrant flowers in autumn. Origin uncertain, perhaps W. Asia.

moschata HORT. See *R. brunonii*.

'La Mortola'. See *R. brunonii 'La Mortola'*.

"Moss Rose". See *R. centifolia 'Muscosa'*.

moyesii HEMSL. & WILS. A medium-sized to large, erect-branched shrub of rather loose, open habit with few-prickled stems and leaves with seven to thirteen leaflets. Flowers rich blood-crimson 6 to 7·5cm. across, either one or two terminating each short spur in June and July. They are followed by equally beautiful large, flagon-shaped, bright crimson fruits. One of the most beautiful species in cultivation and a parent of several lovely hybrids. W. China. Introduced by A. E. Pratt in 1894 and again by E. H. Wilson in 1903. A.M. 1908. F.C.C. 1916. A.G.M. 1925.

fargesii ROLFE. Botanically this tetraploid variety has little to separate it from the type, but as a garden plant it is distinct enough. It has all the attractions of the type, and is similar in fruit, but the flowers are of a glowing, vivid colour, perhaps best described as shining carmine. A.M. 1922.

'Geranium'. Slightly more compact in habit than the type and with flowers of a brilliant geranium-red. The fruits too are slightly larger and smoother. Raised at Wisley in 1938. A.M. 1950. A.G.M. 1969.

ROSA—*continued*

multibracteata HEMSL. & WILS. A very graceful shrub of medium size with stout, prickly stems and attractive, fragrant, fern-like leaves composed of seven to nine leaflets. The bright rose-lilac flowers, 2·5 to 4cm. across, are produced intermittently over a long period. The small, rounded, red fruits are covered with glandular bristles. W. China. I. 1908. A.M. 1936.

multiflora THUNB. (*polyantha*). A vigorous, large shrub or rambler with long stems, which will clamber 6m. into trees if suitably placed. Leaves composed of seven to nine leaflets. Flowers fragrant, white, 2 to 3cm. across, abundantly borne in large, conical heads followed by small, pea-like, bright fruits which last into winter. A dense growing species suitable for hedging and covering ugly banks. An ancestor of the Hybrid Polyantha roses. Japan; Korea. I. 1804.

'Carnea'. Flowers double, pink. A sport of var. *cathayensis*.

'Platyphylla'. The "Seven Sisters Rose". Flowers double, cerise-purple at first changing to mauve-pink and fading to white. An old favourite, vigorous and free flowering. Introduced from Japan by Sir Charles Greville about 1816.

"Musk Rose". See *R. moschata*.

"Musk Rose, Himalayan". See *R. brunonii*.

mutabilis. See *R. chinensis 'Mutabilis'*.

"Myrrh-scented Rose". See *R. arvensis 'Splendens'*.

nitida WILLD. A charming dwarf shrub of suckering habit producing numerous, slender, reddish stems which are densely clothed with fine prickles and bristles. Leaves with seven to nine slender, shining green leaflets which turn crimson and purple in autumn. Flowers rose-red, 5cm. across, followed by slightly bristly scarlet fruits. An excellent carpeting shrub with rich autumn colour. Eastern N. America. I. 1807.

nutkana PRESL. A strong-growing, medium-sized shrub, the leaves with five to nine leaflets. Flowers bright pink, 5cm. across, followed by globose red fruits which persist into winter. Western N. America. Introduced about 1876.

× **odorata** SWEET (*chinensis* × *gigantea*). "Tea Rose". A group of old and variable hybrids raised in Chinese gardens. They are best grown against a sunny, sheltered wall where they will reach several metres high. We offer the clone *'Pseudindica'*.

gigantea. See *R. gigantea*.

'Pseudindica'. "Fortune's Double Yellow", also known as "Beauty of Glazenwood" and "Gold of Ophir". An old rose up to 3m. with semi-double flowers which are salmon yellow or coppery-yellow, flushed coppery scarlet, richly scented. Discovered by Robert Fortune in a mandarin's garden at Ningpo in China and introduced by him in 1845.

omeiensis ROLFE (*sericea omeiensis*). "Mount Omei Rose". An extremely variable species, forming a dense shrub of medium size with usually conspicuously bristly and thorny stems and leaves with usually eleven to fifteen leaflets. The normally white, four-petalled flowers 2·5 to 5cm. across, rather resemble a Maltese Cross and are borne all along the branches in May and early June. They are followed by bright, parti-coloured crimson and yellow, edible, pear-shaped fruits which fall during summer. W. China. I. 1901.

'Atrosanguinea'. Fruits deep crimson.

chrysocarpa REHD. (*xanthocarpa*). Fruits yellow.

'Lutea'. An attractive form with yellow flowers and translucent crimson thorns.

polyphylla. A form with more numerous leaflets and smoother, less spiny stems.

pteracantha REHD. & WILS. A distinct variety, its stems furnished with flat, broad-based, translucent crimson thorns which are particularly pleasing when illuminated by the rays of a winter sun. They are particularly conspicuous on young and vigorous, basal shoots and may be thus encouraged by an annual or bi-annual pruning. W. China. I. 1890. A.M. 1976.

oxyodon. See *R. pendulina oxyodon*.

× **paulii** REHD. (*arvensis* × *rugosa*). A low-growing, mound-forming shrub with extremely thorny, procumbent stems reaching 3 to 4m. in length. Leaves and flowers like those of *R. rugosa*, the latter white and slightly clove-scented. A vigorous shrub excellent as ground cover in sun, or for growing beneath taller shrubs. Garden origin before 1903.

ROSA—*continued*

pendulina L. (*alpina*). A small, semi-erect shrub with smooth or few-thorned green or purplish stems and leaves with five to eleven leaflets. Flowers magenta-pink, 4 to 5cm. across, followed by red, flask-shaped fruits. Mts. of C. and S. Europe.

'Morlettii' (*'Flore Pleno'*). Flowers double, magenta, opening flat and revealing petaloid stamens. Young foliage tinted in spring.

oxyodon REHD. (*R. oxyodon*) (*R. haematodes*). Flowers deep pink; fruits dark red, conspicuous during late summer. Caucasus. C. 1896.

× penzanceana REHD. (*foetida 'Bicolor'* × *rubiginosa*) (*'Lady Penzance'*). A medium-sized shrub with arching branches, fragrant leaves and single flowers which are copper tinted, with bright yellow centre. A.M. 1891. See also Lord Penzance's Briars in our Rose Catalogue.

persetosa ROLFE (*davidii persetosa*). An attractive, medium-sized shrub with densely-bristly stems and leaves with five to nine leaflets. Flowers pink, 2 to 3cm. across, borne in corymbs, followed by red fruits. W. China. I. 1895.

persica MICHX. (*berberifolia*) (*Hulthemia persica*). A rare species of dwarf habit with slender, suckering shoots and simple, greyish-green, downy leaves. The solitary flowers, 2·5cm. across, are brilliant yellow, each petal with a scarlet blotch at its base. The small, globose green fruits are clothed with minute prickles. A difficult plant to establish. It requires perfect drainage and a dry, sunny position. Persia; Afghanistan. C. 1790.

pimpinellifolia L. (*spinosissima*). "Scotch Rose"; "Burnet Rose". A small, native, suckering shrub producing dense, low thickets of slender, erect stems thickly beset with bristles and tiny prickles. Leaves composed of five to nine deep green and glabrous leaflets. The small, white or pale pink flowers, 4 to 5cm. across, are borne in profusion during May and June, followed by rounded, shining black or maroon-black fruits. A common native shrub of coastal sand dunes. Europe; N. Asia. This species has given rise to many forms and hybrids.

altaica REHD. (*R. altaica*). A stronger growing variety up to 2m. high and more across. The large, creamy-white flowers, 5 to 6cm. across, crowd the branches and are replaced by shining maroon-black fruits. An excellent free-flowering rose which, because of its dense, suckering habit makes a useful hedge. Altai Mts. (Siberia). I. about 1820. A.G.M. 1925.

'Canary'. A small, compact shrub intermediate in habit between *altaica* and *'Lutea'*, with comparatively large, single, yellow flowers, intermediate in shade of colour.

Double Pink.

Double Red. See under *'William III'*.

Double White.

Double Yellow. See under *'Williams' Double Yellow'*.

Single Red.

'Glory of Edzell'. A very beautiful, early-flowering shrub reaching 2m. in height. The clear pink, lemon-centred flowers garland the slender branches in May. Possibly of hybrid origin.

hispida KOEHNE (*R. lutescens*). An unusual variety with densely bristly stems up to 1·5m. Flowers creamy-yellow 5 to 6cm. across. Siberia. Introduced before 1781.

'Lutea' (*'Lutea Maxima'*). One of the best single yellow roses. A small shrub with few scattered thorns and bright green foliage, amongst which the buttercup yellow flowers, 5cm. across, nestle. Probably a hybrid between *R. pimpinellifolia* and *R. foetida*.

'William III'. A dwarf, suckering shrub of dense, bushy habit with short branches and greyish-green leaves. Flowers semi-double, magenta-crimson changing to rich plum colour, paler on the reverse. Fruits black. Previously catalogued as *'Double Red'*.

'Williams' Double Yellow'. Rather taller in habit than the type, bearing fragrant double yellow flowers with a central cluster of green carpels. Previously catalogued as *'Double Yellow'*.

pisocarpa GRAY. A dense-growing, medium-sized shrub with leaves composed of five to seven coarsely-toothed leaflets. Flowers fragrant, lilac-pink, 2·5 to 3cm. across, borne in corymbose clusters from June to August. Fruits rounded, to ellipsoid, red. Western N. America. I. about 1882.

ROSA—*continued*

×**polliniana** SPRENGEL (*arvensis*×*gallica*). A rambling shrub forming a low mound up to 1m. high and 3m. across, clambering into trees and shrubs if allowed. Flowers slightly fragrant, 6 to 7·5cm. across, rose-pink in bud, opening blush, with yellow anthers. C. 1820.

polyantha. See *R. multiflora*.

'Polyantha Grandiflora' (*gentiliana*). A climbing or rambling rose reaching 6m. on a suitable support. Leaves glossy, deep green. Flowers strongly fragrant, creamy-white, with orange-yellow stamens, followed by oval, orange-red fruits lasting well into winter. A fine free-flowering rose of uncertain origin. Probably a hybrid of *R. multiflora*. F.C.C. 1888. A.G.M. 1969.

pomifera. See *R. villosa*.

"Prairie Rose". See *R. setigera*.

prattii HEMSL. An exceedingly attractive shrub of medium size with dainty foliage and clusters of deep rose flowers, 2·5 to 3cm. across, in July. The crimson, bottle-shaped fruits are very ornamental. W. China. C. 1908.

primula BOULENGER. A beautiful, medium-sized shrub with arching stems and leaves composed of seven to thirteen dark glossy leaves which emit a strong incense-like odour when crushed. Flowers fragrant, 4cm. across, primrose-yellow passing to white, opening in mid-May. Fruits globose, red. Turkestan to N. China. I. 1910. A.M. 1962.

"Provence Rose". See *R. centifolia*.

×**pruhoniciana** SCHNEID. A strong-growing shrub up to 3m. A seedling of *R. moyesii*, the result of a cross with either *R. multibracteata* or *R. willmottiae*. We offer the following clone:—

'Hillieri' (*R.* ×*hillieri*). A very beautiful rose, raised in our nurseries in about 1924. It resembles *R. willmottiae* in its elegant habit, whilst its flowers recall those of *R. moyesii*, but of a darker shade of crimson. It is perhaps the darkest coloured of all single roses.

"Ramanas Rose". See *R. rugosa*.

"Red Rose of Lancaster". See *R. gallica 'Officinalis'*.

×**reversa** WALDST. & KIT. (*pendulina*×*pimpinellifolia*)) (*rubella*). A small, suckering shrub resembling the "Burnet Rose" in general appearance. The small, semi-double, carmine flowers, white at base, are followed by scarlet fruits. C. 1820.

"Rosa Mundi". See *R. gallica 'Versicolor'*.

'Rose d'Amour' (*virginiana 'Plena'*). "St. Mark's Rose". A medium-sized shrub with almost thornless stems up to 2m. and leaves with five to seven leaflets. Flowers double, fragrant, deep pink, with paler outer petals, continuing over several weeks from mid to late summer. A vigorous, free-flowering rose, a hybrid between *R. virginiana* and another species, possibly *R. carolina*. Garden origin before 1820. F.C.C. 1980.

"Rose des Peintres". See under *R. centifolia*.

roxburghii TRATT. (*microphylla* ROXB.). "Burr Rose"; "Chestnut Rose". A very distinct, viciously-armed shrub of medium size. Leaves composed of nine to fifteen neatly-paired leaflets. Flowers fragrant, 6 to 7·5cm. across, shell-pink, with prickly receptacles, calyces and pedicels, followed by orange-yellow, tomato-shaped fruits covered with stiff prickles. The twisted, spreading, grey to cinnamon-coloured stems with their flaky bark give a gnarled effect to this interesting rose. We grow the wild form *normalis* REHD. & WILS., with single flowers, introduced from China in 1908. The double-flowered form was introduced sometime before 1814.

rubella. See *R.* ×*reversa*.

rubiginosa L. (*eglanteria* L. not MILL.). "Sweet Briar"; "Eglantine". A strong-growing, medium-sized shrub with stout, erect, densely prickly and glandular stems. The deliciously aromatic leaves are composed of five to seven rounded leaflets and the clear pink, fragrant, beautifully formed flowers, 3 to 4cm. across, stud the arching branches during summer. Fruits bright red, oval, lasting well into winter. A lovely native species famed for its fragrance both of flower and foliage. It makes a pleasant if vigorous hedge. Europe. It is a parent of innumerable hybrids and has given rise to several hundred forms, few of which are now in cultivation. Please see our Rose Catalogue under Lord Penzance's Briars. A.M. 1975.

rubra. See *R. gallica*.

ROSA—*continued*

rubrifolia VILL. (*glauca*) (*ferruginea*). A most useful and ornamental species, forming a medium-sized shrub with reddish-violet, almost thornless stems. The great attraction of this rose is its foliage, which is a glaucous-purple in a sunny position and greyish-green, with a mauve tinge when in shade. Flowers clear pink, 2·5 to 5cm. across, followed by ovoid, red fruits. Invaluable for coloured foliage schemes. Mts. of C. and S. Europe. C. before 1830. A.M. 1949. A.G.M. 1969.

rubus LEV. & VANIOT (*ernestii*). A strong-growing, vigorous rambler with good foliage. The long stems possess large prickles and the leaves are composed of usually five leaflets. Flowers fragrant, 3cm. across, pinkish in bud, opening creamy-white with orange anthers, borne in dense corymbs and replaced by dark scarlet, oval fruits. Related to *R. helenae*, but even more vigorous, reaching 9m. in a suitable position. C. and W. China. I. 1907.

rugosa THUNB. "Ramanas Rose". A strong-growing, perpetual-flowering shrub with stout, densely prickly and bristly stems, 1·5 to 2m. high. Leaves up to 18cm. long, composed of five to nine oblong, conspicuously veined, rugose leaflets, downy beneath. Flowers fragrant, 8 to 9cm. across, purplish-rose, followed by bright red, tomato-shaped fruits, 2·5cm. across. A well-known rose, parent of innumerable hybrids, for which see our Rose Catalogue. Its vigorous, suckering habit enables it to form dense thickets and is an excellent hedge plant. In Japan it grows on sandy sea shores and is occasionally found naturalised in similar situations in the British Isles. N.E. Asia. I. 1796. A.M. 1896.

'Alba'. Flowers white, blush tinted in bud. Very vigorous. Exceptional in fruit.

'Blanc Double de Coubert'. Flowers semi-double, white, blush-tinted in bud. Garden origin in 1892. A.M. 1895. A.G.M. 1969.

'Frau Dagmar Hastrop'. A compact shrub up to 1·8m. with lush dark green foliage and flowers of a pale rose-pink, with cream-coloured stamens. Large crops of rich crimson fruits. Makes an excellent hedge. Garden origin 1914. A.M. 1958. A.G.M. 1969.

'Roseraie de l'Hay'. The long, pointed buds are dark purplish-red opening to a rich crimson-purple with cream stamens, expanding 10 to 12cm. across, double. A superb rose of vigorous growth and an excellent hedge. Garden origin in 1901. A.G.M. 1969.

'Rubra'. Flowers wine-crimson, fragrant. Fruits large and conspicuous. A.M. 1955.

'Scabrosa'. A vigorous form with excellent foliage. The enormous violaceous-crimson flowers are up to 14cm. across. Fruits large, like small tomatoes, with persistent sepals. A.M. 1964.

"Sacramento Rose". See *R. stellata mirifica.*

"Scotch Rose". See *R. pimpinellifolia.*

semperflorens. See *R. chinensis 'Old Blush'.*

serafinii VIV. A dwarf shrub, occasionally up to 1m. with densely prickly stems and leaves composed of five to seven rounded, glandular and aromatic leaflets. The small, bright pink flowers are followed by small, bright red, rounded fruits. Mediterranean Region; S.E. Europe. C. 1914.

sericea LINDL. A medium-sized shrub closely related to *R. omeiensis* but rather more erect in growth. Leaves with seven to eleven small, rounded leaflets. Flowers 2·5 to 5cm. across in May, normally white, cup-shaped with four or five overlapping petals. Our stock grown originally from wild-collected seed has lemon-yellow flowers. Fruits small, red, falling early. Himalaya. I. 1822.
omeiensis. See *R. omeiensis.*

setigera MICHX. "Prairie Rose". A small, wide-spreading shrub with long trailing stems and trifoliolate leaves, the leaflets deep green, coarsely-toothed and 5 to 7·5cm. long. Flowers 5cm. across, rose-pink, fading to blush, fragrant, appearing in July and August. Fruits small, globose, red. Useful as a ground cover or for training over bushes and low walls. E. United States. I. 1800.

ROSA—*continued*

setipoda HEMSL. & WILS. A free-growing, medium-sized shrub with stout, erect, few-thorned stems. Leaves composed of seven to nine leaflets which are glandular beneath and possess a delightful sweet-briar-like fragrance when crushed. The clear pink, beautifully-formed flowers 5 to 6cm. across are borne on contrasting purplish pedicels all along the branches and are followed by large flagon-shaped, crimson, glandular-bristly fruits. W. China. I. 1895.

"Seven Sisters Rose". See *R. multiflora 'Platyphylla'*.

'Silver Moon'. A vigorous, rambling rose up to 9m., with glossy, dark green leaves and large creamy-white, richly scented flowers which are butter-yellow in bud. Usually regarded as *R. laevigata* × *R. wichuraiana*, but the "Magnolia Rose" (*R. 'Devoniensis'*) may have also played a part.

sinica AIT. See *R. laevigata*.

sinowilsonii HEMSL. A magnificent climbing species, related to *R. longicuspis*. Its shining, reddish-brown stems are clothed with attractive leaves composed of usually seven, long-pointed, corrugated leaflets which are deep glossy green above, purple-flushed beneath. The white flowers, 5cm. across, are borne in panicles during summer. Superb foliage plant requiring a warm sunny wall in a sheltered garden. Introduced by E. H. Wilson from West China in 1904. The name refers to the collector's nickname "Chinese Wilson".

soulieana CREP. A large shrub with long scandent, pale-spiny stems, forming great mounds. Leaves grey-green, with seven to nine leaflets. Flowers 2·5 to 4cm. across, creamy yellow in bud, opening white, borne on well established, mature plants in large corymbs followed by small, ovoid, orange-red fruits. A strong-growing species requiring plenty of space in which to develop. It looks well covering an old decrepid tree. W. China. I. 1896.

spinosissima. See *R. pimpinellifolia*.

× **spinulifolia** DEMATRA. A hybrid between *R. pendulina* and probably *R. tomentosa*. A small shrub of stiff habit with leaves which are glaucous at first becoming green. Flowers fragrant, 4 to 5cm. across, bright cherry pink, followed by bright red, bottle-shaped fruits.

stellata WOOT. A dwarf shrub with wiry, greyish-green stems forming dense, low thickets. Leaves trifoliolate, with wedge-shaped, coarsely-toothed leaflets. Flowers 5 to 6cm. across, deep pink, with yellow anthers. Fruits small, dull red. Mts. of S.W. Mexico. I. 1902. We offer the following variety:—

mirifica COCKERELL. "Sacramento Rose". A rare shrub, slightly more robust than the type. It also differs in its hairless stems clothed with ivory-coloured prickles and its generally glabrous leaves with three to five, or occasionally seven leaflets. Flowers rose-purple, paling with age, followed by red, top-shaped fruits. It requires a warm sunny position in a well-drained soil. N. Mexico. I. 1916. A.M. 1924.

stylosa DESV. A medium-sized, native shrub with long, arching stems and leaves with five to seven leaflets. Flowers 3 to 5cm. across, pale pink to white followed by ovoid, red fruits. Europe.

"Sweet Briar". See *R. rubiginosa*.

sweginzowii KOEHNE. A strong-growing shrub 3 to 4m. high with strongly thorny stems and leaves with seven to eleven leaflets, in general appearance very like *R. moyesii*. The bright rose pink flowers, 4cm. across, are carried often in clusters on glandular, bristly stalks and are followed by flagon-shaped, bright red, hispid fruits. The latter are about equal in size and colour to those of *R. moyesii*, but ripen earlier. N.W. China. I. 1909. A.M. 1922.

"Tea Rose". See *R.* × *odorata*.

"Threepenny Bit Rose". See *R. farreri persetosa*.

triphylla. See *R. anemoniflora*.

villosa L. (*pomifera*). "Apple Rose". A vigorous, medium-sized shrub with leaves composed of five to seven bluish-green, downy leaflets, fragrant when crushed. Flowers 5cm. across, carmine in bud, opening clear pink followed in early autumn by large, apple-shaped, bristle-clad, crimson fruits. C. and S. Europe; W. Asia. I. 1771. A.M. 1955.

'Duplex'. "Wolley-Dod's Rose". Flowers semi-double, clear pink, fruits dark red. An attractive rose, probably of hybrid origin. Raised in the garden of the Rev. Wolley-Dod. A.M. 1954.

SHRUB ROSES as ground cover

STACHYURUS praecox

SORBARIA arborea

RUBUS Tridel 'Benenden'

SALIX daphnoides

SAMBUCUS racemosa 'Plumosa Aurea'

SORBUS × kewensis

SYCOPSIS sinensis

SORBUS 'Joseph Rock'

ROSA—*continued*

virginiana MILL. (*lucida* EHRH.). A small, suckering shrub forming thickets of slender, erect stems. Leaves composed of seven to nine glossy-green leaflets which turn first to purple then to orange-red, crimson and yellow in autumn. Flowers 5 to 6cm. across, bright pink, deeper in bud, appearing continuously from June or July into August. Fruits small, orange-shaped, bright glistening red. A most attractive species, excellent in sandy soils, particularly by the sea. Eastern N. America. I. before 1807. A.M. 1953. A.G.M. 1969.

'Plena'. See *R. 'Rose d'Amour'*.

wardii MULLIGAN. The type of this rare Tibetan species is thought not to be in cultivation and is represented by the following form:—

'Culta'. A lax-growing shrub up to 2m. with arching branches and leaves similar to those of *R. moyesii*. Flowers also similar to those of the latter, but petals creamy-white, with a mahogany-red disc surrounded by yellow stamens. C. 1924.

webbiana ROYLE. A graceful and slender shrub up to 2m., with arching branches and leaves composed of seven to nine small, rounded leaflets. The clear, almond-pink flowers, 4 to 5cm. across, are carried along the stems creating a charming effect in June. They are followed in late summer by bottle-shaped, shining sealing-wax-red fruits. W. Himalaya. I. 1879. A.M. 1955. A.G.M. 1969.

'Wedding Day'. A vigorous climbing or rambling shrub with red-thorned, green stems reaching 10m. in a suitable tree. Leaves rich green and glossy. Flowers richly scented, in large trusses, deep yellow in bud, opening creamy-white with vivid orange-yellow stamens, fading to pink. Raised before 1950 by the late Sir Frederick Stern at Highdown, Sussex, by selfing a hybrid from the cross *R. sinowilsonii* × *R. moyesii*. A.M. 1950.

"White Rose of York". See *R.* ×*alba*.

wichuraiana CREP. A vigorous, semi-evergreen species with trailing stems up to 6m. long. Leaves small, dark shining green, composed of seven to nine leaflets. Flowers 4 to 5cm. across, white, richly scented, borne in small, conical clusters during late summer, followed by tiny, globose, red fruits. An excellent ground cover, the stems rooting as they grow. Also suitable for clothing tree-stumps and unsightly objects. A parent of numerous hybrids including *'Alberic Barbier'*, *'Albertine'* and *'Dorothy Perkins'*. E. Asia. Introduced from Japan in 1891. A.G.M. 1973. We offer the following:—

'Grandiflora'. A splendid form with larger flowers.

willmottiae HEMSL. An elegant shrub of medium size, with gracefully arching branches and small, sea-green, fern-like leaves composed of seven to nine leaflets, pleasantly fragrant when crushed. Flowers 3 to 4cm. across, lilac-pink, with cream-coloured anthers. Fruits pear-shaped, orange-red. One of the loveliest species, when in flower. Introduced from the Tibetan border region of W. China by E. H. Wilson in 1904, and named after that great gardener and rosarian, Miss Ellen Willmott. A.M. 1958.

'Wisley'. Flowers of a deeper shade of lilac-pink.

× **wintonensis** HILLIER (*moyesii* × *setipoda*). A beautiful hybrid raised in our nurseries in 1928. In general appearance it shows a leaning towards *R. setipoda*, which is apparent in the sweet-brier-like fragrance of the foliage. Flowers rich rose-pink, several in a cluster, with long leafy sepals and very glandular-hairy receptacles.

"Wolley-Dod's Rose". See *R. villosa 'Duplex'*.

woodsii LINDL. A very variable shrub up to 2m., the leaves with five to seven leaflets. Flowers 3 to 4cm. across, lilac-pink, followed by red, globose fruits. C. and W. North America. I. 1815.

fendleri REHD. The most beautiful form of this species and a truly first-class garden shrub. It forms a densely leafy bush to about 1·5m. high and carries bright lilac-pink flowers, followed by conspicuous sealing-wax-red fruits which persist long into winter. Western N. America. C. 1888.

xanthina LINDL. (*xanthina 'Flore Pleno'*). A beautiful, medium-sized shrub with gracefully arching branches and small, dainty, fern-like leaves composed of seven to thirteen rounded leaflets. Flowers semi-double, 4cm. across, golden yellow. A garden form, said to have been cultivated in N. China and Korea for over 100 years. Reintroduced to the Arnold Arboretum in 1907 by that indefatigable collector, Frederick N. Meyer. A.M. 1945.

ROSA—*continued*

xanthina spontanea REHD. The wild form, reaching 3m. in time, the branches clothed with pale sea-green foliage and bedecked in May and early June with single, comparatively large yellow flowers, followed by dark red fruits. A parent of '*Canary Bird*'. N. China; Korea. I. 1907. A.M. 1945. A.G.M. 1969.

xanthocarpa. See *R. omeiensis chrysocarpa.*

"York and Lancaster Rose". See *R. damascena* '*Versicolor*'.

"ROSE OF SHARON". See *HYPERICUM calycinum.*

"ROSEMARY". See *ROSMARINUS.*

***ROSMARINUS—Labiatae**—"Rosemary". A small genus of evergreen, aromatic shrubs, with romantic associations, long cultivated in Western European gardens, thriving in all types of well-drained soil in full sun.

†lavandulaceus TURRILL (*officinalis prostratus* HORT.). A low-growing species forming large, dense, prostrate mats, studded with clusters of blue flowers in May and June. Ideal for draping sunny wall-tops, but somewhat tender.

officinalis L. "Common Rosemary". A dense shrub up to 2m., and as much through, the stems thickly clothed with linear, green or greyish-green leaves, white beneath. Flowers blue, produced in numerous axillary clusters along the branches of the previous year in May. Makes an attractive, informal hedge which may be lightly pruned if necessary, immediately after flowering. S. Europe; Asia Minor. Cultivated in Britain for over four hundred years. The following clones are also available:—

'Albus'. Flowers white.

†'Benenden Blue'. A smaller-growing, distinct form with very narrow, dark green leaves and bright blue flowers. A selected clone of var. *angustifolius.* A.M. 1933.

'Fastigiatus'. Sometimes referred to as "Miss Jessop's Variety". A strong-growing form of erect habit. '*Pyramidalis*' is very similar.

'Majorca'. A lovely clone, with flowers of Bluebird blue, with a dark spot on the lower petals. A.M. 1961.

'Miss Jessop's Variety'. See '*Fastigiatus*'.

prostratus. See *R. lavandulaceus.*

'Pyramidalis'. See under '*Fastigiatus*'.

'Roseus'. A small shrub with lilac-pink flowers.

'Severn Sea'. A dwarf shrub with arching branches and brilliant blue flowers. Raised by that dedicated gardener Norman Hadden, at West Porlock, Somerset.

†'Tuscan Blue'. A small shrub with broader leaves and brighter-coloured flowers than the type.

"ROWAN". See *SORBUS aucuparia.*

RUBUS—Rosaceae—The ornamental brambles are a varied throng, many species thriving in the poorest of soils and other adverse conditions. Several species have attractive flowers and foliage, whilst others have striking white stems in winter, and all have prickles unless otherwise stated. Those grown for their ornamental stems should have the old flowering stems cut down to ground level each year, immediately after flowering. See also under Climbers.

amabilis FOCKE. A small shrub of graceful habit, usually less than 1·2m. Leaves pinnate, with seven to nine, deeply-toothed leaflets, borne along the slender, fairly erect stems. Flowers solitary, 4 to 5cm. across, white, in June and July. Fruits large, red, edible but sparingly produced. W. China. I. 1908.

***australis** FORST. An evergreen climber with long, wiry, prickle-clad stems. Leaves with three to five leaflets, variable in shape and size. Flowers small, dioecious, white, in long panicles, only produced on adult plants. Juvenile plants creep along the ground, forming dense hummocks. Requires a well-drained, sheltered position. New Zealand.

biflorus BUCH.-HAM. A vigorous, medium-sized shrub, the semi-erect, prickly stems are green, but covered with a vivid white, waxy bloom. Leaves composed of five, occasionally three, leaflets, white felted beneath. The small white flowers are produced in small terminal clusters and are followed by edible yellow fruits. Himalaya. I. 1818.

caesius L. "Dewberry". A native species of little ornamental merit, with long, slender, creeping stems, forming extensive carpets. Leaves usually trifoliolate. Flowers small, white, followed by bloomy-black fruits. Europe to N. Asia.

RUBUS—*continued*

***calycinoides** HAY. (*fockeanus* HORT.). A creeping alpine evergreen, forming dense mats of short-jointed, rooting stems. The small, three to five-lobed, mallow-like leaves are glossy green and bullate above, grey-felted beneath. The white flowers are borne singly or in short clusters in summer, but are usually concealed beneath the leaves. A most useful ground cover for the rock garden, scree or peat wall, even in shade. Formosa. The Chinese *R. fockeanus* is very similar.

cissoides pauperatus. See *R. squarrosus.*

cockburnianus HEMSL. (*giraldianus*). A strong-growing species of medium size, the purple arching stems overlaid with a vivid white bloom. The attractively pinnate, fern-like leaves are composed of seven to nine leaflets, white or grey beneath. Flowers small, rose-purple, of little merit, borne in dense terminal panicles and followed by bloomy-black fruits. N. and C. China. I. 1907.

deliciosus TORR. A medium-sized, thornless shrub, the arching branches with peeling bark. Leaves three to five-lobed. Flowers like white dog-roses, 5cm. across, borne in May and June. Fruits purplish but seldom maturing. A delightful flowering shrub and for this purpose, one of the best in the genus. Native of the Rocky Mountains, Colorado (U.S.A.). I. 1870. F.C.C. 1881. A.G.M. 1946.

fockeanus HORT. See *R. calycinoides.*

×**fraseri** REHD. (*odoratus*×*parviflorus*). A vigorous, small, suckering shrub with palmate leaves and comparatively large, fragrant, rose-coloured flowers from June to August. Particularly useful for covering shady areas beneath trees. Garden origin in 1918.

fruticosus L. "Bramble"; "Blackberry". A common and familiar scrambling native which may be found growing in just about every type of soil and situation. It is immensely variable and in the British Isles alone several hundred species or microspecies are recognised. Only a few are of any ornamental merit, for which see *R. laciniatus* and *R. ulmifolius* '*Bellidiflorus*'.

laciniatus. See *R. laciniatus.*

giraldianus. See *R. cockburnianus.*

illecebrosus FOCKE. "Strawberry-Raspberry". A dwarf sub-shrub with a creeping, woody rootstock. Stems erect, bearing pinnate leaves and solitary or terminal clusters of white flowers 2·5 to 4cm. across, in July. Fruits large, red, sweet, but rather insipid. Japan. C. 1895.

laciniatus WILLD. (*fruticosus laciniatus*). "Fern-leaved" or "Cut-leaved Bramble". This bramble is not known in a wild state and yet it breeds true from seed. It is a vigorous species with long scrambling, prickly stems. The leaves are composed of usually five pinnately-lobed leaflets, the lobes incisely toothed, creating an attractive fern-like effect. The rather insignificant flowers are replaced by prolific, sweet, black fruits. Origin before 1770. There is also a similar form with thornless stems.

leucodermis TORR. & GR. A species of medium size with both erect and spreading, glaucous blue stems. Leaves with three to five coarsely-toothed leaflets, white felted beneath. Flowers small, white, borne in terminal clusters in June; fruits purplish-black, edible. Western N. America. Introduced by David Douglas about 1829.

†**lineatus** REINW. In our area a semi-evergreen shrub with rambling, silky-hairy stems, usually less than 1·2m. Leaves unique and beautiful, with five leaflets (compound palmate), dark green above, covered with a shining, silvery, silky down beneath, conspicuously veined. Prickles few or absent. Flowers white in small axillary clusters. Fruits small, red or yellow. Requires a warm sheltered position. E. Himalaya; W. China; Malaya. I. 1905.

linkianus SER. (*thyrsoideus* '*Plenus*'). A robust, medium-sized shrub with long, scrambling stems. Leaves with five leaflets. Flowers double, white, in large, erect, conical panicles in July and August. A conspicuous shrub for the wild garden, also useful in semi-shade. C. before 1770.

mesogaeus FOCKE. A strong-growing shrub producing erect, velvety stems up to 3m. high. Leaves trifoliolate, with large, coarsely-toothed leaflets, grey-tomentose beneath. Flowers small, pinkish-white in June. Fruits black. C. and W. China. I. 1907.

RUBUS—*continued*

microphyllus 'Variegatus'. A small, suckering shrub producing dense mounds of slender, prickly, glaucescent stems. Leaves 4 to 7·5cm. long, prettily three-lobed, green, mottled cream and pink. The type is a native of Japan.

× **nobilis** REG. (*idaeus* × *odoratus*). A small, thornless shrub with erect, peeling stems and large, downy, trifoliolate leaves. Flowers purple-red, in terminal clusters in June and July. A vigorous hybrid with the same potential as *R. odoratus*. C. 1855.

***nutans** WALL. A dwarf evergreen creeping shrub with densely soft-bristly stems and short-stalked, trifoliolate leaves. The attractive, nodding white flowers 2·5 to 4cm. across, are borne on erect, leafy shoots in June, followed by purple edible fruits. A charming carpeting shrub for a shady border or bank. Himalaya. I. 1850.

odoratus L. A vigorous, suckering shrub with erect, peeling thornless stems up to 2·5m. high. Young shoots densely glandular hairy. Leaves large and velvety, palmate. Flowers in branched clusters, 4 to 5cm. across, fragrant, purplish-rose, opening from June to September. Fruits flat and broad, red, edible. An excellent shrub for the wild garden or semi-shade beneath trees. Eastern N. America. I. 1770.

'Albus'. A form with white flowers.

parviflorus NUTT. (*nutkanus*). A strong-growing, suckering shrub with erect, peeling, thornless stems, 1·8 to 2·5m. high. Leaves large, palmate, softly downy. Flowers white, 4 to 5cm. across, in terminal clusters in May and June. Fruits large and flattened, red. Western N. America. I. 1927.

†***parvus** BUCH. A low-growing shrub with long, creeping or semi-climbing stems. Leaves narrow and prickly-toothed, dark or bronze green above, paler beneath. Flowers dioecious, solitary or in small panicles, white, in May and June. Fruits red. Related to *R. australis*, forming attractive ground cover in sheltered places. New Zealand.

phoenicolasius MAXIM. "Wineberry". A conspicuous shrub with reddish, glandular-bristly stems 2·5 to 3m. high. Leaves large, trifoliolate, the leaflets coarsely-toothed, white-felted beneath. Flowers in July, in terminal glandular bristly clusters, small, pale pink. Fruits bright orange-red, sweet and edible. Japan; China; Korea. I. about 1876. F.C.C. 1894.

spectabilis PURSH. A vigorous, suckering shrub, producing erect, finely-prickly stems, 1·2 to 1·8m. high. Leaves trifoliolate. Flowers solitary or in small clusters, 2·5 to 4cm. across, bright magenta-rose, fragrant, in April. Fruits large, ovoid, orange-yellow, edible. Excellent in the wild garden or as ground cover beneath trees. Western N. America. Introduced by David Douglas in 1827.

†**squarrosus** FRITSCH (*cissoides pauperatus*). A curious species, forming a dense, tangled mass of dark, slender stems, bearing numerous, scattered, tiny, ivory-white prickles. Leaves variably shaped, sparse, usually thread-like. Flowers in racemes or panicles, small, yellowish. Fruits seldom seen in this country, orange-red. Normally found in cultivation as a congested mound or scrambling over neighbouring shrubs, but in its native habitat it develops into a tall climber. New Zealand.

thibetanus FRANCH. (*veitchii*). An attractive species with semi-erect, purplish-brown stems covered with a blue-white bloom 1·8 to 2m. high. Leaves pinnate, fern-like, with seven to thirteen, coarsely-toothed leaflets, which are greyish silky hairy above, white or grey felted beneath. Flowers small, purple; fruits black or red. W. China. I. 1904. A.M. 1915.

***tricolor** FOCKE (*polytrichus*). An attractive evergreen ground cover with long trailing, densely bristly stems. Leaves cordate, 7·5 to 10cm. long, dark glossy green above, white-felted beneath. Flowers white, 2·5cm. across, produced singly in the leaf axils in July, sometimes followed by large, bright red, edible fruits. An excellent ground cover in shady places, forming extensive carpets even under beech trees. W. China. First discovered by the Abbé Delavay; introduced by E. H. Wilson in 1908.

RUBUS—*continued*

Tridel (*deliciosus* × *trilobus*). A beautiful hybrid, raised by Capt. Collingwood Ingram, in 1950. A vigorous shrub producing erect, peeling, thornless shoots up to 3m. high. Leaves three to five lobed. Flowers 5cm. across, glistening white, with a central boss of golden-yellow stamens, produced singly all along the arching branches in May. We offer the clone:—

'Benenden'. A.M. 1958. A.G.M. 1962. F.C.C. 1963.

trilobus TORR. A lovely medium-sized shrub with strong, spreading, thornless stems. Leaves resembling those of *R. deliciosus*, but larger and cordate-ovate. Flowers 5cm. across, pure white, with yellow stamens, borne intermittently along the arching stems from May to July. Mexico. I. 1938. A.M. 1947.

ulmifolius SCHOTT. A vigorous shrub with long, scrambling, rambling, plum-coloured stems and leaves with three to five leaflets which are white felted beneath. A common native bramble of which the following is the only form in general cultivation:—

'Bellidiflorus'. Large panicles of showy, double pink flowers in July and August. Too vigorous for all but the wild garden.

"RUE". See *RUTA graveolens.*

***RUSCUS—Liliaceae**—A small genus of evergreen sub-shrubs spreading by underground stems. The apparent leaves are really flattened stems (cladodes), which carry out the functions of the true leaves, these being reduced to tiny, papery scales. The flowers are minute and are borne, during spring, on the surface of the cladodes, male and female on separate plants. Useful plants for dry shady places in all types of soil, the females bearing attractive fruits.

aculeatus L. "Butcher's Broom". A small, erect, native shrub forming thick clumps of green, thick but flexible stems ·5 to 1m. high. Cladodes small, spine-tipped, densely borne on the branches in the upper parts of the stems. Berries resembling bright, sealing-wax-red cherries, sometimes abundantly produced when plants of both sexes are present. Tolerant of dense shade, where few other plants will grow. S. Europe (including Southern England).

hypoglossum L. A dwarf shrub forming broad clumps of green "leafy" stems. The comparatively large, leaf-like cladodes carry a tiny, green flower on their upper surface and on female plants large, red, cherry-like fruits. Excellent ground cover in shade. S. Europe. C. since 16th century.

× **microglossus** BERTOLONI (*hypoglossum* × *hypophyllum*). An interesting hybrid forming extensive suckering patches of erect or ascending stems up to 60cm. high. Cladodes elliptic to obovate, petioled and slender-pointed, smaller and more elegantly posed than those of *R. hypoglossum*. The flower bracts are also much smaller and scale-like. Italy and adjacent parts of France and Jugoslavia. The plants in general cultivation are male and probably belong to a single clone.

racemosus. See *DANAE racemosa.*

RUTA—Rutaceae—A large genus of aromatic shrubs and perennial herbs, thriving in a sunny, well-drained position in almost any soil.

***graveolens** L. "Rue". A small, evergreen shrub up to 1m. with glaucous, much divided, fern-like leaves and terminal corymbs of small, mustard yellow flowers from June to August. A popular "herb", long cultivated for its medicinal properties. S. Europe. Cultivated in England since about 1652, perhaps earlier.

'Jackman's Blue'. A striking form with vivid, glaucous-blue foliage and compact, bushy habit. A.G.M. 1969.

'Variegata'. Leaves variegated creamy-white.

"ST. JOHN'S WORT". See *HYPERICUM.*

SALIX—Salicaceae—The willows are a numerous and diverse genus, varying from tiny, creeping alpines from high northern altitudes, to large, noble lowland trees scattered throughout the temperate regions of the world. All may be grown in ordinary loamy soils and many flourish in damp situations. Only a few are happy on chalky uplands, but almost all except the alpine species are at home in water meadows, chalky or otherwise. Few waterside trees are as beautiful as the weeping willows, despite the attentions of various diseases. Several willows, including *SS. alba 'Chermesina', alba 'Vitellina', daphnoides* and *irrorata* have attractive young stems in winter and to encourage the production of these it is necessary to hard prune each or alternate years in March. The

SALIX—*continued*

willows with coloured stems if planted with silver birches, white-washed brambles, red and yellow-stemmed dogwoods, the snake-barked maples and the mahogany-barked *Prunus serrula*, create an effective winter garden. A number of creeping species and their hybrids are excellent as ground-cover, hiding large, bare or unsightly areas with their dense, leafy stems.

The flowers of the willow are normally dioecious, male and female catkins being borne on separate plants. They generally appear in late winter or early spring, before or with the young leaves. The catkins of *S. bockii* are unusual in appearing in autumn. In the majority of species the male catkins are the more showy.

acutifolia WILLD. (*daphnoides acutifolia*) (*pruinosa*). A very graceful, large shrub, occasionally a small tree, with lanceolate, long pointed leaves and slender, damson-coloured shoots overlaid with a white bloom. Catkins appearing before the leaves. Closely related to *S. daphnoides* from which it differs in its more slender, darker twigs, smaller, narrower catkins and narrower, longer-tapered and more numerously-veined leaves. Russia to E. Asia. C. 1809.

'Blue Streak'. A male clone of Dutch origin, with polished, blackish-purple stems covered with a vivid blue-white bloom.

'Pendulifolia'. A beautiful, male form with conspicuously drooping leaves.

adenophylla HOOK. "Furry Willow". A loosely branched, large shrub or small tree, with densely grey-downy twigs, clothed with ovate, finely-toothed, silky-hairy leaves up to 5cm. long. Catkins before the leaves in early spring. N.E. North America. C. 1900.

aegyptiaca L. (*medemii*) (*muscina* HORT.). A large shrub or occasionally a small tree, with densely, grey-pubescent twigs. Leaves lanceolate, grey pubescent beneath. Its large conspicuous bright yellow male catkins occur in February and March, making this a very beautiful early spring-flowering tree. S. Russia; Mts. of Asia. C. 1820. A.M. 1925 (as *S. medemii*). A.M. 1957 (as *S. aegyptiaca*). A.G.M. 1969.

'Aglaia'. See *S. daphnoides 'Aglaia'*.

alba L. "White Willow". A familiar native species of water meadows and riversides. A large, elegant tree of conical habit, with slender branches, drooping at the tips. The lanceolate, silky-hairy leaves occur in great, billowy masses, creating a characteristic silvery appearance from a distance. The slender catkins appear with the young leaves in spring. A vigorous, fast-growing tree, much planted in moist, sandy areas by the sea. Europe; N. Asia; N. Africa.

'Argentea'. See *'Sericea'*.

'Aurea'. A less vigorous tree with yellowish-green branches and pale yellow leaves.

'Britzensis'. See *'Chermesina'*.

'Caerulea'. See *S. 'Caerulea'*.

'Chermesina' (*'Britzensis'*). "Scarlet Willow". A remarkable form, most conspicuous in winter when the branches are brilliant orange-scarlet, especially if pruned severely every second year. The clone *'Chrysostella'* is similar, if not identical. A.M. 1976.

'Chrysostella'. See under *'Chermesina'*.

'Sericea' (*'Argentea'*) (*'Regalis'*). A smaller, less vigorous, rounder-headed tree with leaves of an intense silvery hue, striking when seen from a distance. A.G.M. 1969.

'Tristis'. See *S.* ×*chrysocoma*.

'Vitellina' (*S. vitellina*). "Golden Willow". A smaller tree than the type. The brilliant yoke-of-egg yellow shoots are made more conspicuous by severe pruning every second year. Male. A.M.T. 1967. A.G.M. 1969.

'Vitellina Pendula'. See *S.* ×*chrysocoma*.

amygdalina. See *S. triandra*.

apoda TRAUTV. A dwarf species with prostrate stems closely hugging the ground and glossy green leaves paler beneath. The erect, silvery-furry, male catkins appear all along the branches in early spring, before the leaves and gradually elongate until 2·5 to 3cm. long, when they are decked in bright, yellow anthers. A superb plant for the rock garden or scree. Both *S. retusa* and *S. uva-ursi* are occasionally wrongly grown under this name. Caucasus. C. before 1939. A.M. 1948. A.G.M. 1969 (male form).

SALIX—*continued*

arbuscula L. (*formosa*). A dwarf, creeping shrub forming close mats of green leaves, glaucous beneath. Catkins long and slender, produced with the young leaves in spring. Scandinavia; N. Russia; Scotland.

'Erecta'. A female clone with erect stems up to 1m.

arbutifolia. See *CHOSENIA arbutifolia.*

atrocinerea. See *S. cinerea oleifolia.*

aurita L. "Eared Willow". A small to medium-sized, native shrub with small, wrinkled, dull green leaves, grey-woolly beneath. Catkins produced before the leaves in early April. A common willow of bogs and streamsides on acid soils. Europe; N. Asia.

babylonica L. "Weeping Willow". An attractive tree of medium size with a wide-spreading head of long, pendulous, glabrous, brown branches. Leaves long and narrow, green above, bluish-grey beneath; catkins slender, appearing with the young leaves in spring. A native of China, but long cultivated in E. Europe, N. Africa and W. Asia. Said to have been first introduced to W. Europe during the late 17th century and into England about 1730. Most of the trees cultivated in this country are said to be female. At one time widely cultivated as a water-side tree, it has now largely been superseded by *S.* ×*chrysocoma*, and other similar hybrids.

'Annularis' (*'Crispa'*) A curious form in which the leaves are spirally curled.

'Ramulis Aureis'. See *S.* ×*chrysocoma.*

×**balfourii** LINTON (*caprea*×*lanata*). A splendid, strong-growing, medium-sized to large bush, intermediate in character between the parents. Young leaves grey-woolly becoming green and downy later in the year. Catkins appearing before the leaves in early April, yellowish and silky-hairy, with tiny red bracts. A remarkable and useful shrub, especially for damp sites. Said to have originated in Scotland. Ours is a male clone.

'Basfordiana' (*fragilis 'Basfordiana'*) (Rubens Group). A medium-sized to large tree with long narrow leaves and conspicuous, orange-red twigs in winter. A male clone with long, slender, yellow catkins appearing with the leaves in spring. Said to have been found originally in the Ardennes, about 1863, by Mr. Scaling, a nurseryman of Basford, Nottinghamshire.

bicolor WILLD. See *S. schraderana.*

×**blanda** ANDERSS. (*babylonica*×*fragilis*). A medium-sized to large tree with a wide-spreading head of weeping branches. Leaves lanceolate, glabrous, bluish-green beneath. Catkins produced with the leaves. C. 1830.

bockii SEEMEN. An attractive small to medium-sized shrub, usually seen as a neat, spreading bush, 1 to 1·2m. high. The numerous, slender, reddish twigs are greyish downy when young and in spring are thickly peppered with the bright-green emerging leaf-clusters. The numerous, small, greyish catkins appear along the current year's growths in late summer and autumn, the only willow in general cultivation to flower at this time of the year. W. China. Introduced by E. H. Wilson in 1908-9.

×**boydii** LINTON (*lapponum*×*reticulata*). A dwarf, erect, slow-growing shrub of gnarled appearance, with rounded, grey-downy leaves becoming green above. A female clone, with rarely produced small, dark grey catkins. An ideal shrub for a trough or for a pocket on the rock garden or scree. Found in the 1870s, only on a single occasion growing in the mountains of Angus in Scotland. A.M. 1958.

'Caerulea' (*alba 'Ceraulea'*) (*S.* ×*caerulea*) (Rubens Group). "Cricket-bat Willow". A large tree of conical habit, with ascending branches and lanceolate leaves which are sea-green above and somewhat glaucous beneath. The best willow for cricket bats and long planted for this purpose in eastern England. The original tree is said to have been found in Norfolk about 1700. It is a female clone of a variable hybrid.

×**calliantha** KERN. (*daphnoides*×*purpurea*). A small tree or large shrub with non-bloomy stems and lanceolate to oblanceolate, serrated leaves, glossy dark green above, sea-green beneath. Ours is a female clone. C. 1872.

caprea L. "Goat Willow" or "Great Sallow". A common and familiar native species, particularly noticeable in early spring when the large, yellow, male catkins are gathered as "Palm" by children. The female form known as "Pussy Willow" has silver catkins. A large shrub or small tree with stout twigs and oval or obovate leaves, grey tomentose beneath. Europe; W. Asia.

SALIX—*continued*

caprea 'Pendula'. "Kilmarnock Willow". A small, umbrella-like, female tree with stiffly pendulous branches; rarely reaching 3m. C. about 1844.

caspica PALL. A large shrub or small tree with long, whip-like, pale grey stems and linear-lanceolate leaves. A rare species from S.E. Russia; W. and C. Asia.

×**chrysocoma** DODE (*alba 'Vitellina'* × *babylonica*) (*alba 'Vitellina Pendula'*) (*alba 'Tristis'*) (*babylonica 'Ramulis Aureis'*). Possibly the most beautiful weeping tree hardy in our climate. A medium-sized, wide-spreading tree producing vigorous, arching branches which terminate in slender, golden-yellow, weeping branchlets, ultimately of great length. Leaves lanceolate; catkins appearing with the leaves in April, both male and female flowers in the same catkin, or occasionally catkins all male or all female. A.G.M. 1931. Unfortunately, subject to scab and canker, which may be controlled on young trees by spraying with a suitable fungicide.

cinerea L. "Grey Sallow". A large shrub or occasionally a small tree. It has stout pubescent twigs and obovate leaves which are grey tomentose beneath. Catkins appearing before the leaves in early spring. Europe (including British Isles); W. Asia; Tunisia.

oleifolia MACREIGHT (*atrocinerea*) (*S. atrocinerea*). "Common Sallow". Similar to the type in general habit, but branches more erect and leaves more leathery, glaucous beneath and with rust-coloured hairs. Perhaps its only claim to cultivation is its toughness and usefulness for planting in derelict areas, such as slag heaps, where it will help in the task of reclamation and reafforestation. Both this species and *S. caprea* are familiar hedgerow shrubs throughout the British Isles. Europe; S. Russia.

'Tricolor'. Leaves splashed and mottled yellow and creamy-white. Perhaps the only form of this species which can claim garden merit.

×**cottetii** KERN. (*nigricans* × *retusa*). A vigorous, low-growing shrub with long trailing stems forming carpets several metres across. Leaves dark, shining green above, paler beneath; catkins before the leaves in early spring. Our plant is a male clone. Too vigorous for the small rock garden, but an excellent ground-cover. European Alps. C. 1905. Formerly wrongly catalogued as *S.* ×*gillotii*.

dahurica TURCZ. A large shrub or small tree with slender branches and linear, serrulate leaves, dull green above, paler beneath.

daphnoides VILL. "Violet Willow". A fast-growing, small tree with long, purple-violet shoots which are attractively overlaid with a white bloom. Catkins before the leaves in spring. Extremely effective in winter especially when hard pruned each or every other year in late March. Female trees are narrower and more columnar in habit than the male. N. Europe; C. Asia; Himalaya. C. 1829. A.M. 1957. A.G.M. 1969.

acutifolia. See *S. acutifolia*.

'Aglaia'. A male clone with large, handsome, bright yellow catkins in early spring.

dasyclados WIMM. A large shrub or small tree with downy young stems and ovate to oblong-lanceolate, sharply pointed leaves, glaucescent and downy beneath. A willow of obscure origin, possibly the hybrid *caprea* × *cinerea* × *viminalis*.

'Decipiens' (*fragilis decipiens*) (Rubens Group). "Cardinal Willow". A small tree or large bush with polished, yellowish-grey branches which are orange or rich red on the exposed side when young. The lanceolate, toothed leaves are shining green above. A male clone.

discolor MUHL. A strong-growing, large shrub, occasionally a small tree with stout, downy shoots, glabrous in the third year. Leaves grey tomentose beneath. Catkins appearing before the leaves in March or early April. Eastern N. America. I. 1811.

×**doniana** SM. (*purpurea* × *repens*). A small to medium-sized shrub with oblong or lanceolate leaves, glaucous beneath. Catkins before the leaves in spring, the males with red anthers, ripening to yellow. Occurs with the parents in the wild. C. 1829.

×**ehrhartiana** SM. (*alba* × *pentandra*) (*hexandra*). A large shrub or small to medium-sized tree with polished, olive-brown twigs and oblong-lanceolate, shining green leaves. Catkins appearing with or after the leaves. Europe (including British Isles). C. 1894.

SALIX—*continued*

elaeagnos SCOP. (*incana*) (*rosmarinifolia* HORT.). "Hoary Willow". A beautiful, medium-sized to large shrub of dense, bushy habit. Leaves linear, like elongated leaves of Rosemary, greyish hoary at first becoming green above and white beneath, thickly clothing the slender, reddish-brown, wand-like stems. Catkins slender, appearing with the young leaves in spring. One of the prettiest willows for waterside planting. C. and S. Europe; Asia Minor. I. about 1820.

'Elegantissima' (Blanda Group). "Thurlow Weeping Willow". A female clone, similar to *S.* ×*blanda* in habit. Both trees are sometimes found in cultivation under the name *S. babylonica.*

×**erdingeri** KERN. (*caprea* × *daphnoides*). An attractive large shrub or small tree, its greenish stems covered with bluish-white bloom. Leaves obovate to oblong, glossy green above, appearing after the catkins in spring. Ours is a female clone. Europe. C. 1872.

eriocephala MICHX. (*missouriensis*). Small to medium-sized tree with slender, spreading, reddish-brown branches, pubescent when young and narrowly lanceolate leaves, hairy at first, later almost glabrous. Catkins before the leaves. United States. I. 1898.

×**erythroflexuosa** RAG. (*chrysocoma* × *matsudana 'Tortuosa'*). A curious, ornamental, small tree discovered several years ago in Argentina. The vigorous, orange-yellow, pendulous shoots are twisted and contorted, as are the narrow leaves.

eucalyptoides. See *CHOSENIA arbutifolia.*

exigua NUTT. "Coyote Willow". A beautiful, large, erect shrub or a small tree with long, slender, greyish-brown branches clothed with linear, silvery-silky, minutely toothed leaves. Catkins slender, appearing with the leaves. Western N. America; N. Mexico. I. 1921.

fargesii BURK. A medium sized to large shrub of rather open habit, with stout, glabrous shoots which are a polished, reddish-brown in their second year. Winter buds reddish, large and conspicuous. Leaves elliptic to oblong-elliptic, up to 18cm. long and deep glossy green with impressed venation. Catkins appearing with or after the leaves, slender and ascending, the females 10 to 15cm. long. C. China. I. 1911. We have only recently acquired true stock of this handsome species, it being confused in cultivation with the closely related *S. moupinensis.*

×**finnmarchica** WILLD. (*myrtilloides* × *repens*). A dwarf shrub, forming a low-wide-spreading patch, with slender, ascending shoots and small leaves. The small catkins crowd the stems before the leaves in early spring. Ours is a female clone. Excellent for the rock garden, or as ground-cover. Found in the wild with the parents in N. and C. Europe.

foetida SCHLEICHER. A dwarf shrub with trailing stems and dark green, sharply-toothed leaves. Catkins produced with the leaves in spring. Mts. of Europe (W. and C. Alps; C. Pyrenees).

formosa. See *S. arbuscula.*

fragilis L. "Crack Willow". A large, native tree with wide-spreading branches, as familiar as the "White Willow", the two often growing together by rivers and streams. Bark rugged and channelled, twigs brittle at their joints. Leaves lanceolate, glabrous, sharply-toothed, glossy dark green above, green or sometimes bluish-green beneath. Catkins slender, appearing with the leaves in spring. Europe; N. Asia.

'Basfordiana'. See *S. 'Basfordiana'.*

decipiens. See *S. 'Decipiens'.*

'Ginme'. See *S.* ×*tsugaluensis 'Ginme'.*

glaucosericea B. FLOD. An attractive grey, dwarf shrub suitable for the rock garden. Leaves narrowly elliptic to elliptic-lanceolate, densely grey hairy at first, less so by autumn. European Alps. Previously distributed as *S. glauca.*

gracilistyla MIQ. A very splendid, vigorous, medium-sized shrub with stout, densely, grey-pubescent young shoots. Leaves silky grey-downy at first, gradually becoming green and smooth, remaining late in the autumn. Catkins appearing before the leaves in early spring, the young males are grey and silky, through which the reddish, unopened anthers can be seen, later they are bright yellow. One of the most effective catkin-bearing shrubs. Japan; Korea; Manchuria; China. I. 1895. A.M. 1925. A.G.M. 1969.

melanostachys. See *S. melanostachys.*

SALIX—*continued*

× **grahamii** BAK. (*herbacea* × *myrsinites*). A dwarf, procumbent shrub forming large patches of slender stems and broad elliptic to oblong-elliptic, shining green leaves, 2·5 to 4cm. in length. Catkins erect, appearing with or after the leaves. Ours is a female clone. Occurring wild with the parents in Sutherlandshire, Scotland, originally found about 1865.

hastata L. A small shrub with obovate to elliptic leaves, which are sea-green beneath. Catkins produced before or with the leaves in spring. C. and S. Europe to N.E. Asia and Kashmir. I. 1780.

'Wehrhahnii' (*S. wehrhahnii*). A slow-growing, small to medium-sized shrub of spreading habit. In spring the stout twigs become alive with pretty, silvery-grey, male catkins which later turn yellow. A.M. 1964. A.G.M. 1969.

helvetica VILL. A small, bushy shrub, the young stems, leaves and catkins clothed in a soft, greyish pubescence. The small, oblanceolate leaves are grey-green above, white beneath. Catkins appearing with the young leaves in spring. An attractive foliage shrub for the rock garden. European Alps. C. 1872.

herbacea L. "Dwarf Willow". A tiny, alpine species and one of the smallest British shrubs, forming mats of creeping, often underground stems. Leaves rounded up to 2cm. long, glossy green and prominently reticulate, borne in pairs or in threes at the tips of each shoot. Catkins up to 2cm. long, appearing with the leaves in spring. Suitable for a moist position in the peat garden or rock garden. Arctic and mountainous regions of Europe and N. America.

'Hippophaefolia' (Mollissima Group). A large shrub or small tree with olive-brown twigs and long, narrow leaves. Catkins similar to those of *S. triandra*, but with reddish anthers. Ours is a male form.

hookerana BARR. A medium-sized to large shrub or small tree with glossy, reddish-brown branches, tomentose when young. Leaves oblong, acute, glossy green above densely felted beneath. Catkins with the leaves. Western N. America. C. 1891.

humilis MARSH. "Prairie Willow". A vigorous, medium-sized shrub. Leaves obovate or oblong-lanceolate, dark green above, glaucous and tomentose beneath. Catkins appearing before the leaves, the males with brick-red, later yellow anthers, the females with brick-red stigmas. Eastern N. America. I. 1876.

incana. See *S. elaeagnos*.

integra THUNB. (*purpurea multinervis*) (*'Axukime'*). A large shrub or small tree of elegant habit. Branches long and slightly drooping, leaves generally in pairs, oblong, bright green, almost sessile. The slender catkins grace the polished stems in early April, before the leaves. A graceful fast-growing species, ideally suitable for waterside planting. Japan; Korea.

irrorata ANDERSS. A vigorous, medium-sized shrub, the long shoots green when young, then purple and covered with a striking white bloom, particularly noticeable in winter. Leaves lanceolate or oblong-lanceolate, glossy green above, glaucous beneath. Catkins appearing before the leaves, the males with brick-red anthers turning to yellow. An attractive species for contrasting with the red and yellow-stemmed clones. S.W. United States. I. 1898. A.M.T. 1967.

japonica THUNB. A large shrub with long, slender, pale stems of elegant disposition. Leaves slenderly pointed, serrulate, bright green above, glaucous beneath. Catkins slender, appearing with the leaves. Japan. C. 1874.

kinuyanagi KIMURA (*'Kishu'*). A strong-growing, large shrub or small tree with long, stout, greyish-brown-felted shoots and long, narrow leaves, silky-hairy beneath. Catkins bright yellow, closely arrayed along the stems in March. Only the male form is known. Native of Japan where it is widely cultivated. It is related to our native "Osier" (*S. viminalis*), which it closely resembles.

'Kishu'. See *S. kinuyanagi*.

koriyanagi KIMURA (*purpurea japonica*). A large, erect-growing shrub or small tree with slender, whip-like stems. The sub-opposite, bright green leaves are suffused an attractive orange-red on emerging. Catkins slender, in rows along the stems, the males with orange anthers. Korea; widely cultivated in Japan for basket-making and furniture.

'Kureneko'. See *S. melanostachys*.

'Kurome'. See *S. melanostachys*.

'Kuroyanagi'. See *S. melanostachys*.

SALIX—*continued*

lanata L. "Woolly Willow". An attractive, slow-growing shrub usually ·6 to 1·2m. high, or occasionally more, with ovate to rounded, silvery-grey-downy leaves and stout, erect, yellowish-grey woolly catkins in spring. The female catkins elongate considerably in fruit, sometimes measuring 10cm. long. A rare native alpine species suitable for the rock garden. N. Europe (including Scotland); N. Asia. A.G.M. 1969.

'Stuartii'. A dwarf, gnarled shrublet, conspicuous in winter with its yellow shoots and orange buds. Its leaves are smaller, but its catkins larger than those of the type. A.G.M. 1969.

lapponum L. "Lapland Willow". A small, densely branched shrub with grey, downy leaves, 2·5 to 5cm. long. The silky, grey catkins are produced before the leaves in spring. Mts. of Europe (including British Isles); Siberia. C. 1789.

lasiandra BENTH. "Pacific Willow". A large, strong-growing tree with the general appearance of *S. fragilis*. Leaves lanceolate, sharply glandular-toothed, glaucous at first beneath. Catkins with the leaves in spring. Western N. America. C. 1883.

lasiolepis BENTH. A large shrub or small tree with linear, toothed leaves dull green above, glaucous beneath. An elegant species, with attractive, grey, female catkins before the leaves in early spring. Western U.S.A.; N. Mexico.

livida. See *S. starkeana*.

lucida MUHL. "Shining Willow". A large shrub or a small to medium-sized tree with glossy young shoots and lanceolate, slender-pointed, glossy green leaves. Catkins produced with the leaves in spring. N.E. North America. C. 1830.

mackenzieana BARR. A small tree of upright habit, with long, slender, pale yellow-green stems and lanceolate leaves. Western North America.

magnifica HEMSL. A large shrub or small tree of sparse habit, bearing large, oval or obovate, magnolia-like leaves up to 20cm. long and 13cm. wide. Catkins produced with the leaves in spring, the females often 15 to 25cm. in length. A most impressive species, native of W. China, introduced by Ernest Wilson in 1909 who, when he first found it thought he had discovered a new magnolia. A.M. 1913.

matsudana KOIDZ. "Pekin Willow". A medium-sized tree of conical habit, with slender stems and long, narrow, slender-pointed leaves which are green above and glaucous beneath. Catkins appearing with the leaves in spring. A graceful species closely related to *S. babylonica*. Only the female form is in general cultivation. N. China; Manchuria; Korea. I. 1905.

'Pendula'. A very graceful tree and one of the best weeping willows, showing resistance to scab and canker.

'Tortuosa'. A curious form with branches and twigs much twisted and contorted.

medemii. See *S. aegyptiaca*.

medwedewii DODE. A small shrub, related to *S. triandra*. Leaves long and narrow, vividly glaucous beneath. Catkins produced with the leaves in spring. Asia Minor. C. 1910.

melanostachys MAK. (*gracilistyla melanostachys*) ('*Kureneko*') ('*Kurome*') ('*Kuroyanagi*'). An attractive and unusual small to medium-sized shrub of Japanese origin. Quite outstanding in the remarkable colour combination of its catkins appearing before the leaves, very dark, with blackish scales and brick-red anthers, opening to yellow. The stout twigs are thickly clustered with oblanceolate leaves which are glaucous beneath at first and sharply serrate. A male clone, known only in cultivation. It is sometimes regarded as a form of *S. gracilistyla*, but differs from this species in its glabrous twigs, non-silky catkins, longer, darker coloured bracts, shorter glands, etc. It is most probably a hybrid. A.M. 1976.

× **meyerana** ROSTK. (*fragilis × pentandra*). A vigorous, medium-sized to large tree with oval, glossy green leaves, glaucescent beneath. Catkins appearing with the leaves in spring. Europe (including British Isles). C. 1829.

missouriensis. See *S. eriocephala*.

miyabeana SEEM. A large shrub or small tree with long, slender, polished-brown stems which, in spring and summer, are heavily clothed with narrow, pale green leaves. Catkins before the leaves. Japan. I. 1897.

SALIX—*continued*

× **mollissima** EHRH. (*triandra* × *viminalis*). A variable hybrid forming a large shrub or small tree, the catkins appearing with the young leaves in spring. See also '*Hippophaefolia*' and '*Trevirani*'.

× **moorei** F. B. WHITE (*herbacea* × *phylicifolia*). A dwarf shrub for the rock garden or scree, forming a low, wide-spreading mound of slender stems. Leaves small, shining green; catkins before the leaves in spring. An excellent ground-cover, not too vigorous. Ours is a female clone. Found wild in Scotland.

moupinensis FRANCH. A very beautiful, medium-sized shrub of great quality, related to and generally resembling *S. fargesii*, with which it has long been confused in gardens. It differs from that species mainly in its slightly smaller, normally glabrous leaves. Both species are extremely ornamental at all times of the year. China. Introduced by E. H. Wilson in 1910.

muscina HORT. See *S. aegyptiaca*.

myrsinifolia. See *S. nigricans*.

myrsinites L. A prostrate, native species forming dense carpets of shortly ascending stems clothed with shining, bright green leaves and bearing large, attractive catkins in April. An ideal species for the rock garden. N. Europe; N. Asia.

nigricans SM. (*myrsinifolia*). A medium-sized to large, native shrub with downy twigs and downy, variably shaped leaves, dark green above, generally glaucous beneath. Catkins appearing before the leaves. N. and C. Europe.

nitida. See *S. repens argentea*.

pentandra L. "Bay Willow". A beautiful small to medium-sized tree, or occasionally a large shrub, with glossy twigs and attractive, bay-like, lustrous green leaves, pleasantly aromatic when unfolding or when crushed. Catkins produced with the leaves in late spring, the males bright yellow. Found wild in northern parts of the British Isles, planted elsewhere. Used as a substitute for "Bay" in Norway. Europe; N. Asia.

phylicifolia L. "Tea-leaf Willow". A medium-sized, native shrub with dark, glabrous twigs and leaves which are shining green above and glaucous beneath. Catkins appearing before the leaves. N. Europe.

× **pontederana** WILLD. (*cinerea* × *purpurea*). A medium-sized to large shrub with branches hairy at first. Leaves obovate-lanceolate, silky-hairy and glaucous beneath. Catkins produced in March, before the leaves. Ours is a male form with yellow anthers prettily red tinted when young. Europe. C. 1820.

pruinosa. See *S. acutifolia*.

purpurea L. "Purple Osier". A graceful, medium-sized to large shrub with long, arching, often purplish shoots. Leaves narrowly oblong, dull green above, paler or glaucous beneath, often in opposite pairs. Catkins slender, produced all along the shoots in spring before the leaves. The wood of the young shoots is a bright yellow beneath the bark, a character which is normally present in its hybrids. Europe (including British Isles); C. Asia.

'Eugenei'. An erect-branched, small tree of slender conical habit producing an abundance of subtly-attractive, grey-pink male catkins, earlier than those of the type.

'Gracilis' ('*Nana*'). A dwarf, compact, slender-branched cultivar. A useful low hedge for a damp site.

japonica. See *S. koriyanagi*.

'Pendula'. An attractive form with long, pendulous branches; trained as a standard it forms a charming, small, weeping tree.

pyrifolia ANDERSS. (*balsamifera*). "Balsam Willow". A large shrub or occasionally a small tree, with shining reddish-brown twigs and red winter buds. Leaves ovate-lanceolate, glaucous and reticulate beneath. Catkins appearing with the leaves in spring. Canada; N.E. United States. I. 1880.

rehderana SCHNEID. A large shrub or small tree with lanceolate, bright green leaves, grey silky beneath. W. China. I. 1908.

repens L. "Creeping Willow". Normally a small, creeping shrub, but in some forms occasionally 1·8 to 2·5m. high, forming large patches or dense clumps of slender, erect stems clothed with small, greyish-green leaves, silvery-white beneath. Catkins small, crowding the naked stems in spring. A common native species of heaths, bogs and commons, particularly on acid soils. Europe; N. Asia.

argentea G. & A. CAMUS (*S. nitida*) (*arenaria*). An attractive, semi-prostrate variety with silvery-silky leaves. Abundant in moist, sandy areas by the sea. Grown as a standard it makes an effective miniature weeping tree. Atlantic coasts of Europe.

SALIX—*continued*

repens subopposita. See *S. subopposita.*

'Voorthuizen'. A charming little plant of Dutch origin, the slender prostrate stems bearing small, silky leaves and tiny female catkins. Suitable for the small rock garden or scree.

reticulata L. A dwarf, native shrub with prostrate stems, forming dense mats. Leaves small, orbicular or ovate, entire, dark green and attractively net-veined above, glaucous beneath. Catkins erect, appearing after the leaves. A dainty, pretty little willow suitable for a moist ledge on the rock garden. Arctic and mountain areas of N. America, Europe and N. Asia. C. 1789.

retusa L. A prostrate species forming extensive carpets of creeping stems and small, notched, polished green leaves. Catkins erect, 12 to 20mm. long, appearing with the leaves. Mts. of Europe. I. 1763.

rosmarinifolia HORT. See *S. elaeagnos.*

× **rubens** SCHRANK (*alba* × *fragilis*) (× *viridis*). A common and variable native hybrid generally intermediate in character between the parents, with some clones leaning more to one than the other. A large, fast-growing tree with lanceolate leaves, green or glaucous beneath. Occuring in the wild either with or without the parents. Several clones have been named including '*Caerulea*', the "Cricket-bat Willow" and '*Basfordiana*'.

sachalinensis F. SCHMIDT. A large shrub or small tree of spreading habit, with young shoots of a polished chestnut brown. Leaves lanceolate, slender-pointed, shining green above, pale or glaucous beneath. Catkins appearing before the leaves, the males large and conspicuous. N.E. Asia. I. 1905. A vigorous, ornamental willow usually seen in the following clone.

'Sekka' ('*Setsuka*'). A male clone of Japanese origin, noted for its occasional curiously flattened and recurved stems, which may be encouraged by hard pruning. Useful when cut for "Japanese" floral arrangements.

× **salamonii.** See *S.* '*Sepulcralis*'.

schraderana WILLD. (*bicolor* WILLD.). A medium-sized shrub, closely related to *S. phylicifolia.* Shoots stout, with yellowish buds in winter. Leaves glossy green above, glaucous beneath. Catkins with reddish anthers, opening to yellow. Mts. of Europe, but not the Alps.

'Sepulcralis' (× *salamonii*) (Chrysocoma Group). A medium-sized tree of weeping habit with long, slender, pendulous stems and linear-lanceolate, glossy-green leaves, glaucous beneath at first. Catkins appearing with the leaves in spring. A vigorous tree resembling *S. babylonica*, but less pendulous. Garden origin before 1864.

× **seringeana** GAUD. (*caprea* × *elaeagnos*) (*salviifolia* LINK.). A large shrub or small tree of erect habit, with grey tomentose stems and lanceolate or narrowly oblong, softly grey-downy leaves, pale beneath. A most ornamental, grey-leaved hybrid. C. 1872.

'Setsuka'. See *S. sachalinensis* '*Sekka*'.

× **smithiana** WILLD. (*cinerea* × *viminalis*). A strong-growing, variable, large native shrub or small tree, with long, stout branches, tomentose when young. Leaves lanceolate, silky-hairy beneath. Catkins produced before the leaves in spring. Ours is a female form. Found in the wild only in the British Isles.

'Spaethii' (Smithiana Group). A small tree with stout, densely hairy shoots, long leaves and female catkins. Of continental origin.

starkeana WILLD. (*livida*). Small to medium-sized shrub with broad elliptic leaves, glossy green above, glaucous-green beneath. Catkins appearing before the leaves. N. and C. Europe; N. Asia. C. 1872.

'Stipularis' (Smithiana Group). A vigorous, small tree or large shrub with tomentose shoots and lanceolate leaves, glaucous and downy beneath. Conspicuous on account of its large foliaceous stipules.

subopposita MIQ. (*repens subopposita*). A rare and very distinct dwarf shrub with slender, erect and spreading stems and small leaves which are opposite or nearly so. Catkins before the leaves in early spring. This unusual little willow has the stance of a *Hebe.* Japan; Korea.

× **tetrapla** WALK. (*nigricans* × *phylicifolia*). Small to medium-sized native shrub of stiff habit with stout, glossy, yellowish-green twigs and oblong-elliptic leaves, glossy green above, glaucous beneath. Occasionally found with the parents in the wild. C. 1829.

SALIX—*continued*

'Trevirani' (Mollissima Group). A vigorous shrub with dark, olive-brown twigs and attractive, yellow, male catkins in April.

triandra L. (*amygdalina*). "Almond-leaved Willow". A large shrub or small tree with flaky bark and lanceolate, glossy green, serrated leaves, glaucous beneath. Catkins produced with the leaves in spring, the males fragrant and almost mimosa-like. Europe to E. Asia. Long cultivated in Europe for basket-making.

hoffmanniana BAB. An uncommon variety with oblong-lanceolate leaves, green beneath.

× **tsugaluensis 'Ginme'.** A medium-sized to large shrub of vigorous, spreading habit. Leaves oblong, bright green, paler beneath and orange tinged when young. Catkins silvery, slender and recurved appearing all along the naked stems in spring. A female clone of Japanese origin, an alleged hybrid between *S. integra* and *S. vulpina*.

uva-ursi PURSH. "Bearberry Willow". A prostrate shrub forming dense carpets of creeping stems clothed with small, glossy green leaves. Catkins appearing with the young leaves in spring. A superb plant for the rock garden or scree. Previously supplied as *S. apoda* with which species and *S. retusa* it is often confused in cultivation. Canada; N.E. United States. I. 1880.

viminalis L. "Common Osier". A large, vigorous shrub or a small tree with long, straight shoots thickly grey tomentose when young. Leaves long and narrow, tapering to a fine point, dull green above, covered with silvery-silky hairs beneath. Catkins appearing before the leaves. A very common native species of rivers, streamsides, lakes and marshes. Long cultivated for basket-making. Europe to N.E. Asia and Himalaya.

× **viridis.** See *S.* × *rubens*.

vitellina. See *S. alba 'Vitellina'*.

wehrhahnii. See *S. hastata 'Wehrhahnii'*.

wilhelmsiana BIEB. A large, elegant shrub with slender, wand-like stems and narrow, obscurely toothed leaves which, like the stems, are silky-hairy at first, later shining green. Catkins appearing with the leaves in spring. S.E. Russia to S. Central Asia. C. 1887.

× **wimmerana** GREN. & GODR. (*caprea* × *purpurea*). A medium-sized shrub with slender branches and oblong to lanceolate leaves, glaucescent beneath. Catkins borne all along the stems before the leaves in early April. The male catkins are very pretty when both brick-red emerging anthers and yellow ripened anthers are apparent at the same time. Ours is a male form. Occurs with the parents in the wild. C. 1872.

yezoalpina KOIDZ. A prostrate shrub with long, trailing stems bearing attractive, long-stalked, rounded or obovate glossy green leaves with reticulate venation. Catkins appearing with the leaves in spring. A rare alpine species, suitable for the rock garden or scree. Japan.

"SALLOW". See *SALIX caprea* and *S. cinerea*.

SALVIA—Labiatae—A large genus of aromatic, flowering plants containing numerous sub-shrubs, of which all but *S. officinalis* are tender in varying degrees. They require a warm, dry, well-drained position in full sun. The more tender species make excellent cool-house subjects. The two-lipped flowers are normally borne in whorls along the stems during late summer or early autumn.

ambigens. See *S. guaranitica*.

†**aurea** L. A small species with round, hoary leaves and rusty yellow flowers. S. Africa. I. 1731.

bethellii. See *S. involucrata 'Bethellii'*.

caerulea. See *S. guaranitica*.

†**fulgens** CAV. "Mexican Red Sage". A small species up to 1m. with heart-shaped leaves and long racemes of showy, densely hairy, scarlet flowers, 5cm. long, in late summer. Mexico. I. 1829. A.M. 1937.

†**gesneriiflora** LINDL. & PAXT. An attractive, small species related to *S. fulgens*, but with even larger, showier flowers of an intense scarlet. Mexico. I. 1840. A.M. 1950.

grahamii. See *S. microphylla*.

†**greggii** GRAY. A small, slender species up to 1·2m., suitable for a sunny south wall, Similar in some respects to *S. microphylla*, but leaves smaller and narrower and flowers rose-scarlet. Texas; Mexico. C. 1885. A.M. 1914.

SALVIA—*continued*

†**guaranitica** ST. HIL. (*ambigens*) (*caerulea*). A small shrub with erect stems up to 1·5m. Softly downy, heart-shaped leaves and long racemes of deep, azure-blue flowers about 5cm. long, during late summer and autumn. S. America. I. 1925. A.M. 1926. A.G.M. 1949.

†**interrupta** SCHOUSH. A small, glandular, hairy sub-shrub up to 1m. Leaves varying from entire, with two basal lobes, to pinnate, with two pairs of leaflets. Flowers violet-purple, with a white throat, produced in loose terminal panicles from late spring to mid-summer. Morocco. I. 1867.

†**involucrata** CAV. Small species with ovate, long-pointed leaves and spike-like racemes of rose-magenta flowers which are sticky to the touch. Late summer to autumn. Mexico. I. 1824.

'Bethellii' (*S. bethellii*). A robust form with large, heart-shaped leaves and stout racemes of magenta-crimson flowers from mid-summer onwards. Garden origin. F.C.C. 1880.

lavandulifolia VAHL. A dwarf species with narrow, grey, downy leaves and spike-like racemes of blue-violet flowers in early summer. Spain.

†**mexicana minor** BENTH. A vigorous, small to medium-sized sub-shrub with large, ovate leaves and terminal spike-like racemes of showy, violet-blue flowers, in late winter. Differing from the type in its smaller calyces. Only suitable for the cool greenhouse. Mexico. I. 1720.

†**microphylla** KUNTH (*grahamii*). A variable, small shrub up to 1·2m. Bright red fading to bluish-red flowers, 2·5cm. long, from June into late autumn. Mexico. I. 1829.

neurepia EPLING (*S. neurepia*). Differs from the type in its larger, paler green leaves 3 to 5cm. long, and showier, rosy-red flowers in late summer and autumn. Mexico.

neurepia. See *S. microphylla neurepia*.

officinalis L. "Common Sage". A well-known, dwarf, semi-evergreen species long cultivated as a herb. Leaves grey-green and strongly aromatic. Flowers bluish-purple, during summer. S. Europe. Cultivated in England since 1597, possibly before.

'Alba'. Flowers white.

'Icterina'. Leaves variegated green and gold.

'Purpurascens'. "Purple-leaf Sage". Stems and young foliage suffused purple. Particularly effective in coloured foliage groups for blending or contrasts.

'Tricolor'. A distinct, compact form with leaves grey-green, splashed creamy-white, suffused purple and pink.

†**rutilans** CARR. A small species up to 1m., suitable for a sunny south wall, with softly downy, heart-shaped leaves, scented of pineapple and loose leafy panicles of magenta-crimson flowers throughout summer. Origin unknown. C. before 1873.

SAMBUCUS—Caprifoliaceae—"Elder". A small genus of generally hardy shrubs, tolerant of almost all soils and situations. Few are eye-catching in flower, but many have ornamental foliage and fruits. All species possess pinnate leaves and serrated leaflets. To encourage the production of large flower-heads or lush foliage the lateral branches may be cut back to within a few cm. of the previous year's growth in March. Ideal subjects for the wild garden.

callicarpa GREENE. A small to medium-sized shrub, the leaves with five to seven leaflets. Flowers whitish, in a round head, 7 to 10cm. across, in June to July, followed by small, scarlet fruits. Western N. America. I. about 1900.

canadensis L. "American Elderberry". A stout, strong-growing shrub of medium to large size, the leaves with five to eleven, usually seven, large leaflets. Flowers white in convex heads, 13 to 20cm. across, appearing in July, followed by purple-black fruits. S.E. Canada; Eastern U.S.A. I. 1761. A.M. 1905. A.M. 1948.

'Aurea'. An unusual form with yellow foliage and red fruits.

'Maxima'. A handsome form with leaves 30 to 45cm. long and enormous flower heads 30cm. or more across. The rosy-purple flower stalks which remain after the flowers have fallen, are an added attraction. A bold shrub which should be pruned each spring to encourage the production of new shoots. A bold subject for the wild garden. A.M. 1951.

'Rubra'. An unusual form with red fruits.

submollis REHD. A variety with leaflets softly greyish pubescent beneath.

SAMBUCUS—*continued*

ebulus L. "Dane's Elder". An unusual species of herbaceous nature, throwing up annually stout, grooved stems 1 to 1·2m. high, in time forming dense colonies. Leaves with nine to thirteen leaflets. Flowers white, tinged pink in flattened heads, 7·5 to 10cm. across, during late summer. Fruits black. Europe; N. Africa; naturalized in the British Isles.

nigra L. "Common Elder". A familiar, native, large shrub or small tree, with a rugged, fissured bark and leaves with five to seven leaflets. The flattened heads of cream-coloured, sweetly fragrant flowers in June are followed by heavy bunches of shining black fruits. Both flowers and fruits are used in country-wine-making. A useful plant for extremely chalky sites. Europe; N. Africa; W. Asia. Long cultivated.

'Albovariegata' (*'Marginata'*) (*'Argenteomarginata'*). Leaflets with an irregular, creamy-white margin. A.M. 1892.

'Aurea'. "Golden Elder". Leaves golden-yellow, deepening with age. One of the hardiest and most satisfactory of golden foliaged shrubs.

'Aureomarginata'. Leaflets with an irregular, bright yellow margin.

'Fructuluteo'. An unusual form with yellow fruits.

'Heterophylla' (*'Linearis'*). A curious shrub with leaflets of variable form, often reduced to thread-like segments.

'Laciniata'. "Fern-leaved Elder". An attractive form with finely divided fern-like leaves.

'Marginata'. See *'Albovariegata'*.

'Plena'. A form with double flowers.

'Pulverulenta'. A form in which the leaves are striped and mottled white.

'Purpurea'. Leaves flushed purple, particularly so when young. A.M. 1977.

'Pyramidalis'. A form of stiff, erect habit, wider above than below; leaves densely clustered on the stems.

pubens MICHX. A large shrub related to *S. racemosa*. Leaves with five to seven leaflets, like the stems pubescent when young. Flowers cream-coloured, borne in rounded or conical heads during May. Fruits red. N. America. I. 1812.

racemosa L. "Red-berried Elder". A medium-sized to large shrub, the leaves with five to seven coarsely-toothed leaflets. Flowers yellowish-white in conical heads, crowding the branches in April followed in summer by dense clusters of bright, scarlet fruits. Europe; W. Asia. Planted as game cover in parts of northern England and Scotland. Cultivated in England since the 16th century. A.M. 1936.

'Plumosa Aurea' (*'Serratifolia Aurea'*). A colourful shrub with beautiful, deeply cut, golden foliage. One of the elite of golden foliaged shrubs; slower growing than the type. Rich yellow flowers. A.M. 1895. A.M. 1956.

'Tenuifolia'. A small, slow-growing shrub forming a low mound of arching branches and finely divided, fern-like leaves. As beautiful as a cut-leaved "Japanese Maple". A good plant for the rock garden. A.M. 1917.

***SANTOLINA—Compositae**—"Lavender Cotton". Low-growing, mound-forming, evergreen sub-shrubs with dense grey, green or silvery, finely divided foliage, and dainty, button-like flower heads on tall stalks, in July. They require a sunny position and well-drained soil. Natives of the Mediterranean Region.

chamaecyparissus L. (*incana*). A charming dwarf species, valued for its woolly, silver-hued, thread-like foliage. Flower heads bright lemon-yellow. S. France; Pyrenees. Cultivated in England since the 16th century. A.G.M. 1969.

corsica FIORI (*'Nana'*). A dwarfer, denser, more compact variety, ideal for the rock garden. Corsica; Sardinia. A.G.M. 1969.

'Nana'. See *corsica*.

incana. See *C. chamaecyparissus*.

neapolitana JORD. A dwarf sub-shrub similar to and perhaps merely a variety of *S. chamaecyparissus*, but rather looser in growth and with longer, more "feathery" leaves. Flowers bright lemon-yellow. N.W. and Central Italy.

'Edward Bowles'. A charming form originally given to us by E. A. Bowles, after whom we have the pleasure of naming it. It is similar to *'Sulphurea'*, but the foliage is more grey-green and the flower heads of a paler primrose, almost creamy-white.

'Sulphurea'. Foliage grey-green; flower-heads pale primrose-yellow.

SANTOLINA—*continued*

pinnata VIV. A dwarf subshrub related to and perhaps merely a variety of *S. chamaecyparissus*. Differing in its longer, finely divided green leaves and flower-heads of an off-white. N.W. Italy.

virens MILL. (*viridis*). An attractive, dwarf species of uncertain origin. Leaves thread-like, of a vivid green colour. Flower-heads bright lemon-yellow.

'Primrose Gem'. A lovely form with flower-heads of a pale primrose-yellow.

viridis. See *S. virens*.

SAPINDUS—Sapindaceae—A small genus of mainly tropical trees and shrubs of which the following are relatively hardy. They require a well-drained soil in sun or semi-shade.

drummondii HOOK. & ARN. "Soapberry". An interesting small tree with pinnate, robinia-like leaves. The tiny, cream-coloured flowers are borne in dense, conical panicles in June. Central S. United States; N. Mexico. C. 1900.

†***mukorossi** GAERTN. A large shrub or small tree with late persisting, pinnate leaves, consisting of eight to twelve leathery, reticulately-veined leaflets. Flowers yellowish-green, in terminal panicles. Japan; Formosa; China to India. C. 1877.

SAPIUM—Euphorbiaceae—A large genus of trees and shrubs almost all of which are found in the tropics.

japonicum PAX. & HOFFN. A rare, small tree or shrub here proving hardy, with greyish, glabrous branches and smooth, dark green, elliptic or obovate-elliptic, entire leaves, turning glowing crimson in autumn. Flowers monoecious, inconspicuous, appearing in June in slender, axillary, catkin-like, greenish-yellow racemes. Capsules like large capers, three-lobed, green, finally brown, pendulous. Japan; China; Korea.

†**sebiferum** ROXB. "Chinese Tallow Tree". A small tree with broadly ovate or rounded, abruptly-pointed leaves and slender racemes of greenish-yellow flowers. The waxy coating of the seeds is used in the manufacture of candles in China. The leaves often turn a brilliant red in autumn. Only suitable for the mildest gardens of the British Isles. China; Formosa. C. 1850.

***SARCOCOCCA—Buxaceae**—"Christmas Box". Attractive, shade-bearing, dwarf or small shrubs, with evergreen, glossy foliage suitable for cutting. The small, white, fragrant, male flowers open during late winter, the tiny, insignificant, female flowers occuring in the same cluster. Succeed in any fertile soil, being especially happy in chalk soils. They slowly attain 1·2 to 1·5m. high unless otherwise indicated.

confusa SEALY. A useful hardy shrub of dense spreading habit. Leaves elliptic, taper pointed; flowers with cream coloured anthers, very fragrant; fruits shining black. Similar in general appearance to *S. ruscifolia chinensis*, but the stigmas vary from two to three, and the berries are black. Origin uncertain, probably China. A.G.M. 1969.

hookerana BAILL. A rare, erect-growing species, with shortly pubescent, green stems, lanceolate leaves and white flowers, the female flowers with three stigmas. Berries black. Not quite so hardy as the var. *digyna*. Himalaya. A.M. 1936.

digyna FRANCH. More slender than the type and with narrower leaves. Female flowers with only two stigmas. Berries black. W. China. I. 1908. A.G.M. 1963. A.M. 1970.

'Purple Stem'. An attractive form with the young stems, petioles and midribs flushed purple.

humilis REHD. & WILS. A dwarf, densely-branched shrub, suckering to form extensive clumps and patches seldom exceeding ·6m. high. Leaves elliptic, shining deep green. Male flowers with pink anthers; berries black. W. China. I. 1907.

ruscifolia STAPF. A small, slow-growing shrub. Leaves broad ovate, thick, shining dark green. Berries dark red. Uncommon in cultivation. C. China. I. 1901. A.M. 1908.

chinensis REHD. & WILS. A more vigorous shrub, commoner than the type in cultivation, differing in its comparatively longer, narrower leaves. It is very similar in general appearance to *S. confusa*, having the same long, slender-pointed leaves and attaining the same dimensions, but the berries are dark red and the female flowers possess three stigmas. C. and W. China.

†**saligna** MUELL.-ARG. (*pruniformis*). A small shrub with erect, glabrous, green stems. Leaves tapering, lance-shaped, up to 13cm. long; flowers greenish-white, with little, if any scent. Berries purple. W. Himalaya; Formosa.

SAROTHAMNUS. See under *CYTISUS.*

‡SASSAFRAS—Lauraceae—A small genus of three species of deciduous trees requiring a lime-free loam and a slightly sheltered position such as in woodland.

albidum NEES. (*officinale*). An attractive and very distinct, aromatic, medium-sized tree of broadly conical habit with flexuous twigs and branches, particularly noticeable in winter. Leaves variable in shape from ovate to obovate, entire or with one or two conspicuous lobes, some leaves resembling those of the "Fig" in outline, dark green above, rather glaucous or pale green beneath, colouring attractively in autumn. Flowers greenish-yellow, inconspicuous, appearing in short racemes in May. Eastern U.S.A. I. 1633.

‡†*SCHIMA—Theaceae—A small genus of uncommon evergreen shrubs and trees requiring a lime-free soil in a sheltered position such as woodland.

argentea PRITZ. A medium-sized to large shrub of erect, bushy habit. Leaves elliptic to elliptic-oblong, tapering to both ends, polished dark green above, usually glaucous beneath. Flowers creamy-white, about 4cm. across, produced on the young wood in late summer. This distinct and attractive member of the Camellia family has been growing successfully here in woodland conditions for over twenty years. Native of W. China, Assam and Formosa, where it is said to attain large tree size. A.M. 1955.

khasiana DYER. A large shrub to medium-sized tree bearing lustrous, dark green, elliptic, serrated leaves, 15 to 18cm. long. Flowers white, 5cm. across, with a central mass of yellow stamens, produced on the young wood during September and October. There are splendid examples in Cornwall, but it is not hardy in our area. Assam; Burma; China. A.M. 1953.

noronhae REINW. A small to medium-sized shrub in cultivation, with oblanceolate or narrow elliptic, acuminate leaves covered above when mature with a bluish bloom. Flowers 4 to 5cm. across, cream coloured, with a central boss of golden stamens produced in the axils of the terminal leaves during late summer and autumn. Only for the mildest areas, but a suitable conservatory shrub. Tropical Asia. I. 1849.

wallichii CHOISY. A small tree in cultivation with elliptic-oblong leaves, pubescent and reticulate beneath. Flowers white, fragrant, 4 to 5cm. across, produced on the young wood in late summer. Not hardy in our area. Sikkim; Nepal; E. Indies.

SCHINUS—Anacardiaceae—A small genus of trees with simple or compound leaves and dioecious flowers.

***dependens** ORT. A medium-sized to large, evergreen shrub, the shoots often spine-tipped. Leaves small, obovate, 1 to 2cm. long. The tiny yellowish flowers crowd the branches in May; fruits purplish, the size of peppercorns. Chile. I. 1790.

†*molle L. "Pepper Tree". A small, evergreen tree with gracefully drooping branches and attractive, pinnate leaves. The small, yellowish-white flowers are borne in short panicles in spring, followed, on female trees, by rosy-red, pea-shaped fruits. Commonly planted as a street tree in S. Europe and best grown as a conservatory tree in the British Isles. S. America.

"SEA BUCKTHORN". See *HIPPOPHAE rhamnoides.*

SECURINEGA—Euphorbiaceae—A small genus of botanical interest related to *Andrachne.* The inconspicuous flowers may be monoecious or dioecious.

suffruticosa REHD. (*ramiflora*). A small, densely-branched shrub with slender stems and oval leaves, 2·5 to 5cm. long. Flowers small, greenish-yellow, produced during late summer and early Autumn. N.E. Asia to C. China; Formosa. I. 1783.

SEDUM—Crassulaceae—A large genus of mainly herbs, well represented in our herbaceous borders and rock gardens. The following is one of the few hardy shrubby species:—

populifolium L. A dwarf sub-shrub of erect habit with reddish-brown bark, peeling on old stems. Leaves with slender stalks, ovate, coarsely-toothed, cordate at base, pale green and fleshy. Flowers sweetly hawthorn-scented, white or pink-tinged, with purple anthers, borne in small, dense, flattened heads in July and August. Siberia. I. 1780.

SENECIO—Compositae—The shrubby members of this vast genus are mostly evergreen and bear heads or panicles of white or yellow daisy flowers during summer. All are sun-lovers and make excellent sea-side shrubs. With rare exception, the woody species will not withstand low continental temperatures but are excellent wind resisters. Unless otherwise stated, the following are natives of New Zealand.

SENECIO—*continued*

***bidwillii** HOOK. f. A striking, dwarf, alpine shrub of compact rigid habit, occasionally very slowly reaching ·75m. Leaves elliptic to obovate, up to 2·5cm. long, remarkably thick, shining above and covered beneath, like the stems in a soft white or buff tomentum. Flowers not conspicuous.

†*compactus T. KIRK. A small, compact, dense-growing shrub attaining ·9 to 1m., like *S. greyi* but less spreading. Leaves oval, 2·5 to 5cm. long, wavy-edged, white-felted beneath, as are the young shoots and flower stalks. Flower-heads bright yellow in few-flowered racemes. Subject to injury in severe winters.

***elaeagnifolius** HOOK. f. A rigid, densely-branched shrub of medium-size with oval, leathery leaves, 7·5 to 15cm. long, glossy above, thickly buff felted beneath, as are the young shoots and flower-stalks. Flower-heads in terminal panicles, of little ornament. An excellent coastal shrub.

buchananii T. KIRK. Smaller in all its parts.

***greyi** HORT. A popular and attractive, grey shrub forming a dense, broad mound up to 1m. high and twice as much across. Leaves silvery-grey when young becoming green above. Flower-heads yellow, in large open corymbs. The plant in general cultivation is a hybrid between the true *S. greyi* and another species possibly *S. compactus*. A.G.M. 1935.

The true species, *S. greyi* HOOK. f., differs from *S. greyi* of gardens most noticeably in its larger leaves and larger, looser corymbs. It is less hardy and requires a sheltered position even in the southern counties.

†*hectoris BUCH. A medium-sized to large, semi-evergreen shrub of erect, rather open habit. Leaves oblanceolate, 13 to 25cm. long, often pinnately lobed at base and conspicuously toothed, white tomentosel beneath. Flower-heads white, 4 to 6cm. across, in large terminal corymbs. H. G. Hillier was first introduced to this unusual Daisy Bush by that great gardener the late Sir Herbert Maxwell, who was growing it in sheltering woodland. Unlike its allies this handsome, large-leaved species cannot be expected to grow in an exposed, windy position. I. 1910.

†*heritieri DC. A small, loose-growing shrub with broadly ovate, toothed or shallowly lobed leaves, 10 to 15cm. long. Both the young stems and the leaf undersurfaces are covered by a dense, white tomentum. Flower-heads white and crimson with purple centres, violet-scented, recalling the popular "Cinerarea", borne in large panicles from May to July. Only suitable for the mildest areas or conservatory. Canary Isles. I. 1774.

†*huntii MUELL. A medium-sized shrub of compact, rounded habit, with glandular-downy young shoots and narrowly obovate leaves up to 11cm. long. Flower-heads yellow, in terminal panicles. Chatham Islands. I. 1909.

†*kirkii HOOK. f. (*glastifolius*). A glabrous shrub of medium size, with brittle stems. Leaves fleshy, varying in shape from narrow-obovate to elliptic-oblong, few toothed or dentate. Flower-heads white, in large, flat terminal corymbs. Only for the mildest areas or conservatory.

***laxifolius** BUCH. A small shrub often confused with *S. greyi*, but rarer in cultivation and with smaller, thinner, pointed leaves. Flower-heads yellow, in loose terminal panicles.

†*leucostachys BAKER. A striking and beautiful, lax, silvery-white shrub of medium size with finely divided pinnate leaves. Its almost scandent branches and tender nature demand a sunny wall. Flowers whitish in summer, not very ornamental. Patagonia. I. 1893. A.M. 1973.

***monroi** HOOK. f. A small shrub of dense habit often forming a broad dome, easily recognised by its oblong or oval, conspicuously undulate leaves which are covered beneath, like the young shoots and flower-stalks with a dense white felt. Flower-heads yellow, in dense terminal corymbs. As attractive and useful in gardens as *S. greyi*.

†*perdicioides HOOK. f. A small to medium-sized shrub, with dull green, glabrous leaves which are finely-toothed and 2·5 to 5cm. long. Flower-heads yellow in terminal corymbs. Only for the mildest areas.

***reinoldii** ENDL. (*rotundifolius*). A medium-sized shrub of dense, rounded habit with thick, leathery, rounded leaves, 5 to 13cm. long, glabrous and shining green above, felted beneath. Flower-heads yellowish in terminal panicles not conspicuous. One of the best shrubs for windswept gardens by the sea. It will take the full blast of the Atlantic Ocean.

rotundifolius. See *S. reinoldii*.

SHEPHERDIA—Elaeagnaceae—A small genus of dioecious shrubs related to *Elaeagnus* and *Hippophae*, differing from both in the opposite leaves. Shrubs for full exposure, excellent in coastal areas.

argentea NUTT. "Buffalo Berry". A slow-growing, occasionally spiny shrub of medium size with oblong, silvery, scaly leaves. The inconspicuous flowers appear in March and are followed, on female plants, by scarlet, edible berries. Central N. America. I. 1818.

canadensis NUTT. A dense, bushy shrub of medium size, with brownish, scaly shoots and elliptic to ovate leaves, which are silvery hairy and speckled with brown scales below. The inconspicuous flowers in spring are followed, on female plants, by yellowish-red berries. N. America. I. 1759.

SIBIRAEA—Rosaceae—A genus of five species closely related to and sometimes included in *Spiraea*, but differing in the entire leaves and various small botanical characters. The following species is best in a well-drained sunny position:—

laevigata MAXIM. (*altaiensis*) (*Spiraea laevigata*). An erect shrub occasionally up to 1·8m. The stout, glabrous branches are clad with narrowly obovate, sea-green leaves, 7·5 to 10cm. long. The panicles of whitish flowers are produced from the tips of the shoots in late spring and early summer, but they are of little ornament. Mts. of C. Asia; S.E. Europe. I. 1774.

croatica SCHNEID. In cultivation smaller in all its parts than the type.

‡SINOJACKIA—Styracaceae—A small genus of deciduous, Chinese small trees or large shrubs, requiring a moist, lime-free soil.

rehderana HU. A very rare, small, styrax-like, loosely branched, small tree or large shrub, with thin, elliptic, alternate leaves. Flowers white, the corolla divided to the base into four to six lobes, appearing singly or in short, axillary racemes in May and June. Alfred Rehder, after whom this species is named, was a giant among botanists. It is to him we all owe a tremendous debt for his "Manual of Cultivated Trees and Shrubs", one of his many works, but like so many botanists he was not "good company" in the garden. E. China. I. 1930.

xylocarpa HU. A small tree differing from *S. rehderana* in its broader leaves; longer-stalked flowers and curious ovoid fruits. E. China. I. 1934.

‡SINOWILSONIA—Hamamelidaceae—A rare monotypic genus related to the witch hazels and mainly of botanical interest. Introduced from China by E. H. Wilson ("Chinese Wilson"), in whose honour it is named. In a walk round the nurseries with Ernest Wilson, it seemed impossible to find a tree, shrub or herbaceous plant with which he was not familiar. A first class botanist, perhaps the greatest of the plant hunters, and like W. J. Bean, a tremendous companion in the garden.

henryi HEMSL. A large shrub or occasionally a small, spreading tree. The large, bristle-toothed leaves, 7·5 to 15cm. long, recall those of a lime and are covered beneath with stellate pubescence. Flowers in May monoecious, small and greenish, the males in slender, pendulous catkins, the females in pendulous racemes lengthening to 15cm. in fruit. C. and W. China. I. 1908.

***SKIMMIA—Rutaceae**—A small genus of slow-growing, aromatic, evergreen shrubs of compact habit. *S. japonica* and *S. laureola* bear male and female flowers on separate plants and both sexes are required for the production of its brightly coloured fruits which persist through the winter. All are tolerant of shade and are excellent shrubs for industrial areas and seaside gardens.

fortunei. See *S. reevesiana*.

japonica THUNB. A variable, small, dome-shaped shrub of dense habit, with leathery, obovate to elliptic leaves. The terminal panicles of white, often fragrant flowers in April and May are followed, on female plants, by clusters of globular, bright red fruits. A most adaptable shrub in all its forms, equally at home on chalk or acid soils. Japan. C. 1838. F.C.C. 1863. A.G.M. 1969.

'Fisheri'. See '*Foremanii*'.

'Foremanii' ('*Fisheri*') ('*Veitchii*'). A more vigorous female clone with distinctly broad-obovate leaves and large bunches of brilliant red fruits. F.C.C. 1888. A.G.M. 1969.

'Fragrans'. A free-flowering male clone of broad, dome-shaped habit with dense panicles of white flowers scented of "Lily-of-the-Valley". A.G.M. 1969.

'Fructu-albo'. A rather weak, low-growing, female clone of compact habit. Leaves small, fruits white.

'Nymans'. An extremely free-fruiting form with oblanceolate leaves and comparatively large fruits.

SKIMMIA—*continued*

japonica repens OHWI. A very slow, low-growing, often creeping form from the mountains of Japan, Sakhalin and Kuriles.

'Rogersii'. A dense, compact, dwarf, female clone of slow growth with somewhat curved or twisted leaves and large, red fruits. A.G.M. 1969.

'Rogersii Nana'. A free-flowering male clone resembling *'Rogersii'*, but more dwarf and compact, slower-growing and with smaller leaves.

'Rubella' (*S.* ×*rubella*). A male clone with large, open panicles of red buds throughout the winter which open in the early spring into white, yellow-anthered flowers. A.M. 1962. A.G.M. 1969.

'Veitchii'. See *'Foremanii'*.

laureola SIEB. & ZUCC. A small, dense growing shrub with lanceolate to obovate dark green leaves, 7·5 to 15cm. long, clustered at the ends of the shoots in the manner of *Daphne laureola*. When crushed they emit a strong pungent smell. The terminal clusters of greenish-yellow flowers borne in spring are, in contrast to the leaves, sweetly fragrant. These are followed on female plants by bright red fruits. Himalaya. C. 1868. A.M. 1977.

‡**reevesiana** FORT. (*fortunei*). A dwarf shrub, rarely reaching ·9m., forming a low, compact mound. Leaves narrowly elliptic, often with a pale margin. Flowers hermaphrodite, white, produced in short, terminal panicles in May, followed by obovoid, matt crimson-red fruits which last through the winter and are usually present when the flowers appear again in spring. It is not satisfactory on chalky soils. China. I. 1849.

×**rubella.** See *S. japonica 'Rubella'*.

"SLOE". See *PRUNUS spinosa*.

"SMOKE TREE". See *COTINUS coggygria*.

"SNOWBALL". See *VIBURNUM opulus 'Sterile'*.

"SNOWBALL, JAPANESE". See *VIBURNUM plicatum*.

"SNOWBERRY". See *SYMPHORICARPOS albus* and *S. rivularis*.

"SNOWDROP TREE". See *HALESIA carolina*.

"SNOWY MESPILUS". See *AMELANCHIER*.

SOLANUM—**Solanaceae**—A large genus of mainly herbaceous plants containing several species of economic importance such as the potato (*Solanum tuberosum*). The following semi-woody species are only suitable for the mildest localities. See also under CLIMBERS.

crispum. See under CLIMBERS.

jasminoides. See under CLIMBERS.

†**laciniatum** AIT. "Kangaroo Apple". A beautiful sub-shrub with purple stems up to 1·8m. high. Leaves lanceolate, usually deeply cut. Flowers comparatively large and very attractive, violet, with a yellow staminal beak, borne in loose, axillary racemes during summer, followed by small, egg-shaped fruits which change from green to yellow. A vigorous species for the very mildest areas or conservatory. Generally confused in cultivation with *S. aviculare* which differs in its lilac or white flowers, with pointed (not notched) lobes. Australia; New Zealand. I. 1772.

†**valdiviense** DUNAL. A vigorous, more or less climbing shrub for a sunny, sheltered wall. The arching shoots lengthen to 2·5 or 3m., bearing entire, pointed leaves. Flowers usually pale mauve or lavender, with a central beak of yellow anthers, borne in axillary racemes during May. Valdivia (Chile). Introduced by Harold Comber in 1927. A.M. 1931.

SOPHORA—**Leguminosae**—A genus of deciduous and evergreen, sun-loving trees and shrubs, much valued for their elegant, pinnate leaves and floral display. Succeeding in all well-drained, fertile soils.

japonica L. "Japanese Pagoda Tree". A medium-sized to large tree, normally of rounded habit. Leaves up to 30cm. long, composed of nine to fifteen leaflets. The creamy-white pea-flowers are produced in large, terminal panicles during late summer and autumn but, unfortunately, not on young trees. It flowers prodigiously in the hot dry summers of S.E. Europe. Native of China, widely planted in Japan. I. 1753.

'Pendula'. A picturesque, small, weeping tree with stiffly drooping branches. An admirable lawn specimen, also suitable for forming a natural arbour.

pubescens BOSSE. Leaflets softly pubescent beneath, up to 8cm. long. Flowers tinged lilac.

'Variegata'. Leaflets mottled creamy-white.

SOPHORA—*continued*

japonica 'Violacea'. A late-flowering form with wing and keel-petals flushed with rose-violet.

†***macrocarpa** SM. (*Edwardsia chilensis*). An attractive evergreen shrub of medium size, flowering at an early age. Leaves up to 13cm. long with thirteen to twenty-five leaflets. Flowers comparatively large, rich yellow, borne in short axillary racemes in May. Chile. I. 1822. A.M. 1938.

†***microphylla** AIT. (*tetraptera microphylla*). A large shrub or occasionally a small tree, closely related to and resembling *S. tetraptera*, but with smaller, more numerous leaflets and slightly smaller flowers. Juvenile plants are dense and wiry in habit. New Zealand. A.M. 1951.

†***prostrata** BUCH. (*tetraptera prostrata*). A small shrub, occasionally prostrate, usually forming a broad, rounded hummock of tangled, interlacing, wiry stems. Leaves with six to eight pairs of tiny leaflets. The small, brownish-yellow to orange pea-flowers are produced singly or in clusters of two or three during May. New Zealand.

†***tetraptera** J. MILL. The New Zealand "Kowhai" is best grown against a south-west-facing, sunny wall in the British Isles. It forms a large shrub or small tree with spreading or drooping branches covered, when young, by a fulvous tomentum. Leaves with twenty to forty ovate to elliptic-oblong leaflets. Flowers pea-shaped, but rather tubular, yellow, 4 to 5cm. long, produced in drooping clusters in May. The curious seed pods are beaded in appearance and possess four broad wings. I. 1772. A.M. 1943. A.M. 1977.

'Grandiflora'. A form with large leaflets and slightly larger flowers.

microphylla. See *S. microphylla*.

prostrata. See *S. prostrata*.

viciifolia HANCE (*davidii*). Small to medium-sized shrub with grey-downy, later spiny branches and leaves with seven to ten pairs of leaflets, silky hairy beneath. The small bluish-white pea-flowers are borne in short terminal racemes in June. China. I. 1897. A.M. 1933.

SORBARIA—Rosaceae—Handsome, vigorous shrubs with elegant, pinnate leaves which serve to distinguish them from *Spiraea*, with which they are commonly associated. All bear white or creamy-white flowers in terminal panicles during summer and early autumn. Even in winter their brownish or reddish stems and seed heads possess a sombre attraction. They thrive in most soils, flowering best in full sun. The old flowering stems may be hard pruned in late February or March, to encourage the production of strong, vigorous shoots with extra large leaves and flower panicles. They look very well in association with water.

aitchisonii HEMSL. A very elegant shrub of medium size, the branches long and spreading, reddish when young. Leaves glabrous, with eleven to twenty-three sharply-toothed and tapered leaflets. Flowers in large, conical panicles, in July and August. Afghan; Kashmir. I. 1895. A.M. 1905. A.G.M. 1969.

arborea SCHNEID. A large, robust shrub with strong, spreading stems and large leaves composed of thirteen to seventeen slender-pointed leaflets which are downy beneath. Flowers produced in large, conical panicles at the end of the current year's growths in July and August. An excellent large specimen shrub for lawn or border. C. and W. China. Introduced by Ernest Wilson in 1908. A.M. 1963.

assurgens VILM. & BOIS. A vigorous shrub of medium size with large leaves composed of thirteen to seventeen sharply, double-toothed leaflets, glabrous or slightly downy on the veins beneath. Flowers borne in dense, erect, terminal panicles in July. China. I. 1896.

sorbifolia A. BR. A small to medium-sized, suckering shrub with erect stems and leaves composed of thirteen to twenty-five sharply-toothed, glabrous leaflets. Flowers produced in narrow, stiffly erect panicles, in July and August. N. Asia. I. 1759. A form in which the leaflets are stellately hairy beneath is distinguished as var. *stellipila* MAXIM. Japan. C. 1900.

tomentosa REHD. (*lindleyana*). A large, strong-growing shrub of spreading habit. Leaves large, composed of eleven to twenty-three deeply toothed leaflets, hairy beneath. Flowers in large, terminal, downy panicles, from July to September. Himalaya. C. 1840.

×**SORBARONIA** (*SORBUS×ARONIA*)—**Rosaceae**—Hardy, slow-growing shrubs or small, spreading trees of a certain quality, intermediate in character between *Sorbus* and *Aronia*. Though of no outstanding ornamental merit, they are interesting on account of their unusual origin and add autumn tints to the garden. Any ordinary soil, in sun or semi-shade.

alpina SCHNEID. (*S. aria×A. arbutifolia*). A medium-sized to large shrub with oval or obovate, finely-toothed leaves, which are usually attractively tinted in autumn. Flowers white, borne in terminal clusters during May; fruits rounded, dark reddish-purple, speckled brown. Garden origin before 1809.

dippelii SCHNEID. (*S. aria×A. melanocarpa*). Similar to ×*S. alpina* in general appearance, but leaves narrower in outline and permanently grey-felted beneath. Fruits dark reddish-purple with an orange pulp. Garden origin before 1870.

fallax SCHNEID. (*S. aucuparia×A. melanocarpa*). A medium-sized shrub or small tree with wide-spreading branches. Leaves elliptic, obtuse or acute, deeply divided below into two or three pairs of serrulate lobes or leaflets, turning to orange and red in autumn. Flowers white; fruits purplish. Garden origin before 1878.

hybrida SCHNEID. (*S. aucuparia×A. arbutifolia*). A wide-spreading shrub or small tree. Leaves variable in form, ovate to elliptic, broader and larger than those of ×*S. fallax*, rounded at the apex, deeply divided into two or three pairs of broad, overlapping leaflets, which give autumn colours of red and orange. Flowers white, hawthorn-like in spring; fruits purplish-black. Garden origin before 1785.

sorbifolia SCHNEID. (*S. americana×A. melanocarpa*). A medium-sized to large shrub similar to ×*S. fallax* in general appearance, but with leaves shortly acuminate and young growths less downy. Fruits blackish. Garden origin before 1893.

×**SORBOCOTONEASTER** (*SORBUS×COTONEASTER*)—**Rosaceae**—A rare, bi-generic hybrid of slow growth, originally found with the parents in pine forests in Yakutskland, eastern Siberia. Two forms are said to occur, one tends towards the *Sorbus* parent and the other to the *Cotoneaster* parent. We offer the former.

pozdnjakavii POJARK (*S. sibirica×C. melanocarpus*). A medium-sized shrub of somewhat erect habit. Leaves ovate, deeply cut into one to three pairs of oval lobes or leaflets, dark green above, densely hairy beneath. Flowers white, up to ten in a corymb. Fruits red. We are indebted for this interesting plant to Dr. D. K. Ogrin of the Faculty of Agriculture, Ljubljana, Jugoslavia who was instrumental in having scions sent to us from Siberia in 1958.

×**SORBOPYRUS** (*SORBUS×PYRUS*)—**Rosaceae**—A rare bi-generic hybrid usually forming a small to medium-sized tree. Any ordinary soil in an open position.

auricularis SCHNEID. (*S. aria×P. communis*). "Bollwyller Pear". A remarkable small to medium-sized tree of rounded habit, with oval or ovate, coarsely-toothed leaves which are grey-felted beneath. Flowers white, produced in corymbs in May. Fruits pear-shaped, 2·5 to 3cm. long, green then reddish, edible. Garden origin before 1619.

'Bulbiformis' (×*S. malifolia*). Probably a seedling of ×*S. auricularis*, differing in its broader, often rounded leaves, heart-shaped at base, its larger flowers in late April and May and its larger pear-shaped fruits 5cm. long which are yellow when ripe. Garden origin in Paris, before 1834.

SORBUS—**Rosaceae**—A large and horticulturally important genus ranging from dwarf shrubs to large trees, the majority of which are quite hardy. Quite attractive in flower, they are mainly grown for their ornamental foliage which, in many species, colours richly in autumn, and for their colourful, berry-like fruits. On average the forms with white or yellow fruits retain their attractions longer into the winter than those with red or orange fruits. Unless otherwise stated, the flowers are white and appear in May and early June. Easily grown in any well-drained, fertile soil. Some of the species and clones of the Aucuparia section are not long lived on shallow chalk soils. The majority of *Sorbus* may conveniently be referred to the first two of three groups—

Aria Section. Leaves simple, toothed or lobed. Excellent on chalky soil.

Aucuparia Section. Leaves pinnate with numerous leaflets.

Micromeles Section. A smaller group differing from the Aria Section in the fruits having deciduous calyces.

SORBUS—*continued*

alnifolia K. KOCH (Micromeles Section). A small to medium-sized tree with a dense head of purplish-brown branches. Leaves ovate to obovate, strongly veined, double toothed, recalling those of the hornbeam. Fruits small, oval, of a bright red. Rich scarlet and orange tints in autumn. Japan. I. 1892. A.M. 1924.

submollis REHD. (*zahlbruckneri* HORT.). Leaves broader, softly pubescent beneath, particularly when young. Japan; Korea; Manchuria; China and Ussuri.

alnifolia × aria. A small to medium-sized tree with glabrous reddish-brown shoots. Leaves elliptic to oblong-elliptic, doubly serrate, dark green and glabrous above, paler and thinly tomentose beneath, grey downy when young.

americana MARSH. (Aucuparia Section). A small tree of vigorous growth, with ascending branches and long-pointed, red, sticky buds. Leaves with thirteen to seventeen sharply-toothed, long-acuminate leaflets. Fruits small, bright red, borne in large, densely packed bunches. Rich autumn tints. Eastern N. America. I. 1782. A.M. 1950.

'Nana'. See *S. aucuparia 'Fastigiata'*.

anglica HEDL. (Aria Section). A medium-sized, native shrub or small bushy tree related to the "Whitebeam" (*S. aria*). Leaves inclined to obovate, shallowly lobed and toothed, glossy green above, grey tomentose beneath, turning golden brown in autumn; flowers white, with pink anthers, followed in autumn by globose, crimson fruits. Found only in western parts of the British Isles (except Scotland) and Killarney.

'Apricot Lady' (Aucuparia Section). A small tree, a seedling of *S. aucuparia* originating in our nurseries. Fruits apricot-yellow, large, in bold corymbs, contrasting with the neatly-cut, bright green foliage which colours richly in autumn. A.M. 1973.

aria CRANTZ. "Whitebeam". A small to medium-size, native tree with a compact, usually rounded head of branches. Leaves oval or obovate, greyish-white at first, later bright green above, vivid white tomentose beneath, turning to gold and russet in autumn when the bunches of deep crimson fruits are shown to advantage. A familiar tree, particularly on chalk formations in the south of England, where it usually accompanies the Yew. One of the best trees for windswept or maritime districts and industrial areas. Europe. A.G.M. 1969.

'Aurea'. Leaves tinted soft yellow-green.

'Chrysophylla'. Leaves yellowish throughout summer, particularly effective in late spring, becoming a rich butter yellow in autumn.

'Cyclophylla'. A form with broad oval or orbicular leaves.

'Decaisneana' (*'Majestica'*). A handsome form with larger, elliptic leaves, 10 to 15cm. long, and slightly larger fruits. A.G.M. 1969.

graeca. See *S. graeca*.

'Lutescens'. Upper surface of leaves covered by a dense creamy-white tomentum, becoming grey-green by late summer. An outstanding tree in spring. A.M. 1952. A.G.M. 1969.

'Majestica'. See *'Decaisneana'*.

'Pendula'. A delightful, small, weeping tree, usually less than 3m. high, with slender branches and smaller, narrower leaves than the type.

'Quercoides'. A small, slow-growing shrub of dense, compact, twiggy and congested growth. Leaves oblong, sharply and evenly lobed, the margins curving upwards.

'Salicifolia'. An attractive form, graceful in habit, with lax branches and leaves narrower and longer than those of the type.

arranensis HEDL. (Aria Section). A large shrub or small tree of upright habit. Leaves ovate to elliptic, deeply lobed, green above, grey tomentose beneath. Fruits red, longer than broad. A rare, native species only found wild in two glens on the Isle of Arran.

aucuparia L. "Mountain Ash"; "Rowan". A familiar, native tree of small to medium size, with greyish downy, winter buds. Leaves pinnate, with eleven to nineteen sharply-toothed leaflets. Fruits bright red, carried in large, dense bunches during autumn, but soon devoured by hungry birds. An easily grown species, quite the equal to its Chinese counterparts, but not long-lived on very shallow, chalk soils. Very tolerant of extreme acidity. A parent of numerous hybrids. Europe. A.M. 1962. A.G.M. 1969.

SORBUS—*continued*

aucuparia 'Asplenifolia' (*'Laciniata'*). An elegant tree with deeply cut and toothed leaflets, giving the leaves a fern-like effect. A.G.M. 1969.

'Beissneri'. An interesting tree with a dense head of erect branches. Young shoots and sometimes the leaf petioles of a dark coral red. Leaves yellow-green, particularly when young, the leaflets varying in form from deeply incised to pinnately lobed, many having an attractive, fern-like appearance. The trunk and stems are a warm copper or russet colour. A.G.M. 1969.

'Dirkenii'. Leaves yellow when young, becoming yellowish-green.

'Edulis' (*'Moravica'*) (*dulcis*). A strong-growing, extremely hardy tree, differing from the type in its larger leaves with longer, broader leaflets, toothed mainly near the apex, and its larger fruits which are sweet and edible and carried in heavier bunches. Originated about 1800.

'Fastigiata' (*S. scopulina* HORT. not GREENE) (*S. americana 'Nana'*) (*S. decora 'Nana'*). A remarkable, slow-growing, columnar shrub or small tree up to 5·5m., with stout, closely erect stems. Leaves large, with eleven to fifteen dark green leaflets. Fruits sealing-wax red, large, borne in large, densely-packed bunches. A distinct plant with a confusing history. A.M. 1924 (as *S. americana nana*). A.G.M. 1969.

'Fructuluteo'. See *'Xanthocarpa'*.

'Moravica'. See *'Edulis'*.

'Pendula'. A small, wide-spreading tree with weeping branches.

'Rossica'. Similar to *'Edulis'*, but leaflets with stronger and more regular teeth.

'Sheerwater Seedling'. A vigorous, upright small tree with a compact, ovoid head of ascending branches, and large clusters of orange-red fruits. Excellent as a street tree.

'Xanthocarpa' (*'Fructuluteo'*) (*'Fifeana'*). Fruits amber-yellow. A.M. 1895. A.G.M. 1969.

bristolensis WILMOTT (Aria Section). A small, native tree with a compact, often rounded head of branches. Leaves oval or rhomboidal, shortly lobed, with a wedge-shaped base, green above, grey downy beneath. Fruits orange-red, carried in dense clusters. Only found wild in the Avon Gorge, near Bristol.

caloneura REHD. (Micromeles Section). A large shrub or small tree with erect stems. Leaves oval to oblong, double toothed and boldly marked by nine to sixteen pairs of parallel veins. Fruits small, brown, globular with a flattened apex. C. China. I. 1904.

cashmiriana HEDL. (Aucuparia Section). A beautiful, small tree of open habit. Leaves composed of seventeen to nineteen strongly serrated leaflets. Flowers soft pink in May. Fruits gleaming-white, 12mm. across. A distinct species with its loose, drooping clusters of fruits like white marbles, remaining long after the leaves have fallen. Kashmir. A.M. 1952. F.C.C. 1971.

chamaemespilus CRANTZ (Aria Section). A small, slow-growing shrub of dense, compact habit up to 1·8m. Twigs stout, bearing elliptic, sharply toothed leaves which are glossy dark green above, paler beneath, turning rich yellow, orange and russett in autumn. Flowers pink, densely packed in terminal corymbs. Fruits 12mm. long, red. A distinct species of neat appearance. Mts. of C. and S. Europe. I. 1683.

commixta HEDL. (Aucuparia Section). A small, variable tree of columnar habit when young, broadening somewhat in maturity. Winter buds long-pointed and sticky. Leaves glabrous, with eleven to fifteen slender-pointed, serrated leaflets, bright, glossy green above, coppery when young, colouring richly in autumn. Fruits small and globular, red or orange-red, borne in large, erect bunches. One of the best species for autumn colour. Japan. C. 1880. A.M. 1979.

× **confusa.** See *S.* × *vagensis*.

conradinae KOEHNE. See *S. esserteauana*.

conradinae HORT. See *S. pohuashanensis*.

cuspidata HEDL. (Aria Section) (*vestita*). "Himalayan Whitebeam". A medium-sized tree of erect habit when young, later spreading. Leaves broad-elliptic, decurrent onto the petiole, 15 to 25cm. long, green above, silvery white or buff tomentose beneath. Fruits green, speckled and flushed warm brown, 15 to 20mm. across, resembling small crab-apples or miniature pears, borne in loose bunches. A magnificent species with bold foliage, quite one of the handsomest of all hardy trees. Himalaya. I. 1820.

'Sessilifolia'. Large elliptic leaves tapering towards base and apex, sea-green above, grey-white tomentose beneath, sessile or very shortly stalked.

SORBUS—*continued*

decora HORT. (Aucuparia Section). An attractive, medium-sized shrub of loose, open growth. Leaves with thirteen to seventeen sea-green, obtuse leaflets. Fruits borne in dense clusters, coloured a conspicuous orange when young, later turning to red. Possibly of hybrid origin.

'Nana'. See *S. aucuparia* '*Fastigiata*'.

decurrens. See *S.* ×*thuringiaca*.

discolor HEDL. (Aucuparia Section). A small tree with an open head of ascending branches. Leaves glabrous with eleven to fifteen toothed leaflets, colouring richly in autumn. Flowers opening generally earlier than the others of the group, in some years by two to three weeks. Fruits creamy-yellow, tinged pink, ovoid to obovoid, carried on red stalks in rather loose clusters. N. China. Introduced about 1883. Apparently a variable species. It is doubtful whether the true species is in cultivation. The plant here described is probably of hybrid origin. See also under *S. hupehensis aperta*.

discolor HORT. See *S.* '*Embley*'.

domestica L. "Service Tree". A medium-sized tree, with open, spreading branches, rough scaly bark and sticky, shining winter buds. Leaves pinnate composed of thirteen to twenty-one leaflets, which are toothed in their upper halves. Fruits pear-shaped or apple-shaped, 2·5 to 3cm. long, green, tinged red on the sunny side, edible when bletted. The form with pear-shaped fruits is sometimes separated as var. *pyriformis*, and the form with apple-shaped fruits as var. *maliformis*. S. and E. Europe. Long cultivated.

'Edwin Hillier'. A slow-growing shrub or small tree. The mother plant was raised from seed received as *S. poteriifolia*, and has the appearance of having a member of the Aria Section as the pollinator. Winter buds rounded and ferruginous. Leaves ovate to elliptic or lanceolate, the lower half divided into one to three pairs of serrated leaflets or lobes, the upper half strongly lobed and toothed, dark green above, densely grey or brownish-grey tomentose beneath. Flowers pink, in terminal corymbs. Fruits oval, rose-red.

'Embley' (Aucuparia Section) (*discolor* HORT.). A small to medium-sized, erect-growing tree. It appears to be closely related to *S. commixta*, having the same pointed, sticky buds, leaves with eleven to fifteen sharply pointed leaflets, and large, heavy bunches of glistening orange-red fruits. It is a superb street tree, with its leaves consistently glowing red in autumn, colouring generally later than those of *S. commixta*, and remaining on the branches longer. A.M. 1971.

It is almost certain that this tree was the recipient of the A.G.M. given in 1930 to *S. discolor*. No doubt this tree was sent home from China by Wilson or Forrest, but has escaped the interest and attention, if not the eye, of an underworked botanist. If the late Dr. Wilfrid Fox had lived to publish his book on Sorbus, it was his intention to describe this most desirable and comparatively widely distributed tree under the name *S. embleyensis*, as it was at Embley Park, Hants., that he first saw this attractive tree in the glory of its autumn colour.

epidendron HAND.-MAZZ (Micromeles Section). A very rare shrub or small tree inclined to the equally rare *S. rhamnoides*, with slightly glaucous shoots. Leaves obovate to narrowly elliptic, long pointed, serrulate dark green above, rusty pubescent beneath. Fruits globose, brownish-green in colour. W. China. Introduced by George Forrest in 1925.

esserteauana KOEHNE (Aucuparia Section) (*conradinae* KOEHNE not HORT.). A small tree of open habit, occasionally up to 11m. Stipules large and leafy. Leaves composed of usually eleven to thirteen, sharply-toothed leaflets, dark matt green above, grey downy beneath. The small scarlet fruits colour later than most other species and are bor nein dense broad clusters. The foliage gives rich autumn tints. W. China. I. 1907. A.M. 1954.

'Flava'. Fruits of a rich, lemon yellow borne in crowded flattened corymbs. A superb clone. A.M. 1934.

'Ethel's Gold (Aucuparia Section). A small tree with bright green, sharply serrate leaflets and bunches of golden-amber fruits. A seedling of hybrid origin which originated in our nurseries. Probably a seedling of *S. commixta*, which it resembles in leaf. The attractively coloured fruits persist into the New Year if the birds allow.

fennica. See *S. hybrida*.

SORBUS—*continued*

folgneri REHD. (Micromeles Section). A graceful, small tree of variable habit, usually with spreading or arching branches. Leaves variable, oval to narrowly so, double toothed, dark green above, white or grey tomentose beneath, often assuming rich autumnal colours. Fruits variable in size, ovoid oı obovoid, dark red or purplish-red, in drooping clusters. C. China. I. 1901. A.M. 1915.

'Lemon Drop'. A graceful tree with slender, arching and drooping branches. Fruits bright yellow, set amid deep green leaves which are white beneath. Originated in our nurseries.

gracilis K. KOCH (Aucuparia Section). A shrub of medium size. Leaves with seven to eleven matt-green leaflets, toothed at the apex, stipules persistent, large and leafy. Flowers in few-flowered corymbs, fruits elongated pear-shape, oblong or obovoid, 15mm. long, orange-red. Japan. C. 1934.

graeca KOTSCH (Aria Section) (*aria graeca*) (*umbellata cretica*). A medium-sized shrub or small tree of dense, compact habit. Leaves obovate or rounded, double toothed, green above, greenish-white tomentose beneath. Fruits crimson. S.E. and E.C. Europe. C. 1830.

†**harrowiana** REHD. (Aucuparia Section). Related to *S. insignis*, this is perhaps the most remarkable and distinct of the pinnate-leaved species. A small tree of compact habit, with stout ascending branches. Leaves 20 to 30cm. long and as much across, pinnate with two to four pairs of sessile leaflets and a long-stalked terminal leaflet; leaflets 15 to 18cm. long by 4 to 4·5cm. across, the lateral ones conspicuously uneven at base, glossy dark green above, pale glaucous-green and slightly reticulate beneath. Flowers small, dull white, borne in large flattened corymbs, followed by equally small pink or pearly white fruits. Discovered by George Forrest in Yunnan in 1912, and later re-introduced by Kingdon Ward. Plants of the latter introduction have survived with little injury the severe winter of 1962-63, whilst those of Forrest's introduction have been killed by severe winters except in the mildest localities. A.M. 1971.

hedlundii HORT. not SCHNEID. (Aria Section). A strikingly handsome, medium-sized tree with large leaves which are silvery-white, tomentose beneath, with rust coloured midrib and veins. The tree in cultivation is merely a selection of *S. cuspidata*.

× **hostii** HEDL. (*chamaemespilus* × *mougeotii*). A small tree or large shrub of compact habit. Leaves oval or obovate, sharply-toothed, green above, grey pubescent beneath. Flowers pale pink, followed by bright red fruits. Occuring with the parents in the wild. C. 1820. A.M. 1974.

hupehensis SCHNEID. (Aucuparia Section). A small, but strong-growing tree developing a bold, compact head of ascending, purple-brown branches. Leaves large, with a distinctive bluish-green cast, easily recognisable from a distance. Leaflets eleven to seventeen in number, sharply toothed in the upper half. Stipules large and leafy. Fruits white or sometimes pink-tinged. Borne in loose, drooping bunches and lasting late into winter. The leaves turn a glorious red in autumn. W. China. Introduced by E. H. Wilson in 1910. A.M. 1955. A.G.M. 1969.

aperta SCHNEID. An elegant tree, smaller in all its parts. Leaves with only nine to eleven pointed leaflets. Fruits white. This very distinct plant, so unlike typical *S. hupehensis*, could possibly be the elusive *S. discolor* HEDL.

obtusa SCHNEID. (*S. oligodonta*). A most attractive form with pink fruits. Leaves with usually eleven leaflets, toothed only near the obtuse apex. Various selections have been named including '*Rosea*' and '*Rufus*', both with pink fruits. F.C.C. 1977.

hybrida L. (Aria Section) (*fennica*). A small to medium-sized, compact tree. Leaves broad ovate, one to one and a half times as long as broad, divided at the base into one or two pairs of long leaflets, the upper half variously toothed and lobed, green above, grey tomentose beneath. Fruits red, globose, almost 12mm. across, in large clusters. Now accepted by many authorities as a species, it is said to have originated as a hybrid between *S. aucuparia* and *S. rupicola*. Wild in Scandinavia.

'Fastigiata'. See *S.* × *thuringiaca* '*Fastigiata*'.

'Gibbsii' (*pinnatifida 'Gibbsii'* HORT.). A selected clone of more compact habit and with larger fruits. A.M. 1925 (as *Pyrus firma*). A.M. 1953.

meinichii. See *S. meinichii*.

× **hybrida** HORT. See *S.* × *thuringiaca*.

SORBUS—*continued*

insignis HEDL. (K.W.7746) (Aucuparia Section). A magnificent, small tree for a reasonably sheltered site, with stout, stiffly ascending, purplish-brown branches. Leaves pinnate, up to 25cm. long, composed of eleven to fifteen oblong-lanceolate, shallowly-toothed leaflets which are dark polished green and reticulate above, glaucous beneath. Petioles with a large, conspicuous clasping base. Fruits small, oval, pink, borne in large heads. They seem to hold little attraction for the birds and persist almost to Easter. In winter the large buds are conspicuous. Related to *S. harrowiana*, but hardier. Introduced by Kingdon Ward from the Naga Hills (Assam) in 1928. Also found in E. Nepal.

intermedia PERS. (Aria Section). "Swedish Whitebeam". A small to medium-sized tree with a dense, usually rounded head of branches. Leaves ovate to broad elliptic, lobed in the lower half, coarsely-toothed above, dark green and glossy above, grey tomentose beneath. Fruits 12mm. across, orange-red, in bunches. N.W. Europe.

japonica HEDL. (Micromeles Section). A rare tree of medium size, the young branches, inflorescence and leaves beneath covered with a dense, white pubescence. Leaves ovate-orbicular to broadly ovate, shallowly-lobed and toothed. Fruits obovoid, red, with brown speckled. Attractive autumn tints. Japan.

calocarpa REHD. An attractive form with leaves whiter beneath and fruits larger, orange-yellow, without speckles. Rich yellow autumn tints. C. Japan. I. 1915.

'Jermyns' (Aucuparia Section) (*aucuparia* × *sargentiana*). A small tree with an upright head of branches. Buds red, glabrous and sticky. Leaves intermediate in shape and size, but without the conspicuous stipules of *S. sargentiana*. Giving good autumn tints. Fruits in large bunches, deep amber turning to orange-red. Originated in our nurseries from seed of *S. sargentiana*.

'Joseph Rock' (Rock 23657) (Aucuparia Section). An outstanding, small tree up to 9m. or more high, with an erect, compact head of branches. Leaves composed of fifteen to nineteen, narrowly-oblong, sharply-toothed leaflets, turning to shades of red, orange, copper and purple in autumn. The rich autumn tints provide an ideal setting for the clusters of globular fruits, which are creamy-yellow at first deepening to amber-yellow at maturity, remaining on the branches well after leaf fall. The origin of this tree remains a mystery. It is thought, by some authorities, to be a hybrid of *S. serotina*, whilst others regard it as a wild species from China. A.M. 1950. F.C.C. 1962. A.G.M. 1969.

keissleri REHD. (Micromeles Section). A very rare and quite distinct small tree up to 12m. or a large shrub, with stiffly ascending branches. Leaves obovate, leathery, glossy green. Flowers greenish-white, sweetly-scented, borne in dense, terminal clusters and followed by small, crab-apple-like fruits which are green, with a bloomy, red cheek. C. and W. China. I. 1907.

× **kewensis** HENSEN (Aucuparia Section) (*pohuashanensis* HORT. not HEDL.). A first class, hardy, free-fruiting rowan, a hybrid between our native species (*aucuparia*), and the best of the Chinese species (*pohuashanensis*). The orange-red fruits are borne in large, heavy bunches, and severely test the strength of the branches, providing in autumn a feast both for the eyes and the birds. It is commonly grown in gardens under the name *S. pohuashanensis* from which it differs mainly in that the leafy stipules below the inflorescence are normally shed before the fruits develop. Raised originally at Kew Gardens. A.M. 1947. A.G.M. 1969 (as *S. pohuashanensis*). F.C.C. 1973 (as *S. pohuashanensis*).

koehneana SCHNEID. (Aucuparia Section). A medium-sized shrub or small, elegant tree. Leaves with seventeen to thirty-three, narrow, toothed leaflets. The small, porcelain-white fruits are borne in slender, drooping clusters. C. China. I. 1910.

lanata K. KOCH (Aria Section). A small to medium-sized tree or large shrub, with vigorous, downy shoots and elliptic-obovate, olive-green leaves, 15 to 23cm. long, white tomentose beneath and grey downy at first above. The attractive, crab-apple-like fruits are green, spotted brown and are borne in loose clusters. A handsome species seen at its best in the milder parts of the British Isles. Himalaya. C. 1870.

latifolia PERS. (Aria Section). "Service Tree of Fountainbleau". A small to medium-sized tree with downy young shoots and shaggy, peeling bark. Leaves ovate or broad elliptic, sharply lobed, glossy green above, grey felted beneath. Fruits globular, russet-yellow with large, brownish speckles. An apomictic species derived from a hybrid between *S. torminalis* and a species of the Aria Section. E.C. Portugal to S.W. Germany.

SORBUS—*continued*

megalocarpa REHD. A remarkable, small tree or large shrub of loose spreading habit. Twigs brown-purple, stout, bearing large, oval to obovate, deep green leaves, 15 to 23cm. long, which sometimes turn to crimson in autumn. The large, terminal flower-buds open before the leaves in early spring, producing a large, conspicuous corymb of cream-coloured flowers which have too pungent a smell for indoor decoration. These are followed by hard, brown fruits, which may be likened in size and colour to small partridge eggs. The large, red, sticky bud scales in spring are often very striking. W. China. Introduced by E. H. Wilson in 1903.

meinichii HEDL. (*hybrida meinichii*). A small, erect tree with a compact head of fastigiate branches. Leaves with four to six pairs of distinct leaflets and a deeply-toothed or lobed terminal portion, green above, grey tomentose beneath. Fruits rounded, red. Now accepted by many authorities as a species, it is said to have originated as a hybrid between *S. aucuparia* and *S. rupicola*, though it resembles more the former. Wild in S. and W. Norway.

meliosmifolia REHD. (Micromeles Section). A small tree or large bushy shrub with stiffly ascending, purplish brown branches. Leaves up to 18cm. long, bright green, with eighteen to twenty-four pairs of parallel veins. One of the first trees to flower once winter has passed. Fruits 12mm. long, brownish-red. A rare species sometimes confused in cultivation with *S. caloneura*, from which it differs in its larger, shorter-stalked, more numerously-veined leaves. W. China. I. 1910.

minima HEDL. (Aria Section). A slender-branched, native shrub of medium size. Leaves elliptic or oblong-elliptic, 5 to 7·5cm. long, shallowly-lobed, green above, grey tomentose beneath. Fruits small, scarlet, with a few speckles. Only found in the wild on limestone crags near Crickhowell, Brecon, Wales.

'Mitchellii' (Aria Section). A handsome, medium-sized to large tree, eventually developing a broad, rounded head. The mature leaves are large, about 15cm. by as much across and remarkably rounded, green above, white tomentose beneath. The original tree from which our stock was raised is growing in the Westonbirt Arboretum, Glos. This tree and others like it are merely selections of *S. cuspidata* which in the wild state varies greatly in leaf size and shape.

mougeotii SOY.-WILLEM. & GODRON (Aria Section). Generally a large shrub or small tree, with ovate or obovate, shallowly-lobed leaves, green above, whitish-grey tomentose beneath. Fruits slightly longer than wide, red, with a few speckles. European Alps (mainly in the west); Pyrenees. C. 1880.

oligodonta. See *S. hupehensis obtusa*.

pallescens REHD. (Aria Section). A beautiful, small tree of upright growth. Leaves narrowly elliptic to elliptic-lanceolate, acuminate, sharply double-toothed, green above, silvery-white tomentose beneath, with conspicuous veins. Older trees have shreddy bark and elliptic to oblong leaves. Fruits pear-shaped or rounded, up to 12mm. long, green with a red cheek, borne in loose clusters. W. China. I. 1908.

'Pearly King' (Aucuparia Section). A small, slender-branched tree with pinnate, fern-like leaves composed of thirteen to seventeen narrow, sharply-toothed leaflets. Fruits 15mm. across, rose at first, changing to white with a pink flush, borne in large, loosely pendulous bunches. A hybrid of *S. vilmorinii*, which originated in our nurseries.

pinnatifida. See *S.* ×*thuringiaca*.

'Gibbsii'. See *S. hybrida 'Gibbsii'*.

pohuashanensis HEDL. not HORT. (Aucuparia Section) (*conradinae* HORT. not KOEHNE) (*sargentiana warleyensis* HORT.). A splendid tree possibly the best Chinese Rowan, attaining up to 11m. with a dense head of spreading and ascending branches. Leaves with usually eleven to fifteen, sharply-toothed leaflets which are green above, grey pubescent beneath. Stipules large and leafy, persistent, especially below the inflorescence even when fruiting. Fruits red, borne in conspicuous bunches, causing the branches to bow under their concentrated weight. One of the most reliable and spectacular of *Sorbus* in fruit. Easily grown and very hardy. A parent of several hybrids, the true plant is rare in cultivation, its place most often being taken by the hybrid *S.*×*kewensis*. N. China. I. 1883. A.M. 1946.

pohuashanensis HORT. not HEDL. See *S.*×*kewensis*.

SORBUS—*continued*

poteriifolia HAND.-MAZZ. (Aucuparia Section). A beautiful, slow-growing, small tree with erect, purplish-brown branches. Leaves composed of fifteen to nineteen sharply-serrate, dark green, downy leaflets. Fruits globular, of a delightful deep-rose-pink, carried in large, loose bunches. China. A.M. 1951.

prattii KOEHNE (Aucuparia Section). An elegant large shrub or occasionally a small tree, with slender branches and leaves composed of twenty-one to twenty-nine coarsely-toothed leaflets. Fruits small, globose, pearly-white, borne in small, drooping clusters all along the branches. W. China. A.M. 1971.

subarachnoidea REHD. A variety in which the leaflets possess a rufous, cobwebby indumentum beneath. W. China. Introduced by E. H. Wilson in 1910.

pygmaea HORT. (Aucuparia Section). The smallest known *Sorbus*. A very rare, tiny shrublet, difficult to cultivate. Leaves composed to nine to fifteen sharply-toothed leaflets. Flowers pale rose to crimson in terminal clusters, followed by globular, white fruits. Related to *S. reducta* and likewise suited to scree or rock garden cultivation. Burma; Tibet; Yunnan.

randaiensis KOIDZ. (Aucuparia Section). A small tree with ascendi.ng branches and arching branchlets. Buds bright chestnut-brown, glabrous and slightly viscid. Leaves with usually thirteen sharply serrated leaflets. Fruits globose, glowing bright red, borne in dense, erect corymbs. A native of Formosa Closely related to the Japanese *S. commixta*.

'Red Marbles' (Aucuparia Section). A small tree with stout twigs which originated in our Eastleigh nurseries in 1961. Leaves with purple stalks and thirteen to fifteen large, broadly and boldly toothed leaflets. Fruits red with pale spots, 12 to 17mm. across, borne in loose, heavy bunches. A magnificent fruiting tree, believed to be *S. aucuparia 'Edulis'* × *S. pohuashanensis*.

reducta DIELS. (Aucuparia Section). A rare and unusual dwarf, suckering shrub forming thickets of slender, erect stems, 30 to 60cm. high. Leaves with red petioles, composed of thirteen to fifteen sharply serrate, dark, shining green leaflets, turning to bronze and reddish-purple in autumn. Fruits small, globular, white flushed rose. A charming species when associated with heathers, dwarf conifers and other dwarf shrubs. N. Burma; W. China. Introduced by Kingdon Ward in 1943. A.M. 1974.

rhamnoides REHD. (Micromeles Section). An extremely rare shrub or small tree of loose habit. Leaves elliptic, 13 to 15cm. long, serrate, slender-stalked, green above, thinly grey-downy beneath at first. Fruits green. Sikkim.

'Rose Queen' (Aucuparia Section) (*'Embley'* × *poteriifolia*). An attractive, small tree raised in our Eastleigh Nurseries in 1963. Leaves composed of thirteen to seventeen sharply serrate leaflets. Fruits of a bright rose-red, produced in large, loose bunches.

rufoferruginea SCHNEID. (Aucuparia Section). A small tree closely related to *S. commixta*, of which it is perhaps merely a variety. It differs from the above species in its slightly villous buds and the presence of soft brown hairs on the inflorescence and along the leaf midrib beneath. Japan. I. 1915.

rupicola HEDL. (Aria Section) (*salicifolia* HEDL.). A medium-sized, native shrub of rather stiff habit. Leaves obovate or oblanceolate, tapering to the base, coarsely-toothed, green above, white tomentose beneath. Fruits broader than long, carmine, with scattered brown speckles. British Isles; Scandinavia.

sargentiana KOEHNE (Aucuparia Section). A magnificent species, slowly developing into a rigidly-branched tree up to 9m. and as much through. Winter buds large and sticky, like those of a horse chestnut, but crimson. Leaves large and attractive, up to 30cm. long, composed of seven to eleven slender-pointed leaflets, each 7·5 to 13cm. long. Leaf-stalks red, stipules large, leafy and persistent. Fruits small, scarlet, late in ripening, produced in large, rounded heads up to 15cm. across. Rich red autumn colour. W. China. Discovered by E. H. Wilson in 1903, and introduced by him in 1908. A.M. 1954. F.C.C. 1956. A.G.M. 1969.

scalaris KOEHNE (Aucuparia Section). A small tree of distinct appearance with wide-spreading branches and neat, attractive, frond-like leaves. They are composed of twenty-one to thirty-three narrow leaflets, which are dark glossy green above, grey downy beneath, turning to rich red and purple in autumn. Fruits small, red, densely packed in flattened heads. W. China. Discovered and introduced by E. H. Wilson in 1904. A.M. 1934. A.G.M. 1969.

SORBUS—*continued*

scopulina HORT. See *S. aucuparia 'Fastigiata'*.

serotina KOEHNE (Aucuparia Section). A small, erect-branched tree related to *S. commixta*. Leaves composed of fifteen to seventeen sharply-toothed leaflets, colouring richly in late autumn. Fruits small, bright orange-red. Korea.

'Signalman'. A small tree of columnar habit raised in our Eastleigh Nursery in 1968 as the result of crossing *S. domestica* with *S. scopulina*. Leaves similar to those of the former parent, but slightly smaller and more densely arranged. Fruits large, bright orange, borne in dense clusters. Should prove to be an excellent tree for the small garden and for street planting.

sitchensis ROEM. (Aucuparia Section). A rigidly-branched shrub, very rare in cultivation. Leaves with seven to eleven elliptic-oblong leaflets colouring richly in autumn. Fruits large, bright red. N.W. North America. I. 1918.

sp. Ghose (Aucuparia Section). A superb, small tree of upright habit showing some affinity to *S. insignis* but hardier. Probably a new species and worthy of extensive planting. Leaves large, composed of fifteen to nineteen oblong, sharply serrate leaflets which are dark, dull green above, glaucescent beneath and rusty pubescent, at least along the midrib. Fruits small, rose-red, produced in large, densely packed bunches which remain on the branches until late in the season. Introduced by us from the Himalayas.

sp. Lowndes. See *S. ursina*.

sp. Yu 8423 (Aria Section). A distinct, slow-growing species which, in our arboretum is an erect, small tree of narrow, columnar habit. Leaves oval to obovate, 10 to 13cm. long, toothed, green above, grey tomentose beneath. Winter buds green and viscid. China.

× splendida HEDL. (Aucuparia Section) (*americana × aucuparia*). A small, robust tree intermediate in character between its parents. Buds sticky but rusty pubescent at tips. Fruits orange-red, in large, dense bunches. Garden origin before 1850.

thibetica HAND.-MAZZ. (K.W. 21127) (Aria Section). A specimen in our arboretum of this rare species is growing strongly and is over 3·6m. high. Its branches are rather stiff and erect, giving the tree a distinct columnar habit. Leaves elliptic to obovate, green and ribbed above, thinly hairy beneath; young leaves grey downy. Fruits in loose corymbs, globular, 12mm. in diameter, amber, speckled greyish-brown. Tibet; Bhutan. A splendid new silvery Whitebeam for sites where space is limited. Introduced by Kingdon Ward.

× thuringiaca FRITSCH (*aria × aucuparia*) (*decurrens*) (*pinnatifida*) (× *hybrida* HORT.). A small tree, developing a dense compact head of ascending branches. Leaves narrowly oval to oblong, one and a half to two and a half times as long as broad, lobed and toothed, divided at the base into one to three pairs of oval leaflets, dull green above, grey tomentose beneath. Fruits rounded, scarlet with a few brown speckles. Occurs rarely with the parents in the wild. Frequently confused with *S. hybrida* in cultivation, it differs in its stricter, more compact habit, and in its slightly larger, more elongated leaves with smaller, oval leaflets. A.M. 1924 (as *S. pinnatifida*).

'Fastigiata' (*hybrida 'Fastigiata'* HORT.). A most distinctive, small tree with an ovoid head of closely packed, ascending branches. Leaves and fruits as in type. A first-class tree possessing most of the qualities sought by those interested in public planting.

tianschanica RUPR. (Aucuparia Section). A slow-growing shrub or low rounded tree up to 3·5 or 4m. high. Leaves pinnate with nine to fifteen sharply-toothed, glossy green leaflets, colouring in autumn. Flowers and fruits are rarely carried on trees in the British Isles, though they are said to be conspicuous on specimens growing in more suitable climes. The flowers are 20mm. across, followed by globular red fruits. Turkestan. I. 1895.

torminalis CRANTZ (Aria Section). "Wild Service Tree". An attractive, medium-sized, native tree with ascending branches, spreading with age, scaly bark and brown twigs, woolly-pubescent when young. Leaves maple-like, ovate, sharply and conspicuously lobed, glossy dark green above, pubescent beneath at first, turning bronzy-yellow in autumn; fruits longer than broad, russety-brown. Europe including England; Asia Minor; N. Africa.

SORBUS—*continued*

umbellata cretica. See *S. graeca.*

ursina SCHAUER. (*sp. Lowndes* (Aucuparia Section). An attractive, small, erect-growing tree with stout, ascending, greyish branches. Buds red, ferruginous hairy at the tips. Leaves composed of fifteen to twenty-one sharply-ttoohed, elliptic-oblong, conspicuously reticulated leaflets. Fruits white or pink-tinged, borne in dense bunches. A very distinct and beautiful new species related to *S. poteriifolia*, introduced by Col. Donald Lowndes from the Himalayas. A.M. 1973.

× **vagensis** WILLMOTT (Aria Section) (*aria* × *torminalis*) (× *confusa*). A small to medium-sized tree of compact habit. Leaves ovate to elliptic, sharply lobed, not as deeply as in *S. torminalis*, glossy green above, thinly grey tomentose beneath. Fruits obovoid; greenish-brown, with numerous brown speckles. Occurs with the parents in the wild, in England only in the Wye Valley.

vestita. See *S. cuspidata.*

vilmorinii SCHNEID. (Aucuparia Section). A beautiful, small tree or medium-sized shrub of elegant, spreading habit. Leaves often in clusters, fern-like, composed of eleven to thirty-one small leaflets, each 12 to 20mm. long, turning to red and purple in autumn. The loose, drooping clusters of fruits are rose-red at first, gradually passing through pink to white flushed rose. A charming species suitable for the smaller garden. W. China. Introduced by the Abbé Delavay in 1889. A.M. 1916. A.G.M. 1953.

'Wilfrid Fox' (Aria Section) (*aria* × *cuspidata*). Named in memory of a generous friend and great gardener who did much to beautify the roadside plantings of England and was the creator of the famous Winkworth Arboretum in Surrey. This handsome hybrid tree has been growing in our nurseries for more than fifty years. It forms a round-headed tree 12m. in height. A broadly columnar tree when young, with densely packed, ascending branches. Leaves elliptic, 15 to 20cm. long, with a slender petiole, 2·5 to 4cm. long, shallowly lobed and doubly serrate, dark glossy green above, greyish-white tomentose beneath. Fruits marble-like, green at first turning to deep amber speckled grey.

'Winter Cheer' (Aucuparia Section) (*esserteauana 'Flava'* × *pohuashanensis*). A seedling of hybrid origin raised in our Eastleigh nursery in 1959. A small to medium-sized, open-branched tree. The large, flat bunches of fruits are a warm, chrome-yellow at first, ripening to orange-red. They begin to colour in September and last well into winter. A.M. 1971.

zahlbruckneri HORT. See *S. alnifolia submollis.*

"SOUTHERNWOOD". See *ARTEMISIA abrotanum.*

†**SPARMANNIA**—**Tiliaceae**—A small genus of tender shrubs and trees natives of Tropical and South Africa.

africana L. "African Hemp"; "House Lime". A large, stellately-hairy, apple green shrub of vigorous habit. Leaves large, often 30cm. or more across, palmately-lobed. Flowers white, 4cm. wide, with sensitive, yellow stamens, borne in conspicuous cymose umbels during spring. An excellent conservatory shrub. This marvellous plant not only tolerates but appears to thrive on the cigarette and cigar ends and tea and coffee dregs of the second class continental cafés. S. Africa. I. 1790. A.M. 1955.

SPARTIUM—**Leguminosae**—A monotypic genus closely related to *Cytisus* and *Genista*, differing in its one-lipped, spathe-like calyx. Thrives in a well-drained, sunny position. An excellent seaside shrub. Specimens drawn up in sheltered gardens are apt to become tall and leggy. These may be hard pruned in March, taking care not to cut into the old hard wood.

junceum L. "Spanish Broom". A strong-growing shrub of loose habit, with erect, green, rush-like stems up to 3m. Leaves small and inconspicuous. The comparatively large, fragrant, yellow, pea-flowers, 2·5cm. long, are borne in loose, terminal racemes throughout summer and early autumn. A wonderful shrub when kept low and bushy by the sea wind's blast. Mediterranean Region; S.W. Europe. Introduced to England about 1548. A.G.M. 1923. A.M. 1968. F.C.C. 1977.

LONICERA tragophylla

SOLANUM crispum 'Glasnevin'

ACTINIDIA kolomikta

CLEMATIS tangutica

PASSIFLORA caerulea

CLEMATIS montana 'Tetrarose'

ABIES koreana

TSUGA canadensis 'Pendula'

METASEQUOIA glyptostroboides

CHAMAECYPARIS lawsoniana 'Minima Aurea'

PINUS wallichiana

SPARTOCYTISUS—Leguminosae—A monotypic genus related to *Cytisus*. Requires a well-drained position in full sun.

nubigenus WEBB. & BERTH. (*Cytisus supranubius*). "Teneriffe Broom". A medium-sized shrub resembling *Spartium* in habit. Leaves small, trifoliolate. Flowers fragrant, milky-white, tinted rose, carried in May in axillary clusters on the previous year's wood. A pretty shrub when in flower. Theoretically a tender shrub it remains uninjured by snow and wind in our relatively cold area. Canary Isles. C. before 1824. A.M. 1924 (as *Cytisus supranubius*).

†*SPHACELE—Labiatae—A small genus of sage-like shrubs and sub-shrubs only suitable for the mildest areas of the British Isles.

chamaedryoides BRIQUET (*campanulata*). A small shrub with wrinkled leaves and loose racemes of pale blue, tubular flowers during summer. It makes a lovely conservatory shrub. Chile. I. 1875.

SPHAERALCEA—Malvaceae—A large genus of mainly tender species requiring a warm, sunny site and a well-drained soil.

†fendleri A. GRAY. A dwarf sub-shrub with downy shoots and three-lobed leaves. The inch wide, mallow-like flowers are pale reddish-orange in colour and are borne in axillary clusters during summer and autumn. A pretty little shrublet, suitable for a sunny border. N. Mexico.

"SPICE BUSH". See *LINDERA benzoin*.

"SPINDLE". See *EUONYMUS*.

SPIRAEA—Rosaceae—A variable and useful genus of hardy, flowering shrubs, many of which are graceful in habit and pleasing in foliage. They are easily grown in any ordinary soil and a sunny position though a few become chlorotic in very shallow chalk soils and are so described. Those of the *bumalda-japonica-douglasii* type which flower on the current year's shoots may be pruned to the ground in March, whilst those of the *henryi-nipponica-veitchii* type which flower on shoots of the previous year may require thinning out and the old flowering shoots cut to within a few centimetres of the old wood, immediately after flowering. Untidy specimens of *S. ×arguta* and *S. thunbergii* may be hard pruned immediately after flowering. *S. douglasii*, *S. salicifolia*, *S. tomentosa* and other thicket-forming species should only be planted where space permits.

aitchisonii. See *SORBARIA aitchisonii*.

albiflora ZAB. (*japonica alba*). A dwarf, "front-row" shrub of compact habit, with angular, glabrous shoots and lanceolate, coarsely-toothed leaves, glaucous beneath. Flowers white, borne in dense, terminal corymbs in late summer, on shoots of the current season. Japan. I. before 1868.

arborea. See *SORBARIA arborea*.

arcuata HOOK. f. A medium-sized shrub related to *S. gemmata*, with pubescent, angular stems and entire leaves. Flowers white, carried in small umbels all along the arching branches in May. Himalaya. C. 1908.

× arguta ZAB. (*multiflora × thunbergii*). "Bridal Wreath"; "Foam of May". A dense-growing, medium-sized shrub with graceful, slender branches. Leaves oblanceolate, to narrowly oval, entire or few-toothed, usually glabrous. Flowers pure white, produced in small clusters all along the branches in April and May. One of the most effective and free-flowering of the early spiraeas. C. before 1884. A.G.M. 1927.

assurgens. See *SORBARIA assurgens*.

baldshuanica B. FEDTSCHENKO. A dwarf shrub of rounded, compact habit, with slender, glabrous, twiggy branches. Leaves small, obovate, sea-green, toothed at the apex. Flowers white, in small, terminal corymbs in summer. S.E. Russia.

bella SIMS. A small shrub occasionally 1·5m. high, with angular branches, downy when young. Leaves broadly ovate, toothed at apex, glaucous beneath. Very attractive when carrying its bright rose-pink flowers in terminal corymbs in June. Not happy in really shallow chalk soils. Himalaya. I. 1818.

betulifolia PALL. A dwarf shrub occasionally up to 1m. high, forming mounds of reddish-brown, glabrous branches and broadly ovate to rounded leaves, 2 to 4cm. long. Flowers white, borne in dense corymbs, 2·5 to 6·5cm. across, in June. Suitable for the rock garden. N.E. Asia; Japan. I. about 1812.

SPIRAEA—*continued*

× **billiardii** HERINQ. (*douglasii* × *salicifolia*). Medium-sized, suckering shrub with erect, hairy stems. Leaves oblong to oblong-lanceolate, sharply toothed, greyish pubescent beneath. Flowers bright rose, borne in narrow, densely crowded panicles throughout summer. Not happy on shallow chalky soils. C. before 1854.

'Triumphans' (*menziesii 'Triumphans'*). A beautiful shrub with dense, conical panicles of purplish-rose flowers during summer. Not happy on shallow, chalky soils.

× **brachybotrys** LANGE (*canescens* × *douglasii*). A strong-growing, medium-sized shrub with gracefully arching branches. Leaves oblong or ovate, toothed at apex, grey downy beneath. Flowers pale rose, borne in dense, terminal panicles during summer. Not recommended for very shallow, chalky soils. C. before 1867.

bracteata. See *S. nipponica.*

bullata. See *S. japonica 'Bullata'.*

× **bumalda** BURVEN. (*albiflora* × *japonica*). A dwarf shrub with glabrous stems and sharply-toothed, ovate-lanceolate leaves. Flowers deep pink, carried in broad, flattened, terminal panicles on the current year's shoots, continuously throughout summer. The leaves are often variegated with pink and cream. C. before 1890.

'Anthony Waterer'. Flowers bright crimson. An excellent, dwarf shrub for the front of borders or for mass effect. The foliage is occasionally variegated cream and pink. F.C.C. 1893. A.G.M. 1969.

'Coccinea'. Flowers of a rich crimson.

'Froebelii'. Flowers bright crimson in July. Somewhat taller growing than the type.

calcicola W. W. SM. A small, graceful shrub with angular, glabrous stems. Leaves very small, fan-shaped, prettily three-lobed and toothed, borne on slender petioles. Flowers white, tinted rose without, produced in numerous small umbels along the arching stems in June. China. I. 1915.

canescens D. DON. A graceful, medium-sized shrub with long, angular, downy branches. Leaves oval or obovate, 1 to 2·5cm. long, toothed at apex, grey downy beneath. Flowers in corymbs, white, wreathing the arching stems in June and July. Himalaya. I. 1837.

myrtifolia ZAB. (*glaucophylla*). Leaves oblong, dark green above, glaucescent beneath.

cantoniensis LOUR. (*reevesiana*). A wide-spreading, graceful shrub up to 1·8m. high, with slender, arching, glabrous branches. Leaves rhomboidal, deeply-toothed or three-lobed, glaucous beneath. Flowers white, borne in rounded clusters along the branches in June. China, long cultivated in Japan. I. 1824.

'Lanceata' (*'Flore Pleno'*). An attractive form with lanceolate leaves and double flowers.

chamaedryfolia L. A suckering shrub, producing erect, angular, glabrous shoots up to 1·8m. high. Leaves ovate to ovate-lanceolate, coarsely-toothed, glaucescent beneath. Flowers white, borne in corymbs along the stems, in May. Widely distributed in the wild from C. and E. Europe to Siberia. C. 1789.

ulmifolia MAXIM. A more robust form with taller stems and ovate, double-toothed leaves. Flowers in large, fluffy heads, in late May or June.

× **cinerea** ZAB. (*cana* × *hypericifolia*). A small, densely-branched shrub with downy, arching stems and narrow, entire leaves, grey-downy when young. The small, white flowers are abundantly produced in dense clusters all along the branches in late April and early May; resembling *S.* × *arguta* in general effect. We offer the following clone:—

'Grefsheim'. A fine-flowering clone of Norwegian origin.

crispifolia. See *S. japonica 'Bullata'.*

discolor. See *HOLODISCUS discolor.*

‡**douglasii** HOOK. A rampant, suckering shrub, forming in time dense thickets of erect, reddish shoots 1·5 to 1·8m. high. Leaves narrowly oblong, coarsely-toothed, grey-felted beneath. Flowers purplish-rose, produced in dense, terminal panicles in June and July. Not recommended for shallow chalk soils. Western N. America. Discovered and introduced by David Douglas in 1827. Naturalised in parts of N. and C. Europe.

SPIRAEA—*continued*

gemmata ZAB. An elegant shrub of medium size, with glabrous, angular stems and characteristic long, slender leaf-buds. Leaves narrowly oblong, entire or three-toothed at apex, glabrous. Flowers white, borne in small corymbs along the arching branches in May. Mongolia. C. 1886.

glaucophylla. See *S. canescens myrtifolia.*

hacquetii. See *S. lancifolia.*

henryi HEMSL. A strong-growing, medium-sized to large shrub of arching habit, with reddish-brown, sparsely hairy stems. Leaves 4 to 8cm. long, narrowly oblong or oblanceolate, coarsely-toothed at apex. Flowers white, produced in rounded corymbs all along the arching branches, in June. C. China. Discovered by Augustine Henry, introduced by Ernest Wilson in 1900. A.M. 1934.

hypericifolia L. A dense, bushy shrub producing graceful, arching branches up to 1·5 to 1·8m. high. Leaves obovate, entire or three-toothed at apex. Flowers white, produced in small clusters along the branches during May. The form in general cultivation is ssp. *obovata.* S.E. Europe. Naturalised in parts of N. America. C. 1640.

japonica L.f. (*callosa*). A small, erect shrub with lanceolate to ovate, coarsely-toothed leaves. Flowers pink, borne in large, flattened heads, from midsummer onwards. A variable species, very popular in gardens. Japan; Korea; China to the Himalayas. Naturalised in parts of C. Europe. C. 1870.

alba. See *S. albiflora.*

'Alpina' (*'Nana'*). A superb dwarf shrub forming a dense, compact mound, 45 to 60cm. high and rather more across. Leaves and flower-heads proportionately smaller than those of the type. Spectacular when closely studded with tiny heads of rose-pink flowers. Worthy of a position in every garden and window-box, and should be mass-planted where space permits. A.G.M. 1969.

'Atrosanguinea'. Young growths red; flowers crimson. A selection of var. *fortunei.*

'Bullata' (*S. crispifolia*) (*S. bullata*). A dwarf, slow-growing shrub of compact habit. Leaves small, broadly ovate, bullate above. Flowers rose-crimson, in terminal, flat-topped clusters in summer. A splendid companion for *'Alpina'.* Garden origin in Japan. C. before 1881. F.C.C. 1884.

'Coccinea'. See *S.* ×*bumalda 'Coccinea'.*

'Fastigiata'. A vigorous, small shrub of stiff, erect habit. Flowers white in exceptionally wide flat heads.

fortunei REHD. The common Chinese form, differing from the type chiefly in its much larger, glabrous, incisely toothed leaves. E. and C. China. I. about 1850.

'Little Princess'. A dwarf, compact form forming a low mound with rose-crimson flowers.

'Macrophylla'. Not the best form in flower, but perhaps the best Spiraea for autumn leaf colour. Leaves large and bullate. A selection of var. *fortunei.*

'Ruberrima'. A dense, rounded shrub with rose-red flowers. A selection of var. *fortunei.*

laevigata. See *SIBIRAEA laevigata.*

lancifolia HOFFMANS (*hacquetii*) (*decumbens tomentosa*). A dwarf, compact, alpine shrub with procumbent, greyish-pubescent stems and ascending branches, up to 20cm. high. Leaves narrow, elliptic, toothed at apex, grey tomentose beneath. Flowers white in small, terminal corymbs, from June to September. A choice little shrub for the rock garden or scree. S.E. European Alps. I. 1885.

latifolia BORKH. (*salicifolia latifolia*). A rampant, suckering shrub producing erect, angular, reddish stems, 1·5 to 1·8m. high. Leaves variable in shape, coarsely-toothed. Flowers white or pale pink, produced in broad, conical, glabrous panicles at the ends of the current year's growths during summer. Not suitable for shallow chalk soils. North America. C. 1789.

lindleyana. See *SORBARIA tomentosa.*

× **margaritae** ZAB. (*japonica* × *superba*). A small shrub with erect, downy, reddish shoots and narrowly oval or oblong, coarsely-toothed leaves. Flowers bright rose-pink, borne in large, flattened heads from July onwards. Foliage brightly tinted in autumn. C. before 1890.

SPIRAEA—*continued*

media FRANZ SCHMIDT (*confusa*). A small shrub of compact habit, with erect, rounded, glabrous stems and ovate to oblong leaves, toothed at the apex or entire. Flowers white, borne in long racemes in late April and May. Widely distributed from E. Europe to Siberia and Japan. I. 1789.

glabrescens SIMONKAI. Differing only in its glabrous or sparsely hairy nature,

‡**menziesii** HOOK. A small to medium-sized, vigorous shrub of suckering habit, with erect, brown stems and lanceolate to oval, coarsely-toothed leaves. Flowers bright purplish-rose, borne in dense, terminal, pyramidal panicles, in July and August. Western N. America. I. 1838.

'Triumphans'. See *S.* ×*billiardii 'Triumphans'*

micrantha HOOK. f. A small to medium-sized shrub related to *S. amoena*. Leaves ovate-lanceolate, 7·5 to 15cm. long, acuminate and toothed. Flowers pale pink, borne in loose, leafy corymbs in June. E. Himalaya. I. 1924.

mollifolia REHD. A pretty, grey-leaved shrub with strongly angled, purplish shoots 1·2 to 1·8m. high. Leaves oval or obovate, silky-hairy. Flowers creamy-white, borne in small corymbs along the arching branches in June and July. W. China. I. 1908.

nipponica MAXIM. (*bracteata*). Among the best June-flowering shrubs. A strong-growing, glabrous, medium-sized shrub of dense, bushy habit. Stems long and arching. Leaves oval or broadly obovate or rounded, toothed at apex. Flowers white, borne in clusters which crowd the upper sides of the branches in June. Each tiny flower is subtended by a small green bract. A bush in full flower is a lovely sight. Japan. Introduced by Siebold, about 1885.

'Rotundifolia'. One of the best June-flowering shrubs, and excellent on chalky soils. A strong-growing form with broader, almost orbicular leaves and slightly larger flowers than the type. This is the form most frequently seen in the older British gardens. I. 1830. A.M. 1955.

tosaensis MAK. (*'Snowmound'*). A small shrub of dense, mound-like habit. Leaves oblong to oblanceolate, entire or crenate at apex. Flowers smaller than those of the type, but just as freely produced, smothering the branches in June. Japan.

×**nobleana.** See *S.* ×*sanssouciana*.

×**oxyodon** ZAB. (*chamaedryfolia* × *media*). A small, suckering shrub developing large patches of erect stems. Leaves small, obovate, toothed at apex, thickly crowding the branches. Flowers white, borne in small umbels along the stems during summer. C. before 1884.

pectinata. See *LUETKEA pectinata*.

prunifolia SIEB. & ZUCC. (*'Plena'*). A dense shrub with arching branches up to 1·8m. high. Leaves ovate, finely-toothed, turning orange or red in autumn. Flowers white, double, borne in tight, button-like, stalkless clusters along the branches in April and May. This form is only known in cultivation and was first introduced from Japan about 1845. Later the wild, single-flowered form was discovered in China and named *simpliciflora* NAKAI, a plant of little horticultural merit.

reevesiana. See *S. cantoniensis*.

salicifolia L. "Bridewort". A vigorous, suckering shrub producing, in time, dense thickets of erect stems. Leaves lanceolate to elliptic, sharply-toothed, green and glabrous on both surfaces. Flowers pink, borne in dense, cylindrical downy panicles in June and July. A good plant for stabilizing poor soils subject to erosion but not satisfactory on shallow chalk soils. C. and E.C. Europe; N.E. Asia; Japan. Naturalised in many parts of Europe, including the British Isles. C. 1586.

latifolia. See *S. latifolia*.

×**sanssouciana** K. KOCH (*douglasii* × *japonica*) (×*nobleana*). A small shrub with erect, brown, grey felted stems and oblong to narrowly oval, coarsely-toothed leaves, grey downy beneath. Flowers bright rose, borne in broad, flattened heads in July. Not recommended for shallow chalk soils. Garden origin before 1857.

sargentiana REHD. A graceful, medium-sized shrub with arching shoots and 2·5cm. long, narrowly oval to narrowly obovate leaves, toothed near the apex. Flowers creamy-white, carried in dense corymbs all along the branches in June. W. China. I. 1908. A.M. 1913.

SPIRAEA—*continued*

'Snowmound'. See *S. nipponica tosaensis.*

sorbifolia. See *SORBARIA sorbifolia.*

splendens K. KOCH. A small shrub with dark red branches and oval or oblong, sharply-toothed leaves. Flowers rose-pink, borne in dense corymbs in June. W. United States. C. 1875.

×**syringiflora** LEMOINE (*albiflora* × *salicifolia*). A small shrub of spreading habit with lanceolate leaves and terminal corymbose panicles of rose-pink flowers. Garden origin before 1885.

thunbergii SIEB. A popular small to medium sized, spreading shrub of dense, twiggy habit, with slender, angular, downy stems and narrow, glabrous, sharply-toothed leaves, 2·5 to 3cm. long. Flowers white, borne in numerous clusters along the branches during March and April. Generally the earliest of the spiraeas in bloom, the pure white flowers often smothering the wiry stems. Native of China, but widely cultivated and naturalised in Japan, from which country it was first introduced about 1863.

tomentosa L. A small, vigorous, suckering shrub, eventually forming a dense thicket of erect, brownish stems which are clothed with brownish felt when young. Leaves ovate, coarsely-toothed, yellowish-grey felted beneath. Flowers purplish-rose, produced in dense, terminal panicles during late summer. Eastern U.S.A. I. 1736.

trichocarpa NAKAI. A vigorous, graceful shrub with glabrous, angular shoots up to 1·8m. high. Leaves apple-green, oblong or oblanceolate, entire or toothed at apex. Flowers white, borne in rounded corymbs along the arching branches in June. Korea. Introduced by Ernest Wilson in 1917. A.M. 1942.

trilobata L. A small shrub of dense, compact habit. Leaves up to 2·5cm. long, rounded in outline and coarsely-toothed, occasionally shallowly three to five lobed. Flowers white, borne in crowded umbels on the previous year's shoots in June. N. Asia. I. 1801.

×**vanhouttei** ZAB. (*cantoniensis* × *trilobata*). A vigorous shrub with gracefully arching branches up to 1·8m. high. Leaves obovate to rhomboidal, coarsely-toothed, sometimes three to five lobed. Flowers white, borne in dense umbels along the branches in June. Excellent for early forcing. Garden origin before 1866.

veitchii HEMSL. A strong-growing shrub up to 3m. high, with long, arching, reddish branches. Leaves oval to oblong, 2·5 to 5cm. long, entire. Flowers white, borne in dense corymbs all along the branches in June and July. A superb species well worth a place in the garden, where space permits. C. and W. China. I. 1900. A.M. 1909.

×**watsoniana** ZAB. (*douglasii* × *splendens*). An attractive shrub with erect, downy shoots to 1·5 to 1·8m. high. Leaves elliptic to oblong, toothed towards the apex, grey downy beneath. Flowers rose, borne in dense, terminal panicles in June and July. Has occurred both in cultivation and with the parents in the wild. (Oregon).

wilsonii DUTHIE. A medium-sized shrub with long, arching shoots. Leaves oval to obovate, 2·5 to 5cm. long, entire or toothed near apex. Flowers white, borne in dense corymbs which crowd the branches in June. Closely related to *S. veitchii*, but never as large and with glabrous corymbs and leaves downy above. C. and W. China. I. 1900.

yunnanensis FRANCH. An elegant shrub up to 1·8m. high, with orbicular-ovate to obovate leaves which are doubly-toothed or shallowly lobed, white or grey tomentose beneath. Flowers white, borne in small, densely pubescent umbels in May or June. W. China. C. 1923.

STACHYURUS—Stachyuraceae—The sole representative of its family, embracing several species, only two of which are hardy throughout the British Isles. The stiffly pendulous inflorescences are formed in the leaf axils before the leaves fall in autumn, but the flowers do not open until the early spring. The individual flowers are normally hermaphrodite, but there are in cultivation clones possessing unisexual flowers. *Stachyurus* will grow in all fertile soils and in sun or semi-shade.

STACHYURUS—*continued*

chinensis FRANCH. A medium-sized to large shrub of spreading habit, with purplish branchlets. Leaves ovate-oblong to elliptic-oblong or oblong-lanceolate, narrowing into a long taper point, dull green and slightly bullate above, shining pale green beneath. Racemes drooping, 10 to 13cm. long, composed of thirty to thirty-five soft yellow, cup-shaped flowers, at Winchester generally opening two weeks later than *S. praecox*. A rare species of considerable merit. Introduced from China by E. H. Wilson in 1908. A.M. 1925.

'Magpie'. A striking, variegated form, the leaves grey-green above with an irregular, creamy-white margin, splashed pale green and tinged rose. Originated in our nurseries about 1945.

†**himalaicus** BENTH. A strong-growing shrub producing long, yellowish-brown shoots up to 3m. high or more. Leaves oblong-lanceolate, slightly bullate above, 13 to 23cm. long, with a long taper point and reddish petiole and midrib. Racemes 4 to 5cm. long, flowers cup-shaped, wine-purple to rose-pink, opening in early April. A rare and unusual species of extremely vigorous habit, worthy of a wall in all but the mildest areas. E. Himalaya to China; Formosa.

japonicus. See *S. praecox*.

†**lancifolius** KOIDZ. (*praecox matzuzakii*). A vigorous, glabrous, medium-sized shrub with long, pale green and glaucescent young shoots. Leaves long-stalked, ovate-oblong to ovate lanceolate, 13 to 25cm. long, tapering gradually to a tail-like point, pale green above, glaucescent beneath. Flowers yellow, opening in early April. A tender shrub usually cut back to ground level each year by frost and, therefore, only suitable for the mildest areas. It is closely related to *S. praecox*, differing in its stouter stems and its long-stalked, larger and longer leaves. Coastal areas of Japan.

praecox SIEB. & ZUCC. (*japonicus*). A medium-sized to large shrub with reddish-brown branchlets. Leaves ovate-oblong to elliptic or broad-elliptic, shortly taper-pointed, larger and broader than those of *S. chinensis*. Racemes stiffly drooping, 4 to 7cm. long, composed of fifteen to twenty-four cup-shaped, pale yellow flowers, opening in March or earlier in mild weather. Differing from *S. chinensis* in its stouter growths, larger leaves and usually shorter racemes. Japan. I. 1864. A.M. 1925. A.G.M. 1964. F.C.C. 1976.

'Gracilis'. A form with female flowers, otherwise differing little from the type.

STAPHYLEA—**Staphyleaceae**—"Bladder Nut". A small genus of hardy flowering shrubs whose seeds are enclosed in curious, inflated, two or three celled bladders. Easily grown in any fertile soil, sun or semi-shade.

bumalda DC. A spreading shrub with glabrous, greyish-brown branches, usually less than 1·8m. high. Leaves trifoliolate. Flowers white, borne in short racemose panicles in May and June. Foliage usually giving attractive red tints in autumn. Japan; Korea; China; Manchuria. I. 1812.

colchica STEV. A strong-growing shrub with erect branches, 2·5 to 3·6m. high. Leaves composed of three to five ovate-oblong leaflets, which are shining green beneath. Flowers white, carried in conspicuous erect panicles up to 13cm. long, in May. Capsules up to 10cm. long. S. Caucasus. I. 1850. F.C.C. 1879.

'Coulombieri'. A form of even more vigorous growth, with larger leaves and smaller capsules. C. 1872. A.M. 1927.

kochiana MEDWED. A minor form distinguished by its hairy filaments.

×**elegans** ZAB. (*colchica*×*pinnata*). A large shrub or occasionally a small tree, the leaves with usually five leaflets. Flowers white, borne in large, drooping panicles in May. Garden origin 1871. A.M. 1961. We offer the following clone:—

'Hessei'. An attractive form with red-purple flushed flowers. A.M. 1927.

holocarpa HEMSL. A beautiful, large shrub or small, spreading tree. Leaves trifoliolate, with oblong-lanceolate leaflets. Flowers white, rose in bud, produced in short, dense, drooping panicles in April and May. First discovered by Augustine Henry in C. China; introduced by Ernest Wilson in 1908. A.M. 1924.

'Rosea'. A lovely spring-flowering shrub or small tree, its spreading branches strung with drooping clusters of soft pink flowers. Young leaves bronze. A.M. 1953.

pinnata L. A large shrub of vigorous, erect habit. Leaves pinnate, composed of usually five, sometimes seven or three leaflets, pale dull green beneath. Flowers white, borne in long, narrow, drooping panicles in May and June. C. Europe. Naturalised in parts of the British Isles, and first recorded as being cultivated in 1596.

STEPHANANDRA—**Rosaceae**—A small genus of shrubs allied to *Spiraea*. Though of subtle beauty in flower, their graceful habit and attractive foliage qualifies them for a place in the garden. They are happy in most soils, in sun or semi-shade. The leaves often give rich tints in autumn. Untidy specimens may be hard pruned in March.

incisa ZAB. (*flexuosa*). A small to medium-sized shrub of dense habit, with slender, warm-brown, zig-zag stems. Leaves 2·5 to 7·5cm. long, ovate, incisely-toothed and lobed. Flowers greenish-white in crowded panicles in June. Japan; Korea. I. 1872.

'Crispa'. A dwarf shrub with small, crinkled leaves forming dense, low mounds. Excellent as ground cover especially in full exposure.

tanakae FRANCH. & SAV. A medium-sized shrub producing long, arching, rich-brown stems. Leaves broadly ovate or triangular, 7·5 to 13cm. long, three to five lobed and incisely toothed. An elegant shrub with stouter growths and larger leaves than *S. incisa*, the flowers also are a little larger though not showy. Japan. I. 1893.

STERCULIA platanifolia. See *FIRMIANA simplex*.

‡**STEWARTIA** (*STUARTIA*)—**Theaceae**—A small but valuable genus of ornamental shrubs and trees allied to *Camellia*, requiring a semi-shaded position and a moist, loamy, lime-free soil, revelling in woodland conditions. All have white or cream flowers which, although soon falling, are produced in continuous succession over several weeks in July and August. Rich autumn colour is another attribute, whilst the beautiful trunks and flaking bark of the older trees is no less attractive. They resent disturbance and, once planted, are best left alone. Like *Eucryphia, Oxydendrum* and *Cornus nuttallii*, they enjoy having their roots shaded from the hot sun.

gemmata. See *S. sinensis*.

koreana REHD. A superb, small to medium-sized tree with glabrous shoots and attractive, flaking bark. Leaves ovate to elliptic, acute, hairy when young, later almost glabrous, giving exceptionally bright autumn colour. Flowers solitary in the leaf axils, resembling those of *S. pseudocamellia* but opening wider, the petals spreading. Korea. Introduced by E. H. Wilson in 1917.

malacodendron L. A large shrub or occasionally a small tree, with ovate to obovate leaves, hairy beneath. Flowers solitary in the leaf axils, 6 to 8·5cm. across, white, with purple stamens and bluish anthers. A beautiful shrub, the purple-eyed flowers studding the branches in July and August. S.E. United States. C. 1742. F.C.C. 1934.

monadelpha SIEB & ZUCC. A large shrub or small tree with ovate to ovate-lanceolate, acuminate leaves which yield attractive autumn tints. Flowers solitary in the leaf axils, 2·5 to 4cm. across, white with spreading petals, the stamens with violet anthers. Japan; Korea (Quelpaert Island). C. 1903.

ovata WEATHERBY (*pentagyna*). A large bushy shrub with ovate to elliptic, acuminate leaves. Flowers solitary in the leaf axils, 6 to 7·5cm. across, cup-shaped, with conspicuous orange anthers. S.E. United States. Introduced before 1785.

pseudocamellia MAXIM. (*grandiflora*). Small to medium-sized tree with attractive flaking bark and glabrous shoots. Leaves ovate to obovate, shortly acuminate. Flowers white, solitary in the leaf axils, 5 to 6cm. across, cup-shaped, anthers bright yellow. The leaves turn to yellow and red in autumn. A free-growing tree of open habit, one of the best for general planting. Japan. C. before 1878. F.C.C. 1888.

†***pteropetiolata** CHENG (*Hartia sinensis*). A very interesting large, semi-evergreen woodland shrub. Leaves dark glossy green, glandular serrate. Stems softly bristly. Flowers white, 3 to 4cm. across, resembling those of *Camellia sinensis*. Only suitable for the mildest localities. Yunnan. I. 1912 by George Forrest.

serrata MAXIM. A small tree with attractive, warm brown stems and ovate-elliptic or elliptic, acuminate leaves which are rather leathery in texture. Flowers solitary in the leaf axils, 5 to 6cm. across, cup-shaped, white, stained red on the outside at base, anthers yellow, opening in June, earlier than other species. Rich autumn tints. Japan. C. before 1915. A.M. 1932.

STEWARTIA—*continued*

sinensis REHD. & WILS. (*gemmata*). A large shrub or small tree with attractive, flaking bark. Leaves elliptic to elliptic-oblong, acuminate. Flowers solitary in the leaf axils, 4 to 5cm. across, cup-shaped, fragrant. Rich crimson autumn colour. C. China. I. 1901.

***STRANVAESIA—Rosaceae**—A small genus of cotoneaster-like, evergreen trees and shrubs, producing clusters of white flowers in June, followed in autumn by bird-proof, red fruits. They make excellent screens and tall hedges and will grow in any well-drained soil in sun or shade. They are also tolerant of atmospheric pollution.

davidiana DCNE. An extremely vigorous, large shrub or small tree with erect branches and dark green, lanceolate or oblanceolate, leathery, entire leaves. The globular, brilliant crimson fruits are carried in conspicuous, pendent bunches all along the branches. In established specimens the oldest leaves turn bright red in autumn contrasting effectively with the still green younger leaves. W. China. First discovered by Perè David in 1869. Introduced by George Forrest in 1917. A.M. 1928. A.G.M. 1964.

'Fructuluteo'. A selected form of var. *undulata*, with bright yellow fruits. A.G.M. 1969.

'Prostrata'. A low growing, more or less prostrate form of var. *undulata*.

salicifolia REHD. (*S. salicifolia*). The most commonly cultivated form differing little from the type. The leaves tend to narrow oblong or narrow lanceolate and are more numerously veined. W. China. Introduced by E. H. Wilson in 1907. A.G.M. 1969.

undulata REHD. & WILS. (*S. undulata*). Less vigorous than the type, usually seen as a shrub of medium size with wide-spreading branches, often twice as wide as high. Leaves as in the type, but generally wavy at the margin. W. China. Introduced by E. H. Wilson in 1901. A.M. 1922. A.G.M. 1922.

†nussia DCNE. (*glaucescens*). A large shrub or, in mild localities, a small tree, with lanceolate to obovate, leathery leaves which are dark glossy green and finely-toothed. Flowers appearing in flattish clusters in July, followed by downy orange fruits. Himalaya. I. 1828.

"STRAWBERRY TREE". See *ARBUTUS unedo*.

STUARTIA. See *STEWARTIA*.

STYRAX—Styracaceae—A very distinguished and beautiful genus of trees and shrubs, thriving in a moist, loamy, lime-free soil, in sun or semi-shade. The name "Snowbell" has been given to them in America, an allusion to their pure white, pendulous flowers which appear in late spring and summer.

americana LAM. A medium-sized shrub with ascending branches and narrowly oval or obovate, minutely-toothed leaves. The slender-stalked, narrow-petalled, bell-shaped flowers hang from the branchlets in June and July. Not one of the easiest species to grow. S.E. United States. I. 1765.

calvescens PERKINS. A rare, small tree or large shrub with minutely and stellately-hairy shoots. Leaves elliptic, acuminate, serrate, lustrous green on both surfaces, rather thin in texture. Flowers borne in short racemes in June or July. China.

†dasyantha PERKINS. A large shrub or small tree. Leaves obovate to broad-elliptic, minutely toothed in the upper half. Flowers pendulous, borne in slender, terminal racemes in July. Not the hardiest species and best grown against a wall except in the mildest areas. C. China. First discovered by Augustine Henry. Introduced by Ernest Wilson in 1900.

hemsleyana DIELS. An attractive, small, openly-branched tree. Leaves broad, elliptic or almost orbicular, oblique at base, 10 to 13cm. long. Flowers white, with a central cone of yellow anthers, borne in long, lax, downy racemes in June. A lovely species similar in some respects to *S. obassia*, but differing in its less downy leaves and exposed chocolate-brown leaf buds. C. and W. China. Introduced by E. H. Wilson in 1900. A.M. 1930. F.C.C. 1942.

STYRAX—*continued*

japonica SIEB. & ZUCC. A very beautiful large shrub or small tree, with wide-spreading, fan-like branches, often drooping at the slender tips. Leaves ovate to narrowly oblong, acuminate. Flowers bell-shaped, white, with yellow, staminal beak, coating the undersides of the branches in June. The commonest species in cultivation and deservedly the most popular, combining daintiness and elegance with a hardy constitution. Best planted where one can admire the flowers from beneath. Japan; Korea. Introduced by Richard Oldham in 1862. F.C.C. 1885. A.G.M. 1969.

fargesii. This variety is more tree-like in habit than the type, with slightly larger, obovate to broad-elliptic leaves. China. I. 1925. A.M. 1945. F.C.C. 1971.

obassia SIEB. & ZUCC. A beautiful, large shrub or small, round-headed tree with handsome, large, broadly ovate to orbicular leaves, 10 to 20cm. long and clothed beneath with a soft, velvety tomentum. The petioles enlarged at the base, enclosing the leaf buds. Bark of second year shoots chestnut and exfoliating. Flowers fragrant, bell-shaped, 2·5cm. long, carried in long, lax, terminal racemes in June. Japan. Introduced by Charles Maries in 1879. F.C.C. 1888.

officinalis L. A medium-sized to large shrub bearing ovate leaves 7 to 9cm. long. The short, drooping clusters of comparatively large, fragrant flowers are borne at the tips of the shoots in June. It requires a warm sheltered position. The gum-like sap of this species is used as incense and the seeds for rosaries. Mediterranean Region.

serrulata ROXB. A densely-branched, wide-spreading shrub of medium to large size. Leaves elliptic-ovate, acuminate, sharply serrulate, dark polished green above, grey or white downy beneath. Flowers bell-shaped, borne in leafy panicles in July. We previously distributed this plant as *S. philadelphoides*. Himalaya.

shiraiana MAK. A large shrub or small tree with stellately hairy young shoots. Leaves obovate to orbicular, coarsely-toothed or lobed in upper half, downy beneath. Petioles swollen at base, enclosing the leaf buds. Flowers funnel-shaped, borne in short, densely hairy racemes in June. Japan. I. 1915.

veitchiorum HEMSL. A very rare large spreading shrub or a small tree with greyish, hairy young shoots. Leaves downy, lanceolate, taper-pointed, 7·5 to 13cm. long. Flowers pendulous, borne in slender panicles up to 20cm. long in June. China. I. 1900.

wilsonii REHD. A beautiful medium-sized shrub of dense, twiggy habit. Leaves tiny, ovate, 1 to 2·5cm. long, toothed or occasionally three-lobed at apex, glaucous and downy beneath. Flowers pendulous, solitary or in clusters, opening in June. A pretty shrub flowering when quite young, but requiring a sheltered position. W. China. I. 1908. A.M. 1913.

***SUAEDA—Chenopodiaceae**—Herbs and sub-shrubs, the majority of no horticultural merit.

fruticosa FORSK. A small, native, maritime sub-shrub of dense habit. Leaves narrow, blue-green and fleshy, semi-evergreen. Flowers inconspicuous. The whole plant sometimes turns a bronze-purple in autumn. It grows best in a sandy soil in full sun and is most suitable for seaside gardens. Sea coasts of S. and W. Europe (including the British Isles).

"SUMACH, STAG'S HORN". See *RHUS typhina.*

"SUMACH, VENETIAN". See *COTINUS coggygria.*

"SUN ROSE". See *HELIANTHEMUM* and *CISTUS.*

†SUTHERLANDIA—Leguminosae—A small genus of which one species is occasionally seen in the British Isles.

frutescens R. BR. A medium-sized to large shrub with downy shoots and pinnate leaves composed of thirteen to twenty-one narrow leaflets. The large, conspicuous, terra-cotta, pea-flowers are carried in axillary racemes in June. Seed pods inflated as in *Colutea*. Suitable for a warm, sunny wall in the mildest areas. S. Africa. C. 1683.

SUTTONIA. See *MYRSINE.*

"SWAMP BAY" or **"SWEET BAY".** See *MAGNOLIA virginiana.*

"SWEET BRIAR". See *ROSA rubiginosa.*

"SWEET CHESTNUT". See *CASTANEA sativa.*

"SWEET FERN". See *COMPTONIA peregrina.*

"SWEET GALE". See *MYRICA gale.*

"SWEET GUM". See *LIQUIDAMBAR styraciflua*.
"SWEET PEPPER BUSH". See *CLETHRA alnifolia*.
"SYCAMORE". See *ACER pseudoplatanus*.

SYCOPSIS—Hamamelidaceae—A small genus of shrubs requiring the same conditions as *Hamamelis*. Only one species is in general cultivation.

***sinensis** OLIV. A medium-sized to large, evergreen shrub or small tree. Leaves elliptic-lanceolate, acuminate, somewhat bullate, leathery and glabrous. Flowers monoecious, without petals, consisting of small clusters of yellow, red-anthered stamens, enclosed by chocolate-brown, tomentose scales, opening in February and March. C. China. Introduced by E. H. Wilson in 1901. A.M. 1926.

***tutcheri** HEMSL. A dense-growing, large shrub differing from *S. sinensis* in its smaller leaves which are elliptic to oblong or oblong-obovate, abruptly short acuminate, and glossy above. Flower-clusters also smaller, with red anthers. The above description is taken from a plant growing in the Royal Botanic Gardens, Kew. S.E. China.

SYMPHORICARPOS—Caprifoliaceae—A small genus of deciduous shrubs. Their flowers are bell-shaped, but small and relatively insignificant. They are mainly grown for their often abundant display of white or rose-coloured berries, which appear in autumn and generally last well into winter, being untouched by birds. Several forms are excellent for hedging and all grow well in shade even among the roots and drip of overhanging trees. They are quite hardy and will grow in all types of soils. Untidy specimens may be hard pruned in March.

albus BLAKE (*racemosus*). "Snowberry". A small shrub with slender, erect, downy shoots, forming dense clumps. Leaves oval to ovate-oblong, downy beneath, lobed on sucker shoots. Berries globose or ovoid, 12mm. across, white. Eastern N. America. I. 1879.

laevigatus. See *S. rivularis*.

× chenaultii REHD. (*microphyllus × orbiculatus*). A dense-growing shrub, ·6 to 1m. high, resembling *S. microphyllus* in general habit. Berries purplish-red on exposed side, pinkish-white elsewhere, carried in clusters or spikes. Garden origin in 1910.

'Hancock'. An outstanding form of dwarf habit. An excellent ground cover, particularly beneath trees.

× doorenbosii KRUSSM. (*× chenaultii × rivularis*). A strong-growing shrub up to 1·8m. high. Fruits white tinged rose. An attractive and very useful hybrid group raised by Mr. Doorenbos of the Hague, one of the greatest Dutch horticulturists of this century. Available in the following clones:—

'Erect'. A vigorous, but compact shrub of erect habit producing trusses of rose-lilac berries. Excellent as a small hedge.

'Magic Berry'. A small shrub of compact, spreading habit, bearing large quantities of rose-pink berries.

'Mother of Pearl'. The first named clone. A small, dense shrub, the branches weighed down by heavy crops of white, rose-flushed, marble-like berries. A.G.M. 1969. A.M. 1971.

'White Hedge'. A small shrub of strong, upright, compact growth, freely producing small, white berries in erect clusters. An excellent, small, hedging shrub.

occidentalis HOOK. "Wolfberry". A small shrub of dense, erect habit with rounded leaves and clusters of globular, white berries. N. America. C. 1880. A.M. 1910.

orbiculatus MOENCH. (*vulgaris*). "Indian Currant"; "Coral Berry". A dense, bushy shrub up to 2m. high, with thin, downy, densely leafy stems. Leaves oval or ovate, glaucescent beneath. Berries purplish-rose, rounded to ovoid, very small but borne in dense clusters along the stems. Eastern U.S.A. I. 1730.

'Variegatus'. Leaves smaller, irregularly-margined yellow. A graceful plant and one of the most pleasing variegated shrubs of medium size but inclined to revert if planted in shade.

rivularis SUKSD. (*albus laevigatus*). "Snowberry". A strong-growing shrub forming dense thickets of erect, glabrous stems up to 1·8m. high. Leaves elliptic to elliptic-oblong, 4 to 7·5cm long, commonly lobed on vigirous, suckering shoots. Berries in great profusion, like large glistening white marbles. The common snowberry of English plantations. Ideal for game cover and for poor soils or dark, shaded corners. Western N. America. I. 1817. F.C.C. 1913. A.G.M. 1931.

vulgaris. See *S. orbiculatus*.

SYMPLOCOS—Symplocaceae—A large genus of evergreen and deciduous trees and shrubs only one of which is generally hardy in the British Isles.

‡**paniculata** MIQ. (*crataegoides*). A deciduous shrub or occasionally a small tree of dense, twiggy habit. Leaves variable in shape, 1·5 to 4·5cm. long. Flowers small, white, fragrant, borne in panicles in May and June, followed by brilliant ultramarine blue fruits in autumn which persist into winter. It is usually necessary to plant two or more specimens in order to achieve successful fertilization; fruits are most abundant after a long, hot summer. A well-berried specimen after leaf fall is quite spectacular. Himalaya; China; Formosa; Japan. I. 1871. A.M. 1938 (flower). A.M. 1947 (fruit). F.C.C. 1954.

SYRINGA—Oleaceae—"Lilac". A genus of hardy, deciduous, flowering shrubs and small trees, containing some of the most elegant and colourful of May and June flowering, woody plants. The flowers of many species and hybrids are accompanied by a delicious fragrance, which has become an inseparable part of their magic. The numerous, large-flowered garden lilacs, hybrids and cultivars of *S. vulgaris*, need no introduction and their continued popularity is ensured. The species are perhaps less well known, and their good qualities deserve much wider recognition. The lilacs are happy in most soils, especially so in those of a chalky nature, and revel in full sun. Unless otherwise stated, it may be assumed that they are strong-growing shrubs of large size, often tree-like, and that they flower in May and June. For "Mock Orange", often wrongly referred to as "Syringa", see *PHILADELPHUS*. Pruning consists of removing the old flowering wood immediately after flowering. Summer pinching of extra strong shoots is often desirable.

affinis L. HENRY. See *S. oblata alba*.

afghanica HORT. See *S. laciniata*.

amurensis RUPR. "Amur Lilac". An elegant shrub with ovate, taper-pointed leaves and large, loose panicles of white flowers in June. The older bark peels, revealing the dark, chestnut-brown, new bark marked with horizontal lenticels. Subject to injury by late spring frost after growth has commenced. Manchuria to Korea. I. 1855.

japonica. See *S. reticulata*.

×**chinensis** WILLD. (*laciniata* × *vulgarsis*). "Rouen Lilac". A medium sized shrub of dense, bushy habit with ovate leaves and large, drooping panicles of fragrant, soft lavender flowers in May. Raised in the Botanic Garden at Rouen about 1777. A.G.M. 1969.

'Alba'. See *S.* +*correlata*.

'Metensis'. Flowers a charming shade of pale lilac-pink. A.G.M. 1969.

'Saugeana' (*'Rubra'*). Flowers lilac-red. A.G.M. 1969.

+**correlata** BRAUN (×*chinensis* +*vulgaris*) (×*chinensis 'Alba'*). This interesting lilac, commonly grown under its synonym has now proved to be a periclinal chimera, composed of an outer layer of *S. vulgaris* (white flowered form), and an inner core of *S.* ×*chinensis*. Its erect panicles of flowers are normally very pale lilac, nearly white, but occasional shoots of typical *S.* ×*chinensis* are produced. A.G.M. 1969.

×**diversifolia** REHD. (*oblata giraldii* ×*pinnatifolia*). A medium-sized to tall shrub with both entire, ovate-oblong leaves and pinnatifid, three to five lobed leaves. Raised at the Arnold Arboretum in 1929. Only the following clone, the type, is available:—

'William H. Judd'. Flowers white, scented; early May.

emodi ROYLE. "Himalayan Lilac". A distinct large shrub of robust habit. Leaves ovate to obovate, 10 to 20cm. long, pale or whitish beneath. Flowers pale lilac in bud fading to white, not very pleasantly scented, borne in erect panicles in June. A noteworthy species claiming a position in every well stocked shrub garden. Himalaya. I. 1838.

'Aurea'. Leaves suffused soft yellow. Best when grown in semi-shade.

'Aureovariegata'. Leaves yellow, with green centre.

'Ethel M. Webster'. A medium to large-size shrub of compact habit. Flowers flesh-pink, borne in broad, loose panicles in May and June. possibly a S. ×*henryi* hybrid. C. 1948.

formosissima NAKAI. See *S. wolfii*.

SYRINGA—*continued*

× **henryi** SCHNEID. (*josikaea* × *villosa*). A tall variable hybrid raised by Mons. Louis Henry at the Jardin des Plantes, Paris, in 1896.

'Alba'. A graceful shrub, more lax in habit than *'Lutece'*. Flowers white.

'Floreal'. See *S.* × *nanceana 'Floreal'*.

'Lutece'. A large, erect shrub with leaves resembling the *villosa* parent. Flowers violet, paling as they age, fragrant, borne in large panicles in June.

'Prairial'. See *S. 'Prairial'*.

× **hyacinthiflora** REHD. (*oblata* × *vulgaris*). An attractive, but variable hybrid first raised by Lemoine in 1876. More recently several clones have been raised by W. B. Clarke of San José, California, using *S. oblata giraldii*. The flowers appear quite early, usually in late April or early May.

'Alice Eastwood'. Claret-purple in bud, opening cyclamen-purple; double. C. 1942 (Clarke).

'Blue Hyacinth'. Mauve to pale blue; single. C. 1942 (Clarke).

'Buffon'. Soft pink, petals slightly reflexed, faintly scented; single, late April to early May. C. 1921 (Lemoine). A.M. 1961.

'Clarke's Giant'. Rosy-mauve in bud, opening lilac-blue, large florets and large panicles up to 30cm. long; single. C. 1948 (Clarke). A.M. 1958.

'Esther Staley'. Buds red, opening pink, very floriferous; single. C. 1948 (Clarke). A.M. 1961. A.G.M. 1969.

'Lamartine'. Flowers blue-lilac, in large panicles; single. Young growths flushed bronze. C. 1911 (Lemoine). A.M. 1927.

'Plena'. Victor Lemoine's original hybrid (*vulgaris 'Azurea Plena'* × *oblata*). Flowers in dense, erect panicles, double, bright purple in bud, opening to a delicate shade of violet. Leaves bronze-tinged when unfolding.

'Purple Heart'. Deep purple; large florets. (Clarke).

japonica. See *S. reticulata*.

× **josiflexa** J. S. PRINGLE (*josikaea* × *reflexa*). A very beautiful race of hybrids raised in Ottawa by Miss Isabella Preston. Medium-sized to large shrubs, with fine, deep green leaves and bearing loose, plume-like panicles of fragrant, rose-pink flowers in May or June.

'Bellicent'. An outstanding clone, the best of this excellent hybrid, with enormous panicles of clear rose-pink flowers. F.C.C. 1946. A.G.M. 1969.

josikaea REICHENB. "Hungatian Lilac". A large shrub related to *S. villosa*. Leaves ovate to obovate, 5 to 13cm. long, glossy dark green above, paler beneath. Flowers fragrant, deep violet-mauve, borne in erect panicles in June. C. and E. Europe. I. 1830.

julianae SCHNEID. A graceful shrub, 1·8 to 2·5m. in height by as much through. Leaves oval, privet-like, grey downy beneath. Flowers in slender, upright panicles, fragrant, pale lilac in May and early June. A choice shrub of free-flowering habit. Ideal for the small garden. W. China. Introduced by E. H. Wilson in 1900. A.M. 1924.

'Kim'. A hybrid of *S. josikaea* with an unknown species. An elegant, medium-sized shrub with dark green, oblong-lanceolate leaves and large, freely-branching panicles of mallow-purple flowers in late May and early June. A.M. 1958.

komarowii SCHNEID. (*sargentiana*). A vigorous, tall-growing shrub with large, deep green, oval or ovate-lanceolate leaves up to 18cm. long. Flowers deep rose-pink borne in nodding, cylindrical panicles during May and early June. China. I. 1908 by Ernest Wilson.

laciniata MILL. (*afghanica* HORT. not SCHNEID.). A beautiful, small shrub with dark, slender stems and small, dainty, pinnately-cut leaves. Flowers lilac in slender panicles in May. W. China.

laciniata HORT. See *S.* × *persica 'Laciniata'*.

meyeri SCHNEID. A dense, compact, rather slow-growing, small-leaved shrub, to about 1·8m. high. Leaves oval or obovate, about 4 to 5cm. long. Flowers violet-purple, in short, dense panicles in May, even on young plants. Sometimes a second crop of flowers appears in September. China. Known only in cultivation. I. 1908.

microphylla DIELS. A very pretty, small-leaved shrub up to 2m. high. Leaves ovate, usually pointed at apex, 1 to 5cm. long. Flowers rosy-lilac, darker externally, fragrant, borne in small panicles in June and again in September. N. and W. China. Introduced by William Purdom in 1910. A.M. 1937. A.G.M. 1955.

'Superba'. A selected form of free-flowering habit. Flowers rosy-pink in May and intermittently until October. A.M. 1957. A.G.M. 1969.

SYRINGA—*continued*

× **nanceana** MCKELVEY (*henryi* × *sweginzowii*). A variable hybrid raised by Lemoine in 1925. We offer the following clone:—

'Floreal' (× *henryi 'Floreal'*). A graceful shrub of lax habit, with panicles of fragrant, lavender-mauve flowers in May.

oblata LINDL. A large shrub or small tree related to *S. vulgaris*, with broadly, heart-shaped or reniform leaves up to 10cm. wide and 7·5cm. long. Flowers lilac-blue, produced in broad panicles in late April or early May. The unfolding leaves are bronze-tinted. Liable to damage by late spring frost. N. China. Introduced by Robert Fortune from a garden in Shanghai, in 1856.

'Alba' REHD. (*S. affinis* L. HENRY). A form with smaller leaves and white flowers.

dilatata REHD. A variety of medium height. Leaves ovate-acuminate, bronze when unfolding, richly tinted in autumn. Flowers violet-purple, in loose panicles. Korea. I. 1917.

giraldii REHD. Differs from the type in its taller, more open habit and the larger, looser panicles of darker (purplish-violet) flowers in late April. N. China. I. 1895.

'Nana'. A dwarf form with bluish flowers.

palibiniana HORT. not NAKAI. See *S. velutina*.

pekinensis RUPR. (*Ligustrina pekinensis*). A small tree with ovate to ovate-lanceolate, long-tapered leaves. Flowers creamy-white, densely crowded in large panicles in June. N. China. Discovered by the Abbé David. Introduced by Dr. Bretschneider in 1881.

'Pendula'. A graceful form with drooping branches.

× **persica** L. (*afghanica* × *laciniata*). "Persian Lilac". A charming, slender-branched shrub of rounded, bushy habit, 1·8 to 2·5m. high and as much across. Leaves lanceolate, entire, 2·5 to 6cm. long. Flowers lilac, fragrant, borne in small panicles in May. Said to have been cultivated in England in 1640.

'Alba'. Flowers white.

'Laciniata' (*S. laciniata* HORT. not MILL.). A graceful form with prettily dissected, three to nine lobed leaves and small panicles of lilac flowers in May. A.M. 1965. Not to be confused with the wild *S. laciniata* MILL., a species which is rare in cultivation.

pinetorum W. W. SM. A medium-sized shrub with ovate to ovate-lanceolate leaves and panicles of pale lavender-rose flowers with yellow anthers, in June. S.W. China.

pinnatifolia HEMSL. An unusual species reaching a height of about 2·5m. Leaves 4 to 8cm. long, pinnate with seven to eleven separate leaflets. Flowers white or lavender-tinted, produced in small, nodding panicles in May. So unlike a lilac as to create an amusing "legpull" or cunundrum for the uninitiated. W. China. Introduced by E. H. Wilson in 1904.

potaninii SCHNEID. An elegcnt, medium-sized shrub with oval, slender-pointed leaves, downy above, grey felted beneath. Flowers white to pale rose-purple, with yellow anthers, fragrant, borne in loose panicles in June. W. China. I. 1905. A.M. 1924.

'Prairial' (× *henryi* × *tomentella*) (× *henryi 'Prairial'*). An elegant shrub producing large panicles of soft lavender flowers in May. Raised by Lemoine about 1933.

× **prestoniae** MCKELVEY (*reflexa* × *villosa*). An extremely hardy race of late-flowering hybrid lilacs, first raised by Miss Isabella Preston at the Central Experimental Farm, Division of Horticulture, Ottawa, Canada, in 1920. Usually referred to as "Canadian Hybrids", they are vigorous, medium-sized to large shrubs, producing large, erect or drooping panicles of flower in late May and June, on shoots of the current year. Red-purple is the dominant colour.

'Audrey'. Flowers deep pink in June. A.M. 1939.

'Elinor'. Flowers dark purplish-red in bud, opening to pale lavender, borne in rather erect panicles in May and June. A.M. 1951.

'Hiawatha'. Flowers rich reddish-purple in bud, opening pale pink.

'Isabella'. Flowers mallow-purple, borne in rather erect panicles in May and June. A.M. 1941.

'Juliet'. Flowers lilac-pink.

'Royalty'. Flowers violet-purple.

'Virgilia'. Flowers deep lilac-magenta in bud, opening pale lilac. Compact habit.

SYRINGA—*continued*

× **prestoniae 'W. T. Macoun'.** Lilac-pink, in large panicles.

reflexa SCHNEID. A distinct, large shrub of considerable quality, bearing large, oval leaves up to 20cm. long and rough to the touch. Flowers rich purplish-pink outside, whitish within, densely packed in long, narrow, drooping panicles, 15 to 20cm. long in late May and June. One of the best of the species and very free-flowering. C. China. Discovered and introduced by E. H. Wilson in 1904. A.M. 1914.

reticulata HARA (*amurensis japonica*) (*japonica*). A robust, large shrub readily trained to a stout, short tree with an attractive trunk. Leaves broad rotund-ovate, reticulate and pubescent beneath. Flowers creamy white, fragrant, borne in large, dense panicles in late June. Japan. I. 1878. F.C.C. 1887.

robusta. See *S. wolfii*.

× **swegiflexa** HESSE (*reflexa* × *sweginzowii*). A beautiful, strong-growing, variable hybrid of open habit with large, dense, cylindrical panicles of usually pink flowers, red in bud. Raised by Messrs. Hesse of Weener, N.W. Germany, about 1934. A.M. 1977.

'Fountain'. A medium-sized shrub of compact habit. Flowers pale pink, fragrant, in long, drooping panicles in May and June.

sweginzowii KOEHNE & LINGELSH. A vigorous, medium-sized shrub of elegant habit. Leaves ovate, acute or acuminate, 5 to 7·5cm. long. Flowers flesh-pink, sweetly fragrant, borne in long, loose panicles in May and June. W. China. Introduced by G. N. Potanin in 1894. A.M. 1915.

'Superba'. A selected form with somewhat larger panicles. A.M. 1918.

tigerstedtii H. SM. A medium-sized shrub related to *S. yunnanensis*. Flowers fragrant, pale or whitish lilac, produced in erect panicles in June. W. China. I. 1934.

tomentella BUR. & FRANCH. (*wilsonii*). A strong-growing, wide-spreading species up to 3·6 to 4·5m. high. Leaves ovate to elliptic, 5 to 13cm. long, dark green and corrugated above, grey-downy beneath. Flowers sweetly scented, deep lilac-pink, white inside, paling with age, produced in broad, terminal panicles in late May and June. W. China. I. 1904. A.M. 1928.

velutina KOMAR. (*palibiniana* HORT. not NAKAI). "Korean Lilac". A small to medium-sized shrub of dense, compact habit. Leaves variable in shape from ovate to rhomboidal or rounded, 4 to 6cm. long, velvety, dark green. Flowers pale lilac or lilac-pink, borne in numerous, elegant panicles in May and June, even on young plants. A lovely species, suitable for the small garden. Korea. I. 1910.

villosa VAHL (*bretschneideri*). A medium-sized to large, erect-branched shrub of compact habit. Leaves oval to oblong, 5 to 15cm. long, dull dark green above, glaucous beneath. Flowers lilac-rose, carried in stiff, compact, erect panicles in late May and early June. N. China. I. 1882. A.M. 1931.

vulgaris L. "Common Lilac". A large, vigorous shrub or small tree of suckering habit. Leaves ovate or heart-shaped. Flowers richly scented, lilac, borne in dense, erect, pyramidal panicles in May. Mountains of E. Europe. A common garden escape readily naturalised. Introduced in the 16th century. Plants raised from seed are variable in colour.

The vast range of garden lilacs have originated from this species. There is probably no other shrub or tree which has given rise to so many cultivars. More than five hundred selections have been named, their differences being confined almost entirely to the colour of their single or double flowers. For a representative selection of the better cultivars see CULTIVARS of SYRINGA VULGARIS.

'Alba'. Flowers white; leaves and winter-buds pale green. Long cultivated.

'Aurea'. Leaves yellow when young, later yellowish green.

wilsonii. See *S. tomentella*.

wolfii SCHNEID. (*formosissima*) (*robusta*). An extremely hardy species related to *S. villosa*. A medium-sized to large shrub, with pale ash-grey branches and elliptic-lanceolate, taper-pointed leaves, 8 to 12cm. long. Flowers fragrant, pale violet-purple, borne in long, wide, loose panicles in June. Korea; Manchuria. I. 1904.

SYRINGA—*continued*

yunnanensis FRANCH. "Yunnan Lilac". A beautiful, medium-sized to large shrub, occasionally up to 4m., of loose, open habit. Leaves elliptic to oblong-lanceolate, glaucous beneath. Flowers fragrant, pink in bud, opening lilac-pink, paling with age, carried in slender panicles in June. Discovered by the Abbé Delavay in 1887, introduced by George Forrest in 1907. A.M. 1928.

'Alba'. Flowers white. A distinct plant, possibly of hybrid origin.

'Rosea'. A superior form or hybrid selected in our nurseries. Flowers rose-pink, in long, slender panicles. In foliage too, it is distinct and attractive.

CULTIVARS of SYRINGA VULGARIS

Medium to large-sized shrubs or occasionally small trees of strong erect habit. Flowers produced in dense, erect, conical panicles in May or early June, varying in colour from white through creamy-yellow to red, blue or purple, single or double. All are sweetly scented. The garden lilacs will always be associated with the names of Victor Lemoine and his son Emile, who raised so many lovely cultivars at their nursery at Nancy, France, towards the end of the 19th century and the early part of the present century. The lover of the lilac also owes a great deal to Alice Harding for her great work and magnificent book on this genus. As with other plants which have become the victims of the specialist, far too many sorts have been selected and named. It requires a highly cultivated imagination to detect the differences in shade of colour, as they vary from hour to hour. The raiser and introducer of each clone will be found in parentheses at the end of each description.

SINGLE

'Ambassadeur'. Azure-lilac with a white eye; large, broad panicles. C. 1930 (Lemoine).

'Blue Hyacinth'. See *S.* ×*hyacinthiflora 'Blue Hyacinth'*.

'Buffon'. See *S.* ×*hyacinthiflora 'Buffon'*.

'Capitaine Baltet'. Light carmine-pink, blue tinged in bud; large panicles. C. 1919 (Lemoine).

'Charles X'. Purplish-red, long, conical panicles. A very popular lilac. C. before 1830.

'Clarke's Giant'. See *S.* ×*hyacinthiflora 'Clarke's Giant'*.

'Congo'. Rich lilac-red in large, compact panicles, paling with age. C. 1896 (Lemoine).

'Esther Staley'. See *S.* ×*hyacinthiflora 'Esther Staley'*.

'Etna'. Deep claret-purple, fading to lilac-pink; late. C. 1927 (Lemoine).

'Firmament'. Clear lilac-blue; early. C. 1932 (Lemoine).

'Glory of Horstenstein'. Rich lilac-red, changing to dark lilac. C. 1921 (Wilke).

'Hugo Koster'. Purple-crimson. C. 1913 (Koster). A.M. 1913.

'Jan van Tol'. Pure white, in long, drooping panicles. C. about 1916 (van Tol). A.M. 1924.

'Lamartine'. See *S.* ×*hyacinthiflora 'Lamartine'*.

'Lavaliensis' (*'Lavanensis'*). Pale pink. C. 1865 (Leroy).

'Madame Charles Souchet'. Soft lilac-blue, large florets and broad panicles; early. C. 1924 (Lemoine).

'Madame Florent Stepman'. Creamy-yellow in bud, opening white. C. 1908 (Stepman).

'Madame Francisque Morel'. Mauve-pink, large florets, enormous panicles. Erect habit. C. 1892 (Morel).

'Marceau'. Claret-purple, broad panicles. C. 1913 (Lemoine).

'Marechal Foch'. Bright carmine-rose, large flowers in broad, open panicles. C. 1924 (Lemoine). A.M. 1935.

'Marie Legraye'. White, creamy-yellow in bud, inflorescences rather small. Popular and much used for forcing. F.C.C. 1880.

'Massena'. Deep reddish-purple, large florets, broad panicles; late. C. 1923 (Lemoine). A.M. 1928. A.G.M. 1930.

'Maud Notcutt'. Pure white, large panicles up to 30cm. long. C. 1956 (Notcutt). A.M. 1957.

'Mont Blanc'. Greenish-white in bud, opening white, long, well-filled panicles. C. 1915 (Lemoine).

'Pasteur'. Claret-red, long, narrow panicles. C. 1903 (Lemoine). A.M. 1924.

SYRINGA—*continued*

'President Lincoln'. Purple in bud, opening light bluish-violet; early. C. about 1916 (Dunbar).

'Primrose'. Pale primrose yellow, small, dense panicles. C. 1949 (Maarse). A.M. 1950.

'Prodige'. Deep purple, large florets. C. 1928 (Lemoine).

'Purple Heart'. See *S.* ×*hyacinthiflora 'Purple Heart'*.

'Reaumur'. Deep carmine-violet, broad panicles; late. C. 1904 (Lemoine). A.M. 1916.

'Sensation'. Purplish-red florets edged white, large panicles. Inclined to revert and lose its marginal variegation. C. 1938.

'Souvenir de Louis Spaeth' ['Andenken an Ludwig Spaeth']. Wine red. Perhaps the most popular lilac, one of the most consistent and reliable. C. 1883 (Spaeth). F.C.C. 1894. A.G.M. 1930.

'Vestale'. Pure white, broad, densely-packed panicles. A magnificent lilac. C. 1910 (Lemoine). A.G.M. 1931

DOUBLE

'Alice Eastwood'. See *S.* ×*hyacinthiflora 'Alice Eastwood'*.

'Ami Schott'. Deep cobalt-blue, with paler reverse. C. 1933 (Lemoine).

'Belle de Nancy'. Purple-red in bud, opening lilac-pink, large panicles. C. 1891 (Lemoine).

'Charles Joly'. Dark purplish-red, late. A reliable and popular lilac. C. 1896 (Lemoine).

'Condorcet'. Lavender, long, massive panicles. C. 1888 (Lemoine).

'Edith Cavell'. Creamy-yellow in bud, opening pure white, large florets. C. 1918 (Lemoine).

'Ellen Willmott'. Cream in bud opening pure white, long, open panicles. C. 1903 (Lemoine). A.M. 1917.

'General Pershing'. Purplish-violet, long panicles. C. 1924 (Lemoine).

'Katherine Havemeyer'. Purple-lavender, fading to pale lilac-pink, broad, compact panicles. Quite first class. C. 1922 (Lemoine). A.M. 1933. A.G.M. 1969.

'Madame Abel Chatenay'. Pale greenish-yellow in bud, opening milk white, broad panicles; late. C. 1892 (Lemoine). F.C.C. 1900.

'Madame Antoine Buchner'. Rose-pink to rosy-mauve, loose, narrow panicles; late. C. 1900 (Lemoine). A.G.M. 1969.

'Madame Casimir Perier'. Cream in bud, opening white. C. 1894 (Lemoine).

'Madame Lemoine'. Creamy-yellow in bud, opening pure white. An old and popular lilac. C. 1890 (Lemoine). A.M. 1891. F.C.C. 1894. A.G.M. 1937.

'Michel Buchner'. Pale rosy-lilac, large, dense panicles. C. 1885 (Lemoine). A.M. 1891.

'Monique Lemoine'. Pure white, large panicles; late. C. 1939 (Lemoine). A.M. 1958.

'Mrs. Edward Harding'. Claret-red, shaded pink, very free-flowering; late. A superb and popular lilac. C. 1922 (Lemoine). A.G.M. 1969.

'Paul Thirion'. Carmine in bud, opening claret-rose, finally lilac-pink; late. C. 1915 (Lemoine). A.G.M. 1969.

'President Grévy'. Lilac-blue, massive panicles. C. 1886 (Lemoine). A.M. 1892.

'President Poincare'. Claret-mauve, large florets. C. 1913 (Lemoine).

'Princesse Clementine'. Creamy-yellow in bud, opening white, very floriferous. C. about 1908 (Mathieu).

'Souvenir d'Alice Harding'. Alabaster-white, tall panicles; late May to early June. C. 1938 (Lemoine).

TALAUMA coco. See *MAGNOLIA coco.*

"TAMARISK". See *TAMARIX.*

TAMARIX—Tamaricaceae—The "Tamarisks" are excellent wind-resisters and are most commonly planted near the sea, but will thrive inland in full sun, and any soil, except shallow chalk-soils. All have graceful, slender branches and plume-like foliage. The tiny pink flowers are borne in slender racemes towards the ends of the branches, the whole creating large, plumose inflorescences which contribute a colourful splash to any landscape. As plants are apt to become straggly in habit, pruning is usually necessary in order to maintain a balance. Those species which flower on growths of the current year should be pruned in late February or March, whilst those which flower on the previous year's wood should be pruned immediately after flowering.

TAMARIX—*continued*

anglica. See *T. gallica.*

caspica HORT. See *T. tetrandra.*

gallica L. (*anglica*). A large, spreading, glabrous shrub or small tree, with dark purple-brown branches and sea-green foliage. Flowers during summer, pink, crowded into lax, cylindrical racemes on shoots of the current year. S.W. Europe. Naturalised along many stretches of the English coast.

germanica. See *MYRICARIA germanica.*

japonica. See *T. juniperina.*

juniperina BUNGE (*japonica*) (*plumosa*) (*chinensis*). A large shrub or small tree of dense habit. Branches extremely slender, clothed with distinctive pale green foliage. Flowers bright pink, opening in May on shoots of the previous year. N. China; Manchuria. C. 1877.

odessana. See *T. ramosissima.*

parviflora DC. (*tetrandra purpurea*). A large shrub or small tree with long, brown or purple branches, clothed with bright green foliage. Flowers deep pink, borne in May on shoots of the previous year. S.E. Europe; W. Asia. Long cultivated and naturalised in C. and S. Europe. C. 1853. A.G.M. 1962.

pentandra PALL. A large glabrous shrub or small tree with reddish-brown branches and attractive, glaucous foliage. Flowers rose-pink borne on shoots of the current year in late summer and early autumn. One of the finest late-flowering shrubs, the whole bush becoming a feathery mass of rose-pink, intermingled with the delightful foliage. W. and C. Asia. C. 1883. A.M. 1933. A.G.M. 1962.

'Rubra'. A splendid selection with darker-coloured flowers. A.G.M. 1969.

plumosa. See *T. juniperina.*

ramosissima LEDEB. (*odessana*). A large, glabrous shrub or small tree with reddish-brown branches. Flowers pink in slender racemes during summer, on shoots of the current year. Caspian Region. I. about 1885. A.M. 1903.

tetrandra PALL. (*caspica* HORT.). A large shrub of loose, open growth, with long dark-coloured branches and green foliage. Flowers in May or early June, light pink, borne in slender racemes on the branches of the previous year, the whole forming long, large panicles. S.E. Europe; W. Asia. I. 1821.

purpurea. See *T. parviflora.*

‡***TELOPEA—Proteaceae**—A small Australasian genus thriving under conditions congenial to Embothriums but welcoming more sun. The "Australian Waratah". requires a warmer clime.

truncata R. BR. "Tasmanian Waratah". A medium-sized to large shrub or occasionally a small tree with stout, downy shoots and rather thick, oblanceolate, evergreen leaves. Flowers rich crimson, borne in dense terminal heads in June. Hardy when planted among other evergreens in moist, but well-drained soil. Thrives in conditions suitable to *Rhododendron*. Introduced by Harold Comber from Tasmania in 1930. A.M. 1934. F.C.C. 1938.

‡***TERNSTROEMIA—Theaceae**—A large genus of evergreen trees and shrubs mainly native to tropical regions. They differ from the closely related *Eurya* in their entire leaves and hermaphrodite flowers and from *Cleyera* in various small floral characters.

gymnanthera SPRAGUE (*japonica*). A medium-sized shrub with stout branches. The thick, leathery, obovate leaves are blunt tipped and generally clustered towards the ends of the shoots. Flowers white, borne in the leaf axils in July. Only suitable for mild areas, requiring a sheltered position in semi-shade. Japan; Korea; Formosa; China; India; Borneo.

'Variegata'. A beautiful form. The dark green leaves are marbled grey and possess a creamy-white margin which turns to rose in autumn.

TETRACENTRON—Tetracentraceae—A rare, monotypic genus of disputable allegiance, included under both *Magnoliacea* and *Trochodendracea* in the past. It bears a superficial resemblance to *Cercidiphyllum*, but its leaves are alternate and its hermaphrodite flowers are borne in catkins. It thrives in woodland conditions, but makes an elegant lawn specimen. It is lime tolerant but grows with greater freedom in an acid or neutral soil.

sinense OLIV. A large shrub or small to medium-sized tree of wide-spreading habit. Leaves ovate or heart-shaped, with a long slender point, red tinted when young. Flowers minute, yellowish, borne in dense, pendulous catkin-like spikes, 10 to 15cm. long, which drape the leafy branches in summer. A graceful tree from C. and W. China; also seen by C. R. Lancaster in East Nepal in 1971. First discovered by Augustine Henry. Introduced by E. H. Wilson in 1901.

TEUCRIUM—Labiatae—The shrubby members of this large genus are useful flowering and foliage plants, requiring a sunny, well-drained position. All have square stems and two-lipped flowers.

***chamaedrys** L. "Wall Germander". A dwarf, bushy, aromatic sub-shrub with creeping rootstock and erect, hairy stems, densely clothed with small, prettily toothed leaves. Flowers rose-pink with darker veins, produced in axillary whorls from July to September. Suitable for walls. C. and S. Europe. C. in England about 1750.

†*fruticans L. (*latifolium*). "Shrubby Germander". A small, evergreen shrub, the stems and the undersides of the ovate leaves covered with a close white tomentum. Flowers pale blue, in terminal racemes, throughout the summer. It requires a sunny, well-drained position with the shelter of a wall. S. Europe; N. Africa. I. 1714.

'Azureum'. A slightly more tender form with darker blue flowers. A.M. 1936.

***polium** L. A dwarf, evergreen shrub with procumbent stems forming low hummocks a few cm. high. Leaves narrow and grey-felted. Flowers white or yellow in terminal heads during summer. Suitable for the rock garden. Mediterranean Region. C. 1562.

***subspinosum** POURR. A dwarf, grey-spiny shrublet of unusual appearance. Flowers mauve-pink, produced in late summer. A worthy plant for the rock garden or scree. Balearic Islands.

THEA sinensis. See *CAMELLIA sinensis.*

"THORN". See *CRATAEGUS.*

"THORN, CHRIST'S". See *PALIURUS spina-christi.*

"THORN, GLASTONBURY". See *CRATAEGUS monogyna 'Biflora'.*

†TIBOUCHINA—Melastomataceae—A large genus of mainly trees and shrubs, natives of Tropical America. None are hardy though several are suitable for walls or pillars in the conservatory.

***urvilliana** COGNIAUX (*semidecandra* HORT.). A large shrub with four-angled stems and velvety-hairy, prominently-veined leaves. The large, vivid royal purple flowers are produced continuously throughout summer and autumn. Old plants tend to become straggly and should be pruned in early spring. S. Brazil. I. 1864. F.C.C. 1868 (as *T. semidecandra*).

TILIA—Tiliaceae—The limes or lindens are all very amenable to cultivation, many growing into stately trees. Because of their tolerance of hard pruning they have been widely used in the past for roadside planting and "pleaching". They will grow in all types of fertile soils and situations. Unless otherwise stated the small, fragrant, creamy-yellow flowers of the "Common Lime" are common to all the species and are borne in numerous clusters in July. The limes are widely distributed, occuring in Europe including the British Isles; Asia and N. America.

alba. See *T. tomentosa.*

americana L. "American Lime". A medium-sized tree with glabrous shoots and enormous broad leaves up to 30cm. long. They are coarsely-toothed, green on both sides, and glabrous, except for minute axillary tufts beneath. It is conspicuous on account of the large leaves but like the American Beech it does not luxuriate in the British Isles. The bark of old trees is rough, almost corky in appearance. E. and C. North America. I. 1752.

'Dentata'. Leaves coarsely-toothed, a striking plant particularly when young.

'Fastigiata'. A narrow, conical form with ascending branches.

'Pendula'. See *T. petiolaris.*

'Redmond'. A selected form said to be of dense conical habit. Garden origin, Nebraska, about 1926. Originally introduced as a form of *T.* ×*euchlora.*

amurensis RUPR. A medium-sized tree related to *T. cordata*, with broadly-ovate, coarsely-toothed leaves. It is unlikely to prove an outstanding tree in the British Isles. Manchuria; Korea. C. 1909.

argentea. See *T. tomentosa.*

caucasica. See *T. dasystyla.*

chinensis MAXIM. A distinct small to medium-sized tree with glabrous, glossy shoots and ovate to broadly-ovate, sharply-toothed, slender-pointed leaves, thinly pubescent beneath. Bark of older trees flaking. China. I. 1925.

TILIA—*continued*

cordata MILL. (*parvifolia*). "Small-leaved Lime". A medium-sized to large, native tree of rounded habit. Leaves heart-shaped, 5 to 7·5cm. long, rather leathery, glossy dark green above, pale green, with reddish-brown axillary tufts beneath. The characteristic spreading inflorescences appear in late July, generally after those of the "Common Lime" and "Large-leaved Lime", flowers ivory coloured and sweetly scented. Europe (including the British Isles).

'Swedish Upright'. A most attractive, columnar form of Swedish origin, with ascending branches. Suitable for planting in broad thoroughfares and city squares.

dasystyla STEV. (*caucasica*) (*begoniifolia*). A medium-sized tree with greenish twigs, pubescent at first and orbicular-ovate, sharply and conspicuously bristle-toothed leaves, dark glossy green above, paler with yellow axillary tufts beneath. S.E. Europe; Caucasus to N. Persia. C. 1880.

×**euchlora** K. KOCH (*cordata* × *dasystyla*). A medium-sized tree with generally glabrous green twigs. Leaves orbicular-ovate, intermediate in size between those of the parents, shining dark green above, paler, almost glaucous, with brown axillary tufts beneath. An elegant tree when young with glossy leaves and arching branches, becoming dense and twiggy with pendulous lower branches in maturity. It is a "clean" lime, being free from aphids, but its flowers tend to have a narcotic effect on bees. C. 1860. F.C.C. 1890. A.G.M. 1969.

×**europaea** L. (*cordata* × *platyphyllos*) (×*vulgaris*) (×*intermedia*). "Common Lime". A familar avenue tree and at least in the past the most commonly planted lime. A large, vigorous tree with glabrous, greenish zig-zag shoots. Leaves broadly ovate or rounded, obliquely heart-shaped at base, sharply-toothed, glabrous except for axillary tufts beneath. A long-lived tree, easily recognised by its densely suckering habit. Occasionally found with its parents in the wild.

'Wratislaviensis'. Leaves golden yellow when young becoming green with age. A sport of the clone '*Pallida*'.

floridana SMALL. A medium-sized tree with glabrous, reddish-brown or yellowish twigs. Leaves broad ovate and coarsely-toothed, dark yellowish-green above, paler beneath. S.E. United States; N.E. Mexico. C. 1915.

grandifolia. See *T. platyphyllos*.

henryana SZYSZ. A very rare, medium-sized tree with broadly ovate leaves up to 13cm. long, oblique at the base and edged with conspicuous, bristle-like teeth. They are softly downy on both surfaces and possess axillary tufts beneath. C. China. Discovered by Augustine Henry in 1888. Introduced by Ernest Wilson in 1901.

heterophylla VENT. A rare tree of medium-size with glabrous branches and large broadly ovate, coarsely-toothed leaves which are dark green above and covered beneath by a close silvery tomentum. Eastern U.S.A. C. 1755.

michauxii SARG. Very similar to the type and the commoner tree in cultivation. It is regarded by some authorities as a hybrid with *T. americana*. Leaves grey-tomentose beneath. Eastern U.S.A. C. 1800.

insularis NAKAI. A large tree with heart-shaped, coarsely-toothed, green leaves, tufted in the vein axils beneath. Korea. I. 1919.

japonica SIMONK. A distinct and attractive, medium-sized, small-leaved tree related to, and resembling our native *T. cordata*, but leaves slightly larger and abruptly acuminate. Japan. I. 1875.

kiusiana MAK. & SHIRAS. A remarkable unlime-like, slow-growing shrub, rarely a "mini" tree, with slender stems and small ovate leaves about 4 to 6cm. long, oblique at base, serrately-toothed, thinly downy on both surfaces and with axillary tufts beneath. One of the most distinct of all limes. Japan. I. 1930.

mandshurica RUPR. & MAXIM. A striking small to medium-sized tree with downy young shoots and large, heart-shaped, coarsely-toothed leaves, which are equal in size to those of *T. americana*, but greyish beneath, both surfaces stellately downy. Subject to injury by late spring frosts. N.E. Asia. I. about 1860.

maximowicziana SHIRAS. A medium-sized to large tree with downy, yellowish shoots and broadly ovate or rounded leaves, 10 to 18cm. long, edged with broad, mucronate teeth. They are stellately hairy above, greyish tomentose beneath, with conspicuous axillary tufts. Flowers appearing in June. Japan. C. 1880. A.M. 1976.

TILIA—*continued*

miqueliana MAXIM. A very distinct, slow-growing tree of small to medium size, with grey-felted shoots. Leaves ovate, tapering to an acuminate apex, coarsely-toothed or slightly lobed, grey-felted beneath, long persisting. Flowers appearing in August, conspicuous and fragrant. E. China. Long cultivated in Japan, particularly around temples. I. before 1900.

× **moltkei** SPAETH (*americana* × *petiolaris*). A strong-growing tree of medium to large size, with arching, slightly pendulous branches. Leaves broad ovate or rounded, 15 to 20cm. long, greyish downy beneath. Raised by Messrs. Spaeth in Berlin.

mongolica MAXIM. "Mongolian Lime". A small tree of compact rounded habit and dense twiggy growth, with glabrous, reddish shoots. Leaves 4 to 7·5cm. long, coarsely-toothed or three to five lobed, particularly on young trees, glossy green and glabrous except for axillary tufts beneath turning bright yellow in autumn. An attractive species with prettily-lobed, ivy-like leaves. Mongolia; N. China. I. 1880.

monticola SARG. Medium-sized tree with reddish young twigs. Leaves ovate, acuminate, deep lustrous green above, pale beneath. Closely related to and, by some authorities, united with *T. heterophylla*. S.E. United States. C. 1888.

neglecta SPACH. A large tree with red, glabrous shoots and broadly ovate, green leaves, stellately hairy beneath. Closely related to *T. americana*. E. and C. North America. C. 1830.

oliveri SZYSZY. An elegant, medium-sized to large tree with glabrous shoots inclined to be pendulous. Leaves broadly ovate or rounded, finely-toothed, dark green above, silvery-white tomentose beneath. Closely related to *T. tomentosa*, but differs in its glabrous young shoots. C. China. Discovered by Augustine Henry in 1888. Introduced by E. H. Wilson in 1900. A.G.M. 1973.

× **orbicularis** JOUIN (× *euchlora* × *petiolaris*). A vigorous, medium-sized tree of conical habit, with somewhat pendulous branches. Leaves large, orbicular, glossy green above, grey tomentose beneath. Raised by Messrs. Simon-Louis, near Metz, N.E. France, about 1870.

parvifolia. See *T. cordata*.

petiolaris DC. (*americana 'Pendula'* HORT.). "Weeping Silver Lime". One of the most beautiful of all large, weeping trees. A large, round-headed tree with graceful, downward sweeping branches. Leaves long-stalked, broadly ovate to rounded, sharply-toothed, dark green above, white-felted beneath, especially attractive when ruffled by a breeze. Flowers richly scented, but narcotic to bees. A tree of uncertain origin, related to *T. tomentosa*. C. 1840. A.G.M. 1969.

platyphyllos SCOP. (*grandifolia*). "Broad-leaved Lime". A large, vigorous tree of rounded habit with downy shoots. Leaves roundish-ovate, sharply-toothed, shortly pubescent above, densely so beneath, especially on veins and midrib. Flowers appearing in late June or early July. A commonly planted tree, especially in parks. Suckers are produced, but not as prolifically as in *T.* × *europaea*. C. and S. Europe to N. France and S.W. Sweden. Possibly native in the Wye Valley and S. Yorkshire. F.C.C. 1892.

'Asplenifolia'. An elegant, small to medium-sized tree with leaves deeply and variously divided into narrow segments. Perhaps a sport of the variable *'Laciniata'*.

'Aurea' (*'Aurantiaca'*) (*grandifolia 'Aurantia'*). Young shoots yellow, becoming olive-green. Most conspicuous in winter.

'Corallina'. See *'Rubra'*.

'Fastigiata' (*'Pyramidalis'*). An erect-branched form of broadly conical habit.

'Laciniata'. A small to medium-sized tree of dense, conical habit. Leaves deeply and irregularly cut into rounded and tail-like lobes.

'Pendula'. Branches spreading, branchlets pendulous.

'Rubra' (*'Corallina'*). "Red-twigged Lime". Young shoots bright brownish-red, particularly effective in winter. The best cultivar for street planting owing to its uniformly, semi-erect habit of branching. Excellent in industrial areas.

spectabilis DIPP. See *T.* × *moltkei*.

tomentosa MOENCH. (*argentea*) (*alba*). "Silver Lime". A handsome, but variable, large tree of stately habit. Branches erect, often pendulous at their tips, shoots white felted. Leaves shortly-stalked, ovate-orbicular, sharply-toothed, dark green above, silvery-white tomentose beneath. They are particularly effective when disturbed by a breeze. S.E. and E.C. Europe. I. 1767.

TILIA—*continued*

× **vulgaris.** See *T.* ×*europaea.*

***TRACHYCARPUS—Palmaceae**—A small genus of palms with very large, fan-shaped leaves, natives of Eastern Asia. The flowers are monoecious. The following species is hardy in the British Isles but it deserves a sheltered position to protect its leaves from being shattered by strong winds.

fortunei WENDL. (*excelsus*) (*Chamaerops excelsa*). "Chusan Palm". A remarkable species of small to medium size, developing a tall, single trunk, thickly clothed with the fibrous remains of the old leaf bases. Leaves large, fan-shaped, 1 to 1·5m. across, borne on long, stout petioles in a cluster from the summit of the trunk, persisting many years. Flowers yellow, small, numerously borne in large, terminal, decurved panicles in early summer; fruits marble-like, bluish-black. C. China. First introduced by Philip von Siebold in 1830 and later by Robert Fortune in 1849. A.M. 1970.

"TREE DAISY". See *OLEARIA.*

"TREE OF HEAVEN". See *AILANTHUS altissima.*

"TREE LUPIN". See *LUPINUS arboreus.*

"TREE POPPY". See *ROMNEYA.*

TRICUSPIDARIA. See *CRINODENDRON.*

‡TRIPETALEIA—Ericaceae—A genus of two species of slow-growing, deciduous shrubs attaining 1·5 to 2m., occasionally more; requiring a moist lime-free soil in semi-shade. The flowers are normally three-petalled.

bracteata MAXIM. A slender shrub with reddish-brown, rounded stems and glabrous, entire, obovate leaves. The greenish-white or pink-tinged flowers are borne in erect, terminal racemes in July and August. Japan. I. 1893.

paniculata SIEB. & ZUCC. An erect shrub with reddish-brown, angular stems. Leaves obovate, minutely pubescent beneath. Flowers white or pink-tinged, with usually three petals, borne in erect, terminal panicles from July to September. Japan. Introduced by Maries in 1879.

‡*TROCHODENDRON—Trochodendraceae—A monotypic genus growing in most fertile soils except shallow chalky soils, in sun or shade. During the severe winter of 1962/63 when most evergreens looked bedraggled, this species was unharmed and quite outstanding.

aralioides SIEB. & ZUCC. A large, glabrous, evergreen shrub or small tree of slow growth and spreading habit, the bark aromatic. The long-stalked, obovate, leathery leaves are bright apple-green or yellowish green in colour and prettily scalloped at the margins. Flowers green, borne in erect, terminal racemes during spring and early summer. A striking and unusual shrub desired by flower arrangers. Japan; Formosa; S. Korea. C. 1894. A.M. 1976.

‡TSUSIOPHYLLUM—Ericaceae—A monotypic genus sometimes united with *Rhododendron*, from which it differs in its three-celled ovary and dehiscent anthers. Requires a moist, lime-free soil.

tanakae MAXIM. (*Rhododendron tsusiophyllum*). A dwarf or small semi-evergreen shrub of dense, twiggy habit, with myriads of tiny leaves, glaucous beneath. The tiny, bell-shaped, white flowers appear in one to three flowered clusters during June and July. A delightful little species. Japan. I. 1915. A.M. 1965.

"TULIP TREE". See *LIRIODENDRON tulipifera.*

"TUPELO". See *NYSSA sylvatica.*

TWEEDIA coerulea. See *OXYPETALUM caeruleum.*

ULEX—Leguminosae—Variously known as "Furze", "Gorse" or "Whin". The three native species are usually found on poor, dry, heath or downland, and are valuable for covering dry banks, and for wind-swept, maritime sites.

If our native gorses were rare exotics, they would be sought alike by connoisseur and garden designer. It would be impossible to imagine in any landscape a richer mass of chrome yellow, intermixed with the occasional splash of deep lemon yellow, than one sees covering the downs around Slieve Donard in Northern Ireland in April. This dazzling feast of colour is provided by *U. europaeus.* In August and September along the Welsh mountain sides, as one approaches central Wales from Herefordshire, the countryside is enriched by lower growing masses of *U. gallii.*

ULEX—*continued*

Many of us have roved those lovely downs which rise from Salcombe harbour in South Devon which, in late summer, become a patchwork quilt of golden gorse and purple heather. In parts of the New Forest we meet *U. minor*, our third native species, which also flowers in the autumn with the heather.

Gorse should be pot grown, otherwise it is difficult to establish. It is not recommended for shallow, chalk soils. Strong growing plants are apt to become leggy and bare at the base. They may be cut to the ground after flowering. Gorse is one of those unusual shrubs which, like heather, grows best in poor, dry, acid soil.

europaeus L. "Common Gorse". A densely-branched, green, viciously spiny, native shrub, 1·2 to 1·8m. high, much more in sheltered or shaded sites. The chrome-yellow, pea-flowers crowd the branches from March to May and intermittently throughout the year. W. Europe extending eastwards to Italy. Extensively naturalised in C. Europe.

'Plenus'. A superb shrub when in April and May its lower growing compact hummocks are smothered in long-lasting, semi-double flowers. A.G.M. 1929. A.M. 1967.

'Strictus' (*'Hibernicus'*) (*'Fastigiatus'*). A slow-growing, unusual form with erect, slender, shortly and softly spiny shoots forming a dense, compact bush. It resembles more a form of *U. gallii* than *U. europaeus* and, though it rarely flowers, makes an excellent low hedge.

gallii PLANCH. A dwarf shrub, often prostrate in maritime areas, usually more robust and stronger-spined than *U. minor*, but much less so than *U. europaeus*. Flowers smaller than those of the "Common Gorse", deep golden-yellow, opening in the autumn from August to October. W. Europe (including the British Isles).

minor ROTH (*nanus*). A dwarf, often prostrate shrub with slender, softly-spiny shoots. Flowers half the size of those of the "Common Gorse", golden-yellow, opening during autumn and particularly spectacular in September. A low-growing species which must be given "starvation diet" to prevent it becoming tall and lanky. S.W. Europe northwards to the British Isles, but not Ireland.

ULMUS—Ulmaceae—A genus which includes some of the noblest, deciduous, hardy trees in this country. They all thrive in almost any type of soil and in exposed positions, the "Wych Elm" being one of the few trees which may be planted near the sea in full exposure to Atlantic gales. The golden and variegated forms are colourful trees in the landscape, while the weeping forms are picturesque and useful for the shade they give. In most species the leaves turn glowing yellow in the autumn sunshine. The flowers of the elm are small and reddish in colour and hermaphrodite; unless otherwise stated, they are borne on the naked twigs in early spring. The fruits (samaras) which follow are greenish, winged and disc-like.

The "English Elm" (*U. procera*) is an inseparable part of the English landscape. Unfortunately its presence in certain areas has, in recent years, been drastically reduced due to the depredations of the Dutch Elm Disease. This disease is caused by a fungus (*Ceratocystus ulmi*), spores of which are transmitted from diseased trees to healthy trees through the agency of various elm-bark beetles. An account of the disease and its occurence in the British Isles is available from the Forestry Commission (Bulletin No. 33). An England devoid of elms would be like Australia without gum trees. In dealing with this serious disease landowners and gardeners are asked to co-operate by checking the condition of all elms (whatever the species) growing on their property. Badly infected trees should be completely removed, but where isolated branches are infected these should be dealt with in the same manner and burnt. To prevent the disease from spreading, it is necessary to remove all possible breeding sites for the elm-bark beetles, and to this end all dead or dying trees and branches should be destroyed. Elm logs or stumps left in the open should have their bark removed.

alata MICHX. "Winged Elm". A small to medium-sized tree developing a rounded head. Branches glabrous or nearly so, with two opposite corky wings. Leaves narrowly obovate to ovate-oblong, glabrous above. Fruits hairy. S.E. United States. I. 1820.

ULMUS—*continued*

americana L. "White Elm". A large, vigorous, attractive tree with ash-grey bark and a wide-spreading head of graceful branches. The ovate to obovate, slenderly-pointed leaves, 10 to 15cm. long, are double toothed along the margins and unequal at the base. Fruits ciliate. E. and C. North America. I. 1752.

angustifolia WEST. (*stricta goodyeri*). "Goodyer Elm". An elegant, medium-sized, native tree with slender branches and small, elliptic or obovate leaves, which are narrower on sucker growths and saplings. Fruits glabrous. The typical tree, which is rare in cultivation, is more spreading in habit than the "Cornish Elm". According to Dr. R. Melville, the type only occurs wild in coastal areas between Christchurch and Lymington in Hampshire.

cornubiensis MELVILLE (*U. stricta*) (*carpinifolia 'Cornubiensis'*). "Cornish Elm". A familiar elm easily recognised by its dense, conical head of ascending branches, eventually attaining a large size and then more open and looser in growth. Leaves small, obovate or ovate; fruits glabrous. Occurs wild in Devon and Cornwall in England, and in Brittany in France, planted elsewhere. An excellent maritime tree.

belgica. See *U.* ×*hollandica 'Belgica'*.

campestris. See *U. procera*.
'Major'. See *U.* ×*hollandica 'Major'*.
stricta. See *U. angustifolia cornubiensis*.
sarniensis. See *U.* ×*sarniensis*.

carpinifolia GLEDITSCH (*nitens*) (*foliacea*). "Smooth-leaved Elm". A large, native tree of graceful, open habit, with slender, often pendulous shoots. Leaves narrowly oval to oblanceolate, markedly unequal at base, double-toothed and rather leathery in texture, glabrous, shining dark green above, hairy in the vein axils beneath. Fruits glabrous. An attractive but variable species, usually developing a conical head, or spreading and round-topped when exposed to gales near the coast, where it is invaluable as a windbreak. Europe; N. Africa.

'Cornubiensis'. See *U. angustifolia cornubiensis*.
'Dampieri'. See *U.* ×*hollandica 'Dampieri'*.
'Italica'. See *U.* ×*hollandica 'Australis'*.
sarniensis. See *U.* ×*sarniensis*.
'Variegata'. Leaves densely mottled white, giving a silvery-grey effect.

chinensis. See *U. parvifolia*.

crassifolia NUTT. A slow-growing, small, round-headed tree in cultivation, with downy young shoots and occasionally opposite or subopposite winter buds. Leaves ovate to oblong, blunt-tipped, leathery, 2·5 to 5cm. long, rough to the touch above, downy beneath. Flowers produced in axillary clusters in late summer and early autumn. Fruits downy. Southern U.S.A.; N.E. Mexico. I. 1876.

davidiana PLANCH. A medium-sized tree with downy shoots and broad, obovate or ovate leaves, pubescent beneath. Fruits hairy in the centre. N.E. Asia. I. 1895.

japonica NAKAI (*U. japonica*). "Japanese Elm". A graceful tree with downy twigs and elliptic or obovate leaves, rough to the touch above. Fruits glabrous. Japan.

effusa. See *U. laevis*.

×**elegantissima** HORWOOD (*glabra* × *plottii*). A natural hybrid occuring with the parents mainly in the Midlands of England. We offer the following clone:—

'Jacqueline Hillier'. A small to medium-sized, suckering shrub of dense habit. The slender, brown pubescent twigs are neatly clothed with small, double-toothed, scabrid leaves 2·5 to 3·5cm. long. An unusual elm which was found in a garden in Birmingham several years ago. Its neat, dense habit lends itself to planting as a low hedge or for bonsai.

exoniensis. See *U. glabra 'Exoniensis'*.

foliacea. See *U. carpinifolia*.

fulva. See *U. rubra*.

ULMUS—*continued*

glabra HUDS. (*montana*). "Wych Elm"; "Scotch Elm". A large native tree, usually developing a dome-shaped crown with spreading branches, arching or pendulous at their extremities. Leaves shortly stalked, large and rough to the touch above, coarsely-toothed, markedly unequal at base, abruptly acuminate. Fruits downy at apex, effective in early spring when they crowd the branches. It is said to be the only native elm which reproduces itself freely and regularly from seed. An excellent tree for planting in exposed situations either inland or along the coast. Many forms have been named. Europe; N. and W. Asia.

'Camperdownii' (*pendula 'Camperdownii'*). "Camperdown Elm". A small, neat and compact tree with pendulous branches, forming a globose or dome-shaped head in marked contrast to the more spreading, stiffer-looking crown of the equally common *'Pendula'*. Suitable as an isolated specimen on a lawn. C. 1850.

'Crispa' (*'Aspleniifolia'*) (*'Urticifolia'*). An unusual form of slow growth and generally loose habit, with narrow leaves which are curiously infolded, with jaggedly-toothed margins.

'Exoniensis' (*'Fastigiata'*) (*scabra 'Pyramidalis'*) (*U. exoniensis*). An erect tree of medium to large size, narrowly columnar when young, broadening with age. Leaves broad, jaggedly-toothed, occurring in clusters on the ascending branches. Found near Exeter, about 1826.

'Fastigiata'. See *'Exoniensis'*.

'Lutescens' (*americana 'Aurea'*). Leaves soft cream yellow in spring, becoming yellowish-green. A very beautiful free-growing tree.

'Pendula' (*'Horizontalis'*). "Weeping Wych Elm". A small tree occasionally reaching 9m., developing a wide head of spreading branches with long pendulous branchlets. Suitable as an isolated specimen for the large garden or park.

'Vegeta'. See *U.* ×*vegeta*.

×**hillieri.** See *U.* ×*hollandica 'Hillieri'*.

×**hollandica** MILL. (*carpinifolia* × *glabra* × *plotii*). An extremely variable, natural hybrid widespread in W. Europe. According to Dr. R. Melville this hybrid, in its numerous forms constitutes almost the entire elm population of Germany, Holland, Belgium and France, as well as being quite abundant in East Anglia and the Midlands. The cultivars described below under this name are of similar parentage, but of independent origin. The majority are very vigorous and, unless otherwise stated, attain a large size.

'Australis' (*procera 'Australis'*) (*carpinifolia 'Italica'*). An interesting tree with conspicuously and numerously veined leaves which are rather leathery in texture. It is said to occur in the wild in S.E. France, Switzerland and Italy.

'Bea Schwarz'. A Dutch selection raised for its resistance to Dutch Elm Disease. First introduced in 1948.

'Belgica' (*U. campestris latifolia*) (*U. belgica*). "Belgian Elm". A natural hybrid strongly resembling *U. glabra*. A vigorous tree forming a broad crown with almost glabrous twigs and obovate-elliptic leaves with a long, serrated point. This is the clone usually grown as *U.* ×*hollandica* in Belgium and Holland where it is commonly planted in parks and along roads. C. 1694.

'Christine Buisman'. An attractive disease-resistant clone of Dutch origin. Introduced in 1937.

'Dampieri'. A narrow, conical tree, with broadly-ovate, double-toothed leaves, densely crowded on short branchlets.

'Hillieri' (*U.* ×*hillieri*). A graceful, compact, slow-growing, miniature, weeping tree or shrub, usually less than 1·2m. high, which originated as a chance seedling in our Pitt Corner nursery, Winchester in 1918. The slender branchlets carry small leaves which, under favourable conditions, turn crimson and yellow in autumn.

'Major' (*U. major*). "Dutch Elm". A large, suckering tree with a short trunk and wide-spreading branches. Young shoots glabrous or almost so. Leaves broad elliptic with a long serrated point and markedly unequal at base. Branchlets often prominently ridged. This is the *U.* ×*hollandica* of England, where it is commonly planted.

'Pendula'. See *'Smithii'*.

'Serpentina'. A remarkable small tree with curved and twisted, zig-zag pendulous branches, forming a dense conical or globose crown.

ULMUS—*continued*

× **hollandica 'Smithii'** (*'Pendula'*). "Downton Elm". An elegant small to medium-sized tree with ascending branches and long, pendulous branchlets. Leaves dark green, smooth and shining above.

'Vegeta'. See *U.* ×*vegeta.*

'Wredei' (*'Wredei Aurea'* HORT.). A narrowly conical tree in which the crowded broad leaves are suffused golden yellow. A sport of *'Dampieri'*. F.C.C. 1893.

japonica. See *U. davidiana japonica.*

laciniata MAYR (*montana laciniata*). A small tree with large, thin, obovate leaves which are usually three to nine lobed at the apex, rough to the touch above and sharply, double-toothed. Fruits glabrous. N.E. Asia. I. 1905.

laevis PALL. (*effusa*) (*pedunculata*). "European White Elm". A large tree with a wide-spreading head and rounded to ovate or obovate, double-toothed leaves, softly-downy below, markedly unequal at base. Fruits ciliate. C.E. and S.E. Europe to W. Asia.

macrocarpa HANCE. "Large-fruited Elm". A small, bushy tree with corky winged branches and roughly hairy leaves. Distinguished from other elms by the large, winged fruits up to 3cm. long, which are bristly, like the leaves. N. China. I. 1908.

major. See *U.* ×*hollandica 'Major'*.

minor. A confused name applied to juvenile forms of *U. angustifolia, U. plottii* and hybrids.

montana. See *U. glabra.*

nitens. See *U. carpinifolia.*

'Stricta'. See *U. angustifolia cornubiensis.*

'Wheatleyi'. See *U.* ×*sarniensis.*

parvifolia JACQ. (*chinensis*) (*sieboldii*). "Chinese Elm". A medium-sized tree with young shoots densely pubescent. Leaves small, 2·5 to 8cm. long, leathery and glossy green. Flowers produced in early autumn. One of the most splendid elms having the poise of a graceful *Nothofagus*, and with small, rich green leaves which persist halfway through the winter. We have never seen this tree affected by disease. N. and C. China; Korea; Formosa; Japan. I. 1794.

'Frosty'. A charming, slow-growing, shrubby form, the tiny, neatly-arranged leaves bearing white teeth.

pinnato-ramosa. See *U. pumila arborea.*

plotii DRUCE. A large, erect tree with short, horizontal or ascending branches and long, pendulous branchlets. Leaves small, smooth above. Differs from the "Cornish Elm" in its looser habit and arching leader, particularly noticeable when young. A native of Central England, being typical of river alluvium, particularly plentiful along the River Trent and its tributaries.

procera SALISB. (*campestris*). "English Elm". A large, stately tree inseparably associated with the English landscape. Shoots downy; leaves appearing earlier than those of the "Wych Elm", oval or rounded, acute, rough to the touch above, sharply double-toothed. Fruits glabrous, but rarely produced. There are few more pleasing sights than a tall mature tree in autumn when the clear, butter-yellow of its fading leaves is intensified by the rays of the setting sun and a background mist. The typical form is known only in England where it is abundant in hedgerows and fields, spreading extensively by suckers but never producing fertile seed.

'Argenteovariegata'. Leaves green, splashed and striped silvery-grey and white. A large tree is particularly conspicuous.

'Louis van Houtte' (*'Van Houttei'*). A handsome tree with golden-yellow foliage throughout the summer.

'Silvery Gem'. Leaves with irregular but conspicuous creamy-white margin.

'Viminalis'. See *U.* ×*viminalis.*

pumila L. "Dwarf Elm"; "Siberian Elm". A variable species varying from a large shrub to a medium-sized tree, the latter being the form in general cultivation. Leaves ovate to ovate-lanceolate, 2·5 to 3·5cm. long, thin in texture simply toothed. Fruits glabrous. N. Asia. I. 1770.

arborea LITV. (*pinnato-ramosa*). A small tree, recognisable by the pinnate arrangement of its small, bright green leaves. W. Siberia; Turkestan. C. 1894.

racemosa. See *U. thomasii.*

ULMUS—*continued*

rubra MUHL. (*fulva*) (*elliptica* KOEHNE). "Slippery Elm"; "Red Elm". A striking, medium-sized tree with a spreading head of branches. Twigs densely pubescent. Leaves large, oval or obovate, velvety-hairy beneath, rough to the touch above. Fruits reddish-brown. Its large velvety leaves make this one of the most distinct elms. C. and E. North America. C. 1830.

× **sarniensis** BANCROFT (*angustifolia* × *hollandica*) (*carpinifolia sarniensis*) (*U. wheatleyi*). "Jersey Elm"; "Wheatley Elm". A large tree of conical habit with strictly ascending branches, developing a narrower, denser crown than the "Cornish Elm". Leaves small, ovate to obovate, broader than those of the "Cornish Elm". Fruits glabrous. One of the finest of all trees for roadside planting, especially near the coast. Occurs in Jersey and along the Channel coast of France. Commonly planted elsewhere. A.G.M. 1969.

'Dicksonii' (*'Aurea'*) (*wheatleyi 'Aurea'*). "Dickson's Golden Elm". A very slow-growing tree with leaves of a beautiful bright golden yellow. A.G.M. 1969.

'Purpurea'. This form differs markedly from the type in its spreading branches, creating a broader crown. The leaves and shoots are suffused dull purple when young. Strong, vigorous shoots on young plants bear large, roughly hairy leaves. Erroneously cultivated in the past under the names *U. glabra 'Purpurea'* and *U. procera 'Purpurea'*.

serotina SARG. A large tree forming a spreading head of drooping branches. Leaves oblong to obovate, slender-pointed, markedly unequal at base, bright glossy green above. Flowers produced during early autumn; fruits ciliate with silvery-white hairs. S.E. United States. C. 1903.

sieboldii. See *U. parvifolia*.

stricta. See *U. angustifolia cornubiensis*.

thomasii SARG. (*racemosa* THOMAS). "Rock Elm". A slow-growing, small to medium-sized tree of conical habit when young. Winter buds large and, like the young shoots, downy. Leaves oval to obovate, unequal at base and abruptly pointed, glabrous and glossy green above, downy beneath. Flowers in short racemes; fruits downy all over. Eastern N. America. I. 1875.

× **vegeta** A. LEY (*carpinifolia* × *glabra*) (× *hollandica 'Vegeta'*) (*U. glabra 'Vegeta'*). "Huntingdon Elm"; "Chichester Elm". A magnificent large tree with a short trunk and long, ascending branches. Young shoots sparsely hairy. Leaves large, elliptic, very unequal at base, long pointed; smooth, shining dark green above, jaggedly-toothed and conspicuously veined. One of the most vigorous elms, raised in a nursery at Huntingdon about 1750.

'Commelin'. A disease resistant clone of Dutch origin differing from the type in its narrower habit and smaller leaves.

villosa BRANDIS. A large, noble tree of vigorous growth and wide-spreading habit with smooth, silvery-grey bark, becoming fissured and greyish-brown. Leaves of a fresh pale green and softly downy. W. Himalaya. A.M. 1974.

× **viminalis** LODD. (*carpinifolia* × *plotii*) (*procera 'Viminalis'*) (*antarctica*). An extremely graceful, medium-sized tree recalling *Zelkova verschaffeltii*, of slow growth, with arching and drooping branches. Leaves small, oblanceolate to narrowly oval, tapered at base, the margins deeply toothed. Long cultivated.

'Argentea'. See *'Marginata'*.

'Aurea' (*'Rosseelsii'*) (*campestris 'Aurea'*). A picturesque form with leaves suffused golden yellow when young, becoming yellowish-green as the summer advances. C. about 1865.

'Marginata' (*'Argentea'*). Leaves mottled greyish-white, especially near the margins.

wallichiana PLANCH. A rare, medium-sized to large tree with downy, red-tinged young shoots and obovate, coarsely toothed leaves ending in a slender point. Himalaya.

wheatleyi. See *U.* × *sarniensis*.

'Wredei Aurea'. See *U.* × *hollandica 'Wredei'*.

***UMBELLULARIA—Lauraceae**—A monotypic evergreen genus resembling the "Bay" in general appearance and requiring a warm, sunny position in a well-drained soil.

californica NUTT. "Californian Laurel"; "Californian Bay". A strongly aromatic, large shrub or small to medium-sized tree of dense leafy habit. One of the largest specimens in the British Isles is at Warnham Court, Sussex. Leaves oblong to oblong-lanceolate, entire, bright green or yellowish-green in colour. Flowers small, yellowish-green, borne in small umbels during April, occasionally followed by oval, green fruits, 2·5cm. long, turning dark purple when ripe. In exposed positions the young shoots are subject to injury by late spring frosts. The pungent aroma emitted by the leaves when crushed has been known to cause a headache when inhaled. The "old school" of gardeners indulged in extravagant stories of the prostrate Dowager overcome by the powerful aroma. California and Oregon. Introduced by David Douglas in 1829.

"UMBRELLA TREE". See *MAGNOLIA tripetala*.

‡VACCINIUM—Ericaceae—A large genus of evergreen and deciduous shrubs widely distributed over the northern hemisphere and on mountains in S. America. They require much the same conditions as heathers, but are more tolerant of shade and moisture. In fact some species demand these conditions. While autumn colour of leaf and berry is their most notable attribute, their flowers and modest beauty at other seasons qualifies them for inclusion in any representative collection of shrubs. Excellent subjects for extremely acid soils.

angustifolium AIT. (*pensylvanicum angustifolium*). "Low-bush Blueberry". A dwarf shrub of compact habit with thin, wiry twigs clothed with bristle-toothed, lanceolate leaves, richly tinted in autumn, sometimes earlier. Flowers cylindrical or bell-shaped, white or red-tinted, produced in dense clusters in April and May. Berries blue-black, "bloomy", sweet and edible. Grown commercially for its fruits in North America. N.E. North America. I. 1772.

laevifolium HOUSE (*pensylvanicum*). A variable form with larger, lanceolate to narrowly oval or oblong leaves. F.C.C. 1890.

arboreum MARSH. "Farkleberry". A medium-sized to large, deciduous or semi-evergreen shrub, said to reach small tree size in some of its native haunts. Leaves ovate to obovate, up to 5cm. long, leathery in texture, glabrous and dark glossy green above, thinly downy beneath giving rich autumn tints. Flowers white, bell-shaped, produced singly or in small racemes during summer, followed by black inedible berries. S. and E. United States. I. 1765.

arctostaphylos L. "Caucasian Whortleberry". A splendid, slow-growing shrub of medium size and loose, wide-spreading habit with reddish young shoots. Leaves large, up to 10 or even 13cm. long, narrowly elliptic to obovate, reticulately veined and finely-toothed, turning purplish-red in autumn and often remaining until Christmas. The waxy, white or crimson-tinted, bell-shaped flowers are carried in conspicuous racemes in summer and again during autumn, followed by rounded, shining black berries. Caucasus. I. 1800. A.M. 1970.

atrococcum HELLER. A small to medium-sized shrub with oval, entire leaves, densely pubescent beneath. Flowers urceolate, greenish-white, tinged red, carried in dense racemes during May, often before the leaves. Berries black and shining. It is closely related to *V. corymbosum* and, like that species, gives rich autumn colours. Eastern N. America. I. before 1898.

***bracteatum** THUNB. A charming evergreen shrub up to 2m. in height with narrowly oval, glabrous leaves, copper-red when young. The cylindrical or ovoid, fragrant, white flowers are borne in numerous leafy racemes during late summer and autumn, sometimes earlier. Berries red. Easily recognised when in flower by the presence of small, leaf-like bracts on the main flower stalk. Japan; Korea; China; Formosa. I. 1829.

corymbosum L. "Swamp Blueberry"; "High-bush Blueberry". A colourful small to medium-sized shrub forming a dense thicket of erect branching stems. Leaves ovate to ovate-lanceolate, up to 8·5cm. long, bright green and reticulate, turning to vivid scarlet and bronze in autumn. The clusters of pale pink or white, urn-shaped flowers are borne in May. Berries comparatively large, black with a blue "bloom", sweet and edible, like small, black grapes. Extensively cultivated in the U.S.A. for commercial fruit production. Eastern N. America. I. 1765. A.G.M. 1936.

VACCINIUM—*continued*

***crassifolium** AIT. A dwarf evergreen shrub of creeping habit, with slender, reddish stems up to 15cm. high. Leaves oval, shining green and leathery, densely crowding the twigs. The small, bell-shaped, rose-red flowers are borne in terminal racemes in May and June. Berries black. S.E. United States. I. 1787.

cylindraceum SM. (*longiflorum*). A superb, more or less semi-evergreen species. An erect, medium-sized to large shrub with bright green, narrow elliptic to oblong-elliptic, finely-toothed and reticulate leaves, often green until the spring days lengthen in the New Year. Flowers cylindrical, 12mm. long, densely packed in short racemes all along the previous year's branchlets during late summer and autumn. In colour they are red in bud, opening to pale yellow-green, tinged red, recalling *Pentapterygium serpens*. They are followed by cylindrical blue-black, "bloomy" berries. The first berries are often ripening when late flowers are still appearing. Azores.

***delavayi** FRANCH. A neat, compact, evergreen shrub slowly reaching 1·8m., densely set with small, box-like, obovate, leathery leaves which are usually notched at the apex. The tiny, pink-tinged whitish flowers are borne in small, hairy racemes terminating the previous year's growth in late spring or early summer. Berries purplish-blue, rounded. In its native state it is said to grow on cliffs and rocks and as an epiphyte on trees. Discovered by the Abbé Delavay in Yunnan; introduced by George Forrest before 1923. A.M. 1950.

deliciosum PIPER. A dwarf, tufted, glabrous shrub, with oval or obovate leaves. The solitary, pinkish, globular flowers in May are replaced by sweet, edible black, "bloomy" berries. N.W. United States. I. 1920.

***floribundum** H.B.K. (*mortinia*). A beautiful, small, evergreen shrub with attractive red young growths and small, ovate, dark green leaves, purplish-red when young, densely crowding the spray-like branches. Flowers cylindrical, rose-pink, carried in dense racemes in June. Berries red, edible. Although its native haunts are close to the equator, it is remarkably hardy in the southern counties. Ecuador. I. about 1840. A.M. 1935 (as *V. mortinia*).

†*gaultheriifolium HOOK. f. A small to medium-sized, evergreen shrub of loose habit with bloomy young shoots. Leaves elliptic, 7·5 to 13cm. long, acuminate, glossy green and attractively veined above, paler and covered by a blue-white bloom beneath, entire or minutely-toothed. Flowers white in corymbs in late summer. Related to *V. glaucoalbum*, but more graceful in habit, and with larger, slender pointed leaves. Himalaya.

***glaucoalbum** CLARKE. An attractive evergreen shrub, suckering and forming patches 1·2 to 1·8m. in height. Leaves comparatively large, oval or ovate, grey-green above, vividly blue-white beneath. Flowers cylindrical, pale pink, borne amongst conspicuous rosy, silvery-white bracts in racemes during May and June. Berries black, blue "bloomy", often lasting well into winter. Liable to damage by frost in cold areas of the British Isles. Himalaya. A.M. 1931.

hirsutum BUCKL. "Hairy Huckleberry". A small, suckering shrub producing dense thickets of slender, hairy stems with ovate or elliptic, entire leaves. Flowers cylindrical, white tinged pink, produced in short racemes during May. Berries blue-black, rounded, covered with tiny, glandular hairs, sweet and edible. Often colouring well in autumn. S.E. United States. I. 1887.

***macrocarpon** AIT. (*Oxycoccus macrocarpus*). "American Cranberry". A prostrate shrublet with slender, creeping, wiry stems and small, delicate, oval or oblong leaves, glaucous beneath. Flowers small, drooping, pink, the petals curving back to reveal a beak of yellow anthers, carried in short racemes during summer. Berries red, globular, 12 to 20mm. across, edible but acid in flavour. Selected clones of this species are the commercially grown "Cranberry" of the U.S.A. It requires a moist, peaty or boggy soil in which to thrive. Eastern N. America. I. 1760.

membranaceum TORR. A small, erect-growing shrub with glabrous, angular branches and ovate to oblong, bright green leaves. Flowers urn-shaped, greenish-white or pink-tinged, produced solitary in the leaf axils in June, followed by purplish-black, edible berries. Closely related to our native "Bilberry" which it much resembles. C. and E. North America. I. 1828.

mortinia. See *V. floribundum*.

VACCINIUM—*continued*

***moupinense** FRANCH. A neat-growing, dwarf, evergreen shrub of dense habit. Leaves narrowly obovate or ovate, 12mm. long, leathery and usually entire, densely crowding the branches. Flowers urn-shaped, mahogany-red, borne on similarly coloured stalks in dense racemes during May and June. Berries purplish-black, rounded. Resembling *V. delavayi* in many ways, differing in its leaves which are rounded, not notched at the apex, and in its glabrous inflorescence. W. China. I. 1909.

***myrsinites** LAM. "Evergreen Blueberry". A dwarf, spreading, evergreen shrub of compact habit with small, neat, oval, finely-toothed leaves. Flowers white or pink-tinged, rose in bud, borne in terminal and axillary clusters during April and May. Berries blue-black. S.E. United States. C. 1813.

myrtillus L. "Bilberry"; "Whortleberry"; "Whinberry"; "Blaeberry". A familiar native species of heaths and moors, forming a dense, suckering patch of slender, bright green, angular stems. Leaves ovate, finely-toothed. Flowers globular, greenish-pink, produced singly or in pairs in the leaf axils from late April to June, followed by "bloomy" black edible berries. Europe to Caucasus and N. Asia.

†*nummularia HOOK. & THOMS. This is probably the most attractive dwarf species in cultivation. A compact, evergreen shrub with bristly-hairy, arching shoots neatly clothed with a double row of small, leathery, dark glossy-green, orbicular-ovate leaves. The small, cylindrical, rose-red flowers are borne in small, dense clusters at the ends of the shoots in May and June, followed by globular, black, edible berries. Athough hardy only in mild localities, this choice little shrub makes an ideal alpine house plant. It is an excellent shrub for a not too dry, sheltered, shady bank. Himalaya. I. about 1850. A.M. 1932.

***ovatum** PURSH. An attractive evergreen shrub of medium size and dense, compact habit. The 1 to 4cm. long ovate to oblong, leathery leaves are bright, coppery red when young, becoming polished dark green, thickly crowding the downy branches. Flowers bell-shaped, white or pink, appearing in short racemes during May and June. Berries red at first, ripening to black. A useful evergreen for cutting. Western N. America. Introduced by David Douglas in 1826.

***oxycoccos** L. (*Oxycoccus palustris*). "Cranberry". A prostrate, native, evergreen shrublet of moorland and mountain bogs, producing far-reaching wiry stems bearing scattered, tiny, silver-backed leaves. The tiny, nodding flowers with pink, recurved petals and a yellow staminal beak are borne on short, erect, thread-like stems and recall those of a *Dodecatheon* ("Shooting Star"), but are much smaller. They appear during May and June and are followed by edible, red, rounded fruits which possess an agreeable acid taste. Requires a moist, peaty soil in which to thrive. Widely distributed in the cooler regions of the Northern Hemisphere, from N. America eastwards to Japan. C. 1789.

padifolium SM. (*maderense*). "Madeiran Whortleberry". A strong-growing, medium-sized shrub of rather stiff, erect growth. Leaves ovate, 2·5 to 6cm. long, serrulate, reticulately veined. Flowers bell-shaped, greenish, appearing in clusters in June. They are small but peculiarly attractive, particularly when viewed from below when the pale brown "eye" of stamens can be seen. Berries globular, purplish-blue. The leaves often remain green until the New Year. Remarkably hardy in view of its origin. Mts. of Madeira. I. 1777.

pallidum AIT. (*vacillans*). A small shrub with arching branches and oval, wavy-edged leaves which are slender-pointed, glaucous beneath. The pale pink, cylindrical flowers in June are followed by round, purplish-black "bloomy" berries, which are sweet and edible. Rich autumn colours. Western N. America. C. 1878.

parvifolium SM. "Red Bilberry". A variable, small to medium-sized shrub, usually of erect habit, with sharply angled stems densely furnished with variably shaped, entire leaves. Flowers globular, pinkish, borne singly in the leaf axils in May and June, followed by conspicuous red berries, edible but acid. Western N. America to Alaska. I. 1881.

pensylvanicum. See *V. angustifolium laevifolium.*

praestans LAMB. A creeping shrub forming dense patches of shortly ascending shoots 3 to 10cm. high. Leaves obovate to broadly ovate, 2·5 to 6cm. long. Flowers bell-shaped, white to reddish, borne single or in clusters of two or three in June. The comparatively large, edible berries which follow are globular, 12mm. across, bright glossy red, fragrant and sweet to the taste. A choice little species for a moist, cool place. Its leaves colour richly in autumn. N.E. Asia; Japan. Introduced by Ernest Wilson in 1914.

VACCINIUM—*continued*

***retusum** HOOK. f. A dwarf evergreen shrub slowly reaching ·6 to 1m., with stiff, downy shoots and small, bright green, oval, leathery leaves which are retuse and mucronate at the apex. The small, urn-shaped, pink flowers are carried in short, terminal racemes in May. Rare and shy flowering. E. Himalaya. I. about 1882.

smallii GRAY. A small, erect-branched shrub with elliptic to broadly ovate leaves. Flowers bell-shaped, greenish-white to pinkish, borne one to three together in clusters in May and June. Berries purple-black, globular. Japan. I. 1915.

uliginosum L. "Bog Whortleberry". An uncommon native species, a dwarf shrub of bushy habit with rounded, brownish shoots and small, obovate or oval blue-green leaves. Flowers ovoid, pale pink, borne single or in clusters in the leaf axils, in May and June. Berries globular, black and "bloomy", sweet to the taste, but said to produce headache and giddiness if eaten in quantity. Cool moorland and mountainous regions of the Northern Hemisphere including N. England and Scotland.

†*urceolatum HEMSL. An evergreen shrub producing strong, downy shoots, 1·2, occasionally to 1·8m. in height. Leaves thick and leathery, ovate-elliptic to oblong-elliptic, slenderly pointed. Flowers urn-shaped, red tinged, borne in axillary clusters in June. Berries globular, black. W. China. I. 1910.

vacillans. See *V. pallidum.*

virgatum AIT. "Rabbiteye Blueberry". An attractive small to medium-sized shrub of loosely erect habit. The long, slender branches arch at their extremities and are clothed with narrow ovate to lanceolate leaves, which turn to rich shades of red in autumn. Flowers white or pink tinged, borne in axillary clusters in May and June. Berries black. A graceful shrub of elegant habit. Eastern N. America. I. 1770.

***vitis-idaea** L. "Cowberry". A dwarf, creeping, evergreen shrub native of moors and woods in the north and west of the British Isles. Leaves small, box-like, obovate, glossy dark green above, paler and gland-dotted beneath. Flowers bell-shaped, white, tinged pink, borne in short, terminal racemes from June to August, followed by globular, red, edible berries, acid to the taste. An excellent ground cover plant in shade. Northern regions of N. America. Europe and Asia; and mountains of C. and S. Europe.

minus LODD. (*'Nana'*). An interesting miniature form with leaves half the size of the type. N. United States; Canada. C. 1825.

'Variegata'. A form with creamy-white margined leaves, not very constant.

VELLA (*PSEUDOCYTISUS*)—**Cruciferae**—A small genus of deciduous and evergreen shrubs; one of the few shrubby members of the cabbage family.

***pseudocytisus** L. (*Pseudocytisus integrifolius*). A small, evergreen shrub suitable for maritime exposure, with spiny-bristly stems and small, obovate, bristly leaves. Long, erect, terminal racemes of small, yellow, four-petalled flowers in late May to early June. Requires a hot, dry, well-drained position to succeed. Spain. C. 1759.

†VERBENA—**Verbenaceae**—A large genus of mostly annual and perennial herbs. The following woody species is quite hardy in most areas of the British Isles, enjoying a warm, sunny position in a well-drained soil.

***tridens** LAG. This very unusual shrub looks like an ungainly tree heath with its stiffly erect, rigid stems thickly crowded with tiny, downy, often spiny leaves. It attains a height of 1 to 1·5m. Flowers white to rosy-lilac, strongly vanilla-scented, produced in terminal spikes in July. In its native land it is often collected and used as fuel. Patagonia. Introduced by Clarence Elliott in 1928. A.M. 1934.

VERONICA—**Scrophulariaceae**—The shrubby members of this large genus may now be found under *HEBE* and *PARAHEBE.*

†*VESTIA—**Solanaceae**—A monotypic genus related to *Cestrum*, requiring the same conditions.

foetida HOFFMANNS. (*lycioides*). A small, evergreen shrub of erect habit, foetid when bruised. Leaves oblong to obovate, 2·5 to 5cm. long. Flowers nodding, tubular, pale yellow, profusely borne in the axils of the upper leaves from April to July, followed by small, yellow fruits. Only suitable for the milder areas of the British Isles, where it requires a warm, sunny position in a well-drained soil. It has succeeded with us for several years planted against a south-east wall. Chile. I. 1815.

VIBURNUM—**Caprifoliaceae**—A large genus of easily cultivated, evergreen and deciduous shrubs containing several of the choicest woody plants in cultivation. Most of the species have white flowers, some very fragrant, in flat heads or rounded corymbs, often followed by brightly coloured fruits. Several of the evergreen species are most effective in leaf whilst many of the deciduous species give rich autumn colour. Generally speaking, those species grown for their fruits give the most satisfactory results when planted two or more together to assist cross pollination.

acerifolium L. "Dockmackie". A small shrub up to 2m. high, bearing three-lobed, maple-like leaves which are coarsely-toothed, and covered with black dots beneath. Flowers white, borne in terminal corymbs in June, but not particularly attractive. Fruits ovoid, red at first turning purplish-black later. The foliage turns a rich dark crimson in autumn. Eastern N. America. I. 1736.

‡**alnifolium** MARSH. "Hobble Bush". A distinct and attractive shrub of medium size, with comparatively large, strongly-veined leaves. In shape they are broadly ovate or orbicular, 10 to 20cm. long, downy above at first, more densely so beneath, turning a deep claret in autumn. The large inflorescences appear in May and June and recall those of a Lacecap Hydrangea, having a marginal row of conspicuous white, sterile florets. Fruits red, turning to blackish-purple. Thrives in woodland conditions. A low suckering shrub as seen in the forests of New England but reaching 2 to 2·5m. in cultivation in this country. Eastern N. America. I. 1820. A.M. 1952.

americanum. See *V. trilobum.*

*'**Anne Russell'** (Burkwoodii Group). A lovely hybrid with clusters of fragrant flowers. The result of a backcross with *V. carlesii.* A.M. and Cory Cup 1957.

***atrocyaneum** C. B. CLARKE. An attractive evergreen introduced by Kingdon Ward and sometimes grown under the name *V. wardii.* A shrub of medium to large size and dense, bushy habit. Leaves ovate, acute, glandular-toothed, dark green above, copper-tinted when young. Fruits small, steely-blue, effective in winter. In habit and leaf this species resembles what one might expect from a cross between *V. harryanum* and *V. tinus.* Himalaya.

betulifolium BATAL. A large, erect-growing shrub with ovate to rhomboid, coarsely-toothed leaves and corymbs of white flowers in June. A magnificent sight in autumn when the long, swaying branches are heavy with innumerable bunches of red-currant-like fruits which persist into the winter. Unfortunately, they are none too freely borne on young plants. One of the finest fruiting shrubs but to ensure fruiting, plant several in a group from different sources. W. and C. China. Introduced by E. H. Wilson in 1901. A.M. 1936; F.C.C. 1957; A.G.M. 1960.

bitchiuense MAK. A medium-sized shrub of slender, open habit similar to *V. carlesii* but rather taller and more lax. Leaves ovate-elliptic, dark metallic green. The sweetly scented, flesh-pink flowers are produced in clusters during late April and May. Japan. I. 1911. A.G.M. 1948.

×**bodnantense** ABERCONWAY (*farreri*×*grandiflorum*). A medium-sized to large shrub of strong, upright habit, producing densely-packed clusters of sweetly-scented, rose-tinted flowers, which are freely produced over several weeks from October onwards. Its flowers are remarkably frost resistant and provide a cheering sight on a cold winter's day. A splendid hybrid, raised at Bodnant about 1935.

'Dawn'. The first-named clone, a vigorous, hardy shrub with leaves approaching those of *V. grandiflorum* and ample clusters of richly fragrant flowers during late autumn and winter. A.M. 1947. A.G.M. 1960.

'Deben'. A lovely clone producing clusters of sweetly-scented flowers which are pink in bud, opening white during mild spells from October to April. A.M. 1962. F.C.C. 1965. A.G.M. 1969.

bracteatum REHD. A rare shrub of medium size, with rounded leaves and cymose clusters of white flowers in May and June, followed by bluish-black fruits. The name refers to the conspicuous bractlets which accompany the flowers. S.E. United States (Georgia). C. 1904.

buddleifolium C. H. WRIGHT. A medium-sized, nearly evergreen shrub of distinctive appearance. Leaves oblong-lanceolate, up to 20cm. long, pale green and softly pubescent above, thickly grey-felted beneath. Flowers white, borne in clusters 7·5cm. across, in June. Fruits red at first, finally black. C. China. I. 1900.

VIBURNUM—*continued*

burejaeticum REG. & HERD. A large shrub with downy young shoots and ovate or elliptic leaves, pubescent beneath. Flowers white produced in downy, cymose clusters during May. Fruits bluish-black. A rare species akin to *V. lantana.* Manchuria; N. China. C. 1900.

***×burkwoodii** BURK. (*carlesii×utile*). A medium-sized, evergreen shrub, taller growing than *V. carlesii,* from which it inherits its clusters of fragrant, pink-budded, white flowers, produced from January to May. Its ovate leaves are dark shining green above and brownish-grey felted beneath. Raised by Messrs. Burkwood and Skipwith in 1924. A.M. 1929. A.G.M. 1956. See also the clones *'Anne Russell'*, *'Chenaultii'*, *'Fulbrook'* and *'Park Farm Hybrid'*.

***calvum** REHD. (*schneideranum*). A medium-sized to large, evergreen shrub, akin to *V. tinus,* with ovate or elliptic, wavy-edged, sage-green leaves. The corymbs of small white flowers appear in June and July, to be followed by glossy, bluish-black fruits. W. China. C. 1933.

canbyi. See *V. pubescens canbyi.*

×carlcephalum BURK. (*carlesii×macrocephalum*). A splendid medium-sized shrub of compact habit, producing rounded corymbs, 10 to 13cm. across, of comparatively large, pink-budded, white flowers in May. The leaves often colour richly in autumn. A.M. 1946. A.G.M. 1969.

carlesii HEMSL. One of the most popular of all shrubs. A medium-sized shrub of rounded habit with ovate, downy leaves which are dull green above, greyish beneath, often colouring in autumn. The rounded clusters of pure white flowers are pink in bud and emit a strong, sweet daphne-like fragrance during April and May. Fruits jet black. Korea. I. 1902. A.M. 1908. F.C.C. 1909. A.G.M. 1923.

'Aurora'. An outstanding selection made by the Donard Nursery, with red flower buds opening to pink and deliciously fragrant. A.G.M. 1969.

'Charis'. Another Donard selection, extremely vigorous in growth, bearing flowers which are red in bud, passing to pink and finally white and richly scented.

'Diana'. A strong-growing clone of compact habit with flower-buds opening red, passing to pink, strongly fragrant. A.G.M. 1969.

‡cassinoides L. A medium-sized shrub of rounded habit with scurvy young shoots. The ovate-elliptic, leathery, dull dark green leaves are bronze-coloured when unfolding and in autumn change to crimson and scarlet. The small, creamy-white flowers in June are replaced by rounded, red fruits changing to metallic blue, finally black. Eastern N. America. Not satisfactory on thin soils over chalk. I. 1761.

'Nanum' (*'Bullatum'*). A remarkable, slow-growing shrub, having large, peculiarly-formed, wavy leaves which colour richly in autumn.

ceanothoides. See *V. foetidum ceanothoides.*

'Chenaultii' (Burkwoodii Group). A medium-sized, semi-evergreen shrub, similar in general appearance to *V. ×burkwoodii* and with the same qualities.

***cinnamomifolium** REHD. A large, handsome, evergreen shrub with large, dark glossy, leathery leaves, similar to those of *V. davidii,* but thinner and entire, or almost so. Flowers small, dull white, carried in cymose clusters, 10 to 15cm. across, in June followed in autumn by small, shining, egg-shaped, blue-black fruits. An imposing species when well grown, it requires a more sheltered position than *V. davidii* and is equally happy in semi-shade. China. Introduced by Ernest Wilson in 1904.

coriaceum. See *V. cylindricum.*

‡corylifolium HOOK. f. & THOMS. A medium-sized shrub with reddish-brown, hairy shoots and broad, ovate or rounded, hairy leaves which colour attractively in autumn. Flowers white, carried in flattened heads during May and June. Fruits bright red, long lasting. E. Himalaya; C. and W. China. I. 1907.

cotinifolium D. DON. A medium-sized to large shrub with densely hairy young shoots and leaf undersurfaces. Leaves broadly ovate to rounded, up to 13cm. long, sometimes turning crimson in autumn and hanging for several weeks. Flowers white, flushed pink, borne in terminal cymes in May; fruits ovoid, red then black. Related to our native *V. lantana.* Himalaya. I. 1830.

VIBURNUM—*continued*

†***cylindricum** D. DON (*coriaceum*). A large, evergreen shrub or occasionally a small tree, with glabrous, warty shoots and comparatively large, narrowly oval or oblong, to broadly ovate, dull green leaves, paler beneath, older leaves tending to hang. The upper surface is covered by a thin, waxy film which cracks and turns grey when bent or rubbed hence an ideal plant on which hooligans may scrawl their names. The characteristic tubular, white flowers have protruding, lilac-coloured stamens and are carried in conspicuous flattened heads, from July to September. Fruits egg-shape, black. Subject to injury in severe winters. Himalaya; W. China. I. 1881.

dasyanthum REHD. A medium-sized shrub of upright habit with ovate, slender-pointed leaves, glabrous except for hairs on the veins and in the vein axils beneath. Flowers white, borne in branched corymbs in June and July, followed by showy bunches of bright red, egg-shaped fruits. Closely related to *V. hupehense*. C. China. I. 1907. A.M. 1916.

***davidii** FRANCH. A small, evergreen shrub of compact habit, generally forming a low, wide-spreading mound and creating good ground cover. The large, narrowly oval, leathery leaves are conspicuously three-nerved and are a glossy dark green above, paler beneath. Flowers small, dull white, borne in terminal cymes in June. The bright turquoise-blue, egg-shaped fruits are never too plentiful but are particularly striking during winter, combining effectively with the lustrous green foliage. Several plants should be planted together to effect cross-pollination. Some plants seem dominantly male and others female whilst others are possibly mules, it is all in the luck of draw. A popular, widely planted species introduced from W. China by Ernest Wilson in 1904. A.M. 1912. A.G.M. 1969. A.M. 1971 (to female plant).

‡**dentatum** L. "Arrow Wood". A medium-sized to large shrub, bearing broad ovate to rounded, coarsely-toothed leaves which are glossy green and glabrous, except for occasional axillary tufts beneath. Flowers white, borne in slender-stalked cymes during May and June. Fruits egg-shaped, blue-black. The strong, straight basal shoots are said to have been used for making arrows by the native Indians. Eastern N. America. I. 1736.

dilatatum THUNB. An excellent shrub of medium size, with downy young shoots and ovate to obovate or rounded, coarsely-toothed leaves, hairy on both surfaces. Flowers pure white produced in numerous trusses in late May and June. Fruits vivid red, borne in heavy bunches and often lasting well into winter. Does particularly well in the Eastern Counties. Japan. I. before 1875. A.M. 1968.

'Xanthocarpum'. A form with yellow fruits. A.M. 1936.

erosum THUNB. A medium-sized, compact shrub with sharply-toothed, rounded, almost sessile leaves. Flowers white, produced in cymes during May, followed in autumn by red fruits. Not as a rule free-fruiting. Japan. I. 1844.

†**erubescens** WALL. A distinct species, a medium-sized shrub or occasionally a small tree with ovate to obovate, acuminate leaves. Flowers fragrant, white, tinted pink, borne in loose, pendulous clusters in July. One of the few viburnums with paniculate flower-clusters. Fruits red then black. A lovely shrub, but too tender for cold or exposed gardens. Himalaya.

gracilipes REHD. A perfectly hardy form with elliptic, usually glabrous leaves and longer panicles of fragrant flowers. Free-fruiting. C. China. I. 1910.

farreri STEARN (*fragrans*). A medium-sized to large shrub with the primary branches stiff and erect but as the shrub ages it forms a broad rounded outline. Leaves oval or obovate, strongly-toothed and with conspicuous, parallel veins, bronze when young. Flowers produced in both terminal and lateral clusters, pink in bud, opening white, sweetly scented. Fruits red, only occasionally produced in cultivation. One of the most popular of all shrubs and a favourite for the winter garden. Its flowers appear in November and continue through winter. N. China. First introduced by William Purdom in 1910, later by Reginald Farrer. A.M. 1921 (as *V. fragrans*). A.G.M. 1923.

candidissimum LANCASTER (*album*). A distinct form with green unfolding leaves and flowers pure white. A.M. 1926.

'Nanum' ('*Compactum*'). A dwarf form of dense mound-like habit; not free flowering. A.M. 1937.

VIBURNUM—*continued*

foetens DCNE. A beautiful, fragrant, winter-flowering shrub of medium size. It is related to *V. grandiflorum*, differing in its looser, more spreading habit, large, smoother leaves and its white flowers which are occasionally pale pink in bud, opening from January to March. Fruits are said to be red turning to black. It is not one of the easiest plants to make happy. It seems to appreciate a good deep moist loam in half shade. Himalaya; Korea. I. about 1844.

foetidum WALL. A medium-sized to large semi-evergreen shrub with oval to oblong leaves which may be entire or coarsely-toothed and are often three-lobed at the apex. Flowers white, with purple anthers, borne in rounded clusters in July. Fruits scarlet-crimson. Large specimens in full fruit are extremely effective in autumn. Plant two or more in close proximity to obtain cross pollination. Himalaya; W. China. I. 1901. A.M. 1934.

ceanothoides HAND.-MAZZ. A rare variety, less spreading in habit than the type, with smaller, usually obovate leaves. W. China. I. 1901.

fragrans. See *V. farreri*.

***'Fulbrook'** (Burkwoodii Group). A medium-sized shrub producing clusters of comparatively large, sweetly-scented flowers which are pink in bud opening white. Like *'Anne Russell'* the result of a backcross with *V. carlesii*. A.M. 1957.

‡furcatum BL. A large shrub closely related to and resembling *V. alnifolium*, but of more upright habit. Leaves broadly ovate or rounded, up to 15cm. long, colouring richly in autumn. Flowers in May, in flattened terminal corymbs, surrounded by several sterile ray florets, resembling a lacecap hydrangea. Fruits red, becoming black at maturity. A beautiful species of elegant charm, an excellent woodland plant. Japan; Formosa. I. 1892. A.M. 1944.

grandiflorum WALL. (*nervosum*). A medium-sized shrub of stiff, upright habit and related to *V. farreri*. Leaves elliptic to ovate, of firm texture with parallel veins. Flowers fragrant, carmine-red in bud, opening deep pink, fading to blush, produced in dense clusters during February and March. It differs from *V. farreri* in its more hairy, multi-veined leaves and slightly larger individual flowers. Himalaya. I. 1914. A.M. 1937.

***harryanum** REHD. A medium-sized shrub of dense, bushy growth. A distinct species on account of its small, neat, orbicular leaves which are dark green above and 1 to 2cm. long. On strong shoots they appear in whorls of three. The small white flowers appear in late spring; fruits ovoid, shining black. Introduced by Ernest Wilson from China in 1904, and named after Sir Harry Veitch who did more than any other nurseryman to introduce new plants to western gardens.

***henryi** HEMSL. A medium-sized, evergreen shrub of open, erect habit with rather stiff branches and narrowly elliptic, glossy green, leathery leaves recalling those of *Ilex fargesii*. Flowers white, fragrant, carried in pyramidal panicles in June, followed by colourful, bright red, then black, ellipsoid fruits. C. China (Hupeh). First discovered by Augustine Henry in 1887. Introduced by E. H. Wilson in 1901. F.C.C. 1910. A.G.M. 1936.

hessei. See *V. wrightii 'Hessei'*.

× **hillieri** STEARN (*erubescens* × *henryi*). A semi-evergreen shrub of medium size with spreading and ascending branches and narrowly oval leaves which are copper-tinted when unfolding and suffused bronze-red in winter. Flowers creamy-white, profusely borne in panicles in June. Fruits red, finally black. An attractive hybrid which originated in our nurseries in 1950. Wilson also reports having seen this hybrid in W. Hupeh (China). We offer the following clone:—

'Winton'. The original selected clone which received the Award of Merit in 1956.

hupehense REHD. A very tough shrub of medium size with broadly ovate, coarsely-toothed leaves. Flowers white in clusters during May and June. The egg-shaped, orange-yellow, finally red fruits are conspicuous in autumn. The leaves colour early in autumn. C. China. I. 1908. A.M. 1952.

ichangense REHD. A small to medium-sized, slender-branched shrub with ovate to ovate-lanceolate, slender-pointed leaves. Flowers white, fragrant, borne in clusters during May. Fruits bright red. C. and W. China. I. 1901.

VIBURNUM—*continued*

***japonicum** SPRENG. (*macrophyllum*). A handsome, medium-sized, evergreen shrub with firm, leathery, often bullate leaves up to 15cm. long and 10cm. wide. They may be entire or undulately-toothed in the upper half and are glossy dark green above, paler and minutely punctate beneath; petioles stout, grooved above. Flowers white, fragrant, borne in dense, rounded trusses in June, but not on young plants; fruits red. Japan. I. about 1879.

***'Jermyns Globe'** (*calvum* × *davidii*). A small, evergreen shrub of dense, rounded habit. Leaves leathery, narrowly-elliptic to lanceolate, 8 to 12cm. long, shallowly and distantly toothed, sometimes twisted or undulate, dark green and reticulate above, borne on slender, reddish petioles. Fruits ovoid, bluish-black.. An interesting hybrid which occured in our West Hill Nursery, Winchester in 1964. It was raised from seed collected from *V. davidii* which grew close to a specimen of *V. calvum*. The habit is intermediate between those of the parents, but much more dense and compact than either.

× **juddii** REHD. (*bitchiuense* × *carlesii*). A delightful small to medium-sized shrub of bushy habit, freely producing its terminal clusters of sweetly-scented, pink-tinted flowers during April and May. A plant of better constitution than *V. carlesii* and less susceptible to aphis attack. Raised in 1920 by William Judd, one time propagator at the Arnold Arboretum. A.G.M. 1960.

kansuense BATAL. A medium-sized, loose growing shrub with deeply lobed, maple-like leaves. The pink-flushed, white flowers in June and July are followed by red fruits. Succeeds best in half shade. Not very lime tolerant. W. China. I. 1902.

lantana L. "Wayfaring Tree". A large, native shrub, a familiar hedgerow plant, particularly on the chalk downs of the south. Leaves broadly ovate, covered beneath as are the young shoots with a dense, stellate tomentum, sometimes turning a dark crimson in autumn. Flowers creamy-white in May and June, followed by oblong fruits which slowly mature from red to black. C. and S. Europe; N. Asia Minor; N. Africa.

discolor HUTER. (*V. maculatum*). An interesting, geographical form from the Balkans with smaller, neater leaves which are white or pale grey tomentose beneath.

'Variegatum' (*'Auratum'*). Young growths yellowish; not very exciting.

lentago L. "Sheep-berry". A strong-growing, large shrub or small tree of erect habit, with ovate to obovate leaves, dark shining green above, giving rich autumn tints. Flowers creamy-white, produced in terminal cymes during May and June. Fruits blue-black and bloomy, like small Merryweather damsons. Eastern N. America. I. 1761.

lobophyllum GRAEBN. A medium-sized shrub allied to *V. betulifolium* and *V. dilatatum*. Leaves variable in shape, usually ovate or rounded with an abrupt point and coarsely-toothed. Flowers white followed by bright red fruits. W. China. Introduced by Ernest Wilson in 1901. A.M. 1947.

macrocephalum FORT. (*macrocephalum 'Sterile'*). A semi-evergreen, medium-sized shrub of rounded habit. Leaves ovate to elliptic, 5 to 10cm. long. Flowers white, sterile, gathered together in large, globular heads, 7·5 to 15cm. across, like the sterile forms of *Hydrangea macrophylla*, giving a spectacular display in May. Best grown against a warm, sunny wall in cold districts. A garden form, introduced from China in 1844 by Robert Fortune. The wild form with fertile flowers is probably not now in cultivation. A.M. 1927.

macrophyllum. See *V. japonicum*.

maculatum. See *V. lantana discolor*.

molle MICHX. A medium-sized shrub with broadly-ovate to rounded, coarsely-toothed leaves. Flowers white in flattened heads in June. Fruits blue-black. The bark of older stems is flaky. N. United States. I. 1923.

nervosum. See *V. grandiflorum*.

‡nudum L. A medium-sized shrub of upright growth, related to *V. cassinoides*, but differing in its dark glossy green leaves, colouring attractively in autumn. Flowers yellowish-white, borne in long-stalked cymes in June. Fruits oval, blue-black. E. United States. I. 1752.

VIBURNUM—*continued*

†***odoratissimum** KER.-GAWL. A large, evergreen shrub of noble aspect, bearing striking glossy green, oval to obovate, leathery leaves on stout, caramel-coloured petioles. They vary in size from 10 to 20cm. long by half as wide and are shallowly serrate in the upper half. Older leaves often colour richly during winter and early spring. The fragrant, white flowers are carried in large, conical panicles during late summer, but not on young plants; fruits red at first finally black. A magnificent species for gardens in mild areas but here best against a south or west facing wall. India; Burma; S. China; C. and S. Formosa; Japan. I. about 1818.

'Oneida' (*dilatatum* × *lobophyllum*). An erect, medium-sized shrub with dark green leaves of variable shape and size. The creamy-white flowers are abundantly produced in May and intermittently throughout summer and are followed by glossy, dark red fruits which persist well into winter. A hybrid of American origin.

opulus L. "Guelder Rose"; "Water Elder". A large, vigorous shrub of spreading habit with long, greyish shoots and three to five-lobed, maple-like leaves which colour richly in autumn. The flattened corymbs of fertile flowers in June or July are surrounded by showy white ray florets, the effect being similar to that of a lacecap hydrangea. These are followed in autumn by copious bunches of glistening red, translucent fruits which persist long into winter. A familiar native of hedgerows and woods, particularly rampant in wet or boggy situations. Europe; N. and W. Asia; N. Africa (Algeria). A.G.M. 1969.

'Aureum'. A striking form of compact habit with bright yellow leaves. Tends to "burn" in full sun.

'Compactum'. A small shrub of dense, compact habit which flowers and fruits freely. A.M. 1962. A.G.M. 1964.

'Fructuluteo'. Fruits lemon yellow, with a strong pink tinge, maturing to chrome yellow with a faint hint of pink.

'Nanum'. A curious, dwarf form of dense, tufted habit, seldom, if ever, flowering but often colouring in autumn.

'Notcutt's Variety'. A selected form with larger flowers and fruits than the type. A.M. 1930.

'Sterile' (*'Roseum'*). "Snowball". One of the most attractive and popular, hardy, flowering shrubs. The flowers are all sterile and gathered into conspicuous, globular, creamy-white heads. A.G.M. 1964.

'Xanthocarpum'. Fruits differing from those of *'Fructuluteo'* in being clear golden yellow at all stages, becoming a little darker and almost translucent when ripe. A.M. 1932. F.C.C. 1966. A.G.M. 1969.

oxycoccus. See *V. trilobum*.

***'Park Farm Hybrid'** (Burkwoodii Group). A strong-growing shrub of more spreading habit than *V.* × *burkwoodii*, and with fragrant, slightly larger flowers produced in April and May. A.M. 1949.

parvifolium HAYATA. A rare, small shrub with small, ovate to obovate, toothed leaves up to 2·5cm. in length. Flowers white, followed by globular, red fruits. Restricted in the wild to Formosa.

pauciflorum RAF. "Mooseberry". A small, straggling shrub with broad, oval or rounded leaves, weakly three-lobed at apex. Flowers white, produced in small clusters during May. Fruits red. Requires a moist, shaded position. N. United States; Canada; N.E. Asia. I. 1880.

phlebotrichum SIEB. & ZUCC. A medium-sized shrub of slender habit, with strong, erect shoots and narrow, ovate-oblong, acuminate, bronze-green leaves which, in the adult state, have spiny teeth and are prettily net veined. Flowers white or pink-tinged in small nodding trusses. Fruits crimson-red. Rich autumn tints. Japan. C. 1890.

plicatum THUNB. (*tomentosum 'Plicatum'*) (*tomentosum 'Sterile'*). "Japanese Snowball". This popular shrub of medium size and dense, spreading habit is in the front rank of hardy, ornamental shrubs. The conspicuous, white sterile florets are gathered into globular heads 5 to 7·5cm. across. They are produced in late May and early June, in a double row along the length of each arching branch, persisting for several weeks. This is a garden form, long cultivated in both China and Japan. It was introduced from the former by Robert Fortune in 1844 several years before the wild form, which is why the name takes precedence over *V. tomentosum*. F.C.C. 1893. A.G.M. 1969.

VIBURNUM—*continued*

plicatum 'Grandiflorum'. A selected form of *V. plicatum*, with larger heads of sterile, white florets flushed pink at the margins. A.M. 1961. A.G.M. 1969.

'Lanarth'. A very fine form resembling '*Mariesii*', but stronger in growth and less horizontal in habit of branching. A.M. 1930. A.G.M. 1969.

'Mariesii'. A superb shrub, a selection of *tomentosum* with a more tabulate arrangement of branching. Its abundance of flower gives the effect of a snow-laden bush. The ray-florets are also slightly larger. A.G.M. 1929.

'Pink Beauty'. A charming selection of *tomentosum* in which the ray florets change to a delightful pink as they age.

'Rowallane'. Similar to '*Lanarth*', but a little less vigorous. The marginal ray florets are larger and it has the added attraction of usually producing a conspicuous show of fruits which very seldom occur on '*Mariesii*'. A.M. 1942. F.C.C. 1956. A.G.M. 1969.

tomentosum REHD. (*V. tomentosum*). The wild form. A wide-spreading, medium-sized to large shrub of architectural value, with a distinctive mode of branching. The branches are produced in layers creating, in time, an attractive and characteristic tiered effect though less horizontal than those of cv. '*Mariesii*'. The bright green pleated, ovate or oval leaves are followed in May and early June by 7·5 to 10cm. wide umbels of small, fertile, creamy-white flowers surrounded by conspicuous, white ray florets. The inflorescences sit in double rows along the upper sides of the branches giving the appearance, from a distance, of icing on a cake. Fruits red, finally black. The leaves are often attractively tinted in autumn. China; Japan; Formosa. I. about 1865. A.G.M. 1969.

***'Pragense'** (*rhytidophyllum* × *utile*). An attractive, spreading, evergreen shrub of medium to large size. The elliptic, corrugated leaves, 5 to 10cm. long, are lustrous dark green above and white-felted beneath. Flowers creamy-white, buds pink, produced in terminal branched cymes during May. This hybrid was raised in Prague and is extremely hardy.

***propinquum** HEMSL. A small to medium-sized evergreen shrub of dense, compact habit. Leaves three-nerved, ovate to elliptic, polished dark green above, paler beneath. Flowers greenish-white, borne in umbellate cymes during summer, followed by blue-black, egg-shaped fruits. C. and W. China; Formosa. I. 1901.

lanceolatum. A form with narrower leaves.

prunifolium L. "Black Haw". A large, erect shrub, or small tree, with shining, bright green, ovate to obovate leaves which colour richly in autumn, and clusters of white flowers in April and May. Fruits comparatively large, bloomy, blue-black, sweet and edible. Eastern N. America. I. 1731.

pubescens PURSH. (*venosum*). A large shrub with broadly oval or rounded, coarsely-toothed leaves often turning rich purple in autumn. The cymes of white flowers in June and July are followed by blue-black fruits. N.E. United States. I. 1731.

canbyi BLAKE (*V. canbyi*). A form differing in its larger, less downy leaves and larger cymes. C. 1884.

rafinesquianum SCHULT. A medium-sized to large shrub with ovate to elliptic, coarsely-toothed, polished leaves. Flowers white, borne in cymes during May and June. Fruits blue-black. The leaves often colour richly in autumn. N.E. United States; E. Canada. C. 1883.

*** × rhytidocarpum** LEM. (*buddleifolium* × *rhytidophyllum*). A large, more or less evergreen shrub, intermediate in habit and leaf between its parents. C. 1836.

× rhytidophylloides SURING. (*lantana* × *rhytidophyllum*). A very vigorous, large shrub with elliptic-ovate to oblong-ovate, rugose leaves and stout cymes of yellowish-white flowers. In general effect intermediate between the parents. A splendid shrub for screen planting. C. 1927.

***rhytidophyllum** HEMSL. A large, fast-growing, handsome, evergreen shrub, with large, elliptic to oblong, attractively-corrugated leaves which are dark glossy green above, densely grey tomentose beneath. The small, creamy-white flowers are produced in stout, tomentose cymes during May. Fruits oval, red, finally black. It is necessary to plant two or more in close proximity, as single specimens do not fruit freely. A magnificent foliage shrub and a splendid chalk plant, creating the effect of a large-leaved *Rhododendron*. C. & W. China. Introduced by Ernest Wilson in 1900. F.C.C. 1907.

'Roseum'. A form with rose-pink tinted flowers. Originated in our nurseries.

VIBURNUM—*continued*

†***rigidum** VENT. (*rugosum*). A medium-sized, evergreen shrub of open habit, perhaps best described as a "maxi" Laurustinus. Leaves ovate to oval, entire, 7·5 to 15cm. long and hairy on both surfaces. Flowers white, borne in flattened corymbs from February to April; fruits egg-shaped, blue, finally black. A tender species for a specially favoured position. Canary Isles. I. 1778.

rufidulum RAF. A large shrub of rigid habit with rusty-tomentose young shoots. Leaves elliptic-obovate, leathery, polished green, often colouring in autumn. Flowers white; fruits blue-black. S.E. United States. I. 1883.

rugosum. See *V. rigidum.*

sargentii KOEHNE. A large, vigorous shrub related to and resembling *V. opulus*, but the maple-like leaves are larger, the bark corky and the flowers have purple anthers (not yellow). The fruits also are a little larger, of a bright, translucent red, lasting well into winter. Rich autumn tints. N.E. Asia. I. 1892. A.M. 1967.

'Flavum' (*'Fructuluteo'*). An unusual form with translucent yellow fruits. The flowers have yellow anthers.

scabrellum CHAPM. Medium-sized shrub with scabrous shoots and ovate to ovate-oblong leaves. The white flowers in June are followed by blue-black, rounded fruits. Eastern U.S.A. C. 1830.

schensianum MAXIM. A medium-sized to large shrub with downy young shoots and ovate to elliptic leaves which are downy beneath. Flowers creamy-white, borne in flattened cymes in May or June followed by red, finally black egg-shaped fruits. It belongs to the same group as *V. lantana.* N.W. China. I. about 1910.

schneideranum. See *V. calvum.*

setigerum HANCE (*theiferum*). A distinct and attractive shrub of medium size and open, lax growth. From time of unfolding until early winter, the ovate-lanceolate to oblong, slender-pointed leaves are constantly changing colour from metallic-blue-red through shades of green to orange-yellow in autumn. Its corymbs of white flowers in early summer are followed by conspicuous clusters of comparatively large, orange-yellow, finally brilliant red, somewhat flattened, oval fruits. C. & W. China. Introduced by E. H. Wilson in 1901. A.M. 1925.

sieboldii MIQ. A vigorous shrub of medium to large size. The unfolding foetid leaves in spring, and the falling leaves in autumn are attractively bronze-tinted and only emit an objectionable smell if crushed. They have a conspicuous impressed venation and throughout the summer are soft yellowish-green. Flowers creamy-white in May and June. The oval, comparatively large fruits are pink, changing to blue-black. Japan. C. 1880.

†***suspensum** LINDL. (*sandankwa*). A medium-sized, evergreen shrub bearing leathery, ovate or rotund, glossy green leaves, 7·5 to 13cm. long. The flat panicles of fragrant, rose-tinted flowers are produced in early spring. Fruits, when produced, globular, red. An attractive species for mild localities where it is best grown against a warm, sheltered wall. Ryukyus; Formosa. Long cultivated in S. Japan from which country it was introduced about 1850.

theiferum. See *V. setigerum.*

***tinus** L. "Laurustinus". One of the most popular evergreens. A medium-sized to large shrub of dense, bushy habit with luxurious masses of dark glossy green, oval leaves. The flattened cymes of white, pink-budded flowers appear continuously from late autumn to early spring. Fruits ovoid, metallic blue, finally black. An excellent winter-flowering shrub for all but the coldest areas. Makes an attractive, informal hedge and is also tolerant of shade and succeeds well in maritime exposure. Mediterranean Region; S.E. Europe. Cultivated in Britain since the late 16th century. A.G.M. 1969.

'Eve Price'. A selected form of dense, compact habit with smaller leaves than the type and with very attractive, carmine buds and pink-tinged flowers. A.M. 1961.

'French White'. A strong-growing form with large heads of white flowers.

† **hirtulum** AIT. (*hirtum*). A distinct form with larger, thicker, densely ciliate leaves. Both shoots, petioles and leaf bases are clothed with bristly hairs. Less hardy than the type, but an excellent shrub for mild maritime areas. A.M. 1939.

VIBURNUM—*continued*

tinus lucidum AIT. A vigorous form with comparatively large, glossy green leaves. The flower-heads too are larger than those of the type, opening white in March and April. A.M. 1972.

'Purpureum'. A form with very dark green leaves, purple-tinged when young.

'Pyramidale' (*'Strictum'*). A selected form of more erect habit.

† **'Variegatum'.** Leaves conspicuously variegated creamy-yellow. Not recommended for cold districts.

tomentosum. See *V. plicatum tomentosum.*

'Plicatum'. See *V. plicatum.*

'Sterile'. See *V. plicatum.*

trilobum MARSH. (*americanum*) (*oxycoccus*). A large shrub, related to and closely resembling *V. opulus*, from which it differs in the usually long terminal lobe of the leaf, the petiole of which is only shallowly grooved and bears small glands. The petioles of *V. opulus* are broadly grooved and bear large, disc-like glands. The red fruits colour in July and persist throughout winter. Rich autumn tints. Northern N. America. I. 1812.

'Compactum'. A smaller form of dense, compact growth.

***utile** HEMSL. A graceful, evergreen shrub of medium size and elegant, rather sparingly-branched habit. The long, slender stems bear narrowly ovate or oblong, glossy dark green leaves which are white tomentose beneath. The white, sweetly-scented flowers are produced in dense, rounded clusters in May. Fruits bluish-black. C. China. Introduced by E. H. Wilson in 1901. A.M. 1926.

veitchii C. H. WRIGHT. A shrub of medium to large size, related to *V. lantana.* Leaves ovate, wrinkled above. Flowers white, borne in flattened heads during May and June. Fruits bright red at first, passing through purple to black. C. China. I. 1901.

venosum. See *V. pubescens.*

wilsonii REHD. A medium-sized shrub related to *V. hupehense*, with oval leaves. Flowers white, appearing in corymbs in June, followed by bright red, downy, egg-shaped fruits. W. China. I. 1908.

wrightii MIQ. A medium-sized shrub with broadly ovate to obovate, abruptly pointed leaves. Flowers white, borne in corymbs in May, followed in autumn by glistening red fruits. The metallic green leaves often colour richly in autumn. Closely related to *V. dilatatum*, from which it differs in its almost glabrous nature. Japan; Sakhalin; Korea; China. I. 1892.

'Hessei'. A dwarf form with broad, ovate, attractively veined leaves. The flowers are followed by conspicuous sealing-wax-red fruits which appear each autumn with remarkable consistency. An excellent shrub for the border front.

†*VILLARESIA—Icacinaceae—A small genus of evergreen trees and shrubs, mainly native of the tropics.

mucronata RUIZ. & PAV. A large, evergreen shrub attaining tree size in favoured areas of the south-west. Leaves ovate, leathery, glossy-green and spine-toothed, rather holly-like on young trees, becoming smooth and entire on older specimens. The small, fragrant, creamy-white flowers are borne in dense panicles in June. The black, egg-shaped fruits, 5 to 7·5cm. long are regularly produced, even on young plants in the nursery. Chile. I. 1840.

***VINCA—Apocynaceae**—"Periwinkle". Vigorous, evergreen, trailing shrubs forming extensive carpets and ideal as ground cover in both shade or full sun. Growing in all fertile soils.

difformis POURR. (*acutiflora*) (*media*). An uncommon species usually herbaceous in cold areas. Leaves ovate, 4 to 7·5cm. long. Flowers solitary in the leaf axils, pale lilac-blue, with rhomboid lobes, resembling a five-bladed propeller, produced during autumn and early winter. In general appearance, it resembles the hardier *V. major*, but is quite glabrous in all its parts. W. Mediterranean Region.

major L. "Greater Periwinkle". A rampant species with shortly ascending shoots which later lengthen and trail along the ground, rooting only at their tips. Leaves ovate, 2·5 to 7·5cm. long, dark glossy green and ciliate. Flowers bright blue, 4cm. across, borne in the leaf axils, produced continuously from late April to June. An excellent shrub for covering unsightly banks or waste ground. C. & S. Europe; N. Africa. Long cultivated and naturalised in the British Isles.

'Elegantissima'. See *'Variegata'.*

hirsuta. See *pubescens.*

VINCA—*continued*

major 'Maculata'. Leaves with a central splash of greenish-yellow, more conspicuous on young leaves in an open position.

pubescens (*hirsuta*). A form with narrower, somewhat pubescent leaves and violet-blue flowers with narrower, pointed lobes.

'Variegata' (*'Elegantissima'*). Leaves blotched and margined creamy-white; a conspicuous plant, as vigorous as the type. A.M. 1977.

minor L. "Lesser Periwinkle". A familiar "cottage garden" plant with long, trailing stems rooting at intervals. Leaves oval or elliptic-lanceolate, 2·5 to 5cm. long. The bright blue flowers, 2·5cm. across, are borne singly in the leaf axils of short, erect, flowering shoots. They appear continuously from April to June and intermittently until autumn. There are numerous named selections. Europe; W. Asia. Doubtfully a British native, though frequently found in woods, copses and hedgebanks.

'Alba'. Flowers white.

'Atropurpurea'. Flowers deep plum-purple.

'Aureovariegata'. Leaves blotched yellow; flower blue.

'Azurea Flore Pleno'. Flowers sky-blue, double.

'Bowles' Variety'. Flowers azure-blue, larger than those of the type.

'Gertrude Jekyll'. A selected form with glistening white flowers. A.G.M. 1962.

'Multiplex'. Flowers plum-purple, double.

'Variegata'. Leaves variegated creamy-white; flowers blue.

VITEX—**Verbenaceae**—Deciduous or evergreen trees and shrubs. The species grown in temperate climes are deciduous shrubs which succeed better in a continental rather than an insular climate. In the British Isles *Vitex* needs good drainage and full sun to ripen growth and produce flower, hence they make excellent subjects for a sunny wall. Pruning consists of the removal of the old flowering shoots in late February or March.

agnus-castus L. "Chaste Tree". An attractive, spreading, aromatic shrub of medium size. The compound leaves composed of five to seven, short-stalked, ovate-lanceolate leaflets, are borne in pairs along the elegant, grey-downy shoots. Flowers violet, fragrant, produced in slender racemes at the ends of the current year's shoots in September and October. Mediterranean Region to C. Asia. Said to have been cultivated in the British Isles since 1570. A.M. 1934.

'Alba'. Flowers white. A.M. 1959.

'Latifolia'. A more vigorous form with broader leaflets. A.M. 1964.

†**negundo** L. A graceful shrub of medium to large size, with long four-angled stems. Leaves compound, with three to five stalked, ovate-lanceolate leaflets. The attractive lavender flowers are borne in loose panicles during late summer or early autumn. India; China; Formosa. I. about 1697.

"WALNUT". See *JUGLANS*

"WATER ELM". See *PLANERA aquatica*.

"WATTLE". See *ACACIA*.

"WAX MYRTLE". See *MYRICA cerifera*.

"WAYFARING TREE". See *VIBURNUM lantana*.

WEIGELA—**Caprifoliaceae**—A small genus of hardy, flowering shrubs differing from the closely related *Diervilla* in the almost regular corolla (two-lipped in *Diervilla*) which is larger and varies in colour from white to pink and red. Very decorative and easily grown shrubs, growing to an average height of 2m. and excellent for town gardens, particularly in industrial areas. The tubular, foxglove-like flowers appear in May and June all along the shoots of the previous year. Occasionally a small second crop is produced in late summer or early autumn. Thin out and cut back old flowering shoots to within a few cm. of the old wood immediately after flowering. The majority of the species and hybrids listed below were previously included under *DIERVILLA*.

amabilis CARR. See *W. coraeensis*.

amabilis HORT. See *W. florida*.

coraeensis THUNB. (*amabilis* CARR.) (*grandiflora*). An elegant shrub of medium size with glabrous shoots and oval to obovate, abruptly pointed leaves. Flowers bell-shaped, white or pale rose at first, deepening to carmine. June. Japan. C. 1850.

'Alba'. Flowers cream changing to pale rose.

WEIGELA—*continued*

decora NAKAI (*nikoensis*). A medium-sized shrub related to *W. japonica*. Leaves obovate-elliptic, abruptly acuminate, slightly glossy above. Flowers white, becoming reddish with age, opening in May and June. Japan. C. 1933.

florida A. DC. (*amabilis* HORT.) (*rosea*). A medium-sized shrub with ovate-oblong to obovate, acuminate leaves. Flowers funnel-shaped, reddish or rose-pink on the outside, paler within, opening during May and June. Perhaps the commonest and most popular species in cultivation. A parent of many attractive hybrids. Japan; Korea; N. China; Manchuria. Introduced by Robert Fortune in 1845.

'Foliis Purpureis'. A slower-growing, dwarfer form of compact habit with attractive purple-flushed leaves and pink flowers.

'Variegata'. A form of more compact habit, the leaves edged creamy-white; flowers pink. One of the best variegated shrubs for general planting. A.M. 1968. A.G.M. 1969.

venusta NAKAI. A free-flowering form, the flowers being a little larger and of a brighter rose-pink than those of the type. Korea. I. 1905.

'Versicolor'. Flowers creamy-white changing to red.

hortensis K. KOCH. A small to medium-sized shrub with ovate-elliptic to obovate, acuminate leaves which are densely white pubescent beneath. Flowers reddish in May and June. The type is rare in cultivation and is less hardy than most other species. Japan. C. 1870.

'Nivea' (*'Albiflora'*). A lovely form with comparatively large white flowers. F.C.C. 1891.

japonica THUNB. Medium-sized shrub with ovate or oval, taper-pointed leaves. The flowers in May are pale rose or nearly white at first, later changing to carmine. Japan. I. 1892.

sinica BAILEY. The Chinese form. A taller-growing variety with pale pink flowers deepening with age. C. China. I. 1908.

maximowiczii REHD. A small shrub of spreading habit, with ovate-oblong to obovate, abruptly-pointed, rather narrow leaves. The greenish-yellow, or pale yellow flowers open in April and May. Japan. I. 1915.

middendorffiana K. KOCH. A small shrub of no mean quality, with exfoliating bark and broader ovate leaves than those of *W. maximowiczii*. They are also more abruptly-pointed. Flowers bell-shaped, sulphur-yellow, with dark orange markings on the lower lobes, produced during April and May. An ornamental species of compact growth, best grown in a sheltered and partially shaded position. Japan; N. China; Manchuria. I. 1850. A.M. 1931.

nikoensis. See *W. decora*.

praecox BAILEY. A vigorous, medium-sized shrub with ovate to ovate-oblong leaves. The comparatively large, honey-scented flowers are rose pink with yellow markings in the throat. They commence to open in early May. Japan; Korea; Manchuria. C. 1894.

'Variegata'. An attractive form with leaves variegated creamy-white.

rosea. See *W. florida*.

CULTIVARS and HYBRIDS OF WEIGELA

A colourful selection of hardy hybrids of medium size, flowering on the old wood during May and June and often a second time in early autumn. Pruning consists of the shortening or removal of the flowering stems immediately after flowering.

'Abel Carriere'. Free-flowering cultivar with large, bright rose-carmine flowers, flecked gold in the throat; buds purple carmine. A.G.M. 1939.

'Avalanche'. A vigorous cultivar with numerous panicles of white flowers.

'Ballet'. A hybrid between *'Boskoop Glory'* and *'Newport Red'*. Flowers dark pinkish-red.

'Bristol Ruby'. Vigorous, erect-growing cultivar, free-flowering with flowers of a sparkling ruby-red. A hybrid between *W. florida* and *W. 'Eva Rathke'*. A.M. 1954. A.G.M. 1969.

'Buisson Fleuri'. Early flowering cultivar with large, fragrant flowers, rose, spotted yellow in throat.

'Conquete'. An old favourite with very large flowers, almost 5cm. long, of a deep rose-pink.

'Esperance'. An early flowering cultivar with large flowers of pale rose-salmon, white within.

WEIGELA—*continued*

'Eva Rathke'. An old favourite and still one of the best reds. A slow-growing cultivar of compact growth. Flowers bright red-crimson, with straw-coloured anthers, opening over a long season. F.C.C. 1893.

'Eva Supreme'. Growth vigorous; flowers bright red. A hybrid between *'Eva Rathke'* and *'Newport Red'*.

'Feerie'. Flowers large and numerous, rose pink, in erect trusses.

'Fiesta'. A hybrid between *'Eva Rathke'* and *'Newport Red'*. Growth lax. Flowers of a shining uniform red, produced in great abundance.

'Fleur de Mai'. Flowers salmon-rose inside, marbled purple-rose outside, purple in bud. Usually the first to bloom.

'Gracieux'. Erect-growing, free-flowering cultivar with large flowers of salmon rose, with sulphur yellow throat. Said to be a selection of *W. praecox*.

'Gustave Malet'. Very floriferous, with long-tubed, deep red flowers. Said to be a selection of *W. florida*.

'Heroine'. An erect-growing cultivar with large flowers of a pale rose.

'Ideal'. Flowers carmine-rose inside, bright carmine outside, in large clusters, early and free-flowering.

'Lavallei'. Crimson, with protruding white stigma.

'Le Printemps'. Large, peach-pink flowers, very floriferous.

'Looymansii Aurea'. Very pleasing in spring and early summer, when the pink flowers enhance the effect of a the light golden foliage. Best in partial shade.

'Majestueux'. An erect, early flowering cultivar producing masses of large, erect flowers, madder pink-flushed carmine in the throat.

'Mont Blanc'. Vigorous cultivar with large, white, fragrant flowers. Perhaps the best of the whites.

'Newport Red' (*'Vanicek'*). A superb cultivar, more upright than *'Eva Rathke'*, with larger flowers of a lighter red.

'Perle'. Vigorous cultivar with large flowers in rounded corymbs, pale cream with rose edges, the mouth clear yellow.

'Styriaca'. Vigorous cultivar with carmine-red flowers produced in great abundance.

†***WEINMANNIA—Cunoniaceae**—A large genus of mainly tropical, evergreen trees and shrubs requiring a loamy soil. The following species are only suitable for sheltered gardens in the mildest areas of the British Isles.

racemosa L. f. "Towai"; "Kamahi". A small, graceful tree or large shrub remarkable on account of the variability of its leaves which, on adult trees, are simple, ovate to oval and coarsely-toothed, and on juvenile specimens vary from simple to three-lobed, or trifoliolate with coarsely-toothed leaflets. Flowers white produced in slender racemes during summer. New Zealand.

trichosperma CAV. A slender, small to medium-sized tree or large shrub, with pinnate leaves composed of nine to nineteen small, neat, oval or obovate, toothed leaflets. The rachis in between each leaflet bears a pair of small, triangular wings. The white flowers, produced in dense racemes during May and June, are succeeded by small, coppery-red capsules. Chile. A.M. 1927.

†***WESTRINGIA—Labiatae**—A small genus of tender, evergreen shrubs native of Australia.

rosmariniformis SM. "Victoria Rosemary". A small to medium-sized shrub bearing whorls of narrow, rosemary-like leaves which, like the shoots are silvery hoary beneath. Flowers white, borne in axillary clusters in July. An interesting shrub for a wall in a warm, sunny, well-drained position in mild areas. E. Australia. I. 1791.

"WHINBERRY". See *VACCINIUM myrtillus*.

"WHITEBEAM". See *SORBUS aria*.

"WHITEBEAM, SWEDISH". See *SORBUS intermedia*.

"WHORTLEBERRY". See *VACCINIUM myrtillus*.

"WINEBERRY". See *RUBUS phoenicolasius*.

"WILD IRISHMAN". See *DISCARIA toumatou*.

"WILLOW". See *SALIX*.

"WING NUT". See *PTEROCARYA*.

"WINTER JASMINE". See *JASMINUM nudiflorum*.

"WITCH HAZEL". See *HAMAMELIS*.

"WYCH ELM". See *ULMUS glabra*.

XANTHOCERAS—Sapindaceae—A monotypic genus related to *Koelreuteria*, but very different in general appearance. The erect flower panicles recall those of the Horse Chestnut.

XANTHOCERAS—*continued*

sorbifolium BGE. A beautiful, large shrub or small tree of upright growth. Leaves pinnate, composed of nine to seventeen sessile, lanceolate, sharply-toothed leaflets. The 2·5cm. wide flowers which are white, with a carmine eye, are borne in erect panicles on the shoots of the previous year in May. Fruit a top-shaped, three-valved, walnut-like capsule containing numerous small chestnut-like seeds. It may be grown in all types of fertile soil, its thick fleshy yellow roots take kindly to a chalk formation. N. China. I. 1866. F.C.C. 1876.

XANTHORRHIZA (*ZANTHORRHIZA*)—**Ranunculaceae**—A monotypic genus belonging to the buttercup family, but very different in general appearance from other members of the family.

simplicissima MARSH (*apiifolia*). "Yellow-root". A small, suckering shrub forming in time a thicket of erect stems up to 1m. The very attractive, pinnate leaves are composed of three to five sessile, deeply-toothed leaflets which turn the colour of burnished bronze, often with a purple cast, in autumn. The tiny, delicate, deep purple flowers are produced in loose, drooping panicles with the emerging leaves during March and April. The roots and inner bark are coloured a bright yellow and are bitter to the taste. Thrives in a moist or clayey soil but is not at home in a shallow chalk soil. E. United States. I. 1776. A.M. 1975 (for foliage effect).

XANTHOXYLUM. See *ZANTHOXYLUM.*

†***XYLOSMA**—**Flacourtiaceae**—Evergreen trees and shrubs, normally with spiny branches and dioecious flowers. All but the following species are found in the tropics.

japonicum A. GRAY (*racemosum*). A large shrub or small bushy tree sparsely armed with axillary spines when young. Leaves ovate to oblong-ovate, leathery and dark glossy green. Flowers dioecious, small, yellow, fragrant, produced in short, axillary racemes in late summer. Berries blackish-purple. Japan; Ryukyus; Formosa; China. We offer the form *pubescens* REHD. & WILS. in which the shoots are hairy.

"YELLOW ROOT". See *XANTHORRHIZA simplicissima.*

"YELLOW WOOD". See *CLADRASTIS lutea.*

***YUCCA**—**Liliaceae**—These remarkable evergreens, with rosettes or clumps of narrow, usually rigid leaves, and tall racemes or panicles of drooping, bell-shaped, lily-like flowers are of great architectural value and help to create a sub-tropical effect in the garden. They are native of Central America, Mexico and southern United States. Several species are hardy in the British Isles where they prefer a hot, dry, well-drained position in full sun.

angustifolia. See *Y. glauca.*

†**arizonica.** A stemless species bearing narrow, rigidly recurved leaves which are chanelled above and clothed with white threads along the margins. Flowers creamy-white, in attractive panicles in late summer. Arizona.

†**brevifolia** ENGEL. "Joshua Tree". A small tree-like species with an erect trunk ending in several stout branches. Leaves green, narrow and recurved, channelled above, margined with fine teeth. Flowers cream to greenish-white, borne in a dense panicle during late summer. S.W. United States.

jaegerana MCKELVEY. Differs from the type in its shorter stature, smaller leaves and panicles. S.W. United States.

filamentosa L. A stemless species producing dense clumps of spreading or erect, lanceolate, slightly glaucous leaves. The leaf margins are clothed with numerous, curly, white threads. The creamy-white flowers, each 5 to 7·5cm. long, are borne in erect, glabrous, conical panicles 1 to 2m. tall, in July and August, even on young plants. S.E. United States. C. 1675. A.G.M. 1969.

'Variegata'. Leaves margined and striped yellow.

flaccida HAWORTH. A stemless species forming tufts of long, lanceolate, green or glaucous leaves. The terminal portion of each leaf bends down and the margins are furnished with curly, white threads. Flowers creamy-white, 5 to 6·5cm. long, borne in erect, downy panicles, ·6 to 1·2m. tall in July and August. As in the related *Y. filamentosa*, this species spreads by short basal side growths. S.E. United States. I. 1816. We offer the following clone.

'Ivory'. Large panicles of creamy-white, green stained flowers. A.M. 1966. F.C.C. 1968. A.G.M. 1969.

YUCCA—*continued*

glauca NUTT. (*angustifolia*). A low-growing, short-stemmed species producing a rounded head of linear, greyish leaves which are margined white and edged with a few threads. The greenish-white flowers, 5 to 7·5cm. long, are carried in an erect raceme, 1 to 1·5m. tall in July and August. The species is hardy in our area but young plants do not flower. South-central United States. I. 1696.

gloriosa L. "Adam's Needle". A small, tree-like species with stout stem, 1·2 to 2·5m. tall, with few or no branches. Leaves straight and stiff, almost dangerously spine-tipped, glaucous-green, ·3 to ·6m. long, by 7·5 to 10cm. wide, gathered into a dense, terminal head. Flowers creamy-white, sometimes tinged red on the outside, borne in an erect, crowded, conical panicle, 1 to 2m. high or more, from July to September. S.E. United States. I. about 1550. A.M. 1975.

'Variegata'. Leaves margined and striped creamy-yellow, fading to creamy-white on older leaves. F.C.C. 1883.

× **karlsruhensis** GRAEBN. (*filamentosa* × *glauca*). A hardy stemless plant with long, linear, greyish leaves and panicles of creamy-white flowers during late summer. It resembles the *glauca* parent in general appearance, but the leaves possess numerous marginal threads.

†**parviflora engelmannii** (*Hesperaloe parviflora engelmannii*). An evergreen, spreading shrub having thick, leathery, linear leaves, 2·5cm. wide and up to 1·2m. long, bright green with white threads hanging from the margins. The aloe-like, tomato-red flowers, golden within, are produced in slender panicles up to 1·2m. long in July. Texas. I. 1822.

recurvifolia SALISB. A medium-sized species, usually with a short stem and several branches. The long, tapered leaves, ·6 to 1m. long, are glaucous at first becoming green with age. All but the upper, central leaves are characteristically recurved. Flowers creamy-white, borne in dense, erect panicles, ·6 to 1m. high during late summer. Perhaps the best species for town gardens. Similar to *Y. gloriosa*, but differing in the recurved leaves. S.E. United States. I. 1794.

'Variegata'. Leaves with a pale green central band.

†**whipplei** TORR. (*Hesperoyucca whipplei*). A stemless species developing a dense, globular clump of long, narrow, rigid, spine-tipped leaves which are finely-toothed and glaucous. The large, fragrant flowers are greenish-white, edged with purple. They are produced in a densely packed panicle at the end of an erect, 1·8 to 3·6m. scape, in May and June. Though able to withstand frost, this magnificent species can only be recommended for sunny places in the mildest counties and requires a very well-drained position. California. I. 1854. A.M. 1945.

"YULAN". See *MAGNOLIA denudata*.

ZANTHOXYLUM (*XANTHOXYLUM*)—**Rutaceae**—A large and rather neglected genus of mainly deciduous trees and shrubs with normally spiny branches and leaves aromatic when crushed. The flowers are small and insignificant but the diversity of the usually compound leaves is always attractive and in some species they are as beautiful as the fronds of a fern and in others, as spectacular as those of the "Tree of Heaven". The fruits too, which may be jet-black or bright red, have a subtle quality rivalling that of the barberries. Easily grown in any ordinary soil, sun or shade.

ailanthoides SIEB. & ZUCC. A very vigorous, sparsely-branched large shrub or small tree with thorny branches and stout, glaucous young shoots. Leaves pinnate, ·3 to ·6m. long, composed of eleven to twenty-three ovate to ovate-lanceolate, acuminate leaflets. The greenish-yellow flowers are produced in flattened heads, 13cm. or more across, during early autumn. An extremely attractive foliage tree of subtropical appearance. Japan; Korea; China; Ryukyus; Formosa.

alatum planispinum. See *Z. planispinum*.

americanum MILL. "Toothache Tree"; "Prickly Ash". A large, rather gaunt shrub or short-stemmed tree with short stout spines and pinnate leaves composed of five to eleven ovate or oval leaflets. The small, yellowish-green flowers are produced in short axillary clusters in spring, followed by conspicuous, capitate clusters of jet-black fruits. The twigs and fruits are said to have been chewed by the North American Indians to alleviate toothache, the acrid juice having a numbing effect. Eastern N. America. I. about 1740.

bungei. See *Z. simulans*.

ZANTHOXYLUM—*continued*

piperitum DC. "Japan Pepper". A medium-sized shrub of neat, compact habit with pairs of flattened spines. The attractive pinnate leaves are composed of eleven to nineteen sessile, broadly lanceolate or ovate leaflets. The small, greenish-yellow flowers are produced on the old wood in May or June and are followed by small, reddish fruits. The black seeds are crushed and used as a pepper in Japan. Leaves turn a rich yellow in autumn. Japan; Korea; Manchuria; China. C. 1877.

planispinum SIEB. & ZUCC. (*alatum planispinum*). A large, spreading shrub with a pair of prominently flattened spines at the base of each leaf. Leaves with three or five ovate or lanceolate, sessile leaflets and a conspicuously winged petiole. The small, yellow flowers in spring are followed by small, red, warty fruits. Japan; Ryukyus; Formosa; China; Korea. C. 1880.

schinifolium SIEB. & ZUCC. A graceful, medium-sized shrub, the branches bearing single thorns and fern-like leaves, which are pinnate and composed of eleven to twenty-one, lanceolate leaflets. The small, flat clusters of green-petalled flowers in late summer, are followed by red fruits. A pretty shrub, resembling *Z. piperitum*, but with solitary spines and flowers on the current year's shoots in August. Japan; Korea; E. China. C. 1877.

simulans HANCE (*bungei*) A medium-sized to large shrub of spreading habit, with spiny branches. Leaves pinnate, composed of seven to eleven, broadly ovate, shining green leaflets. The greenish-yellow flowers, in early summer, are followed by small, reddish fruits. China. I. 1869.

†ZAUSCHNERIA—Onagraceae—A small genus of dwarf sub-shrubs, or perennials, requiring a warm, sunny, well-drained position. They make excellent subjects for the rock garden.

californica PRESL. "Californian Fuchsia". A bushy sub-shrub with several erect, green or grey downy, more or less glandular stems densely clothed with narrow, downy, grey-green leaves. The tubular fuchsia-like flowers are red with a scarlet tube and are borne in long, loose spikes during late summer and autumn. California. I. 1847.

latifolia KECK (*Z. canescens*). More herbaceous in nature, with broader leaves. S.W. United States. A.M. 1928.

cana GREENE (*microphylla*). A grey, dwarf sub-shrub with linear leaves crowding the stems and loose spikes of red, scarlet-tubed flowers during late summer and autumn. California. A.M. 1928 (as *Z. microphylla*).

canescens. See *Z. californica latifolia*.

microphylla. See *Z. cana*.

ZELKOVA—Ulmaceae—A small genus of smooth-barked trees or rarely shrubs allied to the elms, differing in their monoecious flowers and simple (not double) -toothed leaves. The small, greenish flowers and the fruits which follow are of little ornament. They thrive in deep, moist, loamy soils and are fairly tolerant of shade. The zelkovas are trees of considerable quality, their garden value may be paralleled with the deciduous *Nothofagus*.

acuminata. See *Z. serrata*.

carpinifolia K. KOCH (*crenata*) (*Planera richardii*). A long-lived, slow-growing tree eventually attaining a large size. The bark is smooth and grey like a beech, but flakes with age. As seen in the British Isles the trunk is generally comparatively short, soon giving way to numerous, erect, crowded branches which form a characteristic dense, conical head. On old trees the trunk is often buttressed. The hairy shoots bear 4 to 7·5cm. long, ovate to elliptic, coarsely-toothed leaves which are rough to the touch above. Caucasus; N. Iran. I. 1760.

crenata. See *Z. carpinifolia*.

cretica SPACH. A large, wide-spreading shrub with slender twigs and small, ovate to oblong, coarsely-toothed leaves up to 2·5cm. long. The small, whitish flowers are scented. A rare species in cultivation. Mts. of Crete. I. about 1924.

ZELKOVA—*continued*

serrata MAK. (*acuminata*) (*keaki*) (*Planera acuminata*). A medium-sized, occasionally large tree of graceful, wide-spreading habit, forming a rounded crown, with smooth, grey, later flaky bark. The attractive, ovate to ovate-lanceolate, acuminate leaves are 5 to 12cm. long and edged with slender-pointed, coarse teeth. In autumn they turn to bronze or red. Japan; Korea; Formosa; China. I. 1861. This was the largest tree (supplied by us) planted on the Thames embankment site for the Festival of Britain in 1951. It weighed over two tons and had a branch spread exceeding 10m., and throughout its journey from the ancient capital of Winchester to the "new" capital London, it was honoured by a police escort.

sinica SCHNEID. A medium-sized tree with smooth, grey bark flaking with age. Twigs slender and short-pubescent. Leaves small and neat, ovate to ovate-lanceolate, coarsely-toothed, 2·5 to 6cm. long, harsh to the touch. The young growths are pink-tinted in spring. C. & E. China. Introduced by E. H. Wilson in 1908.

verschaffeltii NICHOLS. Normally a splendid large shrub or small, bushy-headed tree of graceful habit, with slender shoots and oval to ovate, conspicuously toothed leaves, rough to the touch above, and in shape recalling those of *Ulmus* ×*viminalis*. In the Westonbirt Arboretum is a large tree which possesses a grey and rich brown, mottled bark and deeply lobed leaves. Although the species has been in cultivation since before 1886, its origin is unknown. It may possibly have originated in the Caucasus. F.C.C. 1886 (as *Ulmus pitteursii pendula*).

‡**ZENOBIA** (*ANDROMEDA* in part)—**Ericaceae**—A monotypic genus requiring a lime-free soil and preferably semi-shade. One of the most beautiful and most neglected of early summer-flowering shrubs. One suspects that this glorious little shrub flowers during the "London Season", how else can it have been so unnoticed.

pulverulenta POLLARD (*speciosa*). A beautiful, small, deciduous or semi-evergreen shrub of loose habit with bloomy young shoots. The oblong-ovate, shallowly-toothed leaves are covered by a conspicuous, glaucous bloom which tends to fade above as the leaves age. The white, bell-shaped flowers, resembling those of a large lily-of-the-valley, are aniseed-scented and appear in pendulous, axillary clusters in June and July. E. United States. I. 1801. A.M. 1932. F.C.C. 1934.

nuda REHD. (*Z. cassinifolia*) (*speciosa nitida*). A form with green, non-glaucous leaves. This variety is said to occur with the type in the wild. Some authorities regard it as a distinct species, but seed-grown plants in cultivation contain forms which appear intermediate between the two. A.M. 1965.

CLIMBERS
(including Wall Shrubs)

This section contains some of the most beautiful of all woody plants. Many of the shrubs described in the foregoing pages are frequently treated as climbers and innumerable shrubs normally too tender in cold gardens are successful when grown against walls. Reference to these is made below.

Climbers may roughly be divided into three main categories, based on their mode of growth, namely:—

Group 1 consists of those climbers which, due to the presence of aerial roots (as in Ivy), or adhesive tendril tips (as in Virginia Creeper), are self-clinging and have the ability to scale a wall or tree trunk without added support.

Group 2 consists of climbers with twining stems (as in Honeysuckle); curling tendrils (as in Vine), or curling petioles (as in Clematis), which require support other than that of a flat surface up which to grow.

Group 3 consists of climbers with hooked thorns (as in Climbing Rose), or with long scandent stems (as in *Berberidopsis*), which require the support of a wall or tree over or into which to scramble.

All climbers require careful attention on a support until established. Even the self-clingers of group 1 usually require the support of a little string or wire until their adhesive organs establish permanent contact with the wall or tree surface.

In the absence of trees or suitable walls the climbers of groups 2 and 3 may be trained up specially constructed wooden supports, or over hedges.

Contrary to their natural inclinations many climbers, particularly those in groups 1 and 3, may be used as ground cover when, particularly on unsightly banks, a rapid and often ornamental effect may be obtained.

Several climbers possess dioecious flowers, the females often followed by attractive fruits. Where fruits are required plants of both sexes are best planted together over or against the same support.

ABELIA floribunda. See Tree and Shrub section.

ABUTILON. See Tree and Shrub section.

ACACIA. See Tree and Shrub section.

ACRADENIA. See Tree and Shrub section.

ACTINIDIA—Actinidiaceae—Vigorous, generally hardy twining climbers with simple leaves, unisexual, bisexual or polygamous flowers and sometimes edible, juicy berries. They are excellent for covering old walls or tall stumps and will grow in most fertile soils in sun or semi-shade. Those grown for their fruits are best planted in pairs.

arguta MIQ. A strong-growing species climbing to the tops of lofty trees in its native land. Leaves broadly ovate, 7·5 to 13cm. long, bristly toothed. Flowers white, with purple anthers, slightly fragrant, 1 to 2cm. across, opening in June and July. Fruits oblong, greenish-yellow, 2·5cm. long, edible but insipid. Japan; Korea; Manchuria. C. 1874.

cordifolia DUNN. A form with heart-shaped leaves.

chinensis PLANCH. "Chinese Gooseberry". A vigorous species reaching a height of 9m. with densely reddish-hairy shoots and large, heart-shaped leaves, 15 to 23cm. long and up to 20cm. wide. Flowers creamy-white, turning to buff-yellow, 4cm. across, fragrant, produced in axillary clusters in late summer. Fruits edible, green then brown, 4 to 5cm. long, resembling a large, elongated gooseberry and with a similar flavour. Selected clones are cultivated for their fruits notably in New Zealand and are available on request. Native of China. I. 1900. A.M. 1907.

'Aureovariegata'. Leaves splashed and marked with cream and yellow.

†**coriacea** DUNN. A vigorous, almost evergreen species with leathery, lanceolate to oblanceolate, slender-pointed leaves, 7·5 to 13cm. long. Flowers 12mm. across, fragrant, an attractive rose-pink in May and June. Fruits brown, spotted white, egg-shaped 2 to 2·5cm. long. Requires a warm, sunny sheltered position. On a west-facing wall at Winchester it survived, in spite of injury, the severe winter of 1962/63. W. China. I. 1908.

giraldii DIELS. A strong-growing species related to *A. arguta* with ovate or elliptic leaves and white flowers during summer. C. China. C. 1933.

ACTINIDIA—*continued*

kolomikta MAXIM. A striking, slender climber reaching 4·5 to 6m. Remarkable on account of the tri-coloured variegation of many of its leaves, the terminal half being creamy-white, flushed pink. The variegation is often not apparent, but may be encouraged by planting against a south or west-facing wall in full sun. Flowers dioecious, white, slightly fragrant, 12mm. across, opening in June; fruits ovoid, 2·5cm. long, yellowish and sweet. The form in general cultivation appears to be a male plant. It is the more ornamental in foliage and may possibly stem from a single clone. Japan; N. China; Manchuria. I. about 1855. A.M. 1931.

melanandra FRANCH. A vigorous species, reaching a great height in a tree. Leaves oblong or narrowly oval, 7·5 to 10cm. long, glaucous beneath. Flowers unisexual, white, with purple anthers, opening in June and July. Fruits egg-shaped, 2·5 to 3cm. long, reddish-brown, covered by a plum-like bloom. C. China. I. 1910.

polygama MAXIM. A slender-branched species up to 4·5 to 6m. in a tree. Leaves broadly ovate to elliptic, 7·5 to 13cm. long, bronze tinted when unfolding. The fragrant white flowers, 2cm. across, are produced in June. Fruits ovoid, beaked, 2·5 to 4cm. long, yellow and edible. C. Japan.

purpurea REHD. Strong-growing species, reaching 6 to 7·5m. in a tree. Leaves oval to ovate-oblong, 7·5 to 13cm. long. Flowers white, 1 to 2cm. across, opening in June. Fruit ovoid or oblong, 2·5cm. long, purple in colour, edible and sweet. W. China. I. 1908.

ADENOCARPUS. See Tree and Shrub section.

AKEBIA—**Lardizabalaceae**—A genus of five species of vigorous, hardy, semi-evergreen, twining plants with attractive foliage and monoecious flowers. Succeeding in most soils, in sun or shade. They are excellent for training over hedges, low trees, bushes or old stumps. A mild spring (for the flowers) and a long hot summer are usually required before the conspicuous and unusual fruits are produced.

lobata. See *A. trifoliata.*

×**pentaphylla** MAK. (*quinata×trifoliata*). A strong-growing, rare hybrid, the leaves with usually five oval leaflets. Flowers similar to those of *A. trifoliata*. Japan.

quinata DCNE. A semi-evergreen climber up to 9 or 12m. in a tree. Leaves composed of normally five oblong or obovate, notched leaflets. Flowers fragrant, red-purple, male and female in the same racemes in April. Fruits 5 to 10cm. long, sausage-shaped, turning dark purple, containing numerous black seeds embedded in a white pulp. Japan; Korea; China. Introduced by Robert Fortune in 1845. A.M. 1956.

trifoliata KOIDZ. (*lobata*). An elegant climber up to 9m. in a tree. Leaves trifoliolate, with broadly ovate, shallowly-lobed or undulate leaflets. Flowers dark-purple, male and female produced in a drooping raceme in April. Fruits sausage-shaped, often in groups of three, 7·5 to 13cm. long, pale violet, containing black seeds in a white pulp. Japan; China. I. 1895.

AMPELOPSIS (*VITIS* in part)—**Vitaceae**—A small genus of ornamental vines climbing by means of curling tendrils. At one time included under *Vitis*, but differing from that genus in having free (not united) petals and usually compound leaves. They are excellent subjects for covering walls, fences, hedges, etc., and with initial support will clamber into trees. Valuable for their attractive foliage and for their fruits which, however, require a long, hot summer and a mild autumn in which to develop. The inconspicuous flowers appear in late summer or early autumn. They will grow in any ordinary soil and in sun or semi-shade, but for those species with attractive fruits a warm sunny, sheltered position is recommended. See also *PARTHENOCISSUS* and *VITIS*.

aconitifolia BUNGE (*Vitis aconitifolia*). A vigorous, luxurious climber. Leaves variable in shape, composed of three or five sessile, lanceolate or rhomboid, coarsely-toothed or lobed leaflets. The whole leaf is 10 to 13cm. across and a deep glossy green above. Fruits small, orange or yellow. N. China. C. 1868.

bodinieri REHD. (*Vitis micans*). A slender climber up to 6m. with smooth, often purplish stems. Leaves simple, triangular-ovate or rounded, 7·5 to 13cm. long, coarsely-toothed and occasionally three-lobed, dark shining green above, somewhat glaucous beneath. The small rounded fruits are dark blue. C. China. I. 1900.

AMPELOPSIS—*continued*

brevipedunculata TRAUTV. (*Cissus brevipedunculata*). A vigorous, luxuriant climber with three-lobed or occasionally five-lobed, cordate leaves resembling those of the "Hop". They vary from 5 to 15cm. across. After a hot summer the masses of small fruits vary between verdigris and deep blue but in the mass are porcelain-blue and are exceedingly attractive. N.E. Asia. C. 1870.

'Citrulloides'. Leaves more deeply five-lobed. An attractive foliage plant. Fruits similar to those of the type. C. 1875.

'Elegans' (*'Variegata'*) (*'Tricolor'*). An attractive form with leaves densely mottled white and tinged pink. Weaker growing than the type and, therefore, useful for planting where space is restricted. An excellent patio plant. Introduced by P. von Siebold before 1847.

'Tricolor'. See *'Elegans'*.

'Variegata'. See *'Elegans'*.

chaffanjonii REHD. (*Ampelopsis watsoniana*). A large-leaved climber suitable for walls and wooden supports. Leaves pinnate, 15 to 30cm. long, composed of five or seven oval or oblong, deep glossy-green leaflets which are purple-tinted beneath, and often colour richly in autumn. Fruits red, later black. C. China. I. 1900. A.M. 1907.

megalophylla DIELS. & GILG. (*Vitis megalophylla*). A strong but rather slow-growing aristocratic climber of considerable quality, reaching 9m. or more in a suitable tree. Leaves bi-pinnate, 30 to 60cm. long, with ovate to ovate-oblong leaflets usually glaucous beneath, coarsely-toothed and 5 to 15cm. in length. The loose bunches of top-shaped fruits are purple at first, finally black. W. China. I. 1894. A.M. 1903.

orientalis PLANCH. (*Cissus orientalis*). A bushy shrub of loose growth or occasionally climbing. Leaves variable, pinnate, bi-pinnate or bi-ternate, with ovate to obovate, coarsely-toothed leaflets. After a hot summer the bunches of red-currant-like fruits are most attractive. Asia Minor; Syria. I. 1818.

sempervirens HORT. See *CISSUS striata*.

veitchii. See *PARTHENOCISSUS tricuspidata 'Veitchii'*.

ANTHYLLIS. See Tree and Shrub section.

†***ARAUJIA**—**Asclepiadaceae**—A small genus of mainly tropical twining climbers requiring full sun.

sericofera BROT. "Cruel Plant". A vigorous evergreen climber with pale green, ovate-oblong leaves, minutely tomentose beneath. The slightly fragrant, creamy-white, salver-shaped flowers are borne in short racemes close to the leaf axils during late summer. These are followed after a long, hot summer by large grooved yellowish-green pods 10 to 13cm. long, containing numerous silky-tufted seeds. Only suitable for the mildest areas of the British Isles. The common name refers to the peculiar fact that in its native habitats, night-flying moths visiting the flowers are held trapped by their long probosces until day-time when they are usually able to release themselves. S. America. I. 1830. A.M. 1975.

ARISTOLOCHIA—**Aristolochiaceae**—A large genus of shrubs, climbers and herbaceous plants, with cordate leaves and peculiarly-shaped flowers. The species here described are excellent, twining plants for covering unsightly walls, fences or stumps and equally effective in trees and on wooden supports such as arbours, archways, etc., and will grow in most fertile soils, in sun or shade.

altissima. See *A. sempervirens*.

durior REHD. not HILL. See *A. macrophylla*.

chrysops WILSON. A rare species up to 6m. with hairy shoots and hairy, auricled, ovate leaves 5 to 13cm. long. Flowers shaped like a small, tubby, greyish saxaphone, 4cm. long, with a flared purplish-brown mouth and a mustard-yellow throat, appearing singly on long, slender, pendulous stalks during late May and June. W. China. I. 1904.

macrophylla LAM. (*sipho*) (*durior* REHD. not HILL.). "Dutchman's Pipe". A vigorous species reaching 9m. in a suitable tree. Leaves heart-shaped or kidney-shaped up to 30cm. long. Flowers tubular, bent in the lower half, like a syphon, 2·5 to 4cm. long, yellowish-green, the flared mouth brownish-purple, produced in June in axillary pairs. Eastern U.S.A. Introduced by John Bartram in 1763.

ARISTOLOCHIA—*continued*

†***sempervirens** L. (*altissima*). An evergreen species with long, lax stems up to 3m., trailing along the ground unless trained up a support. Leaves heart-shaped and slender-pointed, 5 to 10cm. long, glabrous and glossy green. The solitary, yellowish-brown to dull purple flowers are funnel-shaped and curved. They are produced singly in the leaf axils during late spring or early summer. It may be cut to ground level during winter, but invariably appears again the following spring, particularly if given some form of winter protection. E. Mediterranean region; N. Africa. I. 1727.

sipho. See *A. macrophylla.*

tomentosa SIMS. A vigorous species related to and somewhat resembling *A. macrophylla*, but downy in almost all its parts. Its leaves are also smaller and its flowers possess a distinctly three-lobed, yellowish, flared mouth. S.E. United States. I. 1799.

ARISTOTELIA. See Tree and Shrub section.

†***ASTERANTHERA**—**Gesneriaceae**—A genus of only one species of shrubs, climbing by means of aerial roots. They require a cool, leafy soil, preferably neutral or acid, and are happiest in a sheltered woodland or against a north wall in the milder areas of the British Isles.

ovata HANST. A beautiful evergreen trailing creeper which will climb up the trunks of trees or the surface of a wall where conditions are suitable, otherwise it makes a charming ground cover. Leaves opposite, rounded or ovate, 1 to 4cm. long. The tubular, two-lipped flowers are 5cm. long and appear in June. They are red, the lower lip having blood-red veins, accentuated by a white throat. In the forests of the Chilean Andes it adheres closely to the trunks of trees and attains a height of 3 to 6m. Introduced from Chile by Harold Comber in 1926. A.M. 1939.

†***BERBERIDOPSIS**—**Flacourtiaceae**—A monotypic genus requiring an open or sandy loam and a sheltered position in shade, succeeding best in an acid or neutral soil. Correctly sited it is moderately hardy. A shaded site and a moist soil are essential.

corallina HOOK. f. "Coral Plant". A beautiful evergreen, scandent shrub attaining a length of 4·5 to 6m. on a shaded wall. Leaves heart-shaped or ovate, thick and leathery, the margins set with spiny teeth, dark green above, glaucous beneath. Flowers deep crimson, 12mm. across, borne singly on slender stalks or in pendent racemes during late summer. Chile. Introduced by Richard Pearce in 1862. A.M. 1901.

BERCHEMIA—**Rhamnaceae**—A small genus of twining climbers with rather insignificant white or greenish flowers and small fruits which, however, are rarely freely produced in British gardens. Their elegant foliage makes them unusual climbers for walls, hedges, or bushy-headed trees. Easy to grow in most fertile soils in sun or semi-shade.

giraldiana SCHNEID. A graceful species attaining 4·5 to 6m., with reddish-brown shoots and ovate-oblong, parallel-veined leaves 2·5 to 6cm. long, which are dark sea-green above, glaucous beneath. Fruits sausage-shaped, 8mm. long, red at first, then black. C. & W. China. C. 1911.

lineata DC. An elegant climber with neat, elliptic parallel-veined leaves 6mm. to 4cm. long. The tiny fruits ripen to blue-black. China; Formosa; Himalaya.

racemosa SIEB. & ZUCC. A strong-growing, scandent shrub up to 4·5m. with pretty, ovate, parallel-veined leaves 4 to 7·5cm. long, pale or glaucescent beneath. Fruits small, oblong, changing from green to red, then black. A spreading species ideal for growing over hedges, low trees and bushes. The leaves turn clear yellow in autumn. Japan. I. 1880.

'Variegata'. Leaves, particularly when young, conspicuously variegated creamy-white.

***BIGNONIA**—**Bignoniaceae**—As now understood a monotypic genus until recently including *CAMPSIS* and *TECOMA*.

capreolata L. (*Doxantha capreolata*). A vigorous evergreen or semi-evergreen, climbing by means of twining leaf tendrils. Leaves composed of two oblong to ovate-lanceolate leaflets, 5 to 13cm. long. The tubular flowers 4 to 5cm. long, are orange-red, paler within, carried in axillary clusters in June. A rampant climber for a sunny sheltered wall or tree. Hardy in the southern counties. S.E. United States. C. 1653. A.M. 1958.

†***BILLARDIERA—Pittosporaceae**—A small genus of low-growing Australasian twining plants, suitable for a warm, sunny position in the milder areas of the British Isles. It makes an unusual conservatory subject.

longiflora LABILL. A slender climber up to 2m. Leaves lanceolate, 2·5 to 4cm. long. The solitary, bell-shaped flowers hang on slender stalks from the leaf axils during summer and autumn. They are greenish-yellow in colour, 2cm. long and are replaced by brilliant deep blue, oblong fruits 2 to 2·5cm. in length. A charming plant against a wall or clambering over a large boulder on the rock garden or scrambling through a low bush. Tasmania. I. 1810. A.M. 1924.

'Fructu-albo' (*'Alba'*). Fruits white.

"BLUEBELL CREEPER". See *SOLLYA heterophylla.*

BOWKERIA gerardiana. See Tree and Shrub section.

BUDDLEIA (in particular, tender species). See Tree and Shrub section.

BURSARIA spinosa. See Tree and Shrub section.

CAESALPINIA. See Tree and Shrub section.

CALCEOLARIA integrifolia. See Tree and Shrub section.

CALLISTEMON. See Tree and Shrub section.

CAMELLIA. See Tree and Shrub section.

CAMPSIS (*TECOMA*) (*BIGNONIA* in part)—**Bignoniaceae**. A genus of only two species of attractive, deciduous, scandent shrubs related to *Bignonia*, and equally brilliant in flower. Both require a position in full sun to ripen growth and produce flowers. They are excellent when trained over walls or the rooves of out-houses or tree stumps. Specimens which have become too large and tangled may be pruned in late February or March.

chinensis. See *C. grandiflora*.

grandiflora K. SCHUM. (*chinensis*). This beautiful oriental climber will attain a height of 6m. or more in a suitable position. Leaves pinnate, composed of seven or nine ovate, coarsely-toothed, glabrous leaflets. Flowers trumpet-shaped, 5 to 9cm. long, deep orange and red, carried in drooping panicles from the tips of the current year's growths during late summer and early autumn. China. I. 1800. A.M. 1949.

'Thunbergii'. A form with shorter-tubed, red trumpets and reflexed lobes.

radicans SEEM. "Trumpet Vine". A tall, strong-growing species which normally climbs by aerial roots, but is best given a little support until established. Leaves pinnate, composed of nine or eleven, coarsely-toothed leaflets which are downy beneath, at least on the veins. Flowers trumpet-shaped, 5 to 8cm. long, brilliant orange and scarlet, produced in terminal clusters on the current year's growths in August and September. S.E. United States. C. 1640.

'Flava' (*'Yellow Trumpet'*). This attractive form with rich yellow flowers received an A.M. when exhibited by us in 1969.

×**tagliabuana** REHD. (*grandiflora* × *radicans*). A variable hybrid intermediate in habit between the parents. Leaflets varying from seven to eleven, slightly downy on the veins beneath. We offer the following clone:—

'Madame Galen'. A vigorous climber with panicles of salmon-red flowers during late summer. Requires support up which to clamber. I. 1889. A.M. 1959.

CANTUA buxifolia. See Tree and Shrub section.

CARPENTERIA californica. See Tree and Shrub section.

CEANOTHUS. See Tree and Shrub section.

CELASTRUS—Celastraceae—Vigorous twining and scandent climbers with tiny insignificant flowers, followed in autumn by attractive, long persistent capsules containing brightly coloured seeds. The flowers are often unisexual; therefore, when grown for fruit the species are best planted in pairs. Sometimes male and female clones are available. All species are tall-growing, rampant climbers and are best accommodated in an old tree or tall bush. They are also excellent for covering large stumps, hedges, unsightly walls, etc. in full sun or shade.

articulatus. See *C. orbiculatus*.

hypoleucus LOES. (*hypoglaucus*). A large climber, the young shoots covered with a purplish bloom. Leaves oblong or obovate, up to 15cm. long, strikingly glaucous beneath. The yellow-lined green capsules split to reveal the red seeds. A handsome species well distinguished by its terminal inflorescences and the glaucous undersurfaces of its leaves. C. China. Introduced by E. H. Wilson about 1900.

CELASTRUS—*continued*

orbiculatus THUNB. (*articulatus*). A strong-growing climber reaching a height of 12m. or more in a tree. The twining, young shoots are armed with a pair of short spines at each bud. Leaves varying from obovate to orbicular, 5 to 13cm. long, turning clear yellow in autumn. Also in autumn the brownish capsules split open to reveal a yellow lining containing colourful red seeds. A beautiful climber in autumn, when the scarlet and gold-spangled fruits glisten against a backcloth of yellow. The most consistent species for fruiting. N.E. Asia. I. 1860. A.M. 1914. F.C.C. 1958 (for hermaphrodite form).

rosthornianus LOES. A vigorous scandent shrub reaching 5 to 6m. in a tree. Leaves ovate to ovate-lanceolate, 4 to 8cm. long, glossy green above. Capsules orange-yellow, containing scarlet seeds, long persistent. W. China. I. 1910.

rugosus REHD. & WILS. A vigorous climber up to 6m. with warty shoots and ovate or elliptic, strongly-toothed and wrinkled leaves up to 15cm. long. Capsules orange-yellow, containing bright red seeds. W. China. I. 1908.

scandens L. Vigorous climber up to 7m. with ovate to ovate-oblong, sharply-pointed leaves. Female plants produce orange lined capsules containing scarlet coated seeds. Not very free-fruiting in the British Isles. North America. Introduced by Peter Collinson in 1736.

CESTRUM. See Tree and Shrub section.

CHAENOMELES. See Tree and Shrub section.

CHIMONANTHUS. See Tree and Shrub section.

†**CISSUS**—**Vitaceae**—A large genus of shrubs and herbaceous plants, the majority climbing by means of twining tendrils. Only the following species may be grown out-of-doors in the British Isles and then only in the mildest areas.

***antarctica** VENT. "Kangaroo Vine". A strong-growing, vine-like climber with ovate-oblong, cordate leaves, rather leathery in texture, glossy green and 8 to 10cm. long. An excellent climber or trailer for conservatory and a popular house plant, succeeding in sun or shade. Australia. I. 1790.

***striata** RUIZ & PAV. (*Vitis striata*) (*Ampelopsis sempervirens* HORT.). A luxuriant evergreen climber for a sunny wall. Leaves 5 to 7·5cm. across, composed of five obovate or oblanceolate, dark glossy green leaflets which are coarsely-toothed towards the apex. Fruits like reddish-purple currants. Chile and S. Brazil. I. about 1878.

CLEMATIS (including *ATRAGENE*)—**Ranunculaceae**—The species of this most popular genus are, on the whole, much more easy to establish than the large-flowered hybrids, though, like the latter, they thrive best in full sun, with their roots in cool, moist, well-drained soil. The climbing species support themselves by means of their petioles which twine round any slender support available. The stronger-growing species are ideal when grown in trees or over large bushy shrubs and most others are very effective on walls, fences or wooden support. As well as flowers, some species have attractive silken seed-heads. The flower of a clematis is composed of four to eight sepals which are usually large and colourful and sometimes referred to as tepals. The true petals are absent or in a few species (Atragene Section) reduced to small petaloid staminodes.

The only pruning needed is the removal of dead or useless wood, and the shortening of shoots which have extended beyond their allotted space; but, if necessary, the later summer-flowering species may be pruned hard every spring. See also under "Large Flowered Garden Clematis".

afoliata BUCHAN (*aphylla*). A curious species with slender leafless stems up to 3m. long, clambering into bushes or, when no support is available, forming dense mounds. Worth growing for its unusual form, and for the fragrance of its small, dioecious, greenish-white flowers which are borne in May. Requires a warm, sunny position. Hardy in the southern counties when given the protection of a south-facing wall or the support of a dense bush. New Zealand. A.M. 1915.

alpina MILL. (Atragene Section). A lovely species with slender stems up to 2·5m. long. Leaves with nine ovate-lanceolate, coarsely-toothed leaflets. Flowers solitary, 2·5 to 4cm. long, blue or violet-blue with a central tuft of white staminodes. They are borne on long, slender stalks during April and May, followed by silky seed-heads. Superb when grown over a low wall or scrambling over a large rock or small bush. N. Europe; Mts. of C. Europe; N. Asia. I. 1792. A.M. 1894.

CLEMATIS—*continued*

alpina 'Frances Rivis' (*'Blue Giant'*). A vigorous, free-flowering clone with larger flowers, up to 5cm. long, with a contrasting sheaf of white stamens and staminodes in the centre. A.M. 1965 (as *'Blue Giant'*).

'Ruby'. Flowers rose-red, with creamy-white staminodes.

sibirica SCHNEID. (*alba*). Flowers creamy-white. N.E. Europe; Norway; Siberia. I. 1753.

aphylla. See *C. afoliata.*

***armandii** FRANCH. A strong-growing, evergreen climber with stems 4·5 to 6m. long. Leaves composed of three, long, leathery, glossy dark green leaflets. The creamy-white flowers, 5 to 6·5cm. across are carried in axillary clusters during April or early May. A beautiful species; subject to injury in severe winters and best planted on a warm, sunny wall. Seed-raised plants often produce smaller, inferior flowers. C. & W. China. Introduced by Ernest Wilson in 1900. F.C.C. 1914. A.G.M. 1938.

We offer the following clones:—

'Apple Blossom'. A superb form with broad sepals of white shaded pink, especially on the reverse. Leaves bronze-green when young. A.M. 1926. F.C.C. 1936. A.G.M. 1969.

'Snowdrift'. Flowers pure white. A.G.M. 1969.

× **aromatica** LEN. & KOCH (*flammula* × *integrifolia*). A small sub-shrub, dying back to near ground level each winter. Leaves pinnate, with three to seven short-stalked leaflets. Flowers fragrant, dark bluish-violet produced in terminal cymes from July to September.

balearica PERS. See *C. cirrhosa.*

balearica RICH. See *C. cirrhosa balearica.*

†brachiata THUNB. A tender species only suitable for the mildest areas or the conservatory. Flowers greenish-white, deliciously fragrant. S. Africa. A.M. 1975.

campaniflora BROT. A vigorous climber up to 6m. with pinnate leaves, the leaflets in groups of three. Its small, bowl-shaped, blue-tinted flowers borne profusely from July to September, are most effective in the mass. Portugal; S. Spain. I. 1810.

chrysocoma FRANCH. A beautiful species resembling the well-known *C. montana*, but less rampant. Leaves trifoliolate, covered, as are the shoots and flower stalks, with a thick yellowish down. The soft pink flowers are 4 to 6cm. across, generally smaller than those of *C. montana* and carried on usually longer and stouter peduncles. They are profusely borne from early May to June and successionally on the young growths in late summer. W. China. I. about 1890. A.M. 1936.

sericea SCHNEID. (*C. spooneri*). An attractive variety with white flowers produced solitary or in pairs on the older growths in late spring. W. China. I. 1909.

***cirrhosa** L. (*balearica* PERS.). An evergreen species up to 3m. with leaves varying from simple to compound, with three to six leaflets. Flowers 4 to 6·5cm. across, yellowish-white, opening during winter and followed by silky seed-heads. S. Europe; Asia Minor. I. 1596.

balearica WILLK. & LANGE (*C. balearica* RICH.). "Fern-leaved Clematis". An elegant evergreen climber with slender stems, 3·5 to 4·5m. long. Leaves prettily divided into several segments, becoming bronze-tinged in winter. Flowers pale yellow, spotted reddish-purple within, 4 to 5cm. across, produced throughout winter. Balearic Isles. I. before 1783. A.M. 1974.

colensoi. See *C. hookerana.*

× **durandii** KTZE. (*integrifolia* × *jackmanii*). A lovely hybrid up to 3m. Leaves simple, entire, 7·5 to 15cm. long. The dark blue, four-sepalled flowers sometimes exceed 10cm. in diameter and have a central cluster of yellow stamens. They appear from June to September. Garden origin in France about 1870. A.G.M. 1942.

× **eriostemon** DCNE. (*integrifolia* × *viticella*). The original hybrid was raised in France before 1852. We offer the following clone:—

'Hendersonii'. A beautiful clematis, semi-herbaceous in habit, each year throwing up slender stems of 2 to 2·5m. Leaves simple or pinnate. Flowers deep bluish-purple, widely bell-shaped, slightly fragrant, 5 to 6·5cm. across, nodding, borne singly on slender peduncles from July to September. Raised by Messrs. Henderson of St. John's Wood in about 1830. It is best given some support. A.M. 1965.

CLEMATIS—*continued*

fargesii FRANCH. A strong-growing climber up to 6m., with comparatively large, compound leaves. Flowers white, 4 to 5cm. across, produced in the leaf axils continuously from June to September. W. China. It is represented in cultivation by the following variety:—

souliei FINET & GAGNEP. This is the form in general cultivation, differing but little from the type. W. China. I. 1911.

†***finetiana** LEVL. & VAN. (*pavoliniana*). An evergreen climber up to 5m., related to *C. armandii*, but differing in its smaller flowers. Leaves composed of three dark green, leathery leaflets. Flowers white, fragrant, 2·5 to 4cm. wide, borne in axillary clusters in June. Best grown on a warm, sheltered wall except in milder areas. C. to W. China. Introduced by E. H. Wilson in 1908.

flammula L. A strong-growing climber, 4 to 5m. high, forming a dense tangle of glabrous stems clothed with bright green bi-pinnate leaves. From August to October, the loose panicles of small, white, sweetly-scented flowers are abundantly scattered over the whole plant, followed by silky seed-heads. An ideal climber for clothing tall, unsightly walls or hedges. S. Europe. Cultivated in England since the late 16th century.

florida THUNB. An elegant species with wiry stems, 3 to 5m. long, and glossy-green, compound leaves. Flowers 6 to 8cm. across, solitary on long, downy stalks, sepals creamy-white, with a greenish stripe on the reverse, stamens dark purple, opening in June and July. A native of China, long cultivated in Japan and a parent of many garden hybrids. I. 1776. We offer the following clone:—

'Sieboldii' (*bicolor*). A beautiful and striking form recalling a "Passion Flower". Flowers white, 8 cm. across, with a conspicuous central boss of violet-purple petaloid stamens. Introduced from Japan before 1836. A.M. 1914.

forrestii. See *C. napaulensis*.

glauca WILLD. (s. Orientales). A slender climber up to 6m., with pinnate or bi-pinnate, glaucous leaves. The slender-stalked, bell-shaped flowers are 5cm. across, when fully open and deep orange-yellow. They are produced during August and September and are followed by silky seed-heads. W. China to Siberia. C. 1752.

grata WALL. The typical form from the Himalaya is probably not in cultivation. It is represented by the Chinese variety:—

grandidentata REHD. & WILS. A strong-growing climber reaching 9m. in a suitable position. Leaves 15cm. long, composed of three to five, coarsely toothed leaflets. Flowers white, 2·5cm. wide, borne in small axillary and terminal panicles during May and June. It is a hardy species related to *C. vitalba* and was introduced from W. China by E. H. Wilson in 1904.

graveolens. See *C. orientalis*.

***hookerana** ALLAN (*colensoi*). An unusual species of subtle charm, up to 3m., bearing fern-like, compound leaves with glossy-green leaflets. The delightfully fragrant, star-shaped flowers, 4cm. across, have yellowish-green, silky sepals and are borne in profusion during May and June. Succeeds best against a sunny wall. New Zealand. Introduced by Collingwood Ingram in 1935. A.M. 1961.

indivisa. See *C. paniculata* GMEL.

×**jackmanii** MOORE (*lanuginosa* × *viticella*). A superb large-flowered hybrid, raised in the nursery of Messrs. Jackman of Woking in 1860. A spectacular climber, 3 to 4m. high, with pinnate leaves. Flowers 10 to 13cm. across, consisting of normally four conspicuous, rich, violet-purple sepals. They are borne in great profusion singly or in threes from July to October, on the current year's growth. Many clones have been named for which see "Large-flowered Garden Clematis". F.C.C. 1863. A.G.M. 1930.

×**jouiniana** SCHNEID. (*heracleifolia davidiana* × *vitalba*). A vigorous, somewhat shrubby climber up to 3·5m. high. Leaves composed of three to five coarsely-toothed leaflets. Effective in autumn with its profusion of small, white, lilac-tinted flowers. An excellent plant for covering low walls, mounds or tree stumps. Garden origin before 1900.

'Cote d'Azur'. A charming form with azure-blue flowers.

lasiandra MAXIM. An uncommon species, bearing leaves with three to nine, ovate-lanceolate, coarsely-toothed leaflets 5 to 10cm. long. The purple, bell-shaped flowers 12mm. long, are borne in short axillary cymes during autumn. White-flowered forms occasionally appear. Japan; China. I. 1900.

CLEMATIS—*continued*

macropetala LEDEB. (Atragene Section). A charming, slender-stemmed climber up to 2·5m., with prettily divided leaves. Flowers 6·5 to 7·5cm. across, violet-blue, with conspicuous paler petaloid staminodes, giving the effect of doubling, produced from May or June onwards. Seed-heads silky, becoming fluffy and grey with age. A beautiful species for a low wall or fence. N. China; Siberia. Introduced by William Purdom in 1910. A.M. 1923. A.G.M. 1934.

'Markham's Pink' (*'Markhamii'*). A lovely form with flowers the shade of crushed strawberries. A.M. 1935.

maximowicziana FR. & SAV. (*paniculata* THUNB. not GMEL.). A vigorous species up to 10m. often forming a dense tangle of growth. Leaves with three to five long-stalked leaflets. The hawthorn-scented, white flowers, 2·5 to 4cm. wide, are borne in panicles on the current year's growth in autumn. In the British Isles this species only flowers in profusion after a hot summer. Korea; China; Japan. I. about 1864.

†***meyeniana** WALP. A strong-growing evergreen species up to 6m. or more, resembling *C. armandii* in leaf. Flowers white, 2·5cm. across, borne in large, loose panicles during spring. A rare species for a warm, sheltered wall in the milder areas. S. Japan; Ryukyus; Formosa; S. China; Philippines. C. 1821. A.M. 1920.

montana DC. A popular species of vigorous, often rampant growth and strong constitution; stems 6 to 9m. long with trifoliolate, almost glabrous leaves. Flowers white, 5 to 6·5cm. across, borne on long stalks in great profusion during May. A lovely climber for any aspect, excellent for growing in trees, over walls, outhouses and arbours, particularly those with a northern aspect. Himalaya. Introduced by Lady Amherst in 1831. A.G.M. 1930. We offer the following clones:—

'Alexander'. A lovely form with creamy-white, sweetly scented flowers. Introduced from North India by Col. R. D. Alexander.

'Elizabeth'. A lovely clone with large, slightly fragrant, soft pink flowers in May and June. A.G.M. 1969.

grandiflora REHD. A strong-growing, Chinese variety, occasionally up to 12m., producing an abundance of white flowers in May and June. Excellent on a north-facing wall. A.G.M. 1969.

rubens KTZE. A beautiful variety with bronze-purple shoots and leaves and rose-pink flowers during May and June. W. and C. China. Introduced by E. H. Wilson in 1900. A.M. 1905. A.G.M. 1969.

'Tetrarose'. A tetraploid form of Dutch origin, with bronze foliage and lilac-rose flowers up to 7·5cm. across, during May and June.

wilsonii SPRAGUE. A Chinese variety producing masses of fragrant, rather small, white flowers in late June.

†**napaulensis** DC. (*forrestii*). A semi-evergreen climber reaching 6 to 9m., with leaves composed of three to five glabrous leaflets. Flowers cup-shaped, 1 to 2·5cm. long, creamy-yellow, with conspicuous purple stamens. They are produced in axillary clusters on the young growths during winter. Only suitable for the milder areas. N. India; S.W. China. Collected by G. Forrest in 1912. A.M. 1957.

nutans HORT. See *C. rehderana*.

olgae HORT. A slender climber received by us from Russia, a form of *C. integrifolia*. Flowers in threes, bell-shaped with spreading mouth to 6·5cm. across, mauve-blue, borne in August and September.

orientalis L. (*graveolens*) (s. Orientales). A vigorous species up to 6m. often forming a tangled mass of slender shoots clothed with prettily divided, fern-like, glaucescent leaves. The yellow flowers are bell-shaped, slightly fragrant and nodding at first, later expanding to 5cm. across, produced solitary on slender stalks during August and September, followed by silky seed-heads. Caucasus; Persia eastwards through the Himalaya to N. China and Manchuria. I. 1731. A.G.M. 1973. We also offer an unusual form of this plant, or a related species (*L.S. & E.* 13342), collected in S.E. Tibet in 1947. It mainly differs from the type in its remarkably thick, spongy sepals which have given rise to the name "Orange-peel Clematis". It received an A.M. in 1950.

†***paniculata** GMEL. not THUNB. (*indivisa*). A New Zealand species with trifoliolate leaves and dioecious flowers. The male flowers are larger than those of the female, sepals white, stamens yellow, with pink anthers. I. 1840. A tender plant of which we offer the following clone:—

'Lobata'. A juvenile form with coarsely-toothed or lobed leaflets and slightly larger flowers.

CLEMATIS—*continued*

paniculata THUNB. See *C. maximowicziana.*

patens MORR. & DCNE. A slender species up to 3m., closely related to and resembling *C. florida.* The form we offer has flowers 10 to 15cm. across with creamy-white sepals, appearing during late summer and early autumn. Several of the large flowered garden Clematis are derived from this species. Japan; China. I. 1836.

pavoliniana. See *C. finetiana.*

†**phlebantha** L. H. J. WILLIAMS. A recently named species discovered and introduced by O. Polunin, W. Sykes and L. H. J. Williams from Western Nepal in 1952 (under the number P.S.W. 3436). Described as a trailing shrub in the wild. The greatest attraction of this lovely climber is its glistening silvery-silky pinnate leaves and stems. The flowers are 2·5 to 4·5cm. across, with five to seven creamy-white, prettily veined sepals. Borne singly in the leaf axils of the young growths during summer. It is sad that this beautiful plant is not proving more hardy. Planted against a south-east wall in our gardens it is cut back most winters. It is certainly worthy of a selected site in full sun against a south-facing wall or a well-drained sunny bank. An excellent conservatory climber. I. 1952. A.M. 1968.

rehderana CRAIB (*nutans* HORT. not ROYLE). A charming species, reaching 7·5m. in a tree. Leaves pinnate with seven to nine, coarsely-toothed leaflets. The nodding, bell-shaped flowers up to 2cm. long are soft primrose yellow and deliciously scented of cowslips. They are carried in erect panicles 15 to 23cm. long during late summer and autumn. W. China. I. 1898. A.M. 1936. A.G.M. 1969.

serratifolia REHD. (s. Orientales). A slender species up to 3m., related to *C. tangutica*, with prettily divided leaves. Flowers 2·5cm. long, yellow, with purple stamens, borne very profusely in August and September, followed by attractive silky seed-heads. Korea. I. about 1918.

songarica BGE. A low, rambling shrub of greyish-green hue, with narrow, simple leaves up to 10cm. long. Flowers 2·5cm. across, creamy-white, produced during summer and autumn, followed by feathery seed-heads. Siberia to Turkestan. I. before 1880.

spooneri. See *C. chrysocoma sericea.*

tangutica KORSH. (s. Orientales). A dense-growing climber up to 4·5m., closely related to *C. orientalis.* A delightful, easily grown species with prettily divided sea-green leaves and rich yellow, lantern-like flowers, 4 to 5cm. long. They are nodding at first, produced on long, downy stalks during autumn, the later ones intermingled with masses of silky seed-heads. Perhaps the best yellow-flowered species, excellent for low walls, fences, trellises, large boulders and banks. Mongolia to N.W. China. C. 1890. A.G.M. 1934.

obtusiuscula REHD. & WILS. A free-flowering, strong-growing variety differing but little from the type. Introduced by Wilson in 1908. A.M. 1913.

texensis BUCKL. (*coccinea*). A distinct species with pinnate leaves, composed of four to eight, stalked, glaucous leaflets. The red, pitcher-shaped, nodding flowers 2·5cm. long, are produced on peduncles 13 to 15cm. long during the summer and autumn. In the British Isles this attractive climber is usually semi-herbaceous in habit and requires some form of protection in winter. It is a parent of several hybrids. Texas (U.S.A.). I. 1868.

× **triternata** DC. (*flammula* × *viticella*) (× *violacea*). A vigorous climber up to 5m. with leaves pinnate or bi-pinnate. Flowers up to 3cm. wide, pale violet, borne in terminal panicles during late summer. Origin before 1840. We offer the following clone:—

'Rubromarginata'. The fragrant flowers are white, margined reddish-violet, and when borne in masses during late summer give the effect of dark, billowing clouds.

†***uncinata** BENTH. An evergreen climber up to 4·5m., with compound leaves, the leaflets up to 10cm. long, glaucous beneath. Flowers about 2·5cm. across, white, fragrant, borne in large panicles in June and July. A beautiful species requiring a warm, sheltered wall. W. China. First discovered by Augustine Henry in 1884. Introduced by Ernest Wilson in 1901. A.M. 1922.

× **vedrariensis** VILM. (*chrysocoma* × *montana rubens*). A strong-growing climber up to 6m. Leaves trifoliolate with coarsely-toothed, dull purplish-green leaflets. Flowers 5 to 6·5cm. wide, with four to six, broad, delicate rose sepals, surrounding the bunched yellow stamens. Flowering from late May onwards. Raised by Mons. Vilmorin prior to 1914. A.M. 1936.

CLEMATIS—*continued*

veitchiana CRAIB. A strong-growing species closely related to *C. rehderana*, which differs in its pinnate not bi-pinnate leaves. The nodding, bell-shaped flowers are pale yellow and fragrant. They are carried in erect panicles during autumn. W. China. I. 1904.

×violacea. See *C. ×triternata*.

vitalba L. "Travellers Joy"; "Old Man's Beard". A rampant, familiar native climber of hedgerows and roadsides, especially in chalk areas, often clambering high into trees, its rope-like stems forming long columns or dense curtains. Leaves variable in size, pinnate. The small, greenish-white, faintly scented flowers in late summer and early autumn are followed by glistening silky seed-heads which become fluffy and grey with age, remaining throughout winter. Too vigorous for all but the wild garden. S., W. and C. Europe (including British Isles); N. Africa; Caucasus.

viticella L. A slender climber up to 3·5m. with pinnate leaves. The violet, reddish-purple or blue flowers 4cm. across, are profusely borne on slender stalks during summer and early autumn. S. Europe. Cultivated in England since the 16th century.

'Abundance'. Delicately-veined flowers of soft purple. A.G.M. 1973.

'Alba Luxurians'. Flowers white, tinted mauve. A.G.M. 1930.

'Kermesina'. Flowers crimson. A.G.M. 1969.

'Minuet'. Flowers erect, larger than those of the type, creamy-white, with a broad band of purple terminating each sepal.

'Royal Velours'. Flowers deep velvety-purple. A.M. 1948. A.G.M. 1969.

LARGE-FLOWERED GARDEN CLEMATIS

The large-flowered clematis, a selection of which are described below, share with the rose a special place in the garden. They are among the most colourful of flowering plants and when well placed, their effect is charming and often spectacular. Like the species from which they are derived they are fairly adaptable, but being less easily established, require and fully deserve more care in the selection of the site and preparation of the soil.

They are best planted where their "heads" are in the sun and their roots are shaded. They succeed best in a good loamy soil in which well rotted manure plus lime in some form have been mixed. Good drainage is essential They may be trained to wires on a wall or grown over pergolas, trellises, tripods or into shrubs or small trees. They may also be encouraged to grow with wall shrubs or climbing roses, their flowers often combining effectively. When considering training a clematis over or into a tree or bush, care should be taken to plant it, where practicable, well away from the roots of the intended host.

Clematis are gross feeders and respond to an annual mulch of well-rotted manure or compost, plus an ample supply of water.

Generally speaking, clematis flower most abundantly in full sun, but many are almost as prolific in a shady or north-facing position. The paler and more delicately coloured cultivars, such as *'Nelly Moser'*, tend to bleach when exposed to a hot sun.

The large-flowered clematis are sometimes subject to a puzzling disease known as "Clematis Wilt", of which at present there seems to be no known cure. Young plants are mainly affected, the sudden collapse of a single shoot or of the whole plant whilst in full growth is the usual symptom. Unfortunate though this may be, we regret we cannot accept responsibility for failures due to this cause.

Pruning. For pruning purposes the large-flowered clematis can be divided into two groups.

(*a*) Applies to the FLORIDA, LANUGINOSA and PATENS group which flower on the previous year's wood. These normally flower in May and June and the only pruning required is to trim back the old flowering growths immediately after flowering. Old, dense-habited plants may also be hard pruned in February, but the first crop of flowers will thus be lost.

(*b*) Applies to the JACKMANII, TEXENSIS and VITICELLA groups which flower on the current year's shoots. These normally flower in late summer and autumn and may be hard pruned to within 30cm. of the ground in February or March. Old unpruned plants tend to become bare at the base.

The letters in parentheses following the names indicate the groups to which the cultivars belong, viz:—(F)—FLORIDA, (J)—JACKMANII, (L) LANUGINOSA, (P)—PATENS, (T)—TEXENSIS and (V)—VITICELLA.

CLEMATIS—*continued*

'Ascotiensis' (V). Azure blue, pointed sepals, very floriferous; July to September.

'Barbara Dibley' (P). Pansy-violet, with deep carmine stripe along each sepal; May and June and again in September.

'Beauty of Worcester' (L). Blue-violet, with contrasting creamy-white stamens; occasionally produces double flowers; May to August.

'Belle of Woking' (F). Pale mauve, double; May and June.

'Blue Gem' (L). Sky blue, large; June to October.

'Comtesse de Bouchaud' (J). Beautiful soft rose-pink, with yellow stamens, vigorous and free flowering; June to August. A.M. 1936. A.G.M. 1969.

'Daniel Deronda' (P). Large violet-blue, paler at centre, with creamy stamens; flowers often double; June to September.

'Duchess of Albany' (T). Flowers tubular, nodding, bright pink, shading to lilac-pink at margins; July to September. A.M. 1897.

'Duchess of Edinburgh' (F). Large double, rosette-like, white with green shading, scented; May and June.

'Duchess of Sutherland' (V). Petunia-red with a darker bar on each tapered sepal, often double; July and August.

'Ernest Markham' (V). Glowing petunia-red, with a velvety sheen, sepals rounded; June to September. A.G.M. 1973.

'Fairy Queen' (L). Pale flesh pink, with bright central bars; very large; May and June. F.C.C. 1875.

'Gipsy Queen' (J). Rich velvety violet-purple with broad, rounded sepals; vigorous and free-flowering; July to September.

'Gravetye Beauty' (T). Flowers bell-shaped at first, the sepals later spreading, cherry-red; July to September. A.M. 1935.

'Hagley Hybrid' (J). Shell-pink with contrasting chocolate-brown anthers, free-flowering; June to September.

'Henryi' (L). Large, creamy-white, with pointed sepals and dark stamens; vigorous and free-flowering; May and June and again in August and September. A.G.M. 1973.

'Huldine' (V). Pearly-white, the pointed sepals with a mauve bar on the reverse; vigorous and free-flowering; requires full sun; July to October. A.M. 1934.

'Jackmanii'. See *C.* ×*jackmanii* under Species.

'Jackmanii Superba' (J). Large, rich violet-purple with broad sepals; vigorous and free-flowering; July to September.

'King George V' (L). Flesh-pink, each sepal with a dark central bar; July and August.

'Lady Betty Balfour' (V). Deep velvety-purple, with golden stamens; very vigorous, best in full sun; August to October. A.M. 1912.

'Lady Londesborough' (P). Pale mauve at first, becoming silvery-grey, with dark stamens and broad, overlapping sepals; free-flowering; May and June. F.C.C. 1869.

'Lasurstern' (P). Deep lavender-blue, with conspicuous white stamens and broad, tapering, wavy-margined sepals; May and June and again in early autumn. A.G.M. 1969.

'Madame Edouard Andre' (J). Rich crimson, with yellow stamens and pointed sepals; very free-flowering; June to August.

'Marcel Moser' (P). Mauve, each tapered sepal with a deep carmine central bar; May and June. A.M. 1897.

'Marie Boisselot' (P). Large, pure white, with cream stamens and broad, rounded, overlapping sepals; vigorous and free-flowering. May to October.

'Mrs. Cholmondely' (J). Large, pale blue, with long pointed sepals; vigorous and free-flowering; May to August. F.C.C. 1873.

'Mrs. Spencer Castle' (V). Large, pale heliotrope, sometimes double; May and June and again in early autumn.

'Nelly Moser' (L). One of the most popular. Large, pale mauve-pink, each sepal with a carmine central bar; very free-flowering, but best on a north wall or in a shady position to prevent bleaching. May and June and again in August and September. A.G.M. 1969.

'Perle d'Azur' (J). Light blue, with broad sepals; vigorous and free-flowering; June to August. A.G.M. 1973.

'Sensation' (L). Bright satiny mauve; May and June. F.C.C. 1867.

'The President' (P). A popular clematis. Deep purple-blue, with silvery reverse; free-flowering; June to September. F.C.C. 1876.

CLEMATIS—*continued*

'Ville de Lyon' (V). Bright carmine-red, deeper at margins, with golden stamens; July to October. A.M. 1901.

'Vyvyan Pennell' (P). Described by its raisers as the best double clematis yet raised. Deep violet-blue, suffused purple and carmine in centre. Fully double and produced from May to July. Single lavender-blue flowers are also produced in autumn.

'W. E. Gladstone' (L). Very large, silky lavender, with purple anthers; vigorous and free-flowering. June to September. F.C.C. 1881.

'William Kennet' (L). Lavender-blue with dark stamens and sepals with crimpled margins; June to August.

CLEMATOCLETHRA—Actinidiaceae—Twining climbers related to *Actinidia*, but differing in the solid pith and the flowers having ten stamens and a single style (numerous in *Actinidia*). Useful subjects for a wall or tree in sun or semi-shade.

integrifolia MAXIM. A climber up to 7·5m., with ovate-oblong leaves, 4 to 7cm. long, bristle-toothed, glaucous beneath. Flowers solitary or in clusters, small, white and fragrant, produced in June. N.W. China. I. 1908.

lasioclada MAXIM. Attains up to 6m., with downy shoots. Leaves ovate, 5 to 10cm. long, bristle-toothed. Flowers white, borne in axillary cymes in July. W. China. I. 1908.

strigillosa FRANCH. A rare and distinct species with comparatively broad leaves. China.

CLETHRA arborea. See Tree and Shrub section.

CLIANTHUS puniceus. See Tree and Shrub section.

"CLIMBING HYDRANGEA". See *HYDRANGEA petiolaris*.

COCCULUS—Menispermaceae—A small genus of twining climbers suitable for growing into trees, hedges or on trellis-work in sun or semi-shade.

trilobus DC. A variable species up to 4·5m., with long-persistent leaves entire or three-lobed, orbicular to ovate acuminate. Flowers small and inconspicuous, borne in axillary clusters in August. Fruits rounded, black, with a blue bloom. Japan; China. I. before 1870.

COLQUHOUNIA. See Tree and Shrub section.

CORNUS capitata. See Tree and Shrub section.

chinensis. See Tree and Shrub section.

oblonga. See Tree and Shrub section.

COROKIA. See Tree and Shrub section.

CORONILLA glauca. See Tree and Shrub section.

valentina. See Tree and Shrub section.

COTONEASTER. Several species, e.g. *C. franchetii; C. horizontalis* and cvs.; *C. lacteus* and *C. salicifolius* and cvs. See Tree and Shrub section.

CRINODENDRON. See Tree and Shrub section.

CYTISUS battandieri. See Tree and Shrub section.

monspessulanus. See Tree and Shrub section.

'Porlock'. See Tree and Shrub section.

DAPHNE odora. See Tree and Shrub section.

DECUMARIA—Hydrangeaceae—A genus of two perfectly hardy species of shrubs climbing by means of aerial roots. They are related to *Hydrangea*, but differ in that all their flowers are fertile. Like the climbing Hydrangeas and Schizophragmas they succeed in sun or shade on a wall or tree trunk.

barbara L. A semi-evergreen climber up to 9m. Leaves ovate 7·5 to 13cm. long. The small, white flowers are carried in small corymbs in June and July. Native of S.E. United States where it climbs the trunks of trees. I. 1785.

***sinensis** OLIV. A rare evergreen species up to 5m. with obovate or oblanceolate leaves 2·5 to 9cm. long. The small, green and white flowers are profusely carried in corymbs in May and are deliciously honey-scented. C. China. I. 1908. A.M. 1974.

DENDROMECON. See Tree and Shrub section.

DESFONTAINEA. See Tree and Shrub section.

DICHOTOMANTHES. See Tree and Shrub section.

DIOSPYROS kaki. See Tree and Shrub section.

DREGEA. See *WATTAKAKA*.

DRIMYS. See Tree and Shrub section.

ECCREMOCARPUS—Bignoniaceae—A small genus of evergreen or nearly evergreen climbers climbing by means of coiling leaf tendrils. The following species is hardy in a sheltered corner in southern gardens, but in colder areas may be treated either as a conservatory subject or as a half hardy annual.

scaber RUIZ. & PAV. A vigorous, fast-growing climber, quickly covering a support with its angular stems 3 to 4·5m. long. Leaves bi-pinnate ending in a slender tendril. The scarlet to orange-yellow, tubular flowers, 2·5cm. long, are borne in racemes which are continuously produced throughout summer and autumn. Fruit a capsule, packed with small, winged seeds. Chile. I. 1824.

†***ELYTROPUS—Apocynaceae**—A rare, monotypic genus.

chilensis MUELL. A strong-growing, twining, evergreen climber 3 to 4·5m. high, with slender, bristly stems. Leaves opposite, elliptic to elliptic-oblong, acuminate, bristly hairy and conspicuously fringed. The small, white, lilac flushed flowers are produced singly, or in pairs, in the axils of the leaves in spring. Fruits when produced are green, ripening to yellow. A rare climber suitable for a small tree or trellis or against a sheltered wall in milder areas of the British Isles, perhaps preferring semi-shade to full sun. Chile; Argentine.

***ERCILLA—Phytolaccaceae**—A genus of two species of evergreen climbers supporting themselves by means of aerial roots. May be grown on a wall in sun or shade, or as a ground cover.

volubilis A. JUSS. (*spicata*) (*Bridgesia spicata*). A self-clinging evergreen climber with rounded leathery leaves and dense sessile spikes of small, purplish-white flowers during spring. Chile. Introduced by Thomas Bridges in 1840, and more recently by Harold Comber. A.M. 1975.

ERIOBOTRYA. See Tree and Shrub section.

ESCALLONIA. See Tree and Shrub section.

EUONYMUS fortunei radicans. See Tree and Shrub section.

FABIANA. See Tree and Shrub section.

FEIJOA. See Tree and Shrub section.

FENDLERA. See Tree and Shrub section.

FORSYTHIA suspensa and cvs. See Tree and Shrub section.

FREMONTODENDRON. See Tree and Shrub section.

FREYLINIA. See Tree and Shrub section.

GARRYA elliptica. See Tree and Shrub section.

†***GELSEMIUM—Loganiaceae**—A genus of two species of tender evergreen, twining shrubs producing attractive flowers. The following species requires a sunny, sheltered wall.

sempervirens AIT. f. (*nitidum*). A species with stems up to 6m. long bearing oblong or ovate-lanceolate, glossy-green leaves 3·5 to 5cm. long and fragrant, yellow, funnel-shaped flowers 2·5cm. long during late spring or early summer. S. United States.

"GRANADILLA". See *PASSIFLORA edulis.*

GREVILLEA. See Tree and Shrub section.

HEBE hulkeana. See Tree and Shrub section.

***HEDERA—Araliaceae**—"Ivy". A small but familiar genus of evergreen climbers attaching themselves to walls or tree trunks by means of aerial roots. There are no other self-clinging evergreens comparable with the ivies, thriving as they do in almost any soil, or situation, climbing without artificial aid to great heights or clothing bare ground beneath trees or shrubs where not even grass would grow. When large specimens on walls are becoming too dense, they may be pruned severely. The ivies are excellent for industrial sites and for withstanding atmospheric pollution. The leaves of the climbing (sterile) shoots are often markedly different from those of the flowering (fertile) shoots, this is particularly noticeable in the "Common Ivy"—*H. helix*. The flowers of the ivy are small and inconspicuous, borne in greenish umbels and replaced by usually black berry-like fruits.

amurensis. See *H. colchica.*

azorica. See *H. canariensis 'Azorica'.*

canariensis WILLD. (*helix canariensis*) (*algeriensis*) (*maderensis*). "Canary Island Ivy". A strong-growing species with large leaves up to 15cm. or even 20cm. across. Those of the climbing shoots are kidney-shaped, sometimes obscurely three-lobed, those of the flowering shoots rounded with a cordate base. They are a bright green during summer, often turning a deep bronze with green veins in winter, particularly if growing in a dry situation. Azores; Portugal; Canary Isles: N.W. Africa; Madeira. C. 1833.

HEDERA—*continued*

canariensis 'Azorica' (*viridis*) (*H. azorica*). A form with broad leaves of a light matt green, those of the climbing shoots with five to seven blunt lobes.

'Variegata'. See *'Gloire de Marengo'*.

'Gloire de Marengo' (*'Variegata'*). An attractive and colourful form with large leaves, deep green in the centre, merging into silvery-grey and margined white. Admirably suitable for patio gardens and low walls, etc. Less hardy than the type. It is a popular house plant. F.C.C. 1880. A.G.M. 1973.

chrysocarpa. See *H. helix poetica*.

colchica K. KOCH (*amurensis*) (*roegnerana*). "Persian Ivy". A handsome, strong-growing species with leaves the largest in the genus, ovate or elliptic and 15 to 20cm. long or more on the climbing shoots, smaller and oblong-ovate on the flowering shoots; all leaves are dark green, thick and leathery. Caucasus; S. Anatolia. C. 1850.

'Arborescens'. A shrubby form developing into a small, densely leafy mound with large, oblong-ovate leaves. Raised from a cutting of the flowering growth of the type, free fruiting.

'Dentata'. A spectacular climber with leaves even larger than those of the type and somewhat more irregular in outline, slightly softer green and with occasional teeth. A.M.T. 1980.

'Dentata Variegata'. A most ornamental ivy with large, broad, ovate to elliptic often elongated leaves which are bright green shading to grey and conspicuously margined creamy-yellow when young, creamy-white when mature. Hardier than *H. canariensis 'Gloire de Marengo'*, and just as effective in patio gardens, on walls, etc. A.M. 1907. A.G.M. 1969. F.C.C.T. 1980.

'Sulphur Heart' (*'Paddy's Pride'*). An impressive variegated ivy. The large, broadly ovate leaves are boldly marked by an irregular central splash of yellow, merging into pale green and finally deep green. Occasionally almost an entire leaf is yellow. On old leaves the yellow splash becomes pale yellow-green. *'Gold Leaf'* is the same or very similar. A.M.T. 1980.

helix L. "Common Ivy". One of the most adaptable and variable of all plants. It makes an excellent ground cover and is particularly useful where little else will grow. Leaves of climbing shoots variable, three to five-lobed, those of the flowering shoots ovate to rhomboidal, entire. Europe; Asia Minor to N. Persia.

'Arborescens'. A shrubby form developing into a broad, densely-leafy mound. Originated as a cutting from the flowering shoots of the type.

'Atropurpurea'. Leaves entire, or with two short lateral lobes. Dark purplish-green, darker in winter, often with bright green veins. A.M.T. 1980.

'Aureovariegata' (*'Chrysophylla'*). Leaves irregularly suffused soft yellow, but liable to revert.

'Buttercup'. The best golden form of the "Common Ivy". Leaves of a rich yellow, becoming yellowish-green or pale green with age. A.G.M. 1973.

'Caenwoodiana'. A charming form with small leaves regularly divided into narrow lobes, of which the middle lobe is longest.

'Cavendishii'. A pretty form with small, angular green leaves mottled grey and broadly margined creamy-white.

'Chicago'. A form with small, dark green leaves frequently stained or blotched bronze-purple.

'Chrysophylla'. See *'Aureovariegata'*.

'Congesta'. See *'Erecta'*.

'Conglomerata'. A dense, slow-growing form with stiffly erect stems forming a low hummock. Leaves with or without lobes, obtuse at the apex and with a distinct wavy margin. Excellent for rock garden or woodland garden. F.C.C. 1872. A.M.T. 1980.

'Cristata'. A distinct and unusual form with pale green, often rounded leaves which are attractively twisted and crimpled at the margin.

'Deltoidea' (*'Hastata'*). A distinct form of neat, close growth. The leaves possess two basal lobes which are rounded and overlapping. Becoming bronze-tinged in winter.

'Digitata'. Leaves broad, divided into five finger-like lobes.

'Emerald Gem'. See under *poetica*.

'Erecta' (*'Conglomerata Erecta'*) (*'Congesta'*). A slow-growing form with stiffly erect shoots, similar to *'Conglomerata'*. Leaves arrow-shaped with acute apex. An excellent plant for growing by a boulder on the rock garden or against a low tree stump.

HEDERA—*continued*

'Feastii'. See *'Sagittifolia'*.

'Glacier'. Leaves small, silvery-grey with a narrow white margin. A.M.T. 1980.

'Glymii' (*Tortuosa*). Leaves ovate, somewhat curled or twisted, especially during cold weather. Often turning reddish-purple in winter.

'Goldheart'. A most striking form of neat growth, the leaves with a large, conspicuous central splash of yellow. A.M. 1970. Wrongly called *'Jubilee'* in recent years. A.G.M. 1973.

'Gracilis'. A slender form with prettily-lobed leaves.

'Green Ripple'. An attractive form with small, jaggedly-lobed leaves, the central lobe long and tapering. A.M.T. 1980.

'Hastata'. See *'Deltoidea'*.

'Hibernica' (*H. hibernica*) (*H. scotica*). "Irish Ivy". A distinct form with large, dark green leaves 7·5 to 15cm. across, usually five-lobed. A vigorous ivy, particularly useful as a ground cover. The origin of this ivy is rather obscure. It is thought to have arisen in the wild in Ireland early in the 19th century.

'Marginata' (*'Argentea Elegans'*). Leaves triangular-ovate, broadly margined white, often tinged pink in winter.

'Marginata Elegantissima' (*'Tricolor'*) (*'Marginata Rubra'*). A pretty form with small leaves of greyish-green, margined white and edged rose-red in winter. *'Silver Queen'* is a similar clone.

'Marmorata Minor'. An unusual form with small leaves mottled and marbled with cream and grey, occasionally pink tinged during winter.

'Meagheri' (*'Green Feather'*). An unusual cultivar with small, pointed, deeply cut leaves.

'Palmata'. A rather slow-growing form with palmately-lobed leaves.

poetica WEST (*H. chrysocarpa*). "Italian Ivy". An attractive ivy distinguished by its bright green, shallowly-lobed leaves and the yellow fruits of the adult growth. In winter, the older leaves often turn a bright copper colour with green veins. Greece and Turkey (naturalised in Italy and France); N. Africa; S.W. Asia. *'Emerald Gem'* is a named clone.

rhombea. See *H. rhombea*.

'Sagittifolia (*'Feastii'*). A neat-growing form with five-lobed leaves, the central lobe large and triangular.

'Silver Queen'. See under *'Marginata Elegantissima'*.

'Sulphur Heart'. See under *H. colchica 'Paddy's Pride'*.

'Tortuosa'. See *'Glymii'*.

'Tricolor'. See *'Marginata Elegantissima'*.

hibernica. See *H. helix 'Hibernica'*.

nepalensis K. KOCH (*cinerea*) (*himalaica*). "Himalayan Ivy". A strong-growing species with greyish-green, ovate to ovate-lanceolate, taper-pointed leaves, 5 to 13cm. long, occasionally with two basal lobes and several blunt teeth. Fruits usually yellow or rarely red. Himalaya. C. 1880.

rhombea BEAN (*helix rhombea*). "Japanese Ivy". The Japanese equivalent to our native ivy, differing from the common species in its ovate or triangular-ovate leaves with sometimes two shallow lobes. Japan.

HIBISCUS. See Tree and Shrub section.

HOHERIA. See Tree and Shrub section.

***HOLBOELLIA**—**Lardizabalaceae**—A small genus related to *Stauntonia* of luxuriant, evergreen, twining plants with compound leaves and monoecious flowers. Growing in any fertile soil in sun or shade, but requiring sun for flower and fruit.

coriacea DIELS. A vigorous, hardy species up to 6m. or more. Leaves composed of three, stalked, glossy-green leaflets, 7·5 to 15cm. long. Flowers appearing in April and May, the purplish male flowers in terminal clusters, the greenish-white, purplish-tinged, female flowers in axillary clusters. Fruit a purplish, fleshy pod 4 to 7·5cm. long, filled with rows of black seeds. A useful climber for growing on walls, drainpipes or into trees. C. China. Introduced by Ernest Wilson in 1907.

latifolia WALL. (*Stauntonia latifolia*). An attractive, but slightly tender species with leaves consisting of three to seven-stalked leaflets, 7·5 to 18cm. long. The fragrant flowers are borne in short racemes during March, the male flowers greenish-white, the female flowers purplish. Fruit an edible, purple, sausage-shaped, fleshy pod 5 to 7·5cm. long. Hand pollination is usually required to ensure fruiting. May be distinguished from *H. coriacea* by the more pronounced reticulate venation. Himalaya. I. 1840.

"HONEYSUCKLE". See *LONICERA.*
"HONEYSUCKLE, CAPE". See *TECOMARIA capensis.*
"HOP". See *HUMULUS.*

HUMULUS—Cannabidaceae—A small genus of perennial climbers with monoecious flowers. Though herbaceous in nature, the following species and its attractive golden-leaved form are vigorous plants and useful for giving summer clothing to unsightly objects, hedges, etc.

lupulus L. "Hop". A familiar, native climber with long, twining stems 3 to 6m. long. Commonly seen scrambling in hedges and thickets. Leaves 7·5 to 15cm. long, deeply three to five-lobed and coarsely toothed. The female flowers are borne in drooping, yellowish-green, cone-like clusters during late summer, enlarging in fruit. The fruit clusters are a valuable constituent of the best beers, for which purpose this plant is extensively cultivated in certain districts. S. Europe; W. Asia.

'Aureus'. An attractive form with soft yellow leaves. Best grown in full sun. It is most effective when trained on a pergola or a wooden tripod.

HYDRANGEA—Hydrangeaceae—The species here described are climbing shrubs, attaching themselves to trees or walls by means of aerial roots. They are excellent in such positions and are equally happy in sun or semi-shade in all types of soils. They are excellent for industrial sites and withstanding atmospheric pollution.

altissima. See *H. anomala.*

anomala D. DON (*altissima*). A vigorous climber reaching a height of 12m. or above in a suitable tree. Mature bark brown and peeling. Leaves ovate or elliptic, coarsely-toothed. Flowers arranged in slightly domed corymbs, 15 to 20cm. across, in June, small, yellowish-white with several conspicuous, white, sterile florets along the margin. Himalaya to W. China. I. 1839.

integerrima. See *H. serratifolia.*

petiolaris SIEB. & ZUCC. (*scandens* MAXIM. not SER.) (*anomala petiolaris*). "Climbing Hydrangea". A strong-growing, self-clinging species reaching 18 to 25m. in suitable trees and excellent on a north facing or otherwise shady wall; in addition it is very picturesque when grown as a shrub. Leaves broadly ovate, abruptly pointed and finely-toothed. Flowers in corymbs 15 to 25cm. across in June, dull, greenish-white, with several large, conspicuous, white, sterile florets along the margin. Vigorous enough when once established, it may require initial support until its aerial roots become active. Japan; Kuriles; Sakhalin; S. Korea. I. 1865. A.G.M. 1924.

scandens MAXIM. See *H. petiolaris.*

***serratifolia** PHIL. f. (*integerrima*). An evergreen species with stout, elliptic to obovate, leathery leaves which are entire and usually marked with curious, tiny pits in the vein axils beneath. Flowers small, creamy-white, borne in crowded, columnar panicles, 7·5 to 15cm. long, in late summer. Best grown against a wall in sun or shade, though in its native forests it is known to reach 15m. or more in suitable trees. Chile. Introduced by Harold Comber in 1925/27. A.M. 1952.

HYPERICUM leschenaultii. See Tree and Shrub section.

'Rowallane'. See Tree and Shrub section.

ITEA ilicifolia. See Tree and Shrub section.

"IVY". See *HEDERA.*
"IVY, BOSTON". See *PARTHENOCISSUS tricuspidata.*
"JASMINE". See *JASMINUM.*
"JASMINE, CHILEAN". See *MANDEVILLA suaveolens.*

JASMINUM—Oleaceae—"Jasmine"; "Jessamine". A large genus of both twining and scandent shrubs, with small, trumpet-shaped, usually fragrant flowers. Easily grown in most fertile soils, preferring a sunny position. They are excellent for training up walls or pergolas and several are useful for covering unsightly banks. The hardy species are excellent for withstanding industrial sites. See also Tree and Shrub section.

†*angulare VAHL (*capense*). A choice but tender species with rather thickish, dark green, trifoliolate leaves. The sweetly-scented, white flowers, 5cm. long, are borne in large panicles during late summer. Only suitable for the mildest localities, but a beautiful conservatory subject. S. Africa. A.M. 1956.

†*azoricum L. (*trifoliatum*). A beautiful, twining species with trifoliolate leaves and clusters of white, sweetly-scented flowers, purple-flushed in bud, opening in summer and winter. Only suitable for the mildest localities. An excellent conservatory plant. Madeira. I. late 17th century. A.M. 1934.

JASMINUM—*continued*

beesianum FORR. & DIELS. A vigorous, scandent shrub developing a dense tangle of slender stems, 2·5 to 3·5m. long. Leaves tapering to a long point, dark, dull green. Flowers fragrant, rather small, of an unusual deep velvet-red, appearing in May and June; followed by shining black berries which often last well into winter. W. China. I. 1906.

†**dispermum** WALL. A delightful climber with twining stems and leaves varying from trifoliolate to pinnate on the same plant. The fragrant, white, pink-flushed flowers are borne in axillary and terminal cymes during summer. Only suitable for the mildest localities, but admirable as a conservatory plant. Himalaya. C. 1848. A.M. 1937.

diversifolium. See *J. subhumile.*

†***floridum** BGE. (*giraldii*). An evergreen species of scandent growth, with angular shoots and usually trifoliolate leaves. Flowers yellow, appearing in terminal clusters during late summer and early autumn. Requires a warm, sunny wall. W. China. I. 1850.

humile. See Tree and Shrub section.

†**mesnyi** HANCE (*primulinum*). "Primrose Jasmine". A singularly beautiful, almost evergreen species with four-angled shoots and opposite trifoliolate leaves, 2·5 to 7·5cm. long. Flowers bright yellow, 4cm. long, semi-double and produced in succession from March to May. A strong-growing species with scandent stems up to 4·5m. long. Best grown against a warm sheltered sunny wall in favoured localities or in a conservatory. Introduced from S.W. China by E. H. Wilson in 1900. F.C.C. 1903.

nudiflorum. See Tree and Shrub section.

officinale L. "Common White Jasmine". A strong-growing, scandent or twining climber, reaching 6 to 9m. in a suitable tree. Leaves pinnate, composed of five to nine leaflets. Flowers white, deliciously fragrant, borne in terminal clusters from June to September. An old favourite cottage garden plant, said to have been introduced into Britain as long ago as 1548. It requires a sheltered corner in cold northern districts. Caucasus, N. Persia and Afghanistan, through the Himalaya to China. A.G.M. 1973.

'Affine' (*'Grandiflorum'*). A superior form with slightly larger flowers which are usually tinged pink on the outside. Not to be confused with *J. grandiflorum,* a tender species for the greenhouse.

'Aureum' (*'Aureovariegatum'*). Leaves variegated and suffused yellow; a very effective plant.

'Grandiflorum'. See *'Affine'*.

†***polyanthum** FRANCH. A beautiful, vigorous, twining species up to 7·5m., related to *J. officinale,* but tender. Leaves pinnate, composed of five or seven leaflets. The intensely fragrant, white flowers, flushed rose on the outside, are borne in numerous panicles from May until late summer, earlier under glass. Requires a warm wall or trellis in mild localities, but makes an excellent conservatory subject elsewhere providing it is kept under control by rigorous pruning. China. I. 1891. A.M. 1941. F.C.C. 1949.

primulinum. See *J. mesnyi.*

× **stephanense** LEMOINE (*beesianum* × *officinale*). A vigorous climber up to 7·5m., with slender green, angular shoots. Leaves simple or pinnate, with three to ve leaflets. Flowers fragrant, pale pink, borne in terminal clusters in June and July. The leaves of young or vigorous shoots are often variegated creamy-white or creamy-yellow. Interesting on account of it being the only known hybrid Jasmine. It is a beautiful plant where space permits its full development such as when covering an outhouse. It was raised in France just prior to 1920, but similar hybrids are known to occur in the wild in Yunnan (China), where both parent species are found. A.M. 1937.

†**suavissimum** LINDL. (*lineatum*). A tall growing conservatory species with slender twining stems and linear leaves 2·5 to 6cm. long. The white, sweetly-fragrant flowers are borne in loose panicles during late summer. They will perfume the whole conservatory. Australia.

†**subhumile** W. W. SM. (*diversifolium*) (*heterophyllum*). A scandent shrub with purplish young shoots and alternate dark glossy green, leathery privet-like leaves, occasionally with one or two small, slender subsidiary leaflets. Flowers small, yellow, star-like, in slender glabrous cymes during late spring. The form we offer is the variety *glabricymosum,* differing little from type. E. Himalaya. I. 1820.

†***KADSURA**—**Schisandraceae**—A small genus of evergreen twining plants related to *Schisandra*. Flowers dioecious.

japonica DUN. A slender climber up to 3·6m., with dark green, oval or lanceolate leaves, 5 to 10cm. long, glossy green, often turning red in autumn. Flowers solitary, cream coloured 2cm. across, appearing during summer and early autumn. Female plants bear scarlet fruit-clusters. Requires a warm, sheltered wall; best in mild localities. Japan; China; Formosa. I. 1860.

'Variegata'. Leaves with a broad margin of creamy-white.

KERRIA japonica 'Pleniflora'. See Tree and Shrub section.

LAGERSTROEMIA. See Tree and Shrub section.

†***LAPAGERIA**—**Philesiaceae**—A monotypic genus requiring a cool, moist, lime-free soil in shade or semi-shade. Succeeding best on a sheltered wall. It is an excellent conservatory plant, but detests long exposure to strong sunlight.

rosea RUIZ. & PAV. One of the most beautiful of all flowering climbers. An evergreen with strong, wiry, twining stems reaching 3 to 4·5m. on a suitable wall. Leaves ovate-lanceolate to cordate, leathery. The rose-crimson, fleshy, bell-shaped flowers, 7·5cm. long by 5cm. wide, are borne singly or in pendulous clusters from the axils of the upper leaves during most of summer and autumn. A lovely plant for a shaded sheltered wall in the milder counties. Chile; Argentine. I. 1847. F.C.C. 1974.

†***LARDIZABALA**—**Lardizabalaceae**—A genus of two species of evergreen twining plants with compound leaves and dioecious flowers. Suitable for a sheltered wall in sun or semi-shade, but only in mild localities.

biternata RUIZ. & PAV. A fairly vigorous climber with leaves composed of three to nine dark green, glossy, oblong leaves. Flowers chocolate-purple and white, the males in pendulous racemes, the females solitary, appearing during winter. Female plants bear sweet, sausage-shaped, edible, dark purple fruits 5 to 7·5cm. long. Chile. I. 1844.

LONICERA—**Caprifoliaceae**—"Honeysuckle". The climbing species of this large genus contain some of the loveliest and most popular of all twining plants. All are worth cultivating, though none surpass the fragrance of our common native hedgerow species—*L. periclymenum*. They are probably seen at their best when scrambling over other bushes, or tree stumps, trellises or pergolas, but are very adaptable to other purposes and some are even occasionally grown as small standards. Although some flower best with their "heads" in full sun, many honeysuckles luxuriate in half-shade or even complete shade and in such positions are less susceptible to aphis. They are happy in almost all soils. The funnel-shaped or trumpet-shaped flowers are pollinated by hawk-moths and humble-bees, etc.

***acuminata** WALL. A vigorous, even rampant, evergreen or semi-evergreen species related to *L. japonica;* excellent as a rapid ground cover. Himalaya.

***alseuosmoides** GRAEBN. An evergreen species with glabrous shoots and narrowly oblong, ciliate leaves. Flowers small, funnel-shaped, 12mm. long, yellow outside, purple within, carried in short, broad panicles on the young growths from July to October. Berries black, blue-bloomy. W. China. I. by Wilson about 1904.

× **americana** K. KOCH (*caprifolium* × *etrusca*) (*grata*) (*italica*). A magnificent, extremely free-flowering, vigorous climber reaching a height of 9m. under suitable conditions. Leaves broad elliptic to obovate. Flowers 4 to 5cm. long, fragrant, white, soon passing to pale and finally deep yellow, heavily tinged purple outside, appearing in whorls at the ends of the shoots and providing one of the most spectacular floral displays of late June and July. C. before 1730. A.M. 1937. A.G.M. 1955.

× **brownii** CARR. (*hirsuta* × *sempervirens*). "Scarlet Trumpet Honeysuckle". A deciduous or semi-evergreen climber of moderate vigour. Leaves up to 8·5 cm. long, downy and glaucous beneath, the upper leaves perfoliate. Flowers 2·5 to 4cm. long, orange-scarlet, borne in whorls at the ends of the branches in late spring, and again in late summer. Garden origin, before 1850. There are several named clones. See also '*Dropmore Scarlet*'.

'Fuchsoides'. This clone of equal beauty, is scarcely distinguishable from the typical form.

'Plantierensis'. Flowers coral-red, with orange lobes.

LONICERA—*continued*

caprifolium L. (*'Early Cream'*). "Perfoliate Honeysuckle". A fairly vigorous climber up to 6m., with obovate or oval, glaucous leaves, the upper pairs of which are perfoliate. Flowers 4 to 5cm. long, fragrant, creamy-white, very occasionally tinged pink on the outside, borne in whorls at the ends of the shoots in June and July. Berries orange-red. A popular species commonly planted in cottage gardens. The perfoliate upper leaves easily distinguishes it from *L. periclymenum*. C. and S. Europe; Caucasus; Asia Minor. Long cultivated and occasionally naturalised in the British Isles.

'Pauciflora'. Flowers rose-tinged on the outside.

ciliosa POIR. "Western Trumpet Honeysuckle". An American honeysuckle related to *L. sempervirens*, but differing in its ciliate leaves, the upper pairs of which are perfoliate. Flowers 2·5 to 4cm. long, yellow, tinged purple on the outside, borne in whorls at the ends of the shoots in June. Western N. America. I. 1825. A.M. 1919.

'Dropmore Scarlet' (Brownii Group). A tall-growing climber, producing clusters of bright scarlet, tubular flowers, from July to October.

etrusca SANTI. A very vigorous deciduous or semi-evergreen climber with purplish young shoots and oval or obovate, glaucous, usually downy leaves which become perfoliate at the ends of the shoots. Flowers 4cm. long, fragrant, opening cream, often flushed red, deepening to yellow, borne in whorls at the ends of the shoots in June and July, but not on young plants. A superb species revelling in sun and seen at its best in the drier counties. Mediterranean Region. I. about 1750.

flexuosa. See *L. japonica repens*.

***giraldii** REHD. An evergreen species forming a dense tangle of slender, hairy stems. Leaves narrowly oblong, heart-shaped at base, 4 to 9cm. long and densely hairy. Flowers 2cm. long, purplish-red, with yellow stamens, yellowish pubescent on the outside, produced in terminal clusters in June and July. Berries purplish-black. Useful for growing over a low wall or parapet. N.W. China. I. 1899.

glaucescens RYDB. A bushy shrub with twining stems and obovate to narrow elliptic leaves, glaucous and pubescent beneath. Flowers 2cm. long, yellow, borne in terminal whorls in June and July. N. America. C. 1890.

grata. See *L.* ×*americana*.

× **heckrottii** REHD. (*americana* × *sempervirens*) (*'Gold Flame'*). A shrubby plant with scandent branches. Leaves oblong or elliptic, glaucous beneath, the upper ones perfoliate. Flowers 4 to 5cm. long, fragrant, yellow, heavily flushed purple, abundantly borne in whorls at the ends of the shoots from July to August or September. Origin uncertain, before 1895.

***henryi** HEMSL. A vigorous evergreen or semi-evergreen species with downy shoots and oblong, slender pointed, ciliate leaves, 4 to 10cm. long, dark green above, paler and glossy beneath. Flowers yellow, stained red, 2cm. long, borne in terminal clusters in June and July, followed by black berries. W. China. I. 1908.

subcoriacea REHD. The commonest form in cultivation, with larger, ovate-oblong, slightly leathery leaves and slightly larger flowers. W. China. I. 1910.

†*hildebrandiana COLL. & HEMSL. "Giant Honeysuckle". This magnificent species is a giant in every respect. A strong-growing, evergreen climber, in its native forests reaching into lofty trees. Leaves broadly oval, 7·5 to 15cm. long. Flowers 9 to 15cm. long, fragrant, creamy-white at first, changing to rich yellow occasionally flushed orange-yellow, produced in the terminal leaf axils from June to August; berries 2·5 to 3cm. long. This wonderful species is only suitable for the very mildest localities of the British Isles, but makes a spectacular, if rampant, climber for the conservatory. It is the largest in size, leaf, flower and fruit of all the honeysuckles. Shy flowering when young. Burma; Siam; S.W. China. First discovered in the Shan Hills (Burma) by Sir Henry Collet in 1888. F.C.C. 1901.

***implexa** SOL. An evergreen or semi-evergreen climber with glabrous shoots and ovate to oblong leaves, glaucous beneath, the upper ones perfoliate. Flowers 4 to 5cm. long, yellow, flushed pink on the outside, borne in whorls at the ends of the shoots from June to August. Our propagator was shaken when he first received this species as cuttings by air from Mr. H. G. Hillier in 1934, who was then on honeymoon. S. Europe. I. 1772.

italica. See *L.* ×*americana*.

LONICERA—*continued*

***japonica** THUNB. A rampant evergreen or semi-evergreen species reaching 6 to 9m. on a suitable support. Leaves ovate to oblong, often lobed on young or vigorous shoots. Flowers fragrant, 2·5 to 4cm. long, white, changing to yellow with age, produced continuously from June onwards. An excellent climber or creeper for covering and concealing unsightly objects. As a ground-cover it must be kept under control; it is becoming a pest in parts of North America. Japan; Korea; Manchuria; China. I. 1806. A.G.M. 1950. We offer the following forms:—

'Aureoreticulata'. A delightful form of var. *repens*, the neat, bright green leaves with a conspicuous golden reticulation. A.G.M. 1969.

'Halliana'. Flowers white, changing to yellow, very fragrant. Considered by some authorities to be the typical form. A.G.M. 1969.

repens REHD. (*L. flexuosa* THUNB.). A distinct variety, the leaves and shoots flushed purple; flowers flushed purple on the outside, very fragrant. Japan; China. Introduced early in the 19th century.

periclymenum L. "Woodbine". The common honeysuckle of our hedgerows and woods. A vigorous species climbing, scrambling or trailing in habit. Leaves ovate to oblong, glaucous beneath. Flowers 4 to 5cm. long, strongly and sweetly fragrant, creamy-white within, darkening with age, purplish or yellowish outside, appearing in terminal clusters from June to September. Berries red. A pretty climber, long connected with old cottage gardens. Europe; N. and C. Morocco.

'Belgica'. "Early Dutch Honeysuckle". Flowers reddish-purple on the outside fading to yellowish, produced during May and June and again in late summer. Plants under this name have been grown and distributed by British and Continental nurserymen for many years but we have been unable to distinguish any real difference between this clone and '*Serotina*'. Plants received by us from other sources are sometimes one of the other early-flowering honeysuckles such as *L. caprifolium* '*Pauciflorum*'. Cultivated since the 17th century.

'Serotina' ('*Late Red*'). "Late Dutch Honeysuckle". Flowers rich reddish-purple outside, appearing from July to October. A.G.M. 1973.

***sempervirens** L. "Trumpet Honeysuckle". A high climbing, usually semi-evergreen species, with elliptic to obovate, rich-green leaves, glaucous and slightly downy beneath, the upper ones perfoliate. Flowers 4 to 5cm. long, rich orange-scarlet outside, yellow within, borne in axillary whorls towards the ends of the shoots during summer. A striking species, succeeding best on a wall in the British Isles. Eastern U.S.A. I. 1656. A.M. 1964.

***similis delavayi** REHD. (*L. delavayi*). A slender half-evergreen climber with ovate-lanceolate leaves which are white and downy beneath. Flowers fragrant, 3 to 4cm. long, white changing to pale yellow, produced in the axils of the terminal leaves during late summer and early autumn. W. China. I. 1901.

†***splendida** BOISS. A rather fastidious evergreen, or sometimes semi-evergreen, species with oval or oblong, very glaucous leaves, the upper ones perfoliate. Flowers 4 to 5cm. long, fragrant, reddish-purple outside, yellowish-white within, borne in dense terminal clusters during summer. A beautiful climber, succeeding best in the milder areas of the British Isles. Spain. Introduced about 1880.

×**tellmanniana** SPAETH (*sempervirens*×*tragophylla*). A superb hybrid with oval or ovate leaves, the upper ones perfoliate. Flowers 5cm. long, rich coppery-yellow, flushed red in bud, borne in large terminal clusters in June and July. Succeeds best in semi-shade or even in full shade. Raised at the Royal Hungarian Horticultural School, Budapest, sometime prior to 1927. A.M. 1931. A.G.M. 1969.

tragophylla HEMSL. A climber of great ornamental merit. Leaves 7·5 to 10cm. long, oblong to oval, glaucous and downy beneath. Flowers 6 to 9cm. long, bright, golden-yellow produced in June and July, in large terminal clusters. Berries red. An extremely showy species, requiring almost complete shade. Best grown in a tree. W. China. Discovered by Augustine Henry. Introduced by Ernest Wilson in 1900. A.M. 1913. A.G.M. 1928.

LOROPETALUM. See Tree and Shrub section.

LYCIUM. See Tree and Shrub section.

LYONOTHAMNUS. See Tree and Shrub section.

MAGNOLIA, in particular *M. delavayi* and *M. grandiflora*. See Tree and Shrub section.

†**MANDEVILLA—Apocynaceae**—Elegant twining climbers of the periwinkle family, with characteristic milky sap. Mainly natives of Tropical America, the following species requires a warm, sheltered wall and a well-drained soil, in the milder counties. It makes an attractive conservatory plant.

suaveolens LINDL. "Chilean Jasmine". An elegant, sun-loving climber with slender stems 3 to 4·5m. long, or more. Leaves heart-shaped, slender-pointed, bearing tufts of white down in the vein axils beneath. The fragrant, white, periwinkle-like flowers, 5cm. across, are borne in corymbs from the leaf axils during summer. Well worth growing for its sweetly scented flowers. Argentine. Introduced in 1837 by H. J. Mandeville. A.M. 1957.

MELIA. See Tree and Shrub section.

MENISPERMUM—Menispermaceae—A genus of three species of semi-woody, twining, dioecious plants suitable for growing into small trees or over walls, sheds, etc., best in full sun. In cold districts they may be cut to the ground each winter, but will invariably produce new shoots again in spring. They are distinctive in leaf, but to obtain fruit, plants of both sexes are required.

canadense L. "Moonseed". A climber spreading by suckers and making a dense tangle of slender shoots up to 4·5m. long. The conspicuous, long-stalked leaves, 10 to 18cm. across, are ovate to heart-shaped, with five to seven angular lobes. The inconspicuous, greenish-yellow flowers are borne in slender axillary racemes in summer and on female plants are followed by blackcurrant-like fruits, each containing a single, crescent-shaped seed (hence the common name). Eastern N. America. C. 1646.

MICHELIA. See Tree and Shrub section.

MIMULUS. See Tree and Shrub section.

MITRARIA. See Tree and Shrub section.

"MOONSEED". See *MENISPERMUM canadense*.

MUEHLENBECKIA—Polygonaceae—A small genus of creeping or climbing plants of no beauty in flower, but amusing and interesting botanically. *M. complexa* is useful for covering and concealing unsightly objects in mild areas.

axillaris WALP. A hardy, slow-growing, prostrate species forming dense carpets of intertwining thread-like stems clothed with small ovate to orbicular leaves 2 to 5mm. long. Fruits white, bearing a shiny black nutlet. Useful as ground cover on rock gardens and screes. New Zealand; Australia; Tasmania.

†**complexa** MEISSN. A twining species with slender, dark, interlacing stems occasionally up to 6m. or more, forming dense tangled curtains or carpets. Leaves variable in shape and size from 3 to 20mm. long and from roundish or oblong to fiddle-shaped. The minute, greenish, dioecious flowers in autumn are followed on female plants by small, white, fleshy fruits, enclosing a single, black shining nutlet. New Zealand. I. 1842.

trilobata CHEESEMAN (*M. varians*) (*M. trilobata*). A curious and amusing form in which the larger leaves are distinctly fiddle-shaped. In habit it is just as vigorous and as twining as the type, and makes excellent cover for old stumps, walls and banks in mild areas. New Zealand.

varians. See *M. complexa trilobata*.

***MUTISIA—Compositae**—"Climbing Gazania". A large genus of erect or climbing evergreens, the climbing species attaching themselves to a support by means of leaf tendrils. They may be grown on a wall, but are perhaps best planted near an old or unwanted shrub or small bushy tree, so that their stems may be encouraged to grow into the support provided. They require a warm, sunny position in a rich but well-drained soil. The colourful gazania-like flower-heads are produced singly on long stalks.

†**clematis** L. f. A strong-growing species for the conservatory. Leaves pinnate, composed of six to ten oblong-ovate leaflets which are white woolly beneath. Flower-heads pendulous, cylindrical at base, 5 to 6cm. across, with brilliant orange petals, produced in summer and early autumn. Andes of Colombia and Ecuador. I. 1859. A.M. 1926.

decurrens CAV. A rare species up to 3m., with narrowly oblong, sessile leaves 7·5 to 13cm. long. Flower-heads 10 to 13cm. across, with brilliant orange or vermillion petals, borne continuously during summer. A superb but difficult species to establish. It succeeds in a warm, sheltered position such as a partially shaded west wall and in a rich friable sandy loam. Chile. Introduced by Richard Pearce in 1859. F.C.C. 1861.

MUTISIA—*continued*

ilicifolia CAV. A vigorous, hardy species, with stems 3 to 4·5m. long. Leaves sessile, ovate-oblong, the margins strongly toothed, dark green above, pale woolly beneath. Flower-heads 5 to 7·5cm. across, yellow, with lilac-pink petals, borne in summer and early autumn. Chile. I. 1832.

oligodon POEPP. & ENDL. A very beautiful, suckering species usually easy to establish growing through a sparsely branched shrub, forming a low thicket of straggling stems rarely reaching 1·5m. Leaves oblong, sessile, coarsely-toothed, auriculate at base. Flower-heads 5 to 7·5cm. across, with salmon-pink petals, appearing continuously throughout summer and intermittently into autumn. A lovely species more compact in habit than *M. ilicifolia* and with shorter stems. In a sunny site supported by a low trellis or a low to small sized shrub, it is a most attractive plant except that in winter it can look almost dead, with only an occasional green shoot. Chile. Introduced by Harold Comber in 1927. A.M. 1928.

MYRTUS. See Tree and Shrub section.

OLEA. See Tree and Shrub section.

OLEARIA. See Tree and Shrub section.

OSMANTHUS. See Tree and Shrub section.

OSTEOMELES. See Tree and Shrub section.

†OXYPETALUM—Asclepiadaceae—Erect or climbing herbs and sub-shrubs, natives mainly of S. America. The following species may be grown outside only in the very mildest localities. It makes an exceptionally attractive conservatory climber.

caeruleum DCNE. (*Tweedia coerulea*). A beautiful sub-shrub with twining stems and oblong or heart-shaped, sage-green leaves. The remarkable flowers are powder-blue at first and slightly tinged green, turning to purplish and finally lilac. They are freely borne in erect, few-flowered cymes during summer. Temperate S.E. South America. I. 1832. A.M. 1936.

PAEDERIA—Rubiaceae—A small genus of twining plants emitting a foetid smell when bruised. They require a sunny sheltered position in any fertile soil.

scandens MERR. (*chinensis*). A strong-growing climber up to 5m., with ovate, slender-pointed, dark green leaves, often rather downy beneath. Flowers tubular, white, with a purple throat, carried in slender terminal panicles throughout summer, followed by small, orange fruits. China; Japan; Korea. I. 1907.

†*PANDOREA—Bignoniaceae—A small genus of evergreen, twining plants, all native to Australia. They require a warm, sheltered position in very mild localities, but are best grown in a conservatory.

jasminoides SCHUM. (*Bignonia jasminoides*) (*Tecoma jasminoides*). The "Bower Plant" of Australia, a beautiful climber with pinnate leaves composed of five to nine slender-pointed leaflets. The attractive funnel-shaped flowers, 4 to 5cm. long, are white, stained crimson and are borne in panicles during summer.

PARTHENOCISSUS—Vitaceae—A small genus of high climbing vines, previously placed under *Vitis*, attaching themselves to support by means of leaf tendrils which either twine or adhere by adhesive pads. The self-clinging species are excellent on walls or tree trunks whilst those with twining tendrils may be trained over hedges, large coarse shrubs or small bushy trees. The leaves are often richly coloured in autumn. The attractive, small fruits are only produced following a hot, dry summer. See also *AMPELOPSIS* and *VITIS*.

henryana DIELS. & GILG. (*Vitis henryana*). A beautiful, self-clinging species. Leaves digitate, composed of three to five obovate or narrowly oval leaflets, dark green or bronze, with a silvery-white veinal variegation, particularly when growing in half-shade, turning red in autumn. Fruits dark blue. Best grown on a wall. C. China. First discovered by Augustine Henry about 1885. Introduced by Ernest Wilson in 1900. A.M. 1906. A.G.M. 1936.

himalayana PLANCH. (*Vitis himalayana*). A strong-growing, more or less self-clinging climber, differing mainly from the "Virginia Creeper" in its larger leaflets. These turn rich crimson in autumn. Fruits deep blue. Himalaya. C. 1894.

rubrifolia GAGNEP. An attractive variety, leaflets smaller, purple when young. W. China. I. 1907.

PARTHENOCISSUS—*continued*

inserta K. FRITSCH (*Vitis vitacea*). A vigorous vine with twining tendrils climbing into small trees or scrambling over hedges. Leaves with five, stalked, ovate to obovate leaflets, shining green beneath, colouring richly in autumn. Fruits blue-black. Ideal for covering unsightly objects, differing most markedly from the closely related "Virginia Creeper" in its non-adhesive tendrils. Eastern U.S.A. C. before 1800.

quinquefolia PLANCH. (*Vitis quinquefolia*) (*Vitis hederacea*). "Virginia Creeper". A tall-growing, more or less self-clinging vine excellent for high walls, trees, towers, etc. Leaves composed of usually five oval to obovate, stalked leaflets which are dull green and glaucescent beneath, turning brilliant orange and scarlet in autumn. Fruits blue-black. Reaching to the tops of lofty trees in its native habitats. Eastern U.S.A. I. 1629. A.G.M. 1969.

It is unfortunate that in the British Isles we are quite wrongly from childhood brought up to call *Ampelopsis veitchii* (see *Parthenocissus tricuspidata* '*Veitchii*') the "Virginia Creeper". We must try and re-educate ourselves and certainly make sure our children know it as the "Boston Ivy", as the true "Virginia Creeper" is *Parthenocissus quinquefolia*.

sinensis. See *VITIS piasezkii*.

thomsonii PLANCH. (*Vitis thomsonii*). A beautiful vine of slender habit. Leaves composed of five oval or obovate, glossy green leaflets. The young growths in spring are purple, whilst in autumn the foliage turns to rich crimson and scarlet. Fruits black. Himalaya; China. I. 1900. F.C.C. 1903 (as *Vitis thomsonii*).

tricuspidata PLANCH. (*Vitis inconstans* MIQ.). "Boston Ivy". A vigorous, self-clinging vine, almost as ubiquitous as the common ivy. Leaves extremely variable, broadly ovate and toothed, or trifoliolate on young plants, ovate and conspicuously three-lobed on old plants. Turning rich crimson and scarlet in autumn. Fruits dark blue and bloomy. A commonly planted vine, densely covering walls in urban districts and a familiar sight in many of our older cities and towns. Japan; Korea; China; Formosa. Introduced from Japan by J. G. Veitch in 1862. F.C.C. 1868.

'Lowii'. A selection, with small, curiously crisped, palmately, three to seven-lobed leaves and rich autumn colour. A.M. 1907.

'Veitchii' (*Ampelopsis veitchii*) (*Vitis inconstans* '*Purpurea*' HORT.). A selected form with slightly smaller, ovate or trifoliolate leaves, purple when young. A.G.M. 1936.

†**PASSIFLORA** (including *TACSONIA*)—**Passifloraceae**—"Passion Flower". A large genus of mainly climbers, attaching themselves to a support by means of twining tendrils. The majority are too tender for planting outside in the British Isles, but the remaining few contain some of the most beautiful and exotic of flowering creepers. They are best planted on a sunny, sheltered, south-facing wall. The beautiful and fascinating flowers, usually borne singly on long stalks, are composed of a tubular calyx with five lobes or sepals. These are often the same size, shape and colour as the five petals and collectively are referred to as tepals. Inside the tepals are situated rings of "filaments" which are usually thread-like and coloured, collectively referred to as the "corona". The five stamens are carried on a long central column and are topped by the ovary and three nail-like stigmas. The fruits vary in size and shape and contain numerous seeds in an edible, jelly-like pulp. Out-of-doors they are normally only produced after a long, hot summer.

The delightful story connected with the origin of the name "Passion Flower" is worth recounting. According to Dr. Masters it was used originally by the Spanish priests in South America, because of the resemblance their piety led them to detect between the various parts of the flower and the instruments of Christ's Passion. The three stigmas representing the three nails; the five anthers representing the five wounds; the corona representing the crown of thorns or the halo of glory; the ten tepals representing the apostles—Peter and Judas being absent; the lobed leaves and the whip-like tendrils representing the hands and scourges of His persecutors.

'Allardii' (*caerulea 'Constance Elliott'* × *quadrangularis*). A choice hybrid raised at the University Botanic Garden, Cambridge. A strong-growing climber with large, three-lobed leaves. Flowers 9 to 11·5cm. across, tepals white, shaded pink, corona white and deep cobalt-blue, appearing throughout summer and autumn. May be grown outside in the milder counties.

PASSIFLORA—*continued*

antioquiensis KARST. (*Tacsonia vanvolxemii*). A beautiful climber with slender, downy stems and leaves of two kinds—lanceolate, unlobed leaves, and deeply three-lobed leaves, the lobes long and slender-pointed, downy beneath. Flowers pendulous, 10 to 13cm. across, tube 2·5 to 4cm. long, rich rose-red, with a small violet corona, borne singly on long peduncles during late summer and autumn. May be grown outside only in the most favoured localities, otherwise a plant for the conservatory. Colombia. I. 1858.

caerulea L. "Blue Passion Flower". A vigorous, usually rampant species often forming a dense blanket of tangled stems, evergreen in mild localities. Leaves palmately five to seven-lobed. Flowers slightly fragrant, 7·5 to 10cm. across, tepals white or occasionally pink tinged; the conspicuous corona has the outer filaments blue at the tips, white in the middle and purple at base. They appear continuously throughout summer and autumn, often until the first frosts. Fruits ovoid, orange-red, 2·5 to 4cm. long. Hardy on a warm, sunny wall in the south and surviving often many winters in the home counties. S. Brazil. I. 1699.

'Constance Elliott'. A superb clone with ivory-white flowers. F.C.C. 1884.

×caerulea-racemosa SABINE. A vigorous climber with deeply five-lobed leaves. Flowers borne singly, the tepals deeply flushed violet, corona deep violet purple, column apple-green, stigmas purple and green. A free-flowering hybrid, rampant when established. Only suitable for the mildest localities.

edulis SIMS. "Granadilla". A tender, vigorous climber with angular stems and ovate, deeply three-lobed leaves. Flowers 6cm. across, tepals white, green without, corona with curly, white filaments, banded with purple, produced throughout summer. Fruits ovoid, 5cm. long, yellow or dull purple, pulp edible. Commonly cultivated in warmer countries for its fruit which is sometimes produced in the mildest gardens of the British Isles. Tropical S. America. I. 1810.

'Exoniensis' (*antioquiensis × mollisima*) (*Tacsonia 'Exoniensis'*). A beautiful hybrid with downy stems and deeply three-lobed, downy leaves. Flowers pendulous, 10 to 13cm. across, the tube 6cm. long, tepals rose-pink, corona small, whitish, appearing during summer. Only for the conservatory. Raised by Messrs. Veitch of Exeter about 1870. Previously catalogued and distributed wrongly as *P. mixta quitensis*.

mixta quitensis. See under *'Exoniensis'*.

racemosa BROT. (*princeps*). "Red Passion Flower". A climber with ovate, usually three-lobed leaves. Flowers vivid scarlet, with purple, white-tipped outer filaments, borne in drooping, terminal racemes during summer. A magnificent species requiring conservatory treatment., Brazil. I. 1815.

umbilicata HARMS. (*Tacsonia umbilicata*). A fast-growing species with small, violet flowers and round, yellow fruits. Proving one of the hardiest, thriving in the open in the S.W. counties. Bolivia.

"PASSION FLOWER". See *PASSIFLORA*.

PENSTEMON cordifolius. See Tree and Shrub section.

PERIPLOCA—Asclepiadaceae—A small genus of easily grown shrubs and twining climbers, exuding a poisonous, milky juice when cut. Suitable for growing on pergolas, fences, etc., requiring a sunny position in any type of fertile soil.

graeca L. "Silk Vine". A vigorous climber, reaching 9 to 12m., on a suitable support. Leaves ovate or lanceolate, long persistent. Flowers 2·5cm. across, greenish outside, brownish-purple within, possessing a heavy odour, borne in cymes during July and August. Seed-pods in pairs, 12cm. long, packed with small silky-tufted seeds. S.E. Europe; Asia Minor. C. 1597.

†laevigata AIT. (*angustifolia*). A tender, strong-growing, semi-evergreen climber, differing from *P. graeca* in its lanceolate, sessile leaves, subsessile cymes and smaller, greenish-yellow flowers. Canary Isles; N. Africa. I. 1770.

PHILADELPHUS maculatus. See Tree and Shrub section.

PHLOMIS. See Tree and Shrub section.

PHYGELIUS. See Tree and Shrub section.

***PILEOSTEGIA—Hydrangeaceae**—A small genus of evergreen shrubs climbing by means of aerial roots. The following species, the only one in general cultivation, requires a wall or tree trunk in sun or shade, in all types of fertile soil.

PILEOSTEGIA—*continued*

viburnoides HOOK. f. & THOMS. A rather slow-growing, evergreen, self-clinging species reaching 6m. on a suitable surface. Leaves entire, leathery, narrow-oblong to ovate-lanceolate, 7·5 to 15cm. long, strongly veined and minutely pitted beneath. Flowers in crowded terminal panicles, creamy-white, appearing during late summer and autumn. One of the best climbers for any aspect including shady or north-facing walls. Khasia Hills (India); S. China; Ryukyus. The first meeting Mr. H. G. Hillier had with this plant was in 1922 in Orleans when the leading French nurseryman of that time, M. Chenault, proudly pointed to a plant covering the front of his house. Introduced by Ernest Wilson in 1908. A.M. 1914.

PIPTANTHUS. See Tree and Shrub section.

POLYGONUM—**Polygonaceae**—A large genus of mainly perennial and annual herbs. Unless otherwise indicated, the species here described are hardy, twining climbers of vigorous, rampant growth, ideal for covering and concealing unsightly objects. They also look effective when trained into trees and are among the best plants for clothing old stumps, bare banks, etc.

aubertii L. HENRY (*Bilderdykia aubertii*). A rampant climber, with densely twining stems up to 12m. long. Closely resembling and often mistaken in gardens for *P. baldschuanicum* but differing in its white or greenish-white flowers which only become pinkish in fruit, and are borne on short, lateral branchlets. The branches of the inflorescence are minutely scabrid. W. China; Tibet. Occasionally naturalised in Europe (including British Isles). I. 1899. A.G.M. 1928.

baldschuanicum REG. (*Bilderdykia baldschuanica*). "Russian Vine". A rampant climber with stems up to 12m. long. Leaves ovate or heart-shaped, pale-green. Flowers pink-tinged. Though individually small, they are borne in conspicuous, crowded panicles on terminal and short lateral branches throughout summer and autumn. Less common in cultivation than *P. aubertii,* with which it is often confused. The almost smooth branches of the inflorescence contrasts with the scabrid branches of *P. aubertii*. When in flower, covering a 12m. high tree it creates a remarkable picture. S.E. Russia (Tadzhikistan). C. 1883. A.M. 1899. A.G.M. 1928.

multiflorum THUNB. A tuberous rooted, perennial climber with slender, bright red stems up to 4·5m. long. Leaves ovate-heart-shaped, dark shining green. Flowers small, white, borne in loose panicles during summer. The branches of the inflorescence bear a characteristic, dense fringe of hairs. Less hardy than the "Russian Vine" and requiring a warm, sheltered position in full sun. China; Formosa. I. 1881.

PROSTANTHERA. See Tree and Shrub section.

PRUNUS cerasoides rubea, mume and **triloba.** See Tree and Shrub section.

†**PUERARIA**—**Leguminosae**—A small genus of twining climbers with compound leaves and often attractive pea-flowers.

lobata OHWI (*thunbergiana*). "Kudzu Vine". A vigorous species up to 6m., woody at base, stems climbing or trailing. Leaves trifoliolate, the middle leaflets 15 to 18cm. long. Flowers fragrant, violet-purple, borne in long racemes in July and August. The long stems are often cut back during winter, but spring again from the base. Useful for growing over large, unwanted shrubs or old hedges, in full sun. Japan; Korea; China. I. 1885.

PUNICA. See Tree and Shrub section.

"PURPLE BELLS". See *RHODOCHITON atrosanguineum.*

PYRACANTHA. See Tree and Shrub section.

RAPHIOLEPIS. See Tree and Shrub section.

RHAPHITHAMNUS. See Tree and Shrub section.

†**RHODOCHITON**—**Scrophulariaceae**—A monotypic genus requiring conservatory treatment, though it makes an unusual summer creeper.

atrosanguineum ROTHM. (*volubile*). "Purple Bells". A slender plant with stems up to 3m. long, climbing by means of its twining petioles and peduncles. Leaves cordate, few-toothed. The curious flowers, consisting of a broadly bell-shaped, almost black-purple calyx and a long tubular, purplish red corolla are borne in endless succession during summer. Mexico.

RIBES speciosum and **viburnifolium.** See Tree and Shrub section.

ROSA. See Tree and Shrub section, also our Rose Catalogue for a comprehensive selection of Climbing and Rambler Roses.

RUBUS—Rosaceae—The climbing members of this large genus are fairly vigorous shrubs with long, prickly, scandent stems. They may be trained up wooden supports or into small trees or hedges. Of little beauty in flower or fruit, they are mainly grown for their ornamental foliage. Thriving in all types of well-drained soil. See also Tree and Shrub section.

bambusarum. See *R. henryi bambusarum.*

***flagelliflorus** FOCKE. An evergreen species with long, white-felted, minutely-prickly stems. Leaves broad ovate to ovate-lanceolate, 10 to 18cm. long, shallowly lobed and toothed, felted beneath. The small, white flowers are borne in axillary clusters in June, followed by black, edible fruits. Mainly grown for its striking ornamental foliage. China. I. 1901.

***henryi** HEMSL. & KTZE. An evergreen species with long, scandent stems, reaching a height of 6m. on a suitable support. Leaves deeply three-lobed, 10 to 15cm. long, glossy dark green above, white-felted beneath. Flowers pink, borne in slender racemes during summer, followed by black fruits. Both the species and the following variety are grown for their habit and attractive foliage. C. and W. China. First discovered by Augustine Henry. Introduced by Ernest Wilson in 1900.

bambusarum REHD. (*R. bambusarum*). An elegant variety differing most markedly from the type in its leaves, which are composed of three distinct lanceolate leaflets. C. China. I. 1900.

lambertianus SER. A semi-evergreen species with scandent, four-angled, prickly stems which are viscid when young. Leaves ovate, 7·5 to 13cm. long, shallowly three to five-lobed and toothed, glossy on both surfaces. Flowers small, white, borne in terminal panicles during summer, followed by red fruits. C. China. I. 1907.

***parkeri** HANCE. An evergreen species with slender, scandent, biennial stems, densely clothed with greyish hairs. Leaves oblong-lanceolate, with wavy, finely-toothed margins, densely covered with a reddish-brown down beneath. Flowers small, white, produced in panicles during summer, followed by black fruits. C. China. I. 1907.

tricolor. See Tree and Shrub section.

"RUSSIAN VINE". See *POLYGONUM baldschuanicum.*

SALVIA (tender species). See Tree and Shrub section.

SCHISANDRA—Schisandraceae—Deciduous and evergreen twining shrubs of considerable charm and quality, suitable for growing on walls, fences or over shrubs and into trees. Flowers dioecious, borne in clusters in the leaf axils, followed on female plants by long, pendulous spikes of attractive berries.

chinensis BAILL. A high climbing species reaching 9m. on a suitable support. Leaves obovate to oval, 5 to 10cm. long. Flowers fragrant, 1 to 2cm. across, usually white or palest pink, produced on slender, drooping stalks during late spring. Berries scarlet. China; Japan. I. 1860.

grandiflora HOOK. & THOMS. A rare species with obovate, somewhat leathery leaves and conspicuous venation, 7·5 to 10cm. long. Flowers 2·5 to 3cm. across, pale pink, borne on drooping stalks during May and June. Berries scarlet. Temperate Himalaya.

cathayensis SCHNEID. A variety with smaller leaves and clear rose-pink flowers. W. China. I. 1907.

rubriflora SCHNEID. (*S. rubriflora*). Flowers 2·5cm. across, deep crimson, borne on pendulous stalks during late spring. Berries scarlet. W. China. I. 1908. A.M. 1925. A.M. 1978 (for fruit).

propinqua sinensis OLIV. This Chinese variety of a Himalayan species is hardier than the type and is notable for bearing its short-stalked, yellowish terra-cotta flowers during late summer and autumn. Leaves oblong to lanceolate, persistent, 5 to 10cm. long. Berries scarlet. C. and W. China. I. 1907.

rubriflora. See *S. grandiflora rubriflora.*

sphenanthera REHD. & WILS.. A strong-growing climber with noticeably warty shoots. Leaves obovate, 5 to 10cm. long, green beneath. Flowers a distinct shade of orange-red or terra-cotta, borne on slender stalks during May and June. Berries scarlet. W. China. I. 1907.

SCHIZOPHRAGMA—Hydrangeaceae—A small genus of ornamental climbers supporting themselves by means of aerial roots. The small, creamy-white flowers are densely borne in large, flattened cymes, each cyme attended by several conspicuous, cream-coloured, marginal bracts (really enlarged sepals of sterile flowers). Their requirements are similar to those of *Hydrangea petiolaris* and are suitable for north-facing or otherwise shady walls, though flowering best on a sunny wall. They are most effective when allowed to climb a large tree or old stump. Although eventually tall, they are slow starters and need cultural encouragement in their early years.

hydrangeoides SIEB. & ZUCC. A superb climber, reaching 12m. Leaves broadly rotund-ovate and coarsely-toothed (by which it is distinguished from *S. integrifolia*). Flower-heads 20 to 25cm. across, appearing in July, bracts 2·5 to 4cm. long. Native of Japan where it is found in woods and forests in the mountains often accompanied by *Hydrangea petiolaris*. C. 1880. F.C.C. 1885.

'Roseum'. A lovely form with rose-flushed bracts. A.M. 1939.

integrifolium OLIV. A climber reaching 12m. or more under suitable conditions. Leaves broad ovate to elliptic-oblong, slender-pointed, entire or thinly set with small, narrow teeth. Flower-heads often as much as 30cm. across, the bracts 6 to 9cm. long, borne freely in July. A magnificent species, larger in all its parts than *S. hydrangioides*. Native of Central China where it is said to grow on rocky cliffs. Introduced by E. H. Wilson in 1901. A.M. 1936. F.C.C. 1963. A.G.M. 1969.

SENECIO—Compositae—Probably the largest genus of flowering plants in the world. Only a few are climbers and of these the following is the only species likely to be met with in cultivation.

scandens G. DON. A fairly vigorous, half-evergreen, semi-woody climber with long scandent stems 4·5 to 6m. long. Leaves narrowly triangular or ovate, coarsely-toothed, sometimes lobed at the base. The small, bright-yellow, groundsel-like flower-heads are produced in large panicles during autumn. Best planted where it may scramble over bushes, hedges or into small, densely-branched trees. It requires a sunny, sheltered site and though in cold areas it is frequently cut to ground level in winter, it will normally spring up again from the base. Given mild weather, a well established specimen is one of the most conspicuous flowering plants in the garden during October and November. Japan; Formosa; China; Philippines; India; E. Nepal. I. 1895.

SINOFRANCHETIA—Lardizabalaceae—A monotypic genus related to *Holboellia;* with dioecious flowers. It requires a sunny or semi-shady position in any ordinary soil.

chinensis HEMSL. A vigorous, hardy, twining climber reaching a height of 9m. in a suitable tree or on a high wall. Leaves trifoliolate, glaucous beneath. Flowers white, inconspicuous, borne in drooping racemes during May. These are followed, on female plants, by conspicuous, large, elongated bunches of lavender-purple, rounded fruits. C. and W. China. I. 1907. A.M. 1948.

SINOMENIUM—Menispermaceae—A monotypic genus bearing drooping panicles of dioecious flowers. Suitable for growing into a tree or against a large wall in sun or semi-shade; any ordinary soil.

acutum REHD. & WILS. A hardy, twining climber up to 12m. Leaves variable in shape, ovate and entire to kidney-shaped, often shallowly-lobed or more deeply-lobed with three to five lanceolate lobes, shining deep green. Flowers small, yellowish, borne in long, slender, pyramidal panicles in June, followed, on female plants, by small globular, bloomy-black fruits. C. and W. China. I. 1901. We offer the following variety:—

cinereum REHD. & WILS. The form occasionally seen in cultivation, with leaves greyish-pubescent beneath. I. 1907.

SMILAX—Liliaceae—A large genus of evergreen and deciduous, mainly climbing plants. Their often prickly stems are tough and wiry, bearing stipular tendrils by which they are able to support themselves, scrambling over bushes, hedges or similar support. They are normally grown for their rich, often glossy green foliage and are excellent for covering stumps, low walls, etc. Sun or shade in any ordinary soil. Flowers normally dioecious, of little beauty.

SMILAX—*continued*

†*aspera L. An evergreen climber with prickly, angular zig-zag stems and ovate-lanceolate to heart-shaped, glossy green, leathery leaves. The racemes of small, fragrant, pale-green flowers are produced in late summer and early autumn, often followed by small, red fruits. An established plant forms a dense tangle of thorny stems. It requires a warm sunny position and is not suitable for cold areas. S. Europe; N. Africa; Canary Isles. C. 1648. A.M. 1903.

china L. "China Root". A deciduous shrub with rounded, prickly scrambling stems. Leaves variable in shape, usually roundish-ovate with a heart-shaped base, often turning red in autumn. Flowers greenish-yellow in May. Fruits bright red. The large, fleshy root is said to be eaten by the Chinese. It also contains a drug known as "China Root", once valued as a cure for gout. China; Japan; Korea. I. 1759.

discotis WARB. A deciduous species with generally prickly stems up to 3 to 4·5m. long. Leaves ovate, heart-shaped at base, glaucous beneath. Fruits blue-black. W. China. I. 1908.

SOLANUM—Solanaceae—The climbing members of this large genus make spectacular wall climbers for sheltered gardens. They require full sun and a south or west aspect and are not fastidious as to soil.

crispum RUIZ. & PAV. A vigorous, semi-evergreen shrub with scrambling, downy, normally herbaceous stems 4·5 to 6m. long. Leaves ovate to ovate-lanceolate, variable in size, minutely downy. Flowers very slightly fragrant, 2·5 to 3cm. across, resembling those of a potato, but rich purple-blue, with a bright yellow staminal beak, borne in loose corymbs very freely from July to September. Fruits small, yellowish-white. A pleasing species suitable for training on a wall and equally effective when allowed to scramble over small fences, sheds and similar structures. It is hardier than *S. jasminoides* and luxuriates in a chalky soil. Chile. I. about 1830. A.G.M. 1939.

'Glasnevin' (*'Autumnale'*). A selected form with a longer flowering season. A.M. 1955. A.G.M. 1969.

†jasminoides PAXT. A slender, fast-growing, semi-evergreen climber with twining stems in mild areas reaching 6 to 9m. long. Leaves ovate-acuminate, glossy-green and thin in texture. Flowers 2cm. across, pale slate-blue, with a yellow staminal beak, profusely borne in loose clusters from mid-summer until checked by autumn frosts. This species needs the protection of a south or west-facing sunny wall. Brazil. I. 1838.

'Album'. Flowers white, with a yellow staminal beak.

†*SOLLYA—Pittosporaceae—A genus of two species of extremely beautiful evergreen, twining plants only suitable for the mildest localities or for the conservatory. They require a sunny, sheltered position and a well-drained soil. Both the following are natives of Australia and are delightful when grown against a low wall or allowed to scramble over low shrubs.

drummondii. See *S. parviflora*.

heterophylla LINDL. (*fusiformis*). "Bluebell Creeper". A beautiful plant with slender stems up to 2m. or more. Leaves variable, usually ovate to lanceolate, 2·5 to 5cm. long. The nodding clusters of delicate bell-shaped, sky-blue flowers are freely borne during summer and autumn. I. 1830.

parviflora TURCZ. (*drummondii*). A delightful species, differing from *S. heterophylla* in its even more slender shoots, smaller, linear leaves and its smaller darker blue flowers produced usually singly or in pairs during summer and autumn. I. 1838. A.M. 1922.

SOPHORA macrocarpa, microphylla and **tetraptera.** See Tree and Shrub section.

***STAUNTONIA—Lardizabalaceae**—A small genus of evergreen, twining shrubs closely related to *Holboellia*, differing in its united stamens (free in *Stauntonia*). It requires a warm, sheltered wall in full sun or semi-shade. Flowers monoecious.

hexaphylla DCNE. A strong-growing climber up to 10m. or more. Leaves large, composed of three to seven, stalked, leathery, dark green leaflets. Flowers 2cm. across, fragrant, male and female in separate racemes, white, tinged violet, appearing in spring. The egg-shaped, pulpy, purple-tinged fruits, 2·5 to 5cm. long, are edible, but are only produced after a warm, dry summer. Japan; Korea; Ryukyus. I. 1874. A.M. 1960.

latifolia. See *HOLBOELLIA latifolia*.

TACSONIA. See *PASSIFLORA*.

TECOMA. See *CAMPSIS*.

†***TECOMARIA**—**Bignoniaceae**—A small genus of evergreen climbers and shrubs only suitable for mild localities. The following species requires a warm, sunny wall in a sheltered position.

capensis SPACH. "Cape Honeysuckle". A vigorous, self-clinging, twining or scandent shrub with glabrous stems up to 4·5m. long. Leaves pinnate, composed of five to nine toothed leaflets. The brilliant scarlet, trumpet-shaped flowers, 5cm. long, are borne in terminal racemes during late summer. In colder districts it makes an excellent conservatory climber. S. Africa. I. 1823.

TEUCRIUM fruticans. See Tree and Shrub section.

TIBOUCHINA. See Tree and Shrub section.

†***TRACHELOSPERMUM**—**Apocynaceae**—Given a sunny, sheltered wall, these beautiful, self-clinging, evergreen, twining shrubs may be successfully grown in all but the coldest localities. Their attractive, sweetly-scented, jasmine-like flowers are borne in July and August. The stems and leaves exude a milky juice when cut.

asiaticum NAKAI (*divaricatum*) (*crocostemon*). A very beautiful species, when grown on a wall, presenting a dense leafy cover up to 6m. high or more and as much across. Leaves oval, 2·5 to 5cm. long, dark glossy green. Flowers 2cm. across, creamy-white with buff-yellow centre, changing to yellow, fragrant. Hardier than *T. jasminoides* and neater and more compact in growth. It also differs from that species in its smaller leaves and flowers, the latter with exerted stamens and longer-pointed in bud. Japan; Korea.

divaricatum. See *T. asiaticum.*

japonicum. See *T. majus.*

jasminoides LEM. (*Rhyncospermum jasminoides*). A lovely, rather slow-growing climber up to 7m. high or more and as much across. Leaves narrowly oval, 5 to 7·5cm. long, dark polished green. Flowers 2·5cm. across, very fragrant, white, becoming cream with age. It requires a warm, sheltered wall. In cold areas it is a very worthy candidate for the conservatory. C. and S. China; Formosa. Introduced by Robert Fortune from Shanghai in 1844. A.M. 1934.

'Variegatum'. Leaves margined and splashed creamy-white, often with a crimson suffusion in winter. A very pretty plant.

wilsonii HILLIER. An unusual form introduced from China by Ernest Wilson under his number W.776. Leaves varying from ovate to almost linear-lanceolate, with an attractive veining, often turning crimson in winter.

majus STAPF. (*japonicum*). A vigorous climber stated to reach 18m. in its native habitat, but probably half as much in cultivation. Leaves ovate to elliptic, 2·5 to 7·5cm. long, often colouring richly in winter. Taller and larger-leaved than the other species. When established it will clothe a wall as effectively as ivy. Flowers not produced on young plants. Japanese botanists have amalgamated this distinct plant with *T. asiaticum*, but here we retain it as a species. Japan.

TRIPTERYGIUM—**Celastraceae**—A small genus of two interesting species of deciduous, scandent shrubs, requiring a moist loamy soil. They are best planted where they may clamber into a suitable tree or large bush or over a pergola or outhouse. They flower best in full sun, but grow freely in shade.

forrestii. See *T. wilfordii.*

regelii SPRAGUE & TAK. A large, scandent shrub with long, reddish-brown conspicuously warty branches, reaching a height of 6m. in a suitable tree. Leaves ovate or elliptic, slender pointed, up to 15cm. long, dark green above, paler beneath. Flowers small, greenish-white, borne in large, brown-pubescent panicles in late summer, followed by pale-green, three-winged fruits. Japan; Korea; Manchuria. I. 1905.

†**wilfordii** HOOK. f. (*forrestii*). A large, scandent shrub with long, angular, downy stems, up to 6m. long. Leaves ovate or elliptic, 5 to 15cm. long, green above, glaucous beneath. Flowers small, greenish-white, borne in large, rusty tomentose panicles in early autumn. Fruits three-winged, purplish-red. S. China; Formosa; Japan; Burma. Introduced from Yunnan by George Forrest in 1913. A.M. 1952.

TWEEDIA coerulea. See *OXYPETALUM caeruleum.*

VIBURNUM, in particular **japonicum, macrocephalum, odoratissimum** and **suspensum.** See Tree and Shrub section.

"VINE, ORNAMENTAL". See *AMPELOPSIS, PARTHENOCISSUS* and *VITIS.*

"VINE, RUSSIAN". See *POLYGONUM baldschuanicum.*

"VINE, SILK". See *PERIPLOCA graeca.*

"VINE, TRUMPET". See *CAMPSIS radicans.*

"VIRGINIA CREEPER". See *PARTHENOCISSUS quinquefolia.*

VITEX. See Tree and Shrub section.

VITIS (including *SPINOVITIS*)—**Vitaceae**—The ornamental vines are a large genus of climbers, supporting themselves by twining tendrils. They are variable in leaf and several species give rich autumn colour. The majority are of vigorous habit and are most effective when allowed to clamber into a large tree or cover an old hedge or stump. They may also be trained to cover walls, pergolas, bridges and fences. The small, greenish flowers are carried in panicles or racemes during summer and though of little beauty are followed after a hot, dry season by bunches of small grapes. See also *AMPELOPSIS* and *PARTHENOCISSUS.*

aconitifolia. See *AMPELOPSIS aconitifolia.*

amurensis RUPR. A strong-growing species with reddish young shoots. Leaves broadly ovate, 10 to 25cm. across, three to five-lobed, sometimes deeply so. Fruits small, black. Autumn colours of rich crimson and purple. Manchuria; Amur Region. I. about 1854.

betulifolia DIELS. & GILG. A high-climbing vine with ovate to oblong-ovate leaves, 5 to 10cm. long, toothed and occasionally slightly three-lobed, covered with white or tawny floss when young. Rich autumn tints. Fruits small, blue-black. C. and W. China. I. 1907. A.M. 1917.

'Brant' (*vinifera 'Brant'*). One of the most popular of hardy fruiting vines. A vigorous grower, reaching 9m. high or above on a suitable support. It produces numerous cylindrical bunches of sweet, aromatic grapes which are dark purple-black and bloomy when ripe. In addition the attractive, deeply three to five-lobed leaves turn to shades of dark red and purple, with greenish or yellow veins. Often wrongly regarded as a form of the common "Grape Vine" (*Vitis vinifera*), it is in fact a seedling of multiple parentage, *V. 'Clinton'* (*labrusca* × *riparia*) crossed with *V. vinifera 'Black St. Peters'*. It was first raised at Paris, Ontario (Canada) in the early eighteen-sixties by Charles Arnold. A.M. 1970.

coignetiae PLANCH. Perhaps the most spectacular of all vines. A strong-growing species climbing to the tops of lofty trees. The broadly ovate or rounded leaves often measure 30cm. across. They possess a heart-shaped base and three to five obscure lobes, clothed with rust-coloured tomentum beneath. Fruits 12mm. across, black with purple bloom. The large, handsome leaves turn to crimson and scarlet in autumn, giving a magnificent display. Japan; Korea; Sakhalin. C. 1875. A.G.M. 1969.

davidii FOEX (*armata*) (*Spinovitis davidii*). A vigorous climber, its shoots covered with gland-tipped, hooked spines. Leaves heart-shaped, coarsely toothed, 10 to 25cm. long, shining dark green above, glaucous and glandular-bristly beneath, turning a rich crimson in autumn. Fruits black, edible. A luxuriant vine easily recognised by its spiny shoots. China. C. 1885. A.M. 1903.

cyanocarpa SARG. A variety with less prickly shoots, rather larger leaves and bluish, bloomy fruits. Rich autumn colour. A.M. 1906.

flexuosa THUNB. An elegant species with slender stems. Leaves roundish-ovate, 5 to 9cm. across, rather thin in texture, glossy green above. Fruits black. Japan; Korea; China. A variable species; we offer the variety *parvifolia* below.

major. See *V. pulchra.*

parvifolia GAGNEP. A pretty variety with smaller leaves which are a pleasing shade of bronze-green above, with a metallic sheen, purple beneath when young. Himalaya to C. China. I. 1900. A.M. 1903.

henryana. See *PARTHENOCISSUS henryana.*

himalayana. See *PARTHENOCISSUS himalayana.*

inconstans. See *PARTHENOCISSUS tricuspidata.*

'Purpurea'. See *PARTHENOCISSUS tricuspidata 'Veitchii'.*

labrusca L. "Fox Grape". A vigorous, luxuriant vine with woolly young shoots. Leaves broadly ovate or rounded, 7·5 to 18cm. wide, varying from shallowly toothed to three-lobed, normally rather thick in texture, dark green above, white then rusty-pubescent beneath. Fruits black-purple; edible and musky-flavoured. A parent of most of the cultivated American grapes. Eastern U.S.A. I. 1656.

megalophylla. See *AMPELOPSIS megalophylla.*

micans. See *AMPELOPSIS bodinieri.*

odoratissima. See *V. riparia.*

VITIS—*continued*

orientalis. See *AMPELOPSIS orientalis.*

piasezkii MAXIM. (*Parthenocissus sinensis*). A vigorous, but slender species with remarkably variable leaves, 7·5 to 15cm. long. They vary from three-lobed to compound, with three to five oval or obovate leaflets. All are dark green above, brown tomentose beneath. Fruits black-purple. Rich spring and autumn tints. C. China. I. 1900. A.M. 1903.

pulchra REHD. (*flexuosa major*). A climber with reddish shoots and roundish-ovate, coarsely-toothed leaves, 7·5 to 15cm. across. Young leaves reddish, autumn foliage brilliant scarlet. A handsome, vigorous, hardy vine, possibly a hybrid between *V. coignetiae* and *V. amurensis.* C. about 1880.

quinquefolia. See *PARTHENOCISSUS quinquefolia.*

riparia MICHX. (*odoratissima*) (*vulpina* HORT.). "Riverbank Grape". A vigorous, high-climbing species with ovate to broadly ovate, coarsely-toothed and usually three-lobed leaves, 7·5 to 20cm. across. Fruits purple-black, with an intense blue bloom. A useful species worth growing for its attractive bright green foliage and delightfully mignonette-scented male flowers. Eastern N. America. C. 1656.

striata. See *CISSUS striata.*

thomsonii. See *PARTHENOCISSUS thomsonii.*

vinifera L. "Grape Vine". The grape-vine has been cultivated for so long that its native country is now a matter of conjecture. Most authorities regard it as having originated in Asia Minor and the Caucasus Region. Please see our Fruit Tree Catalogue for the best cultivated clones for dessert purposes. The following clones are particularly useful for their ornamental foliage as well as fruits.

'Apiifolia' (*'Laciniosa'*). "Parsely Vine". An attractive form with deeply divided leaves recalling *Ampelopsis aconitifolia.*

'Brandt'. See *V. 'Brant'.*

Fragola. An unusual form with small fruits with a distinct musky flavour, which to some palates is of strawberries, and to others, of gooseberries!

'Incana'. "Dusty Miller Grape". Leaves grey-green, covered with a white, cobwebby down, three-lobed or unlobed. Fruits black. A most effective form when grown with purple-leaved shrubs.

'Laciniosa'. See *'Apiifolia'.*

'Purpurea'. "Teinturier Grape". Leaves at first claret-red, later deep vinous purple, particularly effective when grown with grey or silver foliage shrubs. An attractive combination may be achieved by training a specimen into a weeping willow-leaved pear (*Pyrus salicifolia 'Pendula'*). A.M. 1958. A.G.M. 1969.

vitacea. See *PARTHENOCISSUS inserta.*

vulpina. See *V. riparia.*

†**WATTAKAKA** (*DREGEA*)—**Asclepiadaceae**—A small genus of twining shrubs of which the following species may be grown outside on a warm, sheltered wall, or in a conservatory.

sinensis STAPF. (*Dregea sinensis*). A moderately hardy species with slender stems up to 3m. long requiring some support. Leaves ovate, grey-felted beneath. The deliciously-scented flowers which bear a close resemblance to those of a *Hoya*, are white, with a central zone of red spots. They are borne in long-stalked, downy umbels during summer. Against a west facing wall this climber has here grown successfully for the past eight years. China. I. 1907. A.M. 1954.

WEINMANNIA. See Tree and Shrub section.

WISTERIA (*WISTARIA*)—**Leguminosae**—A small genus of deciduous twiners. There are perhaps no more beautiful climbers than the wisterias, when draped with their multitude of long racemes of white, pink, blue or mauve pea-flowers. May and June is the normal flowering season, but later blooms are often produced. The attractive leaves are pinnate. Planting in full sun is advised, and if the soil is chalky, some good loam should be added. They are excellent subjects for walls, pergolas or for growing into old trees. They may even be trained into small standards by careful cultivation. Large, vigorous specimens on walls, etc., may require an annual hard pruning in late winter to keep them within bounds. A second pruning consists of shortening the leafy shoots in August.

chinensis. See *W. sinensis.*

WISTERIA—*continued*

floribunda DC. "Japanese Wisteria". A lovely climber up to 4m. or more. Leaves composed of thirteen to nineteen ovate, dark green leaflets. Flowers fragrant, violet-blue or bluish-purple, carried in slender racemes, 13 to 25cm. long with the leaves and opening successively from the base onwards. Seed pods velvety. The stems twine in a clockwise direction. Japan. Introduced by Philipp von Siebold in 1830. A.M. 1894.

'Alba' (*multijuga 'Alba'*). Flowers white, tinted lilac on keel, in racemes 45 to 60cm. long. A.M. 1931. A.G.M. 1969.

'Issai'. Flowers lilac-blue, borne in short trusses 18 to 25cm. long, even on young shoots. Possibly a hybrid between *W. floribunda* and *W. sinensis*, the trusses resembling the latter whilst the stems twine in a clockwise direction like the former.

'Macrobotrys' (*W. multijuga*). A magnificent form with racemes ·3 to 1m. long. Racemes up to 1·8m. long have been recorded in Japan. The flowers are fragrant, lilac, tinged blue-purple. Best grown on a wooden bridge, pergola or high arch to allow for the drop of the long racemes. Introduced from Japan to Belgium by Siebold, and thence to England in 1874. A.G.M. 1969.

'Rosea' (*multijuga 'Rosea'*). Flowers pale rose, tipped purple, in long racemes.

'Violacea'. Flowers violet-blue.

'Violacea Plena'. Flowers violet-blue; double.

×**formosa** REHD. (*floribunda 'Alba'* × *sinensis*). An attractive hybrid of American origin; shoots silky downy, flowers pale violet-pink, opening almost simultaneously on racemes 25cm. long. Raised in the garden of the late Professor Sargent of the Arnold Arboretum in 1905.

frutescens POIR. A rare species in cultivation with long climbing stems and leaves composed of five to seventeen ovate leaflets. Flowers fragrant, pale lilac-purple, with a yellow spot, crowded into racemes 10 to 15cm. long which are borne on the current years shoots during summer. Seed pods glabrous. Less vigorous in cultivation than the Asiatic species. S.E. United States. I. 1724.

multijuga. See *W. floribunda 'Macrobotrys'*.

'Alba'. See *W. floribunda 'Alba'*.

'Rosea'. See *W. floribunda 'Rosea'*.

sinensis SWEET (*chinensis*). "Chinese Wisteria". Perhaps the most popular of all wisterias and one of the noblest of all climbers. Reaching 18 to 30m. in a suitable tree. Leaves with nine to thirteen, mostly eleven elliptic to elliptic-oblong leaflets. The fragrant, mauve or deep lilac flowers 2·5cm. long, are carried in racemes 20 to 30cm. long before the leaves, the flowers opening simultaneously. Seed pods velvety. A large specimen in full flower against an old house wall is one of the wonders of May. The stems twine in an anti-clockwise direction. China. First introduced in 1816 from a garden in Canton. A.G.M. 1928.

'Alba'. Flowers white. F.C.C. 1892.

'Black Dragon'. Flowers double, dark purple.

'Plena'. Flowers double, rosette-shaped, lilac.

venusta REHD. & WILS. A strong growing climber up to 9m. or more. Leaves with nine to thirteen oval to ovate, downy leaflets. Flowers, the largest in the genus, white, slightly fragrant, borne in racemes 10 to 15cm. long. Seed pods velvety. C. 1912. Introduced from Japan where it is only known in cultivation. A.M. 1945. F.C.C. 1948.

violacea REHD. The wild form, with violet-coloured flowers. Japan.

CONIFERS

There are few hardy evergreen trees apart from the conifers. Their beauty, wide range of shape, form and colour, plus their adaptability and valuable timber qualities render them indispensable for forest, shelter and ornamental planting. As a general principle it may be stated that, climatic conditions being suitable, they will grow in most soils except very shallow chalky land, pure sand, barren peat or water-logged ground; but there are species adaptable even to these extreme conditions and reference is made to them in the text. Some are excellent for maritime exposures and others lend themselves to hedge-making.

Species, including several from extremely cold arctic conditions, which start into growth very early and are, therefore, subject to injury by spring frosts, are unsuitable for low-lying land and similar "frost pockets". On other sites the risk of injury may be reduced by planting them on the west side of shelter trees, where they are screened from the early morning sun.

The Conifers are mainly distributed in the temperate and subtropical regions of the world (a small proportion occur at high elevations in the tropics). Only three species, namely *Juniperus communis* ("Juniper"), *Pinus sylvestris* ("Scots Pine") and *Taxus baccata* ("Yew") are native to the British Isles, though many foreign species are commonly planted and sometimes naturalised.

The leaves of conifers are, with few notable exceptions, evergreen. They vary from the long, bundled needles of the Pines (*Pinus*) to the shorter, often sharp-pointed leaves of the Firs (*Abies*), Spruces (*Picea*) and Junipers (*Juniperus*). Very different in appearance are the small, scale-like leaves of the Cypresses (*Cupressus*), False Cypresses (*Chamaecyparis*) and Arborvitae (*Thuja*). Of the deciduous conifers the following genera are here described: *LARIX*, *PSEUDOLARIX*, *METASEQUOIA*, *TAXODIUM*, *GINKGO* and *GLYPTOSTROBUS*.

The flowers of conifers are small and primitive and are borne in usually short, catkin-like structures known as strobili. The male and female are borne on separate strobili on the same or on different plants. Pollination is by wind.

The fruits of conifers vary from a woody cone, as in Pine and Larch, to a fleshy, berry-like fruit as in Juniper and Yew.

A great deal of work on the growth and heights of conifers in the British Isles has been carried out by Mr. Alan Mitchell of the Forestry Commission, author of "Conifers in the British Isles" (Forestry Commission Booklet No. 33), published in 1972.

Dwarf Conifers. Recent years have witnessed a tremendous upsurge in the development and interest in miniature to semi-dwarf Conifers of which we now grow about five hundred different sorts. Few species are truly dwarf, they include the creeping or low-growing Junipers, particularly *Juniperus horizontalis* and its clones, *Podocarpus nivalis* and *Dacrydium laxifolium*. Used in a broad sense the term includes all those cultivars which have originated both in the wild and in cultivation as seedling variants, or as sports or mutations; quite a few have come into being as propagations from "Witches Brooms", whilst some prostrate cultivars are the result of vegetative reproduction of horizontally growing side branches.

With the reduction in size of the modern garden there is not room for the large growing timber producing species, but a miniature forest is a thing of beauty and infinite interest for every day of the year. Dwarf Conifers have reproduced in miniature, evergreen trees displaying the full range of colour and contour which exist in the great pinetums and natural forests of the temperate world.

Dwarf Conifers associate well with heathers and many are suitable as specimens on the small lawn or the rock garden. The miniature "bun" forms make excellent subjects for the alpine house or for growing in troughs, etc.

The year in which a cultivar is believed to have arisen or been introduced is indicated at the end of the description, e.g. C. 1876. These dates are often based on the first mention of a name in a book or catalogue and do not necessarily indicate the year of the raising. Often-times descriptions, especially old ones, are quite inadequate and may or may not belong to the plant so named in present-day general cultivation.

HEIGHTS

Trees	Shrubs
Large—Over 18m. (Over 60ft.)	**Large**—Over 3m. (Over 10ft.)
Medium—10 to 18m. (35 to 50ft.)	**Medium**—1·5 to 3m. (6 to 10ft.)
Small—4·5 to 9m. (15 to 30ft.)	**Small**—1 to 1·5m. (3 to 5ft.)
	Dwarf—·3 to ·6m. (1 to 2ft.)
	Prostrate—Creeping

***ABIES—Pinaceae**—The Silver Firs are a beautiful and varied genus of evergreen trees, many of which reach a great size, particularly in the wild. They differ from *Picea* in the disc-like leaf-scars, also in the erect cones which break up whilst still on the tree. The majority of species are conical in outline, at least when young, the branches borne in more or less regular whorls, flattened in a horizontal manner. The leaves are linear and usually flattened, bearing several greyish or white lines of stomata on their lower surface and, in some species, on the upper surface too. On lateral branches they are normally arranged on the branchlets in two opposite ranks or, in some species, are crowded on the upper sides with or without a V-shaped parting. Beneath the branchlets the leaves are generally widely parted (pectinate). Winter buds may be glabrous or resinous, sometimes conspicuously so. Male and female strobili are borne on the same tree during spring. The male strobili are densely clustered along the undersides of the shoots and though partially hidden are often colourful, being most effective when the branchlet sprays are turned over. The erect, usually cylindrical cones are borne on the upper sides of the branchlets and, in many species, are an attractive blue-purple or violet when young.

The Firs require a deep, moist soil if they are to attain their greatest development. The majority dislike industrial atmosphere and shallow chalk soils, the chief exceptions being *A. cephalonica*, *A. pinsapo*, and their hybrid *A.* ×*vilmorinii*.

alba MILL. (*pectinata*). "European Silver Fir". The common species of Central Europe, being particularly predominant in the mountains of France, Switzerland and Germany. A large, or very large tree, with a smooth, grey bark when young. Young shoots greyish, shortly hairy. Winter buds small, pale brown. Leaves 2 to 3cm. long, in two usually horizontal ranks, dark shining green above, marked with two glaucous bands beneath. Cones cylindrical, 10 to 16cm. long, greenish-brown when young, with exerted reflexed bracts. Subject to injury from late spring frosts and one of the least satisfactory species for the southern counties of the British Isles. Europe. I. about 1603.

'Pendula'. An unusual tree of medium size with long, weeping branches, often hanging down the trunk. C. 1835.

'Pyramidalis' (*'Pyramidalis Compacta'*). A medium-sized tree of conical habit, narrower and fastigiate when young, the crowded, ascending branches bearing short, dark shining green leaves. C. 1851.

‡amabilis FORBES. "Red Silver Fir". A beautiful large tree with silvery white bark when young. Young shoots greyish-brown, shortly pubescent; winter buds very resinous, small. Leaves 2·5 to 3cm. long, dark shining green above, white beneath, smelling of oranges when crushed, crowded on the upper sides of the branchlets, pectinate below. Cones ovoid-cylindric, 8 to 15cm. long, purplish when young, bracts hidden. A rare tree in the British Isles and unsuitable for chalky or dry soils. Western N. America. I. 1830.

'Spreading Star' (*'Procumbens'*). A low-growing cultivar up to 1m. high with wide-spreading, horizontally arranged branches. C. 1963.

arizonica. See *A. lasiocarpa arizonica*.

‡balsamea MILL. "Balsam Fir"; "Balm of Gilead". A medium-sized tree common in N. America and extending into the Arctic regions, but not well adapted for our climate. One of the species from which Canada Balsam is obtained. Young shoots softly grey-downy. Winter buds very resinous. Leaves 1·5 to 3cm. long, strongly balsam scented, glossy dark green above except for a patch of glaucous stomata at tip, and with two narrow greyish bands beneath, spreading upwards on the upper-sides of the branchlets, parted beneath. Cones ovoid-cylindric, 6 to 10cm. long, violet-purple when young, bracts usually hidden, sometimes shortly exerted. Not tolerant of chalky soils. I. 1696.

ABIES—*continued*

balsamea 'Hudsonia'. A dwarf shrub. Habit dense and compact with a flattish top. Leaves short and densely arranged on the branchlets. A specimen in our nursery has attained ·75m. × 1·2m. in about thirty years. More lime tolerant than the type. I. before 1810. Clones are sometimes found in cultivation under names such as '*Nana*' and '*Prostrata*' which are insufficiently distinct, even for garden purposes.

'Nana'. See under '*Hudsonia*'.

borisii-regis MATTF. A strong-growing, large tree with pale brown or buff, shortly pubescent young shoots. Winter buds usually thinly resinous. Leaves 2·5 to 3cm. long, dark glossy green above, marked with two glaucous bands beneath, crowded on the upper surfaces of the branchlets, pectinate below. Cones cylindrical, 10 to 15cm. long, bracts exerted and reflexed. A variable species more or less intermediate between *A. alba* and *A. cephalonica*, from which it is perhaps derived as a hybrid. Balkan Peninsular. A.M. 1974.

bornmuellerana MATTF. A large tree resembling *A. nordmanniana* in habit, with branches down to the ground. Young shoots greenish, becoming brown, glabrous; winter buds usually resinous. Leaves densely arranged on the upper sides of the branchlets, up to 2 to 3cm. long, green above, often with stomata at tip, marked with two white bands of stomata beneath. Cones cylindrical, 12 to 15cm. long, bracts exerted and reflexed. Believed to be a natural hybrid between *A. cephalonica* and *A. nordmanniana*, though some authorities regard it as a species related to *A. cilicica*. Asia Minor.

brachyphylla. See *A. homolepis*.

bracteata NUTT. (*venusta*). One of the most outstanding and beautiful of the firs, forming a large tree. Young shoots greenish and glabrous. Distinct on account of its pale-brown, spindle-shaped winter buds up to 2·5cm. long, and its 3·5 to 5cm. long, rigid, spine-tipped dark green leaves which occur on the branchlets in two ranks. Cones ovoid to cylindrical, 7 to 10cm. long, bracts long exerted, spine-tipped, giving the cones a remarkable whiskery appearance. Succeeds on deep soil over chalk. Mts. of S. California. Introduced by William Lobb in 1852. F.C.C. 1915.

cephalonica LOUD. "Grecian Fir". A large, handsome tree with pale brown, glabrous young shoots and resinous winter buds. Leaves rigid, sharp-pointed, shining green, 1·5 to 2·5cm. long, white beneath, spreading more or less all round the branchlets but not so noticeably so as *A. pinsapo*. Cones cylindrical, 12 to 16cm. long, with exerted, reflexed bracts. One of the best species for chalky soils and for freedom from disease, but breaks into growth early and therefore should not be planted in "frost pockets". Mts. of Greece. I. 1824.

'Nana'. A dwarf cultivar with horizontally spreading branches, rigid branchlets and leaves usually shorter than those of the type.

chensiensis VAN TIEGH. (*ernestii*). A medium-sized to large tree with conspicuous rough grey bark. Young shoots yellowish-grey, glabrous; winter buds slightly resinous. Leaves 1·5 to 3·5cm. long, thick and rigid, shining dark green above, marked with two grey or bluish stomatic bands beneath, arranged in V-shaped formation. Cones ovoid-oblong, 5 to 8cm. long, greenish when young, bracts hidden. Very rare in cultivation. It is readily confused with *A. holophylla* and *A. recurvata*. C. China. Introduced by Ernest Wilson in 1907.

cilicica CARR. "Cilician Fir". Medium to large size tree. Bark greyish, deeply fissured on old trees. Young shoots greyish-brown, glabrous or sparsely short pubescent. Winter buds slightly resinous. Leaves 2 to 3·5cm. long, light green above, marked with two narrow, greyish stomatic bands beneath, arranged on the branchlets in a V-shaped formation. Cones cylindrical, 16 to 25cm. long, bracts hidden. Asia Minor; N. Syria. I. 1855.

concolor HILDEBR. "Colorado White Fir". A very beautiful large tree with smooth, grey bark, grooved and scaly on old trees. Young shoots glabrous or shortly pubescent, yellowish-green becoming grey. Winter buds large and thickly resinous. Leaves up to 5·5cm. long, thick, almost round in section, of an attractive blue-green or grey-green colour, arranged mainly in two ranks, but also standing above the shoot. Cones cylindrical, 8 to 14cm. long, pale green when young sometimes purplish bloomy, bracts hidden. S.W. United States. I. 1873.

'Candicans'. A striking cultivar with vivid grey or silvery-white leaves.

ABIES—*continued*

concolor 'Glauca Compacta' (*'Compacta'*). A dwarf shrub of compact but irregular habit, leaves of an attractive greyish-blue colour. A wonderful plant, the most outstanding dwarf Silver Fir, suitable for the large rock garden or as an isolated lawn specimen. A shrub in our arboretum has attained ·75m.×1·1m. in twenty-five years. C. 1891.

lowiana LEMM. (*A. lowiana*). "Pacific White Fir". A large tree, the side-branches are very even in length and short in comparison with the height of the tree and diameter of the trunk. It has greyish-green young shoots and the winter buds are smaller than in the type and the leaves are pectinate above or arranged in V-shaped formation. S.W. United States. Introduced by William Lobb in 1851.

'Violacea'. Leaves glaucous-blue. C. 1875.

'Wattezii'. A small to medium-sized tree, leaves creamy-yellow when young, becoming silvery-white later. C. 1900.

concolor × grandis. A large tree more or less intermediate in character between the parents.

delavayi FRANCH. A medium-sized, handsome tree of somewhat variable nature. Young shoots yellowish-brown or reddish-brown, pubescent or glabrescent. Winter buds large, orange, resinous. The densely set leaves, 2 to 3cm. long, are revolute, bright shining green above and gleaming silvery-white beneath. Cones barrel-shaped, 6 to 10cm. long, dark bluish-violet with very slightly exerted bracts. W. and C. China. I. 1918. Several one-time species are now generally regarded as varieties of *A. delavayi*. A.M. 1980 (to K.W. 21008).

fabri D. R. HUNT (*A. fabri*). A medium-sized tree with brown scaly bark. Young shoots rust-coloured, pubescent. Winter buds orange-brown and slightly resinous. Leaves 2 to 3cm. long, dark green above, gleaming white beneath, with recurved margins, often rather loosely and irregularly arranged. Cones barrel-shaped, 6 to 8cm. long, bluish-black, bracts exerted and reflexed. C. and W. China; Upper Burma. I. 1901.

faxoniana A. B. JACKS. (*A. faxoniana*). A medium-sized tree, differing from the type mainly in its shorter more nondescript flatter leaves and smaller cones. Leaves 1 to 2·5cm. long, marked with two glaucous bands beneath, crowded into two more or less horizontal ranks. Cones barrel-shaped, 6 to 7cm. long, purplish-violet, bracts shortly exerted and reflexed. One of the least satisfactory of the newer Asiatic Firs in cultivation. W. China; Upper Burma. I. 1910.

forrestii A. B. JACKS. (*A. forrestii*). A very distinct and beautiful, small to medium-sized tree with rich, rusty-red, usually glabrous, young shoots. Winter buds conspicuously white resinous. Leaves variable in length and arrangement, but usually 2 to 4cm. long and almost radial, dark green above, conspicuously silvery-white beneath. Cones barrel-shaped, 8 to 9cm. long, sloe-black with exserted bracts. W. China. Introduced by George Forrest about 1910. A.M. 1930.

georgei MELVILLE (*A. georgei*). Closely related to var. *forrestii*, differing in its usually pubescent young shoots and its cones which possess even more conspicuous exerted bracts, with tail-like points. Leaves 3 to 4cm. long. W. China. I. 1923.

'Nana'. A dwarf, slow-growing form of the type. Winter buds orange-brown. Leaves more or less radially arranged, 1 to 1·5cm. long, the margins recurved.

ernestii. See *A. chensiensis*.

fabri. See *A. delavayi fabri*.

fargesii FRANCH. A strong-growing, medium-sized tree with stout, glabrous or slightly hairy, orange-brown or purple young shoots. Winter buds large, conical and very resinous. Leaves loosely two-ranked, 3 to 5cm. long, notched, dark green above, marked with two glaucous bands beneath. Cones 6 to 10cm. long, purplish-brown when young. Bracts shortly exerted and reflexed. A splendid species and one of the best of the newer Asiatic Silver Firs in cultivation. W. and C. China. First discovered by Père Fargès and introduced by Ernest Wilson in 1901.

faxoniana. See *A. delavayi faxoniana*.

ABIES—*continued*

‡firma SIEB. & ZUCC. "Japanese Fir". A large tree with pale, orange-brown, slightly hairy young shoots and small, slightly resinous winter buds. The comparatively broad, stiff, leathery leaves, 1·5 to 4cm. long, are bright, glossy green or yellowish-green above, with two greyish-green, stomatic bands beneath. They are conspicuously notched on the lateral branches, densely crowded, with a V-shaped parting, on the upper sides of the shoots, loosely pectinate below. Cones cylindrical, 8 to 15cm. long, yellowish-green when young. Bracts slightly exerted. A decidedly calcifuge tree. Japan. I. 1861. F.C.C. 1863.

forrestii. See *A. delavayi forrestii.*

fraseri POIR. Medium-sized tree with a slender, conical crown. Young shoots greyish or brownish, pubescent. Winter buds purplish-brown, rounded and resinous. Leaves short, 1 to 2cm. long, crowded on the upper sides of the twigs, pectinate below, dark shining green above, with a few short lines of stomata near the tip, marked with two white stomatic bands beneath. Cones ovoid or cylindrical 3 to 5cm. long, purple when young. Bracts long exerted and reflexed. One of the least satisfactory of the North American Silver Firs in cultivation and very prone to disease. S.E. United States. Introduced by John Fraser in 1811.

gamblei. See *A. pindrow brevifolia.*

georgei. See *A. delavayi georgei.*

grandis LINDL. "Giant Fir". This remarkably fast-growing tree quickly attains a large size. Distinguished by its olive-green, minutely downy young shoots and its horizontally disposed leaves. Winter buds small and resinous. Leaves varying from 2 to 6cm. long, dark shining green above, marked with two glaucous-grey bands beneath. Cones cylindrical 7·5 to 10cm. long, bright green. Grows best in areas with a heavy rainfall and prefers a moist but well-drained soil. A good shade-bearing species and moderately lime-tolerant; the leaves are delightfully fragrant when crushed. Western N. America. Introduced by David Douglas in 1830.

'Aurea'. Leaves yellowish. C. 1891.

holophylla MAXIM. "Manchurian Fir". A large tree, rare in cultivation. Young shoots yellowish-grey and glabrous. Winter buds resinous. Leaves 2·5 to 4cm. long, bright green above, with two greyish-green stomatic bands beneath, densely arranged on the upper-sides of the shoot, pectinate below. Cones cylindrical, 10 to 13cm. long, green when young. Closely related to *A. homolepis*. Manchuria; Korea. I. 1908.

homolepis SIEB. & ZUCC. (*brachyphylla*). "Nikko Fir". A very splendid, large tree, with light brown, buff or sometimes white, deeply grooved, glabrous young shoots. Winter buds resinous. Leaves 1·5 to 3cm. long, green above, with two chalk-white, stomatic bands beneath, crowded on the upper sides of the branchlets, pectinate below. Cones cylindrical 7·5 to 10cm. long, purple when young. A tough, adaptable tree which will even tolerate a certain amount of atmospheric pollution, and succeeds where many other species would fail. Japan. I. 1861.

intermedia. See *I. pindrow intermedia.*

kawakamii ITO. A very rare, small to medium-sized tree with very pale or whitish bark. Young shoots yellowish-white, orange pubescent in grooves. Winter buds pale orange, thinly resinous. Leaves 1·5 to 3cm. long, "bloomy" at first above, later green, marked with two pale bands beneath, crowded and curved on the upper sides of the branchlets, loosely spreading below. Cones cylindrical, 5 to 7·5cm. long, purple when young. Formosa. I. before 1930.

koreana WILS. A small, slow-growing tree of neat habit. Young shoots pale brown or buff, glabrous. Winter buds small, white resinous. Leaves 1 to 2cm. long, dark green above, gleaming white beneath, radially arranged on strong shoots, loosely arranged on others. An interesting species, producing its violet-purple, cylindrical cones, 5 to 7·5cm. long, even on specimens half a metre high. S. Korea. I. 1905.

'Compact Dwarf'. A small, compact form, spreading horizontally, without a leader. Non-coning.

lasiocarpa NUTT. "Alpine Fir". A medium-sized tree with ash-grey, minutely-pubescent young shoots and small resinous winter buds. Distinct on account of its pale greyish-green leaves, 1·5 to 3·5cm. long, densely but irregularly arranged on the branchlets in two ranks. Cones cylindrical, 5 to 10cm. long, purple when young. Moderately lime-tolerant. Western N. America.

ABIES—*continued*

lasiocarpa arizonica LEMM. (*A. arizonica*). "Cork Fir". A medium-sized tree with greyish or buff-coloured, shortly pubescent branchlets and thick, soft, corky bark. Winter buds very resinous. Leaves 2·5 to 3·5cm. long, silvery-grey. Cones smaller than those of the type. Arizona. I. 1903.

'Compacta' (*arizonica 'Compacta'*). A slow-growing shrub of compact, conical habit, leaves of a conspicuous blue-grey. C. 1927.

lowiana. See *A. concolor lowiana.*

‡magnifica A. MURR. "Californian Red Fir". A beautiful large tree of slender, cone-shaped habit, attaining 60m. in its native habitats. Bark of young trees whitish. Young shoots shortly reddish-brown pubescent. Winter buds resinous. Leaves long and curved, 2 to 4cm. long, grey-green or blue-green on both surfaces, densely clothing the upper sides of the branchlets, pectinate below. Cones cylindrical, 15 to 22cm. long, purple when young. Not suitable for chalk soils. Western U.S.A. I. 1851.

'Glauca'. Leaves of a deep glaucous-green. C. 1891.

'Nana'. A dwarf form with wide-spreading branches.

‡mariesii MAST. "Maries' Fir". Medium-sized to large tree with persistently reddish-brown, downy young shoots. Winter buds very resinous. Leaves 1·5 to 2·5cm. long, shining dark green above, with two conspicuous white bands of stomata below, crowded on the upper sides of the branchlets, pectinate below. Cones 7·5 to 10cm. long, violet-purple when young. Japan. Introduced by Charles Maries about 1879.

marocana TRABUT. "Maroc Fir". A medium-sized tree closely related to *A. pinsapo*. Young shoots yellowish-grey and glabrous. Winter buds resinous. Leaves 1 to 1·5cm. long, green above, with white stomatic bands beneath, arranged in two horizontal ranks. Cones cylindrical, 12 to 15cm. long, pale brown. Rare in cultivation. Morocco. I. about 1905.

nebrodensis MATTEI. A small to medium-sized tree, related to *A. alba*, but differing in its smaller size and the broader, flatter crown of mature specimens. The leaves are also stiffer and slightly shorter and densely arranged on the upper sides of the branchlets. Cones cylindrical, 2·5 to 3·5cm. long, with exerted bracts. A very rare species almost extinct in the wild and now restricted to a few trees in the mountains of Northern Sicily.

nobilis. See *A. procera.*

nordmanniana SPACH. "Caucasian Fir". A noble species of great ornamental value. A large to very large tree reaching 50 to 60m. in its native habitats, with tiered branches sweeping downwards. Young shoots greyish-brown, shining but shortly hairy. Winter buds reddish-brown. Leaves 2 to 3cm. long, shining green above, marked with two white stomatic bands beneath, densely arranged on the branchlets, pointing forwards and overlapping above, pectinate below. Cones oblong-ovoid to cylindrical 15 to 20cm. long, greenish when young, scales long-exerted and reflexed. A very satisfactory, generally disease-resistant species. W. Caucasus. I. 1840.

'Aureospica'. Growth irregular. Leaves tipped golden-yellow. C. 1891.

'Golden Spreader' (*'Aurea Nana'*). A dwarf, slow-growing cultivar with wide-spreading branches. Leaves 1 to 2·5cm. long, light yellow above, pale yellowish-white beneath. C. 1960.

'Pendula'. A wide-spreading, semi-prostrate form, the branchlets with pendulous tips. C. 1870.

numidica CARR. "Algerian Fir". A large tree of conical habit, with shining-brown, glabrous young shoots. Winter buds large, resinous when young. Leaves radially arranged, but all curving upwards, averaging 1 to 2cm. long, dark green above, with a greyish stomatic patch near the apex, marked with two white bands beneath. Cones cylindrical, 12 to 18cm. long, brown. Only native in a small mountainous area of Eastern Algeria. I. 1861. A.M. 1976.

'Pendula'. A slow-growing form with pendulous branchlets.

†oaxacana MARTINEZ. A rare, medium-sized tree with conspicuous glabrous, orange-brown young shoots. Leaves 2 to 4cm. long, dark green above, marked with two glaucous, stomatic bands beneath. Cones 8 to 11cm. long, bracts exerted. Resembles both *A. religiosa* and *A. vejari*, at least when young. Mexico.

pectinata. See *A. alba.*

ABIES—*continued*

pindrow SPACH. "West Himalayan Fir". A rare and beautiful large tree of slender, conical habit. Young shoots stout, greyish-brown and glabrous. Winter buds large and conspicuous, orange-brown, thinly resinous. Leaves normally 3 to 6cm. long, bright shining green above, with two greyish-white, stomatic bands beneath, loosely arranged but concealing the branchlets above, pectinate below. W. Himalaya, where it forms mixed forests with *Cedrus deodara* and *Picea smithiana* and ranges into *A. spectabilis*. Introduced by Dr. Royle, about 1837.

brevifolia DALLIM. & A. B. JACKS. (*A. gamblei*). A very distinct tree differing markedly from the type in its pale brown or reddish-brown shoots and its shorter leaves, 2 to 3·5cm. long. C. 1860.

intermedia HENRY. A very distinct variety with stout, pale buff-coloured young shoots which have darker-coloured pubescence in the grooves. Winter buds as in the type. Leaves 4·5 to 6cm. long, dark green above, gleaming silvery-white beneath, loosely two ranked. A striking fir of uncertain origin. A beautiful and remarkable tree possessing the longest leaves of the genus, vividly white beneath, possibly a species or maybe a hybrid with *A. spectabilis*. C. 1870. A.M. 1944.

pinsapo BOISS. "Spanish Fir". A medium-sized to large tree, easily recognised by its short, rigid, dark green leaves up to 1·5cm. long which radiate from all sides of the branchlets. Young shoots cinnamon-brown, smooth and glabrous. Winter buds thinly resinous. Cones cylindrical, 10 to 15cm. long, purplish-brown when young. One of the best species for chalk soils and one of the only two species with radially spreading leaves, the other being *A. cephalonica* although *A. numidica* and some forms of *A. delavayi forrestii* approach this condition. Mts. of S. Spain. I. 1839.

'Aurea'. Leaves suffused golden yellow. Usually a medium to large shrub of rather poor constitution. C. 1868.

'Glauca'. A large tree selected for its striking blue-grey leaves. C. 1867.

‡**procera** REHD. (*nobilis*). "Noble Fir". A most beautiful, large to very large tree. Young shoots clothed with short rusty-brown down. Winter buds resinous, with a basal collar of long-pointed scales. Leaves 2·5 to 3·5cm. long, bluish-green above, with two narrow, glaucous bands beneath, crowded on the upper sides of the branchlets, pectinate and decurved below. The magnificent cylindrical cones are 16 to 25cm. long, green when young, with long-exerted, reflexed bracts. Not suitable for chalk soils. W. United States. Introduced by David Douglas in 1830. A.M. 1973.

'Glauca'. A selection with blue-grey leaves. C. 1863.

'Glauca Prostrata' (*'Prostrata'*). A low bush with spreading or prostrate branches and glaucous leaves. Originated in our Shroner Wood Nursery in about 1895.

recurvata MAST. A medium-sized tree closely resembling *A. chensiensis* but with shorter leaves. Young shoots pale brown and glabrous. Winter buds pale orange and thinly resinous. Leaves 1·5 to 2·5cm. long, thick and rigid, those on the upper sides of the terminal branchlets strongly recurved, dark shining green or sometimes slightly glaucous above, paler beneath. Cones oblong-ovoid, 5 to 10cm. long, violet-purple when young. W. China. I. 1910.

†**religiosa** SCHLECHT. "Sacred Fir". A rare tree of small to medium size with downward-sweeping stems. Young shoots reddish-brown, shortly pubescent. Winter buds resinous. Leaves 1·5 to 3·5cm. long, peculiary tapered and curved, dark green above, marked with two greyish stomatic bands beneath, densely arranged and forward-pointing on the upper sides of the branchlets, pectinate below. Cones cylindrical, 10 to 15cm. long, bluish when young, bracts exerted and reflexed. In Mexico the branches are used to decorate mission buildings during religious festivals. Reasonably lime tolerant, it has grown in our nursery for more than fifty years. Mexico; Guatemala. I. 1838.

sachalinensis MAST. "Sachalin Fir". A medium-sized tree with greyish young shoots, pale brown pubescent in grooves. Winter buds small but conspicuously bluish-white resinous. Leaves very dense, 1·5 to 3·5cm. long, light green above, marked with two greyish bands beneath. Cones cylindrical 7 to 8cm. long, olive-green when young, bracts exerted and reflexed. Less susceptible to spring frosts. Differs from the closely related *A. sibirica* in its furrowed shoots not densely white pubescent. N. Japan; Sakhalin; Kurile Isles. I. 1878.

ABIES—*continued*

sachalinensis mayriana MIYABE & KUDO. A Japanese variety differing mainly in its shorter leaves, 1·5 to 2·5cm. long and slightly larger cones.

spectabilis SPACH (*webbiana*). "Himalayan Fir". A magnificent large tree closely resembling forms of *A. delavayi*. Young shoots reddish-brown, stout and rough, downy in the grooves. Winter buds large and globular, very resinous. The densely two-ranked leaves 1·5 to 5cm. or occasionally 6cm. long, are shining dark green above and gleaming silvery-white beneath. Cones cylindrical, 14 to 18cm long, violet-purple when young, bracts hidden or slightly exerted. Unfortunately, this striking species is susceptible to spring frosts. Nepal; Sikkim; Bhutan. I. 1822. A.M. 1974.

squamata MAST. "Flaky Fir". A very rare, small to medium-sized tree with conspicuous shaggy, peeling, purplish-brown bark. Young shoots dark reddish-brown, downy. Winter buds white resinous. Leaves 1 to 2·5cm. long, greyish green above with two greyish bands beneath, sharply pointed, densely arranged on the upper sides of the branchlets. Cones ovoid-cylindric, 5 to 6cm. long, violet, the bracts with exerted, reflexed tips. Our largest tree measured 12m. in 1970. Introduced by E. H. Wilson from W. China, in 1910.

sutchuenensis REHD. & WILS. "Szechwan Fir". A very rare, medium-sized tree with usually glabrous, shining purplish-brown or plum-purple, sometimes almost chocolate brown, young shoots. Winter buds stout and resinous. Leaves pungently scented when crushed, 1 to 2·5cm. long, green above, marked with two glaucous bands beneath, crowded on the upper sides of the branchlets and forming a V-shaped parting, loosely pectinate below. Cones ovoid-oblong, 5 to 7·5cm. long, dark violet or purplish-black, bracts with exerted, reflexed tips. W. China. First discovered by William Purdom and introduced by him in 1911. It was again introduced by Joseph Rock in 1925.

×**vasconcellosiana** FRANCO (*pindrow*×*pinsapo*). A very rare, medium-sized tree which occurred in a park in Portugal in 1945. Resembling *A. pindrow* in general habit. Young shoots pale brown, winter buds very resinous. Leaves 1 to 3cm. long, slightly curved, glossy dark green above, prominently marked with two greyish stomatic bands beneath. Cones cylindrical, 12 to 15cm. long, dark purple when young.

‡**veitchii** LINDL. A beautiful, large, fast-growing tree. Young shoots brown, smooth and glabrous, or minutely pubescent. Winter buds purplish, very resinous. The densely-arranged, upcurved leaves, 1 to 2·5cm. long, are glossy dark green above and silver-white beneath. Cones cylindrical, 5 to 7cm. long, bluish-purple when young, tips of bracts exerted. This handsome species thrives better in the vicinity of large towns than most others, but is not happy on chalk soils. C. Japan. First discovered by John Gould Veitch on Mt. Fuji in 1860; introduced by Charles Maries in 1879. A.M. 1974.

†**vejari** MARTINEZ. A newly introduced small to medium-sized tree with glabrous or minutely pubescent, light olive-brown young shoots. Leaves up to 3·5cm. long, dark green above, marked with two grey stomatic bands beneath. Cones 5 to 8cm. long, purple when young, bracts with exerted tips. Young specimens resemble *A. religiosa*. Mexico. I. 1964.

venusta. See *A. bracteata*.

×**vilmorinii** MAST. (*cephalonica*×*pinsapo*). A medium-sized to large tree with stout, yellowish-brown young shoots. Leaves 2 to 3cm. long, marked with two grey bands beneath, radially-arranged but more densely so on the upper sides of the branchlets. Cones cylindrical, 14 to 20cm. long, bracts exerted and reflexed at tips. An intentional cross raised in 1867 by Maurice L. de Vilmorin, whose arboretum at Les Barres was and still is one of the largest and richest in Europe. It was to Mons. Vilmorin that the plant-collecting French missionaries such as David, Delavay and Farges sent from China seed of so many new and exciting woody plants. This same hybrid frequently occurs where the two parent species are growing in close proximity.

webbiana. See *A. spectabilis*.

†***AGATHIS**—**Araucariaceae**—Large, evergreen trees with massive trunks, related to *Araucaria*. Only one species is in cultivation and is only suitable for the mildest localities. The thick, scaly, resinous bark emits a thick, milky liquid when wounded. Male and female strobili are normally borne on the same tree.

AGATHIS—*continued*

australis SALISB. "Kauri Pine". An exotic-looking tree with thick spreading branches. Leaves variable, on young trees they are narrowly lanceolate, 2·5 to 8cm. long, spreading, leathery and lime-green in colour, on old trees they are shorter, oblong and sessile. Young plants are bronze or purple flushed. Cones 6 to 8cm. across, subglobose. These are produced on a tree growing on chalk soil in our home nursery in a cold house. It attains small tree size in the British Isles, but in New Zealand giants of 45m. high with trunks 6 to 7m. in diameter are recorded. Native of New Zealand (North Island) where it is of economic importance for its timber and resin. I. 1823.

***ARAUCARIA—Araucariaceae**—Evergreen trees found only in the southern hemisphere. Young trees remarkable for their symmetrical habit, with branches usually borne in whorls down to ground level. The long-persistent, spirally-arranged leaves are usually leathery and overlapping, but vary in size and shape often on different parts of the same tree. Male and female strobili normally borne on different trees, occasionally on different branches of the same tree. The globular or ovoid cones break up while still on the tree. The following is the only hardy species.

araucana K. KOCH (*imbricata*). "Chile Pine"; "Monkey Puzzle". A medium-sized to large tree of unique appearance with long spidery branches and densely overlapping, rigid, spine-tipped, dark green leaves. Cones globular, 11 to 18cm. long, taking three years to mature. One of the few South American trees hardy in the British Isles and an excellent wind resister. It grows best in a moist, loamy soil. In industrial areas it loses its lower branches and becomes ragged in appearance. Extensively planted in Victorian times. Chile; Argentine. First introduced by Archibald Menzies in 1795 and later by William Lobb in 1844. A.M. 1980.

***ATHROTAXIS—Taxodiaceae**—The "Tasmanian Cedars", with their small cones and usually short, thick, imbricated leaves, are unique in appearance and slow growing. Male and female strobili borne on the same tree. Cones small, ripening the first year. Leaves of the main branchlets are larger than those of the subsidiary branchlets. All three species are native to Tasmania and require a warm, sheltered position. *A. cupressoides* and *A. laxifolia* have grown successfully here without injury for more than fifty years, but *A. selaginoides* is less hardy and is injured or killed in a severe winter.

cupressoides D. DON. A small, erect tree with very small, closely-imbricated, dark-green, scale-like leaves, obtuse at the tips and pressed close to the stems. Cones 8 to 12mm. across. I. 1848.

laxifolia HOOK. A small to medium-sized tree differing from *A. cupressoides* in its laxer habit and larger, usually pointed leaves which are slightly spreading. Cones 16 to 18mm. across. I. 1857.

†selaginoides D. DON. A small to medium-sized tree larger in all its parts than the other two species. Closer to *A. laxifolia*, but leaves larger—up to 12mm. long, more spreading, showing the conspicuous glaucous bands above, and with a long pointed apex. Cones up to 18mm. long and broad. I. about 1857. A.M. 1931.

***AUSTROCEDRUS—Cupressaceae**—A monotypic genus closely related to and sometimes united with *LIBOCEDRUS*. Leaves scale-like, borne in unequal opposite pairs, marked with glaucous stomatic bands, forming flattened sprays. Male and female strobili borne on the same tree. Cones small, solitary.

chilensis FLORIN & BOUTELJE (*Libocedrus chilensis*). "Chilean Cedar". A remarkably beautiful and distinct species, here slow-growing, but hardy and making a small, columnar tree. The branchlets are flattened and beautifully moss-like or fern-like in their ultimate divisions. Leaves in V-shaped pairs, of a pleasant shade of sea-green. This tree has grown successfully in our nursery for forty years. Chile; Argentine. I. 1847.

'Viridis'. Leaves bright green, lacking the glaucous, stomatic bands.

†*CALLITRIS—Cupressaceae—The Cypress Pines of Australia and Tasmania are evergreen trees and shrubs thriving in dry, arid conditions. Their branchlets are long and thread-like, densely clothed with small, narrow or scale-like leaves. Male and female strobili borne on the same tree. The globular, ovoid or conical cones, with six to eight scales, are often borne in clusters and persist for several years. All species are tender and should be grown in the conservatory or in sheltered woodland in mild localities.

CALLITRIS—*continued*

oblonga RICH. "Tasmanian Cypress Pine". An erect bush of medium size. The densely-arranged, spray-like branchlets bear short, appressed, scale-like leaves. Cones up to 2·5cm. long, woody, with clawed scales; produced singly or in clusters. Tasmania. A.M. 1931.

rhomboidea L. C. RICH (*cupressiformis*) (*tasmanica*). "Oyster Bay Pine". A rare species in cultivation attaining small tree size. Branchlets finely divided, clothed with bright green or glaucous scale-like leaves. Cones ovoid, 8 to 13mm. across, purplish brown. E. Tasmania; Australia (Queensland; New South Wales; Victoria).

tasmanica. See *C. rhomboidea.*

***CALOCEDRUS** (*HEYDERIA*)—**Cupressaceae**—A small genus of evergreen trees allied to *Thuja* and, by many authorities, united with *Libocedrus.* The branchlets are arranged in broad, flattened sprays. Leaves scale-like, flattened, densely borne in opposite pairs. Male and female strobili borne on different branches of the same tree. Cones woody, ripening the first year.

decurrens FLORIN (*Libocedrus decurrens*). "Incense Cedar". A large tree with a conical head of spreading branches in the wild state. Most cultivated trees belong to the form '*Columnaris*'. The characteristic columnar habit renders it unmistakable among cultivated trees and ideal as a single specimen or for grouping for skyline or formal effect. The long-decurrent, dark green leaves are crowded into dense, fan-like sprays. Cones ovoid, pendulous, up to 2·5cm. long. S.W. United States. I. 1853.

'Aureovariegata'. A cultivar in which sprays of golden leaves occur irregularly about the branches. An attractive, slow-growing, medium-sized tree. C. 1904.

'Fastigiata'. See '*Columnaris*' under *C. decurrens.*

'Nana' ('*Intricata*'). A remarkable dwarf form with thick, flat and twisted recurving branchlets. Our specimen has made a dense, rigid column, 1·2m. high by ·6m. wide after 20 years. C. 1923.

†**formosana** FLOR. (*Libocedrus formosana*). A distinct species. A small treeof open habit showing kinship with *C. macrolepis*, but differing in its more slender branchlets and bright green leaves, yellowish-green beneath. Only suitable for the mildest localities. Plants have survived several winters here, growing among shelter trees. Formosa.

†**macrolepis** KURZ (*Libocedrus macrolepis*). A beautiful, small, open-branched tree with broad, elegant, fan-like sprays of flattened branchlets. The large, flattened leaves are sea-green above and glaucous beneath. Only suitable for the mildest localities. S.W. China; E. Burma. Introduced by Ernest Wilson in 1900. F.C.C. 1902. (as *Libocedrus macrolepis*).

***CEDRUS**—**Pinaceae**—"Cedar". A small genus of four species of evergreen trees, renowned for their grandeur and longevity. Young trees are conical in outline, developing often a massive trunk and large horizontal branches as they age. They are among the most popular of all trees for specimen planting, but owing to their eventual size are only suitable for parks, open areas and large gardens.

The narrow, needle-like leaves are sparsely arranged in spirals on the terminal shoots and borne in rosettes on the numerous, spur-like side growths. Male and female strobili are borne usually on the same tree, the bright yellow males peppering the flattened branchlets in autumn. Cones, barrel-shaped, erect, maturing in two years and breaking up while still on the tree. *C. atlantica* and *C. libani* are very closely related and differ only in small details. Some authorities regard all of the following as geographical forms of one species.

atlantica MANETTI. "Atlas Cedar". A large or very large tree of rapid growth when young. Leaves 2 to 3·5cm. long, green or grey-green, thickly covering the long branches which, though somewhat ascending at first, eventually assume the horizontal arrangement generally associated with *C. libani.* Cones 5 to 7cm. long. The "Atlas Cedar" is said to differ from the "Cedar of Lebanon" in a number of characters such as hairier shoots, larger leaf rosettes, etc., but these minor differences are not consistent, varying from tree to tree. It is perhaps best considered as a geographical subspecies of *C. libani.* Atlas Mts. in Algeria and Morocco (N. Africa). I. about 1840.

'Aurea'. A medium-sized tree; leaves shorter than in the type, distinctly golden yellow. Not always a satisfactory grower. C. 1900.

'Fastigiata'. A large, densely-branched tree of erect habit, the branches sharply ascending, branchlets short and erect. Leaves bluish-green. C. 1890.

CEDRUS—*continued*

atlantica glauca BEISSN. "Blue Cedar". Perhaps the most spectacular of all "blue" conifers and a very popular tree for specimen planting. Leaves silvery-blue, extremely effective. It occurs both in the wild and in cultivation. F.C.C. 1972. A.G.M. 1973.

'Glauca Pendula'. A superb small tree with weeping branches and glaucous leaves. Most effective when well positioned. C. 1900.

'Pendula'. A small, weeping tree with green or greyish-green leaves. C. 1875.

brevifolia HENRY. "Cyprian Cedar". A rare species of slow growth, but eventually making a tree of medium size. The arrangement of the branches is similar to that of *C. libani*, but the usually green leaves are much smaller—1 to 1·25cm. long, or up to 2cm. on young trees. Mts. of Cyprus. I. 1879.

deodara G. DON. The "Deodar" is a most beautiful, large tree of somewhat pendant habit. The leaves are glaucous when young, soon deep green. It is readily distinguished from all other species by its drooping leader and by its longer leaves which occasionally measure 5cm. long. Cones 7 to 10cm. long. W. Himalaya. I. 1831.

'Albospica'. Tips of young shoots creamy-white. An elegant tree, particularly effective in late spring. C. 1874.

'Aurea'. "Golden Deodar". A tree with leaves golden-yellow in spring, becoming greenish-yellow later in the year. C. 1866.

'Aurea Pendula'. Branches weeping; leaves yellow during late spring and summer, yellow-green during winter.

'Pendula' (*'Prostrata'*). A form with pendulous branches spreading over the ground, eventually growing too large for the rock garden. C. 1900. Attractive as a wide-spreading low bush if controlled by pruning, but if permitted to develop unchecked it tends to produce a leader and lose its dwarf habit.

'Pygmy' (*'Pygmaea'*). An extremely slow-growing, dwarf form increasing at about 1·5cm. per year. It is of American origin, making a tiny hummock of blue-grey foliage. C. 1943.

'Robusta'. A wide-spreading tree of medium height with irregular drooping branches and long, stout, dark blue-green leaves up to 8cm. long. C. 1852.

'Verticillata Glauca'. A dense-growing, small bushy tree with horizontal branches and almost whorled (verticillate) branchlets. Leaves dark glaucous-green. C. 1887.

libani A. RICH. "Cedar of Lebanon". A large, wide-spreading tree, slower-growing than *C. atlantica* and, like that species, conical when young, gradually assuming the familiar, picturesque, flat-topped and tiered arrangement of a mature tree. Leaves green or greyish-green, 2 to 3·5cm. long. Cones 8 to 10cm. long. This interesting tree has innumerable scriptural and historical associations. It is a native of Asia Minor and Syria and is thought to have been first introduced into England sometime before 1650, possibly 1645.

'Aurea Prostrata' (*'Golden Dwarf'*). A slow-growing, horizontal, dwarf bush with yellow leaves. Stems sometimes prostrate.

'Comte de Dijon'. A slow-growing, conical form of dense, compact growth, eventually making a medium-sized bush. C. 1908.

'Nana'. A very slow-growing, dense, conical bush of medium size, similar to *'Comte de Dijon'*, but with slightly broader, shorter leaves, 1 to 2·5cm. long. C. 1838.

'Sargentii' (*'Pendula Sargentii'*). A slow-growing, small bush with a short trunk and dense, weeping branches; leaves blue-green. A superb plant, ideal for the rock garden. C. 1923.

stenocoma DAVIS. A conical or broadly columnar tree, intermediate in leaf and cone between *C. atlantica* and *C. libani*. A geographical form native to S.W. Anatolia. I. about 1938.

***CEPHALOTAXUS—Cephalotaxaceae**—A small genus of shrubs or shrubby trees, best described as large-leaved yews. Like the latter they grow well in shade and in the drip of other trees, even coniferous ones, and thrive on calcareous soils. The plants are normally dioecious, the females producing large, olive-like fruits ripening the second year. They differ from *Taxus* both in their fruits and in their longer leaves which have two broad, silvery bands beneath. From the closely related *Torreya* they are distinguished by their non-spine-tipped leaves.

drupacea. See *C. harringtonia drupacea*.

CEPHALOTAXUS—*continued*

fortuni HOOK. "Chinese Plum Yew". A handsome, large shrub or small bushy tree wider than high, with daık glossy green, lanceolate leaves, 6 to 9cm. long, arranged spirally on the erect shoots and in two opposite rows along the spreading branchlets. Fruits ellipsoid or ovoid, 2 to 3cm. long, olive-brown. An excellent shade-bearing evergreen. C. and S.W. China. Introduced by Robert Fortune in 1849. A.M. 1975.

'Grandis'. An attractive female form with long leaves.

'Prostrata' (*'Prostrate Spreader'*). A low-growing shrub with wide-spreading branches and large, deep green leaves. A superb ground-cover plant, eventually covering several yards. It originated in our nurseries before the first world war as a side cutting. The original plant is ·8m. high × 4·5m. across.

harringtonia K. KOCH (*C. pedunculata*) (*drupacea pedunculata*). A large shrub or small bushy tree of dense growth. Leaves 3·5 to 6·5cm. long, densely arranged along the spreading branchlets in two irregular ranks, usually shorter and stiffer than those of *C. fortuni*, also rather paler green. Fruits ovoid to obovoid, 2 to 2·5cm. long, olive green, borne on drooping peduncles 6 to 10mm. long. Origin unknown, probably China, but cultivated in Japan for many years. I. 1829.

drupacea KOIDZ. (*C. drupacea*). "Cow's Tail Pine"; "Japanese Plum Yew". In cultivation a medium-sized shrub rarely above 3m., of dense, compact habit. This is the wild form native to Japan and Central China. It differs from *C. harringtonia* in its smaller size (in cultivation) and in its smaller leaves 2 to 5cm. long, which are ascending, creating a V-shaped trough on the upper sides of the branchlets. Large plants develop into beautiful large mounds with elegant, drooping branchlets. Fruits obovoid 2 to 3cm. long, olive-green. I. 1829.

'Fastigiata'. An erect-branched shrub of medium to large size, resembling the "Irish Yew" in habit. Leaves almost black-green, spreading all round the shoots. Probably derived as a sport from *C. harringtonia*. Garden origin in Japan. I. 1861.

'Gnome'. A dwarf form with shortly ascending stems, and radially-arranged leaves, forming a flat-topped dome. A sport from *'Fastigiata'*, raised in our Crookhill Nursery in 1970.

'Prostrata' (*drupacea 'Prostrata'*). A dwarf form with low-spreading branches. Similar to *drupacea* except in habit. Originated in our West Hill Nursery as a sport from *'Fastigiata'* before 1920.

pedunculata. See *C. harringtonia*.

***CHAMAECYPARIS—Cupressaceae**—"False Cypress". A small genus of evergreen trees differing from *Cupressus* in their flattened frond-like branchlets and smaller cones. Young trees are conical in outline, broadening as they mature. Leaves opposite, densely arranged, awl-shaped on seedling plants, soon becoming small and scale like. Male and female strobili borne on the same tree, the males minute but usually an attractive yellow or red. Cones small, globose, composed of six to twelve shield-like scales, usually maturing during the first year. They thrive best in a moist, well-drained soil, being slower growing on a dry, chalk soil. Unlike *Cupressus* they do not resent disturbance and may be moved even as small specimen trees.

Though the species are few in number they have given rise in cultivation to an astonishing number of cultivars covering a wide range of shapes and sizes, with foliage varying in form and colour. A few are really dwarf, others are merely slow-growing, whilst many are as vigorous as the type. Forms with juvenile foliage (awl-shaped leaves) were formerly separated under the name *RETINISPORA*.

formosensis MAXIM. "Formosan Cypress"; "Formosan Cedar". In its native land a giant of up to 60m.; in the British Isles a medium-sized tree of loose conical or bushy habit. Young trees are most attractive in their bright green foliage which becomes darker and bronzed in autumn. Leaves sharp pointed making the sprays rough to the touch, sometimes whitish beneath, smelling of sea-weed when bruised. Slow-growing in our climate; established trees are proving hardy. Formosa. I. 1910.

CHAMAECYPARIS—*continued*

henryae LI. This interesting, medium-sized tree, previously included under *C. thyoides*, has recently been described as a distinct species. It inhabits the Gulf coast plains of Florida, Alabama and Mississippi and is said to differ from *C. thyoides* in its smoother bark, less flattened branchlets and the much lighter yellowish-green foliage especially pronounced on young specimens. The leaves also differ in being slightly larger and more appressed. Juvenile leaves are green, not glaucous beneath. The male strobili are pale not dark in colour and the cones are slightly larger and green, or only slightly glaucous. Large specimens are said to resemble more *C. nootkatensis* than *C. thyoides*. Named after that indefatigable traveller and collector of American plants the late Mrs. J. Norman Henry, who first collected it.

lawsoniana PARL. "Lawson Cypress". A large conical tree with drooping branches and broad fan-like sprays of foliage, arranged in horizontal though drooping planes. Leaves pointed, green or glaucous-green, marked with indistinct white streaks beneath. Male strobili usually pinkish or red in spring. Native of S.W. Oregon and N.W. California where trees of 60m. have been recorded. It was first introduced in 1854 when seeds were sent to Lawson's nursery of Edinburgh.

It is a most useful and ornamental tree and makes an excellent hedge or screen even in exposed positions and shade. Its numerous cultivars vary from dwarf shrubs suitable for the rock garden to stately, columnar trees in many shades of green, grey, blue and yellow, also variegated.

'Albospica'. A slow growing, small conical tree. Foliage green, speckled white, with tips of scattered shoots creamy-white. F.C.C. 1869.

'Allumii'. A medium-sized tree of columnar habit; branches dense, compact and ascending; foliage blue-grey, soft, in large, flattened sprays. A popular and commonly planted cultivar. C. 1891.

'Argenteovariegata'. A strong-growing, broadly columnar tree of medium size with green foliage interspersed with creamy-white patches. C. 1862.

'Aurea Densa'. A small, slow-growing, conical bush of compact habit, eventually up to 2m. Foliage golden-yellow in short, flattened, densely-packed sprays, stiff to the touch. One of the best golden conifers for the rock garden. Raised by Messrs. Rogers Ltd., of Red Lodge Nurseries, Southampton, who produced many excellent dwarf conifers during the early part of the present century. C. 1939.

'Aureovariegata'. A small to medium-sized tree. Foliage in flattened sprays, green with scattered patches of creamy yellow. C. 1868.

'Backhouse Silver'. See *'Pygmaea Argentea'*.

'Blom'. A dense columnar bush of medium size with ascending branches and vertically-flattened sprays of glaucous foliage. A sport of *'Allumii'*, raised about 1930.

'Bowleri'. A dense, globular, small bush; branches very slender, spreading, drooping at the tips; foliage dark green. C. 1883.

'Caudata'. A small, curious, rather flat-topped shrub. The crowded branches bear apical tufts of green stems and occasional long, tail-like stems. C. 1934.

'Chilworth Silver'. A slow-growing, broadly columnar bush, with densely packed, silvery-blue juvenile foliage. A sport of *'Ellwoodii'*.

'Columnaris' (*'Columnaris Glauca'*). A small, narrow, conical tree with densely-packed, ascending branches and flattened sprays which are glaucous beneath and at the tips. One of the best narrow growing conifers for the small garden. Raised by Jan Spek of Boskoop about 1940. A.G.M. 1961.

'Darleyensis'. A medium-sized tree of conical habit; branches open, loosely held; leaves with a pale yellow or cream overlay, borne in large, flattened sprays. C. 1880.

'Depkenii'. Medium-sized tree of slender, conical habit; branches slender; foliage yellowish white, becoming green in winter. C. 1901.

'Duncanii'. A small bush of compact habit forming a wide-based, flat-topped dome; branches narrow, thread-like; leaves glaucous-green. C. 1953.

'Elegantissima'. A beautiful, small tree of broadly conical habit, with pale yellow shoots and broad, flattened, drooping sprays of silvery-grey or greyish-cream foliage. Raised in our nurseries before 1920. A.G.M. 1969.

CHAMAECYPARIS—*continued*

lawsoniana 'Ellwoodii'. A slow-growing, columnar bush of medium to large size. The short, feathery sprays of grey-green foliage are densely arranged and become steel blue in winter. A deservedly popular and commonly planted conifer, excellent as a specimen for the lawn or large rock garden. A juvenile form of garden origin. C. 1929. A.M. 1934. A.G.M. 1969. The selection known as '*Kestonensis*' hardly differs from the typical plant. It is usually broader, with many tops.

'Ellwood's Gold'. A neat, compact, columnar form of slow growth. The tips of the sprays are yellow-tinged giving the whole bush a warm glow. A sport of '*Ellwoodii*'.

'Ellwood's White' ('*Ellwoodii Variegata*'). A sport of '*Ellwoodii*', with creamy-white or pale yellow patches of foliage. Slow growing.

'Erecta' ('*Erecta Viridis*'). A medium-sized to large tree of dense, compact growth, columnar when young, broadening in maturity. Foliage bright, rich green, arranged in large, flattened, vertical sprays. It normally forms numerous long, erect branches which require tying-in to prevent damage by heavy snow. An old but still very popular cultivar. F.C.C. 1870.

'Erecta Alba'. A medium-sized to large, conical tree with stout, shortly spreading branches, foliage grey-green; tips of young growths white. F.C.C. 1882.

'Erecta Aurea'. A slow-growing, eventually medium-sized or large bush of dense, compact habit with erect sprays of golden foliage which tends to scorch in full sun. C. 1874.

'Erecta Filiformis' ('*Masonii*'). Medium-sized tree of dense, conical habit; branches ascending with long, spreading and drooping thread-like tips, foliage bright, rich green. C. 1896.

'Erecta Witzeliana'. See '*Witzeliana*'.

'Erecta Viridis'. See '*Erecta*'.

'Filifera'. A large shrub or small tree of loose habit, with slender green, drooping, filiform branchlets. Less strong growing than '*Filiformis*' and without the long projecting terminals. A.M. 1896.

'Filiformis'. A medium-sized to large tree of broadly conical habit; branches whip-like, drooping, with thread-like sprays of green foliage and long, slender, projecting terminals. The branches of mature trees form enormous hanging curtains. C. 1884.

'Filiformis Compacta' ('*Globosa Filiformis*'). Dwarf bush of globular habit; branchlets thread-like, drooping, with dark green foliage. C. 1891.

'Fletcheri'. A well-known and commonly planted cultivar, forming a dense, compact column up to 5m. or more. Normally seen as a broad, columnar bush with several main stems. The semi-juvenile foliage is similar to that of '*Ellwoodii*', but more greyish-green in colour, becoming bronzed in winter. Because of its slow growth it is often planted on the rock garden where it soon becomes too large. A specimen in the Bedgebury Pinetum was 11m. high in 1971. F.C.C. 1913. A.G.M. 1969.

'Fletcheri Somerset'. See '*Somerset*'.

'Fletcher's White' ('*Fletcheri Variegata*'). A large, columnar bush with greyish-green, close foliage, boldly variegated with white or creamy-white.

'Forsteckensis'. A small, slow-growing bush of dense, globular habit; branchlets short, in congested fern-like sprays; foliage greyish-blue-green. A specimen in our nursery is ·9m. × 1·2m. after 30 years. Recalling '*Lycopodioides*' but branchlets not so cord-like and twisted. C. 1904.

'Fraseri'. Medium-sized tree of narrowly conical or columnar habit; branches erect; foliage grey-green, in flattened, vertically arranged sprays. Similar to '*Allumii*' and, like that cultivar, commonly planted. It differs, however, in its greener foliage and neater base. C. 1893.

'Gimbornii'. A dwarf, dense, globular bush of slow-growth; foliage bluish-green, tipped mauve. Suitable for the rock garden. C. 1937.

'Glauca'. A dense, broadly columnar tree with glaucous foliage. Similar forms commonly turn up in seedbeds and occur in the wild. A selected form is known as '*Blue Jacket*'.

'Golden King'. A medium-sized, conical tree with rather sparse spreading branches and large, flattened sprays of golden-yellow foliage, becoming bronzed in winter. A seedling of '*Triomf van Boskoop*, raised before 1931.

CHAMAECYPARIS—*continued*

lawsoniana 'Gracilis Nova'. Medium-sized tree of conical habit, branches slender, foliage bluish-green, in whorled sprays. C. 1891.

'Gracilis Pendula' Small tree with slender, thread-like, pendulous branches, foliage dark green, with a bluish bloom. C.1881.

'Grayswood Pillar'. A medium-sized tree of narrow columnar habit, with tightly packed, ascending branches and grey foliage. It occurred as a sport of '*Blue Jacket*' and the original tree is now approx. 9m. × ·5m. after 16 years. A.M. 1969.

'Green Hedger'. An erect, medium-sized to large tree of dense conical habit with branches from the base; foliage rich green. Excellent for hedges and screens. A.G.M. 1973.

'Headfort'. A medium-sized tree of graceful habit with spreading branches and large, loosely-borne, flattened sprays of blue-green foliage, silvery white beneath. Named after the late Lord Headfort, one of the most enthusiastic growers of this century, who planted a very complete pinetum at "Kells", County Meath and staged an outstanding exhibit at Westminster at the Conifer Conference of 1930.

'Hillieri'. Medium-sized tree of dense, conical habit; foliage in large, floppy, feathery sprays, bright golden yellow. Selected by Edwin Hillier before 1920.

'Hollandia'. A medium-sized to large tree of conical habit; branches thick, spreading, bearing flattened sprays of dark green foliage. C. 1895.

'Intertexta'. A superb large tree of open, ascending habit. Branches loosely borne, with widely spaced, drooping branchlets and large, thick, flattened, fan-like sprays of dark glaucous-green foliage. A most attractive conifer of distinct growth resembling a columnar form of *Cedrus deodara* from a distance. C. 1869. A.G.M. 1969.

'Kilmacurragh'. A medium-sized to large tree of dense, narrow, columnar habit. The short, ascending branches bear irregular sprays of dark green foliage. A superb tree similar to the "Italian Cypress" in effect and perfectly hardy and due to the angle of branching remarkably resistant to snow damage. A.G.M. 1969.

'Knewefieldensis'. A dwarf, dense, flat-topped, dome-shaped bush; foliage deep sea-green, in short, overlapping, plumose sprays. C. 1911.

'Kooy' ('*Glauca Kooy*'). Medium-sized, conical tree with spreading branches and fine sprays of glaucous-blue foliage. C. 1925.

'Krameri'. A semi-dwarf, globular, rather flat-topped bush with densely and irregularly arranged branches, cord-like terminal growths and dark green foliage. C. 1909.

'Krameri Variegata'. A sport of '*Krameri*', with silver or cream variegated growths.

'Lane' ('*Lanei*'). A columnar tree of medium size; thin, feathery sprays of golden-yellow foliage. One of the best golden Cypresses. C. 1938.

'Lutea'. A medium-sized tree of broad columnar habit, with a narrow, drooping spire-like top; foliage golden-yellow in large, flattened, feathery sprays. An old and well tried cultivar. F.C.C. 1872. A.G.M. 1955.

'Lutea Nana'. A small, slow-growing bush of narrowly conical habit, eventually attaining 2m. in height. Foliage golden yellow, densely arranged in short, flattened sprays. C. 1930.

'Luteocompacta'. A small to medium-sized tree of dense, conical habit; foliage golden yellow in loosely held sprays. C. 1938.

'Lycopodioides'. A slow-growing, broadly conical, medium-sized to large bush eventually a small, fat tree. The curious grey-green branchlets are cylindrical in form and become twisted and tangled like whipcord. C. 1890.

'Minima'. A small, slow-growing, globular bush, eventually about 2m. high with numerous ascending stems and densely packed, often vertically arranged, neat sprays of green foliage. Suitable for the rock garden. C. 1874.

'Minima Aurea'. A dense-growing, dwarf, conical bush with often vertically held sprays of golden-yellow foliage, soft to the touch. One of the best golden conifers for the rock garden. Specimens in our nursery have attained 1·1m. × ·8m. in 30 years. C. 1929. A.G.M. 1969.

'Minima Glauca'. A dense, globular, small bush of slow growth. Foliage sea-green, borne in short, densely packed, often vertically arranged sprays. A specimen in our nursery has attained 1m. × 1·2m. in 25 years. C. 1874.

CHAMAECYPARIS—*continued*

lawsoniana 'Naberi'. Medium-sized tree of conical outline; foliage green with sulphur-yellow tips, paling to creamy-blue in winter. A very distinct shade of colour. C. 1929.

'Nana'. A small, dense, semi-globular bush, slowly growing to 2m. and developing a thick central trunk in later years; foliage dark glaucous-green, in short, generally horizontal sprays. A specimen in our nursery has attained 2m. × 1·5m. in about 35 years. It differs from the rather similar *'Minima'* in its generally pointed top, thick and obvious central trunk (on old plants) and rather horizontally held branchlets. C. 1861.

'Nana Argentea'. A remarkably attractive, dwarf, slow-growing bush. The inner previous year's foliage is cream, whilst the current season's growth is silver-grey, with an occasional cream fleck. C. 1884.

'Nidiformis'. A slow-growing form of dense habit, ultimately a small tree. Foliage green, borne in large horizontally flattened sprays, drooping gracefully at the tips. A specimen in our arboretum is 6m. high by 3·5m. wide. Not to be confused with *C. 'Nidifera'* which is a form of *C. nootkatensis.*

'Parsons'. A beautiful, dense, compact, dome-shaped bush, eventually of medium size; foliage green in large, flattened, arching and drooping, overlapping, fern-like sprays. One of the most graceful of the smaller Lawson cultivars.

'Patula'. A graceful, conical tree of medium size; foliage greyish dark green in narrow, outward-curving sprays. C. 1903.

'Pembury Blue'. A medium-sized, conical tree with sprays of silvery-blue foliage. A very striking cultivar. Perhaps the best blue "Lawson Cypress". A.G.M. 1969.

'Pena Park'. An attractive, slow-growing, wide-spreading bush with glaucous-green foliage. The original plant in Portugal was stated to measure 2·5m. high × nearly 35m. in circumference after approx. 80 years.

'Pendula'. A medium-sized, rather open tree of conical shape; branches pendulous; foliage dark green. C. 1870. F.C.C. 1870.

'Pottenii'. A medium-sized, columnar tree of dense, slow growth; foliage sea-green partly juvenile, in soft crowded, feathery sprays. Very decorative. A.M. 1916.

'Pygmaea Argentea' (*'Backhouse Silver'*). A dwarf, slow-growing bush of rounded habit; foliage dark bluish-green with silvery-white tips. Suitable for the rock garden. Perhaps the best dwarf, white variegated conifer. C. 1891. A.M. 1900. A.G.M. 1969.

'Pyramidalis Alba'. A small to medium-sized tree of narrow columnar habit; branches erect, foliage dark green, with creamy-white tips. C. 1887.

'Robusta Glauca'. A large tree of broadly columnar habit; branches stout, rigid and spreading; foliage in short, thick, greyish-blue sprays. C. 1891.

'Rogersii' (*'Nana Rogersii'*). A small, slow-growing bush of dense, globular habit, old specimens are broadly conical, foliage grey-blue, in thin, loose sprays. Eventually attains a height of about 2m. C. 1930.

'Shawii'. Dwarf, globular bush of slow growth, foliage light glaucous green, in loose sprays. Suitable for a large rock garden. C. 1891.

'Silver Queen'. Medium-sized to large conical tree with elegantly spreading branches; foliage greyish-green, creamy-white when young, in large, flattened sprays. Not one of the best variegations, *'Elegantissima'* is much better. C. 1883.

'Smithii' (*'Smithii Aurea'*) (*'Lutea Smith'*). Medium-sized conical tree of slow growth; branches spreading, foliage golden yellow, in large drooping horizontal sprays. C. 1898.

'Somerset' (*'Fletcheri Somerset'*). A densely columnar, small tree or large bush, a sport of *'Fletcheri'*. The blue-grey, feathery foliage is yellowish-tinged during summer, becoming bronze-tinged in winter.

'Stardust'. An outstanding, columnar or narrowly conical tree with yellow foliage suffused bronze at the tips.

'Stewartii'. A medium-sized to large tree of elegant, conical habit; branches slightly erect bearing large, flattened sprays of golden-yellow foliage, changing to yellowish-green in winter. A very hardy, popular cultivar and one of the best "Golden Lawsons" for general planting. C. 1920.

'Tabuliformis'. A small to medium-sized shrub of dense spreading habit with overlapping, flattened sprays of green foliage.

CHAMAECYPARIS—*continued*

lawsoniana 'Tamariscifolia'. Slow-growing, eventually medium-sized to large bush with several ascending and spreading main stems, flat-topped and spreading when young, eventually umbrella-shaped; foliage sea-green in horizontally arranged flattened fan-like sprays. One of many fine conifers raised by James Smith and Son at their Darley Dale nursery, near Matlock in Derbyshire. There are several large attractive specimens in the Bedgebury Pinetum including one at 5·5m. high and 4·5m. across. C. 1923.

'Tharandtensis Caesia'. Dwarf to medium-sized bush of globular habit when young, broadly conical and sometimes flat-topped when older; branches short; foliage glaucous, in dense, curly, moss-like sprays. C. 1890. Very similar to '*Forsteckensis*'.

'Triomf van Boskoop' ('*Triomphe de Boskoop*'). A very popular cultivar, growing into a large tree of open, conical habit; foliage glaucous-blue, in large, lax sprays. Needs trimming to obtain density. C. 1890.

'Versicolor'. A medium-sized tree, broadly conical in outline, with spreading branches and flattened sprays of green foliage, mottled creamy-white and yellow. C. 1882.

'Westermannii'. Medium-sized tree of broadly conical habit, branches loose and spreading; foliage in large sprays, light yellow when young becoming yellowish-green. C. 1880.

'Winston Churchill'. A dense, broadly columnar tree of small to medium size; foliage rich golden yellow all the year round. One of the best "Golden Lawsons". C. 1945.

'Wisselii'. A most distinct and attractive, fast-growing tree of medium to large size. Slender and conical with widely spaced, ascending branches. The stout, upright branchlets bear crowded, short, fern-like sprays of bluish-green foliage. The rather numerous red male strobili are very attractive in the spring. C. 1888. A.M. 1899. A.G.M. 1969.

'Witzeliana' ('*Erecta Witzeliana*'). A small, narrow, columnar tree with long, ascending branches and vivid green, crowded sprays. An effective cultivar, like a slender green flame. Probably a sport of '*Erecta*'. C. 1934.

'Youngii'. A beautiful, medium-sized to large, conical tree, with loosely spreading branches and long, frond-like firm sprays of shining dark green foliage. One of the best of the green clones. C. 1874.

nootkatensis SPACH. "Nootka Cypress". A large tree of conical habit often broadly so. Branchlets drooping, with long, flattened sprays of green, rank-smelling foliage which is rough to the touch due to the sharp pointed, scale-like leaves. A handsome specimen tree differing from *C. lawsoniana* in its coarser, stronger smelling, duller green foliage and the yellow male strobili in May. The cone scales also possess a pointed boss which is absent in the commoner species. Western N. America. First discovered by Archibald Menzies in 1793. I. about 1853. A.M. 1978.

'Aureovariegata'. A medium-sized tree with conspicuous deep yellow variegated foliage. C. before 1872. F.C.C. 1872.

'Compacta'. A medium-sized to large bush of dense, globular habit; foliage light green, in crowded sprays. C. 1873.

'Glauca'. A medium to large, conical tree with dark sea-green foliage. C. 1858.

'Lutea' ('*Aurea*'). Medium-sized, conical tree; foliage yellow when young, becoming yellowish-green. C. 1891.

'Pendula'. A superb specimen tree of medium to large size. Branchlets hanging vertically in long, graceful streamers. C. 1884.

'Variegata' ('*Argenteovariegata*'). A medium-sized tree, foliage with splashes of creamy-white. C. 1873.

obtusa ENDL. (*Retinospora obtusa*). "Hinoki Cypress". A large tree of broad, conical habit. Branches spreading horizontally, foliage deep shining green, in thick, horizontally-flattened sprays. Differing from other species in its unequal pairs of usually blunt tipped leaves, with white, X-shaped markings below and in its larger cones. One of the most important timber trees in Japan and held to be sacred by followers of the Shinto faith. It was introduced by both P. F. von Siebold and J. G. Veitch in 1861. The garden cultivars of this species, including many of Japanese origin, are almost as numerous as those of *C. lawsoniana* and include several excellent dwarf or slow-growing forms.

CHAMAECYPARIS—*continued*

obtusa 'Albospica'. Small tree of compact habit; young shoots creamy-white changing to pale green. C. 1874.

'Aurea'. A conical tree with flattened sprays of golden-yellow foliage. Introduced by Robert Fortune in 1860. See also *'Crippsii'*.

'Bassett' (*'Nana Bassett'*). A very dwarf bush similar to *'Juniperoides'*, but taller growing and foliage a darker green. A rock garden plant.

'Caespitosa' (*'Nana Caespitosa'*). A slow-growing, miniature bush of dense bun-shaped habit, a gem for the alpine garden or trough; foliage light green, in short, crowded, shell-like sprays. One of the smallest conifers, raised by Messrs. Rogers and Son of the Red Lodge Nursery, Southampton, sometime before 1920, from seed of *'Nana Gracilis'*.

'Chabo-yadori'. A dwarf or small bush of dome-shaped or conical habit. Both juvenile and adult foliage are present in irregular fan-like sprays. A most attractive clone, recently imported from Japan.

'Compacta'. Medium-sized to large bush of dense, compact, conical habit; foliage deep green. C. 1875.

'Coralliformis'. Small to medium-sized bush, with densely arranged, twisted, cord-like branchlets; foliage dark green, branchlets brown. A specimen in our nursery has attained 1·5m. × 1·5m. after 30 years. C. 1903.

'Crippsii'. A small, slow-growing, loosely conical tree, with spreading branches and broad, frond-like sprays of rich golden-yellow foliage. One of the loveliest and most elegant of small golden conifers. C. before 1899. F.C.C. 1899.

'Densa' (*'Nana Densa'*). A slow-growing, miniature bush of dense, dome-shaped habit; foliage in densely crowded and congested cockscombs. Suitable for the rock garden or trough. A specimen in our nursery has attained ·6m. high by a little greater width after 35 years.

'Filicoides'. "Fern-spray Cypress". A bush or small tree of open, irregular, often gaunt habit, branches long and straggly, clothed with dense pendulous clusters of fern-spray, green foliage. A specimen in our nursery has reached 2·4m. high by as much through in 25 years. C. 1868.

'Filicoides Compacta' (*'Compact Fernspray'*). A miniature, rather stunted form of *'Filicoides'*.

'Flabelliformis' (*'Nana Flabelliformis'*). A miniature bush of globular shape, with small, fan-shaped branchlets of slightly bloomy, light green foliage. Very similar to *'Juniperoides'*. Suitable for the alpine house or trough. C. 1939.

formosana REHD. A rare, small to medium-sized tree in cultivation, smaller in all its parts than the type. Distinct in its Thuja-like foliage, green beneath. One of the most important timber trees in Formosa. I. 1910.

'Hage'. Dwarf, slow-growing bush of dense, compact, conical habit; foliage bright green in crowded, twisted sprays. C. 1928.

'Intermedia' (*'Nana Intermedia'*). A miniature, slow-growing bush of slightly loose, conical habit, with short, loose sprays of green foliage. Regarded as intermediate between *'Caespitosa'* and *'Juniperoides'*. Suitable for the alpine house or trough. C. 1930.

'Juniperoides' (*'Nana Juniperoides'*). A miniature bush of very slow growth; globular habit, with loose branches and small cupped sprays of foliage. Suitable for alpine house or trough. C. 1923.

'Juniperoides Compacta'. Similar to *'Juniperoides'* in general appearance, but slightly more compact and dense as an old plant. C. 1939.

'Kosteri' (*'Nana Kosteri'*). A dwarf bush, intermediate in growth between *'Nana'* and *'Pygmaea'*. Conical in habit with flattened and mossy sprays of bright green foliage, bronzing in winter. Suitable for the rock garden. C. 1915.

'Lycopodioides'. A medium-sized bush of informal habit often gaunt with age; branches sparse, heavy with masses of dark bluish-green, mossy foliage becoming particularly congested towards the ends of the branches. A specimen in our nursery has attained 1·8m. × 2·4m. in about 30 years. Introduced from Japan in 1861.

'Lycopodioides Aurea'. A slower-growing form of *'Lycopodioides'* with soft, yellow-green foliage. Introduced from Japan in about 1890.

'Magnifica'. Small, broadly conical tree with broad, fan-shaped, heavy sprays of deep green leaves. C. 1874.

CHAMAECYPARIS—*continued*

obtusa 'Mariesii' (*'Nana Variegata'*). Small, slow-growing bush of cone-shaped habit and open growth. Foliage in loose sprays, creamy-white or pale yellow during summer, yellowish-green during winter. A specimen in our nursery has attained ·6m. × ·75m. in 25 years. C. 1891.

'Minima' (*'Nana Minima'*). Miniature bush, forming a moss-like, flat pin-cushion; foliage green, in tighly packed, erect, quadrangular sprays. Perhaps the smallest conifer of its kind. Suitable for the alpine house or trough. Raised by Messrs. Rogers and Son. C. 1923.

'Nana'. A miniature, flat-topped dome, comprising tiers of densely packed, cup-shaped fans of black-green foliage. One of the best dwarf conifers for the rock garden. A specimen in our nursery has attained ·75m. high by 1m. wide at base in 40 years. Introduced from Japan by Philip von Siebold in about 1861. The stronger-growing plant found under this name in many collections throughout Europe is *'Nana Gracilis'*.

'Nana Aurea'. A looser, slightly taller-growing plant than *'Nana'* with golden-yellow foliage. Perhaps the best dwarf golden conifer. Ideal for the rock garden. Introduced from Japan. C. 1875. A.G.M. 1973.

'Nana Gracilis'. A conical bush or eventually a small tree of dense, compact habit; foliage dark green, in short, neat, shell-like sprays. Perhaps the most commonly planted "dwarf" conifer, eventually attaining several metres in height. C. 1874. A.G.M. 1969. It was from seeds of this cultivar that Messrs. Rogers & Son of Southampton, England, raised a whole selection of dwarf and miniature bun-shaped conifers which included *'Caespitosa'*, *'Juniperoides'*, *'Minima'* and *'Intermedia'*.

'Nana Pyramidalis'. Dwarf bush of dense, conical habit; foliage dark green in short, shell-like sprays. Suitable for the rock garden. C. 1905.

'Nana Rigida' (*'Rigid Dwarf'*). A small, slow-growing bush of stiff, rigid, almost columnar habit; foliage almost black-green, with conspicuous, white markings beneath, in shell-like sprays. Most effective amongst the bun-shaped clones.

'Pygmaea'. A small, wide-spreading bush with loose sprays of bronze-green foliage, tinged reddish-bronze in winter, arranged in flattened tiers. Introduced from Japan by Robert Fortune in 1861.

'Pygmaea Aurescens'. Resembling *'Pygmaea'* in growth, but foliage permanently yellow-bronze, richer in winter. C. 1939.

'Pygmaea Densa'. A smaller, more compact form of *'Pygmaea'*.

'Repens' (*'Nana Repens'*). Dwarf bush with prostrate branches and loose sprays of bright green foliage, yellow-tinged in winter. A sport of *'Nana Gracilis'*. A most attractive clone of spreading habit. C. 1929.

† **'Sanderi'** (*Juniperus sanderi*) (*Retinispora sanderi*). A dwarf, slow-growing, juvenile form with short, thick leaves. The whole bush is delightfully sea-green in summer, becoming plum-coloured in winter. It is somewhat wind tender and requires a sheltered, well-drained position or a pot in the alpine house. It was originally introduced from Japan in 1894 and for many years was considered to be a Juniper. Sometimes found in cultivation under the name *'Ericoides'*, which name rightly belongs to another, rarer cultivar.

'Spiralis' (*'Contorta'*) (*'Nana Spiralis'*). A dwarf, ascending bush with attractively twisted branchlets, resembling *'Nana'* as a young plant. A specimen in our nursery has attained ·75m. × ·45m. in about 30 years. C. 1930.

'Suiryuhiba'. Medium-sized shrub of loose habit with long cord-like branchlets which are often curiously twisted and contorted.

'Tempelhof'. A dense, conical bush of small to medium size. Foliage deep green, in broad, dense, shell-like sprays.

'Tetragona Aurea'. An unusual large shrub or small tree of angular appearance. Branches sparse, usually wide-spreading, thickly covered with golden-yellow, moss-like sprays of foliage. A very distinct and attractive clone which associates well with heathers. Introduced from Japan in about 1870. The green form *'Tetragona'*, which is said to have been introduced at the same time, now appears lost to cultivation. In our opinion both may have arisen as sports of cv. *'Filicoides'*, the "Fern-spray Cypress". F.C.C. 1876.

'Tonia'. A dwarf, white-variegated sport of *'Nana Gracilis'*. C. 1928.

'Tatsunami'. A dwarf, globular bush of loose habit, with slender, thread-like branchlets and drooping sprays of foliage.

CHAMAECYPARIS—*continued*

pisifera ENDL. (*Retinispora pisifera*). "Sawara Cypress". A large tree of broadly conical habit, with spreading branches and horizontally flattened sprays of dark green foliage. The sharply-pointed, scale-like leaves, with white markings below, plus its small cones 6mm. across, distinguish it from other species. It has given rise to numerous cultivars, many of which have juvenile foliage. Japan. Introduced by Robert Fortune in 1861. F.C.C. 1861.

'Argenteovariegata' (*'Albovariegata'*). A medium-sized tree with foliage speckled silvery-white. Introduced from Japan in 1861.

'Aurea'. Young foliage yellow, passing to soft green during summer. Introduced from Japan in 1861. F.C.C. 1862.

'Aurea Nana'. Dwarf, slow-growing form of flattened, globular habit. One of the most consistent rich yellow, dwarf conifers; suitable for the rock garden. C. 1891. F.C.C. 1861.

'Aureovariegata'. A slow-growing, small tree or large bush with golden variegated foliage. C. 1874.

'Boulevard' (*'Cyanoviridis'*). An outstanding, medium-sized bush of dense, conical habit. The steel-blue foliage is soft to the touch, becoming attractively purple-tinged in winter. A juvenile form which originated as a sport of *Squarrosa'* in the U.S.A. about 1934. It has now become one of the most popular of all conifers and is suitable even for the small garden. A.G.M. 1973.

'Cyanoviridis'. See *'Boulevard'*.

'Filifera'. A small to medium-sized tree or large shrub of broadly conical habit, usually broader than high. Branches spreading, with long, drooping, whip-like branchlets and string-like sprays of green foliage. Introduced from Japan in 1861.

'Filifera Aurea'. Smaller and slower-growing than *'Filifera'*, making a medium-sized to large bush with attractive golden-yellow foliage. C. 1889. A.G.M. 1973.

'Filifera Aureovariegata'. A small to medium-sized bush. The whip-like branches and branchlets are splashed with sections of yellow foliage.

'Filifera Nana'. A dense, rounded, flat-topped, dwarf bush with long, string-like branchlets. Suitable for the rock garden. C. 1897.

'Filifera Nana Aurea' (*'Golden Mop'*). Small, dense-growing, bright golden form of *'Filifera Nana'*.

'Gold Spangle'. Small, densely conical tree with both loose and congested sprays of golden yellow foliage. A sport of *'Filifera Aurea'*. C. 1900.

'Nana'. A dwarf, slow-growing bush forming a flat-topped dome with crowded flattened sprays of dark green foliage. Old specimens will form a top tier, resembling a cottage loaf. A very consistent cultivar. A specimen in our nursery has attained ·6m. × 1·4m. after about 30 years. C. 1891.

'Nana Aureovariegata'. Similar in habit to *'Nana'*, but foliage possessing a golden tinge. Excellent for the rock garden. C. 1874.

'Nana Variegata' (*'Compacta Variegata'*). Similar to *'Nana'*, but foliage flecked with a creamy-white variegation. C. 1867.

'Parslorii' (*'Nana Parslorii'*). A dense, dwarf shrub of flattened, bun-shaped habit, with foliage in short crowded sprays. Suitable for the rock garden.

'Plumosa'. A small to medium-sized conical tree or large, compact bush with densely packed branchlets and plumose sprays of bright green, juvenile foliage, soft to the touch. Introduced from Japan in 1861. F.C.C.1866.

'Plumosa Albopicta'. Foliage speckled with white, otherwise similar to *'Plumosa'*. C. 1881.

'Plumosa Aurea'. Young growths bright yellow deepening with age to soft yellow-green, stained bronze-yellow.

'Plumosa Aurea Compacta' (*'Plumosa Nana Aurea'*) (*'Plumosa Aurea Nana'*). Dwarf, dense, conical bush of slow growth; foliage soft yellow, more especially in spring. C. 1891.

'Plumosa Aurescens'. A small conical tree with plumose branchlets, the tips of which are light yellow in summer, changing to bluish green in autumn. C. 1909.

'Plumosa Compressa'. A dwarf, slow-growing, rather flat-topped bush, usually forming a tight, rounded bun with both *'Plumosa'* and *'Squarrosa'* foliage, which, on young plants is crisped and moss-like. C. before 1925. A.M. 1925.

'Plumosa Compressa Aurea'. Similar to *'Plumosa Compressa'*, but foliage gold tinged in summer.

CHAMAECYPARIS—*continued*

pisifera 'Pygmaea' (*'Plumosa Pygmaea'*). Small, slow-growing bush of compact, conical habit with densely crowded juvenile foliage.

'Snow' (*'Squarrosa Snow'*). A dwarf, bun-shaped bush with mossy, blue-grey foliage tipped creamy-white. Tends to burn in full sun or cold wind.

'Squarrosa'. A small to medium-sized tree of broadly conical outline with spreading branches and dense, billowy sprays of glaucous juvenile foliage, soft to the touch. A commonly planted cultivar. Introduced from Japan in 1861. F.C.C. 1862.

'Squarrosa Aurea Nana'. A dwarf, slow-growing form of dense, compact habit with yellow foliage paling in winter.

'Squarrosa Intermedia' (*'Squarrosa Minima'*) (*'Squarrosa Argentea Pygmaea'*) (*'Dwarf Blue'*). A dense, dwarf, globular bush with densely-packed and congested, greyish-blue; juvenile foliage through which occasional longer shoots protrude. An unsatisfactory plant unless one is prepared to trim annually. C. 1923.

'Squarrosa Boulevard'. See *'Boulevard'*.

'Squarrosa Sulphurea'. Similar to *'Squarrosa'* in habit; foliage sulphur-yellow, especially in spring. C. before 1894. A.M. 1894.

‡thyoides BRITT., STERNS & POGG. "White Cypress". A small to medium-sized tree in the British Isles, of conical habit. Branchlets bearing erect, fan-shaped sprays of aromatic, glaucous green foliage. Cones small and bloomy. Unsuitable for shallow chalk soils. Eastern U.S.A. Introduced by Peter Collinson in 1736.

'Andelyensis' (*'Leptoclada'*). Generally a medium-sized, slow-growing bush of dense, narrowly-columnar or narrowly-conical habit, with crowded branchlets and short sprays of dark bluish-green adult and juvenile foliage. Attractive in late winter when peppered with its tiny red male strobili. A specimen in the Bedgebury Pinetum was 6m. high in 1971. F.C.C. 1863.

'Andelyensis Nana' (*'Leptoclada Nana'*) (*'Conica'*). A small shrub of slow growth with mostly juvenile foliage, forming a dense, rather flat-topped bush. A specimen in our nursery has attained 1·1m. × ·9m. after about 30 years. C. 1939.

'Ericoides'. An attractive, small, compact, conical form with sea-green juvenile foliage, soft to the touch, becoming bronze or plum purple in winter. C. 1840.

'Glauca' (*'Kewensis'*). A glaucous-blue form of the type. C. 1897.

'Variegata'. Similar in habit to the type; foliage speckled with yellow. C. 1831.

***CRYPTOMERIA—Taxodiaceae**—A monotypic genus. Male and female strobili borne on the same tree, the males orange or reddish in March. Cones solitary, globular, maturing the first year.

japonica D. DON. "Japanese Cedar". A large, fast-growing tree of broadly columnar habit with reddish shredding bark and spreading or decurved branches. Leaves awl-shaped, densely crowded on long slender branchlets. It resembles in some ways the "Wellingtonia" (*Sequoiadendron*), but its leaves are longer and its bark has not the spongy thickness of the American tree. Easily cultivated and thriving best in moist soils. Many cultivars are in cultivation. Japan; C. China. I. 1842.

The Chinese form var. *sinensis* SIEB. & ZUCC. is said to be the common tree in cultivation, differing from the Japanese tree in its looser habit, slender, more drooping branches and fewer-scaled cones.

'Araucarioides'. See under *'Viminalis'*.

'Bandai-sugi'. A small, slow-growing compact bush becoming more irregular in old age. Foliage in congested, moss-like clusters with intermittent normal growth. C. 1939.

'Compressa'. A dwarf bush of very slow growth similar to *'Vilmoriniana'*, forming a compact, rather flat-topped globe. Foliage densely crowded, turning reddish-purple in winter. Suitable for the rock garden or scree. C. 1942.

'Cristata'. A conical bush eventually making a small to medium-sized tree. Many of the branches are flattened (fasciated) into great cockscomb-like growths. C. 1901.

'Dacrydioides'. See under *'Viminalis'*.

'Elegans'. A beautiful clone of tall bushy habit, eventually making a small tree. The soft, feathery juvenile foliage is retained throughout life and becomes an attractive red-bronze during autumn and winter. Introduced by Thomas Lobb from Japan in 1854. F.C.C. 1862.

CRYPTOMERIA—*continued*

japonica 'Elegans Compacta'. A somewhat slow-growing and smaller shrub than *'Elegans'*, with even softer, more plumose foliage, forming a medium-sized "billowy" bush. Leaves turn rich purple in winter. A sport of *'Elegans'*. C. 1881.

'Globosa' A small, dense, dome-shaped bush of neat and compact habit. Foliage adult, rust-red in winter. Ideal for the large rock garden attaining about ·6 by ·8m. in 15 years. C. 1923.

'Globosa Nana'. A dwarf, dense, flat-topped bush of slow growth. Branchlets and foliage agreeing with *'Lobbii'*. Numerous, somewhat arching branchlets fan out to make a perfect low dome, previously listed as *'Lobbii Nana'*.

'Jindai-Sugi'. A small, dense, slow-growing bush developing an irregular but rather flattened top. Foliage of a cheerful bright green, densely crowded. A specimen in our nursery has attained 1·2m.×1·2m. in twenty-five years. C. 1939.

'Knaptonensis'. See under *'Nana Albospica'*.

'Lobbii'. A very desirable medium-sized to large conical tree, differing from the type in its longer branchlets more clustered at the ends of the shorter branches. Leaves deep rich green and more apressed to the shoots. Introduced by Thomas Lobb in about 1850.

'Lobbii Nana'. See under *'Globosa Nana'*.

'Lycopodioides'. See under *'Viminalis'*.

'Midare-sugi'. A small bush of loose growth resembling *'Elegans'* in foliage, except for scattered bunches of congested growths at the base of shoots.

'Monstrosa'. A medium-sized bush up to 3m. Growth irregular, shoots long at first, then becoming dense and crowded, forming large, congested clusters over the whole bush. C. 1909.

'Nana'. A small, slow-growing, compact bush with slender branchlets ending in recurved tips.

'Nana Albospica' (*'Albovariegata'*) (*'Argenteovariegata'*). A dwarf, slow-growing, flat-topped bush; foliage green, young growths creamy-white. The creamy tips are often browned by sun or frost and a sheltered position is desirable. The clone *'Knaptonensis'* is very similar in general appearance, being perhaps a little more compact and slower-growing.

'Pygmaea'. A slow-growing, eventually compact, rounded bush of about 2m., forming intermittent clusters of congested branchlets, with short needle-like, apple green leaves. A most attractive shrub, suitable for the large rock garden or as a lawn specimen.

'Pyramidata'. A conical bush or small tree of rather open growth with small, densely-packed leaves concealing the slender branchlets.

'Selaginoides'. See under *'Viminalis'*.

'Spiralis'. "Grannies Ringlets". There is a large tree of this clone in the gardens at Nymans in Sussex and at Fota in S.W. Ireland, but as grown in general cultivation, it forms a small, slow-growing bush of dense, spreading habit. The leaves are spirally twisted around the stems. The whole bush is a pleasant, bright green in colour. Introduced from Japan in 1860.

'Spiraliter Falcata' (*'Spiralis Elongata'*). Similar in effect to *'Spiralis'*, but with longer, thinner, almost whipcord-like branchlets with pendulous tips. A medium sized bush of loose growth. C. 1876.

'Vilmoriniana'. An exceedingly slow-growing, dwarf bush with very small, crowded branchlets and leaves, forming a dense, rigid globe. Turning reddish-purple in winter. One of the most popular dwarf conifers for the rock garden, very similar to *'Compressa'*, but leaves a little shorter and more congested on the branchlets. A specimen in our nursery attained ·6m.×1m. in about 30 years. A.G.M. 1973.

'Viminalis'. A large, irregular bush with long, slender, whip-like branches bearing terminal whorls of elongated branchlets. A specimen in our nursery has attained 4·6m.×4·6m. in about 40 years. The following clones *'Araucarioides'*, *'Athrotaxoides'*, *'Dacrydioides'*, *'Lycopodioides'* and *'Selaginoides'* are very similar, some appearing identical.

***CUNNINGHAMIA—Taxodiaceae**—A small genus comprising two known species of very distinct trees recalling *Araucaria*. They are fairly hardy, but thrive best in a sheltered position. Male and female strobili are borne on the same tree. The whorled branches are densely clothed with spirally arranged leaves which are twisted at the base so as to appear in two ranks.

CUNNINGHAMIA—*continued*

†konishii HAYATA. A small tree mainly differing from *C. lanceolata* in its smaller leaves and cones. Young plants of both species are very similar. As may be expected this tree is less hardy than the "Chinese Fir" and is not suitable for the colder areas of the British Isles. Formosa. I. 1910.

lanceolata HOOK f. (*sinensis*). "Chinese Fir". A small to medium-sized, exotic-looking, hardy tree. Leaves lanceolate, 3 to 7cm. long, irregularly arranged, emerald green above, marked with two white bands of stomata beneath, becoming dark and bronzy by autumn. Cones usually in clusters, ovoid or rounded, 3 to 4cm. across. It would be unwise to plant this tree in a windswept site. C. and S. China. First introduced by William Kerr in 1804. A.M. 1977.

'Glauca'. Leaves with a conspicuous glaucous bloom.

* × **CUPRESSOCYPARIS** (*CUPRESSUS × CHAMAECYPARIS*)—**Cupressaceae**—Interesting bi-generic hybrids, all of which have arisen in cultivation. They are extremely fast-growing trees with many uses, and are rapidly becoming one of most popular conifers. Their requirements are similar to those of *Chamaecyparis*.

leylandii DALLIM. (*Cupressus macrocarpa × Chamaecyparis nootkatensis*). "Leyland Cypress". A large noble tree of dense columnar habit, extremely vigorous in growth. Foliage borne in flattened or irregular, slightly drooping sprays, similar to those of *C. nootkatensis*, but less strong smelling when bruised. In general appearance it resembles more the *Chamaecyparis* parent, the cones are intermediate. It is the fastest-growing conifer in the British Isles, indeed the fastest-growing evergreen, apart from some *Eucalyptus* species. Even on a relatively poor site plants from cuttings have reached a height of 15m. in 16 years. Such is its vigour and adaptability that it is unsurpassed for tall hedges and screens and is tolerant of a wide range of conditions including coastal areas and chalk soils.

First originated at Leighton Hall, Montgomeryshire, Wales in 1888 (6 seedlings) and again in 1911 (2 seedlings), also in a garden at Ferndown, Dorset in 1940 (2 seedlings). A.M. 1941. A.G.M. 1969. Several clones are in cultivation, of which we offer the following:—

'Green Spire' (Clone 1). A dense, narrow column of bright green foliage, arranged in irregular sprays. Eventually very similar to '*Haggerston Grey*'.

'Haggerston Grey' (Clone 2). Perhaps the commonest clone in cultivation, more open in growth than '*Leighton Green*'; foliage green or with a slight pale grey cast, arranged in dense, irregular sprays.

'Leighton Green' (Clone 11). One of the clones most commonly propagated. It forms a tall column of green foliage arranged in more or less flattened fern-like sprays. Cones often present.

'Naylor's Blue' (Clone 10). A narrow columnar tree with greyish-green foliage most noticeably glaucous during winter, arranged in more or less irregular sprays.

'Stapehill'. A dense columnar tree with more or less flattened sprays of green foliage.

notabilis MITCHELL (*Chamaecyparis nootkatensis × Cupressus glabra*). A recently introduced hybrid raised at the Forestry Commission's Research Station at Alice Holt Lodge, Surrey. The original seed was collected in 1956 from a specimen of *Cupressus glabra* growing at Leighton Hall, Montgomeryshire. In 1970 the original two seedlings were reported as being 9m. and 7·5m. respectively, and growing fast. They are described by Mr. A. F. Mitchell as having sinuous, upswept branches draped with flattened sprays of dark grey-green foliage. It promises to be an attractive conifer and should eventually attain a medium size.

ovensii MITCHELL (*Chamaecyparis nootkatensis × Cupressus lusitanica*). An interesting new hybrid raised by Mr. H. Ovens in his nursery at Talybont, Cardiganshire, from seed collected in 1961 from a specimen of *Cupressus lusitanica* growing in Silkwood, Westonbirt Arboretum, Gloucestershire. This hybrid exhibits a strong influence of the "Nootka" parent and produces large flattened sprays of drooping dark, glaucous green foliage. It promises to reach a medium size.

***CUPRESSUS—Cupressaceae**—A genus of evergreen trees of mostly conical or columnar habit. Male and female strobili borne on the same tree, the males often quite effective in the mass. Cones globular, composed of six to twelve shield-like scales, maturing during their second year, becoming woody and remaining on the branches often for several years.

The species of *Cupressus* differ from those of *Chamaecyparis* in their irregular, rounded or quadrangular branchlet systems and larger cones, and on the whole they are less hardy. They do not transplant easily from the open ground, hence young trees are pot grown. They are tolerant of a wide range of soil conditions (excepting wet soils) and several species will grow even in shallow chalk soils.

abramsiana C. B. WOLF. "Santa Cruz Cypress". A fast-growing, symmetrical tree of dense, columnar habit. Branches ascending bearing both ascending and spreading, finely divided branchlets clothed with green foliage. Similar in general effect to a narrow-growing "Monterey Cypress". Cones irregularly globose, 2 to 2·5cm. long, scales with a slight boss. A remarkably vigorous species related to *C. goveniana*, but much more dense and compact in habit and with larger cones. A specimen in our arboretum, grown from seed received in 1950, was 18·5m. in 1971. Santa Cruz Mts. (California). C. 1935.

arizonica GREENE. not HORT. (*arizonica bonita* LEMM. not HORT.). A small to medium-sized tree of dense conical or broadly columnar habit with grey and brown, stringly and slightly ridged bark. Foliage green. Cones 1 to 2·5cm. across, globose, the scaleswith prominent bosses. Arizona; New Mexico; North Mexico. A rare and graceful species in cultivation but most trees grown under this name are the related *C. gubra*, which also see.

bonita. See *C. arizolnica* and *C. glabra*.

bakeri JEPS. "Modoc Cypress". A small to medium-sized tree of loose conical habit, with reddish-grey, flaking bark. Branches spreading, branchlets drooping, much divided into greyish-green, thread-like sections, liberally speckled with resin. Cones globular 1·25cm. across, scales with prominent bosses. California. C. 1930.

matthewsii C. B. WOLF. "Siskiyou Cypress". In the wild a taller tree than the type and with longer branches. Small specimens passed the severe winter of 1962-63 without injury. California; Oregon. I. 1917.

†cashmeriana CARR. (*pendula*). "Kashmir Cypress". One of the most graceful and beautiful of all conifers. A small to medium-sized tree of conical habit. The branches are ascending and are draped with long, pendulous branchlets. Foliage a conspicuous blue-grey, in flattened sprays. We have here grown this plant out-of-doors for twenty years, but it is only seen at its best in the mildest parts of the British Isles. It makes an excellent specimen for the large conservatory. Origin unknown. It has variously been regarded as a juvenile form of both *C. funebris* and *C. torulosa*. I. 1862. F.C.C. 1971.

duclouxiana HICKEL. A graceful, small to medium-sized species forming a conical tree with reddish-brown bark. Branchlets finely divided into greyish-green, thread-like segments. Cones globular and smooth, 2 to 2·5cm. across, like miniature footballs. S.W. China.

†dupreziana CAMUS. An extremely rare relative of *C. sempervirens*, of which it is probably a geographical form, differing from that species in a few minor points, including its flattened branchlets and smaller, longer cones. Only found in the Tassile Mountains in the Sahara, where it is now almost extinct, only fourteen or so ancient trees surviving in a remote valley there.

forbesii JEPS. A rare and little-known species proving hardy here. A small, slender tree with attractive brown and red flaking bark, resembling a *Stewartia* in this respect. Branches spreading, with loose and irregular branchlet systems and green foliage. Cones irregularly globose, 2 to 2·5cm. across. California. C. 1927.

funebris ENDL. "Mourning Cypress"; "Chinese Weeping Cypress". An elegant, small to medium-sized tree, erect in growth when young, becoming more open and pendulous with age. Branches spreading, eventually drooping, branchlets pendulous; adult foliage sage-green in flattened sprays. Until it forms its adult leaves it makes a very attractive pot plant with soft glaucous-green juvenile foliage. In this form before the last world war it was often used as the central table piece in cafes and restaurants in London and other large cities and was dispensed by growers as *Juniperus bermudiana*. A native of C. China where it reaches a large size and is commonly found near temples and monasteries. I. 1849.

CUPRESSUS—*continued*

glabra SUDW. (*arizonica* HORT. not GREENE) (*arizonica bonita* HORT. not LEMM.). "Smooth Arizona Cypress". A small to medium-sized tree of dense, conical habit with ascending branches and an attractive, peeling, red bark, blistering and purple with age. Foliage greyish-green or grey, resin-speckled. Cones globular, 2 to 3cm. long, with prominent bosses. A common tree in cultivation, usually under the name *C. arizonica*, a somewhat similar but rarer species which differs mainly in its usually green foliage and less attractive bark. Central Arizona (U.S.A.). I. 1907.

'Aurea'. A broadly conical form. Leaves suffused yellow during summer, paling towards winter. Originated in Australia.

'Compacta' (*'Nana'*) (*arizonica 'Compacta'*). A beautiful, dwarf, globular bush with attractive grey-green adult foliage and red-brown branchlets. Suitable for the rock garden or scree. C. 1913.

'Hodgins'. A strong-growing tree with ascending and spreading branches covered with silvery-grey foliage which is conspicuously resin-speckled, strong-smelling when bruised and rough to the touch.

'Pyramidalis' (*arizonica 'Pyramidalis'*) (*arizonica 'Conica'*). A dense, compact, conical tree of medium size, with blue-grey foliage. The small, yellow male strobili pepper the branchlets during late winter. Cones freely produced. One of the best formal "blue" conifers in cultivation. C. 1928. A.G.M. 1969.

'Variegata'. A slow-growing, conical tree with blue-green foliage interspersed with creamy white growths. Requires a sheltered position.

goveniana GORD. "Gowen Cypress"; "Californian Cypress". A small to medium-sized tree of conical or broadly columnar habit with loosely-arranged, ascending branches and long, drooping, irregularly-divided branchlets; foliage dark green, fragrant when crushed. Cones globular, 2cm. long, the scales with prominent bosses. Restricted in the wild to Monterey (California) where it occurs with *C. macrocarpa*. I. 1846.

pygmaea LEMMON (*C. pygmaea*). A small tree with greyish-brown shreddy bark. Foliage dark green. Cones 1·5cm. across, the scales with inconspicuous bosses. We are indebted to Mr. Brian Mulligan of the University of Washington Arboretum, Seattle, for this rare variety. California.

guadalupensis S. WATS. "Tecate Cypress". A very beautiful, fast-growing tree of medium size, with attractive, peeling, cherry-red bark. Branches ascending, with finely divided crowded branchlets and greyish-green foliage. Cones globular, 3 to 4·5cm. across, the scales with conspicuous bosses. Proving hardy in the home counties. Guadalupe Island (Mexico). I. 1880. A.M. 1978 (for foliage and fruit).

†**lusitanica** MILL. "Mexican Cypress"; "Cedar of Goa". A medium-sized to large, graceful tree with rich brown, peeling bark. Branches spreading, with pendulous branchlets and greyish-green foliage. Cones glaucous, globular 12mm. across, the scales with slender, pointed bosses. Though surprisingly hardy, it cannot be recommended for cold districts. Mexico; Guatemala. C. 1682.

benthamii CARR. A very distinct tree of narrowly conical habit, in which the bright, shining green branchlet systems are decidedly flattened, giving an attractive fern-like appearance. Not recommended for cold areas. Mexico. I. about 1838.

'Flagellifera'. A rare form. A small to medium-sized tree with long, pendulous, cord-like, green branchlets. Cones up to 2cm. across. C. 1927.

'Glauca'. Similar in habit to the type, but foliage an attractive bluish-green. C. 1910.

'Glauca Pendula'. A beautiful form selected by Edwin Hillier, with a spreading crown and graceful, drooping, glaucous-blue branchlets. Makes a small, wide-spreading tree. C. 1925. A.M. 1944.

lusitanica × macrocarpa. A strong-growing tree of graceful habit with spreading branches, drooping branchlets and green foliage. Eventually attaining a large size.

macnabiana MURR. "McNab's Cypress". A small tree or large shrub with comparatively wide-spreading branches, conspicuous, red-tinged branchlets and pale glaucous-green foliage. Cones 2 to 2·5cm. across the scales with conical curved bosses. A rare tree in cultivation and one of the hardiest cypresses, even on shallow chalk soils. California. I. 1854.

CUPRESSUS—*continued*

macrocarpa GORD. (*lambertiana*). "Monterey Cypress". A popular, very fast-growing tree of medium to large size, conical or broadly columnar in habit when young, becoming broad-crowned with age when it resembles almost a Lebanon Cedar in outline. Foliage bright green, in densely packed sprays. Cones 2·5 to 3·5cm. across, the scales with a short boss. A valuable shelter tree in coastal districts. Young plants are subject to damage in cold areas. The yellow-foliaged forms colour best in an open position, becoming green when in shade. California. I. about 1838.

'Conybeari'. A small, wide-spreading tree of loosely conical habit, bearing drooping branches and long filiform yellow or yellowish-green branchlets. An unusual form of Australian origin, recalling *Chamaecyparis pisifera 'Filifera'* in habit.

'Crippsii' (*'Sulphurea'*). A form with stiffly spreading, horizontal branches and short, stiff branchlets which are cream-yellow at the tips when young. C. 1874.

'Donard Gold'. A conical or broadly columnar tree of medium size. Foliage rich deep golden-yellow. An improvement on *'Lutea'*. C. 1946.

'Globosa'. A dwarf, globular bush of dense, compact habit, with scale-like leaves. If reversions occur they should be removed.

'Goldcrest'. A medium-sized tree of narrowly columnar form and dense, compact habit. Feathery juvenile foliage of a rich yellow. Raised by Messrs. Treseder's of Truro about 1948. One of the best of its colour.

'Lutea'. A tall, broadly columnar tree of medium size and compact growth. Foliage soft yellow, becoming green. C. before 1893. F.C.C. 1893.

'Minima' (*'Minimax'*). A dwarf, slow-growing, low bush of mainly juvenile foliage. If reversions occur they should be cut away. Raised by Mr. R. Menzies at the Golden Gate Park, San Francisco, and sent to the late Alfred Nisbet of Brooker's Farm, Gosport, Hants., who, until his death, had gathered together one of the best collections of dwarf conifers in the British Isles.

'Pendula'. A broad tree of medium size. The wide-spreading branches droop at their extremities. The original tree at Glencormac, Bray, Co. Wicklow is now 15m. in height (1971).

'Pygmaea' (*'Woking'*). The best miniature of the species. The tiny scale-like leaves are in four ranks, very closely set, concealing the stem and recalling *Pilgerodendron*. This remarkable dwarf plant was raised in 1929 by the late Mr. Marcham of Carshalton Nursery, Surrey.

'Variegata' (*'Lebretoni'*). Foliage with irregular creamy-white variegation. C. 1866. F.C.C. 1867.

pygmaea. See *C. goveniana pygmaea*.

sargentii JEPS. "Sargent Cypress". A small to medium-sized tree, with dark coloured bark and soft green foliage. Cones 2 to 2·5cm. long, scales with inconspicuous bosses. This tree is succeeding here where it has been growing for five years. California. C. 1908.

sempervirens L. "Italian Cypress" or "Mediterranean Cypress". The "Cypress" of the ancients. A medium-sized tree of narrow columnar habit, with strictly ascending branches and dark green foliage. Cones 2 to 3cm. across, the scales with small bosses. A familiar tree in the Mediterranean Region where it is widely distributed and cultivated. Young plants are subject to injury in cold areas. The form described above, *'Fastigiata'* or *'Stricta'*, is unknown in the wild state. Mediterranean Region; W. Asia.

'Gracilis'. A narrowly columnar form of dense, compact growth raised in New Zealand.

horizontalis GORD. The wild form, differing from the above in its more spreading branches, forming a conical crown. East Mediterranean Region.

'Swane's Golden'. A compact, columnar form with golden tinged foliage. Raised in Australia.

†stephensonii C. B. WOLF. "Cuyamaca Cypress". A rare, small tree related to *C. glabra*. Smooth cherry-like bark and grey-green foliage. Cones globose, scales with inconspicuous bosses. This tree has been growing successfully here for the past five years. California.

torulosa D. DON. "Bhutan Cypress". A graceful, usually small to medium-sized tree, but occasionally attaining large proportions. It is conical in habit, with horizontal branches and flattened sprays of whip-like branchlets and dark green foliage. Cones 1 to 2cm. across, dark brown with a violet bloom, the scales with small boses. N. Himalaya; W. China. I. 1824.

corneyana CARR. Branchlets pendulous; sprays more spreading. I. about 1847.

'Majestica'. A distinct, slow growing form with thickened branches and rather congested moss-like foliage. C. 1855.

"CYPRESS". See *CUPRESSUS* and *CHAMAECYPARIS*.

***DACRYDIUM—Podocarpaceae**—A small genus of evergreen trees allied to *Podocarpus* and natives mainly of Australasia. The leaves are scale-like on adult trees and awl-shaped on juveniles. Male and female strobili are normally borne on different trees. Fruits consist of an ovoid nut-like seed seated in a cup-like aril. The only species which here survives our severest winters outside is *D. laxifolium*.

†biforme PILGER (*colensoi* KIRK not HOOK.). A rare species recently received by us from Messrs. Duncan & Davies of New Plymouth, New Zealand, who describe it as a slow-growing, alpine conifer up to 6m. The leaves of juvenile plants are likened to those of a Yew, spreading in two opposite ranks. Leaves of adult plants are smaller and scale-like. New Zealand.

†colensoi HOOK. not KIRK. "Westland Pine". A small, conical tree of rather loose habit, branchlets long and slender. The wood is highly prized in New Zealand where it is a native.

†cupressinum LAMB. "Rimu" or "Red Pine". A small, graceful, conical tree with arching branches and pendulous string-like branchlets. Considered by the botanist Cheeseman to be "as beautiful and attractive as any tree in New Zealand". Slow growing in the British Isles even in a sheltered position. It makes a charming specimen for the conservatory. New Zealand.

†franklinii HOOK. f. The "Huon Pine" of Tasmania. In the milder parts of this country forms a large, graceful shrub or small conical tree. The slender, drooping branches are clothed with bright green, scale-like leaves. Subject to injury in severe winters. The wood is highly prized for furniture and cabinet work in Tasmania.

†intermedium KIRK. A small tree or large bush with spreading branches. Widely distributed in New Zealand where its wood is used for railway sleepers, boat building and telegraph poles.

laxifolium HOOK. f. "Mountain Rimu". A prostrate or scrambling conifer forming mats of slender, wiry stems and tiny scale-like leaves which turn plum-purple in winter. Perhaps the smallest conifer in the world, coning at 8cm. high; it is found in mountain districts of New Zealand.

***DISELMA—Cupressaceae**—A monotypic, Tasmanian genus related to *Fitzroya*. Male and female strobili are borne on separate plants. The cones are small and composed of two pairs of scales.

archeri HOOK. f. A beautiful, medium-sized to large bush of lax habit. Leaves scale-like, appressed to and concealing the slender branchlets. This species was lost to cultivation until recently re-introduced by Lord Talbot de Malahide to whom we are indebted. Lord Talbot is growing a great collection of Tasmanian plants in his garden near Dublin.

"FIR". See *ABIES*.

***FITZROYA—Cupressaceae**—A monotypic genus, closely allied to *Diselma*. Male and female strobili borne on the same or on separate plants.

cupressoides JOHNSTON (*patagonica*). The only species is a beautiful shrub of cypress-like habit and in cultivation forms a surprisingly hardy, graceful, large shrub or small, dense tree with scale-like leaves borne in threes, banded white, carried on drooping branchlets. Cones small consisting of nine scales. Chile; Argentina. Introduced by William Lobb in 1849 and later by Richard Pearce. There is a splendid tree of this species at Killerton near Exeter. This magnificent collection was planted by the late Sir Francis Acland, and is now maintained by the National Trust.

***FOKIENIA—Cupressaceae**—A genus of one, possibly two species, related to both *Cupressus* and *Calocedrus*. Resembling *Calocedrus macrolepis* in foliage. Male and female strobili are borne on the same plant. The cones, up to 2·5cm. long, are similar to those of a *Chamaecyparis*, ripening the second year. The following species is best given a sheltered position in woodland.

hodginsii HENRY & THOMAS. A small to medium-sized shrub of very slow growth. The very distinct and characteristic spine-tipped, paired, scale-like leaves are bright, glossy green above, marked with conspicuous silvery-white bands of stomata beneath. They are borne in large, flattened sprays somewhat resembling those of a *Thujopsis*, but more delicate and graceful. Probably the best specimen in cultivation is at Borde Hill, planted by that great amateur gardener the late Col. Stephenson Clarke. This rare and remarkable conifer is a native of S.E. China and was first discovered in the province of Fokien (Fukien) by Captain Hodgins in 1908, and was introduced the following year by Sir Lewis Clinton-Baker. A.M. 1911.

GINKGO—Ginkgoaceae—A remarkable and distinct, monotypic genus of great ornamental, botanical and geographical interest. *G. biloba* is the sole living survivor of an ancient family whose ancestors occurred in many parts of the world (including the British Isles) about 160 million years ago. Male and female strobili occur on separate plants. The yellow, plum-shaped fruits are produced in pairs or threes at the end of a slender stalk, ripening and falling in autumn, when, if crushed, they emit a strong offensive odour. It is regarded as a sacred tree in the east and is commonly planted in the vicinity of Buddhist temples. Long considered to be extinct in a wild state, it is now known to have survived in Chekiang Province, Eastern China.

biloba L. (*Salisburia adiantifolia*). "Maidenhair Tree". A medium-sized to large, deciduous tree of conical habit when young. Easily recognised by its peculiar fan-shaped, undivided leaves which turn a beautiful clear yellow before falling in autumn. Perfectly hardy and suitable for most soils. It is tolerant of industrial areas and is magnificent either as a single specimen or as an avenue tree. It was first introduced in about 1727 and to England in about 1758. Small grafted plants of both sexes are offered. A.G.M. 1969.

'Fastigiata'. A striking columnar form with semi-erect branches.

'Pendula'. A remarkable selection with spreading or weeping branches.

'Tremonia'. We are indebted for this conical form to the late Dr. G. Krussmann, once director of the celebrated gardens at Dortmund. Dr. Krussmann was a very rare example of a botanist who was also a horticulturist.

†GLYPTOSTROBUS—Taxodiaceae—A monotypic genus related to *Taxodium*. Male and female strobili are borne on the same plant. Cones pear-shaped, 2cm. long, borne on long stalks. Not recommended for cold localities.

lineatus DRUCE (*pensilis*) (*sinensis*). An extremely rare, deciduous conifer, attaining a large bush or small tree. The soft sea-green, narrow leaves turn a rich brown in autumn. This remarkable species has grown slowly in our arboretum without protection for the past fifteen years. It is a native of the province of Canton, S. China, where it is often found on the banks of streams and similarly moist situations.

"HEMLOCK". See *TSUGA*.

***JUNIPERUS—Cupressaceae**—"Juniper". A large genus of trees and shrubs, ranging from prostrate or creeping alpines to dense bushy shrubs and tall, conical or columnar trees. The leaves of juvenile plants are awl-shaped and usually pungently pointed, those of adult plants are normally scale-like and densely crowded, although in some species they retain their juvenile form. The awl-shaped leaves of the Juniper bear white or glaucous stomatal bands above (i.e. on the inner surface) but because of the often horizontal disposition of the branches the bands appear to be on the lower surface. Male and female strobili are borne on the same or on separate plants. The fruits are usually rounded or ovoid, becoming fleshy and berry-like.

The junipers are a most versatile race, containing plants for most soils and situations. They are amongst the most suitable conifers for calcareous soils though such are not essential to their well-being. They range in colour from green to yellow, grey and steel-blue. The prostrate forms are excellent as ground cover in sun and several of the small, columnar forms are effective in the heather garden.

†ashei BUCHH. (*monticola*). A large, slow-growing, dioecious shrub or occasionally a small tree of conical habit. Foliage awl-shaped and sage-green on young plants, scale-like and dark green on mature plants. Fruits rounded, 6 to 8mm. across, deep blue and covered with a glaucous bloom, sweet and aromatic to the taste. A rare species for a sheltered site in the milder counties. It occurs with *J. virginiana* in the wild. S. United States; Mexico. I. 1926.

†californica CARR. "Californian Juniper". A large bush or small tree; foliage yellowish-green, scale-like. Fruits reddish-brown, bloomy. Only for mild areas. California; Oregon. Introduced by William Lobb in 1853.

canadensis. See *J. communis depressa*.

JUNIPERUS—*continued*

†**cedrus** WEBB & BERTH. "Canary Island Juniper". An erect-growing, dioecious, small tree of graceful habit, with slender, drooping, whitish branchlets densely clothed with sharply pointed awl-shaped leaves which are arranged in whorls of three. Fruits 10 to 12mm. across, reddish-brown, bloomy. A tender species closely related to *J. oxycedrus*. Native of the Canary Isles where it is now very rare. Large trees are still to be found on the island of Palma growing in inaccessible parts of the volcanic crater. It has been grown outside in the home counties for many years.

chinensis L. "Chinese Juniper". An extremely variable, dioecious species distributed in the wild over a wide area. In cultivation it is typically a tall, conical or columnar, grey or greyish tree of medium size and dense, compact habit, with both awl-shaped juvenile and scale-like adult foliage on the same plant. Fruits rounded or top-shaped, 5 to 7mm. across, glaucous, ripening in the second year. It is one of the most important ornamental junipers, having given rise to innumerable garden forms. See also *J. davurica* and *J. ×media*. Himalaya; China; Japan. Originally introduced before 1767. Introduced into England by William Kerr in 1804.

'Albovariegata'. See *'Variegata'*.

'Ames'. Medium-sized bush of rather spreading growth; leaves awl-shaped, bluish-green at first later green. C. 1935.

'Armstrongii'. See *J. ×media 'Armstrongii'*.

'Aurea'. "Young's Golden Juniper". A tall, slender, slow-growing conical or columnar tree with golden foliage, inclined to burn in full sun. A male clone exhibiting both juvenile and adult foliage. C. 1871. F.C.C. 1871.

'Columnaris Glauca'. Small tree of dense, columnar habit, slightly broader at base and tapering gradually to summit. Leaves awl-shaped, sharply-pointed and glaucous. Sometimes wrongly referred to under the name *'Pyramidalis Glauca'*. A seedling selected at the U.S. Dept. of Agriculture from seed collected by Frank N. Meyer in Hupeh, China. C. 1920.

'Echiniformis'. A dwarf, tight ball of prickly leaves. Previously thought to be a form of *J. communis*. Not one of the easiest plants to grow. A.M. 1961.

'Excelsa Stricta' HORT. See *'Pyramidalis'*.

'Expansa'. See *J. ×davurica 'Expansa'*.

'Fairview'. Small to medium-sized tree of narrow habit; leaves bright green, mostly juvenile. Raised from seed in 1930.

fortunei HORT. See *J. sheppardii*.

'Globosa Cinerea'. See *J. ×media 'Globosa Cinerea'*.

'Iowa'. Medium-sized shrub of spreading habit; leaves green, slightly bluish, both scale-like and awl-like present on the same plant. Female. C. 1935.

'Japonica Oblonga'. See *'Oblonga'*.

'Kaizuka' (*torulosa*) (*J. sheppardii torulosa*). A large, erect-growing shrub, eventually a small tree, with long, spreading branches clothed with characteristic dense clusters of scale-like, bright green foliage. A very distinct form, particularly effective in the heather garden or as an isolated lawn specimen. Introduced from Japan in about 1920.

'Kaizuka Variegata'. Foliage green splashed creamy-white. Slower growing than *'Kaizuka'*. C. 1958.

'Keteleeri' (*virginiana 'Keteleeri'*). Small, conical tree of dense habit; crowded masses of vivid green, scale-like leaves and an abundance of small, light green fruits. C. 1910.

'Maney'. Medium-sized shrub with ascending branches; leaves bluish bloomy, awl-shaped. C. 1935.

'Mountbatten'. Medium-sized bush or small tree of columnar habit; leaves greyish-green, awl-shaped. Raised by the Sheridan Nurseries, Ontario, Canada. C. 1948.

'Obelisk'. Medium-sized shrub of erect, columnar habit; foliage bluish-green, awl-shaped, densely packed. Raised from seed in 1930.

'Oblonga' (*'Japonica Oblonga'*). A small shrub of irregular, rounded habit with densely crowded branches, those in the lower part of the bush bearing prickly, dark green, awl-shaped leaves, those in the upper part projecting and clothed with scale-like leaves. A sport of cv. *'Japonica'*. C. 1932.

'Olympia'. Medium-sized shrub or small tree of columnar habit; leaves glaucous both scale-like and awl-shaped. C. before 1956.

'Parsonsii'. See *J. ×davurica 'Expansa'*.

JUNIPERUS—*continued*

chinensis 'Pfitzerana'. See *J.* ×*media 'Pfitzerana'*.

'Plumosa'. See *J.* ×*media 'Plumosa'*.

procumbens. See *J. procumbens*.

'Pyramidalis' (*'Excelsa Stricta'* HORT.) (*'Glauca'*). A dense, slow-growing, conical bush with almost entirely juvenile, prickly, glaucous leaves. F.C.C. 1868 (as *J. excelsa stricta*).

'San José'. Dwarf shrub with prostrate branches; leaves grey-green, mostly juvenile. C. 1935.

sargentii. See *J. sargentii*.

'Sheppardii'. See *J. sheppardii*.

torulosa. See *'Kaizuka'*.

'Variegata' (*'Albovariegata'*). Usually a large conical bush of dense, compact habit. Leaves mostly juvenile, glaucous, with scattered sprays of white variegation. Introduced from Japan about 1860.

communis L. "Common Juniper". A variable species, usually found as a medium-sized to large shrub. Its silver-backed leaves are awl-shaped, prickly to the touch and arranged in whorls of three. Fruits rounded, 5 to 6mm. across, black, covered by a glaucous bloom, ripening during the second or third year and are sometimes used to flavour gin. This species has probably a wider distribution than any other tree or shrub, occurring from N. America eastwards through Europe and Asia to Korea and Japan. It is one of our three native conifers, being particularly plentiful on the chalk downs of the south of England. It is one of the most accommodating of conifers, its prostrate forms especially being useful as ground cover in sun, whilst the slender columns of the "Irish Juniper" are a conspicuous feature of many gardens. A.M. 1890.

'Compressa'. A gem for the rock garden or scree. A dwarf, compact, slow-growing column. Resembling a miniature "Irish Juniper". Several specimens planted with variously coloured prostrate junipers creates a charming miniature landscape. C. 1855.

'Cracovia'. A conical or broadly columnar geographical form of Polish origin with ascending branches and branchlets with drooping tips. C. 1855.

depressa PURSH (*J. canadensis*). "Canadian Juniper". A dwarf, wide-spreading variety to about ·6m., forming large patches of densely packed, slightly ascending stems clothed with comparatively broad, yellowish or brownish-green, silver-backed leaves which are bronze-coloured above during winter. A wild variety from the mountains of North America and one of the best of all dwarf carpeting conifers, excellent as ground cover in sun.

'Depressa Aurea'. Leaves and young shoots golden yellow during early summer. Growth as in var. *depressa*. C. 1887.

'Dumosa'. A dwarf spreading shrub forming large patches. Leaves green, silvery-white beneath, turning coppery bronze or brown in winter. A form of *depressa* which originated in Holland. A splendid ground cover for an open situation. A specimen in our arboretum has attained ·6×1·5m. in fifteen years. C. 1934.

'Effusa'. A wide-spreading, semi-prostrate form. The leaves green above, silvery-white beneath, point forward and lie along the branches, which they more or less conceal. An excellent dwarf carpeting conifer, its leaves usually remaining green in winter contrasting effectively with the bronze of *depressa* and *'Dumosa'*. C. 1944.

'Hibernica' (*'Stricta'*) (*J. hibernica*). "Irish Juniper". A dense-growing, compact form of slender, columnar habit attaining 3m. or occasionally 5m. in height. Leaves densely arranged. A very popular conifer, excellent for use in formal landscapes and gardens. To some extent the counterpart of the "Italian Cypress" of the warmer S. European gardens though never so tall. C. 1838.

'Hornibrookii' (*'Prostrata'*). A dwarf, creeping ground cover taking on the shape of the object over which it creeps. Leaves comparatively small, loosely spreading, sharply-pointed, silvery-white beneath. A seedling collected in Co. Galway, Ireland, by that great authority on dwarf conifers, Murray Hornibrook. C. 1923. A clone *Hornibrookiana Nana'* (*'Prostrata Nana'*) is slower-growing and more compact. A.G.M. 1973.

jackii REHD. A geographical variety from the Rocky Mts. A prostrate shrub with long slender branches lying on the ground in all directions; leaves sea-green. C. 1904.

JUNIPERUS—*continued*

communis montana. See *J. nana.*

nana SYME (*montana*) (*saxatilis*) (*J. nana*) (*J. sibirica*). A slow-growing, prostrate form, its densely-packed stems hugging the ground and forming mats or carpets of dark green leaves. In the wild it is found on rocks, mountains and moors and in the north of Scotland may be seen draping sea-cliffs in the teeth of cold, briny winds. Western N. America; Greenland; British Isles and through Europe, the Himalayas to Japan.

'Oblonga Pendula'. An elegant, erect shrub of compact habit up to 3 to 5m., with slightly ascending branches drooping at the tips, branchlets pendulous. Leaves sharply pointed bronze during winter. Recalling *J. oxycedrus*, but with rounded shoots. C. 1838.

'Prostrata'. See *'Hornibrookii'*.

'Repanda'. A dwarf, carpet-forming shrub with densely-packed, semi-prostrate stems and forward-pointing, loosely arranged leaves which sometimes become slightly bronze tinged in winter. Although of different origin this cultivar is for garden purposes identical with *'Effusa'*. Both make excellent ground cover in full sun. *'Repanda'* was discovered in Ireland by the late Maurice Prichard. C. 1934.

saxatilis. See *nana.*

'Stricta'. See *'Hibernica'*.

suecica BEISSN. (*J. suecica*). A medium-sized shrub similar to *'Hibernica'* in habit, but the ascending branches are open and drooping at the tips. Occurs wild in Scandinavia. C. 1768.

'Vase' (*'Vase Shaped'*). Dwarf shrub up to ·7m. with low, obtusely spreading branches and leaves turning bronze in winter. C. 1936.

conferta PARL. (*littoralis*) (*rigida conferta*). "Shore Juniper". A prostrate species with shortly ascending branches, forming large patches of bright green, prickly leaves which possess a white stomatal band on the upper surface. Fruits globose, 8 to 12mm. across, purplish-black and bloomy. An invaluable ground cover species, its dense prickly carpets of apple-green foliage contrasting effectively with the prostrate dark green forms of *J. communis* and the blue and grey forms of *J. horizontalis*. A native of Japan and Sakhalin where it is found on sandy sea-shores. Introduced by Ernest Wilson in 1915.

×**davurica** PALL. (*sabina* × *sheppardii*). Regarded by the botanist Van Melle as an extremely variable hybrid with a distribution through northern Asia. It is represented in cultivation by the following clones:—

'Expansa' (*chinensis Parsonsii'*) (*chinensis 'Expansa'*). A dwarf shrub with rigid, wide-spreading, almost horizontal, thick branches, eventually developing into a low mound up to 1m. high in the centre and 3m. or more across. The scale-like, sage-green leaves are arranged in attractive dense, spray-like heavy clusters along the branches. Introduced from Japan by the Parsons Nursery of New York State in 1862.

'Expansa Aureospicata'. Smaller and slower-growing than the type, with predominantly juvenile leaves. Greyish-green, with scattered yellow splashes. C. 1940.

'Expansa Variegata' (*chinensis 'Parsonsii Variegata'*). Similar to the type in habit and foliage, but with scattered, creamy-white sprays. C. 1933.

'Parsonsii Variegata'. See *'Expansa Variegata'*.

deppeana STEUD. A small, dioecious tree of conical habit, with reddish-brown bark deeply furrowed into square plates. Leaves glaucous; fruits globular, 10 to 12mm. across, reddish-brown and bloomy. Mexico. I. 1904.

pachyphlaea MARTINEZ (*J. pachyphlaea*). "Chequer-barked" or "Alligator Juniper". Differing from the type in its attractive, flaky bark and denser blue-white foliage, particularly conspicuous as a young plant when it is the most vividly silver-blue of all junipers. Not an easy subject to cultivate coming as it does from the dry mountain slopes of Arizona, Texas and New Mexico.

distans FLORIN. A rare, large shrub or small tree of loosely columnar habit with drooping branchlets. Leaves mainly juvenile, awl-shaped, grey-green; fruits ovoid, 8 to 12mm. long, reddish-brown. S.W. China. I. 1926.

JUNIPERUS—*continued*

drupacea LABILL. "Syrian Juniper". A striking and distinctive dioecious species of narrow columnar habit, at least in cultivation. A small tree, branches short and densely crowded with sharply pointed, awl-shaped leaves which are fresh green, broadly banded white on the inner surface. Fruits ovoid or globose, 2 to 2·5cm. across, bluish-black and bloomy, ripening during the first season when they are edible. So far fruits have not been reported in the British Isles. A remarkable species easily recognised in gardens by its habit, together with its comparatively broad, prickly leaves. Asia Minor; Syria; Greece. I. in about 1854.

excelsa BIEB. "Greek Juniper". Small tree or large shrub of conical or loosely columnar habit, with long sprays of thread-like branchlets densely clothed with tiny grey-green leaves spreading at tips. Fruits ripening the second year, globose, 9 to 12mm. across, deep purplish-brown and bloomy. Asia Minor; Balkans; Caucasus to Persia. I. 1806.

'Stricta'. A columnar form with mainly juvenile foliage. Unfortunately this name has been erroneously used in gardens for *J. chinensis 'Pyramidalis'*.

†**flaccida** SCHLECHT. "Mexican Juniper". A small tree with attractive scaly bark, slender branches and pendulous branchlets; leaves scale-like, grey-green, bright grass-green on mature trees. Fruits ripening the second year, globose, 10 to 15mm. across, reddish-brown, bloomy. This species has reached 3m. outside in our arboretum but has not yet had to withstand a really severe winter. Mexico; Texas. I. 1838.

†**formosana** HAYATA. "Prickly Cypress". A beautiful, small, dioecious tree of loose elegant habit with drooping branchlets. Leaves awl-shaped, in whorls of three, sharp pointed, glaucous above. Fruits sub-globose, 6 to 12mm. across, olive-green, with three conspicuous white grooves at the apex, ripening to dark brown the second year. A graceful but tender species similar in aspect to *J. oxycedrus*. China; Formosa. I. about 1844.

'Grey Owl' (*virginiana 'Grey Owl'*). A splendid medium-sized, vigorous shrub with widely spreading branches; foliage soft silvery grey. It is thought to be a hybrid between *J. virginiana 'Glauca'* and *J.* ×*media 'Pfitzerana'*, possessing a habit similar to the latter but in other respects appears typical *J. virginiana*. Originated in 1938. A.M. 1968.

hibernica. See *J. communis 'Hibernica'*.

hispanica. See *J. thurifera*.

horizontalis MOENCH. "Creeping Juniper". A dwarf or prostrate shrub with long, sometimes procumbent branches, forming in time carpets several metres across. Leaves on cultivated plants mostly juvenile crowding the branchlets, glaucous green, grey-green or blue, varying in intensity and often plum purple in winter. Fruits rarely produced in cultivation. One of the best species for use as ground cover, contrasting effectively with the green prostrate forms of *J. communis*. It is a native of North America where it inhabits sea-cliffs, gravelly slopes, even swamps. C. 1830. A.G.M. 1969.

'Alpina'. A form with prostrate branches and ascending branchlets up to ·6m. high. Leaves greyish-blue, purple-tinged during autumn and winter. C. 1836.

'Bar Harbor'. A prostrate form with branches closely hugging the ground and spreading in all directions. The shortly ascending branchlets are clothed with glaucous, grey-green, scale-like leaves. C. 1930.

'Blue Rug'. See *'Wiltonii'*.

'Coast of Maine'. Low-growing form forming flattened mounds. Leaves awl-shaped, grey-green, purple tinted in winter.

'Douglasii'. "Waukegan Juniper". A low-growing, procumbent form up to ·5m. high with long, spreading branches and sprays of both adult and juvenile leaves. The whole plant is a bright, glaucous, grey-green in summer, purple-tinged in autumn and winter. C. 1916.

'Glauca'. Prostrate, branches long with slender "whipcord" tips hugging the ground. Leaves steel-blue in slender sprays. C. 1939.

'Montana'. A prostrate form with long branches, slender and filiform at their tips. Branchlets shortly-ascending, plumose and densely packed, bearing scale-like leaves of an intense glaucous blue. In our opinion, one of the best forms.

'Plumosa'. A dense, procumbent form of compact habit with ascending, plumose branchlets up to ·6m. high. Leaves awl-shaped, grey-green, becoming purple-tinged in winter. C. 1919.

JUNIPERUS—*continued*

horizontalis 'Prostrata'. A prostrate form with shortly-ascending branchlets clothed with awl-shaped and scale-like, glaucous leaves, bronze-tinted in winter. C. 1938.

'Wiltonii' (*'Blue Rug'*). One of the best forms, its branches long and prostrate, forming flattened, glaucous-blue carpets. C. 1914.

indica BERTOL. A rare species in cultivation, varying in the wild from a small, spreading shrub to a small, conical tree. Foliage dense and crowded, varying from deep green to grey-green. From high altitudes in the Himalaya.

japonica HORT. See *J.* ×*media 'Plumosa'*.

macrocarpa. See *J. oxycedrus macrocarpa*.

× **media** VAN MELLE (*chinensis* × *sabina*). A variable hybrid which, according to the author, occurs in the wild in N.E. Asia. Van Melle was of the opinion that four commonly cultivated junipers previously regarded as forms of *J. chinensis* belonged to this hybrid group and existed in a wild state. Whilst agreeing with his concept of their hybrid origin, we prefer here to treat them as clones originally selected from wild material rather than varieties having a distinct geographical distribution. We also regard *J. chinensis* in its broader concept as a parent rather than Van Melle's *J. sphaerica*. Many authorities disagree with Van Melle's conclusions, whilst others prefer to remain neutral until such time that the whole of the *J. chinensis* complex has been thoroughly studied and unravelled.

'Armstrongii' (*chinensis 'Armstrongii'*). In habit resembling a dense and compact "Pfitzer Juniper". Leaves mainly scale-like, greyish. The juvenile leaves are mostly confined to the centre of the bush. A sport of *'Pfitzerana'* introduced in 1932 by the Armstrong Nurseries of California.

'Blaauw'. A strong-growing shrub up to 1·5m. with strongly ascending main branches and shorter outer branches, all densely clothed with feathery sprays of mainly scale-like, greyish-blue leaves. It is often confused in gardens with *'Globosa Cinerea'* which it resembles as a young plant, but is stronger and much more irregular in habit when older. C. 1924.

'Blue Cloud'. Similar in habit to *'Pfitzerana'*, but lower growing and less vigorous, with slender, almost thread-like branchlets and glaucous-blue foliage. C. 1955.

'Globosa Cinerea' (*chinensis 'Globosa Cinerea'*). A strong-growing, small to medium-sized shrub with ascending branches, clothed with blue-grey, mostly adult leaves. C. 1923. It is very similar to the clone *'Blaauw'*.

'Hetzii'. A medium-sized to large, wide-spreading shrub similar to *'Pfitzerana'*, but stems more ascending. The glaucous, mainly adult foliage is also softer to the touch. C. 1920.

'Kosteri' (*virginiana 'Kosteri'*). A small shrub with prostrate and ascending, plumose branches clothed with grey-green, scale-like and awl-shaped leaves, sometimes purple-tinged in winter. C. 1884.

'Old Gold'. A sport of *'Pfitzerana Aurea'*, from which it differs in its more compact habit, and bronze-gold foliage which does not fade in winter. C. 1958.

'Pfitzerana' (*chinensis 'Pfitzerana'*). "Pfitzer Juniper". One of the most popular and commonly planted of all conifers. A small, eventually medium-sized, wide-spreading shrub with stout, arm-like branches, ascending at an acute angle and drooping at the tips. Leaves mainly green and scale-like, but with scattered sprays of juvenile leaves with glaucous upper surfaces, particularly in the centre of the bush. An excellent conifer either as a lawn specimen or when used to break the regular outline of a border or bed. It makes an excellent ground cover for large areas and is remarkably shade-tolerant even between beech trees. The "Pfitzer Juniper" is a friend of the landscape gardener, it never lets him down, it marries the formal into the informal, it embellishes his layout and hides his errors. (For an equally good friend see *J. sabina 'Hicksii'*). It is often used effectively to cover unsightly structures of low stature such as manhole covers and inspection pits. C. 1896. A.G.M. 1969.

Its true origin has given rise to much wrangling amongst botanists and horticulturists. It was first mentioned by the great German nursery firm of Spaeth who named if after W. Pfitzer, a nurseryman at Stuttgart. Van Melle suggested that it was a wild form from the Ho Lan Shan Mountains, Inner Mongolia, and may possibly have been introduced by the French missionary, Armand David in about 1866.

JUNIPERUS—*continued*

×**media 'Pfitzerana Aurea'.** "Golden Pfitzer". Terminal shoots and foliage suffused golden yellow in summer, becoming yellowish-green in winter. A sport of '*Pfitzerana*' which originated in the U.S.A. in 1923.

'Pfitzerana Compacta'. A sport of '*Pfitzerana*', more dense and compact in habit, with a preponderance of juvenile awl-shaped leaves. C. 1930.

'Pfitzerana Glauca'. A sport of '*Pfitzerana*' raised in the U.S.A. It is a little denser in habit than the type, with mainly awl-shaped, grey-glaucous leaves. It may be described as a glaucous '*Pfitzerana Compacta*'. C. 1940.

'Plumosa' (*chinensis 'Plumosa'*) (*J. japonica* HORT.). A low-growing male shrub with wide-spreading branches bearing crowded plume-like sprays of densely set, green, scale-like leaves. Occasionally a few sprays of juvenile awl-shaped leaves are present in the centre of the bush. Originally introduced from Japan as *J. japonica*, under which name it was commonly grown in cultivation. *J. japonica* of Carriere becomes *J. chinensis 'Japonica'*. C. before 1920.

'Plumosa Albovariegata' (*J. japonica 'Albovariegata'*). Dwarf spreading shrub of slow growth; foliage scale-like, deep-green speckled white. C. 1867.

'Plumosa Aurea' (*J. japonica 'Aurea'* HORT.). A most attractive and ornamental form of '*Plumosa*', with ascending branches arching at the tips, densely clothed with plumose sprays of yellow, scale-like leaves which ripen to bronze-gold in winter. C. 1885.

'Plumosa Aureovariegata' (*J. japonica 'Aureovariegata'*). Similar in habit to '*Plumosa Aurea*', but lower and slower growing, its green foliage irregularly variegated deep yellow. C. 1873.

'Reptans' (*virginiana 'Reptans'* HORT). A low-growing shrub with rigid, slightly ascending branches. Leaves both scale-like and awl-shaped, grey-green. The foliage is rough to the touch. C. 1896.

†**monosperma** SARG. "Cherrystone Juniper". A large, densely-branched shrub or small tree, with fibrous reddish-brown bark and greyish-green, scale-like foliage. S.E. United States; N. Mexico. I. about 1900.

monticola. See *J. ashei*.

morrisonicola HAYATA. "Mount Morrison Juniper". A medium-sized to large shrub of usually dense, erect habit with bluish-green, awl-shaped leaves crowding the short branchlets. Fruits single-seeded, 6mm. long, black when ripe. A rare species restricted in the wild to Mount Morrison, Formosa, where it forms impenetrable scrubby thickets on rocky slopes, reaching small tree size in more sheltered ravines. Botanically it is close to *J. squamata*.

nana. See *J. communis nana*.

†**osteosperma** LITTLE (*utahensis*). "Utah Juniper". Small, monoecious, conical tree with brown fibr ous bark, and green, scale-like leaves. Fruits rounded, 6 to 16mm. long, reddish-brown and bloomy. S.W. United States. I. 1900.

oxycedrus L. "Prickly Juniper". A large dioecious shrub or small tree of open, drooping habit. Leaves in threes, awl-shaped, ending in a sharp point, green above marked with two white stomatic bands beneath. Fruits ovoid or globose, 9 to 13mm. long, shining reddish-brown when ripe in the second year. A variable species widely distributed in Southern Europe where it shows much the same kinds of variation in growth and size as *J. communis* in the British Isles. The fragrant wood produces an "Oil of Cade" which is used medicinally, particularly in the treatment of certain skin diseases. Mediterranean Region; W. Asia. C. 1739.

macrocarpa BALL (*J. macrocarpa*). A large shrub or small tree, occasionally prostrate in the wild. It differs from the type in its larger fruits. Its distribution follows that of the type.

pachyphlaea. See *J. deppeana pachyphlaea*.

phoenicea L. "Phoenicean Juniper". A large shrub or small tree of dense, rounded or broadly conical habit. Leaves green, awl-shaped on juvenile plants. Fruits rounded, 6 to 14mm. across, ripening the second year. It has been growing successfully here for several years without protection. Mediterranean Region. I. 1683.

turbinata PARL. Differing in its egg-shaped or top-shaped fruits. Occurs on hills and by the sea in Spain; Italy; Sicily; Dalmatia and Algeria.

†**pinchotii** SUDWITH. A rare, large shrub with wide-spreading branches; leaves dark yellowish-green, awl-shaped on juvenile plants, scale-like on adult plants. W. Texas.

JUNIPERUS—*continued*

†**procera** ENDL. "East African Juniper". A tall tree in Eastern Africa where it occurs at high elevations in the mountains. In cultivation it is usually seen as a large shrub or small tree with green, scale-like leaves, awl-shaped on juvenile plants. Fruits rounded, 5mm. across, glaucous. Only suitable for the mildest localities.

procumbens MIQ. (*chinensis procumbens*). "Creeping Juniper". A dwarf, procumbent species with long stiff branches, forming carpets up to 30cm. high (in the centre) and several metres across. The tightly packed branchlets are crowded with awl-shaped, glaucous green, sharply-pointed leaves. An excellent ground cover for an open, sunny position on a well-drained soil. A native of Japan where it is said to inhabit seashores. I. 1843.

'Bonin Isles'. See '*Nana*'.

'Nana' ('*Bonin Isles*'). A more compact plant with shorter branches. Introduced from Japan in about 1922.

pseudosabina HOOK. f. not FISCH. & MEY. See *J. wallichiana*.

recurva D. DON. "Drooping Juniper". A large shrub or small tree of broadly conical habit, with stringy, shaggy bark and drooping branchlets. Leaves awl-shaped, in threes, green or greyish-green, usually with white stomatal bands above, occasionally green. Fruits ovoid, 7 to 10mm. long, glossy olive-brown, ripening to black, containing a single seed. It is an extremely variable species and in the wild appears to intergrade with *J. squamata*. Some forms in cultivation seem intermediate in character between the two species though they always retain their characteristic drooping habit. The wood of *J. recurva*, particularly that of the variety *coxii* is burned for incense in Buddhist temples in the eastern Himalaya. E. Himalaya, from Nepal to Yunnan and Upper Burma. I. about 1822.

'Castlewellan'. A small tree of loose open habit, the branches lax, like fishing rods, the branchlets drooping in long, slender sprays of soft, threadlike foliage.

coxii MELVILLE. An elegant, small tree with gracefully drooping branchlets which are longer and more pendulous than those of the type. Leaves also more loosely arranged, sage-green in colour. Introduced from Upper Burma in 1920 by E. H. M. Cox and Reginald Farrer.

'Embley Park' (*viridis* HORT.). A very distinct, small, spreading shrub with reddish-brown, ascending branches clothed with rich grass green, awl-shaped leaves. Raised at Exbury and Embley Park, Hampshire, from seed collected by George Forrest in China.

'Nana'. A dwarf form of spreading habit, the branches strongly decurving; foliage greyish-green.

viridis. See '*Embley Park*'.

rigida SIEB. & ZUCC. An elegant, large, dioecious shrub or small tree, bearing spreading branches and gracefully drooping branchlets. Leaves rigid, awl-shaped and sharply pointed, marked with glaucous bands above, bronze-green during winter. Fruits globose, 6 to 8mm. across, black and bloomy, ripening the second year. A lovely species, native of Japan, Korea and N. China. Introduced by John Gould Veitch in 1861.

sabina L. "Savin". A common and extremely variable, usually dioecious species of spreading or procumbent habit. In its typical form it is a low, wide-spreading shrub, with primary branches extending 2 to 3m. and slender, ascending, plumose branchlets. Its exceptionally pungent, disagreeable smell when crushed will usually separate this species from forms of *J. virginiana*, with which it can sometimes be confused. Leaves green or grey-green, mostly scale-like, but scattered sprays of paired, awl-shaped leaves occur even on old plants. Fruits ovoid or globose, 5 to 7mm. across, bluish-black and bloomy. Widely distributed in the wild, from the mountains of Southern and Central Europe to the Caucasus. It is said to have been cultivated since ancient times and has been known in England since 1548.

'Arcadia'. A dense, dwarf shrub with short branchlets clothed with predominantly scale-like, greyish-green leaves. Similar in effect to *tamariscifolia*. A plant in our garden has attained 30 to 45cm. by 1m. after ten years. C. before 1949.

'Blue Danube'. A low-growing shrub with spreading branches and crowded branchlets. Leaves mostly scale-like, grey-blue. C. 1956.

JUNIPERUS—*continued*

sabina 'Cupressifolia'. A low-growing form throwing out long, more or less horizontal branches seldom exceeding ·6m. above ground, clothed with mostly adult, dark green leaves. A female clone. C. 1789.

'Erecta'. A strong-growing, medium-sized, female shrub with ascending branches clothed with predominantly scale-like, green leaves. This is the form usually distributed as *J. sabina*. It is also sometimes wrongly grown as *'Cupressifolia'* which is lower-growing. C. 1891.

'Fastigiata'. A large shrub of dense, columnar habit with tightly packed, ascending branches; leaves dark green, mainly scale-like. A most unusual form. C. 1891.

'Hicksii'. A strong-growing shrub with spreading or ascending, later procumbent branches and semi-erect, plumose branchlets crowded with greyish-blue, awl-shaped leaves. A most splendid and vigorous semi-prostrate shrub, to all practical intents and purposes a blue "Pfitzer". It soon reaches 1·2m. and sends out its 3 to 4m. long, plumose steely grey-blue branches. C. 1940.

'Mas'. A male clone, similar in habit to *'Cupressifolia'*. Leaves mainly awl-shaped, dark green. C. 1940.

'Skandia' (*'Scandens'*). An excellent, low, creeping shrub with dark green, mainly awl-shaped leaves. A plant in our garden has attained 20cm. by 2m. after ten years. C. 1953.

tamariscifolia AIT. A low-growing, compact variety with horizontally-packed branches, forming in time a wide-spreading, flat-topped bush. Leaves mostly awl-shaped, bright green. An extremely popular juniper of architectural value, equally suitable for clothing dry banks, wall tops or the edges of lawns. Mts. of Southern Europe. In the Spanish Pyrenees large carpets several metres across are occasionally met with. Long cultivated. A.G.M. 1969.

'Tripartita' (*virginiana 'Tripartita'*) (*lusitanica* HORT.). A strong-growing, medium-sized shrub, with strongly-ascending, nearly erect branches densely clothed with both green, scale-like leaves and glaucous, awl-shaped leaves. It is a juniper of rather heavy, ponderous habit which has now been superseded by the many forms of the "Pfitzer Juniper". C. 1867.

'Variegata'. A small shrub with low, slightly ascending branches and dark green, adult foliage flecked with white. C. 1855.

'Von Ehren'. A strong-growing shrub up to 1·25m. high, with wide, horizontally spreading, slender branches forming a unique plateau 5m. or more across. Branchlets ending in slender sprays; leaves awl-shaped green. C. 1912.

sanderi. See *Chamaecyparis obtusa 'Sanderi'*.

sargentii TAK. (*chinensis sargentii*). A prostrate shrub slowly forming dense carpets two metres across. Leaves mostly scale-like, green and bloomy. Fruits blue. A pleasing ground cover in an open position. It is regarded by many authorities as a variety of *J. chinensis*. Native of Japan, S. Kuriles and Sakhalin where it inhabits rocky mountain cliffs and sea-shores. Introduced by Prof. Sargent in 1892.

'Glauca'. A slower-growing form with glaucous grey-green foliage. A good small rug for the scree.

scopulorum SARG. "Rocky Mountain Juniper". A small cypress-like tree of conical habit, often with several main stems. Bark red-brown and shredding. Branches stout and spreading, with slender branchlets and tightly appressed scale-like leaves, varying in colour from light green to bluish-green and glaucous. Fruits rounded, 6mm. across, dark blue and bloomy. A native of the Rocky Mountains from British Columbia to Arizona and Texas. It has given rise to many forms. I. 1839.

'Erecta Glauca'. An erect, loosely columnar form with ascending branches and both scale-like and awl-shaped, silvery-glaucous leaves becoming purple-tinged in winter.

'Glauca Pendula'. Dwarf to medium-sized shrub of loose, open habit, branches ascending, branchlets drooping; foliage awl-shaped, greyish-green. With us forming a plant of rather weak constitution.

'Hillburn's Silver Globe'. Small, dense shrub of irregular, rounded habit with silvery blue, mainly awl-shaped leaves.

'Hill's Silver'. A compact, narrowly columnar form with silvery, grey-blue foliage. C. 1922.

JUNIPERUS—*continued*

scopulorum 'Pathfinder'. A small, narrow, conical tree with flat sprays of bluish-grey foliage. C. 1937.

'Repens'. A dwarf, carpeting shrub with prostrate branches clothed with bluish-green, awl-shaped leaves. C. 1939.

'Springbank'. Small tree of erect, columnar habit; branches ascending and spreading, branchlets slender; foliage silvery grey-green.

sheppardii VAN MELLE (*chinensis 'Sheppardii'*) (*chinensis fortunei* HORT.) (*J. fortunei* C. DE VOS). A large, usually multi-stemmed shrub with orange-brown, peeling bark and loose, bushy growth. Branches ascending and gracefully spreading at the tips. The branches of older plants become rather congested, with characteristic projecting filiforme shoots. Leaves green, mainly adult with occasional small sprays of juvenile leaves. S.E. China. According to Van Melle, probably first introduced by Robert Fortune in about 1850. Ours is a male clone and in late winter and early spring is rendered easily recognisable by its multitudes of male strobili.

torulosa. See *J. chinensis 'Kaizuka'*.

sibirica. See *J. communis nana*.

sp. Forrest. A rare, medium-sized, densely branched, rather rigid shrub suggesting kinship with *J. squamata*. It has bright, apple-green, awl-shaped leaves. Apart from its fruits it recalls a juvenile form of *Cupressus macrocarpa*.

sp. Yu. A beautiful, small tree of conical habit, the spreading branches pendulous at the tips. Leaves of a striking rich green. Our plant is a female clone, bearing quantities of small, but conspicuous, nodding, blue-bloomy fruits. A wild species collected in China it answers the description of Van Melle's *J.* ×*media* var. *arbuscula*, and appears very similar to the plant grown in cultivation as *J. virginiana 'Pendula Viridis'*.

sp. Yu 7881. See *J. squamata 'Chinese Silver'*.

squamata D. DON. An extremely variable species ranging in habit from a prostrate shrub to a small bushy tree. Approaching some forms of *J. recurva* in characters. All forms have characteristic nodding tips to the shoots and short, awl-shaped leaves which are channelled and white or pale green above. Fruits ellipsoid, 6 to 8mm. across, reddish-brown becoming purplish-black, containing a single seed. The old leaves tend to persist, turning brown. It is widely distributed in the wild throughout Asia, from Afghanistan eastwards to China. I. 1824. The form we offer under this name is a low growing plant which forms a dwarf, dense, spreading little bush with shortly ascending branches, sometimes found in cultivation under the name *'Pygmaea'*.

'Blue Star'. A low-growing bush of dense habit with comparatively large, silvery-blue, awl-shaped leaves. A very desirable new cultivar.

'Chinese Silver' (*Yu* 7881). A beautiful, medium-sized to large, multi-stemmed shrub of dense habit with recurved terminal shoots. Leaves awl-shaped of an intense silvery blue-green.

fargesii REHD. & WILS. An erect-growing variety slowly attaining small tree size. Bark greyish-brown peeling in long strips. Branches ascending, branchlets drooping, densely packed, clothed with awl-shaped, apple green leaves. It is said to be the arborescent form of the species, occurring in woodlands throughout the China-Tibet borderland, closely approaching forms of *J. recurva*. I. 1908.

'Loderi'. See under *'Wilsonii'*.

'Meyeri'. A popular and easily recognised juniper of semi-erect habit, with stout, ascending, angular branches and densely packed, glaucous-blue, awl-shaped leaves. Although usually seen as a small to medium-sized shrub it will eventually reach a large size. Introduced from a Chinese garden by Frank N. Meyer in 1914. A.M. 1931.

'Pygmaea'. See under *J. squamata*.

'Wilsonii'. A small, slow-growing shrub of dense, compact, usually conical habit, eventually reaching 3m. The branchlets nod at their tips and are densely set with short, awl-shaped leaves which are marked with two white bands above. As a young plant it is an ideal subject for the rock garden. This is one of several seedlings raised from seed, collected by E. H. Wilson in W. China in 1909. The form known as *'Loderi'* raised by Sir Edmund Loder at Leonardslee, Sussex, in 1925 appears identical, although it is no doubt a distinct clone.

suecica. See *J. communis 'Suecica'*.

JUNIPERUS—*continued*

thurifera L. (*hispanica*). "Spanish Juniper". A large, dioecious shrub or small tree of tight, columnar habit. In the wild developing a rounded or spreading head and stems with a large girth. Adult leaves scale-like, greyish-green borne on slender, thread-like branchlets. Fruits globose, 7 to 11mm. across, blue, ripening to black, bloomy. A rare species in cultivation and unsuitable for the coldest areas. Mts. of S., C. and E. Spain; French Alps; N.W. Africa (Atlas Mts.). C. 1752.

utahensis. See *J. osteosperma*.

virginiana L. "Pencil Cedar". One of the hardiest and most accommodating of conifers, forming a medium-sized to large tree of broadly conical habit. Branches ascending on young trees, becoming horizontal on old trees. Branchlets slender; clothed with small, sharp-pointed, scale-like leaves and scattered patches of awl-shaped, glaucous, juvenile leaves. Fruits rounded or ovoid, 5mm. across, brownish-purple and bloomy, ripening the first year. A variable species which can be confused with *J. chinensis* but the latter has broader juvenile leaves. There are numerous cultivars. E. and C. North America. C. 1664.

'Burkii'. A columnar form of dense, compact habit, with ascending branches and both scale-like and awl-shaped, steel-blue leaves which are bronze-purple in winter. An excellent clone. C. 1932.

'Canaertii'. Small, conical tree of rather dense habit. Foliage bright green, very attractive when peppered with small, cobalt blue to purple-bloomed, violet fruits. C. 1868.

'Chamberlaynii' (*'Pendula Nana'*). A female clone of dense habit. A dwarf, spreading or prostrate shrub with drooping branchlets and glaucous, mainly awl-shaped leaves. C. 1850.

'Cupressifolia'. A dense, conical or columnar form with densely-packed, slender, fastigiate branches clothed with dark green, scale-like foliage. C. 1932.

'Elegans'. A small tree of graceful habit. Branches ascending, drooping at the tips, branchlets spreading or arching. Leaves scale-like, bright green. F.C.C. 1875.

'Glauca'. A dense, columnar form with spreading branches clothed with silvery-grey, mainly scale-like leaves. A most attractive small to medium-sized tree. C. 1855.

'Globosa'. Dwarf shrub of dense, rounded habit. The densely packed branches are clothed with mainly scale-like, bright green leaves. C. before 1904.

'Grey Owl'. See *J. 'Grey Owl'*.

'Hillii' (*'Pyramidiformis Hillii'*). A slow-growing, columnar form of dense, compact habit up to 4m. Leaves awl-shaped, glaucous or bluish-green, turning to purplish-bronze in winter. C. 1914.

'Keteleeri'. See *J. chinensis 'Keteleeri'*.

'Kosteri'. See *J.* ×*media 'Kosteri'*.

'Manhattan Blue'. A small, conical, male tree of compact habit, foliage bluish-green. C. 1963.

'Nana Compacta'. Dwarf shrub, similar to *'Globosa'*, but less regular in shape and bearing mainly juvenile leaves of a greyish-green, becoming purple-tinged in winter. C. 1887.

'Pendula'. An elegant, small tree with spreading or arching branches and drooping branchlets. Leaves mainly awl-shaped, green. C. 1850.

'Pendula Nana'. See *'Chamberlaynii'*.

'Pseudocupressus'. Slender, columnar form of compact habit. Leaves awl-shaped, light green, bluish-green when young. C. 1932.

'Reptans'. See *J.* ×*media 'Reptans'*.

'Pyramidiformis Hillii'. See *'Hillii'*.

'Schottii'. Small tree of dense, narrowly-conical habit; foliage scale-like, light green. C. 1855.

'Skyrocket'. A spectacular form of extremely narrow columnar habit. Our tallest specimen measured 5m. high by 30cm. in diameter in 1970. Foliage blue-grey. One of the narrowest of all conifers and as such an excellent plant for breaking up low or horizontal planting schemes. Particularly effective in the heather garden. It was found in the wild as a seedling. C. 1949. A.G.M. 1973.

'Tripartita'. See *J. sabina 'Tripartita'*.

JUNIPERUS—*continued*

wallichiana PARL. (*pseudosabina* HOOK. f. not FISCH. & MEY.). A dioecious, large shrub or small tree of densely, narrowly conical habit when young. Branches ascending, densely packed, bearing dense bunches of scale-like, green leaves and scattered sprays of juvenile leaves, the latter more apparent on young plants. Fruits ripening the second year, ovoid 6mm. long, black when mature. Himalaya. Introduced by Sir Joseph Hooker in 1849. Sometimes found in cultivation under the name *J. pseudosabina* which is an irregular shrub with smaller, often rounded fruits.

***KETELEERIA—Pinaceae**—A small genus of evergreen trees related to *Abies* and resembling them in general appearance. Young trees are rather conical in habit, gradually becoming flat-topped with age. The oblong-lanceolate or linear leaves are arranged in two ranks on the lateral shoots, leaving a circular scar (as in *Abies*) when they fall. Leaves of juvenile plants are usually spine-tipped. Male and female strobili are borne on the same tree, the males in clusters. The erect cones ripen during the second year, falling intact.

davidiana BEISSN. A small to medium-sized tree, old specimens developing buttess-like roots. Young shoots bristly hairy or glabrous. Leaves dark shining green or sometimes yellowish-green, sharply pointed and 4 to 6cm. long on young trees, blunter and 2 to 4cm. long on adult trees. The shortly-stalked terminal cones are cylindrical, 12 to 20cm. long, reddish when young, maturing pale brown. Perhaps the hardiest species, although the young shoots are subject to damage by late spring frosts. C. and W. China; Formosa. Discovered by Père David in 1869; introduced by Augustine Henry in 1888.

†fortunei CARR. A small tree in cultivation, resembling *K. davidiana*, but with shorter leaves and larger seeds. It requires a sheltered position and is subject to damage by late spring frosts. S.E. China. First introduced by Robert Fortune in 1844.

LARIX—Pinaceae—"Larch". A small genus of mostly fast-growing, deciduous, monoecious trees combining utility and beauty. The branches are borne in irregular whorls ending in long, slender, flexible branchlets which, on older trees tend to droop or hang in a graceful manner. Leaves linear, borne in dense rosettes on short spurs on the older wood, bunched on short side shoots and spirally-arranged on the young growing shoots. They are generally of a bright green or occasionally blue-green during spring and summer, turning to butter yellow or old gold in autumn. In early spring the attractive red, pink, yellow or green female strobili and the more numerous but smaller yellow male strobili stud the, as yet, leafless branchlets. The small, erect, rounded or oblong cones which follow, shed their seed usually in the autumn of the first year, but remain intact for an indefinite period and as such are commonly made use of for Christmas decoration in the home.

Several of the larches are extremely valuable for their timber which is strong, heavy and durable. They are adaptable to most soils, though wet sites and dry shallow chalk soils are best avoided. There is no more refreshing tint of spring than the pale green of their awakening buds, or a more mellow shade than the autumn colour of their foliage.

americana. See *L. laricina*.

dahurica. See *L. gmelini*.

decidua MILL. (*europaea*). "European Larch"; "Common Larch". A large tree with a slender, cone-shaped crown when young. Branches and branchlets drooping on old specimens. Shoots yellowish or grey, glabrous. Rosette leaves 1·5 to 3·5cm. long, light green. Cones ovoid, 2 to 4cm. long, bracts hidden. One of the most important afforestation trees. Native of the European Alps and Carpathians. Commonly planted elsewhere. Long cultivated; perhaps first introduced into the British Isles in about 1620.

'Corley'. A slow-growing, small, leaderless bush of rounded habit. Propagated from a "Witches Broom" found by Mr. R. F. Corley.

'Fastigiata'. A narrow, conical form with short, ascending branches. C. 1868.

'Pendula'. A tall tree of irregular habit; branches arching downwards, branchlets pendulous. C. 1836.

'Repens'. A form in which the lower branches elongate and spread out along the ground. C. 1825.

LARIX—*continued*

×**eurolepis** HENRY (*decidua*×*kaempferi*). "Hybrid Larch"; "Dunkeld Larch". A vigorous large tree of great commercial value. It differs from *L. decidua* in its faintly glaucous shoots and its slightly broader, somewhat glaucous leaves. From *L. kaempferi* it differs in its less glaucous, brown or pale orange shoots and shorter, less glaucous leaves. This important hybrid forest tree is less susceptible to disease than the "Common Larch". It originated at Dunkeld, Perthshire, in about 1895.

europaea. See *L. decidua*.

gmelini KUZENEVA (*dahurica* TURCZ.). "Dahurian Larch". A variable species of medium size in cultivation, with usually glabrous, yellowish shoots which may be reddish during winter. Leaves 2 to 3cm. long, bright green. Cones 1·5 to 3cm. long. Not one of the best species for the British Isles, being liable to damage by spring frosts. N.E. Asia. I. 1827.

japonica PILG. "Kurile Larch". A medium-sized tree differing from the type in its denser branching system, shorter leaves and smaller cones. Shoots reddish-brown and downy. Slow growing and liable to injury by late spring frosts. Sakhalin; Kurile Isles. I. 1888.

olgensis OSTENFELD & LARSEN. Similar in growth to var. *japonica*, but shoots even more densely reddish hairy and both leaves and cones smaller. Like its relatives this larch is conditioned to much longer and severer winters than are experienced in the British Isles and is too easily tempted into premature growth by warm periods and then damaged by subsequent inclement conditions. E. Siberia. I. about 1911.

principis-ruprechtii PILG. A more vigorous form of the type with reddish-brown, glabrous shoots, much longer bright green leaves, up to 10cm. long on vigorous shoots, and larger cones. Korea; Manchuria; N.E. China. I. 1903.

†**griffithii** HOOK. f. (*griffithiana*). "Himalaya Larch". A beautiful tree of medium size with long, drooping branchlets and downy shoots which turn reddish-brown the second year. Leaves 2·5 to 3·5cm. long, bright green. Cones large, cylindrical, 7 to 10cm. long, with exerted, reflexed bracts. A graceful species for the milder districts easily distinguished by its weeping branchlets and large cones. E. Nepal; Sikkim; Bhutan; S.E. Tibet. Introduced by Sir Joseph Hooker in 1848. A.M. 1974.

kaempferi CARR. (*leptolepis*). "Japanese Larch". A vigorous tree of large size, with reddish shoots. Leaves 2 to 3·5cm. long, sea-green, broader than those of *L. decidua*. Cones ovoid, 2 to 3cm. long with scales turned outward and downward at tips. A commonly planted larch used extensively for afforestation, withstanding exposure well. The reddish twigs appear to create a purple haze above a plantation on a sunny afternoon in late winter. Japan. Introduced by John Gould Veitch in 1861.

'Blue Haze'. A selected clone with leaves of an attractive glaucous-blue.

'Pendula'. A beautiful, tall, elegant tree with long weeping branches. C. 1896. '*Dervaes*' is very similar.

laricina K. KOCH (*americana*). "Tamarack". A small to medium-sized tree, vigorous when young. Shoots glabrous and glaucous at first, later reddish-brown. Leaves 2 to 3cm. long, bright green. Cones cylindric-ovoid, 1 to 1·5cm. long. Though of great value in N. America it is less successful in the British Isles and has been little planted. It is interesting on account of its small, neat cones. Eastern N. America. I. about 1760, possibly before (see note under *L.* ×*pendula*).

leptolepis. See *L. kaempferi*.

lyallii PARL. A small to medium-sized tree in its native habitat, often forming a gnarled, wind-swept, small tree or shrub. It is easily recognised by its densely felted young shoots and its four-angled, greyish-green leaves, 2·5 to 3·5cm. long. Cones oblong-ovoid, 3·5 to 5cm. long. with conspicuous, long-pointed, exerted bracts. Regarded by some authorities as an alpine form of *L. occidentalis*. One of the least adaptable species for the British Isles and appears to require a colder climate. Western N. America. I. about 1904.

occidentalis NUTT. "Western Larch". A large tree, attaining 60m. in its native habitat. Young shoots pale straw, hairy in the grooves, pale orange-brown and glabrous the second year. Leaves 2·5 to 4cm. long, greyish-green. Cones ovoid, 2·5 to 3·5cm. long, with long-pointed, exerted bracts. N. America. Originally discovered by David Douglas. C. 1880.

LARIX—*continued*

×**pendula** SALISB. "Weeping Larch". A large tree with long branches, pendulous branchlets and shoots which are glabrous and pinkish when young, becoming purple in summer.

The origin of this attractive larch has long been obscure. It was first recorded in cultivation in Peter Collinson's garden at Peckham where it had been planted in 1739. It was at that time claimed to be growing wild in America, but no-one since then has found any evidence of its existence there. Most authorities favour the explanation of its origin as a hybrid between *L. decidua* and *L. laricina*. Mr. Desmond Clarke has recently pointed out that the tree originally described by the botanist Solander was not the Peckham tree but a tree growing in Collinson's garden at Mill Hill which some authorities assumed was the same tree which Collinson had simply transplanted from one garden to another. From this it seems highly probable that Collinson's original tree at Peckham was in fact *L. laricina* and that the later, Mill Hill tree (*L.* ×*pendula*) was a seedling, the result of a cross with *L. decidua*.

potaninii BATAL. (*thibetica*). "Chinese Larch". A beautiful, medium-sized tree with comparatively long, blue-green leaves and graceful, drooping branchlets and orange-brown or purplish, usually glabrous shoots. Leaves four-angled, 2 to 3cm. long. Cones oblong-ovoid, 2·5 to 5cm. long, with long-pointed exerted bracts. The common larch of W. Szechwan and said to be the most valuable coniferous timber tree in W. China. Unfortunately, it is not a tree of robust constitution in the British Isles. Introduced by E. H. Wilson in 1904.

russica. See *L. sibirica*.

sibirica LEDEB. (*russica*). "Siberian Larch". A medium-sized tree of conical habit when young. Shoots yellow, hairy or glabrous. Leaves 2 to 4cm. long, sharply pointed. Cones conical, 3 to 4cm. long. Like several of its relatives this species requires a colder more even climate than can be expected in the British Isles. The young shoots are very subject to damage by spring frost. N.E. Russia; W. Siberia. I. 1806.

thibetica. See *L. potaninii*.

"LEYLAND CYPRESS". See ×*CUPRESSOCYPARIS leylandii*.

***LIBOCEDRUS—Cupressaceae**—A small genus of ornamental trees allied to *Thuja*. In accordance with current opinion a number of species are now included under the genera *CALOCEDRUS* and *AUSTROCEDRUS*. *LIBOCEDRUS* as it now stands is a small genus of evergreen trees and shrubs from the southern hemisphere. The branches are regularly divided into flattened fern-like sprays of scale-like leaves. Male and female strobili occur on the same plant. Cones short-stalked, ripening the first year. The following species are only suitable for the mildest areas of the British Isles.

bidwillii HOOK. f. "Pahautea". A rare species differing from *L. plumosa* in its smaller leaves and cones and the four-sided character of the branchlets. This fastigiate tree is hardier than *L. plumosa* and has here survived outside uninjured for eight years. New Zealand.

chilensis. See *AUSTROCEDRUS chilensis*.

decurrens. See *CALOCEDRUS decurrens*.

doniana. See *L. plumosa*.

formosana. See *CALOCEDRUS formosana*.

macrolepis. See *CALOCEDRUS macrolepis*.

plumosa SARGENT (*doniana*). "Kawaka". A small tree often shrubby in cultivation with peculiar flattened, fern-like branchlets clothed with bright green, scale-like branchlets clothed with bright green, scale-like leaves. Cones ovoid, 1 to 2cm. long. This unusual tree has been growing slowly in our nurseries for several years, with but little frost damage. New Zealand.

tetragona. See *PILGERODENDRON uviferum*.

"MAIDENHAIR TREE". See *GINKGO biloba*.

METASEQUOIA—Taxodiaceae—The first specimen of this monotypic genus was found by Mr. T. Kan in a village in Central China in 1941. Not until 1944 were further trees discovered and specimens collected and in the following year the sensational news was released that a living relic of a fossil genus had been discovered. Not unlike *Taxodium* in general appearance it differs in several botanical characters, including its leaves and ultimate branchlets, both of which are oppositely arranged.

METASEQUOIA—*continued*

glyptostroboides HU & CHENG. "Dawn Redwood". A strong-growing, vigorous, deciduous tree of conical habit when young, with shaggy, cinnamon-brown bark. Leaves linear, flattened, borne in two opposite ranks on short, deciduous branchlets, the whole resembling a pinnate feathery leaf. They are bright larch green during summer, becoming tawny pink and old gold in autumn. Male and female strobili borne on the same tree, the males in large racemes or panicles. Cones pendulous, on long stalks, globose or cylindrical, 15 to 20mm. across, dark brown and mature the first year.

The ease with which it is propagated and its rapid growth, plus its ornamental qualities have combined to make this perhaps the most popular coniferous species in the shortest possible time. In this respect it has certainly beaten the potato *'King Edward'*, the strawberry *'Royal Sovereign'*, and the apple *'Cox's Orange Pippin'*. It thrives best in moist but well-drained conditions. On chalk soils it is slower-growing. It has proved quite hardy and is equally successful in industrial areas. Trees growing in the British Isles from seeds received from the Arnold Arboretum in 1948 have already exceeded 17m. in height. Mature trees in its native habitat were reported to be 28 to 35m. in height with rounded crowns. Native of S.E. China (N.E. Szechwan and W. Hupeh). First seen in 1941, and introduced in 1947. A.M. 1969. A.G.M. 1973.

'National'. A more narrowly conical form, selected by the National Arboretum, Washington, in 1958.

***MICROBIOTA—Cupressaceae**—A new monotypic genus related to *Juniperus*, differing in its fruits which possess hardened, almost woody scales, breaking up when mature. Male and female strobili are borne on separate plants.

decussata KOMAR. An extremely rare, dwarf, densely branched, evergreen shrub, bearing small, opposite, almost scale-like leaves, although awl-shaped leaves are present on some branches. Fruits very small, berry-like, 3mm. long. It is confined in the wild to the Valley of the Suchan, to the east of Vladivostock, E. Siberia. A.M. 1973.

***MICROCACHRYS—Podocarpaceae**—A hardy, monotypic genus related to *Podocarpus*, with slender stems and scale-like leaves. Male and female strobili are borne on the same plant.

tetragona HOOK. f. A splendid prostrate bush with snake-like, four-angled, arching branches clad with minute, scale-like leaves arranged in four ranks. Both male and female strobili are conspicuous when present. Fruits egg-shaped, bright red, fleshy and translucent. A rare conifer, restricted in the wild to the summits of two mountains in Tasmania. I. 1857. A.M. 1971. F.C.C. 1977.

†*MICROSTROBOS—Podocarpaceae—Two species of very rare evergreen shrubs related to *Microcachrys*. The adult leaves are scale-like and spirally-arranged along the slender stems. Male and female strobili are borne on the same plant. Cones about 2mm. long, containing several pale brown or greyish seeds. Both species are found in moist conditions in the wild.

fitzgeraldii GARDEN & JOHNSON (*Pherosphaera fitzgeraldii*). A small, semi-prostrate, densely-branched shrub with slender stems, clothed with tiny, olive-green, scale-like leaves. Differs from *M. niphophilus* in its looser growth and longer, less congested leaves. Usually only found at the foot of waterfalls in the Blue Mountains of New South Wales, Australia.

niphophilus GARDEN & JOHNSON (*Pherosphaera hookerana*). A slender-branched, small to medium-sized shrub with short, stiff branches, densely clothed with tiny green, overlapping, scale-like leaves. Resembles *Dacrydium franklinii* in general appearance. Only found in high alpine regions in Tasmania, normally frequenting the margins of lakes, streams and waterfalls. Rare, even in the wild.

"MONKEY PUZZLE". See *ARAUCARIA araucana*.

***PHYLLOCLADUS—Podocarpaceae**—A small genus of evergreen trees and shrubs of unusual appearance, suggesting a primitive origin. The branches are normally arranged in whorls and bear peculiar and attractive leaf-like, flattened branchlets (cladodes), which perform the functions of the true leaves, these being scale-like and found mainly on seedlings. Male and female strobili are found on the same or on separate plants, the males produced in clusters at the tips of the shoots, the females borne on the margins of the cladodes. Fruits consisting of one to several seeds, each in a cup-like, fleshy receptacle. Suitable only for the mildest districts, except *P. alpinus*, which has grown here successfully for twelve years and was uninjured by the severe winter of 1962-63, when we lost all other species of the genus.

PHYLLOCLADUS—*continued*

alpinus HOOK. f. "Alpine Celery-topped Pine". A small to medium-sized shrub, often dwarf and stunted, usually with a single main stem. We offer an erect form of narrowly conical habit bearing numerous, small, green, diamond-shaped cladodes up to 3·5cm. long. The clusters of reddish male strobili are small, but attractive. This species is perfectly hardy here and is a splendid miniature tree for the rock garden. New Zealand.

'Silver Blades'. A small to medium-sized shrub of slow growth. Small, neat, diamond-shaped cladodes of silvery-blue. The best colour is retained on plants under glass.

†**asplenifolius** HOOK. f. (*rhomboidalis*). "Celery-topped Pine". A small tree with glaucous, fan-shaped cladodes up to 2·5 to 5cm. long, usually toothed or lobed. Suitable only for the conservatory or sheltered corners in the mildest areas. Tasmania.

†**glaucus** CARR. "Toatoa". An attractive, small tree bearing cladodes of two kinds. Those of the main stem are solitary and fan-shaped with coarsely-toothed margins. On the branchlets they are arranged in whorls and resemble pinnate leaves 10 to 25cm. long, with nine to seventeen coarsely-toothed, fan-shaped or diamond-shaped "leaflets". Male and female strobili are borne on separate plants. New Zealand.

rhomboidalis. See *P. asplenifolius*.

†**trichomanoides** D. DON. "Tanekaha". A large shrub or small tree with fan-shaped or ovate, entire or lobed, green cladodes which are pinnately arranged in attractive "fronds". The young emerging cladodes are a reddish-brown in colour. New Zealand.

***PICEA—Pinaceae**—"Spruce". A large genus of evergreen trees, usually of conical habit, with branches borne in whorls. The shoots and branchlets are rough to the touch due to numerous, tiny, peg-like projections left by the fallen leaves. The leaves are short and needle-like, flattened or quadrangular and arranged spirally or in two ranks. Stomata may occur on the upper surface (seemingly beneath on leaves arranged pectinately) or rarely on all surfaces. The ovoid or conical winter buds may be resinous or glabrous. Male and female strobili are produced on the same tree, the male axillary and the often colourful females, terminal. Cones pendulous varying from ovoid to cylindrical, ripening in the autumn of the first year, remaining intact and falling usually late in the second year.

The spruces are an extremely ornamental group of trees, containing a wide range of shapes and sizes with foliage varying in shades of green and grey. They thrive in a variety of soils, but cannot be recommended for really poor, shallow, chalky or dry soils, nor as single isolated specimens or narrow shelter belts in very exposed places. As a group they are widely distributed over the temperate regions of the northern hemisphere. They differ from the superficially similar *Abies* in their plug-like leaf scars and pendulous cones which fall intact

abies KARSTEN (*excelsa*). "Common Spruce"; "Norway Spruce". The commonest spruce in general cultivation and the species popularly known as the "Christmas Tree". A large tree with orange or reddish-brown, usually glabrous shoots. Leaves 1 to 2·5cm. long, shining dark green, densely clothing the upper sides of the branchets, pectinate below. Cones cylindrical, 10 to 15cm. long. This species is elxtensively used for afforestation and the white or cream-coloured wood for a wide variety of articles. The young shoots and leaves are the basis of "Spruce Beer". Widely distributed in the wild over N. and C. Europe, often in large forests. Introduced to the British Isles about 1500.

Under cultivation it has given rise to numerous forms, differing mainly in size and habit. Most of the "dwarf" forms are extremely slow-growing and suitable for the large rock garden.

'Acrocona'. A large, spreading bush or small tree with semi-pendulous branches which, even at an early age, usually terminate in a precocious cone. C. 1890.

'Aurea'. Unfolding leaves bright yellow, changing as they age to soft yellow-green. C. 1838. F.C.C. 1862.

'Capitata'. Dense, small, globular bush with clustered terminal branches. Terminal buds large, more or less concealed by the erect leaves. A specimen in our collection has attained 1·2×1·2m. after thirty-five years. C. 1889.

'Cincinnata'. A small tree with weeping branches. C. 1897.

PICEA—*continued*

abies 'Clanbrassiliana'. A dense, small, flat-topped bush, wider than high. In the dormant season it is conspicuous by its innumerable brown winter buds and small crowded leaves on branchlets which are noticeably variable in vigour. A specimen in our collection has attained 1·2×2·4m. after forty years. One of the oldest cultivars, originally discovered in Northern Ireland about 1790.

'Cranstonii'. A curious, small, irregular tree of loose, open habit with long, lax branches often without branchlets. C. 1855.

'Cupressina'. A medium-sized tree of columnar habit, with ascending branches. An attractive form of dense growth. C. 1855.

'Doone Valley'. A remarkable, extremely slow-growing clone forming a minute bun of tightly congested growth. Almost unrecognisable as a spruce. Suitable for the scree or the alpine trough garden. Named after "Doone Valley" the one time garden of Mr. W. Archer.

'Echiniformis'. An exceedingly slow-growing, little hummock of dense, congested growth. It may be confused with *'Gregoryana'*, but is slower-growing, never so large and its leaves are more rigid and prickly. A specimen in our collection has attained 23×53cm. after twenty years. Most suitable for the rock garden. C. 1875.

'Effusa'. A dense, compact, dwarf bush of irregular dome-shaped habit. Suitable for the rock garden.

'Fastigiata'. See *'Pyramidata'*.

'Finedonensis' (*'Argentea'*). Small tree with spreading branches and silver foliage. Tends to scorch in strong sun. Originally found as a seedling at Finedon Hall, Northamptonshire. C. 1862.

'Gregoryana'. A dense, compact, dwarf bush developing into a somewhat billowy, rounded, flat-topped dome. Its radially arranged sea-green leaves are conspicuous. A specimen in our collection has attained ·5×1·2m. after thirty years. One of the most popular dwarf forms. C. 1862.

'Humilis'. A dwarf, slow-growing bush of dense, compact, conical habit with crowded and congested branchlets. Suitable for the rock garden. Differs from the very similar *'Pygmaea'* in its pale or yellowish-brown winter buds. C. 1891.

'Inversa' (*'Pendula'*). An unusual form usually seen as a large shrub with depressed branches. It is taller, less rigid and softer to the touch than *'Reflexa'*. A magnificent specimen exceeding a hundred years old is growing in the celebrated garden of Mr. and Mrs. de Belder, at Kalmthout, Belgium. C. 1855.

'Little Gem'. A dwarf, slow-growing bun of globular habit with tiny, densely crowded leaves. Originated as a sport of *'Nidiformis'* in the nurseries of F. J. Grootendorst of Boskoop.

'Maxwellii'. A squat, dwarf, rounded, slow-growing dome with coarse, rigid, spine-pointed, sea-green leaves. C. about 1860.

'Nana'. A slow-growing, dwarf bush of conical habit with densely crowded branches and sharply pointed, small leaves. C. 1855.

'Nidiformis'. A very popular and commonly planted clone of German origin, making a dwarf, dense, flat-topped bush of spreading habit, the branches forming a series of tight, horizontal layers. A specimen in our collection has attained ·6×1·8m. after thirty years. C. 1907.

'Ohlendorffii'. Small, conical bush of dense habit; leaves yellowish-green, rather small, recalling those of *P. orientalis*. Freer-growing than most it will reach 1·8×1·2m. after thirty years. C. about 1845.

'Pachyphylla'. Dwarf, slow-growing bush with few short, stout branches and exceptionally thick, forwardly-directed, rigid leaves. An excellent specimen of this distinct clone is growing at Glasnevin Botanic Garden, Ireland. C. 1923.

'Pendula'. See *'Inversa'*.

'Pendula Major'. A strong-growing, conical tree with mainly spreading branches, some decurving and pendulous bearing branchlets which are also decurving or pendulous. C. 1868.

'Phylicoides'. A slow-growing, medium-sized to large shrub of irregular growth, conspicuous by its short, thick, distantly-spaced leaves. A specimen in our collection has attained 1·8×1·5m. after thirty years. C. 1855.

'Procumbens'. A dwarf, flat-topped, wide-spreading bush with densely layered branches, the branchlets ascending at the tips. A specimen in our collection has attained ·6×3m. after 30 years. C. 1850.

PICEA—*continued*

abies 'Pseudoprostrata' (*'Prostrata'*). Dwarf, broad-spreading shrub with flattened top. Denser growing than *'Procumbens'*. A specimen in our collection has attained ·6×1·5m. after 25 years. C. 1923.

'Pumila'. A dwarf, slow-growing, flat topped bush of spreading, compact but irregular habit. Branches and branchlets densely packed and congested. A specimen in our collection has attained ·6×1·5m. after thirty years. C. 1874.

'Pumila Nigra'. Dwarf bush, similar to *'Pumila'*, but leaves shining dark green. The clone *'Pumila Glauca'* is almost if not identical.

'Pygmaea'. A dwarf, extremely slow-growing form of globular or broadly dome-shaped habit, with tightly congested branchlets forming a neat, compact but irregular outline. It is one of the slowest-growing of all *P. abies* cultivars, attaining 45×30cm. in about thirty years. It is also one of the oldest, having been known since about 1800.

'Pyramidata' (*'Fastigiata'*) (*'Pyramidalis'*). A strong-growing, narrowly conical tree with strongly ascending branches. Excellent where space is limited. C. 1853.

'Reflexa'. A dense, rigid, more or less prostrate or creeping bush of irregular habit with normal-sized branchlets and leaves. Unless it is trained to a single upright stem it forms a low dome with long prostrate branches extending carpet-like for several metres. A specimen in our collection, 25 years old, is ·5m. high at the raised centre and measures 4m. across. An excellent ground cover. C. 1890.

'Remontii'. A dense, slow-growing, conical bush, similar to *P. glauca albertiana 'Conica'* in shape, eventually attaining 2 to 2·5m. high. C. 1874.

'Repens'. A slow-growing, dwarf, flat-topped bush with branches in layers. A low, wide-spreading clone suitable for the large rock garden. It appears very similar to *'Pseudoprostrata'*. C. 1898.

'Tabuliformis'. A small, slow-growing bush with tabulated growth and flattened top. A specimen in our collection has attained 1·75×3·5m. after 30 years. C. 1865.

'Virgata'. A medium-sized tree of curious habit, with long, whorled, sparsely produced branches. They are undivided and snake-like in appearance or with a few pendulous branchlets. The leaves are radially arranged. C. 1853. A.M. 1978.

'Waugh'. Medium-sized, sparsely-branched bush with thick shoots and thick, widely-spaced leaves.

alba. See *P. glauca*.

ajanensis. See *P. jezoensis*.

alcockiana. See *P. bicolor*.

asperata MAST. A medium-sized tree similar to and resembling *P. abies* in general appearance, with pale yellowish-brown, usually glabrous young shoots. Buds resinous. Leaves more or less radially arranged or loosely pectinate below, 1 to 2cm. long, four-angled, dull greyish-green sometimes bluish-green, rigid and sharply pointed. Cones cylindrical, 7·5 to 13cm. long. This very hardy, lime-tolerant species is the Chinese counterpart of the European *P. abies*. W. China. I. 1910.

notabilis REHD. & WILS. A variety with slightly longer, glaucous-green leaves and rhombic-ovate cone scales.

retroflexa BOOM (*P. retroflexa*). Differing but little from the type, the leaves green and pectinate below.

bicolor MAYR (*alcockiana*) (*alcoquiana* in part). A medium-sized to large tree of broad conical shape, with long branches upcurved at tips and with yellowish-brown to reddish-brown, glabrous or hairy young shoots. Leaves four-sided, but compressed, 1 to 2cm. long, green or bluish-green above, somewhat glaucous beneath, densely crowded on the upper surfaces of the branchlets, less so below or loosely pectinate. Cones ovoid-cylindric, 6 to 12cm. long, reddish-purple when young. Japan. Introduced by John Gould Veitch in 1861.

acicularis SHIR. & KOYAMA. An uncommon variety differing in its more densely arranged leaves. Japan. I. 1868.

reflexa SHIR. & KOYAMA. An obscure variety from Japan in which the cone scales are elongated and reflexed. It is the most ornamental form, with more conspicuous stomatic lines.

PICEA—*continued*

brachytyla PRITZ. (*sargentiana*) (*ascendens*). A beautiful, medium-sized to large tree, conical when young but developing a rounded head in maturity. The long, spreading branches are gracefully ascending, then arching at the tips. Young shoots shining pale brown, buff or almost white and usually glabrous, bearing attractive chestnut-brown, slightly resinous buds in winter. Leaves flattened, 12 to 20mm. long, green or yellowish-green above, vividly white beneath, crowded and overlapping on the upper surface of the branchlets, pectinate below. Cones oblong-cylindric, 6 to 9cm. long, greenish or purple-tinged when young. A most ornamental species with its slenderly upcurved branches and drooping branchlets. W. and C. China. I. 1901.

complanata CHENG. Differing from the type in its slightly longer, sharply-pointed leaves, up to 2·5cm. and its brown or purplish-brown young cones.

brewerana S. WATS. "Brewer's Weeping Spruce". Perhaps the most beautiful of all spruces and one of the most popular of all ornamental conifers. A small to medium-sized, broadly conical tree, with spreading or decurved branches from which hang slender, tail-like branchlets, 1·8 to 2·5m. long. Young shoots brown and hairy; buds smooth or slightly resinous. Leaves flattened, radially arranged, 1·5 to 3cm. long, shining dark blue-green above, marked with two white bands beneath. Cones narrowly cylindrical up to 10cm. long, green at first, turning purple later. F.C.C. 1974.

There are few more breathtaking sights than a fine specimen of this spruce with its curtained branches, rising like a majestic green fountain. It is sometimes confused with *P. smithiana*, particularly when young, but differs from this species in its smaller, flattened, dark blue-green leaves, smaller, dome-shaped buds and hairy shoots. It is a rare tree in the wild state, being confined to a few isolated localities in the Siskiyou Mountains of N.W. California and S.W. Oregon. I. 1891. A.M. 1958.

‡**engelmannii** ENGELM. "Engelmann Spruce". A small to medium-sized tree with usually finely-downy, pale yellowish-brown young shoots. Buds resinous. Leaves four-angled, 1·5 to 2·5cm. long, sharply pointed, greyish-green, emitting a pungent odour when bruised, crowded on the upper surfaces of the branchlets, pectinate below. Cones oblong-cylindrical, 4 to 7·5cm. long. Not suitable for dry or shallow chalk soils. Western N. America. I. 1862.

glauca BEISSN. Leaves glaucous.

excelsa. See *P. abies*.

gemmata REHD. & WILS. A slow-growing, small to medium-sized tree of broadly conical habit, very similar to *P. asperata*, differing in various minor characters. W. China. I. 1908.

glauca VOSS (*alba*). "White Spruce". A large tree of dense, conical habit, with decurved branches, ascending at the tips. Young shoots pale brown, often white, usually glabrous, often glaucous but darkening with age. Leaves four-angled, 12 to 20mm. long, glaucous-green, emitting a foetid odour when bruised, densely arranged and standing above the upper surfaces of the branchlets, pectinate below. Cones oblong-cylindric, 3 to 6cm. long. A very hardy species, useful for planting in cold, exposed positions. Canada. N.E. United States. I. 1700.

albertiana SARG. "Alberta White Spruce". An uncommon variety, differing from the type in its less upright habit, slightly longer leaves which are less glaucous beneath and its smaller, ovoid cones. Central N. America. Introduced by H. J. Elwes in 1906. A.M. 1920.

'Conica'. A slow-growing, perfectly cone-shaped bush of dense, compact habit with leaves of a bright grass green. A deservedly popular cultivar, in thirty years making a pointed cone of symmetrical shape, 2m. high × 1·2m. at base. Originally found in the Canadian Rockies, near Alberta in 1904 by Dr. J. G. Jack and Prof. Alfred Rehder. A.M. 1933. A.G.M. 1969.

'Aurea' HORT. See *P. mariana 'Aurea'*.

'Caerulea'. An attractive form with densely-arranged, silvery, grey-blue leaves. C. 1866.

'Densata'. A slow-growing, eventually large shrub or small tree of dense, compact habit. C. 1920.

'Echiniformis'. Dwarf, slow-growing, globular bush of dense habit; leaves glaucous grey-green, forward pointing, concealing both branchlets and buds. A first-class miniature conifer for the rock garden. C. 1855.

PICEA—*continued*

glauca 'Nana'. A dwarf or small, slow-growing bush of dense, globular habit, with radially arranged, greyish-blue leaves. A specimen in our collection has attained 1·4×1·8m. after thirty years. C. 1828.

glehnii MAST. "Sakhalin Spruce". A small to medium-sized, slender, conical tree with reddish or chocolate-brown, flaking bark. Young shoots conspicuously reddish-orange and shortly hairy. Leaves bluish-green above, glaucous beneath, four-angled, 1·5cm. long, green, densely arranged on the upper surfaces of the branchlets, loosely pectinate below. Cones oblong-cylindric, 4 to 8cm. long, violet when young. Similar in effect to *P. abies*, but less vigorous and with shorter leaves. S. Sakhalin; E. and N. Hokaido (Japan). I. 1877.

×**hurstii** DE HURST (*engelmannii*×*pungens*). A vigorous, medium-sized tree, more or less intermediate in character between the parents. Young shoots pale orange, usually glabrous. Buds slightly resinous. Leaves four-sided, 10 to 12mm. long, greyish-green, spreading all round the branchlets or loosely parted below.

jezoensis CARR. (*ajanensis*) (*alcoquiana* in part). "Yezo Spruce". A medium-sized to large tree with deflexed branches and shining pale brown to yellowish-brown, glabrous, young shoots. Leaves flattened, 1 to 2cm. long, glossy dark green above, silvery-white beneath, densely crowded and overlapping on the upper surfaces of the branchlets, pectinate below. Cones cylindrical, 5 to 7·5cm. long, reddish when young. The young growths are subject to injury by late spring frosts. N.E. Asia; Japan. Introduced by John Gould Veitch in 1861.

hondoensis REHD. "Hondo Spruce". A variety with shorter leaves, dull green above. In cultivation less susceptible to damage by spring frosts. Mts. of Hondo (Japan). I. 1861. A.M. 1974.

koyamae SHIRAS. A small to medium-sized tree of narrowly conical habit, with reddish-orange, glabrous or sparsely hairy young shoots and resinous buds. Leaves four-angled, 8 to 12mm. long, green or slightly glaucous, densely packed on the upper surfaces of the branchlets, pectinate below. Cones ovoid or ovoid-oblong, 5 to 10cm. long, pale green when young. A rare tree both in the wild and in cultivation. Distinguished from all other Japanese species by its resinous buds. Found in the wild only on Mount Yatsuga in Central Japan. Discovered by Mitsua Koyama in 1911. Introduced by E. H. Wilson in 1914.

likiangensis PRITZ. A most ornamental, vigorous and accommodating tree of medium size, showing considerable variation within the species. Upper branches with ascending terminals. Young shoots pale brown or reddish, hairy or occasionally glabrous. Buds resinous. Leaves flattened, 1 to 2cm. long, green or bluish-green above, glaucous beneath, loosely packed on the upper surfaces of the branchlets, pectinate below. Cones oblong-ovoid, 6 to 10cm. long, reddish-pink when young. In April and May when loaded with its male flowers and brilliant red young cones it is spectacularly beautiful. W. China. C. 1910. A.M. 1961. F.C.C. 1974.

balfouriana CHENG. A variety with densely hairy branchlets, dark green or glaucous, obtuse leaves and violet-purple young cones.

purpurea DALLIM. & JACKS. (*P. purpurea*). A distinct variety developing a narrower more pointed upper crown than the type, the upper branches with erect terminals. Leaves also darker green, smaller and more closely pressed on the upper surfaces of the branchlets. Cones smaller, violet-purple. W. China. I. 1910.

×**lutzii** LITTLE (*glauca*×*sitchensis*). A medium-sized tree intermediate in character between the parents. Young shoots yellowish and glabrous. Leaves slightly four-angled, greyish-green. Cones oblong-cylindric, 3 to 6cm. long. Found in the wild with the parents in S. Alaska in 1950. It has also been artificially raised in cultivation in Europe.

mariana B. S. & P. (*nigra*). "Black Spruce". A medium-sized, rather narrowly conical tree with brown, densely glandular-hairy young shoots. Leaves four-sided, 6 to 12mm. long, dark bluish-green, densely crowding the upper surfaces of the branchlets, loosely pectinate below. Cones ovoid, 2·5 to 3·5cm. long, produced in large quantities, dark purple when young. N.W. North America. C. 1700.

'Aurea' (*glauca 'Aurea'* HORT.). Leaves yellow when young, becoming glaucous green later. Tends to lose its colour when growing in shade. C. 1891.

'Doumetii'. Eventually a large bush of dense, rather irregular but somewhat globular habit. C. 1850.

PICEA—*continued*

mariana 'Nana'. A slow-growing, dwarf, globular bush of dense, compact habit, with grey-green leaves. A good dwarf conifer, suitable for the rock garden. C. 1884. A.G.M. 1973.

× **mariorika** BOOM (*mariana* × *omorika*). A medium-sized tree intermediate in character between the parents, with some forms closer to one parent than the other. Resembles *P. omorika* in general appearance, but usually broader in habit with narrower, more sharply-pointed leaves, and smaller cones 3·5 to 4·5cm. long. Raised in the nurseries of G. D. Boehlje at Westerstede, Germany in 1925.

maximowiczii MAST. A small to medium-sized, densely-branched tree of conical habit with yellowish-brown or reddish, glabrous young shoots and white resinous buds in winter. Leaves four-sided, 10 to 15mm. long, dark shining green, densely arranged above, pectinate below. Cones cylindrical, 3 to 6cm. long, pale green when young. It resembles an intermediate between *P. abies* and *P. orientalis*. Mts. of Japan. First discovered on Mt. Fujiyama in 1861. Introduced in 1865.

morinda. See *P. smithiana*.

morrisonicola HAYATA. "Mount Morrison Spruce". A rare and graceful, small to medium-sized tree with white or pale-brown, glabrous shoots. Leaves four-sided, 1 to 2cm. long, green, very slender, sharply pointed, crowded forward on the upper surfaces of the shoots, loosely pectinate below. Cones oblong-cylindric, 5 to 8cm. long. Formosa.

nigra. See *P. mariana*.

obovata LEDEB. "Siberian Spruce". A medium-sized to large tree often a large bush, closely related to *P. abies*, but differing in its usually shorter, duller leaves and smaller cones, 6 to 8cm. long. Rare in cultivation. N. Europe; N. Asia. I. 1852.

omorika PURKYNE. "Serbian Spruce". One of the most beautiful and adaptable spruces in cultivation, quickly forming a tall, graceful, slender tree. A medium-sized to large tree with relatively short, drooping branches which curve upwards at the tips. Young shoots pale brown and hairy. Leaves flattened, 1 to 2cm. long, dark green above, glaucous beneath, densely arranged on the upper surfaces of the branchlets, loosely parted below. The leaves of young plants are narrower, sharply-pointed and more spreading on the shoots than those of the adult. Cones ovoid-conic, 4 to 6cm. long, bluish-black when young. It is one of the best spruces for industrial areas and chalk soils and would make an excellent evergreen street tree. A superb species, native of Yugoslavia where it inhabits limestone rocks on both sides of the River Drina. It was first discovered in 1875 and introduced to England in 1889. A.G.M. 1969.

'Expansa'. A low, wide-spreading bush with shortly ascending branches up to ·8m. C. 1940.

'Nana'. A small, densely conical bush of compact habit. The conspicuous stomatal bands add considerably to its attraction. A specimen in our collection has attained 1·2 × 1·2m. after fifteen years. C. 1930.

'Pendula'. A very beautiful, slender tree with drooping, slightly twisted branches displaying the glaucous upper surfaces of the leaves. C. 1920. A.G.M. 1969.

orientalis LINK. "Oriental Spruce". A large, densely-branched tree of broadly conical habit, with branches to ground level. Young shoots pale brown and densely hairy. Leaves four-sided, 6 to 8mm. long, with blunt tips, dark shining green, densely pressed on the upper surfaces of the branchlets, pectinate below. Cones ovoid-cylindric, 5 to 9cm. long, purple when young. One of the best and most adaptable species in cultivation, easily recognised by its dense, conical habit and small, closely-pressed leaves. Asia Minor; Caucasus. I. about 1839.

'Aurea' (*'Aureospicata'*). Young shoots creamy-yellow, becoming golden yellow later, finally green. A spectacular shrub or small tree in spring. C. 1873. F.C.C. 1893.

'Gracilis' (*'Nana Gracilis'*). A slow-growing, rounded bush of dense habit, eventually developing into a small, conical tree up to 5 or 6m. A specimen in our collection has attained 2·4 × 1·8m. after twenty-two years. C. 1923.

'Pendula'. A compact, slow-growing form with weeping branches.

PICEA—*continued*

polita CARR. "Tiger-tail Spruce". A medium-sized to large tree of dense, broadly conical habit, with nearly horizontal branches. Young shoots stout and glabrous, of a shining yellowish-brown, often white. Leaves four-sided, 1·5 to 2cm. long, green, sickle-shaped and spine-pointed, stiffly spreading all round the branchlets. Cones ovoid to cylindrical, 8 to 10cm. long, yellowish-green when young. A distinct species, easily recognised by its stout, prickly leaves which are more difficult to handle than any other species. Japan. Introduced by John Gould Veitch in 1861. F.C.C. 1873.

pungens ENGELM. "Colorado Spruce". A medium-sized to large tree of conical habit, with stout, glabrous, orange-brown young shoots, which are glaucous at first. Leaves four-angled, stout and rigid, 1·5 to 3cm. long, sharply-pointed (hence the name), varying in colour from green to grey, spreading all round the branchlets, but denser on the upper surfaces. Cones cylindrical, 5 to 10cm. long, green when young. The type is uncommon in cultivation due to the popularity of its glaucous-leaved forms of which there are a considerable number. S.W. United States. I. about 1862. F.C.C. 1877.

'Compacta'. A medium-sized, flat-topped bush of dense, compact habit, with horizontally spreading branches and grey-green leaves. C. 1874.

glauca BEISSN. "Blue Spruce". A medium-sized to large tree with glaucous leaves. A variable form occurring both in the wild and in cultivation. The leaves tend to lose their intensity as they age, those at the base of the branches being greyish-green or green. In cultivation the most glaucous forms are usually small to medium-sized trees. F.C.C. 1890.

'Globosa' (*'Glauca Globosa'*) (Glauca Group). Dwarf, flat-topped, globular bush of dense habit; leaves glaucous-blue. C. 1937.

'Hoopsii' (Glauca Group). An excellent small to medium-sized tree of densely conical habit, with vividly glaucous-blue leaves. C. 1958.

'Koster' (Glauca Group). The most popular form of "Blue Spruce". A small to medium-sized, conical tree with leaves of an intense silver-blue. C. 1885.

'Moerheimii' (Glauca Group). A small to medium-sized tree of dense, conical habit with intensely glaucous-blue leaves. One of the most satisfactory of the group. C. 1912.

'Montgomery' (Glauca Group). A dwarf, slow-growing bush of compact habit. The sharply-pointed leaves are greyish-blue. C. 1934.

'Pendula' (Glauca Group). A slow-growing small tree with down-swept branches and glaucous-blue leaves. F.C.C. 1898.

'Procumbens' (*'Glauca Procumbens'*) (Glauca Group). Dwarf shrub with low, spreading branches in all directions; branchlets pendulous. Leaves glaucous-blue. If terminal reversions occur they should be removed. C. 1910.

'Spekii' (Glauca Group). Small to medium-sized, conical tree with glaucous-blue leaves. Introduced by the Jan Spek nurseries of Boskoop in about 1925.

'Thomsen' (Glauca Group). A beautiful, conical tree of small to medium-size bearing leaves of a striking silvery-blue. C. 1928.

purpurea. See *P. likiangensis purpurea.*

retroflexa. See *P. asperata retroflexa.*

‡**rubens** SARG. (*rubra* LINK not A. DIETRICH). "Red Spruce". A medium-sized to large tree with reddish-brown, scaly bark. Youngshoots light reddish-brown. Leaves four-sided, 1 to 1·5cm. long, yellowish-green or grass-green, incurved and twisted, densely set on the upper surfaces of the branchlets, pectinate below. Cones ovoid-cylindric, 3 to 5cm. long, green or purple when young. At its best in moist conditions and unsuitable for chalk soils. N.E. North America. I. before 1755.

rubra LINK not A. DIETRICH. See *P. rubens.*

schrenkiana FISCH. & MEYER. "Schrenk's Spruce". A medium-sized tree with greyish, glabrous or sparsely hairy young shoots and resinous buds. Leaves obscurely four-sided, 2 to 3cm. long, sage green, rigid and sharply pointed, arranged all around the branchlets, but more densely above than below. Cones cylindrical, 7 to 9cm. long. It resembles *P. smithiana* in its leaves which, however, are slightly shorter, more glaucous and less radially arranged. C. Asia. I. 1877.

PICEA—*continued*

sitchensis CARR. "Sitka Spruce". A fast-growing, large to very large, broadly conical tree primarily of economic importance. Young shoots light brown, glabrous. Leaves flattened, 15 to 18mm. long, rigid and sharply-pointed, green above marked with two glaucous bands beneath, spreading all round the branchlets, or sometimes loosely parted below. Cones oblong-cylindric, 6 to 10cm. long, yellowish-brown when young. A remarkable, prickly-leaved spruce, thriving particularly well in damp sites.

It is one of the most important afforestation trees and is the most commonly planted conifer for this purpose in the British Isles, particularly in the north and in Wales. It is a native of Western N. America, occuring from California north to Alaska. Originally discovered by Archibald Menzies in 1792, and introduced by David Douglas in 1831.

smithiana BOISS. (*morinda*). "West Himalayan Spruce". A large and extremely beautiful tree with branches, upcurved at tips, and long, pendulous branchlets. Young shoots glabrous and shining, pale brown or greyish, with spindle-shaped, shining, chestnut-brown buds. Leaves four-sided, 2·5 to 4cm. long, dark green, needle-like and flexible, spreading all round the branchlets. Cones cylindrical, 12 to 17cm. long, green when young, becoming purplish. An attractive and ornamental tree recognisable at all ages by its drooping branches, long leaves and glabrous shoots. Young plants are occasionally subject to injury by late spring frosts, but established trees are quite hardy and develop into a specimen second only in elegance to *P. brewerana*. W. Himalaya. I. 1818. A.M. 1975.

spinulosa HENRY. A medium-sized to large tree, reaching heights of 60m. and above in its native environs. Branches spreading, branchlets pendulous. Young shoots glabrous, yellowish or pale orange-brown at first, later greyish. Buds rather large, slightly resinous. Leaves flattened, 2 to 3·5cm. long, green below, glaucous above, spreading all round the branchlets. Cones oblong cylindric, 6 to 10cm. long, green or reddish-grey when young. A rare and remarkable semi-weeping tree but perhaps a little gaunt and sparsely branched when compared with *P. brewerana* or *P. smithiana*. E. Himalaya. I. about 1878.

wilsonii MAST. (*watsoniana*). A small tree remarkable on account of its conspicuous marble white, glabrous, young shoots, attractive buds and narrow leaves. Leaves four-sided, 1 to 2cm. long, dark green, densely clothing the upper surfaces of the branchlets, pectinate below. Cones oblong-cylindric, 4 to 5cm. long. C. and W. China. Introduced by Ernest Wilson in 1901.

***PILGERODENDRON—Cupressaceae**—A monotypic genus differing from the closely related *Libocedrus* in its uniformly four-ranked leaves. Male and female strobili are borne on the same plant.

uviferum FLORIN (*Libocedrus tetragona*). "Alerce". A rare, small, slow-growing tree of stiff, upright habit when young. The small, green, scale-like leaves are borne in four ranks, giving the shoots a quadrangular appearance. Cones ovoid, 8 to 13mm. long, with four, woody, brown scales. This remarkable tree, a native of Chile, is proving hardy in our arboretum. I.1849.

***PINUS—Pinaceae**—A large genus of evergreen trees widely distributed in the temperate regions of the northern hemisphere and in subtropical regions of both hemispheres. Young trees are normally conical in habit, broadening and becoming bushy or flat-topped with age. The leaves are long and needle-like, borne in bundles of from 2 to 5, densely clothing the ends of the branches. They vary from semi-circular to triangular in section. Male and female strobili are borne on the same tree and are often attractive in late spring and early summer. Cones varying in shape from rounded and conical to banana-shaped, ripening at the end of the second year. In most species the cones release their seed on ripening, but in a few species the cones remain intact until they fall. Under natural conditions certain species such as *P. radiata* retain their cones intact on the tree for many years until forced to open by forest fires.

The pines serve a great variety of purposes, many being highly ornamental as well as useful Some species will succeed in the poorest soils whether alkaline or acid but as a rule the five-needled species are not long satisfactory on shallow chalk soils, whilst others are invaluable as windbreaks, especially in coastal districts. All species dislike shade and very few will tolerate smoke-polluted air. Numerous dwarf or slow-growing clones have appeared in cultivation, many of which are suitable for the rock garden where they combine effectively with dwarf spruces, firs and junipers.

PINUS—*continued*

albicaulis ENGELM. A small tree related to *P. flexilis* from which it differs in its dense, short leaves and its cones which do not open when ripe. Young shoots reddish-brown, sparsely downy or glabrous. Winter buds ovoid, sharply pointed. Leaves in fives, 4 to 6·5cm. long, entire, green or greyish-green. Cones sessile, ovoid, 4 to 7·5cm. long, falling intact. Seeds edible. A rare species in cultivation. Western N. America. Introduced by John Jeffrey in 1852.

'Nana' (*'Noble's Dwarf'*). A dwarf shrubby form of compact habit. Our plant was propagated from material received from the late Mr. Nisbet of Gosport who in turn received his plant from the late Mr. Noble of California.

aristata ENGELM. A small tree or large shrub, with stout, reddish-brown, hairy young shoots. Leaves in fives, 2 to 4cm. long, lined with glaucous bands and flecked with white resinous exudations, tightly bunched and closely pressed to the branchlets. Cones sessile, ovoid to rounded, 6 to 9cm. long. the scales with slender-spined, bristle-like bosses. Native of the S.W. United States (Colorado; Arizona; New Mexico), where trees aged up to 2,000 years have been recorded. I. 1863.

Specimens of the recently separated *P. longaeva* D. K. BAILEY, of California, Nevada and Utah, have been proved to be much older, up to 5,000 years in the White Mountains of California. In the wild it differs in its leaves which lack the white specks of *P. aristata*. Both these species are known as "Bristlecone Pines".

armandii FRANCH. "Armand's Pine". An attractive tree of medium size with usually glabrous young shoots and slightly resinous, cylindrical, winter buds. Leaves in fives, 10 to 15cm. long, glaucous. Cones usually borne in clusters of two or three, barrel-shaped, 14 to 19cm. long, becoming pendulous. A very ornamental species with its drooping, glaucous leaves and decorative cones. It grows well in the British Isles. W. China; Formosa; Korea. I. 1895.

attenuata LEMM. (*tuberculata*). "Knobcone Pine". A small to medium-sized tree with an open, upswept crown of long branches. Young shoots furrowed, glabrous, orange-brown. Winter buds cylindrical, resinous. Leaves in threes, 10 to 18cm. long, greyish-green, densely crowding the branches. Cones short-stalked, variable in shape, usually conical, 7·5 to 13cm. long, the scales armed with sharp prickles, appearing singly or in whorls of two to four. They remain intact for many years and in the wild are usually opened as a result of forest fires. Closely related to *P. radiata*. S.W. United States. I. about 1847.

ayacahuite EHREN. A large tree with a spreading head of branches and stout, pale brown or greyish, normally pubescent young shoots. Winter buds conical and resinous. Leaves in fives, slender and spreading, 10 to 20cm. long, glaucous-green. Cones broadly cylindrical, 10 to 20cm. long, sometimes longer. They are pendulous and borne singly or in clusters of two or three towards the ends of the branches, even on quite young trees. An attractive and ornamental species with its long greyish leaves and resin-smeared cones. It is more suitable for the warmer, sheltered gardens of the south and west. Mexico and Central America. I. 1840. A.M. 1960. F.C.C. 1961.

‡**banksiana** LAMB. "Jack Pine". A very hardy tree of medium size, occasionally gnarled and shrubby. Young shoots yellowish-green and glabrous; winter buds cylindrical and resinous. Leaves in pairs, 2 to 4cm. long, curved or twisted. Cones usually in pairs, irregular in shape, ovoid-conical, curved, 3 to 5cm. long. It is adaptable to most soils except shallow chalk soils and is particularly good in moist soils. It is an easily recognised species on account of its characteristic crooked branches and uneven cones. It occurs further north than any other American pine. N. United States; Canada. C. 1783.

bungeana ZUCC. "Lace-bark Pine". A small to medium-sized tree or a large shrub, typically branching from near the base. On trees in cultivation the smooth, grey-green bark flakes away creating a beautiful patchwork of white, yellow, purple, brown and green. Specimens in the wild are reported to have almost white bark. Young shoots greyish-green and glabrous; winter buds spindle-shaped. Leaves in threes 5 to 10cm. long, rigid. Cones ovoid, 5 to 7cm. long, the scales with a short reflexed spine. One of the most ornamental of all pines, easily recognised by its usually low branching and attractive, flaky bark. It is closely allied to *P. gerardiana*. China. First discovered by Dr. Bunge in a temple garden near Peking in 1831. Introduced by Robert Fortune in 1846.

PINUS—*continued*

†canariensis C. SMITH. "Canary Island Pine". A very beautiful tree reaching a large size in its native habitats, but smaller and only suitable for the mildest localities in the British Isles. A graceful pine with spreading branches and drooping branchlets. Young shoots yellow and glabrous, strongly ridged, winter buds large and ovoid, pointed. Leaves in threes, 20 to 30cm. long, conspicuously glaucous on very young plants, bright green later. Cones cylindrical-ovoid, 15 to 23cm. long, solitary or in clusters, deflexed. Small plants in pots are excellent for conservatory decoration. Canary Isles.

†caribaea MORELET. "Caribbean Pine". In the British Isles a small tree suitable only for the most sheltered positions in the mildest areas. Young shoots orange-brown at first, winter buds cylindrical Leaves in threes, occasionally in fours or fives, 15 to 23cm. long, crowded at the ends of the branchlets. Cones reflexed, conical, 5 to 10cm. long. Bahamas to C. America.

cembra L. "Arolla Pine". A small to medium-sized tree of characteristic, dense, conical or columnar habit in cultivation. Young shoots clothed with dense, orange-brown pubescence; winter buds ovoid, resinous. Leaves in fives, 5 to 8cm. long, densely crowded and of a dark blue-green with blue-white inner surfaces. Cones deep blue, short-stalked, erect, ovoid, 5 to 8cm. long, never opening, the seeds being liberated due to the scales rotting or by the attentions of squirrels or birds. An ornamental tree of almost formal aspect which has distinct landscape possibilities. Mountains of C. Europe and N. Asia. C. 1746.

'Aureovariegata'. A pleasing form with yellow-tinged leaves. C. 1865.

'Jermyns'. An exceedingly slow-growing, compact bush of dwarf, conical habit, raised in our nurseries.

pumila. See *P. pumila*.

'Stricta' (*'Columnaris'*). A columnar form with closely ascending branches. C. 1855.

cembroides ZUCC. "Mexican Nut Pine". A small, short-stemmed tree or large bush with a dense, rounded head of branches. Young shoots glaucous, glabrous or shortly pubescent, winter buds ellipsoid. Leaves normally in threes, but varying from two to five on some trees, sickle-shaped, 2·5 to 5cm. long, with a sharply pointed apex. Cones globular or ovoid, 2·5 to 6cm. long, containing large, edible seeds. It is a variable species and several varieties have been named. S. Arizona to Mexico.

edulis VOSS (*P. edulis*). "Two-leaved Nut Pine". A variety with leaves in pairs, occasionally in threes. Arizona to Mexico. I. 1848.

monophylla VOSS (*P. monophylla*). "One-leaved Nut Pine". An unusual variety in which the stiff, glaucous-green leaves occur singly, or occasionally in pairs. S.W. United States to Mexico. I. 1848.

†chihuahana ENGELM. (*leiophylla chihuahana*). A small to medium-sized, tender tree, closely related to *P. leiophylla*, and resembling it in most characters. Leaves in threes or fours, occasionally in pairs or fives, 7 to 10cm. long. S. Arizona and New Mexico.

‡contorta LOUD. "Beach Pine". A medium-sized to large tree, occasionally a large bush, with short branches. Young shoots green and glabrous; winter buds cylindrical and resinous. Leaves in pairs, 4 to 5cm. long, characteristically twisted and yellowish-green in colour. Cones ovoid, 2·5 to 5cm. long, occurring in pairs or clusters, the scales bearing a slender recurved spine. Not adaptable to chalky soils, but a suitable species for light stony or sandy land. It is a vigorous species, used for fixing sand-dunes in maritime areas. Western N. America. Introduced by David Douglas in 1831.

latifolia S. WATTS. "Lodgepole Pine". A medium-sized tree, less vigorous than the type and with slightly broader leaves 6 to 8·5cm. long and larger cones. The common name derives from its use by the North American Indians as the central pole of their huts. Mountains of Western N. America. Introduced by John Jeffrey in about 1853.

PINUS—*continued*

coulteri D. DON. "Big-Cone Pine". A remarkable and striking tree of medium to large size. Young shoots stout and prominently ridged, glaucous and glabrous; winter buds orange, large, ovoid, long-pointed and resinous. Leaves in threes, 15 to 30cm. long, stiff and curved, pale bluish-grey-green. Cones very large and heavy, ovoid or oblong-ovoid, 25 to 35cm. long, each scale with a strongly curved hook or claw. The largest cones may weigh between 4 and 5lbs. (about 2kgs.) when still green. S. California; N. Mexico. Discovered by Dr. Coulter in 1832 and intioduced by David Douglas in the same year. It was given an A.M. by the R.H.S. when shown by us in 1961.

‡**densiflora** SIEB. & ZUCC. "Japanese Red Pine". A medium-sized to large tree. Young shoots green and shortly pubescent or pink and bloomy at first; winter buds oblong-ovoid, sharply pointed and resinous. Leaves in pairs, 5 to 12cm. long, twisted. Cones shortly stalked, solitary or in clusters of two or three, conical-ovoid, 3·5 to 5cm. long. It is the Japanese counterpart to our native "Scots Pine" and has similar reddish young bark. Japan. I. 1852.

'Oculus-draconis'. "Dragon-eye Pine". A curious form whose branches, when viewed from above, show alternate yellow and green rings, hence the name. C. 1890.

'Pendula'. A dwarf shrub with prostrate branches. C. 1890.

'Umbraculifera'. A miniature tree of extremely slow-growth, with a dense umbrella-like head of branches, bearing tiny cones. Our largest specimen attained 2m. × 2·4m. in thirty years. C. 1890.

‡**echinata** MILL. "Short-leaf Pine". A small to medium-sized tree with green, violet-flushed young shoots which are glabrous and bloomy, winter buds ovoid, resinous. Leaves usually in pairs, sometimes in threes or fours, 7·5 to 13cm. long, twisted, dark grey-green. Cones ovoid, usually clustered, 4 to 6cm. long, normally remaining on the branches after the seeds have been shed. Best suited to well-drained soils. E. and S.E. United States. I. 1739.

‡†**elliottii** ENGELM. "Slash Pine". A small tree in cultivation only suitable for the mildest areas of the British Isles. Young shoots orange-brown at first, rough and scaly, winter buds cylindrical, large. Leaves in pairs or threes, 18 to 25cm. long, occasionally longer. Cones conical, 6 to 14cm. long, the scales armed with a stout prickle. S.E. United States.

excelsa. See *P. wallichiana.*

flexilis JAMES. "Limber Pine". A medium-sized tree of conical outline. Young shoots glabrous or shortly pubescent; winter buds broad ovoid, slender-pointed. Leaves in fives, 3·5 to 7·5cm. long, crowded towards the ends of the branches, entire, or almost so. Cones conic, 8 to 15cm. long, spreading. Rocky Mts. of Western N. America. I. 1861.

gerardiana WALL. "Gerard's Pine". A rare, small tree in cultivation, its main attraction being the beautiful patchwork bark which is greyish-pink, flaking to reveal green, yellow and brown new bark. Young shoots olive-green, ridged and glabrous; winter buds spindle-shaped. Leaves in threes, 5 to 10cm. long. Cones ovoid, 15 to 20cm. long, the scales with a short recurved spine. An extremely ornamental tree, allied to *P. bungeana* from which it mainly differs in its longer leaves and larger cones. N.W. Himalaya; Afghanistan. First discovered by Captain Gerard of the Bengal Native Infantry. Introduced by Lord Auckland in 1839.

greggii ENGELM. A medium-sized tree thriving best in a sheltered position. Young shoots glabrous, glaucous at first; winter buds cylindrical, bright deep chestnut, sharply pointed. Leaves in threes, bright green, 7·5 to 15cm. long. Cones ovoid-conic, shining creamy-brown, 8 to 15cm. long, borne in reflexed clusters. A beautiful pine rendered conspicuous at all times of the year by the bright grass-green of the younger leaves. It has grown here for four years without winter damage. Mexico.

griffithii MCCLELLAND not PARL. See *P. wallichiana.*

halepensis MILL. "Aleppo Pine". A medium-sized tree with glaucous, glabrous young shoots; winter buds conic. Leaves in pairs, very distant, sparse, slightly twisted, 5 to 10cm. long, bright fresh-green. Cones ovoid-conic, stalked and deflexed, 8 to 10cm. long. Naturally found in warm, dry regions this species is suitable for maritime areas in the south. It will also grow on dry, shallow chalk soils. Mediterranean Region; W. Asia. C. 1683.

PINUS—*continued*

halepensis brutia HENRY. A variety differing mainly in its orange-brown, young shoots. Leaves 12 to 16cm. long, oblong winter buds and almost sessile, spreading cones. Distribution as the type.

× **holfordiana** A. B. JACKS. (*ayacahuite* × *wallichiana*). A large, fast-growing tree with wide-spreading branches and pubescent young shoots. In leaf and cone characters it is close to *P. wallichiana* and resembles that species in general appearance. A most ornamental hybrid with its long, silvery-green leaves and long, banana-shaped, resin-flecked cones. Originated in the Westonbirt Arboretum about 1906. A.M. 1977.

× **hunnewellii** A. G. JOHNSON (*parviflora* × *strobus*). A vigorous, medium-sized tree of loose, open habit, similar in some respects to *P. strobus*, but with larger cones and hairy young shoots. Leaves 7·5 to 8·5cm. long, grey-green. Originated in the Hunnewell Arboretum, Wellesley, Massachusetts in 1949.

insignis. See *P. radiata*.

jeffreyi MURR. (*ponderosa jeffreyi*). A large, imposing tree with a conical or spire-like crown. Young shoots stout, glaucous and glabrous; winter buds cylindric-conic, acute. Leaves in threes, 18 to 22cm. long, dull bluish-green or pale grey, crowded towards the ends of the branchlets. Cones terminal and spreading, conical-ovoid, 13 to 20cm. long, the scales with a slender recurved spine. The species is similar in many respects to *P. ponderosa*, differing mainly in its black or purple-grey bark and its stouter, longer, bluish-green leaves which are invariably in threes. S.W. United States. I. 1852, possibly earlier.

†**kesiya** GORD. (*khasia*). A small tree in cultivation, with glabrous, pale brown young shoots and oblong-conic winter buds. Leaves in threes, very slender, green or greyish-green, 13 to 23cm. long. Cones ovoid, 5 to 7·5cm. long. A rare species only suitable for the mildest areas. N. Burma; Philippines.

koraiensis SIEB. & ZUCC. "Korean Pine". A medium-sized tree of loose, conical habit. Young shoots green, covered by a dense, reddish-brown pubescence; winter buds cylindric-ovoid, shortly pointed and resinous. Leaves usually in fives, 6 to 12cm. long, stiff and rough to the touch, blue-green. Cones short-stalked, cylindric-conic, 9 to 14cm. long. Closely related to *P. cembra* from which it differs in its openly branched habit and its usually longer, more glaucous leaves which are toothed to the apex and possess three as against two resin canals. E. Asia. Introduced by J. G. Veitch in 1861.

'Compacta Glauca' (*cembra 'Compacta Glauca'* HORT.). A strong-growing, compact form with short, stout branches and attractive, densely-packed, conspicuously glaucous leaves. C. 1949.

'Winton'. A large, bushy form wider than high, with glaucous leaves. It possesses characters intermediate between the above species and *P. cembra*. The leaves are not toothed to the apex and the resin canals vary from two to three. A specimen in our collection attained 2m. × 4·5m. in thirty years.

lambertiana DOUGL. "Sugar Pine". The largest of all pines, attaining a height of 75m. or more in its native habitats. In the British Isles it is a medium-sized tree with minutely, brown, pubescent young shoots and oblong-ovoid, resinous winter buds. Leaves in fives, 7 to 14cm. long, sharply pointed and conspicuously twisted. Cones pendulous, cylindrical, 30 to 50cm. long (the longest in the genus). A sweet exudation from the heartwood has in the past been used as a substitute for sugar. Oregon and California. Introduced by David Douglas in 1827 and later by William Lobb in 1851.

laricio. See *P. nigra maritima*.

‡†**leiophylla** SCHL. & CHAM. "Smooth-leaved Pine". A small tree in the mildest areas of the British Isles. Young shoots glaucous. Leaves in fives, 7·5 to 10cm. long, slender and greyish-green. Cones stalked, solitary or in clusters, ovoid, 4 to 6cm. long. Mexico.

leucodermis ANT. (*heldreichii leucodermis*). "Bosnian Pine". A medium-sized tree with smooth greenish-grey bark, possessing a dense, ovoid habit. Young shoots glabrous and glaucous; winter buds ovoid-oblong or cylindrical, shortly and sharply pointed. Leaves in pairs, 6 to 9cm. long, rigid and erect, dark almost black-green. Cones ovoid-conic, 5 to 7·5cm. long, bright blue the first year. It is sometimes regarded as a mountain form of *P. nigra* and though slower-growing is very distinct and pleasing in appearance. Particularly suitable for dry soils and shallow soils over chalk. Italy; Balkan Peninsula. I. 1864.

PINUS—*continued*

leucodermis 'Pygmy' ('*Pygmaea*') ('*Schmidtii*'). A slow-growing, dwarf or small form developing into a dense, compact mound. Discovered in the wild by the late Mr. Schmidt of Czechoslovakia. C. 1952.

longaeva. See under *P. aristata*.

longifolia. See *P. palustris* and *P. roxburghii*.

‡†**luchuensis** MAYR. "Luchu Pine". A rare, small to medium-sized tree with characteristic smooth, greyish bark. Leaves in pairs, 15 to 20cm. long. Cones ovoid-conic, 5cm. long. Luchu Isles (Japan).

maritima POIR. See *P. pinaster*.

†**massoniana** LAMB. A small to medium-sized tree with reddish young bark and glabrous young shoots; winter buds conic-cylindric, resinous. Leaves in pairs, 14 to 20cm. long, very slender. Cones ovoid, 3·5 to 6cm. long. S.E. China; N. Formosa. I. 1829.

†**michoacana** MARTINEZ. A small to medium-sized tree in the mildest areas of the British Isles, closely related to *P. montezumae*. Leaves in fives, 25 to 43cm. long, spreading and drooping. Cones oblong-ovoid, 25 to 30cm. long. Mexico.

montana. See *P. mugo*.

†**montezumae** LAMB. "Montezuma Pine". A magnificent, medium-sized to large tree with rough and deeply fissured bark and a large domed crown. Young shoots glabrous, stout, orange brown; winter buds ovoid, pointed. Leaves usually in fives but varying from three to eight on some trees, 18 to 25cm. long, bluish-grey, spreading or drooping. Cones varying from ovoid-conic to cylindrical, 7·5 to 25cm. long. A bold and imposing tree, suitable only for the milder counties. Mts. of Mexico. I. 1839.

hartwegii ENGELM. (*P. hartwegii*). The hardiest variety in cultivation in the British Isles. Leaves often in threes or fours, greener than the type. In Mexico it grows at higher altitudes than other varieties.

† **lindleyi** LOUD. (*P. lindleyi*). A beautiful variety with slender, drooping, apple-green leaves, 15 to 25cm. long, and pale brown cones. Not so hardy as the type.

† **rudis** SHAW (*P. rudis*). Leaves generally six or seven in a cluster, 10 to 15cm. long. Cones smaller than in the type, 5 to 6cm. long, bluish-black when young. It is found in warmer regions of Mexico and is only likely to succeed in the milder counties. Mts. of Mexico.

‡**monticola** D. DON. "Western White Pine". A medium-sized to large tree of narrowly conical habit, with minutely pubescent young shoots; winter buds cylindrical-ovoid. Leaves in fives, 8 to 10cm. long, dark blue-green with white inner surface. Cones solitary or in clusters, ovoid-cylindrical, stalked, 10 to 25cm. long, usually clustered at ends of branches, pendulous after the first year. Western N. America. I. 1831.

mugo TURRA (*mughus*) (*montana*). "Mountain Pine". A very hardy, large shrub or small tree of dense, bushy habit. Young shoots light green, ridged and glabrous; winter buds cylindric, very resinous. Leaves in pairs, 3 to 4cm. long, rigid and curved, dark green. Cones solitary or in clusters, ovoid to conic, 2 to 6cm. long. A variable species in the wild, all forms succeeding in almost all soils. Very lime tolerant. Several of the smaller forms are excellent in association with heathers, whilst the dwarf, slow-growing clones are suitable for the rock garden or scree. Mts. of Central Europe.

'Gnom'. A small, compact selection forming a dense, dark green, globular mound. C. 1927.

'Mops'. Dwarf, globular bush of dense, slow growth. C. 1951.

pumilio ZEN. A dwarf form often prostrate, but occasionally reaching 2m. Alps of C. Europe.

rostrata. See *P. uncinata*.

‡**muricata** D. DON. "Bishop Pine". A very picturesque, medium-sized to large tree forming a dense, rather flat head of branches. Young shoots green at first, glabrous; winter buds cylindrical, deep purple-brown, very resinous. Leaves in pairs, 10 to 15cm. long, stiff and curved or twisted, dark bluish-grey or yellowish grey-green. Cones solitary or in clusters, ovoid, 5 to 9cm. long, the scales armed with a stout recurved spine; often remaining unopened on the branches for many years. In the wild the cones have been known to remain intact for thirty or forty years, the seeds eventually being liberated by forest fires. This species is suitable for exposed areas, but not on chalk soils. California. I. 1848.

PINUS—*continued*

nigra ARNOLD (*nigra austriaca*). "Austrian Pine". A commonly planted and familiar large tree with rough, greyish-brown or dark brown bark and a dense head of large branches. Young shoots yellowish-brown, ridged and glabrous; winter buds ovoid-oblong to cylindrical, resinous. Leaves in pairs, dark green, 8 to 12cm. long, stiff and stout, densely crowded on the branchlets. Cones solitary or in clusters, ovoid-conic, 5 to 8cm. long, the scales ending in a small prickle. All forms of *P. nigra* are excellent for maritime areas and are tolerant of most soils. The "Austrian Pine" here described thrives better than any other in chalky soils and in bleak exposures. It makes an excellent wind-break. It is a native of Europe, from Austria to Central Italy, Greece and Yugoslavia. Introduced to Britain by Messrs. Lawson of Edinburgh in 1835.

calabrica. See *maritima*.

caramanica REHD. (*pallasiana*). "Crimean Pine". A large tree of broad, conical habit, with usually many long, stout, erect branches; leaves 13 to 18cm. long. Cones ovoid, 6 to 10cm. long. Rarer in cultivation than the "Austrian Pine" from which it mainly differs in its more compact, conical habit, longer, thicker leaves and usually larger cones. Balkan Peninsula; S. Carpathians; Crimea; W. Asia. I. 1798.

cebennensis REHD. (*salzmannii*). "Pyrenees Pine". A medium sized tree with drooping branches forming a widely spreading, low-domed crown. Leaves 10 to 15cm. long, greyish-green, very slender and soft to the touch. Cones 4 to 6cm. long. Cevennes, Pyrenees and C. and E. Spain. I. 1834.

'Hornibrookiana'. A dwarf form of very slow growth. Originated from a "witches broom" on an "Austrian Pine" in Seneca Park, Rochester (U.S.A.) before 1932.

maritima MELV. (*calabrica*) (*P. laricio*). "Corsican Pine". A large tree with a straight main stem to summit of crown, more open and with fewer, shorter, more level branches than the "Austrian Pine". It also differs in the more slender and flexible, grey-green leaves which occur less densely and more spreading on the branchlets. The "Corsican Pine" is extensively used for forestry purposes and is happy in almost any soil or situation. The wood is used throughout the Mediterranean region, especially for general construction purposes. S. Italy and Corsica. Introduced by Philip Miller in 1759.

pallasiana. See *caramanica*.

'Pygmaea'. A very slow-growing, miniature tree of dense, globular or ovoid shape, the leaves turning yellow green in winter. It is a form of var. *maritima* collected from the upper regions of Mt. Ansaro, Italy. C. 1855.

†oocarpa SCHIEDE. A rare and beautiful, small to medium-sized tree allied to *P. patula*. Young shoots glaucous. Leaves variable in number, in threes, fours or fives, 25 to 30cm. long, sea-green. Cones long-stalked, broadly ovoid, 5 to 9cm. long. A tender species only suitable for the very mildest areas. Central America.

‡palustris MILL. (*longifolia* SALISB.). "Southern Pitch Pine". A slow, erect-growing, small to medium-sized tree requiring a warm, moist soil, void of free lime. Young shoots stout, orange-brown and glabrous; winter buds large, cylindrical. Leaves in threes, 20 to 25cm. long, up to 45cm. long on young, vigorous plants, flexible, densely crowded on the branchlets. Cones cylindrical, 15 to 25cm. long, the scales with a reflexed spine. Eastern U.S.A. I. 1730.

parviflora SIEB. & ZUCC. "Japanese White Pine". A small to medium-sized tree, conical when young, flat-topped in maturity. Young shoots sparsely short, pubescent; winter buds ovoid, slightly resinous. Leaves in fives, 5 to 7·5cm. long, slightly curved, deep blue-green with blue-white inner surfaces. Cones solitary or in clusters, erect or spreading, 5 to 8cm. long. This picturesque Japanese tree or large shrub is the pine of the "Willow Tree" pattern and is commonly cultivated in that country, particularly for bonsai purposes. Introduced by John Gould Veitch in 1861. A.M. 1977.

'Adcock's Dwarf'. A dwarf bush of slow, rather compact growth. Leaves 1·5 to 2·5cm. long, greyish-green, produced in congested bunches at the tips of the shoots. A seedling raised in our Jermyn's Lane Nursery in 1961. Named after our propagator, Graham Adcock.

PINUS—*continued*

parviflora 'Brevifolia' ('*Pentaphylla*'). A small tree with tight bunches of short, stiff, blue-green leaves. C. 1900.

'Tempelhof'. A vigorous form, faster-growing than the type, otherwise similar.

‡†patula SCHL. & CHAM. An extremely beautiful, small to medium-sized tree of graceful habit, with reddish bark, long spreading branches and pendulous, glaucous-green, glabrous young shoots; winter buds cylindrical, long-pointed. Leaves bright green, usually in threes, occasionally in fours or fives, 15 to 30cm. long. Cones in clusters, ovoid-conic, curved, 7·5 to 10cm. long. An elegant species with gracefully drooping foliage. This lovely tree has grown uninjured in our nurseries for thirty years, but is not recommended for the coldest northern areas. Mexico.

‡peuce GRISEB. "Macedonian Pine". An attractive, medium-sized to large tree, recalling *P. cembra* in its narrowly conical habit. Young shoots shining green and glabrous; winter buds ovoid, resinous. Leaves in fives, 7 to 10cm. long, deep blue-green with white inner surfaces, densely packed on the branchlets. Cones almost cylindrical, curved, 10 to 15cm. long. Balkan Peninsula. I. 1864.

pinaster AIT. (*maritima* POIR). "Maritime Pine"; "Bournemouth Pine". Usually a sparsely-branched, medium-sized tree but occasionally a large tree with a bare stem and thick, reddish-brown or dark purple bark in small squares. Young shoots pale brown, glabrous; winter buds large, spindle-shaped. Leaves in pairs, 18 to 25cm. long, rigid and curved, dull grey. Cones deflexed, solitary or in clusters, ovoid-conic, 9 to 18cm. long, rich shining brown, often remaining intact on the branches for several years.

An excellent species for sandy soils and seaside districts, particularly in the warmer parts of the British Isles. It is commonly planted along the south coast, especially in the Bournemouth area. It is an important source of resin and the chief centre of the industry is in Western France, from whence large quantities of turpentine and resin are distributed. W. Mediterranean Region. Cultivated since the 16th century.

pinea L. "Umbrella Pine"; "Stone Pine". A very distinct tree of small to medium height developing a characteristic dense, flat-topped or umbrella-shaped head of spreading branches. Young shoots greyish-green and glabrous; winter buds ovoid, pointed. Leaves in pairs, 10 to 15cm. long, stiff and slightly twisted, sharply pointed, rather distant. Cones stalked, ovoid or nearly globose, 8 to 15cm. long, shining nut brown. Seeds large and edible. A picturesque pine of distinct habit, particularly suitable for sandy soils and maritime areas. Mediterranean Region.

ponderosa LAWSON. "Western Yellow Pine". A large tree of striking appearance with usually a tall, clear trunk, scaly cinnamon bark and stout, spreading or drooping branches. Young shoots stout, orange-brown or greenish, glabrous; winter buds cylindrical and pointed, resinous. Leaves in threes, 12 to 26cm. long, stiff and curved, spreading and crowded at the ends of the branchlets. Cones ovoid, 12 to 26cm. long, the scales armed with a small spine. A variable species with several named varieties. Western N. America. Introduced by David Douglas in 1826. A.M. 1980.

arizonica SHAW. "Arizona Pine". A variety with deeply fissured, almost black bark, glaucous young shoots and leaves in bundles of five or occasionally in threes or fours. S. Arizona; N. Mexico.

jeffreyi. See *P. jeffreyi*.

scopulorum ENGELM. A variety with usually drooping branches, shorter leaves, 7·5 to 15cm. long, and smaller cones, to 7·5cm. long. Dakota; Nebraska and E. Wyoming.

‡†pseudostrobus LINDL. A tender tree of small to medium size, only suitable for the mildest areas of the British Isles. Young shoots glaucous; winter buds ovoid, pointed. Leaves usually in fives, apple-green, 18 to 25cm. long, pendulous. Cones ovoid, 8 to 14cm. long. It is closely allied to *P. montezumae*, differing in its glaucous shoots and smooth bark. Mexico; Central America. I. 1839.

oaxacana HARRISON. A variety with leaves 20 to 30cm. long, and cones 13 to 14cm. long. Mexico.

PINUS—*continued*

‡**pumila** REG. (*cembra pumila*). "Dwarf Siberian Pine". Variable in habit, usually a dwarf shrub of spreading growth, occasionally a dense, medium-sized bush. Young shoots densely clothed with a reddish-brown pubescence; winter buds narrowly conical, sharply pointed and resinous. Leaves in fives, 4 to 7 or occasionally 10cm. long, blue-white on the inner surfaces, densely bundled and crowding the branchlets. Cones ovoid, 5cm. long. Closely related to *P. cembra* and often difficult to distinguish from dwarf forms of that species. *P. pumila* and its forms is an excellent conifer for the heather garden and the large rock garden. Widely distributed in E. Asia, usually growing in cold, exposed places high in the mountains. I. about 1807.

'Compacta'. A small shrub up to 2m. of dense, erect, bushy habit; the branches crowded with large bunches of glaucous leaves. Very effective on a large rock garden or border edge.

‡**pungens** MICH. "Hickory Pine". A small to medium-sized tree, often of bushy habit, with thick, reddish-brown bark. Young shoots green at first, soon dark red-brown, glabrous; winter buds cylindrical, shortly pointed. Leaves in pairs or occasionally in threes, 5 to 7·5cm. long, rigid and twisted, sharply pointed, densely crowded on the branchlets. Cones ovoid or conical, 5 to 9cm. long, the scales with a stout recurved spine, often remaining intact on the tree for several years. Eastern N. America. I. 1804.

‡**radiata** D. DON (*insignis*). "Monterey Pine". A large tree with deeply fissured, dark brown bark and a dense head of branches. Young shoots glabrous; winter buds ovoid, resinous. Leaves in threes, 10 to 15cm. long, bright green, densely crowded on the branchlets. Cones obliquely ovoid, 7·5 to 15cm. long, with smoothly rounded protruding scales, borne in whorls along the branches, often remaining intact for many years. An attractive, rapid-growing tree for mild inland and coastal areas. Excellent for withstanding sea winds. Monterey Peninsula (California). Introduced by David Douglas in 1833.

‡**resinosa** AIT. "Red Pine". Small to medium-sized tree of rather heavy appearance, with a broad, conical head of branches. Young shoots pale brown or orange, glabrous; winter buds narrowly conical, resinous. Leaves in pairs, 12 to 18cm. long, slender and flexible. Cones ovoid-conical, 4 to 6cm. long. An important timber tree in North America. Eastern Canada; N.E. United States. C. 1736.

‡**rigida** MILL. "Northern Pitch Pine". A medium-sized tree with strongly ridged, green young shoots; winter buds cylindrical or conical, sharply pointed and resinous. Leaves in threes, 8 to 10cm. long, thick, stiff and spreading. Cones usually in clusters, short cylindric to conic, 3 to 9cm. long, the scales with a reflexed spine. A peculiarity of this species is the tendency to produce tufts of leaves on the trunk. It is not tolerant of chalk soils. Eastern N. America. C. 1759.

†**roxburghii** SARG. (*longifolia* ROXB.). "Long-leaved Indian Pine". A small tree in cultivation. Young shoots clothed with scale-like leaves; winter buds small, ovoid. Leaves in threes, 23 to 33cm. long, light green. Cones ovoid, 11 to 20cm. long, borne on short, stout stalks. A rare species, only suitable for the milder areas of the British Isles. Himalaya. I. 1807.

sabiniana DOUGL. "Digger Pine". A remarkable pine, related to *P. coulteri*. A medium-sized tree usually of gaunt open habit, with straggly branches. Young shoots prominently ridged, glaucous and glabrous; winter buds narrowly cylindric, resinous. Leaves in threes, 20 to 30cm. long, spreading or drooping, glaucous green, sparsely arranged on the branchlets. Cones ovoid, reflexed, 15 to 25cm. long, the scales tipped with a stout, claw-like hook. The edible seeds were once an important article of food for the American Indians. California. Introduced by David Douglas in 1832.

‡×**schwerinii** FITSCH. (*strobus* × *wallichiana*). A large tree resembling *P. wallichiana* in general appearance. Young shoots glaucous and densely pubescent; winter buds cylindric-conic, long pointed and very resinous. Leaves in fives, 7·5 to 13cm. long, loose and pendulous, glaucous green. Cones slightly curved, 7·5 to 15cm. long. It differs from *P. wallichiana* mainly in the densely hairy shoots and shorter leaves. An attractive hybrid which originated on the estate of Dr. Graf von Schwerin, near Berlin, in 1905.

PINUS—*continued*

‡**strobus** L. "Weymouth Pine"; "White Pine". A large tree of conical habit when young, later developing a rounded head. Young shoots slender, greenish, with short hairs usually below the leaf bundles; winter buds conic, sharply pointed and resinous. Leaves in fives, 7·5 to 15cm. long, somewhat glaucous-green. Cones cylindrical, 8 to 20cm. long, pendant on slender stalks, liberally flecked with resin. Once the most commonly planted of the five-needled pines, due to its ornamental habit and fast growth. It owes its English name to Lord Weymouth, who made extensive plantings of this species at Longleat, Wiltshire, in the early 1700's. Eastern N. America. Cultivated since the mid 16th century.

'Compacta'. A dwarf, slow-growing bush of dense habit.

'Contorta' ('*Tortuosa*'). A curious form, developing twisted branches and densely-set, conspicuously twisted leaves. C. 1932.

'Densa'. A dwarf bush of dense habit. Similar to '*Nana*'.

'Fastigiata'. An erect-branched form of conical or broadly columnar habit. C. 1884.

'Nana'. A small form developing into a dense bush. There are several slight variations of this form, some of which are more vigorous and larger growing.

'Nivea'. An attractive form in which the glaucous leaves are tipped milky-white, giving the whole tree an unusual silver-white colour.

'Pendula'. A form with long, drooping branches.

'Prostrata'. A remarkable prostrate form, the branches lying flat on the ground or shortly ascending and forming a low mound. Originally found by Dr. Alfred Rehder in the Arnold Arboretum. C. 1893.

sylvestris L. "Scots Pine". Our only native pine. A familar tree usually seen as a large, tall-stemmed tree and, occasionally, a low, picturesque, spreading tree. It is easily recognised by its characteristic and attractive, reddish young bark. Young shoots greenish and glabrous; winter buds oblong-ovoid. Leaves in pairs, 3 to 10cm. long, twisted, grey-green or blue-green. Cones ovoid-conic, 2·5 to 7·5cm. long, on short stalks.

A common tree which combines beauty with utility. In the British Isles, truly wild stands of this species may only be found in parts of Northern Scotland, but it was once found naturally throughout England and Wales. Due to extensive planting in the past it is becoming naturalised in many areas, particularly on heaths and moors. There are numerous geographical variants of which our native form is var. *scotica*. Many garden forms have arisen, several of which are suitable for the rock garden. The Scots Pine may be grown in all types of soil but does not reach its maximum proportions or maximum age either in damp acid soils or shallow dry chalk soils. A.G.M. 1969.

'Argentea'. We offer a beautiful form selected by Edwin Hillier with silvery-blue-green leaves and reddish stems. A.G.M. 1969.

'Aurea'. A slow-growing, small tree with leaves of a striking golden yellow in winter. A.M. 1964.

'Beuvronensis'. This miniature "Scots Pine" forms a small, compact, dome-shaped shrublet. A superb subject for the rock garden. C. 1891. A.M. 1968. A.G.M. 1969.

'Compressa'. A dwarf bush of conical habit, with short, crowded, glaucous leaves. C. 1867.

'Doone Valley'. A dwarf form of compact, somewhat conical habit. Leaves glaucous. Named after "Doone Valley", the one-time garden of Mr. W. Archer.

'Fastigiata'. A remarkable "Scots Pine", the shape of a "Lombardy Poplar". C. 1856.

lapponica FRIES. A geographical variety, usually developing a narrow head of branches. Lapland; C. and N. Scandinavia; N. Finland.

'Nana'. Dwarf, bushy form of slow growth; differing from the very similar '*Beuvronensis*' in its non-resinous winter buds. C. 1855.

'Pumila'. See '*Watereri*'.

'Pygmaea'. A rare, slow-growing, dwarf form of dense, rounded habit. C. 1891.

rigensis ASCH. & GRAEBN. A geographical form with a slender trunk and a conical head of branches. Baltic Coast.

'Viridis Compacta'. Dwarf bush of conical habit, superficially resembling a dwarf form of *P. nigra*, with its long, vivid, grass-green leaves. C. 1923.

PINUS—*continued*

sylvestris 'Watereri' (*'Pumila'*). A slow-growing, medium-sized bush or rarely a small tree, conical in habit at first, later becoming rounded. It is suitable for the heather garden, but eventually becomes too large for the normal rock garden. Found on Horsell Common, Surrey, by Mr. Anthony Waterer in about 1865. The original plant in the Knap Hill Nursery is approximately 7·5m. high. A.G.M. 1969.

'Windsor'. Dwarf, bun-shaped form of slow growth. Leaves very small, greyish-green. Originated as a "witches broom".

tabuliformis CARR. (*sinensis* MAYR.). "Chinese Pine". An uncommon species varying in habit from small and flat-headed, to tall and shapely. Young shoots glabrous, glaucous at first, then pale yellow; winter buds oblong and pointed. Leaves in pairs or threes, 10 to 15cm. long, densely crowding the branchlets. Cones ovoid, 4 to 6·5cm. long. China; Korea. C. 1862.

yunnanensis SHAW (*P. yunnanensis*). Differs from the type in its stout, glabrous shining pink shoots, its longer, more slender and drooping leaves, 20 to 30cm. long, borne usually in threes, and in the larger, darker brown cones up to 9cm. long. A very distinct, rather sparsely-branched tree creating the effect of *P. montezumae*. By some authorities given specific rank which indeed it seems to merit. W. China. I. 1909.

taeda L. "Loblolly Pine". A small to medium-sized tree with glabrous and glaucous young shoots; winter buds conic, long-pointed. Leaves in threes, 15 to 25cm. long, slender and flexible and slightly twisted. Cones ovoid-oblong, 7 to 10cm. long, the scales with a stout, recurved spine. Suitable for southern and drier parts of the British Isles. S. and E. United States. A distinct and effective tree which should be in every pinetum. I. 1741.

†**taiwanensis** HAYATA. A rare tree of small to medium size; leaves in pairs. Only suitable for the conservatory or sheltered sites in mild areas. Formosa.

thunbergii PARL. "Black Pine". A distinct and splendid large tree with stout, twisted branches. Young shoots light brown, ridged and glabrous; winter buds ovoid, sharply pointed, conspicuously silky silvery-white. Leaves in pairs, 7 to 18cm. long, rigid and twisted. Cones ovoid-conic, 4 to 6cm. long, borne singly or in large clusters. The "Black Pine" is one of the most important timber trees in Japan, where it often occurs by the seashore. In the British Isles it is useful as a windbreak in maritime areas and for growing in poor, sandy soils. Japan; Korea. I. 1852.

'Compacta'. A dense-growing large bush.

'Oculus-draconis'. An unusual form in which the leaves are marked with two yellowish bands.

†**torreyana** CARR. A small tree or a gnarled bush, sometimes prostrate in the wild. Young shoots green and bloomy at first; winter buds cylindrical, long pointed. Leaves in fives, 20 to 30cm. long, borne in dense bunches at the ends of the branchlets. Cones broadly ovoid, 10 to 13cm. long, stalked. Seeds sweet and edible. Only suitable for the milder, drier areas of the British Isles. California. I. 1853.

tuberculata. See *P. attenuata*.

uncinata MIRBEL (*mugo rostrata*). "Mountain Pine". A medium-sized tree, closely related to *P. mugo*, differing in both its habit and its larger cones, 5 to 7cm. long. A splendid dense, bushy, broadly conical tree for creating shelter against the coldest winds. Succeeding in all types of soil including shallow chalk soils. Pyrenees to Eastern Alps.

‡**virginiana** MILL. "Scrub Pine". Small to medium-sized tree with purplish, bloomy young shoots; winter buds ovoid, resinous. Leaves in pairs, 4 to 6cm. long, stiff and twisted. Cones oblong-conical, 4 to 7cm. long, the scales ending in a short, recurved prickle. It dislikes shallow, chalk soils. Eastern U.S.A. I. 1739.

wallichiana A. B. JACKS. (*griffithii* MCCLELLAND not PARL.) (*excelsa*). *M* "Bhutan Pine". An elegant, large, broad-headed tree, retaining its lowest branches when isolated. Young shoots glaucous and glabrous; winter buds cylindric-conic, resinous or glabrous. Leaves in fives, 12 to 20cm. long, blue-green, slender and drooping with age. Cones stalked, solitary or in bunches, banana-shaped, 15 to 25cm. long. A most attractive species with its graceful foliage and ornamental, resin-smeared, pendulous cones. Moderately lime-tolerant but not recommended for shallow chalk soils. Temperate Himalaya. I. about 1823. A.M. 1979.

PINUS—*continued*

wallichiana 'Nana'. A small, dome-shaped, glaucous bush of slow growth and dense habit.

'Zebrina'. Leaves with a creamy-yellow band below the apex. C. 1889.

‡**washoensis** MASON & STOCKWELL. A rare, medium-sized tree allied to *P. jeffreyi* from which it differs mainly in its smaller leaves, 10 to 15cm. long and smaller cones, 5 to 7·5cm. long. Nevada and California.

yunnanensis. See *P. tabuliformis yunnanensis*.

***PODOCARPUS—Podocarpaceae**—A large genus of evergreen trees and shrubs mainly confined in the wild to the southern hemisphere in warm temperate and tropical countries. Leaves are variable in shape usually spirally arranged. Fruits consist of a fleshy, coloured, usually red, receptacle in which the seed is inserted. Several species are suitable for the milder areas of the British Isles and a few may be classed as hardy. The Podocarpus succeed in most types of soil whether acid or alkaline.

acutifolius KIRK. A small to medium-sized, moderately hardy shrub usually of dense, prickly habit. Leaves linear, 1 to 2·5cm. long, sharply pointed, bronze-green. Although it reaches small tree size in its native habitat it remains dense and slow-growing in cultivation and, as such, is an interesting plant for a prominent position on the large rock garden. This plant has grown successfully on our scree garden for the past eight years. New Zealand.

alpinus HOOK. f. A remarkably hardy, dwarf species, forming a low, densely-branched mound or a creeping carpet extending 1 to 2m. or more across. Leaves yew-like, narrow, blue or grey-green, crowding the stems. Suitable for the rock garden or as ground cover. In its native habitat it is often found on stony mountain sides and helps to prevent erosion. S.E. Australia; Tasmania.

andinus ENDL. (*Prumnopitys elegans*). "Plum-fruited Yew"; "Chilean Yew". A small to medium-sized tree or large shrub somewhat resembling a yew in habit. Leaves linear, 1 to 2·5cm. long, bright green above, twisted to reveal the glaucous-green undersurface. Fruits like small damsons, glaucous black, borne on slender scaly stalks. This species grows excellently on good soils over chalk. It is a native of the Andes of S. Chile and was introduced by Robert Pearce for Messrs. Veitch in 1860. F.C.C. 1864.

chilinus. See *P. salignus*.

cunninghamii. See *P. hallii*.

†**dacrydioides** A. RICH. An extremely beautiful small tree in the mildest areas of the British Isles, but reaching 45m. and above in its native habitat. The long, slender, gracefully drooping branchlets are clothed with small, narrow, bronze-green, two-ranked leaves, which on young trees are scale-like, spirally-arranged on older trees. An elegant species which makes an attractive conservatory specimen. New Zealand.

†**elatus** R. BR. A small to medium-sized tree of elegant habit, its branches clothed with narrowly-oblong, bright green leaves varying from 5 to 15cm. long, or longer on young vigorous specimens. Only possible in the mildest areas, but suitable for the conservatory. S.E. Australia.

†**falcatus** R. BR. A small to medium-sized tree; leaves long and narrow, variable in length and arrangement, up to 13cm. long on young plants. Suitable only for the mildest areas or for the conservatory. S. Africa.

†**ferrugineus** D. DON. A graceful small tree. Leaves rather yew-like in shape but a softer yellow-green, arranged in two irregular ranks along the slender branches which are pendulous at their extremities. This rare and attractive species is doing well in the beautiful garden made by Mrs. Vera Mackie at Helen's Bay, N. Ireland. Native of New Zealand where it is an important timber tree.

†**gracilior** PILGER. An attractive and elegant, small to medium-sized tree with willow-like leaves, up to 10cm. long on young plants. An important timber tree in its native land. Only suitable for the mildest gardens in the British Isles or the conservatory. E. Africa.

†**hallii** KIRK (*totara hallii*) (*cunninghamii*). A small tree or large, bushy shrub, related and similar to *P. totara*, but differing in its longer leaves, 2·5 to 5cm. on young plants, and its thin papery, peeling bark. There is a good specimen growing very well at Castlewellan in that splendid pinetum planted by Mr. Gerald Annesley in N. Ireland. New Zealand.

'Aureus' (*totara 'Aureus'*). Leaves, yellow-green.

PODOCARPUS—*continued*

‡**macrophyllus** D. DON. "Kusamaki". One of the hardiest species, forming a shrub or small tree of very distinct appearance. Leaves 10 to 13cm. long, up to 18cm. on vigorous plants, 12mm. wide, bright green above, glaucous beneath, arranged in dense spirals on the stems. Not suitable for chalky soils. It has withstood 28 degrees of frost in our arboretum. Native of China and of Japan where it is occasionally grown as an unusual and effective hedge.

'Angustifolius'. A form with narrower leaves than the type. C. 1864.

'Argenteus'. A slow-growing form, its narrow leaves with an irregular white border. C. 1861. F.C.C. 1865.

†**nagi** MAKINO. A small, slow-growing tree or large, bushy shrub. Leaves opposite or nearly so, ovate or broadly lanceolate, 4 to 5cm. long, leathery, dark green above, paler below. Not hardy enough to survive long in the home counties. Japan; China; Formosa.

nivalis HOOK. "Alpine Totara". One of the hardiest species succeeding throughout the British Isles and doing well in chalky soils. Normally seen as a low, spreading mound of shortly erect and prostrate stems, densely branched and crowded with small, narrow, leathery, olive-green leaves, 6 to 20mm. long. An excellent ground cover. A large plant growing in shade in the Bedgebury Pinetum, Kent, has formed a carpet 2 to 3m. across. Native of New Zealand where it is found on mountain slopes, fulfilling the same purpose there as *P. alpinus* in Tasmania and Australia.

'Aureus'. Leaves bronze tinged, more noticeable in the young growths.

nubigenus LINDL. A distinct, slow-growing, beautiful shrub rarely reaching the size of a small tree. The usually spirally-arranged, sharply pointed, narrow leaves are 3·5 to 4·5cm. long, deep green above and glaucous beneath. Here uninjured by winter cold during the past thirty years. Mts. of Chile; Patagonia; Valdivia and Chiloe.

†**salignus** D. DON (*chilinus*). A most attractive and elegant, small tree or large shrub, with drooping branches and long, narrow, bright grey-green leaves, 5 to 15cm. long. A well-grown specimen creates an almost tropical effect with its lush piles of glossy evergreen, willow-like foliage. Hardy in the south-west when given the shelter of other evergreens. Chile.

†**spicatus** MIRBEL. The "Matai" or "Black Pine" of New Zealand. An interesting small tree in the mildest areas of the British Isles. Young trees possess numerous, slender, drooping branches and branchlets, towards the tips of which occur the small, narrow, bronze-tinted leaves.

†**totara** D. DON. A tall tree in New Zealand, but usually a slow-growing large shrub in this country. Leaves yellowish-green, scattered or two-ranked, up to 2cm. long on adult plants, 2·5cm. long on young plants, leathery, stiff and sharply pointed. Correctly sited among sheltering evergreens this unusual shrub is more or less hardy in the home counties.

'Aureus'. See *P. hallii 'Aureus'*.

hallii. See *P. hallii*.

PRUMNOPITYS elegans. See *PODOCARPUS andinus*.

‡**PSEUDOLARIX—Pinaceae**—A very hardy, monotypic genus differing from *Larix* in several small botanical characters. The linear leaves which are borne in dense clusters on short spurs on the older wood, are spirally-arranged on the young shoots. Male and female strobili are borne on the same tree. It requires a lime-free soil.

amabilis REHD. (*fortunei*) (*kaempferi*). "Golden Larch". A beautiful, slow-growing, deciduous, medium-sized tree of broadly conical habit. The long, larch-like, light green leaves, 3 to 6cm. long, turn a clear golden yellow in autumn. Cones ripening the first year. On a large tree they stud the long, slender branches, resembling small, pale-green artichokes, bloomy when young, reddish-brown when ripe. Eastern China (Chekiang and Kiangsi). Introduced by Robert Fortune in 1852. A.M. 1976.

‡***PSEUDOTSUGA**—**Pinaceae**—A small genus of evergreen trees of broadly conical habit, with whorled branches and spindle-shaped buds recalling those of the Common Beech. The leaves are linear, soft to the touch and marked with two glaucous, stomatic bands beneath. Male and female strobili are borne on the same tree. Cones pendulous, ripening in one season. The members of this genus may be distinguished from *Abies* by the pendulous cones which fall intact, and from *Picea* by the shortly-raised leaf-scars and conspicuous three-lobed cone-bracts. The majority of species dislike chalky soils, thriving best in moist, but well-drained soils. *P. menziesii* is of great economic importance.

douglasii. See *P. menziesii.*

glauca. See *P. menziesii glauca.*

japonica BEISSN. The "Japanese Douglas Fir" is rare in cultivation and makes a small, bushy tree. Young shoots grey and glabrous. Leaves 2 to 2·5cm. long, notched, pale green, arranged on the branchlets in two ranks. Cones ovoid, 4 to 5cm. long, bracts exserted and reflexed. A rare species in cultivation, distinguished from other species by its glabrous shoots, smaller cones and shorter leaves. S.E. Japan. I. 1898.

macrocarpa MAYR. "Large-coned Douglas Fir". A rare, medium-sized tree, growing well in our arboretum. Young shoots reddish-brown, hairy or glabrous. Leaves 2·5 to 3cm. long, usually horny-pointed, arranged on the branchlets in two ranks. Cones 10 to 18cm. long (the largest in the genus) with slightly protruding bracts. Native of S. California. Introduced by H. Clinton-Baker in 1910.

menziesii FRANCO (*taxifolia*) (*douglasii*). "Oregon Douglas Fir". A fast-growing, large tree. The lower branches of large specimens are characteristically downswept and the bark thick, corky and deeply furrowed. Young shoots yellowish-green, shortly pubescent. Leaves 2·5 to 3cm. long, blunt or shortly pointed at apex, arranged on the branchlets in two, usually horizontal ranks, fragrant when crushed. Cones oval-ovoid, 7 to 10cm. long, with conspicuous exerted bracts. This well-known conifer is an important timber tree both here and in North America. It is one of the stateliest conifers, being particularly effective when planted in groups, as in the New Forest and at Knightshayes Court in Devon. It is unsatisfactory on chalk soils. It is a native of Western N. America, reaching its finest proportions in Washington and British Columbia where specimens of 90m. and above are recorded. It was originally discovered by Archibald Menzies in about 1792 and introduced by David Douglas in 1827.

'Brevifolia'. A small, shrubby form, occasionally a miniature tree up to 2m., with leaves only 6 to 15mm. long, densely spreading all round the shoots. It differs from the similar '*Fretsii*' in its narrower leaves, and is less lime tolerant. F.C.C. 1886.

caesia FRANCO. "Fraser River Douglas Fir" or "Grey Douglas Fir". Differs from the type in its slower growth and grey-green leaves which are arranged in two ranks, with a V-shaped parting above. Because of its extreme hardiness it has been used for afforestation purposes in Finland and similar Arctic climates. It is found wild in British Columbia.

'Densa'. Dwarf, slow-growing, shrubby form of dense habit, with spreading branches and green leaves to 2cm. long. C. 1933.

'Elegans'. See under '*Glauca Pendula*'.

'Fletcheri' (*P. glauca 'Fletcheri'*). A slow-growing, shrubby form developing into an irregular, flat-topped, globular bush, eventually reaching 1·5 to 2m. in height. Leaves blue-green, 2 to 2·5cm. long, loosely arranged. Originated as a seedling of var. *glauca* in 1906. A.M. 1912.

'Fretsii'. An unusual, slow-growing form. The short, broad, obtuse, leaves, 10 to 12mm. long, resemble those of a *Tsuga*, but the arrangement is radial. Specimens in our nurseries at thirty years are irregular bushes about 1·2m. high by 1·8m. across. More lime-tolerant than '*Brevifolia*'. The colour of the leaves suggests kinship with var. *caesia*. C. 1905.

glauca FRANCO (*P. glauca*). "Blue Douglas Fir". A medium-sized tree of narrow conical habit. Leaves shorter than in the type, glaucous above, smelling of turpentine when crushed. Cones 6 to 7·5cm. long, the bracts reflexed. Hardier than the type, but slower growing and more lime-tolerant. Native of the Rocky Mountains, from Montana to N. Mexico.

PSEUDOTSUGA—*continued*

menziesii 'Glauca Pendula'. A small, weeping tree of graceful habit. Branchlets ascending, clothed with bluish-green leaves, 3 to 5cm. long. C. 1891. We have ascending, clothed with bluish-green leaves, 3 to 5cm. long. C. 1891. F.C.C. 1895. We have received plants under the name *'Elegans'* which appear identical with this clone.

'Holmstrup'. A small to medium-sized shrub or miniature tree of rather compact, upright habit, with green leaves 1 to 1·5cm. long, densely and radially-arranged on the branchlets.

'Nana' (*P. glauca 'Nana'*). Small to medium-sized bush, conical when young. Leaves 2 to 2·5cm. long, glaucous-green, almost radial. Originated as a seedling of var. *glauca*, in 1915.

'Pendula'. An unusual form with weeping branches, a clone of var. *caesia*. C. 1868.

sinensis DODE. A small tree in cultivation, with reddish-brown, young shoots. Leaves 2·5 to 3·5cm. long, notched at apex, arranged in two ranks. Cones ovoid, 4 to 5cm. long, with shortly exerted reflexed bracts. This rare, slow-growing species is susceptible to damage by spring frost. S.W. China. I. 1912.

taxifolia. See *P. menziesii*.

"REDWOOD". See *SEQUOIA sempervirens*.

RETINISPORA. An obsolete generic name which was at one time used to cover those forms of *CHAMAECYPARIS* with permanently juvenile (awl-shaped) foliage.

SALISBURIA adiantifolia. See *GINKGO biloba*.

***SAXEGOTHAEA—Podocarpaceae**—A monotypic genus resembling *Podocarpus andinus* in general appearance. The branchlets are arranged in whorls of three or four. Male and female strobili borne on the same plant. The genus is named in honour of Prince Albert, consort of Queen Victoria, after the Prussian Province from which he came. It forms a connecting link between *Podocarpaceae* and *Araucariaceae*, resembling a *Podocarpus* in foliage and an *Araucaria* in the female strobili. It occurs in dense forests in Chile and Patagonia.

conspicua LINDL. "Prince Albert's Yew". An unusual large shrub or small tree of loose habit, with laxly spreading branches and drooping branchlets. Leaves linear, 1·5 to 2cm. long, dark green above, marked with two glaucous bands beneath, rather twisted and arranged on the lateral branches in two ranks. Fruits 12 to 20mm. across, soft and prickly. An attractive conifer and botanically very interesting. Introduced by William Lobb in 1847.

‡*SCIADOPITYS—Pinaceae—A hardy, monotypic genus of unique appearance, thriving in a lime-free soil. It should be planted in every representative collection of conifers. It does well in partial shade.

verticillata SIEB. & ZUCC. "Umbrella Pine". A slow-growing, monoecious tree of medium-size. Dense and conical when young usually with a single trunk, although a form exists with several main stems. Bark exfoliating to reveal the reddish-brown new bark. Branches horizontal, bearing lush clusters of rich, glossy green foliage. The apparent single linear leaves, 5 to 13cm. long, are, in fact, fused pairs and are arranged in characteristic dense whorls like the spokes of an umbrella, hence the English name. The attractive ovoid, short-stalked cones, 6 to 10cm. long, are green at first, ripening to brown the second year. Native of Japan where it is restricted in the wild to two small areas in Central Honshu. The wood is durable and fairly water-resistant. First introduced as a single plant by Thomas Lobb in 1853, later more successfully by both Robert Fortune and J. G. Veitch in 1861. A.M. 1979.

***SEQUOIA—Taxodiaceae**—A well-known monotypic genus named after Sequoyah (1770-1843), a Cherokee half-breed of Georgia, who invented the Cherokee alphabet. An interesting character is that the butt of a felled tree will produce a sheaf of suckers, which is unusual in a conifer. Given ·6m. depth of soil, it will succeed in chalk areas.

gigantea. See *SEQUOIADENDRON giganteum*.

SEQUOIA—*continued*

sempervirens ENDL. (*Taxodium sempervirens*). "Californian Redwood". A very large, evergreen, monoecious tree, reaching over 100m. tall in its native forests, possessing a thick, fibrous, reddish-brown outer bark which is soft and spongy when struck. Branches slightly drooping, yew-like, bearing two-ranked, linear-oblong leaves, 1 to 2cm. long, dark green above, marked with two white stomatic bands beneath. Leaves on leading shoots and fertile shoots smaller and spirally arranged. Cones pendulous, ovoid to globose, 2 to 3cm. long, ripening the first season.

This majestic tree is a native of California and Oregon where it is found on the seaward side of the coastal mountain range. It was first discovered by Archibald Menzies in 1794 and first introduced into Europe (St. Petersburg) in 1840. Three years later Hartweg sent seed to England. The Redwood has the distinction of being the world's tallest recorded tree, the record at present being held by the "Howard Libbey" tree in the Humbolt State Redwood Park which, in 1968, measured 110m. (366ft.). The tallest tree in the British Isles is found on an estate in North Devon, which in 1970 measured 41m. (138ft.). It is also a long-lived tree, the average age being 500 to 700 years. Several trees have reached 2,000 years and the oldest known specimen, felled in 1934, was dated at 2,200 years.

'Adpressa' (*'Albospica'*). The tips of the young shoots are creamy-coloured, and the short leaves regularly disposed in one plane. It is often grown as a dwarf shrub but usually reverts, producing tall stems which eventually develop into a normal size tree. C. 1867. F.C.C. 1890.

'Prostrata' (*'Cantab'*) (*'Nana Pendula'*). A most remarkable dwarf form with spreading branches thickly clothed with comparatively broad, glaucous-green, two-ranked leaves. Originated as a branch sport on a tree at the University Botanic Garden, Cambridge. We have a specimen in our arboretum which has produced a terminal leader and has every appearance of making a tree. C. 1951. A.M. 1951.

wellingtonia. See *SEQUOIADENDRON giganteum.*

***SEQUOIADENDRON—Taxodiaceae**—A monotypic genus, until recently included under *SEQUOIA*, differing in its naked winter-buds, awl-shaped leaves and larger cones, ripening during the second year. It is quite hardy and reasonably lime-tolerant but will not succeed on thin chalky soils.

giganteum BUCHOLZ (*Sequoia gigantea*) (*Sequoia wellingtonia*). "Wellingtonia", "Mammoth Tree". The "Big Tree" of California attains a very large size. The deeply furrowed, reddish-brown outer bark is similar to that of *Sequoia sempervirens* in texture. As a young tree it develops a densely-branched, conical habit. On older trees the branches are more widely spaced and conspicuously down-swept. Sometimes the lower part of the trunk is clear of branches for several metres, revealing the ornamental bark. Leaves awl-shaped, 6 to 12mm. long, bright green, spirally-arranged, persisting for up to four years. Cones ovoid, 5 to 7·5cm. long, green at first maturing to reddish-brown the second year. It is a familiar tree of parks and estates and resembles no other hardy cultivated conifer, except perhaps *Cryptomeria japonica* which has similar leaves and similarly coloured bark. I. 1853.

It is a native of California where it grows on the western slopes of the Sierra Nevada. Although never as tall as the "Redwood", in its native state it attains a greater girth and the "General Sherman" tree, with a height of 81m. (272ft.), a girth of 24m. (79ft.), at 5ft., and a total trunk volume of 50,000 cubic feet, is generally acknowledged to be the world's largest living thing. Specimens of 30m. and above are not uncommon in the British Isles, the record being held by a specimen at Endsleigh, Devon which, in 1970, measured 49m. (165ft.), with a girth (at 5ft.) of 6·71m. (22ft.). The "Wellingtonia" is regarded as one of the oldest living things in the world (see also *Pinus aristata*). The oldest authenticated age of a felled tree is about 3,200 years, whilst several standing trees appear to be about 1,500 to 2,000 years old.

'Glaucum'. Leaves glaucous. A narrower tree than the type. C. 1860.

'Pendulum'. A tree of unique appearance often assuming the most fantastic shapes, but usually forming a narrow column with long branches hanging almost parallel with the trunk. C. 1863. F.C.C. 1882.

'Pygmaeum'. Small to medium-sized bush of dense, conical habit. If reversions occur they should be removed. C. 1891.

SEQUOIADENDRON—*continued*

giganteum 'Variegatum'. Resembling the type in habit. Leaves flecked with a white variegation. Not a beauty. C. 1890.

"SPRUCE". See *PICEA*.

***TAIWANIA—Taxodiaceae**—A genus of only two species of remarkable conifers both rare in cultivation, related to and somewhat resembling *Cryptomeria* in general appearance. Male and female strobili are borne on the same tree.

†cryptomerioides HAYATA. A rare tree of conical habit, attaining heights of 50m. or more in its native habitats. In cultivation it forms a small, sparsely-branched tree with slender, drooping, whip-like branchlets, densely clothed with glaucous-green, linear, sickle-shaped, sharply pointed leaves which become shorter and more scale-like on adult trees. Cones cylindrical, 12mm. long. This unusual conifer requires a moist but well-drained soil and a sheltered site to succeed. Western slopes of Mount Morrison, Formosa. I. 1920. A.M. 1931.

flousiana GAUSSEN. "Coffin Tree". An attractive species closely resembling *T. cryptomerioides*, but with greener, slightly longer, less rigid leaves, softer to the touch. In our arboretum it has proved a hardier tree. A specimen in our Chandler's Ford Nursery has been growing slowly for the past fourteen years uninjured by severe winters. It is a native of S.W. and C. China and also N. Burma, where it was discovered by Kingdon Ward. Its wood is used in China for making coffins and it is this species rather than *J. recurva coxii* which is in danger of extinction through over-felling.

‡TAXODIUM—Taxodiaceae—A small genus of deciduous trees with ascending or spreading branches. Leaves linear and flattened or awl-shaped, arranged alternately in two opposite ranks on short, deciduous branchlets, the whole resembling a pinnate leaf. On persistent branchlets they are radially arranged. Male and female strobili are borne on the same tree, the males in long, drooping, terminal panicles. Cones shortly stalked, with thick woody, shield-like scales, ripening during the first year. These beautiful North and Central American trees, with their attractive frond-like foliage, can be successfully grown in all soils other than chalky soils. They are remarkable on account of their adaptability for growing in water-logged conditions, but it is essential that they be "mound planted" in such sites.

ascendens BRONGN. A small to medium-sized tree of narrowly conical or columnar habit, with spreading branches and erect branchlets. Leaves awl-shaped, 5 to 10mm. long, incurved and appressed, bright green. Cones globose, 1 to 3cm. across, purplish and resinous when young. In cultivation in the British Isles it tends to be slower-growing than *T. distichum*, but it is worth growing for its habit and rich brown autumn foliage. Native of swampy places in the S.E. United States. We offer the following form:—

'Nutans'. A beautiful columnar tree with shortly spreading or ascending branches. The thin, crowded branchlets are erect at first, later nodding, clothed with appressed, awl-shaped leaves up to 5mm. long. C. 1789.

distichum RICH. "Deciduous Cypress"; "Swamp Cypress". A strikingly beautiful tree and the most suitable conifer for wet soils. A large tree with fibrous, reddish-brown bark and strongly buttressed trunk. Branches spreading or ascending. Leaves linear and flattened, 1 to 1·5cm. long, grass green, pectinate on short, deciduous shoots, spirally arranged on the persistent branchlets, turning bronze-yellow in autumn. Cones globular or obovoid, 2 to 2·5cm. across, purple and resinous when young. When grown by water, large specimens produce peculiar "knee-like" growths from the roots, which project above ground. Native of wet places, rivers and swamps in the southern U.S.A., and the dominant tree in the famous Everglades region of Florida. In America it is known as the "Bald Cypress". It was first introduced by John Tradescant about 1640. A.M. 1973.

'Hursley Park'. A dwarf, dense bush which originated from a "witches broom" on a tree at Hursley Park, Hampshire, in 1966.

'Pendens'. A form with drooping branchlets and branch tips. C. 1855.

†mucronatum TENORE. "Mexican Cypress". A small to medium-sized tree, closely resembling *T. distichum*, but leaves semi-persistent in warm areas. It is too tender for all but the mildest areas of the British Isles. Native of Mexico where specimens of great size and age are said to occur.

sempervirens. See *SEQUOIA sempervirens*.

***TAXUS**—**Taxaceae**—"Yew". A small genus of evergreen trees and shrubs bearing linear, two-ranked or radial leaves which are marked by two yellowish-green or greyish-green bands beneath. Male and female strobili borne during spring, usually on separate plants. Fruits with a fleshy, often brightly-coloured cup (aril) containing a single poisonous seed. The yews are of great garden value, tolerant of most soils and situations, including dry chalk soils and heavy shade. They are very useful for hedges and the columnar forms for formal planting.

baccata L. "Common Yew"; "English Yew". One of our three native conifers, usually found in the wild on chalk formations. A small to medium-sized tree or large shrub with dark, almost black-green leaves, yellowish-green beneath and 2 to 3cm. long. Fruits with a red aril. A well-known tree, a common and familiar resident of churchyards where venerable specimens of great age may occasionally be found. The low prostrate forms make wonderful ground-cover plants, even in dense shade. The yew has given rise to numerous forms varying in habit and colour. Given good drainage the yew will grow on almost pure chalk or in very acid soils. Europe; N. Persia; Algeria. A.G.M. 1969.

'Adpressa'. A large shrub or small tree, a female clone of dense, spreading habit, with ascending branches and short crowded branchlets clothed with small, dark, pectinately-arranged, green leaves, 5 to 10mm. long. C. 1828.

'Adpressa Aurea'. See under *'Adpressa Variegata'*.

'Adpressa Erecta' (*'Adpressa Stricta'*). A taller female form with more ascending branches, forming a broad shrub with dark green leaves up to 1·5cm. long. C. 1866. F.C.C. 1886.

'Adpressa Variegata'. A male form of *'Adpressa'*. The unfolding leaves are old gold, passing to yellow, a colour which is confined to the margin as the leaves age. This is the form usually grown wrongly under the name *'Adpressa Aurea'*. C. 1866. F.C.C. 1889.

'Amersfoort'. A curious, small to medium-sized shrub of open habit. The stiffly ascending branches are clothed with numerous, small, radially-arranged, oblong-ovate leaves, 5 to 7mm. long. A botanical conundrum quite un-yew-like in appearance, and recalling *Olearia nummulariifolia*. The mother plant, of French origin, is growing at the Psychiatric Hospital of Amersfoort, Holland.

'Argentea'. See *'Variegata'*.

'Argentea Minor' (*'Dwarf White'*). A delightful dwarf, slow-growing, female shrub with drooping branchlets. The leaves have a narrow, white margin.

'Aurea'. "Golden Yew". A large shrub of compact habit, with golden-yellow leaves turning green by the second year. This name is usually used to cover several golden-foliaged forms, the most popular of which is *'Elegantissima'*. C. 1855.

'Cavendishii'. A low-growing, female form less than 1m. high, with wide-spreading branches drooping at the tips. In time forming a semi-prostrate mound several metres across. An excellent ground cover, even for heavy shade. C. 1932.

'Cheshuntensis'. An erect-growing, female clone, in habit intermediate between the Common and Irish Yews. It was raised as a seedling of the latter in Messrs. Paul's Nursery at Cheshunt about 1857.

'Decora'. A dwarf, slow-growing shrub forming a low, flat-topped hummock with arching branches and dark, polished-green, upward-curving leaves which are 3cm. long and 3 to 4mm. broad.

'Dovastoniana'. "Westfelton Yew". A very distinct, wide-spreading, small, elegant tree with tiers of long, horizontal branches and long, weeping branchlets. Leaves blackish-green. It is normally female. The original tree, planted in 1777, is at Westfelton, Shropshire. Plants which have lost their leader when young form wide-spreading, shallowly vase-shaped bushes several metres across. A.G.M. 1969.

'Dovastonii Aurea'. Similar to *'Dovastoniana'* in habit, but leaves margined yellow. A male clone raised in France. C. 1891. A.G.M. 1969.

'Elegantissima'. The most popular of the golden yews. A dense growing, large bush with ascending branches and yellow young leaves, which later pass to straw-yellow when the colour is confined to the margin. Female. C. 1852. A.G.M. 1969.

'Erecta'. "Fulham Yew". An erect-branched, broadly-columnar, open-topped, female bush, eventually of large size. Raised from seed of the "Irish Yew". C. 1838.

TAXUS—*continued*

baccata 'Ericoides'. A medium-sized to large, slow-growing bush of erect habit; leaves narrow and spreading. C. 1855.

'Fastigiata'. "Irish Yew". A female clone of erect habit, forming a dense, compact, broad column of closely-packed branches. As a young specimen it is narrowly columnar. Leaves black-green, radially arranged. A very popular Yew and a familiar resident of churchyards. Originally found as two plants on the moors in County Fermanagh in 1780: There is also a male form of slightly broader habit. F.C.C. 1863. A.G.M. 1969.

'Fastigiata Aureomarginata'. "Golden Irish Yew". A male form, similar in appearance to '*Fastigiata*', but leaves with yellow margin. C. 1880.

'Fructoluteo'. See '*Lutea*'.

'Glauca' ('*Nigra*'). "Blue John". A male form of loose yet upright habit with leaves a characteristic dark bluish-green almost black-green above, paler below. One of the most easily recognised forms particularly in early spring when the male strobili crowd the sombre foliage. C. 1855.

'Lutea' ('*Fructoluteo*') ('*Xanthocarpa*'). "Yellow-berried Yew". An unusual and attractive form, the fruits with yellow arils are often abundant and then quite spectacular. C. about 1817. A.M. 1929. A.G.M. 1969.

'Nana'. A dwarf, slow-growing bush of compact habit. C. 1855.

'Nigra'. See '*Glauca*'.

'Nutans'. A small, flat-topped bush. Leaves irregular in shape often small and scale-like. A specimen in our collection has attained 1m. × ·8m. after thirty years. C. 1910.

'Pygmaea'. An extremely slow-growing, dwarf shrub of dense conical or ovoid habit, bearing small, polished, black-green, radially arranged leaves. C. 1910.

'Repandans'. A low-growing, often semi-prostrate, female bush, with long spreading branches, drooping at the tips. A splendid ground-cover plant doing well in sun or dense shade. C. 1887. A.G.M. 1969.

'Repens Aurea'. A low, spreading, female bush with leaves margined with yellow when young, turning to cream later. Recalls a low form of '*Dovastonii Aurea*'. Like all golden-foliaged plants it loses its colour when in deep shade.

'Semperaurea'. A slow-growing, male bush of medium size with ascending branches and short, crowded branchlets well clothed with foliage. The unfolding leaves are old gold, passing with age to rusty yellow, a colour which they retain throughout the year. C. 1908. A.G.M. 1969. A.M. 1977.

'Standishii' ('*Fastigiata Standishii*'). A slow-growing, female form of '*Fastigiata Aurea*'. It is of dense, columnar habit with erect, tightly packed branches and radially arranged, golden-yellow leaves. The best of its colour and habit, but slow in growth. C. 1908. A.G.M. 1969.

'Variegata' ('*Argentea*'). A female form with obtusely ascending branches, in habit simulating the "Pfitzer Juniper". The unfolding leaves are creamy-yellow, maturing to a slender marginal band of greyish-white. C. 1770.

'Washingtonii'. A vigorous, female form with ascending branches forming a broad, medium-sized bush. Young leaves rich yellow, ageing to yellowish-green, becoming bronzed during winter. C. 1874.

'Xanthocarpa'. See '*Lutea*'.

canadensis MARSH. "Canadian Yew". A small, erect-growing, monoecious shrub up to 1·8m. high, with crowded branches and irregularly-arranged, often two-ranked leaves, 1 to 2cm. long. Fruits with a red aril. In the wild the main shoots are loose, often becoming semi-prostrate and taking root, in time forming extensive carpets. Canada: N.E. United States. I. 1800.

celebica LI (*chinensis*). "Chinese Yew". A splendid large shrub or small tree of loose, spreading habit easily confused with *Torreya grandis*. Leaves two-ranked, 1 to 3cm. long, of a characteristic yellowish-green or pale green colour. Fruits with a red aril. S.E. Asia.

chinensis. See *T. celebica*.

cuspidata SIEB. & ZUCC. "Japanese Yew". In its native habitats a small to medium-sized tree, but usually shrubby in cultivation. Leaves 1 to 2·5cm. long, dark green above, yellowish-green beneath, ascending from the branchlets. Fruits with a red aril. In colder climes it proves hardier than our native yew. Japan. Introduced by Robert Fortune in 1855.

'Aurescens'. A low-growing, compact form with deep yellow young leaves changing to green the second year. C. 1920.

TAXUS—*continued*

cuspidata 'Densa'. A dwarf, compact, female shrub forming a mound of crowded, erect stems. C. 1917.

'Minima'. An extremely slow-growing, dwarf bush of irregular habit. C. 1932.

'Nana'. A dense, small, male bush with ascending branches, nodding at the tips. Leaves radially arranged. Old specimens in cultivation have attained 1·2 to 1·5m. high by 3m. or more across. C. 1861.

floridana CHAPMAN. "Florida Yew". Medium-sized to large shrub with crowded, ascending branches and dark green, sickle-shaped leaves, 2 to 2·5cm. long. Fruits with a red aril. Rare in cultivation. Florida.

× **hunnewelliana** REHD. (*canadensis* × *cuspidata*). A vigorous, large, very wide-spreading shrub with obtusely-ascending branches and an open centre. It resembles one of the wide-spreading forms of *T.* × *media* from which it differs in its longer, narrower, deep green leaves. A specimen in our arboretum planted in 1954 is now 3m. high and 6m. across. Raised in the Hunnewell Pinetum, Wellesley, Massachusetts. C. 1900.

× **media** REHD. (*baccata* × *cuspidata*). A vigorous, medium-sized to large shrub of spreading habit, more or less intermediate between the parents. Leaves usually two ranked. Raised by T. D. Hatfield at the Hunnewell Pinetum, Wellesley, Massachusetts about 1900. There are several named clones in cultivation. Some of the wide-spreading clones develop a peculiar twisting character in the branches, shoots and older leaves.

'Brownii'. A broadly columnar male form with semi-erect branches. Excellent as a hedge. C. 1950.

'Hatfieldii'. A dense, compact, male form with sharply ascending branches. An excellent subject for hedging. C. 1923.

'Hicksii'. A broadly columnar, female bush. It makes an excellent hedge. C. 1900.

'Nidiformis'. A dense, broad, open-centred, male bush with obtusely ascending branches. C. 1953.

'Sargentii'. An erect-growing, female form of dense habit, excellent for hedging.

'Thayerae'. A broad, vigorous, male shrub with widely-ascending branches and open centre. In habit somewhat like *T.* × *hunnewelliana* but with shorter, broader leaves and probably not so tall. C. 1930.

†*TETRACLINIS—Cupressaceae—A monotypic genus related to *Callitris*, only suitable for the conservatory or outside in the mildest localities. Male and female strobili borne on the same plant.

articulata MAST. A rare evergreen species attaining tree-size in its native environs, but generally shrubby in the British Isles. Branches dense and ascending, terminating in flat, jointed, spray-like branchlets clothed with scale-like leaves which are decurrent at the base and arranged in fours. Cones solitary, rounded, 8 to 12mm. across, composed of four, thick, woody, glaucous scales. Both the wood and resin are of commercial importance. Native to Algeria; Morocco; Mogador; Malta and S.E. Spain, in which countries it grows in dry places and withstands considerable periods of drought.

***THUJA** (*THUYA*) (including *BIOTA*)—**Cupressaceae**—"Arbor-vitae". A small genus of hardy, evergreen trees and shrubs differing from the superficially similar *Chamaecyparis* in the usually pleasantly aromatic foliage and cones with overlapping scales. Most form trees of attractive conical habit with small, scale-like, overlapping leaves arranged in four-ranks and borne in often large, flattened, fan-like sprays. Male and female strobili are borne on the same tree in early spring, the males reddish. Cones small, oblong or subglobose, and composed of three to ten pairs of woody, overlapping scales which are attached at their base, maturing the first year. The Thujas will thrive in almost any soil, providing it is well-drained.

Two species (*T. occidentalis* and *T. plicata*) are invaluable for hedges and screens, whilst a good number of cultivars are dwarf or slow-growing and thus suitable for the rock garden. There are several excellent coloured forms though the range is less than in *Chamaecyparis*.

japonica. See *T. standishii.*

koraiensis NAKAI. "Korean Arbor-vitae". A striking species, usually densely shrubby in habit, but occasionally a small tree with decurved branches and dark brown, peeling bark. Foliage borne in large, flattened, frond-like sprays, green or sea-green above, conspicuously white beneath, pungently aromatic when crushed. Korea. Introduced by Ernest Wilson in 1917.

THUJA—*continued*

lobbii. See *T. plicata.*

occidentalis L. "American Arbor-vitae". An extremely hardy, medium-sized tree of columnar habit with reddish-brown, peeling bark. Branches horizontally spreading, upcurved at the tips. Leaves with conspicuous resin glands, dark green above, pale green beneath, borne in numerous, much-divided, flattened sprays, usually bronze coloured during winter. A commonly planted species differing from the closely related *T. plicata* in the pale green undersurface to the leaves and cones with only four, fertile scales. Like that species the foliage possesses a pleasant fruity odour when crushed. An important timber tree in the U.S.A. As a hedging subject it is less good than *T. plicata* but in colder climes than in Britain it succeeds where *T. plicata* is killed by extreme cold. Eastern N. America. I. about 1534. Innumerable forms have arisen in cultivation.

'Aurea' (*'Mastersii Aurea'*). A broadly conical, medium-sized to large bush with golden-yellow leaves. C. 1857.

'Aureospicata'. An erect-growing form with the young shoots becoming yellow, intensified in winter to a rich burnished old gold.

'Beaufort'. An open, slender-branched, large shrub or small tree with leaves variegated white. C. 1963.

'Bodmeri'. Medium-sized bush of open, conical habit. Branches thick and stout; foliage dark green, in large, monstrous sprays. C. 1877.

'Buchananii'. Small tree of narrow, conical habit, with ascending branches and long branchlets with sparse foliage. C. 1887.

'Caespitosa'. A dwarf, slow-growing bush forming a rounded hummock, wider than high. Foliage irregular and congested. Excellent for the rock garden. C. 1923.

'Cristata'. A slow-growing, dwarf bush with short, flattened, crest-like branchlets, recalling those of the "Fern-Spray Cypress". C. 1867.

'Danica'. A dwarf bush of dense, compact, globular habit. Foliage vertically held in erect, flattened sprays.

'Ellwangerana Aurea'. See under *'Rheingold'*.

'Ericoides'. A small, dense, rounded or cone-shaped bush with soft, loose branchlets and dull green, juvenile foliage which becomes donkey-brown in winter. Very liable to damage by snow. C. 1867.

'Fastigiata' (*'Columnaris'*) (*'Pyramidalis'*) (*'Stricta'*). A narrowly conical or columnar form of dense, compact growth. An excellent small, formal tree. C. 1865.

'Filiformis'. A slow-growing, fairly compact bush with drooping "whipcord" branchlets. In thirty years reaching 2m. × 1·2m. C. 1901.

'Globosa'. A compact, globular bush, slowly reaching about 1·3m. high by 2m wide. C. 1875. The clones *'Globularis'* and *'Tom Thumb'* are almost, if not identical.

'Hetz' Midget'. An extremely slow-growing, dwarf bush of globular habit. Perhaps the smallest form of all. C. 1928.

'Holmstrupii' (*'Holmstrupensis'*). A slow-growing, medium-sized to large, narrowly conical bush of dense, compact habit with rich green foliage throughout the year in vertically arranged sprays. C. 1951.

'Hoveyi' (*'Froebelii'*) (*'Spihlmannii'*). A slow-growing bush of globular or ovoid habit, eventually reaching a height of 3m. The yellowish-green foliage is arranged in vertically held sprays. C. 1868.

'Indomitable'. A large shrub or small tree with spreading branches and dark green foliage, rich reddish-bronze in winter. C. 1960.

'Little Gem'. Dwarf, globular bush of dense, slightly flat-topped habit; foliage deep green, in crowded crimpled sprays. The clone *'Recurva Nana'* is very similar. C. 1891.

'Malonyana'. A striking small to medium-sized tree of narrow, columnar habit, leaves a uniform rich green, borne in short, dense, crowded sprays. This architectural tree forms a perfect avenue in the late Count Ambroze's garden, Arboretum Mlynany, Czechoslovakia.

'Mastersii' (*'Plicata'*). A small, conical tree with large, flat sprays of foliage, arranged in a vertical plane and tipped old gold in the spring. C. 1847.

THUJA—*continued*

occidentalis 'Ohlendorffii' (*'Spaethii'*). One of the most distinct and curious of dwarf or semi-dwarf conifers, carrying dense clusters of soft juvenile foliage, and long, erect, slender, whipcord-like branches, clothed with adult foliage. C. 1887.

'Pendula'. "Weeping American Arbor-vitae". Small tree with openly ascending branches and pendulous branchlets. C. 1857.

'Pygmaea' (*'Plicata Pygmaea'*) (*'Mastersii Pygmaea'*). A dwarf bush of dense but irregular growth, with crowded sprays of sea-green foliage.

'Recurva Nana'. A low-growing, flat-topped dome, the branchlets noticeably recurved at the tips. *'Little Gem'* is very similar.

'Rheingold'. A slow-growing bush of ovoid or conical habit eventually making a large shrub. Foliage mainly adult, of a rich deep old gold, shaded amber. A very popular plant, perhaps the richest piece of radiant old gold in the garden in the dead of winter. It is an excellent companion to heathers and heaths and contrasts most effectively with darker conifers. C. before 1902. A.M. 1902 (as *T. occidentalis 'Ellwangerana Pygmaea Aurea'*). A.G.M. 1969.

The name *'Rheingold'* is sometimes retained for small plants raised from cuttings of juvenile shoots. In the course of time these revert to the plant here described and appear inseparable from the cultivar *'Ellwangerana Aurea'*.

'Spiralis'. A narrowly columnar small tree of densely-branched habit with, short, pinnately-arranged sprays of dark green foliage. A splendid formal tree. C. 1923.

'Vervaeneana'. A large bush or small tree of dense, conical habit, with crowded sprays of light green and yellow foliage, becoming bronzed in winter. C. 1862.

'Wareana' (*'Robusta'*). A compact, slow-growing, small bush of conical habit with short, thickened sprays of green foliage. Raised in the nursery of Messrs. Weare, at Coventry in about 1827.

'Wareana Lutescens' (*'Lutescens'*). Similar to *'Wareana'*, but more compact and with pale yellow foliage. C. 1884.

'Wintergreen' (*'Lombarts' Wintergreen'*). Small to medium-sized tree of columnar habit, foliage green throughout the year.

'Woodwardii'. A dense, ovoid bush, taller than broad, eventually reaching 1m. in height, with typical *T. occidentalis* foliage remaining green in winter.

orientalis L. (*Biota orientalis*). "Chinese Arbor-vitae". A large shrub or small tree of dense, compact, conical or columnar habit when young. Branches and branchlets erect, the leaves very small and green, borne in flattened, frond-like, vertical sprays. This species is distinct in its formal habit, its foliage less aromatic than others and its cone scales which have conspicuous recurved hooked cups. There are several forms suitable for the rock garden. N. and W. China. I. about 1690.

'Athrotaxoides'. An extremely slow-growing, small shrub with noticeably thick branches and branchlets, lacking the spray-like foliage typical of the species. Originated in the Jardin des Plantes, Paris, in 1867.

'Aurea Nana'. A dwarf, globular bush of dense habit, with crowded, vertically arranged sprays of light, yellow-green foliage. C. 1804. A.G.M. 1969.

'Compacta'. See *'Sieboldii'*.

'Conspicua'. A medium-sized to large bush of dense, compact, conical habit. The golden yellow foliage is retained longer than in most other forms of similar colour. C. 1804.

'Decussata'. See *'Juniperoides'*.

'Elegantissima'. A medium-sized to large bush of dense columnar habit. Foliage golden-yellow, tinged old-gold, becoming green in winter. C. 1858. A.G.M. 1973.

'Filiformis Erecta'. An unusual form of ovoid habit forming a large bush or small tree, with erect, whip-like stems, clothed with yellowish green leaves, bronzed in winter. C. 1868.

'Hillieri'. A small to medium-sized bush of dense, compact, ovoid habit. Leaves soft yellow-green, becoming green in winter. Raised in our nurseries prior to 1924.

'Juniperoides' (*'Decussata'*). A dwarf, rounded bush with soft, juvenile foliage which is greyish-green in summer turning a rich, purplish-grey in winter. It is a most attractive form requiring shelter from cold winds. C. 1850. A.M. 1973.

'Meldensis'. A dwarf bush of dense, globular habit. The semi-juvenile foliage is sea-green in summer turning a delightful plum-purple in winter. Raised in 1852.

THUJA—*continued*

orientalis 'Minima Glauca'. A beautiful, dwarf bush of dense, globular habit. Foliage semi-juvenile, sea-green in summer, turning a warm yellow-brown in winter. C. 1891.

'Rosedalis' (*'Rosedalis Compacta'*). A dense, ovoid bush with soft juvenile foliage which, in early spring, is a bright canary yellow, changing by midsummer to sea-green, and in winter glaucous plum-purple. In fifteen years it will attain ·8m. in height. Its soft-to-the-touch foliage and its spring colour distinguish it from the similar *'Meldensis'*. C. 1923.

'Semperaurea'. A dense, rounded bush of medium size with foliage yellow throughout summer, becoming bronzed later. C. 1870. F.C.C. 1870.

'Sieboldii' (*'Nana'*) (*'Compacta'*). A small, rounded bush of dense, compact habit. Foliage golden yellow at first, turning to mid-green later, borne in delicate lace-like, vertical sprays. C. 1859.

plicata D. DON (*lobbii*) (*gigantea*). "Western Red Cedar". A large, fast-growing, ornamental tree with light brown or cinnamon-red, shredding bark and spreading branches. Leaves of a bright glossy green above, faintly glaucous beneath, carried in large, flattened, drooping sprays and emitting a pleasant, fruity odour when crushed. An important timber tree in North America. It makes a splendid hedge or screen, withstanding clipping well; it is also tolerant of shade and shallow chalk soils. Western N. America. Introduced by William Lobb in 1853. The clone we grow is sometimes listed under the name *'Atrovirens'*.

When planting a formal or trimmed hedge of this or almost any other subject, light trimming or pruning, or maybe only pinching of terminal growths should commence as soon as the plants are sufficiently established to make normal growth, and under favourable conditions this means the second growing season. The best time for this cutting is about the first half of August when there is still sufficient time for late new growth to be made and ripened before frost. Such control encourages density of growth which may not be achieved by decapitating when the plants have attained the desired height. If possible always allow a very small annual increment even when the plants have reached the size wanted.

'Aureovariegata'. See *'Zebrina'*.

'Aurea'. An outstanding form with foliage of a rich, old gold. F.C.C. 1897.

'Cuprea'. A dense, very slow-growing, conical bush, the growths tipped in various shades of deep cream to old gold. A splendid plant for the rock garden. Raised by Messrs. Rogers and Sons of Southampton about 1930.

'Fastigiata' (*'Stricta'*). A tall-growing, narrowly columnar form with densely arranged, slender, ascending branches. Excellent as a single specimen tree or for hedging when only the minimum of clipping is necessary. C. 1867.

'Gracilis'. A large bush of conical habit with finely-divided sprays of green foliage. C. 1923.

'Gracilis Aurea'. Medium-sized, slow-growing bush with slender branchlets and yellow-tipped foliage. A sport of *'Gracilis'*. C. 1949.

'Hillieri' (*'Nana'*). A slow-growing, dense, compact, rounded bush of medium size. The green foliage is arranged in curious moss-like clusters on branchlets which are thick and stiff, with irregular crowded growths. Our original plant, which occurred in our Shroner Wood Nursery before 1900, had attained 2·4×2·1m. when it was sold about 1925.

'Rogersii' (*'Aurea Rogersii'*). A slow-growing, dwarf, compact bush of conical habit, with densely crowded gold and bronze-coloured foliage. It will attain about 1·2×1m. in thirty years. Raised by Messrs. Rogers of Southampton about 1928.

'Semperaurescens'. An extremely vigorous, large tree worthy of inclusion in any pinetum or as a tall screen where colour variation is desired. Young shoots and leaves tinged golden-yellow, becoming bronze-yellow by winter. C. 1923.

'Stoneham Gold'. A slow-growing, small bush of dense, conical habit. Foliage bright gold, tipped coppery-bronze. A superb plant for the large rock garden. C. 1948.

'Zebrina' (*'Aureovariegata'*). A conical tree, the sprays of green foliage banded with creamy-yellow. A strong-growing, large tree, certainly one of the best variegated conifers, the variegations being so crowded as to give a yellow effect to the whole tree. C. 1868. F.C.C. 1869.

THUJA—*continued*

standishii CARR. (*japonica*). "Japanese Arbor-vitae". A small to medium-sized tree of conical habit with loosely spreading or upcurved branches and drooping branchlets. Leaves yellowish-green above, slightly glaucous beneath, carried in large, gracefully drooping sprays. An attractive species, easily recognised by its characteristic yellowish-green appearance and loose habit. The foliage when crushed smells of Lemon Verbena. Central Japan. Introduced by Robert Fortune to the Standish Nurseries, Bagshot in 1860.

***THUJOPSIS—Cupressaceae**—A monotypic genus related to *Thuja*, differing in its broader, flatter branchlets and larger leaves. It thrives in all types of well-drained soil including shallow chalk soils. Male and female strobili are borne on the same tree.

dolabrata SIEB. & ZUCC. (*Thuja dolabrata*). A distinctive small to medium-sized tree or large shrub of dense, broadly conical habit. Branchlets flattened, bearing sprays of large, four-ranked, scale-like leaves, the outer ones boat-shaped, shining dark green above, marked with conspicuous silver-white bands of stomata beneath. Cones ovoid, 12 to 20mm. long. An attractive conifer easily recognised by its large, flattened sprays of silver-backed leaves. Japan. I. 1853. F.C.C. 1864.

'Aurea'. Leaves suffused golden yellow. A splendid yellow conifer which deserves to be much more frequently planted. C. 1866.

hondai MAKINO. The northern form of the species, attaining 30m. in its native habitat. It tends to be more compact in habit, with smaller, blunter leaves.

'Nana' (*laetevirens*). A dwarf, compact, spreading, flat-topped bush, smaller than the type in all its parts. I. 1861.

'Variegata'. A strong-growing clone with scattered patches of creamy-white foliage. Not very stable. I. 1859.

THUYA. See *THUJA*.

***TORREYA—Taxaceae**—A small genus of evergreen trees and shrubs allied to *Cephalotaxus*. Leaves linear, rigid and spine-tipped, marked with two glaucous bands beneath, spirally arranged on leading shoots, twisted to appear in two ranks on the lateral shoots. Male and female strobili are sometimes borne on the same tree in cultivation, although they are dioecious in the wild. Fruits plum-like, fleshy, containing a single seed. They are excellent trees for chalk soils and are good shade-bearers.

californica TORR. (*myristica*). "Californian Nutmeg". A small to medium-sized, broadly conical tree, well furnished to ground level, like a majestic "Yew". Leaves rigid, 3 to 7·5cm. long, shining dark green above, spine-tipped. Fruits ovoid or obovoid, 3 to 4cm. long, green, streaked with purple when ripe. Native of California. Discovered and introduced by William Lobb in 1851.

'Spreadeagle'. A low-growing form with long, spreading branches. Originated in our Crook Hill Nursery in 1970.

grandis FORTUNE. A rare small tree or large shrub in cultivation, the least "grand" in the genus. Leaves spine-tipped, 2 to 2·5cm. long, yellowish-green above. Fruits broad ellipsoid, 2·5 to 3cm. long, brownish when ripe. A species similar to *T. nucifera*, differing in its paler green, slightly smaller leaves which lack the familiar aromatic scent of the Japanese species and may be confused with those of the "Chinese Yew" (*Taxus celebica*). China. Introduced by Robert Fortune in 1855.

nucifera SIEB. & ZUCC. Although a large tree in its native habitat, in the British Isles it is usually seen as a large shrub or occasionally a small, slender, thinly-foliaged tree. Leaves smaller than those of *T. californica*, 2 to 3cm. long, sickle shaped and spine-tipped and rather more consistently in a flat plane, pungent when crushed. Fruits oblong to obovate, 2 to 2·5cm. long, green, clouded purple when ripe. Japan. I. 1764.

taxifolia ARNOTT. A small tree, rare in cultivation. It most resembles *T. californica* but has smaller leaves, 2 to 4cm. long. Fruits obovoid, 2·5 to 4cm. long. N.W. Florida. I. 1840.

***TSUGA—Pinaceae**—A small genus of extremely elegant, evergreen trees of broadly conical habit with spreading branches and gently drooping or arching branchlets. The leaves are short and linear, arranged on the branchlets so as to appear two-ranked, except in *T. mertensiana*. Winter buds small. Male and female strobili are borne on the same tree. The cones are small and pendulous, ripening during the first year, but remaining until the second year. The Tsugas are good shade-bearers and thrive best in a moist, but well-drained, loamy soil. *T. canadensis* may be grown in moderately deep soils over chalk.

albertiana. See *T. heterophylla*.

brunoniana. See *T. dumosa*.

canadensis CARR. "Eastern Hemlock". A broad tree which may usually be distinguished by its trunk, being forked near the base. The best species for limey soil. A large tree often with several main stems from near the base. Young shoots greyish-brown, densely pubescent. Leaves 5 to 15mm. long, marked with two whitish bands beneath. Cones ovoid, slender stalked, 1·5 to 2·5cm. long. It has given rise to innumerable cultivars, a selection of which are here listed, many of them suitable for the rock garden and stone troughs. It differs from the closely related *T. heterophylla* in its usually forked trunk and its leaves which are more tapered to the apex and not so noticeably banded beneath. Another characteristic is the line of leaves lying undersides uppermost, along the uppersides of the branchlets. Eastern N. America. I. 1736.

'Albospica'. A slower-growing, more compact form in which the growing tips of the shoots are creamy white. Particularly effective during spring and summer. C. 1884.

'Armistice'. A slow-growing, dwarf form developing into a flat-topped mound.

'Aurea'. A slow-growing, dwarf form of compact, conical habit. Leaves rather broad and crowded, golden yellow when unfolding, becoming yellowish-green later. C. 1866.

'Bennett' (*'Bennett's Minima'*). A slow-growing, dwarf shrub of spreading habit and dense, crowded growth. C. 1920.

'Cinnamomea'. Dwarf, slow-growing bush of dense, congested, globular habit. Young stems densely covered with a cinnamon pubescence. C. 1929.

'Cole' (*'Cole's Prostrate'*). A remarkable prostrate plant with long branches flattened along the ground, in time forming extensive carpets. Similar in habit to *'Prostrata'*.

'Compacta'. Dwarf bush with short, crowded branchlets. C. 1868.

'Curly'. A curious dwarf form in which the young leaves are crowded and curled around the shoots.

'Dwarf Whitetip'. A small, broadly conical bush, the young shoots creamy white, changing to green in late summer. C. 1939.

'Fantana'. A small bush as broad as high, with wide-spreading branches. C. 1913.

'Fremdii'. A small, slow-growing, eventually broadly conical, small tree of compact, bushy habit, with crowded branchlets and leaves. C. 1887.

'Globosa'. Dwarf, globose bush with pendulous tips to the branchlets. C. 1891.

'Greenwood Lake'. Slow-growing, medium-sized to large bush with crowded branchlets and no definite leader. C. 1939.

'Horsford' (*'Horsford's Dwarf'*). A dwarf, globular bush with congested branchlets and small, crowded leaves.

'Hussii'. Medium-sized to large bush of slow growth. Habit dense and irregular with no definite leader. C. 1900.

'Jervis'. An extremely slow-growing, dwarf bush of compact but irregular habit, with crowded, congested growths. A gem for the rock garden.

'Macrophylla'. Large, bushy shrub or small, densely-branched tree with leaves larger than in the type. Inclined to revert to typical growth. C. 1891.

'Many Cones'. A slow-growing bush of open habit with gracefully arching branches, free coning.

'Microphylla' (*'Parvifolia'*). A distinct and interesting large bush or small tree with tiny heath-like leaves. C. 1864.

'Minima'. A slow-growing, wide-spreading, small bush with arching and drooping branches. C. 1891.

TSUGA—*continued*

canadensis 'Minuta'. An extremely slow-growing, miniature bun of tightly congested growth, with small, crowded leaves. I. 1927.

'Nana'. A small, slow-growing bush of graceful, spreading habit. Suitable for the large rock garden. C. 1855.

'Nana Gracilis'. Dwarf, mound-forming bush of graceful habit with slender, arching stems.

'Pendula'. A most attractive form developing into a low mound of overlapping, drooping branches. A superb plant for a prominent position on a large rock garden or isolated on a lawn. In forty years it has here reached about 2m. by 3·7m. I. before 1876. A.G.M. 1973.

'Prostrata'. A rather slow-growing, prostrate form with stems which press themselves to the ground and lie in all directions, eventually forming large mats. C. 1933.

'Pygmaea'. A dwarf, irregular globe, with short, congested growths.

'Rugg's Washington Dwarf'. A dwarf, globular or mound-forming bush with dense, congested growth.

'Stranger'. Small, slow-growing tree of compact habit; leaves rather broad and thick. C. 1939.

'Taxifolia'. Dwarf to medium-sized, irregular bush of compact habit, the leaves crowded at the ends of each year's growth, longer than in the type. C. 1938.

'Warner's Globe' (*'Warner Globosa'*). A globular bush with shorter, broader leaves than those of the type.

‡caroliniana ENGELM. "Carolina Hemlock". Although a handsome, large, conical tree in its native habitats, it is rarely more than a compact, small tree or large shrub in this country. Young shoots grey, yellow-brown or red-brown and shining, with short pubescence scattered along the grooves. Leaves 1 to 1·2cm. long, soft yellowish-green, marked with two white bands beneath. Cones ovoid or oblong, 2 to 3·5cm. long. S.E. United States. I. 1881.

chinensis PRITZ. Usually a small tree in cultivation. Young shoots yellowish. Leaves 1 to 2·5cm. long, comparatively broad, blunt or shallowly notched at apex, marked with two inconspicuous, greyish-green bands beneath. Cones ovoid, 2 to 2·5cm. long. A distinct hardy species not subject to damage by spring frost and to a considerable degree lime tolerant. It most resembles *T. heterophylla*. C. and W. China. I. 1900.

‡diversifolia MAST. "Northern Japanese Hemlock". In cultivation a small horizontally-branched tree. Young shoots reddish-brown, pubescent. Leaves glistening deep green, 5 to 15mm. long, notched at the apex, marked with two chalk-white bands beneath, oblong, very regular. Cones ovoid, 2cm. long. An attractive species easily distinguished by its combination of hairy shoots and leaves with entire margins. Japan. Introduced by J. G. Veitch in 1861.

†dumosa EICH. (*brunoniana*). "Himalayan Hemlock". A distinct tender species only likely to be confused with *T. yunnanensis*, scarcely more than shrubby in most districts, but has attained about 21m. in Cornwall. Branches gracefully drooping. Young shoots light brown, pubescent. Leaves 2·5 to 3cm. long, tapering to an acute, recurved apex, marked with two vivid, silvery-white bands beneath. Cones ovoid, sessile, 2 to 2·5cm. long. A beautiful species when growing well, but very subject to injury by spring frosts. It is moderately lime-tolerant. Native of the Himalaya where it attains heights of over 30m. in sheltered valleys. First introduced by Captain Webb in 1838. A.M. 1931.

†formosana HAYATA. "Formosan Hemlock". A rare species in cultivation allied to *T. sieboldii*, differing in its shorter leaves and smaller cones. It had appeared hardy here for more than twenty years until being badly mauled by the severe winter of 1962-63. Formosa. I. about 1934.

forrestii DOWNIE. The tree received under this name from Borde Hill is quite different from *T. chinensis*, a species to which it is referred by some botanists. In its longer, narrower leaves, white beneath, it approaches *T. dumosa*, but is decidedly hardier.

TSUGA—*continued*

‡**heterophylla** SARG. (*albertiana*). "Western Hemlock". A large, fast-growing tree with gracefully spreading branches. Young shoots greyish, pubescent. Leaves narrowly oblong, 5 to 20mm. long, marked with two bright white bands beneath. Cones oblong-ovoid, sessile, 2 to 2·5cm. long. A beautiful conifer, particularly when grown as a single specimen, developing into an elegant tree with a spire-like crown. It is an important timber tree in North America and is becoming extensively planted in the British Isles. It is not suitable for chalk soils but is tolerant of shade. It makes a better specimen tree than the allied *T. canadensis*, but unlike that species it has given rise to few cultivars. Western N. America. First discovered by David Douglas in 1826, it was introduced by John Jeffrey in 1851. A.G.M. 1969.

'Conica'. A medium-sized bush of dense, conical or ovoid habit, the branches ascending, drooping at the tips. Raised in the arboretum of van Gimborn, Doorne, Netherlands, about 1930.

'Greenmantle'. A graceful, tall, narrow tree with pendulous branches, which originated at Windsor Great Park.

'Laursen's Column'. A striking tree of loosely columnar habit, recalling *Podocarpus andinus* in general appearance. Leaves irregularly, almost radially-arranged on the ascending branches. A seedling found by Mr. Asger Laursen in 1968.

× **jeffreyi** HENRY (*heterophylla* × *mertensiana*). A comparatively slow-growing, eventually medium-sized to large tree, first raised at Edinburgh in 1851.

mertensiana CARR. (*pattoniana*). A beautiful species, a large tree of spire-like habit. Young shoots brownish-grey and densely pubescent. Leaves radially arranged, 1 to 2·5cm. long, pointing forwards, greyish-green or blue-grey on both surfaces. Cones sessile, oblong-cylindrical, 5 to 8cm. long. A distinct species easily recognised by its radially arranged leaves and comparatively large cones. Western N. America. Introduced by Jeffrey in 1851.

'Glauca'. A beautiful form with glaucous leaves. C. 1850.

pattoniana. See *T. mertensiana.*

sieboldii CARR. In the British Isles usually a small to medium-sized, dense tree or large bush, but reaching greater proportions in the wild. Young shoots light shining brown and glabrous. Leaves 1 to 2·5cm. long, notched at apex, glossy green above, marked with white bands beneath. Cones ovoid, 2·5 to 3cm. long. S. Japan. Introduced by Philip von Siebold in about 1850.

†**yunnanensis** MAST. A rare and rather tender, small tree with reddish-grey, densely pubescent young shoots. Leaves serrated, 1 to 2cm. long, marked with two broad, vividly chalk-white bands beneath. Cones ovoid, 1 to 2cm. long. Subject to injury by spring frosts. Yunnan and W. Szechwan (China). I. 1906. A.M. 1931.

"WELLINGTONIA". See *SEQUOIADENDRON giganteum.*

†***WIDDRINGTONIA**—**Cupressaceae**—A small genus of evergreen, cypress-like trees from Central and Southern Africa. Male and female strobili normally borne on the same tree. Leaves are spirally arranged and linear on young plants, scale-like on adult trees. The erect, woody cones remain for some time after shedding their seed. All are tender and require conservatory treatment except in the mildest areas. They are excellent conifers for hot, dry climes.

cupressoides ENDL. "Sapree Wood". A shrubby species of medium size. Branches ascending bearing soft, loose sprays of linear, glaucous-green leaves up to 12mm. long on juvenile plants. Those of adult plants are scale-like, triangular and closely pressed. Closely related to *W. juniperoides*, differing in its dwarfer habit and somewhat shorter, juvenile leaves. S. Africa.

juniperoides ENDL. "Clanwilliam Cedar". A small tree with elegant sprays of linear, glaucous-green juvenile leaves, 1 to 2cm. long, soft to the touch. Adult leaves scale-like closely pressed. S. Africa.

schwarzii MAST. "Willowmore Cedar". A small tree, but reaching 27m. in its native habitat. Leaves scale-like, glaucous, in closely-pressed pairs. An attractive tree. Young plants growing under glass differ strikingly from the three other species here described, in their conspicuously glaucous and scale-like leaves. S. Africa.

whytei RENDLE. "Mlanji Cedar". A small tree of conical habit when young, reaching 42m. with a spreading crown in its native habitat. Juvenile leaves linear, up to 2·5cm. long, sea-green and soft to the touch. Adult leaves scale-like and closely pressed. S. and E. Africa.

"YEW". See *TAXUS.*

BAMBOOS

(Gramineae)

Members of the Grass family, some of the most beautiful and elegant of all evergreens, are included under this heading.

The majority of the species described below are perfectly hardy, but they are not suitable for wind-swept sites and it is a mistake to imagine that, because they are moisture lovers, they will grow in permanent wet land. Many are excellent for growing in shade and all succeed in good soils over chalk.

When skilfully placed they are amongst the most ornamental features of any planting scheme, but it is as water-side plants that they show to their best advantage.

Though the transplanting period need not be restricted, early autumn and late spring are usually the most satisfactory times.

The flowering of Bamboos is still not completely understood. Most species will live a great many years before flowering, whilst some flower over a period of years. Contrary to what is often said, death does not always follow flowering.

In their native habitats many of the following species reach great heights, but the ultimate heights quoted below are approximate under average conditions of soil and aspect in the British Isles. The leaves of most species are long and narrow, rich green above, pale green or greyish green beneath.

It is important to avoid using near bamboos any selective weed killer designed to destroy Couch Grass or other grasses.

The species sometimes included under *CHIMONOBAMBUSA*, *PLEIOBLASTUS*, *PSEUDOSASA*, *SEMIARUNDINARIA*, *SINOARUNDINARIA*, *TETRAGONOCALAMUS* and *THAMNOCALAMUS* are included here.

We strongly recommend the publication "Bamboos" (by A. H. Lawson, 1968) as an excellent guide to the hardy species and their cultivation in the British Isles. We would also here like to express our appreciation to Dr. C. E. Hubbard for his kind suggestions regarding the nomenclature of bamboos in the following account.

† Indicates that these species are too tender for all but the mildest localities, but are ideal for the cool house or conservatory.

ARUNDINARIA. A large genus of Bamboos of tufted growth or with creeping underground stems. Many species form extensive patches or thickets and should only be planted where space permits. Differing from *Phyllostachys* and *Sasa* in the usually more numerous branches to each cluster and also from *Phyllostachys* in the rounded (terete) internodes, those of the latter being flattened or broadly grooved on alternate sides.

†amabilis MCCLURE. A little known species suitable for sheltered gardens in the mildest parts of the British Isles, where it will reach a height of 2·4 to 4·6m. Leaves variable in size from 10 to 35cm. long by 1 to 4cm. wide. China.

anceps MITF. A beautiful but rampant species, ideal for screens and hedges and the mature canes for use in the garden. The straight, erect, deep, glossy green canes reach a height of 3 to 3·5m. or more in mild localities. The arching tips bear masses of glossy green leaves, 10 to 15cm. long by 12mm. wide. Has flowered in various parts of the British Isles. N.W. Himalaya. I. 1865.

'Pitt White'. A vigorous form which, in the garden of Dr. Mutch at Pitt White, Lyme Regis, Dorset has reached a height of 9m., the canes bearing great plumes of small, narrow leaves, 7·5cm. long by 1·25cm. wide. It was originally misidentified as *A. niitakayamensis*, a dwarf species native to Formosa and the Philippines which is not in cultivation.

angustifolia DE LEHAIE (*Bambusa angustifolia*) (*Bambusa vilmorinii*). A rampant species, forming dense clumps or small thickets. Canes slender, dark purplish-green, reaching 2 to 2·5m. in height. Leaves bright rich green on both surfaces, 5 to 15cm. long by 6 to 8mm. wide. Japan. I. about 1895.

auricoma. See *A. viridistriata*.

chino MAK. (*simonii chino*) (*Pleioblastus chino*). An erect-growing bamboo with a creeping root-stock and dark green, purple-flushed canes, 1 to 2m. high. Leaves 10 to 25cm. long by 2 to 2·5cm. wide, borne in stiff, plume-like clusters. Possibly only a form of *A. simonii*. Has flowered several times in cultivation without any ill-effect. China. I. 1876.

ARUNDINARIA—*continued*

chrysantha MITF. (*Sasa chrysantha*). A fast-growing species forming dense thickets. Canes 1 to 2m. high, deep olive green. Leaves 7·5 to 18cm. long by 1·5 to 2·5cm. wide, bright green, striped yellow, not very constant. A vigorous bamboo, useful as a ground cover. Japan. I. 1892.

†**falconeri** DUTHIE (*nobilis*) (*Thamnocalamus falconeri*). A strong-growing, but tender species forming dense clumps up to 6m. or more in sheltered gardens, but normally 1·8 to 3m. Canes olive green, maturing to dull yellow in a sunny position, thin and pliable. Leaves 5 to 10cm. long by 12mm. wide, delicate and paper-thin. Distinguished from the closely related *A. falcata* by the purple-stained nodes of the canes. Flowered during 1875-77, 1903-07 and again profusely during 1966 and 1967 producing large, gracefully branched panicles of chocolate-red spikelets. All clumps subsequently died, but seed was produced and we are now building up fresh stocks. Formerly distributed wrongly as *A. pantlingii*. Himalaya. Introduced by Col. Madden in 1847.

fastuosa MAK. (*Semiarundinaria fastuosa*). An extremely hardy, vigorous bamboo of stiff, erect habit, forming tall, dense clumps of deep glossy green canes, 4·5 to 7·5m. high which are useful as stakes. Leaves 10 to 25cm. long by 1·5 to 2·5cm. wide. A handsome species of distinct habit which has been flowering sporadically in cultivation for several years. The young shoots in spring are edible. An excellent screen or tall hedge. Japan. I. 1892. A.M. 1953.

fortunei. See *A. variegata.*

'Gauntlettii' (*Sasa gauntlettii*). A small clump-forming bamboo with bright green, later dull purple canes up to ·8m. high. Leaves 7·5 to 18cm. long by 1 to 2cm. wide. An uncommon bamboo of obscure, possibly Japanese origin. It was named by Messrs. Gauntlett of Chiddingfold, Surrey, and is closely related to *A. pumila.*

gigantea CHAPM. (*macrosperma*). "Cane Reed". A strong-growing bamboo, forming dense thickets under suitable conditions, but rarely invasive. Canes 4·5 to 6m. or above in sheltered gardens, but usually 2·5 to 3m., dull greenish-yellow in colour. Leaves variable in size, 10 to 30cm. long by 2 to 4cm. wide. Native of the S.E. United States where it frequently forms dense thickets known as "Cane Brakes" on the swampy margins of rivers. It requires a sheltered position and is not suitable for cold areas.

graminea MAK.. (*Pleioblastus gramineus*). A fast-growing species forming dense clumps or patches. Canes up to 3m. tall, pale green, maturing to dull yellowish-green. Leaves very narrow in proportion to their length, 10 to 25cm. long by 8 to 12mm. wide. An excellent screening plant and one of the few hardy bamboos that prefers shade. It has flowered in several localities in recent years and good seed is usually produced. Ryukyus (Japan). I. 1877.

hindsii MUNRO (*Pleioblastus hindsii*). A strong-growing species forming dense thickets of erect, olive-green canes, 2·5 to 3·5m. high. Leaves variable in size, 15 to 23cm. long by 1·5 to 2·5cm. wide, of a rich sea-green, thickly clustered towards the summits of the canes. A useful bamboo which is equally happy in sun or dense shade and makes an excellent hedge or screen. China. Long cultivated in Japan. I. 1875.

†**hookerana** MUNRO. An attractive but tender bamboo suited for the conservatory, or outside only in the mildest localities. Canes up to 3·5 to 5·5m. in height, golden-yellow when mature, with deep striations. Leaves 7·5 to 30cm. long by 1·25 to 3·75cm. wide, glaucous when young. Sikkim; Bhutan. Plants flowered, seeded then died at Kew in 1899.

humilis MITF. (*Pleioblastus humilis*). A rampant species forming low patches or thickets. Canes slender, dark green, ·6 to 1·8m. high, but usually under 1·2m. Leaves 5 to 20cm. long by 1 to 2cm. wide, slightly downy beneath. An excellent ground cover beneath trees or for covering unsightly banks or waste places. A few canes have flowered at their tips in several localities in recent years without any apparent ill-effect. Japan. I. about 1892.

†**insignis** HORT. A tall species, with dark green 4·5 to 6m. canes wreathed in whorls of soft green leaves; a rather tender species. A bamboo of puzzling origin, said to have been introduced from the Himalaya.

†**intermedia** MUNRO. A vigorous but tender species with erect, green canes, 2·5 to 3·5m. high, forming a dense clump. Leaves 7·5 to 20cm. long by 1·5 to 2·5cm. wide. Only suitable for the mildest localities, but an attractive tub plant for the conservatory. E. Himalaya. Flowered and died at Kew in 1899.

ARUNDINARIA—*continued*

japonica SIEB. & ZUCC. (*Pseudosasa japonica*) (*Bambusa metake*). This extremely adaptable and very hardy species is the Bamboo most commonly cultivated in the British Isles. It forms dense thickets of olive-green canes, 3 to 4·5m., occasionally up to 6m. high, arching at the summit and bearing lush masses of dark glossy-green leaves 18 to 30cm. long by 2 to 5cm. wide. The greyish undersurface of the leaf has a characteristic greenish marginal strip. Branches borne singly from each of the upper nodes. Isolated plants and odd canes have flowered sporadically in cultivation. Japan. I. 1850.

macrosperma. See *A. gigantea.*

marmorea MAK. (*Chimonobambusa marmorea*). A normally low-growing bamboo forming clumps or patches of 1 to 2m. canes which are green at first maturing to deep purple when grown in a sunny position. The new shoots are an attractive pale green, mottled brown and silvery-white, tipped and striped pink. Leaves 5 to 15cm. long by 1 to 1·5cm. wide. A few canes have flowered on old clumps in recent years. Japan. I. 1889.

murieliae GAMBLE (*Sinoarundinaria murieliae*). An elegant species forming graceful arching clumps 2·5 to 3·5m. high or more. Canes bright green at first, maturing to a dull yellow-green. Leaves 6 to 10cm. long by 1 to 2cm. wide, of a bright pea-green. This beautiful bamboo, which is undoubtedly one of the best species in cultivation, was introduced from China in 1913 by Ernest Wilson, after whose daughter it was subsequently named. Excellent as an isolated specimen plant or in a large tub. A.G.M. 1973.

nitida MITF. (*Sinoarundinaria nitida*). This beautiful clump-forming species is often confused with *A. murieliae*, but differs most noticeably in its purple flushed canes and narrower leaves. It is one of the most elegant and ornamental of all bamboos, with canes 3 to 3·8m. high, or more, arching at the summit under the weight of foliage. Leaves 5 to 8cm. long by 6 to 12mm. wide, thin and delicate. It thrives best in a little shade and makes an excellent specimen plant. It may also be grown most effectively in a large tub. China. C. 1889. F.C.C. 1898. A.G.M. 1930.

nobilis. See *A. falconeri.*

pumila MITF. (*Pleioblastus pumilus*). A very hardy, dwarf bamboo forming dense carpets of slender, dull purple canes ·3 to ·8m. in height, with conspicuously hairy nodes. Leaves 5 to 18cm. long by 1 to 2cm. wide. A far-creeping species, useful as a ground cover. Japan. I. late 19th century.

pygmaea MITF. A dwarf species with far reaching rhizomes forming carpets of slender stems up to 25cm. long, taller in shade. Leaves up to 13cm. long by 2cm. wide. Our stock is a glabrous form. An excellent ground cover plant. Japan.

quadrangularis MAK. (*Tetragonocalamus quadrangularis*). "Square-stemmed Bamboo". A rare species with a creeping root-stock. The bluntly four-angled canes reach 2·5 to 3m. in height and in colour are dark green, occasionally splashed purple. The young shoots in spring are edible. Leaves 7·5 to 23cm. long by 2·5 to 3cm. wide. An attractive and unusual bamboo, only succeeding in a sheltered position. Not suitable for cold areas. China. Long cultivated and naturalised in Japan.

racemosa MUNRO. A rare bamboo with a creeping root-stock. Canes brownish-green at first, maturing to dull brown, 2·5 to 3·5m. high or more. Leaves 5 to 15cm. long by 12mm. wide. Similar to *A. spathiflora* in general appearance, but habit more robust and foliage of a darker green. The internodes are extremely rough to the touch. Nepal; Sikkim; Bhutan.

ragamowskii. See *SASA tesselata.*

simonii A. & C. RIV. (*Pleioblastus simonii*). A vigorous bamboo of erect habit, forming dense clumps or patches of tall, olive-green canes up to 4·5m. high or more. The first-year canes are liberally dusted with a white bloom. Young shoots in spring edible. Leaves 7·5 to 30cm. long by 1 to 3cm. wide. The leaf undersurface is green down one side, greyish-green down the other. A hardy species with luxuriant foliage, useful as a hedge or screen. It has flowered in several localities in recent years and good seed produced. China. I. 1862.

chino. See *A. chino.*

'Variegata' (*Bambusa albostriata*). Some of the smaller leaves striped creamy-white, not consistent.

ARUNDINARIA—*continued*

spathiflora TRIN. (*Thamnocalamus spathiflorus*). A beautiful clump-forming species of neat, erect habit. Canes densely packed, up to 4·5m. high, but more usually 2·5 to 3m., bright green ripening to a pinkish-purple shade on the exposed side, white bloomy during their first season. Leaves 7·5 to 15cm. long by 6 to 12mm. wide. A lovely bamboo, thriving best in a little shade and shelter. Himalaya. I. 1882.

tecta MUHL. A rare species in cultivation, regarded by some authorities as a variety of *A. gigantea*. Canes up to 2m. high bearing coarsely textured leaves up to 25cm. long by 2cm. wide. A rambling species of no outstanding merit. S. and S.E. United States.

tessellata MUNRO. A rare species, not to be confused with *Sasa tessellata*, forming clumps or patches. Canes 2·5 to 3·5m. high, pale green at first, darkening and maturing to a deep purple. Cane sheaths conspicuous, white the first year, cream later. Leaves 5 to 14cm. long by 1cm. wide. The only bamboo native to S. Africa, where it occurs in the mountains from Table Mountain northwards. The canes are said to have been used by the Zulus in the construction of shields, etc.

vagans GAMBLE (*Pleioblastus viridistriatus vagans*). A dwarf, creeping species, quickly forming extensive carpets of bright green foliage. Canes ·4 to 1·1m. high, bright green at first, becoming deep olive green, bearing solitary branches from each node. Leaves 5 to 15cm. long by 1 to 2cm. wide, downy on both surfaces. Too rampant for most gardens, but an excellent ground cover where little else will grow, even in dense shade. Japan. I. 1892.

variegata MAK. (*fortunei*) (*Pleioblastus variegatus*). A low-tufted species forming dense thickets of erect, zig-zag, pale green canes ·8 to 1·2m. high. Leaves 5 to 20cm. long by 1 to 2·5cm. wide, dark green, with white stripes, fading to pale green. The best of the white variegated bamboos and suitable for the rock garden or tub culture. Japan. C. 1863.

veitchii. See *SASA veitchii*.

viridistriata ANDRÉ (*auricoma*) (*Pleioblastus viridistriatus*). A very hardy species with erect, purplish-green canes 1 to 2m. high, forming small patches. Leaves variable in size, 7·5 to 20cm. long, 1 to 4cm. wide, dark green, striped rich yellow, often more yellow than green. The best of the variegated bamboos, quite small when grown in shade and an excellent tub plant. Old canes may be cut to ground level in autumn to encourage the production of new canes with brightly coloured young foliage. It has flowered at the tips of the canes in several localities over a considerable period (since 1898) without any ill effect. Japan. I. about 1870. A.M. 1972.

BAMBUSA albostriata. See *ARUNDINARIA simonii 'Variegata'*.

angustifolia. See *ARUNDINARIA angustifolia*.

metake. See *ARUNDINARIA japonica*.

vilmorinii. See *ARUNDINARIA angustifolia*.

CHIMONOBAMBUSA marmorea. See *ARUNDINARIA marmorea*.

CHUSQUEA. A rare genus of graceful, mainly South American bamboos, distinguished from *Arundinaria* by the even more numerous, densely clustered branches, and from all cultivated hardy bamboos by their solid stems. Because of this latter characteristic Chusqueas are useful for cutting, as their leaves do not flag as easily as do those of the hollow-stemmed bamboos.

breviglumis PHIL. A very distinct and ornamental, small bamboo with numerous, erect olive-green canes. Leaves more or less parallel-sided, 8 to 12cm. long by 7 to 8mm. wide, the tessellated venation conspicuous when held against the light. The leaves are collected towards the ends of the branches and this coupled with the fact that only the upper branch clusters remain leafy give to the plant an almost palm-like effect. This rare bamboo was introduced from Chile by Harold Comber. A plant growing in the woods at Exbury, Hants. from Comber's seed has formed a clump of approximately 1·2m. high by 2·5m. across. It is also in cultivation in the gardens at Wakehurst, Sussex.

couleou E. DESV. A hardy species, forming broad dense clumps. The deep olive-green canes, 2·5 to 3·5m. high or occasionally up to 9m. produce dense clusters of slender, short, leafy branches along their entire length, giving them a characteristic bottle-brush effect. The first-year canes possess conspicuous white sheaths at each node. Young shoots in spring, edible. Leaves 2·5 to 7·5cm. long by 6 to 10mm. wide, slender pointed. Chile. I. 1890 and again by Harold Comber in 1926. A.M. 1974.

PHYLLOSTACHYS. Tall, graceful bamboos usually less invasive than many of the Arundinarias from which they differ most markedly in the usually zig-zag stems, the internodes of which are flattened or shallowly grooved on alternate sides. Branches normally in pairs at each node.

aurea A. & C. RIV. (*Sinoarundinaria aurea*). A very graceful species, forming large clumps 2·5 to 3·5m. high. Canes bright green at first, maturing to pale creamy-yellow, dull yellow in full sun. Leaves 7·5 to 18cm. long by 1 to 2cm. wide. A hardy bamboo characterized by the peculiar crowding of the nodes at the base of each cane and the curious swelling beneath each node. Young shoots in spring, edible. The canes are used in the Far-east for walking sticks, umbrella handles, etc. and in America for fishing rods. It has flowered on several occasions. China. Long cultivated in Japan. I. before 1870.

bambusoides SIEB. & ZUCC. (*quilioi*). A very hardy and highly ornamental bamboo forming large clumps. Canes 3 to 4·5m. high, deep shining green at first becoming deep yellow-green and finally brown at maturity. Leaves 5 to 19cm. long by 1·5 to 3cm. wide. In warmer countries canes are known to grow as much as 23m. high and almost 15cm. in diameter. In China, Japan and the U.S.A. it is cultivated on a commercial scale and its canes put to a wide range of uses. Young shoots in spring, edible. China. I. 1866.

'Sulphurea' (*P. sulphurea*) (*'Allgold'*). A very attractive bamboo, differing from the type in its generally smaller leaves and its rich yellow canes, which are sometimes striped with green along the internodal grooves. C. 1865.

boryana. See *P. nigra 'Boryana'*.

flexuosa A. & C. RIV. A graceful Bamboo, 2·5 to 3m. high, throwing up slender, somewhat wavy canes which are bright green at first, becoming darker at maturity. In time large thickets are formed. Young shoots in spring, edible. Leaves 5 to 13cm. long by 1 to 2cm. wide. Extensively cultivated in France for use as fishing rods. Excellent as a screening plant. Strong shoots are noticeably zig-zag at base. China. I. 1864.

henonis. See *P. nigra 'Henonis'*.

heterocycla MATSUM. (*mitis heterocycla*). "Tortoise-shell Bamboo". An unusual bamboo of vigorous growth closely related to *P. pubescens*, of which it is said by some authorities to be merely a form. It differs from that species in the curious appearance of the cane base caused by the alternate swelling of the internodes. China; Japan. I. 1893.

mitis A. & C. RIV. A strong-growing species with bright green, later dull yellow canes up to 4·5m. high. Young shoots edible and much prized for this purpose in warmer climes. Leaves 7·5 to 10cm. long by 2cm. wide. A clump-forming species, forming thickets in warmer countries. Best grown in a sheltered position. China.

nidularia MUNRO. A rare, recently introduced Chinese species with tall canes up to 6m. in sheltered positions.

nigra MUNRO (*niger*). "Black Bamboo". A beautiful clump-forming bamboo of gracefully arching habit. Canes normally 2·5 to 3·5m. ,green the first year becoming mottled dark brown or black and finally an even jet black. In colder gardens the canes often remain a mottled brownish green. Young shoots in spring, edible. Leaves 5 to 13cm. long by 6 to 12mm. wide. This distinct and attractive species enjoys a sunny position. China; Japan. I. 1827. A.M. 1975.

'Boryana' (*'Bory'*) (*P. boryana*). An elegant bamboo producing luxuriant masses of arching, leafy stems. Canes 2·5 to 4m. high, green at first, changing to yellow and splashed purple. Young shoots in spring, edible. Leaves 5 to 9cm. long by 6 to 12mm. wide. A magnificent specimen plant in isolation. Originated in Japan.

'Henonis' (*'Henon'*) (*P. henonis*). A handsome Bamboo throwing up tall, graceful canes, 2·5 to 4m. high, swathed in dark green clouds of shining leaves. Canes bright green at first maturing to brownish-yellow. Young shoots in spring, edible. Leaves 7·5 to 11cm. long by 1 to 2cm. wide. One of the best species for planting as a specimen in a lawn or similarly prominent position. Originated in China. Long cultivated in Japan. C. about 1890.

'Punctata' (*P. punctata*). Similar in habit to the type, but less effective. Canes 2·5 to 3·5m. high, green, mottled black, never wholly black as in *P. nigra*. Young shoots in spring, edible. Leaves 5 to 10cm. long by 6 to 12mm. wide. Originated in China.

punctata. See *P. nigra 'Punctata'*.

PHYLLOSTACHYS—*continued*

quilioi. See *P. bambusoides.*

ruscifolia. See *SHIBATAEA kumasasa.*

sulphurea. See *P. bambusoides 'Sulphurea'.*

viridi-glaucescens A. & C. RIV. A graceful, extremely hardy clump-forming species. Canes 4 to 6m. high, green at first changing to dull yellowish green. Leaves 7·5 to 15cm. long, 1 to 2cm. wide, brilliant green above, glaucous beneath. Forms a thicket in ideal conditions, but otherwise an attractive specimen plant in isolation. China. I. 1846.

vivax MCCLURE. An erect-growing species of compact, clump-forming habit. The tall green, thin-walled canes will attain 8m. in mild areas and bear heavy drooping foliage. It resembles *P. bambusoides*, but is faster growing. China.

PSEUDOSASA japonica. See *ARUNDINARIA japonica.*

SASA. A genus of small, thicket-forming Bamboos differing from most species of *Arundinaria* in their typically low habit and the usually solitary branches arising from each node and in the relatively broader oblong or ovate-oblong leaves. See also *ARUNDINARIA.*

albomarginata. See *S. veitchii.*

palmata E. G. CAMUS (*Bambusa palmata*). A rampant, large-leaved bamboo forming extensive thickets of bright green canes 2 to 2·5m. high. Leaves up to 35cm. long by 9cm. wide, the margins often withering during a hard winter. It has been flowering profusely for several years now. Although too invasive for the small garden it provides an excellent shelter plant where space permits. Japan. I. 1889. F.C.C. 1896.

'Nebulosa'. This is usually grown and sold as the type and is common in cultivation. It is distinguished by its purple blotched stems.

tessellata MAK. & SHIB. (*Arundinaria ragamowskii*). Not to be confused with the rare South African *Arundinaria tessellata*, q.v. This remarkable species forms dense thickets of slender, bright green canes up to 2m. tall. The shining green leaves up to 60cm. long by 5 to 10cm. wide are the largest of all hardy bamboos and such is their collective weight that the canes bend down, giving the clump an almost dwarf habit. China. I. 1845.

veitchii REHD. (*albomarginata*) (*Arundinaria veitchii*). A small, dense-growing species forming large thickets of deep purplish-green, later dull purple canes ·6 to 1·2m. high. Leaves 10 to 25cm. long by 2·5 to 6cm. wide, withering and becoming pale straw-coloured or whitish along the margins in autumn, providing an attractive and characteristic variegated effect, which lasts throughout winter. Japan. I. 1880. A.M. 1898.

SEMIARUNDINARIA fastuosa. See *ARUNDINARIA fastuosa.*

SHIBATAEA. A genus of only two species. Low growing bamboos with a creeping root-stock. Stems flattened on one side between the nodes. Branches short and leafy, borne in clusters of three to five at each node.

kumasasa MAK. (*kumasaca*) (*Phyllostachys ruscifolia*). A very distinct bamboo of dwarf, compact habit. Canes ·5 to ·8m. high characteristically zig-zag and almost triangular in outline, pale green at first, maturing to dull brownish. Leaves broadly lanceolate to ovate-oblong, 5 to 10cm. long by 2 to 3cm. wide. It has flowered in recent years with no apparent ill effect. A charming species forming dense leafy clumps, particularly happy in a moist soil. Japan. I. 1861. F.C.C. 1896 (as *Phyllostachys kumasasa*).

SINOARUNDINARIA aurea. See *PHYLLOSTACHYS aurea.*

murielae. See *ARUNDINARIA murielae.*

nitida. See *ARUNDINARIA nitida.*

TETRAGONOCALAMUS quadrangularis. See *ARUNDINARIA quadrangularis.*

THAMNOCALAMUS falconeri. See *ARUNDINARIA falconeri.*

spathiflorus. See *ARUNDINARIA spathiflora.*

BOTANICAL NAMES

To many people botanical names are at best an inconvenience and at worst an annoying and sometimes confusing barrier to a better understanding of plants. Why can't plants be known only by English names? Botanical names are written in Latin and are accepted the world over. Vernacular or common names are often easier to remember and pronounce but they can be a source of much confusion and misunderstanding. For example, the names "Bilberry", "Whortleberry", "Blaeberry", "Huckleberry" and "Whinberry" are all English names used in different parts of the British Isles for the same plant—*Vaccinium myrtillus*. Mention "Huckleberry" to an American gardener and he would probably think of a *Gaylussacia*. Mention any of the above to a Russian, Chinese, French or any other non-English-speaking horticulturist and he would shake his head, but mention the botanical name and there is a reasonable chance that he would understand. Another example is the "Swamp Honeysuckle" of the United States. An English gardener would probably imagine this to be a species of *Lonicera* and be surprised to learn that it is in fact the American name for *Rhododendron viscosum*. Thus it will be seen that botanical names are worth learning and using. They need not be tiresome and boring; on the contrary botanical names usually tell us something about a plant.

Generic Names. These are always nouns. Their origins and meanings are occasionally obscure, but the majority are derived from older names in Greek, Latin, Arabic and other languages.

Some generic names are based on characters in Greek mythology, e.g.

DAPHNE named after the river god's daughter

ANDROMEDA named after the daughter of Cepheus and Cassiope

PHYLLODOCE name of a sea nymph

whilst others commemorate people, such as botanists, patrons, etc., e.g.

BUDDLEIA named after Rev. Adam Buddle

DEUTZIA named after J. Deutz

ESCALLONIA named after Signor Escallon

FUCHSIA named after Leonard Fuchs

LONICERA named after Adam Lonicer

Specific Epithets. The names used to describe species are varied and fall into four main categories (see also under "Nomenclature and Classification", page 3) namely:—

A. Names which indicate the origin of a plant, e.g. continent, country, region, etc.

B. Names that describe the habitat of a plant (where it grows in the wild), e.g., in woods, on mountains, by rivers, etc.

C. Names that describe a plant or a particular feature, such as size, habit, leaf shape, colour of flower, etc.

D. Names which commemorate people, e.g., botanists, plant collectors, patrons, famous horticulturists, etc.

Those wishing to pursue this subject may be interested in the following books:—

"Plant Names Simplified" by A. T. Johnson and H. A, Smith, first published in 1931, and since revised and enlarged;

"Botanical Latin" by William T. Stearn, 2nd revised edition published in 1973; a book which can be thoroughly recommended to all interested in botanical names, be he botanist or gardener;

"A Gardener's Dictionary of Plant Names" by A. W. Smith; revised and enlarged by William T. Stearn, and published in 1972.

The following lists are merely a selection of the most commonly used names (specific epithets) and their meanings.

Names which are Geographical

atlantica(um)(us)	(*Cedrus atlantica*)	—of the Atlas Mountains (North Africa)
australe(is)	(*Cordyline australis*)	—southern
boreale(is)	(*Linnaea borealis*)	—northern
californica(um)(us)	(*Fremontodendron californicum*)	—of California
capense(is)	(*Phygelius capensis*)	—of the Cape (South Africa)
europaea(um)(us)	(*Euonymus europaeus*)	—of Europe
himalaica(um)(us)	(*Stachyurus himalaicus*)	—of the Himalaya
hispanica(um)(us)	(*Genista hispanica*)	—of Spain
japonica(um)(us)	(*Camellia japonica*)	—of Japan
lusitanica(um)(us)	(*Prunus lusitanica*)	—of Portugal
nipponica(um)(us)	(*Spiraea nipponica*)	—of Japan
occidentale(is)	(*Thuja occidentalis*)	—western
orientale(is)	(*Thuja orientalis*)	—eastern
sinense(is)	(*Wisteria sinensis*)	—of China

Names describing Habitat

alpina(um)(us)	(*Daphne alpina*)	—alpine, of the Alps or growing in alpine regions
arvense(is)	(*Rosa arvensis*)	—of fields or cultivated land
aquatica(um)(us)	(*Nyssa aquatica*)	—of water, or growing by water
campestre(is)	(*Acer campestre*)	—of plains or flat areas
littorale(is)	(*Griselinia littoralis*)	—of sea shores
maritima(um)(us)	(*Prunus maritima*)	—by the sea
montana(um)(us)	(*Clematis montana*)	—of mountains
palustre(is)	(*Ledum palustre*)	—of swamps or marshes
rivulare(is)	(*Symphoricarpos rivularis*)	—of streams and brooks
rupestre(is)	(*Daphne rupestris*)	—of rocks or cliffs
sylvatica(um)(us)	(*Fagus sylvatica*)	—of woods

Names describing Habit

arborea(um)(us)	(*Rhododendron arboreum*)	—tree-like
fastigiata(um)(us)	(*Cassiope fastigiata*)	—erect, the branches
fruticosa(um)(us)	(*Bupleurum fruticosum*)	—shrubby
horizontale(is)	(*Cotoneaster horizontalis*)	—horizontally spreading
humile(is)	(*Chamaerops humilis*)	—low growing
major(us)	(*Vinca major*)	—greater
minor(us)	(*Vinca minor*)	—lesser
nana(um)(us)	(*Betula nana*)	—dwarf
pendula(um)(us)	(*Betula pendula*)	—pendulous, weeping
procera(um)(us)	(*Abies procera*)	—very tall, high
procumbens	(*Juniperus procumbens*)	—procumbent, creeping
prostrata(um)(us)	(*Ceanothus prostratus*)	—prostrate, hugging the ground
repens	(*Salix repens*)	—creeping and rooting
suffruticosa(um)(us)	(*Paeonia suffruticosa*)	—woody at base

Names describing Leaves

Many names describe shape and toothing of leaves, e.g., ovata, lanceolata, rotundifolia, serrata, crenata, laciniata for which see Glossary pp. 8 to 10.

(**phylla(um)(us)** and **folia(um)(us)** = leaf)

angustifolia(um)(us)	(*Arundinaria angustifolia*)	—narrow-leaved
arguta(um)(us)	(*Spiraea × arguta*)	—sharp
coriacea(um)(us)	(*Holboellia coriacea*)	—coriaceous, leathery
crassifolia(um)(us)	(*Hymenanthera crassifolia*)	—thick-leaved
decidua(um)(us)	(*Larix decidua*)	—deciduous, dropping its leaves
glabra(um)(us)	(*Elaeagnus glabra*)	—glabrous, without hairs
heterophylla(um)(us)	(*Osmanthus heterophyllus*)	—variable-leaved
hirsuta(um)(us)	(*Vaccinium hirsutum*)	—hairy
incana(um)(us)	(*Alnus incana*)	—grey-downy

Names describing Leaves—*continued*

integerrima(um)(us)	(*Schizophragma integerrima*)	—without teeth
laevigata(um)(us)	(*Rosa laevigata*)	—smooth and polished
latifolia(um)(us)	(*Ilex latifolia*)	—broad-leaved
macrophylla(um)(us)	(*Acer macrophyllum*)	—large-leaved
maculata(um)(us)	(*Elaeagnus pungens* 'Maculata'	—spotted, blotched
marginata(um)(us)	(*Ulmus × viminalis* 'Marginata'	—margined
microphylla(um)(us)	(*Azara microphylla*)	—small-leaved
molle(is)	(*Hamamelis mollis*)	—soft
nitida(um)(us)	(*Lonicera nitida*)	—shining
parvifolia(um)(us)	(*Ulmus parvifolia*)	—small-leaved
picta(um)(us)	(*Kalopanax pictus*)	—painted, coloured
pinnata(um)(us)	(*Psoralea pinnata*)	—pinnate
platyphylla(os)(um)(us)	(*Tilia platyphyllos*)	—broad-leaved
reticulata(um)(us)	(*Salix reticulata*)	—net-veined
sempervirens	(*Buxus sempervirens*)	—always green, evergreen
splendens	(*Cotoneaster splendens*)	—glittering, shining
tomentosa(um)(us)	(*Tilia tomentosa*)	—covered with a short dense pubescence
variegata(um)(us)	(*Cornus mas* 'Variegata')	—variegated, two coloured
velutina(um)(us)	(*Syringa velutina*)	—velvety

Names describing Flowers

(**flora(um)(us)** = flower)

campanulata(um)(us)	(*Rhododendron campanulatum*)	—bell-shaped
floribunda(um)(us)	(*Dipelta floribunda*)	—free-flowering
grandiflora(um)(us)	(*Viburnum grandiflorum*)	—large-flowered
macropetala(um)(us)	(*Clematis macropetala*)	—many-petalled
nudiflora(um)(us)	(*Jasminum nudiflorum*)	—naked, without leaves
nutans	(*Rubus nutans*)	—nodding
paniculata(um)(us)	(*Koelreuteria paniculata*)	—flowering in panicles
parviflora(um)(us)	(*Aesculus parviflora*)	—small-flowered
pauciflora(um)(us)	(*Corylopsis pauciflora*)	—few-flowered
polyantha(um)(us)	(*Jasminum polyanthum*)	—many-flowered
racemosa(um)(us)	(*Berchemia racemosa*)	—flowers in racemes
spicata(um)(us)	(*Corylopsis spicata*)	—flowers in spikes
stellata(um)(us)	(*Magnolia stellata*)	—starry
triflora(um)(us)	(*Abelia triflora*)	—flowers in threes
umbellata(um)(us)	(*Berberis umbellata*)	—flowers in umbels
uniflora(um)(us)	(*Crataegus uniflora*)	—one-flowered

Names describing Colours

alba(um)(us)	(*Populus alba*)	—white
argentea(um)(us)	(*Shepherdia argentea*)	—silvery
aurantiaca(um)(us)	(*Mimulus aurantiacus*)	—orange
aurea(um)(us)	(*Salvia aurea*)	—golden
bicolor	(*Picea bicolor*)	—two-coloured
carnea(um)(us)	(*Aesculus × carnea*)	—flesh-coloured
caerulea(um)(us)	(*Passiflora caerulea*)	—blue
cinerea(um)(us)	(*Erica cinerea*)	—ash grey
coccinea(um)(us)	(*Quercus coccinea*)	—scarlet
concolor	(*Abies concolor*)	—of the same colour
discolor	(*Holodiscus discolor*)	—two-coloured
ferruginea(um)(us)	(*Rhododendron ferrugineum*)	—rusty brown
flava(um)(us)	(*Rhododendron flavum*)	—pale yellow
glauca(um)(us)	(*Picea glauca*)	—sea-green
lactea(um)(us)	(*Rhododendron lacteum*)	—milk white
lilacina(um)(us)	(*Paulownia lilacina*)	—lilac
lutea(um)(us)	(*Cladrastis lutea*)	—yellow
nigra(um)(us)	(*Sambucus nigra*)	—black
punicea(um)(us)	(*Mimulus puniceus*)	—crimson
purpurea(um)(us)	(*Malus × purpurea*)	—purple
rosea(um)(us)	(*Lapageria rosea*)	—rose-coloured

Names describing Colours—*continued*

rubra(um)(us)	(*Quercus rubra*)	—red
sanguinea(um)(us)	(*Ribes sanguineum*)	—blood red
tricolor	(*Rubus tricolor*)	—three-coloured
variegata(um)(us)	(*Weigela florida* 'Variegata')	—variegated—two coloured
versicolor	(*Cytisus × versicolor*)	—variously coloured, or changing colour
violacea(um)(us)	(*Jovellana violacea*)	—violet
viride(is)	(*Alnus viridis*)	—green

Names describing Aromas and Scents

aromatica(um)(us)	(*Laurelia aromatica*)	—aromatic
citriodora(um)(us)	(*Lippia citriodora*)	—lemon-scented
foetida(um)(us)	(*Viburnum foetidum*)	—strong-smelling, unpleasant
fragrans	(*Viburnum fragrans*)	—fragrant
fragrantissima(um)(us)	(*Lonicera fragrantissima*)	—most fragrant
graveolens	(*Ruta graveolens*)	—smelling unpleasantly
odorata(um)(us)	(*Rubus odoratus*)	—sweet-scented
odoratissima(um)(us)	(*Viburnum odoratissimum*)	—sweetest scented
moschata(um)(us)	(*Olearia moschata*)	—musk-scented
suaveolens	(*Datura suaveolens*)	—sweet-scented

Names alluding to Other Plants

bignonioides	(*Catalpa bignonioides*)	—Bignonia-like
jasminea	(*Daphne jasminea*)	—Jasmine-like
liliiflora(um)(us)	(*Magnolia liliiflora*)	—Lily-flowered
pseudoplatanus	(*Acer pseudoplatanus*)	—False Plane
salicifolia(um)(us)	(*Cotoneaster salicifolius*)	—Willow-leaved
tulipifera(um)(us)	(*Liriodendron tulipifera*)	—Tulip-bearing

Names which are Commemorative

delavayi	(*Abies delavayi*)	—after the Abbé Delavay
harryana(um)(us)	(*Viburnum harryanum*)	—after Sir Harry Veitch
henryana(um)(us)	(*Parthenocissus henryana*)	—after Dr. Augustine Henry
hookeri	(*Acer hookeri*)	—after Sir Joseph Hooker
thunbergii	(*Spiraea thunbergii*)	—after Carl Peter Thunberg
williamsiana(um)(us)	(*Rhododendron williamsianum*)	—after Mr. J. C. Williams
willmottiana(um)(us)	(*Ceratostigma willmottianum*)	—after Miss Ellen Willmott
wilsoniae	(*Berberis wilsoniae*)	—after Mrs. E. H. Wilson

Miscellaneous Names

affine(is)	(*Cotoneaster affinis*)	—related (to another species)
alata(um)(us)	(*Euonymus alatus*)	—winged
amabile(is)	(*Kolkwitzia amabilis*)	—lovely
ambigua(um)(us)	(*Ribes ambiguum*)	—doubtful (identity?)
amoena(um)(us)	(*Lonicera amoena*)	—charming, pleasing
bella(um)(us)	(*Spiraea bella*)	—pretty
commune(is)	(*Juniperus communis*)	—common, occuring in plenty
confusa(um)(us)	(*Sarcococca confusa*)	—confused (identity?)
dulce(is)	(*Prunus dulcis*)	—sweet
edule(is)	(*Passiflora edulis*)	—edible
florida(um)(us)	(*Cornus florida*)	—free-flowering
formosa(um)(us)	(*Leycesteria formosa*)	—handsome, beautiful
hybrida(um)(us)	(*Deutzia × hybrida*)	—hybrid
insigne(is)	(*Sorbus insignis*)	—outstanding
intermedia(um)(us)	(*Eucryphia × intermedia*)	—intermediate
media(um)(us)	(*Mahonia × media*)	—middle, midway between
officinale(is)	(*Rosmarinus officinalis*)	—of the shop (herbal)
praecox	(*Chimonanthus praecox*)	—early
pulchella(um)(us)	(*Barosma pulchella*)	—beautiful

Miscellaneous Names—*continued*

speciosa(um)(us)	(*Callistemon speciosus*)	—showy
sativa(um)(us)	(*Castanea sativa*)	—sown, planted or cultivated
utile(is)	(*Viburnum utile*)	—useful
vernale(is)	(*Hamamelis vernalis*)	—spring
vulgare(is)	(*Calluna vulgaris*)	—common

TREES and SHRUBS for LANDSCAPE and GARDEN DESIGN

The approach to the choice of trees and shrubs is naturally varied. The nature of the job, public or private, town or country, the individual taste of the landscape designer or garden maker, the labour available for maintenance, all these factors and more affect the decision as to what trees and shrubs to use and all must be influenced by the nature of the soil and situation. Having produced a wide selection of woody plants we are anxious that they should be used to the best possible advantage, suited both to the chemical and physical conditions of the soil and the particular job in hand.

In addition to the symbols used in the text indicating the likes and dislikes of the plants the following lists are intended to serve as a guide to, or perhaps merely a reminder of species of trees and shrubs suitable for some of the many different soils and situations found in the British Isles and even within one site. The lists of trees and shrubs with distinctive habit or bark, leaf-shape or colour, etc., may be helpful to both the professional and amateur.

We wish to emphasize that the trees and shrubs mentioned in each list are merely a selection and there are numerous other examples. We would also point out that we have listed plants which are suitable for a particular situation and are not necessarily recommending them to be planted only in that situation. A great many plants grow quite happily in a variety of situations.

For further details of the plants in these lists, please refer to the individual descriptions in the text.

cvs. = cultivars (See under "Nomenclature and Classification", page 3).

INDEX of LISTS

The three main factors controlling the growth of a plant and consequently its selection for the garden are soil, situation and hardiness.

To most gardeners soil is either clayey, sandy or chalky, and wet or dry. These are basic conditions but there are obviously many variations. There are many trees and shrubs which, weak and miserable in a *shallow* soil over chalk, will grow well in a *deep* soil over chalk.

Soil pH and the Plant

pH is the term used to designate the acid or alkaline reaction of the soil. A pH reading of seven is neutral and below this the soil becomes increasingly acid and above it progressively alkaline.

Most ornamental plants thrive best in soils with a pH between 5·7 and 6·7, but in the cultivated trees and shrubs are found plants which tolerate the most extreme conditions at either end of the scale. For example, in the Ericaceae occur species which flourish in soils with a pH as low as three, whereas in some families such as Rosaceae, Oleaceae etc., are found species thriving in soils with pH readings as high as 8·5. In some cases, for example Holly, Beech and Yew, plants are able to thrive in soils which show a pH range from 3·6 to above 8.

The relationship between soil pH and plant growth is extremely complex and no hard and fast rules can be made. A Rhododendron which is able to grow well on one type of soil with a pH of 6·5 may well fail on a different type of soil with the same pH reading. Secondary factors undoubtedly play an important part in a plant's reaction to soil pH.

Themost profound influence of pH on plant growth is through its effect on the availability to the plant of soil chemical elements.

In the pH range between 5·7 and 6·7 the greatest number of nutrients are held in a soluble state and are, therefore, available to the plant.

As the pH rises such important major elements as Nitrogen, Phosphorus and Potassium gradually become less available and the minor elements such as Iron become increasingly unobtainable. As the pH lowers and the soil becomes more acid the three major elements again become less available and the important minor element Calcium is deficient, while other minor elements such as Iron, Manganese and Aluminium become available in excess, giving rise to toxic symptoms.

Generally speaking there is little point in struggling to grow plants in soils greatly unsuited to their growth, but excessively acid soils may be improved by the addition of chalk or limestone and the pH of alkaline soils may be lowered by applying Iron sulphate, ammonium sulphate or Flowers of Sulphur. Normally a radical change in soil pH cannot be achieved quickly without causing harm to the chemical constitution of the soil and gardeners wishing to grow acid loving plants on alkaline soils can often obtain satisfactory results by applying the missing elements in chelated form, i.e. as Iron Sequestrene.

Hardiness. The hardiness of plants is something about which the gardener is forever wondering. It is a subject full of pitfalls, surprises, disappointments and exceptions to the rule.

"Why?" he may ask, "should trees from the harsh climes of Northern Europe, Russia and Siberia prove unsatisfactory in the comparatively warmer, less extreme conditions of southern England". Our treacherous springs, with mild spells followed by sharp frosts trick these unsuspecting trees into early growth only to cut them back again, and again until the tree is exhausted and dies. Plants from the milder countries of New Zealand and Chile are not so easily duped. They wait for the settled weather of late spring before making their move.

As past events have proved, few plants may confidently be described as being able to withstand any condition in any position in any part of the British Isles. On the other hand, it is surprising the number of "suspect" plants one may grow with the minimum of protection.

Generally speaking, it is a known and accepted fact that the milder, moister areas in the west of the British Isles offer a more congenial home to tender plants than do the often colder or drier areas of central and eastern regions. What is not always appreciated is that many tender plants may be grown, indeed, are grown, in central, eastern and northern gardens where careful positioning or happy chance has provided suitable protection.

ATMOSPHERIC POLLUTION may occur wherever there are factories, works or railways, but only in large industrial areas does its effect have any serious consequence. Smoke and fumes belching out from countless chimneys contain numerous impurities and noxious gases, the chief of which is sulphur dioxide. Leaves become coated with pollution and the soil becomes defiled by it. In such areas, evergreens are frequently deciduous or partly so, the leaves of deciduous trees commonly fall early, growth is often restricted and resultant plants stunted, flowering is sometimes late and less abundant and the leaves and stems of larger plants are coated with an unsightly layer of dirt. A similar state of affairs exists along many of our roads and highways where exhaust fumes are continually present.

A depressing picture it would seem, but these extremes are mainly existent in the larger industrial areas and even here the situation is fortunately changing for the better. Smokeless fuels, electrification of industrial power and the decline of the steam engine are all helping towards a cleaner atmosphere. This, together with an adventurous and imaginative gardening public should go a long way towards putting gardens in industrial areas on the same basis as those in more favoured areas.

TREES and SHRUBS suitable for CLAY SOILS (neutral to slightly acid)

Trees

Acer (all)
Aesculus (all)
Alnus (all)
Betula (all)
Carpinus (all)
Crataegus (all)
Eucalyptus (all)
Fraxinus (all)
Ilex (all)
Laburnum (all)
Malus (all)
Populus (all)
Prunus (all)
Quercus (all)
Salix (all)
Sorbus (all)
Tilia (all)

Shrubs

Abelia (all)
Aralia elata and cvs.
Aronia (all)
Aucuba japonica and cvs.
Berberis (all)
Chaenomeles (all)
Choisya ternata
Colutea (all)
Cornus (all)
Corylus (all)
Cotinus (all)
Cotoneaster (all)
Cytisus (all)
Deutzia (all)
Escallonia (all)
Forsythia (all)
Genista (all)
Hamamelis (all)
Hibiscus syriacus and cvs.
Hypericum (all)
Lonicera (all)
Mahonia (all)
Magnolia (all)
Osmanthus (all)
Philadelphus (all)
Potentilla (all)
Pyracantha (all)
Rhododendron Hardy Hybrids
Ribes (all)
Rosa (all)
Senecio greyi
Skimmia (all)
Spiraea (all)
Symphoricarpos (all)
Viburnum (all)
Weigela (all)

Conifers

Abies (all)
Chamaecyparis (all)
Juniperus (all)
Larix (all)
Pinus (all)
Taxodium distichum
Taxus (all)
Thuja (all)

Bamboos

Arundinaria (all)
Phyllostachys (all)
Sasa (all)

TREES and SHRUBS suitable for DRY ACID SOILS

Trees

Acer negundo and cvs.
Ailanthus altissima
Betula (all)
Castanea (all)
Cercis (all)
Gleditsia (all)
Ilex aquifolium and cvs.
Populus alba
canescens
tremula
Robinia (all)
Ulmus pumila

Dry Acid Soils—Shrubs

Shrubs

Acer ginnala
Berberis (all)
Calluna vulgaris and cvs.
Caragana arborescens
Cistus (all)
Colutea arborescens
Cotoneaster (all)
Elaeagnus angustifolia
commutata
Ephedra (all)
Erica (all)
Genista (all)
Hakea microcarpa
Halimodendron halodendron
Helianthemum (all)
Hibiscus (all)
Ilex crenata and cvs.
Indigofera (all)
Kerria japonica and cvs.
Ligustrum amurense
Lonicera (all)
Lycium barbarum
Pernettya mucronata and cvs.
prostrata
Physocarpus opulifolius
Rosa pimpinellifolia and cvs.
Salix caprea
cinerea oleifolia
repens
Tamarix (all)
Ulex (all)
Viburnum lentago

Conifers

Cupressus glabra and cvs.
Juniperus (all)
Pinus (all)

TREES and SHRUBS suitable for SHALLOW SOIL OVER CHALK

Trees

Acer campestre
negundo and cvs.
platanoides and cvs.
pseudoplatanus and cvs.
Aesculus (all)
Carpinus betulus and cvs.
Cercis siliquastrum
Crataegus oxyacantha and cvs.
Fagus sylvatica and cvs.
Fraxinus excelsior and cvs.
Fraxinus ornus
Malus (all)
Morus nigra
Populus alba
canescens
Prunus "Japanese Cherries"
Sorbus aria and cvs.
hybrida
intermedia
Ulmus (all)

Shrubs

Aucuba japonica and cvs.
Baccharis halimifolia
patagonica
Berberis (all)
Buddleia davidii and cvs.
Buxus sempervirens and cvs.
Caragana arborescens and cvs.
Ceanothus (all)
Cistus (all)
Colutea (all)
Cornus mas and cvs.
Cotoneaster (all)
Cytisus nigricans
Deutzia (all)
Dipelta floribunda
Elaeagnus (deciduous species)
Euonymus (all)
Forsythia (all)
Fuchsia (all)
Genista cinerea
Hebe (all)
Hibiscus syriacus and cvs.
Hypericum (all)
Laurus nobilis
Ligustrum (all)
Lonicera (all)
Mahonia aquifolium and hybrids
Olearia (all)
Paeonia delavayi
lutea
Philadelphus (all)
Phillyrea (all)
Photinia serrulata
Potentilla fruticosa and cvs.
Rhus (most)
Rosa (most)
Rosmarinus (all)
Rubus tricolor
Sambucus (all)
Sarcococca (all)
Senecio (all)
Spartium junceum
Spiraea japonica and cvs.
nipponica and forms
Stachyrus (all)
Symphoricarpos (all)
Syringa (all)
Vinca (all)
Weigela (all)
Yucca (all)

Shallow Soil over Chalk—Conifers—*continued*

Juniperus communis and cvs.
× media and cvs.
Pinus mugo and forms
nigra
Taxus baccata and cvs.
Thuja occidentalis and cvs.
plicata and cvs.
Thujopsis dolabrata and cvs.

Bamboos

Arundinaria japonica
vagans

TREES and SHRUBS tolerant of both extreme ACIDITY and ALKALINITY

Trees

Betula papyrifera and forms
pendula and cvs.
platyphylla and vars.
pubescens
Crataegus monogyna and cvs.
Fagus sylvatica and cvs.
Populus alba
Populus canescens
tremula
Quercus cerris
robur and cvs.
Sorbus × hybrida
intermedia

Shrubs

Berberis vulgaris
Ilex aquifolium and cvs.
Ligustrum ovalifolium and cvs.
Lycium barbarum
chinense
Rhamnus frangula
Salix × balfourii
caprea
cinerea oleifolia
Sambucus nigra and cvs.
racemosa and cvs.
Viburnum opulus

Conifers

Juniperus communis and cvs.
Pinus nigra
Pinus sylvestris and cvs.
Taxus baccata and cvs.

TREES and SHRUBS suitable for DAMP SITES

Trees

Alnus (all)
Amelanchier (all)
Betula × koehnei
nigra
pendula
pubescens
Crataegus oxyacantha and cvs.
Magnolia virginiana
Mespilus germanica
Populus (all)
Pterocarya (all)
Pyrus betulifolia
communis
Quercus palustris
Salix (all)
Sorbus aucuparia and cvs.

Shrubs

Amelanchier lamarckii
stolonifera
Aronia (all)
Calycanthus floridus
Cephalanthus occidentalis
Clethra (all)
Cornus alba and cvs.
baileyi
stolonifera and cvs.
Gaultheria shallon
Hippophae rhamnoides
Ilex verticillata
Lindera benzoin
Myrica cerifera
gale
Neillia longiracemosa
Photinia villosa
Physocarpus opulifolius and cvs.
Prunus spinosa and cvs.
Salix × balfourii
caprea
humilis
integra
purpurea and cvs.
repens and cvs.
many other bush species
Sambucus (all)
Sorbaria (all)
Spiraea × billiardii 'Triumphans'
× sanssouciana
trichocarpa
× vanhouttei
× veitchii
Symphoricarpos (all)
Vaccinium (all)
Viburnum dentatum
lentago
opulus and cvs.

Damp Sites—Conifers

Metasequoia glyptostroboides
Picea sitchensis
Taxodium ascendens and forms
distichum

Bamboos

Arundinaria (all)
Phyllostachys (all)
Sasa (all)

TREES and SHRUBS suitable for INDUSTRIAL AREAS

Trees

Acer (many, but not Japanese Maples)
Aesculus (all)
Ailanthus altissima
Alnus cordata
glutinosa and cvs.
incana and cvs.
Amelanchier (all)
Betula papyrifera and forms
pendula and cvs.
platyphylla and vars.
pubescens and cvs.
Carpinus betulus and cvs.
Catalpa bignonioides
ovata
Crataegus (most)
Davidia incolucrata and var.
Eucalyptus (most)
Fagus (all)
Fraxinus (all)
Ilex × altaclarensis and cvs.
aquifolium and cvs.
+ Laburnocytisus adamii
Laburnum (all)
Ligustrum lucidum and cvs.
Liriodendron tulipifera and cvs.
Magnolia acuminata
denudata
× soulangiana and cvs.
kobus
Magnolia × loebneri and cvs.
Malus (all)
Mespilus germanica
Morus nigra
Platanus (all)
Populus (most)
Prunus amygdalo-persica 'Pollardii'
avium
cerasifera and cvs.
dulcis
"Japanese Cherries"
padus and cvs.
Pterocarya (all)
Pyrus (most)
Quercus × hispanica
ilex
× turneri
Rhus (most)
Robinia pseudoacacia and cvs.
Salix (most)
Sorbus aria and cvs.
aucuparia and cvs.
Tilia × euchlora
× europaea
platyphyllos and cvs.
Ulmus carpinifolia
glabra and cvs.
hollandica and cvs.
procera and cvs.
× sarniensis and cvs.

Shrubs

Acanthopanax (all)
Amelanchier (all)
Aralia elata
Arbutus unedo and cvs.
Aucuba japonica and cvs.
Berberis (all)
Buddleia davidii and cvs.
Buxus sempervirens and cvs.
Camellia japonica and cvs.
× williamsii and cvs.
Ceanothus × delinianus and cvs.
Ceratostigma willmottianum
Chaenomeles (all)
Cistus (all)
Clethra (all)
Colutea arborescens
× media
Cornus alba and cvs.
stolonifera and cvs.
Cotoneaster (most)
Cytisus (most)
Daphne mezereum
Deutzia (many)
Elaeagnus × ebbingei
glabra
pungens and cvs.
Escallonia (all)
Euonymus fortunei and cvs.
japonicus and cvs.
Fatsia japonica
Forsythia (all)
Garrya (all)
Genista (many)
Hibiscus sinosyriacus and cvs.
syriacus and cvs.
Hydrangea macrophylla and cvs.
Hypericum (all)
Ilex aquifolium and cvs.
cornuta and hybrids
Kerria japonica and cvs.
Leycesteria formosa

Industrial Areas—Shrubs—*continued*

Ligustrum involucrata
japonicum
ovalifolium
Lonicera pileata
Lycium (all)
Magnolia grandiflora and cvs.
×soulangiana and cvs.
stellata and cvs.
Mahonia aquifolium and hybrids
japonica
lomariifolia
×media and cvs.
pinnata
'Rotundifolia'
Olearia avicenniifolia
×haastii
Pernettya mucronata and cvs.
Osmanthus (all)
×Osmarea burkwoodii
Pernettya mucronata and cvs.
Philadelphus (all)
Phillyrea (all)
Physocarpus (all)
Prunus laurocerasus and cvs.
Pyracantha (all)
Rhododendron caucasicum
Hardy Hybrids
(Knap Hill Azaleas)
luteum
ponticum
Rhodotypos scandens
Rhus glabra
typhina
Ribes (all)
Rosa (most)
Salix (most)
Sambucus canadensis 'Maxima
nigra and forms
Sarcococca (many)
Senecio greyi
monroi
Skimmia japonica and cvs.
Sorbaria (all)
Spartium junceum
Spiraea (all)
Staphylea (all)
Stranvaesia davidiana
Symphoricarpos (all)
Syringa (all)
Tamarix tetrandra
Ulex (all)
Viburnum (many)
Vinca major and cvs.
minor and cvs.
Weigela florida and cvs.
Hybrids

Climbers

Ampelopsis (most)
Hedera (all)
Parthenocissus (all)

Conifers

Cephalotaxus fortuni
harringtonia and forms
Fitzroya cupressoides
Ginkgo biloba
Metasequoia glyptostroboides
Taxus baccata and cvs.
cuspidata and cvs.
×media and cvs.
Torreya californica

TREES and SHRUBS suitable for COLD EXPOSED AREAS

Trees

Acer pseudoplatanus and cvs.
Betula (most)
Crataegus monogyna and cvs.
Fagus sylvatica and cvs.
Fraxinus excelsior and cvs.
Laburnum (all)
Populus 'Robusta'
'Serotina'
Populus tremula
Quercus robur and cvs.
Sorbus aria and cvs.
aucuparia and cvs.
intermedia
Tilia cordata
Ulmus angustifolia cornubiensis
×sarniensis

Shrubs

Arctostaphylos uva-ursi
Calluna vulgaris and cvs.
Chamaedaphne calyculata
Cornus alba and cvs.
baileyi
stolonifera and cvs.
Cotinus coggygria and cvs.
Elaeagnus commutata
Euonymus fortunei and cvs.
japonicus robustus
×Gaulnettya wisleyensis and cvs.
Gaultheria shallon
Hamamelis virginiana
Hippophae rhamnoides
Hydrangea paniculata 'Grandiflora'

Cold Exposed Areas—Shrubs—*continued*

Kalmia angustifolia
latifolia
Kerria japonica 'Variegata'
Lavatera olbia
Ledum groenlandicum
Leucothoe fontanesiana
Lonicera involucrata
pileata
Mahonia aquifolium
Myrica gale
Pachysandra terminalis
Pernettya mucronata and cvs.
Philadelphus (many)
Pieris floribunda
Prunus spinosa
Rhododendron caucasicum
Hardy Hybrids
ponticum
yakushimanum
Salix (most)
Spiraea (most)
Tamarix (all)
Ulex (all)
Viburnum opulus and cvs.

Conifers

Chamaecyparis nootkatensis and cvs.
obtusa and cvs.
pisifera and cvs.
Cryptomeria japonica and cvs.
Ginkgo biloba
Juniperus communis and cvs.
×media and cvs.
Larix decidua
Picea abies and cvs.
Pinus banksiana
nigra
maritima
ponderosa
sylvestris and cvs.
Taxus baccata and cvs.
Thuja occidentalis and cvs.
standishii
Tsuga canadensis and cvs.

TREES and SHRUBS suitable for SEASIDE AREAS

Trees

Acer pseudoplatanus
Arbutus unedo and cvs.
Castanea sativa
Crataegus (all)
Eucalyptus (many)
Fraxinus angustifolia and cvs.
excelsior and cvs.
Griselinia littoralis
Ilex ×altaclarensis and cvs.
aquifolium and cvs.
Laurus nobilis and cvs.
Phillyrea latifolia and cvs.
Populus alba
canescens
tremula
Quercus cerris
ilex
petraea
robur
×turneri
Salix (most)
Sorbus aria and cvs.
aucuparia and cvs.

Shrubs

Atraphaxis frutescens
Atriplex canescens
halimus
Baccharis halimifolia
patagonica
Bupleurum fruticosum
Cassinia fulvida
Chamaerops humilis
Choisya ternata
Colutea (all)
Coprosma lucida
Cordyline australis
indivisa
Corokia cotoneaster
×virgata
Cotoneaster (many)
Cytisus (many)
Diostea juncea
Elaeagnus ×ebbingei
glabra
pungens and cvs.
Ephedra (many)
Erica arborea 'Alpina'
lusitanica
×veitchii
Escallonia (most)
Euonymus fortunei and cvs.
japonicus and cvs.
Fabiana imbricata 'Prostrata'
Fuchsia magellanica and cvs.
Garrya elliptica
Genista (most)
Halimium (all)
Halimodendron halodendron
Hebe (all)
Helianthemum (most)
Helichrysum (many)
Hippophae rhamnoides
Hydrangea macrophylla and cvs.
Ilex aquifolium and cvs.
Lavandula spica and cvs.
Lavatera olbia
Leycesteria formosa
Lonicera pileata
Lycium (all)

Seaside Areas—Shrubs—*continued*

Myrica cerifera
Olearia (most)
Ozothamnus (many)
Pachystegia insignis
Parahebe (all)
Phlomis (most)
Phormium (all)
Pittosporum (most)
Prunus spinosa
Pyracantha (all)
Rhamnus alaternus
Rosa (many species)
Rosmarinus officinalis and cvs.
Salix (many)
Sambucus racemosa
Santolina (all)
Senecio (most)
Sibiraea laevigata
Spartium junceum
Spiraea (many)
Suaeda fruticosa
Tamarix (all)
Ulex (all)
Viburnum, many, especially evergreen spp.
Yucca (all)

Climbers

Muehlenbeckia complexa
varians
Polygonum aubertii
baldschuanicum

Conifers

×Cupressocyparis leylandii
Cupressus (many)
Juniperus (most)
Pinus contorta
mugo and forms
muricata
nigra
Pinus nigra maritima
pinaster
pinea
radiata
thunbergii
Podocarpus alpinus
nivalis

Bamboos

Arundinaria (many)
Sasa (all)

SHRUBS suitable for HEAVY SHADE

Arctostaphylos uva-ursi
Aucuba japonica and cvs.
Buxus sempervirens and cvs.
Camellia japonica and cvs.
×williamsii and cvs.
Cornus canadensis
Daphne laureola
pontica
Elaeagnus (evergreen)
Euonymus fortunei and cvs.
×Fatshedera lizei
Fatsia japonica
Gaultheria (all)
Gaylussacia (all)
Hedera helix 'Arborea'
Hypericum androsaemum
calycinum
Ilex ×altaclarensis and cvs.
aquifolium and cvs.
Leucothoe fontanesiana
Ligustrum (many)
Lonicera nitida and cvs.
pileata
Mahonia aquifolium
Myrsine africana
Osmanthus heterophyllus and cvs.
Pachysandra terminalis
Pachystima canbyi
myrsinites
Phillyrea decora
Prunus laurocerasus and cvs.
lusitanica
Rhododendron Hardy Hybrids
ponticum
Rhodotypos scandens
Ribes alpinum
Rubus odoratus
spectabilis
tricolor
Ruscus (all)
Sarcococca (all)
Skimmia (all)
Symphoricarpos (all)
Vaccinium vitis-idaea
Viburnum acerifolium
davidii
Vinca (all)

Conifers

Cephalotaxus (all)
Juniperus ×media 'Pfitzerana'
Podocarpus alpinus
Podocarpus andinus
nivalis
Taxus (all)

Bamboos

Arundinaria (most)
Phyllostachys (most)
Sasa (all)

SHRUBS and CLIMBERS suitable for NORTH and EAST-FACING WALLS

Shrubs

Acradenia frankliniae
Azara microphylla
petiolaris
Berberis ×stenophylla
Camellia 'Inspiration' (North Walls only)
japonica and cvs. (North Walls only)
reticulata (North Walls only)
saluenensis (North Walls only)
sasanqua (North Walls only)
×williamsii and cvs. (North Walls only)
Carpodetus serratus
Chaenomeles (most)
Choisya ternata
Crinodendron hookeranum
patagua
Daphne gnidium
×hybrida
odora
Desfontainea spinosa
Dichotomanthes tristaniicarpa
Drimys winteri
Eriobotrya japonica
Eucryphia cordifolia
×intermedia
×nymansensis and cvs.
Euonymus fortunei and cvs.
Garrya elliptica
Garrya ×thuretii
Grevillea rosmarinifolia
Ilex corallina
georgei
insignis
latifolia
Illicium anisatum
Jasminum humile and forms
nudiflorum
Kerria japonica 'Pleniflora'
Lomatia myricoides
Mahonia japonica
lomariifolia
×media and cvs.
Mitraria coccinea
Osmanthus yunnanensis
Pentapterygium serpens
Photinia serrulata
Piptanthus laburnifolius
Pyracantha (all)
Ribes laurifolium
Rubus henryi
lambertianus
Schima argentea
Viburnum foetens
grandiflorum

Climbers

Akebia quinata
Berchemia racemosa
Celastrus orbiculatus
Hedera colchica and cvs.
helix and cvs.
Hydrangea anomala
Hydrangea petiolaris
Muehlenbeckia complexa
varians
Parthenocissus (all)
Schizophragma hydrangeoides
integrifolium

SHRUBS suitable for GROUND COVER

Arctostaphylos nevadensis
uva-ursi
Aucuba japonica 'Nana Rotundifolia'
Berberis tsangpoensis
wilsoniae
Buxus microphylla
sempervirens 'Prostrata'
Calluna vulgaris and cvs.
Ceanothus gloriosus
divergens
Coprosma propinqua
Cornus canadensis
Cotoneaster—several including:
adpressus
dammeri
horizontalis
'Hybridus Pendulus'
microphyllus and cvs.
salicifolius 'Repens'
'Skogholm'
'Valkenburg'
Cytisus ×beanii
decumbens
×kewensis
scoparius prostratus
Daboecia cantabrica and cvs.
Dryas octopetala
Empetrum nigrum
Ephedra andina
distachya
Erica (most)
Euonymus fortunei and cvs.
Gaultheria (most)
×Gaulnettya wisleyensis
Hebe, many, especially
albicans
'Carl Teschner'
carnosula
pinguifolia 'Pagei'
rakaiensis
Hedera (all)
Helianthemum (all)
Hypericum calycinum
×moseranum
Jasminum nudiflorum
parkeri
Leptospermum humifusum
Leucothoe fontanesiana
keiskii

Ground Cover—Shrubs—*continued*

Lithospermum diffusum and cvs.
Lonicera acuminata
Mahonia nervosa
repens
Mitchella repens
Muehlenbeckia (all)
Pachistima myrsinites
Pachysandra terminalis
Pernettya buxifolia
ciliata
prostrata
Pimelia prostrata
Potentilla fruticosa 'Beesii'
mandschurica
Rhododendron (many, especially members of the Lapponicum series and Saluenense series)
Evergreen Azaleas, many, including
'Arendsii'
'Hatsugiri'
'Izayoi'
'Kure-no-yuki'
'Leo'
'Miyagino'
'Rosebud'
Ribes alpinum 'Pumilum'
henryi
laurifolium
Rosa 'Max Graff'
nitida
× paulii
× polliniana
'Raubritter'
wichuraiana
Rosmarinus lavendulaceus
Rubus calycinoides
tricolor
Salix—several, including:
cottetii
× finnmarchica
× grahamii
myrsinites
repens and cvs.
uva-ursi
Santolina (all)
Sarcococca humilis
Stephanandra incisa 'Crispa'
Symphoricarpos × chenaultii
'Hancock'
Vaccinium, many, especially
delavayi
glaucoalbum
moupinense
myrtillus
vitis-idaea
Viburnum davidii
Vinca (all)

Conifers

Cephalotaxus fortuni 'Prostrata'
harringtonia 'Prostrata'
Juniperus communis, several forms, including—**depressa**
'Effusa'
'Hornibrookii'
'Repanda'
conferta
horizontalis and forms
× media (several cvs.) including—**'Kosteri'**
'Old Gold'
'Plumosa'
Juniperus sabina tamariscifolia
Picea abies 'Repens'
Pinus strobus 'Prostrata'
Podocarpus alpinus
nivalis
Taxus baccata 'Cavendishii'
'Repandens'
'Repens Aurea'

Bamboos

Arundinaria vagans
Sasa tessellata
Sasa veitchii
Shibataea kumasasa

TREES of PENDULOUS HABIT

Acer saccharinum 'Pendulum'
Betula pendula 'Dalecarlica'
'Tristis'
'Youngii'
Buxus sempervirens 'Aurea Pendula'
'Pendula'
Crataegus monogyna 'Pendula'
'Pendula Rosea'
Fagus sylvatica 'Aurea Pendula'
'Pendula'
'Purpurea Pendula'
'Tortuosa'
Fraxinus angustifolia 'Pendula'
excelsior 'Pendula'
Gleditsia triacanthos 'Bujoti'
Laburnum × watereri 'Alford's Weeping'
Malus prunifolia 'Pendula'
Parrotia persica 'Pendula'
Populus 'Hiltingbury Weeping'
tremula 'Pendula'
tremuloides 'Pendula'
Prunus mahaleb 'Pendula'
subhirtella 'Pendula'
× yedoensis 'Ivensii'
'Shidare Yoshino'

Pendulous habit—Trees—*continued*

Pyrus salicifolia 'Pendula'
Quercus pyrenaica 'Pendula'
robur 'Pendula'
Salix babylonica
×blanda
×chrysocoma
'Elegantissima'
×erythroflexuosa
matsudana 'Pendula'
'Sepulcralis'
Sophora japonica 'Pendula'
Tilia petiolaris
Ulmus glabra 'Camperdownii'
'Pendula'
×hollandica 'Serpentina'
'Smithii'

Conifers

Cedrus atlantica 'Glauca Pendula'
'Pendula'
Chamaecyparis lawsoniana 'Intertexta'
'Pendula'
nootkatensis 'Pendula'
Cupressus lusitanica 'Glauca Pendula'
macrocarpa 'Pendula'
Dacrydium franklinii
Larix decidua 'Pendula'
kaempferi 'Pendula'
Picea abies 'Inversa'
brewerana
omorika 'Pendula'
smithiana
spinulosa
Taxodium distichum 'Pendens'
Taxus baccata 'Dovastoniana'
Tsuga canadensis 'Pendula'
heterophylla 'Greenmantle'

The ultimate height of the underlisted trees is largely dependent on the stem height at which they are grafted.

Caragana arborescens 'Pendula'
Cornus florida 'Pendula'
Corylus avellana 'Pendula'
Cotoneaster 'Hybridus Pendulus'
Ilex aquifolium 'Argenteomarginata Pendula'
'Pendula'
Laburnum alpinum 'Pendulum'
anagyroides 'Pendulum'
Malus 'Elise Rathke'
Morus alba 'Pendula'
Prunus cerasifera 'Pendula'
Prunus fruticosa 'Pendula'
'Hilling's Weeping'
'Kiku Shidare Zakura'
mume 'Pendula'
persica 'Crimson Cascade'
'Windle Weeping'
subhirtella 'Pendula Rubra'
Salix caprea 'Pendula'
purpurea 'Pendula'
Sorbus aria 'Pendula'
aucuparia 'Pendula'

TREES and SHRUBS of UPRIGHT or FASTIGIATE HABIT

Trees and Shrubs

Acer ×lobelii
platanoides 'Columnare'
pseudoplatanus 'Erectum'
rubrum 'Scanlon'
saccharinum 'Pyramidalis'
saccharum 'Temple's Upright'
Aesculus hippocastanum 'Pyramidalis'
Betula pendula 'Fastigiata'
Carpinus betulus 'Columnaris'
'Fastigiata'
Corylus colurna
Crataegus monogyna 'Stricta'
Fagus sylvatica 'Cockleshell'
'Dawyck'
Ilex aquifolium 'Green Pillar'
Laburnum alpinum 'Pyramidale'
anagyroides 'Erect'
Liriodendron tulipifera 'Fastigiata'
Malus ×micromalus
prunifolia 'Fastigiata'
tschonoskii
Morus alba 'Pyramidalis'
Populus alba 'Pyramidalis'
nigra 'Italica'
'Thevestina'
simonii 'Fastigiata'
Prunus 'Amanogawa'
×hillieri 'Spire'
lusitanica 'Myrtifolia'
'Pandora'
×schmittii
'Taizanfukun'
'Umineko'
Ptelea trifoliata 'Fastigiata'
Quercus castaneifolia 'Green Spire'
petraea 'Columnaris'
robur 'Fastiata'
'Fastigiata Purpurea'
Robinia pseudoacacia 'Pyramidalis'
Sambucus nigra 'Pyramidalis'
Sorbus aucuparia 'Fastigiata'
commixta
'Joseph Rock'
meinichii
scopulina
×thuringiaca 'Fastigiata'
Tilia cordata 'Swedish Upright'
Ulmus angustifolia cornubiensis
glabra 'Exoniensis'
×sarniensis
'Dicksonii'

Upright or Fastigiate Habit—Conifers

Austrocedrus chilensis
Calocedrus decurrens
Cedrus atlantica 'Fastigiata'
Cephalotaxus harringtonia 'Fastigiata'
Chamaecyparis lawsoniana 'Allumii'
'Columnaris'
'Ellwoodii'
'Erecta'
'Fraseri'
'Kilmacurragh'
'Pottenii'
'Robusta Glauca'
'Wisselii'
'Witzeliana'
Cryptomeria japonica 'Lobbii'
× Cupressocyparis leylandii and cvs.
Cupressus abramsiana
glabra 'Pyramidalis'
goveniana
sempervirens
Ginkgo biloba 'Fastigiata'
Juniperus chinensis 'Keteleerii'
'Pyramidalis'
virginiana 'Hillii'
'Skyrocket'
Picea abies 'Pyramidata'
omorika
Pinus sylvestris 'Fastigiata'
Sciadopitys verticillata
Taxodium ascendens 'Nutans'
Taxus baccata 'Fastigiata'
'Fastigiata Aureomarginata'
'Standishii'
× media 'Hicksii'
'Sargentii'
Thuja occidentalis 'Fastigiata'
'Malonyana'
'Spiralis'
plicata 'Fastigiata'
Tsuga heterophylla 'Laursen's Column'

TREES and SHRUBS with ORNAMENTAL BARK or TWIGS

Trees

Acer davidii
griseum
grosseri
hersii
negundo 'Violaceum'
palmatum 'Senkaki'
pensylvanicum and cvs.
Arbutus × andrachnoides
menziesii
Betula (most)
Carya ovata
Eucalyptus (most)
Fraxinus excelsior 'Jaspidea'
Lagerstroemia indica
Lyonothamnus floribundus aspleniifolius
Myrtus apiculata
Parrotia persica
Platanus (all)
Prunus dawyckensis
maackii
× schmittii
serrula
Salix alba 'Chermesina'
'Vitellina'
acutifolia and cvs.
× chrysocoma
daphnoides and cvs.
× erythroflexuosa
matsudana 'Tortuosa'
Stewartia (most)
Tilia platyphyllos 'Aurea'
'Rubra'

Shrubs

Abelia triflora
Arctostaphylos (most)
Clethra acuminata
barbinervis
delavayi
Cornus alba and cvs.
baileyi
officinalis
stolonifera 'Flaviramea'
Corylus avellana 'Contorta'
Deutzia several spp.
Dipelta floribunda
ventricosa
Euonymus alatus
phellomanus
Hydrangea aspera
bretschneideri
sargentiana
villosa
Hypericum kalmianum
prolificum
Kerria japonica and cvs.
Leucothoe grayana
oblongifolia
Leycesteria formosa
Philadelphus (several)
Prunus canescens
Rhododendron Barbatum Series
glaucophyllum
thomsonii
Ribes lacustre
Rosa omeiensis pterocantha
roxburghii
setigera
virginiana
Rubus biflorus
cockburnianus
leucodermis
phoenicolasius
thibetanus
Salix irrorata
moupinensis
Stephanandra tanakae
Syringa reticulata
Vaccinium corymbosum

Ornamental Bark or Twigs—Conifers

Abies squamata
Cryptomeria japonica
Cupressus forbesii
guadalupensis
Juniperus deppeana pachyphlaea
recurva
Juniperus wallichiana
Pinus bungeana
gerardiana
sylvestris
Sequoia sempervirens
Sequoiadendron giganteum

TREES and SHRUBS with BOLD FOLIAGE

Trees

Acer japonicum 'Vitifolium'
macrophyllum
Ailanthus altissima
Aralia (all)
Catalpa (all)
Cordyline australis
Firmiana simplex
Griselinia lucida
Gymnocladus dioicus
Idesia polycarpa
Juglans cinerea
sieboldiana
Kalopanax pictus
Magnolia macrophylla
obovata
officinalis biloba
tripetala
Melia azedarach
Meliosma oldhamii
veitchiorum
Morus alba 'Macrophylla'
Paulownia (all)
Platanus (all)
Populus lasiocarpa
szechuanica
wilsonii
Pterocarya (all)
Quercus dentata
macrocarpa
pontica
velutina 'Rubrifolia'
Sorbus cuspidata
harrowiana
insignis
'Mitchellii'
Tilia americana
× moltkei
Trachycarpus fortunei
Zanthoxylum ailanthoides

Shrubs

Alangium chinense
platanifolium
Aralia (all)
Chamaerops humilis
Entelea arborescens
Eriobotrya japonica
× Fatshedera lizei
Fatsia japonica
Gevuina avellana
Hydrangea quercifolia
sargentiana
Ilex latifolia
platyphylla
Magnolia delavayi
grandiflora and cvs.
Mahonia acanthifolia
japonica
lomariifolia
× media and cvs.
Mallotus spp.
Melianthus major
Osmanthus armatus
yunnanensis
Phormium tenax
Pseudopanax arboreus
davidii
laetus
Rhododendron, several including
fictolacteum
grande
macabeanum
rex
sinogrande
Sambucus canadensis 'Maxima'
Sorbaria (all)
Viburnum rhytidophyllum
Yucca gloriosa
recurvifolia

Climbers

Actinidia chinensis
Ampelopsis megalophylla
Aristolochia macrophylla
tomentosa
Hedera canariensis and cvs.
Hedera colchica and cvs.
Holboellia latifolia
Vitis amurensis
coignetiae

Bamboos

Sasa palmata
Sasa tessellata

TREES and SHRUBS for AUTUMN COLOUR

Trees

Acer, many, especially
  capillipes
  nikoense
  platanoides and cvs.
  rubrum and cvs.
  triflorum
Aesculus, several, including
  flava
  glabra
  neglecta
Amelanchier laevis
  lamarckii
Betula (most)
Carpinus (all)
Carya (all)
Cedrela sinensis
Cercidiphyllum japonicum
Cercis canadensis
Cladrastis (all)
+Crataegomespilus dardarii
Cornus controversa
Crataegus, many, especially
  coccinioides
  nitida
  pinnatifida major
  prunifolia
×Crataemespilus grandiflora
Fagus (most)
Fraxinus excelsior 'Jaspidea'
  oxycarpa 'Raywood'
Gymnocladus dioicus
Liquidambar (all)
Malus, several, including
  florentina
  prattii
  transitoria
  trilobata
  tschonoskii
Nothofagus antarctica
Nyssa (all)
Parrotia persica
Phellodendron (all)
Photinia beauverdiana
  villosa sinica
Picrasma quassioides
Populus, several, including
  alba
  canescens
  'Serotina Aurea'
  tremula
  trichocarpa
Prunus, many, including
  ×hillieri
  ×juddii
  litigiosa
  sargentii
Quercus, many, including
  coccinea
  palustris
  phellos
  rubra
Rhus potaninii
  succedanea
  sylvestris
Sassafras albidum
Sorbus, many, including
  alnifolia
  americana
  commixta
  'Embley'
  'Joseph Rock'
  scalaris
Stewartia (all)
Ulmus, several, including
  carpinifolia
  procera

Shrubs

Acer, many, especially
  ginnala
  japonica and cvs.
  palmatum and cvs.
Aesculus parviflora
Amelanchier florida
Aronia (all)
Berberis, many, including
  aggregata
  dictyophylla
  morrisonensis
  thunbergii
  wilsoniae and vars.
Callicarpa (all)
Ceratostigma willmottianum
Clethra (all)
Cornus alba
  baileyi
  florida and cvs.
  officinalis
Corylopsis (all)
Cotinus (all)
Cotoneaster, many, including
  adpressus
  ambiguus
  bullatus
  divaricatus
  horizontalis
Disanthus cercidifolius
Enkianthus (all)
Eucryphia glutinosa
Euonymus, many, inclnding
  alatus
  grandiflorus
  latifolius
  oxyphyllus
Fothergilla (all)
Gaylussacia brachycera
Hamamelis (all)
Hydrangea 'Preziosa'
  quercifolia
  serrata

Autumn Colour—Shrubs—*continued*

Lindera (most)
Parabenzoin praecox
Photinia koreana
villosa
Prunus, several, including
besseyi
incisa
Ptelea trifoliata
Rhododendron (several of the Azalea series) including
arborescens
calendulaceum
luteum
occidentale
quinquefolium
reticulatum
Rhus, several, especially
copallina
glabra
typhina
Ribes americanum
odoratum
Rosa nitida
rugosa and cvs.
setigera
virginiana
Sorbaria aitchisonii
Spiraea prunifolia
Stephanandra (all)
Vaccinium, several, including
corymbosum
praestans
virgatum
Viburnum, many, including
carlesii and cvs.
furcatum
opulus
prunifolium
trilobum
Zanthoxylum piperitum

Climbers

Actinidia arguta
Ampelopsis (all)
Celastrus (all)
Parthenosiccus (all)
Vitis (all)

Conifers

Ginkgo biloba
Larix (all)
Metasequoia glyptostroboides
Pseudolarix amabilis
Taxodium (all)

TREES and SHRUBS with RED or PURPLE FOLIAGE

Trees

Acer campestre 'Schwerinii'
palmatum 'Atropurpureum'
'Heptalobum Elegans Purpureum'
platanoides 'Crimson King'
'Schwedleri'
Betula pendula 'Purpurea'
Catalpa × erubescens 'Purpurea'
Fagus sylvatica purpurea
'Riversii'
'Rohanii'
'Roseomarginata'
Malus 'Aldenhamensis'
'Echtermeyer'
'Jay Darling'
'Lemoinei'
'Profusion'
× purpurea
Pittosporum tenuifolium 'Purpureum'
Prunus × blireana
'Moseri'
cerasifera 'Diversifolia
'Hessei'
'Nigra'
'Pissardii'
'Rosea'
'Trailblazer'
× cistena
padus 'Colorata'
persica 'Foliis Rubis'
Quercus petraea 'Purpurea'
robur 'Atropurpurea'

Shrubs

Acer palmatum 'Dissectum Atropurpureum'
'Linearilobum Purpureum'
Berberis × ottawensis 'Purpurea'
thunbergii atropurpurea
'Atropurpurea Nana'
'Rose Glow'
Brachyglottis repanda 'Purpurea'
Corylopsis willmottiae 'Spring Purple'
Corylus maxima 'Purpurea'
Cotinus coggygria 'Royal Purple'
'Rubrifolius'
Euonymus europaeus 'Atropurpureus'
Phormium tenax 'Purpureum'
Prunus spinosa 'Purpurea'
Sambucus nigra 'Purpurea'
Weigela florida 'Foliis Purpureis'

Climbers

Vit is vinifera 'Purpurea'

TREES and SHRUBS with GOLDEN or YELLOW FOLIAGE

Trees

Acer cappadocicum 'Aureum'
negundo 'Auratum'
pseudoplatanus 'Worleei'
saccharinum 'Lutescens'
Alnus glutinosa 'Aurea'
incana 'Aurea'
Catalpa bignonioides 'Aurea'
Fagus sylvatica 'Aurea Pendula'
'Zlatia'
Gleditsia triacanthos 'Sunburst'
Ilex aquifolium 'Flavescens'
Laburnum anagyroides 'Aureum'
Laurus nobilis 'Aurea'
Populus alba 'Richardii'
'Serotina Aurea'
Quercus robur 'Concordia'
rubra 'Aurea'
Robinia pseudoacacia 'Frisia'
Sorbus aria 'Aurea'
'Chrysophylla'
aucuparia 'Dirkenii'
Tilia ×europaea 'Wratislaviensis'
Ulmus glabra 'Lutescens'
×hollandica 'Wredei'
procera 'Louis van Houtte'
×sarniensis 'Dicksonii'

Shrubs

Acer japonicum 'Aureum'
Berberis thunbergii 'Aurea'
Buxus sempervirens 'Latifolia Maculata'
Calluna vulgaris 'Aurea'
'Golden Feather'
'Gold Haze'
'Joy Vanstone'
'Serlei Aurea'
Cornus alba 'Aurea'
mas 'Aurea'
'Elegantissima'
Corylus avellana 'Aurea'
Erica carnea 'Aurea'
cinerea 'Golden Hue'
Euonymus japonicus 'Ovatus Aureus'
Ilex aquifolium 'Flavescens'
Ligustrum ovalifolium 'Aureum'
'Vicaryi'
Lonicera nitida 'Baggesen's Gold'
Philadelphus coronarius 'Aureus'
Physocarpus opulifolius 'Luteus'
Pittosporum tenuifolium 'Warnham Gold'
Ptelea trifoliata 'Aurea'
Ribes alpinum 'Aureum'
sanguineum 'Brocklebankii'
Sambucus canadensis 'Aurea'
nigra 'Aurea'
racemosa 'Plumosa Aurea'
Syringa emodii 'Aurea'
'Aureovariegata'
vulgaris 'Aurea'
Viburnum opulus 'Aureum'
Weigela 'Looymansii Aurea'

Climbers

Hedera helix 'Buttercup'
Humulus lupulus 'Aureus'

Conifers

Cedrus deodara 'Aurea'
'Aurea Pendula'
Chamaecyparis lawsoniana, many cvs., including
'Golden King'
'Lanei'
'Lutea'
'Lutea Nana'
'Stewartii'
'Winston Churchill'
obtusa, several cvs., including
'Crippsii'
'Nana Aurea'
'Tetragona Aurea'
pisifera, several cvs., including
'Aurea'
'Filifera Aurea'
'Golden Mop'
'Plumosa Aurea'
Cupressus macrocarpa, several cvs., especially
'Donard Gold'
'Goldcrest'
Juniperus chinensis 'Aurea'
×media 'Old Gold'
'Pfitzerana Aurea'
'Plumosa Aurea'
Taxus baccata, several cvs., including
'Dovastonii Aurea'
'Elegantissima'
'Standishii'
'Washingtonii'
Thuja occidentalis, several cvs., especially
'Rheingold'
orientalis, several cvs., especially
'Aurea'
'Aurea Nana'
plicata 'Aurea'
Thujopsis dolabrata 'Aurea'

TREES and SHRUBS with GREY or SILVER FOLIAGE

Trees

Eucalyptus, many, including
  coccifera
  globulus
  gunnii
  niphophila
Populus alba
  canescens
Pyrus, several, especially
  × canescens
  elaeagrifolia
  nivalis
  salicifolia 'Pendula'
Salix alba 'Sericea'
  exigua

Shrubs

Artemisia (all)
Atriplex canescens
  halimus
Berberis dictyophylla
  temolaica
Buddleia, several, including
  alternifolia 'Argentea'
  fallowiana
  tibetica
Calluna vulgaris 'Silver Queen'
Caryopteris × clandonensis
  incana
Cassinia vauvilliersii albida
Cistus, several, including
  albidus
  × canescens
  × glaucus
  laurifolius
Convolvulus cneorum
Cytisus battandieri
Elaeagnus, several, including
  angustifolia
  commutata
  macrophylla
Erica tetralix 'Alba Mollis'
Euryops acraeus
  pectinatus
Fejoia sellowiana
× Halimiocistus wintonensis
Halimium atriplicifolium
  halimifolium
Halimodendron halodendron
Hebe, several, including
  albicans
  colensoi 'Glauca'
  glaucophylla
  pinguifolia 'Pagei'
Helianthemum apenninum roseum
  nummularium, several cvs. including
    'Mrs. Croft'
    'Rhodanthe Carneum'
    'The Bride'
Helichrysum (all)
Hippophae rhamnoides
Lavandula spica (several cvs., including
    'Grappenhall'
    'Hidcote'
    'Vera'
  stoechas
Leptospermum cunninghamii
  lanigerum
Marsdenia erecta
Olearia, several, including
  mollis
  moschata
  × scilloniensis
Pachystegia insignis
Perovskia (all)
Phylica superba
Potentilla arbuscula 'Beesii'
  fruticosa 'Mandshurica'
    'Vilmoriniana'
Romneya (all)
Rosa rubrifolia
Ruta graveolens and cvs.
Salix × balfourii
  elaeagnos
  exigua
  glaucosericea
  gracilistyla
  lanata
  lapponum
  repens argentea
  seringeana
Salvia lavandulifolia
  officinalis and cvs.
Santolina chamaecyparissus
  neapolitana
Senecio, several, especially
  greyi
  leucostachys
Shepherdia argentea
Sibiraea laevigata
Teucrium fruticans
Zauschneria cana

Conifers

Abies concolor 'Candicans'
  'Glauca Compacta'
  'Violacea'
  lasiocarpa arizonica
  magnifica 'Glauca'
  pinsapo 'Glauca'
Cedrus atlantica glauca
Chamaecyparis lawsoniana, many cvs., including
  'Columnaris'
  'Ellwoodii'
  'Fletcheri'
  glauca
  'Pembury Blue'

Grey or Silver Foliage—Conifers—*continued*

Chamaecyparis lawsoniana 'Robusta Glauca'
'Triomf van Boskoop'
pisifera 'Boulevard'
'Squarrosa'
Cupressus cashmeriana
glabra and cvs.
lusitanica 'Glauca'
'Glauca Pendula'
Juniperus chinensis (several cvs.)
'Grey Owl'
horizontalis and cvs. especially **'Plumosa'**
'Wiltonii'
× media, several cvs., including **'Blue Cloud'**
'Pfitzerana Glauca'
Juniperus procumbens
sabina 'Hicksii'
scopulorum, several cvs., including **'Pathfinder'**
'Springbank'
squamata 'Meyeri'
virginiana, several cvs. including **'Glauca'**
'Manhattan Blue'
Picea glauca
× hurstii
pungens glauca and cvs.
Pinus koraiensis 'Glauca Compacta'
pumila and cvs.
wallichiana
Pseudotsuga menziesii glauca
Tsuga mertensiana 'Glauca'

Climbers

Lonicera caprifolium and cvs.
× splendida
Vitis vinifera 'Incana'

TREES and SHRUBS with VARIEGATED FOLIAGE

Trees

Acer negundo 'Elegans'
'Variegatum'
platanoides 'Drummondii'
pseudoplatanus several cvs. especially **'Leopoldii'**
'Nizetii'
rufinerve 'Albolimbatum'
Buxus sempervirens 'Aurea Pendula'
Castanea sativa 'Albomarginata'
Cornus controversa 'Variegata'
mas 'Variegata'
Crataegus monogyna 'Variegata'
Fagus sylvatica 'Luteovariegata'
Fraxinus pensylvanica 'Aucubifolia'
'Variegata'
Ilex × altaclarensis, several cvs., including **'Golden King'**
'Silver Sentinel'
Ligustrum lucidum 'Excelsum Superbum'
'Tricolor'
Liquidambar styraciflua 'Aureum'
Liriodendron tulipifera 'Aureomarginatum'
Platanus × hispanica 'Suttneri'
Populus × candicans 'Aurora'
Quercus robur 'Variegata'
Ulmus procera 'Argenteovariegata'

Shrubs

Abutilon megapotamicum 'Variegatum'
× milleri 'Variegatum'
Acanthopanax sieboldianus 'Variegatus'
Acer palmatum, several cvs., especially **'Albomarginatum'**
'Dissectum Variegatum'
Aralia elata 'Aureovariegata'
'Variegata'
Aucuba japonica, several cvs., especially **'Crotonifolia'**
'Gold Dust'
Azara microphylla 'Variegata'
Berberis thunbergii 'Rose Glow'
Buddleia davidii 'Harlequin'
Buxus sempervirens, several cvs., especially **'Elegantissima'**
Cleyera fortunei
Cornus alba 'Elegantissima'
'Spaethii'
'Variegata'
alternifolia 'Argentea'
mas 'Variegata'
Coronilla glauca 'Variegata'
Cotoneaster horizontalis 'Variegata'
Crataegus oxyacantha 'Gireoudii'
Daphne odora 'Aureomarginata'

Variegated Foliage—Shrubs—*continued*

Elaeagnus pungens 'Dicksonii'
'Maculata'
Euonymus fortunei 'Silver Queen'
'Variegatus'
japonicus, several cvs. especially
'Aureopictus'
'Macrophyllus Albus'
Fatsia japonica 'Variegata'
Fejoia sellowiana 'Variegata'
Fuchsia magellanica 'Variegata'
'Versicolor'
Griselinia littoralis 'Variegata'
Hebe ×andersonii 'Variegata'
×franciscana 'Variegata'
glaucophylla 'Variegata'
Hibiscus syriacus 'Meehanii'
Hydrangea macrophylla 'Maculata'
'Tricolor'
Hypericum ×moseranum 'Tricolor'
Ilex aquifolium, many cvs., especially
'Argenteomarginata'
'Aureomarginata'
'Golden Milkboy'
'Grandis'
'Handsworth New Silver'
'Ovata Aurea'
Kerria japonica 'Variegata'
Leucothoe fontanesiana 'Rainbow'
Ligustrum sinense 'Variegatum'
Myrtus communis 'Variegatus'
Osmanthus heterophyllus
'Aureomarginatus'
'Latifolius Variegatus'
'Variegatus'
Pachysandra terminalis 'Variegata'
Philadelphus coronarius 'Variegatus'
Phormium tenax 'Variegatum'
'Veitchii'
Pieris japonica 'Variegata'
Pittosporum eugenioides
'Variegatum'
tenuifolium, several cvs., including
'Silver Queen'
'Variegatum'
Prunus laurocerasus 'Variegata'
lusitanica 'Variegata'
Rhamnus alaterna
'Argenteovariegata'
Rhododendron ponticum
'Variegatum'
Rubus microphyllus 'Variegatus'
Ruta graveolens 'Variegata'
Salvia officinalis 'Icterina'
'Tricolor'
Sambucus nigra 'Albovariegata'
'Aureomarginata'
'Pulverulenta'
Stachyurus chinensis 'Magpie'
Symphoricarpos orbiculatus
'Variegatus'
Syringa emodii 'Aureovariegata'
Vaccinium vitis-idaea 'Variegata'
Viburnum tinus 'Variegata'
Vinca major 'Maculata'
'Variegata'
minor 'Variegata'
Weigela florida 'Variegata'
praecox 'Variegata'

Conifers

Calocedrus decurrens
'Aureovariegata'
Chamaecyparis lawsoniana, several cvs., including
'Albospica'
'Argenteovariegata'
'Aureovariegata'
nootkatensis 'Aureovariegata'
'Variegata'
pisifera 'Nana Variegata'
Juniperus ×davurica 'Expansa Variegata'
×media 'Plumosa Albovariegata'
'Plumosa Aureovariegata'
Taxus baccata 'Variegata'
Thuja plicata 'Zebrina'
Thujopsis dolabrata 'Variegata'

Climbers

Actinidia kolomikta
Ampelopsis brevipedunculata
'Elegans'
Hedera canariensis 'Variegata'
colchica 'Dentata Variegata'
'Paddy's Pride'
helix, several cvs., including
'Glacier'
'Goldheart'
'Marginata'
Jasminum officinale
'Aureovariegatum'
Kadsura japonica 'Variegata'
Lonicera japonica 'Aureoreticulata'
Trachelospermum jasminoides
'Variegatum'

Variegated Foliage—Bamboos

Arundinaria chrysantha
variegata
Arundinaria viridistriata
Sasa veitchii

TREES and SHRUBS bearing ORNAMENTAL FRUIT

Trees

Acer pseudoplatanus erythrocarpum
Ailanthus altissima
Arbutus (all)
Catalpa bignonioides
Cercis siliquastrum
Diospyros kaki
Euodia (all)
Fraxinus ornus
Gleditsia triacanthos
Halesia (all)
Ilex, many, including
×altaclarensis 'Balearica'
'Camelliifolia'
'Wilsonii'
aquifolium 'J. C. van Tol'
latifolia
Koelreuteria paniculata
Maclura pomifera
Magnolia, several, including
campbellii mollicomata
obovata
tripetala
Malus, many, including
'Cashmere'
'Chilko'
'Dartmouth'
'Golden Hornet'
'John Downie'
Prunus cornuta
serotina
virginiana
Pterocarya (all)
Robinia fertilis
kelseyi
Sorbus, most, including
aucuparia and cvs.
commixta
'Joseph Rock'
pohuashanensis
scalaris
vilmorinii
'Winter Cheer'
Trachycarpus fortunei
Xanthoceras sorbifolium

Shrubs

Acanthopanax henryi
Aucuba japonica (female cvs.)
Berberis (most, especially deciduous)
Callicarpa (all)
Cercis siliquastrum
Chaenomeles (most)
Citrus 'Meyer's Lemon'
Clerodendrum trichotomum
Colutea (all)
Coriaria (all)
Cornus, many, especially
amomum
baileyi
mas
Cotinus coggygria
Cotoneaster (all)
Crataegus, most, especially
azarolus
durobrivensis
×grignonensis
mollis
orientalis
tanacetifolia
Cydonia oblonga
Daphne mezereum
Decaisnea fargesii
Dipteronia sinensis
Eriobotrya japonica
Euonymus, many, including
cornutus
grandiflorus
Euonymus latifolius
oxyphyllus
sachalinensis
Garrya elliptica (female)
×Gaulnettya wisleyensis
Gaultheria, many, including
cuneata
forrestii
miqueliana
procumbens
Hippophae rhamnoides
Ilex, most, including
aquifolium 'Amber'
'Bacciflava'
'Pyramidalis'
cornuta 'Burfordii'
serrata
verticillata and cvs.
Leycesteria formosa
Ligustrum chenaultii
confusum
Mahonia aquifolium
japonica
lomariifolia
Mespilus germanica
Myrica californica
cerifera
pensylvanica
Ochna serrulata
Paliurus spina-christi

Ornamental Fruit—Shrubs—*continued*

Pernettya buxifolia
ciliata
mucronata and cvs.
Poncirus trifoliata
Prinsepia (all)
Prunus, several, including
lauroceracus and cvs.
Ptelea (all)
Pyracantha (all)
+**Pyrocydonia danielii**
×**Pyronia veitchii**
Rehderodendron macrocarpum
Rosa, many, including
'Arthur Hillier'
'Highdownensis'
macrophylla and cvs.
moyesii and forms
setipoda
webbiana
Rubus phoenicolasius
Ruscus aculeatus
Sambucus (most)
Skimmia (all)
Staphylea (all)
Stranvaesia davidiana and cvs.
Symphoricarpos (most)
Symplocos paniculata
Vaccinium, several, including
corymbosum
cylindraceum
praestans
Viburnum, many, including
betulifolium
opulus and cvs.
setigerum
wrightii and cv.
Zanthoxylum planispinum

Climbers

Actinidia chinensis
Akebia quinnata
trifoliata
Ampelopsis, several, especially
brevipedunculata
Billardiera longiflora
Celastrus (all)
Clematis, several, especially
orientalis
tangutica
Lardizabala biternata
Parthenocissus, several, including
himalayana
Passiflora caerulea
edulis
Schisandra (all)
Sinofranchetia chinensis
Tripterygium (all)
Vitis, several, especially
'Brant'

Conifers

Abies, many, including
delavayi and vars.
koreana
procera
Picea, many, including
likiangensis
smithiana
Pinus, many, including
ayacahuite
wallichiana
Taxus baccata 'Lutea'

TREES and SHRUBS with FRAGRANT or SCENTED FLOWERS

The scents of flowers are a wonderful part of garden enjoyment as well as being a delightful extra attraction in a flowering plant. Just as a sense of smell differs from person to person, so scents vary from flower to flower. The positioning of a plant is of importance if its scent is not to be lost to the wind. Even if the position is right weather conditions can make all the difference to the strength or carrying power of delicate scents.

Trees

Acacia dealbata
Aesculus hippocastanum
Azara microphylla
Cladrastis lutea
sinensis
Crataegus monogyna
Drimys winteri
Eucryphia billardieri
Fraxinus mariesii
Gordonia chrysandra
Laburnum alpinum
×**watereri**
Magnolia fraseri
kobus
macrophylla
obovata
salicifolia
Malus angustifolia
baccata mandshurica
coronaria 'Charlottae'
floribunda
×**hartwigii**
'Hillieri'
'Hopa Crab'
hupehensis
ioensis

Fragrant or Scented Flowers—Trees—*continued*

Malus 'Profusion'
×robusta
spectabilis
zumii
Michelia doltsopa
figo
Myrtus apiculata
lechlerana
Pittosporum eugenioides
Plagianthus divaricatus
Poliothyrsis sinensis
Prunus, many, including
conradinae
'Jo-nioi'
Prunus lusitanica and cvs.
mahaleb
serrulata 'Albida'
'Taki-nioi'
yedoensis and cvs.
Robinia pseudoacacia and cvs.
Styrax japonica
Tilia ×euchlora
×europaea
oliveri
petiolaris
platyphyllos

Shrubs

Abelia chinensis
triflora
Alangium chinense
Azara lanceolata
petiolaris
Berberis buxifolia
sargentiana
vulgaris
Bruckenthalia spiculifolia
Buddleia, many, including
alternifolia
asiatica
auriculata
crispa
davidii and cvs.
fallowiana
farreri
forrestii
'Lochinch'
officinalis
'West Hill'
Buxus sempervirens and cvs.
Camellia sasanqua and cvs.
vernalis
Ceanothus 'Gloire de Versailles'
Chimonanthus praecox and cvs.
Chionanthus virginicus
Choisya ternata
Citrus (all)
Clerodendrum bungei
trichotomum
Clethra acuminata
alnifolia and cvs.
barbinervis
fargesii
Colletia armata
cruciata
Corokia cotoneaster
Coronilla glauca
valentina
Corylopsis (all)
Cytisus battandieri
maderensis magnifoliosus
monspessulanus
'Porlock'
praecox
purgans
Damnacanthus indicus
Daphne, many, including
alpina
arbuscula
blagayana
'Burkwoodii'
cneorum and forms
collina and vars.
gnidium
×hybrida
mezereum and cvs.
odora and cvs.
pontica
Datura suaveolens
Deutzia 'Avalanche'
compacta and cvs.
×elegantissima and cvs.
sieboldiana
Edgworthia papyrifera
Elaeagnus angustifolia
commutata
×ebbingei
glabra
macrophylla
umbellata
Erica arborea
'Alpina'
×darleyensis and cvs.
lusitanica
×veitchii
Escallonia 'Donard Gem'
pterocladon
Eucryphia milliganii
Euonymus sachalinensis
Eupatorium ligustrinum
Fothergilla gardenii
major
Freylinia cestroides
Gaultheria forrestii
fragrantissima
Genista aetnensis
cinerea
monosperma
virgata
Hakea microcarpa
Hamamelis mollis and cvs.

Fragrant or Scented Flowers—Shrubs—*continued*

Hoheria glabrata
lyalii
Itea ilicifolia
virginica
Jasminum humile 'Revolutum'
wallichianum
Ligustrum, all, including
quihoui
sinense
Lomatia myricoides
Lonicera angustifolia
fragrantissima
myrtillus
×purpusii
rupicola
standishii
syringantha
Luculia grandifolia
gratissima
pinceana
Lupinus arboreus and cvs.
Magnolia denudata
grandiflora and cvs.
sieboldii
sinensis
×soulangiana and cvs.
stellata and cvs.
×thompsoniana
virginiana
×watsonii
wilsonii
Mahonia japonica
×media and cvs.
Marsdenia erecta
Myrtus communis and cvs.
Olearia ×haastii
ilicifolia
macrodonta
odorata
rani
Osmanthus (all)
×Osmarea burkwoodii
Osmaronia cerasiformis
Paeonia ×lemoinei and cvs.
Paulownia fargesii
lilacina
Petteria ramentacea
Philadelphus, many, including
'Belle Etoile'
'Bouquet Blanc'
coronarius
delavayi
'Etoile Rose'
×lemoinei
'Sybille'
'Virginal'
Phillyrea decora
Phylica superba
Pimelea prostrata
Pittosporum patulum
tobira
undulatum

Poncirus trifoliata
Prunus mume
Ptelea trifoliata
Pterostyrax hispida
Pyracantha (all)
Rhododendron, many, including
'Albatross'
'Altaclarense' (Deciduous Azalea)
arborescens
'Argosy'
atlanticum
auriculatum
'Balzac' (Deciduous Azalea)
calophytum
canescens
'Countess of Haddington'
'Daviesii' (Deciduous Azalea)
decorum
diaprepes
discolor
'Exquisitum' (Deciduous Azalea)
fortunei
'Fragrantissimum'
'Irene Koster' (Deciduous Azalea)
'Isabella'
'July Fragrance'
Lodauric
Loderi and cvs.
luteum
'Magnificum' (Deciduous Azalea)
'Midsummer Snow'
nudiflorum
nuttallii
occidentale
'Polar Bear'
roseum
scottianum
'Superbum' (Deciduous Azalea)
viscosum
Ribes alpinum
fasciculatum
gayanum
odoratum
Romneya (all)
Rosa, many, including
acicularis
'Albert Edwards'
'Andersonii'
banksiae (single forms)
bracteata
brunonii
cinnamomea
×dupontii
filipes
foliolosa
helenae
laevigata
longicuspis
'Macrantha'
moschata
multiflora

Fragrant or Scented Flowers—Shrubs—*continued*

Rosa × odorata and forms
pisocarpa
primula
roxburghii
rubus
setigera
soulieana
wichuraiana
Sarcococca (all)
Skimmia japonica 'Fragrans'
'Rubella'
laureola
Spartium junceum
Spartocytisus nubigenus
Syringa, many including
× chinensis and cvs.
× henryi and cvs.
× josiflexa and cvs.
julianae
× persica and cvs.
Syringa sweginzowii
wolfii
yunnanensis and cvs.
Vulgaris Hybrids
Ulex europaeus
Viburnum, many, including
bitchiuense
× bodnantense and cvs.
× burkwoodii and cvs.
× carlcephalum
carlesii and cvs.
erubescens
farreri and cvs.
grandiflorum
japonicum
× juddii
odoratissimum
Yucca filamentosa
flaccida
Zenobia pulverulenta

Climbers

Actinidia chinensis
polygama
Akebia quinata
Clematis armandii and cvs.
cirrhosa balearica
flammula
montana and forms
paniculata
pavoliniana
rehderana
uncinata
× violacea 'Rubro-marginata'
Clematoclethra integrifolia
Decumaria sinensis
Holboellia latifolia
Jasminum azoricum
beesianum
officinale
polyanthum
× stephanense
Lardizabala biternata
Lonicera × americana
caprifolium and cvs.
etrusca
× heckrotii
japonica and cvs.
periclymenum and cvs.
Mandevilla suaveolens
Pueraria thunbergiana
Stauntonia hexaphylla
Trachelospermum (all)
Vitis riparia
Wattakaka sinensis
Wisteria (all)

TREES and SHRUBS with AROMATIC FOLIAGE

Aromatic plants and those with scented leaves or wood play an important part in the make-up of a garden. Whether they give off their aroma freely or only as a result of a gentle bruising, they contribute much to the appreciation of a living plant.

Trees

Atherosperma moschatum
Cercidiphyllum japonicum (in autumn)
Cinnamomum glanduliferum
Clerodendrum (all)
Eucalyptus (all)
Juglans (all)
Laurelia serrata
Laurus nobilis and cvs.
Phellodendron (all)
Populus × acuminata
balsamifera
trichocarpa
Salix pentandra
triandra
Sassafras albidum
Umbellularia californica

Aromatic Foliage—Shrubs

Artemisia arborescens
Barosma pulchella
Camphorosma monspeliaca
Caryopteris (all)
Cistus, many, including
 ×**aguilari**
 ×**cyprius**
 ladanifer
 ×**loretii**
 palhinhae
 'Pat'
 ×**purpureus**
 ×**verguinii**
Clerodendrum bungei
Coleonema album
Comptonia peregrina
Drimys lanceolata
Elsholtzia stauntonii
Escallonia illinita
 laevis
 macrantha and hybrids
 punctata
 rubra
 viscosa
Gaultheria procumbens
Hebe cupressoides
Helichrysum plicatum
 serotinum
Hypericum hircinum
Illicium (all)
Lavandula spica and cvs.
Leptospermum liversidgei
Lindera (all)
Lippia citriodora
Myrica (all)
Myrtus communis and cvs.
Olearia ilicifolia
 mollis
 moschata
Orixa japonica
Perovskia (all)
Prostanthera (all)
Ptelea polyadenia
 trifoliata
Rhododendron, many, including
 augustinii
 cephalanthum
 cinnabarinum and hybrids
 concatenans
 glaucophyllum
 Hybrid Mollis (Azaleas)
 'Pink Drift'
 saluenense
Ribes sanguineum
 viburnifolium
Rosmarinus officinalis and cvs.
Ruta graveolens
Salvia (all)
Santolina (all)
Skimmia (all)

Conifers

Most conifers, particularly the following
Calocedrus decurrens
Chamaecyparis (all)
Cupressus (all)
Juniperus (all)
Pseudotsuga menziesii and forms
Thuja (all)

FLOWERING TREES and SHRUBS for EVERY MONTH

A month by month selection of flowering trees and shrubs. Many subjects flower over a long period, but only under the months during which they provide a reasonable display are they mentioned.

JANUARY

Trees

Acacia dealbata

Shrubs

Camellia sasanqua and cvs.
Chimonanthus praecox
Erica carnea and cvs.
 ×**darleyensis** and cvs.
Garrya elliptica
Hamamelis (many)
Jasminum nudiflorum
Lonicera fragrantissima
 standishii
 ×**purpusii**
Sarcococca (several)
Viburnum ×**bodnantense** and cvs.
 farreri
 tinus

FEBRUARY

Trees

Acacia dealbata
Magnolia campbellii and forms
Populus tremula
Prunus conradinae
 davidiana
Prunus incisa 'Praecox'
 mume and cvs.
Rhododendron arboreum and forms
Sorbus megalocarpa

February—Shrubs

Camellia sasanqua and cvs.
Cornus mas
officinalis
Daphne mezereum
odora
Erica carnea and cvs.
×**darleyensis** and cvs.
Garrya elliptica
Hamamelis (many)
Jasminum nudiflorum
Lonicera fragrantissima
setifera
standishii
Lonicera×**purpusii**
Mahonia japonica
Pachysandra terminalis
Rhododendron dauricum
mucronulatum
Sarcococca (several)
Ulex europaeus
Viburnum×**bodnantense** and cvs.
farreri
tinus and cvs.

MARCH

Trees

Acer opalus
rubrum
Magnolia (several)
Prunus (several)
Rhododendron (several)
Salix (many)
Sorbus megalocarpa

Shrubs

Camellia japonica (several cvs.)
sasanqua and cvs.
Chaenomeles (several)
Corylopsis pauciflora
Daphne mezereum
Erica carnea and cvs.
×**darleyensis** cvs.
lusitanica
mediterranea and cvs.
×**veitchii**
Forsythia (several)
Hamamelis japonica 'Zuccariniana'
Lonicera setifera
Magnolia stellata
Mahonia aquifolium
japonica
Osmanthus (several)
Pachysandra terminalis
Prinsepia utilis
Prunus (several)
Rhododendron (several)
Salix (many)
Stachyurus praecox
Ulex europaeus
Viburnum tinus and cvs.

APRIL

Trees

Acer platanoides
Amelanchier (several)
Magnolia kobus
×**loebneri** and cvs.
Magnolia salicifolia
Malus (several)
Prunus (many)
Pyrus ussuriensis

Shrubs

Amelanchier (several)
Berberis darwinii
linearifolia
×**lologensis**
Camellia japonica and cvs.
×**williamsii** and cvs.
Chaenomeles (many)
Corylopsis (several)
Cytisus (several)
Daphne (several)
Erica (several)
Forsythia (many)
Kerria japonica and cvs.
Magnolia ×**soulangiana** and cvs
stellata
Mahonia aquifolium
pinnata
Osmanthus delavayi
×**Osmarea burkwoodii**
Phillyrea decora
Pieris floribunda
japonica and cvs.
Prunus (many)
Rhododendron (many)
Ribes (many)
Spiraea×**arguta**
thunbergii
Viburnum (many)

Climbers

Clematis alpina
armandii
Holboellia coriacea

MAY

Trees

Aesculus (many)
Cercis (several)
Cornus nuttallii
Crataegus (many)
Davidia involucrata
Embothrium coccineum and cvs.
Fraxinus (Ornus Section)
Halesia (all)
Laburnum anagyroides
× watereri
Malus (many)
Paulownia tomentosa
Prunus (many)
Pyrus (all)
Sorbus (many)
Xanthoceras sorbifolium

Shrubs

Camellia japonica and cvs. (several)
Ceanothus (several)
Chaenomeles (many)
Choisya ternata
Cornus florida and cvs.
Cotoneaster (many)
Crinodendron hookeranum
Cytisus (many)
Daphne (many)
Dipelta floribunda
Enkianthus (all)
Erica (several)
Exochorda (all)
Genista (many)
Halesia (all)
Helianthemum (all)
Kerria japonica and cvs.
Kolkwitzia amabilis
Ledum (all)
Lonicera (many)
Magnolia liliiflora
× soulangiana
Menziesia (all)
Neviusia alabamensis
Paeonia (many)
Piptanthus laburnifolius
Potentilla (many)
Pyracantha (many)
Rhododendron (many)
Rosa (many)
Xanthoceras sorbifolium

Climbers

Clematis (many)
Lonicera (many)
Schisandra (all)
Wisteria (all)

JUNE

Trees

Aesculus (several)
Crataegus (many)
Embothrium coccineum and forms
Laburnum alpinum
× watereri
Magnolia, several, including
'Charles Coates'
Magnolia
cordata
fraseri
obovata
Malus trilobata
Robinia (several)
Styrax (several)

Shrubs

Abelia (several)
Buddleia globosa
Cistus (many)
Colutea (all)
Cornus kousa
Cotoneaster (many)
Cytisus (many)
Deutzia (most)
Erica ciliaris and cvs.
cinerea and cvs.
tetralix and cvs.
Escallonia (many)
Genista (many)
× Halimiocistus (all)
Halimium (all)
Hebe (many)
Helianthemum (all)
Hydrangea (several)
Kalmia (all)
Kolkwitzia amabilis
Lonicera (several)
Magnolia, several, including
× thompsoniana
virginiana
Neillia (several)
Olearia (several)
Ozothamnus (all)
Paeonia (all)
Penstemon (several)
Philadelphus (many)
Potentilla (all)
Rhododendron (many)
Rosa (many)
Rubus (many)
Spartium junceum
Spiraea (many)
Staphylea (several)
Syringa (many)
Viburnum (many)
Weigela (all)
Zenobia pulverulenta

June—Climbers

Clematis (many)
Jasminum (several)
Lonicera (many)
Schisandra (several)
Wisteria (all)

JULY

Trees

Aesculus indica
Castanea sativa
Catalpa (all)
Cladrastis sinense
Cornus macrophylla
Eucryphia (several)
Koelreuteria paniculata
Liriodendron tulipifera
Magnolia delavayi
grandiflora and cvs
Stewartia (several)

Shrubs

Buddleia davidii and cvs.
Calluna vulgaris and cvs.
Cistus (many)
Colutea (all)
Daboecia cantabrica and cvs.
Desfontainea spinosa
Deutzia setchuenensis
Erica ciliaris and cvs.
cinerea and cvs.
tetralix and cvs.
vagans and cvs.
Escallonia (many)
Fuchsia (many)
Grevillea sulphurea
Halimodendron halodendron
Hebe (many)
Hoheria (several)
Hoheria (several)
Holodiscus discolor
Hydrangea (many)
Hypericum (many)
Indigofera (several)
Lavandula spica and cvs.
Magnolia virginiana
Microglossa albescens
Olearia (several)
Penstemon (several)
Philadelphus (several)
Phygelius (all)
Potentilla (many)
Rhododendron (several)
Romneya (all)
Yucca (several)
Zenobia pulverulenta

Climbers

Clematis (many)
Eccremocarpus scaber
Jasminum (several)
Lonicera (many)
Mutisia (several)
Passiflora (several)
Polygonum (all)
Schizophragma (all)
Solanum (all)
Trachelospermum (all)

AUGUST

Trees

Catalpa bignonioides
Cornus macrophylla
Eucryphia (several)
Koelreuteria paniculata
Ligustrum lucidum
Magnolia delavayi
grandiflora and cvs.
Oxydendrum arboreum
Stewartia (several)

Shrubs

Buddleia (many)
Calluna vulgaris and cvs.
Caryopteris (several)
Ceanothus (several)
Ceratostigma willmottianum
Clerodendrum (all)
Clethra (several)
Colutea (all)
Daboecia cantabrica and cvs.
Desfontainea spinosa
Deutzia setchuenensis
Elsholtzia stauntonii
Erica ciliaris and cvs.
cinerea and cvs.
tetralix and cvs.
vagans and cvs.
Fuchsia (many)
Genista tinctoria and cvs.
Grevillea sulphurea
Hibiscus (several)
Hydrangea (many)
Hypericum (many)
Indigofera (several)
Itea ilicifolia
Lavandula spica (several cvs.)
Leycesteria formosa
Myrtus (several)
Olearia (several)
Perovskia (all)
Phygelius (all)
Potentilla (all)
Romneya (all)
Rosa (many)
Yucca (several)
Zenobia pulverulenta

August—Climbers

Berberidopsis corallina
Campsis (all)
Clematis (many)
Eccremocarpus scaber
Jasminum (several)
Lonicera (many)
Lapageria rosea
Mutisia (several)
Passiflora (several)
Pileostegia viburnoides
Polygonum (all)
Solanum (all)
Trachelospermum asiaticum

SEPTEMBER

Trees

Eucryphia ×nymansensis and cvs.
Magnolia grandiflora and cvs.

Shrubs

Abelia chinensis
×grandiflora
Aralia elata
Buddleia (several)
Calluna vulgaris and cvs.
Caryopteris (several)
Ceratostigma griffithii
willmottianum
Clerodendrum bungei
trichotomum
Colutea (several)
Daboecia cantabrica and cvs.
Elsholtzia stauntonii
Erica ciliaris and cvs.
cinerea (several cvs.)
terminalis
tetralix and cvs.
vagans and cvs.
Fuchsia (several)
Grevillea sulphurea
Hebe (several)
Hibiscus (several)
Hydrangea (several)
Hypericum (several)
Genista tinctoria and cvs.
Indigofera (several)
Lespedeza thunbergii
Leycesteria formosa
Magnolia cordata
Perovskia (all)
Potentilla (most)
Romneya (all)
Vitex (all)
Yucca gloriosa
Zauschneria

Climbers

Campsis (all)
Clematis (several)
Eccremocarpus scaber
Jasminum (several)
Lapageria rosea
Mutisia (several)
Passiflora (several)
Pileostegia viburnoides
Polygonum (several)
Solanum crispum 'Glasnevin'

OCTOBER

Trees

Magnolia grandiflora and cvs.

Shrubs

Abelia ×grandiflora
Calluna vulgaris (several cvs.)
Ceratostigma griffithii
willmottianum
Erica carnea 'Eileen Porter'
vagans (several cvs.)
Fatsia japonica
Fuchsia (several)
Hibiscus (several)
Hydrangea (several)
Hypericum (several)
Lespedeza thunbergii
Mahonia ×media and cvs.
Potentilla (several)
Vitex (all)
Zauschneria (all)

Climbers

Clematis (several)
Eccremocarpus scaber
Lapageria rosea
Polygonum (several)

NOVEMBER

Trees

Prunus subhirtella 'Autumnalis'

Shrubs

Calluna vulgaris 'Durfordii'
Erica carnea 'Eileen Porter'
Jasminum nudiflorum
Lonicera standishii
Mahonia acanthifolia
× media and cvs.
Viburnum ×bodnantense and cvs.
farreri

DECEMBER

Trees

Prunus subhirtella 'Autumnalis'

Shrubs

Erica carnea (several cvs.)
×darleyensis 'Silberschmelze'
Hamamelis mollis
Jasminum nudiflorum
Lonicera fragrantissima
×purpusii
Lonicera standishii
Mahonia ×media and cvs.
Viburnum ×bodnantense and cvs.
farreri
foetens
tinus

PLANTS RAISED or SELECTED by HILLIER and SONS

(Dates in parentheses represent the approximate year of raising or selection)

Abutilon ×suntense 'Jermyns' (1967)
Acer ×hillieri (before 1935)
palmatum 'Heptalobum Lutescens' (before 1935)
'Silver Vein' (1960)
Apple 'Easter Orange' (before 1897). A.M. 1897.
Aucuba japonica 'Hillieri' (before 1930)
Berberis ×stenophylla 'Etna' (before 1935)
×wintonensis (before 1955)
Buddleia 'West Hill' (before 1967)
Camellia ×heterophylla 'Barbara Hillier' (1960)
×williamsii 'Jermyns' (1960)
Caryopteris incana 'Peach Pink' (1960)
Ceanothus 'Blue Mound' (1960)
Cephalotaxus fortuni 'Prostrata' (before 1920)
harringtonia 'Gnome' (1970)
'Prostrata' (before 1930)
Chamaecyparis lawsoniana 'Elegantissima' (before 1930) A.G.M. 1969
'Hillieri' (before 1930)
Chrysanthemum 'Hillier's Apricot' (1919) A.M. 1921
Cistus 'Silver Pink' (1910) A.M. 1919. A.G.M. 1930
Corylopsis willmottiae 'Spring Purple' (1969)
Cotoneaster prostratus 'Eastleigh' (1960)
'Salmon Spray' (before 1940)
Cupressus lusitanica 'Glauca Pendula' (before 1914) A.M. 1944
Cytisus ×versicolor 'Hillieri' (1935)
Deutzia chunii 'Pink Charm' (1960)
×hillieri (1926)
Escallonia 'Wintonensis' (before 1921)
Fagus sylvatica 'Cockleshell' (1960)
×Gaulnettya wisleyensis 'Pink Pixie' (1969)
×Halimiocistus wintonensis (1910) A.M. 1926
Hamamelis ×intermedia 'Carmine Red' (1934)
'Hiltingbury' (1934)
vernalis 'Red Imp' (1966)
'Sandra' (1962)
'Squib' (1966)
Helianthemum nummularium 'Coppernob' (1968)
Hibiscus sinosyriacus 'Autumn Surprise' (1936)
'Lilac Queen' (1936)
'Ruby Glow' (1936)
Hypericum 'Eastleigh Gold' (1964)
Ilex ×altaclarensis 'Purple Shaft' (1965)
aquifolium 'Amber' (1950)
'Jermyns Dwarf' (before 1955)
Iris chrysographes 'Purple Wings' (1962)
Kniphofia 'St. Cross' (before 1935)
Laburnum anagyroides 'Erect' (1965)
×watereri 'Alford's Weeping' (1968)
Linum flavum 'Saffron' (1967)
Lupinus 'Broadgate Yellow' (1962)
Magnolia campbellii 'Ethel Hillier' (1927)
salicifolia 'Jermyns' (1935)

Plants raised or selected by Hillier and Sons—*continued*

Pernettya mucronata 'Cherry Ripe' (1965)
'Mulberry Wine' (1965)
'Pink Pearl' (1965)
'Rosie' (1965)
'Sea Shell' (1965)
'White Pearl' (1965)
Phyllocladus alpinus 'Silver Blades' (1968)
Pieris formosa forrestii 'Jermyns' (1950) A.M. 1959
Pinus cembra 'Jermyns' (1929)
koraiensis 'Winton' (1929)
parviflora 'Adcock's Dwarf' (1965)
sylvestris 'Argentea' (1920) A.G.M. 1969
Populus 'Hiltingbury Weeping' (1962)
Potentilla 'Eastleigh Cream' (1969)
'Elizabeth' (1950) A.M.T. 1965. A.G.M. 1969
'Milkmaid' (1960)
'Ruth' (1960)
Primula sinensis flore pleno 'Annie Hillier' (1875) F.C.C. 1880
Prunus ×hillieri (before 1928) A.M. 1959
'Spire' (1937)
incisa 'Praecox' (before 1938) A.M. 1973
×yedoensis 'Ivensii' (before 1929)
Quercus castaneifolia 'Green Spire' (1948)
Rhododendron campylogynum 'Crushed Strawberry' (1955)
kaempferi 'Highlight' (1955)
kiusianum 'Hillier's Pink' (1957)
tosaense 'Barbara' (1958)
'April Chimes' (1938)
'Arthur J. Ivens' (1938) A.M. 1944
'Arthur Stevens' (1960)
Fittra (1938) A.M. 1949
'July Fragrance' (1955)
'Midsummer Snow' (1955)
(**Knap Hill Azalea**) **'Dracula'** (1965)
'Orange Truffles' (1966)
Robinia ×hillieri (1933) A.M. 1962
Rosa 'Albert Edwards' (1937)
'Arthur Hillier' (1938)
×pruhoniciana 'Hillieri' (1926)
×wintonensis (1928)
Santolina virens 'Primrose Gem' (1960)
Schizophragma hydrangeoides 'Roseum' (1933) A.M. 1939
Sorbus 'Apricot Lady' (1960)
'Autumn Glow' (1967)
'Eastern Promise' (1967)
'Edwin Hillier' (1947)
'Ethel's Gold' (1960)
folgneri 'Lemon Drop' (before 1950)
'Jermyns' (1955)
'Pearly King' (1959)
'Red Marbles' (1961)
'Rose Queen' (1959)
'Signalman' (1963)
'Sunshine' (1968)
'Tundra' (1968)
'Vesuvius' (1960)
'Winter Cheer' (1959) A.M. 1971
Stachyurus chinensis 'Magpie' (1948)
Syringa yunnanensis 'Alba' (1946)
'Rosea' (1946)
Thuja orientalis 'Hillieri' (1920)
plicata 'Hillieri' (1880)
Torreya californica 'Spreadeagle' (1965)

Plants raised or selected by Hillier and Sons—*continued*

Ulmus ×hollandica 'Hillieri' (1918)
Verbascum 'Golden Bush' (1962)
Viburnum ×hillieri 'Winton' (1949) A.M. 1956
'Jermyns Globe' (1964)
rhytidophyllum 'Roseum' (before 1935)

PLANTS NAMED by HILLIER and SONS

(Dates in parentheses represent the approximate year of naming)

Acaena 'Blue Haze' (1965)
Aucuba japonica 'Lance Leaf' (1968)
'Speckles' (1968)
Betula 'Jermyns' (1974)
Camellia Cornish Snow 'Winton' (1948)
Cornus mas 'Hillier's Upright' (1974)
Cotinus coggygria 'Flame' (1964) A.G.M. 1969
Cotoneaster conspicuus 'Highlight' (1965)
×watereri 'Pink Champagne' (1965)
Deutzia compacta 'Lavender Time' (1969)
Escallonia 'E. G. Cheeseman' (1948)
Eucryphia ×hillieri 'Winton' (1953)
×Gaulnettya wisleyensis 'Ruby' (1967)
Foeniculum vulgare 'Smoky' (1964)
Genista tenera 'Golden Shower' (1973)
Griselinia littoralis 'Dixon's Cream' (1969)
Hamamelis ×intermedia 'Moonlight' (1960)
Hedera colchica 'Paddy's Pride' (1970)
Helxine soleirolii 'Golden Mat' (1963)
Hydrangea heteromalla 'Snowcap' (1970)
Hypericum olympicum 'Sunburst' (1974)
Ilex ×altaclarensis 'Silver Sentinel' (1970)
aquifolium 'Green Pillar' (1970)
Larix decidua 'Corley' (1971)
Ligustrum lucidum 'Excelsum Superbum' (1908)
Magnolia campbellii 'Sidbury' (1970)
'Werrington' (1970)
×loebneri 'Snowdrift' (1969)
Malus 'Hillieri' (1928)
Olearia avicenniifolia 'White Confusion' (1969)
Pernettya leucocarpa 'Harold Comber' (1965)
mucronata 'Edward Balls' (1965)
Phlomis 'Edward Bowles' (1967)
Pinus sylvestris 'Windsor' (1971)
Pittosporum tenuifolium 'Warnham Gold' (1969)
Prunus 'Pink Shell' (1969) A.M. 1969
serrulata 'Autumn Glory' (1969) A.M. 1966
'Snow Goose' (1970)
Quercus ilex 'Bicton' (1971)
Reynoutria compacta 'Pink Cloud' (1964)
Rhododendron 'Cool Haven' (1969)
'Lorien' (1973)
'Mrs. Edwin Hillier' (1933)
Santolina neapolitana 'Edward Bowles' (1968)
Sarcococca hookerana digyna 'Purple Stem' (1968)
Sorbus alnifolia 'Skyline' (1976)
'Chinese Lace' (1973)
'Embley' (1971)
'Wilfrid Fox' (1964)
Taxodium distichum 'Hursley Park' (1970)
Trachelospermum jasminoides wilsonii (before 1935)
Tsuga heterophylla 'Laursen's Column' (1971)
Ulmus ×elegantissima 'Jacqueline Hillier' (1967)
parvifolia 'Frosty' (1970)

VENTNOR BOTANIC GARDEN

Since 1969, with the permission and kind assistance of the South Wight Borough Council, and co-operation of the Superintendent, Mr. R. J. Dore, Mr. H. G. Hillier, C.B.E., has interested himself in the planting of a garden on the site of the old Royal National Hospital at Ventnor, on the south coast of the Isle of Wight.

It is hoped within the next few years that this planting will make an attractive and very interesting garden within the mature setting which was originally planted at the turn of the century. We believe within the limits set by the alkaline nature of the soil it will be possible to grow plants which hitherto have been confined to Cornwall and the South West of England and Ireland, and the west coast of Scotland. If our surmise is correct there will be a Mediterranean garden within forty miles of our nurseries.

Most of the lime tolerant plants marked as tender in this Manual will be grown in the Ventnor Botanic Garden. There will also be a few calcifuge plants growing in a natural peat deposit over hard limestone.

CONVERSION TABLES

Heights and Lengths

approx.
·3m.= 1ft.
·5m.= 1½ft.
·6m.= 2ft.
·7m.= 2ft.
·8m.= 2½ft.
·9m.= 3ft.
1m.= 3ft.
1·5m.= 5ft.
2m.= 6ft.
2·5m.= 8ft.
3m.= 10ft.
3·5m.= 11ft.
4m.= 13ft.
4·5m.= 15ft.
5m.= 16ft.
5·5m.= 18ft.
6m.= 20ft.
7m.= 23ft.
8m.= 26ft.
9m.= 30ft.
10m.= 33ft.
11m.= 36ft.
12m.= 40ft.
13m.= 43ft.
14m.= 45ft.
15m.= 50ft.
18m.= 60ft.
20m.= 65ft.
21m.= 70ft.
25m.= 80ft.
28m.= 90ft.
30m.= 100ft.
40m.= 135ft.
50m.= 160ft.

approx.
6mm.= ¼in.
8mm.= ⅓in.
12mm.= ½in.
20mm.= ¾in.
·5cm.= ¼in.
·75cm.= ⅓in.
1cm.= ⅓in.
1·5cm.= ½in.
2cm.= ¾in.
2·5cm.= 1in.
3cm.= 1in.
3·5cm.= 1¼in.
4cm.= 1½in.
4·5cm.= 1¾in.
5cm.= 2in.
6cm.= 2¼in.
7cm.= 2¾in.
8cm.= 3in.
9cm.= 3½in.
10cm.= 4in.
11cm.= 4⅓in.
12cm.= 4¾in.
13cm.= 5in.
14cm.= 5½in.
15cm.= 6in.
18cm.= 7in.
20cm.= 8in.
23cm.= 9in.
25cm.= 10in.
28cm.= 11in.
30cm.= 12in.
35cm.= 14in.
38cm.= 15in.
40cm.= 16in.
45cm.= 18in.
50cm.= 20in.
60cm.= 24in.
70cm.= 28in.

1m.= 39·4in. (3·3ft.)
1 kilometre = 1094yds.

Temperature

°C	°F	
30	86	
25	77	
20	68	
15	59	
10	50	
5	41	
0	32	Freezing
—5	23	
—10	14	
—15	5	

Area

1 sq.m. = 10·8sq. ft.
1 hectare = 2½ acres (approx.)
10 hectares = 24½ acres (approx.)

cm ins

cm	ins
18	7
17	
16	
15	6
14	
13	5
12	
11	
10	4
9	
8	3
7	
6	
5	2
4	
3	
2	1
1	½
0	0